The Macintosh Bible

6th Edition

Edited by Jeremy Judson

Sharon Zardetto Aker, Ted Alspach,
John Christopher, Michael E. Cohen,
Don Crabb, Bart Farkas, Joseph O. Holmes,
Ted Landau, Maria Langer, Steve Schwartz,
Kathleen Tinkel, and Bob Weibel

Peachpit Press

The Macintosh Bible, 6th Edition

Edited by Jeremy Judson

Peachpit Press
2414 Sixth Street
Berkeley, CA 94710

510 548-4393
fax: 510 548-5991

Find us on the World Wide Web at: http://www.peachpit.com

Peachpit Press is a division of Addison Wesley Longman

Copyright © 1996 by Peachpit Press

Copyeditor: Jackie Dove
Page layout & production: David Van Ness
Editorial Assistant: Karla Huebner
Technical reviewer: Dennis Cohen
Cover/interior design: YO, San Francisco
Cover/technical illustration: Bud Peen
Margin icons: Joe Crabtree, Art Parts
Index: Steve Rath

Notice of Rights

Notice of Liability

ISBN 0-201-88636-7

9 8 7 6 5 4 3 2 1

Printed and bound in the United States of America

If there were no Macintosh,
it would be necessary to invent one.

২৯

—*Michael E. Cohen*

Acknowledgments

Those deserving of the Peachpit Purple Heart of Valor for laughing in the face of harrowing deadlines include:

"The Dirty Dozen." The twelve editors of this book who painstakingly crafted their chapters (between smart whipcracks) to inform, enlighten, and even entertain.

David Van Ness, Production Czar extraordinaire, whose familiar refrain, "I'll make it happen," never ceased to be a sound for sore ears. He added quality to this book that I'm sure I've yet to realize.

My humble sidekick, **Karla Huebner**, for her hard work and commonsense suggestions throughout this project.

Illustrator, and now Webmaster, **Bud Peen**, whose unique way of looking at—and drawing—things made even a SCSI cable seem interesting!

Maria Giudice and **Lynne Stiles** and the good folks at **YO, San Francisco**, whose designs continue to put Peachpit's best face forward.

I couldn't chirp louder for **Lizzie** and **Stumpy** who remained a calming influence when chaos reigned supreme.

Special thanks to publisher, **Ted Nace**, for entrusting me with one of Peachpit's most enduring titles, and to **Darcy DiNucci**, whose work on the fifth edition provided a firm foundation upon which to build this edition.

Table of Contents

PART 3: EXTENDING YOUR REACH

Introduction

by Jeremy Judson

Welcome to the only Macintosh book that's been around practically since the dawn of the Mac's creation. This edition marks ten years that *The Macintosh Bible* has been lighting the way for people like you through the sometimes dark and perplexing catacombs of computing.

What's the secret to its longevity? Commitment.

This sixth edition carries forward our longstanding commitment to you in delivering accurate and timely Macintosh information in an accessible and usable way. We do this by finding experts especially well-suited to write about the specific topics, and who use their Macs in much the same way you do (or will). In all, 13 editors and over 70 contributors have had a hand in the creation of this book, with each one bringing their own expertise into the mix by providing hard-earned knowledge and hot, step-saving tips. This multiple-voice approach promotes differing views and perspectives throughout, ultimately benefiting you, the reader. (Pity's the writer who's asked to write a 1000-plus page book by himself on all things Mac.)

So what's so good about our writers? Well, who better to write about storage and peripheral devices than John Christopher, for example, who makes a living recovering peoples' data (and who had a hand in saving 12 episodes of "The Simpsons," which, to my mind, makes him a hero of sorts)? Or Joseph Holmes, an award-winning Web page designer, who can gently shuttle you up into cyberspace (and help you avoid crashing and burning upon re-entry) even as he makes you hep to the Internet jive. But don't take my word for it; have a looksee and see what I mean.

Additions to This Edition

The new, updated, and revised information in this edition of *The Macintosh Bible* includes:

- The Internet—getting on it with your Mac and a modem; creating your own Web page; sending and receiving electronic mail.

- The Mac Home Office—why you need one and how to equip it with the right hardware and software.

- Troubleshooting—including what the error codes mean (and don't mean).

- Software—covers the latest versions of popular software including Word 6, Excel 5, and ClarisWorks 4; System 7.5 updates, fonts, utilities, and the latest in multimedia and CD-ROM technology.

- Hardware—covers Power Macs, PowerBooks (5000 series), and peripheral devices such as monitors, keyboards, and mice.

The Mac Bible Editors

Here are the editors of *The Macintosh Bible*, sixth edition. Look for their initials and opinions throughout the book.

Sharon Zardetto Aker (SZA) had a Macintosh on (or near) Day One, and has been making her living writing about it ever since, with more than a dozen books (including *The Macintosh Bible, 3rd Edition*), hundreds of magazine articles, and a contributing editorship at *MacUser*. She lives in New Jersey with her two kids, PowerBook expert Richard Wolfson, and their seven Macintoshes.

Ted Alspach (TA) is the author of several books, including the best-selling *Macworld Illustrator 6 Bible* and *Illustrator Filter Finesse*. Considered to be one of the foremost experts on digital imaging and graphics, Ted speaks all over the country on various topics. When he isn't editing chapters of *The Macintosh Bible*, Ted fights the menace of pixel-based images from deep within the desert of Cave Creek, Arizona, population 327 ... including cattle.

John Christopher (JC) is a data recovery engineer at DriveSavers in Novato, California. He writes for various publications and has been a Mac fanatic for over ten years. John can be reached by e-mail at: datadoc@linex.com.

Michael E. Cohen (MEC) has produced and programmed a number of multimedia products at Voyager (most notably, Voyager's *Macbeth*), and is currently the senior tech-nomancer at Calliope Media. He has been using computers since the standard input device was a card reader.

Don Crabb (DC) is a contributing editor and columnist for *MacToday*, *MacWEEK*, *Mobile Office*, *MacUSER*, *Digital Chicago*, *MacTech*, *Win95User*, *ComputerUser*, *The Chicago Sun-Times Features Syndicate*, *The Springfield Union-News*, *PC Magazine*, and many other publications. Don welcomes comments at his Internet address: decc@cs.uchicago.edu. You can also check out his WWW home page at <http://www.cs.uchicago.edu/~decc/>.

Bart Farkas (BF) is the co-author of *The Macintosh Bible Guide to Games* and is the games editor for *MacSense* magazine. From his northern roost in Canada he writes game-related articles for *Inside Mac Games* magazine and *MacHome Journal*.

Joseph O. Holmes (JH) writes a monthly how-to section on designing a home page for *MacAddict* magazine. His Web site, Space Age Bachelor Pad Music <http://www.interport.net/~joholmes/index.html>, has received accolades from such magazines as *Entertainment Weekly*, *MacUser*, the *Net*, the *Village Voice*, and *Yahoo! Internet Life*.

Jeremy Judson (JJ) is an editor on staff at Peachpit Press whose specialty is aiding new computer users in the digestion of techno-babble. He is also co-creator of the popular *"...For Dummies"* line of books from IDG Books Worldwide (of which he edited the very first one: *DOS For Dummies*).

Ted Landau (TL) is the author of the best-selling Macintosh troubleshooting book: *Sad Macs, Bombs, and Other Disasters*. He has been writing about the Macintosh since 1987, when he was a contributing editor for the now-defunct *MACazine*. A contributing editor for *MacUser* since 1992, he has most recently written a series of troubleshooting articles for the magazine's "Hands On" section. His articles have also appeared in *Macworld*, *Mac Home Journal* and *A+*. In his "other life," he is a professor of psychology at Oakland University in Rochester, MI.

Maria Langer (ML) Maria Langer is the author of 15 computer books, including two Macintosh Bible series books (*Word 6* and *Excel 5*) and seven Visual QuickStart Series books (*AOL 3 for Windows*, *PageMill 1 for Mac*, *Excel 5 for Mac*, and *Excel for Windows 95*). She is a frequent reviewer for *MacWEEK* magazine, and is the *Publisher of Macintosh Tips & Tricks*, a popular news and productivity newsletter. In addition to writing, Maria works as a consultant, Webmaster, and applications trainer.

Steve Schwartz (SS) is the author of more than 30 books, including *Macworld ClarisWorks 4.0 Bible*, *Macworld FileMaker Pro 3.0 Bible*, and *Treasure Quest: The Official Resource Guide*.

Kathleen Tinkel (KT) bought a 128K Macintosh in April 1984 and never looked back—within three years, her studio was doing all its in-house production on the Mac. She started writing about design and typography for *Personal Publishing* and the new *Step-by-Step Electronic Design* newsletter in 1989, co-edited the weekly fax newsletter MacPrePress, and now spends her time writing for such graphic design and computer publications as *x-Height*, *Step-by-Step Graphics*, *Adobe Magazine*, *MacWEEK*, *MacUser*, and others.

She's also a sysop on the Desktop Publishing and Professional Publishing forums on CompuServe.

Bob Weibel (BW) is a former senior technical editor for *Publish* magazine, and is now the "Publishing Advisor" columnist for *Computer Currents* magazine and a frequent guest on Gina Smith's "On Computers" radio show. With over 200 computer magazine articles to his credit, you may have read Bob's work in *Publish*, *PC/Computing*, *PC World*, *MacWorld*, *MacWeek*, *Photo District News*, *c\net online*, and other 'zines. He's also coauthor of *Desktop Publishing Secrets*, *The QuarkXPress Book: Windows Edition*, and a contributor to *The Macintosh Bible: fifth and sixth editions*, all published by Peachpit Press.

What to Look For

One look at this edition and you'll see some major differences from—and lots of similarities to—earlier editions of the *Mac Bible*.

- **Who wrote what.** As always, you'll see the initials of the people who wrote each entry in the entry head. In this edition, the main contributors for each chapter are introduced on the table of contents page for that chapter. To avoid redundancy, some sections don't have initials—they were written by the chapter editor.

- **Icons to help you find specific kinds of information.** As in earlier editions, you can use the margin icons to find hot tips, good features, and other types of information. A guide to the icons is provided on page xvi.

- **Editors' Polls.** As with the previous edition, there are editors' polls, which let you know what the *Mac Bible* editors think on topics of importance—like what's the best screensaver out there, or whether it really is important to have a color monitor.

Each editor had a pretty free hand in determining how to approach the topics he or she was responsible for. We just asked everybody to use the pages they were allotted to say the most important things about that topic they could think of. Generally, though, each chapter includes a basic introduction to the topic, pointers to any products you should know about in that category, and hot tips that should make your life easier. The chapter intros and tables of contents will give you an overview of what each editor decided to highlight.

We've included a *big* index and glossary in the back of the book. We try to explain Macintosh terms the first time they come up, but come on: Who knows in what order you're going to read the book, and we can't define every term *every* time. So if you hit a term you're not familiar with (well, a *computer* term you're not familiar with), look it up in the glossary. And if you want to know more about any topic, turn to the index first. I bet you'll find what you're looking for.

Guide to the Icons

All those little icons in the margin of this book aren't just for show. They're there to help you find information you may be particularly interested in. (Okay, and for show, too; we especially like the beach bum and the grim reaper.)

HOT TIP

Every time you see this, you'll find out how to make your life a day at the beach. Sometimes, we have so many tips in a row that we just use one of these icons for a whole bunch of tips and add squiggly lines to show you how far the tips extend.

BAD FEATURE

Sometimes a product does some really dumb stuff. This warns you.

POWERBOOK

The information labeled with this icon should be particularly interesting to people who work on PowerBooks.

GOOD FEATURE

Features of a product that have earned this icon will make you howl and wag your tail.

POWER MAC

Buckle your seatbelt because something set off with this icon was meant to take advantage of the Power Mac's muscle.

WARNING

You won't die—usually—if you ignore this icon, but some nastiness could befall you or your Mac if you do.

PART

1

The Mac Itself

Editors' Poll: What Makes a Mac a Mac?

BW: Its pleasing, upscale, suburban exterior design, and a user interface that looks simpler than it really is, along with the fact that it doesn't have to say it's sorry when it bombs.

TA: A Mac is simplicity and gracefulness. In no other system will you find such incredible ease of use and ease of setup and maintenance. Likewise, a Macintosh system feels united, as if all the parts within make it one. The original all-in-one Macs had this quality, and the top-of-the-line Power Macs and PowerBooks have it as well.

JH: This sounds like a copout: everything. Everything from the Chicago typeface to the Apple Menu. From the desktop to the incredible consistency among applications to the arrow cursor to the OK button to the zoom rectangles to the Finder to the startup chimes. They're all what makes a Mac a Mac and no imitation comes close to the real thing.

JJ: For me, the Mac represents computing without commitment. I don't have to commit myself to hours of slogging through manuals to get things done on it, and like many of my recent dates, the Mac's "got a great personality," too—it smiles at you when you start it up! This must be the reason my Mac's the only appliance I own that I've named (with the possible exception of my four-slice toaster, "Burnie").

KT: From a user's point of view, *consistency* is what makes a Mac a Mac. The Mac is the first (and so far the only) really consistent computer. It provides the same interface and set of menus, tools, and dialogs for all applications. It's easy to add scanners, monitors, printers, hard drives, and other third-party hardware because of the Mac's consistent standards. The use of a common PostScript driver makes it easy to use a variety of output devices.

JC: I could use terms such as "interface" and "plug and play" but that's not what the Mac is about. I bought a Saturn a couple of months ago (that's a car, not a computer), and it reminded me of what I like about the Mac. It's knowing that you got something good and being really satisfied. The Mac is like that. *[I swell with pride reading this, but don't expect an invitation from Apple to one of those folksy company barbecues anytime soon ...—JJ]*

TL: The Mac OS, with its desktop metaphor and consistent interface and that fact that there is no DOS layer (or anything like it) underneath it all. The Mac interface *is* the underlying system. This is at the heart of what makes the Mac great. When the Mac is working at its best, you can accomplish a task so simply and easily that there is almost no learning curve required. For example, deleting a file simply by dragging the file's icon to a Trash icon has become so common that we don't think of it as special anymore. But compared to how this used be done (and still is done on UNIX systems), this was a major breakthrough. Others can try to imitate this approach, sometimes with partial success, but it is still what defines the Mac. That's why when someone tries to praise Windows 95, the highest praise they can give it is "It works like a Mac."

1 | Working With Your Mac

The Macintosh's graphical interface is more than just good-looking: It's also designed to make working with a computer as easy as possible. And while many of its features have been adopted by other operating systems, only the Mac has staked its existence on being the best at them.

The Mac may be easier to use than any other computer in history, but that's not really saying much. The interface is "intuitive" only after you've learned the basics; so, we cover those basics in this chapter. And if you're an experienced Mac user, you still might want to check the tips at the end of the chapter.

Contributors

Sharon Zardetto Aker (SZA) is the chapter editor.

Darcy DiNucci (DD) is a Mac writer and editor who runs *To the Point Publishing* in San Francisco; she was the editor of this chapter for the fifth edition of this book.

John Kadyk (JK) has been involved with all six editions of this book. When he's not working with the Mac, he likes playing music and biking.

Contents

On the Desktop

When you first turn on your Macintosh, you see the famous Mac *desktop*, the home base for all your computer activities. At the top is the *menu bar*, displaying individual *menu titles*. The little pictures on the desktop are *icons*; there are miniature icons in the menu bar, too. (If your screen doesn't look like the following figure, see the "If Your Desktop Looks Different..." sidebar.)

The program that actually provides the desktop and its operations is the *Finder*, so the terms *desktop* and *Finder* are used pretty much interchangeably.

The Pointer and the Mouse

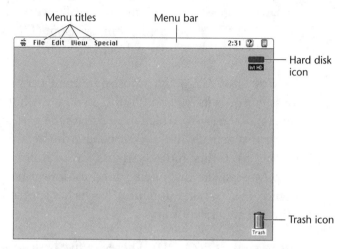

The Mac desktop, with its menu bar and icons, is what you see when you first start the computer.

When you move the mouse around on your desk, an arrow moves around on the screen. The arrow is called the *pointer*, reasonably enough, since you point to things with it. But it takes other shapes, too, and you don't always just *point* with it, so it's also generally referred to as the *mouse cursor*, or simply the *cursor*.

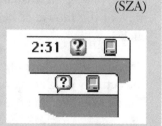

Common cursors (SZA). The two most common mouse cursors are the pointer and the *text* (or *I-beam*) cursor which appears when you're dealing with text. But you'll see an amazing variety of cursors as you work with the Mac.

The pointer and the I-beam (top) are the most common mouse cursors. The watch and the beachball (bottom) are "wait" cursors that tell you the Mac is busy.

A "wait" cursor tells you the Mac is busy and you'll have to wait until it's finished. It was originally a static wristwatch, later replaced by one with spinning hands so you could tell if the computer was really working on something or if it had frozen up for some reason. The spinning "beachball" is another system-level wait signal.

The hot spot (SZA). The most important part of any mouse cursor is its *hot spot*. On the pointer, the hot spot is the tip of the arrow, which means that's the part of the pointer that actually has to be touching the item you're pointing to. Other mouse cursors have different hot spots: A crosshairs that's being used to draw a box, for instance (as shown in this figure), has its hot spot in the center, so that's where the lines of the box are drawn from.

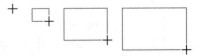

Because the center of the crosshairs cursor is its "hot spot," that's where the lines for the box are drawn from.

Mouse moves (SZA/DD). There are five basic mouse actions:

- *Pointing* is simply rolling the mouse to move the cursor to a specific spot.

- *Pressing* is holding the mouse button down while pointing to something.

- *Clicking* is a quick press-and-release of the mouse button; you usually click on something, which means you point to an object before you click.

- *Double-clicking* means clicking twice in a row, at just the right speed and without moving the mouse in between (so that the Mac doesn't interpret it as two single clicks).

- *Dragging* means keeping the button down while you move the mouse. Sometimes you actually drag an item; sometimes the drag operation doesn't move anything but is used to define an area of the screen.

There are other "mouse moves," too. Some programs—including the Finder—let you perform special operations by combining the basic mouse moves with the press of a key. So, holding down ⌘ while dragging a desktop icon (a "command-drag") makes the icon snap to the invisible desktop grid when you let it go; holding down Option while you drag an item (an "option-drag") usually makes a copy of the item in the new location.

Working With Desktop Icons (SZA)

Icons represent various things on your desktop, such as disks, folders, and files. (A *file* is any discrete collection of information—a program like a word processor, a memo you wrote with the word processor, or a component of the system software.)

Icons. There are many different types of icons on the Mac. There are three common types of disk icons for the desktop (for hard disks, floppy disks, and CDs), and other icons for other types of storage volumes. Each application has its own distinctive icon, and a document icon is usually visually related to the "parent" application. If the Mac can't figure out which application created a document, it uses the *generic* icon, which looks like a blank piece of paper with its upper-right corner turned down.

A document icon is usually visually related to the application that created it. When the Mac doesn't know about the "parent" application, it uses a generic document icon for the file.

Each type of storage volume has a different icon on the desktop. Even though the Mac desktop has been "colorized" for years, basic disk icons are still only black-and-white.

There are lots of special folders and files used by the Mac's operating system, and most get special icons. There is, for instance, a common element in the design of all control panels, and of all extensions.

The icons at the left are all control panels, and include the "slider" control in the icon design. The icons in the middle group, using the puzzle-piece design, are all extensions. The group at the right consists of special system folders.

Folders. A *folder* can hold files and other folders, so you use folders to organize what's on your disks. You create a new folder with the New Folder command in the File menu. You can put folders within folders within folders to your heart's content—whatever you need to organize your work and make things easy to find.

Using the New Folder command creates a new folder in the active window, with the default name "untitled folder."

Selecting icons (SZA/DD). To select a single icon, click on it; it reverses colors or is darkened in some way to show that it's selected. To select multiple icons, click on one and then shift-click (hold down Shift while you click the mouse button) on the others. Or, drag a rectangle around the icons you want: Start in any corner of an imaginary box that surrounds the icons and drag to the opposite corner. You'll see a dotted line defining the rectangular area that you've dragged.

To *deselect* an icon, select another one or click someplace where nothing will be selected. You can shift-click on a single icon to deselect it from a group of selected icons.

Renaming icons. To rename an icon, first select its *name* by clicking directly on the name (not on the picture); a selected name is highlighted inside an editing rectangle. There's a brief delay from the time you click to the time the editing rectangle appears, so be patient—click again too soon and the Mac thinks you've double-clicked and will open the icon. If the icon itself is already selected and your hands are on the keyboard instead of the mouse, you can press Return or Enter to select the name.

HOT TIP

untitled folder   untitled folder

Clicking on the name of an icon puts an editing rectangle around it; when the cursor is inside the rectangle, it changes to the text cursor.

Basic text-editing techniques (covered in Chapter 8) work in the editing rectangle. You can use icon names of up to 31 characters long, and include any character except the colon (:).

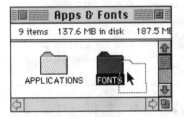

Apps & Fonts
9 items   137.6 MB in disk   187.5 MB

APPLICATIONS   FONTS

When you drag an icon, an outline of the item moves with the pointer until you let go of the mouse button, at which point the icon moves to the new location.

Moving icons. Move an icon by dragging it to a new position. An outline of the icon moves along with the pointer until you release the mouse button, at which point the icon jumps to its new location.

Dragging an icon from one place to another on the same disk just changes its location. But dragging an icon from one disk to another leaves the original intact and puts a copy onto the other disk. For example, dragging a file from a floppy disk to your hard drive means there are then two copies of the file: the original on the floppy, and a duplicate on your hard drive.

final note   Trash   final note   Trash

When you're putting one icon into another, the "target" darkens when you're in the right area. In the picture on the left, the document won't be in the Trash if the mouse button is released, but the one on the right will.

When you're dragging one icon into another— putting something into a folder, or into the Trash— the "target" icon darkens when you've moved the icon into the right position.

Opening icons. The basic way to open an icon is to double-click on it. You can also select an icon and then choose Open from the File menu or press ⌘O. An opened icon is filled with a dark dotted pattern to show that it's open.

What happens when you open an icon depends on what the icon represents: Opening a disk, a folder, or the Trash, opens a window; opening an application icon launches the program; opening a document icon launches its parent application and then opens the document.

Starting Up and Shutting Down　　(SZA)

We started this chapter assuming that you were looking at your Mac's desktop, with the computer already on. But there are a few things to know about the startup procedure, and there's more than one way to shut down.

If you have an external storage device, such as a hard drive or CD-ROM drive, turn it on *before* you start the computer. Monitors, printers, and modems can be turned on at any time.

When you turn on your Mac, you'll first see the famous "Happy Mac," an icon of a smiling Mac. Next you get the friendly "Welcome to Macintosh" dialog box, followed by the Mac OS logo if you're running System 7.5.1 or later. You'll see a series of icons appear across the bottom of the screen—these are extensions and controls panels that are loading into memory. Finally, you get to your desktop.

Shutting off the Mac incorrectly—just turning it off with a power switch—can lead to the loss of some of your work. Even if you've saved all your documents and quit all applications, the Mac has to do several "housekeeping" chores before you turn it off; without the housekeeping, some things you think are finished are only in memory and not yet stored on the disk.

In System 7.1 and earlier, you use the Shut Down command in the Finder's Special menu. System 7.5 added a second Shut Down command, listed as •Shut Down in the menu. Starting with System 7.5.1, there's a third option: Press the Power On key on the keyboard to get a dialog that asks if you want to shut down, restart, or cancel. You can use any of the three methods available to you at any time: If any unsaved documents are open, you'll be asked if you want to save them before the Mac shuts down.

HOT TIP

Using the Trash. To erase a file, you drag it into the Trash can. But items just sit in the Trash until you use the Special menu's Empty Trash command. You'll know when the Trash needs emptying because it bulges whenever there's something inside it.

Trash　　Trash

The "normal" Trash icon is on the left; when there's something inside, the can bulges, as on the right.

To take something out of the Trash before it's erased, double-click on the Trash icon to open it, and drag the file out of the Trash's window. Or, just select the icon in the window and use the Put Away command from the Special menu—the icon zooms back to wherever it was before you trashed it.

HOT TIP

Ejecting disks. Selecting a disk and using the Special menu's Eject Disk command—as obvious and logical as that seems—leaves a "ghost" icon of the disk on the desktop (the icon is somewhat darkened). The Mac is still keeping track of the disk's contents, and you might get repeated requests to reinsert the disk.

As odd as it seems, you can eject a floppy disk or CD by dragging its icon to the Trash. Don't worry—nothing will be erased! Or, you can select a disk and choose the File menu's Put Away command. Either of these methods ejects the disk and also erases its ghost from the desktop.

Working With Windows (SZA)

When you open a disk, a folder, or the Trash on the desktop, you get a *window* that shows what's inside. When you open a document inside an application, the contents of the document are displayed in a window. Windows are your work areas when you're using the Mac, and although Finder windows have some special properties to make file-handling easier, most Mac windows behave in the same way and have common controls.

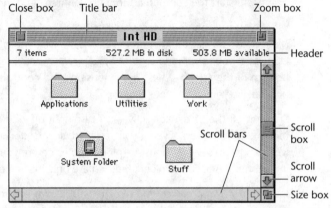

All Finder windows and most document windows share the same basic "parts" and controls.

Opening and closing. When a window first opens on the desktop, it is *active:* It's on top of any other open windows, and any window commands, such as "Close," apply to only this window. Only one window is active at a time; you can tell which it is by its striped title bar. If you want to activate a window that's already open, all you have to do is click anywhere in it.

To close a window, click its *close box* at the left end of the title bar. Or, choose the Close command from the File menu or press ⌘W.

Moving and resizing. To move a window, you drag it by its *title bar;* you change its size by dragging the *size box* in its lower-right corner.

To quickly change the size and position of a window, click in its *zoom box*

The active *window—shown in the front here—has a striped title bar and visible scroll controls. An inactive window, such as the* Int HD *window in this picture, has a blank title bar and scroll areas.*

in the upper-right corner: The window will zoom back and forth between the size you created and a size that's just large enough to display all its contents.

Scrolling windows. Blank scroll bars in an active window mean everything that's in the window is displayed. When either or both scroll bars are a dotted gray, there are items in the window that aren't showing.

The position of the scroll box in the scroll bar indicates what part of the window you're looking at: If it's at the top, for instance, you're viewing the uppermost items in the window.

- Click on a *scroll arrow* to scroll the window in that direction; press on an arrow (that is, keep the mouse button down) for continuous scrolling.

The vertical scroll bar shown here is a dotted gray pattern, which means there are items down below the ones displayed. Since the horizontal scroll bar is blank, there are no items to the left or right of the ones that are showing.

- Click in the *scroll bar* above or below the scroll box to scroll the window contents in larger increments—the width or height of the window itself.

- Drag a *scroll box* into a position that corresponds to the area of the window you want to see.

The View menu lets you change how the contents of Finder windows are displayed.

Changing window views. Use the View menu to change a window's display from large icons to something more convenient for viewing lots of files. There's a Small Icon view in which you can still drag icons around. There are also several list views which differ only in the order in which the items appear—according to Name, or Size, or Kind, and so on. The techniques you use on icons (like double-clicking to open, clicking to select, or dragging to select multiple items) work on items in list views, too.

Hierarchical views. When a Finder window is in a list view, each folder in it is marked with a triangular arrow. Click on the arrow, and the folder *expands* to list what's in it; click again, and the folder *collapses* to hide its contents. (The terms *expand* and *collapse* differentiate these procedures from *opening* and *closing* folders.) You can also expand and collapse the folders inside the expanded folders to as many levels as you want.

Clicking on a folder's arrow in a list view (background) expands the folder, listing what's inside.

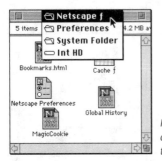

The Path menu. Point to the title of an active window, hold down ⌘, and press the mouse button. The Path menu pops up, showing what folder the window belongs to, which folder *that* one's in, and so on, all the way back to the disk. Choosing an item from the Path menu opens that window.

Point to the title of a window, hold down the ⌘ key, and press the mouse button; you'll see the Path menu that shows all the folders that the window is in.

Menus and Dialogs

There are lots of ways of telling the Mac what you want it to do. So far, we've concentrated on manipulating icons on the desktop; in this section, we get into detail about menus and dialog boxes.

Using Menus   (SZA)

Using menus is a cinch: You press on the menu title to open the menu, slide the pointer down to the command you want (each command is highlighted as you touch it), and release the mouse button. If the menu's open and you decide you don't want any of the commands, simply move the pointer off the menu and let go—you don't have to go back up to the menu title.

To select from a menu, press on the menu title, slide down to the command you want, and then let go of the mouse button.

Dimmed commands. Sometimes a command is *dimmed* in the menu—its name is gray instead of black, like the Paste command in the last picture. A dimmed command can't be used because it doesn't apply at the time you open the menu.

For further info... When a menu command is followed by an ellipsis (three dots, like this...) that means the Mac needs more information before the command can be executed, so a dialog box opens when you select the command.

Application and system menus. Most menu titles are words, and "belong" to whatever application you're working in. You'll see these titles in the menu bar change as you move from one application

Apple menu   Help menu   Application menu

System menus are tiny icons, like the ones at the far ends of the menu bar.

to another (although most programs include a File and Edit menu). Menu titles that are icons, though, are *system* menus, and they stay on the menu bar no matter what program you're in. There are three basic system menus:

- The menu (called the *Apple* menu, since so few people can pronounce) at the far left of the menu bar lists whatever you put in the Apple Menu Items folder inside the System Folder.

- The Application menu at the far right of the menu bar lists all open applications so you can easily move from one to another.

- The Help menu provides access to Balloon Help, Apple Guide, and whatever help system might be available for a particular program.

Submenus. A triangular arrow to the right of a menu item means there's a submenu; pause on the main menu command, and the submenu appears. To choose from the submenu, slide the pointer into it, to the command you want; if you're fast enough, you can slide diagonally from the main menu command directly to the submenu command without the submenu's closing.

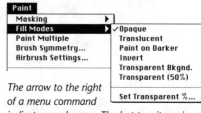

The arrow to the right of a menu command indicates a submenu. The last two items in this truncated main menu are each followed by an ellipsis (those three dots...), which means a command opens a dialog box.

Scrolling menus. When a menu has so many items on it that they can't all fit on the screen, the menu can scroll to show you all the choices. A downward-pointing arrow at the bottom of a menu indicates that there are items off in that direction; slide down to the arrow, and the menu starts to scroll. Once it's scrolling, there'll be an upward-pointing arrow at the top to show that there are now choices off in *that* direction; slide the pointer back up to scroll in that direction.

Toggle commands. Some "commands" are actually choices that stay in effect until you turn them off—a Bold command in a Style menu, for instance, will turn selected text bold but can also keep you typing in bold text until you turn it off. This kind of command is called a *toggle* because if you choose it when it's turned off, it gets turned on, and vice versa. A toggle command sometimes has a check mark in front of it to show that it's in effect (like the Opaque item in the top figure) Some change the wording, for example, Show Balloons and Hide Balloons.

A menu with too many items to display at once has an arrow at the bottom (left). Hold the pointer at the bottom of the menu, and the menu scrolls; an arrow appears at the top of the menu to show that it can scroll in that direction, too (right).

PlainTalk (DD)

PlainTalk is a system extension that lets you give voice commands to your Mac. Instead of using the mouse to move the pointer to the close box of a window and clicking, for instance, you can just say, "Computer: Close." You can give many different kinds of commands this way, including any menu or dialog box command. If you want to get more creative and sound less like Captain Picard, you can choose a name other than "Computer" for your Mac.

PlainTalk lets you choose from among several voices and then name your character. Your commands and the Mac's replies are listed in the window.

If you're running PlainTalk and voice recognition is turned on, there will be a small PlainTalk window at the bottom of the screen. The window displays a cartoonish character and the text of what you say and how the Mac responds. By default, the character is an ear called Vincent (get it?) but you can choose from a half-dozen characters.

Not all check marks in a menu are toggles. The Application menu, for instance, puts a check mark in front of the currently running application; you don't choose it to turn it off—you choose another application to move there, and then *that's* the checked item in the menu.

Keyboard commands. Many menu commands have *keyboard equivalents*, which means you can give the command without opening the menu at all, but just by holding down ⌘ while you press a letter (whatever's listed in the menu next to that command). So, pressing ⌘O is the same as choosing Open from the File menu. (The ⌘ key—on some keyboards there's no apple on it, but just the cloverleaf squiggle—is called the *command* key.)

Key Symbols in Menus (SZA)

The ⌘ symbol is easy to display in a menu because it's also a symbol on the keyboard. But the other modifier keys—Shift, Option, and Ctrl—need special symbols in a menu because they appear as words on the keyboard. The cryptic symbols Apple picked are shown here.

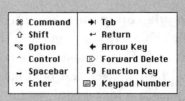

And what happens when a keyboard command involves some other nonprinting key (such as Tab, Enter, or Return) that has to show in a menu? They, too, have their own symbols.

⌘	Command	⇥	Tab
⇧	Shift	↩	Return
⌥	Option	←	Arrow Key
^	Control	⌦	Forward Delete
_	Spacebar	F9	Function Key
⌤	Enter	⌨9	Keypad Number

Modifier keys, and nonprinting keys, use the special symbols shown here when they appear in a menu.

Keyboard commands are often simply ⌘ plus the first letter of the command name. Sometimes other *modifier keys* in addition to ⌘ (such as [Shift], [Option], and even [Ctrl], alone or in combination) are used so you'll have more keyboard combinations available.

Although the letter listed in a menu for a keyboard command is in uppercase, you don't press [Shift] to use it—in fact, adding [Shift] to the combination can change the command entirely.

Dialog Boxes and Alerts

(SZA)

Choosing a command with an ellipsis after it (those three dots...) opens a *dialog box* where you enter information—which document to open, for instance, or how many copies to print. (It's called a dialog because the Mac is telling you something and asking for a response.) Dialog boxes have all sorts of controls—buttons, boxes, lists, and menus—that let you easily input information and give commands.

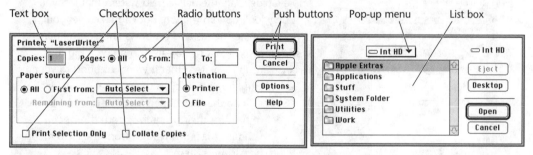

Two typical Mac dialog boxes and their standard components.

Text boxes and lists. A *text box* is a frame where you type in information, such as the name for the document or the number of pages you want to print. To move from one text box to another, you can click in a box, or press [Tab] to move to the next box and [Shift][Tab] to move to the previous one.

HOT TIP

A *list box* has a scrollable list from which you make a choice by clicking on the item, or sometimes by typing one or more letters to identify the item you want.

Buttons. Buttons are the quickest way to input dialog box information. There are three basic types:

- Standard buttons, called *push buttons*, are rounded rectangles with commands inside them; click a button to execute the command. When a button is highlighted with a thick frame, it's the *default* button—you can "click" it by pressing [Return] or [Enter].

- *Radio buttons* come in groups, for options that are mutually exclusive: choosing one of them means you can't have any of the others. When you click on a radio button (it fills in to show it's been selected), the previously chosen button is deselected.

Getting Help   (SZA)

On the Mac, help is never more than a few mouse moves away. In the Help menu at the right of your menu bar, you'll find not one, but two, help systems: Balloon Help (introduced in System 7) and Apple Guide (introduced in System 7.5).

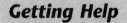

Trash

To discard an item or eject a disk, drag it to the Trash. To get an item back, open the Trash icon and drag the item out of the Trash window.

The Trash is bulging because there is something in it.

When Balloon Help is on, pointing to any item gets you an information-filled balloon.

Turn on Balloon Help by choosing Show Balloons in the menu. Then point to something—you don't even have to click the mouse—to get information about it, which shows up in a little balloon. The information in the balloon comes from the program you're using, so the actual helpfulness of Balloon Help really depends on the programmer's thoroughness.

About Apple Guide
Show Balloons
Macintosh Guide   ⌘?
Shortcuts

The Help menu is always available at the far right of the menu bar. It lets you access both the Balloon Help and Apple Guide help systems.

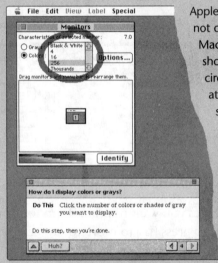

Apple Guide is an interactive help system that lets you not only look up information, but can take over your Mac, opening menus and windows and control panels, showing you what to do—it even draws a big red circle around any item that it wants to bring to your attention! "Apple Guide" is the general name for the system, one that developers can use to make interactive help for their programs; from the Finder, you choose Macintosh Guide from the Help menu to access the system.

Apple Guide, the interactive help system, takes you step-by-step through anything you need to know. The circle in the Monitors control panel shown here is drawn slowly on the screen in red to catch your eye.

• *Checkboxes* can be used singly, but often come in groups for items that are *not* mutually exclusive: you can check any, all, or none of the checkboxes in a group. Clicking in the box puts an X in it, which indicates the option is on; clicking in it again turns it off.

Pop-up menu. You'll find a variety of *pop-up menus* when you're working with the Mac: menus that show up someplace other than in the menu bar at the top of the screen. In dialog boxes, the standard pop-up menu is a shadowed box with a triangular arrow at its right. Press on a pop-up menu, and it—well, it pops up and lets you select something by dragging the pointer up or down.

Dismissing dialogs. When you're finished setting options in a dialog box you have to get it off the screen. All you have to do is click an OK button for the dialog to go away and the original command to be carried out using the parameters in the dialog box. If you want to forget about the whole thing, you can go back to where you were before you chose the command that opened the dialog: Click the Cancel button in the dialog (or press ⌘., which most dialogs interpret as a Cancel command).

Alerts. An *alert* is a special kind of dialog box, one with just a statement or a warning in it, such as: *Using Revert will cancel all the changes you've made since you opened the document.* Alerts have a minimum of buttons—usually just OK

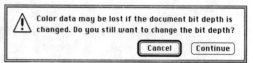

An alert warns you about something you're about to do, providing minimal options from that point.

and Cancel, or sometimes just the OK button so you can acknowledge the warning and dismiss the dialog.

Beyond the Desktop

So far, we've talked mostly about working on the desktop, but if you stay there, you'll never get any work done. The most common operations you'll perform include launching applications, moving from one application to another, creating and saving documents, and moving information from one place to another by using the Clipboard.

Applications and Documents (SZA)

Applications are programs that enable you to get work done; *documents* are the files you create with applications.

Launching and quitting applications. To use an application, you *launch* it, which is another way of saying you open it. Opening an application (the same way you open any desktop icon) gives you a whole new environment to work in, where the basic rules you've learned still apply, but a wealth of other capabilities await you.

Every application provides a Quit command in its File menu, and its keyboard equivalent (⌘Q) won't vary from program to program. Quitting an application automatically closes any open documents, first giving you the option to save any changes you might have made.

At Ease (DD)

At Ease is a replacement for the Finder that first shipped with early Performa models. It's still shipped with some models but is also available separately.

When At Ease is installed, most of the screen is taken up by a stack of giant file folders. The folders are covered with buttons that you click on to launch the item in the button (similar to the Launcher's buttons).

At Ease is designed so that whoever sets up the system can assign different levels of

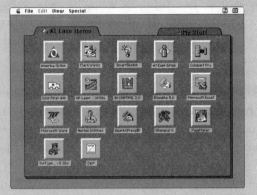

The At Ease screen replaces the normal desktop view.

access to different users, so you may have to sign on before you even get to the At Ease desktop. At Ease may also restrict you from saving or opening files in certain folders.

The Launcher. Although double-clicking on an application icon is an easy way to launch it, sometimes it's not so easy to get to the icon—it might be buried in one, two, or even three (or more!) folders. The Launcher control panel, included in System 7.5,

is an easy way to launch programs that you'd otherwise have to open folders to get at. You simply click once on the icon button in the Launcher window to open the program.

Any item or *alias* (a sort of "pointer" to a file, covered in Chapter 3) you put in the Launcher Items

Click on a button in the Launcher window to launch the item that the button represents.

folder appears as a button in the Launcher window. Open the Launcher window by opening the Launcher control panel; you can make it open automatically on startup by checking the Open Launcher at Startup button in the General Controls control panel (control panels are covered in Chapter 3).

Moving between applications. As long as you have enough memory (discussed in Chapter 4), you can run more than one program at a time. The Application menu at the far right of the menu bar lists all applications that are open; selecting one from the list moves you to that program.

The Application menu lists all the open applications.
Choosing one from the menu moves you into that program.

Any windows that belong to inactive but open applications hang around in the background, coming forward when the application is selected from the menu. Clicking anywhere in a background window is another way to move into an application. If you don't want the background applications' windows showing while you're working, use the Hide/Show commands in the Application menu.

Opening and creating documents. To open a document, use the Open command from the application's File menu. If you're on the desktop, you can double-click on the document: The application that created it launches and opens the document. If the application is already running, the Mac switches from the Finder to the application and opens the document.

File	
New...	⌘N
Open...	⌘O
Close	⌘W
Save	⌘S
Save As...	

Selecting the New command gives you a new, blank document in any application.

Most applications start up with an empty document window for you to work in. But if you don't have an empty window, or if you've used the initial one, you can get a new blank document by using the application's New command.

Saving and closing documents. A document exists only in the computer's memory and disappears when you close it unless you've stored it on the disk, using the application's Save command. Changes to an existing document also have to be explicitly saved.

When you use Save on a new document, you'll get a Save dialog where you can name the document and show where on the disk you want it stored. When you use Save on a document that's been saved before, no dialog appears—the Mac just goes ahead and saves the edited version of the document, replacing the previous version on the disk. Most applications provide a Save As command so you can save an edited document as a separate document, with a different name, so the original document stays intact.

Don't wait until you're finished working on a document to save it; instead, save every five or ten minutes to guard against mishaps such as a power failure or a computer crash that could cause you to lose the work you've done.

HOT TIP

The Open and Save dialogs. The dialog boxes you'll see when you're opening or saving documents (cleverly referred to as the Open and Save dialogs) have many features in common, since both let you navigate around disks and through folders. A Save dialog, though, has to provide at least one more option—that of naming the current document. The dialogs in the following figure are the basic ones; many programs provide extra controls, such as checkboxes and pop-up menus, depending on the features the program provides. You might, for instance, be able to specify what kind of files will show in the list, or a special format in which the document will be saved.

The list shows   The pop-up menu   The disk icon shows   Use the pop-up menu
the items in the   shows the folder   which disk you're   to move to a folder
current folder.   that you're in.   looking at.   "above" the current one.

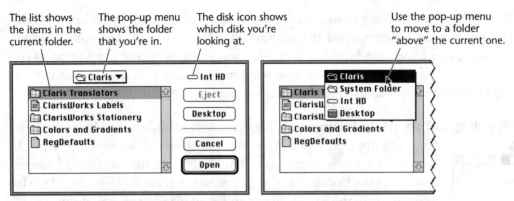

The basic Open dialog box lets you navigate through the folders of your disk to find the document you want to open.

In the Open dialog box:

- The *pop-up menu* shows the current folder. To move "up" to one of the listed folders, select it from the menu.

- The *list* shows the files and folders in the current folder. To open something in the list, click on it and then click the Open button, or just double-click on the name in the list.

- The *disk icon* shows which disk the current folder is on.

- The *Eject* button is available when the current folder is on a floppy disk.

- The *Desktop* button jumps you right up to the top level, listing the files and folders that are out loose on the desktop.

- The *Cancel* button dismisses the dialog without opening anything.

- The *Open* button (because it's the default button, you can press [Return] instead of clicking it) opens the item you've selected in the list.

The basic Save dialog box has three additional features:

- The *text box* is where you type the name of the document you're saving.

- The *New Folder* button (it doesn't say "Folder," but uses an obvious icon) lets you create a new folder inside the current folder.

- The *Save* button, which you click after you've picked a location for the document and given it a name, changes to Open if you've selected a folder in the list.

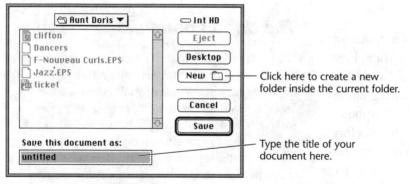

Click here to create a new folder inside the current folder.

Type the title of your document here.

The basic Save dialog lets you name your document and choose a place for it to be stored.

Cutting, Copying, and Pasting

(SZA)

One of the most elegant and useful tools on the Mac is the *Clipboard*—a temporary holding place for material that you *cut* or *copy* from one place to *paste* in another. The Clipboard can hold material of almost any length, and it's an easy way to move material inside a document, between documents, or even between applications.

You'll find Cut, Copy, and Paste commands in the Edit menu of every Mac program. The keyboard shortcuts for these commands are practically sacred and don't change from one program to another as other keyboard equivalents do: ⌘X is Cut, ⌘C is Copy, and ⌘V is Paste. Together with the ⌘Z shortcut for the Undo command, these four fixtures of the Edit menu use the first four keys on the bottom row of the keyboard.

Nearly every Edit menu starts with these four commands, and the keyboard equivalents for them never vary.

The Cut and Copy commands. Using Cut or Copy on selected material places the selection on the Clipboard; with Cut, the selection disappears from the document, while Copy leaves the original in place. (The Finder and many other programs let you check the contents of the Clipboard by choosing a Show Clipboard command.)

If you want to delete something from a document without moving it someplace else, there's no need to put it on the Clipboard: just use Delete.

The Paste command. To put something from the Clipboard into a document, you use the Paste command. If you're working with text, the pasted material appears at the insertion point or replaces selected text. In graphics programs, a pasted item usually appears in the center of the window and stays selected so you can move it wherever you want.

The Clipboard

The Clipboard is a *temporary* holding place in two ways. First, because it can hold only one item at a time, putting something new on the Clipboard replaces what was there before. Second, the Clipboard contents disappear entirely when you shut down the computer.

HOT TIP

Using the Paste command doesn't empty the Clipboard, so you can continue using the command to put multiple copies of the Clipboard contents anywhere you want them.

The Undo Command   (SZA/DD)

The Undo command in the Edit menu was introduced with the very first Mac; the first time you accidentally delete ten paragraphs of text, you'll appreciate the concept. If you use the Undo command twice in a row (without doing anything in between), you can undo the undo, putting things back the way they were before the first undo. In fact, after you've used Undo, the command in the Edit menu often changes to Redo.

Undo is restricted to *editing* actions, so you won't, for instance, be able to undo saving a document or opening a new window. It's also restricted to a single action, the last one you took; so, use it immediately or lose the opportunity for a quick fix. Some programs implement a "multiple undo" feature so you can reverse, step-by-step, the work that you've done.

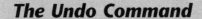

Finder Tips

HOT TIPS

General Tips

Keyboard cancel (SZA). In most situations, ⌘. will cancel what you're doing— printing, for instance, or copying a file from one disk to another. It will also "push" the Cancel button in most dialog boxes. Esc also works, in most instances, as a substitute for ⌘..

Restoring Clipboard contents (SZA). If you cut or copy something and then realize you still need what was previously on the Clipboard, use the Undo command. When it undoes the Cut or Copy command, it also restores the Clipboard to its previous state.

Shortcuts in the Save and Open dialogs (SZA). Because you use the Open and Save dialog boxes all the time, there are plenty of shortcuts available to get you through them quickly. They're rounded up in the following table.

HOT TIPS

Open and Save Dialog Shortcuts

To "click" buttons:

Cancel	⌘[.] or [Esc]
Desktop	⌘[D] or ⌘[Shift][↑]
Save	[Return] or [Enter] or ⌘[S]
Open	[Return] or [Enter] or ⌘[O] or double-click on an item in the list
New Folder	⌘[N]
Eject	⌘[E]
To move through folders and disks:	
To the next available disk	⌘[→]
To the previous available disk	⌘[←]
Up one folder level	⌘[↑] or click on the disk icon
Down into the folder	⌘[↓] (or [Return] or [Enter] to trigger the Open button)
To move through the list:	
To move up and down through the list	[↑] and [↓]
To jump to a specific file	Type as many letters as necessary to differentiate the file from the ones before and after it alphabetically

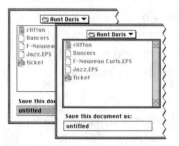

The background shows the standard state of the Save dialog. In the foreground, the list box is activated so that typing selects an item in the list rather than names the document.

In a Save dialog, only the text box or the list box is active at any one time (since typing could be naming the file or selecting from the list). To activate one box or the other, click in it or use [Tab] to move back and forth.

When the text box is active, either the cursor is blinking or text is selected; when the list box is active, there's a dark frame around it.

Using special characters to sort files (SZA/JK). File names are alphabetized in both list views on the desktop and in list boxes inside Open and Save dialogs. If you know the Mac's alphabetizing rules, you can force any document or folder you want to the top (or bottom) of any list by changing its name slightly.

Numbers come before letters, so *9* is sorted before *A*. Punctuation marks are sorted before, after, or between the numbers and letters, according to their ASCII codes (a standard for all computers that assigns a number to every character).

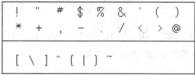

The punctuation symbols you can use to sort files before alphabetic characters (top) and the ones that sort after alphabetic characters (bottom).

Option characters—the ones you get by holding down Option or Shift Option when you type—are also sorted before, after, or between alphanumeric characters, depending on the character.

The startup screen (SZA). Replace the boring "Welcome to Macintosh" box at startup with a graphic of your choice. Take any PICT-type graphic (covered in Chapter 15) and name it StartupScreen—capitals don't matter, but be sure to leave out the space. Drop it in your System Folder (*not* in the Startup Items folder) and you'll see that picture instead of the Welcome dialog next time you start up.

Turning off the Trash warning (SZA/Charles Rubin). When you use the Empty Trash command, the Mac asks you if you're sure you want to proceed. If you find this tiresome, you can disable the warning. Select the Trash icon and use the Get Info command (⌘ I); uncheck the Warn Before Emptying checkbox in the Trash's Info window. If you like the warning in most cases (because it gives the total number of files in the Trash and the space they take up on the disk) but want to turn it off temporarily, hold down Option while you select the Empty Trash command from the menu (this actually reverses the Warn Before setting in the Info window).

Startup order (SZA). The icon in the upper-right corner of your desktop is that of the *startup disk*, the one with the System Folder on it—usually, it's your internal hard drive. But you might have more than one device with a System Folder available to the Mac at startup—a floppy disk, a CD, an external hard drive, and so on. Here's the order in which the Mac scans its devices for a startup folder—the first one it finds "wins"!

1. floppy drives (first, the internal; then it checks for a second internal drive and then an external drive)

2. the device identified in the Startup Disk control panel

3. internal hard drive

4. external SCSI devices, starting with the one with the highest ID number

5. back to the floppy drive (in case you didn't get that disk in fast enough at startup)

When the Mac can't find a startup disk at all, it puts up a disk icon with a flashing question mark in it.

On the Desktop

The drag-launch (SZA/Nicholas Lavroff/JK). You can open a document from the desktop by dragging its icon onto an application icon; if the application is capable of opening the document, it will. This doesn't sound any easier than double-clicking on the document icon, but the trick is that you can drag a document onto an application *other* than the one that created it—drag a plain text file onto Word, for instance, for it to open there instead of in SimpleText, as it would otherwise. (SimpleText comes with your system software—it's described in Chapter 3.)

The Option**-copy option** (SZA/DD). As mentioned before, dragging an icon from one folder to another on a disk (or between the disk and the desktop) moves the icon from one location to another. But if you hold down Option while you drag an icon, a *copy* is placed in the new location while the original stays put. (This copy operation is automatic if you're dragging from one disk to another.)

Desktop patterns (SZA). Even a color Mac starts out with a gray screen (actually, it's a black-and-white pattern that looks gray), but you can change it with the Desktop Patterns control panel. Click through the selections and when you find one you like, click the Set Desktop Pattern button. Hold down Option, and the button changes to Set Utilities Pattern: click it, and the current pattern will be used as the background for desk accessories such as the Calculator.

Launcher folders (SZA). Create subsets of your Launcher items by creating folders inside the Launcher Items folder and giving each a name that begins with the bullet character (•) or Option 8. Each of the folder names (minus the bullet) appears at the top of the Launcher window as a button; click on a button and the window displays the contents of the folder.

Group your Launcher items by creating special subfolders inside the Launcher Items folder.

Icons

Selecting icons from the keyboard (SZA/JK). You can select an icon in a Finder window without scrolling around to find it first. Type the first few letters of its name—just enough to differentiate it from any other icon in the window (sometimes you'll need only one letter)—and the icon gets selected. You can also select icons in alphabetical order by pressing Tab, and in reverse-alphabetical order by pressing Shift Tab. As if that weren't enough, you can select the next item in any direction by using the appropriate arrow keys. These keyboard-selection techniques work in both icon and list views.

Locking files (SZA). A locked file can't be deleted or modified, although a locked document can be opened for reading. To lock a file, select its icon on the desktop, choose the Get Info command, and click in the Locked checkbox. To unlock a file, uncheck the checkbox.

On the desktop, it's easy to tell if an icon is locked without opening the Info window: A locked file's name can't be changed, so you won't be able to select its name for editing.

Cleaning up windows and the desktop (SZA). Use the Clean Up command on the Special menu to neatly align your icons to the invisible grid in icon-view windows. If no windows are active, the command changes to Clean Up Desktop and will neaten the loose icons you have hanging around. Change the grid from straight to staggered with the Views control panel.

Hold down Option while you choose the Clean Up command, and it changes to Clean Up by Name, or Clean Up by Size, or another choice—whatever sorting criterion you last used for that window in a list view.

Faster name editing (SZA). Sometimes it takes two or three seconds for an icon's name to be ready for editing after you click on it. But you can have instant access by moving the mouse even slightly as soon as you click on the icon's name.

Trashing locked icons (SZA). Normally, a locked icon can't be erased; if you put it in the Trash and use the Empty Trash command, you'll get a dialog telling you so. But you don't have to unlock the item: Hold down Option while you choose Empty Trash and locked items will be erased.

Windows

HOT TIPS

Zooming to fill the screen (SZA/DD). If you want a window to open to the full screen instead of just enough to display its contents, hold down (Option) while you click in the zoom box. A full-screen size on the desktop is one that leaves a strip of desktop along the right edge so you can see the disk and Trash icons.

Automatic window closing (SZA/JK). There are several ways you can close windows automatically on the desktop:

- Hold down (Option) while you click in a close box, or when you use the Close command, or while you press (⌘)(O), and all desktop windows close.

- Press (Option) while you double-click any Finder item; as the item opens, its window closes.

- Hold down (Option) when you choose something from a window's Path menu, and the current window closes as the new one opens.

Automatic window hiding (SZA). Hold down (Option) while you move from one application to another (by selecting from the Application menu or by clicking in an exposed window), and windows belonging to the application you're leaving are all hidden. (*Hiding* a window is different from *closing* it: When you close a window, you have to save its contents or lose them, but hiding a window means it's just out of sight temporarily.)

To automatically hide the Finder's windows, as well as loose desktop icons, uncheck the Show Desktop When In Background option in the General Controls control panel.

Keyboard window scrolling (SZA). You can scroll desktop windows without touching the mouse by using (Pg Up) or (Pg Dn) which is like clicking in the vertical scroll bar above or below the scroll box; pressing (Home) or (End) is like dragging the scroll box to the top or bottom of the scroll bar.

Moving inactive windows (SZA). You can move an inactive window *without* making it the active one by holding down (⌘) as you drag the window's title bar.

List Views

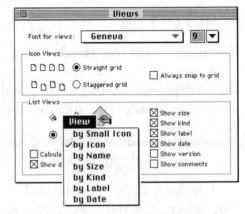

The checkboxes you select in the Views control panel (at the lower right) determine the choices in the View menu.

Changing your point of views (SZA). The choices listed in the View menu for sorting in text views match the columns of information showing in the Finder's windows. You can add or delete those columns by using the checkboxes in the Views control panel: Any checked item appears both as a column in the windows and a choice in the View menu.

Sorting by different categories (SZA). You don't have to use the Views menu to sort a window's contents: Just click on the column name in the window's header (beneath the title bar). The column that the window is currently sorted by is underlined in the header.

Expanding and collapsing list views (SZA/JK). When you expand a folder in a list view by clicking on its arrow, the level of expansion inside that folder matches however you left it last. If you want it to expand as far as possible—with all its inner folders expanded—hold Option as you click on the arrow. Holding Option as you collapse a folder collapses its contents so that the next time you expand it, you'll see only a single level of its contents.

2 | The Macintosh Family

The Mac is no one-size-fits-all computer. With new models introduced every six months or so, and dozens of discontinued ones on the used market, it's hard to decide what's right for you. The good news (unless you're trying to sell a used Mac) is that each year's new Macs nearly always do more, work faster, and cost less than the ones introduced in the previous year.

In this chapter, we explain what makes a Mac, so you'll understand what makes one model different from another—to help you if you're looking for a new Mac, or just better understand the one you have.

Contributors

Sharon Zardetto Aker (SZA) is the chapter editor.

David Hauer (DH) is a Macintosh consultant and BMUG helpline staffer. When that gets old, he plays notes, or writes them.

John Kadyk (JK) has been involved with all six editions of this book. When he's not working with the Mac, he likes playing music and biking.

Richard Wolfson (RW) is a college professor who teaches, among other things, educational technology, and is the co-author of *The PowerBook Companion*.

Contents

The Inside Story

It used to be easy to buy a Mac—for years, the single current model was replaced by a new one. When Apple first offered a multi-model Mac line, it was still simple because the differences were so obvious ("Oh, you want *color?*"). But in the years since, Apple has created—and killed—many Mac product lines, and most included several models whose differences were quite minor. To add to the confusion, lines were not only added and dropped, they were also sometimes blended (Centris and Quadra) or given a new niche (Performa).

So, unfortunately, it becomes more and more important that you understand the basics of the Mac's component parts. That way, when you read a description of some model or another, you can judge whether it adds up to what you want and need. That's what this section's all about.

Processors and Clocks   (SZA)

At the very heart of the computer is—to mix a metaphor—its brain, which goes by many names: *CPU, central processing unit, microprocessor, processor chip, processor,* or, simply, *chip* (although there are other kinds of chips, too, including memory chips). Just what does a processor chip process? Instructions—many millions are sent to the chip every second by applications and system software.

CPU and CPU. The CPU is the central processing unit, but ever since the modular Mac II came out, "CPU" has also referred to the actual box that holds the CPU (and the motherboard, and slots, and other things).

The PowerPC processor. Most current Macs—that is, the ones currently being sold—are based on the PowerPC chip made by IBM and Motorola. These chips use a special technology called *RISC (reduced instruction set computing)* to churn out more raw power than the previous chip technology, *CISC (complex instruction set computing)*. So far, there are four different PowerPC chips in use: the 601 in the original Power Macs; the 603, a lower-cost version of the 601; the 603e, a version for the PowerBook with a low power draw; and the 604.

The 68000 family. Until the introduction of the PowerPC chip, Macs used processing chips from the Motorola 68000 series, starting with the 68000 itself, and progressing through the 68020, 68030, and 68040. The PowerBook 190 was the last model to be manufactured with a Motorola 68000-series processor.

A quick look at some of the capabilities of the chips in this family shows how technology continually improves and speeds a computer's performance. You can skip this list if you hate the technical stuff—but you'll find all the terms explained later in this chapter.

- The 68000 was given that name because it has 68,000 transistors on it (the 68040 has well over a million!). Although it was considered a 32-bit chip, it handles only 16-bit chunks of information internally.

- The 68HC000 is a special low-power version of the 68000 chip. ("Low-power" refers to the electricity needed to keep it running, not to its capabilities; it was used in the battery-powered PowerBook 100.)

- The 68020, introduced in the Mac II, deals with 32-bit chunks internally and has a 256-byte instruction cache to hold frequently accessed information.

- The 68030 includes a 256-byte data cache in addition to the instruction cache and provides two 32-bit data paths instead of one so it can handle twice the information traffic. The '030 includes a *paged memory management unit*, known as a PMMU, something that's necessary for System 7's virtual memory feature.

- The 68040 has instruction and data caches 16 times larger than the ones in the '030, and has built-in capabilities for most of the functions of the math coprocessor that had to be added separately to earlier machines.

- The 68LC040 is a special, low-cost version of the 68040 that doesn't include the math coprocessor functions.

Clock speed (SZA/JK/DH). Information marches through a processor chip to the beat of a very special drum: a quartz crystal that vibrates in response to an electric current. The pulses are so rapid that they're measured in *megahertz*—millions of cycles per second. A chip that runs at 80MHz is beating 80 million times a second. *[So, in one minute it beats more often than your heart will in your entire lifetime!—SZA]* This crystal "clock" determines the *clock rate*, or *clock speed*, or simply, the *speed* of your processor.

Nicknames   (SZA)

The 68000 chip is called the "sixty-eight thousand," but other chips in the series aren't pronounced as real numbers; the 68020, for instance, is "sixty-eight oh-twenty." But that's a mouthful, so the chips are abbreviated, in writing and speaking, to the numbers that differentiate them: '020 ("oh-twenty"), '030 ("oh-thirty"), and '040 ("oh-forty"). If you're referring to a 68000-series chip without meaning any specific one, you use the number 680x0 or the abbreviation 68K (the K is for the "kilo" prefix that means 1000).

Clock speed is useful as a measure of relative speed only between processors of the same type: All other factors being equal, a Mac with a 601 chip running at 80MHz is faster than a 601 running at 60MHz. But a more advanced chip can outperform an earlier one even if the clock speed on the new chip is slower than the older one.

Coprocessors

A *coprocessor* is a secondary processor that specializes in a specific kind of computation, relieving the main processor of some work, and speeding up the tasks it's specifically designed for. A computer can have more than one kind of coprocessor.

FPU (SZA/JK/DH). The most common coprocessor used on 68K Macs is the *math coprocessor*, also called a *floating-point unit*, or *FPU*. (The *floating-point* part of the phrase refers to a type of number.) It's so common, in fact, that if someone refers to "the coprocessor," that means the FPU, even though there are other coprocessors. The fancy math handled by an FPU doesn't make a difference to basic spreadsheet calculations, but it greatly accelerates the kind of sophisticated calculations used in programs like three-dimensional modeling and animation. In addition to the speed benefit, an FPU keeps things more accurate, working with up to 18 places after the decimal point instead of the basic processor's 14-place accuracy.

A Mac's FPU is a Motorola chip; the Mac II uses the 68881 coprocessor, while the '030 Macs use its successor, the 68882. Macs with '040 processors don't need FPUs because the coprocessor's functions are built into the '040 itself. Power Macs don't need FPUs either.

PMMU (SZA). A *PMMU (paged memory management unit)* is a coprocessor whose functions were built into the 68030 and later chips, so you don't hear much about it anymore. But because the Mac II, the first color model, had a 68020, it used to be a big deal. Since System 7's virtual memory feature needs PMMU functions to work, the phrase "an '030 or a Mac II with a PMMU" as a system requirement description was widespread for awhile.

SoftwareFPU   (RW/JK)

Some programs need an FPU to run at a reasonable speed; some need an FPU to run at all. If your 68K Mac doesn't have an FPU, John Neil's shareware SoftwareFPU can usually take care of the problem. (Although some applications check the hardware environment for an actual FPU and won't run unless it's found, SoftwareFPU is effective in the majority of cases.)

And, if you're running a 68K version of an FPU-needy program on a Power Mac, you can upgrade SoftwareFPU to a special "fat" version that includes the native PowerPC code.

DSP (JK/DH). The '040-based AV Macs include a *digital signal processor* chip—a DSP—that some programs use to allow or expedite the processing of certain types of data (typically, sounds or images). To get the full benefit of the DSP, software has to be designed to take advantage of it. There's a plug-in file available on-line, for example, called **AV DSP Power** that enables Adobe's PhotoShop (there's lots about that in Chapter 15) to use the DSP chip. With the plug-in, screen redraws and filters are 10 to 30 percent faster.

General Terminology

Here are a few miscellaneous, but important, hardware concepts.

ROM (SZA/JK). ROM stands for *read-only memory*. It's like software that's hard-wired into your Mac—basic, permanent information that tells it things like how to load up the operating system when you turn it on. As Macs evolve, new capabilities—like the ability to display colors—get added to their ROMs.

The ROMs in the Mac have grown from storing 64K of information in the first Mac to 4MB (megabytes) in the Power Macs. In some cases, installing a system specifically made for an older Mac will let that Mac fake the capabilities of a newer one because the later ROM information goes into the System file. In other cases, a separate file can be added to the System Folder to provide capabilities not in the older Mac's ROMs. Of course, in many cases, you're just out of luck and can't get the capabilities of a newer machine no matter what.

Clean and Dirty ROMs   (SZA)

Starting with the Mac II, Macs were theoretically able to address more than eight megabytes of memory. But it was in theory only for that model, as well as for the Mac II, IIx, and IIcx because of their ROMs—later known as "dirty" ROMs. For these machines to use more than 8MB of RAM, you need an extension called Mode32. (This is covered in more detail in Chapter 4.)

Logic, mothers, and daughters (SZA/JK). There are many things inside a Mac's case, but none so important as the all-important *logic board*, or *motherboard*. The "board" part of each phrase comes from *printed circuit board*, which is a board with silver tracings (the circuits); the little black boxes on these boards are chips. The logic board is what makes a computer a computer. Continuing the matriarchal metaphor, a board connected to motherboard—either soldered directly onto it or inserted in a slot—is called a *daughterboard*.

The data bus (SZA/JK). Macs have an internal pathway—called the *data path* or *data bus*—for shuttling data around. The wider and faster this path is for a given processor and clock speed, the faster the Mac can handle tasks that require a lot of data transfer. A Mac's data path usually performs at the same speed as its processor, but sometimes it's slower, which slows down the overall operation of the computer.

A narrow data path can cripple a computer, no matter what its speed. For example: The LC had an '020 processor running at 16MHz, while the LC II had a much improved '030 processor at 16MHz. The LC II should have been faster because of its better processor, but the two machines had almost identical performance because they both had 16-bit data buses.

The 68000-based Macs have a data path that's either 16 or 32 bits wide; the Power Macs use a 64-bit-wide bus.

Memory

One of the most essential computer components—*memory*—is so important that it's always included in the specs when a computer is being sold.

RAM (SZA/JK). A computer's *RAM (random access memory)*, usually referred to simply as *memory*, is an electronic work space. Whenever the Mac is on, it keeps at least part of its system software and any opened programs and documents

An insect-like memory chip, and chips mounted on a SIMM.

in memory. So, the amount of RAM in a Mac determines how many files and applications you can have open at once, and how large they can be. All Macs come with some RAM inside, but you can buy and install more.

Physically, RAM comes as little black memory chips soldered directly to the motherboard (for built-in memory) or onto little boards called *SIMMs* or *DIMMs* (for memory that you add). There's lots more about memory in Chapter 4.

Memory caches (SZA/JK). A *memory cache* (pronounced "cash," not "ca-shay" or "catch") increases a Mac's performance by storing frequently used instructions either in the processor itself or in high-speed memory outside the processor; that way, they don't have to be fetched from regular RAM (which is slow in comparison) every time they're needed. A *Level 1* cache is one built into the processor; a *Level 2*, or *secondary*, cache is an external one installed in a slot on the motherboard. Most Power Macs come with secondary caches.

GOOD FEATURE

The DMA chip (JK). Processors spend a lot of time supervising the transfer of data between memory and hard drives, floppy drives, and other devices; that's time taken

Bits, Bytes, and Beyond   (SZA)

The units of measure used in computerdom are based on the binary numbering system that's at the heart of the computer's processor (in contrast to the human-friendly *decimal*, or *base 10* system). Both memory and disk space (and, therefore, file size) are measured in these binary-based units.

The smallest unit of information a computer deals with is a *bit*, a word that comes from the phrase *binary digit*. Eight bits together make a *byte*, but the measurements we use after that are a sometimes confusing blend of binary numbers and the words we use in our decimal system of numbering.

The prefix *kilo*, for instance, stands for *thousand*, but a *kilobyte* is not 1,000 bytes: It's 1,024 bytes, the closest "round" number to a thousand in binary. The kilobyte, abbreviated as *K*, is something you're probably familiar with as a unit measurement for file sizes.

With *mega* standing for million, a *megabyte* is roughly a million bytes. Just as 1,000,000 in decimal is actually 1,000 thousands, the megabyte (abbreviated *MB*) is 1,024 kilobytes. The amount of memory in your computer, and the size of many hard drives are usually given in terms of megabytes, or *megs*.

The next unit is the *gigabyte*, which—as you may have anticipated—is 1,024 megabytes. The term is often shortened to *gig,* and is abbreviated *GB.* Many hard drives now offer a gig of storage; in fact, drives that offer about 500 megabytes of room are sometimes referred to as a "half gig" in size.

Here's a quick review:

```
        8 bits = 1 byte
    1,024 bytes = 1 kilobyte
      1,024K = 1 megabyte
    1,024MB = 1 gigabyte
```

away from other things the processor could be doing. Some Macs—including Power Macs and the AV Macs—have *direct memory access* (DMA) chips, which handle this processing, either for specific types of devices (like disk drives) or for input and output from all sources.

VRAM (SZA/JK). It takes a lot of memory to keep a display going. Back when Mac screens were black-and-white, 9-inch displays, this wasn't such a problem. But the bigger a display is, and the more colors you want showing at one time, the more memory you need. Early Macs grabbed screen memory from the general system memory, but later Macs use separate, specialized memory called, logically enough, *video memory*, or *VRAM*.

Older models like the IIsi and IIci, and the Performa 630 and 6100, Quadra 630, and Power Mac 6100 still use part of regular memory (DRAM) instead of VRAM for the screen. This can noticeably slow down the performance of the non-PowerPC models because memory is being shared between the monitor and whatever software is running. The PowerPC is generally fast enough that you won't notice the penalty being extracted for DRAM-based video support.

BAD FEATURE

Storage

In the beginning, Macs came with a single storage device: a 400K floppy drive and disk. The first Mac hard drive from Apple was an external 20-megabyte model (which, by the way, cost $1,500 and couldn't act as the startup disk—you had to start with a floppy and then turn control over to the hard drive!). Current models still have only a single floppy drive, but the floppies now hold 1.4MB of information. Internal hard drives of 700 to over 1,000 megabytes are the norm. And a third storage option—the CD-ROM drive—is standard equipment now.

Floppy drives (SZA/JK). Floppy drives use 3.5-inch floppy disks whose metal-shuttered plastic cases don't look all that floppy because the flimsy part is stored inside the case. Since 1990, the standard built-in floppy drive uses high-density 1.4MB floppy disks; Apple calls it the *FDHD*, for Floppy Drive High Density, but it's commonly known as the *SuperDrive*.

Hard drives (SZA/JK). The hard drive (or *hard disk*—the terms are interchangeable) is the Mac's large storage area for all your applications, files, and system software. When you're working, the computer copies data it needs from the hard disk into RAM, where the data can be accessed and manipulated much more quickly.

CD-ROM drives (SZA/JK). Unlike floppies and hard drives, which let you both store your information and get it back, a CD-ROM drive offers a one-way capability, evidenced in its very name: *compact disk read only memory*. A CD—the same shiny disc used for audio—can store as much as a large hard drive: 600 megabytes. The selection of CDs for your computer is vast; because they can store so much information, and because high-quality graphics take so much room on a disk, you'll find the fanciest, most involved game software on CDs now. On the serious side, reference materials like encyclopedias and dictionaries are also proliferating on CD. (See Chapter 18 for more on education and reference CDs.)

Expansion

No matter what basic hardware is included with your Mac, you can always add more, both inside and out.

Internal (SZA)

The earliest Macs weren't made to be opened by their owners—not that that stopped everybody! Later, the modular Macs were designed not only for a pick-and-choose approach to putting together a Mac system, but also for easy opening so a user could add internal components. As the Mac evolved, it has, for the most part, stayed modular and "openable," whether you can do it yourself or need professional help.

Slots and cards. An expansion *slot* is a connector inside the Mac where you plug in a *card* or *board* (that's the same board as in "logic board" and "motherboard"—a printed circuit board). There are many different types of slots inside an expandable Mac, but they're not always so easy to get at. Just to install memory in the 7100, for instance, requires removing the power supply, the internal hard drive, the floppy drive, and the CD-ROM drive—not a process for the faint-of-heart! So, while the illustration here is a good representation of how you might install a card into a Mac, it's not always so simple.

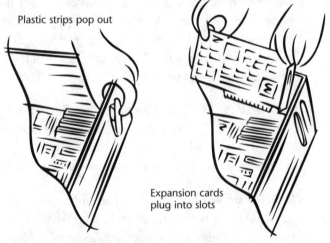

Plastic strips pop out

Expansion cards plug into slots

Installing a card in an internal slot isn't always this easy, because some slots are hard to get at, but the basics remain the same.

Basic slots. Most of the Mac's expandability comes from slots for general-purpose cards that range from processor accelerators to video controllers to an entirely different computer from the one you bought originally. There are three types of general-purpose slots:

- *PDS (Processor Direct Slot)* is a direct connection to the computer's processor. A Mac can have only a single PDS. ("PDS slot" is an accepted phrase, but it actually translates to "processor direct slot slot.")

- *NuBus* was, until fairly recently, the basic expansion slot for the Mac, with anywhere from one to six of them in an expandable Mac. NuBus is an elegant standard for handling add-in boards, with the Mac directing the signals from multiple boards. But NuBus has served its purpose and can no longer keep up with the demands of the fastest Mac models.

- *PCI (Peripheral Component Interconnect)* slots are the new standard, replacing the slower NuBus technology. Many current models use PCI slots, and all future ones will.

The type and number of these slots vary from one model to another. Some models need 7-inch NuBus cards, others take 14-inch ones; there are different kinds of PDS cards too, named for the machines in which they first appeared—SE PDS, LC PDS, and LC III PDS, for instance. In some models, using a PDS card blocks one of the NuBus slots. Then again, some models have a PDS slot that takes an adapter so you can plug in a NuBus card instead!

Specialized slots. There are a variety of specialized slots that might be inside a Mac. In addition to memory slots, which are in every Mac, you might also find a slot for a *cache card* (described a little earlier), for a DAV card (*digital audio video*, for AV Macs), or for an internal modem (referred to as a *communications slot*).

Expansion bay and PCMCIA slots. PowerBooks have two special expansion capabilities not found on desktop Macs: the expansion bay and the PCMCIA slot. The expansion bay is *not* the same thing as a "storage bay" in tower-design desktop Macs, which is merely a space (and waiting cables) to add internal storage devices. (Both the bay and PCMCIA are covered in "PowerBooks" later in this chapter.)

External

You don't need to open the Mac to add hardware. In fact, the most common and useful hardware add-ons are, by their very name—*peripheral*—outside the Mac: modems,

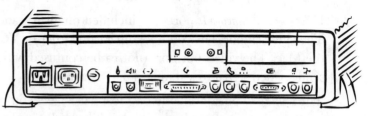

The exposed backside of a Mac. The number and position of ports vary from one Mac to another, but most are easy to identify, and only the modem and printer ports accept the same cable, so it's hard to attach something incorrectly.

printers, keyboards, scanners, and so on. The socket where you plug in a peripheral's cable is called a *port*, and there's a wide variety of them on the back of the Mac. They're sometimes referred to as *I/O ports*, for Input/Output.

The basic ports (SZA/JK). Not all Macs have all the ports listed here. In fact, if you include PowerBooks, there are some Macs with only a single port available. But most Macs provide about a half-dozen ports for standard peripherals.

✄	🖶	✆	◇	▢	◁)))
ADB	printer	modem	SCSI	monitor	sound out
🎤	‹••›	🎧	📹 IN	📹 OUT	⊕ ⊖
sound in	Ethernet	headphone	video-in	video-out	stereo in

The ports on every Mac are labeled with icons.

- The *ADB* port (*Apple Desktop Bus*—a bus being something that information travels on in a computer) is for your keyboard and mouse, and anything that replaces one or the other—a trackball, for instance. Most Macs have a single ADB port, since you can plug the keyboard into it and then plug the mouse into the keyboard.

- The *printer* port accommodates not only printers, but also serves as the main connector for Apple's AppleTalk network.

- The *modem* port is used, of course, for modems, but can also handle other serial devices, like printers. (But not printers which require AppleTalk connections, as do most LaserWriters.)

- The *SCSI* port is for external SCSI devices like hard drives, CD-ROM drives, removable storage (SyQuest and magneto-optical, for instance), and scanners. Desk Macs use a 25-pin SCSI connector; PowerBooks use a more compact one called HDI-30.

- The *display*, or *monitor port*, is on Macs that provide support for a monitor. But keep in mind that there are different levels of "support": few models can run an extra-large display from their internal video, and many are limited in the number of colors they can display on even a standard-size screen.

- *Video-in* and *video-out* ports are included on all AV and some Power Mac models. The video-in port lets you hook up a camcorder or VCR to play into a window on the Mac. The video-out port (not to be confused with the monitor port) lets you send a video signal to a standard TV or a VCR.

- The *sound out* port, available on most Macs, lets you plug in headphones or small speakers that use a standard miniplug (like Walkman headphones). All Macs already have built-in speakers.

- The *sound input* port accepts an Apple microphone (some models just have built-in mikes so you wind up talking to the screen). Some Macs have, in addition, *stereo sound input*, with separate ports for left and right input.

- The *Ethernet* port, available at least as an option on most new Macs, is for Ethernet network connections.

- There's a separate *headphone* port on some later Mac models, conveniently located on the front of the case rather than on the back.

SCSI and IDE (SZA). The internal hard drive on most Macs is a SCSI device, but some lower-priced models (to date, the LC 580, Quadra and Performa 630, Power Mac 5200, and PowerBook 150) have an IDE interface for their internal drives; IDE *(Integrated Drive Electronics)* drives are less expensive than SCSI drives. Models with IDE drives still provide an external SCSI port so you can use other SCSI devices.

If you have an IDE drive and you're not using Apple's formatting software, make sure the third-party utility you're using can handle IDE drives and not just SCSI ones.

HOT TIP

Serial and parallel (SZA). Ports can be divided into two general categories: *serial*, where the information travels in a stream of data pretty much single file, one bit at a time; and *parallel*, which is more like a multi-lane highway, letting the information march along at least eight bits abreast. Parallel, of course, is a much faster connection; the Mac's modem and printer ports are serial, while the SCSI port is parallel.

The GeoPort (SZA). The GeoPort isn't a separate port at all, but a specialized version of a serial (modem or printer) port. This port provides extra speed, so that it can be used for multiple purposes—sending a fax, printing a document, maintaining a network connection—all at the same time. The modem port on Quadra AV models is a GeoPort, and both the modem and the printer ports on Power Macs are GeoPorts. GeoPorts have room for a 9-pin connector instead of the standard 8-pin serial connector, so you can tell something's a GeoPort just by looking at it. Because the GeoPort difference is an extra hole, it can still function as a standard serial connector.

GeoPort and Telecom Adapter   (SZA/JK)

A Mac with a GeoPort can function as a speakerphone, an answering machine, and a fax modem if you get Apple's **GeoPort Telecom Adapter** ($130) so you can hook it to a phone line. The Adapter comes with the software you need for all of this, including MegaPhone from Cypress and SITcomm from Aladdin Systems. If you like to type while you talk, the **Jabra** is a headset and software necessary to use any Mac with a GeoPort as a hands-free telephone (from Jabra, $100 for standard, $170 for Quadra AV/Power Mac version).

The high-density display port (JK). Many PowerPC-based Macs have a special, over-sized display port called the *AV* or *high-density* port. The AV port is actually a combination monitor, ADB, sound, and video port that was designed for multimedia monitors like Apple's AudioVision 14 Display, which has built-in speakers, a microphone, and places to plug in a keyboard and other peripherals. It supports monitors up to mid-size or portrait, but not large 19- to 21-inch models. You need a **Power Mac Display Adapter** ($30) to connect any other monitor to an AV high-density port.

Video support and port names (SZA/JK). Macs vary in their built-in ability to support a monitor. Some can't do it at all; some have built-in video support for a screen of up to a certain size for a certain number of colors; a limited number of models actually provide support for two monitors.

Whatever the built-in support, you can always add a video card that will let you hook up a monitor that the Mac can't handle by itself, whether that means it's your only monitor, or a second one in addition to the one that the Mac runs by itself. On a smaller scale, adding more *video RAM (VRAM)* on models that are upgradable in that area will let you display more colors on the screen.

The name of the port for built-in monitor support has been gradually evolving; it's generally called the *video port*, although sometimes it's called the *monitor port*. Apple has begun referring to it as the *display port* since it introduced Macs with ports for hooking up video equipment like TVs and camcorders. If you see or hear the term *video port* or *video support*, you'll have to judge from the context whether it's referring to a monitor display or the more general video capability.

Current Model Lines

Mac model lines appear, disappear, and get reorganized more often than departments at Apple Computer—and that's quite frequently! At this writing, there are three major product lines: Power Macs, Performas, and PowerBooks. In addition, there's what you might call the "sideline": WorkGroup Servers for a special niche market.

And then there's the growing clone market: You don't have to buy a Macintosh to get a Macintosh. That is, you don't have to buy an Apple-brand Macintosh computer to have a computer that works just like a Macintosh. Of course, that's what a lot of Windows 95 users say, but that's not what we mean—we mean the genuine Macintosh OS!

Power Mac

The Power Mac line was launched in March 1994 as the first branch of the Mac family to use the new, more powerful RISC technology of the PowerPC processor chips. The first group of machines (the 6100, 7100, and 8100, using the 601 chip) was barely in the stores before they were each upgraded to faster speeds. The next round (the 5200, 6200, and 7200) included two machines with the less-expensive 603 PowerPC chip instead of the 601. A year later, the newest group (the 7500, 8500, and 9500), included two machines with the 604 processor.

The Power Macs don't have a lock on the PowerPC processor: Many Performa models use it too. In fact, it's the only processor Apple's going to be using in every Mac from now on.

Power Mac names (SZA/JK). Don't rely on the model number to tell you what's what on a Power Mac. The only number you can count on is the one after the slash in the model name (9500/120 versus 9500/132), which tells you the speed of the processor. The rest of the numbers aren't directly related to the machine's capabilities—what processor it uses, for instance, or what kind of internal expansion it provides.

So far, the only meaningful grouping is that the 6000s use a single-slot case; the 7000s provide three slots in a larger box; and, the 8000s use a 3-slot tower design. The 9500 (the only one in the 9000 series at this writing) provides six slots in a tower.

In addition, a 500 is still significant at this point: The 7500, 8500, and 9500 all use PCI slots instead of NuBus. But folks at Apple never plan ahead on model numbers, or, if they do, they seldom stick to the plan, so always check the specs of any machine instead of making assumptions based on model names.

Native and emulation modes (SZA). A Power Mac can work in two different modes: *native*, which means it's using software made to take advantage of the PowerPC chip, and *emulation*, which means it's pretending to be a 68000-based machine, running software made for earlier Macs. These modes are invisible to the user: The Mac works in whatever mode is necessary to get the job done, switching back and forth without your telling it to—in fact, without your even knowing.

Many programs still come in only a 68K version, since that runs on both types of Macs; soon, though, the high-end graphics and layout programs will be available in only PowerPC versions. Some programs actually have separate

> ### *WorkGroup Server*   (SZA/JK)
>
> A WorkGroup Server is basically a Quadra or Power Mac that's been souped up to work better as a *server*—a Mac that provides a central location for resources accessed by a network of other Macs. They're sold without monitors or keyboards. Any Mac can be used as a file server, but these machines are customized with file-server software and hardware enhancements for particularly demanding networks; some even include tape backup units.

versions, one each for 68000-based and PowerPC-based machines. Others come as something called *fat binary*, which contains instructions for both types of processors, using whatever's necessary for the machine you install it on.

The emulator slowdown (JK). Since the 68K and PowerPC processor families each have their own language for communicating with software, and neither can run programs written for the other, Apple built an interpreter (the *emulator*) into the Power Mac's ROM. This translates instructions from 68K software for the PowerPC chip and interacts with 68K software the way a 68K processor would.

BAD FEATURE

The result is that most 68K programs will run on a Power Mac, but only about as fast as they would on an '040 Mac because the translation slows things down. Also, since the emulator doesn't include an FPU, it won't let you run 68K programs that require one.

Power Mac AVs (SZA/JK). Power Mac AV models include an AV card in the PDS slot instead of an accelerated display card. The AV card (which you can order separately for some Mac models) provides a second display port and video-in and video-out ports; it gives you (not surprisingly, considering its name—the AV stands for *audio-visual*) all the special video capabilities of a 68K AV Mac, but on a faster machine.

Forms and Functions

The Mac has evolved both inside and out over the years. The familiar compact original went through only very minor changes for many models. The modular approach that started with the Mac II has many variations: the CPU box that usually sits under the monitor varies in height, width, and depth (one was so slim it was christened the "pizza box"), while the tower design, meant to stand on the floor (so much for desktop computing!), also comes in different heights.

Some later models went back to an all-in-one design, with a built-in 14-inch color monitor on top of what would normally be the CPU box. And, of course, there's the line of PowerBooks with its diversity—including the Duo model which, when inserted in its Duo Dock, looks like another style of desktop Mac.

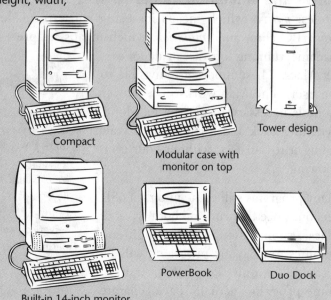

Compact

Modular case with monitor on top

Tower design

Built-in 14-inch monitor

PowerBook

Duo Dock

The body types in the Mac family are about as varied as those in the human family!

There's no DSP chip on the card (as there is in the AVs) because the PowerPC chip can handle all its functions at speeds rivaling that of a dedicated chip. There is a DAV slot on the AV board that you can use to add cards that extend the audio and video capabilities of the computer.

Performa   (SZA)

Performas were originally marketed as Apple's consumer machine: bottom-of-the-line power, prepackaged with a keyboard and not-so-great monitor, bundled with software, given a special set of "extra-easy" system software, and sold through general stores like Sears and K-Mart. In fact, to get around Apple's original agreements with its dealers, which prevented it from selling Macintoshes except through them, these machines were named "Performa" with no "Macintosh" anywhere in the name.

But everything changes: Current Performas aren't underpowered by any means; they use standard Mac software, and even the name is, officially, "Macintosh Performa."

Performa names (SZA). Performa model names are probably the worst of any in the Mac family. Sometimes the only difference from one model to another is the inclusion of a CD-ROM drive or a modem; sometimes it's an even simpler matter of the size of the hard drive. So, we wind up with model numbers like 460, 466, and 467, and 5200, 5215, and 5216! Who can keep track? We've put all the specs in the chart at the end of the chapter but there are bound to be more models every year, so make sure you figure out what you want and check the particulars of the models you're looking at. In general, the last number of a three-digit

Macintosh DOS   (SZA)

Mac models with "DOS Compatible" in their names are two, two, two computers in one. The Power Mac 6100/66 DOS Compatible, the LC 630 DOS Compatible, and the Performa 630 and 640CD DOS Compatibles each has a 486DX2 processor on a separate card inside. But that processor is to the PC world what the '040 is to the Mac world; perhaps by the time you read this, you'll find that there are Pentium-based compatible cards available for the Mac.

model number (460, 466, 467) means a minor difference like a different hard drive or modem configuration, while the major components—processor, speed, slots—are the same. For a four-digit model number, the last two digits (6200, 6215) are the ones that indicate minor component differences.

Performa system software (SZA). Performa models up until the 580 were released with a special version of the system software, the "P" version of System 7 and System 7.1. The major differences between the P and standard versions are the inclusion of At Ease (a Finder replacement), a special Launcher window, and a different General

Controls control panel. But Performas are still Macs, and the standard versions of the system software can be installed on those early models.

There's no P version of System 7.5, because the Performa is now a mainstream Mac. At Ease is still, as of this writing, included on Performas, and the Launcher is now standard system software.

Performa equivalents (SZA/JK). Because of the original marketing idea for Performas (mainstream versus Apple dealer), many of the early Performa models are basically the equivalent of some other Mac (see table).

Performa "P" system software is identified in the About This Macintosh dialog from the Finder's Apple menu.

Performa	Equivalent Mac Model
200	Classic II
400	LC II
405, 410, 430	LC II (plus modem and larger drive)
450	LC III
460, 466, 467	LC III (with faster clock speed)
550, 560	LC 550
575, 577, 578	LC 575
600, 600CD	IIvx (without cache card and FPU)
630	LC 630
630 DOS	LC 630 DOS

Mac Clones

(SZA)

In early Mac days, a *clone* was definitely a Bad Thing: an illegal (and therefore behind-the-times and/or very glitchy) copy of the Mac's ROMs and supporting hardware in a cheaper setup than you could get from Apple. Now a clone is a Good Thing, because Apple has licensed its technology to a limited number of vendors who can build Macs (under another name) with Apple's blessing and support.

Send in the clones. Clone manufacturers generally target the two extremes of the market. On the low end, they'll put together hardware bundles cheaper than those Apple offers; on the high end, they'll put together "scream machines" whose power and speed are needed by only a relatively small group of users.

The fact that so many clones are available at lower prices than the comparable Apple models is not necessarily because the units use cheaper materials (although that's a possible factor for some machines); clone manufacturers can generally offer good deals because they're not hampered by big Research and Development budgets.

Should you buy a clone? Maybe. The cautionary tone of that answer is not because a clone isn't as good as a genuine Macintosh, because it truly is a Mac under the skin. But the problem lies in the manufacturer's longevity. We're reasonably sure Apple's going to be around to support its machines years down the road, but the same can't be said of the clone manufacturers. If your clone falls apart next year and the manufacturer is out of business—who you gonna call?

As of this writing, only Power Computing has shown any staying power. Radius, originally known for its great monitors, announced high-end clones that it couldn't deliver, and the company itself is not likely to survive much longer. DayStar, known mostly for its accelerators, sells a high-priced multi-processor model that hasn't yet found its market.

In all, getting a clone in what is still the earliest stage of the Mac clone marketing is a gamble; make sure the price break you're getting is worth the gamble.

DayStar. DayStar has cloned a Monster Mac. Its flagship Genesis MP 600 uses the 150MHz PowerPC 604 processor—*four* of them! The multiple-processor approach supplies nearly three times the speed of Apple's fastest 604-based Mac. But the unit is priced at nearly $11,000, and comes with no keyboard, no internal hard drive, and no RAM. The Genesis MP 528, for $9,000, is the same setup with the processors running at 132MHz, while the $6,000 MP 300 uses two 150MHz chips.

But the real problem with the Genesis is not the price. It's the fact that unless software is specifically written to take advantage of multiple processors, they don't give you any advantage at all—and Adobe's Photoshop is the only program, at this time, that knows how to do that.

PowerComputing. PowerComputing is clone-making the right way: It offers systems configured any which way (the customer chooses the speed, the size of the internal drive, the amount of RAM, and so on), bundled with get-started software and utilities, and offered at a price below a comparable Apple-brand machine. So, the cases are clunky PC-style boxes—you want *everything?*

In fact, PowerComputing offers several options Apple doesn't. How about a built-in Iomega Zip drive that stores 100MB of information on a removable, floppy-sized cartridge? Or a model that offers both PCI and NuBus slots? (See Chapter 2 for more about slot types.)

Because PowerComputing pretty much lets you "roll your own" system, it's difficult—in fact, nigh unto impossible—to make a chart to round up its models. But here's a short list of typical late-'96 configurations and prices. (As with Mac model names, the numbers after the name indicate the processor chip and its speed; if you need help deciphering any of the other specs, such as *4x CD-ROM drive* or *1GB hard drive*, check Chapters 2 and 5 for more information.)

- *PowerCurve 601/120*, 8MB RAM (expandable to 256MB), 850MB hard drive, 3 PCI slots, 1MB VRAM, Ethernet, keyboard, and mouse: $1800. With 4x CD-ROM drive and monitor: $2300.

- *PowerWave 604/120*, 8MB RAM (expandable to 512MB), 850MB hard drive, 4x CD-ROM drive, 3 PCI slots, 2MB VRAM, Ethernet, keyboard, and mouse: $2,500. With 16MB RAM, 1GB hard drive, internal Iomega Zip drive, and monitor: $3,257.

- *PowerWave 604/132*, 24MB RAM (expandable to 512MB), 1GB hard drive, 4x CD-ROM drive, 3 PCI slots, 2MB VRAM, Ethernet, keyboard, mouse, and monitor: $4,050.

- *PowerWave 604/150*, 32MB RAM (expandable to 512MB), 1GB hard drive, 4x CD-ROM drive, internal Iomega Zip drive, 3 PCI slots, 4MB VRAM, Ethernet, keyboard, mouse, and monitor: $5,150.

PowerBooks

Although Apple's first "portable" computer—the Portable—was a joke because of its weight, the PowerBook line truly deserved to be in the then-new category of *laptop* computer: everything you need in a package small enough and light enough to fit on your lap, powered by a battery so you don't have to sit near an electric outlet.

Components and Capabilities

The PowerBook generations so far have offered four different battery technologies, three different types of screens, four different processors, and several different form factors; they've even introduced new types of connectors and connectivity.

Screen technology (RW/JK). The big division between types of PowerBook displays is not color versus black-and-white, as you might expect, but between two types of *LCD* (liquid-crystal display) technologies: *active* and *passive matrix*. Active-matrix screens provide crisp, sharp images when viewed from any angle, under any lighting condition.

**BAD
FEATURE**

Passive-matrix screens are less bright and sharp, have a narrow viewing angle, and are relatively slow to react: Drag an object on the screen, or move the cursor at a normal speed, and you'll see a trail of images left behind—move the cursor too quickly, and it totally disappears. (This is known as *submarining* because you see the cursor in its original spot, and again in its final position, but in between, where it disappears, it seems to have dipped beneath the surface of the screen.) While it's obvious that active-matrix displays are far superior, they have two major drawbacks: they're heavy, and they're expensive (on the order of $1,000 to $1,600 more for a color display).

While active-matrix displays remain the screen of choice for those who can afford it, passive-matrix technology has improved: *Dual-scan* passive-matrix displays redraw the top and bottom halves simultaneously, for double the refresh rate.

The first PowerBooks were strictly black-and-white, regardless of the screen technology. Later models offered four, and then 16 shades of gray. Finally, color showed up on PowerBooks, first on the washed-out 165c passive-matrix screen and then in the superb 180c active-matrix one. Aside from the premium you pay for color, you also pay in terms of battery power—color screens need higher backlighting, which eats up power. But with battery technology improving, a color display is a more practical option now than it was in previous years.

Screen size (SZA/JK). PowerBook screens range from 8.4 to 10.4 inches on a diagonal measurement, but, as with desktop monitors, the measurements can be deceiving. It's a screen's *pixel resolution*—how many pixels are used horizontally and vertically—that determines how much information it can actually display. The 8.4-inch screen on the 180c, for instance, displays just as much as a 14-inch monitor—640 pixels across by 480 down; things just look much smaller because the pixels themselves are tinier. By contrast, the 10-inch screen on the 180 has a resolution of 640 by 400—one-sixth less information vertically—but at a more readable size.

There's a trade-off between the number of pixels on a screen and the color depth of the display due to memory constraints; so, models like the PowerBook 5300c provide 256 colors on the standard 640-by-480 display, but let you switch to thousands of colors in a 640-by-400 display.

Note that many games assume a 640-by-480 display, so older PowerBooks, even if they're capable with their memory, hard drive, and processor speed constraints, may not be able to run many games because of the dimensions of the screen.

BAD FEATURE

Keyboards, trackballs, and trackpads (SZA). PowerBook keyboards are cramped affairs that make users guiltily dream about IBM's "butterfly" laptop keyboard that expands to full size when the case is opened. PowerBook keyboards are missing numeric keypads, of course, and models before the 500 series don't have any function keys, or even a Power On key.

Although most PowerBooks have an ADB port where you can plug in a mouse if you want to, the built-in pointing device is either a trackball or a trackpad. Trackballs come in three different sizes: one for the 100, another for all the 100-series PowerBooks, and the tiny one used in the Duo.

Trackpads were introduced with the 500s and slowly improved. The one on the 190 takes taps and double-taps right on the pad instead of your having to use the button for clicking. Oddly enough, the most expensive PowerBooks (as of this writing) have

GOOD FEATURE

> ### *The Little Things Mean a Lot* (SZA)
>
> Some of my favorite PowerBook products are tiny and relatively unimportant. **PowerBalls** ($5 each, $7 to $12 a four-pack) replace the old gray trackball with a variety of colors (or an eight-ball); mine's DayGlo Orange. Have a trackpad? Try a "tattoo," a thin mylar skin with nifty graphics ($7 for a sheet of 20 different ones). And don't forget the **PowerDoor**, a replacement I/O door for the one that constantly breaks off the back of 140–180 models; it has an opening for the phone jack, so you won't have to open the entire door (and break it off) so often. All these items are available from APS Technologies.
>
> And if you travel outside the country, you'll be boggled by the wide variety of phone jacks used around the world, but you can stay on-line if you choose one of TeleAdapt's hundreds of international phone plug adapters. They are available individually ($30) or in multipacks ($50 to $450) for various geopolitical regions. And if you don't know what you need, don't worry—TeleAdapt seems to know it all!

slightly behind-the-times trackpads that don't understand tapping, although Apple sort of promised an upgrade for them. It looks like trackpads are the only pointing device available now on any new PowerBooks, which is a shame for those of us who just don't like them.

Batteries (RW). The continuing quest for inexpensive, lightweight, but long-lasting batteries for laptop computers has resulted in five distinct battery technologies for PowerBooks (so far).

- *Lead acid*, the same type of battery as in your car, was used only for the PowerBook 100. It's particularly unfriendly (that is, *toxic*) to the environment when disposed of.

- *Nickel-cadmium (NiCad)* batteries are used by the 100-series PowerBooks.

- *Nickel-metal-hydride (NiMH)* batteries are used in the Duos and in the 500-series PowerBooks. The original one, now referred to as Type I, recharges faster and lasts longer than a NiCad. It was followed by (what else?) Type II and then Type III, which provide even more staying power.

- The *intelligent battery* in the 500-series PowerBook is a NiMH battery, but it includes a special chip to help the PowerBook manage its power needs more efficiently and provide a more accurate charge reading than is available from other, "dumb" batteries.

- *Lithium-ion (LiIon)* batteries were originally slated for use in the 5000-series PowerBooks. Now they're set for the newest PowerBook line (which isn't even announced as I write this, but should be out by the time you read this).

SCSI connections (RW/JK). PowerBooks have a different type of SCSI port than desktop Macs because there's not much room at the back of a PowerBook; it's called the *HDI-30* (for *high-density interface*, with 30 pins). To connect a standard SCSI device, you need the HDI-30 SCSI cable, which plugs into the back of the PowerBook and provides a standard 25-pin SCSI connector at the other end.

All PowerBooks except the 140, 145, 145B, and 170 provide a unique feature called *SCSI disk mode*, where you can use the PowerBook itself as an external SCSI drive. You use the **HDI-30 SCSI Disk Adapter** cable ($30, from Apple—not the same as the SCSI cable) to attach a PowerBook to a desktop Mac. You turn on the PowerBook and then the desktop Mac, and voilà: The PowerBook's internal drive shows up as an icon on your desktop Mac. The transfer of files across a SCSI connection is much faster than using a network connection.

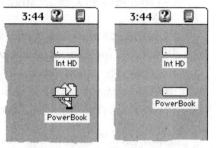

At left, a PowerBook that's connected to a desktop Mac on a network. At right, the PowerBook has been connected in SCSI Disk Mode and is treated as an external hard drive.

Sleep (RW/JK). PowerBooks use a special power-saving mode called *sleep* which drastically cuts down on battery drain. You can put a PowerBook to sleep manually (there are several ways—the Sleep command in the Finder's Special menu is the most self-evident, and later models go to sleep when you close the cover), or set it to go to sleep after a particular interval of inactivity. In sleep, the screen goes blank and the hard disk stops spinning, but those are only the most obvious results; all sorts of internal components are also powered down during sleep. A touch of a key wakes up a sleeping PowerBook instantly.

Putting a PowerBook to sleep is the usual way to turn it off rather than actually shutting down; newer models, as a matter of fact, go to sleep if you just shut the case. While Apple has always recommended shutting down a PowerBook when you're transporting it, few, if any, users ever bother—and you shouldn't, either.

Sleeping Desk Macs (David Ramsey)

PowerBooks are no longer the only Macs that go to sleep. Power Mac models 7200, 7500, and 8500 (so far) also have a sleep mode that saves energy: The screen blanks and the hard drive spins down. Only the 7200, though, also powers down parts of the logic board and meets the EPA's "Energy Star" rating of using less than 30 watts of power in its sleep state.

Video output (RW/JK). With the exception of the PowerBook 100, every black-and-white and grayscale PowerBook still "thinks" in color, and can provide color information for an external color monitor. But the 140, 145B, and 170, despite their hidden color capabilities, have no video port to accommodate a monitor hookup. Some third-party adapters were available in the first heady year of PowerBook existence, but none is available now. Other all-in-ones have video ports available, although the level of support they provide (how large a monitor, or how many colors) varies from model to model. The Duos, of course, can support a monitor when inserted into a Dock or attached to a mini dock.

PCMCIA cards (SZA). The 500-series PowerBooks introduced a new type of slot: *PCMCIA* (for *Personal Computer Memory Card International Association*). To use the slot, though, you need Apple's **PCMCIA Expansion Module** (commonly known as the "card cage," $200) to replace the left-hand battery. The 190 and the 5000-series PowerBooks have built-in, accessible PCMCIA slots.

The PCMCIA acronym is such a mouthful that the cards for the slot are commonly referred to as simply PC cards. They come in three sizes: Type I, Type II, and Type III. They all have the same surface area but their thicknesses vary. PCMCIA slots usually come in pairs, but can accommodate only one Type III card because its girth blocks the second slot.

An amazing amount of functionality can be built into a PC card: Modems, memory, Ethernet connections, and combinations thereof are all on PC cards for PowerBooks, from such trustworthy vendors as VST Systems, Dayna, Farallon, and Global Village.

The expansion bay (SZA). The 5000-series PowerBooks, and the look-alike 190, include an *expansion bay*, which comes with a floppy drive in it. Pop out the floppy drive and insert hard drives, memory modules and even magneto-optical drives for the bay from third-party developers like VST Systems and APS Technologies.

Infrared networking (SZA). Everyone's getting tired of wires, and infrared is the coming thing. The 5000 PowerBooks introduced yet another new feature: infrared capability. (It's optional on the 190.) You set up an infrared network connection much the same way you work with AppleTalk, and

The Next Round of PowerBooks   (RW)

As of this writing, the PowerBook 5300 is the newest and the top-of-the-line model, but rumors run rampant about what's next. Disregarding the ones that are more wishful thinking than anything else, we're left with one very significant feature: a redesign of the expansion bay so that it can accommodate a drive for a standard CD-ROM. But the new bay will have a "double door" setup so that you can still use modules designed for the smaller expansion bay in the 5000-series PowerBook.

it's intriguing to see the network window acknowledge an interrupt of the signal and then pick it up again without having lost a bit of the data transfer.

And if you're enamored of a wireless office, check out VST's **AIRPlex** modem ($600, including the base unit), a PC-card based modem that connects by infrared to a base unit (that's plugged into a phone line) up to 50 feet away!

PowerBook Models

The 15-pound Mac Portable was Apple's humorous first entry into the portable market; it had a full-size keyboard, a trackball off to the right, and a beautiful active-matrix screen (although only a few late units came with backlighting). Now, onto the 7-pound (and less) wonders!

The PowerBook 100 (SZA). One of the three original models, the PowerBook 100, stood out not only because of its light weight (5.1 pounds) and the lack of an internal floppy drive, but also because it used the 68000 processor, a chip that had long been abandoned in desktop models. Its display is a slow passive-matrix one; it's the only PowerBook to use a lead-acid battery.

The 100-series models (SZA). The 100-series PowerBooks (with the exception of the 100 itself) are referred to as "all-in-ones" because they include an internal floppy drive; all but the 190 use the 68030 processor, and all use NiCad batteries.

- The PowerBook 140 and 170 were in the original group of PowerBook offerings. The 170 was the top-of-the-line primarily because of its beautiful active-matrix screen which, of course, added to its weight. But it bettered the 140 in several other ways, too: a faster '030 processor and an FPU. The 145 replaced the 140, its single difference being a faster clock speed. The 145B is identical—it was just redesigned internally for cheaper manufacturing. All these models have black-and-white displays and are limited to 8MB of RAM.

- The PowerBook 160 introduced the grayscale passive-matrix screen; the 165 is its twin except for a faster processor. The 165c was the first color PowerBook, but its passive-matrix screen displayed washed-out colors. The 180 was the first PowerBook to use the standard 640-by-480 pixel proportions of a desktop monitor, in a grayscale active-matrix screen. The 180c had a tiny but beautiful active-matrix color screen. All these second-round PowerBooks have a 14MB RAM limit.

- The PowerBook 150 was positioned as an entry-level PowerBook at a point when the first PowerBook models were out of production and the price tags of current models were prohibitive. At heart, it's just a 145B with a 40MB RAM limit and four levels of gray in a 600-by-480 screen—and a severely limited set of I/O ports, not even including video out.

- The PowerBook 190, released at the end of 1995, is the last of the 68K Power-Books. While it uses the low-power '040 chip, it shares most of its design with the 5000-series PowerBooks released at the same time: infrared capability, PCMCIA slots, and an expansion bay. The 190c is the color version.

The 500 series (SZA). The 500-series PowerBooks (four models offering different types of screens) provide '040 power in an all-in-one laptop design. The 68LC040 chip used in these PowerBooks (and in the Duo 280 and 280c) is a special low-power version of the chip so it uses less battery power; it's missing some of the built-in FPU functions of the standard '040 chip. The 500 PowerBooks introduced the double-battery approach, and use special "intelligent" batteries that keep track of the charge and time that's left. You can replace one of the batteries with a PCMCIA adapter (described earlier in "Components and Capabilities").

The Duos (RW). The Duos introduced a new concept in take-it-with-you computing. For traveling, you have a lightweight laptop, but back at the desk, it slips into a docking station and performs as the brains of a desktop system that includes a standard monitor and keyboard, and even slots for expansion. To keep the Duo small and light, the design called for no internal floppy drive and few ports—in fact, there's only a single serial port (for an external modem or printer), a connector for a dock, and the option of a phone jack for an internal modem. To hook up anything else to a Duo when it's not in its Duo Dock, you need a mini-dock that provides extra ports. So, the thrill of traveling light is often mitigated by the necessity of schlepping a bag full of extras for either planned activities (a presentation, say) or in case of emergencies (you need the **Floppy Adapter** [$95] and an external floppy drive to reinstall a corrupted system from floppies).

Duo Docks (RW). Apple's Duo Docks turn a laptop Duo into a desktop Mac. The Duo slides in the front of the Dock, creating a setup that includes an internal floppy drive, a complete set of I/O ports, NuBus slots, and a connection for an internal hard drive.

The Duo Dock II was introduced to accommodate the thicker, color Duos (although you can upgrade the original with a new top). Additional features included a math coprocessor (optional on the original), a 32K memory cache, an Ethernet port, and support for a 20-inch monitor (the original was limited to a 16-inch monitor).

Then there's the Duo Dock II+ which really should be called a "minus" instead of a "plus" because it doesn't have the math coprocessor—it's made for '040 and PowerPC Duos, which don't need an FPU.

If you don't need a full Duo Dock (and you don't *want* it when you're traveling), there are a variety of mini docks available from Apple and Newer Technologies. These small docks let you hook up a duo to floppy drives, hard disks, Ethernet networks, monitors, and other external devices.

PowerBook Specs

Model	Chip[1]	Speed (MHz)	FPU[2]	Max. RAM (MB)	Screen	Display size (diag. in.)	Colors	Pixel Resolution	Battery	PCMCIA slots	Infrared	Weight (lbs.)	"Mouse"
100	68000	16	no	8	passive	10	b&w	640x400	lead-acid			5.1	trackball
140	68030	16	no	8	passive	10	b&w	640x400	NiCad			6.8	trackball
145	68030	25	no	8	passive	10	b&w	640x400	NiCad			6.8	trackball
145B	68030	25	no	8	passive	10	b&w	640x400	NiCad			6.8	trackball
150	68030	33	no	40	passive	9.5	4 grays	640x480	NiCad			5.5	trackball
170	68030	25	yes	8	active	10	b&w	640x400	NiCad			6.8	trackball
160	68030	25	no	14	passive	10	16 grays	640x400	NiCad			6.8	trackball
165	68030	33	no	14	passive	10	16 grays	640x400	NiCad			7	trackball
165c	68030	33	yes	14	passive	10	256	640x400	NiCad			6.8	trackball
180	68030	33	yes	14	active	10	16 grays	640x400	NiCad			6.8	trackball
180c	68030	33	yes	14	active	8.4	256	640x480	NiCad			7.1	trackball
190	68LC040	33	no	40	passive, dual-scan	9.5	16 grays	640x480	NiCad[3]	2	(opt)	6	trackpad
190cs	68LC040	33	no	40	passive, dual-scan	10.4	256 colors	640x480	NiCad[3]	2	(opt)	6.3	trackpad
520	68LC040	25	no	36	passive	9.5	16 grays	640x480	NiMH	(cage)		6.3	trackpad
520c	68LC040	25	no	36	passive	9.5	256 thousands	640x480 640x400	NiMH	(cage)		6.4	trackpad
540	68LC040	33	no	36	active	9.5	16 grays	640x480	NiMH	(cage)		7.1	trackpad
540c	68LC040	25	no	36	active	9.5	256 thousands	640x480 640x400	NiMH	(cage)		7.3	trackpad
5300	603e	100		64	passive, dual-scan	9.5	16 grays	640x480	NiCad[3]	2	yes	5.9	trackpad
5300cs	603e	100		64	passive, dual-scan	10.4	256	640x480	NiCad[3]	2	yes	6.2	trackpad
5300c	603e	100		64	active	10.4	256 thousands	640x480 640x400	NiCad[3]	2	yes	6.2	trackpad
5300ce	603e	117		64	active	10.4	thousands	800x600	NiCad[3]	2	yes	6.2	trackpad
Duos													
210	68030	25	(Dock)	24	passive	9	16 grays	640x400	NiMH			4.2	trackball
230	68030	33	(Dock)	24	passive	9	16 grays	640x480	NiMH			4.2	trackball
250	68030	33	(Dock)	24	active	9	16 grays	640x400	NiMH			4.2	trackball
270c	68030	33	yes	32	active	8.4	256 thousands	640x480 640x400	NiMH			4.8	trackball
280	68LC040	33	no	40	active	9	16 grays	640x480	NiMH			4.2	trackball
280c	68LC040	33	no	40	active	8.4	256	640x480	NiMH			4.8	trackball
2300c	603e	100		56	active	9.5	16 grays	640x400	NiMH			4.8	trackpad

Notes:

1 6xx is PowerPC chip; others are Motorola

2 Not an issue for '040 and PowerPC chips

3 Can run on, but not charge, LiIon batteries

The 5000 series (SZA). The four models of the 5000 series got off to a bumpy start: Consumers complained about the absence of a CD-ROM drive, the supply fell far short of demand, and a few early problems with lithium-ion batteries cast a pall over the new lineup. But the 5000-series machines are cutting edge as of this writing, incorporating all the best of the features described earlier in "Components and Capabilities": PowerPC processors, 64MB RAM expansion, 10.4-inch screens (on three of the four), infrared capability, PCMCIA slots, and an expansion bay.

Apple is backtracking on the battery issue for these models and will supply only NiCads for them. LiIons will come with the newest PowerBook models and, although the new battery will run a 5000 PowerBook, the 5000 models won't be able to recharge them.

Older Macs

You don't need the latest technology (they don't call it the *cutting* edge for nothing!) to get a lot of productive work done. There's plenty of life left in the pre-Power Mac models. (For more on this issue, see "Is an Older Mac Usable?" in Appendix C.)

The Previous Generation (SZA)

The generation of Macs before whatever is the current model line always includes perfectly fine, workable machines that, for the most part, can run current software, even if they can't match the newest speed demons. With the exception of software written especially for PowerPC-based Macs (and that includes the long-awaited System 8 operating system), '040-based machines can still handle all your needs.

Centris. The short-lived Centris line debuted in early 1993, in the midst of a veritable explosion of new Mac models; it was the first to use the '040 processor. The 610 runs at 20MHz, has no FPU, and offers a single slot that can be used for either a NuBus or a PDS card. The original 650 version runs at 25MHz, has an FPU, and offers one PDS and three NuBus slots. Within a year, these models were sucked into the Quadra line in Apple's effort to streamline its offerings.

Quadra. The Quadras derived their name from the '040 chip. They introduced the "tower" style case that offers bays for extra internal storage devices; they were also the first Macs to include Ethernet network connections.

Quadra/Centris. The Centris 650, introduced with a 25MHz processor, got a boost to 33MHz and was rechristened the Quadra 650 less than a year later. So, you'll often see the name Quadra/Centris used to refer to it and to the 610, which was also renamed a Quadra after a speed boost to 25 MHz.

But in both cases there are also some other minor differences between the Centris and the Quadra models. For the 650, the Quadra offers an FPU as standard instead of optional, includes an Ethernet port, and has a 132MB instead of a 136MB memory limit. (In fact, the Centris 650 is actually closer in specs to the Quadra 800 because they have the same RAM limit.) For the 610, the Quadra provides an optional FPU (instead of no possibility) and Ethernet capability.

Ephemeral Macs   (SZA)

Did you ever hear of the Mac TV? An all-in-one design, 32MHz-'030 with an 8MB RAM limit, a CD-ROM drive, a 14-inch color monitor, stereo speakers—and a TV tuner, all in a consumer-electronics black casing? It was an odd animal, with very limited availability during its short lifetime, so don't be surprised if you never knew of its existence.

There are other Mac models whose names are sometimes bandied about, yet it's hard to find solid information about them. This is usually because the model was strictly for the overseas market. The IIvi, for instance, was basically the same as the IIvx; the Color Classic II was a slightly improved version of the now-defunct compact unit; and, the 5300 (not to be confused with the PowerBook 5300) is a 100MHz Performa 5200.

The Centris 660AV and the Quadra 660AV, on the other hand, are absolutely identical.

The AV models (SZA/JK). The Quadra and Centris AV models have special features related to audio and video, and telephone communications, made possible by their DSP coprocessor (described earlier). They can record and play back video and CD-quality stereo sound, making them well-suited to people who design multimedia presentations, or those who like experimenting with digital audio and video recording. They can output directly to TV or tape using NTSC, PAL, or S-video signals.

Oldies But Goodies   (SZA)

A fast '030-based machine is still viable, as long as you up the memory and get a larger hard drive to accommodate memory- and space-hungry applications.

The II Line. The Mac II line started with, what else—the Mac II, which was the first *modular* Mac. It had no built-in screen but came with slots so you could add a video card of your choice (not that there was much choice then) and other cards as they became available. The Mac II was the first to go beyond the 68000 processor chip; it uses the 68020, while all the other Macs in the line use the '030 chip.

Just for Fun   (SZA)

There are lots of nifty little things hidden in the older Mac models. (Maybe there are things in the newer Macs too, but we haven't found them yet.)

- There's a secret message in the Mac Plus. Press the interrupt switch at the left side of the computer. Type *G 40E118* (type the space and use a zero, not the letter O), then press `Return`.

- The SE has the same secret message. Press the interrupt switch and type *G 40E118* and press `Return`.

- The SE also has a built-in slide show. Press the interrupt switch, type *G 41D89A*, then press `Return`.

- For the SE/30's secret message, press the interrupt switch and type *DM 4082E853 20* (type both spaces!) and press `Return`.

- The IIci doesn't have a message—it has a picture of the design team buried in it, and it's more complicated to find. Set the Mac's date to 9/20/89, set the monitor to 256 colors, and restart while holding down `⌘``Option``C``I`.

- The IIfx design team left its picture inside, too: Set the clock to 3/19/89, the monitor to 256 colors, and then restart holding down `⌘``Option``F``X`.

In each case, restart the Mac by using the reset switch.

During the five-year life span of the II line, six other models came out:

- The IIx introduced the '030 chip and included an FPU; it also was the first to use 1.4MB floppy drives.

- The IIcx was a slightly faster IIx, with three NuBus slots instead of six.

- The IIci ran at 25MHz instead of its predecessors' 16MHz, and was the first Mac to have a built-in video card and a cache card slot.

- The IIsi, meant as a low-cost alternative to the IIci, introduced the "pizza box" case, RAM on the motherboard, and a sound input port with a microphone.

- The IIvx replaced the IIci, and provided an innovation that's now standard: an internal CD-ROM drive.

- The top of the II line was the IIfx, with its 40MHz processor and six NuBus slots.

The LC line. The LC line was meant to be the low-cost alternative to other Macs (that's what the "LC" stands for) and they were, for a while. But once the Performas—that other low-cost alternative—were no longer limited to stores like Sears, the LC family became an educational-institution-only line before it just faded away.

The LC models range from the original LC with its 16MHz '020 chip to the later '040 models, but they're all severely limited in expansion possibilities, with no NuBus or PCI slots.

Classics. The first Mac Classic was a throwback in more than just the return to a compact case: It also returned users to a 9-inch black-and-white screen and the pokey 68000 processor, with no FPU and a 4MB RAM limit—hardly better than the long-dead Mac Plus. The Classic II bettered the situation with a 16MHz '030 chip and the ability to address up to 10MB of memory. The Color Classic finally put a color screen into a classic case, allowed for an optional FPU, and provided a PDS slot. But to no avail: Performa models were finally offered as all-in-one units with larger screens, and no one wanted a compact after that!

The Classic has a unique feature: a *ROM disk* that lets you start up the machine with the built-in System 6.0.3 without any disk. To access it, you start up while holding down ⌘ Option X O .

HOT TIP

Ancient History (SZA)

How can we not mention, at least in passing, the Macs that started it all, and their immediate successors?

- The original Mac, which we retroactively refer to as the 128K, was ground-breaking in concept, design, and execution—all in 128K of memory, with a single, 400K floppy drive. The so-called Fat Mac, with quadruple the memory (all of 512K), was introduced about 10 months later. (The upgrade to 512K of RAM for the original model cost $1,000—for 384K of memory! That's over $2,600 per meg!) The 512Ke, released the following year, offered an 800K drive.

- The Mac Plus came out two years after the first Mac, with an 800K floppy drive, a SCSI port for a hard drive (even though there was no hard drive available), and a full megabyte of memory, expandable to 4MB.

- The Mac SE showed up more than a year after the Plus, with an internal slot (that you couldn't get at), the ADB connector for keyboard and mouse, and a second floppy or an internal hard disk; later production models included the SuperFloppy drive. The SE/30 introduced the '030 chip and the FPU, and was the first compact Mac to break the 4MB RAM barrier.

~~~~~~

Upgrades

"Upgrading" really refers to any hardware improvement—adding memory, getting a larger (or second) hard drive, adding a CD-ROM drive if there wasn't one included originally. But in this section we're referring to more gut-level upgrades: getting more processing power with new or accelerated processor chips.

Keep in mind that changing any specific component of one Mac model to match another doesn't necessarily mean that you then have all the capabilities of the better model; there's internal circuitry and speeds to consider, as well as a model's internal expandability and external ports.

PowerPC Upgrades

I've never been one to insist that the latest and greatest Mac is always the one to get, but the truth is that non-PowerPC Macs, at this point, have an extremely limited life span because so much software, and even the newest operating system (System 8) will run only on the PowerPC chip. Luckily, the later 68K models can be upgraded to a PowerPC chip. There are two basic approaches to turning your 68K Mac into a PowerPC Mac: add a card with a PowerPC processor, or replace the current 68K logic board with a PowerPC logic board.

Upgrade cards (SZA/JK). For the most part, an added PowerPC card goes into the PDS slot of an '040 machine, and gives you two computers in one case (you have to restart to switch from one to the other). This flexibility is an advantage if you're going to keep using 68K applications, since they'll often run faster on your old processor than under the upgrade card's 68K emulator.

In the evolving world of software, however, issues like this—how to bridge the "old" and "new" machines, processors, or even operating systems—fade in importance as time goes on and everything is made to work on the newer system. In fact, Apple seemed to make the issue fade a lot faster than many users did, discontinuing certain PowerPC upgrade cards only months after announcing them. Luckily, third-party vendors like DayStar have stepped into that particular void.

Board replacement (SZA/JK). Many later-model 68K Macs which have the same "body" as certain PowerPC models can be turned into the PowerPC model by a logic board swap (strictly an Apple product). This is more expensive than an upgrade card, but you get all sorts of PowerPC-based capabilities that you don't get with the simple upgrade card approach: GeoPorts, CD-quality sound recording and playback, and voice recognition. Also, you should note that while the processor on Apple's PowerPC upgrade card runs at twice the speed of the computer's original processor (giving you speeds of 40 to 66MHz), a new logic board has a *minimum* speed of 66MHz, and it can be upwards of 100MHz and more. At this stage of Mac development, if you're going to upgrade at all, the logic board swap is the better approach.

HOT TIP

PowerPC for PowerBooks (RW). Apple promised that the 500-series PowerBooks and the Duo 200s would be upgradable to PowerPC, but it hasn't kept its word, *exactly*. The 500-series upgrade (from Apple and from Newer Technologies) is on a daughtercard, and at this writing the word is that Apple engineers are not going to be spending enough testing time on it to warrant that the upgraded PowerBook, though it will run at PowerPC speeds, will be able to run System 8—the long-awaited new system software. It's certainly not much of an upgrade if you're locked out of the system software meant for the upgraded machine.

The Duo upgrade, on the other hand, because it's a new logic board (only available from Apple), will be totally compatible with system upgrades.

Other Upgrades

Most computer upgrades are for increasing the speed of your Mac, so it's no surprise that many of the upgrades concentrate on changing the CPU itself, or its *clock rate*. Since those aren't the only speed factors in a computer, you'll find a variety of other options as well. But think carefully before spending too much money on accelerating or otherwise enhancing an older Mac; it may be all you need to keep your system humming for a couple of years—or you may decide after only a few months that you really need a PowerPC-based Mac, and all its trimmings, after all.

Accelerators (SZA/JK). One of the basic approaches for accelerating a Mac's abilities is an *accelerator card*, which either supplants the original CPU with something faster or adds a specialized coprocessor that handles only certain specific tasks. An accelerator card usually plugs into a PDS slot; sometimes you get a CPU replacement that goes into the CPU socket or clips onto the original CPU's legs. The new CPU usually totally supplants the old one, taking over all its tasks.

But an '030 machine usually just gets a faster '030 chip (or, at best, an '040 chip), and an '040 machine a faster '040 chip. Since an '030's top speed is 50MHz and an '040's is 40MHz, that's the maximum improvement you can expect in an accelerated version.

Coprocessors (SZA/JK). Another way of accelerating a Mac is to give it a coprocessor to take some of the burden off the main processor for certain tasks, the way the FPU takes over certain math functions. A *coprocessor accelerator* (that is, a coprocessor that accelerates the Mac, not an accelerator that makes a coprocessor work faster) specializes in one area and does certain work much more efficiently than the CPU. In most cases, a coprocessor accelerator works only with an application that's been designed to use it; if your needs are very specific and there's an accelerator designed to meet them, this is definitely a way to go.

Choosing an accelerator (DH). Many accelerators come with, or can be upgraded with, additional memory, memory caches, FPUs, or other specialized acceleration. It's worth paying attention to such features, because they can have a significant impact on performance. For example, a memory cache can add another 50 percent to the speed of an '040 accelerator card but costs only about 20 percent of its price.

Speed differences between comparable accelerators from different manufacturers are likely to be slight. More important are the cards' compatibility and expandability, and the companies' customer support and trade-up policies. DayStar has the best reputation in most of those areas; its accelerators are also the only ones that let you use Apple's virtual memory.

QuickDraw acceleration (SZA). Sometimes the real bottleneck of a Mac system is not its processing speed, but how long it takes to draw information on the screen. A QuickDraw accelerator doesn't make the processor work faster but it makes the screen draw faster (QuickDraw is the set of routines in the Mac's ROM that draws things on the screen). Many video cards include QuickDraw acceleration.

Increasing clock speeds (SZA/JK). A few years back, some intrepid soul discovered that you could make a Mac IIsi run about as fast as a IIci by replacing its clock crystal with a faster one—a job that costs less than $10 in parts if you're good with soldering equipment. Now you can find upgrades—through kits or mail-in services—that do the same for the many other Mac models, including Power Macs and PowerBooks.

Such boosting depends on the fact that the processors in most of these Macs can handle a speed higher than the one for which they're rated. Boosting the clock rate isn't always a miracle: Sometimes a chip can't work faster than it was meant to; sometimes a speedier chip is crippled by slow memory; sometimes the extra heat generated by the faster chip can cause problems. A good upgrade will let you revert to the original chip speed; it might even include a fan or a heat sink that conducts extra heat away from the processor.

One company that provides these speed boosts is Newer Technologies, whose **Variable Speed Overdrives** ($150) for some of the older II models and some Quadras allow the user to fine-tune the oscillator speed until a stable level is reached; their **PowerClips** ($100 to $150) are for different Power Mac models.

Cache cards (DH). As mentioned earlier, cache cards speed up the Mac by providing a small amount—typically 32K to 512K—of high-speed RAM where the processor can quickly store and access data while it's working. (Don't confuse these with DayStar's PowerCache cards, which are actually full-blown accelerators.) Cache cards don't provide as big a speedup as accelerators, but they're less expensive. The Power Macs, '040 Macs, and the IIci, IIsi, and LC III all show significant performance improvement with the addition of a cache card.

Adding an FPU (JK). On 68K Macs, certain programs perform dramatically better with an FPU—and some require one to run at all. If you use this type of software (programs that handle sophisticated math functions, three-dimensional modeling, or high-end graphics) on a 68K-based Mac that doesn't have an FPU, you may be able to add one. The table at the end of the chapter shows which Macs have a built-in FPU; you can add one to many '020 and '030-based models.

While FPU functions are built into the standard '040 chip, the 68LC040 chip doesn't have all the FPU functions, nor can it cooperate with an external FPU; but, some companies provide a replacement for the CPU itself, to a full-fledged '040.

Apple provides FPU upgrades for the LC II, the Color Classic, and the IIsi (there's an FPU built into the adapter cards that are required to use the IIsi's expansion slot). You can also get FPU upgrades for earlier LCs (about $100) from third-party vendors like Digital Eclipse and Shreve Systems.

Adding slots and ports (JK). If your Mac is meeting your needs except that it doesn't let you add peripherals that you'd like, it's possible to add ports and slots. Most "boxes" that provide additional serial ports, like Momentum's **PortJuggler** ($100), don't let you use all the new ports at the same time—you flip a switch to activate whichever device you want at the moment. Creative Solutions' **Hurdler** NuBus cards, on the other hand, provide two ($300) or four ($380) serial ports that can be used simultaneously.

For a Mac that doesn't supply enough slots, you can try products like DGR Technologies' **Max** and Sonnet Technologies' **Twin Slot LC** which provide an LC or LC II extra PDS slots for $200 to $350; Second Wave has a line of products that expand PDS and NuBus options for other Mac models.

Apple provides NuBus adapter cards for the IIsi, Centris and Quadra 660AV, Centris 610, and Power Mac 6100; the adapter fits into the Mac's PDS slot and lets you plug in a NuBus card instead.

Apple CPU upgrades (SZA). Although Apple is no longer providing logic board upgrades for older Macs (except those which can move up to a PowerPC), they did

More Mac Than Meets the Eye

Original model	changed to this	with part number
Mac Classic	Mac Classic II	M1545LL/A
Mac LC or LC II	Mac LC III	M1386LL/A
Performa 400, 405, 410, 430	Performa 450	M0375LL/A
Mac II or IIx	Mac IIfx	M1330LL/A
Mac IIvx, Performa 600, 600CD	Quadra 650	M1421LL/A
Quadra 900	Quadra 950	M6940ZA

provide upgrades for a short time to several different models. If you're buying or dealing with used equipment whose owners insist that there's a different machine "inside" than the one identified on the outside, the table "More Mac Than Meets the Eye" of past Apple CPU upgrades may be helpful.

For PowerBooks (SZA). There are several options for squeezing more speed out of an early 100-series PowerBook. For instance, the 140 can be enhanced with an FPU and new clock chip at 25MHz; the 160 can get an FPU and a 33MHz clock; the 160 and the 145 can get FPUs. Digital Eclipse and Shreve Systems both specialize in these kind of PowerBook upgrades. But think twice, or thrice (I've always wanted to use that word) before sinking a few hundred dollars in an old PowerBook for what will amount to perhaps only a few minutes saved each day (how fast can you type, anyway?).

Hardware Tips

Inside and Out

HOT TIPS

Numbers in names (SZA/JK). A set of slashed numbers (8/230 or 7100/80, for instance) can stand for one of two things. As a rule of thumb, when the first number is smaller than the second (8/230), the numbers stand for the amount of memory (8MB of RAM) and the size of the hard drive (230MB). For Power Mac models, the first number (7100/80) is larger and is the model number; the second number is the speed of the processor.

ADB cable (SZA). The ADB cable used on the Mac is the same as Super VHS cabling—even the connectors are the same. So if you want an extra-long or extra-short custom ADB cable, you can get one at a local electronics store.

ADB chains (SZA). You can create a *chain* of ADB devices—a keyboard, a trackball, and a mouse, for instance. But because the mouse presents a dead end, it always has to be the last device. There are T- and Y-connectors available that let you branch two items (a mouse and a trackball, for instance) from a single ADB connector. And many devices, especially trackballs, come with "pass-through" connectors so you can plug in the new device and then the mouse.

ADB devices can be connected in a chain. At the top, the trackball is a "pass-through" device, which lets you attach the mouse to it. At the bottom, the trackball and mouse are both attached to the keyboard by means of a Y-connector.

There's a theoretical limit of 16 ADB devices for the Mac, because there are 16 different "addresses" that can be assigned internally to ADB devices to keep track of them. But you can really use only three or four in a chain (which, face it, ought to be plenty) because with more than that, the signal from the last device is too weak to reach the Mac. That's probably because the other ADB chain limitation kicks in—the total length of the chain shouldn't exceed five meters (about 16 feet).

Live ADB unplugging (David Ramsey). Although it's generally believed that plugging or unplugging an ADB connector while the Mac is turned on is a dangerous thing, it was a problem that first surfaced on the Mac II and was also present only on the IIx and, to a lesser degree, on the IIcx.

There was nothing inherently dangerous about the ADB per se on these machines, but the design of the logic board was such that a minor flexion of the board could occur if the ADB plug was inserted or removed a little too vigorously—resulting in a short from the ADB power line to the metal shielding on the inside of the case.

Later Macs have thermal, self-resetting fuses which prevent this problem. *[But you are left with this minor annoyance: If you have to connect your mouse after the computer's on, it's going to move the cursor very slowly, and using the Mouse control panel to reset the tracking speed isn't going to help much. You need to restart the Mac to get the mouse to behave correctly.—SZA]*

Not always a GeoPort (SZA). The external difference between a GeoPort and a standard serial port is the presence of a ninth pin. The Power Mac 5200 and the Performa 5200 and 6200, however, have a ninth pin on their modem ports—but they are *not* GeoPorts.

Power Macs

Monitor slowdown (JK). The high-density monitor port on some PowerPC Macs, which runs Apple's AV Display (or, with an adapter, standard monitors) uses the Power Mac's system memory, and not separate VRAM as do other video setups on the Mac. This slows down the display considerably.

Acceleration by system software upgrade (JK). Power Macs come with a PowerPC version of System 7, but in fact, only part of the system software has been translated into PowerPC code.

With any Mac or system version, applications make heavy use of a part of the system called the *Toolbox*, a collection or pre-written routines that perform common tasks. Programs use only about 20 percent of the routines 80 to 90 percent of the time. Those are the routines Apple optimized for the PowerPC chip, with the rest left in 68K code that would be translated a little more with each new system release. Consequently, if you upgrade a Power Mac's system software when new releases come out, when more of the system software has been converted to native PowerPC code, the computer should actually run faster.

No DSP software on a Power Mac (JK). Software written to take advantage of the DSP chip in the Quadra AVs won't work on a Power Mac because there is no DSP— its functions are handled by the PowerPC chip.

Old extension problem (JK). Some older extensions and control panels have a serious negative impact on the performance of native applications on the Power Mac, because extensions written for a 68K machine force the Power Mac to continually switch between the emulator and the PowerPC.

Old drives are slow (JK). Some older hard drives, whose drivers don't support SCSI Manager 4.3, slow down dramatically when used with a Power Mac. If you have an old Apple drive, you can update its drivers with HD SC Setup 7.3 or later to speed things up. For a non-Apple drive, find the latest formatter and updater from its manufacturer, or get a general hard disk formatter like La Cie's Silverlining or Casa Blanca Works' Drive7.

PowerBooks

No burn-in (SZA). Although screen burn-in was never an issue for PowerBook screens, as it was for early phosphor-coated monitors, a PowerBook screen is subject to a shadowing effect if you leave it on and unchanged for, say, 24 hours. To cure the shadowing, put the PowerBook to sleep; the longer the screen was on, the longer a sleep period it needs to cure the shadows.

Battery protectors (Susan McCallister). It's important to use the case Apple provides for the 100- and 200-series PowerBook batteries, or to buy, or create one yourself. The batteries' contacts can accidentally short if they're bridged by a metal object such as a paper clip, keys, or a metal pen barrel. A short could cause a fire or burns and, of course, ruin the battery. *[If you travel, you'll find that the "shoe-polish mitt" provided by many hotels along with their other bathroom paraphernalia is the perfect size for a battery cover.—SZA]*

Conserving battery power (SZA/JK). Keeping the power drain to a minimum lets you work longer on a single battery charge. Here are some things you can do to maximize your battery life:

- Keep AppleTalk turned off (in the Chooser).

- Keep the backlight turned down as far as possible.

- Keep hard disk access to a minimum: don't use virtual memory; allocate *lots* of memory to an opened application so it won't go to the disk so often; and use a RAM disk whenever possible.

- Keep *processor cycling* turned on in the PowerBook control panel.

- Put the PowerBook to sleep whenever you're not using it for more than two minutes.

- Keep the settings in the PowerBook control panel at maximum conservation settings.

- If yours is an older model that lets you run the CPU at two different speeds, set it to run at the slower speed.

Color and contrast don't count (SZA). Color PowerBook screens eat up more battery power than do their grayscale and black-and-white counterparts. But it's not the color itself that's drawing the power—it's the extra backlight needed on these screens that eats up power. So, running a color PowerBook in black-and-white won't conserve any battery power—and changing the contrast settings makes no difference on any screen.

NiCad reconditioning (RW). NiCad batteries need occasional reconditioning in order to hold a complete charge. If you continually charge a NiCad, then use it for awhile, then recharge it, use it for awhile, and so on, without ever totally draining the charge, a "full" charge won't last very long.

Occasionally recondition the battery by running it down totally. The best way to get a complete discharge is to use an external charger/reconditioner, but the easiest way is to use something like VST System's **PBTools** software or Jeremy Keizer's shareware **DeepDischarge**. A deep discharge can bring an anemic battery back to life.

Later batteries better (SZA). NiCad batteries have gone through two subtle revisions, each one providing longer-lasting power. The original one, whose model number is #5417, is a 2.3 amp-hour model labeled 140/170. The second-generation NiCad is 2.5 amp-hours, model #5653; the third one is #5654, a 2.9 amp-hour version. When you buy a new, or second, battery, make sure you get the latest model.

Later adapters better, too (RW). The power adapters for the 100-series Power-Books were quietly improved over time, with the later ones able to recharge your battery in a shorter time. The first model (#M5140) is a 15-watt version with a dangerous propensity: The black ring at the tip of the plug was prone to hairline cracks which could result in serious damage to the motherboard. The second version is a 17-watt model (#M5651); the best is the third model (#M5652), a 24-watt version. (The 500-series PowerBooks use 40-watt adapters, sending 20 watts to each battery.)

Rechargeable, not immortal (SZA). Rechargeable batteries have a limited *life cycle*—the number of times the battery can be drained and recharged. NiCads, for instance, have an average of 500 life cycles which translates to two to three years of use. If your battery just won't recharge anymore, it may be really and truly dead.

The stupid smart battery (SZA). The "intelligent battery" in the 500-series Power-Books has a chip whose memory is easily corrupted, especially when left uncharged for a long period of time. Symptoms of this stupidity include: the battery can't be charged in the PowerBook or externally; the battery isn't recognized by the battery icon; the battery completely discharges in a sleeping PowerBook in a day or two (instead of a week); and the battery is extremely hot to the touch when removed from the PowerBook.

There are two cures for a dumbed-down smart battery. Apple provides a free fix with its later system software, Intelligent Battery Reconditioner; **EMMpathy** (the Energy Monitoring Module controller in the battery is what's at fault), put out as freeware from VST Systems, also fixes the problem.

HOT TIPS

SCSI cables (RW). There are two PowerBook SCSI cables used for two very different purposes. The HDI-30 SCSI System Cable is used for connecting SCSI peripherals to the PowerBook; the HDI-30 SCSI Disk Adapter Cable is used to connect the PowerBook *as* a SCSI device to another Mac. These two cables are often confused, but there are several differences between them:

	System Cable	Disk Adapter Cable
PowerBook connector:	HDI-30	HDI-30
Pins (on HDI-30):	29	30
Second connector:	50-pin male	50-pin female
Length:	18 inches	10 inches
Color:	light gray	dark gray

But if you're connecting SCSI devices to the PowerBook, the best way to go is something called **SCSI Doc** ($40, APS Technologies). It plugs into the HDI-30 connector on the PowerBook and provides a standard 25-pin SCSI connector on the other end—with a switch that lets you choose standard SCSI or SCSI-mode connection.

PowerBook to PowerBook connection (RW). You can't just connect one PowerBook in SCSI disk mode to act as an external hard drive for another PowerBook, even if you have all the right cables. A PowerBook in SCSI disk mode doesn't provide any termination *power,* usually provided by the desk Mac on a normal hookup. To make a reliable PowerBook-to-Power-Book SCSI connection, you need this chain:

1. The first PowerBook

2. HDI-30 SCSI System Cable

3. Pass-through SCSI 50-pin terminator with power supply

4. HDI-30 SCSI Disk Adapter Cable

5. PowerBook in SCSI mode

APS Technologies' **SCSI Sentry** ($40) is the perfect product for the center of this chain: it works as an end-of-chain or a pass-through device that detects and solves many SCSI signal problems. You can get a separate termination power supply ($20) for situations like this PowerBook chain.

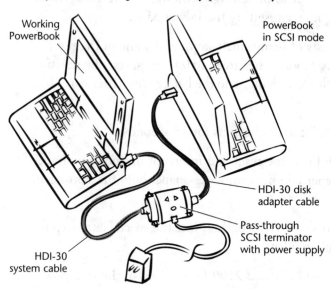

Working PowerBook

PowerBook in SCSI mode

HDI-30 disk adapter cable

Pass-through SCSI terminator with power supply

HDI-30 system cable

Hooking up a PowerBook in SCSI disk mode to another PowerBook.

HOT TIPS

Alternative power sources (SZA/JK). You don't have to stick with the AC adapter that came with your NiCad-based PowerBook, or depend solely upon the internal battery for any PowerBook model. A number of companies make products like: special power adapters that let you recharge your PowerBook from, say, a car's cigarette lighter; external battery chargers that let you charge two batteries at a time; and, best of all, external batteries for the NiCad-based PowerBooks to double their unplugged run time. Based on weight, price, length of charge, and included software (because a PowerBook doesn't know anything about external batteries), VST Power Systems' **ThinPack** external batteries are the best.

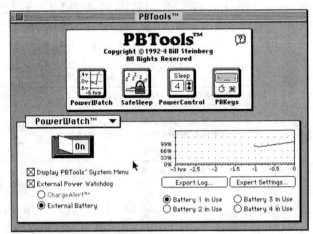

VST's PBTools makes a PowerBook "aware" of an external battery; it's also the perfect PowerBook utility for anyone from a casual user to a true wirehead.

Resetting the Power Manager (SZA/RW). Resetting the Power Manager is a panacea for all sorts of ills on a PowerBook—much like zapping PRAM is for all Macs. When your battery isn't charging, or it's not lasting too long, or the PowerBook thinks you didn't even put a battery in, try resetting the Power Manager.

Resetting the Power Manager consists of many small steps, and some of them differ from one model to another. For any model other than a 500-series, start by shutting down the computer, and removing the AC adapter and the battery (or batteries). Then do the following:

- *For the 100:* Hold in the reset and interrupt buttons for 15 seconds.

- *For the 140, 145, 145B, and 170:* Press the reset and interrupt buttons simultaneously by pushing them with a paper clip bent into a U-shape; hold the buttons in for 30 seconds.

- *For the 150:* Hold in the reset button for 30 seconds. (Note the special later step for this model, in the following numbered list).

- *For the 160, 165, 180 PowerBooks* and *200 and 2300 Duos:* Hold in the rear power button for 30 seconds.

- *For the 5300-series* and *190:* Hold in the reset button for 30 seconds.

After the appropriate procedure listed above, do these steps in this order (which is *not* the order you'd normally follow!):

1. Reconnect the AC adapter.

2. Plug in the PowerBook.

3. For all but the 150: Turn on the PowerBook.
    or
    For the 150: Briefly press the reset button again. You might hear a pop from the speaker, and the PowerBook may start up. If it doesn't, press the main power button in back.

4. *Now*, reinsert the battery.

For the 500 series, all you have to do is just shut down the computer, hold down ⌘ Option Ctrl and Power On for a few seconds, and turn it back on.

X-ray away (RW). You can't damage your PowerBook by putting it through the x-ray machine at an airport. Honest. X-rays are a form of light; it's magnetic waves that might erase your disk or otherwise damage something in your computer.

Quadra and Centris (SZA)

Greenish screen fix (SZA). If you're using the Apple Basic Color Monitor on a Centris or Quadra, you may find the screen is greenish or washed-out blue. Use the Apple Basic Color Monitor extension to clear it up.

Quadra RAM disk problem (SZA). A Quadra 950 filled to its maximum 256MB of RAM can't use a RAM disk. Honest!

Quadra 950 display problem (SZA). If you use the built-in video card and set the monitor to millions of colors, you may find that many graphics images don't display correctly. Use the 950 Color Addition extension to clear it up.

The II Line (SZA)

Speeding up the IIci. The IIci uses system RAM instead of separate video RAM for its display when you use the internal video card, which slows things down. Using a separate video card speeds things considerably.

If you're running on the internal video in anything but black-and-white *and* you have four 256K SIMMs in Bank A *and* you have a total of 5, 9, or 11MB, you can get a

Desktop Mac Specs

Model	CPU[1]	Speed (MHz)	FPU[2]	Max RAM (MB)	Level 2 Cache	PCI slots	NuBus slots	Other slots[3]	GeoPort	Built-in Ethernet
PowerMacs										
9500/120, 9500/132	604	120, 132		768	512K	6			yes	yes
8500/120	604	120		512	256K	3			yes	yes
8100/80, 8100/100, 8100/110	601	80, 100, 110		264	256K		3			yes
7500/100	601	100		512	256K or 512K	3			yes	yes
7200/75, 7200/90	601	75, 90		256	256K or 512K	3			yes	yes
7100/66, 7100/80	601	66, 80		136	256K		3			yes
6200/75	603	75		64	256K			LC PDS, CS, video		yes
6100/66 DOS Compatible	601[4]	66		722	256K					yes
6100/60, 6100/66	601	60,66		72	256K		(1)[6]	(PDS)[6]		yes
5200/75 LC	603	75		64	256K			LC PDS, CS, video		(opt)
Performas										
200	68000	16	no	10						
400, 405, 410, 430	68030	16	no	10				LC PDS		(opt)
450	68030	25	(opt)	36				LC III PDS		(opt)
460, 466, 467	68030	33	(opt)	36				LC III PDS		(opt)
475, 476	68030	25	no	36				LC III PDS		(opt)
520	68030	25	(opt)	36				LC III PDS		
550	68030	33	(opt)	36				LC III PDS		
560	68030	33	(opt)	36				LC III PDS		(opt)
575, 577, 578	68LC040	66/33	no					LC PDS, CS		(opt)
600, 600 CD	68030	32	(opt)	68			2	LC PDS		
630	68LC040	66/33	no	36				LC PDS, CS, video		(opt)
630 and 640CD DOS Compatible	68LC040[4]	66	no	52[5]				CS, video		(opt)
5200CD	603	75		64			0	LC PDS, CS, video		(opt)
6100	601	60		72			(1)[6]	(PDS)[6]		yes
6200CD	603	75		64			0	LC PDS, CS, video		(opt)
Quadra & Centris										
Centris 610	68040	20		136			(1)[6]	(PDS)[6]		
Centris 650	68040	25		136			3	PDS		
Quadra 605	68LC040	25	no	20				LC III PDS		
Quadra 610	68040	25		68			(1)[6]	(PDS)[6]		
Quadra 630	68040	66/33		36				LC PDS, CS, video		(opt)
Quadra 650	68040	33		132			3	1		
Quadra 700	68040	25		64			2	PDS		
Quadra 900	68040	25		256			5	PDS		
Quadra 950	68040	33		256			5	PDS		

Model	CPU[1]	Speed (MHz)	FPU[2]	Max RAM (MB)	Level 2 Cache	PCI slots	NuBus slots	Other slots[3]	GeoPort	Built-in Ethernet
Quadra & Centris (continued)										
Quadra 800	68040	33		136			3	PDS		
Quadra/Centris 660AV	68040[7]	50		68			(1)[6]	(PDS)[6]	yes	yes
Quadra 840AV	68040[7]	80		128			3			
WorkGroup Servers										
60	68040	25		68				040 PDS		
80	68040	33		136				040 PDS		
95	68040	66		256	256K or 512K		5	040 PDS		yes
6150/66	601	66		72	256K		(1)[6]	(PDS)[6]		yes
8150/110	601	110		264	256K		3	PDS		yes
9150/120	601	120		264	1MB		4	PDS		yes
The II Line										
Mac II	68020	16	(opt)	20			6			
Mac IIx	68030	16	yes	32			6			
Mac IIci	68030	25	yes	32			3			
Mac IIcx	68030	16	yes	32			3			
Mac IIsi	68030	20	yes	17			(1)[6]	(PDS)[6]		
Mac IIvx	68030	32	yes	68			2			
Mac IIfx	68030	40	yes	32			6	1		
The LC's										
LC	68020	16	no	10				LC PDS		
LC II	68030	16	yes	10				LC PDS		
LC III	68030	25	(opt)	36				LC PDS		
LC 475	68LC040	50/25	no	36				LC III PDS		
LC 520	68030	25	(opt)	36				LC PDS		
LC 550	68030	33	(opt)	36				LC PDS		
LC 575	68040	66/33		36				LC PDS, CS		(opt)
LC 580	68LC040	66/33	no	52				LC PDS, CS, video		(opt)
LC 630	68LC040	66/33	no	36				LC PDS, CS, video		(opt)
LC 630 DOS Compatible	68LC0401	66	no	52[5]				CS, video		(opt)
Compacts										
Classic	68000	8	no	4						
Classic II	68030	16	no	10						
Color Classic	68030	16	opt	10				LC PDS		
Color Classic II	68030	33	opt					LC III PDS		

Notes:

1 6xx is PowerPC chip; others are Motorola
2 not an issue for 68040 or PowerPC processors
3 CS = communications slot
4 DOS Compatibles include 486DX2/66 processor
5 32MB limit for DOS
6 1 NuBus OR 1 PDS
7 Also includes DSP processor

HOT TIPS

speed increase by setting the Disk Cache in the Memory control panel to 768K.

For an all-round, but small, speed increase, keep 32-bit addressing turned on in the Memory control panel even if you don't have more than 8MB of memory.

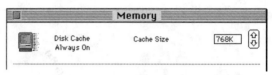

Setting the Memory control panel's disk cache to 768K can, under some circumstances, speed up a IIci or a IIsi.

Finally, if yours is an early IIci that doesn't have a cache card, see if you can get one—they were originally $70 but if you can find one at all, it will only be about $20 now. It's well worth it if you're sticking with the IIci. It's easy to see if you have one: Open the case and look at the motherboard—the cache slot is right in the center.

Speeding up the IIsi. If you use the internal video support on the IIsi, you can almost double its speed by switching the monitor to black-and-white. For any color setting, you can get a little speed boost by keeping the Disk Cache setting in the Memory control panel at 768K. Finally, a separate video card gives the best speed boost of all.

Sound on the IIsi. The IIsi has a finicky connection between the motherboard and the speaker; sometimes the sound output quits until you restart. Here are some things you can do about it: Open the Sound control panel, set the volume to maximum, and then reset it to the volume you want. Or, attach an external speaker to the sound port, because the problem is the connection to the internal speaker. Or, open the case, unplug the speaker cable, clean the contacts, and plug the cable back in.

1984

Apple's award-winning introductory commercial for its new Macintosh computer aired only once: during the 1984 SuperBowl. Its theme: why 1984 (the year) wouldn't be like 1984 (the book). Hundreds of brain-washed workers trudged into an auditorium to listen to a televised lecture, until the screen was smashed by a slow-motion sledge hammer throw. Most people have no idea just what propaganda was being spouted by that talking head, but here it is:

> Each of you is a single cell in the great body of the State. And today, that great body has purged itself of parasites. We have triumphed over the unprincipled of facts. The thugs and wreckers have been cast out. Let each and every cell rejoice! For today we celebrate the first glorious anniversary of the Information Purification Directive. We have created, for the first time in all history, a garden of pure ideology where each worker may bloom secure from the pests purveying contradictory and confusing truths. Our unification of thought is more powerful a weapon than any fleet or army on earth. We are one people. With one will. One resolve. One cause. Our enemies shall talk themselves to death, and we will bury them with their own confusion. We shall prevail!

3 | System Software

When you first buy a computer, it's the hardware that gets all the attention. But what really makes the Mac what it is—an easy-to-use and highly customizable personal computer—is the system software. The system software creates the desktop, lets you organize your files in folders, and gives you capabilities—such as cutting and pasting text and graphics—that work in virtually any Mac program.

In this chapter, we describe the basic components of the Mac system software. You'll also find advice on system software installation and modification.

Contributors

Sharon Zardetto Aker (SZA) is the chapter editor.

John Kadyk (JK) has been involved with all six editions of this book. When he's not working with the Mac, he likes playing music and biking.

Charles Rubin (CR) is a Mac writer who has contributed to previous *Mac Bible* editions.

Contents

~~~~~~

The Operating System

The hardware components that make up your computer system aren't enough to make the computer work; it's the software that makes things really happen. Without software, a computer is like a terrific stereo system with no tapes or CDs: You have the potential, but you don't have the music. But on the computer, before you can run any programs to get any work done, you need the *system software*—the stuff that gets the computer working at its most basic level. The system software creates the desktop and provides across-the-board capabilities such as cutting and pasting and program launching.

Together with the routines built into the Mac's ROM, which provide the lowest-level essentials such as window- and menu-handling, the system software provides the Mac's *operating system*.

System Software

The Mac's system software is inside the System Folder on your hard drive. When you buy a Mac, the most recent version of the system software is already installed on it, but you can continually upgrade it as new system releases become available.

System, system (SZA). The word *system* in this chapter usually refers to your system software, but can be used in several different ways: the version of the system software you're using *(What system are you running?)*; your system software in general *(The system crashed)*; or your hardware configuration *(Which Mac system do you have?)*. The phrase *System file* (with a capital S) refers specifically to the suitcase-icon System file in your System Folder. Without the capital, *system file* refers to any file inside your System Folder or its subfolders. Likewise, the *System Folder* (capitalized) is that special System Folder; a *system folder*, uncapitalized, refers to one of the System Folder's subfolders.

System version numbers (SZA). As with other software, system software continually evolves, with higher numbers indicating later versions. A double-decimal system is used so that you can tell the difference between major and minor changes.

When the main number changes (such as System 6 to System 7), that indicates a major change, with totally new approaches to the system environment—so major that often older hardware can't handle it and older software can't run under it. A change in the first decimal place (such as System 7.0 to System 7.1), usually means some significant component was changed or added, but you won't have to relearn anything or change your hardware or software.

A change to the second decimal place (such as System 7.5.1 to System 7.5.2) can mean one of two things. First, it might be the newest version of the current system that has a few minor tweaks so it works on Mac hardware that was developed after the system was released. Or, it can indicate that there were some bug fixes and/or enhancements to minor system components such as printer drivers. Or, it can be both—a fix for existing Macs through an updater, while those fixes are rolled into the version of the system that's shipping on new Macs.

To see what version of the system you're running, use the About This Macintosh command in the Finder's menu.

```
┌──────────────────── About This Macintosh ────────────────────┐
│                                                               │
│     ┌─┐              System Software 7.5.1                    │
│    ⟨─┘      Power Macintosh   © Apple Computer, Inc. 1983-1995 │
│                                                               │
```

To check what version of the system software is on your Mac, use the Finder's About This Macintosh command in the menu.

This book assumes you're using System 7.5 or some "tweak" of it, such as 7.5.2 or 7.5.3. (As I write this, 7.5.3 is just about out.) But almost everything in this chapter (and others) also applies to System 7.0 and System 7.1, and the text usually mentions when there's a significant difference between System 7.5 and the two earlier versions.

Hardware requirements for system software (SZA/JK). You can't run just any system on any Mac. Older Macs sometimes can't run a newer system because it takes too much memory or hard disk space, or because it absolutely requires certain support from a processor chip or the ROMs in the newer machines. (The next generation operating system, for instance, is planned strictly for PowerPC chips.) Newer Macs won't run at all on systems earlier than the one that was current when the hardware was released.

In addition, later systems need a lot more memory to run effectively—or at all. Here's Apple's recommended memory requirements for System 7.5:

Basic System 7.5	4MB
Basic System 7.5 on Power Mac	8MB
System 7.5 with QuickDraw GX	8MB
System 7.5 with QuickDraw GX on Power Mac	16MB

System 7 flavors (SZA). System 7 was introduced, to much fanfare, back in 1991; since then it has had several minor updates and two distinct version changes (7.1 and 7.5). Here's a roundup:

- *System 7 Pro*, a ridiculously marketed upgrade, included a few enhancements (such as a scriptable Finder, QuickTime, and PowerTalk) that didn't make it into the System 7 package; while System 7 was free, you had to buy the Pro version. All of its capabilities were later added to the standard system software.

- *System 7.1's* most obvious improvement over 7.0 was the way it handled fonts, providing a Fonts folder inside of the System Folder. There were also more subtle differences, such as how memory is allocated to an application in its Get Info window. It was the first system to include WorldScript, a technology that lets a single application work in many different languages as long as the correct language kit from Apple is used. It was the system that introduced the can of worms known as *enablers* (which we'll get to later) and is also infamous for being the first system upgrade that had to be (gasp!) *paid* for.

- *System 7.0.1P* and *System 7.1P* were the 7.0 and 7.1 systems that came on Performas. As mentioned elsewhere, early Performas came with modified systems to make the machine even easier to use.

- *System 7.5* ushered in features such as QuickDraw GX, AppleScript, QuickTime, PowerTalk, and more. It's the biggest—in terms of both memory and disk space needed—operating system ever seen on a Mac. Everyone learns to live with it, and most learn to love it. There are new control panels with better capabilities, and old desk accessories have been updated. Some of its more minor features are the most appreciated: a terrific Find File utility, a hierarchical menu, and drag-and-drop capability (all of which are covered later in this chapter).

Performa system software (SZA/JK). Prior to System 7.5, Performas came with their own special system software (versions 7.0.1P and 7.1P) which were standard Mac systems modified slightly to be even easier for beginners. System 7.1P went through several modifications—7.1P1 through 7.1P6—which included many bug fixes and added a few new features (such as the Shut Down desk accessory on the menu). System 7.5 took most of the Performa system's special options—such as the special desktop patterns, the Launcher, and default Applications and Documents folders—and made them part of standard system software.

Don't upgrade (SZA). At least, don't upgrade right away. Wait about six months after a major system release before you upgrade; by then, all—or almost all—of the bugs will have been worked out.

HOT TIP

Updates, Tune-Ups, and Enablers (SZA)

In between major system upgrades, Apple releases minor updates to fix bugs and to run new hardware. For System 7.0, these updates were called *Tune-Ups;* for System 7.1, bug fixes were called *Hardware* or *System Updates,* and changes for new hardware came in *enablers.* Bug fixes and enhancements that come in minor updates are almost always rolled into the next version of the system software.

The System 7.0 Tune-Up. System 7 was a very buggy system release. Apple tried to get away from interim system release numbers with second decimal places by introducing the Tune-Up approach, and provided Tune-Up 1.0 to fix the major bugs. Unfortunately, Apple also introduced some new machines with System 7.0.1—which had the 1.0 Tune-Up features incorporated into it—at the same time. So, people moved to System 7.0.1 (not realizing it was simply to work with the new machines), and *then* used the Tune-Up, which wasn't necessary at that point. Of course, later, there were revisions to the Tune-Up!

HOT TIP

System 7.0.x is the only system that uses Tune-Ups for fixing bugs. If you're using System 7.0, switch to System 7.0.1, which incorporates very important bug fixes—such as the one that keeps folders from disappearing! And, make sure you use Tune-Up 1.1.1 with it, which takes care of some other very serious system problems. (To use the Tune-Up, all you have to do is run the Installer that comes with the disk; it will replace all problem files and add the new ones you need.)

You can tell if a Tune-Up is being used because when you check the system version number in the About This Macintosh box (under the menu in the Finder), it will have a bullet (•) following the system number.

System 7.1 Updates. For System 7.1, Updates replaced the Tune-Up approach for bug fixes and minor enhancements. The 1.0 Update was entitled *Hardware System Update;* by version 3.0, the name was shortened to *System Update.* Running the Update installer is a cinch; it places and replaces files in your system folder, and adds an update extension (its icon is a too-cute Mac with a screwdriver) to the Extensions folder. There's no indication in the About This Macintosh box regarding whether or not you're using an Update; you have to check the Extensions folder.

If you're using System 7.1, make sure you have the 3.0 System Update, which has been the latest update for nearly a year as of this writing, so it's reasonably safe to assume it's the last one.

System 7.5 Updates. The Update approach has continued with System 7.5, with a minor, and sometimes confusing, difference: installing the Update changes the system software version number. So, if you're working with System 7.5 and use the 1.0 Update, your system software version is then System 7.5.1. What's confusing? When someone is running System 7.5.2 on her machine, you have no way of knowing if there's a 2.0 Update, or if she has a machine that needed the more advanced version of the system when she bought it—unless you search through the System Folder on that machine for an Update file. And then you still have the *version* problem: the 1.0.2 version of the 1.0 Update, for instance.

Enablers. An *enabler* is a system file that enables a current system to work with Mac models that came out after the system was introduced. Before enablers—that is, before System 7.1—a new version of the system software, with a second decimal number, had to be used for new machines.

But this seemingly simple idea got confusing very quickly. The first problem was the names: System Enabler 040 and 088, for instance. And changes: Enabler 111 and 121 were both replaced by Enabler 131. And then there are the fixes to buggy enablers—such as System Enabler 131 version 1.0.3. Talk about intuitive! And with so many Mac models coming out during the course of System 7.1 and System 7.5's lifetimes, it was a Mac tech support person's nightmare!

For a while, things cleared up a little. First of all, at least some enablers wound up with "real" names, such as *PowerBook Duo Enabler* and *PowerPC Enabler*. Also, many different enablers were combined so that several machines could use the same enabler. Finally, *all* the enablers for System 7.0 and System 7.1 were rolled into the main System 7.5 technology. But the calm was short-lived, as new machines introduced after System 7.5 required enablers of their own.

System 7.1 Enablers. First, a quick list of which machines don't need an enabler when running System 7.1:

- Mac Plus, SE, SE/30

- Classic, Classic II

- LC, LC II, LC 580

- Mac II, IIx, IIcx, IIsi, IIci, IIfx

- PowerBook 100, 140, 145, 170

- Quadra 700, 900, 950

- Performa 200, 400, 405, 410, 430, 580, 640, 6110-series

For machines running System 7.1, the table "System 7.1 Enablers" on the next page shows what you need.

System 7.5 Enablers. Listing the enablers needed under System 7.1 is relatively easy, since it's a static system—there aren't any more revisions being made to it. For System 7.5, it's a different matter. Not only were all the previous enablers rolled into the system or into a single "universal enabler" that was then made part of the System file, but some enablers required under System 7.5 were included in System 7.5.1, some needed under System 7.5.1 were included in System 7.5.2, and, as I write this, *all* the 7.5-based

System 7.1 Enablers

Model	Enabler	Version
IIvi, IIvx	System Enabler 001	1.0.1
LC III	System Enabler 003	1.1
Color Classic	System Enabler 401	1.0.5
LC 520, 550	System Enabler 403	1.0.2
Quadra 605, LC 475, 575	System Enabler 065	1.2
Macintosh TV	System Enabler 404	1.0
Quadra/Centris 610, 650, Quadra 800	System Enabler 040	1.1
Quadra/Centris 660AV, Quadra 840AV	System Enabler 088	1.2
Performa 450, 460–467	System Enabler 308	1.0
Performa 475–476, 575–578	System Enabler 364	1.1
Performa 550, 560	System Enabler 332	1.1
Performa 600	System Enabler 304	1.0.1
Performa 630	System Enabler 406	7.1.2P
PowerBook 160, 165c, 180, 180c	System Enabler 131	1.0.3
PowerBook 520, 520c, 540, 540c	PowerBook 500 Series Enabler	1.0.2
PowerBook Duo 210, 230, 250, 270c, 280, 280c	PowerBook Duo Enabler	2.0
Power Mac 6100, 7100, 8100	PowerPC Enabler	1.0.2
PowerPC Upgrade Card	PowerPC Upgrade Card Enabler	1.0.1

enablers are reportedly being rolled into System 7.5.3. And, of course, there will be System 7.5.3 enablers for the machines introduced after that. So, making a list of System 7.5 enabler needs is more difficult than shooting at a moving target.

The following table notes both the system version and the enabler you need for the later-model Macs.

System 7.5 Enablers

Model	System	Enabler	Version
PowerMac 6100/66, 7100/80, 8100/100, 8100/110	7.5	PowerPC Enabler	1.1.1
PowerMac 5200, Performa 6200	7.5.1	System Enabler 406	1.0
PowerMac 7200, 9500	7.5.2	System Enabler 701	1.1
PowerMac 7500, 8500	7.5.2	System Enabler 701	1.2
PowerBook 190, 2300, 5300 series	7.5.2	PowerBook 5300/2300/190 Enabler	1.2.1

Keeping track. How can you keep track of system software upgrades, updates, tuners, and so on? Well, the easiest way is to let someone else do it for you: Join a user group—there's *always* someone who has the latest information. Don't count on the major Mac magazines—information is three to four months old by the time you see it. Hanging around on-line is one of the best ways to keep abreast of system software changes.

Although Apple no longer provides the main system software for free (System 7.1 was the last free operating system, not counting the latest system that comes with the computer), updates are provided for free. If you belong to a major on-line service, you'll probably find system updates available; most user groups are authorized to hand out the updates, too.

System Installation   (SZA)

When you buy a Mac, there's a System Folder on the hard drive. But there are lots of times when you have to install system software yourself: You might reformat the hard drive and have to start with a complete system installation; you might have to reinstall the same system version because yours has become corrupted; you might update the current system to fix some bugs; or, you might want to install an alternate, complete system on an external hard drive.

System disks. Current system software comes in two formats: on a CD or on lots of floppies. If you have no CD-ROM drive, or if you have an older Mac that can't start up from a CD, you need the floppies, because you'll have to start up from the disk that's doing the installation.

But even if you have a CD-ROM drive, you'll want a set of floppy installation disks: Someday, your Mac will be so messed up that you'll need to reinstall the system, but the Mac won't be able to read anything in the CD-ROM drive—really, it happens. There's an option on a CD system disk that allows you to make a set of floppy system disks: The Disk Copy utility in the CD's Applications folder can be used to create disks from the *disk images* in the Disk Images folder. Use it!

Clean installations. The philosophy of a "clean install" is one that should be your guiding principle. A clean install puts all your old System Folder contents in a separate folder and creates a new System Folder for the new system. Then, you get to check all your old non-Apple extensions, control panels, and other system files one at a time (or, more practically, in batches) to see if they work with the new system.

Starting with the System 7.5 installer, there's a quick trick to make the Installer do a clean install: Press ⌘Shift K when the Installer window is open, and you'll get the dialog box shown here. Click the Install New System Folder button and proceed.

Clicking the Install New System Folder button lets you do a "clean" install.

For systems prior to System 7.5, you have to set up a manual clean install: Drag the System file out of the System Folder, leaving it on the desktop; then, rename the System Folder something like *(Old) System Folder.* Then go ahead with the installation—a new System Folder will be created for you instead of the old one being updated.

Reinstalls. When you reinstall a system because it's been giving you trouble (constant crashing, perhaps, or weird printing problems), make sure you do a clean install even though the new system is the same version number as the one you're already using. The installer checks if you have the most recent version of a system file; it doesn't check to see if that file's intact. So, for instance, if it sees the current version of a printer driver, it won't replace it—and that might be the component giving you problems.

The installation. Here are the basic steps for a system installation:

1. Run Disk First Aid to check that your hard drive is in good shape—it's on the system disks that came with your computer.

2. If you're changing system version numbers (such as 7.0 to 7.1 or either of those to 7.5, not a simple update or second-decimal change), update the hard drive driver on your hard disk. There's more about this in the chapter on storage but, in brief: The *driver* is a very small piece of software that controls the communication between the Mac and the drive. To update the driver, use the HD SC Setup utility with the new system disks. Use the Update button to update the driver; although this won't affect the information on your drive, it's always a good idea to back up everything before you do system installations anyway.

3. If the Installer you're using doesn't support the automatic Clean Install option, set up a clean install as described previously.

4. Restart the Mac with the Install disk as the startup.

5. Double-click on the Installer icon and choose your options (as described following).

6. If the Install disk includes an Update Installer, run that next.

7. Restart the Mac.

8. Look through your Old System Folder (created by the Clean Install option), and drag your non-Apple items into the new System Folder. If you're moving up from System 7.0 or System 7.1, you'll have to open the System file itself to take out fonts and sounds you store in there.

The Installer

(SZA)

It's imperative that you use the Installer for putting a new or updated system on your hard disk—don't just drag a System Folder, or the System file or Finder, from the Install disk and expect things to work. The Installer not only makes sure you have exactly what you need, it also does all the drudgery of putting things in the various folders where they belong. The Installer window provides a pop-up menu that lets you choose between an Easy (automatic) or Custom installation; in Custom mode, you can pick and choose from among various options.

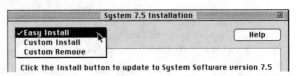

Use the Installer's pop-up menu to choose the Easy or Custom install option.

If you're using floppies, you'll find the Installer on the first disk of the set. On the system CD, you'll find the Installer, as well as any available Update Installer, in the folder named System Software Install.

PowerTalk and QuickDraw GX aren't installed with the general system installation. You'll find separate Installers for those options in subfolders inside the System Software Install folder. But don't expect to set up the installation and walk away, as you can with the system installation; both these installers contain dialogs plugging the other option (suggesting that you install it) right in the middle of the installation process—which halts the process until you click OK.

BAD FEATURE

The Installer used prior to System 7.5 provides basically the same options for system installation (not, of course, those unique to System 7.5), but it is more difficult to use because there's no hierarchical setup and you have to shift-click to select multiple items rather than using checkboxes.

Easy Install. The Easy Install option installs system software to run your specific model of Macintosh. It's smart enough to look inside the existing System Folder to see what printer driver's already there and install the new version of it; but, if you're doing a clean install, as is always recommended, you'll wind up with every conceivable printer driver. Easy Install also gives you every Network option. You may wind up cleaning out some of the System Folder's inner folders when you use Easy Install. But, it is the easy—and sure—way to go.

System 8   (SZA)

Waiting for the next-generation operating system, code-named Copland, is like waiting for System 7 all over again, except the wait is longer and the hype is bigger. At this point, the target release is "some time" in 1997. (All the information in this box is subject to change, at Apple's whim.)

The biggest surface change is definable window and icon styles, with things such as metallic 3-D window frames. This goes along with an official nomenclature change: out with "user interface" and in with "user experience." But that's nothing compared to what's going to be underneath: protected memory (so an application crash can't bring down the whole system) and preemptive multitasking, a more efficient way of doling out processor time to concurrently running programs.

We'll also get new Open and Save dialogs, with an easier way to navigate among folders on the disk, and a special way to view files according to category rather than by what folders they're in. And we'll have better ways to handle windows on the desktop—such as a "drill" option that lets you get at inner folders just by holding down the mouse button while pointing to an outer folder.

Sure, this all comes at a price. First, System 8 will run only on PowerPC-based Macs. It will, no doubt, take more disk space and memory. Extensions written for System 7 will have to be entirely rewritten to work in the new environment. And there will be all the normal upgrade headaches of getting applications and utilities to work properly. But then, we practiced all this stuff when we moved to System 7!

Custom installs. You can save disk space, and even wind up with a system that uses less memory, by using the Custom Install option. You get to choose from these major categories:

- *System Software:* Choose between standard system software or minimal system software for "this Mac" or for "any Mac." Use the standard system option, not the minimal one; if you're putting it on your internal drive, use the "this Mac" option. The "any Mac" option sets up a System Folder that can start up any Mac, so it's much bigger than you need; if you're putting a system on an external hard drive that might be used as the startup for more than one Mac, use the "any Mac" option.

- *Printing:* Check only the printers that you'll actually be using. If you have a LaserWriter and the model isn't listed separately in the list, choose the Laser-Writer 8 option; and, always choose the LaserWriter Utility option, too.

- *Networking:* Even if you aren't on a network, choose the File Sharing option—you never know when you might need it (if, for instance, someone drops by with a

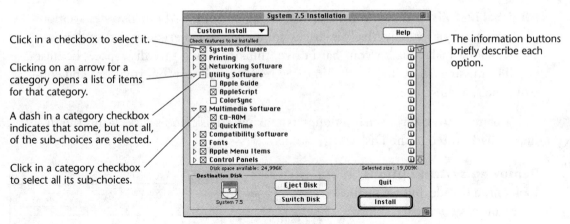

Click in a checkbox to select it.

Clicking on an arrow for a category opens a list of items for that category.

A dash in a category checkbox indicates that some, but not all, of the sub-choices are selected.

Click in a category checkbox to select all its sub-choices.

The information buttons briefly describe each option.

The Custom Install option lets you pick and choose what's going in your system.

PowerBook and plugs in to your setup). You'll know if you need EtherTalk or TokenTalk; check MacTCP if you're going to be accessing the Internet.

- *Utility Software:* Apple Guide is a good thing to check unless hard drive space is really at a premium; without it, Guide material supplied with other programs won't run. AppleScript doesn't take much room on the disk, and none at all in memory when it's not in use; if you think you might be running other people's scripts, or use any of the useful little ones that Apple provides, install it. Check the monitor information in Chapter 6 and decide if you need ColorSync software or not.

- *Multimedia Software:* If you have a CD-ROM drive, just check the main box, because you'll want both the CD-ROM and QuickTime software sub-options. If you have no CD-ROM but play QuickTime clips, you'll need the QuickTime software.

- *Compatibility Software:* Macintosh Easy Open should be installed, since it lets you specify which application should open documents whose "parent" application isn't around. PC Exchange lets you format and read PC disks.

- *Fonts:* Just check the main box; you should have each and every one of these basic fonts.

- *Apple Menu Items:* You might as well check the main box here. If you want to pick and choose, you absolutely need Chooser and Find File; the rest are more expendable.

- *Control Panels:* This list needs a little more attention; you should skip the items that don't work on your system. CPU Energy Saver, for instance, is for certain monitors only, the Cache Switch is for '040 machines only, and the Control Strip is for PowerBooks.

Minimal installs and startup floppies. Using one of the Minimal System options (for "this Mac" or for "any Mac") is strictly for making an emergency startup floppy—you shouldn't make one on your hard drive, thinking you'll save disk space, because you'll be missing *lots* of stuff by the time you're done—all sorts of extensions and control panels, for instance.

But a better choice for a startup floppy is making a Disk Tools disk, using the disk image that's stored in the Disk Images folder.

HOT TIP

Removing system options. It took only a decade, but we finally have an easy way to remove certain system components: just use the Remove option in the Installer. If you're only getting

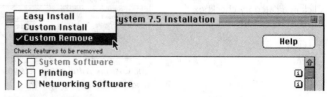

Remove system components with the Installer's Remove option.

rid of a few control panels, it's easier to just drag them out of their folders and trash them. But if you want to remove, say, AppleScript, using the Installer is easier because there are so many components scattered around the disk. If you want to remove PowerTalk or QuickDraw GX, you have to run their Installers and use the Remove option there.

〜〜〜〜〜〜〜〜〜〜〜〜〜〜〜〜〜〜〜〜〜〜〜〜〜〜〜〜〜〜〜

The System Folder

System Folder

The special System Folder is stamped with an icon.

The System Folder is the most important folder on your hard drive, because it contains the software-based portions of the Mac's operating system. And just to prove that it's special, it's stamped with a tiny Mac icon.

You'll find a few "loose" files in the System Folder, among them the System and the Finder. In addition, you'll find lots of special subfolders that hold other pieces of the system software.

The System and Finder Files   (SZA)

There are only a few files in the System Folder that aren't buried in some subfolder or other. The two most important of all are the System and Finder files.

The System file. The System file contains the core of the software-based instructions that run the Mac; they work in conjunction with the hardware-based instructions in the Mac's ROM. (Many of the other files in the System Folder's subfolders also add to the Mac's operating system.) The System file has a suitcase-style icon because it's a

Suitcase Files (SZA)

The System file is a special type of file called a *suitcase,* not only because of the shape of its icon, but because of the way it behaves; screen fonts are also stored in suitcase-type files. A suitcase isn't the same as a folder, despite some surface similarities (you double-click on the icon to open its window and you can drag things in and out).

A suitcase is very particular about the kinds of things it can hold: resources only—screen fonts (which are a type of resource) in a font suitcase, and special system resources for the System file. When you drag something in or out of a suitcase window (which is branded in the upper left with a tiny suitcase icon), you're not just moving it from one place to another on a disk. Items in a folder still exist as separate files, but when you put something in a suitcase it becomes an integral part of that suitcase file and is no longer a separate file on the disk.

The "loose" files in a typical System Folder include the all-important System and Finder, as well as other system files shown in the top two rows here. The bottom row consists of typical files from sloppy applications which don't put their support files in one of the System Folder's subfolders.

special type of file—a suitcase file, which has some special properties, described in the sidebar, "Suitcase Files."

System resources. In addition to zillions of lines of programming code that you can't (and shouldn't want to!) get at, the System file contains many different kinds of *resources* (dialog boxes, cursors, and icons) that give the Mac its Macness. But it also includes a few types of resources that are easy for any user to install and remove.

To see these files, just double-click on the System file: a window opens to show the user-configurable resources. Depending on your system, you'll see any or all of these:

- *Sounds:* The basic system beep is built-in so deeply that you can't get at it, but the other sounds are there as separate files.

- *Keyboard layouts:* There's usually only a single one besides the "buried" standard one, but you can add more. These are the layouts that are listed in the Keyboard control panel.

- *Language scripts:* You probably don't have any of these—they're for non-Roman alphabet languages such as Hebrew and Japanese.

The opened System file (note the suitcase icon in the upper left) displays user-configurable resources. In this system, there's one extra keyboard resource and five sounds.

System 7.0's System file also holds bitmapped fonts, which are stored in the Fonts folder in System 7.1 and later.

To remove a resource from the System file, just drag it out. To add one to the System file, drag it into the System file's open window, or onto the closed System file icon. You can't add or remove resources while any applications are running.

The Finder. The Finder file is what provides the Finder's capabilities—it's your desktop, with all its menus and abilities squeezed into this file. While the Finder used to be more independent—before System 7, it was a separate application that you could allocate memory to, for instance—it has become more and more closely aligned with the System file. It may be totally rolled into the System file by the next system revision.

Other "loose" files. Besides the System and Finder files, you may see several other files out "loose" in the System Folder instead of inside one of the subfolders. Some programs are less fussy about where they go and may drop some preferences or support files right inside the System Folder, and many control panels and extensions can work from this top level instead of inside their own folders. Here are the items you're most likely to see:

- *Clipboard.* Although the Clipboard (covered in detail in Chapter 2) is actually a RAM-based file, when memory's tight and you cut or copy something large to the Clipboard, the item is temporarily written to the disk, in this file.

- *Notepad File* and *Scrapbook File.* These are the files that hold the material you put in these desk accessories.

- *Updates* and *Enablers.* System updates and system enablers are usually stored in the top level of the System Folder.

The Inner Folders   (SZA)

The collection of folders inside your System Folder depends to some extent on which Mac you have, which system version you're running, and what programs you use: Some system folders (Speakable Items and Fonts, for instance) depend on your hardware and software setup, and other folders are put there by some applications.

"The System Folder's Subfolders" table gives a quick rundown of the basic system folders. Some of them are described later in this section, and some are covered in detail in "Control Panels" later in this chapter.

The System Folder's Subfolders

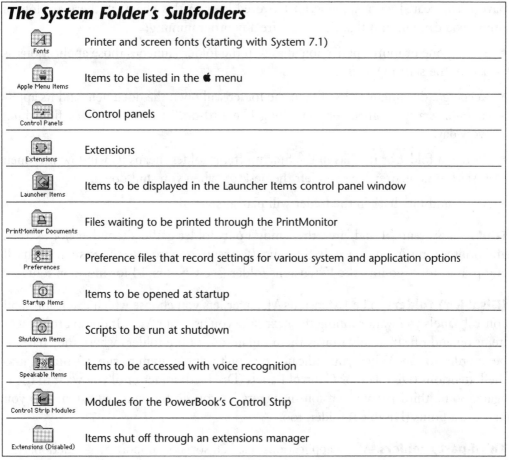

Icon	Description
Fonts	Printer and screen fonts (starting with System 7.1)
Apple Menu Items	Items to be listed in the menu
Control Panels	Control panels
Extensions	Extensions
Launcher Items	Items to be displayed in the Launcher Items control panel window
PrintMonitor Documents	Files waiting to be printed through the PrintMonitor
Preferences	Preference files that record settings for various system and application options
Startup Items	Items to be opened at startup
Shutdown Items	Scripts to be run at shutdown
Speakable Items	Items to be accessed with voice recognition
Control Strip Modules	Modules for the PowerBook's Control Strip
Extensions (Disabled)	Items shut off through an extensions manager

The smart System Folder. The System Folder is pretty smart—it can route certain items to some of its inner folders. If you drag a control panel, extension, or font onto the System Folder icon (the icon, not the opened window), you'll get a dialog telling you where the item belongs, and you can let the Mac put it there. If you drag a group of items at the same time, you'll get a dialog afterward telling you what went where.

Startup Items. Anything in the Startup Items folder opens when you start your Mac, right after the desktop appears. Although it can be used for storing scripts that

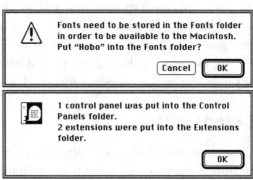

Dragging a special item into the closed System Folder gives you a dialog offering to place the item in the correct subfolder (top). If you drag a combination of items into the System Folder, you'll get a report telling you what went where (bottom).

have been created with AppleScript (covered later in this chapter), there are lots of things you can put in it that don't require any programming:

- Storing one or more application aliases in the folder launches those applications as part of the startup routine.

- Keeping a document or its alias in the folder will open the document and its application at startup—great for something like a to-do list that you check first thing every day.

- Putting a folder or its alias in the Startup Items folder means its window will open at startup no matter how you left the desktop when you shut down.

- Any sound file that's in the folder will play at startup.

Fonts. In System 7.1 and later, the handy Fonts folder gathers together both screen and printer fonts in one place. In System 7.0, screen fonts go into the System file itself and printer fonts go into the Extensions folder (see Chapter 14 for more on fonts).

(Disabled) folders. The Extensions Manager lets you choose which extensions and control panels you want running the next time you use your Mac. It doesn't turn these items on and off: It simply moves them in and out of the folders where they have to be in order to run. When you indicate you don't want an item to run, it's moved into the Extensions (Disabled) or Control Panels (Disabled) folder until you want to use it again. Some third-party extension managers let you do the same with fonts, so you may see a Fonts (Disabled) folder, too.

Third-party folders. Many applications need all sorts of support files—dictionaries, glossaries, import/export filters, and so on—in order to work. Sometimes these are stored in the application's folder, but when a company makes more than one Mac product, shared support files are often stored in the System Folder instead. My System Folder, for instance, has folders named Aldus, Claris, EfiColor, and Microsoft, as well as single-application support folders such as AppleLink OutBasket and Thunder Folder.

Extensions   (SZA)

Extensions extend the capability of the system software by loading into memory at startup, right there along with the system software. *Extension conflicts*—two or more extensions fighting over the same piece of memory—is one of the most common system problems, and is discussed further in Chapter 7.

There's quite a variety of items in the standard System Folder: the extensions themselves (which come in three varieties), support documents for extensions, various subfolders, and even an application (the PrintMonitor). In the table "Inside the

Extensions Folder," we list common contents according to category, and note what type of file each item is.

Extensions and memory. Because extensions load into memory, using lots of extensions eventually eats up lots of memory—you can't just keep adding extensions without eventually paying a price. And, since they load into memory at startup, when you add a new extension to your collection, you have to restart the Mac in order for it to take effect.

Kinds of extensions. When we talk about extensions, we're usually referring to what's more accurately defined as a *system extension*—the kind that has, or should have, a puzzle-piece type of icon, and loads into memory at startup. But there are two other kinds of extensions, too, which you'll notice if you put your Extensions folder window into a list view (that's covered in Chapter 1) and take a look at the Kind column.

Chooser extensions are the items that show up in the Chooser for printing, networking, and faxing. Many of the Chooser extensions are named for various printers and have icons that look like little printers; these are the *printer drivers*, software that lets a Mac and a printer talk to each other. The drivers for the GX printing technol-ogy (covered in Chapter 21) are a combination of the printer icon and the extension puzzle-piece design.

Standard printer dri-ver icons (top) and their GX equivalents (bottom).

Another class of extension is the *communications tool*. You might have the Apple Modem Tool and the Serial Tool extensions installed with your basic system, but many others are available and usually get installed when you install a telecommunications program.

Extensions versus control panels. At first it seems easy to differenti-ate between extensions and control panels, because they're in different folders and because a quick definition says extensions load into memory and control panels change some system feature. But, in fact, the dividing line isn't always so clear.

Yes, an item is either an extension or a control panel; some utilities even have two components, one an extension and one a control panel. But some extensions—the Chooser extensions for printer drivers, for instance—don't load into memory. And some control panels have components that *do* load into memory at startup—that's why you'll see their icons during the "parade" at startup.

The pre-System 7 term *init* is often used instead of *extension*, but also refers to control panels that load into memory at startup.

The icon parade. During startup, you see a parade of icons across the bottom of the screen; sometimes there are so many that they wrap up to a second line. These are

Inside the Extensions Folder

	Type*	Description	Machine-Specific
Apple Guide/Balloon Help			
Apple Guide	E	Enables Guide help	
Finder Help	D	Balloon Help info	
About Apple Guide	D	Apple Guide info for About command	
Macintosh Guide	D	Apple Guide info for Macintosh	
Shortcuts	D	Apple Guide info for Finder	
Speech Guide Additions	D	Apple Guide info for Speech Recognition	AV, PowerMac
Video Guide Additions	D	Apple Guide info for Video Player	AV
PowerBook Guide Additions	D	Apple Guide info for PowerBooks	PowerBook
PowerTalk Guide	D	Apple Guide info for PowerTalk	AV, PowerMac
CD-ROMs			
Apple Photo Access	E	For viewing Kodak CD images	
Audio CD Access	E	For playing audio CDs	
Apple CD-ROM	E	Enables CD mounting	
Foreign File Access	E	Allows mounting of "foreign" format CDs on desktop	
High Sierra File Access	E	Works with Foreign File Access	
ISO 9660 File Access	E	Works with Foreign File Access	
Printing			
StyleWriter II	C	Printer driver for StyleWriter I and II	
ImageWriter, LaserWriter 8, etc.	C	Printer drivers for various printers	As named
Printer Share	E	Enables non-network printers to be shared through a central Mac	
PrintMonitor	A	Monitors and controls background printing	
Printer Descriptions	F	Info for LaserWriter 8 driver for various printers	
Networks			
AppleShare	C	For accessing network volumes	
File Sharing Extension	E	For sharing folders and disks on AppleTalk network	
Network Extension	E	For filesharing	
EtherTalk Phase 2	E	For Ethernet network connections	
MacTCP Token Ring Extension	E	For TCP/IP on Token Ring	
TokenTalk Prep	E	Support for TokenTalk	
TokenTalk Phase 2	E	Support for Token Ring Card	
Graphics, Sound, Video			
ColorSync	E	For matching colors from monitor to printer (and from scanner)	
Color Picker	E	Lets you set current color for control panel use	
Record Button	E	For recording of sound with Apple Adjustable Keyboard; built into AV and PowerMac ROMs	
Apple Basic Color Monitor	E	Fixes green- or blue-cast video for this monitor	Centris, Quadra
950 Color Addition	E	Fixes display problems with internal video and monitor set to millions of colors	Quadra 950
IIci Monitor, PowerPC Monitors Extension, etc.	E	Info for Monitors control panel for named Mac using internal video	As named
QuickTime			
QuickTime	E	Provides QuickTime capabilities	
QuickTime PowerPlug	E	Native-code support, improved compression	PowerPC
QuickTime Musical Instruments	E	For embedding MIDI tracks in QuickTime movies	
Voice Recognition/Speech			
Speech Manager	E	For PlainTalk text-to-speech	AV, PowerPC
Speech Recognition	E	Support for speech recognition	AV, PowerPC
SR Monitor	E	Monitors and interprets speech with PlainTalk microphone	AV, PowerPC
System Speech Rules	D	Support for speech recognition	AV, PowerPC
Voices	F	Voice files for PlainTalk	AV, PowerPC

	Type*	Description	Machine-Specific
Voice Recognition/Speech (continued)			
MacinTalk Pro	E	Lets the Mac read text documents in various voices (stored in Voices folder)	
My Speech Macros	D	Support for Speech Macro Editor	AV, PowerPC
PowerBooks			
Assistant Toolbox	E	Provides syncing capabilities and several ⌘-key sleep options	PowerBook
Caps Lock	E	Puts Caps Lock mode indicator in menu bar	PowerBook
PowerBook Monitors Extension	E	Info for Monitors control panel when used on PowerBook	PowerBook
Duo Battery Patch	E	For Duos under System 7.1 with Type II batteries; rolled into Duo Enabler 2.0 for System 7.1.1	Duo
Type III Battery Patch	E	For Duos with Type III batteries; rolled into System 7.5	Duo
AppleScript			
AppleScript	E	For basic AppleScript capability; Apple Event Manager built into 7.5's version	
Finder Scripting Extension	E	Still needed, even for 7.5 scriptable Finder	
InLine Filter	E	Lets AppleScript and PlainTalk work together	
AppleScriptLib	D	Native-code AppleScript support	PowerPC
Scripting Additions	F	Scripting files for extending AppleScript capabilities	
PowerTalk			
PowerTalk Manager	E	PowerTalk support	
PowerTalk Extension	E	For PlainTalk capability	
Catalogs Extension	E	For catalog support	
Mailbox Extension	E	For mailbox support	
Serial Tool	T	Modem tool for PowerTalk	
Updates and Fixes			
!PowerAV Update	E	For problem with Apple 21" monitor; replaces !TTY extension	PowerMac AV
040 Update	E	For '040 machines that freeze when using virtual memory	'040 models
630 SCSI Update	E	For 630-series Macs that freeze during large file transfers	630-series
Apple Multimedia Tuner	E	Fixes minor QuickTime 2.0 problems	
AV Serial Extension	E	Fixes printing problems	Quadra AV
MathLib	E	Improves performance of math operations	PowerMac
PowerPC Finder Update	E	Support for native PowerPC code; doesn't make the Finder itself native	
Finder Update	E	In 1.0 System Update for System 7.5; replaces PowerPC Finder Update	
Miscellaneous			
Apple Modem Tool	T	Basic telecom support	
Find File Extension	E	Allows keyboard launch of Find File DA	
EM Extension	E	Works with Extensions Manager control panel, lets you interrupt extension loading	
A/ROSE	E	Machines using NuBus cards running Apple Real-Time Operating System	
ObjectSupportLib	D	Helps applications to send and receive Apple Event	PowerMac
ThreadsLib	D	Special info for programmers	PowerMac
Clipping Extension	E	Enables dragging clippings to the desktop surface	
Macintosh Drag-and-Drop	E	Enables Drag-and-Drop under System 7.0, 7.1; rolled into System 7.5	
Dragging Enabler	E	Replaced Macintosh Drag-and-Drop; rolled into System 7.5	
WorldScript Power Adapter	E	Support for Language Kits	PowerPC
SCSI Manager 4.3	E	Faster SCSI for Quadra and Centris; updates ROM info in AVs, PowerMac Upgrade Card	Quadra, Centris, AV, PowerMac Card

*Notes:
E = System Extension; **C** = Chooser Extension; **T** = Communication Tool; **D** = Document; **F** = Folder; **A** = Application

Now You See Them...   (SZA)

And now you don't. Some extensions, and other system files that you get used to seeing under one system version, aren't necessary under another because they've been rolled into the main system software or replaced by something else. Here's what disappeared between System 7.0/7.1 and System 7.5:

Extensions:

- *Apple Event Manager:* rolled into AppleScript extension
- *Drag-and-Drop, Sound Manager, Thread Manager, 040 VM Update:* rolled into System file
- *EM Sound Update, Mount IDE Extension, PowerBook 150 Update:* rolled into Update 1.0

Enablers:

- 7.1 enablers rolled into System file
- early 7.5 enablers rolled into 1.0 Update
- all 7.5 enablers to date rolled into System 7.5.3.

Puzzle: replaced by Jigsaw Puzzle

Alarm Clock: dropped

An X through an icon at startup means the extension or control panel has been turned off.

the items that are loading into memory—extensions and control panels.

If you see an X through one of the icons, that means it's not loading but it's still in the Control Panels or Extensions folder: It may be turned off from within the control panel, it may be a demo that's reached its expiration date, or it might not be able to load because another extension that it depends on didn't load first.

Trashing extensions. It's not so easy to trash an extension because you're not allowed to erase any file that's in use—and most extensions, since they load into memory at startup, are flagged as "in use" even if you're not using their particular capabilities at any given time.

So, trashing an extension is usually a two-step process. First, drag it out of the Extensions folder or use Extensions Manager to disable it. Then, after you restart the Mac, you can drag it to the Trash.

Control Panels   (SZA)

It's getting almost impossible to keep up with all the control panels that Apple provides. Some of them are covered elsewhere in this book, where the related topics are being covered: Network, Sharing Setup, Users & Groups in Chapter 24; Memory in Chapter 4; Extension Manager in Chapters 8 and 13; and Speech in Chapter 17. The Apple Menu Options control panel is covered later in this chapter under "The Hierarchical Apple Menu."

Cache Switch. The Cache Switch control panel turns the '040 "processor caching" on and off so that older programs that aren't compatible with the caching operation can run on '040 (and 'LC040) machines. Because the caching is something that speeds up the Mac, turning it off can cut its speed in half.

HOT TIP

If you option-click on the Faster or More Compatible button, the changes take effect immediately instead of after restart.

Color. Use the Color control panel to set the highlight color used for text, and the color of window frames on the desktop. There are nine choices for the window frame, and eight colors and "Other" for the highlight. "Other" opens the Color Picker that lets you choose the exact shade you want.

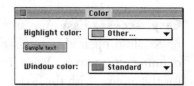

The Color control panel lets you customize your desktop's windows.

If you're using an older machine and want to speed up Finder operations, set the window color to black and white—windows will open, close, and scroll faster. (It's just the frames that will be black and white—the window contents are still full color.)

HOT TIP

Click on one of these icons to choose the Color Picker mode.

Drag this crosshairs, or simply click in a new spot in the color wheel to choose a new color (changing the hue and saturation).

This shows the color that was current when you opened the Color Picker.

This shows the new color you're choosing.

These numbers change as you reposition the crosshairs in the color wheel, but you can use the arrows to change the numbers, or type in numbers, and the crosshairs will move to match them.

Change this number manually instead of using the slider on the Lightness bar.

This toggles to More Choices; use it to show or hide the mode icons at left.

Drag the slider to a position on the bar to change the percentage of black in the colors; the number in the Lightness box changes accordingly.

The Color Picker can be accessed from several different control panels and has two distinct modes: HSL (Hue-Saturation-Light), shown here, and the RGB (Red-Green-Blue) mode where you use sliders to set the colors.

Date & Time. The Date & Time control panel lets you set the date, time, and time zone for your Mac's clock; you can also choose the date and time formats that will be used by the system.

But the handiest option in the control panel is the Menubar Clock, which puts a digital clock in your menu bar; you can turn it on or off, specify the font, size, color, and type of readout, and so on.

These are the options available through the Date & Time control panel for the Menubar Clock.

Easy Access. Easy Access is a way for physically impaired persons to bypass difficult mouse and keyboard operations by defining alternatives. *Mouse Keys* lets you substitute the keys on the numeric keypad for the mouse, with the ⑤ key acting as the button. *Slow Keys* adds a delay to each key press so an accidental press won't register, and disables the normal key repeat feature. *Sticky Keys* lets you press a modifier key (such as ⌘), release it, and then press another key (such as Ⓟ), and have it register as the ⌘Ⓟ combination; a modifier can be locked down for multiple key presses, too.

General Controls. The General Controls control panel that showed up in System 7.5 was a total redesign that incorporated features first found in Performa system software, and banished the desktop patterns to its own control panel. In fact, the only things left from the original version are the blink rates for the insertion point and menu blinking!

Unchecking this hides desktop windows and icons when you're in other applications; you won't be able to click on the desktop surface to move to the Finder, either. (If you use the Application menu's Hide command, the Finder's windows are hidden, but its icons are not.)

This controls how fast the text insertion point blinks; most find the middle setting fine.

Checking this opens the Launcher window automatically at every startup.

Avoid that annoying "The Mac was shut down improperly" dialog at startup after a crash by unchecking this option.

Turning on protection means items inside the folders can't be renamed or deleted.

The Applications folder is created on your desktop when you check this button.

This controls how many times the highlight on a selected command blinks when you release the mouse button. Try turning it off—you'll see how important that feedback is!

Sets the default folder for the Open and Save dialogs (although some applications override this setting). Choosing Documents folder as the default creates a Documents folder on your desktop.

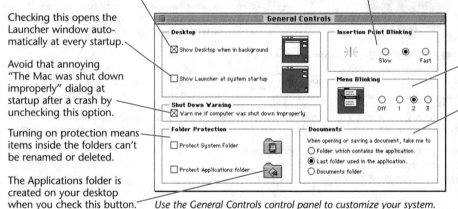

Use the General Controls control panel to customize your system.

Keyboard. The Keyboard control panel lets you set how fast a character is typed if you hold down a key, and how long you must hold it down before the repeat kicks in. It also lets you choose a keyboard layout, supplying two to start with (in U.S. systems, that is): U.S., which is built-in and can't be removed, and U.S.-System 6, which is visible in the opened System file as a resource that you can remove. (There were some slight changes in the position of some option-key characters from System 6 to System 7.)

Use the Keyboard control panel to set keyboard options.

Why would you want to switch keyboard layouts (which you can find on various on-line services and through user groups)? Well, if you get tired of typing N>Y> as the abbreviation for New York because your finger doesn't come off the shift key fast enough, there are layouts that "remap" the keyboard so the shifted character is still the period. Or, for PowerBook users, there are layouts that include key combinations that substitute for the missing numeric keypad.

POWERBOOK

Starting with System 7.5, pressing ⌘Option Spacebar switches from one keyboard layout to another—without asking your permission or letting you know it was done. But the 1.0 Update, and System 7.5.1, provide a checkbox in the control panel so you can turn this off—and start out with it off as the default.

HOT TIP

Labels. Applying a label to an icon is a simple matter of selecting the icon and then choosing from the Label menu; both the name and the color are applied to the icon. Because you can search and sort according to labels, and the color provides a visual clue, using labels is an easy way to organize some of the information on your disk.

The settings in the Labels control panel affect the Label menu. If there's a dash in front of a menu item, like the ones shown here, it means that one or more items in a multiple selection have that label.

But you're not stuck with the labels that are in the Label menu: Use the Labels control panel to alter the choices in the menu. To change a name, just type it in the box; to change a color, double-click on it and use the Color Picker that opens to assign a new color. When you change the name of the available labels, all the icons you labeled with the former name are relabeled with the new name.

Avoid using light colors; although they look nice on full-size folders because the inside of the icon is filled with it, in list views (in desktop windows and inside Open and Save dialogs) the color is used only for the outline, which makes the icon practically disappear.

HOT TIP

Launcher. The Launcher control panel (also discussed in Chapter 1) lets you simply click a button to launch an application or open a document instead of hunting through folders to find it. To create a button, you put an item (or, more practically speaking, an item's alias) inside the Launcher Items folder. Starting with the 2.7 version of this control panel (in System 7.5's 1.0 Update, and with System 7.5.1 and later), you can simply drag an icon into the Launcher window, and an alias will automatically be created inside the Launcher Items folder.

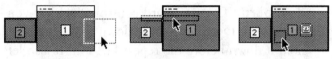

Using the Monitors control panel for double-monitor setups.
Left: Drag the screen icons to define the relative positions of the monitors so the mouse cursor will slide from one to the other naturally.
Center: Drag the menu bar from one screen icon to another to choose the monitor that should have the real menu bar.
Right: Hold down option and drag the Happy Mac icon that appears to choose which monitor should display the Welcome dialog at startup.

Monitors. Use the Monitors control panel to adjust the number of colors being displayed on your monitor—it will list choices up to the maximum available for your hardware setup. The options available through the Options button depend on your video card and monitor—and on whether the information is in the Extensions folder.

HOT TIP

This control panel also provides several ways to configure a double-monitor setup, as shown in the figure above.

Mouse. The Mouse control panel lets you set the *tracking speed* for the cursor: the relationship between how fast you move the mouse and how far the mouse cursor travels on the screen. You can also adjust the double-click speed setting: how close together two clicks have to be to count as a double-click instead of two single clicks.

The double-click speed also controls the edit delay on the desktop—how long it takes from the time you click on an icon's name to when the editing rectangle appears around it.

PC Exchange. PC Exchange gives you three capabilities:

• It lets you see a PC-formatted disk (one formatted on a DOS or Windows machine) on your desktop; all you have to do is insert the disk and, if PC Exchange is installed, the disk shows up on the desktop. Whether or not you can read the files on it depends on what the files are and what applications you have.

• You can format a blank disk for a DOS or windows machine. If PC Exchange is installed, every time you erase a disk or put in a blank disk, you'll be given the option to format it as a Mac or PC disk.

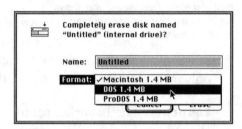

• You can, through the control panel's window, define which Mac application should open when you double-click on specific types of PC files.

PC Exchange gives you a choice for floppy disk formatting.

Sound. The Sound control panel lets you select an alert sound (also known as the *system beep*), record sounds (if your hardware supports a microphone), and set volumes for the alert as well as for the headphone jack (if you have one).

The sounds in the list are the ones inside the System file. You can cut or copy any sound in the list, and you can paste in new ones.

Startup Disk. The Startup Disk control panel lets you select the disk that you want as a startup disk, overriding the normal SCSI ID-based order for looking for a start-up disk. (You might want to do this to temporarily run your Mac from a different system, one that's on an external drive.)

The control panel shows all mounted volumes and doesn't know if the disk you choose actually has a System Folder on it, so you have to make sure that the selected volume can actually act as a startup. Disk partitions show up as separate volumes, but some versions of the system software keep track only of the SCSI ID of the volume you choose, and can't differentiate among partitions on a drive.

Views. The Views control panel provides lots of control over the look of your desktop windows, starting with the text used for the icon names. You can use it to customize your desktop and keep it obsessively neat, too. (Note that there's a minor controversy as to whether the Calculate Folder Sizes setting *actually* slows things down in the Finder or just *seems to* slow things down because you're waiting for the figures to show up.)

Holding down ⌘ while dragging an icon temporarily reverses the Snap To Grid setting in this control panel.

HOT TIP

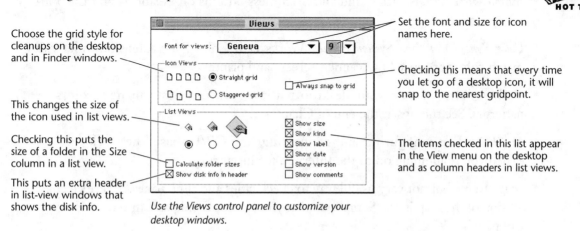

Choose the grid style for cleanups on the desktop and in Finder windows.

Set the font and size for icon names here.

This changes the size of the icon used in list views.

Checking this puts the size of a folder in the Size column in a list view.

This puts an extra header in list-view windows that shows the disk info.

Checking this means that every time you let go of a desktop icon, it will snap to the nearest gridpoint.

The items checked in this list appear in the View menu on the desktop and as column headers in list views.

Use the Views control panel to customize your desktop windows.

WindowShade. This nifty control panel is one that's often overlooked, but it provides a wonderful way to cut down on screen clutter: It lets you shrink a window down to just a title bar—so, it hangs around and is immediately available but doesn't take up

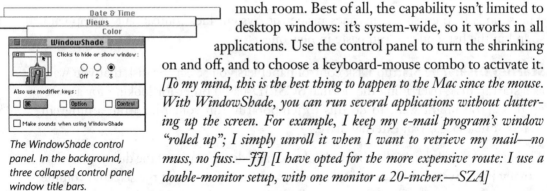

much room. Best of all, the capability isn't limited to desktop windows: it's system-wide, so it works in all applications. Use the control panel to turn the shrinking on and off, and to choose a keyboard-mouse combo to activate it. *[To my mind, this is the best thing to happen to the Mac since the mouse. With WindowShade, you can run several applications without cluttering up the screen. For example, I keep my e-mail program's window "rolled up"; I simply unroll it when I want to retrieve my mail—no muss, no fuss.—JJ] [I have opted for the more expensive route: I use a double-monitor setup, with one monitor a 20-incher.—SZA]*

The WindowShade control panel. In the background, three collapsed control panel window title bars.

Ad Infinitum. Finally, here's a quick take on the control panels that aren't covered elsewhere and don't require too much in the way of explanation:

- *ATM GX:* Adobe Type Manager for QuickDraw GX shipped with System 7.5; there's a special version (3.8) that's PowerPC native. (See Chapter 14 for more information about ATM.)

- *Auto Power On/Off:* Shuts down the Mac after a specified idle time or at a defined time; you can identify special circumstances that keep it from shutting down automatically.

- *Brightness:* Adjusts brightness of screen on Classic and Classic II models.

- *Button Disabler:* Disables sound and brightness buttons on Performa and LC 500-series models.

- *Color Sync, Color Sync System Profile:* Works with Color Sync extension to let you match colors produced by scanner, screen, and printer.

- *Desktop Patterns:* Sets your desktop pattern (you can paste in new colors or patterns). See the tips at the end of Chapter 1.

- *MacTCP:* For configuring and connecting to TCP/IP-based network services (when you're jumping on to the Internet, for instance).

- *Map:* A cute but not very useful way to check cities and time zones. There's a color version of the map in the Scrapbook that you can copy and paste into the Map control panel.

- *Numbers:* Set the number formatting for system use—you'll see your formatting choice in Finder windows and dialogs.

- *PowerTalk setup:* Configures PowerTalk settings.

- *Serial Switch:* For Mac IIfx and Quadra 950 only, for compatibility for programs that use printer or modem ports.

- *Text:* Sets the sorting order and script behavior based on country/language.

System Components for PowerBooks (SZA)

Although Apple touts something called its "mobile operating system," it's the basic Mac system software with a few special extensions, control panels, and utilities for **POWERBOOK** PowerBook users.

Extensions. There are a few extensions that are specific to the PowerBooks:

- *Assistant Toolbox:* Provides syncing capabilities for File Assistant application, and keyboard options for sleep commands.

- *Battery Patch:* For Duos using System 7.1 and Type II batteries.

- *Caps Lock:* Puts Caps Lock mode icon in menu bar.

- *PowerBook Guide Extension:* Provides information for Apple Guide help system.

- *PowerBook Monitors Extension:* Provides information for the Options button in the Monitors control panel.

- *Type III Battery:* For Duos using Type III batteries and systems previous to System 7.5.

Control panels. PowerBook control panels have been evolving along with the PowerBooks themselves. They include the following:

- *AutoRemounter:* For PowerBooks, it automatically remounts a network server when coming out of sleep.

- *Control Strip:* Provides the Control Strip technology (see "The Control Strip"); included in some System 7.1 versions that shipped with PowerBooks, and with all System 7.5 installations.

- *Date & Time:* This has special features for PowerBooks—battery indicator and click-sleep control in menu bar.

- *Portable:* Left over from the old Portable Mac, this shipped with the first round of PowerBooks and was replaced by the PowerBook control panel.

- *PowerBook:* Shipped with System 7.1, redesigned in the 3.0 update, this gives you control over the basics of sleep intervals and battery conservation.

- *PowerBook Setup:* For PowerBook models that support it, this lets you set the ID for SCSI disk mode and a wakeup time.

- *PowerBook Display:* Contains settings for working with an external monitor.

- *Trackpad:* Configures trackpad behavior.

The Control Strip. The Control Strip is a control panel with a modular approach: Items in the Control Strip Modules folder (inside the System Folder) appear as icons in the strip itself. The system comes with quite a few modules, but you'll find others on-line and in packages such as VST's PBTools (covered in Chapter 13).

Desk Accessories   (SZA)

Desk accessories (often referred to as DAs) are little applications with narrowly focused capabilities. Prior to System 7, they were part of the System file itself, but now they're stand-alone items. They're not exactly applications—you'll see that they're listed as a "desk accessory" type in a list view window, for instance, and they handle memory a little differently—but you don't have to worry about the behind-the-scenes stuff like that.

Chooser. The Chooser is for letting you *choose*—printers, file servers, and even fax modems—and then set options. Clicking on an icon in the left pane lists options on the right; just which options you get depend on what you've selected. Click on a LaserWriter driver on the left, and you'll see the available LaserWriters; clicking on the AppleShare icon gets you a list of file servers and shared network volumes. The Chooser is also where you can turn two special things on and off: AppleTalk and Background Printing.

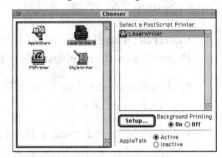

The Chooser window, with the left pane active (there's a dark frame around it). Selecting a different icon on the left lists different options on the right.

The awkward thing about using the Chooser is that there's no OK button; things happen when you select them, even though you don't get any feedback most of the time.

There are a few keyboard shortcuts available in the Chooser. Pressing ⟨Tab⟩ alternately activates the left or right pane. Inside the active pane, you can type a few letters to identify the item you want selected, or you can use the ⟨←⟩⟨→⟩⟨↓⟩⟨↑⟩ keys to select the item adjacent to the currently selected item.

HOT TIP

Note Pad. System 7.5's Note Pad was finally updated from the archaic version that's been with the Mac since forever, but it's still not beefy enough to serve any practical purpose. New features include: a three-dimensional look and sound effects when you flip a page; a resizable window; scrollable text on each page; your choice of font and size for text; and, a Find function.

To flip between pages, click on the corner, or the upturned corner, in the lower left of the Note Pad. But for all its little improvements, this version lost a major one: You can't flip from page 8 (the last one) right around to page 1 anymore—you have to flip every page to get back to the first.

Scrapbook. The Scrapbook was updated for System 7 and again for System 7.5; the improvements are enough to make it a reasonably useful little utility. The window is resizable and displays information for each page. The Scrapbook can store text, graphics of all types, sounds, and QuickTime movies. It also stores all sorts of special things, such as HyperCard buttons including their scripts, and PageMaker or Quark page elements. *[If I had a dime for everyone I know who uses the Scrapbook, I might be able to afford calling the three of them from a public phone booth!—JJ]*

To put something into the Scrapbook, you put it on the Clipboard and then choose the Paste command in the Scrapbook; the item appears on a newly created page. To copy or cut something, you don't have to select it—you just flip to its page and choose the command from the Edit menu. (You can also use Drag-and-Drop to add items to or to remove them from the Scrapbook.)

The Scrapbook doesn't do any "converting" of information, so whether or not the information you put in from one application can transfer to another depends on the application. A HyperCard button with a script can be copied and pasted into any stack, but if you try to copy from the Scrapbook and paste it someplace else, you'll get only the graphic part of the button and not its attached script.

Others. There are a few other desk accessories included in the system software, ranging from somewhat useful to totally whimsical:

- *Calculator:* Just what it looks like; you can paste in problems such as *16*42+8*, and the Copy command copies the results in the Calculator's window to the Clipboard.

- *Key Caps:* You can check out all the characters in any font by looking at them here (use the Key Caps menu); type by using the keyboard or by clicking the keys in Key Caps. You can select and copy the text in the Key Caps window.

- *Jigsaw Puzzle:* A pleasant diversion, but less puzzling than the Mac's original Puzzle. Paste in a new picture if you want (try the color map that's in the Scrapbook).

- *AppleCD Audio Player:* Lets you play audio CDs on your Mac, and even set up "play lists" for them.

- *Shut Down:* You never get to open this DA—select it and the Mac shuts down. Since it's in the menu, you don't have to go back to the desktop to use the Shut Down command in the Special menu.

Special System Features

The list of system features grows with every new system version. In this section, we cover some that deserve special attention and round up the rest with brief descriptions.

The Hierarchical Apple Menu   (SZA)

The hierarchical menu that debuted in System 7.5 is provided by the Apple Menu Options control panel. Unfortunately, this control panel was the cause of so many conflicts, problems, and system slowdowns that early adopters of 7.5 soon dragged it out of their Control Panels folders. It's been improved with each system update, but many users still don't trust it entirely, especially on systems that are running lots of extensions, and prefer to use a utility such as Now Utilities' NowMenus to provide hierarchical menus.

Apple Menu Options. The main function of the Apple Menu Options control panel is right at the top of its window, where you turn the hierarchical menu on or off. This has an immediate effect—you don't have to wait until you restart. In the lower section, you specify how many items should be listed in the "recent" folders, or turn them off completely.

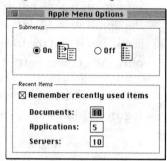

Use the Apple Menu Options control panel to turn the hierarchical menu on and off.

With the hierarchical menu turned on, folders listed in the menu (because they're in the Apple Menu Items folder) have submenus that list their contents. Your system starts out with one for the Control Panels folder, and one called Automated Tasks (if you've installed AppleScript).

HOT TIP

Using the hierarchical function makes things a lot easier. Instead of having desk accessories, control panels, applications, and documents collated into an alphabetical list for your menu, you can organize the inside of the Apple Menu Items folder with subfolders so that similar items are grouped together. Create folders when you need them, and use aliases of existing folders where you can. Aliasing your hard drive icon and putting it in the menu gives you five-folder deep access to its contents.

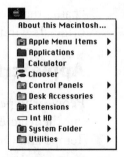

Recent folders. Using the Recent Items options creates up to three folders inside your System Folder: Recent Documents, Recent Appli-

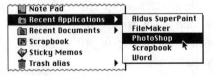

cations, and Recent Servers. The menu will keep track of the items in those categories that you used most recently by creating aliases that go into the Recent folders. If you want some of the recent folders, but not others, put a zero in the Apple Menu Options control panel for the Recent folder you don't want.

Use the Recent Applications folder to re-launch an application.

Organizing your Apple Menu Items folder can do wonders for your hierarchical Apple menu.

Aliases   (SZA)

Aliases, introduced with System 7, are among the most useful and yet perhaps most underutilized features of the system software. An *alias* is a "pointer" to an icon—it's a copy of just the icon, not the file, folder, or disk that the icon represents. Double-click on the alias, and the original item opens. So? So you can put an alias of an application out on the desktop, or in a special window, even though the real application has to be inside a folder with its support files. Using aliases is like having a single icon exist in more than one place at a time.

ClarisWorks   ClarisWorks alias

The original application icon (left) and its alias.

Creating an alias. Creating an alias is simple: Select the item and choose Make Alias from the Finder's File menu. The alias shows up as an identical icon, with its italicized name the same as the original's except for the "alias" appended to it. You can rename it (the name stays in italics) or move it anywhere you want. If you move or rename the original item, the alias still finds it.

Put an alias anywhere it's convenient for you to open the file or folder it represents. The menu is a popular spot for folders, applications, and documents that you access often—especially if you utilize the hierarchical menu setup.

Open only. You can't do anything to the original file with an alias except open it. If you trash an alias or copy it to another disk, it's only the alias that's erased or copied; the original stays untouched.

Finding the original. An alias can almost always find its original—but what if you want to find the original file without opening it? Get Info on the alias and check the "path" that's described under "Original." Or, click the Get Original button for the original's window to be opened with the item selected in it.

AppleScript

People who perform routine tasks repeatedly on the Mac can save a lot of time by having the Mac execute those tasks automatically. And while macro programs such as Tempo and QuicKeys (covered in Chapter 13) have provided a way to automate small tasks, AppleScript provides a way for a user to do sophisticated *scripting* (it's really *programming*, but nobody wants to scare you away with that word).

AppleScript was first introduced with System 7 Pro, but became part of the standard system software in 7.5.

Creating scripts (SZA/Ken Maki/JK). You can use AppleScript to create a script that does something simple, such as emptying the Trash at shutdown, or something as complicated as one that prepares a weekly report by retrieving data over a network from database or spreadsheet files on colleagues' disks, copying it into the appropriate places in a word processor file, saving the new report, and e-mailing copies to a list of recipients. How you use AppleScript depends on your own needs and imagination—and your scripting skills.

You use the Script Editor application to create *scripts*—a series of instructions for the Mac to follow. A script can send instructions to the Finder or to any application that "understands" AppleScript commands.

A few applications, including the Finder, are "recordable," which means you can create scripts the same way you record macros in QuicKeys or Tempo—just by telling the Script Editor to watch and record what you're doing. But even recorded scripts usually need some tweaking, so unless you're willing to learn some scripting (and if you've used HyperTalk, you're halfway there), AppleScript isn't for you.

Running scripts (SZA). Scripts can be run from the Script Editor window, or they can be "compiled" into stand-alone applications that run when you double-click on them. If you put scripted applications in the Apple Menu Items folder, or in a subfolder that's in the menu, you can run the script by simply selecting it from the menu. In fact, when you choose to install AppleScript in System 7.5, your Apple Menu Items folder is set up with an alias to the Automated Tasks folder which contains some ready-made scripts.

One of the most convenient places for storing certain compiled scripts is in the Startup Items or Shut Down Items folders in the System Folder so that the script will be executed when you start up or shut down the Mac. You can have a script automatically launch a telecom program and pick up your mail each time you start up, or automatically empty the Trash before you shut down for the night.

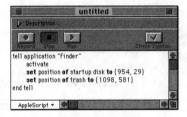

The scripted results of recording something in the Finder—the relocation of the startup disk and trash icons.

You can also save a script as a special kind of application—a *droplet*—that goes into action when you drag an icon onto it. The script in the droplet acts on whatever item(s) you've dragged onto it. It could, for instance, lock or unlock the documents you've dragged there, or compress each one and move it into a special folder so it can be backed up later. There are countless tasks you can automate this way.

Instant translation (Ken Maki/JK). Scripts transcend the language of the computer they're run on—when you put a script written in English on a computer using KanjiTalk, it runs normally. The script itself is actually translated and can be edited in the new language.

Find File (SZA)

It was only with System 7 that there was actually a Find command in the Finder, but System 7.5 leaped ahead with a much more full-featured Find command. The Find File application lets you use all sorts of criteria, alone or in combination, to find a misplaced file.

The Find command. The basic Find command opens a dialog that lets you search an entire hard drive for a file, even if you can't remember its complete name. And if you strike out on the name, you can search by all sorts of criteria. If, say, you created a report in ClarisWorks some time in the middle of last week, you can set up the

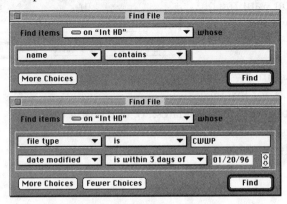

The standard Find File window (top) can be expanded with the More Choices button (bottom) so you can specify multiple criteria for the search.

search criteria to be "file type" of CWWP (that's the ClarisWorks word processor file type) and a date "within 2 days of" the date you think you last modified it—that should be enough to pinpoint the file. To use multiple criteria, use the More Choices button in the Find File window; click it again for each set of search parameters you want to set and the window keeps expanding to accommodate your needs.

HOT TIP

If you want to search something other than the internal hard drive, use the pop-up menu in the window to specify the disk you want to search in. To search inside a specific folder, first select it on the desktop and then choose In Finder Selection from the menu.

The Items Found window. After Find File searches for your file, it opens the Items Found window. In the upper area, it lists the "hits"; the lower area shows the complete path to the item you've selected in the upper pane.

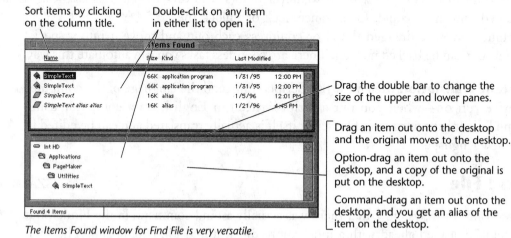

Sort items by clicking on the column title.

Double-click on any item in either list to open it.

Drag the double bar to change the size of the upper and lower panes.

Drag an item out onto the desktop and the original moves to the desktop.

Option-drag an item out onto the desktop, and a copy of the original is put on the desktop.

Command-drag an item out onto the desktop, and you get an alias of the item on the desktop.

The Items Found window for Find File is very versatile.

Find File provides an amazing number of options once you've found the file: Look through its menus and you'll see commands for opening, printing, and even getting info on a selected item, as well as for opening the folder that the selected item is in. There are some capabilities—such as changing the sizes of the upper and lower panes—that aren't so obvious; they're described in the above figure.

Using the old Find command. If you want the old Find command and dialog, hold down (Shift) as you choose Find from the File menu (or press ⌘(Shift)(F)).

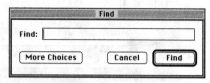

The old Find command is still available.

Further evolution. The Find File utility keeps evolving. A system update for System 7.5, for instance, added the "within" options for the created and modified dates; so, don't forget to check the details anytime you update your system. The table "Search Criteria in Find File" lists the search options available as of this writing.

Search Criteria in Find File

Search for a file whose...	Choices	Match*
name	contains starts with ends with is is not doesn't contain	[*text*]
size	is less than is greater than	[*number*]K
kind	is is not	alias application clipping file document folder font sound stationery
label	is is not	None (label list)
date created	is / before / after / not is within 1/2/3 days of is within 1/2/3 weeks of is within 1/2/3/6 months of	[*month/date/yr*]
date modified	*(same as date created choices)*	[*month/date/yr*]
version	is is not	[*text*]
comments	contain do not contain	[*text*]
lock attribute	is	locked unlocked
folder attribute	is is not	empty shared mounted
file type	is is not	[*text*]
creator	is is not	[*text*]

*Item in [*brackets*] is what you fill in.

Drag-and-Drop   (SZA)

System 7.5's Drag-and-Drop capability gives you an extra-easy way to move information from one place to another: just select it and drag it. Even if you're dragging a block of text, or a grouping of graphics, and you're dragging it from one window to another, or one application to another, or right out onto the desktop, all you do is select and drag. But remember that Drag-and-Drop, while a system-level capability, is one that has to be implemented by each individual application, so it won't always work.

There's occasionally some confusion about what "drag and drop" really is. Apple first used the phrase in System 7 to refer to the desktop feature that lets you drag a document icon onto an application icon and have the document open inside the application. (You can still do this, but it's not called "drag and drop" anymore.)

Then there's "drag-and-drop editing," introduced by Microsoft Word and copied by many applications since: you can drag selected text to a new spot in a document. This actually fits the definition of the system-level drag-and-drop capability, of course, but the difference is that it works only within the application itself, and not between applications or onto the desktop.

Basic drag and drop. You can check out the drag-and-drop process using two of the desk accessories that come with your system: the Note Pad and the Scrapbook (it works with SimpleText, too). Open both DAs and type something into the Note Pad. Select it, and drag it into the Scrapbook—right across any intervening space. Let it go on top of the Scrapbook, and there it is! The original item is still in place, and a copy is in the new spot.

Clippings. When you don't have two applications open and can't drag and drop between them, you don't have to store the transfer material in an interim application or desk accessory like the Scrapbook: You can just drop the selection onto the desktop. Later, you can drag it into the document where you want it.

text clipping   picture clipping

The icon for a clipping file changes according to the type of clipping it is.

A dropped selection is called a *clipping;* its icon is that of a page torn out of a notebook, but changes according to whether the clipping is text, graphics, or a sound. The default name is simply *text clipping* or *picture clipping,* so you should rename it right away in order to keep track of what it really is. Double-clicking on a clipping icon opens a window that displays the text or graphic (double-clicking a sound clipping merely plays it).

If you have a clipping that you want to use in a document, but that application doesn't support Drag-and-Drop, open the clipping window and copy the item so you can paste it in instead.

No clippings. If you just can't drop a clipping on the desktop but Drag-and-Drop is working from one supporting application to another, you're missing the Clipping Extension from your Extensions folder. You should be able to find it on your system disks.

Other

Apple Events (SZA/JK/CR). Apple Events are part of an underlying technology through which applications can communicate, and even control one another; an *event* is a command sent from one application to another. For this to work, an application has to be "aware" of events—it has to be designed to take advantage of Apple Events. Apple Events can work on one Mac, or even between Macs on a network, or over a modem line. AppleScript uses Apple Events to control the Finder and other "pliable" programs.

Publish and Subscribe (SZA/CR/JK). Publish and Subscribe, introduced in System 7, works like an automatic cut-and-paste feature, allowing you to link data so that changing it in one place also changes it anyplace else you've put it. The data is *published* from one document, creating a separate file, the *edition*. Another document *subscribes* to the edition and can be set to automatically update if the edition changes.

It's a great idea that has not really caught on or received support from both users and software companies that it needs to become an important part of Mac computing.

Stationery (SZA). Stationery is another System 7 feature that never quite made it to the mainstream. Despite the fact that so few applications provide a Stationery button in the Save dialog—which is what the Apple guidelines called for—you can still use the feature, albeit a little awkwardly.

Stationery lets you create a *template*, a document with a format that you use repeatedly—one with your letterhead in it, for instance, so you don't have to re-create the letterhead every time you need it.

You can set up your document with all the formats you want included and save it under a name like MemoForm. Then, on the desktop, Get Info on the document and check the Stationery Pad checkbox in the window. The next time you open the document, the Mac creates a copy of it, leaving the original untouched. (Although different applications handle this type of document in different ways.)

HOT TIP

QuickTime (SZA). QuickTime lets you cut and paste still or animated images, with or without sounds; as a matter of fact, it lets you handle the sounds without the images, too. QuickTime is both the name of the technology and the name of the extension that lets you use it.

To see a QuickTime movie, you need not only the QuickTime extension (which came with system software starting with System 7.1, but works with systems back through 6.0.7), but also some application that lets you play the movies. (See Chapter 17 for more on QuickTime.)

Actually, there is one way you can see a QuickTime movie without any kind of player: Name the file *Startup Movie* and leave it in your System Folder. When you start your Mac, the movie plays. (Press ⌘. to stop it if it's too long!)

QuickDraw (SZA). QuickDraw is the set of graphics routines built into the Mac's ROMs that control how things are drawn on the screen. "Drawn" doesn't mean just pictures, though—characters in fonts are "drawn" on the screen, too. This leads to the misnomer "QuickDraw printer" for a non-PostScript printer, since the Mac's Quick-Draw routines do all the formation of letters and then send the images to the printer.

QuickDraw GX (SZA). QuickDraw GX, part of System 7.5, provides great potential for improved font handling and printing on the Mac. But so much of its capabilities depend on using GX-compatible fonts, and Adobe has such a lock on computer font technology with millions of users adhering to its PostScript specs, that it's been rough going for GX.

WorldScript (Elizabeth Castro). The Mac has been able to write in different languages and alphabets for quite some time. But with WorldScript, the Mac provides programmers with a standardized approach to different alphabets and supports "double-byte" languages such as Japanese and Chinese.

Although WorldScript is built into system software version 7.1 and later, to actually type something in a foreign alphabet you'll need one of Apple's Language Kits (the Japanese Language Kit goes for about $250) and a program that supports WorldScript, such as Nisus or WordPerfect.

PowerTalk (JK). PowerTalk puts a universal mailbox on your desktop, from which you can exchange messages, faxes, and files with others across a network or via on-line services. You save people's contact information as "business cards," and send a document by dragging its icon onto the appropriate business card. *[Yet another system feature that developers declined to support.—SZA]*

PlainTalk (JK/Michael Santiago/Elizabeth Castro). PlainTalk, available on the Quadra AVs and Power Macs, actually consists of two parts. *Text-to-speech* enables applications that support it to read aloud in a human-like voice, while *voice recognition* works in conjunction with AppleScript to let you give voice commands to the Mac.

The text-to-speech feature gives you a choice of voices of varying quality. Although all of them sound like a computer talking, the high-quality voices' pronunciation is impressively close to human speech, complete with inflections around punctuation. PlainTalk is even smart enough to pronounce words and abbreviations differently based on context—saying *dr* as *doctor* when it's in a name but *drive* when it's part of an address.

GOOD FEATURE

OpenDoc (JK)

At this writing, Apple is revising the system software to support a revolutionary new document format called OpenDoc, which takes interapplication communication a step beyond what Apple events makes possible. OpenDoc will allow you to use several applications to work on different types of data within a single document (called a *compound document* because of the multiple formats it contains). Parts of a document that would normally be separate documents from different applications could be part of a single file, eliminating the need to cut and paste between applications or re-importing into a central document every time it needs editing. *[It's interesting or frustrating to note that as I write this for the Sixth Edition, John's "at this writing" from the Fifth Edition doesn't get changed. We're still waiting for OpenDoc; it's closer, but not here "at this writing."—SZA]*

The voice-recognition part of PlainTalk is designed to open files and activate menu commands; you can also teach it special commands or set it to activate AppleScript scripts. Any menu item in the current application can be invoked using speech (in this limited sense, all applications support voice recognition). Applications that respond to Apple Events can be more fully controlled by PlainTalk.

Many users say they sometimes have to repeat commands several times before the computer responds, and when it does, there may be a long delay before the command is executed. Sometimes the computer may even execute the wrong command, or take an action when you don't expect it to (because you were talking to someone else, but the computer "heard" you). Despite the various "tolerance" settings available in the Speech Setup control panel, it's often difficult to get the Mac to truly cooperate with spoken commands.

Stickies (SZA). Stickies is a little application that lets you make the electronic equivalent of Post-it notes. It also lets you clutter up your screen, the same way you can with the paper version. A sticky memo is a little window with minimal controls (a title bar, close box, and zoom box). Use Stickies menus to change the color of the note, and the font used in it.

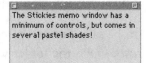

A Stickies memo is a window with minimal controls.

Unfortunately, a note sticks to a spot on a screen, and not to anything particular, such as a window or an icon. And, since Stickies is an application, it has to be the active one for its notes to show up on top of other windows on the screen.

BAD FEATURE

TeachText and SimpleText (SZA/JK). TeachText has almost always been a part of system software: a tiny application that opened text files. It was a handy vehicle for

Readme files, those late-breaking news reports that are shipped with software whose documentation is printed before everything's ironed out. But TeachText was replaced by SimpleText starting with the System Update 3 for System 7.1. It supports multiple fonts, sizes, and styles in a document, can record and play back sounds, and open more than one document at a time.

SimpleText is installed on the main level of your hard drive when you install system software. If you put it away in some folder, and reinstall your system software, you'll get another copy right out there in the open. You should try using the Find command occasionally to weed out multiple copies of SimpleText.

System Tips

HOT TIPS

General

Creating a disk-space monitor (JK). You don't have to add a header to every list-view window if all you want to keep track of is how much space is on your hard disk. Create a folder called Disk Space, set its window to display by icon, and put it in the Apple Menu Items folder. Whenever you want to check your available disk space, choose Disk Space from the menu and the window that opens will have that information.

Replace folder contents, not folders (SZA). If you drag a folder from one disk to another, and the destination disk already has a folder on it with the same name, the contents of the folder you're dragging completely replace the contents of the existing folder. This can be a big problem, since you may be wiping out files in the destination folder that don't exist in the copied-over folder.

To be safe, never replace one folder with another. Instead, work with the folder *contents*. Open the folder you want to copy, select its contents with (⌘A), and drag the items into the destination folder. Files with the same name will be replaced, but extra files won't be touched. (But watch out for any folders inside that folder!)

Stopping extensions and startups (SZA). Hold down (Shift) at startup to prevent extensions from loading—a step that's necessary when you're troubleshooting an extension problem.

You can also hold down (Shift) *after* the extensions are loaded, just before your desktop shows up, and it will prevent items in the Startup Items folder from opening.

Silencing the Mac (SZA/Eric Apgar). If you don't want to hear any system beeps, move the slider bar in the Sound control panel to zero; instead of making sounds, the Mac will flash the menu bar when it wants your attention. To silence the startup chord, though, you have to plug something into the audio-out port on the back of the Mac.

Control Panels

Label sorting (SZA). Labels aren't the handiest of functions in the Mac system, but if you use them, you'll be surprised at how they get sorted in list-view windows. Labels are sorted according to their position in the Label menu! So, don't count on names such as A Priority and B Priority unless you put them in the right spot on the menu.

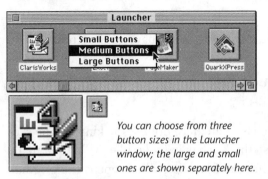

You can choose from three button sizes in the Launcher window; the large and small ones are shown separately here.

Launcher buttons (SZA). The 2.7 version of the Launcher control panel that comes with the 1.0 System Update for System 7.5 contains a few little tweaks that add to its versatility. My favorite: Hold down ⌘ and press the mouse button while pointing to the window background, and you'll get a menu that lets you choose from three button sizes.

Pasting sounds into the System file (SZA). You can't directly transfer a sound from the Clipboard into the System file, where you'd be able to use it as a system beep. But you can use the Sound control panel as an intermediary and accomplish the transfer.

Open the Scrapbook and copy a sound from it (there's one there when you install your system). Then, open the Sound control panel and choose Paste. The pasted sound—with the name you specify in the dialog that pops up—appears in the control panel's list of available sounds. And, it's now in the System file, too.

Control Strip tricks (SZA). The PowerBook's Control Strip is at first a seemingly immovable object, only shrinking and stretching when you click on the tab. But the Option key is the key to everything:

Hold Option while you drag the tab, and the Control Strip can be positioned anywhere, although one end is always stuck to the left or right side of the screen. Holding down Option also lets you drag the icons inside the strip to a new position.

Aliases

Folder hopping (SZA/CR/JK/Nicholas Lavroff). One of the best uses for an alias is to use it as a shortcut from one folder to another. Whether you're working in desktop windows or inside an Open or Save dialog, just double-clicking the folder alias will open that folder for you.

Trash aliases (SZA/CR/JK/Nicholas Lavroff). Making aliases of the Trash can come in handy. (When you drag something into a Trash alias, the icon doesn't plump—the item just zooms right to the real Trash.)

Put one in the Apple Menu Items folder. You can use it to open the Trash if the icon is covered by windows, or, with a hierarchical menu, you can check the Trash contents without even moving to the desktop.

Put some in the windows that you use the most; you won't have to drag items far to erase them.

Scatter Trash aliases around large screens or double-monitor setups so you won't have to drag icons too far to get them to the Trash.

Alias of an alias (SZA). If you make an alias of an alias, double-clicking on the second alias still opens the original—at least that's what it looks like. What's actually happening is that the second alias is opening the first alias, which opens the original. What difference does that make? If you erase the first alias, the second alias won't work, because it was never pointing directly to the original. So, if you want multiple aliases for an item, make them all directly from the original.

A Show Clipboard command (SZA). If you double-click on the Clipboard file in the System Folder, a window opens showing what's on the Clipboard. Some applications include a Show Clipboard command, but you can make one that's always available:

Make an alias of the Clipboard file and name it Show Clipboard. Put it in the menu. To check the Clipboard, select the "command" from the menu.

Cataloging files (JK/Darcy DiNucci). If you sometimes have trouble remembering which floppy disk or cartridge you've backed up a file onto, here's an easy way to catalog them. Make aliases of every file on every backup disk and put them in a folder on your hard disk. When you double-click on one of the aliases, the Mac will ask for—by name—the disk that contains it.

Mounting shared disks (CR). Normally, mounting a shared disk or folder on your Mac is a nine-step process through the Chooser. But once the item's mounted, if you make an alias of it, double-clicking on the alias will automatically remount the item with no more than an OK button click.

4 | Memory

Much like a person, a computer with no memory would be helpless. Before your Mac can run a program, or even display icons on the desktop, it has to load instructions into memory. Before you can edit a report, change the figures in a spreadsheet, or retouch an image, the Mac has to read the file into memory. And when you create a new document, it exists only in memory until you save it on disk.

The more memory you have available, and the more efficiently you use however much you have, the more you can do with your Mac: start up more programs, open bigger files, install more system extensions, look at more elaborate screensavers. And more memory makes many operations faster.

Fortunately, Macs are free of most of the arcane and archaic memory restrictions that bedevil users of DOS and DOS/Windows PCs. Unfortunately, the Mac memory story has become pretty convoluted in its own right. The aim of this chapter is to help you through this maze. You'll find out what memory is and what it can do for you, how to determine how much you need, how to make the most of what you have, and how to add more if you need it.

Contributors

Ted Alspach (TA) is the chapter editor.

Gene Steinburg (GS) is a contributing editor to *Macworld,* and the author of *Using America Online* (Que).

Rob Teeple (RT) is president of Teeple Graphics, an Apple VAR and WWW services company.

Henry Norr (HN) contributed to earlier editions of *The Macintosh Bible,* from which parts of this chapter were taken.

Contents

Memory Basics

Macs have several kinds of memory, but what people normally mean when they talk about a computer's memory is its *random access memory*, a term that's generally abbreviated to *RAM*. When the clerk at Sears, say, tells you the Performa 475 comes with 4 megabytes of memory, or when you try to open a scanned image in Adobe Photoshop and instead you get a dialog box informing you that there isn't enough memory, it's RAM you're dealing with.

Physical Foundations (HN)

Physically, RAM is made up of a bunch of silicon chips designed to serve as a temporary holding place for digital information; inside these chips are thousands of microscopic switches, which the Mac turns on and off in particular patterns to represent words, numbers, pictures, sounds, and program code. This kind of memory is called *dynamic* because the Mac can change what's there at any time, adding, deleting, or moving information as it sees fit.

Most, but not all Macs have some memory chips soldered onto their main logic board at the factory; the rest come on small green plastic strips that plug into special slots on the logic board. You can add memory to the Mac by plugging in more of those cards (or replacing the old ones with new ones that have more memory capacity). Traditionally, these cards have been called *SIMMs* (single in-line memory modules), but PowerBooks and a few other models require different kinds of plug-in cards. Newer Power Macintosh models now use *DIMMs* (dual in-line memory modules).

Memory versus Storage (RT)

One of the most confusing issues you'll ever have to deal with regarding your Macintosh is discerning between memory and storage. At first glance, the two seem very similar, but the differences far outweigh the similarities.

To your Macintosh, *memory* is a temporary holding place. It is where information is kept that needs to be retrieved quickly or constantly changed or updated. *Storage* is more permanent, where information can be kept for long periods of time. For instance, while you are working in your word processor, typing a document, the document is being written into RAM. When you save the document, that information currently in RAM is placed onto a hard drive. When you switch off your computer, RAM information is gone, but the information on the hard drive remains.

RAM Speed versus Drive Speed (RT)

Memory (RAM) speed is measured in *nanoseconds*, which is billionths of a second. Older Macintosh models used 100- to 150-nanosecond RAM. A typical Power Macintosh 8100 uses 60- to 80-nanosecond RAM. This means that a typical piece of information travels from the computer CPU to the RAM in about 60 billionths of a second.

Storage (hard drive) speed is measured in *milliseconds*, which is thousandths of a second. A fast hard drive may be rated at 9 milliseconds, which means information travels from the CPU to the storage device in about 9 thousandths of a second.

To put this speed issue in perspective, let's assume that RAM and a hard drive are going to have a race. Where would you put your money? Well, in the time it takes the hard drive to travel one mile, RAM would have lots of round-the-world travel stickers, as it would have traveled 111,111 miles.

My favorite memory analogy: Memory is a chalkboard; you can quickly add information (with chalk), subtract information (with an eraser), but the amount of information is limited to the size of your chalkboard.

Storage is a filing cabinet initially filled with blank pieces of paper; you can add information by writing on those pieces of paper and then you can file them away. To remove information, you simply tear up the pieces of paper you no longer want and throw them out. The amount of information you have is limited to the size of your filing cabinet.

Of course, it takes longer to retrieve information from the filing cabinet, as you have to open the correct drawer and folder and pull out the right papers and read them; retrieving information from the chalkboard requires merely a glance in the direction of the information.

The main similarity between memory and storage is in the way they are measured. Both mediums' capacities are measured in numbers of bytes. Usually this number is many, many bytes, so terms that reflect this are used: *kilobytes* (K) are 1,000 bytes; *megabytes* (MB) are 1 million bytes, or 1,000K; *gigabytes* (GB) are 1 billion bytes, or 1 million K, or 1,000MB. See "Measuring Memory Size" later in this section for more information on memory-specific measurements.

The three major differences between the two media are polar opposites of each other; one's strength is the other's weakness.

Speed. Memory is much faster than storage (see the "RAM Speed versus Drive Speed" sidebar). The reason for this drastic speed difference is due to the mechanical nature of storage versus the electronic nature of memory.

Volatility. Memory is terribly volatile. Most types of RAM can only hold information while power is supplied to them. When the power is removed, the information is gone. Storage information exists regardless of whether power is supplied to it or not; power is only needed to move information to and from the storage medium.

Price. The price of memory versus storage is in proportion to their respective speeds. Memory costs more than 100 times as much as storage per megabyte. For instance, as of this writing, 8MB RAM SIMMs were priced at about $250, which works out to about $31.25 per megabyte. A 1GB internal hard drive was running about $250, which works out to about $.25 per megabyte.

Other issues cloud the differences as well, such as *virtual memory* (storage masquerading as memory, discussed in the section "Virtual Memory"), and *RAM disks* (memory pretending to be storage, discussed in the section "RAM Disks").

Measuring Memory Size (RT)

Every internal computer size measurement is built upon the concept of on or off. When you start adding many of these on or off switches together, you begin to have something that the computer can understand. This on or off switch is represented by a *bit* (*b*inary dig*it*). Each bit is on or off, according to the computer. The common way for us to represent on or off is by using the number 1 as on and 0 as off. So the numbers 10011011 would be interpreted by the computer as "on off off on on off on on."

Why Does it Say I'm Out of Memory When There's Still Plenty of Room on My Hard Disk? (HN)

That's a question almost every new computer user poses sooner or later.

The fact is that the Mac, left to its own devices, is very clear about the distinction between storage and memory, and it won't substitute one for the other unless you give it some special instructions (described later in the section on RAM disks and virtual memory). The processor in the machine can't work on information that's only on disk; it must first load that information into memory so it can have quick access to it. If there's no room in memory for the application you want to start up or the big document you're trying to open, all the disk space in the world won't help (unless you've set up virtual memory). And if, conversely, your hard disk is full, you can't save a file there, even if half your memory is free.

HOT TIP

A string of eight of these bits is a *byte*. A byte can be one of up to 256 different combinations, from 00000000 (zero), 00000001 (one), 00000010 (two), 00000011 (three), 00000100 (four), all the way up to 11111110 (254), and 11111111 (255). You can also think of a byte as 2 to the eighth power (2^8). But this unit is still much too small to use for measuring.

A *kilobyte* is about 1,000 bytes. Actually, it's 1,024 bytes, because it's 2^{10} bytes. When you multiply 2 times itself you get the numbers 2, 4, 8, 16, 32, 64, 128, 256, 512, 1,024. Kilobytes are usually referred to as "K." You can say "That file is 25K" instead of "That file is 25 kilobytes."

Memory is measured in the next major increment, a *megabyte*. There are 1,024K in 1 megabyte. Unlike K, however, don't say the popular written abbreviation "MB" but instead say "meg." So you would say that your Mac came with 8 "megs" of RAM. Most Macintosh models come with either 8MB or 16MB of RAM, though some are configured with more. The table "RAM Configurations by Model," at the end of this chapter, shows how much memory can be put into all Macintosh and Mac clone computers.

Hard Drives are becoming larger and larger, and it's not too unusual to find hard drives as large as several *gigabytes*. A gigabyte is 1,024MB, or about a billion bytes. Gigabytes are commonly written as GB and spoken as "gigs."

Even bigger and undoubtedly on the near horizon are *terabytes*, 1,024GB. Terabytes are still relatively uncommon, and thus no "official" way to write or say them is in computer vogue. Maybe a terabyte is big enough to demand full pronunciation of the term.

How Much Memory? (HN)

In theory, memory is one of those good things you can't really have too much of. But your Mac will set some limits for you, and so will your budget.

How Much Do You Need? (RT)

The old saying, "You can never have too much money or too much RAM" is still a good rule of thumb, though Macintosh computers are limited to the maximum amount of RAM that can be installed (see "How Much Memory Can You Have?").

The money part of that saying is true, especially when it comes to buying RAM. RAM costs amount to a large percentage of your overall system investment, sometimes costing as much as or more than the rest of the entire system. Usually, the more RAM you have, the better off you'll be when it comes to speed and productivity, but you might have to hold off on that new addition to the house for a few years.

The more realistic question for most of us, on a fairly rigid budget, is to determine the exact amount needed, so none of your hard earned (or easily inherited) money is spent on RAM you aren't really taking advantage of. This is a tough question, and the answer may not be as obvious as you'd like.

If you have an old, all-in-one Mac (Plus, SE, or Classic), you've got a low RAM limit anyway, and you may find that your budget for memory outweighs your machine's capacity.

The 32-Bit Problem on Older Macs   (RT)

When the first Macintosh computers were made, no one envisioned that the Macintosh would be around for a dozen years, or that anyone would ever have a need for more than about 8MB of RAM (which in 1984 wasn't just excessive, but downright silly). So the architects of the original Mac (and the Lisa before it) engineered the Macintosh to recognize 24-bit-long addresses, which translates into about 16 million different addresses. Of course, not all of these could be used for memory, and it turned out that only about half of those addresses could be used for memory; about 8 million addresses. Doing the math, you would discover that this is roughly 8MB, the "ceiling" of memory which no Macintosh could exceed.

When the Mac II shipped, a few things started changing. Color required more memory than before, and the applications using the new, 68020 processor were bigger and more complex, also requiring more memory. Programs such as PageMaker and Photoshop started to suck quite a bit of memory from the total available. And the popularity of MultiFinder, which allowed more than one program to run at a time, increased dramatically the need for more than 8MB of RAM.

Apple responded by inserting new hardware into newer Macintosh computers, and upgrading the software to take advantage of more memory. The switch was from 24-bit to 32-bit, which worked out to a total of 4GB of address space, with 1GB of that space available for RAM.

Problems started occurring when new Macintosh computers designed to take advantage of 32-bit addressing had 24-bit software running on them. Although this problem has almost been entirely eliminated (the last non-32-bit system was the Mac IIcx, made in 1989) due to the widespread use of new machines, the problems may linger on existing older machines that are still in use.

To remedy this problem, owners of Mac IIs and the SE/30 can use either MODE32 (available from most on-line services) or Apple's 32-bit Enabler. But this is a software solution to a hardware problem; thus many problems may still occur, and your best bet is to upgrade to a machine that is *32-bit clean*.

Of course, if you have a more recent Macintosh or Power Macintosh, the upward limit of 768MB or more of RAM is costly enough to wonder how Junior is ever going to be able to go to college.

The minimum amount of RAM as of this writing, for your Macintosh to be usable and functional is not 8MB of RAM, but 16MB. Some software programs need more than the 5MB left over after your system software takes its chunk out of the original 8MB. And 16MB is the minimum, which over the next few years will become harder and harder to survive with, as software begins to take up more and more of your precious RAM. Even games are starting to require more and more RAM; in 1989 I could play every game available on a 2MB Mac II, while several games now *require* 10MB of application memory.

HOT TIP

Now, how far above the minimum should you go? The best thing to do is to figure out which software you'll be using with your computer, and how many programs you'll need open at the same time. For instance, I use Adobe Photoshop, Adobe Illustrator, Microsoft Excel, and Microsoft Word every day; often I'll switch to one and then back to another. I need enough RAM to run all four of these programs. But then sometimes I'll run America Online, or Netscape, or I'll want to play a quick game of Strategic Conquest or Marathon 2: Durandal. And I don't want to quit Word to play a game (Word takes about 10 to 15 years to load, it seems, with time off for good behavior or few fonts). So I've figured out how much RAM I need for my main four programs and the system software (about 30MB), and multiplied that times 1.5, for a total of 45MB. There isn't a Macintosh available that'll take 45MB, so instead I've got to round it to the nearest number my Mac will take: 48MB in my case. If I'm using RAM compression software like RAM Doubler, I can get away with less (see "RAM Doubler" later in this chapter), for a modest performance gain.

This isn't an exact science, and it's better to err on the low side when doing your initial figuring. You can always buy more memory. The only problem you might run into is when you have a limited number of SIMM slots, and you fill them up with low-capacity SIMMs. In this case, you'll have to replace some SIMMs to upgrade, which will cost more than if you had the right capacity SIMMS to start with.

The industry doesn't see any dramatic decline or increase in the future of RAM prices over the next three years, unlike most other system components where prices seem to be eternally dropping.

How Much Memory Can You Have?   (TA/HN)

No matter what Mac model you have, there's a built-in limit on how much memory you can install. You can't add extra memory at all to the original 128K Mac or to the

512K or 512K Enhanced models (unless you get some unauthorized modifications made to your hardware). And the Plus, the SE, and the original Classic are limited to a maximum of 4MB of RAM.

Early Mac II models, such as the II, IIx, and IIcx, as well as the closely related SE/30, had the hardware to handle more memory, but System 6 and code in the machines' *ROMs* (Read Only Memory chips) imposed an artificial limit of 8MB (see the sidebar "The 32-Bit Problem on Older Macs").

The ROMs in newer Macs theoretically support up to 1GB of RAM—more than you can probably afford (unless your name is Bill Gates, at which point you probably have minimal interest in having a souped-up Macintosh) and, with current RAM chips, more than would fit in any desktop computer. That means the main limiting factor is the number of SIMM slots Apple builds into each model, although there are some products becoming available that double the number of SIMMs you can place in each slot. Another limitation is the size of the largest SIMMs available. Most current desktop models allow much more memory than most users need, but the range varies widely. Although the Quadra 650, for example, can handle up to 136MB of RAM, the 605 has only one SIMM slot, which can hold up to 32MB on top of the 4MB soldered to the logic board.

PowerBook memory capacities are also limited by space—there simply isn't room for a lot of extra chips inside the notebooks' cramped cases. (See the sidebar "Adding Memory to PowerBooks," later in this chapter.)

POWERBOOK

A summary of how much memory each Mac model can handle is supplied in the table "RAM Configurations by Model" at the end of this chapter.

Virtual Memory (TA/HN)

Virtual memory, as its name implies, isn't real memory—it's hard disk space that's used as temporary memory. In effect, VM (as techies call it) enables your machine to work as if, or *almost* as if, it had more RAM than it really does, so you can open more programs and larger files.

Unfortunately, though, virtual memory doesn't replace real, physical RAM SIMMs. Instead, it adds to what already exists. A notable limitation to any virtual memory scheme (including RAM Doubler) is that you never want to allocate more memory to an application than you have in physical RAM. Doing so will usually result in disaster.

Virtual memory software comes free with System 7. All you have to do to turn it on is click a few buttons in the Memory control panel and reboot. But as you'll learn in this section, virtual memory has significant downsides as well as upsides.

Using Your Mac's Virtual Memory (RT)

The Mac's built-in virtual memory is a quick fix to low memory problems, but not a very good overall solution to the not-enough-memory woes. Virtual memory uses a hard drive as RAM, fooling the CPU into thinking that there's much more space available for short-term memory than there really is. The downside, if you've been paying attention, is quite obvious: A hard drive is just awfully slower than your memory. To further confuse the situation, Power Mac models require less memory for their applications if virtual memory is on.

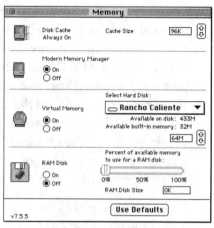

Fortunately, the Mac does a bit of magic shuttling things around to prevent those types of enormous delays, but you can expect a slowdown of on the average of 300 to 1,000 percent. That's usually unacceptable in all but the most extreme circumstances.

HOT TIP

To set up virtual memory, open the Memory control panel from the Control Panels folder in your System Folder. Turn on Virtual Memory, and pick the fastest hard drive you have from the pop-up list. The faster your hard drive, the faster it'll

You can turn virtual memory on and off in the Memory control panel. It's best to select the fastest hard drive you have when turning on VM.

seem to make your system when you're using VM. Then allocate the amount of virtual memory you'd like to use. Apple recommends using no more than the amount of installed memory as virtual memory, but you can get away with much more for a slight performance penalty (at this point, it doesn't much matter if it's a wee bit slower). When you restart your Mac, you'll have that memory added to the installed "real" memory for running software.

RAM Doubler (RT)

If there's one utility everyone should own, Connectix's RAM Doubler would be it. RAM Doubler does some fancy footwork to double the amount of RAM without having to use a hard disk as RAM. RAM Doubler achieves this seemingly incredible magical feat by using compression techniques to compress what is currently being spit out by the CPU, on the fly, while the information is going into RAM, and decompresses it on the way out from memory.

A performance hit is the penalty, but it's slight enough (5 to 10 percent) to not be a burden. And all you do is install it and forget about it. It's that simple.

Many users, upon upgrading their memory to the amount they need, keep RAM Doubler installed because it is "like an addiction." After all, if you're used to 64MB with RAM Doubler, and then you buy 32MB RAM, wouldn't it be amazing to have 128MB of RAM with RAM Doubler? Sure.

Applications' Virtual Memory Schemes (RT)

Some applications, like Adobe Photoshop, contain their own virtual memory schemes. Oftentimes this is a fallback for when the program knows there won't be enough memory allocated to it to perform a certain task, so instead of just stopping you from doing that particular thing, it uses a hard drive as temporary, virtual RAM.

Unfortunately, many programs that have their own virtual memory schemes have either serious conflicts (serious being a locked system or a bomb window) or tremendous slowdowns when Apple's VM is on.

WARNING

Managing Your Memory (HN)

You probably don't think much about how your Mac uses memory, and ordinarily there's no reason you should. But if you find yourself unable to open as many programs as you think you should be able to, or if your programs are crashing or telling you they don't have sufficient memory, knowing what's going on back there can sometimes help you solve the problem.

How the Mac Divvies Up Its RAM (HN)

Some of your RAM is consumed by the Mac operating system; the rest is available for applications.

What the system takes is called the *system heap*. Its size depends on many factors, including the version of the system you are running; the extensions, cards, and other add-ons you've installed; and the size of the Disk Cache setting in the Memory control panel. (For more on the disk cache setting see "The Memory Control Panel Cache," later in this chapter.)

What RAM is left over after all that is called the *application heap*. As you launch programs you want to work with, each lays claim to a chunk of the application heap, on a first-come, first-serve basis, and programs don't give up what they've claimed until you quit.

About This Macintosh...   (HN)

To see where your RAM is going, go to the Finder and choose About This Macintosh from the menu. In addition to detailing how much total memory is available and

the size of the largest unused block of memory (see the figure at right), this screen shows with numbers and bar graphs how much memory the system and open applications have claimed. The filled-in part of each bar represents the portion of reserved memory actually in use.

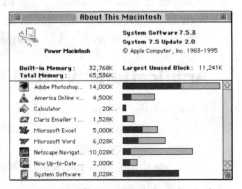

HOT TIP

The About This Macintosh dialog box can be a useful tool for tuning and troubleshooting your system. If you find that an application's bar has a lot of unfilled white space—more than a third of the bar's total length, say—when you are using the program in the normal way (typical number and complexity of documents open, typical range of features in use), it may be taking more memory

Choosing About This Macintosh from the Apple menu displays a wealth of memory-related information. Note that the version of system software is 7.5.3, which uses more RAM than any previous version.

than it really needs. Conversely, if an application's bar is almost entirely filled, it's running low on free memory—a condition that can cause crashes.

Changing Applications' Memory Usage   (HN)

How much RAM a program normally takes is determined by information provided by the developer and stored inside a part of the program called the *SIZE resource*. But if your analysis of About This Macintosh suggests that some programs should be taking more or less RAM, you can easily change these settings.

HOT TIP

To do this, close the program whose memory you want to change (if it's open). Then click on the program's icon on the desktop, and press ⌘Ⅰ or choose Get Info from the Finder's File menu. In the lower-right corner of the Get Info box that appears you will see a box called Memory Requirements containing (under System 7.1 and later) three items: suggested size, minimum size, and preferred size. The suggested size is the developer's advice about how much RAM the program needs. The minimum size is the minimum RAM the program requires; if that much isn't available, you won't be able to launch the program. The preferred size item determines how much memory the program will grab if it can. (System 6 has just one "application memory size" field, and System 7 doesn't display the "minimum" field.)

You can control how much memory your applications use by editing the values in the minimum and preferred fields. My advice is to never reduce the minimum value

Selecting an application and choosing Get Info from the File menu displays the application's Get Info dialog box. You can use the Get Info dialog box to change the amount of memory that the application requests in the Preferred size text field.

at all: Doing so would only increase the risk of poor performance and crashes. I'd also hesitate before setting the preferred amount to less than the developer's suggestion, even if About This Macintosh shows some memory going to waste (represented by white space within the bar). If, however, the preferred value is far above the suggested size, and you consistently see a lot of white space in the bar when you're using the program normally, you should be able to reduce the preferred setting safely, thus freeing up some memory for other programs.

If you've got the memory to spare, however, it's often a good idea to increase the settings. I routinely increase both the preferred and minimum memory sizes for each new program I install by about 25 percent. In some cases that's probably an unnecessary extravagance, but in my experience it tends to reduce the number of crashes I suffer, and I'm willing to sacrifice some RAM in the interest of stability. This is an especially good idea for Power Mac users running 68K applications.

HOT TIP

Don't Let the System Take It All! (HN)

No matter how you slice it, System 7 needs a good bit of RAM—usually at least 2MB, and up to 8MB in System 7.5.3. But if you want to preserve as much as possible for applications, here are several things to check:

- *The Disk Cache setting in the Memory control panel.* The disk cache is a section of your system heap the Mac operating system sets aside for holding (caching) information you've recently read from disk, so it can be retrieved quickly if it's needed again (for more details see "The Memory Control Panel Cache," later in this chapter). If you prefer to have the RAM free for other purposes, you can reduce the cache setting.

- *The RAM Disk setting in the Memory control panel.* Memory set aside for a RAM disk (see "RAM Disks," later in this chapter) reduces the amount available for applications. (It is counted as part of the system's memory allocation in About This Macintosh.) If you are not using your RAM disk, shut it off via the Memory control panel and reboot so you can use the memory for other things.

- *The amount of memory you're devoting to extensions.* Unfortunately, the Mac alone doesn't give you that information, and neither do the developers of most extensions. But most of the leading commercial and shareware extension managers (with the exception of Apple's own Extensions Manager that ships with System 7.5 and later)—utilities that let you monitor and control the loading of extensions—provide information on the amount of memory each extension requests as it loads. (Extension managers are described in Chapter 13.) Another option is **TattleTech,** a utility from Decision Maker's Software that reports detailed information about all aspects of your system. It's "good-causeware" (the author, John Mancino, asks you to make a donation to a nonprofit organization of your choice), and it's excellent. Each extension might not take up a lot of memory, but taken together, they add up.

- *The number of fonts you are using.* The number of fonts you use can have an effect on the amount of memory your system consumes (see Chapter 14 for more on how to handle fonts).

Why Won't My Program Open When About This Macintosh Says I Have Enough Free Memory?   (HN)

Occasionally, if you've opened and closed several applications, you may find yourself unable to open another program, even though you think you should have enough RAM available for it. That's usually due to a condition called *memory fragmentation,* which can leave parts of your free memory inaccessible.

Suppose you start a session with 4MB of free memory. You open a program that takes 1MB, then another that takes 2MB, then a third that takes the remaining 1MB. After work-ing for awhile you close the first and third appli-cations. That leaves you with a total of 2MB free, but in two separate 1MB chunks, separated by the 2MB allocated to the application that's still open.

If you should now try to open a fourth program, one that requires 2MB of

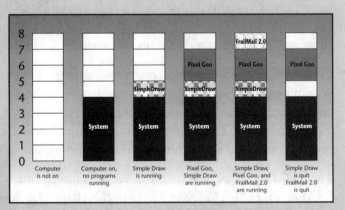

RAM, you'll run smack into a "not enough memory" dialog because the Mac requires a con-tiguous block of memory for each application.

The only solution I know of is to close the 2MB application, so you're back to having 4MB of free memory. Then you should be able to reopen that program, plus the second 2MB application that wouldn't open earlier.

Using Memory to Improve Performance (HN)

If you are fortunate enough to have a surplus of memory and you're looking for a little extra performance, there are several ways you can use some of the former to add to the latter.

The Memory Control Panel Cache (HN)

Because RAM is speedier than any disk, your Mac should work faster when it can get the data it needs from memory instead of storage. That's why Apple built a *disk cache* (sometimes known also as a *RAM cache*) into the Mac operating system.

The cache is a portion of your Mac's memory set aside to hold information you have recently read from disk. How does this help performance? The answer is that, statistically speaking, there's a significant probability that data you've just read from disk will be needed again soon. That's not always true, of course, but it's true often enough to make the cache worthwhile. Under System 7 you can't even shut it off (though you can control how much RAM it gets).

WARNING

The problem is that Apple's caching algorithms are not very efficient, so the disk cache provides only a slight performance boost, at best. And the larger the cache, the longer it takes to search it, so more time goes to waste when there's a *miss* (the desired data isn't there), and it takes longer to find it even when it is there.

The optimal point depends on your work habits and the software you're using, but most users find that a setting of 96K or 128K works best; some argue for 256K. Higher amounts slow performance, so you should reset it even if you have RAM to burn.

It's especially important to set the cache to the minimum level if you're using Adobe's Photoshop, because interactions between the disk cache and Photoshop's own built-in virtual memory system can cause serious delays.

Alternate Caches (HN)

Some hard disk drivers implement their own caching schemes, and they do a better job than Apple does. (Hard disk drivers and what they do are described in Chapter 5.) **Spot On** ($100, MacPeak Research) and version 3 of **Drive7** ($90, Casa Blanca Works) let you turn on caching and choose among several configuration options in their control panels. It's hard to know just how much good all this does, but in my experience it provides a small but perceptible performance boost.

RAM Disks   (RT)

If you feel the need for speed, and you have some extra RAM lying around in your system, not being used by your applications, then you're a candidate for a RAM disk. RAM disks are really your RAM pretending to be a disk drive; they even appear on your desktop like any other disk.

HOT TIP

RAM disks can improve your system performance to such an extreme state that your computer will be waiting for you, instead of the other way around. When you start up your system from a RAM disk, it takes a few seconds, even if you have half a screen full of extensions. It takes more time to double-click an application than it does for it to launch. And saving 10MB files is a snap. And why not? The information isn't going anywhere; it's just being redistributed around your RAM SIMMs.

Of course, there are a few drawbacks:

RAM disks are expensive. This is the big one. In order to have a 32MB RAM disk (big enough for a small System Folder and a few tiny applications), you need to have 32MB of *extra* RAM. Now, I don't know about you, but I've never had any "extra" RAM…. I always seem to be wanting more than I currently have. And 32MB of RAM will run you about $800 to $900. Considering you could get a 4GB drive for that amount, you might have second thoughts.

RAM disks are cumbersome. Because the information on a RAM disk only exists while power is supplied to the CPU, when you shut down the CPU, the RAM disk contents are toast. This is especially annoying if you have your System Folder on the RAM disk. The other problem is that files you save to the RAM disk will eventually have to be moved to a hard disk to permanently store them. One little plus is that a hangup or restart won't disturb the RAM disk contents, as long as power isn't cut off from the CPU.

POWERBOOK

PowerBooking With RAM Disks   (RT)

On a PowerBook, you can run your system off a RAM disk, saving to it and starting up from it, never having to spin up the hard drive, making your battery sessions longer than you ever dreamed. This keeps the PowerBook nice and quiet as well.

If you have a PowerBook 100, you have a slow PowerBook. *But,* you have the only computer ever made by Apple that retains what is on the RAM disk when you shut down. As long as the battery isn't entirely drained, the RAM disk contents are still on the RAM disk the next time you start up the PowerBook (which almost makes up for the incredibly slow processor).

There are several RAM disk programs which work better than the built-in RAM Disk of the Memory control panel. The shareware program **RamDisk+** by Roger Bates has many useful features that make up for many of the cumbersome disadvantages of RAM disks. Other commercial RAM disk utilities include **Atticus RAMDiskSaver** ($70) and **Maxima** ($100) from Connectix.

Adding More Memory (HN)

The earliest Macs, back in 1984 and 1985, had their meager memory soldered to their logic boards and no slots for adding more. Fortunately, Apple came to its senses before too long, and since 1986 almost every new Mac has had slots that make it easy to add more memory.

Except in the case of the Mac Portable, PowerBooks, and some versions of the original Mac Classic (all of which require specially designed memory cards), adding memory means plugging in extra SIMMs or DIMMs.

Buying Memory (RT)

If you can install memory yourself (see "Installing Memory Yourself," later in this chapter), consider ordering memory via a company such as Newer Technology. Newer's reliability and customer service is top-notch, and its technical support is the best I've ever encountered. The prices are usually a bit higher than some other memory mail order suppliers, but that's a small price to pay for peace of mind in the murky world of RAM.

Be careful if you choose a different vendor, as they may not know their products and the Macintosh line as well as the experts at Newer. Make sure you have your Mac model's requirements handy (see the table "RAM Configurations by Model," at the end of the chapter) and specify not just the pins and the capacity, but the speed as well. Oftentimes slower RAM will appear to work fine in a machine requiring faster SIMMs, but the machine will be plagued with crashes and other problems.

If you're a little uncertain of your installation abilities, you can take your Mac to a computer store such as CompUSA, where they'll install memory for you. Usually they'll guarantee their service and maybe do some quick testing of the RAM before you pick up the machine. Of course, for this personal service you'll pay a premium, both for the RAM and the installation. (If you've blown all your cash just getting the memory and don't want to pay to have it installed, try bribing your local Mac guru with a bag of Skittles.)

Investing in Memory   (RT)

OK, the bad news: Memory is a terrible investment. While you don't use it up, and there are precious few (if any) reports of memory going bad after it's been used too much, memory just doesn't hold its value. Used memory sells for about 25 percent less than the current market price, and memory prices rarely go up, but instead hover at

POWERBOOK

Adding Memory to PowerBooks   (TA/HN)

Boosting the memory in Apple's notebook models presents some special problems. RAM for PowerBooks tends to be more expensive than for desktop Macs, since the notebooks require lower-power chips and specially designed memory expansion cards rather than standard SIMMs. To compound the problem, the design seems to change with each new model. Apple makes its specs available to selected outside manufacturers, but sometimes not in final form until just before or even after new models are released; the manufacturer then has to design the card and find sources for the necessary components.

For all these reasons, RAM expansion cards for new PowerBook models are often scarce and expensive when the machines first ship. Several times, third-party RAM vendors, unable to get adequate supplies of Apple-spec components (because Apple is taking everything available), have come out with alternative technologies. Sometimes they work fine, but there have been cases where vendors have had to stop shipments and make changes in their cards after problems cropped up.

I don't ordinarily advise people to buy memory from Apple, because it usually costs too much, but if you are buying a brand-new notebook, consider ordering it with a full complement of RAM, or else plan to wait a few months while the dust settles (and prices come down) before buying from a third party.

Fortunately, things have changed in the past few years. Current PowerBooks, following the example of Apple's Newton MessagePad and many PC laptops, have a new type of slot that makes it much easier to install extra memory (as well as tiny hard disks, modems, or other add-ons). Without even opening the case, you can just slide a credit-card-shaped circuit board into the system. It's known as a PCMCIA slot, because it's based on a standard set by an industry group called the Personal Computer Memory Card International Association, but computer industry wags have come up with lots of alternative interpretations of the name—my favorite is People Can't Memorize Computer Industry Acronyms.

about the same rate for several years. PowerBook memory is worse, because it's bought in entire chunks at a time.

By the time your 16MB SIMM is worth more than what you paid for it, that *type* of SIMM probably won't be used anymore. All those people with thousands of dollars invested in 30-pin SIMMs for their Quadra 950s can't sell it to anyone, and there are less and less of those machines around for the memory to be used in.

Make sure you're going to use the RAM you buy, and get the most out of it.

Installing Memory Yourself (RT)

Installing RAM SIMMs in most desktop Macs isn't too difficult, and poses relatively little danger to the motherboard and the SIMMs themselves. PowerBooks can be a little more difficult, depending on the model, since there are tighter quarters and less room to maneuver around in, and they require a special tool to open them up. The all-in-one Macs of the '80s (Mac Plus, SE, SE/30, and Classics) are a different matter; the copper tube of the monitor is exposed during the installation, which can provide enough of a charge to send you to the emergency room, or worse. In addition, the compact Macs require a special tool to open; unless you have several to do at once, it's cheaper and easier to pay a qualified technician to add RAM to these machines.

Apple states that you are voiding your warranty by adding memory yourself, instead of taking it to an authorized technician (but then again, if you don't tell them *you* put in extra memory, they probably won't even ask).

Most RAM you can buy comes with basic installation instructions, but there are a few things you should always do:

- *Unplug the Mac and any attached devices.* For PowerBooks, remove the battery.

- *Carefully remove the cover and any components obstructing the SIMM slots.*

- *Before handling the memory, touch the Mac's power supply.* This will discharge any static you and/or the Mac have built up.

- *Ensure a proper fit.* SIMMs only go in one direction! Look for the little hole in the one end of the SIMM, and make sure it matches the SIMM bracket on the motherboard.

- *Never force the SIMMs into position;* you can damage both the SIMM and the socket this way.

Where Did All My New Memory Go? (HN)

With the latest Mac models you don't have to do anything special to take advantage of any amount of memory your Mac can handle. But with older machines there is a small but easily overlooked extra step required: opening the Memory control panel, clicking on one radio button to switch from 24-bit addressing to 32-bit addressing, and restarting your Mac.

The way Macs used to keep track of what was in memory, 24-bit addressing imposes a limit of 8MB on system memory, regardless of how much is installed. Switching to 32-bit mode removes that limit. (For more on 24- and 32-bit addressing, see the sidebar "The 32-Bit Problem on Older Macs," earlier in this chapter.)

If your older Mac came with 8 or fewer megs of RAM, it is probably set to run in 24-bit mode. If you forget to change it, you can spend $300 for another 8 megs, install it, and find that you don't have any more memory available than before. (If you are in 24-bit mode, About This Macintosh depicts any installed memory beyond 8 megs as part of what the Mac system takes up.)

Finding Out More (HN)

As you've undoubtedly figured out by now, the Mac memory story is pretty complicated. Connectix, in addition to developing a whole series of useful, memory-related utilities, has done the Macintosh community a major service by producing a comprehensive handbook on the subject called the *Macintosh Memory Guide*. It contains a detailed history of Mac memory, along with tables detailing everything you need to know about memory options and requirements for all Mac models past and present.

Connectix used to give the booklet away free. Now it only distributes and updates it in electronic form, via user groups and on-line services. But if you prefer hard copy, you can get an up-to-date version of much of the same material in booklet form from Technology Works (see Appendix D for contact information). Ask for the *Memory Solutions Guide*.

Another information resource along the same lines is *SimmStack*, a HyperCard stack developed and regularly updated by Apple's Mark Hansen. It, too, is available free from on-line services and user groups.

SIMM Nitty Gritty

In the remaining pages of this chapter, we give you the lowdown info on memory. This is the Cliff-Claven type of information to know if you want to get into a conversation with a Mac-head who *really* knows his or her technical stuff. At the end of this chapter, there's a handy table detailing all the existing Macintosh models (as of this writing) and what memory configurations are present in each one.

Where Are All Those Pins?   (GS)

When you read an ad or a product description for memory chips, no doubt you see the reference to pins—30-pin, 72-pin, 168-pin, that sort of thing. But when you look at the RAM module itself, there are no pins, just little rectangular strips all in a row at one end. Well it's those metallic strips that manufacturers call *pins*, and they are used to make electrical contact between the RAM board and your Mac. The older type of Mac RAM has 30 pins. More recently Apple briefly standardized on 72-pin SIMMs. But to make matters more confusing, the newest generation of Macs and compatibles use still another kind of RAM, called DIMMs, which contain 168 pins.

When you buy RAM for your Mac, you need to know what kind fits the model you have; otherwise, it's like putting a square block into a round hole. It just won't fit.

Here's the basic rundown of the kinds of RAM available for your Mac:

SIMMs. A *SIMM* is a *single-inline memory module*, and it's the form in which most memory upgrades for Macs are supplied. Basically, it's a printed circuit card containing a bunch of memory chips. The chips may all be on one side or on two sides (depending on how much RAM the module contains).

DIMMs. *DIMM* stands for *dual-inline memory module* and it's the form in which RAM is supplied for all the latest Macs. A single DIMM supports a 64-bit *data path* (the amount of information that can simultaneously travel to and from the DIMM) and you can install just one, but some of the new Macs can deliver faster performance if you install DIMMs in identical pairs, because both modules are addressed at the same time by a process called *interleaving*.

DRAM. Short for *dynamic random access memory*, this is the kind of RAM found not only in Macs but in PCs as well.

Flash RAM. This is a kind of RAM that is designed to work just like a hard drive, only much, much faster. This sort of RAM is considered "nonvolatile," meaning the data you store in Flash RAM can last up to ten years. You can buy Flash RAM in PC card form for the newest PowerBooks, but they're very expensive for the amount of storage capacity they offer.

SRAM. Your basic PowerBook contains another type of RAM, called *static RAM* which requires very little power. Another advantage is that SRAM will hold data for long periods of time, which explains how you can awaken your PowerBook from the sleep mode and find all of your open programs and open documents intact.

VRAM. *VRAM* is a high-speed form of RAM that is used on a Mac's video card (the "V" is for video). It is ideally suited to the fast screen refresh and huge data movement needed for good video performance.

PRAM. Your Mac's *PRAM*, or *parameter RAM*, is a small amount of memory that holds your basic system settings, such as mouse tracking speed, monitor resolution, network selection (LocalTalk or Ethernet, for example), and screen depth (the number of colors displayed) and so forth. It's powered by a small lithium battery. "Zapping the PRAM" (holding down the ⌘Option P R keys when your Mac starts) quite often clears up odd behavior and unexplained crashes. (See Chapter 7 for more details on zapping the PRAM.)

All RAM is Not Alike!   (GS)

From dealer to mail order catalog to magazine ad, if you want to buy more RAM for your Mac or compatible, you are confronted with a bewildering array of choices and prices. You can save hundreds of dollars if you just do a little shopping around.

But just how real are those ultra-cheap prices you see advertised? Are they run by firms who will disappear with your money and not deliver—or deliver a bad product? If you've got any doubts whatever about the reliability of a firm, call the Better Business Bureau or consumer protection agency in their city and see how they rate. Ask your friends, check the chatter in the message boards of the on-line services or Usenet newsgroups (see Chapter 23) and see how others have fared with these firms.

Or stick with the tried and true. You may pay a little more to buy your RAM from a firm such as Newer Technology or TechWorks, but you'll get a lifetime warranty, prompt technical support, and high quality merchandise. And if you truly want to save as much as possible, give The Chip Merchant a call. They won't give you any installation instructions with their memory chips, but I've always found their products of high quality, and they are absolutely reliable in delivering exactly what they promise at the advertised price.

Stay away from *composite* SIMMs or DIMMs. Composite SIMMs/DIMMs use lots of low-density memory chips on a module, to save a few bucks. But they can also create logic board timing problems, and cause crashes and general grief. The most likely composite memory modules are 16MB and 32MB types. If the 16MB module has 8 or 9 memory chips, you're doing okay. If it has twice that many, stay away. A noncomposite 32MB SIMM will have the same layout as the 16MB version, but it'll have two sides (the same number of chips on each side).

WARNING

If your Mac suddenly starts crashing repeatedly, displays a Sad Mac or occasional multiple startup notes from time to time after installing new RAM, you can bet something is wrong with the installation or the performance of your RAM upgrade. Try reinstalling your memory upgrade, or ask your dealer for assistance (and replacements if need be).

HOT TIP

RAM Configurations by Model   (GS)

Mac Model	RAM soldered on (MB)	RAM Slots	Available Sizes (MB)	Maximum RAM (MB)	RAM Speed	Notes
128*	128K	0	N/A	128K	N/A	
512K/512Ke*	512K	0	N/A	512K	N/A	
Plus*	0	4	256K, 1	4	150 ns	1, 4
SE*	0	4	256K, 1	4	150 ns	1, 4
SE/30*	0	8	256K, 1, 4	32	120 ns	4
Classic*	1	2	256K, 1	4	150 ns	1, 2
Classic II	2	2	1, 2, 4	4	150 ns	1, 2
Color Classic	4	2	1, 2, 4	10	100 ns	3
LC*	2	2	1, 2, 4	10	100 ns	3
LC II*	4	2	1, 2, 4	10	100 ns	3, 8
LCIII, Performa 450/550*	4	1	1, 2, 4, 8, 16, 32	36	80 ns	3, 8
Performa 200*	2	2	1, 2, 4	10	100 ns	3
Performa 400*, 405*, 430*	4	2	1, 2, 4	10	100 ns	3, 8
Performa/LC 475, 476*	4	1	4, 8, 16, 36	36	80 ns	
Performa 600*	4	4	256K, 1, 2, 4, 16	68	80 ns	3, 10
Performa/LC 550*	4	1	1, 2, 4, 8, 16, 32	36	80 ns	
Performa/LC 550*	4	1	1, 2, 4, 8 16, 32	36	80 ns	

RAM Configurations by Model (continued)

Mac Model	RAM soldered on (MB)	RAM Slots	Available Sizes (MB)	Maximum RAM (MB)	RAM Speed	Notes
Performa/LC 575*	4	1	1, 2, 4, 8 16, 32	36	80 ns	
LC 580	4	2	1, 2, 4, 8 16, 32	52	80 ns	
Performa/LC 5200/5300	0	2	4, 8, 16, 32	64	80 ns	
II*	0	8	256K, 1, 4	20	120 ns	1, 4, 5, 6, 7
IIx*	0	8	256K, 1, 4 16	32 128	120 ns	1, 4 5, 6, 7
IIcx*	0	8	256K, 1, 4	32	120 ns	4
IIci*	0	8	256K, 512K, 1, 4	32	80 ns	3
IIfx*	0	8	1, 4, 16	32	80 ns	3, 9
IIsi*	1	4	256K, 512K, 1, 2, 4	17	100 ns	3
IIvi/IIvx*	4	4	256K, 1, 2, 4, 16	68	80 ns	3, 10
Macintosh TV	4	1	1, 4	8	80 ns	3
Centris/Quadra 610, WS60*	4	4	4, 8, 16, 32	68	80 ns	3
Centris/Quadra 650*	8	4	4, 8, 16, 32	132	80 ns	3, 13
Centris/Quadra 660AV*	4	4	4, 8, 16, 32	68	80 ns	3, 13
Quadra 605*	4	1	48, 8, 16, 36	36	80 ns	3,
Quadra 700*	4	4	1, 4	20	80 ns	3
Quadra 900/950, WS95*	0	16	1, 4, 8, 16	256	80 ns	3
Quadra 800/840AV, WS80*	8	4	4, 8, 16, 32	136	60 ns	3, 13
Power Mac 6100/6100AV*	8	2	4, 8, 16, 32	72	80 ns	14
Power Mac 7100/7100AV*	8	4	4, 8, 16, 32	136	80 ns	14
Power Mac 8100/8100AV*	8	8	4, 8, 16, 32	264	80 ns	14
Performa 6200/6300	0	2	4, 8, 16, 32	64	80 ns	
Power Mac 7200	0	4	4, 8, 16, 32, 64	264	70 ns	15
Power Mac 7500	0	8	4, 8, 16, 32, 64	512	70 ns	15, 16
Power Mac 8500	0	8	4, 8, 16 32, 64	512	70 ns	15, 16
Power Mac 9500	0	12	4, 8, 16, 32, 64, 128	1536	70 ns	15, 16
Portable*	1	1	N/A	9	100 ns	4, 11, 12
Portable* (backlit)	1	1	N/A	8	100 ns	4, 11, 12
PowerBook 100*	2	1	N/A	8	100 ns	

RAM Configurations by Model (continued)

Mac Model	RAM soldered on (MB)	RAM Slots	Available Sizes (MB)	Maximum RAM (MB)	RAM Speed	Notes
PowerBook 140*, 145*	2	1	N/A	8	100 ns	
PowerBook 145B*	2	1	N/A	8	100 ns	
PowerBook 150*	4	1	4, 8, 12 20, 28, 36	40	100 ns	
PowerBook 170*	2	1	N/A	8	100 ns	
PowerBook 160*	4	1	4, 8	14	85 ns	
PowerBook 165*	4	1	4, 8	14	85 ns	
PowerBook 165c*	4	1	4, 6, 8, 10	14	85 ns	
PowerBook 180*	4	1	4, 8	14	85 ns	
PowerBook 180c*	4	1	4, 6, 8, 10	14	85 or	
PowerBook 500 Series	4	1	4, 8, 12, 20, 32	36	70 ns	
PowerBook 5300 Series	8 or 16	1	4, 8, 12, 16, 32, 48	64	70 ns	
PowerBook 190 Series	4 or 8	1	4, 8, 16, 32	36 or 40	70 ns	
PowerBook Duo 210/230*	4	1	4, 6, 8, 10, 12, 16, 20	24	70 ns	
PowerBook Duo 250/270c*	4	1	4, 6, 8, 10, 12, 16, 20	24	70 ns	
PowerBook Duo 280/280c*	4	1	4, 6, 8, 10, 12, 16, 20, 24, 36	40	70 ns	
PowerBook 2300 Series	8	1	4, 8, 12, 16 20, 24, 32, 36, 48	56	70 ns	
Macintosh Compatibles						
DayStar Genesis MP 132/150	0	12	4, 8, 16, 32, 64, 128	1536	70 ns	15, 16
Power Computing Power 100/120	8	8	4, 8, 16, 32	200	80 ns	14
Power Computing PowerWave 120/132/150	0	8	4, 8, 16 32, 64	512	70 ns	15, 16
Radius System 100	8	8	4, 8, 16, 32	264	80 ns	14
Radius 81/110	8	8	4, 8, 16, 32	264	80 ns	14

Notes

* No longer being manufactured.

1 Third-party 1MB SIMMs with only two chips are incompatible with these computers. Apple two-chip 1MB SIMMs may be found, however, in the SE/30, IIci, IIsi, LC, and Quadra 950.

2 The computer has 1MB of RAM soldered to its logic board. Additional RAM requires an expansion card. Apple's Macintosh Classic 1MB Memory Expansion Card has 1MB of additional RAM and two SIMM connectors.

RAM Configurations by Model (continued)

Notes *(continued)*

3 These systems have 32-bit-clean ROMs. Computers with 32-bit-clean ROMs can take advantage of more than 8MB of physical RAM under System 7.

4 The ROMs in these systems are not 32-bit-clean, but with the 32-Bit System Enabler under System 7.1, or Connectix MODE32 with System 7.0 through 7.5.1, they can run in 32-bit mode and can take advantage of more than 8MB of physical RAM.

5 The Mac II and IIx require special 4MB SIMMs. Be sure to specify your Macintosh model when ordering these SIMMs and make certain the vendor knows the difference. The Mac II requires the Macintosh II FDHD Upgrade to use 4MB SIMMs.

6 To take advantage of more than 8MB of physical RAM, the Macintosh II must have a PMMU installed and Apple's 32-bit System Enabler or MODE 32, as described in Note 4.

7 The Macintosh II won't start up if you install 4MB SIMMs in Bank A. Install 4MB SIMMs in Bank B, and use 256K or 1MB SIMMs in Bank A.

8 These systems can address a maximum of 10MB of RAM. When the SIMM slots are filled with 4MB SIMMs, the lower 2MB of RAM on the logic board isn't recognized.

9 Requires 64-pin SIMMs.

10 Only 8-chip, 16MBx1 SIMMs have been tested on the Mac IIvi and IIvx.

11 The Macintosh Portable has 1MB of RAM soldered to the main logic board. You can add more RAM using an expansion card, which can have from 1MB to 4MB of RAM or, in the case of the backlit Portable, 1MB to 3MB of RAM.

12 If the processor-direct slot (PDS) is used for other peripherals, the maximum RAM is 5MB for the portable and 4MB for the backlit version.

13 These systems use memory interleaving when SIMMs in identical pairs are used (for example: two 8MB SIMMs). This can improve performance 5 to 10 percent.

14 These Power Macs use 32-bit, 72-pin SIMMs, and they must be installed in identical pairs.

15 The latest Power Macs use 64-bit, 168-pin DIMMs. They may be installed one at a time.

16 Installing two DIMMs in identical pairs (same size and capacity) in the corresponding A and B memory banks will offer memory interleaving. You can expect a performance improvement of 5 to 10 percent.

17 First two slots must each contain 4MB SIMMs.

5 Storage

If you're like most computer users, you aren't much more interested in computer storage than in bookcases. After all, hard disks, floppies, CD-ROM drives, and tape backup units don't actually do much—they just provide a place to leave the files you've created and collected when you're not using them.

In fact, nothing is more critical to the performance and reliability of your computer system than your storage devices. If your drive is slow, you'll be staring at the wristwatch pointer and twiddling your thumbs when you should be working or having fun. If your hard disk crashes, you could lose hours or years of your work, and if you haven't taken the necessary precautions, you may never get those files back. Problems like those can make you rue the day you ever heard of high technology.

No one can guarantee you'll never have such hassles. In this chapter, we provide background information and tips that will help you understand how storage devices work; show you what to look for when purchasing a new drive; and show you how to manage your devices effectively.

Contributors

John Christopher (JC)
is the chapter editor.

Kristina De Nike (KD)
is a Senior Project
Leader at MacUser Labs.

Henry Norr (HN),
Arthur Naiman (AN),
and **Sharon Zardetto
Aker (SZA)** were edi-
tors of previous editions
of *The Macintosh Bible*,
from which parts of this
chapter were taken.

Randy B. Singer (RS)
is a practicing attorney
and an Apple Legal
Fellow. He writes for
Law Office Computing
and *Law Technology
Product News*, runs a
Macintosh user group
for attorneys, and hosts
the yearly MACLO
(Macintosh in the Law
Office) show.

Contents

How Disks Work

The most common Mac storage technologies, including *hard disks*, floppies, tape, and most other removable media, are magnetic; bits of data are recorded by changing the magnetic polarity of small areas on the surface of the storage media.

Comparing Floppy and Hard Disks

(AN/SZA/RS/Susan McCallister/HN/JC)

Magnetic media consists of an iron-oxide coating (more commonly known as rust), that is adhered to a foundation layer. In the case of floppy disks, the foundation layer is…well…floppy. It's a flexible plastic similar to recording tape, only slightly more durable. The disk itself is housed inside a rectangular, hard plastic shell to protect it from damage.

With hard disks, the foundation material is usually made of aluminum that is man-ufactured as a hard disk (hence the name hard disk drive). Typically, a drive has several separate hard disks, or *platters*, that are stacked on top of each other on a center spindle with a motor attached that spins them rapidly.

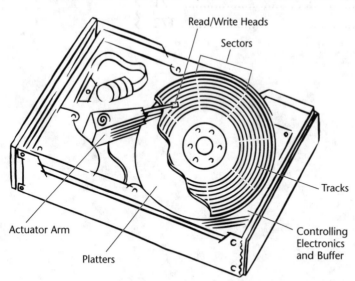

Inside a hard disk mechanism. The platters are stacked on a spindle that spins rapidly as the read/write heads, attached to the actuator arm, move back and forth.

On hard disks and floppies, read/write heads store data by giving bits of the iron-oxide coating a positive or negative magnetic charge, correspond-ing to the 1's and 0's of digital data; they read the data by checking to see what the charges are.

Modern floppy drives have heads that read and write data on both sides of the media.

Hard disks have a pair of read/write heads for each platter. The heads are mounted on arms in much the same way that needles are mounted on the tone arms of record turntables, and move rapidly in toward the center and out toward the edge as the platters spin.

Floppy drives rotate the disk at 300 rpm; in a hard disk the platters spin at speeds ranging from 3,600 rpm to 7,200 rpm. While the read/write heads of floppy disk drives actually touch the disk, in hard disks they float over the platters on a cushion of air at a distance less than the width of a human hair. The tolerance is so fine that the hard disk housing is sealed to prevent dust from getting in. Even the tiniest speck of dust could cause serious damage if it came in contact with the read/write heads.

Macintosh hard disks, whether internal or external, have a printed circuit board that contains the electronics that control the drive and manage its communications with the Mac. External drives also include a fan, connectors, a power supply, and of course, the outer case.

In recent years, several technologies that use light as well as magnetism in the process of reading and writing data have become common on the Mac. (For a description of how they work, see "Removable Media" and "CD-ROM," later in this chapter.)

Formatting and Initializing Disks (JC)

To keep track of the files you store on a disk, the Macintosh uses its own filing method known as the Hierarchical File System (HFS). Every type of storage media that is used on the Mac must be formatted (sometimes called *initializing*) to set up the filing system and keep track of stored data.

A *hard disk formatter* is required to *format* hard disks and removable media. Typically new hard disks are preformatted by vendors so they can be used right out of the box.

The process of formatting a disk breaks down roughly into three steps: There is the actual formatting which erases the entire surface of the disk, maps out any bad blocks that cannot reliably store data, and creates *tracks* (concentric rings that run around the disk) and *sectors* (small sections that divide the tracks). The next step is the installation of the disk driver so the Macintosh can communicate with the newly formatted drive. Last is initialization which creates the HFS partitions that will be used to store the data.

Disk Drivers (JC)

One of the most important elements on a hard disk is software known as the *disk driver*. It is an invisible program that is written to a hard disk or removable cartridge when it is formatted or initialized. The disk driver on your hard disk is loaded into the Mac's memory whenever you start up—it mounts the hard disk on the desktop and displays its icon.

Disk drivers are extremely important because they are used to transfer data between the Mac's memory and all storage devices. Anytime you open or save a file, the driver is used to transfer the data.

HOT TIP

Upgrading a disk driver is important when moving up to a new Macintosh, changing operating systems, or adding new storage devices. To upgrade disk drivers you must use a hard disk formatter.

Hard Disk Formatters   (JC)

A hard disk formatter isn't something you'll need to use every day but you should keep a copy around on a floppy disk. Besides formatting and initializing, formatters can test the media and map out *bad blocks*. They can usually install a new disk driver without reformatting a drive or losing data. In addition, formatters can divide a disk into sections called partitions that help organize files and use space more effectively. (We'll explore partitioning in "Getting the Most Out of Your Hard Disk," later in this chapter.)

HOT TIP

Several companies publish universal hard disk formatters that work with virtually every kind of drive and most removable media. The best of the formatter crop are FWB's **Hard Disk ToolKit** ($200) and **Hard Disk ToolKit Personal Edition** ($80), La Cie's **Silverlining** ($150), CharisMac's **Anubis** ($130), and Casa Blanca Works' **Drive7** ($80). All of these programs offer very reliable disk drivers and are updated regularly by their publishers whenever new system software or storage devices are introduced.

Apple's Hard Disk Formatters   (JC)

Apple includes its own hard disk formatter on the Disk Tools disk included with the set of System 7 installer floppies or on *CD-ROM*. Apple's **HD SC Setup** program is used for all Apple hard disks except those installed in Power Macs and Macs with *IDE* hard disks (see the sidebar "A Look at Macintosh IDE Drives," later in this chapter. **Drive Setup** works for both Power Macs and IDE hard disks. It is the first Apple formatter that can partition a hard disk.

```
▓▓▓▓▓▓▓▓  Drive Setup  ▓▓▓▓▓▓▓▓

List of Drives

Volume Name(s)              Type Bus ID LUN
<not supported>             SCSI  0   0   0
<CD-ROM drive>             SCSI  0   3   0
Macintosh HD               SCSI  0   6   0

┌──────────────────────────────────┐
│ This disk can be initialized.     │
└──────────────────────────────────┘

                        [ Initialize... ]
```

Apple's formatters only work on "Apple drives" which are drives specifically installed by Apple, that have an Apple logo sticker attached, and that come with your Macintosh as original equipment.

Dealing With Floppy Disks

Almost everyone has to deal with *floppies* sometime. New software usually comes on floppies, and they remain a convenient medium for moving files between your computer and someone else's.

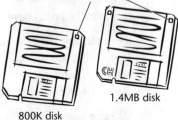

You can lock a floppy disk by flipping the tab up so the hole is open.

1.4MB disk

800K disk

1.4MB floppy disks have two square holes and the letters "HD" on the plastic case.

400K, 800K, and 1.4MB Disks (HN/JC)

The earliest Macs had single-sided 400K *floppy* drives. The second generation, starting with the Mac Plus, used double-sided, double-density disks, with a capacity of up to 800K. In 1988 Apple introduced the SuperDrive, a drive that can read and write 1.4MB high-density disks, 800K disks, and 720K or 1.4MB disks formatted for PCs.

Formatting Floppy Disks (SZA/AN/RS/HN/JC)

The first time you insert a new floppy disk into your drive, you'll get a dialog box that reads, "This disk is unreadable: Do you want to initialize it?" If you click Initialize, you'll get a series of dialog boxes leading you through the process.

You can save a little time if you purchase Macintosh preformatted floppy disks. They often cost a dollar or two more but you won't have to go through the initialization process, waiting around staring at your screen. If you buy preformatted floppies be sure they specifically say "Macintosh" (not IBM PC). Otherwise you'll have to initialize as usual and have spent the extra money for nothing.

HOT TIP

Sometimes when you insert a floppy that you know is already formatted, you get the same dialog box or one that begins, "This is not a Macintosh disk." Several things can cause this problem: The disk's directory may be damaged; the floppy drive may be dirty or out of alignment; or you may have inserted a high-density disk formatted for 1.4MB into an 800K drive. If the contents of the disk are important, click Eject and try the methods described in "Unreadable Floppies," in Chapter 7.

WARNING

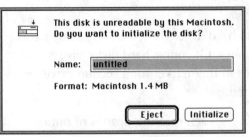

This disk is unreadable by this Macintosh. Do you want to initialize the disk?

Name: untitled

Format: Macintosh 1.4 MB

Eject   Initialize

To initialize or not? Think twice before you click Initialize. Any information already on the disk will be erased and data recovery utilities won't be able to retrieve anything.

Floppy Disk Safety Tips   (SZA/RS/AN/HN/JC)

Get sloppy with your floppies and you and your data may unexpectedly part ways. Using the following safety tips will go a long way toward safeguarding your work.

Lock Your Floppy Disks

When a floppy is locked, nothing can be written, changed, or trashed. To lock, or write-protect a disk simply slide the tab in the upper-right corner so the square hole is open. In the Finder, locked disks have a padlock in the upper-left corner of their directory windows.

Keep Floppy Disks Away From Magnetic Fields

Floppy disks are susceptible to magnetic fields that can demagnetize the media. Magnetic fields are found in common office items including paper clip holders, radio and cassette player speakers, and telephone handsets.

Use the Erase Disk Command to Reinitialize

Floppy disk media break down faster than other storage types so bad blocks (demagnetized areas) tend to appear more frequently. Using the Erase Disk command in the Special menu to reinitialize a floppy will reformat the disk and map out any bad blocks that may develop through constant use.

Use Virus Protection

A good number of viruses are passed around by sharing floppy disks. Invest in a virus protection utility and configure it to scan floppy disks whenever they are inserted into the Macintosh.

Floppy Disk Jams

When a floppy disk does not eject, try restarting your Mac while holding down the mouse button. Or, insert the end of an unfolded paper clip (use a heavy-duty one) into the small hole to the right of the disk slot until the disk pops out.

Choosing a Hard Disk

For several years all new Macs have had internal hard disks pre-installed, so buying a Mac means owning one of the drives Apple includes. Of course hard disks have a way of filling up fast, and many users find themselves in the market for a second drive, or a bigger replacement sooner than they anticipated.

With scores of vendors in the Mac storage business, each offering dozens of options, choosing a drive can be a daunting task. Fortunately, you have to go out of your way to buy a bad drive these days. If you shop from an established vendor and choose a mechanism from a well-known manufacturer, chances are you'll wind up satisfied.

Capacity (JC)

One of the first things to think about when buying a new hard disk is its capacity. This is the amount of storage space you will need for your current data and free space you need to expand for the future. First and foremost, purchase the largest capacity drive you can afford, especially if you work with graphics, databases, or sound files. Buying a hard disk with more space than you currently need is actually a good thing since you'll always need more.

The capacity of current new hard disks on the market start as small as 540MB and go as large as 9 gigabytes. For basic home or business use such as word processing or spreadsheets, an 840MB or 1 gig will do.

When looking at the capacity of a new hard disk, keep in mind that some areas of the disk are used for directories and the disk driver so you never get to use the entire capacity of the drive. It's not uncommon to lose about five percent of the drive's total capacity when it is formatted. The larger the drive, the more directory space needed, so the percentage of lost space may be even higher.

Because drive manufacturers have no common way of expressing drive capacity, ask your vendor if the capacity listed is for a formatted or unformatted drive.

HOT TIP

Sizes and Shapes (HN/JC)

Drives are commonly categorized by two physical dimensions: the diameter of the platters inside and the height of the whole sealed mechanism. Known as the *form factor*, these dimensions are the basis for size standards that make units from different manufacturers interchangeable.

There are five different form factors: Full Height 5.25-inch; Half Height 5.25-inch; Half Height 3.5-inch; Low Profile 3.5-inch; and Low Profile 2.5-inch.

Most modern hard disks are 3.5-inch Low Profile models that are only 1 inch high and can be used in virtually any Mac. Removable-cartridge devices such as CD-ROM and SyQuest drives are Half Height 5.25-inch devices.

Internal versus External Hard Disks (AN/RS/HN/JC)

An *external drive* is one that comes in its own box and plugs into the Macintosh via a SCSI cable. An internal hard disk is one that's mounted inside the Mac itself. Internal drives use the Mac's fan and power supply, so they're typically about $100 cheaper than the equivalent external hard disk.

There are a few advantages to external drives. Servicing or replacing an internal drive requires opening the computer or taking the Mac to a dealer. If you are going to work at different Macs from time to time, it's easier to bring an external drive than the whole Mac. Later, if you trade in your Mac for a newer model, it's also easier to connect an external drive to the new computer.

Drive Performance   (HN/JC)

There's no single index for measuring the performance of hard disks. If you care about maximum speed, you need to pay attention to several variables and weigh them differently depending on your Mac and what you do with it.

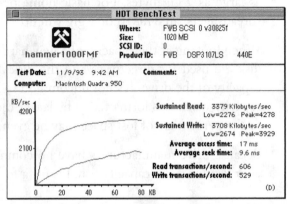

Seek and access times. The simplest variable is *average seek time* or *average access time*. Both are measured in milliseconds (thousandths of a second, abbreviated ms). Technically, average seek time is how long it takes the heads to move to the desired track; nowadays, it's usually somewhere between 8 and 20 ms. Average access time is the sum of that figure plus an additional, smaller

Curious about hard disk performance? Chart your drive's statistics with HDT BenchTest, part of FWB's Hard Disk ToolKit.

amount (normally about 6 or 8 ms) for *latency*, the average wait for the desired sector to come around under the heads once they get to the right track.

Unfortunately, many vendors are sloppy and inconsistent in their use of these terms; some will even tell you they mean the same thing. If milliseconds matter to you, be sure you're using the same standard when comparing products: A drive with an average access time of 15 ms is actually faster than one with an average seek time of 12 ms.

Throughput or transfer rate. The *data transfer rate* is a measure of how fast a drive can deliver data to the Mac once it gets to the sectors it's looking for. The transfer rate is counted in megabytes per second (or sometimes, just to confuse things, megabits per second). Today's drives have transfer rates of between 1.5 and 5MB per second.

If you deal mostly with small files or database records, transfer rate is less important than seek or access time, because your drive will spend more time getting to the data you need than transferring it to the Mac. When you open a letter created in Word, say, or look up a customer's record in a FileMaker database, you don't read in large amounts of data, so even large differences in actual transfer rate have negligible consequences. But if you work with large scanned images in Adobe Photoshop, for example, or big QuarkXPress layouts, or giant QuickTime files, transfers actually take whole seconds, so differences in the transfer rate matter—much more than a difference of a few thousandths of a second in seek or access time.

There's also a difference between *burst transfer rates* and *sustained transfer rates*. The former measures how fast a drive can pump out a small amount of data loaded into memory buffers on the drive controller; the latter is how fast it can deliver larger amounts, even after the buffers are empty. Burst rates are much higher, so some vendors focus on those, but for most purposes the sustained rate is more important.

And no matter how fast your drive can deliver data, it won't do you much good unless your Mac can receive the information at the same speed. The SCSI ports on most pre-Quadra Macs couldn't handle more than about 1 to 1.5MB per second, so drives with faster transfer capabilities didn't do much good. Centris/Quadra and Power Mac models have improved SCSI systems that can handle about 5MB per second. Dual SCSI channel Power Mac models such as the 7500, 8500, and 9500 have an internal bus capable of 10MB per second. So drives that are slower than the Mac's data transfer speed can be a bottleneck.

Spindle speed. The standard *spindle speed*—the rate at which a hard disk's platters rotate—used to be 3,600 rpm. In the last few years drive manufacturers have begun delivering drives that spin at 4,500, 5,400, even 7,200 rpm. The extra rotation speed reduces latency, but its main value is to boost sustained transfer rates: The faster the disks are spinning, the faster the drive should be able to read in all the data it's after. You'll notice the difference mainly with big files.

Reliability. No matter how fast a drive may be, you don't want it if it's not reliable. Fortunately, today's hard disks are less likely to experience hardware failures than those built a few years back.

Drive manufacturers measure the durability of their drives in terms of *mean time between failures*, or MTBF—the number of average power-on hours a drive will last before some component gives out. For most new drives the figure runs around 200,000 hours to 800,000 hours.

Now, 200,000 hours works out to almost 23 years and 800,000 hours to more than 91 years, so these claims are not based on actual field experience—they're derived by running a bunch of drives simultaneously in a lab and somehow extrapolating from the rate of breakdown during the test period.

A Look at Macintosh IDE Drives (KD)

Years ago, Apple pioneered ease-of-use by including a SCSI bus on all its computers. In recent years it has deviated from this technology by including Integrated Drive Electronics or IDE drives in a few models.

IDE drives have long been the standard on PC and Windows machines and they have a few advantages. They are slightly cheaper and easier to find, especially 2.5-inch drives for PowerBooks.

Apple isn't dodging its commitment to SCSI. All Macintoshes will continue to have an external SCSI bus connection. IDE drives will only come internally, and support only one drive.

Apple is using IDE drives in models it doesn't expect users to typically open themselves. This includes new PowerBooks, starting with the PowerBook 150 and 190, and the Duo 2300, and 5300 series; also some of the lower end Macs and their Performa cousins including the Quadra 630, LC 630, and Power Mac 5200 series.

IDE has a reputation for being slower, but in fact having a single drive on the bus gives it a performance advantage. In most respects IDE drives work and feel just like SCSI drives. The only exception is that some older disk utilities may not see the drive.

Still, MTBF probably means something, at least as an indicator of relative reliability, so it's worth considering when you are choosing a product. But try to supplement it with reviews in Mac publications and first-hand reports from users.

Warranty. Next to reliability, the length of time a drive is covered by warranty is extremely important. You can expect the warranty period to be at least one year for drives with a capacity of less than 500MB. One-gigabyte drives and larger tend to have longer warranty periods that can last as long as five years.

Should the drive mechanism or any components inside an external case fail (power supply, fan, and so on), the vendor will typically replace the drive at no charge. They will not, however, cover the cost to recover or re-create any data lost as a result of a drive failure, so be sure you back up religiously.

Choosing a Good Brand (HN)

Almost all storage vendors get their drive mechanisms from the same manufacturers: Quantum, Seagate, Conner, Maxtor, Micropolis, Fujitsu, and IBM. All of these manufacturers provide high-quality drives, so it may not appear to make much difference where you buy, and price may seem to be the only consideration. This simply isn't true.

Sure, the mechanism is the single most important variable in a storage product. But between two drives with the same mechanism, the bundled formatter and any additional utility software and, in the case of external drives, the quality of the other components, such as the fan, power supply, case, connectors, cables, and shielding, can make a huge difference in performance and reliability. Even if the hardware and software are identical, warranties, service, and support vary widely for each vendor.

The Formatter and Disk Driver (HN/JC)

Whether or not they ship their drives preformatted, nearly all Mac storage vendors include a formatting utility. For most users the formatter that comes with their drive is good enough. But the various packages do differ, in features as well as performance and reliability. Most formatters, for instance, let you partition a drive into separate volumes, but not all let you password-protect a volume.

The quality of the disk driver can also make a real difference in the performance you get out of a given disk. You can always upgrade your formatter if you don't like the one you got with your drive. (See "Hard Disk Formatters," earlier in the chapter.)

Recommended Drive Vendors (HN/JC)

It's difficult to recommend specific mechanisms because they change so fast. But generally speaking, Quantum drives tend to be among the best in relatively low capacities (500MB or less); they're usually quick, quiet, and reliable. In the mid range (500MB to 1.2GB), Quantum and Seagate make good drives. At higher capacities, Seagate, with its Elite and Barracuda lines, has been the dominant supplier in the Mac market, but Quantum and Micropolis are coming on strong, and Fujitsu has its fans too. Many multimedia users recommend Micropolis's AV drives, which are specially designed to ensure good performance with long sound and video files.

As for vendors, two of the largest and most respected in the mail-order category are APS Technologies and La Cie. APS offers a wide variety of storage products and accessories, its prices are competitive, and its products are solid and well-made. It provides a toll-free support number, which is staffed by knowledgeable, friendly people. The company is celebrated for near-heroic feats of service and repair.

GOOD FEATURE

La Cie specializes in many types of storage devices including tape drives, removable-media devices, and other peripherals. Like APS, La Cie provides good prices, solid if not chart-topping performance, and attractive and innovative case designs. La Cie drives come with the excellent Silverlining formatter.

GOOD FEATURE

At the high end, MicroNet and FWB are regularly on the leading edge in performance. Both provide good technical support and update their formatters regularly.

There are many other fine companies in the Mac storage market, so don't take these as exclusive recommendations. Ask around, read the reviews, and check the ads that appear in various Mac publications. Just remember how dependent on your hard disk you're likely to become; buy from a vendor you have reason to believe is worthy of your trust, and hope the company doesn't change.

Getting the Most Out of Your Hard Disk

Ordinarily, you shouldn't have to think about your hard disk—just turn it on and it should do its thing. But to get all the performance and capacity you paid for, you do need to pay some attention to setup and maintenance.

The Interleave Ratio (HN/JC)

Because older Macs couldn't digest data as fast as it could be read off a hard disk, you had to tell your formatting software to go through some special tricks to give the Mac a little time to catch up between each bit it read from the disk. This process was called setting the *interleave ratio*, or just the *interleave*.

Using an interleave of 3:1, for example, allows the Macintosh to skip over two sectors and read every third sector on the disk. This gives the Macintosh enough time to swallow the data before the next sector passes underneath the read/write head.

Setting the Disk Cache (JC)

You can get a slight boost in your Mac's performance by setting the Disk Cache in the System 7 Memory control panel. The Disk Cache sets aside a portion of the Mac's memory to store directories and commands. This helps the Mac run faster because data held in the cache doesn't have to be read repeatedly from the hard disk.

The rule of thumb for setting the correct cache size is 32K for each megabyte of RAM installed in your Mac. The Memory control panel in System 7 includes a Use Defaults button that sets the proper size for you based on the amount of RAM installed in the Mac.

The Memory control panel in System 7.5.

The Mac Plus required an interleave ratio of 3:1; for the SE, the Classic, and the PowerBook 100, the requisite ratio is 2:1.

All recent Macs however, have been able to handle a 1:1 ratio, which makes performance much better. An interleave of 1:1 means that every consecutive sector is read with no "digestion time" required.

Most formatters now suggest or automatically set the optimal ratio, so you shouldn't have to think about the issue at all—if you confront a choice, just leave it at 1:1 unless you're working with one of the earlier models mentioned.

Partitioning Your Hard Disk (HN/JC)

Partitioning means dividing a single physical disk into two or more logical volumes—separate sections that look to the Mac like completely separate disks. Partitioning allows you to minimize the amount of space a file uses on a drive and configure options that let you control access to specific data.

Allocation block size. The most popular reason to partition a drive is to reduce the *allocation block size*. This is basically the size of the blocks recorded on the media that are used to store your files.

Normally your hard disk icon appears alone on the desktop.

After partitioning the drive a separate icon appears on the Mac's desktop for each partition. Each of these icons represents a separate partition on a single hard disk.

The allocation block size grows larger for every 32MB of hard disk capacity. On a drive that holds less than 60MB, each allocation block occupies 1K; on an 80MB drive, they're each 1.5K; on a 300MB drive, they're 5K each; and so on, all the way up to 32K on 2GB drives. The Mac permits only one file in an allocation block. So if the file is small but the allocation block is big, the rest of the allocation block goes to waste. Because partitioning a drive divides it into smaller volumes, each partition has its own smaller allocation blocks so small files use up less space.

Partition sizes. What's the optimal partition size? It all depends, but on my 1GB drive I usually don't make any volume smaller than about 200MB. If you make too many volumes, you'll have too many icons cluttering your desktop, and you are apt to run out of space on the individual volumes.

If your drive's capacity is 400MB or larger and you use your Mac for mostly small files such as text or spreadsheets, you could be wasting space if you don't partition. If your drive is smaller than, say, 300MB, the space savings probably won't justify partitioning. Likewise, if you mostly have big files, partitioning is not necessary since big files are spread over many allocation blocks; the percentage of capacity going to waste will be small.

Partition options. Even if you're not worried about wasting space, there may be other reasons to partition your drive: You can, for example, create separate partitions for your personal or work files and your children's games. Depending on the options your formatter offers, you may be able to set a volume not to appear on the desktop automatically at startup, but only when you explicitly call it up; for even stronger protection, some formatters provide a measure of security by requiring anyone trying to mount your volume to enter a password.

Fighting Fragmentation (HN/JC)

Whenever you save a new file, the Mac attempts to write it in the largest contiguous space it can find on your hard disk. When it can't, it breaks the file up into pieces or fragments and writes them wherever the Mac finds empty spaces. The problem is called *fragmentation*, and it can slow down your hard disk because it takes longer to retrieve all the fragments that are scattered around the media. (Databases are frequently fragmented because data is constantly being added or changed.)

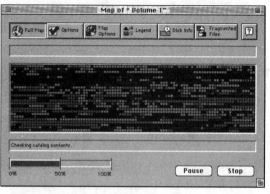

Defragmenters or *optimizers* (because they optimize disk performance) are utility programs that work by analyzing your disk and shuffling fragments of files around until each forms a neat, contiguous whole.

Using the optimizer in Symantec's MacTools Pro reveals a heavily fragmented hard disk.

The best of the bunch is Alsoft's **DiskExpress II** ($90). DiskExpress can do its thing on command or whenever your Mac is sitting idle, any time or during hours you specify. Besides defragmenting, it can track what files you use most often and group them at the most accessible parts of the disk. Altogether, it's a great tool for the compulsive hard disk jockey.

You'll find simpler optimizers in the leading disk-utility packages: Symantec's **Norton Utilities** or **MacTools Pro**. (Disk-utility packages are discussed in Chapter 7 and Chapter 13.) Owning one of these packages is a good precaution anyway; the optimizers are an extra bonus. (There's also an optimization command in La Cie's Silverlining disk formatter.)

All of the optimization programs take precautions to ensure your disk won't be scrambled if there's a crash or a power outage during the defragmentation process. But it's always a good idea to make sure you have an up-to-date backup before letting an optimizer loose.

Removable Media

If you're in the market for a second drive, it might make sense to consider a *removable-media* drive—a SyQuest, Iomega, or a *magneto-optical* drive. These very different storage technologies have one thing in common: They all put your data on cartridges that can be easily removed and replaced. That means you can lock up the data at night, carry it with you to a service bureau, mail it to a client, or simply put it aside while you work on something else. It also means you can expand your storage capacity just by adding more cartridges—in many cases a much more economical approach than buying another hard disk.

SyQuest Drives (HN/JC)

SyQuest drives (or just SyQuests, in everyday usage) were the first popular removable-media devices for the Mac, and they remain the most common. They are so named because they all incorporate mechanisms manufactured by one company, SyQuest Technology, but virtually every vendor that sells Mac storage products sells them.

SyQuest technology is close to that of ordinary hard disks, except that there's only one platter and it's encased in a plastic cartridge. When you insert the cartridge, a shutter door opens up to give the read/write heads access to the recording surface.

The original SyQuests used 5.25-inch cartridges and had a capacity of 44MB. SyQuest now makes drives that use 5.25-inch cartridges with capacities of 88MB and 200MB, and has added 3.5-inch versions with cartridge capacities of 105MB, 135MB, and 270MB.

Among the various SyQuest models, the 3.5-inch units (especially the EZ135 drive) are the fastest and, on a per-megabyte basis, cheapest; they are the best bet if you are buying for only personal use or for exchanging data with others who have a similar drive.

GOOD FEATURE

If you plan to use the cartridges to carry your images or layouts to a service bureau, you should go with a 5.25-inch unit. The 200MB version offers the best performance and is backward compatible with 44MB and 88MB cartridges.

HOT TIP

Pursuing the old Gillette razor strategy, SyQuest prices its drives low and makes its money on cartridges. At this writing, mail-order prices run about $400 for an external 200MB, 5.25-inch, or 270MB, 3.5-inch model. Cartridge prices range from as little as $25 up to $100.

Iomega Drives   (HN/JC)

The Iomega Corporation is best known for its **Bernoulli** drive, a device that uses special 5.25-inch cartridges. In the last couple of years, Iomega has made big advances in storage technology by introducing low-cost removable storage devices such as the **Zip** and **Jaz** drives.

Iomega's Bernoulli drives were first introduced in 1980. Since then, the drives have graduated up through various cartridge capacities which currently peak at 230MB.

Bernoulli drives do not use a rigid disk platter like a hard disk—the medium inside the cartridge is floppy. The disk itself floats on a cushion of air as it spins, making the media immune to the head crashes (physical contact between the head and media) that can ruin a standard hard disk.

Iomega currently sells two models of Bernoulli drives, the **MultiDisk 150** ($470) and **230** ($500). Since earlier models are no longer made, the 150 and 230 are capable of reading and writing 150, 105, 90, 65, and 35MB Bernoulli disks. The 150 model can also read 44MB cartridges. 230MB and 150 cartridges run about $100 and smaller capacity cartridges are still available.

The main disadvantage of the Bernoulli drives is they are less common than SyQuests. If you need to send large amounts of data to a service bureau or any other company that depends on the Mac, you should check in advance if they have a Bernoulli drive. These days they probably have a 5.25-inch SyQuest drive and a Zip drive on hand; the odds that they'll have a Bernoulli drive are much slimmer.

GOOD FEATURE

With the 100MB Zip drive, Iomega broke the removable drive price barrier down to a mere $200. The Zip has been well-received, gained a loyal following, and forced competitors to introduce comparable products such as SyQuest's **EZ135**. (See how the Zip stacks up against the EZ in the sidebar, "Storage Wars".)

GOOD FEATURE

Iomega's latest feat is the Jaz drive ($600), a high-capacity removable that uses 1 gigabyte and 540MB cartridges with two platters inside. The Jaz is as fast, if not faster than an average hard disk with a seek time of 12ms. The drive's design is compact for easy transport and it's lightweight. Cartridges cost $120 for the 1GB, and $70 for the 540MB.

The Jaz is good for backing up if you have a large capacity hard disk, and is the perfect solution for transporting large files like sound and video. Because the drive is fast it can be used to run multimedia presentations that often require high data transfer rates.

Storage Wars: Iomega ZIP versus SyQuest EZ135 (KD)

Removable storage manufacturers have been battling each other, producing some great bargains. Iomega started the fight with the ZIP drive; SyQuest retaliated with the EZ135 drive. Both of these new generation small, easy-to-use removable drives cost about $200, with cartridges for about $20. They are particularly useful for single-user backups and both come with software to help automate the task.

Iomega has been touting the ZIP drive as the next floppy. It may never become that universal, but it has been selling well. When the drives were first introduced, Iomega was scrambling to keep up with demand. The more popular the ZIP drive is, the more likely it is you'll be able to use a ZIP cartridge to send data to a friend.

The ZIP drive is lighter and smaller than the SyQuest drive. The cartridges are also more likely to survive being dropped. Like a floppy, the cartridge pops out when you drag it to the trash. One drawback is that Iomega cut corners on the SCSI ID switch; it only lets you set the drive to ID 5 or 6.

The SyQuest EZ135 has only one weapon, but it's a doozy. The EZ135 is the fastest removable drive on the market. It's twice as fast as the Zip drive. SyQuest has dramatically increased the reliability of its cartridges in recent years. They are still somewhat susceptible to damage if dropped, but each cartridge comes in a cushioned case to protect it.

Either of these drives is a good choice as a backup device. If speed is your main concern, go with the EZ135. Otherwise the ZIP drive is a better choice for transportability and ease of use. Besides, the ZIP drive is just plain cool.

Magneto-Optical Drives (HN/JC)

Magneto-optical (MO) drives—also known as *erasable optical* drives—read and write 5.25-inch or 3.5-inch removable disks enclosed in a hard plastic case. The media inside consists of a rigid plastic or glass substrate coated by several kinds of metallic alloy, in layers. One of the characteristics of the coating is that its polarity can be changed only at very high temperatures. When you write data to an MO disk, a laser heats a tiny spot on the media to about 150° C, at which point the polarity of that spot can be changed by an electromagnet located underneath it. Areas of the surface with different polarities reflect light differently, and that's how the laser reads the information.

First-generation MO drives used 5.25-inch cartridges, and most used a standard format that allowed up to 650MB of data per cartridge (325MB per side—you have to flip them over). The latest drives from most vendors support a 1.3GB or 2.6GB format, but as time marches on capacities are expanding. Pinnacle Micro recently introduced an MO capable of storing 4.6GB on a two-sided cartridge.

The original MO drives were painfully slow, but the new ones alleviate that problem. The fastest of them, from Pinnacle Micro, are almost as fast as a mid-range hard disk. Most 5.25-inch MO drives cost between $1,400 and $1,700. Cartridges cost about $100 to $300—not bad if you need to archive gigs of data in an easily readable format.

In recent years, 3.5-inch MO drives using cartridges only a little thicker than a floppy have appeared on the market. The most common capacity currently is 230MB per (single-sided) cartridge. The drives are available from many Mac storage vendors, at prices ranging from $460 to $500; extra cartridges are around $30 to $50.

MO performance levels are in the hard disk range. They are too slow to make a good primary working drive, but they're not bad as a place to put files and projects you don't require regularly—those you open up occasionally or might need for reference or reuse in the future. Because the cartridges show up on your desktop just like a hard disk and the files are stored in standard format, it's easy to open them from the MO or drag them to your hard disk; you don't have to run a special program to retrieve the file, as you ordinarily do if you use a tape drive for backup.

CD-ROM

A few years ago *CD-ROM* (compact disk, read-only memory) drives were a specialty item mainly used in libraries. Today they are standard equipment built into new desktop Macs.

A CD-ROM drive (sometimes called a player) isn't essential to the functioning of your computer in the way that a hard disk and a floppy drive are; if you use your machine for word processing, spreadsheets, and communications, and the like, you can get along fine without one. But if you hope to take advantage of the increasing wealth of multimedia reference and entertainment titles available on the Mac, you're missing the boat if you don't equip your system with this third kind of drive.

What's It For? (HN)

CD-ROMs are the ideal medium for products that involve quantities of data so vast they can't practically be distributed on floppies and stored on your hard disk: games and encyclopedias that incorporate lots of graphics, music, and video; collections of high-resolution images; ZIP code directories; research databases; and technical manuals.

Even with files that have to be installed on your hard disk before you can use them—system software, development tools, and major applications—it's easier, and better for the environment to use a single CD instead of a mountain of floppies.

CD-ROM Hardware: What to Look For (HN)

As their name suggests, CD-ROM drives read discs that look like standard audio CDs. The technologies are so similar that most CD-ROM drives can also play audio CDs. In both cases, the 5-inch disks are made of an aluminum inner layer with a rigid plastic outer coating. Information is stored on these disks in the form of tiny pits, which reflect light differently from the nondented portions. Audio CD players and CD-ROM drives read the discs by shining a laser beam on the surface and interpreting the pattern of reflection.

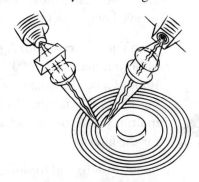

CD-ROM drives connect to the Mac via the SCSI port. Drives can be installed internally in most recent Macs (except PowerBooks and other small-case Macs), or you can hook up an external drive. As with hard disks, each approach has its pros and cons: internal mechanisms cost less and take up no desk space; external drives are easier to move around.

Light produced by a laser beam is reflected off the surface of a compact disc and collected by a photocell detector.

GOOD FEATURE

Current CD-ROM drives can read Photo CD discs, a format developed by Kodak for storing digitized photographs; most drives offer multisession Photo CD support, meaning they can read all the images on a disc even if they were recorded at different times. You can get your family photos developed on disc, so you can use programs such as Adobe Photoshop to retouch them. If you're a graphic designer, you can take advantage of stock photo collections in Photo CD format. There's no significant price premium for a drive with Photo CD capability, so you don't have anything to lose by getting it, and it just might come in handy some day.

CD-ROM Speed (HN/JC)

CD-ROM technology is intrinsically slow: Access times and data transfer rates are more like those of floppies than hard disks. As of this writing, state-of-the-art drives offer average access times of between 140 and 300 ms.

For years, single-speed CD-ROM drives were limited to a transfer rate of 150K per second, the standard set for music CDs. But a few years ago manufacturers figured out a way to make their drives spin faster and thus deliver higher throughput. The fastest CD-ROM drives on the market are 6x and 4x drives. These drives spin six times and four times faster respectively, than the original single-speed drives.

At this writing, Sony, NEC, and Apple all market quadruple-speed CD players. NEC also has a sextuple-speed unit and other manufacturers are likely to follow. The faster spindle speeds do make copying files faster, but the performance of current games and other programs played directly from the CD don't benefit appreciably. That won't happen until the software is rewritten to take advantage of the extra speed.

Brand Names   (HN/JC)

Over the years, most Apple-brand storage products have been mediocre at best; people bought them because they came with the Mac, not because of their merits.

HOT TIP

That's not the case with Apple's recent CD-ROM drives: the **CD 600e** (external) and **600i** (internal). The 600 model offers excellent performance, supports multisession Photo CDs, and comes with good software for playing audio CDs and manipulating Photo CD images. In its efforts to establish the Mac as the leading platform for multimedia, Apple has set a surprisingly low price, just $330 for the external and $250 for the internal.

Some Toshiba and top-of-the-line NEC mechanisms may be a tad faster; NEC's low-end drives are cheaper; and many users report satisfaction with **Plextor** drives. On the whole, when it comes to CD-ROM, there's no reason not to buy Apple.

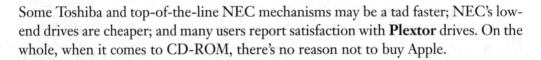

Riding the SCSI Bus

SCSI is the standard bus, or electrical communications channel, for connecting storage devices and other peripherals to the Mac. It works well if you follow the rules, use quality cables, and properly terminate devices. (For the complete rundown see "Termination" later in this chapter.)

A word of caution: Never change any SCSI addresses, or plug or unplug any SCSI cables, without turning off the Macintosh and all the devices on the chain.

WARNING

SCSI ID Numbers   (Michael Bradley/SZA/AN/Chris Allen/HN/JC)

A SCSI chain can contain seven devices. Each device on the chain gets a SCSI ID number (also known as an address), from 0 to 6. The Mac itself, acting as the SCSI host, is assigned ID number 7 and cannot be changed. Apple's internal hard disks are always set to address 0. ID numbering has no necessary relationship to the physical order of the devices on the chain.

Most external SCSI devices provide switches that make it easy to change the ID number. Before you add a new peripheral to your system, check the numbers and, with all devices powered off, make the changes necessary to eliminate any conflicts. If any two

WARNING

devices on the chain have the same ID, your system will crash, and you may even wipe out data on one or more hard disks.

SCSI address switches are almost always tiny and in the back of the drive (and therefore hard to get to). If you write the ID number on a sticker or spot of masking tape and place it on the front of each device, you can see at a glance which addresses are used and which are free. (You can also determine the SCSI ID of any device with your disk formatting software or with SCSIProbe, an invaluable freeware device-management utility.)

HOT TIP

SCSIProbe displays all the devices attached to your Mac's SCSI bus and can mount removable cartridges and hard disks too.

SCSI Connectors

(HN/JC)

Desktop Macs have a 25-pin DB-25 SCSI port for connecting external devices. To add a single external SCSI device to your Mac you typically need a (male) DB25-to-50 pin (male) Centronics cable (Apple calls it a system cable).

To connect (or daisy-chain) two external devices you need a 50-pin (male) Centronics cable to 50-pin (male) Centronics cable. Apple calls this one a SCSI Peripheral Interface Cable.

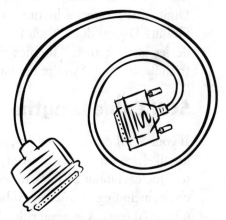

Some external SCSI devices have a smaller 25-pin port, and some recent ones use a newer, smaller 50-pin connector design called Micro-SCSI or

You'll need this DB25-to-50-pin Centronics cable if you want to connect an external SCSI device.

MicroD. High performance add-on SCSI cards that support Fast/Wide SCSI have a 68-pin micro connector.

PowerBooks have a rectangular SCSI port that requires a special cable called HDI-30 that comes in two forms. The Apple **HDI-30 SCSI System Cable** is used for connecting to an external SCSI device. The other cable is the Apple **HDI-30 SCSI Disk Adapter** that allows PowerBooks to be connected to a desktop Mac using the SCSI ports. This lets your PowerBook appear like an external drive on a desktop Mac. The PowerBook must support the SCSI disk mode feature for this to work. Don't try it if you're not sure as you could permanently damage both Macs! Check your PowerBook manual or contact your local Apple dealer.

POWERBOOK

Cable Quality (RS/HN/JC)

The quality of your cables can make the difference between constant hassles and a bus that hums along smoothly. It may seem silly to spend $40 or $50 for a few feet of wire, but if you are building a complex SCSI chain, this is not the place to economize—especially if you are working with one of the Macs noted for its SCSI sensitivities, such as the Quadra AV models and the Power Macs. Look for double-shielded cables—they're usually thick and heavy because they have lots of shielding around the separate wires inside the cable to minimize the possibility of signals on one line generating noise on another. We recommend gold-plated connectors.

The cables Apple sells are pretty good quality, and many peripheral vendors supply good cables. But few, if any, match the extra-high-quality cables offered by a small company called Berkeley Data Access. It offers old-fashioned personal service and very reasonable prices. The only catch is that the minimum order is four cables.

Other excellent sources for high-quality cables are APS Technologies and Granite Digital. APS offers a lifetime warranty on cables sold through its quarterly catalog. Granite Digital doesn't sell its cables direct but instead will refer you to the nearest dealer in your area. The nice thing about these companies is that they are all Mac friendly, so even if you're not sure what you need they'll go the distance to help.

SCSI Cable Lengths (HN)

If your SCSI chain is too long, signals may be too weak to be received clearly and you are likely to experience a variety of problems. Theoretically, the chain can extend up to 7 meters (about 23 feet), measured from your computer to the last device in a SCSI chain, including all internal ribbon cables. Apple recommends a maximum of 6 meters (about 20 feet). A general rule: The shorter, the better.

HOT TIP

As for the length of individual cables, that's one of the murkiest areas in SCSI. Some people have problems with long cables; still others have trouble with very short ones (about 12 to 18 inches is the shortest available). If you are buying new cables, you might as well stick to the middle ground: 3-foot lengths.

Termination (HN)

The electrical signals that race up and down your SCSI cables generate electrical echoes, or *noise*. If they're not suppressed, these reflections can be strong enough to confuse devices on the bus. That can cause an array of problems, including slow-downs, data errors, drives refusing to appear on the desktop, and crashes.

That's why you need *terminators*, or *resistors*, at either end of the SCSI chain. Terminators can be internal (attached to a drive's circuit board) or external (plugged into one of the device's SCSI ports). They require a small amount of electrical power—termination power—which is supposed to be, but is not always, provided by the SCSI device. The rules for termination vary according to the Mac model you're using.

For most Macs. Generally speaking—here's one of those rules that usually works—the first and last devices on the SCSI chain should be terminated. The first device is the Mac: If you have an internal hard disk, it should be terminated with resistors installed on the drive's circuit board (if it's a factory-installed drive, or if it's dealer-installed, it will come with terminators). If you don't have an internal drive, most Macs require a special terminator for the internal SCSI port. (If you normally have an internal drive but have to remove it for servicing, don't forget to have your dealer add termination.)

HOT TIP

The last device—the one at the other end of the SCSI chain—should also be terminated. In between—normally—the other devices on the chain should not be terminated. If you have an external device with internal termination, put it at the end of the chain, if that's convenient; if not, or if you have more than one internally terminated device, you or a technician will probably have to remove the terminating resistor from one of them.

The Mac Plus. Because the Mac Plus has no internal SCSI connector, your first external device (the one closest to the Mac) is considered the first device and should be terminated, as should the last device on the chain. If you have only one drive on the chain, it should be terminated.

The Mac IIfx. The Mac IIfx follows the general rules above, but it requires a special terminator at the end of the chain. It's black, and Apple calls it the SCSI Terminator II. One should have come with your IIfx.

PowerBooks. PowerBooks are something else again. Hard-drive-equipped Power-Books have a small internal terminator, but if you are connecting external devices, Apple recommends adding two more terminators: One should go between the HDI-30 cable attached to your PowerBook and the first device. If only one external device is connected, the other should go on the device's unoccupied SCSI port; if there are several, the terminator should go on the last device in the chain.

If you are planning to connect a PowerBook to a desktop Mac in SCSI disk mode—setting up the PowerBook's hard disk to function as an external drive attached to your desktop machine—the termination rules are hopelessly complicated. Fortunately, they are very clearly illustrated in Apple's PowerBook manuals. Check there.

POWERBOOK

Backing Up

According to an ancient saying, there are two kinds of computer users: those who've had a hard disk crash and those who are about to. All computer storage devices, for now and for the foreseeable future, are inherently unreliable—they're susceptible to directory corruption, electrical glitches, and mechanical breakdown. And don't forget the risk of human error: Almost everyone who has used a computer has at one time or another inadvertently trashed some important file.

Nevertheless, most computer users don't bother to back up their data—they just don't think about it, or they decide it's not worth the hassle, or they say they'll get to it later. It's your choice, of course, but remember the bottom line: If you don't have a good— i.e., recent and complete—backup, the odds are great that sooner or later you will lose documents that are important to you.

If you do decide to make *backup*s, you need to choose media, software, and a strategy.

Backup Media   (HN/JC)

In reviewing your options for backup media, having an extra hard disk is the fastest and easiest choice—you can simply drag files and folders to it to make a backup, and back again to restore. But this approach also has clear disadvantages: doubling your disk capacity is expensive, and the second drive is as vulnerable to breakdown, fire, or theft as the first.

Floppies are the other obvious choice, and on the face of it the most economical, since you already have the drive. But you should factor in the cost of your time, since backing up to floppies requires near-constant attention over at least several hours (depending, obviously, on the size of your backup). In an era when 500MB are standard and gigabyte drives are common, floppies just won't do for full backups. They remain a good choice for quick backups of a select group of critical files—your tax return, say, or your dissertation.

The other choices are removable cartridges and tape. Using removable-media drives from Iomega or SyQuest, or magneto-optical disks offer many of the advantages of using an extra hard disk: You can back up and restore directly from the Finder, and you have the added advantages of expandability (if you run out of space, just get another cartridge) and portability (you can easily take a cartridge off site for safekeeping).

The only real disadvantage of these options is the cost of media. Buying multiple cartridges to do a complete backup of a 500MB drive can get expensive. If you want the added security of duplicate copies, or your drive is bigger than that, media costs go up proportionately. And if you want to preserve archives of files no longer on your hard disk—copies you keep in reserve in case you ever need them again for reference, recycling, or updating—along with backups of your current files, the expense can go through the roof.

That leaves tape. In many ways it's the most un-Mac-like medium, since you can't ordinarily mount tape drives on your desktop, and you have to run special software to copy or restore your files or even to see what's on a tape. And the drives aren't cheap: At this writing the least expensive *digital audio tape* (DAT) drives using the latest DDS-2 technology are about $800.

But tape has one huge advantage: The cost per megabyte is infinitesimal. With DAT, you can store anywhere from 1 to 2GB of data (depending on tape length and whether the drive supports compression), on a tape that costs about $9; if you buy one of the latest models you can store up to 8GB on one $25 tape.

In addition to DAT, low-cost tape drives that have been used commonly on PCs are beginning to be made available for the Mac market. As of this writing, APS offers a tape drive that uses QIC (quarter-inch cartridge) media. The **APS HyperQic** ($500) can store as much as 4GB of data using software compression. Tapes run about $35.

Backup Software (HN)

If you are using a tape drive, you have only a couple of choices for backup software, and if you're like most other Mac tape users, you'll end up choosing Dantz Development's **Retrospect** ($150, but often bundled free with many tape drives). It supports almost every backup medium known to humankind, it offers an amazing array of features, it's exceptionally well-supported, and though it's not exactly uncomplicated, version 3 provides an appealing interface and simplifies things enough so it's not hard to use. If you are on a network, you can get **Retrospect Remote** ($270 for ten Macs) and have every drive on the net automatically backed up overnight.

If you are using any media you can mount on the desktop—floppies, hard disks, or cartridges—you don't need anything except the Finder to make copies. But you'll probably want to do *incremental backups*—backups that encompass only the files that have been created or modified since the last backup—between more time-consuming full backups of everything on your disk, and for that purpose (among others) a good backup utility makes life much simpler.

If you've already invested in a disk utility package like Symantec's **MacTools Pro** ($95) or **Norton Utilities** ($95) (covered in Chapter 7), you already own a backup

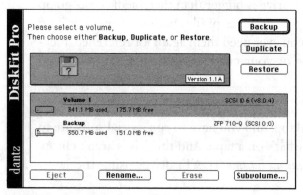

utility. These programs are good, but they may not offer the features you want. Many users, once they get serious about backup, invest in a specialized utility. In this category, too, the best-sellers come from Dantz: **DiskFit Direct** ($50) is the easiest to use, while **DiskFit Pro** ($125) offers more features. Also **Personal Backup** ($50) from SunStar Publishing is extremely easy to use and currently comes bundled with Iomega's Zip drives.

You're just a few mouse clicks away from an automatic backup with Dantz Development's DiskFit Pro.

Backup Strategies   (HN)

The best way to get yourself to back up is to make it a routine that demands little if any effort or attention. Many of the backup utilities have a scheduling option, so all you have to do is set up the program and make sure media is available.

I don't do that (why not? I don't know), but I do leave my DAT drive on my SCSI chain almost all the time, and I keep two tapes, Odd and Even, close at hand. When I'm winding up a serious work session, I fire up Retrospect, pop in a tape (Odd or Even depending on the date), and let her fly. With two recent backups, I'm pretty well protected even if one tape should get damaged or corrupted. (I've had several tapes go bad over the years.)

HOT TIP

If your backup software has a verification option, as Retrospect does, turn it on. That way the software will read back every file it's backed up and check it against the original to make sure the copy is accurate. It can double the time required to complete a backup, but it's worth it. (Besides, the sensible way to do a backup is to start it at the end of your computing day or schedule it to start automatically during the night. That way, who cares if it takes a few extra hours?)

However diligent you are in making incremental backups, it's a good idea to do a new full backup from time to time. And it's plain common sense to keep a backup off site, to protect you from such threats as fire or theft.

6 } Basic Peripherals

To operate your Mac, you need a few essential pieces of equipment besides the computer itself. You need input devices (a keyboard and a mouse, generally) to control the computer, and a monitor to see what you're doing.

Monitors and keyboards are provided with new Performa model Macs. Most of the time these devices meet your needs, but you may want more features to do more work (or have more fun). Perhaps you want a bigger monitor, or you've grown tired of that broken key in the middle of your keyboard.

Maybe you're uncomfortable with your mouse and have considered your options. (How about a trackball instead of a mouse?)

And what about purchasing a scanner to get pictures and documents into your Mac?

This chapter is about all these basic peripherals and we'll provide you with all the answers.

Contributors

John Christopher (JC) is the chapter editor.

Brad Bunnin (BB), principal author of *The Writer's Legal Companion*, is an attorney who practices literary law.

Andreu Cabré (AC) is a Catalan designer living in Northampton, Massachusetts.

Joe Matazzoni (JM), a former *Macworld* editor, writes about desktop publishing and interactive media.

Randy B. Singer (RS) is a practicing attorney, an Apple legal fellow, and a contributor to *Law Technology Product News* and *Law Office Computing*.

Arthur Naiman (AN), **Sharon Zardetto Aker (SZA)**, **Susan McCallister (SM)**, and **John Kadyk (JK)** edited earlier editions of *The Macintosh Bible*, from which sections of this chapter were taken.

Contents

Monitors

(JC)

Not all monitors are made alike. The choices you make when choosing a monitor will determine whether you see your work in 256 colors or a million, and the quality of the screen will determine whether you get a headache after an hour, or work comfortably all day. In this section, we'll describe what to look for in a monitor (often called a *display*), find out which ones will work with your Mac, and run through some of the many choices on the market.

Finding What You Need

Choosing a monitor is one of the most important decisions you'll make when setting up your computer system. In this section, we'll discuss important points to consider when shopping for a monitor.

Monitor sizes (JK/BB). Most monitors fall into one of four size categories, based on their shape and diagonal screen measurement. Don't attach too much importance to a screen's physical size (it rarely matches the actual viewable image area).

- Small (12-inch to 15-inch) monitors are fine for typical home uses: writing letters, using personal accounting software, playing games, and so on.

- Mid-size (16-inch or 17-inch) monitors allow you to display quite a bit more, but they're not quite tall enough to show the full length of a letter-size page with margins, or wide enough to show two adjacent pages.

- Full-page or portrait monitors (15-inch, but shaped differently than "small" 15-inch monitors) are designed to show a full letter-size page, with a little room next to it to leave the disk and Trash icons showing. The word *portrait* indicates the monitor's tall, rectangular shape (the term *landscape* is sometimes used to describe the shorter, wider shape of ordinary monitors).

- Two-page (19-inch to 21-inch) monitors display two full letter-size pages side by side, so they're great for desktop publishers. They're also useful for graphic artists and people who create spreadsheets or keep a lot of documents open.

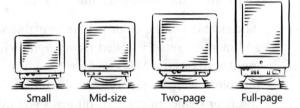

Small   Mid-size   Two-page   Full-page

The size of the monitor you choose depends on the kind of work you do, as well as the amount of space you have available on your desk.

Pixels and resolution (JK). The image you see on a Mac's screen is made up of many tiny dots called *pixels*. The amount of information that fits on a screen depends on how many pixels it displays, which is called the screen's *resolution*. For example, Apple's standard resolution for small external monitors is 640 pixels across the screen and 480 from top to bottom; for mid-size monitors, it's 832 by 624; for portrait monitors, it's 640 by 870; and for large monitors, it's 1,024 by 768 or 1,152 by 870.

When you set a mid-size monitor to a resolution of 1,152 by 870, you're putting a lot more pixels in the same area, so the monitor uses smaller pixels, and everything on the screen looks smaller. The size of the pixels used at a given resolution is measured in pixels per inch, usually expressed as *dpi* (dots per inch).

GOOD FEATURE

Monitors of the same general size and pixel dimensions often have different dpi because they have different-size image areas. Macs are designed so a 72-dpi screen displays at actual size. This means a one-inch line on the screen will print out as a one-inch line on paper.

Many monitors can be set up to display several different resolutions—depending on the capabilities of the Mac they're hooked up to—so you either cram more information onto the screen or blow everything up to a more readable size. Such monitors are called *multisync* or *multiscan* monitors and can usually be used with PCs as well as Macs. You generally need to get a special adapter plug from the monitor's manufacturer—usually for free or cheaply—to make a particular resolution work, but if you've installed a display card, you should be able to make the switch in the Monitors control panel. Most manufacturers make software that allows their monitors to make the switch without even restarting.

Richness of colors or grays (JK/AN/SZA/SM/Mac Kenny). On color monitors, each pixel can be black, white, or any of over 16.7 million colors, including grays—an image of almost photographic quality. You select which level of color you want in the Monitors control panel.

Black and white in color. Changing the resolution in the Monitors control panel to grayscale or black & white will give your color monitor a slight boost in the speed that graphics appear on the screen, and scrolling through a large graphic will also be improved.

The richness of the color palette available with a given Mac and monitor setup is called its *bit depth*, which refers to the number of bits the Mac's memory assigns to each pixel. One-bit color gives you just black and white; 8-bit gives you 256 colors or shades of gray; 16-bit gives you over 32,000 colors or shades of gray; and 24-bit gives you over 16.7 million.

The bigger the monitor, the more pixels it has, and the more memory is required for a given bit depth. The number of colors you can actually get out of your machine depends on the video capabilities of your Mac. So, for example, a Mac's built-in video support may be able to put 32,000 different colors or grays at once on a 16-inch screen, but only 256 at once on a 21-inch screen, because it has so many more pixels. With a 24-bit display card installed, the same Mac can produce 16.7 million colors on either of those monitors.

Video support, display cards, and acceleration (JK). Current Macs have some level of built-in video support, which means you can connect a monitor directly to the Mac's video port. But the level of support varies quite a bit between models, so don't assume you'll be able to plug any monitor into any Mac. Generally, the more recent and expensive the Mac model, the more kinds of monitors it will support. See Chapter 2 for a partial list of which Macs support which monitors.

On some Macs, you can expand the video support by buying a VRAM upgrade (see Chapter 4 for more on VRAM), which will allow you to hook up a larger monitor or get more colors on a small one. Otherwise, you'll have to buy a display card (which plugs into one of your Mac's expansion slots).

GOOD FEATURE

If you work with large, full-color (24-bit) images, you may find that it takes forever for the screen to redraw whenever you make a change or even drag an image a couple of inches. If that's the case, you'll probably want to invest in a display card that includes graphics acceleration. Some graphics accelerator cards can make changes appear several times faster than they would without acceleration, but they can also cost several times more than a regular display card.

Two Monitors, One Mac (JC)

Sometimes, having one monitor attached to your Macintosh isn't enough. You might be working on a large page layout and want to see it all. Having two monitors lets you spread your work out across two displays. To accomplish this you need to install a video card inside your Mac to support a second monitor.

The Monitors control panel lets you adjust the position of the second monitor, and its Identify button displays a number on the corresponding monitor's screen in case you get confused. Other options let you specify which monitor will be used during startup and which will display the menu bar.

Image quality (JK/AN/BB). A monitor's *refresh rate*—how often it redraws the image on the screen—helps determine how steady and solid the image looks. (Don't confuse the refresh rate with the screen's ability to keep up with the mouse when you move a graphic around on the screen; the latter depends on the speed of the Mac and its graphics acceleration, if it has any.)

The refresh rate is measured in *Hertz* (times per second)—abbreviated Hz. If a screen refreshes too slowly, you get *flicker* (also called *strobe*). The larger the screen, the more flicker is likely to bother you, so larger monitors usually have higher refresh rates. (Actually, the refresh rate is linked to the monitor's resolution, so a given monitor can have different refresh rates depending on which resolution is being used.)

Generally, any monitor that's connected to the Mac's video port and operates at a resolution of 640 by 480 pixels has to run at 67 Hz; if the resolution is any higher, it runs at 75 Hz. The main exceptions are VGA monitors and SVGA monitors, which were developed for PCs but can run on most current Macs. They can run as low as 60 Hz or even 56 Hz, although some Macs let you increase the refresh rate of SVGA monitors up to 70 Hz or 72 Hz in the Monitors control panel by clicking the Options button.

Peripheral vision is particularly sensitive to flicker, so if you're in doubt about a screen, turn away from it and see how it looks out of the side of your eye.

Several other factors contribute to image quality. *Dot pitch*, which is the distance between individual dots of phosphor on the screen, affects the overall clarity of the image. Generally, anything below .30mm (millimeters) is acceptable, and most Mac monitors fall within that range. With color monitors, sharpness depends partly on the ability of the display tube to focus the three color beams to hit the right spots on the screen (this is called *convergence*, and a few monitors let you adjust for it—a very good feature). *Distortion* refers to a screen's tendency to misrepresent shapes—to display straight lines as bowed, for example. It's often most noticeable at the edges and corners of the screen, and it's more common on large monitors.

Emissions and MPR II (JK). Monitors produce electromagnetic emissions—called *ELF* and *VLF* (extremely low frequency and very low frequency) radiation—that, according to some research, may increase your risk of cancer (for more on this subject, see Appendix A). There's no conclusive evidence that a risk exists, and no level of exposure that has been determined to be safe. The Swedish government has produced a set of low-emissions guidelines called MPR II, and most current monitors adhere to those standards.

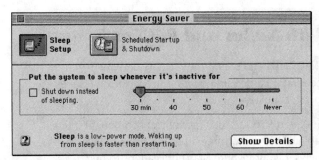

The Energy Saver control panel can be configured to switch an Energy Star–compliant monitor into low-power mode and dim the screen to black. It works in a similar way to the sleep mode built into PowerBooks and supports any Quadra/Centris, LC III, or Power Mac running system 7.1 or above. It can also be configured to turn the Mac on and off at specific days and times so you can, for example, call in and connect to your desktop Mac using your PowerBook.

Energy Star (JK). To cut down on energy consumption, the Clinton administration set up the Energy Star program. Energy Star requires all computer equipment sold to the U.S. government to drop its power consumption below 30 watts when it's not being used.

Equipment manufacturers don't want to be excluded from selling to the Feds (they're the world's biggest customer, after all, accounting for ten percent of all computer equipment sales in the United States), so most of them are changing their products to meet the standards. As a result, a lot of hardware is being designed to go automatically into a low-power mode or turn itself off when it's not being used.

Energy Star–compliant monitors from Apple, NEC, and Radius have a screen-saver-like feature that not only dims their screens, but reduces their power consumption by 50 to 85 percent when the Mac is not being used for a given length of time. To bring one of these monitors back up to full power, you just move the mouse or hit any key.

GOOD FEATURE

Small Color Monitors (JC)

Most people opt for small color monitors—they're reasonably priced, they don't take up too much space on the desk, and they meet the needs of the typical user. For a quick glance at all the monitors mentioned here see the table "Comparing Monitors," later in this chapter.

The **Apple Multiple Scan 14** ($360) packs a lot of features into a small display. This model represents Apple's low end, yet it has front panel controls, a 12.4-inch viewable image size, front-mounted stereo speakers, and a headphone jack. If you want a slightly larger viewable image size you should definitely consider Apple's **Multiple Scan 15** Display ($480). It has all the features of the Multiple Scan 14 but its speakers are side-mounted and it gives you 13.3 inches of viewable image area. Apple monitors carry a one-year replacement warranty.

Accelerating Graphics With NuBus and PCI Cards   (JC)

For boosting the speed that graphics are displayed and seeing more colors on screen, you might look into purchasing a graphics accelerator card. Starting with the Macintosh II series, most desktop Macs have NuBus expansion slots built-in.

Power Macs (such as the 7200, 7500, 8500, and 9500 use *PCI* (peripheral component inter-connect) cards which are reportedly capable of delivering three times the performance of the NuBus type. Be sure to check the reviews in your favorite Mac publications to find out which cards are the peak performers. (See Chapter 2 for more tips on installing NuBus and PCI cards.)

POWER MAC

NEC Technologies makes some excellent displays and consistently scores high in reviews from Mac publications. The NEC **MultiSync C400** ($330, average street price) is an excellent basic monitor and has a 13.2-inch viewable image with no black border, front panel controls, and a tilt-and-swivel stand. For color, clarity, and price, it rivals Apple's Multiple Scan 14.

GOOD FEATURE

For a few dollars more NEC's **MultiSync XV15+** ($500, average street price) gives you control of the display's settings through the aid of an on-screen help manager. NEC has an outstanding three-year warranty period which covers parts, labor, and—most importantly—the picture tube (*cathode ray tube*) itself.

Sony's Trinitron picture tube is almost legendary for quality and sharpness. With Sony's Trinitron Color Display **CPD-1425** ($380) you get high quality at a decent price. Like the other monitors mentioned here, it comes on a tilt-and-swivel base and offers 13.1 inches of viewable image area. This is a nice monitor for the price, but the adapter necessary to connect it to the Mac will cost you an additional $15.

Another excellent monitor from Sony is the **Multiscan 15SX** ($550). It provides a slightly larger viewable image area (13.9 inches) and front panel digital controls. All of Sony's monitors have a three-year warranty on parts and labor and two years on the CRT.

So which one should you buy? Well, ultimately the decision will depend on your budget and the particular features you're looking for.

Personally, I like the fact that NEC monitors have a long warranty period, and that coverage includes the CRT. In the 15-inch size my first pick is the NEC MultiSync XV15+, followed closely by the Apple Multiple Scan 15 Display (I like its integration of speakers so I can listen to CDs).

In the 14-inch size I like the price of the NEC MultiSync C400, and again the long and thorough warranty. My second pick here is the Apple Multiple Scan 14 because it's full of high-end features and comes at a decent price.

Medium-Size Color Monitors   (BB/JC)

Not only are 16- and 17-inch color monitors bigger in screen size, but they are also bigger in *footprint* (the space they take up on the desktop), weight, and bulk than the 14-inchers, and they cost more, yet they display less than twice as much information. Despite the fact that they generally offer more controls over color and image, their image quality usually isn't as good as that of the smaller monitors. But if you need one, here are a few recommendations.

Leading the pack is the affordable Apple **Multiple Scan 1705** Display ($820 without speakers, $850 with speakers). It features 15.8 inches of viewable image area and has an anti-static and anti-glare screen.

Next up is NEC **MultiSync XV17+** ($850, average street price). This model features NEC's Opticlear screen surface which gives it an anti-glare and anti-static coating. Like its little brother (the XV15+), the XV17+ utilizes an on-screen help manager and is covered by NEC's three-year warranty.

If you need a monitor to help you create or use multimedia applications, the **AppleVision 1710AV** Display ($1,160) is the one to get. It has front-mounted speakers, a built-in microphone, headphone and external microphone jack, and ADB ports. A non-AV model is also available with fewer ports for $1,040.

The Radius **PrecisionView 17** ($1,100) uses a Sony Trinitron picture tube for high image quality. It displays resolutions of up to 1,024 by 768, and is covered by Radius' premium warranty with 24-hour replacement.

Sony's **Multiscan 17SF2** Trinitron Graphic Display ($1,100) has an on-screen display with digital controls to adjust the picture within its 16-inch viewable image area. Sony designed this model with home and corporate users in mind.

The NEC MultiSync XV17+ and the AppleVision 1710AV Display are my favorites in this category. I prefer the MultiSync XV17+ for its picture clarity, advanced user controls, and warranty coverage. The AppleVision 1710AV is also exceptional for all its bells and whistles, and quality sound. For more details on the monitors mentioned here see the table "Comparing Monitors."

Portrait Display Labs's Color Pivot Monitor   (JC)

Ever wish you could see the entire page of the document you're working on without scrolling up and down? Portrait Display Labs has the answer with its two-in-one monitor the **Pivot 1700** ($1,100).

In portrait mode, the Pivot displays a complete 8.5-by-11 page (perfect for Web surfers and designers). With a quick swivel of the display (without shutting down or quitting the application you're working in) you get a superb landscape view just right for large spreadsheets and multimedia presentations.

Large Color Monitors   (JK/BB/JC)

You can now buy 19-, 20-, and 21-inch color monitors for under $2,000, but unless you have a high-end Mac (one of the top Quadra or Power Mac models), you'll have to spend several hundred dollars more on a VRAM upgrade or a display card to get decent color richness. If you have an older Mac, it probably won't support this size monitor at all, so you'll have to buy a display card to use it at its intended resolution.

HOT TIP

Only buy a large monitor if you genuinely need the large screen and have a place to put it; you'll find its presence overwhelming unless you can sit well back from it.

Sony's **Multiscan 20SF** Trinitron Graphic Display ($2,300) is a top-of-the-line monitor with a 19.1-inch viewable screen area and front-panel digital controls. It is designed for graphics professionals who need high resolutions for CAD, desktop publishing, and imaging applications.

The NEC **MultiSync XE21** ($1,900, average street price) is loaded with high-end features such as NEC's Opticlear coating; a multilingual on-screen help program; a large 19.8-inch viewable screen area, and it's covered by a three-year warranty.

The Apple **Multiple Scan 20** Display ($2,150) features a 19.1-inch viewable image area. It uses a Sony Trinitron picture tube and has an anti-glare screen and integrated ADB ports.

In the expensive-but-worth-it category is the Radius **MultiView 21** ($2,150). It has a .25mm dot pitch that makes text and images appear incredibly clear onscreen and comes with its own Dynamic Desktop software that lets you switch resolutions without restarting the Mac or quitting applications. For an easy reference to all monitors discussed in this section, see the following table.

Comparing Monitors

Model	Viewable Image Area	Outstanding Features	Price
Small Color Monitors			
Apple Multiple Scan 14	12.4 inches	Stereo speakers, headphone jack	$360
Apple Multiple Scan 15	13.3 inches	Stereo speakers, headphone jack	$480
NEC MultiSync C400	13.2 inches	Front panel controls, tilt-and-swivel stand	$330
NEC MultiSync XV15+	13.8 inches	On-screen help manager	$500
Sony Multiscan 15SX	13.9 inches	Front panel controls, tilt-and-swivel stand	$550
Sony Trinitron CPD-1425	13.1 inches	Front panel controls, tilt-and-swivel stand	$380
Medium-Size Color Monitors			
Apple Multiple Scan 1705	15.8 inches	Stereo speakers, anti-static, anti-glare screen	$850
AppleVision 1710AV	16.1 inches	Stereo speakers, microphone, ADB ports	$1,160
NEC MultiSync XV17+	15.6 inches	Opticlear anti-static, anti-glare screen	$850
Radius PrecisionView 17	16 inches	Sony Trinitron picture tube	$1,100
Sony Multiscan 17SF2	16 inches	Digital controls	$1,100
Large Color Monitors			
Apple Multiple Scan 20	19.1 inches	Anti-glare screen, ADB ports	$2,150
NEC MultiSync XE21	19.8 inches	Opticlear anti-static, anti-glare screen	$1,900
Radius MultiView 21	19.8 inches	Sony Trinitron picture tube	$2,150
Sony Multiscan 20SF	19.1 inches	Front panel digital controls	$2,300

Keyboards (JC)

When you buy a modular Mac, the keyboard usually isn't included. Most people will automatically buy an Apple keyboard, even though there are plenty of others on the market that might suit a particular purpose much better. Here are some hints on what to look for and which products provide it.

Evaluating Keyboards (JK/JC)

Keyboards may seem generic, but there are plenty of differences to consider. To do a worthwhile comparison, use the information here to think about what you want. Then find a keyboard in a store or catalog that seems to meet your needs. If you can, try it out, or get a money-back guarantee; you won't really be able to judge its performance until you've used it with your own Mac for awhile.

Key feel. Every keyboard has a slightly different feel. Do you prefer a hard, solid keystroke or a softer, mushier one? You'll need to do some hands-on testing to decide.

Ergonomics. Using a keyboard a lot can also put you at risk for various injuries, some of which can become permanent disabilities (see Appendix A for more on this). If you're constantly typing, you should seriously consider getting one of the specially built ergonomic keyboards on the market designed to avoid injuries.

The numeric keypad. Most keyboards come with a numeric keypad, or at least have an option to add one. The keypad saves a huge amount of time for people who enter numbers a lot and can touch-type the ten-key layout. For people who don't use it, the keypad is just an obstacle on their hand's way to the mouse.

HOT TIP

You can assign other functions to the keypad. If you hit the [Clear] or [Num Lock] key while using Microsoft Word, the number keys become controls for moving the insertion point up or down, or to the start or end of a line. If a disability prevents you from using the mouse, you can use the Easy Access control panel to make the number keys on the keypad move the pointer.

HOT TIP

Function keys and other controls. Apple's extended and AppleDesign keyboards, and many third-party keyboards, include 15 function keys, which some programs (Microsoft Word and Excel, for example) use as shortcuts for standard commands. You can also use macro programs like QuicKeys (described in Chapter 13) to assign any function you want to these keys.

Built-in trackballs. Some keyboards have built-in trackballs, which save you the expense of buying one separately. But don't assume the keyboard's trackball will work the same way as others you might have used. Built-in trackballs tend to be smaller and hard to control, which makes some of them virtually unusable.

Key arrangement. Some keyboards have unique layouts you may find very convenient or very annoying. You might, for instance, prefer a larger [Return] or [Delete] key. Again, it's ideal to try before you buy, or at least get a money-back guarantee.

Compatibility. Some early third-party keyboards were not fully compatible with the Macintosh. These keyboards simply did not work for Mac-unique procedures such as holding down the [Shift] key to disable extensions, or zapping the PRAM ([⌘][Option][P][R]), during startup. (The fine art of PRAM zapping and extension disabling is covered in Chapter 7.)

Fortunately most (if not all) non-Apple manufactured keyboards currently being sold work as they're supposed to. If you should happen to purchase one that doesn't, promptly return it.

The Cheap Keyboard Challenge (JC)

Mom always said, "cheaper isn't always better" and in most cases the old adage remains true. Yet as consumers, we never stop looking for products that are high in quality and low in price even though the two almost never go hand in hand. Bearing this in mind I set out on a mission in search of the cheapest, high-quality keyboard I could find through three mail-order catalogs.

Shopping for anything through a catalog can be challenging, especially since you don't know what you're getting until it arrives. Fortunately purchasing through mail-order has an advantage; a good number of products that are sold have a 30-day money-back guarantee so they can be returned if they don't meet your expectations.

All three of the keyboards I ordered were the extended type with 105 keys, an ADB cable was included, and each tested fully Mac-compatible.

At $60 the MacWarehouse **PowerUser 105 Extended** was the most expensive model I looked at. It has a durable design, carries a one-year warranty, but has no height adjustment, and pressing the keys down required some extra effort. I also didn't like the small Delete key; other keyboards feature one that is typically at least twice as wide. My advice is to stay away from this keyboard as it is too expensive for what you get.

The best thing about Mac Zone's **Performantz Soft Touch Extended** ($50) is the feel of the keys. Although it may be a bit mushy for some, typing on this keyboard was virtually silent and effortless. The warranty period is impressive—it's covered for three years. This is a good keyboard if you prefer the soft-touch feel.

Surprisingly, the cheapest keyboard, the **MDS Mac-105M** ($40, PC & MacConnection) was the one I liked the best. It was the only one to come with an instruction manual, a two-year warranty, and a nice, stylish design. The key feel was just about right—not too mushy with a nice solid "click" as the keys are pressed. If you don't want to invest big bucks to buy an Apple brand keyboard, get this one.

GOOD FEATURE

Standard and Extended Keyboards (AN/BB/JK/JC)

Not long ago Apple offered two styles of keyboard. The standard model had only 81 keys; the extended model featured 105 keys and a row of 15 function keys.

Apple no longer manufactures the 81-key model but currently makes two extended keyboards: the **AppleDesign** (about $90 mail-order) and the **Apple Extended Keyboard II** ($170 mail-order). Both of these keyboards are virtually identical except the Extended II includes a plastic template that fits over the row of function keys that serves as a reference for shortcuts. The AppleDesign is included with Performa model Macs and has a nice contoured shape.

A number of companies besides Apple make extended keyboards. DataDesk was one of the first. I find their **Mac101E** ($120) lighter yet more satisfying to the touch than Apple's or other companies' boards.

MicroSpeed's **Keyboard Deluxe Mac** ($125) is certainly worth checking out as is the **Soft Touch Plus** (about $50 mail-order) from Adesso.

Ergonomic Keyboards   (RS/JC)

As we mentioned earlier, heavy keyboard use can put you at risk for some very serious and permanent injuries (to find out more, see Appendix A). People should be concerned enough over this issue to look for products that will protect rather than harm them, and companies are beginning to develop keyboards for healthy computing.

GOOD
FEATURE

Most new keyboards on the market have some form of ergonomic support built-in such as height adjustment or softer keys. But, the **Kinesis Ergonomic Model 130** ($275, Kinesis) is really the only keyboard made that can be considered 100 percent ergonomic. It's designed to correct the awkward postures that can lead to repetitive stress injuries, and according to independent studies cited by Kinesis, and reports from users, it really works.

The Kinesis left- and right-hand keys are set in two concave bowls that are separated by several inches of empty surface. The keys are arranged so your thumbs are higher than the rest of your hand, and palms face each other slightly. The result is that your hands and arms remain in a natural position while using

The Kinesis Keyboard is split down the middle and curved to fit the shape of your hands.

the keyboard, and very little finger movement is necessary to push down each key.

Some keys have been relocated, so you have to do a little relearning, but the keyboard also has the ability to be remapped if necessary. Using the Kinesis requires much less effort than a standard keyboard. I highly recommend trying one, even if you don't (yet) suffer from any kind of repetitive stress injury.

Another finger-friendly option, the **Tru-Form Keyboard** ($90 mail-order, Adesso), features an ergonomically contoured design with a split keyboard layout and built-in wrist support.

Type It For Me, Will You Mac? (JC)

Wouldn't it be nice if your Mac automatically typed the date or added your name at the close of a letter or e-mail message? Well it can by using either of three different programs that create scripts or shortcuts.

TypeIt4Me ($20) is a fantastic shareware program that maintains a list of words or entire paragraphs you use frequently. By invoking certain keyboard or mouse combinations the desired text appears instantly.

If you want to automate your Mac beyond merely typing, CE Software's **QuicKeys** ($119) program is definitely for you. QuicKeys pretty much does it all and you can create a different set of shortcuts for every application you use. For more on QuicKeys see Chapter 13.

One Click ($129, WestCode) takes the idea of QuicKeys further by displaying customizable button palettes to run the shortcuts and scripts you create. It's extremely Mac-like and easy to use.

Keyboards With Trackballs (JC)

The latest trend these days seems to be keyboards with either a built-in trackball or touch-sensitive trackpad. For roughly the same price as an extended keyboard, you get built-in cursor control and save space on your desk. *[While some may enjoy having their left hand know what their right hand is doing by using the built-in cursor controls, asking others of us to forsake our mouse is outright Mac-blasphemy!—JJ]*

Currently two manufacturers sell keyboards with built-in trackballs: DataDesk makes the **TrackBoard** ($150); and there's also the **TrakPro** ($250) from Key Tronic.

Unfortunately built-in trackballs rarely work as well as their external cousins. The feel, position of the clicking buttons, and movement of the built-in trackballs we've tried were disappointing, so do go for a test drive before buying one.

Your best bet for a keyboard with built-in cursor control is **TouchBoard** ($180, DataDesk) which features a touch-sensitive pad similar to those found on newer PowerBooks. The TouchBoard's pad offers better, more accurate control of the mouse than a built-in trackball. It lacks a numeric keypad but you can add one for $70 if you find you really miss it.

Non-English Keyboards (JK)

Apple makes standard and extended keyboards for all the major Western European languages, plus Japanese, Korean, Russian, Persian, Hebrew, Greek, Turkish, Icelandic, Finnish, and Flemish. To use them properly, you need the corresponding version of the system software. You can order both the keyboard and the system software through Apple dealers.

A Chord Keyboard (Caleb Clark)

The **BAT Personal Keyboard** ($199, Infogrip) is a seven-button keyboard that lets you type one-handed: there's one key for each of your four fingers and three for your thumb. You hit combinations ("chords") of the seven keys to produce all the various keyboard characters. For example, the chord for the letter *g* is the middle thumb and ring finger keys pushed down simultaneously.

Standard keyboards are faster than the BAT for straight typing, but the BAT is convenient for things such as layout or text editing, because you can keep one hand on the keyboard and one on the mouse, and never look away from the screen. I put the BAT to the left of my standard keyboard so I can type on either one according to the situation, and it works great.

The BAT has a palmrest and ergonomically designed keys, and it didn't take long to learn.

~~~~~~

Mice and Other Pointing Devices

Mice are one of the Mac's great innovations. They give you much more direct control over what's on the screen than any keyboard can. The mouse controls the pointer, which gives you the ability to select objects on the screen and control cursors in word processors, paintbrushes in art programs, and paddles in shuffleboard games.

Mice

There's certainly nothing wrong with the mouse that comes with your Mac, but someday you may have to replace it, or there may be a substitute that would better fit the way you use your Mac. For example, some mice and trackballs have extra buttons that lock down for dragging objects, or for other purposes that you can assign. Here are several alternative mice you might consider.

Mouse Cleaning   (SZA/SM/AN/RS/JK)

Over time, gunk builds up on the rollers inside a mouse, making it feel rough and causing the pointer to skip jerkily around the screen. Luckily, there's an easy way to fix it.

Remove the ring at the bottom of the mouse by turning it (or sliding it, on some older mice) and drop the ball out into your palm. Then, using a penknife or pencil eraser, scrape or rub off the track of crud that you'll see on the rollers inside. Wipe the ball with a cloth, and put the mouse back together. This little chore is really worth the time it takes. The difference between a gunky, rough mouse and a clean, smooth mouse is astounding.

Ergonomic mice (JC). Apple's **Desktop Bus Mouse II** ($80) is ergonomically designed and comes standard with new Macs. The Mouse II is molded to fit into your hand and requires less effort to click the mouse button, which can help prevent injury.

For a fraction of the price, Kensington's **Mouse in a Box** ($40) gives you a similar design and shape as Apple's but comes with a five-year warranty and an amazing 90-day no risk trial. If you have an older mouse or need more ergonomic support this is a good one to get.

The Kensington folks also make the two-button **Kensington Mouse** ($60) and programmable, four-button **Thinking Mouse** ($90). Both have a symmetrical shape and allow their buttons to be configured to reduce repetitive tasks.

A cordless mouse (AN/JC). I've often found the cord on my mouse getting in my way as I make the big, sweeping arm movements so typical of people with my particular constellation of neurological defects. The solution is a cordless mouse that transmits its motion to the Mac using either an infrared beam or through radio waves.

Logitech's cordless **MouseMan** ($90) is molded to fit your palm and has three buttons—one to click and two that can be programmed to issue different commands for specific applications. The MouseMan uses radio waves to transmit up to six feet away from a receiver plugged into the Mac's ADB port, and does not require them to be lined up with each other like infrared devices. Four separate channels can be used to eliminate interference from other radio devices.

Trackballs

Trackballs are a bit like upside-down mice. You roll a ball that sits inside a stationary holder, so they require less desk space than mice. Trackballs control the pointer more precisely than a mouse does (which is particularly important for graphics). They all have at least two buttons: one that's like a normal mouse button, and one that can lock in the down position so you can drag objects or menus without holding the button down with your finger.

The **TurboMouse** ($110) from Kensington is the best-known trackball; year after year, Mac magazines give it top review ratings and "Best Of" awards and it remains one of our favorites as well.

The TurboMouse's ball is much larger and heavier than other trackballs, so it has more inertia. The four buttons' position, size, and feel are excellent. They require enough pressure to keep you from accidentally clicking, without making you aware of a need to press hard.

GOOD FEATURE

To control the TurboMouse, Kensington includes its own software that has many advanced features. For example, you can select spots on the screen and make the pointer jump to them by clicking both TurboMouse buttons and rolling the ball in the proper direction.

GOOD FEATURE

CoStar's **Stingray** ($100) has a small ball that's easy to control; its two buttons take the form of a pair of sloping wings, which surround the ball. They're so sensitive you have to be careful not to click them accidentally. You can alter pointer speed and select which button you want to use as the normal click and which to use as the click-lock—a boon to lefties.

The **Trackman Marble** ($100, Logitech) is a highly ergonomic trackball that fits comfortably into the palm of your hand. It has three buttons at the end of a large, curved palmrest, and the trackball is off to the side for your thumb to control. You can program two of the three buttons using the MouseKey software for custom shortcuts.

Touchpads

If you're familiar with Apple's newest PowerBooks you've probably noticed the small square *touchpad* below the keyboard used to move the cursor. Touchpads have become a popular item and several manufacturers make external models that plug into any Mac with an ADB port.

Guiding the cursor is accomplished by using one finger and applying very little pressure. Because they're touch-sensitive using a touchpad requires little effort, but does involve some getting used to.

A couple of the most popular touchpads available are the **Adjustable Glidepoint** ($80, Alps) and the **QuePoint II** ($75, MicroQue). Both of these touchpads feature programmable buttons—the Glidepoint has three and the QuePoint has four. You can also tap the surface of these touchpads to double-click on an icon.

A nice feature of the Glidepoint is the ability to adjust its base for more comfort.

Besides one additional button, the **QuePoint** also scores for its pass-through connector which allows other ADB devices to be connected to it.

When choosing one of these pads it's really best to try before you buy, especially in the rare event that you don't like, or can't get used to using one.

Me and My QuickCam   (JC)

Okay, so you spent several hours on your tax return, then worked up a few spreadsheets and answered some e-mail. You and your Mac are probably ready for some fun. What's that? You're bored with the latest shoot-'em-up space game? You say you've discovered all the secrets in Brøderbund's Myst? Allow us to introduce you to the Connectix **QuickCam** (about $100 for the grayscale version, $230 for the color model).

Slightly smaller than a billiard ball, with a tiny lens and built-in microphone, the QuickCam captures 4-bit grayscale or 24-bit color QuickTime video, and takes still pictures, too.

It's an addictive little product, in fact you'll be amazed at all the ways you'll discover to use it. On the practical side you can use the QuickCam to add pictures to documents, newsletters, genealogy programs, databases, and even an address book using a program such as TouchBase Pro.

Create QuickTime video of yourself and your friends with the QuickCam.

Most of all, the QuickCam is fun. Just doing your best contorted, Jim Carey-like faces in front of it can waste an entire afternoon. Beyond that, if you have kids—or pets—you really should get a QuickCam. Imagine capturing video of your child, pet, friend, relative or significant other, playing it back on your Mac at work when you're feeling down. It could certainly brighten your day and make everyone else in the office envious, or maybe a little jealous.

The QuickCam is also the perfect low-cost solution for videoconferencing. Used in conjunction with the free **CU-SeeMe** program from Cornell University, you can transmit video and sound with others over the Internet.

For videoconferencing within the boundaries of your home, office, or over high-speed ISDN phone lines, Connectix makes a program called **VideoPhone** ($150), which can be purchased separately or bundled with the QuickCam.

Pressure-Sensitive Tablets

(AC/JC)

Pressure-sensitive tablets let you imitate traditional painting media, such as brushes or charcoal, by changing the thickness, color, or opacity of a line in proportion to the pressure you apply with the stylus as you draw. A good tablet can recognize at least 120 pressure levels (although a lot of software still can recognize only 60). A stylus should also be light, cordless, and responsive. Many styluses offer buttons to which you can assign specific functions.

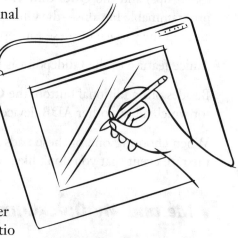

Some tablets also let you trace images placed under a transparent sheet of plastic, control the ratio between the active area of the tablet and the screen area where you want to draw, and create macros, which can be activated by the menu bar or stylus button.

Pressure-sensitive tablets let you create and manipulate art the old-fashioned way—by hand.

Wacom ArtZ and ArtPad tablets. Wacom, the industry leader for some time, carries the **ArtPad II** ($150) and **ArtZ** ($390 for the 6- by 8-inch tablet) tablets which can interpret as many as 256 pressure levels. Their stylish, featherweight stylus, the **UltraPen**, has a programmable side switch you can use to assign different functions and macros.

The best thing about the ArtZ tablets is that you can completely customize the performance of the stylus and the tablet, and save different sets of preferences for each program you work with, so you don't have to waste time switching them back and forth. My favorite adjustment is the Custom Pressure Curve, which lets you control the tablet's response to different pressure levels, so you can, for example, obtain a softer and more sensitive "brush".

The ArtPad II tablet takes the economical route and offers a small 4- by 5-inch active area. It's great if you're just getting started, or on a tight budget.

DrawingSlate II. The **CalComp DrawingSlate II** ($200 for the 6- by 9-inch tablet), features a cordless stylus, and although it's a little heavier than the Wacom's, it's very responsive, and the tip has a great feel to it. The stylus has two buttons for defining actions or commands that, together with the 18-function menu on the tablet, make DrawingSlate a useful tool for working with macros.

Expanding Serial Ports (JC)

If you're running out of places to plug in serial devices (such as modems, additional printers, or graphics tablets) you have a couple of expansion options.

The least expensive route is an A/B switch box (for DIN8 pin devices) that you can purchase from a local computer dealer or mail-order company for about $25, which allows the connection of one additional serial device. You'll also need a serial cable that runs about $10.

Using a switch box lets you share one of the two serial ports on the Macintosh with an additional device. The only disadvantage is you can only use one of the two devices connected through the switch box at a time. You could also potentially run into a problem with any system extensions or control panels that need to communicate with the particular serial device you have switched off on the A/B box.

A better solution is the **Port Juggler** ($95, Momentum, Inc.). Using a combination of hardware and software, Port Juggler handles up to four additional serial devices and automatically switches between them as needed. It also never loses communication with devices such as modems that require constant communication with the Mac. For the convenience Port Juggler is well worth its price.

Scanners

Scanners are devices that convert images—typically photographs or other artwork—into digital form so they can be stored and manipulated by computers. When used in conjunction with *OCR* (optical character recognition) software, they can also convert a page of text into an editable document on your computer.

Mac-compatible scanners range in price from a few hundred dollars to a hundred thousand dollars. The ones under $10,000 are great for jobs that don't require precise detail or color reproduction, but they can't compete with high-end equipment when it comes to demanding jobs like color photographs in slick publications.

There are more than 100 scanners on the market today. The models change frequently and there are often variations even between one individual unit and another. So in addition to the reviews of particular models in the next section, we've explained, in general terms, what to look for when evaluating scanners. For more details on scanning, see Chapter 15.

How Scanners Work   (JM)

During scanning, light is reflected off (or passed through) the artwork and focused onto *CCDs* (charge-coupled devices—basically, light sensors) that convert the light energy to electricity. Color scanners use colored filters (or sometimes a prism) to read red, green, and blue values separately, and then combine the three single-color scans to yield a full-color image. Though the principle is the same for all scanners, units differ in how many readings per inch they take (the scanner's resolution), how much color information they capture at each reading (the scanner's bit depth), whether they take separate passes of the light source to read the red, green, and blue values (three-pass scanners) or take all the readings in a single pass (minimizing the chance for misregistration and speeding up the scanning process), and the quality of the scanning software that comes with the machine.

Bit depth (JM). One-bit scanners read all sample points as either black or white. There aren't very many of these around anymore. Most people use 8-bit grayscale scanners (for 256 shades of gray) or 24-bit color scanners (256 shades each of red, green, and blue, for a total of more than 16 million colors).

Some scanners read 36 or 48 bits of information at each sample point, even though their final product is a 24-bit file. Doing this reduces the amount of *noise* (inaccurate data) that CCDs inherently produce. (The less noise there is in relation to total data collected, the more usable information the scanner can deliver.)

This extra information doesn't go to waste. A common problem when you alter scans is that you lose information—if you brighten colors, for example, you might lose image detail. But when you scan 48 bits, you can tell the scanner to digitally convert only the brightest 16 million colors, say, so that its final 24-bit image contains the best information.

Resolution (JM/AN). A scanner's resolution refers to the number of sample points per inch it's capable of capturing (often expressed as dpi, although spi is more accurate). Some scanners are also rated in terms of total resolution, the maximum number of points they can sample. To compare these two figures, divide the total resolution by each dimension of your intended output, then average the two figures. For example, a scanner whose total resolution is 2,000 by 3,000 dots can output a 5- by 7-inch image at a resolution of about 415 dpi (2,000/5 = 400; 3,000/7 = 428.6; (400+428.6)/2 = 414.3).

Types of Scanners

(JM)

The two most common types of scanners are:

- *Flatbed scanners.* These operate like photocopiers; you place the artwork on a glass surface, and a scan head and light source move across it under the glass. Flatbeds can scan almost anything that has at least one flat side, even a slab of marble. Most of them can't scan transparencies or slides, but a growing number of manufacturers offer attachments for that purpose. All flatbeds will scan up to at least 8.5 by 11 inches, and some go up to 11 by 17 inches.

- *Transparency scanners.* As their name suggests, transparency scanners scan transparent materials such as 35mm slides, negatives, and larger photographic transparencies (4 by 5 inches or 8 by 10 inches).

A flatbed scanner is the perfect solution for getting flat and not-so-flat art into your Mac.

Evaluating Scanners

(JM)

Evaluating scanners is easy if your scanned images will only be displayed on the screen; just do some test scans and compare the results on a monitor like the one you'll be using. The best images to use for tests contain fine detail and a mix of bright and muted colors; a human face is ideal, since small tonal shifts can make it look totally wrong.

If you're going to print your scanned images, don't try to evaluate them on a screen. Scans that look dull on a screen may actually contain better data for printing than those that look bright and colorful. It usually isn't possible to make a scan and then print it on the output device you're planning to use, but you can at least avoid some of the most obvious and common problems by making a few test scans and analyzing them with Photoshop's Levels chart (other image-editing programs have similar capabilities).

HOT TIP

In the end, the quality of your scans will depend just as much on your skill in processing them as on how good a scanner you used. Just about every scan needs to be brightened and sharpened in software, and no scanner program can take the place of a good image-editing program like Photoshop (which comes bundled with many scanners). Also remember that, for most people, differences in quality won't matter as much as differences in convenience. Small color imbalances probably won't bother you if you're producing newsletters, but a slow scanner will annoy you every time you use it.

The scanner should provide a Photoshop plug-in or some other software that enables you to scan directly into your image-editing package. Because all scans need correction, most people find this the most convenient way to work.

The Visioneer PaperPort   (JC)

Several years ago when computers were first introduced they were touted as a way to eliminate paper in the office. Today we are still buried in stacks of paper that move from left to right on our desks as we search for enough free space to work. The folks at a company called Visioneer got a brilliant idea and developed the PaperPort, a small desktop scanner, to finally get paper off our desks and into our Macs.

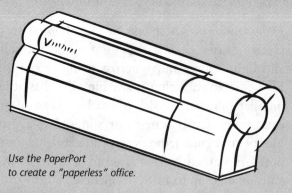

Use the PaperPort to create a "paperless" office.

GOOD FEATURE

The **PaperPort Vx** ($300) uses virtually no space on your desk. The unit measures just 12 inches long and 3.75 inches high, and is specially designed to set up directly in front of most Macs without blocking access to the floppy drive. Because it utilizes rollers, the PaperPort can only be used for flat objects such as documents and photographs. It supports 8-bit grayscale (256 shades) and up to 400 dpi.

The bundled software is excellent and includes everything you need to become a PaperPort fanatic. Visioneer includes versions of OmniPage Lite, OCR software to convert scanned images into text, Corex CardScan for storing scanned business cards, and PictureWorks copier software that prints documents using features similar to those of a copy machine.

You can feed the PaperPort pretty much anything cluttering your desk: newspaper clippings, receipts, invoices, reports, recipes, and of course, business cards. After a recent Macworld Expo I decided to put the PaperPort to work on the stack of business cards I collected. I had high hopes it would save me hours of manually typing each entry and indeed it did. Each card was quickly input into the Mac, processed by the CardScan software, and converted into text which I then imported into my address book program. The PaperPort got all the cards (about 70 of them) into my Mac in just a couple of hours.

If you receive documents on your Mac through a fax modem the PaperPort is the ultimate complement. It essentially acts like the input slot of a standard fax machine so you can immediately fax back contracts or other documents that require your signature or notations.

The only drawback to the PaperPort is it requires the use of one of the Mac's serial ports which are typically occupied by a modem and printer. Fortunately the Visioneer folks realize this and now have a SCSI upgrade kit ($70) so your PaperPort can be daisy-chained with other SCSI devices. The PaperPort Vx costs less than a flatbed scanner, is faster, takes very little space, and most importantly gets all those scraps of paper off your desk.

Color Flatbed Scanners (JC)

With nearly an infinite number of choices available we managed to whittle our picks for scanners down to the following, based on reviews in Mac publications and through word of mouth.

At the top of the heap is the **Silverscanner DTP** ($800, La Cie) which competes and wins in both price and quality against other scanners on the market. The Silver-Scanner has an optical resolution of 400 by 800 dpi and a maximum bit depth of 30.

La Cie also makes the **Silverscanner PRO** ($600), a low-cost model designed for home users and web-page creators. It supports 24-bit color and 300 by 300 dpi. With its low price and La Cie's reputation for quality, it is definitely worth checking out.

The **ES-1200c** ($1,300, Epson) is no slouch either. It's competitively priced and is often sold through mail-order catalogs for under $1,000. It comes with Adobe Photoshop and is covered by a two-year warranty. It supports a resolution of 600 by 1,200 dpi with 30 bits.

Rounding out our top picks is the **ScanTouch AX-1200** ($1,720, Nikon). It features a resolution of 565 by 1,200 and a maximum depth of 30 bits. The ScanTouch costs a little more than other scanners but the quality is superb.

The Apple Color OneScanner 600/27 (JC)

As we were going to press, Apple announced the **Color OneScanner 600/27** ($600). Like its predecessor, the Color One is a "one-pass" scanner (meaning that it scans the original just once, rather than once each for red, green, and blue).

The centerpiece of the product is the OneScanner Dispatcher software which integrates image and document processing features into a single program. This allows you to organize, edit, print, fax, and archive documents and images.

A plug-in included with the OneScanner lets you scan directly into an image editing program like Adobe Photoshop. Also included is Xerox's TextBridge OCR software for converting scanned documents into editable text form.

The Color One is smaller than most flatbed scanners measuring just 11 by 16 inches. It has an optical resolution of 300 by 300 dpi, and enhanced resolution of 1,200 by 1,200 dpi. A cool Xenon bulb keeps heat-sensitive originals from being damaged during scanning.

Editors' Poll:
If You Were on a Desert Island and Could Have
Only One Peripheral, What Would it Be? Why?

BF: A joystick. What's a Mac without games? Of course, this is coming from the games editor. If not a joystick, a Wacom tablet to allow drawing.

BW: Assuming I had a functional Mac/Monitor/mouse and power source: A video camera and capture board, so I could produce my own shows and do stop-action animation with bits of coral and dead crabs. Production would keep me busy during the day, and playback would entertain me during the lonely nights.

JH: I'd take a CD-ROM player and a copy of the Myst sequel—when it's released.

TL: No contest. A (wireless?) modem. That way, I could still surf the Web while I was marooned and I could even send a message for help! (I am assuming that an internal hard drive does not count as a peripheral here.)

JC: Probably a mouse with a long cord that I could use for fish bait!

JJ: A large speaker with mounds of spaghetti cable so I could enjoy listening to my CDs while stretched out serenely on my SCSI-cable hammock.

SZA: Definitely a printer, for producing all the little notes I'd put in bottles that would say: "If you're reading this, you're too close to my island!"

7 Preventing and Solving Problems

If you are in a panic because your hard drive seems to have died or because your favorite application won't open or because your cursor has frozen solid or because a message appeared on your screen that said you had a Type 11 error, here is where you'll learn how to get your Mac running smoothly again (see "When Trouble Strikes" for immediate help). Solving these types of problems is what this chapter is all about. So welcome to the least fun chapter in this book. It's the stuff you need to know so that you can have fun the rest of the time.

And make no mistake about it: You will have problems using your Mac. This is a given. Whether you are a novice user running a new Mac straight out of the box or a seasoned pro running a top-of-the-line Mac that has been modified, expanded, and customized more times than a car buff's '57 Chevy, you will have problems.

The best way to solve problems is to avoid them. That's why our first aim in this chapter is to prescribe some preventive medicine—helpful hints on how to stop problems before they happen. Next, we review the tools of the trade, those software utilities that you'll need to make your problem solving as painless as possible. Finally, we present a survey of the most common maladies you will face and what to do to cure them.

Contributors

Ted Landau (TL) is the chapter editor.

Randy B. Singer, Esq. (RS) is a longtime contributor to *The Macintosh Bible* and also answers the technical questions posed in the Mac Bible forum on America Online.

Lisa Lee (LL) is a Macintosh engineer, has written *Upgrading and Repairing your Mac,* and can be found at AFC Lisa@aol.com.

Henry Norr (HN) edited the Preventing & Solving Problems chapter in the previous edition of *The Macintosh Bible,* from which parts of this chapter were taken.

Contents

Preventive Medicine for Hardware (LL)

Hardware precautions tend to be simple and painless—and definitely worth doing. The problems they prevent are ones that could otherwise be fatal to your Mac.

Your Setup Makes a Difference

How you set up your Mac can prevent unnecessary hardware problems from occurring and provide prolonged, efficient use of your Macintosh computer. Your setup includes where your Mac is located, as well as the location of all its hardware peripherals.

Surge Protectors. Surge protectors (a power strip with a buffer to protect your equipment if the voltage suddenly changes) are an essential part of a computer system. Plugging all of your computer components into a surge protector can protect your hardware from unnecessary or unexpected power surges or electrical damage from lightning or local power source. During storms, to be extra safe, unplug your computer equipment altogether. *[If you are going to get a surge protector, spend the extra bucks to get a good one. In general, any surge protector that costs less than $20 is not really offering the protection you should expect. Figure on spending $40 or more.—TL]*

Accidents. Be sure your Mac setup is away from extreme heat, cold, water, or unstable environments. All of these elements can permanently damage your Mac's internal components. Place your Mac, peripherals, monitor, and keyboard on a table with a strong base, and on a stable, flat floor. Try to keep the computer away from high-traffic areas to minimize having things or people bumping into your computer, or jarring the table. You may also want to consider adding your computer and related equipment to your home insurance policy.

Moisture and Static. Macs, like other computer hardware and electrical components, are not made to be water or static friendly. Put your Mac in a location furthest from water, moisture, mildew, or steam. Water on your Mac or peripherals can create an electrical short on your motherboard, which can be a costly replacement.

The most common source of static in a home or office is a carpet. Moving your feet across a carpet can generate enough of a static shock, so that you could damage your Mac's microcircuit components just by touching them. That's why, before opening your Mac's case or any other hardware product casing, you should ideally be in a static-free area and grounded. Professionals use grounding straps to do this. However, in most cases, it is sufficient to discharge your static electricity by touching a piece of metal (such as the casing of the Mac's power supply) before working with any other components.

Magnetic incompatibilities. Be sure to keep your Mac and its monitor at least a few feet away from other magnetic sources, such as a stereo speaker, television, telephone, or power line. Magnetic sources can affect the consistency of your screen display, video input or output quality, or audio input and playback quality.

Dustability. Try to avoid dust build-up on the outside and inside of your Macintosh. Keep your Mac in a well-ventilated area, leaving at least a few inches around the ventilation slits on the case open so air circulation is not hampered and to avoid overheating the internal hardware pieces in your Mac. Dust build-up on your Mac's logic board (the main component board inside your Mac) can cause your Mac to have slightly slower performance, and can also be a factor in overheating a chip or solder on your motherboard.

If you do not use your computer frequently, or if you have to unavoidably locate it in an overly dusty, windy or congested environment, consider purchasing a plastic cover for the Mac (use only when it is not on) and the keyboard to protect it from unnecessary exposure to computer-unfriendly environmental elements.

When to Save Energy

For desktop Macs or PowerBooks, you can leave your Macintosh turned off if it is not used daily. If you plan on using the Mac over several days, leave it on until you and other users have completed work. Then shut if off until you plan on using it again. If you use your Mac daily, we recommend leaving your Mac on all the time. With the possible exception of the monitor, many people believe that frequently turning your equipment on and off shortens the life of its electrical components.

PCI Power Macintoshes and PowerBooks have a *sleep* feature, which puts your Mac in low-power mode until you press the space bar. You can put your Mac to sleep automatically by adjusting settings in the PowerBook control panel or (with desktop systems) the Energy Saver control panel. Sleep mode allows you to bypass the start-up process which occurs when you power up your Mac from the keyboard or switch on your Mac's case. Any applications open before Sleep mode begins remain open when your Mac awakes from sleep. We recommend you use sleep mode if you use your Mac daily and wish to preserve the longevity of your Mac hardware.

For most other Macs, Apple has one of a myriad of Energy Saver control panels that at least put the monitor to "sleep." Screen saver utilities, such as After Dark (see Chapter 13), remain another popular way of doing this. However, most monitors available today don't require a screen saver since they are energy saver-aware and will power down if not in use for a predetermined amount of time. Screen savers are not harmful, though, and can be fun to watch. *[With newer monitors, screen savers are also no longer needed to protect against burn-in (where a monitor develops a permanent "ghost" of an image that was left on the screen for too long).—TL]*

Before Moving Your Hardware

Before moving your Mac or any peripherals, always turn off the power and disconnect power cables from the electrical power source (from the wall, or surge protector). Doing this reduces the possibility of static electricity-induced damage, and data corruption due to electrical, hardware, or software errors caused by moving hardware while the computer is on. While your computer is powered on, never disconnect or move hardware peripherals or internals as this can damage your equipment or affect the efficiency of the device if it has moving parts (such as a hard drive).

[The same goes for Apple Desktop Bus (ADB) cables. Even though the cables that go to your mouse and keyboard carry only a small amount of power, unplugging one can blow a fuse on some Mac logic boards. I know—I fried a Mac II (at the beginning of one of the busiest weeks of the year for me) by disconnecting a keyboard.—HN]

WARNING

[On the other hand, I connect and disconnect devices attached to my serial ports (printers and modems) all the time and have never had a problem.—TL]

Before moving or disconnecting cables, follow each cable connection visually or physically to avoid selecting the wrong cable (i.e. the cable to another Mac or computer). Disconnect and move cabling slowly to avoid damaging the pins inside the cable, as well as other clips or cables surrounding it.

If you are adding a new hardware product to your Mac configuration, make sure all hardware, cabling, and connection pieces are present before disconnecting or moving existing hardware. Before attempting installation, be sure you have cables with the correct length, and ample room on your table for housing the hardware.

Preventive Medicine for Software (TL)

Whenever something on a Mac fails to work, too many users immediately assume that the hardware is at fault. If a system crash occurs twice in one day, they are already packing up their Mac to take it to the repair shop. Happily, this is rarely needed. Most Mac problems are software-based. Many of them can be easily prevented by following the prescriptions in this section. And most other problems can be fixed by the software cures described in the remaining sections of this chapter.

Get Those Updates

The vast majority of the freezes, crashes, and other types of failures your Mac is likely to have are ultimately due to software bugs. The bug may be in the application you are using, a third-party extension, or some component of the system software. It may even be some mysterious combination of these causes.

Whatever the ultimate source of the bug, you cannot fix it. Let me repeat: you cannot eliminate a bug yourself. That is a task for the people who wrote the software. However, what you can do is find out if a bug-fixed version of the software is already available (and if not, when it will be) and what work-around solutions may be possible while you are waiting for the upgrade to arrive.

Read before you use. Check out the packaging that comes with your software. It should describe the minimum requirements to use it. Pay attention. There's no point in buying software that only runs on a Power Mac if you are using a Mac II. While this sort of incompatibility is technically not a "bug" (that is, it isn't something wrong with the software that needs to be fixed), it amounts to the same thing for you: without the right hardware you won't be able to use the software.

Similarly, check out any Read Me file that comes on the program disk or that is installed when you install the software on your hard drive. You will likely learn about such things as specific extension conflicts, known bugs that have not been fixed in the current version of the program, and special circumstances where the program may be incompatible with Apple's system software.

Macintosh magazines, such as *MacUser* and *Macworld*, also routinely report known bugs and compatibility problems.

Register your products. Send back the registration card that came with your product. That way, when a bug-fixed upgrade comes out, the company will typically notify you about it. They may even send it to you for free!

Check online for upgrades and conflicts. Get online. If a bug-fixed upgrade is free (and many are), the company is almost certain to post the upgrade on some on-line service. Your best bet these days is to find the Web site (see Chapter 23) of the company (every company has one now, trust me) and check it out. There are also numerous on-line Web sites devoted to listing conflicts and bugs. One of the best is the Complete Conflict Compendium <http://www.islandnet.com/~quill/c3data.html>.

Get help from technical support. If you have a problem with a specific program and you are in desperate need of immediate help, call the vendor's technical support line. You'll find the number somewhere in the documentation that came with your software. For Apple, it's 1-800-SOS-APPL.

If you are not in a panic for an immediate answer (which may not be so immediate anyway, as many technical support lines are notorious for keeping you on hold indefinitely), your software's documentation probably lists on-line locations where you can leave messages or check for technical support tips. User-supported Mac forums and newsgroups are also a good place to leave requests for help (see Chapters 22 and 23 for more on this).

Can you really do it all? Does all of this seem too time-consuming? Does it seem like keeping up with all of this can be a full-time job in itself? Of course it does. That's because it is. Nobody really does *all* of these things *all* of the time. Well, okay, I do, but I write about the Macintosh for a living. Just do what you have the time for. Whatever effort you expend, it will rarely be wasted.

Speaking of myself, I would be remiss if I did not recommend my own troubleshooting book, *Sad Macs, Bombs, and Other Disasters* ($35, Addison-Wesley), and my Web page <http://www.oakland.edu/~landau/sadmacs/> for those times when you want more help.

Managing Your Memory (TL/HN)

Shortages of memory are one of the biggest sources of instability on the Mac: the less free RAM available, the greater the risk of a crash or freeze. And that rule holds for individual applications as well as the whole system: Each program you launch gets a certain memory *allocation* or *partition*, and if you fill that up, you could have problems even if there's plenty of memory lying idle on your system—the Mac doesn't normally redistribute memory dynamically among open applications.

Developers don't want their products perceived as memory hogs, so they tend to set the Minimum and Preferred memory amounts (the data the system uses to allocate memory to a program when you launch it) to levels that may be too low for real-life usage. You can give your programs a safety cushion by increasing these amounts: Simply go to the Finder, select the program's icon (when it's not running) and press ⌘I or select Get Info from the File menu. Under current versions of the system software, you can change Preferred and Minimum values. Hit Enter or just close the Get Info window, and the new numbers will be saved and used the next time you launch the program. There are also several programs, included **AppSizer** (shareware, Pierce Software), that let you make these adjustments at launch, bypassing the need to go to the Get Info window.

For more specific advice regarding memory management problems, see "Not Enough Memory" later in this chapter.

Save Your Work

If you learn nothing else from this chapter, learn this: With depressingly few exceptions, if you get a system freeze or crash while you are working on a document, any unsaved changes you made to the document are lost—forever! So remember to routinely press the ⌘S keys as you work. The few seconds it takes to save your document can save you hours of frustration down the road.

Back Up Your Work

Even if you saved a document, danger still lurks. A file could become hopelessly corrupted or a hard disk crash could wipe out the entire contents of your disk (don't get too alarmed; this happens only rarely, but it does happen). To prevent thoughts of suicide at such times, make sure all of your data are backed up to some other location.

These days the most popular choice of backup medium is removable cartridges, such as Iomega's **Zip drive** and **SyQuests' EZ135**. Removable cartridges are as convenient as floppy disks but hold many times more information (from 100MB to over 1GB, depending upon which model you get). And the least expensive models are relatively cheap (less than $200), which is very important because users are generally resistant to spending their hard-earned cash on something as unglamorous as a backup device. Resist this resistance and get a backup device. Otherwise, it's like saving money by getting a car that doesn't include an airbag in the hopes that you never have an accident. It isn't worth the risk (see Chapter 5 for more on backup devices).

The Finder is great for making frequent backups of a few critical documents, but for full disk backups you'll want a more heavy-duty program, such as Retrospect (see "Troubleshooting Tools" later in this chapter).

HOT TIP

[If you have some disk space to spare, it's a good idea to keep an extra, up-to-date copy of your System and Finder (or even your whole System Folder) online—if your main system gets corrupted, switching to this backup is easier than doing a complete reinstall. But compress the backup with a utility such as StuffIt, DiskDoubler, or Compact Pro; that way, there's no danger that it could be confused for the active system, and it won't take up so much space. (If your original system software gets badly damaged, boot from a floppy, decompress the backup, throw away the damaged original files, and reboot.)—HN]

Have Emergency Startup Disks Ready (TL/HN)

Right after your hard drive has crashed and your Mac won't start up is not the best time to discover that you don't have an emergency startup disk handy. Right now is the best time to prepare a set of startup disks.

If you got a set of Apple floppy disks with your machine, you can always use the original Disk Tools disk as your emergency disk. Better yet, prepare your own emergency disk. First make a copy of the Disk Tools disk using a utility such as Apple's Disk Copy (which is now included on the CD-ROM that comes with most Macs). Make sure it's the Disk Tools disk that came with your Mac or it may not work with your Mac. Alternatively, if you have a CD-ROM that came with your computer, there should be a file on it called Disk Tools.image. Double-click it and it will open Disk Copy. Now all you have to do is insert a fresh floppy disk and you are ready to make a copy. After you have the copy made, you can add one or two small utilities to it or delete existing files from it to make room for other files. You can do this to make as many emergency disks as you need. Finally, slide the tab to lock the disk and test it to see if it really works as a startup disk.

Alternatively, if your Mac came with a CD-ROM drive, remember that the CD-ROM that came with your Mac can act as a startup disc itself! It already contains Disk First Aid, Drive Setup (or Apple HD SC Setup), and a complete set of Installation disk files. Even better, when booting from the CD-ROM, you can still insert a floppy disk for access to additional software.

To start up with these special CD-ROMs in an internal CD-ROM drive, insert the disc, select Restart and hold down the ⓒ key until you see the Welcome to Macintosh message. If you have an external CD-ROM drive, press the ⌘ Shift Option Del keys at startup. This should bypass the internal hard disk so that you boot from the CD.

If you have a second hard drive (especially a removable cartridge drive) you can set it up as an alternative startup disk. The advantage here is that there is no worry about fitting everything you want onto the disk. You select which disk to start up from by using the Startup Disk control panel (or to simply bypass the internal drive, press ⌘ Shift Option Del at startup).

Your emergency tool set should at least include: a disk-formatting utility, a utility that can check the status of all of your SCSI devices (such as SCSI Probe), and a data recovery/repair utility (such as Norton Utilities). Check out "Troubleshooting Tools" for more details. You should also have handy the floppy or CD-ROM disks that came with your Mac (as well as the disks you used the last time you upgraded to a new system version). You'll need these to do a clean reinstall of your system software.

System 8 Alert

By mid-1997, Apple expects to ship a major upgrade to its operating system, code-named *Copland*. Although it will only run on Power Macs, it will have a profound effect on much of the troubleshooting advice in this chapter. Here's two particularly noteworthy tidbits:

- Extensions and desk accessories will no longer work in System 8. All of this software will be rewritten to conform to the new technology. This will radically change the whole concept of dealing with extension conflicts.

- Protected memory, a new feature of System 8, should reduce the effect of many types of system crashes and freezes by preventing a crash in one program from leading to a system-wide crash that necessitates restarting your Mac. This is a good thing.

GOOD FEATURE

Know Your System

(HN/TL)

If and when you ever call a vendor's technical support, they will almost certainly ask you about the details of your Mac configuration, including both hardware issues (model number, processor speed, total memory, installed cards, and so on) and software particulars (system version, names and version numbers of the applications you use, the extensions and control panels you have installed, and so on). If you don't have this information handy, get it and print it out now, before your Mac goes down and you can't get at it. Fortunately, there are utilities that make collecting these data a breeze. If you own Now Utilities (described in Chapter 13), use Now Profiler. More limited, but still useful, is a new utility from Apple (included with System 7.5.3) called Apple System Profiler. A variety of other shareware and commercial alternatives exist.

HOT TIP

Troubleshooting Tools

(RS)

When it comes to troubleshooting your Mac, some of the best help you can get comes in the form of troubleshooting utilities. Here's a short list of the cream of the crop (see Chapter 13 for more on these utilities).

Tools to Try First

Before you run out and purchase an expensive software diagnostic package to try to cure your Mac's problem, possibly save yourself some bucks and first try these free or inexpensive shareware tools (available from user groups or from on-line services).

TechTool. **TechTool** (freeware, MicroMat) is a utility that every Macintosh owner should have. TechTool rebuilds your desktop from scratch, eliminating problems with desktop files that are so corrupted that they cannot be rebuilt in the normal fashion. TechTool also zaps the PRAM (see "Zapping the PRAM" later in this chapter) in a more thorough way than Apple's standard method. It also allows you to save and restore your current PRAM settings so that you don't have to go back and do it manually. The most recent versions of TechTool also test for damaged System files. *[And it does this all without you having to remember any special keyboard combination shortcuts—TL].*

GOOD FEATURE

SCSIProbe. This essential freeware control panel scans your SCSI bus, provides name and SCSI ID information on attached SCSI devices, and allows you to mount devices that did not show up (or were not present) at startup. Several other utilities can do this just as well, but **SCSIProbe** set the standard.

Font Box. Insider Software's **Font Box** ($30) is a shareware diagnostic utility that solves many of the mysteries of font management. It checks for corrupted fonts, font ID conflicts, incorrectly installed fonts, and more. A similar utility, though not shareware anymore, is **theFONDler** ($70, Rascal Software).

Save a BNDL. Problems with a file's BNDL resource can lead to incorrect icons in the Finder. Rebuilding the desktop often, but not always, fixes these problems. For problems with one or two specific files, a faster and more reliable method is to use the freeware **Save a BNDL** utility. Just drag and drop the problem file to the Save a BNDL icon, restart, and you are done.

Extension Informant. Wondering what a particular extension does, whether it runs on your machine, or if you can afford to trash it? Then just drag the mysterious extension's icon over to **Extension Informant** ($10, shareware), a nifty utility that reveals the inside scoop on all of these files. *[However, this program has so far not been updated in a timely manner. A more up-to-date source of this information can be found on the Web at* http://www.AmbrosiaSW.com/DEF/—*TL]*

Extension Managers

Extensions managers are an invaluable aid in tracking down extension conflicts (see "Solving Extension Conflicts" later in this chapter). You can use them to selectively turn on and off individual extensions, reorder the loading sequence, and even perform tests to identify a problem extension. Apple includes its own version of this type of utility named, aptly enough, **Extension Manager.** It lacks many of the

GOOD FEATURE

features of its competitors, but at least it is free. The two best known of the commercial bunch are **Startup Manager** ($90, part of Now Utilities) and **Conflict Catcher 3** ($100, Casady & Greene). Conflict Catcher is the class leader here. One of the coolest things that only Conflict Catcher can do is to have extensions and control panels display their names, rather than just their icons, as they dance across the screen at startup. (For more details on utilities, see Chapter 13.)

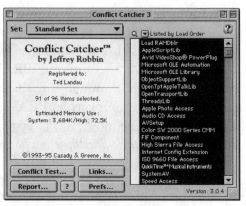

Clicking the Conflict Test button of Conflict Catcher sends it on a hunt for extension conflicts.

Data Recovery Tools/Hard Drive Repair

Norton Utilities and MacTools Pro. You may not need a repair utility often, but when you do need one, it is a lifesaver. The field of commercial hard drive repair packages has narrowed down to two: **Norton Utilities for Macintosh** ($150, Symantec) and **MacTools Pro** ($150, also from Symantec via its Central Point division). Each one has devoted fans that swear by it. The truth is that each can do some things better than the other, but the debate as to which one is best may soon be moot. The folks at Symantec say that the two will eventually be merged into one product. *[I have always liked MacTools Pro better, although I use both. I especially like MacTools' TrashBack extension for recovering accidentally deleted files. No other program does it better (as long as TrashBack doesn't cause an extension conflict).—TL]*

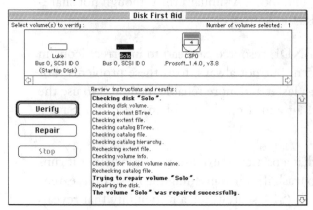

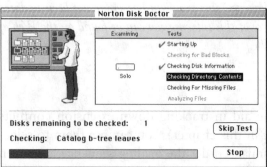

After repairing a disk with Disk First Aid (top), Norton Utilities checks over the same disk (bottom). When it has finished, it confirms that no more problems were found.

Norton Utilities and MacTools Pro are collections of utilities that include hard drive diagnostic and repair software (their premiere function), hard

Getting Help From Apple Guide (TL)

Are you having trouble figuring out how to get your Mac to play an audio CD? Are you unsure how to get file sharing up and running? For the answers to these and dozens of other basic questions about your Mac, I'd like to say just check the printed documentation that came with your Mac. Unfortunately this won't always help. Apple's current printed documentation is so skimpy that it is almost an embarrassment.

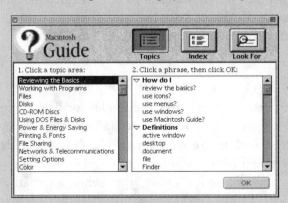

However, Apple has not completely abandoned its responsibility here. It now supplies Apple Guide (included as part of System 7.5). To use Apple Guide, choose the ? menu from the Finder (it's near the right hand end of the menubar) and then select

For general help instructions, check out Apple Guide when Apple's documentation comes up short.

Macintosh Guide (when using other applications, you may find they have their own Guide files). If all you want is a quick read, Apple Guide can be frustratingly tedious to use. But for interactive walk-through advice, it can't be beat.

drive defragmenters (utilities that combine the fragmented segments of a program as it is stored on a disk and combine them into a single segment, supposedly leading to improved performance of your drive), utilities that recover files which have accidentally been deleted or otherwise lost, and a host of other features. But no matter how good these programs are, don't use them as a substitute for backing up the contents of your disk!

[Norton Utilities and MacTools Pro both come with an emergency startup disk. If it fails to run on your Mac (typically because it is missing a needed machine-specific enabler file or needs a more recent version of the system software), these programs also include a special feature for creating customized startup disks. MacTools Pro can even create a startup RAM disk (a portion of RAM that the Mac is fooled into thinking is a physical disk), if you have enough RAM available. If none of this seems to work, contact the software's technical support for additional advice.—TL]

Disk First Aid. Even if you choose not to buy one of the commercial data recovery packages, you still have an important repair utility at your disposal: Apple's **Disk First Aid**. It comes with all versions of the system software (it's on the Disk Tools disk).

It is more limited in what it can do. In particular, there are several problems that Disk First Aid can identify, but which it cannot repair. For that you *will* need either Norton Utilities or MacTools Pro. But it's fast, free, easy to use, and Apple regularly updates it.

CanOpener. For files that cannot open because they appear to be corrupted in some way, your best defense is **CanOpener** ($65, Abbott Systems, Inc.). If there's a way to recover corrupted text, graphics, sounds, or movies, CanOpener will find it.

Backup Utilities

When you finally realize you need something more than the Finder for backing up your files, it's time for a specialized backup utility. **Retrospect** ($50, Dantz Development) is the premier package for business, and for use on networks. It is scriptable, works with just about any storage medium, and includes compression. Retrospect Remote includes client software for network nodes. Other worthwhile alternatives for personal use include **DiskFit** ($50, Dantz Development) and **Redux Deluxe** ($80, Focus Enhancements). Norton Utilities and MacTools Pro also both include backup utilities as part of their software suite. (See Chapter 13 for more details on backup utilities.)

Disk Formatting Utilities   (RS/TL)

Although basic information about disk formatting utilities is covered in Chapter 5, be aware that these are useful troubleshooting tools. Most notably, they are used to replace or update the *driver* software on your hard drive. A corrupted or out-of-date driver can cause a host of problems, including system crashes and the inability to even start up your Mac. Because updating the driver is a simple and painless procedure, it is almost always worth a try. They can also test the media of your hard drive for defects. If a defect is found, they can lock out that defective area so that it isn't used. Using these utilities to actually reformat your disk (after you've backed it up first!) may solve problems that nothing else can fix. But save this radical surgery as a last resort.

For drives that come directly from Apple, the formatting utility is either **Drive Setup** (for Power Macs and for Macs that have IDE drives) or **Apple HD SC Setup** (for all other Macs). Other drive manufacturers typically ship with their own formatting utilities that work only with their drives. A few utilities such as **Drive7** ($90, Casa Blanca Works) and **Hard Disk ToolKit** ($199, FWB) are designed to work with virtually any drive. This makes them especially useful for Macs that use several drives from different manufacturers. Using the same universal driver on all your drives can eliminate

GOOD FEATURE problems all by itself.

Anti-Virus Utilities   (RS/TL)

To check for a possible virus invasion, you need an anti-virus utility. The three most well known are **Disinfectant** (freeware), **Symantec AntiVirus for Macintosh** ($100, Symantec), and **Virex** ($100, Datawatch). The latter two do the better job of proactively preventing a virus infection (such as preventing an infected floppy disk from even mounting on your desktop). *[However, this checking can slow down your Mac or otherwise cause conflicts with other software. Personally, I don't use this feature any more. The threat of a virus is too small to compensate for the downside of using it—HN]* All three are equally fine at detecting and eradicating existing infections, as long as you make sure you regularly update the programs (the latest update files for Disinfectant and SAM are available free online; Virex charges for updates). Out-of-date versions will be unable to recognize newly discovered viruses.

Despite the publicity they have received, viruses are not a common threat on computers, especially on a Macintosh. There are only about 36 viruses that infect Macs (compared to well over 100 for IBM-compatibles) and few of them are intentionally malicious (though they all can cause operating problems or data loss). Still, it is a good idea to periodically scan for viruses, especially if your Mac develops symptoms that suggest an infection (all the anti-virus utilities describe what these symptoms are). Be especially wary if you copy files from public computers (such as in schools and universities) or from unmonitored sites on the Internet *[I downloaded an infected file from the Internet while working on this chapter!—TL]* In contrast, the chance of getting a virus from commercial on-line services is quite low, as these files are always checked for viruses before they become available.

WARNING

Virex (version 5.6 or later) can automatically scan files as they are downloaded.

GOOD FEATURE

Hardware/Software Diagnostics

This class of software tests the performance of your Mac and points out problems or impending problems. They have no ability to repair any problems they find. I would *not* really recommend most of the programs for ordinary users, except in special circumstances (such as trying to track down an existing problem that would be expensive to have a technician look at) or if they are particularly paranoid. These utilities *are* extremely useful for a system administrator or a shop technician.

Help! Help! ($50, Teknosys) is primarily a huge database with thousands of rules that define the specific requirements for an impressive variety of Mac software. This database is kept up to date via a paid subscription updater service. The program looks at your Macintosh system and then gives you a report about such things as damaged files, incompatible programs and extensions, and improperly installed or configured software. Look for a union between Help! and Peace of Mind (described next) in the near future.

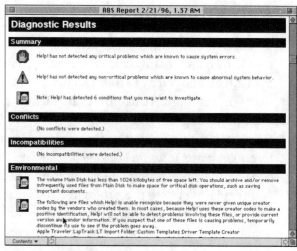

Help! analyzes your disk and reports back to you with a list of potential compatibility problems.

Hardware Diagnostics. Peace of Mind ($100, Diagsoft) and **MacEKG** ($150, MicroMat) both perform a series of diagnostic tests that check the performance and integrity of your Mac's hardware. They test the CPU, memory, hard and floppy disks, keyboard, mouse or trackball, system clock, sound capabilities, ROM, PRAM, modem, printer, and add-in cards.

I recommend Peace of Mind over MacEKG, assuming Peace of Mind has been upgraded to work with the latest Power Mac CPUs by the time you read this. MacEKG just isn't as comprehensive, although its interface is way cool!

*[MicroMat has now released **TechTool Pro** ($150). Although the MacEKG control panel conducts brief tests at startup as a means of detecting changes in performance that could sig-*

TechTool Pro checks your hardware and software for problems that you probably didn't even know existed.

nal some problem, TechTool Pro is an application that is best used to check for specific suspected problems or to conduct a much wider range of tests. Integrating and extending features from TechTool (the freeware version), MacEKG, and DriveTech (MicroMat's floppy disk diagnostic software), TechTool Pro checks just about every imaginable aspect of your hardware (as well as a few aspects you probably never imagined!)—TL]

Apple's diagnostic utility, **Apple Personal Diagnostics** ($99), hasn't been updated since August of 1995 and only covers Macintosh models up to and including the Power Macintosh 9500. The development team for this product no longer exists and word is that the program is up for sale to another publisher.

When Trouble Strikes (TL)

Okay, you've followed all of the advice in the previous parts of this chapter and you are as prepared as a Boy Scout with a shirt full of merit badges. Or maybe you haven't had time to check out the advice yet because you are too panicked about your current Mac crisis. In either case, something is definitely wrong with your Mac.

Been there. Done that.

You've come to the right place. Here's a wealth of tips, tricks, and solid advice that should get you through most of your troubled times.

The Frozen Mac

You're merrily working along when WHAM! everything halts. If you are lucky, the cursor may still move when you move your mouse, but that's it. Pressing keys does nothing, and clicking the mouse button does nothing. Nothing does anything. Your Mac screen is now a frozen still life. Here's how to thaw it out.

Force Quit.

1. Before doing anything else, Press ⌘S. If you had unsaved work at the time of the freeze, this might still save it (doubtful really, but worth a try) even though it won't help you recover from the freeze.

2. Press ⌘Option Esc. This is called a *force quit*. With some luck (and you can't be having a lot of luck here or you wouldn't have had this problem to begin with), you will get a message with a button that says "Force Quit." Now click the Cancel button. I know. Officially, this should do nothing at all. But occasionally it wakes up the Mac and gets things rolling again. I also have had similar success

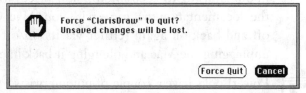

When your Mac is frozen, pressing ⌘Option Esc brings up this Force Quit alert box.

(even before doing a Force Quit) by moving the cursor to the desktop and clicking on an icon there and then switching back to the frozen application. If this works, immediately save all your data. Then, to minimize the chance of another freeze returning all too soon, restart your Mac.

3. If, as is more likely, your Mac is still frozen, click the Force Quit button. You still have to hope for some luck here, because this button only works maybe 70 percent of the time. If it fails, either nothing will happen or the situation will get worse (such as the cursor, which had been responding to your mouse movements, no longer doing so).

4. If the Force Quit succeeds, the program named in the Force Quit dialog box (presumably the one most responsible for the freeze) will quit and you will most likely be dumped into the Finder. Your Mac should now be behaving fairly normally and any work you had going in other programs (aside from the one you quit) should still be available to be saved. As for whatever unsaved work you had in any documents you were working on in the application that quit, well, my condolences to you.

WARNING

5. Once you are back in business and have saved all that could be saved, select Restart from the Finder's Special menu. This is just to be safe. You can continue working without restarting, but you are courting disaster. Another freeze is likely to occur soon, especially if you return to the application you force quit from.

Reset. If the Force Quit failed at any point in the previous steps (or you were never able to get the force quit alert box at all), press ⌘Control-Power (the Power key is the one on your keyboard with the triangle symbol on it). This is called a *reset*. On most recent Mac models, this should restart the Mac.

If this key combination does nothing, it is probably because you have a Mac model that uses a physical reset button somewhere on the Mac itself, rather than using this key combination. It is usually one of a pair of buttons on the front or rear of the machine (If you press the "wrong" one of the pair of buttons, don't fret. Whatever happens, press the other button next and the restart will happen.)

Finding the exact location of the reset button can be a bit tricky, as the folks at Apple find it amusing to keep finding new places to hide it. If you can't find it, check with the documentation that came with your Mac. Otherwise, you can simply turn the Mac off and back on again (either via its on/off button or, if absolutely necessary, by unplugging the Mac and plugging it back in again).

POWERBOOK

PowerBooks have a couple of unique twists to this reset drama:

• On 100-series PowerBooks (except the Model 100) and most 200-series Duos, the reset button is recessed and you can only access it by using something like an unbent paper clip; in this case it's easier to use the on/off button. However, after a system freeze or crash, you'll have to hold the on/off button for about five seconds or so before it actually shuts down the PowerBook.

- If ⌘Control-Power should ever fail to reset your PowerBook, and your PowerBook model does not have an on/off switch (such as for the 500-series PowerBooks), press ⌘ControlOption-Power. This should shut down the PowerBook. Then turn it back on as normal.

After resetting. After resetting, you may get a message during startup saying you did not shut down the Macintosh properly. This is true. Shutting down by any method other than selecting the Restart or Shut Down command from the menu bar is considered improper. But don't worry. It doesn't mean anything bad has happened. Just dismiss this message and proceed as normal. Still, if you want to prevent this message from reappearing the next time you have a problem, go to the General Controls control panel and uncheck "Shut Down Warning."

HOT TIP

After you reach the desktop, you'll probably find a folder called "Rescued Items…" in the Trash. If you had some unsaved work that was lost in the freeze, there is a rat's whisker of a chance that a file in here contains the lost data. To find out, open the file(s) in the application(s) that you were working on at the time of the crash. Most likely, you'll find that the files are worthless. It's not a coincidence that these files are in the Trash. It's a hint as to what you should do with them!

Permanent solutions. Finally, you're back in business and your Mac should now be running fine again. But what if the freeze returns the next time you do whatever caused it to occur the first time? How do you figure out what is causing the freeze, so that it doesn't happen again? The depressing answer to that question is that there is no easy answer to the question. The happy answer (and I am sure the one you would rather hear) is that most freezes are due to just a few possible causes. The following steps should solve most freezes for you:

1. Check for an *extensions conflict* (see the "Solving Extensions Conflicts" sidebar).

2. Check for problems with the program. If it's not an extension conflict, it's probably a problem with the program itself (in which case you'll have to contact the vendor to see if they have a bug-fixed upgrade) or with the application's preferences file (see "When Programs Don't Work" later in this chapter). Occasionally, increasing the application's memory Suggested Size (as described in "Not Enough Memory" later in this chapter) may reduce the risk of a freeze, but don't bet on it.

3. Make sure you have the latest version of Apple's system software. Also check if Apple has released any special updates that fix your problem. For example, Apple

Solving Extension Conflicts

Extensions are those files whose icons appear along the bottom of the Welcome to Macintosh screen at startup. They are usually found in the Extensions (of course!) and Control Panels folders.

Extensions may conflict with each other or with open applications. The first step to diagnosing an extension conflict is to start up with extensions off, by holding down the [Shift] key at startup until the words "Extensions Off" appears. If the symptoms disappear, you have an extension conflict.

The problem now is to figure out what the problem extension is. If you just added a new extension, that's the likely culprit. Otherwise, especially with dozens of extensions that have proliferated in most users' System Folders, the only sane way to approach this is with an extension management utility. Apple includes one with System 7.5 called **Extensions Manager**.

Use the manager to remove and reinstall extensions in a systematic fashion until you locate the one that appears to trigger the conflict. Far better is to use either Casady & Greene's **Conflict Catcher 3** or the **Startup Manager** that is part of Now Utilities (see "Troubleshooting Tools"). Both utilities include a conflict isolation feature that automatically takes you through the process of identifying the problem extension. No thinking is required on your part! These utilities also have a feature to quickly identify an extension that causes a crash at startup.

After you identify the problem extension, you can install a fresh copy to see if that helps. You might also delete its preferences file, if it has one. Otherwise, disable or delete the extension to eliminate the conflict (and try to find out if an upgrade exists that resolves the conflict).

has a special set of printing update files to fix freezes and crashes that occur when printing from System 7.5.2.

4. Beyond this, you'll have to resort to the tried-and-true collection of possible cures. Most likely to be helpful is reinstalling your system software (see the "Reinstalling System Software" sidebar, later in this chapter). You might also update your disk driver using your formatting utility as well as check for disk damage with Disk First Aid or other data recovery utilities (as described in "Troubleshooting Tools").

5. Finally, while not really a freeze, if your application suddenly quits without warning and an alert box appears that includes the words "unexpectedly quit," treat this as a sort of automatic Force Quit (see the previous "Force Quit" section).

System Crashes and Bombs

If you're wondering what could be worse than a system freeze, here's one answer: a *system crash* (or, as it is sometimes called, a *bomb*). Typically, an alert box appears with an icon of a bomb in it. The message starts off by apologizing for the intrusion, "Sorry…" But I doubt if that will make you feel any more kindly toward it.

Don't worry, the bomb icon does not mean your computer is in danger of exploding. You may laugh, but I know someone who, after getting their first bomb alert, refused to touch their computer for the next several hours, until she could get a hold of me on the phone, fearful of what might happen if she tried to use it further.

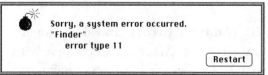

Sorry, a system error occurred.
"Finder"
error type 11

Restart

Uh-oh. Some call this a "bomb." Others call it a "crash." Call it what you will, it is not a welcome sight.

As with the freeze, the bomb puts an end to whatever you were doing. Actually, dealing with bombs is quite similar to dealing with freezes, except that the force quit option is so unlikely to ever work, I wouldn't even bother trying it (the Restart button that may appear in the bomb box also only works sporadically).

Your first step should be to restart your Mac. If you are lucky, the system crash won't repeat. If it does, the most likely cause of recurring crashes remain extension conflicts and buggy or corrupted software. Overall, the logic is similar to what was described for diagnosing system freezes (see the previous section, "The Frozen Mac").

If a crash occurs after all the extensions have loaded, but before the desktop finishes loading, try restarting from another startup disk. If you succeed, go to the Preferences folder inside your startup hard disk's System Folder, and throw away the Finder Preferences file.

HOT TIP

What Are All Those Error Codes?

When you get a system crash or an unexpected quit, you'll often find that the accompanying error message lists a code number (such as "error Type 1") or an equally mysterious expression (such as "unimplemented trap" or "FPU not installed"). You may well wonder: What the heck does all of this mean?

More printer's ink has been wasted answering this question than any other troubleshooting question about the Macintosh. I have seen books devote dozens of pages listing the meaning of almost every imaginable error code number. The information in these tables typically isn't any easier to understand than the error codes themselves. And they almost never contain any useful advice as to what to do if you get a specific error.

The plain truth is that these messages are meant to be used as guides to programmers who routinely get these messages while debugging their software. They have little usefulness for the rest of us. Still, I know you won't be satisfied until you learn more about what these messages mean (and, yes, you can occasionally glean some helpful information from them). So here's my sixty-second tutorial on the subject.

First, it helps to know that these error codes (or IDs) come in two flavors: positive and negative. Positive error codes most often accompany system crashes or unexpected quits. Negative error codes occur after a variety of less disruptive problems, such as a failure to copy or delete a file.

Positive error codes: 01 (Bus Error), 02 (Address Error), and 03 (Illegal Instruction). These are the most common errors on Macs with 68000-series processors. To technogeeks, they mean that your Mac either tried to access a memory location that does not exist or tried to execute an improper program instruction. Sometimes, you can prevent further errors of this type by increasing the memory allocation of the application in use at the time of the crash.

Otherwise, the exact cause varies with when the error occurs. If it occurs right as startup begins, it's probably a problem with an externally connected SCSI device (possibly an incompatible disk driver). If it occurs while the extensions are loading during startup, it's probably due to an extension conflict (typically the extension that is trying to load when the crash occurs). If it happens while in the Finder, it's probably due to corrupted system software. Should you get the error while in any other application, it's probably due to a bug in the application itself.

After you diagnose the problem, solve these errors by isolating the extension conflict (see "Solving Extensions Conflicts" sidebar), determining the SCSI problem (see the "SCSI Troubleshooting" sidebar), updating the disk driver (by using your disk formatting utility), doing a clean reinstall of the system software (see "Reinstalling System Software"), or contacting the vendor for information on patches or updates for the problem software (or, if that is impossible, stop using the software altogether).

Error Type: 09, 10 (Unimplemented Trap; No FPU Installed; Bad F-Line Instruction) and 11 (Miscellaneous Hardware Exception) These are the most common errors on Power Macs. The "No FPU Installed" and "Bad F-line Instruction" messages may appear if the software mistakenly calls for a floating point unit (FPU) while running in emulation mode on a Power Mac (as there is no FPU in emulation mode). It also may appear whenever the Mac can't figure out what the actual correct error message should be. The Type 11 error typically occurs anytime a Power Mac is running a native application and an error occurs that would have caused a Type 01–03 error on a Mac with a 68000-series processor.

POWER MAC

In most cases, if the problem is specific to a single application, it again means there is a bug or corruption in some software. Try the solutions previously described. Otherwise, for more randomly occurring Type 11 errors, zapping the PRAM (see the "Zapping the PRAM" sidebar) sometimes helps. Defective memory (SIMMs, DIMMs, and especially RAM caches) is also a common source of Type 11 errors. To check for this, you'll have to remove the suspected memory cards and see if the errors go away.

Error Type: 25 (Memory Full) and 28 (Stack Ran into Heap) As their name implies, these are often memory related errors. See "Not Enough Memory" later in this chapter.

Error Type: 26 (Bad Program Launch) Occurs when there is a bug in the application itself or the application is damaged. Try replacing it.

Other positive errors. Errors between 04 and 14 are most likely due to bugs in application software. Other errors between 15 and 31 are most often due to a corrupted System file.

Negative Error Codes. If you are lucky (and most often you won't be), these codes may point you in the right direction. For example, if you get a message that says you can't copy a file because of a –34 (disk is full) error, this does suggest why the copy attempt failed. While we can't list every negative error code here (there are hundreds of them), we can supply a list of common category divisions. File system errors (33–61) are probably the most common category. These include: –39 (unexpected end of file), –41 (memory full), and –42 (too many files open). Several shareware utilities, such as **MacErrors**, provide a complete list of all error code numbers and their technical names.

> 0–8: General System Errors
> 9–21: Color Manager Errors
> 17–30: I/O System Errors
> 33–61: File System Errors
> 64–66: Font Manager Errors
> 64–90: Disk, Serial Ports, Clock Specific Errors
> 91–99: AppleTalk Errors
> 100–102: Scrap Manager Errors
> 108–117: Storage Allocator Errors
> 120–127: HFS Errors
> 126–128: Menu Manager Errors
> 130–132: HFS Errors (again)
> 147–158: Color QuickDraw and Color Manager Errors (again)
> 170–182: ColorSync errors
> 185–199: Resource Manager Errors (other than I/O)
> 200–232: Sound Manager Errors
> 250–261: MIDI Manager Errors

The Blinking Question Mark Disk Icon

Nothing can throw you into a panic quicker than when you turn on your Mac and you are greeted with a disk icon that has a blinking question mark inside it. Nothing else happens. The Mac seems to be saying everything on your hard drive is lost and you will never be able to start up your Mac again, so what are you going to do?

Fortunately, in most cases, things are not nearly as bad as they seem. What's happening is that the Mac is unable to locate a suitable startup drive, so it doesn't start up. The mystery of course is why your internal hard drive (which is typically the startup drive in question here), which was working just fine as a startup drive moments before, now seems to be on vacation. The answer is usually that some critical data on your drive, called the *boot blocks*, have gotten messed up so that the Mac no longer recognizes the drive as a startup drive. Here's what to do:

1. If you can get your Mac to start from a floppy disk (such as your Disk Tools disk) or a startup CD-ROM, cross your fingers and hope your hard disk(s) appear on the desktop (it may take a long time). If not, and if you have SCSIProbe or a similar utility on your startup disk, check whether it can see and mount your problem drive. If you succeed, back up any critical files immediately.

2. Next, find the System Folder on your startup volume (disk or partition) and drag the System file out of it. Close the System Folder's window, then drag the System file back into it. This may seem like pointless fiddling, but in fact moving the System and Finder will make the Mac update the volume's boot blocks, and that in itself is sometimes enough to make it bootable again.

3. Whether or not your disk mounted, run Disk First Aid. Hopefully, the problem disk will be listed there. If so, select the disk's icon, click the Repair button, and hope for the best. If Disk First Aid reports damage that it could not fix, start up from a disk that has Norton Utilities or MacTools Pro installed and use it to check the disk.

4. Run your disk formatting utility and update the hard disk's driver.

5. Restart your Mac and see if it now starts up okay.

6. If it doesn't, try zapping the PRAM (see the "Zapping the PRAM" sidebar).

7. If you have external SCSI devices connected to your Mac, check for SCSI-related problems (see the "SCSI Troubleshooting" sidebar for more advice).

8. Occasionally, the problem may be corrupted system software. To solve this, simply restart with your system software Installer disk and do a clean reinstall of the system software (see the "Reinstalling System Software" sidebar later in this chapter).

9. If you are still unable to start up, now is the time to panic. You may have a hardware problem and you may be in danger of losing the files on your disk. This may be a good time to call a company, such as DriveSavers (see Appendix D), which is known for resuscitating drives that others have given up for dead.

SCSI Troubleshooting (HN)

WARNING

SCSI problems can cause a variety of symptoms, ranging from inability to start up your Mac or use some of your peripherals to sporadic, unpredictable crashes or data corruption. To check for this, try the following (just remember to never connect or disconnect SCSI cables while the Mac is on):

- Make sure that no two devices on the chain have the same ID number and that the chain had proper termination. If you have no idea what this means, check Chapter 5 for more information.

- If you've just added a new device, power down, take it off the chain, and restart. If everything else works normally, you know the problem is with the newcomer or its relationships with its neighbors.

- Otherwise, disconnect the SCSI cable attached to the Mac, and restart. If you've still got a problem, it's probably not a SCSI issue but one that involves system software or drivers. If you can boot up normally with no SCSI connection, you have confirmed your suspicions that the problem lies somewhere on the chain.

- Vary anything and everything (as long as the power is off when you are changing things). Swap cables, reverse the order of the devices on the chain, add an extra terminator, or take one away. If you can stand it, make these changes one at a time, restarting and testing after each change. You can save time by restarting with the Shift key down, or (better yet) setting your extension manager to skip all, so you won't have to wait for extensions to load. It will take time, but at least you can tell what variable has produced a change.

- Some combinations of devices (particularly if an older SyQuest drive or a scanner is involved) simply never work well, no matter how you organize things. In such cases, you have no choice but to remove one of the conflicting devices from your SCSI chain, at least temporarily, in order to use the other.

POWERBOOK

PowerBooks That Won't Start Up on Battery Power

Suppose you can start up your PowerBook when it is plugged in but not when you are using battery power. What to do?

One obvious cause is that your batteries are dead. If so, replace them.

A less obvious cause is that the data in the Power Manager (a small area of memory in which the Mac stores power-related settings) has gotten corrupted and needs to be reset. For most recent models of PowerBooks, you reset the Power Manager by shutting down the PowerBook and then pressing the ⌘Control Option-Power keys. In some cases, you may also have to remove the battery for a few minutes. For any variations on this theme, specific to your model, check the manual that came with your PowerBook or look it up in Apple Guide. Actually, I prefer to use a freeware utility called **RstPwrMgr** that seems to work just fine on all PowerBooks and saves me from trying to remember all the different procedures.

The Sad Mac and the Chimes of Death   (HN/TL)

Rarely, your Mac may halt its startup routine even before it gets a chance to show a blinking question mark. When this happens, your Mac typically plays an unusual startup chime (called the Chimes of Death—although on Power Macs the sound is that of a car crash) and/or you get the dreaded Sad Mac icon. When this happens, it may mean you have a hardware problem (most often with defective or improperly installed RAM). But this is not a foregone conclusion. Before you open your Mac or start calling your service dealer, there are several steps you can take.

If you're greeted with the Sad Mac icon, a hardware repair may be in your future. But if the last digit on the first line is an "F," it's more likely a software problem.

1. Try to start up with a startup floppy disk. If this works, make sure you have the correct version of the system software installed on the problem disk. Do a clean reinstall of the software to be safe.

2. If that doesn't work, shut off your Mac and make sure all your cables are connected. If you have external SCSI devices attached, check out the "SCSI Troubleshooting" sidebar for more advice.

3. Try zapping the PRAM (see the "Zapping the PRAM" sidebar).

4. Reformat any suspect hard drive (internal or external).

5. If nothing has worked, it's almost time to call for help, but if you are even a little comfortable working with hardware, try opening the case of your Mac, touching

Reinstalling System Software   (HN/TL)

If your Mac won't boot up or is acting erratically, you may be able to cure it by replacing your system software with a clean version.

If you have a compressed backup copy of your System Folder that is not itself corrupted (see "Back Up Your Work" earlier in this chapter), use it to replace your active files.

Otherwise, you'll need to boot from a set of Apple system floppies or CD-ROM (the one(s) that came with your Mac or newer one(s) that are compatible with your hardware). Then run the Installer.

Using the Installer correctly can be a little trickier than it seems, because it doesn't recognize many kinds of corruption. If it finds System and Finder files already present in a valid System Folder, it may update them (if it's installing a newer version) or just leave them alone. Either way, the damage you are trying to get rid of may remain.

To make sure you get a clean version of the system software when you reinstall it, you can't just do an ordinary reinstall. You have to do what is called a clean reinstall. With recent versions of Apple's Installer, you do this by pressing ⌘ Shift K at the Installer window and then selecting the "Install New System Folder" option. Complete details can be found in Chapter 3 under "Clean installations" in the "System Installation" section. Doing this ensures that the Installer creates virgin, uncorrupted copies of all the required files from scratch.

After you are done with your reinstall, you will still have to separately reinstall any other Apple system software you had previously added that is newer than the basic system software you just reinstalled. This could include, for example, updated printer drivers, display software, or networking software.

HOT TIP

the metal power supply casing (to discharge your static electricity), and then check to make sure that all cards and SIMMs are *seated* properly—that is, that they don't seem loose in their slots. Then put everything back together and try again. If you still get the chimes and the Sad Mac, and you know what you are doing, try experimenting with removing individual RAM cards to check if they are defective. If you remove defective RAM (assuming you still have sufficient RAM remaining), the Mac should start successfully. Otherwise, now is the time to call your dealer.

Not Enough Memory

You go to launch an application and you get a message that says: "There is not enough memory to open [your application]." This is one of the most common problems a Mac user faces—especially since application developers seem to double the minimum amount of memory their programs require every time they come out with a new version.

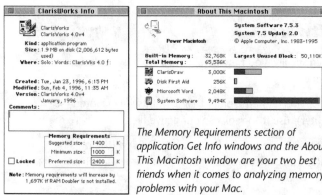

The Memory Requirements section of application Get Info windows and the About This Macintosh window are your two best friends when it comes to analyzing memory problems with your Mac.

What can you do about this? First, it helps to understand exactly why you got this message and how much more memory you need to get the application to open. To do this, click on the application's Finder icon and select Get Info from the Finder's File menu ($\boxed{\text{⌘}}\boxed{\text{I}}$ is the shortcut). From here, note the Minimum size listed in the Memory Requirements box. Next, while still in the Finder, select About This Macintosh from the top of the ⌘ menu. From the box that appears, note the size of the Largest Unused Block. If this number is smaller than the Minimum size, you don't have enough memory to open the application. What to do next depends upon how much more memory you need and what you currently have running on your Mac. Here are some guidelines that should get you through most memory hassles:

1. Quit all open applications. Close all open Finder windows. Actually, the alert message you get, indicating a lack of available memory, probably advises you to do this. Doing so frees up additional memory, which may be all you need to open that pesky application. It should also resolve problems with *memory fragmentation* (where unused memory is divided into several small chunks rather than one large one).

2. If you still can't get the program to open, go back to the About This Macintosh window and sum the Largest Unused Block and the System Software allocations. They should add up to approximately the same number as the Total Memory. If not, you may have a *memory leak* (where an application does not release its memory allocation after you quit the program). Programs that make use of *shared library* extensions may result in a similar problem. Whatever the cause, the surest way to fix it is quite simple: restart. If that seems too time-consuming, you can try a Force Quit (press $\boxed{\text{⌘}}\boxed{\text{Option}}\boxed{\text{Esc}}$). This usually works although it may leave your Mac in a state that is more prone to system freezes and crashes. Another alternative is to try to free up memory via a freeware utility such as **Mac OS Purge**.

3. If you are still stuck, you can reduce the amount of memory used by the system software by starting up with all nonessential extensions disabled. To start with *all* extensions off, simply restart by holding down the $\boxed{\text{Shift}}$ key. Of course, you may want (or even need) to keep some extensions enabled in order to use a memory hungry application (RAM Doubler is an obvious example here). Here's another

Should You Ever Turn Virtual Memory Off? (TL)

You may wonder, given all of the advantages of virtual memory (especially for Power Mac users), why anybody would not use it. First, certain programs do not run with virtual memory on (especially games and high-end graphics and multimedia programs). Second, virtual memory can slow down your Mac especially when using programs that require so much memory that you can't even open them unless virtual memory is on. You may have similar problems with RAM Doubler. For these situations, there is no substitute for more physical RAM.

place where an extensions manager (see "Extension Managers," earlier in this chapter) comes in real handy. You can make a minimal extensions set and shift to it for just these sorts of occasions. However, to load just RAM Doubler without any other extensions, hold down the [Shift][Option] keys at startup.

HOT TIP

4. Still not successful? Go to the Memory control panel. Make sure 32-bit addressing is turned on (on Power Macs you don't have this option; it is always on). Reducing the size of the disk cache also frees up extra RAM, but unless you have it set quite high, this is unlikely to be a critical factor. You'll have to restart after making these changes.

5. If all of this fails, your remaining option is to increase the total amount of memory you have available. If you are using System 7, you can do this by turning on virtual memory from the Memory control panel (though there are some potential downsides to doing this, including the fact that some programs will not work with virtual memory on, as explained in the "Should You Ever Turn Virtual Memory Off?" sidebar). Otherwise, go out and get Connectix's RAM Doubler (it works on all PowerPC, 68040, and 68030 Macs). Or, if you can afford it, simply buy more memory and install it in your Mac. (See Chapter 4 for more on virtual memory and RAM Doubler).

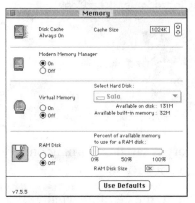

Changing settings in the Memory control panel, such as turning down the disk cache and turning up virtual memory, can let you open applications that otherwise would not have enough memory to open.

By the way, turning on virtual memory (or using RAM Doubler, which has the same effect) is especially helpful if you have a Power Mac. Turning on virtual memory, to even as little as 1MB, not only gives you more memory, but dramatically reduces the amount of memory needed by all applications that are "Power Mac native." You can tell that an application is in *native code* by opening its Get Info window.

POWER MAC

Installing System 7.5 Update 2.0 (System 7.5.3)   (TL)

The most recent incarnation of Apple's System 7.5 software is System 7.5.3. Users who have bought a Mac in recent months will find it already installed on their hard drive. The rest of us need to upgrade to it via a set of floppy disks (or CD-ROM) called *System 7.5 Update 2.0*.

Even though this update fixes more bugs and incompatibilities than any one user will ever experience in a lifetime (which is why the update is definitely recommended), it also introduces a few new problems of its own. To help you sort it out, here are four things you should absolutely know before you install System 7.5.3:

- It pays to do a clean reinstall of your original system software before installing the update. To do that, you'll need to find your original system software disks. The Update cannot do a clean install. After doing the clean reinstall, you'll also have to reinstall certain software, such as AppleVision software (if you have an AppleVision monitor) that the clean install does not include. Then, finally, run the Update. Keep extensions *on* when updating.

POWER MAC

- If you have a Power Mac with an Apple hard drive, it's especially important that you also update your disk driver with the new version (1.0.4) of Drive Setup that is included as part of the Update.

- The Update includes a new networking architecture called Open Transport (for more details, see Chapter 24). The old software is called "Classic AppleTalk." Most non-PCI-based Mac models can run either software (PCI-based Macs must use Open Transport). A utility called Network Software Selector (NSS) is included with the Update to allow you to shift back and forth. But note that when one system is active, control panels (such as MacTCP or TCP/IP) used by the other system are made temporarily invisible. They are still on your disk. They will reappear when you switch back again.

WARNING

- If anything you expected to find was not installed by the Easy Install, go back and look for it via a Custom Install. You'll probably find it. Install it.

- If you have an AppleVision monitor, you are especially likely to have things go wrong with the Update's installation of AppleVision-related software. Apple has a file called AppleVision Fix that makes things go right again. Run it after you have completed all other installations described here.

At the bottom a note will indicate exactly how much memory is saved by turning on virtual memory or RAM Doubler. Non-native programs do not have this note.

If you are fortunate enough to have the memory to spare, go to the Get Info window of your commonly used applications and increase their Suggested Size by as much as 50 percent. This will usually result in your applications running faster, make them less

Five Ways Installers Could Be a Lot Better (TL)

Personally, I have a strong distaste for most Installer utilities. True, an Easy Install could not be simpler to do. But often, I am looking for something more than sheer simplicity. So in case any developers are listening, here's my wish list for how Installers *should* work:

- When the Installer is used to install applications, such as word processors, many files are quietly installed in the System Folder rather than the folder where the application resides. Users should be clearly informed that this will happen, with details of what is going where. Even better, give me the option to install these files in a special folder called "Put These in the System Folder." That way, I can control what gets placed in my System Folder. Too often, these files are unnecessary for my use or are older versions of files I already have.

- Allow each separate component of the software to be separately installed. It's frustrating when I want to replace a corrupted copy of a single extension that the Installer forces me to reinstall all of its several dozen extensions. Granted, Apple does provide some control here via the Custom Install option, but it is not as complete as it could be. For companies other than Apple, too often the Custom Install option (if it even exists) is relatively useless.

- A Custom Remove option should always be included. That way, even if I used an Easy Install, I am certain that I can later uninstall everything that was added.

- Allow users to complete an installation even if it seems that their machine does not have the correct hardware or software for what is being installed. I hate messages that say you need 16MB of RAM or you need System 7.5. or later to do this installation. Warn me, but don't prevent me. Maybe I have a good reason for overriding your warning.

- Don't force users to restart their computer after the Installation is complete. I know that installed extensions will not be active until after I restart, but I may want to do other work before I restart and activate the extension. Give me the choice.

likely to cause system freezes or crashes, and will allow you to open a greater number and/or larger sized documents from within each application (though it also means you will be more limited in how many applications you can have open at one time). As a partial check as to how likely this is to be helpful, go back to the About This Macintosh window when a troublesome application is open. Pay special attention to the bars next to each application listed: The length of the bar represents the size of the program's memory partition; the darker, filled-in section represents what it is actually using at that moment. If it is almost full, it is a good sign that increasing its memory allocation would be helpful.

Documents That Won't Open

Another all too common problem is when you double-click a document icon to open it from the Finder and you get a message saying that the document would not open because the "creating application could not be found." Most of the time, the document is just fine. Run through the following checklist, and you will almost certainly succeed in opening it:

- If this is a document that you created yourself, presumably the creating application is on your disk somewhere. If it isn't, that's your problem right there.

- If the creating application *is* on the disk but the document still doesn't open, try opening it from within the application itself, via its Open dialog box. As a possible long term solution you might try rebuilding the desktop (see "Desktop Icon Problems" later in this chapter). Now the document will probably open from the Finder.

- In the remaining cases, you are probably working with a document created by someone else (maybe you downloaded it from an on-line service) and you don't have the needed creating application. Not to worry. If the file is a plain text file, you may be able to open it in TeachText or SimpleText. In fact, the alert message you get when the document refuses to open may even ask if you want to try this. Go ahead. Unfortunately, if the file is more than 32K, it still won't open.

- Most word processors can open a variety of text file formats. Claris applications, in particular, include special files (called XTND files) that are located in the Claris folder in the System Folder, that allow Claris applications to open almost any type of document. The simplest way to test this is to drag the document's icon to the application's icon. Otherwise, you'll have to import the file from within the application, typically from the application's Open dialog box.

- Macintosh Easy Open, PC Exchange, and MacLink Plus software (all included with System 7.5) can also help to open foreign files (although Macintosh Easy Open causes so many other problems that I never use it).

- Make sure you are not trying to open a compressed or encoded file. Use a utility such as StuffIt Expander to check for this.

- If you are still having trouble opening a graphics, sound, or movie file, it is probably because the file is in some special format that none of your applications can understand. This is often the case for files that you download from on-line services or that you try to view on the World Wide Web. To solve this, you could get shareware applications that are designed to solve this problem.

For example, programs like **JPEGView** or **Sparkle** are useful for graphics and movies. Commercial programs such as **DeBabelizer** and **Photoshop** are also good. **SoundApp** and **SoundMachine** are particularly good for opening sound files.

Can't Empty the Trash

The Trash can is bulging, but when you go to empty it, it refuses to cooperate. Calling your local sanitation department won't help you. However, one of the following solutions is almost certain to fix this glitch.

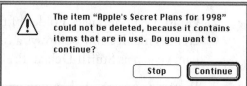

In the best of times, this annoying message is eliminated simply by quitting all open applications. In the worst of times, you may have to ultimately reformat your disk.

- If the problem is that the file is simply locked, the Macintosh informs you of this when you try to delete it. It should also suggest the simplest solution: hold down the ⌜Option⌟ key when choose the Empty Trash command.

- If a message says that the file/folder can't be deleted because there is not enough memory to complete the operation, just restart your Mac and try deleting again. It will succeed.

- If a message says that the file/folder can't be deleted because it is "in use," quit all your open applications and try deleting again. If this fails, create a dummy file in another location on your disk and give it the same name as the problem file. Now try to replace the problem file. If it succeeds, try to delete the replaced file. Otherwise, restart and try again.

- If even this fails, start up with another startup disk and try to delete the file.

- Whether or not you finally succeed in deleting the file/folder, you may still have underlying corruption of your disk's *directory*, which is the underlying cause of the problem. Left alone, the problem may return or get worse. To fix things, run Disk First Aid from an emergency startup disk and make repairs as needed. If you have **Norton Disk Doctor** or **MacTools Pro's Disk Fix**, use them as well.

- If none of the preceding steps have worked, you'll have to reformat the disk.

Problems Deleting Fonts (TL)

If you are trying to delete a font file, the Mac may refuse to let you drag it out of the System Folder. If this happens, drag the entire Fonts folder out of the System Folder and restart. Now delete whatever fonts you want. Then return the Fonts folder to the System Folder, replacing the new one that was just created, and restart again.

HOT TIP

When Programs Don't Work

Basically, this is a catch-all category that covers those occasions when some command or some feature of a program doesn't work the way that it should. To be honest, there are dozens of possible explanations for why this might happen. Still, most of the time the following few steps will lead you to a cure:

1. Quit the problem program. If your problem program is a control panel, also restart the Mac with the control panel disabled.

2. Go to the Preferences Folder of the System Folder and locate the program's Preferences file. It's almost always a file that has the name of the program as part of its name (such as StuffIt Deluxe Prefs for StuffIt Deluxe). Delete the Preferences file.

3. Restart as normal. When you next use the program, it will re-create a new Preferences file. Ideally, your problem will now be gone. However, you may have to reset any changes you made to the program's default preference settings.

4. If deleting the Preferences file did nothing, delete the entire application software. Reinstall it from its original disks.

5. If you still have no success, check for extension conflicts (see the "Solving Extension Conflicts" sidebar earlier in this chapter).

6. If the problem persists, there is probably some bug in the program you are using. Contact the vendor for assistance. In the meantime, although not an ideal permanent cure, turning off one or more features of Apple's system software can sometimes act as a work-around. The most common culprits here are: Virtual Memory, Modern Memory Manager, AppleTalk, and File Sharing.

Corrupted Files   (HN/TL)

Occasionally, when you try to open a document file, you may get a message that it is corrupted or damaged or that a "disk error" has occurred. Don't despair. You may still be able to save the contents of the file. (For corrupted applications, just trash and reinstall them.)

*   Duplicate the file in the Finder (select the file and press ⌘D) and try to open the copy.

*   If the file in question is a Microsoft Word or Excel file, the FileFix module from MacTools Pro may be able to fix it. Many databases and some other applications come with special utilities to repair damaged files.

- CanOpener can extract text, PICT images, icons, and sounds from files of almost any format, including from many damaged files. The recovered data may not look the way it did in its native application, but at least you can recover some of its main components. Otherwise, Norton Utilities' Disk Doctor or MacTools Pro's DiskFix may be able to recover the file.

- If the file is on a floppy disk, you might first try to copy the entire disk, using the copy utilities that come with MacTools or Norton Utilities. Then try to open the file on the newly copied disk. If this succeeds, discard the problem disk; it is probably damaged.

- If the damaged file is on a hard disk, check it for media damage (bad blocks) with Norton Utilities, MacTools Pro, or your disk formatting utility. If damage is found, you will either have to lock out the block (to prevent data from being written there) or reformat the entire disk (check with your utility's documentation for more help).

Desktop Icon Problems   (TL/HN)

If some of your files have lost their usual desktop icons in favor of those boring generic document and application icons, or if you double-click on a document icon and get a message that says the application that created it can't be found even though you know it's around, it's probably time to *rebuild the desktop*—the invisible files in which the Mac stores icons and comments associated with files, including the application to be launched when a document is double-clicked.

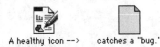

A healthy icon --> catches a "bug."

When interesting icons (left) suddenly transform into generic icons (right), it's time to rebuild your desktop.

- Even before rebuilding the desktop, select Get Info for the file and then close the Get Info window. Sometimes this alone does the trick, saving you the trouble of a rebuild.

- Rebuild your desktop. This fixes and updates special invisible Desktop files that are used to keep track of all the icons and file and folder location information. To do this, restart and hold down the ⌘Option keys until you get a message asking whether you want to rebuild the desktop. Click OK. Alternatively, you can use TechTool to rebuild the desktop (see "TechTool," earlier in this chapter). In either case, your custom icons should now be restored (except those for documents created by applications not presently installed on any mounted volumes).

- To be extra safe, Apple recommends that you rebuild the desktop with Extensions Off. To do this, hold down the Shift key at startup until the words "Extensions Off" appear; then press the ⌘Option keys.

- If you have several hard disks or partitions that appear when you start up, the Mac will ask you about rebuilding the desktop for each volume in succession. True, your Mac has only one desktop, but every disk or partition has its own Desktop files. Rebuild all volumes that are giving you trouble.

- One of the longest standing complaints of the Mac operating system is that rebuilding the desktop erases any text in the Comments boxes of Get Info windows. If preserving these comments is important to you, several utilities (such as CommentKeeper and Norton Utilities) can do this. However, the happy news is that with System 7.5.3, the system software finally preserves Comments text after a standard desktop rebuild.

- If you have just one or two files that seem resistant to all the previous methods, try this almost never-fail technique: Launch Norton Utilities' Disk Doctor. Select the "Add File To Desktop" command from the Tools menu and select the problem file. Restart when you are done.

- If none of the preceding has worked, and especially if you also have trouble getting the document to open, the document itself or the disk's directory may be corrupted in some way. Use Norton Utilities or MacTools Pro to make any needed repairs.

Zapping the PRAM   (HN/TL)

Another time-honored folk remedy for Mac ills is *zapping the PRAM*—clearing the *parameter RAM*, a small area of memory in which the Mac stores settings such as the preferences you select in the General Controls and Sounds control panels. (It's nonvolatile memory, kept alive by battery, so these settings will survive when the Mac is shut down.)

Just how the PRAM gets corrupted and what effects this has is something of a mystery, but clearing it can sometimes cure a variety of otherwise inexplicable problems.

It used to be that to zap the PRAM under System 7, you would just hold down ⌘ Option P R as you boot up and wait for the Mac to restart a second time. These days, Apple recommends keeping those keys down until the Mac restarts itself two or three times! Alternatively, you can use TechTool to reset your PRAM. In either case, after your zap, you'll need to reset the Apple control panels the way you want them.

HOT TIP

If you have a PCI Power Mac, you need to reset both the Parameter RAM (PRAM) and the nonvolatile video RAM (NVRAM). This is because PCI-based Macs store display settings in NVRAM rather than in PRAM. To do this double reset: shut down the Mac (don't use Restart); *immediately* hold down the ⌘ Option P R keys at startup; wait for the Mac to chime twice; release the keys and let startup proceed. If you don't hold down these keys immediately, you will only reset the PRAM. You should also trash the Display preferences file after starting up with extensions off.

BAD FEATURE

The Desktop Rebuilds At Every Startup   (TL)

If your Mac rebuilds the desktop whenever you start up after having previously started up with Extensions Off, this is almost certainly because you have Macintosh Easy Open control panel installed. If you don't use this control panel, drag it out of your System Folder and delete it. Otherwise, other than never starting up with Macintosh Easy Open disabled, there is no way to prevent this problem. You just have to live with it.

The Printer Won't Print

When your printer mysteriously refuses to cough up your output, the fault almost always lies with the Macintosh, not with the printer.

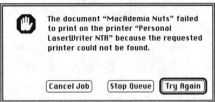

If your document fails to print, you'll most likely see this message on your screen (you may need to go to the Finder to see it).

- Make sure your printer is on and its cable is connected to your Mac. For a laser printer, give it about a minute or so to warm up before trying to print. If you have a problem here, you will get an alert message that asks if you want to try printing again. If so, after making sure everything is ready, go ahead and click Try Again. It should work.

- For AppleTalk connected printers, make sure AppleTalk is turned on. In most cases, you turn this on from the Chooser or the AppleTalk control panel. If you have a Mac that uses a Control Strip, you can turn it on from there.

- If you have an AppleTalk printer and a PCI Power Mac or other model that uses the new AppleTalk control panel, make sure that the control panel's selected port (printer or modem) is the same one that your printer cable is connected to. For other Macs, connect the printer only to the printer port.

- Go to the Chooser and select the printer driver for your printer. If the printer driver for your printer should somehow not be in the Chooser's window, check if it got moved to the "Extensions (disabled)" folder. If so, move it back to the Extensions folder. Otherwise, you'll probably have to reinstall the printer software. For AppleTalk printers, your printer's name should appear in the Chooser window after you select the driver. Click on the name.

- If you are trying to connect to a printer via PrinterShare, make sure that both the printer and the Mac that is connected to the printer are on. Then check that the PrinterShare extension is installed and that PrinterShare has been turned on from the Chooser's Setup options.

PostScript Errors (TL)

If you get a message that say, that a PostScript error occurred while printing, this almost always means either that you have a corrupted document (or your document uses a font that is corrupted) or that you ran out of memory while trying to print.

One simple cure that often works for corrupted word processing documents is to Select All and then change the font of the document to some other acceptable font. Try printing again. If this works, you can try reselecting your original font. It may work now. If the problem is specific to a certain page, you can limit these font changes to just that page.

To solve PostScript errors due to memory problems, the easiest thing to do is to shorten the document (by breaking it into two or more separate documents, for example) or simplify it (by using fewer fonts, for example). Also, turn off background printing from the Chooser. Then try printing again.

- If you are using LaserWriter 8.x, and everything else you have tried has failed, go to the Preferences folder, locate the LaserWriter 8 Prefs file and delete it. Now go back to the Chooser and select Setup for the printer.

- With computers running Open Transport, starting up with extensions off will prevent you from running any AppleTalk-connected printer (such as most Laser-Writers). If you try to select such a printer from the Chooser, you will get an error message saying that "The printer port is in use. AppleTalk cannot be made active now." You need the Open Transport extensions re-enabled in order to print.

- If you start up with extensions off and you use the *desktop printer* extensions (see Chapter 21), the desktop printer icons on the desktop will appear with X's over them. You can still print, but you don't have access to the special desktop printer features.

- Similarly, if you have installed QuickDraw GX, starting up with extensions off disables it.

POWERBOOK

- Working with PowerBooks that have only one serial port can be a bit of a pain, especially if you also have an external modem. For example, to print to an AppleTalk connected printer, you have to turn AppleTalk on. To use an external modem, you have to turn AppleTalk off again. For problems with non-AppleTalk printers and/or with internal modems (such as Apple's Express Modem), check the documentation that came with your printer and your modem. Exactly what to do keeps changing as software gets upgraded.

- Zapping the PRAM sometimes helps solve these sorts of printing problems. Try it.

- If all of the previous steps still fails to get your Mac to print, you may have corrupted printer software. Reinstall the software and try again. (For more troubleshooting advice on printing, see Chapter 21.)

Unreadable Floppy Disks

If you insert a floppy disk and the Mac says it is unreadable and offers you the option to initialize it, don't panic—and don't initialize it. As long as you don't erase the data on the disk, the odds are generally good that you can recover the data, even if the disk itself turns out to be unsalvageable.

If this message appears when you insert a floppy disk that you know has data on it, don't click the "Initialize" button! Doing so will erase the data on it, preventing you from any chance of recovery.

- Eject the disk. If it isn't already write-protected, do so now (slide the plastic tab on the disk until you can see through the hole). Once it's protected, try inserting it in another Mac (if you have one available)—often the alignment of the heads in two floppy drives is just different enough to make a disk that's unreadable in one drive readable in another. If the disk was last used in a Mac other than yours, try that drive in particular if it's nearby. If another drive can read the data, copy the files to the hard drive and then to a new floppy.

- Some newer models of Mac have trouble reading mass-produced 800K disks. If this happens, and you don't have another Mac around that can read the disk, starting up with extensions off or zapping the PRAM may solve the immediate problem.

- To read PC-formatted disks, make sure PC Exchange is installed (it comes with System 7.5).

- If the unreadable disk is an HD (1.44MB) disk that you are inserting into an old 800K drive (such as on a Mac Plus), the drive can't read the disk. You will need to use a newer SuperDrive floppy disk drive (used on all current Mac models).

- Failing all this, it's likely that the disk really is damaged. If you want to try to recover data from the disk, your best bet is to first make a copy of the disk using Norton Utilities' **Floppier** or MacTools Pro's **FastCopy**. The copied disk will probably mount now with most or all files on it accessible. Copy the files to your hard drive. If the copied floppy disk is also unreadable, or you still can't locate or open a particular file, try using file recovery features of Norton Utilities or MacTools Pro. In any case, when you are done with your recovery, discard the unreadable disk. Don't bother trying to reformat it and use it again. It's not worth the risk.

- Occasionally, a floppy disk is unreadable because the floppy disk drive itself is dirty or malfunctioning. Disk cleaning kits manufactured by 3M (available separately or as part of MicroMat's DriveTech software) may fix this. From my experience, this will only rarely help, but it's cheaper to try this first than to take your drive in for an unneeded repair.

Floppy Disk and CD-ROM Disc Jams

You selected the Eject and/or Put Away commands but your disk refuses to budge. Try each of these in turn until one works.

1. Quit all open applications. Try again to eject the disk, typically by dragging the disk icon to the Trash icon.

2. Turn off file sharing (especially if it is a CD-ROM you are trying to eject). Try again to eject the disk. (Turning off file sharing should not be necessary if you are using System 7.5.1 or later, but try it anyway.)

3. For floppy disks, press ⌘ Shift 1 .

4. Restart and hold down the mouse button. Wait for the disk to eject.

5. For CD-ROMs, restart and immediately press the drive's eject button. Note that this button will not eject a disc at any other time. Normally, the button only opens the tray when there is no disc in it.

6. For CD-ROMs, if you started up with extensions off and got an ID=-50 error when trying to eject the disc, restart with extensions on. The disc should now eject normally.

7. If all else has failed, manually eject the floppy disk or CD by inserting an unbent paper clip into the hole adjacent to the drive and pushing in gently. If it only comes partially out when trying this, you can gently pull it out the rest of the way. But don't try to force it too much or you may do more damage. If it seems hopelessly stuck, take the drive in for repair.

Some floppy disk jams can be caused by a floppy disk with a bent metal shutter or a partially unglued label. Check for these problems before inserting the disk.

Dealing With Hardware Problems   (LL)

Okay, so not all your problems will turn out to be due to software. Sometimes, it really is a hardware problem. Here are some tell-tale signs that the insides of your Mac may need rehabilitation and what to do when disaster strikes.

No sign of life. You should hear your Mac's startup chimes and hard drive running when you start up your Mac. You should also see the green power light come on. If you see no sign of life at all, try plugging your Mac into a different surge protection device or wall outlet. Check if the surge protector is off, or if your wall outlet's fuse is out. Consider swapping power cables to see if this helps your Mac start up. If you have

Mac peripherals, such as a monitor or hard drive, turn them on to see if they are able to receive power successfully. Check for disconnected or incorrectly connected cables to all components of your system. Doing all this will help isolate whether the problem is just with your Mac (a bad motherboard, power supply, or hard drive), with your power connection (to the wall outlet or surge protector) or perhaps not even a hardware problem at all.

Isolating dysfunctional hardware. If you have largely ruled out software as the cause of your problem, you need to isolate which part of your Mac's hardware is not functioning. If your motherboard is the main problem, you naturally will not be able to do this because you will be unable to start up at all. However, if your power supply, hard drive, monitor, and motherboard are working properly, chances are you have enough of a computer functioning to help you isolate other dysfunctional hardware connected to your Mac.

Basic hardware components which may have failed include the following: CD, floppy, clock/battery, DRAM, display card, network ports or connecting cables and transceivers, and serial port. Generally, computer hardware failures will be symptomatic to the functionality you lose. For example, if you have your CD software properly installed, but the CD cannot be read by the drive, there's a good chance you may need to clean your CD-ROM drive, or have it serviced. For Macs that have been running for a few years, it is common for the battery (located on the motherboard) to run out of juice. Symptoms can include incorrect clock times, the clock not remembering the time you input, or other clock-related problems.

Replacing internal bad parts. If a part is removable from the Mac's motherboard (such as DRAM or cards), you can buy a replacement from a Mac vendor. Batteries for the motherboard can be found or ordered at Radio Shack. Removing and installing some parts may be difficult, especially if you are not familiar with electronics or handling computer hardware (for example, in some Mac models, the motherboard needs to be removed from the Macintosh case before the part can be replaced). *[For peripheral components other than the Mac itself, it rarely if ever pays to try to open them up at all—TL]*

If a damaged part cannot be removed from the motherboard or is otherwise inaccessible, you'll probably need to go to a Apple certified repair shop. If the Mac or other Apple component is still under warranty, contact Apple at 800/SOS-APPL. For third-party products, contact the vendor directly.

Editors' Poll: What's the Most Recent Problem You Have Had With Your Mac?

SZA: Super-bad disk directory damage that caused files and folders to disappear and which required reformatting of the hard drive to eliminate; luckily, it's the first time in 12 Mac years that I've had such a serious disk problem.

JC: Installing Apple's System 7.5, 2.0 update has been my latest challenge. As is the case with all updates, there are bound to be some incompatibilities so backing up the current System Folder before installing it is imperative.

TL: Problems with freezes and broken connections while online. It happens more often since I switched to Open Transport.

ML: A conflict between Microsoft Word 6.0.1 for Power Mac and Global Village Fax software. The problem was solved by installing a Microsoft patch to Microsoft Office.

SS: My optical discs would only mount if they were in the drive at startup. After several hours of playing with SCSI cables and moving the drives around, I discovered that the problem was caused by a corrupted extension.

What's the Most Common Recurring Problem You Have With Your Mac?

JC: Open Transport has been a real pain. Version 1.1 has cleared up a lot of problems but its components seem very sensitive and easily corrupted if the system crashes.

MEC: Extension conflicts ... but I try out a lot of shareware and freeware extensions, so I expect this sort of thing.

DC: Type 11 errors. Increasing application memory size usually solves it.

JH: I've never known why, but for six or seven years I've had to run Norton or another utility almost daily on my various Macs running various systems. B-tree problems have haunted my Macs, even while friends run fine for months without ever launching Norton. I have no idea what I do that's so tough on those B-trees...

TL: If I lumped every system freeze or crash I've had into one group, regardless of their cause, this would be my number one problem. Otherwise, I'm with Joe Holmes on this one. It seems no matter how many times I check my directory, chances are there is some problem with it.

ML: "Not Enough Memory" errors caused by fragmented RAM or applications occupying the RAM space next to the System Heap, preventing the heap from growing when it needed to. Solution: Restart.

2

Macintosh Software

Editors' Poll:
What Programs Do You Use All the Time?

MEC: Eudora: I *need* my e-mail.

ClarisWorks: It does most of what I need it to do.

BBEdit: I write a lot of code, and BBEdit really *doesn't* suck.

JH: MS Word 5.1a: I use it because I can't stand Word 6.

Claris Emailer: It handles all my e-mail needs—I really use all of its features. Right now it's picking up messages containing a particular subject, filing them in a folder, mailing an automatic reply, and forwarding a copy to someone else!

Netscape Navigator.

Compuserve Navigator: I use it because off-line is the only way to work!

ML: Microsoft Word: I am a writer.

QuarkXPress: Peachpit makes me lay out the books I write.

Photoshop: I need to crop and otherwise manipulate screen shots I put in my books.

ScreenShot: I need to take screen shots for my books.

PageMill: I maintain several Web sites and have grown tired of manually coding in HTML.

StuffIt Expander & DropStuff: When sending files online, they've got to be small.

TL: Netscape: I use it because I am on the Web all the time, maintaining my own Web site and checking on others.

Claris Emailer: I use it because when I am not on the Web, I am checking my e-mail or writing to people (such as sending Mac Bible editors this poll).

Microsoft Word 5.1: It's still what I use to do all of my serious writing.

Now Up-to-Date and Now Contact: It keeps track of what I would otherwise forget.

ClarisWorks: I use it for just about anything else I need to do. It's versatile and easy to use.

SiteMill: I am currently using it a lot to design my Web site.

KT: CompuServe Information Manager: I use it because it makes it easy to chat with forum members if need be and has good tools for marking and capturing messages and other information.

Microsoft Word 5.1: I use it because I'm a writer and always have something approaching (or past deadline).

PageMaker and/or QuarkXPress: I use them because I need to create new projects, or because I also do my correspondence, invoicing, and so on in these programs (I can't stand the wretched typographic control in Word).

QuickDEX II: I use it because I always need to phone someone or look up something (I use it for stashing all sorts of information, not just names and addresses).

ATM and Suitcase: Of course.

8 Working With Words

Text is everywhere on the Mac—on the desktop, in dialog boxes, in desk accessories, and even in many graphics programs. It's comforting to know that the basics of text entry and editing work in every one of these places.

But when you think *words* and *computer*, you think *word processor*—that ultimate writer's tool. The ease of editing in a word processor, whether it's reorganizing sentences and paragraphs or letting the Mac correct your spelling, can make anyone a better writer.

Contributors

Sharon Zardetto Aker (SZA) is the chapter editor.

Elizabeth Castro (EC) fell in love with the Mac while living in Barcelona, and founded the publishing house *Pagina Uno*. She was this chapter's editor for the fifth edition.

Rick Casreen (RC) is a writer and the source of *The Pelorian Press*.

Contents

The Basics of Text Handling

The basics of handling text are the same everywhere on the Mac, no matter where you're working. But many programs go beyond the basics (like, say, triple-clicking to select a sentence or paragraph), so make sure you check the details of each program.

Text Entry and Selection (SZA)

Entering text is just a matter of typing, keeping in mind this basic rule:

Everything happens at the insertion point.

The *insertion point* is the vertical bar that blinks on and off in the text you're working on. Typing or using Delete takes place at the insertion point; if you paste text, it appears at the insertion point. Clicking with the mouse repositions the insertion point, although for small moves using the arrow keys (→ ← ↑ ↓) is more convenient.

Selecting and deselecting. The basic way to select text is to simply drag across it. Take the shortest route from the beginning to the end of the selection, dragging down across lines of text. Keep in mind that you can drag backwards, too.

To select large, irregular segments of text, click at the beginning of the text block and shift-click at the other end. Just as on the desktop, a shift-click also modifies the selection, adding to or subtracting from it.

Double-clicking selects a whole word; it also usually selects the trailing space, too, so that if you press Delete, you're not left with two spaces between the adjacent words.

Control Panels and Text (SZA)

Basic text-entry settings are scattered through three different control panels:

- Set the blink rate for the insertion point in the General Controls control panel.

- Set the key repeat rate (how fast repeated characters are typed when you keep a key pressed down) and the repeat delay (how long you have to hold down a key before the repeating starts) in the Keyboard control panel.

- Choose the highlight color in the Colors control panel.

Adjust the blink rate (top) in the General Controls control panel. The key repeat controls (bottom) are in the Keyboard control panel.

To deselect text, click someplace that won't select anything, or select something else. Typing to replace the selection leaves you with unselected text, too. But often the most convenient way of deselecting text is pressing ⬅ or ➡ to move to the beginning or end of the selection.

Selection units. Using a shift-click to extend a selection (that is, holding down Shift and clicking at a spot in the text to add to the original selection) usually works in the "unit" of the original selection. So, if you double-click to select a word, shift-clicking someplace else selects up to and including the nearest whole word, even if the shift-click spot is in the middle of a word.

A simple drag operation for the original selection doesn't define a unit for this shift-click operation. But if you use a special function to select another unit of text (command-clicking for a sentence works in some word processors, for instance, or triple-clicking to select a paragraph), a shift-click will select to the end of that unit.

Caps Lock **is not** Shift **lock.** On a typewriter, locking down Shift gives you the shifted character for every key, so that if you hit 8, for instance, you get an asterisk. But the Caps Lock on a keyboard is just that: It locks for *capital* letters, and all other keys you hit still type their unshifted characters.

The Don'ts of Word Processing   (SZA)

You'll find that some habits you've brought to the Mac from your old typewriter days (if you're old enough to have had typewriter days, that is) just don't cut it in the computer age.

- Don't press Return at the end of a line unless you're ending a paragraph.

- Don't use double spaces after a sentence (or semicolon). That spacing requirement—which made things easier to read in the days of typewriting monotype—is unnecessary with word processors.

- Don't press Tab to indent the first line of a paragraph. Instead, set a *first line indent* for the paragraph so that it's automatically indented.

- Don't use tabs to center a title on the page; use a center paragraph alignment.

- Don't use multiple spaces instead of tabs. If you change the size or font of the text, the size of the spaces also change, disrupting the alignment you wanted. (And repositioning tabbed text is so much easier than working with spaces!)

- Don't use multiple tabs to get somewhere on a line: Set a tab where you need it. The only exception: When you've set tabs for columns of text and you have to leave a blank in one of the rows, you use two tabs to get past the blank column.

Formatting and Special Characters

It's hard to believe now, more than ten years after its creation, the Mac was not only the first computer to let you use different fonts, it was the first to let you see *character formatting* on the screen—genuine underline, bold and italics, instead of some combination of slashes, brackets, and codes to indicate the formatting.

Character and paragraph formatting (SZA). *Formatting* characters means applying a font, a size, and a style (like bold, underline, or italic) to text. You can apply formatting "after the fact" to selected text, but the easiest way to format small chunks of text is on the fly, using keyboard commands to turn character formatting on and off as you type.

Type ⌘B here to turn on bold formatting.

Type ⌘B here to turn off bold formatting.

This is bold text

Using keyboard commands to turn formatting on and off as you type is the easiest way to format small chunks of text.

Formatting a paragraph means setting all the options that affect the text in a paragraph, such as margins, indents, line spacing, and tab stops. Depending on your word processor, a paragraph format can also include things like extra space before the paragraph, or preceding each paragraph with a number. When applying paragraph formatting to a single paragraph, you don't have to select the paragraph first—whichever paragraph contains the insertion point is considered selected.

HOT TIP

Hyphens and dashes (SZA). A *hyphen* should be used only as a character that either splits a word or joins multiple words. An *em dash* is what people normally call a dash—there's one right there. An *en dash* is half the length of an em dash and is used as a minus sign or to indicate ranges of numbers. (They get their names from their widths: more or less that of a capital *M* and lowercase *n*.)

Here's a comparison of the three, and how to type them. You'll find that the length of the hyphen in relation to the en dash varies from one font to another.

hyphen	-	[-]
en dash	–	[Option][-]
em dash	—	[Shift][Option][-]

Hard spaces, hard and soft hyphens (SZA). Most programs interpret the [Option][Spacebar] character as a *hard space*, which glues together the words on either side of it so they won't be split at the end of the line. (Some fonts, such as Zapf Dingbats, have a character for the [Option][Spacebar] keystroke.)

Removing Blanks and Returns (SZA/Dale Coleman/Paul Hoffman)

Many word processor documents imported from other computers and programs open with multiple spaces in the place of tabs and a Return at the end of every line. Here's how to clean them up:

First, the spaces: Do a search and replace, changing every occurrence of double spaces to a single space. You'll have to do this several times until all the multiple spaces are gone.

Next, the returns. You have to first mark every instance of *two* return characters, because that's where a paragraph really ends. Do a search and replace, replacing every double return (^p^p is the code in Word) with something like ##. Then replace every single return (^p in Word) with a single space. Finally, replace each ## occurrence with a single paragraph mark to restore the paragraph breaks.

If your word processor has macro capability (that's described later in this chapter), you might be able to string all these operations into a single command.

The *hard*, or *nonbreaking*, *hyphen* is a related concept: You use it when you don't want the words on either side of it to be separated at the end of a line. The *soft*, or *optional*, *hyphen*, on the other hand, is used to show where the word should break if it falls at the end of a line—but it shows only if it's needed. The key combinations you need to type these characters can vary from one program to another, but you'll usually get the hard hyphen using ⌘ Shift -, and the soft hyphen using ⌘ -.

HOT TIP

Smart quotes and inch marks (SZA). All word processors let you automatically type "curly" or "smart" quotes and apostrophes—the ones that actually curl towards the right or left to surround text. But remember to turn them off when you're typing something like 6' 10" for six feet, ten inches—which needs straight apostrophes and quotes. (And we'll see if, by the time what I typed goes through several computers and programs for editing and layout, if some clever Mac program "fixes" those straight symbols by substituting curly ones when no one's looking.)

Word Processors

The spreadsheet was the application that launched the personal computer revolution, but if there's a single application that every computer owner uses sooner or later, it's a word processor.

The Features

All word processors let you do the basics of character and paragraph formatting, and they always have. Years ago, though, other capabilities we now think of as basic weren't available in every program: headers and footers, spelling checkers, word count, print previews, multiple columns … the list goes on and on.

Some special word processor.features are still available in only some programs, and the extent to which a feature is implemented varies from one program to another. Here's a brief roundup of some special word processing features.

Word's multiple undo feature provides a menu listing the actions available for undoing.

Multiple undo (SZA/EC). Nisus was the first program to expand on the beloved Undo command by letting you go back more than one step—a feature not truly appreciated until you use it. Microsoft finally picked up on the idea for Word 6, and other word processors will eventually all fall in line.

Page layout and graphics (EC). In line with the "one program to do everything" syndrome, some word processors provide features normally found in page layout and graphics programs, such as multiple columns of text, creating and placing images in a document, wrapping text around graphics, and drawing and cropping images. If you need these extras, make sure they're not too watered down to be of use. *[On the other hand, if you need all these features on a powerful level, you probably should be looking at a page-layout program.—SZA]*

Outlining (SZA). Good writing means putting your thoughts in order; since they seldom come out in the correct order, re-ordering is what outlining is all about. But outlining isn't just a straight roster of items that you drag into various positions until they make perfect sense. An outline is a hierarchical listing that lets you use headings and subheadings and sub-subheadings as far as you need to sort things out. And, with the capability to collapse or expand headings to hide or show what's beneath them, you can concentrate on one section of your outline at a time or get a quick overview of the whole thing any time you want.

Styles (SZA/EC). A *style* is a collection of character and paragraph formats that you can apply in one fell swoop. You can, for instance, define a *Title* style that applies three character formats (Palatino, 14, bold) and two paragraph formats (centered, blank line after) at one time.

The great thing about styles is that if you change a definition, every paragraph tagged as that style changes automatically. You want those subtitles in 12-point Schoolbook? You don't have to find each one—you just change the style definition.

Styles can also be based on other styles, letting you change all the styles in your document just by changing the primary style. You can also define which style should be applied automatically to a following paragraph, which lets you format as you write—press ⌐Return⌐ and the new style is automatically applied.

A *style sheet* is the collection of styles used in a document. Some programs confuse things by calling the definitions for a single style its style sheet. And, to muddy the waters a little further, some programs have separate *character styles* and *paragraph styles*. And some programs that claim they offer styles give you only character styles, which lets you apply a combination of character styles in one action—handy, but nowhere near as convenient as paragraph-based styles.

Macros (SZA). A macro lets you string together a series of commands that can be played back with a single keystroke. A macro might be as simple as one that combines the Save and Close commands, or it could perform more complicated editing combinations like finding every graphic in a document, resizing it, formatting the line following it as a caption, and saving the changes.

Nisus, WordPerfect, and Word all provide macro capability. But because Word incorporates Microsoft's BASIC programming language for its macros, it is both more complicated (beyond the simple recording level) and far more powerful than the macro abilities you'll find in other programs.

Other special features to look for (SZA). If you know what you'll be using a word processor for, then you know what components you need in your documents—and you should know what special features to look for in a word processor:

- A good spelling checker is a must-have. It should let you create custom dictionaries of words you use in your field.

- For anything beyond simple columns of single-line text and numbers, which can be adequately formatted with tabs, look for a good table feature that lets you work with cells that have text wrap and can be outlined and shaded.

- Footnotes are more than just superscripted numbers in body text. If you need them, make sure your word processor automatically renumbers footnotes if you add or delete any, lets you easily edit the footnote text, and can put the footnotes on each page or all together at the end of the document.

- For a table of contents or index, you tag the words or phrases you want included and let the word processor create the page number directory. An advanced program will keep the page numbers "hot," changing them if the referenced page numbers change when you edit the document instead of making you recompile the index.

The Programs

Here's a roundup of the most popular word processor programs. Although it's unlikely a totally new program will join the fray, these programs keep evolving, so make sure you keep reading ads and reviews to keep track of the latest developments.

Microsoft Word (SZA). For years, Microsoft Word has been the program users love to hate, and **Microsoft Word 6** ($340) continues the tradition of mixing incredible power with interface oddities that drive you crazy. But for the first time, Word has a basic *performance* problem, too: On anything less than a fast Quadra model, it's just too sluggish for regular use. (It's fine on a PowerPC-based Mac.) This version also introduces the Microsoft Windows environment to Mac users, with the program mimicking the PC version at every turn. Even if you finally accept the less-than-elegant *look* of this program with all its gray dialogs, the clunky setup of, say, needing to go through three levels of dialog boxes just to change the font in a style definition continually grates on your nerves.

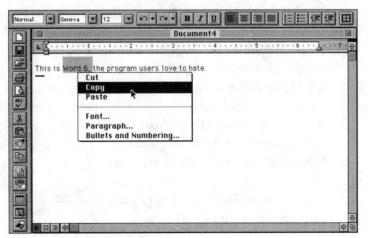

A Word window surrounded by two toolbars. In the center, the pop-up menu that's accessed by clicking with [Control] down; its contents change depending upon where you click.

But Word is Word: a leader in the marketplace, a strong cross-platform product, and, finally, the most powerful word processor around. It has everything but the kitchen sink—and I wouldn't be surprised if even that is buried in a dialog somewhere. It's totally customizable in the way of menus, keyboard commands, and toolbars. The macro language is incredibly robust—I swear that one of these days I'll figure out how to program it to write a book for me.

Word has more formatting options than any one person could possibly use. The template-based document approach means that it's easy to attach certain style sheets and macros to specific documents. Tables are easier to use in this version, and can handle basic spreadsheet-like formulas. Page layout capabilities are advanced, if a little ungainly. Word includes, of course, spelling and grammar checking and a thesaurus. AutoText lets you call up prestored words or phrases at a keystroke. AutoCorrect watches as you type and corrects misspellings and typos automatically; because you can teach it what's "correct" for a typo, you can type in shorthand by defining, say, *word processor* as the correction for *wp*.

Just listing other features that Word includes would take a few more pages. But, in short: If your Mac is fast and you're willing to trade in a little elegance for a lot of power, Word is what you need. I hate the fact that I can't live without it.

Nisus (Adam C. Engst). Unlike kitchen-sink programs such as Word 6.0, Nisus Software's **Nisus Writer 4.1** ($250) doesn't attempt to be all things to all people. Instead, Nisus Writer provides a powerfully quirky set of tools that you can customize heavily.

Useful touches abound. Discontiguous select enables you to select multiple words or phrases and make them all bold, for instance. Nisus Writer has unlimited undos, ten editable clipboards, drag-and-drop editing, multiple key shortcuts, and a spelling checker that works with an "Ignore Spelling" style to permanently ignore words in a specific document. Graphics and sound layers enable some multimedia capabilities, and Nisus Writer can read aloud text in other languages with appropriate intonations.

A clunky external table editor provides rudimentary table functionality. Styles operate at the character level instead of the more common paragraph level, and named rulers provide paragraph formatting.

Foremost among Nisus' tools is its unparalleled PowerFind, which simplifies finding text such as phone numbers by searching for wildcards like "any letter" or "any digit" in a specific pattern. Then, PowerFind's

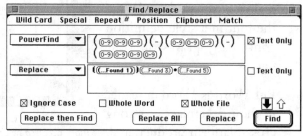

Nisus Writer's PowerFind command lets you do special reformatting in a single swoop. The setup in this dialog box will find phone numbers formatted in plain text with hyphens after the area code and exchange and substitute a bold-formatted area code in parentheses followed by the main number with a bullet character after the exchange: from 201-555-1212 to (201) 555•1212.

"Replace with Found" capability could reformat those phone numbers in bold with parentheses around the area code. You can search in a single file, through all open files, or through a set of files. Nisus Writer's macro capabilities extend PowerFind by enabling you to string multiple Find commands together along with anything else you can do in Nisus Writer. This program is a copy editor's dream.

Nisus Writer is the most WorldScript-savvy word processor, which is great for people who use other script systems, such as Japanese, Chinese, Arabic, Hebrew, and Cyrillic. Unfortunately, you need a hardware *dongle*—a stupid little piece of hardware that plugs into one of the Mac's ports—to use Nisus Writer with some script systems such as Arabic and Hebrew (but not English or Japanese).

With included macros for creating HTML documents for the Web utilize discontiguous select, PowerFind, character styles, and the "Ignore Spelling" style, Nisus Writer is perhaps the most powerful HTML editor available.

On the downside, Nisus Writer continues to increase its size and memory requirements, and its previously blinding speed has slowed significantly. It's still RAM-based, so opening very large documents can be a problem if you don't give the application a lot of memory. Still, Nisus Writer is the only word processor I'd consider using.

WordPerfect (Gregory Wasson). Sporting one of the most elegant interfaces of any Mac word processor, it's not surprising that **WordPerfect** ($190), after years of just surviving in the shadow of Microsoft Word, caught the attention of Mac users soon after the release of what wags dubbed "Microsoft Word 6.0 for Windows for the Mac." WordPerfect is subtle techno-jazz to Microsoft Word's in-your-face baroque.

The main window lets you work in three layers: watermark, text, and overlay. Watermark is for text and graphics that you want to appear under the main text on every page. Overlay contains graphics and text you want on top of the text. Headers, footers, footnotes, and endnotes appear in separate editing windows. You must use a print preview feature to see these items in place.

The program's cleverly designed ruler bar area gives access to button bars for ruler, layout, font, styles, tables, and other options. An icon bar to the left of the main window contains icons for common commands; you can customize it at will.

WordPerfect offers the usual writing tools: spelling/grammar checker, thesaurus, paragraph (but not character) style sheets, tables (with some basic math support), outlining (substandard), and word count (including counting inside selected text only). QuickCorrect corrects common mistakes (double spaces, punctuation peccadilloes, and so on) as you type. It doubles as a low-end glossary: It expands abbreviations to words or paragraphs (254-character maximum). A great macro feature lets you record or write macros. The macro language isn't as robust as WordBasic, but its simplicity does make the language more practical to use with a minimal learning curve.

The 3.5 release also has bookmarks and a Print To Fit option that squeezes or expands text onto a specific number of pages. (Need a ten-page report from only five pages of information? You got it!) WordPerfect also offers hypertext, so you can create interactive documents that let you launch macros or navigate to other documents, and so on, by clicking on HTML-like links. Speaking of which, the program doubles as an HTML editor, with access to HTML formatting right from the ruler bar.

WordPerfect 3.1 and 3.5 offered me enough power and elegance to abandon Word. Unfortunately, the program's future is now uncertain, because it's once again up for sale as of this writing.

POWERBOOK

WriteNow (Kristi Coale). My word processor of choice has been **WriteNow** ($250, SoftKey International) for a number of years, and what endears it to me most is its svelteness (it takes up a mere 595K of RAM), particularly because I use a PowerBook. (In fact, there's a collection of PowerBook Extras with this program, including cursor helpers and efficient battery usage.)

Version 4 lets you add tables to your documents and convert tab-delimited tables into the WriteNow table format; you can easily create and edit tables. Another welcome feature is the ability to insert PICT, EPS, and MacPaint graphics into a document; you can resize, crop, and reposition the graphics.

What should be a relief for WriteNow loyalists is that even though the program has changed owners (T/Maker used to sell the package), it's basically the same. It's the same program that years ago let you add and copy rulers throughout a document— and it's also the same program that only in the last two years added style sheets to its feature set. The biggest relief for me is knowing that it still has its great thesaurus.

MacWrite Pro (Lofty Becker). MacWrite has always been the easiest word processor to learn and use, but for a long time it lagged behind in features. But **MacWrite Pro 1.5** ($50, Claris) includes a powerful set of formatting tools so elegantly implemented that you'll actually *use* the features, not just *have* them. *[And what a price! But check out Claris' wonderful integrated program, ClarisWorks, before deciding on this program.—SZA]*

MacWrite Pro's basic orientation is a page, and what you see is precisely what prints. Fonts, sizes, and character or paragraph styles can be selected from a menu or a window. Columns (equal or variable width) and tables are a breeze, though tables can't cross page boundaries.

When you write by hand, you can scribble anywhere on the page—scrawl in the margins, or stick a headline at the top. In most word processors, placing that text (or a picture) just where you want it is an exercise in frustration, but MacWrite does this right. Headers and footers show up in the right spot. Add a footnote, and you're typing at the bottom of the page. For anything else, just insert a *frame* (containing text, a table, graphics, or even a QuickTime movie) and drag it where you want.

For all its ease of use, MacWrite Pro still lacks features some users want. It will create a table of contents but not an index, and there's no outliner or macro facility. If you don't like the keyboard shortcuts, too bad—you can't customize them. And if you regularly deal with plain text files, MacWrite won't cut it, since it insists on translating those files into its own formats.

Still, the current version of MacWrite Pro is an impressive tool, particularly strong in ease of use and formatting power.

Writing Tools

Writing doesn't always begin and end in a word processor. There are other tools, too, which can fill in the blanks of your word processor's feature list.

Spelling and Grammar

Whether you're a miserable speller or just a bad typist, it's getting harder and harder for mistakes to slip through to a final printout, what with all the spelling checker options around: Every word processor has one built-in, and there are stand-alone products available, too. Getting the grammar down pat is a more difficult problem.

Built-in spell checkers (SZA). A good spelling checker is an absolute necessity—there's just no reason for any misspellings in any computer-generated document. (Although there is *one* good excuse—such as when your misspelling creates a valid word that's spelled correctly. Way back in the third edition of this book, for instance, I dropped the letter *l* from the first word in the phrase *public domain*. The spelling checker let it through. But don't go back and look for it in that book, because a final eagle-eyed read-through caught the mistake.)

The only way you're going to use a spelling checker for every document, though, is if there's one built into your word processor—after all, it's unlikely you're going to bother running a separate program to check a single-page cover letter.

Stand-alone spell checkers (RC). Here's a quick roundup of spelling checker programs:

Spelling Coach Professional ($200, Deneba) comes as close as any spelling checker to doing it all. Batch-check selections or let Coach Pro watch for errors while you type. A pop-up menu gives you options for correct spellings, and if none seems appropriate, you can ask for phonetic guesses. It includes a 95,000-word main spelling dictionary (about 90 percent with definitions) and legal, technical, and medical supplements. It also includes the terrific BigThesaurus (described in "Other Tools," later in this chapter).

Spellswell ($75, Working Software) is more than a spelling checker but not quite a grammar checker. It catches things like incorrect capitalization, missing apostrophes, and double words. It also looks for "poor word choices," explaining the difference between "among" and "between," for instance; this was the first feature I turned off!

Lookup ($40, Working Software) is a fast and elegant little interactive DA spelling checker. It checks a highlighted selection, but only one word at a time—a major limitation. For more power, use the program with its bigger companion checker Spellswell; it can share Spellswell's 93,000-word dictionary, or use its own.

Grammar checkers (SZA). Let me be blunt: There's not a good grammar checker available anywhere yet. English grammar is much too complicated and subtle to be helpfully analyzed by some computer program—at least, by any program yet invented. Sure, it can flag problem words for you—but how many times do you want to be queried as to whether you meant to use *to*, *too*, or *two?* I even had one grammar checker ask me, at every instance of the word *the*, if perhaps, just maybe, might I have meant *thee*, the archaic form of *you?* Give me a break! (And how might *that* sentence be interpreted?) Of course, you can train most grammar checkers to ignore certain things and look for others, but then you can train yourself to do that, too. Grammar checkers that also check style can be useful—letting you know, for instance, that all your sentences are way too long—but nothing even approaches the skills of a real-life editor.

Here, for instance, are five sentences, each incorporating a common grammatical error—the ones that most grate on my nerves:

Sentence	*Correct form*
They divided the cake between the four guests.	*among* the four guests
He gave it to the student that deserved it.	*who* deserved it
The movie only played for one night.	played for *only* one night
None of them want to continue reading the book.	*wants* to continue
I was impressed by him refusing the reward.	by *his* refusing the reward

I ran all five sentences through both a built-in grammar checker (Word's) and a stand-alone product (Grammar Checker), with identical results. Both flagged the *between* problem in the first sentence, explaining the difference between *between* and *among;* both were smart enough to ignore the sentence if it contained the phrase "between the *two* guests" instead. But neither caught any of the other mistakes, although both queried the use of the passive voice ("was impressed") in the last sentence.

So there.

Grammar checker programs (EC). Serious grammarians will appreciate **Correct Grammar's** ($100, SoftKey International) 135,000-word spelling dictionary and the fact that the program lets you write your own grammar or style rules to "conform to a corporate or personal standard." A tutorial button gives you rule explanations, and a Help button turns Balloon Help off or on. *[More than a year after Word 6's release, however, Correct Grammar can't open Word 6 files.—SZA]*

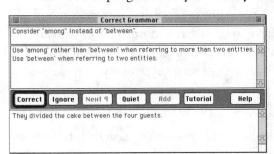

A grammar lesson in Correct Grammar's working window.

RightWriter ($50, Que Software) offers powerful style analysis, well-designed filter sets, and excellent on-screen help. But it has a glaring interface error: Press [Return] to activate the highlighted Next button to move on to the next questioned text, and the return character replaces the highlighted text in the document instead of triggering the button—and you can't Undo the action. *[As far as I'm concerned, that one glaring error is so blinding that you shouldn't touch this program with a ten-foot ADB cord.—SZA]*

BAD FEATURE

Other Tools

This section covers a few miscellaneous writer's tools you should know about. (CD-based dictionaries and thesauruses, by the way, are covered in Chapter 18.)

Spell Catcher (SZA). Previously incarnated as Thunder 7, **Spell Catcher** ($60, Casady & Greene), is one utility I absolutely can't live without—in fact, I delayed moving to System 7 until a compatible version of Thunder 7 was available. Its menu stays on the menu bar no matter where you're working, so it's always available.

For me, the crux of this program's usefulness is its watch-as-you-type approach: Spell Catcher is always in the background keeping track of your keyboard activity. You can set it to beep or flash immediately for all sorts of typos (misspellings, double words, no capital at the beginning of a sentence); it can make corrections automatically or

GOOD FEATURE

wait for your approval. Spell Catcher's glossary function lets you "teach" it the correct spelling for common misspellings; so, *hte* changes to *the* as soon as it leaves your fingertips, and something like *amif* expands to *Apple Menu Items folder*. You don't have to do anything special to trigger the corrections and expansions—as soon as you type the space that signifies the end of a word (or a punctuation mark), Spell Catcher jumps into action. (Word 6 gives me this capability, too, but Spell Catcher makes it available everywhere.) Spell Catcher can also check spelling in an after-the-fact "batch" mode.

Although the spell-checking and glossary expansion functions are enough to keep this on my top-ten utility list, there's more. Spell Catcher's Thesaurus is expansive and includes lots of synonyms as well as related words, and even antonyms—all grouped by meaning and with definitions; all you have to do is click on the word you want substituted for what you typed, and it's automatically entered in your document. Could you ask for anything more? You don't have to ask: there's more. There's a group of little "extras," like curly quote substitution and em-dash insertion when you type a double-hyphen. And there's GhostWriter, which saves every keystroke you make so that if you crash without saving a document, you can reconstruct it from the separate file GhostWriter compiled.

All these functions come in a smooth, unobtrusive utility with an elegant interface that's totally customizable—you can have it on or off in any application, and you can define which functions work in which program. It's an absolute must-have for anyone who does anything more than the most casual of writing on the Mac.

BigThesaurus (RC). This is one of the most seamlessly designed utilities in any category. A **BigThesaurus** ($100, Deneba) menu automatically appears in the menu bar of all your programs. Highlight a word, and a keystroke or a menu click opens the thesaurus window. You can easily open additional windows for any words you see in the first window. This multiple-window scheme comes close to Roget's index in that when several windows are arranged to be simultaneously visible, glancing from one to the other increases your chances of finding just what you need. Although available separately, BigThesaurus is also part of Deneba's Spelling Coach Professional.

Little thesaurus and lots of style (Charles Seiter). Microlytics offers both **Word Finder Plus** ($40), which has one million synonyms and 50,000 definitions, and an electronic version of **The Elements of Style** ($30), with all the text from Strunk and White's classic book.

MagicTypist (RC). This utility watches as you type and "guesses" the word you're typing before you're finished; if the word you want is in its list of suggestions, you don't have to finish typing it yourself. Unless you remove a lot of the magic suggestions from the control panel, you'll find the constant flashing in the menu bar and the pop-up suggestion list a real annoyance. You can teach **MagicTypist** ($130, Olduvai) words not in its dictionary, of course, and a well-trained MagicTypist can save you lots of typing time and effort.

Sonar Bookends (EC). You can create indexes in unique ways with **Sonar Bookends** ($130, Virginia Systems). It indexes any word that appears more than ten times in a document, or any word that you've defined in a special list. The program disk includes indexing and table of contents functions in an Addition for PageMaker and an XTension for Quark.

DocuComp (EC). This utility is essential for anyone who works with various versions of a document—lawyers and editors, for instance. **DocuComp** ($180, Mastersoft) compares any two documents and then shows what text has been added, deleted, or moved.

Zillion Kajillions (SZA). *If you write in iambic pentameter*
But can't find a rhyming parameter,
If you wish you were nimble and quick
In completing a new limerick,
You can find what it is that you need
With ease and incredible speed
One, two, or a million times
With a Zillion Kajillion Rhymes.

A Zillion Kajillion Rhymes ($50, Eccentric Software) contains an extensive dictionary of common, technical, and slang terms. Its companion, **A Zillion Kajillion Clichés** ($50), makes finding just the right (if trite) expression as easy as… pie, falling off a log, duck soup, taking candy from a baby, A-B-C, 1-2-3, shooting fish in a barrel…

Word 6 Tips

Basics

Creating new documents (EC). You wouldn't think that you'd need a tip to create a new document, but that's Word for you. Press ⌘N and you get a new document, no questions asked. But use New from the File menu, and you'll get a dialog box that lets you pick a template for the new document to be based on.

Double-click shortcuts (SZA). Word's document window has several "hot spots" that you can double-click to get dialog boxes or perform actions, as shown in the following picture. And, if you double-click in the status bar at the bottom of the screen, the Go To dialog opens.

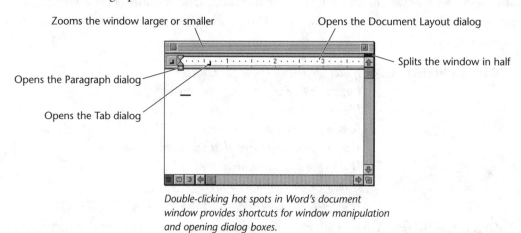

Double-clicking hot spots in Word's document window provides shortcuts for window manipulation and opening dialog boxes.

Shortcut menus (SZA/EC). One of Word's cleverest, but most hidden, features is the shortcut menu. Hold down ⌘ and Option and click the mouse, and you get a menu with special options. What special options? That depends on where you click. Click in some text and you get Cut, Copy, Paste, and some basic editing commands. Click in a table and you'll get table commands such as Insert Column. Click in a cell where you've defined a formula, and you'll get formula commands.

The Repeat command (SZA). The Repeat command (⌘Y) repeats the last command, your last edit, or the last thing you typed. If you've just applied a style to a paragraph, you can click in another paragraph and use Repeat to apply the style there, too.

If you want to use Repeat for a group of character or paragraph formats (bold, outline, and italic, say, or justified, indented, and double-spaced), use the Font or Paragraph commands to apply all the formats at once instead of keyboard or toolbar commands to apply them individually. That way, the Repeat command will include all the formats, instead of just the last one you applied.

Footnote shortcuts (SZA). The Footnotes command in the View menu splits the document window so you can review the text of the footnote entries, but there are two other ways to open the footnote *pane*. Hold Shift while you drag the window's split bar, and you'll get the footnote pane instead of a regular split window. Or, simply double-click on a footnote reference mark and the window splits to display that footnote.

To close the footnote pane, you can drag the split bar back to the top of the scroll bar, or press ⌘Shift S. But to close the pane and jump to a specific footnote reference at the same time, double-click on the reference mark next to the footnote itself in the lower pane.

Keyboard control (SZA). You can control everything from the keyboard if you want to in Word; this is no big surprise in a program that was created for the Windows

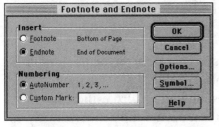

An underlined letter in a button name signifies the key you press to activate it.

world, but sometimes it really is convenient to ignore the mouse.

To activate the keyboard control, press ⌘Tab. For menus, you'll see that every title will have a single letter underlined; press that letter (no ⌘ key necessary) and the menu drops down. Every menu command will have a single underlined letter; press the letter, and the command is executed. You can use ← and → to move from one menu to another once a menu's open; ↑ and ↓ move you up and down inside an opened menu.

Dialog boxes that open after you've pressed ⌘Tab will have all their controls marked so that you can press the ⌘ key and the underlined letter to choose the option.

The keyboard control mode turns off automatically after you've used it for a command or dialog box. You can cancel it manually by pressing Esc.

Help (SZA). Clicking on the Help icon in a toolbar changes your mouse pointer to a Help pointer; clicking on something or selecting from a menu opens the Help window to that topic, or pops up a balloon of pertinent information.

But when you need help for a more general topic, double-click on the Help button: You'll get the Help window's Search dialog, where you can type in what you're looking for.

If you're working on a macro and need help with a command, select the command in the macro window and press ⌘?; the Help window opens to the WordBasic area and displays the command you selected in the macro window.

Find and Replace

Finding again (SZA). To find another occurrence of the last item you searched for, you don't have to open the Find dialog again: just press ⌘ Option Y. Combining Find Again with Repeat (⌘ Y) lets you find something, apply a format to it (if that's what you did to the found text), find the next occurrence, apply the format to it, and so on, all without a dialog box in the way.

Replacing with more than 255 characters (SZA). The Replace With box in the Replace dialog has a limit of 255 characters. If you want to specify a larger block of text as the replacement, copy the block to the Clipboard and type ^c in the Replace With box. (If you can't remember that special code, choose Clipboard Contents from the Special menu at the bottom of the dialog.)

Replace formatting shortcut (SZA). You can specify character or paragraph formatting for the Find or Replace text in the Replace dialog, but it's a multistep process: Select the category (font, paragraph, styles, and so on) from the dialog's Format menu, then specify the formats in the dialogs that open—and do it separately for each category. But you don't have to do all that. First, click in either the Find What or the Replace With box—whichever one you're defining the format for. Then use the Formatting toolbar to define the format (click on the Bold button, select a style, choose a font and/or size), and the formatting selections go into the Format definition in the dialog.

Searching for case (EC). If you're searching with the Match Case option checked in the Find or Replace dialog box, you won't find text that's been formatted with the All Caps or Small Caps options, since these don't truly change the case of the text, but only its outward appearance.

Finding and replacing for format (SZA). If you simply want to find and replace for character or paragraph formats (like changing all the blue double-underlined text to red dotted-underlined text), set up the Replace dialog for the formats without putting any text in the Find What and Replace With boxes.

If you want to find specifically formatted text and return it to whatever is normal for the paragraph style that contains it, leave Replace With blank but use the Style command from the Format button to set the style to *Default paragraph font*.

Tables and Columns

Using tabs inside tables (EC). Since Tab moves you to the next cell in a table, how do you actually enter a tab in a table? Well, if you're doing it a lot, you probably need another column. But for that occasional predicament, use Option Tab.

Selecting a table (SZA). Select a row or column in a table by putting the pointer at the top or side of the table, where it will change to a thick arrow, then click.

To select an entire table, double-click anywhere inside it while pressing Option, or press Option Clear (on the keypad) when the insertion point is anywhere in the table.

Creating uneven columns (EC). When you drag the column markers on the ruler, you don't just change one column, you change them all. How do you create two columns that have different widths? In the Columns dialog box, check Left or Right for the automatic settings, or click Two or Three Columns and uncheck Equal Column Width. Then enter the widths you want for your columns. Now when you drag the column markers in the ruler, it will affect only one column.

Adding lines between columns (EC). Okay, this isn't really a trick, but since you might spend a while using the Borders command or some such thing to place lines between your columns, I'll give you this hint: Use the Line Between option in the Columns dialog box.

Styles

Recognizing character and paragraph styles (EC). Word combines both the character and paragraph styles in a single menu. How do you tell them apart? Paragraph styles are in bold, and character styles are in plain text.

Quickly redefining styles (SZA). You can quickly redefine a style by applying it and then making changes to a paragraph. Then, select the entire paragraph by double-clicking on it from the selection bar. Next, click in the Style menu in the Formatting toolbar, and press Return twice: the first time opens a dialog box, and the second okays the redefine option.

Customizing

Toolbar tricks (SZA). Here are four quick tips for working with toolbars:

- Control-click anywhere to see a menu of toolbars; select one from the menu to open it.

- Reposition a button on a toolbar by holding down ⌘ while you drag the button.

- To remove a button from a toolbar, hold down ⌘ and drag the button off. Let it go on another toolbar to move it there; let it go anywhere else, and it just disappears.

- To make a copy of a button, hold down Option while you drag it. Let it go over another toolbar to put the copy on that toolbar. Let it go anywhere else on the screen, and you'll get a new toolbar holding that button.

Creating keyboard commands (SZA). To change an existing keyboard equivalent or create a keyboard combination for a command that doesn't have one, use the Customize command from the Tools menu. Click on the Keyboard tab, and find the command you want in the Commands list. Then click in the Press New Shortcut Key box and press the combination you want; finally, click the Assign button.

Creating a document menu (SZA). You can create a menu that lists the documents that you work on often. First, create the menu itself: Choose Customize from the Tools menu, and click on the Menus tab. Click the Menu Bar button, and in the dialog that opens, name your new menu and show where you want it to appear on the menu bar. Close all the dialogs and you'll see your new (empty) menu.

The easiest way to add documents to the menu is to start by opening them. Then go to the Menus tab again in the Customize dialog. Choose your new menu from the Change What Menu list, and show where in the menu you want the document listed. Select *FileOpenFile:* from the Commands list, and then select your document from the pop-up menu that appears in the lower-right corner.

When you're working with menu and menu item names, the letter following the ampersand (&) is the one that will be underlined when you're working in keyboard mode, so put it in a good spot or delete it entirely.

9 Spreadsheets

The first software package for the personal computer, VisiCalc, was a spreadsheet program. It became wildly successful and made people realize that perhaps there was money in selling software. Twenty years later, spreadsheets have grown up quite a bit. Used for more than just addition and subtraction, spreadsheets now solve complex financial analysis problems, create 3-D graphs, and automatically generate monthly reports. We'll tell you just what you can expect from today's spreadsheets, get you started with some spreadsheet basics, and give you a collection of tips you can use with your favorite spreadsheet software package.

Contributors

Maria Langer (ML) is the chapter editor.

Christian Boyce (CB), a former rocket scientist, is widely known as The Macintosh Consultant to the Stars. His published works include *Your Mac Can Do That!*, *Macs 4 Morons*, and *Everything you Wanted to Know About the Mac* (all Hayden books).

Eve Gordon (EG) is an applications trainer and science fiction writer whose life wouldn't be complete without Excel.

Dennis Cohen (DC) is a senior software engineer at Claris Corporation and a long-time forum consultant on America Online's Macintosh Developer Forum. He writes occasionally for *MacTech* (formerly *MacTutor*) and performs technical editing and review work for a number of Macintosh publishers.

Elizabeth Castro (EC) was the chapter editor for the 5th edition of *The Macintosh Bible*, from which parts of this chapter were taken.

Contents

What's All This About Spreadsheets?

Imagine an accountant's worksheet filled with columns and rows of numbers. Now put that worksheet inside a computer, add the ability to change inputted and calculated values instantly, and throw in a few extra features—such as built-in formulas, charting capabilities, and database sorting. What you'll have when you're finished is a spreadsheet.

Spreadsheets Explained (ML)

Spreadsheet software is like a word processor for numbers. You use it to neatly organize, calculate, and present numerical information. The resulting document is usually a spreadsheet—sometimes called a *worksheet* file—but it can also be a chart.

Like a paper worksheet, an electronic worksheet is laid out in a grid. *Rows*, which are labeled with numbers, and *columns*, which are labeled with letters, intersect at *cells*. Each cell has an *address* or *reference* that consists of the letter of the column and the number of the row. So you'd find cell C16 at the intersection of column C and row 16.

To use a spreadsheet you enter *values* and *formulas* into cells. A value can be text, a number, a date, or a time. It's often called a *constant value* because it won't change unless you change it. A formula is a calculation that you want the spreadsheet to perform for you. You begin a formula with an equals sign (=) and follow it with a combination of values, cell references, operators, and functions—more on those later.

The beauty of a spreadsheet is that if it's properly constructed, it can calculate the results of complex formulas in less time than it takes to bat an eye. And if you change any of the values that are referenced by a formula, the results change instantly. It sure beats an accountant with pencil-stained fingers and a 10-key calculator.

"Real-World" Spreadsheets

The best way to see what spreadsheet software is all about is to look at some real-life examples. With spreadsheets like the ones on the next few pages, you can calculate totals and averages, create a loan amortization table, perform a "what-if" analysis, manage and report data, and create charts. These examples are just a small sampling of what's possible—with a little imagination and practice, you'll soon be taking spreadsheets to their limits.

Totals column adds the numbers from January, February, and March. The formula in cell E2, for example, is =B2+C2+D2.

The Averages column computes the average of the values in the white cells, row by row, with a formula like the one in F2: =AVERAGE(B2..D2). The "dot-dot" notation means "and everything in between." Thus, B2..D2 means "B2, C2, and D2." Note that this is only true for ClarisWorks; Microsoft Excel denotes the same range of cells as "B2:D2." It's still "dot-dot" notation, except these dots are stacked vertically.

1st Quarter Expenses (SS)

	A	B January	C February	D March	E Totals	F Averages	G
1		January	February	March	Totals	Averages	
2	Dining	$109	$62	$37	$208	$69	
3	Hotels	$269	$301	$67	$637	$212	
4	Car rentals	$121	$209	$125	$455	$152	
5	Airfare	$633	$541	$344	$1,518	$506	
6	Telephone	$287	$198	$174	$659	$220	
7	Postage	$46	$95	$61	$202	$67	
8	Totals	$1,465	$1,406	$808	$3,679	$1,226	
9							

The formulas in the Totals row add the cells above them. But rather than use a formula in B8 like =B2+B3+B4+B5+B6+B7, we used a shorter one: =SUM(B2..B7). As you can see, the dot-dot notation can save some typing.

This simple ClarisWorks spreadsheet calculates totals and averages for the numbers entered into the white cells.

Simple calculations (CB). Here's a simple little spreadsheet that does some straight-forward mathematics. When you enter expense information into the white cells, the spreadsheet calculates totals and averages for each category (the light gray cells), and totals for each month (the darker gray cells).

Complex calculations (EG/ML). Not every formula you write or spreadsheet you create will be simple. By combining simple formulas and more advanced functions, you can create more complex spreadsheet models, such as the following loan amortization table.

	A	B	C	D
1		Car Loan Payments		
2	Loan Amount			$15,000.00
3	Annual Interest Rate			8%
4	Number of Years			2
5	Monthly Payment			$ 678.41
6				
7	Pmt#	Interest	Payment	Balance
8	0			$15,000.00
9	1	100.00	$678.41	$14,421.59
10	2	96.14	$678.41	$13,839.33
11	3	92.26	$678.41	$13,253.18
12	4	88.35	$678.41	$12,663.12
13	5	84.42	$678.41	$12,069.13
14	6	80.46	$678.41	$11,471.19
15	7	76.47	$678.41	$10,869.25
16	8	72.46	$678.41	$10,263.30
17	9	68.42	$678.41	$ 9,653.32
18	10	64.36	$678.41	$ 9,039.26
19	11	60.26	$678.41	$ 8,421.11
20	12	56.14	$678.41	$ 7,798.85
21	13	51.99	$678.41	$ 7,172.43
22	14	47.82	$678.41	$ 6,541.84
23	15	43.61	$678.41	$ 5,907.04
24	16	39.38	$678.41	$ 5,268.01
25	17	35.12	$678.41	$ 4,624.72
26	18	30.83	$678.41	$ 3,977.14
27	19	26.51	$678.41	$ 3,325.25
28	20	22.17	$678.41	$ 2,669.01
29	21	17.79	$678.41	$ 2,008.39
30	22	13.39	$678.41	$ 1,343.37
31	23	8.96	$678.41	$ 673.92
32	24	4.49	$678.41	$ (0.00)
33				

Using good spreadsheet design, this one includes an input or assumption area where you enter the amounts you already know: the amount or principal of the loan, interest rate, and loan term.

The monthly payment formula in cell D5 uses one of Excel's built-in financial functions: PMT. The formula is: =PMT(D3/12,D4*12,D2). This says to find the periodic payment for a loan based on its interest rate, number of periods, and principal. Because we want a monthly payment amount, we divide the interest rate by 12 and multiply the number of periods by 12.

The rest of the table calculates and displays the interest, payment, and ending balance for each period of the loan. Cell D8 carries forward the principal in cell D2 with the formula =D2. Cell C10 carries forward the monthly payment calculated in cell D5 with the formula =D5. By using formulas rather than values, we can change the loan amount in one cell (D2) and the rest of the spreadsheet will change automatically.

Cell B9 calculates the interest for the first month with the formula =D8*(D3/12).

Cell D9 calculates the ending balance with the formula =D8–(C9–B9). This takes the principal and subtracts the difference between the payment and the interest, which is the amount of principal paid.

You can build a loan amortization table by combining simple and complex formulas, taking advantage of Excel's built-in financial functions.

Using Data Tables for What-If Analyses   (EG)

Another way to approach the car loan scenario is to build a data table showing ranges of interest rates and different terms. The following spreadsheet, for instance, shows different monthly payments for a car loan based on interest rates ranging from 5 percent to 15 percent, and loan terms ranging from one year to five years.

A data table is based on a formula—in this example, the one in cell B8 which calculates monthly loan payments.

The loan term and interest rate in cells E5 and E4 don't change ...

... but you can change the loan amount in cell E3, the rates in cells B9 through B17, or, terms in cells C8 though G8, and the table will update based on the new information.

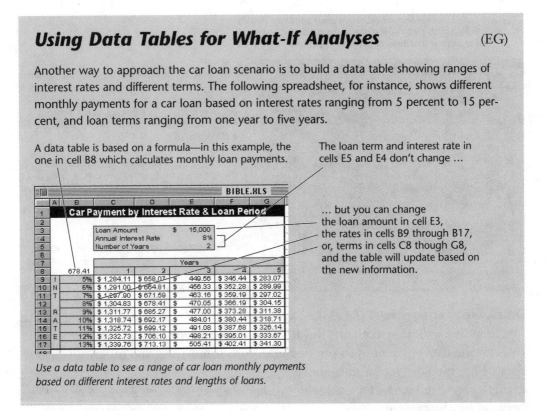

Use a data table to see a range of car loan monthly payments based on different interest rates and lengths of loans.

What-If analysis (EG/ML). Probably the most powerful feature of a spreadsheet is its ability to recalculate results quickly when you make changes to it. This is known as *what-if analysis* because by changing a value, you're saying, "*What* happens *if* this number changes?"

Based on the previous loan amortization table, what if you decide to buy a cheaper car? Or change the loan term? Or find a better interest rate?

It's easy to see how these changes will affect the monthly payment. Just change the information in the appropriate cell and—presto!—your change is reflected throughout the spreadsheet.

Playing "what if," if you change the amount of the loan in cell D2, the entire worksheet changes instantly.

Excel's outline feature adds buttons to hide or display detail. In this example, Excel automatically created the outline structure based on the subtotals.

	A	B	C	D	E	F	G
1	The Pinheads - Bowling Stats						
2							
3	Name	Date	Game 1	Game 2	Game 3	Series	Avg
4	Cohen	5-Jan	184	201	173	558	186
5	Cohen	12-Jan	167	186	184	537	179
6	Cohen	19-Jan	213	195	197	605	202
7	Cohen	26-Jan	175	175	171	521	174
8	Cohen Total		739	757	725	2,221	
9	Cohen Average		185	189	181	555	
10	Langer	5-Jan	178	176	200	554	185
11	Langer	12-Jan	177	185	180	542	181
12	Langer	19-Jan	169	161	189	519	173
13	Langer	26-Jan	182	180	170	532	177
14	Langer Total		706	702	739	2,147	
15	Langer Average		177	176	185	537	
16	Gordon	5-Jan	177	177	174	528	176
17	Gordon	12-Jan	186	200	183	569	190
18	Gordon	19-Jan	195	165	198	558	186
19	Gordon	26-Jan	202	185	187	574	191
20	Gordon Total		760	727	742	2,229	
21	Gordon Average		190	182	186	557	
22	Team Total		2,205	2,186	2,206	6,597	
23	Team Average		184	182	184	550	

Each unique column heading is a field name.

Each row contains a record—information about one thing. In this case, each record is the bowling scores for a particular player on a particular day.

By sorting the records by player name (and date), Excel's subtotal feature can be used to quickly calculate totals and averages. These subtotals can be quickly removed with an option in the Subtotals dialog box.

This Excel worksheet contains a database of scores for members of a bowling league. By using database features such as sorting and subtotaling, you can quickly analyze information.

Database management (DC/ML). Spreadsheets are also useful for simple database functions. By setting up columns for different categories or *fields* of information and rows for the data or *records*, you can organize, sort, summarize, and otherwise analyze data. The spreadsheet in the above example shows the scores for the members of a bowling league.

Charting (CB). A picture's worth a thousand words, and when the picture stands in for numbers it's probably worth even more. You can use the charting features of spreadsheet software to make sense of what could otherwise be just a bunch of numbers. The column and pie charts shown here illustrate two examples of how you can graphically display a spreadsheet's results.

Because most spreadsheet packages can create several kinds of charts, you can use different charts for different purposes. It's usually as easy as selecting the data you want to chart and clicking a chart button on a toolbar.

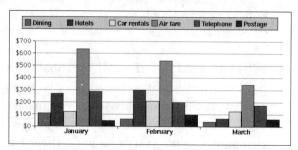

The column chart quickly tells you that Air fare is the biggest expense, that telephones and hotels are the next biggest, and that the rest of the expenses hardly make a difference. Try getting information like that as quickly from raw numbers!

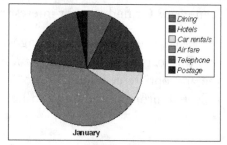

The pie chart makes it easy to see that Air fare is nearly half of the total expenses for January.

Using Spreadsheets   (CB)

"Fine," you're saying. "I'm sold. But how do I make the dang thing work?" Read this section and you'll soon be using spreadsheets with style and verve, at least to the point that you'll impress your friends and pets.

Moving around. You can't put anything into a cell until you select it. You can tell that a cell is selected by noticing the border around it. When the border is thick, the cell is selected. When it isn't, it isn't. Selecting a cell can be accomplished in two ways:

- Position the mouse pointer over a cell and click once. You have to click. Just moving the mouse pointer over a cell does not select it.

- Use a keyboard key to move to a cell. Here are the most commonly used keystrokes; they should work in most spreadsheet programs:

This key...	Selects this cell...
→ or Tab	The cell to the right of the current cell
← or Shift Tab	The cell to the left of the current cell
↓ or Return	The cell below the current cell
↑ or Shift Return	The cell above the current cell

Cell references. When you select a cell the spreadsheet program dutifully reports the cell reference in the upper-left corner of the window. As mentioned earlier, the cell reference consists of the letter (or letters) of the cell's column and the number of the cell's row.

Despite the ability to select more than one cell at a time by dragging through several cells at once, only one cell is active at a time. The cell reference area never displays the reference for more than a single cell.

There are alternative ways to describe cell locations but nobody uses them because they confuse the issue. We'll stick with the standard notation here.

Entering information. There are two kinds of entries: the kind that you merely type in (values), and the kind that compute values (formulas).

Entering values is easy: just select the cell you want to put information into, type what you want to put in the cell, and then do one of the following:

- Press Return. The value is entered and the next cell down becomes selected.

- Press Enter. The value is entered and the cell remains selected.

When You Enter Too Much ... (CB/ML/DC)

For long entries, the cell width determines what appears in the cell:

- If you type a number (or date or time) that doesn't fit into a cell, the cell's contents turn into repeated pound signs (#####).

- If you type more text than can fit in the cell and there is nothing in the cell to its right, the text overflows to the right so you can see all of it. Even if text appears to overflow into other cells, that text is still contained in only one cell.

- If you type more text than can fit in the cell and there is something entered into the cell to its right, the text appears truncated in the cell in which you entered it. This doesn't mean the text is cut off—it isn't. It just doesn't show.

In most cases you can properly display lengthy numbers or text by making the column wider. Just drag the right boundary of the column heading at the top of the column.

Another way you can make lengthy text fit in a cell is to turn on the word wrap feature for that cell. Although not all spreadsheets offer this feature, both Excel and ClarisWorks do.

HOT TIP

- Press ⌷Tab⌷. The value is entered and the next cell to the right becomes selected.

- Click the check mark button next to the X near the top of the window. That's the Enter button and it's the same as pressing ⌷Enter⌷. The value is entered and the cell remains selected.

HOT TIP

If you make a mistake while entering a value (or a formula, for that matter) you can start over by clicking the X button beside the check mark near the top of the window. That's the Cancel button. If you prefer keyboard keys, ⌷Esc⌷ does the same thing.

Editing entries. You can change the contents of a cell in two ways:

- Select the cell and type something different into it.

- Select the cell, click in the *formula bar* at the top of the window where the cell's contents are displayed, and use standard word processing techniques to edit what's there.

No matter how you edit an entry, don't forget to press ⌷Return⌷ or ⌷Enter⌷ or click the Enter button to complete it.

Creating formulas. Putting numbers and words into neat rows and columns is fine, but spreadsheets are built to compute. You can tell your spreadsheet to add two cells, calculate sales tax, or figure out what day of the week it will be 100 days from now.

In fact, you can do just about anything that involves math—and some things that don't. But to do these fancy things, you must know how to create formulas.

There's one thing you must remember to successfully enter a formula: All formulas start with an equals sign (=). No exceptions!

To enter a formula, select the cell where you want the formula's results displayed, type an equals sign, type the formula, and complete the formula by pressing [Return] or [Enter], or by clicking the Enter button.

Here's an example. Let's say you have a number in cell A1 and another number in cell A2. You want to add them and put the answer in cell A3. Here's what you do: Select cell A3, type *=A1+A2* (no spaces), and press [Return]. As soon as you press [Return], the result appears in cell A3.

There are other ways to enter the parts of formulas. For example, if you like clicking, you can enter a cell reference in a formula by clicking it. To write the above formula by clicking, do this: Click in cell A3, type an equals sign, click on cell A1, click on cell A2, and click the Enter button. The answer appears in cell A3.

This method is especially useful for preventing typing errors—the less you type, the less chance you have of making a typo!

As you may have noticed, the plus sign is added by default if you click a cell without first specifying an operator. What you may also notice is that if you forget to complete the formula by *not* pressing [Return] or [Enter] or clicking the Enter button, any cell you click on will be added to the formula in the formula bar. That's why it's important to complete each entry properly before continuing to other cells.

Those Darned Error Messages   (EC/ML)

When you write a formula incorrectly, the spreadsheet program usually tells you by displaying a dialog box with an error message or an error message within the cell. Here's a table of some of Excel's error messages—other spreadsheets offer similarly vague messages.

#DIV/0!	Your formula is trying to divide by zero, which is a no-no.
#N/A	One of the referenced values is not available.
#NAME?	You've used a cell or range name that isn't recognized. If you didn't mean to use a name, you've probably spelled a function name incorrectly.
#NUM!	Your formula uses a number incorrectly.
#REF!	Your formula references an invalid cell. This can happen after the formula has been written if you've deleted cells.
#VALUE!	Your formula uses an incorrect argument or operator. Check for extra or missing commas and parentheses and for proper function name.

2 + 3 + 5 * 10 = ?   (EG/ML)

The answer is 55. Why? Well, mathematical operations don't happen in the order of appearance—they have a specific order, which is shown in the table below. In the example above, the spreadsheet multiplies 5 by 10 first, then adds 2 and 3 to get 55.

Operation	Operator
Parentheses	( )
Exponents	^
Multiplication	*
Division	/
Addition	+
Subtraction	–

To force an operation to occur first, put it in parentheses. In the example above, to add 3 and 5 first, the formula would be 2+(3+5)*10. The spreadsheet would first add 3 and 5 to get 8, multiply that by 10, and then add 2. The result: 82. See what a difference the parentheses can make?

HOT TIP

Beyond the Basics

So far, we've given you enough information to get you started with just about any spreadsheet program. But here are a few additional techniques and concepts to consider as you hone your spreadsheet skills.

Functions (CB). Remember high school math? No? Fortunately, the people who make spreadsheet software do remember, and they've loaded their programs with handy calculations called *functions*. Here are some of my favorites, the ones I use over and over again. You saw some of them in action earlier in this chapter.

- *SUM* sums (adds) a bunch of numbers. It's especially handy for totaling a column or a row.

- *AVERAGE* calculates the average of a range of cells. As with most functions, it's a lot easier to use the function than to calculate averages yourself.

- *MAX* looks at a range of cells and returns the largest value. You could do this by looking at the cells yourself, but the MAX function is faster, and it never makes mistakes.

- *MIN* determines which cell in a range is the smallest.

- *IF*—my favorite—gives you supreme power and flexibility. It evaluates a condition (such as, "Is B10 greater than 5,000?") and performs a calculation (or returns a result) based on whether the condition is met (true) or not met (false). Using this function creatively can add intelligence to your spreadsheets.

- *PROPER* changes the first character of text to a capital letter.

- *SIN*—as in "sine," not "Thou Shalt Not." It's trigonometry, the high school math subject you either understood completely or not at all. Fortunately, spreadsheets excel (hey, a spreadsheet pun!) at trigonometry. Given an angle, the sine is a function away. COS gives you cosines, and TAN produces tangents.

- *WEEKDAY* returns the day of the week that a certain date falls on. The answer you'll get is a number from 1 to 7 that represents the day of the week. (The actual result depends on the settings in the Date & Time control panel.)

- *SQRT*—that's "square root," not "squirt"—a function that calculates square roots.

- *PMT* figures out how much the periodic payments will be when you borrow a certain amount of money at a certain rate of interest for a certain length of time.

Why Use Cell References? (ML)

HOT TIP

A well-constructed spreadsheet includes cell references whenever possible in its formulas. Why? So the spreadsheet is easier to modify.

The two samples below illustrate how cell references in formulas can make it easier to modify spreadsheets.

You can write formulas that include the percentage rate as a constant within the formula, like this: =B2*15%.

	A	B Sales Amount	C Commission
1	Name		
2	Christian	145.00	21.75
3	Eve	95.00	14.25
4	Dennis	79.00	11.85
5	Maria	130.00	19.50
6	Jeremy	201.00	30.15
7	Roslyn	138.00	20.70
8	Nancy	123.00	18.45
9			

If you want to change the commission rate in this spreadsheet, you need to edit the contents of the formulas in cells C2 through C8. That's seven changes! And if you forget to make a change, the spreadsheet's results will be incorrect!

But it's a lot more convenient to write formulas that reference a cell containing the percentage rate, like this: =B4*C1.

	A	B Sales Amount	C Commission
1	Commission Rate:		15%
2			
3	Name		
4	Christian	145.00	21.75
5	Eve	95.00	14.25
6	Dennis	79.00	11.85
7	Maria	130.00	19.50
8	Jeremy	201.00	30.15
9	Roslyn	138.00	20.70
10	Nancy	123.00	18.45
11			

In this spreadsheet, you'd only have to change the contents of cell C1 to properly recalculate all commissions in column C. That's one change that's impossible to miss. Which would you prefer?

Copying formulas (ML). You can create a spreadsheet like the expense summary or loan amortization table shown earlier without entering each and every formula down the columns. How? By copying similar formulas. The spreadsheet software automatically changes cell references as necessary so the copied formulas are correct. Of course, there are limitations to this (see the "Absolute References" sidebar), so check the formulas you copy to make sure they're correct.

Macros (EG). Many spreadsheet packages give you the ability to write and use macros that automate repetitive tasks or create custom functions.

Here's an example. Say you've been keeping track of the scores for your bowling league. Each week, you create a stacked bar graph that puts each bowler's scores into a bar and color codes the scores for each game. Rather than go though the steps to create the chart manually each week, you can create a macro to do it automatically.

> ### *Absolute References*   (EG)
>
> You can use two kinds of references in your formulas: *relative* (such as D5) or *absolute* (such as D5). The only time the kind of reference matters is when you copy a formula. A relative reference will automatically change relative to where you paste it. An absolute reference will always refer to the same cell no matter where you paste it. This is probably the most complex concept when dealing with spreadsheets, but once mastered, it can help you create error-free spreadsheets very quickly.

HOT TIP

When you first get started with macros, use the software's macro recorder to have it write the macro for you. This is a nice—although limited—use of macros that can help familiarize you with the macro language.

Formatting (ML). Of course, all spreadsheet software offers the ability to format your spreadsheets and charts with different fonts, colors, styles, borders—you name it. The spreadsheets shown throughout this chapter offer good examples. With a little creativity, you can make a spreadsheet look like a million bucks—even if it's reporting a $68 million loss.

Printing (ML). When you print a spreadsheet, what emerges from your printer depends on several factors:

- Did you specify a print area? A *print area* is the rectangular selection of cells that will print. If you don't specify a print area, most spreadsheet packages will print the entire spreadsheet, inserting page breaks wherever necessary to get it all on paper.

- Did you insert manual page breaks? You can specify where you want one page to end and the next to begin to eliminate page break surprises.

- Did you set page orientation, margins, or scale? By fiddling around with these page setup options, you can squeeze a relatively large spreadsheet onto standard-size paper—or magnify spreadsheet cells for use in a presentation.

- Did you turn off gridlines and headings? Some spreadsheets, such as Excel, will print spreadsheet gridlines unless you manually turn them off.

- Did you set print titles? If your spreadsheet is lengthy it may include *print titles* that you want to print on each page. Unless you tell the spreadsheet software which column(s) or row(s) to use as titles, it will only print them on the first page.

These options vary from one spreadsheet package to another. Explore the Page Setup and Print dialog boxes of your spreadsheet software to see how their settings affect your printouts.

Spreadsheet Software

Contrary to popular belief, there is more than one program out there that can create spreadsheets and charts. (There used to be a lot more, but let's not dwell on the past.) Let's take a look at them.

Microsoft Excel   (ML)

Microsoft Excel ($300) is undoubtedly the most feature-packed spreadsheet software package around. It goes beyond the basics of spreadsheets and charts by offering hundreds of built-in functions, extensive database features, drawing tools, a wide range of formatting capabilities, and a comprehensive macro language.

The power of Excel goes beyond what it *can* do to *how* it does it. It is a well-thought-out package that includes many features to make data entry easier or more error-free. Its dialog boxes are well organized and easy to use and understand (with a few exceptions that aren't worth detailing here). It includes extensive on-line help with hypertext links, making it easy to navigate from topic to topic to find the information you need. And unlike another Microsoft product (which I won't mention by name), its heavy load of features does not affect its performance.

Although some people think I'm partial to Excel because I wrote three books about it in a year, that's not true. I can objectively look at Excel and its alternatives and tell you that Excel is the best and most powerful spreadsheet package around. But is it for everyone? Of course not! The vast majority of folks who use their Macs at home or

Spreadsheet Templates (EC/ML)

Companies like Baarns Publishing offer spreadsheet templates that you can use even if you haven't fully figured out your spreadsheet program. Each template is a spreadsheet file created to perform a specific function. You simply enter the information in the spaces provided and the predefined formulas, charts, and macros do the rest. Although the templates are usually in Excel format, you can often open them with other spreadsheet software. Why reinvent the wheel when someone with experience has already built a good one for you?

school don't need even half of Excel's bells and whistles. If you're one of these folks, be sure to read about the other packages in this section. But if you're in corporate finance, science, or other industries where heavy-duty number crunching and presentation is a must, I doubt if you'll find a better spreadsheet software package for your needs than Excel.

However, the power of Excel will cost you in terms of dollars, disk space, and RAM. You'll pay about $300 for the software, which will take up at least 10MB of hard disk space and 4MB of RAM. But for serious number crunchers, this is a small price to pay for Excel's power.

Let's Keep It Simple Spreadsheet (ML)

A newcomer to the spreadsheet market is **Let's Keep It Simple Spreadsheet** (Let's KISS) by Casady & Greene. Although still in the final stages of beta testing when this book was in production, I got a chance to work with it—and liked what I saw.

Let's KISS is a spreadsheet package that lets you create documents by dragging components into a blank window. You start by adding a grid to the window and sizing it to contain your data. Then drag Top and Side labels onto the grid to add cells for descriptive text. Type the labels and values into the cells. To total a row, drag a Column part into position in the window and add a Top label to it. Then drag a

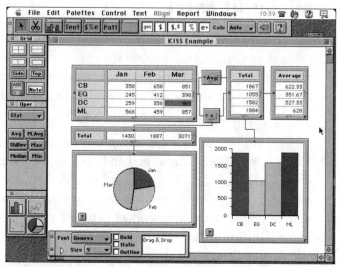

With *Let's Keep It Simple Spreadsheet*, all formulas are "written" with your mouse pointer—just drag and drop spreadsheet and chart parts on a window and connect them to create relationships, total columns and rows, or perform other calculations.

Plus operator into the window. Using your mouse, connect the grid containing the rows you want to total to the Plus operator and then connect that to the Column part. The totals appear instantly. No formulas, no cell references, no calculation errors due to typos.

Although KISS might not appeal to experienced spreadsheet users who have already mastered and grown comfortable with cell references, formulas, and functions, it's sure to be a hit with folks who are intimidated by these things. Its drag-and-drop techniques make it easy to solve problems, create spreadsheet models, make charts, apply formatting, and prepare nice-looking reports. And it's kind of *fun* to use, too!

While lighter in features than a spreadsheet king like Excel, KISS is also lighter in price—the expected retail price is $130. It requires a Mac with a 68020 or better processor running System 7 or later and uses 3.5MB of RAM.

BiPlane Deluxe (EC/ML)

BiPlane Deluxe is a great little spreadsheet package from Night Diamonds Software. It has all the standard spreadsheet features, including over 100 functions, formatting control, and charting capabilities. It can read Excel 4 and SYLK format spreadsheet files. It should meet the needs of most users and you certainly can't beat the price: $60.

POWERBOOK

BiPlane Deluxe is especially good for folks with older Macs or PowerBooks with limited RAM or disk space because it fits on one 800K disk, uses only 1MB of RAM, and is compatible with System 6.

Spreadsheets and Charts Without Spreadsheet Software (ML)

Spreadsheet software packages aren't the only products that create spreadsheets and charts. You'll find mathematical and charting capabilities in a wide variety of packages. **Claris Impact** ($90) and **Microsoft PowerPoint** ($300) are two presentation software packages that include spreadsheet-like tables and charts. Microsoft Word and WordPerfect are two word processing packages with table and math capabilities that you can use to make simple spreadsheets. Even database applications such as FileMaker Pro offer mathematical features that make them handy for creating calculated tables of data.

If all you're after is charts, check out DeltaPoint's **DeltaGraph Pro** ($140). This charting package offers more kinds of charts than most people will use in a lifetime—including many chart types you won't find anywhere else.

Integrated Software (DC/ML)

An important component of any integrated software package is its spreadsheet module. Here are some spreadsheet specifics for the top two contenders, ClarisWorks and Microsoft Works (see Chapter 12 for more details on integrated software).

- ClarisWorks' spreadsheet is fast, versatile, and powerful. It provides basic spreadsheet capability, a large number of built-in functions, nicely integrated 2- and 3-D charting capabilities, and extensive formatting control.

- Microsoft Works' spreadsheet is a scaled-down version of Excel with Excel's look and feel and many of its features.

Tips

Because there's more than one spreadsheet package out there, we've done our best to come up with a few generic tips that you can use with any software package. But Excel and ClarisWorks users won't be disappointed with the application-specific tips we've rounded up.

Generic Spreadsheet Tips

HOT TIPS

Use arrow keys to change the active cell but use the scroll bar to change the view of the spreadsheet (ML). Although you can use the scroll bars to change your view of a spreadsheet, using the scroll bars does not change the active cell.

Pay attention to the mouse pointer (CB/ML). Spreadsheets change the mouse pointer to provide visual clues about things you can do.

- The mouse pointer appears as a white cross (or plus sign) when it's in the spreadsheet area—click to select a cell, row, or column; drag to select multiple cells; or click to add a cell to a formula if the formula bar is active.

- The mouse pointer appears as a standard I-beam when it's in the formula bar—click to edit the contents of the formula bar.

- The mouse pointer appears as a thick black bar with arrows when it's between column or row headings—drag to change the width of the column or height of the row.

- The mouse pointer appears as a standard arrow pointer when you move it out of the spreadsheet window—use it to pull down a menu, scroll with a scroll bar, move or resize a window, or switch to another open window or application.

Turn a formula into a text value (CB). If you're having trouble entering a formula correctly and your spreadsheet keeps beeping at you each time you try to move on to another cell, delete the equals sign from the beginning of the formula and press ⏎Enter. The spreadsheet accepts what remains as mere text, allowing you to move on to other things. Later, you can come back (older and wiser) to fix the thing up. Why not just delete the formula and start from scratch later? Because often you'll get very close to getting a formula right—to throw it all away is to waste the time and effort you've already put into it.

Use shift-click to select cells (CB). Select the first cell of a range, then hold down ⇧Shift and click in the last cell of the range or use the arrow keys to extend the selection.

Create a data entry area (CB/ML). Select the range of cells in which you want to enter data. Then, when you complete an entry by pressing ⏎Return or ⏎Enter, you'll automatically move to the next cell in the selection. This is quicker than selecting each cell, one at a time.

Understand the difference between relative and absolute references (ML). You indicate that all or part of a cell reference is absolute by putting a dollar sign ($) before it. To help remember what that symbol means in a cell reference, think of the word *always*. So, for example, D5 can be thought of as *always D always 5*—or *always D5!*

Use drawing tools to annotate spreadsheets and charts (DC). You can draw attention to spreadsheet results by drawing circles and arrows right on the spreadsheet. Use a text box tool, if available, to add notes.

Excel Tips

Edit directly in the cell (EC). If you want to change the contents of a cell without having to use the formula bar, double-click the cell.

Move cells with drag and drop (EC). You can drag a cell or a range of cells by its border to move it to a new position. Hold down ⇧Shift while dragging to insert it between other cells. Hold down ⌥Option while dragging to copy it to the new location.

Use AutoFill to enter data into adjacent cells (EC/ML). Enter a value or formula into the first cell, press ⏎Enter to complete the entry, and then drag the fill handle (the little box in the bottom-right corner of the cell) to extend a box around the other cells you want to contain the same value or formula. If the original cell contains a day, month, or other familiar series, Excel completes the series for you.

Enter the current time or date quickly (EC). To enter the current time in a cell, press ⌘-. To enter the current date, press ⌘;.

Use AutoSum to add columns or rows (EC/ML). Select the cell at the bottom of a column or the right side of a row you want to total. Then double-click the AutoSum button (the one with the sigma (Σ) on it). Excel "guesses" which cells you want to total and writes a formula with the SUM function and references to the cells. You can use this feature in a variety of ways—even to total more than one column or row at a time.

Use the Function Wizard to write complex formulas (EG/ML). The Function Wizard not only provides on-line help to help you understand functions, but it takes you every step of the way through the creation of a formula with one or more functions.

Change relative references to absolute references with a keystroke (EC). If you've already entered a cell reference in a formula and want to change the reference type, select the cell reference and press ⌘T until Excel places the absolute reference dollar sign(s) where you want them.

Split the screen so headings stay put (CB). Excel has a little black bar at the very top of the vertical scroll bar. Drag the bar down as far as you wish to split the screen— you can then scroll either the top *or* bottom half of the window. Splitting the screen into left and right sections works the same way—look for the split bar to the left of the horizontal scroll bar.

Use shortcut menus (CB/ML). Hold down the ⌘ and Option keys at the same time and click on a selection. A pop-up menu with commands that can be used on the selection appears. If you hold down ⌘ and Option and click on a toolbar, you'll get a pop-up menu of other toolbars you can display.

Float a toolbar (CB). Position the mouse pointer anywhere on a toolbar other than on a button and drag the toolbar down from the top of the screen. You'll get a floating toolbar that you can put anywhere you like. Drag it back up (or down or to the side) to "dock" it again.

Make a column the best width (CB). To automatically make a column just wide enough to display the longest item in the column, double-click on the line to the right of the column letter in the column heading area.

Rename sheets (EC). You can change the name of a worksheet in an Excel workbook by double-clicking the sheet tab for the sheet and then entering a new name in the Rename dialog box that appears.

ClarisWorks Tips

(CB)

Put some color in your spreadsheets. Select a range of cells to color, then use the color pop-up (next to the paint bucket in the toolbar) to choose a color. Can't see black text against your colored background? Pick a text color for selected cells with the Text Color command from the Format menu.

Show the Shortcuts palette. There are all kinds of time-saving buttons on it: one to format numbers as currency, another to format them as percentages, another to add them up. Choose Shortcuts from the File menu.

Zoom out to see more of your work at once. Click the small mountains button at the bottom left of a spreadsheet window to zoom out; click the big mountains button to zoom in. In addition to displaying your current magnification level, the number in the bottom left corner of the window lets you zoom as far as you want to in a single move. Just click on the number, hold the mouse button down, slide to the desired zoom percentage, and let go.

Use the Fill Special command to type stuff for you. Need to enter a series of months into adjacent cells? Click in a cell that contains the first month of the series and drag to the right or down as far as you want to go. Then choose Fill Special from the Calculate menu. This works for all kinds of series.

Copy and paste formatting. Select a cell with formatting you want to copy to other cells. Then choose Copy Format from the Edit menu. Now select the cells you want to copy the format to and choose Paste Format from the Edit menu. The formatting of the first cell is copied to the other cells. This is much easier than choosing formatting options such as font, size, color, or style by hand and it always works perfectly.

Split the screen, so headings stay put when you scroll. ClarisWorks, like Excel, has a little black bar at the very top of the vertical scroll bar. Drag the bar down as far as you wish—whatever is above the bar will be frozen as everything else scrolls below. Horizontal splitting works similarly—look for the split bar to the left of the horizontal scroll bar.

Make a column the best width. This works just like Excel—to automatically make a column just wide enough to display the longest item in the column, double-click on the line to the right of the column letter in the column heading area.

Use the Lock Title Position command to keep column titles in sight (DC). Not only does this prevent column titles from scrolling out of the window, but it ensures that column titles print on each page. It's also a handy way to identify a range of cells.

Editors' Poll: For What Do You Use Spreadsheet Software Most Often?

SA: Quick budget-type things (for both work and home stuff); recently, a more complex worksheet to calculate promotion rankings for a university promotions committee!

TA: Keeping track of my comic books, income status, and invoicing.

DC: Keeping my laboratory and tutor/TA ledgers (at the University of Chicago Department of Computer Science).

JC: I use ClarisWorks spreadsheets for various things—almost none of them financial. I've used it to create a quick sign-up form. Also for creating home budgets and even for creating lists of things to do. You gotta love those nice clean lines!

MC: Keeping track of assets in the multimedia project on which I'm working.

BF: I don't use a spreadsheet.

KT: I use spreadsheets for two completely different sorts of tasks.

1. The normal stuff—I have a complex estimating sheet for quoting design jobs; it took years to develop. I also keep other financial information in other spreadsheets—cost basis for inherited stocks, for example.

2. As an interim tool for doing database publishing. Export data from a d/b program as tab-delimited text, set it up in a spreadsheet, introduce new columns of cells and use them to enter style tags, export again as tab-delimited text, delete the tab character between the tag delimiters (>) and tagged text, and place the text in QuarkXPress or, now, at last, PageMaker.

JH: I don't use Spreadsheets.

ML: Tracking telephone expenses and business miles.

SS: Two things: tracking personal tax data and cleaning up address data before importing it into yet another PIM.

BW: I use Excel mainly to create product/feature tables for magazine articles and books. I also use it to keep a running tally of my estimated State and Federal income taxes. With the spreadsheet, I don't estimate my tax, I *know*, day by day, and I pay what I *owe*, not what I'm supposed to have estimated based on previous years.

10 Personal & Business Management

When it comes right down to it, managing your life and your business is about getting access to the right information when you need it, in a form that is instantly usable. Welcome to personal and business management software, designed to help you manage your time, your schedule, your money, and your personal and business contacts.

Many of those tasks belong to a category of software called *personal information managers,* or PIMs. They combine the functionality of address books, calendars, schedulers, and to-do lists, among other things.

For financial management, there are many accounting packages for the Macintosh. We've divided this category into software that makes sense for individuals and for small businesses.

Finally, there are also many other programs that are equally useful to businesses but have nothing to do with money, contacts, or time management. We provide information on a pair of useful business programs in the "More Business Software" section at the end of the chapter.

Contributors

Steve Schwartz (SS)
is the chapter editor.

Maria Langer (ML)
is the author of ten
Macintosh books and
numerous articles and
reviews. She is the pub-
lisher of the *Macintosh
Tips & Tricks* news and
productivity newsletter
and was an accountant
in a former life.

Crosby! (C!) earns his
living as a graphic de-
signer, commercial pho-
tographer, print broker,
consultant, and author.
He is also a top sales
professional and credits
using his computers to
keep on top of things as
a major reason for his
success. His motto:
"You can never have
too many Macs."

**Connie Guglielmo
(CG)** was this chap-
ter's editor for the fifth
edition.

Arthur Naiman (AN),
Scott Beamer (SB),
and **Rochelle Garner
(RG)** were all contribu-
tors to earlier versions
of *The Macintosh Bible*,
from which parts of this
chapter were taken.

Contents

Managing Time and Contacts (RG)

In recent years, *personal information managers* (PIMs) have grown. Now a single program (or an integrated *pair* of programs) is designed to tackle the all-encompassing job of keeping track of your working life.

Take address books, for example. For the most part, these handy electronic card files have been superseded by a genre of PIM software called *contact managers*. Not content to simply track names and numbers, contact managers are true databases that let you organize, sort, and arrange every person in your life by whatever criteria you choose. Most also let you write letters, create faxes, and print on a variety of envelopes and labels. No wonder many people consider contact managers their most important software. Calendar programs also have assumed larger roles—scheduling and reminding you of weekly meetings, appointments, and to-do items.

The latest twist in PIMs though, is a merging of contact managers with schedulers that have been linked with system software to automatically update and attach shared information. So when your calendar tells you that you've promised to have a conference call with Wilma and Fred on Friday, a mouse click not only finds their phone number but also dials the number for you. Thus, you'll find that most of the PIMs are either all-in-one programs or they pair a contact manager with a calendar program, offering them as a bundle.

ACT! (C!)

ACT! 2.5 ($200, Symantec) doesn't make coffee, but if you need to keep track of people, appointments, phone calls, correspondence, and things to do, it can increase your productivity. ACT! is not a basic PIM nor a replacement for that paper calendar you've been carrying around—although it can print out enough different styles of calendar pages to make buying refills for paper calendars a thing of the past. ACT! is an industrial strength, multi-

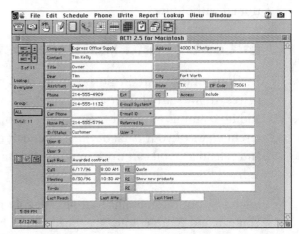

Act! records can display standard address and phone information, scheduled meetings and phone calls, and a record of previous contacts.

platform (Macintosh, Newton, PC, and several brands of palmtop computers) contact, correspondence, and schedule management system.

With ACT! you won't have to worry about people getting misplaced or events falling through the cracks. You can have an unlimited number of databases for contacts (prospects, club members, and so on) or a huge database with everyone in it that you can narrow down by using lookups.

ACT! has a full-featured word processor with mail merge capabilities. Date-stamped notes help refresh your memory concerning what was said and done. A calendar (day, week, month) with alarms makes sure that you make those appointments and calls when you said you would. ACT! also has an auto-dialer with call timer and call status (attempted, completed, and so on), a report generator, and a macro recorder with clickable icons to speed up repetitive tasks. Mobile professionals will love the ability to synchronize their contact data with co-workers, the home office, or their desktop computer.

There are 15 user fields that you can change to suit your needs. You can also change the labels and data types (be careful!) for all the other fields, too. ACT! can fax documents, create custom templates, send and receive e-mail, attach documents to e-mail letters using PowerTalk, and integrate data with other applications using AppleScript.

All of this power comes with a steep learning curve. ACT! is not really an install-and-get-right-to-work application, but the time taken to master it is well spent. The manual is rather thick, but it's well-written and easy to understand. An Apple Guide-based Quick Start Guide, on-line help, and an easy-to-follow tutorial get you quickly started. Once you've mastered ACT!, you'll wonder how you ever functioned without it.

In Control and FastPace Instant Contact   (SS)

In Control ($85, Attain Corporation) is an organizer/planner/list manager extraordinaire. Attain started with a familiar tool—an outliner—and made it more useful by adding columns to it and then linking it to a calendar. In Control provides four different views of your data: outline, calendar, day, and combo (displays both the outline and calendar). You can work in whatever views are appropriate for the task or project at hand.

Each new outline contains four default columns: Description, Start, End, and Priority. You can add more columns as needed and hide or delete others that aren't essential. In addition to main outline headings, you can also have multiple outline levels—each indicated by indenting. You can rearrange outline items—moving them from one spot to another or changing their indent level—by simply clicking and dragging. You can add items or move them between views in the same way. For example, to associate a to-do item with a particular day, you can just drag it from the outline to the calendar.

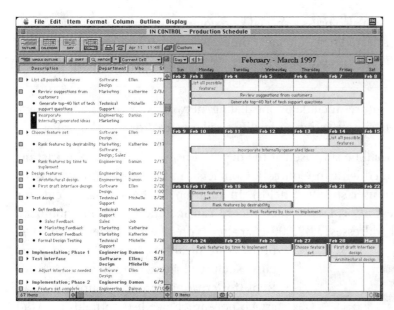

In Control's Combo view is used to examine and work with information in both the outline and calendar at the same time.

You can schedule events by typing them into a day in the calendar or by entering a start date for them in the outline. If you precede an outline item with a time (as in, "9a Meeting with Bob"), it is set as an appointment in that day's calendar. If no time is specified, it automatically is treated as a to-do item for that day. You can automatically move uncompleted to-do items to the following day.

Scheduled events can also have alarms (called "reminders") associated with them. If you install the In Control Reminder control panel, reminders are triggered whether In Control is currently running or not. Otherwise, they only appear when In Control is active.

You can sort an outline (or part of an outline) based on the contents of any of the outline columns. The Match command makes it simple to see just the outline information that is important to you at the moment. For instance, in the outline made to handle assignments for this chapter of *The Macintosh Bible*, I can select any contributor's name, click Match, and immediately see the status of that person's assignments.

GOOD
FEATURE

In Control 4 includes two useful features for working with the Internet. First, any outline item can be linked to a Web site. Once linked, there are several simple procedures and commands for connecting to the site. You must also, however, obtain and install **Internet Config**, a freeware utility, for this to work. (Outline items can also be linked to particular programs or documents, too.) Second, In Control can import Netscape Navigator bookmarks and extract all URLs from HTML documents, creating links to each one. In Control 4 also has extensive support for drag-and-drop editing. For example, you can create new outline items by dragging text selections in from other applications. You can also press a special key sequence in other programs to create a "clipping" of the selected text. The next time you open an In Control file—even after shutting down the Mac—all new clippings are automatically added to the first outline you open.

Other useful program features include phone dialing, network support for shared outlines, and QuickSteps (a simple scripting facility similar to that of FileMaker Pro).

For a low-cost PIM, you'll be surprised at the depth of features in **FastPace Instant Contact** ($50, or bundled with In Control). Contacts can be viewed individually or as a scrolling list (with user-specified fields). In addition to the standard fields for work and home address information, each record can include ten phone numbers, pager IDs, and e-mail addresses; a 32,000-character Notes field; a dozen or so additional customizable fields; and user-defined tags, such as Friend, Medical, and Sales Reps (for creating contact groups). You can attach pop-up choice lists to fields to avoid repetitive typing (for salutations, such as Mr. and Ms., for example). You can dial any phone number in a record by simply clicking the telephone icon beside the number. And if you're on a network, you can use FastPace to share a company- or department-wide contact file.

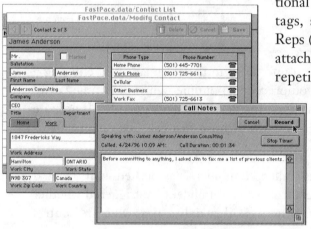

You can set FastPace to automatically display a Call Notes window (lower-right) whenever a call is dialed through the program. The date, time, and duration are saved as part of the call notes.

While FastPace's powerful search capabilities enable you to perform complex searches based on the contents of one or several fields (this is great for creating mailing list groups), and you can save searches that you use frequently, this flexibility can get in the way if all you need to do is find Sam Jensen's phone number. If your contact list doesn't contain thousands of people, you may find it easier to just keep your database sorted, bring it up in list view, and scroll to the name you want. (When I need a phone number, I want it *now*!) You can sort contacts in from one to three fields.

HOT TIP

FastPace has the most extraordinary printing capabilities of any PIM that I've seen! With its built-in, full-featured word processor, you can create and print address books, faxes, letters, labels, and envelopes. You can pull merge data from fields in your contact database.

GOOD FEATURE

FastPace also has impressive import capabilities that work like those of FileMaker Pro. After selecting options and previewing the incoming data, you can save the import instructions as a reusable template. If you use a spreadsheet to clean up address data before importing, you'll really appreciate FastPace's ability to strip out the quotation marks that often surround address fields and company names.

In Control is integrated with FastPace Instant Contact in precisely the same manner as it is with FileMaker Pro, Dynodex, TouchBase Pro, and Now Contact. That is, you can define lookups that copy information from a single field in a contact database into the current In Control document. While impressive-sounding, this feature has some limitations. First, only *exact* matches are identified, so you must be sure to type the match data exactly the way that it was entered in your database. Second, only the *first* match is found. If you have 25 entries for "Apple Computer," you'll never see the last 24. If your contact database has an Entire Name field (combining first and last names), you'll have better luck finding the right record than by basing lookups on Last Name or Company.

Now Up-to-Date and Now Contact   (ML)

Now Up-to-Date and **Now Contact** ($100 as bundle or $75 each, Now Software) are a feature-packed scheduling and contact management duo. Although they're avail-

able separately, you'll probably want to use them together to take advantage of their complete feature sets. Both have an intuitive interface and features that make it quick and easy to add, edit, and find information.

Now Up-to-Date is the scheduling application—you use it to add events to your calendar file. An event can be a to-do item, appointment, meeting, special event, or another kind of event (the type of event you choose determines how it appears on your calendar and what time and date options are available).

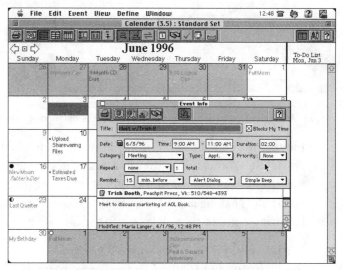

In Now Up-to-Date, you schedule events such as appointments. You can link events to records in Now Contact so contact information appears in the Event window.

For example, if you add an appointment to your calendar, you can specify a start and end time; if you add a to-do item, you can tell Now Up-to-Date to forward it automatically to the next day if you don't complete it. You can code events with categories, set them to repeat, and create reminders. Your calendar can appear in a variety of customizable views, including month, week, multi-day, day, and List views. You can also have the day's events appear on a QuickDay menu that you can put in your menu bar.

Now Contact is a contact management application. You use it to record the names, addresses, and other contact information for individuals and organizations. It offers separate fields for each piece of information, including two separate groups of fields for work and home addresses, four telephone fields, and eight custom fields you can use for whatever information you like. An area at the bottom of the Detail View window for a contact includes space for entering time- and date-stamped notes and attaching documents. You can assign categories and keywords to contacts to put them in various groups, search the contact database by any field, and print information in a wide variety of completely customizable print formats, including labels, envelopes, and address books. You can also add the people you call most to a QuickContact menu on the menu bar.

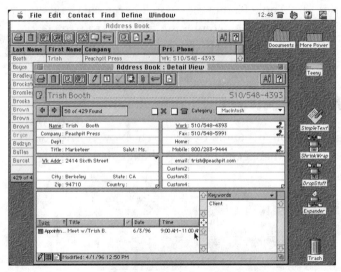

In Now Contact, you can enter a wide variety of information about a contact. Any linked events appear in a list at the bottom of the window.

To tap the full power of Now Up-to-Date and Now Contact, you can use them together to create links from your calendar file to your contact file. For example, say you add an appointment event to your calendar file. You can link that event to the contact records of the person you plan to meet. This way, that person's contact information is readily available, right in your calendar file. Making a link this way also adds an appointment to the contact file, so when browsing contact records, you can quickly access the appointments attached to them.

With version 3.6, Now Up-to-Date and Contact became "Internet aware." The Public Event and Public Contact Servers can automatically create linked Web pages that show events and contacts in all kinds of ways. While browsing the World Wide Web, if you see a Now Up-to-Date or Contact Web page with an event or contact that you want to add to one of your files, just drag it from the Web page to the appropriate Now application. It'll be added instantly.

Now Up-to-Date and Contact, which include the Server applications, are available separately for about $75 each or together as a bundle for about $100. When used in a networking environment, each user can link his events and contacts to the public calendar and contact file. This makes it easy to check the availability of co-workers, schedule meetings, and keep track of company-wide events. Because each network user must have his own version of the client application, Now offers multiuser packs and site licensing. The Web Publishing version of the Now Up-to-Date and Contact bundle costs about $300, but if you plan to publish events or contacts on the Internet, its automatic Web page creation capabilities will make your life a lot easier.

One more thing … if you're a Newton user, be sure to check out **Now Synchroniz**e ($30). This package lets you synchronize the Names and Dates file on your Newton with the Contact and Calendar file on your desktop Mac.

Now TouchBase and DateBook Pro (ML)

The **TouchBase and DateBook Pro** ($50, Now Software) organizer package has changed hands more times in the past few years than any other package I know. Developed years ago by After Hours Software (you might remember the ads with Guy Kawasaki), it went to Aldus, which was purchased by Adobe, and finally ended up at Now Software. Along the way, the package was revised and updated several times.

Now TouchBase and DateBook Pro have the same generous feature sets as Now Contact and Now Up-to-Date. Their interfaces, however, are quite different, giving the packages a different look and feel. To me, Contact and Up-to-Date have a cleaner, less cluttered interface. But certain features of TouchBase and DateBook—such as the Alphabetical Index Tabs in the List view of the contact file and the graphical Time Bar in Detail view of the calendar file—can be very useful at times.

A strength of TouchBase is its FastLetter feature, which offers fully customizable, built-in mail merge functions. When combined with the powerful search engine, this feature makes sending out form letters a breeze.

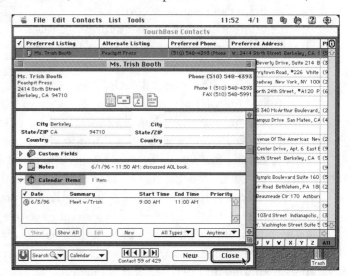

Use TouchBase to enter contact information and link it to your DateBook calendar file.

DateBook offers categorization of events by project, helping you keep tasks organized by their related projects. Unlike Contact and Up-to-Date, however, neither TouchBase nor DateBook have networking capabilities, so they're best suited for individual users.

A CD-ROM of Now TouchBase and DateBook Pro sells for $70 and includes 45 City Guides. PowerBook users who are constantly on the go may find the City Guides very useful—they contain restaurant, hotel, museum, and other city information in contact files that you can take on the road.

InTouch and DateView   (SS/RG)

You want simple? The venerable address book **InTouch** ($70, Prairie Group) fits that description. You launch it from the menu. That approach buys you speed—for quickly calling up that phone number you need while working on your research report, for instance. What you see when you call up InTouch is a Rolodex-size screen that

sports a colorful, immediately understandable interface for working with names and addresses. InTouch lets you type in free-form information, an approach that's comfortable to use, although it poses problems if you want to export your information into another program that uses fields.

Although data entry is free-form, InTouch 2.5 can sort the records based on the contents of one or two address lines. You also associate each record with groups, so you can view just local merchants or Las Vegas hotels, for example. One of InTouch's strongest

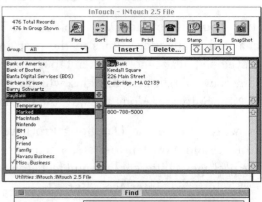

This simple interface makes InTouch one of the easiest-to-use address books.

GOOD FEATURE

features—the one that's kept me as a faithful customer for all these years—is its blindingly fast search capabilities. In most other contact managers, you can only execute a search after setting criteria for it—the particular field to be searched; whether the text is at the beginning, end, or just contained in the field; and the text string to find. Because InTouch is not a field-oriented program, the entire record is automatically searched—there're no fields you have to specify. You can even set InTouch to automatically display the Find window whenever it's launched. That way, you can immediately type the search string, click Find (or press Return), and quickly locate the person, phone number, or address needed.

Beyond the address book, InTouch 2.5 sports an appointment/calendar reminder, a phone dialer, and a print facility for envelopes, labels, address books, and fax cover sheets. With an included control panel called Snap*, you can even print envelopes using selected text in your word processor or automatically create a new InTouch record without first having to launch InTouch.

InTouch also has a companion appointment book—**DateView 2.6** ($70), a desk accessory that works with InTouch or by itself. (The two programs can be purchased as a bundle for $100.) As with InTouch, figuring out DateView is simplicity itself. Buttons and dialog boxes are self-explanatory. You create an event (for a point in time, a block of time, a date, or a to-do item) by double-clicking on a day or by clicking and dragging to the displayed beginning and end times. You can optionally set a priority for each event, as well as set an alarm to remind you when it's going to come due.

InTouch and DateView easily share their data. Any DateView event can be linked with an InTouch record. To create the link, you click the Link button in DateView, type the InTouch text you want to find (a person's name or company, for example), and then you are shown a list of all matches. Pick the correct one, and the link is established. To view the linked record (to see the person's phone number, for instance), you just click the appropriate button in the reminder when it pops up. Linking is simple and effective.

By comparison, DateView isn't as full-featured as many of the competing calendar programs. But it is fast and easy to use, and—for many people—that will be all that's needed.

Claris Organizer (SS)

Claris Organizer ($50, Claris Corporation) offers the basic features of most PIMs, including a contact database, appointments and alarms, to-do items, attachments (notes or documents from other programs, for example), and phone dialing. However, Claris Organizer distinguishes itself from the pack when it comes to intelligence.

That's right, Organizer is smarter than the average PIM. When you create an appointment or to-do that mentions someone's name or a company, the program quickly lists all potential matching contact records. To associate one of them with the event, it only takes a button click. For instance, if the event is "Call Jim," Organizer displays all Jim contact records. If you're more specific and say "Call Jim at Claris," Organizer only shows the records of people named Jim who happen to work at Claris. There are other instances of intelligence, too. Organizer can automatically complete contact record entries as you type and—instead of having to scroll through your contact list—

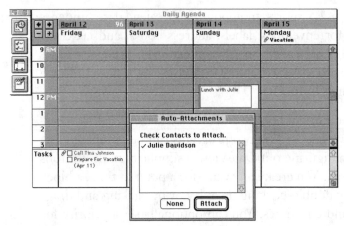

Claris Organizer is a bright program. If you create an event with a person's or company's name in it, Organizer automatically presents an appropriate list of contact records that you may wish to attach to the event.

you can just press a letter and Organizer chooses the first contact record whose last name begins with the letter.

Other notable features of Claris Organizer include color-coded categories for contacts, a note window that automatically appears whenever you dial a phone number through the program, a fast and simple Find feature (you don't have to specify a field to search), and customizable contact fields and categories.

CAT IV   (C!)

CAT IV (Contacts Activities and Time) is a very different kind of contact manager ($495, Chang Labs). It is document-based, fully relational, and *fast*! CAT combines the capabilities of a contact manager, word processor, database, spreadsheet, and forms program into one neat package.

You work in CAT with Name Cards, Documents, and Templates. *Name Cards* contain the names and addresses of your accounts (companies). You can have an unlimited number of contacts per company, avoiding unnecessary duplication. *Documents* are anything you attach to an account, such as phone notes, faxes, letters, contracts, and so on. *Templates* are documents that you create to use over and over. There are also basic drawing tools that you can use to create complex forms with shading, math functions, and cross-links to other forms.

CAT uses a clairvoyant method of looking up account and contact information. Click in the Account or Contact area, and start typing the company name you want to find. CAT immediately starts searching for companies with names that match what you're typing. Often, a letter or two is all that's needed.

Clicking on the New box brings up the list of templates that you've created (from a simple letter format to complex forms); all the pertinent company and contact information is automatically entered. Type any necessary text and click Print. CAT automatically saves the document with a date/time stamp so you know when you created it and then prints it. (Changes are automatically saved to a special CHG file, but you have to tell CAT to save the file to your disk.)

BAD FEATURE

All Name Cards, Documents, and Templates are saved in *one* file—so there's only one to back up! My data file is almost six years old, has 928 accounts, and contains many letters, faxes, contracts, quotes, invoices, and phone notes. Yet it still fits on a single floppy! This data file not only gives you a time- and date-stamped list of everything you've ever done with a particular account, but you can also view any original item in its entirety.

CAT lets you sort and view Name Cards by using groups called Views. A View can be created using almost any criteria you can think of: everyone in Washington State,

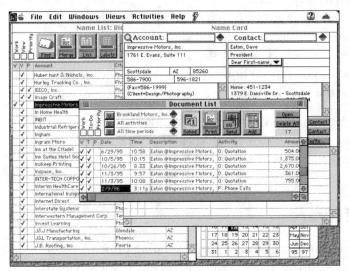

In CAT IV, windows is the name of the game.

all prospects, all directors of marketing, or all prospects in Washington State who are not directors of marketing, for example. Once you group the appropriate accounts into a View, you can merge them with any document that you'd like to send as a mass mailing.

Another unique feature of CAT is *tactics*. CAT allows you to trigger the automatic creation of up to four activities per document. For example, you might send out a brochure and want to be reminded to follow up in a week with a phone call, a week later with a letter, and three days later with another call.

Don't get the impression that everything about CAT is perfect. The manuals are thin and not as comprehensive as they should be. Although the Name Card note areas will hold a lot of data, they're very small and you can end up scrolling your life away. You're better off creating a separate Notes template and appending it as needed. And although CAT will show you your daily, weekly, or any other date range of to-do items, it does not have alarms or an integrated calendar. One particularly bad design element is that if you enter a lot of data on a Name Card and forget to click the Enter box before continuing, you lose all of the changes.

CAT has a loyal following despite these problems. Personally, I've experimented with just about every contact manager on the market and CAT IV is the one I still use. It does far too much and operates too fast for me to replace it.

Managing Your Finances

Financial management applications run the gamut from low-cost programs designed to automate your checkbook, manage your investments, and help you prepare your taxes, to multimodule integrated applications for managing the books of companies ranging in size from mom-and-pop stores to large corporations.

Personal finance programs, designed to help individual users get a grip on their personal expenses, generally rely on a very simple interface (often based on a checkbook). Once entered and categorized, information can be retrieved and viewed in a variety of ways. Every time you "write" a check, for instance, you can assign it a category (such as food or entertainment). With a few clicks, you can see how much you've spent on food that month, for several months, or for the year to date.

The *small-business programs* are the next step up, based on the double-entry accounting system of debits and credits and offering more sophisticated account tracking and reporting capabilities, including balance sheets, profit and loss statements, and amortization schedules.

Personal Finance Software

Many families manage their personal finances with a simple guiding principle: "Am I spending less than I make? Yes—then my finances must be in order." If you would like a little more control over your spending and a lot more information about exactly where your money is going, the programs we discuss in this section may be just what you need. Quicken and Managing Your Money are popular personal finance programs, MacInTax can help you make short work of your federal and state tax returns, and WealthBuilder simplifies investment tracking and management.

Quicken (ML). For the accounting-phobic, there's **Quicken** ($45, Intuit), an entry-level bookkeeping package. This inexpensive program—which is updated annually to add features—uses a checkbook-like interface to record transactions. But Quicken is far more than a checkbook program. It includes comprehensive budgeting, loan and investment tracking, and reporting features. A QuickFill feature keeps track of all information related to transactions, so you don't have to enter a recurring transaction more than once. The Quicken Financial Calendar lets you schedule transactions and have Quicken either remind you about them or automatically record them for you. Quicken also supports on-line banking, so you can make transactions via a modem.

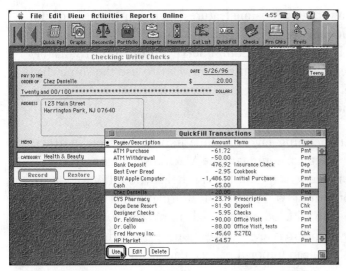

Quicken's QuickFill feature makes it easy to record recurring transactions. Either begin typing the payee name and let Quicken complete the entry or choose an entry from the QuickFill List window.

My favorite feature is Quicken Quotes, which uses my modem to connect to CompuServe and retrieve the current prices of stocks and bonds I own or want to monitor. With the click of a button, I can update the market value of my investments, so I know just how much I've gained (or lost!) on each stock. Quicken can also produce line graphs of an investment's price levels, making it easy to see performance. Of course, you must have an account on CompuServe or use the Quicken Quotes Hotline 900 number to use this feature. If you prefer to handle your investments off-line, you can enter investment value information manually and have Quicken track it for you.

Managing Your Money (ML). For Mac users on a tight budget, there's **Managing Your Money** ($20, MECA Software). This basic personal and business accounting package helps you keep track of the money you spend, as well as plan for the future.

Managing Your Money's interface is referred to as the SmartDesk window, a graphical representation of an office with a desk, bookshelf, and wall charts. You click on an element to record a transaction or perform a task. For example, when you click the Register on the desk, the checkbook register appears and displays your transactions; when you click the Mortgage book on the shelf, a Mortgage Refinancing form appears, ready to calculate interest and payments. The SmartFill feature completes transactions based on previous entries. The Report and Graph Galleries make it easy to get information about your financial status or spending patterns.

Managing Your Money, the least expensive personal and business accounting package we found, uses an office-like interface to access its features.

Managing Your Money supports a variety of on-line features, including electronic bill-paying with CheckFree, portfolio pricing with QuoteLink, and VISA card balance monitoring with CompuServe. It comes with CompuServe Information Manager, so you can set up a CompuServe account—assuming you want to use the somewhat costly on-line features. Of course, you don't *have* to use any of these features to get the most out of Managing Your Money.

MacInTax (SS/SB/CG). An overwhelming favorite since its introduction in 1985, **MacInTax** ($40, Intuit) helped define tax planning on the Macintosh. This easy-to-use program, continually updated to reflect changes in tax law, helps you fill out your tax forms. To simplify the process of putting your financial information in digital form, MacInTax provides solid on-line help—including material from various IRS publications. A feature called "The EasyStep Interview" guides you through the process of selecting and filling out tax forms. You can import financial data from Quicken to save some typing time.

On screen you see exact replicas of IRS forms, but there's an important difference: The forms do the calculations for you, and they're linked so that a figure you enter (or that is calculated) on one form automatically appears wherever you need it on other forms (and changes if the first figure changes). In addition to its ability to print your return on facsimiles of IRS-approved forms, MacInTax returns can also be filed electronically (for an additional fee), or you can print a 1040ES (an abbreviated, numbers-only tax form that can reduce a 15-page return to just a couple of sheets of paper). If you run a small business, you may want to check out the new **MacInTax for Business** ($80); it offers additional filing help for sole proprietors, partnerships, corporations, and S-corporations.

The changes in the current version of MacInTax are minor. Perhaps the biggest are the multimedia features available in **MacInTax Deluxe** ($50). A pair of tax advisors appears in an extensive series of QuickTime movies, offering tax information, strategies, and advice. The text of two tax books is also included: *How to Pay Zero Taxes* and *The Money Income Tax Handbook*. If you've never done your own taxes, you'll find this material invaluable. On the other hand, if you've done your taxes for years (like me), you can save a few bucks by sticking with the standard version of MacInTax. There's little new information for the tax-savvy.

HOT TIP

Nobody's perfect, though. For the past two years, MacInTax (and most other tax programs) has been plagued by reports of calculation errors. Most users, however, have little to fear. The types of situations that trigger errors are usually *very* obscure—along the lines of a self-employed organ grinder who had casualty losses in the previous year and is depreciating his monkey over a three-year period rather than five years. Besides, if MacInTax is responsible for a calculation error, Intuit will pay the IRS penalty and interest.

Although I'm perfectly capable of doing my own taxes, I've entrusted this task to MacInTax for the last four years. On average, it has reduced the time needed to prepare my taxes from two weeks (doing it manually) to under three days. If you value your time and your return can't be handled by a simple 1040EZ, you're a good candidate for MacInTax.

WealthBuilder (SS). Although programs like Quicken can track what you've done with your money, **WealthBuilder** ($50, Reality Online) focuses on taking the money you have and helping you increase it. Unlike the personal finance programs, WealthBuilder isn't concerned with bill paying and credit card tracking. It's a financial planning and investment management program designed to handle the big bucks and the big picture.

WealthBuilder can calculate your net worth; assist with budgeting; help plan for future objectives, such as retirement or financing your child's college education; and track investments. It includes a series of financial calculators that you can use for insurance and estate planning, determining how expensive a house you can afford, and calculating loan and mortgage details.

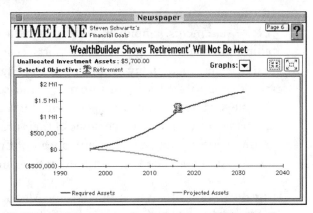

In combination with an account with Reuters Money Network ($7 to $20 per month), WealthBuilder users can get stock quotes; perform on-line trades; update the program's extensive research databases for stocks, bonds, and mutual funds; get the latest news on their investments through a clippings service; download historical data and obtain detailed company reports; and subscribe to investment newsletters. Unlike most on-line ser-

In WealthBuilder, you can plan for the future with the Objective Manager. As this chart graphically illustrates, however, not only will I not meet my retirement goals, I'll be half a million in debt! (Send contributions in care of Peachpit Press.)

vices, you don't interact with this one at all. Before connecting, you simply tell WealthBuilder what information and updates you want. After you click the Connect button, the data is fetched for you and the modem automatically disconnects. You never have to worry about wasting time on-line.

One of WealthBuilder's strengths is how it helps you select new investments from its databases. To do this, you create *filters* (formulas that set criteria for selecting investments). You might, for example, create a filter that chooses only stocks with a *P/E ratio* (price to earnings) below 12 and a five-year record of increased earnings. You apply the filter, and WealthBuilder presents a list of investments that meet the criteria. Similar formulas can be created for *alerts* that you can use as buy or sell indicators. (An alert can be a notification that a specific stock or bond price has been reached or that an important financial event has occurred.)

Small Business Accounting Software

Keeping a good set of books can sometimes make the difference between survival and failure for a small business. Remember, though, that someone has to be responsible for learning the software, setting it up, and using it on an ongoing basis. There's also no benefit in having the data in electronic form and generating lots of reports if no one uses the reports to make informed management decisions.

Small-business accounting packages are aimed at companies that have to keep track of the finances and costs associated with a few employees and numerous suppliers and clients. These applications provide the kinds of reports that investors, banks, and the IRS require of businesses, including comprehensive balance sheets, profit and loss (P&L) statements, employee tax and benefit calculations, client records (including billing and receivables), inventory reports, cost of goods sold, and the like. You'll often find that the functionality needed to do these tasks is relegated to various modules that are designed to work in an integrated and seamless environment (changes in one module for one account are reflected in the account records in other modules). Many companies offer free demo versions of their programs, allowing you to see what you're getting yourself and your staff into ahead of time. If you don't take the time to investigate first, it could end up costing you time and money later.

Big Business (ML). A newcomer to the Mac accounting software arena, **Big Business** ($400 single user/$800 network, Big Software) is billed as a *"complete management system."* It combines standard accounting functions found in other accounting packages with some contact management, marketing, and sales tools. The result: All business information is stored in one file that is handled by one program.

You access Big Business features with a customizable toolbar and card windows. Clicking buttons or tabs displays different options and forms. The interface is very easy

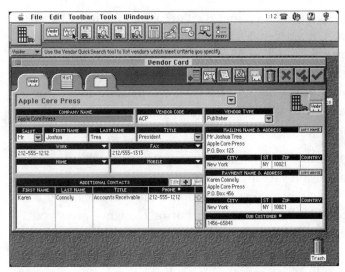

In Big Business, you access options and features by clicking buttons and tabs. Information is logically organized, making it easy to enter and find data.

to use and the feature set is well thought out. For sales and marketing, Big Business can keep track of customers, generate quotes, create and place sales orders, and track customer history. For inventory, it keeps track of vendors, creates purchase orders, monitors inventory levels, and supports bundled inventory items. For finance and accounting, it creates a wide range of reports, reconciles account balances, schedules vendor payments, and tracks receivables. The

BAD FEATURE

only glaring omission (and it's a big one) is payroll capabilities. But an upgrade with payroll features was in progress at the time of this writing.

One very cool feature of Big Business is its communication capabilities, enabling you to exchange messages (with or without card attachments) with other Big Business users. This feature, however, is only useful with the network version. And Big Business is a big program—you'll need 40MB of disk space and at least 8MB of RAM to run the single-user version.

GOOD FEATURE

M.Y.O.B. (ML). **M.Y.O.B. Small Business Accounting** ($80/$140 with payroll, Best!Ware) is an easy-to-use small business accounting package. (In case you're wondering, M.Y.O.B. stands for "Mind Your Own Business.") M.Y.O.B. includes general

ledger, invoicing, inventory and purchasing, accounts payable and receivable tracking, bids and estimates, job tracking, and contact management, all for a bargain price. If you need a program with payroll capabilities, **M.Y.O.B. with Payroll** is available.

M.Y.O.B.'s interface features Command Centers, each of which displays a window full of flowchart buttons. You click a button to enter transactions and perform tasks.

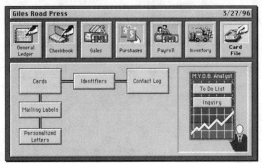

Use M.Y.O.B.'s Command Center to enter transactions, get information, and perform all basic tasks.

M.Y.O.B.'s forms are easy to understand and use, since they're based on familiar paper forms such as checks and invoices. The Easy-Fill feature offers automatic entry based on information you've entered previously. The M.Y.O.B. Analyst has buttons that make it simple to get financial information. There's plenty of on-line help, including a Getting Started videotape and a video help CD-ROM. I especially like "The World's Shortest Accounting Course" portion of the video. It makes me wonder why I spent four years to get an accounting degree.

M.Y.O.B.'s strength is its customizability. The setup process is a good example —M.Y.O.B. includes 100 different business templates that cover a wide range of business types. No matter which one you choose, you can customize the chart of accounts to include just the ones you need. The built-in Custom Forms Designer gives you complete control over the appearance of forms, such as checks and check stubs, invoices, and purchase orders. This level of flexibility is not often found in low-cost accounting software.

Peachtree Accounting for Macintosh (ML). Another easy-to-use accounting software package, **Peachtree Accounting for Macintosh** ($100, Peachtree Software), is for small- to medium-size businesses. It offers integrated general ledger, purchases and payment, sales and receipts, inventory, job tracking, and payroll features.

Peachtree Accounting for Macintosh (PAM) provides two ways to enter transactions and access program features. The Tasks menu on the menu bar lists basic categories of functions. Once you choose a task, a window with an Icon Bar for specific functions

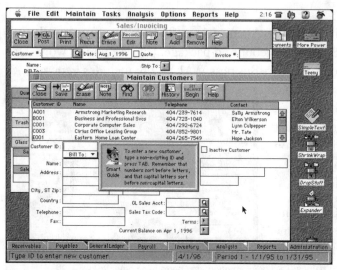

appears. The Navigation Aid—a row of folder tabs along the bottom of the window—also offers access to functions. You click a tab to display icons for different functions or lists. Then click the icon for the desired item to display an entry window or list. The entry windows represent commonly used paper forms, such as invoices and checks. Unfortunately, the inability to resize windows limits the amount of information you can see in a form. The Invoice form is a good example—it shows only two line items at a time.

Peachtree Accounting for Macintosh offers real double-entry accounting, made easy with forms and lists. Just try not to be frustrated by small windows that won't resize.

PAM is real double-entry accounting that is simplified through its forms. Accountants can still create entries by entering them into a general ledger. Batch entry posting is one example of a feature that's hard to find in accounting software packages. When combined with PAM's password-protection feature and multiuser capabilities, it provides a great way to set up an inexpensive, decentralized accounting system.

PAM includes a variety of on-line help features that make it easy to learn. Smart Guides are small help windows that appear when you activate certain form fields. You can click a Help icon in the Icon Bar of any window to display context-sensitive help. The Status Bar at the bottom of the screen also displays help messages, depending on the current task. PAM includes a tutorial, but it does little to teach you how to use PAM—instead, it simply illustrates and describes features. (It ran very slowly on my Power Mac.) You'll probably find the sample data file a lot more helpful if you'd like to learn PAM by experimentation.

Timeslips (ML). For people or organizations that bill based on time, **Timeslips** ($200, Timeslips Corporation) is the ultimate software. This package offers more time-based billing options than I thought existed, so I'm sure it'll meet the billing needs of the most demanding professionals, and the invoicing requirements of the pickiest clients. It also enables you to bill for expenses that you incur on behalf of a client, with or without a markup.

You access Timeslips' commands through the TSReport application's Timeslips Navigator window. (It reminds me a lot of the Control Center window in M.Y.O.B.) Set up users, clients, activities, and expenses. When it's time to record an activity or expense, create a new Time Slip. This launches the TSTimer application, displaying a form you can fill out for the activity or expense. You choose the user, client, activity, or expense from pop-up menus, and then enter the time or cost. If you're entering an activity that you're working on right now—such as a phone call or task performed at your desk—you can use the built-in timer to track the time spent.

When you're ready to create bills, you can choose which ones to print based on the user, client, activity, date, or other criteria. Timeslips' invoices are completely customizable, so you can modify them to fit on letterhead or existing forms. A built-in receivables feature lets you track payments, so you know what's outstanding and what's not. If you prefer, you can use **Timeslips Accounting Link** ($60) to transfer Timeslips data into your accounting program—it works with M.Y.O.B. and Peachtree Accounting, as well as a few others.

More Business Software   (C!)

Of course, there are many other types of programs for managing other types of business information. To give you a taste of what's out there, this section provides information on BizPlan Builder (a program for designing business plans) and Informed Designer/Manager (a pair of programs for designing and filling in business forms).

BizPlan Builder

"Plan your work and work your plan" is one of the axioms to running a successful business. Yet few small- to medium-size businesses invest the time to create the road map to their goal of business success—a business plan. Enter **BizPlan Builder** ($140, Jian), a set of word processing and spreadsheet templates and a comprehensive manual designed to painlessly take you step-by-step through the process of creating an effective professional business plan.

BizPlan Builder will help you take a good hard look at your business. You'll see where your company (or projected company) is now, create a vision statement, perform market analysis, plan your marketing, make financial projections, set realistic business goals, and look at methods of getting needed funds. You'll plug in your own figures, see the possible results of doing things in different ways, and determine what offers the greatest future potential. When you're done, you'll be able to confidently discuss with your banker or investors where the business is now and where it can go—in detail.

Included is 90 pages of pretyped and preformatted material (more than most businesses will ever need), allowing you to customize your plan by picking and choosing those items that relate to your business now and updating as things change and goals are realized. The templates are designed to be used with your existing word processing and spreadsheet software, letting you focus on creating a business plan without the burden of learning new software or spending hours typing and formatting text.

Informed Designer/Informed Manager

Remember all the talk about the "paperless office" and the promises of how—through the use of computers—our future would be free of all the paper that now clutters our lives? Seen or heard much about it lately? If Shana Corporation continues on the path they're on, we may actually get there. **Informed Designer** ($295, download it for free from their Web site, or get a special CD for the cost of shipping) and **Informed Manager** ($195) go a long way toward making forms design and management easy, interesting, and fun.

Informed Designer is an advanced page layout application specifically for forms. Creating complex multicolumn forms with colors and shaded areas, variable line thicknesses, checkboxes, social security and credit card number columns, and so on is a breeze. Informed Designer includes all the tools you'll need to re-create any form you've ever seen or can imagine.

With Informed Designer, you can develop detailed forms such as this one.

Informed Designer makes the design task easy. Select the Table Tool, click and drag, and you have a basic table. Click inside of the table and drag to create the number and width of desired columns. Control size and shape either by eye (with numeric feedback) or by using the Specs palette, where you can type in the sizes you want. A few more clicks and drags, the addition of some fill shading, and a logo, and you've painlessly created a professional-looking form.

From there you can print out the form for hand filing or use the advanced features of Designer to set the tab order, incorporate math functions, set defaults, and create lookups that link to other forms. To aid others in filling out the forms, you can create help messages that clarify what the desired input is or point to where the data can be found. Test mode allows you to do a thorough dry run to make sure the form functions to your satisfaction—without having to run Informed Manager (the companion form-filling program).

Once you're happy with the form, Informed Manager will automate the process of quickly and accurately filling it out. The program supports lookups, choice lists, calculations, form numbering, error-checking, password protection, AppleScript, text notes, voice annotation, and more. Completed forms can be searched, sorted, grouped, and batch processed. Informed Manager also supports most popular Mac e-mail systems. Newton owners will be happy to know that there's an Informed Filler for Newton that allows you to do remote data collection and then send the collected data to the desktop machine for processing.

[At this writing, Shana is completing Informed Designer/Manager 2. New features will include form attachments, buttons, Drag-and-Drop support, a customizable menu bar, routing lists, scrollable fields and tables, and spell checking. The programs will also run under Windows (providing cross-platform support) and be Power Mac native.—SS]

Editors' Poll:
Which PIM Do You Use and Why?

DC: I use Now Contact and Now Up-to-Date, along with Now Synchronize, so I keep my appointments and to-do's both on my Macs and my Newton. Very handy. The public events calendar in Now Up-to-Date 3.5 is particularly good for managing a group calendar, and the beta of 4.0, which works over the Web, is even handier. The Now stuff also has the big advantage of working with Windows versions.

JC: I've been using TouchBase Pro since version 1.0! It's a great program with a very clean interface and some excellent features.

TL: My favorite is Now Up-to-Date/Now Contact. There's nothing mysterious about why I like it best. No other program combines the ease-of-use, an attractive user interface, and the features that I crave as much as these do. I especially use its multitude of different types of events (from appointments to to-do's to banners) and the quick access to its databases via its Quick add-on menus.

MEC: I use Claris Organizer, because it is simple to use and I don't have very complex PIM needs. Also, it was a birthday present.

JH: Ah, I miss my favorite, DayMaker, long gone. I now use Now Contact and Now Up-to-Date, but only because they sync with my Newton MessagePad—or they would if the Sync utility didn't crash.

SS: I use a *lot* of programs. For quickly finding phone numbers, nothing beats InTouch. I use Expresso for its calendar and reminders, In Control for project planning (dealing with these chapters, for instance), and FileMaker for project record-keeping.

ML: I like Now Contact and Now Up-to-Date. They do everything I need, *including* sychronizing with my Newton Names and Dates files.

SZA: For heavy-duty work, such as product and vendor information for the chapters of this book that I worked on, I use FileMaker to keep track of things.

BW: I don't use any form of PIM. I realized I'd spend more time getting one set up and keeping it up to date than it would take to just get my projects finished. However, I do use Word as my PIM, on a project-by-project basis. Word Bookmarks serve as a sort of database index, and I keep a to-do list at the top of each project document.

11 Databases

If you're still keeping track of important names and addresses, recipes, or a CD collection using a word processor, you're a prime candidate for a database program.

In this chapter, we'll show you how databases organize information and explain the differences between flat-file and relational database programs. We'll also give you a rundown on the most popular software available so that you can decide which database program is right for you. Finally, at the end of the chapter, you'll find a collection of tips so you can get the most from your database program.

Contributors

Steve Schwartz (SS) is the chapter editor.

Jay Lee (JL) spent many years in technical support and is a veteran Mac user. He is currently working as a computer consultant and multimedia designer/producer in Silicon Valley.

Don Crabb (DC) is a well-known writer and *MacWEEK* columnist.

Elizabeth Castro (EC), Arthur Naiman (AN), Robert Lauriston (RL), John **Kadyk (JK),** Sharon **Zardetto Aker (SZA),** and **Susan McCallister (SM)** were all contributors to earlier versions of *The Macintosh Bible,* from which parts of this chapter were taken.

Contents

What Is a Database?   (SS/EC)

A database organizes information by dividing it up into small, discrete pieces called *fields*. An address book might be divided into name, address, and phone number fields; a checkbook into check number, payee, description, and amount fields. A computer can use these fields to help it quickly sift through huge amounts of data, perhaps in order to find a certain name (or check number or entry word) or to arrange a client list by ZIP code (or other criteria).

Spreadsheets versus Databases   (EC)

Spreadsheet and database programs provide similar ways of looking at information and, in fact, can perform many of the same functions. Each row of a spreadsheet contains a collection of pieces of information, each with its own label (the column label). You can think of the columns as *fields* and the rows as *records*. (If you don't know what fields and records are, don't worry, we explain them in "Parts of a Database File".)

And although you can create a database file with a spreadsheet program, and can search, sort, and perform calculations, you will be severely limited with respect to reports, entry forms, and other types of specialized layouts.

On the other hand, you can use a database as a spreadsheet, keeping track of monthly and yearly totals, for example, but you will have limited means of charting and creating what-if scenarios—a spreadsheet's most powerful feature.

The address book and checkbook mentioned above are all *database files* (or simply, *databases*). You create, view, and manipulate databases with a *database program* (also called a *database manager*), such as FileMaker Pro, Visual FoxPro, 4D, Helix Express, or Panorama. The tricky part is that many people use the term *database* when speaking about both the files and the programs. (To make things easy for you, we'll just refer to the files as *databases* and the applications as *database programs*.)

All of the programs discussed in this chapter can be used to create custom databases, enabling you to organize and present your information in any way you like. Some examples of home-grown databases are recipe files and videocassette catalogs, but many people also create contact managers, checkbook registers, and bookkeeping databases. If you'd rather just concentrate on entering data—leaving the design work to others—you'll be pleased to learn that most database programs include a variety of *templates* (preformatted databases that you can immediately put to use in your home or business).

Some stand-alone programs such as Now Contact and Act! are actually single-purpose database programs, usually marketed as "personal information managers." Using one of these programs may save you some time, effort, and money when compared to buying and working with a full-fledged database program.

HOT TIP

What Can You Do With a Database Program?   (SS/EC)

Word processors can also hold information such as names and addresses, recipes, and the contents of your CD collection. So why would you want to use a database program to organize that information? The answer lies in the way information is stored in a database. The information for each person, place, or thing within the database is stored as a discrete piece of information, such as a first name, check number, or recipe ingredient. This data segmentation allows the database program to access and manipulate the information quickly and easily, which in turn allows you to consult individual parts of your data, order it, and then output portions of it (or the whole thing).

Storing information in a database lets you view the same information in many ways, selected and ordered according to your current needs. For example, suppose you have a list of names and addresses. A database will allow you to order (that is, *sort*) the list by last name in order to create a printed phone directory, and later by ZIP code, so you can print labels for a bulk mailing. You can also quickly find the portions of your data you want to work with—say, all of your clients in the northeast, or just those who haven't placed an order in the last six months. These tasks would be much more difficult with a list stored in a word processing document.

Parts of a Database File   (SS/SZA/AN/SM/JK)

Here are some basic terms you need to know when using a database program. To help make them clearer, we'll compare each with a concrete, real-world example that you're undoubtedly familiar with—a Rolodex file.

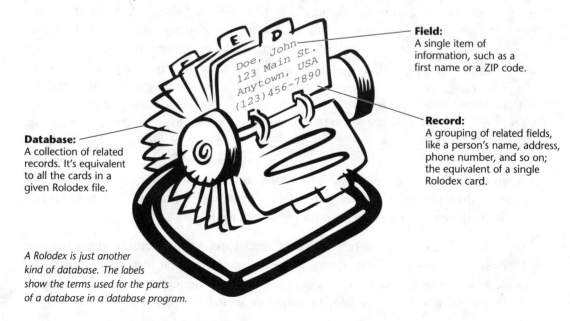

Field:
A single item of information, such as a first name or a ZIP code.

Record:
A grouping of related fields, like a person's name, address, phone number, and so on; the equivalent of a single Rolodex card.

Database:
A collection of related records. It's equivalent to all the cards in a given Rolodex file.

A Rolodex is just another kind of database. The labels show the terms used for the parts of a database in a database program.

Flat-File versus Relational (SS/EC)

The main difference between the two major kinds of database programs—*flat-file* and *relational*—is in their information-sharing capabilities. Suppose you have a database that you use to do invoicing. In order for the name and address of your client to appear on an invoice, the database must already contain fields for recording this information or there must be a link to another database that stores client addresses.

In a flat-file database program (such as Panorama), you normally include all necessary fields in one database. Thus, the address information would be an integral part of the invoicing database. In a relational database, a link (based on a key field such as an ID number) can be made to information in a Client database in which the address data is stored. Whenever you look at or print an invoice, the program consults the Client file and displays the latest address information.

The primary advantage of a flat-file database is ease of learning. Understanding how relations work, on the other hand, can be conceptually difficult. Advantages of relational databases include speed and the avoidance of duplicate data. Instead of copying or retyping address information into every database where it's needed, you can place it all in a single file and then simply *refer* to it.

Now that FileMaker Pro has become a full-fledged relational database program, the distinction between flat-file and relational programs has blurred considerably. Keep the following in mind, though: You can create flat-file databases in *any* database program. Just because a program has relational capabilities doesn't mean that you have to use them.

Choosing a Database Program

In this section, we review several of the leading database programs.

FileMaker Pro (JL)

Claris has finally released the long-awaited upgrade to **FileMaker Pro** ($200), the popular database program that many users favor for its ease of use and power. FileMaker Pro 3 adds many important new features, such as relational capabilities, more scripting options, improved text handling, and integrated mail merges (a real time- and sanity-saver for anyone who has to do this on a regular basis). Forty templates are provided for business, education, and home use that can either be used as is or modified to suit your needs. And for users who have made the jump to the Power PC, version 3 is accelerated for the Power Macintosh.

While some of the new capabilities increase the program's complexity, the basic features still work the same way. This means that it remains easy to use and is a good first program for database novices, but also gives previous users the ability to go relational without the steep learning curve associated with switching to a new program.

FileMaker Pro 3 can open files created by earlier versions and automatically convert them to the current format. Text, ClarisWorks 2 and 3, Excel 3 and 4, SYLK, DBF, and other file types can also be opened directly, bypassing the old method of creating a new database and then importing the old data.

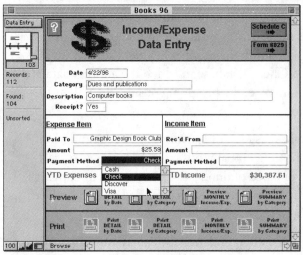

FileMaker Pro layouts can include graphics, pop-up lists, and buttons that execute a series of actions, such as printing a report or displaying it on screen.

Making the leap to relational databases is straightforward. You create a relational database by defining *relationships* between files—two fields (one in each file) which contain a matching value (a customer ID number, for example). When a matching value is entered in a record, the data from one database is displayed in the other. Any changes made to that data are reflected in both files. In other words, when a customer number is entered in an invoice, information (such as an address and credit card number) from the related database is shown. If this information is changed in either database, the record in the other database can automatically be updated.

Earlier versions of FileMaker Pro accomplished file linking by means of *lookups*, where the data was actually pasted from one database into another. Not only was the data duplicated, but changes made to the data were not automatically updated. This meant that if you weren't careful, you could have two different addresses for the same customer, for instance.

HOT TIP

FileMaker Pro's scripting capabilities have also been beefed up. Conditional tests (If..Then, If..Then..Else) and loops are now supported. A new Dial Phone script step lets you dial a telephone through your modem or the Mac's speaker (an extremely handy feature for contact databases). The new Button tool makes it easy to create 3-D buttons to which scripts can be attached, enabling you to select a particular subset of records, sort, and then print a report with just a single mouse click, for example.

To sum up, FileMaker Pro 3 still provides an easy-to-use solution for the beginning database user, while offering plenty of opportunity for growth. For the experienced FileMaker user, the new features solve many issues associated with earlier versions and provide enough new tools to take their databases to new levels. And dedicated users finally have what they've craved: true relational capabilities.

4D First (EC/SS)

For a relational database at a bargain price, try **4D First** ($100, ACI US). Designed as an entry-level database with many automatic features, 4D First is a pared-down version

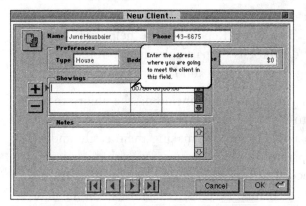

You can add your own Balloon Help to any 4D First layout to help remind you or data entry operators what and how information should be entered in each field.

of 4th Dimension (4D) that can stand on its own or be used as a run-time version to open 4D files. This means that you can not only use the hundreds of 4D templates that are already available, but you can also create new databases as you need them.

Although 4D First is slightly more difficult to learn than a flat-file database program, the relational strength and automated features it offers may be worth it. For example, 4D First automatically creates input and output

GOOD
FEATURE

layouts, and its QuickReport and Graph features make analyzing your information easier than with FileMaker Pro.

4D First has two nice features that help you prepare your database for other users. First, you can add balloon help to the fields in a layout. If you (or your data entry operator) forget what goes in a field, simply activate balloon help and point to the field with the mouse. Second, you can create a whole set of custom menus for your users so that they have access to all the commands (and only those commands) that you want them to use.

Finally, if you ever need a really powerful database, you can upgrade directly to 4th Dimension. And every database you've developed will still work.

4th Dimension (JL)

4th Dimension ($895, ACI US) is a full-featured relational database that is well suited for even the most demanding applications. Users can start by creating basic databases with limited functionality and still have plenty of room for change as their needs and proficiency grow. For experienced users and developers, there is a wealth of tools and features—including a high-powered programming language—for creating sophisticated custom applications. 4th Dimension (4D) databases can also be compiled into run-time versions for distribution.

4D has many features to solve problems that database administrators face, including data validation (making sure that items such as phone numbers are formatted correctly), a robust search editor, and password protection. Scripting can be done in the traditional text mode or you can use a graphical flowchart-style interface. Procedures (scripts) can be global or associated with a particular layout or file, adding to 4D's flexibility.

HOT TIP

Generating reports is another task that can be troublesome for a database administrator, but 4D handles it with aplomb. The QuickReport feature helps you set up meaningful reports with breakdowns and subtotals by particular fields. You can also chart your data in 4D rather than having to export it to another program.

4D has all of the relational capabilities you could want, including the ability to do one-to-many, many-to-one, and many-to-many joins. Relationships are drawn (using a connect-the-dots metaphor) and displayed graphically, making them easily understood. You can also create *subfiles* (a separate file that is associated with a particular record). This means you can keep track of performance reviews, revisions, or other data that may be present on some records but absent on others.

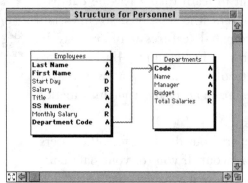

You can create and display relationships graphically in 4th Dimension.

One of the most significant changes to occur in the latest release (version 3.5) is the addition of cross-platform compatibility. This is especially important in corporate settings where acceptance of a Macintosh-only solution is fast becoming a rarity.

4D is part of a comprehensive product family including 4D Server, a software development kit, and a unique (for a database product) suite of utilities that enable you to integrate word processing, spreadsheet, drawing, and charting capabilities into your database applications.

4th Dimension is not a program for novices, but that isn't necessarily bad. Any program with the power to handle complex data requirements sometimes suffers in ease of use. There's no mistaking that 4D requires an investment on the part of the user, but—given its rich feature set—this investment is sure to pay off in the long run.

Helix Express (DC)

In the world of Mac databases, **Helix Express** ($590, Helix Technologies) lives about as far from the mainstream as can be. While many folks worry about procedural data languages, SQL, ODBC, and other relational and client/server technologies, Helix Express users command an icon-laden, object-oriented database unlike any other on the Mac (or on Windows, for that matter). Although Helix Express is fully relational and supports its own client/server multiuser architecture, learning to use it is nothing like learning other Mac relational database programs.

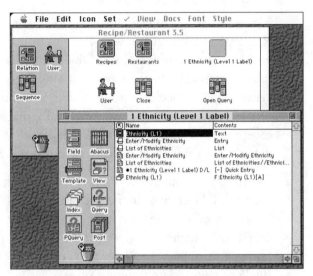

When you fire up Helix Express, you're faced with a mini-desktop holding four icons (Trash, Relation, Sequence, and User) and desktop space in which to place them—which is the first step in building an application. Relation icons define fields and form templates, views, and queries. Sequence icons allow you to set up simple procedures to interact with Relations. The User icon defines passwords, permissions, and related access parameters. You build your Helix application by placing these icons on the desktop and by opening them and using the tools and commands they provide.

In Helix, you can define and modify databases by manipulating icons.

Like its competitors, Helix Express provides a programming language to tie together actions and results. Unlike its competitors, the language of Helix is less richly defined, lacking basic looping and branching structures. Still, once you understand how to use the basic and subsidiary icons (Field, Abacus, Template, View, Index, Query, PQuery, and Post), you can build Helix Express applications that work well—making Helix Express a reasonable choice for building small business applications.

To help with its rather underpowered development environment, Helix Express now fully supports a color development environment, as well as conditional macros, conditional buttons, a fixed-point data format, faster query technology, and improved performance. The latest release also adds support for Publish and Subscribe, and Apple Events, although it does not support AppleScript, QuickDraw GX, or PowerTalk. Helix Express has improved its operating speed so that it's now in the middle of the pack when it comes to sorting, searching, writing to disk, and related tasks. And its multiuser performance remains strong.

What Helix Express lacks is mainstream connectivity with other Mac databases and development environments, a procedurally driven interface that most users are familiar with, and a large enough user base to make it a comfortable choice for many potential users. If you need a Mac relational database and don't mind living outside the mainstream, Helix Express is competent and worth a closer look.

Phyla (DC)

Mainstay calls **Phyla** ($300) an object-oriented database—and for good reason. Rather than come at you with flat files or tables related via common fields, Phyla uses an object-based architecture. Object classes substitute for flat files or for relational tables; attributes do the work of fields. But in many ways, this is simply a nomen-clature issue. Once you are using Phyla to build mailing lists, invoice files, customer reports, and inventories, it won't really matter to you that these are Phyla objects, except that—because of its object-orientation—it takes less effort to manipulate your data than is sometimes the case with procedurally driven programs.

If you've cut your teeth doing C++ programming with Metrowerks CodeWarrior, then you'll be right at home with Phyla's class definitions. Phyla makes it easy to cre-ate an object—simply give it a name and a set of attributes. You could create an object called My Clients and give it these attributes: name, address, phone number, credit rating, and so on. Then later you could add other attributes, as needed. Unlike C++, Phyla can also relate different objects easily—just by drawing a relational arrow con-necting them and then typing the relational definition.

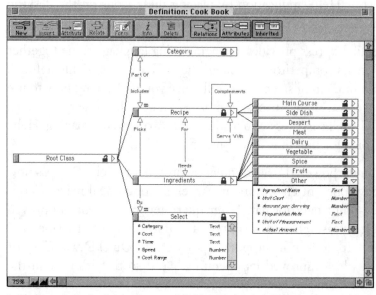

In Phyla, each application has its own definition window in which you can graphically create and display relations and attributes.

Because of Phyla's object orientation, drag-and-drop database creation and editing is possible. You can also bring non-Phyla files into Phyla, or export file types that other database programs can use. Phyla updates all its objects as a background activity. This means speed, speed, speed when it comes to searching, sorting, reporting, and other tasks.

Although you don't *have* to know anything about C++ or other OOP languages to use Phyla, knowing such things helps you get the hang of the system quicker, since the program bears little resemblance to others for the Mac. And although Phyla is fast and easy to use once you get the hang of its object orientation, getting that "hang" is likely to be harder than with traditional programs like FileMaker Pro. Phyla also suffers from being on the periphery of Mac databases, making it harder to find Phyla gurus to help you. But having said all that, Phyla is still a solid effort and worth checking out.

Panorama (DC)

Like Helix Express, **Panorama** ($395, ProVue Development) marches to the beat of a different database drummer. And good for them. The latest version of Panorama takes its spreadsheet-style interface and adds full multiuser capabilities, an integrated word processor, a snappy forms generator, real security, AppleScript awareness, and an improved programming language (including a much-needed interactive debugger).

Panorama's long-standing claim to fame is its speed. It loads the entire database into RAM, even though it's a fully relational program. The new version's multiuser capabilities come as a result of licensing a version of EveryWare's Butler SQL server. This gives individual users the ability to work on a part of a large database while on the road or at home, and then automatically synchronize those changes with the host copy whenever you reconnect to the server. The program also supports record locking when used in client/server mode. And whenever you want to convert an existing single-user Panorama database into a multiuser version, the program will create the necessary SQL code automatically.

GOOD FEATURE

Using Panorama's new client-server model also helps fix a problem that the previous versions suffered from—you couldn't build a database larger then available RAM. Now, subsets of databases can be loaded into RAM on a local Mac, while the rest of the database lives on the server.

The new security scheme is very "AppleShare-ish" in implementation. You get users and groups, 255 different access levels, and data-access restrictions on a record-by-record and field-by-field basis. While this security is not as complete as what 4th Dimension offers, it's pretty good for a product in this class.

While not a relational database program, Panorama can link databases via procedures. Clicking an item in the price list (right) automatically generates a new line item in the current invoice in the Invoices database (left).

Each database field can be edited with the program's word processor. You can format and style text to your heart's content. This makes it easier to build meaningful forms and reports, as well as fancier interfaces. Interfaces are further improved thanks to an interface engine that ProVue calls SuperObject. You can use it to create lists, menus, scalable text and pictures, buttons, and matrix objects (like schedules, multiple column lists, or calendars) without having to program. Just select the kind of SuperObject you want (or create your own), and then plug in the particulars. Panorama will resize, redraw, reposition, and color the objects and windows on your forms to match the available color depth and size of your screen. This makes it very handy for exporting databases to Macs whose characteristics are unknown.

Panorama's spreadsheet-like interface, coupled with its new client-server features, make it a powerful tool for the SOHO crowd, as well as for mid-sized companies.

Visual FoxPro (SS)

Long known as the speed demon of Mac database programs, FoxPro is currently undergoing a major transformation. The resulting cross-platform program will be **Visual FoxPro 3.0** (Microsoft), a 32-bit application-development tool with full object-orientation and integrated client-server capabilities.

Visual FoxPro allows users to build reusable *components* (objects). Visual design tools and wizards can be used to design forms, queries, and reports, as well as create classes and subclasses. The Visual Class Designer enables users to create classes without having to learn the syntax for the new object model. You can also build full-featured, distributable applications.

Among the new and improved visual design tools included in Visual FoxPro are the Project Manager, Database Designer, and Form Designer. The new version promises blinding speed, reusability of components, and enhanced development tools. If you're considering any of the other high-end programmable databases, Visual FoxPro should certainly be on your list.

Working With a Database Manager   (SS/EC)

Work with a database program is generally divided into two parts: designing databases and entering and viewing the information.

Creating a Database

When you create your own database, it is up to you to decide how to divide up the information, how it will be entered, and how it will be output. If this is done with a little thought and planning, entering and using the information should be easy.

Defining fields. The fields in a database serve to divide the information into smaller pieces so the program can sift through the information more efficiently. You should create a field for each category of information; that is, each piece of information that will be similar among many records but different in some way from the rest of the information within a single record.

Should You Do It Yourself, Buy a Canned App, or Hire a Programmer?   (RL)

For simple tasks like address books and recipe collections, it's fairly easy to make your own databases using FileMaker Pro or Panorama. For more complex tasks, like inventory tracking or accounts receivable, however, the do-it-yourself approach may be crazy, since even professional database developers may need weeks or months to create such complex applications.

When a job's too big to do yourself, the main decision is whether to buy an off-the-shelf application for the task (an accounting program, for instance) or hire a developer to create a custom database. If you can find a canned application that meets your needs, it's likely to be a lot less expensive than a custom job. On the other hand, it may not do exactly what you want, and you may end up having to figure out workarounds for those limitations. Ask other people in your line of business what programs they use and how satisfied they are, or check trade publications for ads. Check out the vendors' on-line support forums on CompuServe and America Online to get an idea of the problems their users might be facing.

If you *can't* find an off-the-shelf solution, check the same sources for referrals to database programmers. You want to find people who understand not just programming, but also the needs of your particular business. Before hiring anyone, check their references carefully. It's best to choose a programmer or company with a long history of customer satisfaction. Make sure your developers fully document their work, including extensive "comments" in the database code so that you are not dependent on them for future modifications.

The classic example is a Last Name field. In an address database, all your records will have one, and the last name is clearly distinguishable from the other information in the record (Street, ZIP code, Telephone number, and so on).

Another example might be the Category field in a Recipe database. Each recipe will be of a certain type (Dessert, Main Course, Appetizer, and so on), and this information is clearly different from the other fields (Ingredients, Directions, Prep time, Cooking time, and so on).

Database Templates (EC/SS)

If your heart doesn't skip a beat at the thought of calculated fields, procedures, and subtotals, but you'd still like to use a database, consider buying a *database template*—a ready-to-use database that someone has already created with a particular database program.

Sometimes the database already holds information you can use or add to (a list of U.S. ZIP codes and matching cities, for example); other times you simply enter your own data (keeping track of items in your stamp collection, for example). In many cases, you can modify the database's structure, adding fields and layouts when necessary.

Even if you're looking for a specialized database with which you can run your business, such as a dental office or video rental store, you don't have to rush out and hire a database programmer. Vertical applications of this sort are commonly available—although they're often quite expensive.

If you have a limited budget, you can start by looking at the many freeware and shareware templates that are available online. Claris, for example, provides a FileMaker Pro forum on America Online (Keyword: Claris) that is chock full of database templates. Software publishers' Web sites are often another good source of templates. *[Beware, though. The quality of shareware and freeware database templates ranges from extraordinary to pure garbage. And you'll find plenty of examples of the latter. Plan on lots of fruitless downloads before discovering the gems.—SS]*

There are developer associations for almost every database program, where you can find out about templates for your program. For FileMaker database templates, call the Claris Solutions Alliance (408/727-8227). For Panorama templates, contact ProVue (714/892-8199). There are more than 1,200 4D developers; call ACI US for a catalog (408/252-4444).

Database programs often come with several templates. In addition to helping you better understand how to create your own databases, some of them are actually quite useful. *[For the last several years, for example, I've done all my invoicing in a database that came with FileMaker Pro.—SS]*

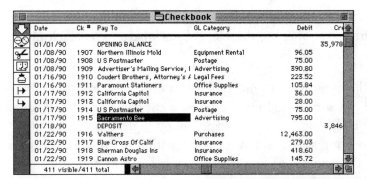

Different layouts present the same information (or parts of the same information) in different ways. Information viewed in a check register layout (left) looks completely different when viewed as an individual check (below).

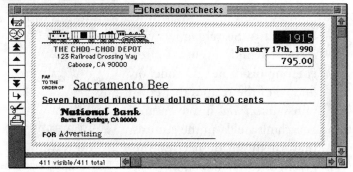

Creating layouts. The second step in creating your own database is designing layouts. You should create different layouts for different purposes: one for data entry, one for viewing lists on screen, one for mailing labels, one for the annual sales report, and so on. You'll have to decide which fields to put in each layout and where to place them. You will often put field labels next to the fields so that you can remember what information is contained (or needs to be contained) in each field.

Depending on the database program, creating layouts is often similar to using a graphics program. It involves dragging elements around the screen, changing their size, drawing lines, and aligning objects.

Using a Database Program

Once you've defined your fields and created the layouts, you can begin to enter information, search or sort the information that the database contains, and output it in practically any way you need.

Entering information. Of all the tasks involved with databases, entering the information is by far the easiest—and the dullest. You simply create a new record and start typing. When you have filled in the information for one record, you create a new record and start again. Most databases save your data automatically whenever you create a new record.

Many database programs allow you to import existing information from word processors, spreadsheets, and other databases so that you can keep typing to a minimum.

The original information must be divided into fields (usually by commas or tabs) and records (generally with returns) so that the database knows where to put each piece of information.

Sorting. All databases allow you to put your records in order, according to your criteria. For example, you can sort an address database by last name or by ZIP code (or by last name *and* ZIP code), or sort your recipe file by ingredients, prep time, or category. In addition to using any criterion (or combination of criteria), you can usually sort in ascending, descending, or in a custom order (such as high, medium, and low).

Searching. Searching lets you instantly find a client after entering his or her ID code, or find all of the recipes that contain salmon *and* heavy cream. Searching yields all the records that satisfy all or part of the given criteria, depending on the logical operators used.

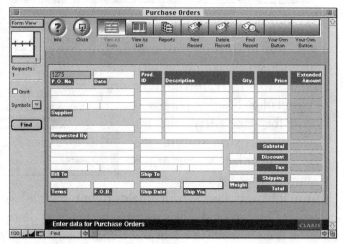

Previewing and printing data. The simplest way to output data is to show it on screen (called *previewing* in FileMaker

FileMaker Pro's Find request form looks exactly like the layout when viewed in Browse mode. To begin a search, you type the information you're looking for in the appropriate fields (in this case, a P.O. number) and click Find.

Pro). For example, you can examine an individual record or preview a multipage report. Databases are especially useful because they also allow you to *print* your data in almost any way you can imagine. You can create mailing labels, directories, monthly summaries, form letters, or fax templates, for example.

Summary reports are one of the more complicated but powerful features of a database. (Ain't that always the case?) For example, you can list your baseball cards by Card Type and then by Year, and have the database calculate the value of each year's collection.

Using macros or scripts. Most database programs let you create macros or scripts to speed up and automate your work. For example, to create your monthly mailing labels, suppose you normally search for all your active clients, sort them by ZIP code and last name, and then print them using a layout called Mailing Labels. You can create a macro or script named Print Monthly Mailing to perform all of these steps automatically. The next time you need to print mailing labels, you just run the script.

Database Tips

Database Design

How you organize your databases can mean the difference between having information, and having information at your fingertips. For the latter, read on.

Use all the data entry control available (EC). Almost all databases offer some help in keeping your data accurate and consistent. Use data entry control options to let you select values from a list, mark checkboxes or radio buttons, automatically enter default data, restrict data to a certain value or range, or insist that a field contain an entry.

Different layouts for different uses (EC). Even if your monitor is so big it touches both sides of your room, you shouldn't try to put every single field in each layout. Instead, create a different layout for each use—one for data entry, one for creating a phone book printout, one for address labels, and so on—and show only the fields that are necessary.

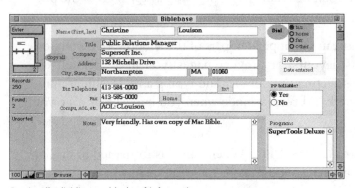

By visually dividing up blocks of information, you can put more on a data entry layout without confusing your data entry operators.

If you do have many fields in a layout, use background color (or gray shades) to distinguish different areas.

Making menus (SS). If your database is so complex that it requires more than a couple of layouts, consider adding a main menu layout that lets you (or others) choose what to do next. At its simplest, a menu layout might contain buttons for data entry, reports, and help information, for example. A more complex menu system could incorporate several submenus, enabling you to select specific types of reports, execute searches, and so on.

Formatting ZIP code and telephone fields (SS/SZA/AN/EC). Make sure that ZIP code and telephone fields are defined as text rather than number fields. A numeric ZIP code field will strip the leading zero from ZIPs like 07461 and may perform a subtraction on 07461-8976. Since text fields can contain text *or* numbers, you don't have to worry that leading zeros will disappear.

Formatting ZIP codes and telephone numbers as text fields also makes it easier to find a group based on the first few numbers. If you search for 9 in a text ZIP code field, you'll get all those that *begin* with a 9. You'll get all those ZIP codes that are *equal* to 9 if you search for 9 in a *numeric* ZIP code field, which—in this country—wouldn't yield many.

Duplicate files before working on them (Steve Michel). It's good practice to keep at least two copies of any database file. But if you're too lazy to do that, at least do yourself the favor of duplicating a database file before launching the application to work on it. Most databases keep their files on disk and automatically save changes to them while you work. So the file you had on disk when you began to work is not the file you'll return to when you're done.

FileMaker Pro Tips

Getting around (EC/SS). You can use the keyboard shortcut ⌘Tab to go to the next record, find request form, layout, or report page, or ⌘Shift Tab to go to the previous one.

The number below the little book, in the upper-left part of the window, tells you how many records (or find requests, layouts, or preview pages) you have created. Go directly to the one you need by selecting the number and typing a replacement number. This is an especially good trick in Preview mode when you know what page you want to look at.

Selecting from a list of values (SZA/SM/EC). When a field is formatted to display a set of values, either in a list or with checkboxes or radio buttons, you can use the arrow keys to move through the values, or you can type the first few letters of the word you want. Then hit Return (not Enter)to accept the entry. The moral of the story? Set up your lists so that each value begins with a different letter and don't ever use pop-up menus—they can't be accessed from the keyboard but are identical to pop-up lists in every other way.

Choosing "None of the above" (EC). FileMaker Pro lets you add an "Other" option to pop-up menus, checkboxes, and radio buttons (select Field Format and then check Include "Other…" item). However, if you format your field as a pop-up list, you don't need an Other option. Simply press Enter or Esc instead of selecting a value from the list, or press Delete if you've already selected something, and type a new value or leave it blank.

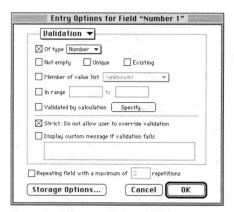

Check the "Strict" option to prevent users from overriding the validation options you've set for a field.

"Strict" field validation (SS). In previous versions of FileMaker Pro, you could specify loads of field validation criteria, but the user could freely override them. While this was useful for dealing with exceptions (a Canadian Postal Code contains more characters than a U.S. ZIP, for example), it also meant that your data could be easily compromised. In FileMaker Pro 3, you can make sure that the right type of data is *always* entered into an important field. Just set validation options and then click in the "Strict: Do not allow user to override validation" checkbox.

Bypassing the Delete alert (SZA/JK). When you use Delete Record to remove a record from your file, FileMaker asks you if you're sure you want to delete it. This is a normal Mac touch—giving you a chance to change your mind before an irreversible operation is performed. But if you're *sure* you want to delete the record, Option ⌘ Enter will avoid the dialog box. *[This command also works for deleting find requests.—SS]*

Looking for empties and nonempties (EC). The best way to find empty fields is by typing an equal sign (=) in the field in Find mode. To find nonempty fields, type an equal sign in the field, check the Omit box, and then click Find.

On the other hand, the fastest way to find empty *records* is to sort your file in order of a field that should never be empty—such as a client's name. All the empty records will appear at the top of the list.

Eliminating duplicate records (EC). First and foremost, *don't* use the duplicate operator to look for duplicates. Because of the way FileMaker creates its index, analyzing each individual word of a field, it would flag *Claris Corporation* and *Microsoft Corporation* as duplicates, but not *MS Corp.* and *Microsoft Corporation*.

A good way to find and eliminate duplicates in an address database is to sort by ZIP code, address, and name—in that order—and view them as a list. The real duplicates are those that are at the same address, with *almost* the same name but not quite. You'll be able to identify and get rid of them quickly.

Ask for a little and you'll get a lot (SS/EC). You're Ronald Reagan and you're looking up your old friend, the former leader of the Soviet Union, in your database. You know his name is Gorbachoff or Gorbichef, or something like that. Don't tax yourself;

just search for "Gorb." Any name (or word in a name) that begins with those letters will appear in the found set. Even if you know how to spell it, you should search for as little as possible. This saves you the trouble of entering more than is necessary and gives you a better chance of finding the information, even if it was entered incorrectly.

Holding on to a tool (SS/EC). Generally, after you use a tool in Layout mode, it automatically switches back to the Pointer tool. FileMaker Pro will let you hang on to a tool indefinitely by double-clicking to select it. If you want tools to be locked with a single click, check "Always lock layout tools" in the Layout Preferences dialog.

Fast sizing and styling in layouts (SZA/JK). Create a copy of any object on a layout by holding down Option and dragging. This is a fast way to create text labels with the same fonts, size, and style—just make several copies and then edit the text.

When you drag a single *field* this way, you get a dialog box that lets you choose which field you want to appear in the new spot—it doesn't have to be the one you moved.

This is an easy way to add new fields with the same size and attributes.

Magic menus (JL). FileMaker Pro 3 provides a new way to modify layout elements and field data. Holding down Control while clicking on a field or object displays a pop-up menu for changing attributes of data in that field or the selected object (such as font, style, fill color, and so on). This trick can be used in both Layout and Browse modes.

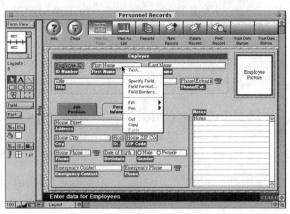

Control-clicking a field or other element when in Layout mode displays this handy menu of formatting options.

Dotted lines (EC/SS). You can create dotted lines by selecting a 2- or 3-point width line and then applying a zigzag line pattern to it. They're great for separating subsummaries.

Selecting tricks (SS/EC). Press ⌘ while selecting objects and fields, and anything the selection marquee touches will fall into its grip. Without ⌘ you will have to completely surround the objects you wish to select.

Click any tool before choosing Select All to select all the objects created with that tool.

Select one field, press Option, and then choose Select All to select all fields.

Restraining yourself in one or more directions (EC). You probably know that if you hold down Shift while resizing an object or field, your movement is restricted to just one direction, horizontal or vertical. If you hold down (Option), your movement is restricted in *both* directions, and the object becomes a perfect square or circle.

A database with moving parts (SS/EC). You can delete any empty part (that's Part with a capital *P*, as in Body, Footer, and so on) in a layout by dragging the bottom border up to the next part or by selecting the part's tag and pressing (Delete).

If the part contains objects or fields, you can still delete it by clicking its label and pressing (Option)(Delete). Its objects are automatically added to the part immediately below it. (Note that this tip cannot be applied to the bottom-most part on a layout.)

You can change a part's identity by double-clicking its tag and selecting a different part type. This won't affect its contents.

Get rid of the body (EC). When you're creating summary reports—say, to count your baseball cards to check how much the collection is worth—don't forget that you don't need a body. The body contains information about each card that may distract you from the totals that the report is designed to show (like the fact that your Topps collection is worth $26,457).

Cheat sheets (EC/SS). Since FileMaker Pro lets you create scripts, you don't have to remember how to sort, search, or print your report. But how do you remember what a particular script was for? Write a short description at the top of the report, format it in red, and then select "Do not print the selected objects" from the Slide Objects dialog box (select Sliding/Printing in the Format menu). *[In FileMaker Pro 3, there's a way to do this that doesn't mess up your layouts. You can use the new Comment script step to document the script.—SS]*

Copying layouts (SS). FileMaker Pro 3's support for Drag-and-Drop allows you to copy a layout from one database to another by simply changing to Layout mode in both databases and then dragging fields, text, and graphics into the receiving database. Fields dragged in this manner however, will be undefined in the new database (unless you've already created fields by the same name).

Relookup of just some of the records (SZA/EC). If you've changed information in a file that's used as a lookup (say, you've updated names and addresses that are looked up by your invoicing file), the Relookup command in the Edit menu can update all, some, or just one of your records.

To update all your records, choose Find All in the Select menu, place the cursor in the lookup field, and select Relookup. If you want to update a group of records, select those records with the Find command before using the Relookup command.

To force an update for only the current record, move to the field that does the lookup. Make a minor change to it—say, add a space and then delete it. When you move out of the lookup field, the "new" information in it will force a lookup and the rest of the record will be updated.

Creating automatic serial numbers with letters (SS/EC). If the serial numbers in your company happen to start with or include embedded letters, you can still get FileMaker to fill the information in automatically. Choose Define Fields from the File menu, select the serial number field (a Number field), and then click Options. In the Auto Enter section of the dialog box that appears, type the starting serial number, such as B17-6A1. When each new record is created, only the numeric portion of the number will be increased, producing B17-6A2, B17-6A3, and so on.

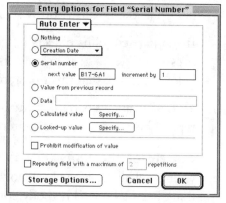

Creating a serial number that contains numbers and letters is easier than you'd think.

Checking for length (EC). When entering names and addresses into your database, your assistant often puts in the first three digits of the ZIP code but sometimes forgets to look up the rest. You want to check and make sure each record in your database has a five- or nine-digit ZIP code. Create a Calculation field (Ziplength) with the following formula:

```
Ziplength = Length (Zip code)
```

Now search the Ziplength field, omitting all those records with five or ten (nine digits plus a hyphen) characters. You'll immediately find which ZIP codes have been entered incompletely.

Creating relational value lists (JL). Once you've taken the plunge and created a relationship between files, the next issue is how do you display this information? One way is to have a field value list comprised of records from the related file. This is a good idea when the items in your value list change frequently. Examples of this include client names in your daily planner, product lists in an invoice, or tasks in a project database. To do this:

1. Create the field on your layout, and select Field Format from the Format menu.

2. Choose Pop-up list from the Style box and select Define Value Lists.

3. Give your value list a name, and click Create.

4. Click "Use values from a field," and click Specify Field.

5. Choose the file and field you want to display as your value list, and click OK.

6. Click Done when you're finished, set any other attributes you'd like, and click OK.

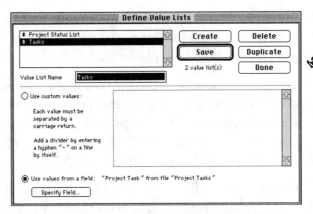

When you switch to Browse mode and tab into or click in this field, you'll see a list comprised of records from the related file that you specified.

Although value lists are commonly created by just typing the words for the items, you can also base a value list on the contents of a field—in either the current database or a related one.

Creating portals (JL). Suppose you want to look at more than one field from a related file, such as item description, price, and stock number. That's where *portals* come in. A portal is similar to the relational value list described in the last tip, but allows you to display multiple related fields per record. To set up a portal, follow these steps:

1. Switch to the Layout mode, and select the Portal Tool.

2. Click and drag a rectangle where you want the related fields to be displayed.

3. In the Portal Setup dialog box, choose the relationship you want to use. (You can create a new relationship if one doesn't already exist.)

4. Choose Options from the Format section of the dialog box, and click OK. You'll see a rectangle with the number of repetitions you specified.

5. Drag the fields you want to use into the top row of the portal. Select related fields in the Specify Field dialog box that appears. (Names of related fields are preceded by two colons, as in ::Last Name.)

You use the Portal Setup dialog to specify the relationship on which the portal will be based, as well as set display options for the portal.

When you switch to Browse mode, you'll see fields from the records of the related file you specified.

Cross-platform printing (DC). Scripts that include Page Setup/Print Setup and Print steps are not totally cross-platform compatible—even if you're printing to the same printer from both platforms.

The Print steps in ScriptMaker rely on the current printer driver in order to find out what paper sizes, orientation, and so on are available. Even if Macintoshes and PCs are connected to the same printer, the drivers can be significantly different, so FileMaker is unable to totally restore page setup and print options cross-platform. To work around this, you have three options:

1. Create a conditional test in your scripts that uses Status (CurrentPlatform) to determine what computer is being used and Status (CurrentPrinterName) to select the needed print script for either Macintosh or Windows 95. In order for this to work, you must create the Macintosh script on the Mac and the Windows 95 script on the PC.

```
If ["Status(CurrentPlatform) = 1"]
  If ["PatternCount(Status(CurrentPrinterName), "LaserWriter")>0"]
    Go to Layout ["LaserWriter Layout"]
    Page Setup [Restore, No dialog]
  Else
    If ["PatternCount(Status(CurrentPrinterName), "ImageWriter") > 0"]
      Go to Layout ["ImageWriter Layout"]
      Page Setup [Restore, No dialog]
    Else
      If ["PatternCount(Status(CurrentPrinterName), "StyleWriter") >0"]
        Go to Layout ["StyleWriter Layout"]
        Page Setup [Restore, No dialog]
      End If
    End If
  End If
End If
```

2. Create separate scripts for Macintosh and Windows 95.

3. Do not select Perform Without Dialog. This will allow you to change the setup options before you print as part of the script.

12 | Integrated Software

If you're looking for the Swiss Army knife of Macintosh applications—one program that does it all—*integrated software* is it. The programs described in this chapter combine the basic software tools most people use everyday. These tools include a word processor, a spreadsheet, a database, drawing tools, and a communications program.

We'll spell out why you might choose an integrated application instead of investing in several separate, specialized applications. You'll find out who's who in the market, as well as get a quick overview of which combination of tools each package offers.

If you've already bought one of the two most popular integrated applications on the Macintosh—ClarisWorks or Microsoft Works—we've compiled a list of tips, tricks, and shortcuts that should help you get the most out of these leading programs.

Contributors

Steve Schwartz (SS) is the chapter editor.

Jay Lee (JL) spent many years in technical support at Claris and is a veteran Mac user. He is currently working as a computer consultant and multimedia designer/producer in Silicon Valley.

Connie Guglielmo (CG), **Charles Rubin (CR)**, and **Carolyn Said (CS)** were all contributors to earlier versions of *The Macintosh Bible*, from which parts of this chapter were taken.

Contents

Getting the Works (CG)

Integrated applications offer one-stop shopping to Macintosh users who may not want or need separate specialized applications for some of the basics. The basics we're talking about are word processing, database management, spreadsheets, telecommunications, and drawing.

Integrated applications (each component of which is usually called a *module* or an *environment*) offer several advantages over many individual programs:

- *Price*. These programs range in price from $55 to $500. You don't have to be a financial wizard to figure out that buying an integrated application is often less expensive than buying a stand-alone word processor, drawing program, spreadsheet, and so on.

- *Program size*. If you want or need to keep the number of applications on your hard disk to a minimum, then having one application rather than several saves space. An integrated application may be ideal if you have a PowerBook or Duo and want to pack a lot of functionality into limited hard disk space.

POWERBOOK

- *Integration*. Because all the tools are integrated, sharing data between them and moving among them is, for the most part, a snap.

The trade-off is that these programs often offer a limited set of features compared to the leading stand-alone applications. Yes, the basics are here, but if you need to automate your accounts receivable department or plan to write a textbook complete with footnotes and indexes, you may need the more specialized features that stand-alone applications offer.

Choosing an Integrated Package (SS/CS)

The players in this software category have changed considerably since the last edition of *The Macintosh Bible*. GreatWorks (Symantec) and WordPerfect Works no longer exist. And if RagTime and HandiWorks are still around, you can't tell by looking at ads and mail-order catalogs. Thus, there are now only two serious contenders in the Mac integrated software market: ClarisWorks (which is bundled with Apple's Performas and several Macintosh clones) and Microsoft Works.

Although Microsoft Works owned this category for years, Works (now in version 4) hasn't been updated since mid-1994. Introduced in 1991, ClarisWorks has virtually taken over this market, and has released major updates on an annual basis. And of the two programs, only ClarisWorks has a native version for Power Macintoshes.

POWER MAC

In this chapter, you'll also find a discussion of Microsoft Office, a *suite* of programs that Microsoft sells as an integrated package. Unlike ClarisWorks and Microsoft Works, the modules in Microsoft Office are complete copies of three best-selling Microsoft applications: Word, Excel, and PowerPoint.

Regardless of which integrated package you choose, there's extensive support available, including books, training services, libraries of macros—and the tips at the end of this chapter. Choosing a program will depend on the combination of modules that you need (the following table shows what features the leading integrated packages offer).

GOOD FEATURE

ClarisWorks   (JL)

Already the leading integrated application for the Macintosh, **ClarisWorks 4** ($130, Claris) continues its evolution with the addition of powerful new features that beg the question, "Do I really need to buy a Microsoft Office type of product?" By requiring less memory and hard disk space, yet giving users features and power that they'll actually use, it becomes harder for many to justify the expense and overhead of a full-blown suite.

All of the environments (with the exception of communications) offer something new, but it's the word processor that receives the most attention in version 4. Style sheets enable users to format their documents much faster than before. Styles can be edited, saved, and then applied to text, paragraphs, outlines, and tables. Users can easily access the styles via a pop-up menu on the text ruler or by using the floating style sheet

Integrated Offerings

	Word processing	Spreadsheet	Database	Communications	Drawing	Painting	Page layout	Other
ClarisWorks 4	•	•	•	•	•	•	some	
Microsoft Works 4	•	•	•	•	•	•	some	address book, calendar
Microsoft Office 4.21	•	•						presentations, data queries, programming

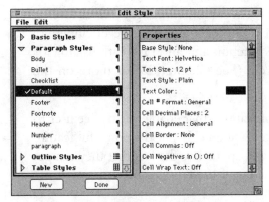

In ClarisWorks, you can create, edit, and apply styles to text, paragraphs, outlines, and tables.

window. Also new is the ability to have multiple sections in a document. For instance, you could have a single column at the top of the page and multiple columns on the lower half. Other new layout options include end notes and multiple headers and footers in a document.

As more features are added, one common concern is that ease of use may suffer. Because many new Macintosh users get their first taste of computing with ClarisWorks, *Assistant* technology has been added to help them create more complex documents like newsletters and home-finance spreadsheets. When creating a new document using an Assistant, you are asked a series of questions concerning the layout and content. After the Assistant gathers the required information, it creates a new formatted document for you, ready to receive information. And Assistants aren't just for new users; experienced users can also save time by not having to set up documents manually. ClarisWorks also includes many stationery documents that can be quickly modified for common and not-so-common tasks.

The database environment now has a feature that most Microsoft Works users have taken for granted (and have often requested after making the switch): an automatic List view. New field types have been added to make data entry faster and more accurate. Although true scripting isn't available,

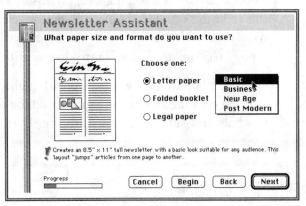

ClarisWorks 4 Assistants help you quickly create complex documents such as newsletters.

a feature called FastReports lets you store sets of find and sort instructions and later re-execute them (so you don't need to recreate them each time). Users will appreciate the Assistant that helps set up the dreaded mailing labels, too.

The draw environment includes a drag-and-drop art library with 500 clip art images that you can easily add to any document. The spreadsheet environment gets a graphic makeover with the addition of cell shading. Another nice feature is a Fill Special command that automatically fills in day names, months, quarters, and so on, as row or column headings. Claris finally decided to add some scripting capabilities via

AppleScript and now supports WorldScript, too. (In combination with various foreign language kits, WorldScript enables users to create foreign language documents.) Other features of note are a new mail merge function and an HTML translator for creating documents for the World Wide Web. (See Chapter 23 for more on the World Wide Web.)

Overall, ClarisWorks 4 provides a robust set of features that enable the novice user to grow with the program. More experienced users will quickly put the powerful feature set to use. But most of all, just about everyone will appreciate the fact that they can get all of this functionality without having to buy a bigger hard disk or more memory.

Microsoft Works (CS)

Microsoft Works 4 ($55 disk version; $80 CD version, includes Microsoft Bookshelf) addresses some major problems with the previous version. In fact, some users of Works 3 "backtracked" to version 2 because they preferred the way some of the features in that version worked. Works 4 integrates its modules using Microsoft's *Object Linking* and *Embedding* (OLE) technology. This approach works well; you simply click a button and draw a rectangle to, say, insert a spreadsheet in a word processor. You can then edit the embedded object by double-clicking it, and you can also embed objects from other OLE programs within Works. (OLE is Microsoft's version of the same type of technology Apple is introducing with OpenDoc, described in Chapter 3.)

Microsoft beefed up the software with plenty of new features, such as a slide show; a tool for creating tables; an equation editor for editing equations with mathematical symbols and subscripts; an AutoSum button for calculating totals automatically; multi-level database sorting; and drag-and-drop editing that lets you move or copy a selection by just dragging it to the desired location. It ships with a selection of clip art and a Gallery for organizing clip art images, and it now comes with about 36 file-conversion filters.

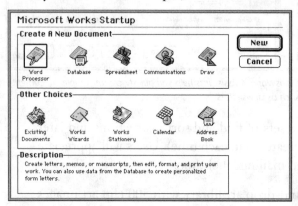

To choose a module in Microsoft Works 4, you click on an option in the opening dialog box. Because all the modules are integrated, it's easy to share data among the word processing, database, spreadsheet, and drawing modules and to make sure that changes made to information in one module are reflected in the others.

Works 4 also adds a new calendar and address book, as well as a new paint tool that has features such as gradient fills, rotation, filters for creating special graphical effects, and support for Adobe Photoshop plug-in tools and filters.

Microsoft's WordArt includes TrueType fonts and provides tools for different shadow effects, shapes, and text and line rotations. You can also use WordArt to create fancy headlines and banners.

Works 4 offers some features that simplify common tasks such as writing letters, generating reports, and designing newsletters. A feature called WorksWizards helps create documents such as greeting cards and newsletters by posing simple questions that users answer. Almost 40 *stationery documents* templates (called AutoStart in Works) provide a quick starting point for creating different types of documents (such as a Grade Book, Cash Flow Projection, and Home Inventory) designed for teachers, business users, and home users.

Microsoft Office (SS)

Microsoft Office ($500) combines three best-selling Microsoft applications in one convenient package: Microsoft Word 6 (word processing), Excel 5 (spreadsheets), and PowerPoint 4 (presentations). Because many businesses have standardized on Word and Excel, buying Office is a commonsense move. It costs only a little more than the combined prices of Word and Excel. As a bonus, Microsoft tosses in a single workstation license for Microsoft Mail (although server software must be purchased separately), as well as the ability to query databases.

Microsoft Office adds its own ever-present icon to the menu bar. Click it to expose a menu from which you can launch installed Microsoft applications, as well as other programs that you've added to the menu.

Even though Office contains only three programs (plus a single workstation license for Microsoft Mail), a complete installation requires massive amounts of disk space—over 90MB! Office comes with a thorough setup program that you use to install, remove, or reconfigure its components. And it's a good thing because Office is finicky about how it's set up. If you move or rename any folders or forget to enable any of its two dozen or so extensions, there's a good chance that you'll receive a nasty surprise.

WARNING

Because Microsoft Office is billed as an integrated package, you may well be wondering what this integration consists of. Information can be shared between applications by standard Mac methods: copy and paste, Publish and Subscribe, and importing. None of these techniques, however, is new or earthshaking. Office provides two additional data-sharing techniques: *embedding* and *linking*. Suppose, for example, you want to include an Excel chart in a Word document. If you embed the chart in the Word document, no link is kept with the spreadsheet in which it was created. But if you ever need to edit the embedded chart, you can just double-click it. Doing so launches Excel and opens the original spreadsheet. Linking, on the other hand, works like Publish and Subscribe: When you link an object (such as a chart) and later edit it, all linked copies are automatically updated.

GOOD FEATURE

Do-it-yourselfers will be excited by the package's new scripting capabilities. Word 6 includes a macro recorder, as well as its own scripting language called WordBasic (long available in Word for Windows). And you can now script Excel using the Visual Basic language. (At some point in the near future, *all* Microsoft applications will be scriptable using Visual Basic, so here's your chance to get a head start.)

Other important new features include the following:

- Drag-and-Drop support (within and between programs)

- *OLE* (Object Linking and Embedding) support

- AutoCorrect (a revised glossary feature for inserting lengthy text strings and automatically correcting common typos and misspellings)

- AutoFormat (choose from a set of document formatting styles)

- Wizards (step-by-step guidance for common tasks such as making charts, tables, mailing labels, and designing presentations)

- Improved table handling and formatting

- Excel's "drag and plot" (automatic chart modification by dragging data)

- Workgroup features for collaborating on documents over a network

- TipWizard (watches you work and offers suggestions for easier, more efficient ways to accomplish tasks)

One of the main selling points for Office is its cross-platform compatibility. If your business has standardized on these Microsoft applications, you can readily share your data between Macs and PCs, and users can easily switch from one platform to another (the programs work the same). Of course, the *main* reason for buying Microsoft Office rather than ClarisWorks or Microsoft Works is power, power, power! If you make your living as a writer or a number cruncher, you won't have to worry about constantly bumping into the limitations of typical integrated packages. If Word, Excel, and PowerPoint can't do it for you, it probably can't be done.

ClarisWorks Tips

These tips are for ClarisWorks 4, although many of them will also work in earlier versions of ClarisWorks.

General

Saving memory (CR/SS). ClarisWorks can run short of memory during long communications sessions or when using the paint environment. Here are a few ways to maximize memory when using these document types:

- Use the Communication preferences to change from an unlimited scrollback area to one of a small fixed size, and use the Capture Text command to store communications data in a file on your disk instead of in memory.

- To free up more memory for paint documents, use the Resolution & Depth command to set the pixel depth to Black & White, 4 colors, or 16 colors, instead of using thousands or millions of colors.

- Because ClarisWorks' Paint environment demands a lot of memory, Claris recommends increasing the memory allocation before using it.

Which shortcut is which? (CR/SS). If you can't remember what each button on the Shortcuts palette does, you can display the shortcuts as names instead of icons. Just change the Shortcuts preferences to Show Names. To find out what one specific button does, choose Edit Shortcuts, click the button in the dialog box, and look in the Description area.

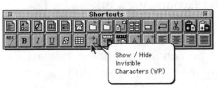

ClarisWorks' Shortcuts palette gives you access to commonly used functions (represented by icons) with one mouse click.

If you regularly forget what the buttons mean, you can also set the Automatic Balloons option in the Shortcuts preferences. Then whenever the cursor rests over a Shortcuts button for a second or two, a help balloon appears that identifies the button.

Recycling macro keys (CS). If you create lots of macros and find yourself running out of macro keys, try assigning macros to specific ClarisWorks document types instead of creating macros that work everywhere. For example, you could use Option ⌃⌘ 2 to double-space a word processing document, and use the same keys to choose a fixed-number format with two decimal places in the spreadsheet. Just be sure to check the document type you want in the Record Macro dialog box as you define each macro.

Wrapping text around a graphic (CS). You can wrap text around a graphic even when you're not in the word processing environment. Turn Frame Links on for the frame containing your text. ClarisWorks will wrap text around graphics that were created with the drawing tools or were pasted in PICT format. If you need to wrap around other objects (e.g., bitmapped graphics, EPS files, and so on), draw a border-less white object that is slightly larger than your graphic and move it behind the pasted-in graphic (Send to Back).

Creating slide presentations (CS). A nice feature in ClarisWorks is the ability to create on-screen slide presentations. There are several different ways to do this; in fact, any environment in ClarisWorks can be turned into a slide presentation. Some of the less obvious ways to do this include:

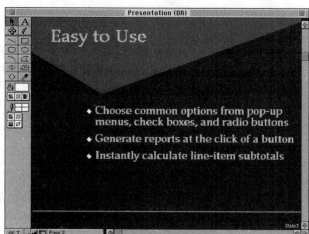

You can create slides like this in ClarisWorks' draw module using the Presentation Assistant.

- From the Draw environment, insert text frames and organize them as outlines. Use outline formats to define the fonts, sizes, and styles for each level in your presentation. (You can have multiple levels, so the first level could be 36-point bold Times; the second level 30-point Times Roman, and so on.) *[If you need help, you can use the Presentation Assistant to quickly design basic presentations.—SS]*

- From the Database environment, set up a Database layout with a title and a few bullet points. You can then enter data to create a very quick presentation.

Creating predefined formats (CS). You can create predefined document formats such as a fax cover sheet, a standard memo, or a presentation. The format will have all the type styles and other formatting you've defined. Choose Save As from the File menu and click the Stationery radio button. This will save a template with your for-matting; you can then select it whenever you create a new document of that type.

Creating default formats (CS/SS). You can create a default document for each of the ClarisWorks environments; then every time you make a new document in that environment, it will automatically default to your predefined formatting. To do this, create a stationery document and, for the word processor, name it *ClarisWorks WP Options* (for the draw module, substitute *DR*; for the paint module, *PT*; for the database module, *DB*; for the spreadsheet module, *SS*; and for the communications module, *CM*).

In ClarisWorks 4, you must keep these documents inside the ClarisWorks Stationery folder (which is chosen automatically when you click the Stationery radio button in the Save As dialog box).

Automating text searches (SS). To conduct a search without having to deal with the normal Find/Change dialog box, select the search text in the document (*Apple Computer*, for example), and then choose Find Selection rather than Find/Change. ClarisWorks takes you directly to the next instance of the selected text string.

Using AppleScripts (JL/SS). Several AppleScript examples are included in the ClarisWorks Scripts folder of ClarisWorks 4. For example, by dragging files or folders onto the Convert Documents AppleScript icon, you can quickly convert foreign files (such as Microsoft Word documents) to ClarisWorks 4 format. Read the *About the AppleScripts* document for instructions.

In the same folder, Claris also includes a database of available AppleScript commands (called ClarisWorks AppleEvents List) so you can get started writing your own scripts. This is a great way to get started with AppleScript.

Word Processing

Inserting graphics (SS/CS). There are two ways to add graphics to a word processing document:

- If the cursor is an I-beam and you have a blinking insertion point in your document, pasting will bring in the graphic as a (usually) large character in the line with the previous characters.

- If you Show Tools, select the Pointer tool, and then choose Paste from the Edit menu, your graphic will appear as a completely separate object from the text. Inserting or changing text will not affect its position. You can then choose Text Wrap from the Options menu and wrap the text around your graphic.

The second method is preferable if you're trying to do any kind of page layout. Use the first method if you want to make sure the graphic stays tied to a particular text section. *[Rather than leave the graphic embedded in the middle of a line of text—usually resulting in horrid between-line spacing—you can use the first method and put the graphic on its own line. You can then apply alignment options (left or centered, for example) and set the line spacing before and after (choose the Paragraph command from the Format menu) to position the graphic exactly where you want it.—SS]*

Toggling invisible characters on and off (CS). Pressing ⌘; toggles invisible characters, such as paragraph and return symbols, on or off.

Creating a custom style (JL). You can create your own custom styles to help you quickly and consistently format documents. Choose Show Styles from the View menu, and click New. Choose the type of style you want to create (basic, paragraph, outline, and so on) and then click OK. You can modify and add attributes by clicking the Edit button and then selecting options from the text ruler or menus. When you've got the style the way you want it, click Done. You can later reuse the style by either creating a stationery document or by exporting the style and then importing it into your other documents.

Creating tables (CS). You can easily create tables in a word processing document by using spreadsheet frames. Like a graphic, the table can be free-floating (easily moved around within the document) or tied to a specific section of text.

Paint and Draw

Using a draw document for page layout (CR). It may seem best to use the word processor for newsletters, but creating text frames in a Draw document gives you much more flexibility for arranging blocks of text and graphics on a page. After you create text frames, you can link them (so text flows from one frame to another in the same story). And because frames are objects, you can select them and use the draw document's alignment commands to precisely align columns and graphics.

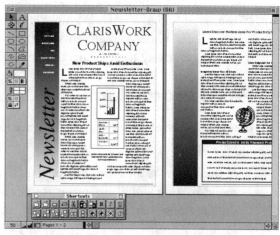

You can use text frames in a ClarisWorks draw document to create page layouts.

Using a draw document for multipage printing (CR). Paint documents in ClarisWorks can be only one page long. To create a multipage paint document, open a draw document, add the number of pages you want, and then create one or more paint frames on each page.

Selecting images precisely without the Lasso (CR). Using the Lasso tool is the most common way to select an image without selecting white space around it. But you can do the same thing more quickly by holding down the ⌘ key while dragging the selection rectangle around the image(s) you want to select. To select all the images on a document without any white space around them, double-click on the selection rectangle tool while holding down the ⌘ key.

Spreadsheet

Saving paper (CS/SS). Before printing a spreadsheet, drag to select the range you want to print, choose Set Print Range from the Options menu, and click OK. At this point, select Page View from the View menu to see how it will print. Because you can keep working in this view, you can adjust the column widths so pages break the way you want them to.

Making big chart changes (CR). If the chart formatting options in the spreadsheet aren't flexible enough for you, copy the chart to a draw document, select it, and then use the Ungroup Picture command to break up the chart into its components. After you use Ungroup Picture, you can select different chart elements like the legend or a group of bars, and then use the Ungroup command to break up elements further. For example, you could ungroup a series of bars to select and change the fill pattern in one bar. Unfortunately, once you paste a chart into a draw document, it becomes unlinked from the original spreadsheet, so make sure the chart shows exactly the data you want before modifying it in a draw document.

Inserting multiple rows or columns (CR). The Insert Cells command in the spreadsheet takes awhile to work, and using it repeatedly to insert several rows or columns seems particularly slow. You can speed things up by selecting as many rows or columns as you want to insert and then using the Insert Cells command. ClarisWorks will then insert as many rows or columns as you have selected.

Moving data between databases and spreadsheets (CS). You can move data from a database to a spreadsheet—or vice versa—by selecting all of the records (by choosing Select All from the Edit menu) and copying that data into a new spreadsheet. You can go the other direction as well, but you'll need to re-create the field names and definitions.

For better-looking spreadsheets that are suitable for presentations, use the Shortcuts palette to turn grids on and off and to automatically size rows and columns. You can also insert graphics and text balloons.

Shortcuts for formatting spreadsheets in presentations (CS). After you put data into a spreadsheet, you can do a lot to dress it up and format it exactly the way you want it. In the Shortcuts palette, you can access commands to automatically size rows and columns, turn on and off row and column headers, and specify whether grid lines should be solid or dashed, for example. Because it's still a spreadsheet, you can also make a chart out of it.

Database

Using two windows to design layouts (SS). One of the frustrating things about creating layouts is that you constantly have to switch back to Browse mode to see the effects of your changes. That's where the New View command comes in handy. Next

time you need to change a layout, start by selecting New View from the View menu, and then select Tile Windows from the same menu. Make sure that a filled-in record is displayed, and then switch to Layout mode in one of the two windows. As you change the layout—by moving and resizing fields, changing field formatting, and so on—you can instantly see the effects of your modifications in the other window.

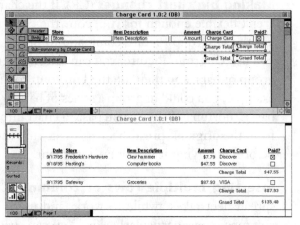

When modifying a layout, you can see the effects of changes—as they are made—if you keep one window open in Layout mode (top) and a second window open in Browse mode (bottom).

Setting up labels (CS). When setting up labels, getting fields to line up next to each other can be tricky. Say you have two fields: First and Last. You'd like Last to slide next to First when it prints. Three things must be true: the *tops* of the fields must be exactly lined up (use 400 percent view so you can see what you're doing, or use the Align Objects command in the Arrange menu); the fields can be very close but they *cannot* touch; and the height of the fields cannot increase as you go from left to right.

Creating reusable sorts, finds, and reports (JL). ClarisWorks 4 lets you save search and sort criteria so you can use them over and over. Click the Search or Sort tool in the toolbar on the left and then choose the New command from the pop-up menu. After giving a name to the action, generate the search or sort. It is now recorded for use at a later time. You can string these commands together by using the FastReport function that lets you select a layout, search instructions, sort instructions, and then print the resulting report.

Communications

Capturing sessions (CS). Capturing information in a session is most reliably done with Capture Data rather than by saving the communications document itself. Saving the document is best used only to retain the settings for calling a particular service or bulletin board. To keep the file small, save it before using it.

Microsoft Works Tips

These tips are for Microsoft Works 4, although many of them will also work in Works 3.

General

Embedding objects (CS). You can add a graphic, spreadsheet, or table to a document without ever leaving the word processor (actually, the same holds true for *any* document—not just word processing documents). From the tool palette, select the appropriate tool by clicking on it, and then draw a rectangle where you would like the object to appear in your document. The appropriate tools for the object you have chosen will appear. To edit that object later, simply double-click it. Using the same steps, you can add any number of OLE objects, including a Microsoft Excel spreadsheet or chart, a Microsoft Word document, WordArt, clip art, or an Equation Editor formula.

Using AddressBook for fast searches (CS). If you type a name in the word processor and then open the AddressBook, the name will automatically appear in the Match Records dialog box, ready to be matched to a record in the database.

Opening multiple documents as one Workspace (CR). If you regularly work with two or more Works documents at a time, you can save the documents as a set, called a *Workspace*, so they're easier to open. Just open all the documents you need to work with (a database file and a form letter, for example), and then use the Save Workspace command on the File menu to save the documents with a project name. Works creates a *workspace document*. The next time you double-click on the workspace document, all the documents saved with it will open at the same time.

Getting to Balloon Help (CS). Hold down [Shift][⌘][Option] to get instant access to Balloon Help for descriptions of the items on the toolbar and palette.

Word Processing

Zooming (CS). Formatting changes and alignment of graphics and text will be a lot easier to see if you zoom in on your document. Documents can be magnified up to 800 percent using the magnifying glass buttons on the ribbon, or you can zoom to a particular percentage by clicking on the down arrow at the bottom of the window. The percentage will show next to the arrow.

Automating search text entry (CS). To speed search and replace, select text before you choose the Find or Replace command (both on the Search menu). The selected text is automatically entered into the Find What text box.

Optimizing spell checking (CR). You can make Works' spelling checker run a little faster by resetting some of the standard spelling options. First, choose the Spelling command from the Document menu and click the Options button. Then click the Ignore Words In All Caps and Ignore Words With Digits boxes (so an X appears in each of them). If you don't need Works to help you with alternate spellings, click the Always Suggest box to remove the checkmark from it—it takes extra time for Works to look up and display alternate spellings.

Accessing the thesaurus quickly (CR). You can use Works' built-in thesaurus to find synonyms whenever you want, not just when you select a word in a document. Just choose the Thesaurus command from the Document menu, type the word whose synonyms you want to look up into the With box, and click the Look Up button.

Paint and Draw

Resizing paint frames (CS). While resizing a paint frame (with the frame handles), hold down the ⌘ key. This resizes the frame without scaling (and distorting) the contents.

Making a discontiguous selection (CS). If you need to change the colors, for instance, in some but not all parts of an image, you can select several different (discontiguous) sections of a paint frame by pressing Shift while using the Selection tool.

Selecting colors (CS). Hold down the ⌘ key and click on the paint selection with the Wand tool to select all occurrences of a particular color throughout an image.

Rotating text (CS). You can rotate text created in the Draw module by any degree by clicking on the Rotate Text button on the toolbar and selecting the number of degrees for rotation.

Rearranging pages (CS). Instead of using Copy, Cut, and Paste to move pages of text in a Draw document, you can easily rearrange pages by dragging and dropping them in the Page Sorter. This view shows all the pages in a Draw document side by side in a thumbnail preview. Select Page Sorter from the Views submenu of the View menu.

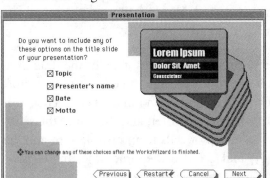

When creating a slide show presentation, use the Master Slide feature to place elements, such as your name or logo, on every slide.

Creating master slide elements (CS). Use the Master Slide feature to automatically insert a graphic or title onto all slides in a presentation. Access the Master Slide through the toolbar, or in the Format menu select Master Slide Attributes, or in the View menu, scroll to Views.

Working along straight lines (CR). You can force Works to draw straight lines at 45- or 90-degree angles by holding down [Shift] as you draw with the Straight Line tool. To move an object along a straight 45- or 90-degree line, select the object and hold down [Shift] as you drag it.

Embellishing lines with arrows (CR). You can add an arrow to one or both ends of any straight line you draw in Works. To move an arrow from one end of a line to the other, just flip the line around: Select the line, choose Rotate from the Draw menu, click the Horizontal Flip or Vertical Flip checkboxes, and then click the OK button.

Creating identical columns (CS/CR). Instead of trying to re-create similar-sized columns one at a time (and then spending time trying to align them), you can create multiple (one, two, three, or four) identically sized columns by clicking on the New Columns button on the Column tool in the floating tool palette. After you've selected the number of columns you want, drag out a rectangle on the page and Works will automatically create the desired number of equally sized columns within that rectangle.

To create a group of identical columns in Works 3, make one column the size you want, select it, duplicate it, and then drag the duplicate to the proper location. This is much faster than trying to draw identical columns from scratch.

Spreadsheet

Selecting areas to be printed (CS). If you have more than a single cell selected in a spreadsheet, when you choose the Print command, Works will print the range you have selected, not the entire spreadsheet.

Moving spreadsheet cells in groups (CR). By taking advantage of the drag-and-drop functionality added in Works 4, you can move a range of cells faster and more easily than you can with the Move command: Simply select a range of cells, click near the edge of the selection when the cursor becomes a pointer, and then drag the selection to the desired new location. To move a group of cells from one place to another in Works 3, select the cells, hold down ⌘ and Option at the same time, and click on the upper-right cell in the area where you want the selection to move.

Using ranges in formulas (CR). After you begin a formula, you can specify a range of cells by simply holding down the mouse button and dragging the mouse pointer across a group of cells. As you do this, the range address appears in the formula.

Getting to cell notes (CR). Cell notes are incredibly handy for inserting backup or explanatory information about numbers in your spreadsheets. To open a cell note quickly, hold down the ⌘ key and double-click on the cell whose note you want to display.

Creating new charts (CR). Instead of using the New Chart command to make a chart, select the data you want in the chart, click the Chart tool in the tool palette, and then hold down the mouse button as you drag an outline where you want the chart to appear. When you release the mouse button, the chart will be drawn inside the outline.

Database

Counting records (CS). You can automatically count the number of records in a field by creating a *serialized field*. To do that, choose Field from the Insert menu and click on Serialized in the dialog box that appears.

Printing selected records (CS). Use the Mark Records for Printing option (in the Tools menu) to print selected records. For instance, if the printer misprints a few labels (or you put them on the wrong envelope), you can mark those records to be reprinted.

Creating new fields (CR). When you're in Design view and need to add a new field to your file, hold down ⌘ and then press the mouse button to drag an outline where you want the field to appear. When you release the mouse button, the New Field dialog box will appear, and you can then type a name for the new field. (In Works 3, oddly enough, you don't have to hold down the ⌘ key.)

Changing field names and formats (CR). The fastest way to make field name or format changes is to double-click anywhere on the field in List or Design view. This brings up a Field Format dialog box where you can change the field name or format. In Works 3, changing the field name and its format requires you to go to two different dialog boxes: You'll need to double-click on the field's name to display the Field Name dialog box and double-click on the field's data space to display the Field Format dialog box.

Entering data in a form (CR). When you enter data on a Data view form, the selection moves from one field to another in the order in which you added fields to the form. In Works 4, to change the tab order all you have to do is choose Tab Order from the Format menu. In other versions, make a new form and add the fields in the tab order you want.

Communications

Automating sign-on (CS). Microsoft Works will record your sign-ons to automatically log onto commonly used services. To record a sign-on sequence, select Sign-On

If you use on-line services a lot, you may find it easier to record and save the sign-on sequence. When you need to sign on, just choose Play and the program executes the sign-on script for you.

from the Tools menu, and then select Record from the submenu. When you finish your recording, you will be prompted to name your sign-on sequence and save it. In future communications sessions, you can simply select Play and your script name, and Works will automatically sign onto the service.

Tracking time and costs (CS). Works now has a timer that keeps track of time spent on-line and the charges for the session. Make sure to reset the timer and charges log whenever you begin a new communications session.

Optimizing communications documents (CR). It takes forever to close a communications document when you have Works set to use an overflow area. To speed up communications documents, choose Preferences and click None in the Overflow Area Size box, and then click the Always Capture Text option.

Continuing to work during file transfers (CR). Works can maintain a connection during a long file transfer even if you activate another Works document. Just start sending or receiving, and then switch to the other document and continue working. When the file transfer is complete, Works will beep twice to let you know so that you can return to your communications document.

Calendar

Changing appointments (CS). Move appointments quickly by using drag and drop (instead of deleting and retyping the information). Select the appointment to be moved, hold down the mouse button as you move the selected text to the new location, and then release the mouse button to move the appointment.

Keeping track of To Do items for individual projects (CS). Display all the To Do items for a particular project by assigning each item a keyword (such as Report, Meeting, and so on) on which you can sort.

13 Utilities

It's always been a little difficult to define *utility*. A small program? One that doesn't make its own documents? One that serves as a supplement to another, full-fledged application? None of these definitions actually works because a utility can be quite large and intricate, create documents, and work as a stand-alone program.

But it's safe to say that a utility is a program that you wouldn't need unless you were also using your Mac for other things. You don't need a spelling checker unless you do word processing; you don't need a disk repair utility unless you're using that disk to store applications and documents; and you wouldn't need a utility that fancies up your desktop if you had no reason to be on the desktop!

We can't, of course, cover *every* Mac utility in this chapter—there are just too many. Utilities are mentioned in many chapters throughout this book; font utilities, for instance, are covered in Chapter 14. But we've tried to cover a good sampling of general-interest utilities in this chapter.

Contributors

Sharon Zardetto Aker (SZA) is the chapter editor.

Elizabeth Castro (EC) fell in love with the Mac while living in Barcelona, and founded the publishing house *Pagina Uno*. She was this chapter's editor for the fifth edition.

Kristi Coale (KC) has held staff positions at *InfoWorld* and *MacUser* and now freelances for Mac publications.

Rick Casreen (RC) is a writer, and the source of *The Pelorian Press*.

Ken Maki (KM) is a Macintosh consultant and author in Portland, Oregon.

Contents

~~~~~~

Power Tools

You may not think of yourself as a power user, but that definition is open to interpretation. Anyone who goes beyond using one or two applications and adds a few extra extensions might qualify for the title—and might find that some of the power tools discussed here come in handy.

Macros

A *macro* is a series of commands or actions that's invoked with a single key combination or a menu selection. On a simple level, you can use a *macro editor* to assign a keyboard equivalent to a menu command that doesn't have one, or combine two menu commands into a single one—putting Save and Quit onto ⌘ Option Q, for instance.

But that doesn't even scratch the surface of a macro program's power. As I wrote this chapter, for instance, I put the figures and their captions in the Word document as footnotes. When I was finished, I used a macro that went to each footnote reference mark, cut out the related picture, put it into a Photoshop document, and saved it as a PICT file, asking me to name the document; next, it came back to Word, cut the caption out of the footnote, and put it into the body of the chapter, formatting it the way the layout people needed it—applying the right style, typing "CAPTION:" in front of it, and marking it with the figure number.

I hope that description intrigues you, not frightens you away. Because although you can wind up doing some complicated programming—such as a list of commands for an intricate macro, the majority of macros—even those that play back a long series of actions—can be simply recorded by telling the macro editor to watch you while you do something.

QuicKeys (EC). I've used CE Software's **QuicKeys** ($120) macro-creating control panel for years to create keyboard equivalents for menu commands. It's performed flawlessly, and I've gotten so I can barely work without it (as I realized when I upgraded my system software and didn't have a compatible version of QuicKeys for a few days).

I found earlier versions of QuicKeys a bit complex and hard to use, but the current version is pretty intuitive. It may not be the most powerful macro program, but I don't use ten percent of QuicKeys' power as it is, and neither will most Mac users.

QuicKeys 3 has a whole slew of extensions, which let you, say, dial your telephone through your modem or select a printer from the Chooser. It also supports Apple events and AppleScript (described in Chapter 3).

Tempo (EC). The most powerful macro utility you can get is **Tempo II Plus** ($180, Affinity Microsystems). One of the most important benefits it has over QuicKeys is that it's smart—it can assess the contents of a field in a database, the codes that precede paragraphs, or part of a file's name in order to decide what action it should perform next.

Suppose you want to sharpen the images in a group of Photoshop files. You'll need to open each one, apply the filter, gaze off into space as the filter is applied, save the document, and open the next one. Because Tempo can choose files by name, you can have Tempo process each file sequentially, while you either find something better to do or just gaze off into space the *entire* time.

Tempo has an incredible array of *Externals*. You can use them in macros to check how much free space you have on a disk, assign and use variables, find out how long a particular string is, repeat a macro a given number of times, and much more. You can automate practically any Mac function with Tempo.

If all you want to do is assign keyboard shortcuts to a few menu commands and programs, you'll find all you need in **TempoEZ** ($80, Affinity Microsystems), the scaled-down version of Tempo II Plus, discussed above. TempoEZ also lets you play more complicated macros created with Tempo II Plus.

QuicKeys versus Tempo (SZA). I've always preferred Tempo, but for the sake of this chapter, I gave it up and worked exclusively with QuicKeys for three months. I used it for everything from simple keyboard equivalents for menu commands that didn't have them to more complicated tasks such as the Word/Photoshop figure-processing procedure described earlier.

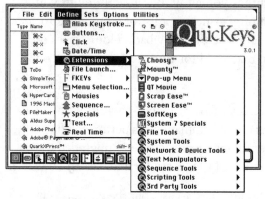

Despite the confusing plethora of options and menu icons in the QuicKeys dialog, you can save lots of time by using macros you create with it.

And how do I feel about QuicKeys after putting it through its paces? I feel that it's still awkward and ungainly—too many windows, too many menus, too many labels (a macro can be a sequence, a mousie, an extension, and so on), too many steps in what should be a simple recording. (The 3.5 version, due out about the same time as this book, will address all these issues. CE promises a totally reworked interface, as well as some new capabilities, such as the ability to create application-specific toolbars and a batch-processing mode which will let you execute a macro on a collection of files.)

The current version has too many glitches: Sometimes a macro works flawlessly ten times and then chokes on the eleventh, leaving the QuicKeys icon blinking at the top of the Apple menu until you restart the computer. View what you've recorded for a QuicKeys macro, and you'll find a dozen surprises: multiple listings of *pause .5 seconds* and *wait watchcursor* which, if you delete, rarely prevent the macro from working.

At the same time, on its simpler levels, it's a cinch to use and is a boon to every Mac user. It handles some things that Tempo balks at—such as working with pop-up menus inside dialog boxes—and does most of its chores smoothly. But its dominance in the marketplace is due to better marketing, not inherent superiority or simplicity.

I'm glad to get back to Tempo, though my love for it isn't blind. It occasionally slips up in the order of

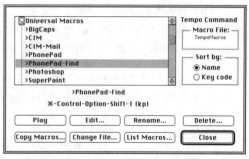

Two of Tempo's dialog boxes.
Top: The Tempo Command dialog where you can edit and rename, or even trigger, existing macros.
Bottom: The editing window, where you can alter, delete, or add steps to an existing macro.

commands—record a switch to a desk accessory followed by a Find command, play it back in, say, Word, and the Find command may be executed (in Word) before the desk accessory opens. But Tempo's overall power, its capability to branch to a specific series of commands based on the specifics at the time of the macro playback (for instance, depending on what's on the Clipboard), its ability to present a dialog box and act on user input, the ease with which you can request that an existing macro be repeated a specific number of times, and its less obtrusive interface makes it, for me, far superior to QuicKeys.

Compression

Compression is making a file smaller so you can squeeze more information into a smaller space on a disk. Only a few short years ago, when hard drives were relatively small and expensive, compressing even active files (the ones you were still working on) was important. Although that's less of an imperative now, compressing archival files (ones that you want to save just in case you ever need them again) is still an issue. And, of course, if you want to e-mail a file, smaller ones transmit more quickly, so file compression is always a major concern for telecommunication.

File-level compression (SZA/KC). A *file-level* compression package lets you select individual files, folders, or groups of files and folders to compress. A compression utility might let you do any or all of the following:

- Choose between compressing your files quickly but not as compactly, or compressing more tightly but taking more time to do so.

- Select groups of files for compression according to their labels, file types, prefixes or suffixes in their names, or according to a list of what should be included or excluded.

- Segment a large file into pieces to fit on floppy disks.

- Add a password to restrict access to a compressed file.

- Use a special menu in the Finder to compress files directly on the desktop.

- Translate files compressed in a variety of compression formats.

- Create a *self-extracting archive* which can be expanded without the compression software.

Some compression utilities offer "on-the-fly" compression: As you save a document, it's automatically compressed, and if you open it, it's automatically expanded without your having to do anything (except keep the compression extension running in the background). Some even work constantly in the background on

> ### Lossless versus Lossy Compression (KC)
>
> Whether file- or disk-level, the compression programs described in this chapter use *lossless compression*—the files retain all of their information after compression. You can compress and then extract a file as many times as you need to, and you will always have exactly the same file. *Lossy compression,* on the other hand, is employed by utilities that perform JPEG compression and other such methods used in compacting video files, for example, where some information is lost during compression.

any or all files on your drive to keep free space at a maximum; these utilities usually let you define which files can be compressed (documents not modified in the last two months, for instance) and how long your computer should be idle before the *idle time compression* kicks in.

StuffIt Deluxe (SZA/KC/EC). Even if **StuffIt Deluxe 3.5** ($130, Aladdin Systems) weren't the most powerful compression program for the Mac, it would still be the sentimental favorite: first, for having been around so long, and second, because it started out as a shareware program written by high school student Raymond Lau (who's been out of college for a while now). In fact, the utility's very name is used in the Mac world to refer to compressed files—*stuffed* files. Its age is something of an advantage: The majority of the files you find on-line have been compressed—and, more importantly,

G Ch1.sit					
9 items	"Ch1 .sit " is 50K		545,672K free on " Int HD "		
Name	Kind	Date	Expanded	Stuffed	Saved
1.1	Adobe Photoshop™ 3...	1/28/96	16K	4K	75%
1.2	Adobe Photoshop™ 3...	1/28/96	10K	4K	54%
1.3	Adobe Photoshop™ 3...	3/13/96	7K	4K	49%
1.4	Adobe Photoshop™ 3...	1/28/96	12K	5K	57%
1.5	Adobe Photoshop™ 3...	2/26/96	14K	8K	40%
1.6	Adobe Photoshop™ 3...	1/28/96	21K	8K	63%
1.7	Adobe Photoshop™ 3...	1/28/96	12K	5K	60%
1.8	Adobe Photoshop™ 3...	1/28/96	10K	4K	61%
1.9	Adobe Photoshop™ 3...	1/28/96	15K	6K	57%

Stuff UnStuff New Delete Info View Launch Move

☐ Self-Extracting ✎ Comments...		117K	49K	58%

StuffIt Deluxe's main window and control palette. You can see the sizes of the original files, and their compressed sizes in the window; the statistics for the entire archive are at the bottom of the window.

can be decompressed—with StuffIt. Any time you see a file with a *.sit* suffix (like *QReport.sit)*, it's a file that's been stuffed with StuffIt.

StuffIt compresses your files—either manually through the main program or automatically with the included module when your Mac is idle—in *archives*, separate documents that may contain any number of your original files. You can segment large archives into two or more pieces to fit on floppy disks. The ingenious View option lets you peek at text and images inside your compressed files. You can protect your archives from inquiring minds with encryption and a password (see "Levels of Security" later in this chapter). And, StuffIt provides the capability of expanding many other compression formats, ones used by other compression programs. One quick tip: In the main StuffIt dialog box, the Open button is the default when a folder is selected in the left panel. If you don't want to open the folder, but instead want to add it to the panel on the right, hold down ⌘ to make Add the default button so you can activate it with Return or Enter instead of reaching for the mouse.

HOT TIP

StuffIt's Magic Menu, which is added to the menu bar in the Finder, and its drag-and-drop compression options let you compress files right from the desktop.

StuffIt's completeness comes at a price, and it occupies 2MB on your hard disk. A shareware version, **StuffIt Lite** ($25), limits you to stuffing and unstuffing but that may be all you need. The automatic compression module, **SpaceSaver**, can also be purchased separately for $80.

Compact Pro (EC). My personal favorite in the file-compression field is **Compact Pro**, a shareware program by Bill Goodman. It doesn't work automatically, nor does it have a Finder menu, but it can compress and expand, add passwords, and split large files with the best of them. Compact Pro is fast and reliable and worth every penny of the $25 it costs.

More Disk Space (KC). Other than the flexibility it gives you when compressing files, **More Disk Space** ($100, Alysis) doesn't distinguish itself much from the other programs mentioned here except for its operation along a network. Network administrators will be happy to know that MDS can be installed onto other Macs on the network from a central location; it can also be set up on a server to automatically compress files that are added to it.

Self-Extracting Archives (Darcy DiNucci/EC)

Older versions of compression software often can't read files that have been compressed with newer versions. If you're not sure whether the recipient will be able to open the file, make it a *self-extracting archive,* which can decompress itself.

A self-extracting archive is actually an application, and it uses memory like any other application. If you get an "insufficient memory" message when you double-click on a self-extracting archive, give it more memory (with the Get Info command).

If you are compressing a very small document (say, under 25K), it usually doesn't make sense to make it self-extracting: Compression programs add from 18K to 25K of instructions to the file so it knows how to decompress itself. Instead, use a compression program that the recipient has, or send the file uncompressed.

Driver-level compression (KC). Driver-level compression utilities are supposedly easier to use than file-level packages because they compress your entire disk and carry out expansion and recompression without any user intervention. All files remain compressed and are decompressed only when the Mac reads them from the disk.

Use caution when using driver-level compression utilities. They replace your Mac's hard disk driver, which controls how the Mac and all its applications handle files. Before installing any driver-level utility you should make sure your hard disk is completely backed up. *[Let me reword that in much stronger language. Don't use driver-level compression software. It's not worth the risk. File recovery from a damaged disk that's been compressed is nearly impossible. Why spend $150 on questionable software when for $200 you can get an 800MB hard drive?—SZA]*

If I were to use a driver-level compression program, it would be **Stacker** ($100, Stac Electronics). It's the least intrusive disk-level utility, since it merely attaches itself to your existing disk driver instead of replacing it. It also lets you use other programs such as Disk First Aid and Norton Utilities.

I can't recommend Alysis' **eDisk** ($150), which is much more intrusive than Stacker, since it replaces the hard disk's driver—and erases your hard disk in the process, so you have to reinstall your system software and applications after the disk is compressed.

Security　(KM)

Unfortunately, we live in a world where sometimes we must be concerned about safeguarding computer data so it doesn't fall into the wrong hands.

Levels of Security (SZA/KM). There are several different ways to secure your data, each of which may be available separately or as part of a larger software package.

Data encryption is at the extreme end of the security spectrum: Encryption programs secure your data by scrambling and unscrambling it when you provide the proper password. Basic encryption programs are generally secure; only someone who is very knowledgeable and determined could get to your data after it's been encrypted.

For medium-level security, try a utility that can lock a folder. The contents of a locked folder cannot be accessed without a password, but the items in the folder are not encrypted. This is a good method for keeping people from casually browsing through your data.

Exaggerate the locked folder idea, and you get a locked hard disk. You can lock a disk so that only someone with the password can access its data; more secure programs also encrypt the drive's data.

Unless you absolutely need high-level security, avoid encryption programs like the plague. If you forget a password, there is *no* way to get at your files—even the company that made the program won't be able to help you. If you store encrypted files and a year or two later want to get at them, you may be using newer encryption software

HOT TIP

Is Big Brother Watching?　(KM)

There are several data encryption methods, but DES *(Data Encryption Standard)* is generally considered the most secure. It was established by the National Bureau of Standards and is supposedly impossible to break unless you possess the *encryption key.* But not everyone thinks DES is all it's cracked up to be.

Many believe that the code was written so that NSA agents could break it. Bell scientist Michael Wiener introduced a paper at Crypt93 (a conference for cryptographers) describing a microprocessor chip that will enable the NSA to break any DES-encrypted message in two minutes.

There is, however, a solution called Pretty Good Privacy (PGP), a *public key cryptography* application, although many—including the government—are unhappy about the existence of this program because its encryption seems to be unbreakable. Despite the opposition, **ViaCrypt PGP for Macintosh** is available from ViaCrypt for $135.

by then—which won't open the old files, even with the password. And, to top it all off, encrypted files usually can't be recovered from a hard disk when disaster strikes.

FileGuard and TrashGuard (KM). ASD Software provides two security packages. **FileGuard** ($250) is a comprehensive security package that provides disk-, folder-, and file-level security. It will automatically encrypt your data as it is saved to the hard disk; you can also use it to prevent files from being copied off your hard drive. For Macs that are used by several people, you can set up a security system that allows access using an AppleShare-like privilege setup.

TrashGuard ($80) is a simple utility that completely erases a file when it's placed in the trash. The space the file occupied is overwritten, making it unrecoverable.

The Kent Marsh collection (KM). Kent Marsh makes a line of security products that can be used to encrypt files, lock up your hard drive, lock folders, or prevent casual access to your Macintosh. While each is a stand-alone product providing a certain level of security, they are also made to work with each other to provide a complete security system. One of the unique features of the Kent Marsh system is the use of an Administrator's disk, which allows access to your data even if you forget your password.

NightWatch II ($160) locks your hard drive without encrypting files. Access to the hard disk can be gained with a password or with a key disk. NightWatch II also includes a security screensaver that prevents someone from accessing open files on your Mac when you leave it unattended.

FolderBolt Pro ($130) is used to manage access to folders. You can determine the level of access someone has to your folders by making them read-only, write-only, or completely locked. FolderBolt also lets you lock the trash so only someone with the password can delete files.

CryptoMatic ($100) is a complete encryption package that lets you use a variety of standards to encrypt files or folders. If you have to send a file to someone else, you can create a self-deciphering file that the recipient can open without the CryptoMatic extension, as long as he or she has the proper password. CryptoMatic also allows you to erase files so that they are unrecoverable, even with data recovery software.

QuickLock ($30) is a screensaver that prevents others from using your Mac without the proper password.

A.M.E. (KM). **Access Managed Environment**, or **A.M.E.** ($160, Casady & Greene), is a multilevel security package providing varying levels of access to different users. It offers disk-, folder-, or file-level security, and can even be set up to reject floppy disks so that nothing can be copied from your disk. A.M.E. includes a secure delete feature so that trashed files cannot be recovered.

A.M.E. is very comprehensive, providing tools for almost every security need. It can even be used to prevent desktop modification and setup—ideal for multiuser access where each user has his or her own secure folder. A.M.E. can also be used in an AppleShare environment to restrict access to AppleShare volumes or other AppleTalk devices.

Critical warning! Do not use any hard disk utility programs or update the hard disk drivers on a drive protected by A.M.E.. Doing so will destroy the data on your hard drive or cause your hard disk to crash.

WARNING

Other Must-Haves

Your arsenal of Mac utilities wouldn't be complete without at least some of the programs described in this section.

Managing extensions (SZA). An *extension manager* helps solve startup conflicts by letting you determine which extensions and control panels should load, and in what order. (Extension conflicts—which can involve both extensions and control panels—are covered in Chapter 7.) Full-featured managers handle more than just extensions and control panels; some offer control over fonts and items in the Startup Items and Apple Menu Items folders.

An extension manager utility basically does its work by moving things in and out of the Extensions and Control Panels folders. If you use an extension manager, you'll find folders inside your System Folder named something like *Control Panels (disabled)* and *Extensions (disabled)* that are used to hold the items you've turned off.

The straightforwardly named **Extensions Manager** was, for a long time, a no-frills freeware control panel. It has a few frills now, and it's freeware of a different sort: it's included in System 7.5. You can create various "sets"—groups of extensions—and choose a set for a restart. It lets you run or disable extensions, control panels, fonts, and even items in the Startup Items folder, but it doesn't let you change the order in which they load. Now Utilities, described later in this chapter, includes **Now Startup Manager** which offers a few more features than the Extensions Manager.

Catching conflicts (SZA). **Conflict Catcher 3** ($100, Casady & Greene) retains its predecessor's claim to being the best extensions manager around. The program goes beyond simple management both in function and interface. You can define sets of extensions to use under certain circumstances, handle fonts and Apple Menu items, and get information about the function of each item in every list. (For common items, Conflict Catcher uses a description from its own database of information; for others, the embedded Balloon Help information is displayed.) Conflict Catcher puts its own menu up in the menu bar so you can easily open the control panel or select a set of extensions to use at the next startup.

GOOD FEATURE

One of Conflict Catcher's neatest features is the Linking option, which lets you define groups of extensions which should always run together (like Apple's handful of CD-ROM extensions) or never run together (such as two screensavers). With links defined, turning one item on or off affects the others in the link automatically. And, of course, there's Conflict Catcher's original claim to fame: It helps you track

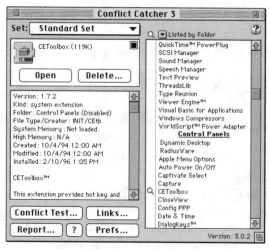

Conflict Catcher manages your Mac's extensions and also provides little extras such as information about the items listed in its window.

down the troublemaker(s) in an extension conflict by shuffling items around and asking you to restart the Mac, as many times as necessary, until the culprit is isolated.

Speed bump (SZA). Accelerate your Mac without touching the hardware—just install Connectix's **Speed Doubler** ($100). While the name is a slight exaggeration—you won't *double* the speed of your machine—you will see a significant increase in its performance.

POWER MAC

Speed Doubler's main module is for Power Macs; it boosts the speed of non-native code (instructions written for the 68K-based Macs instead of for the PowerPC chip) considerably. Because the Finder is still not entirely native for PowerPC Macs, Speed Doubler helps even users who are using native applications. The speed increase you get depends on your Mac, and your software, but you can generally assume you'll be bumped up a little past the capabilities of the model that's one step beyond yours; so, a Power Mac 6100 with Speed Doubler can perform a little better than a Power Mac 7100.

Speed Doubler also includes a module for 68K Macs that increases their performance, although not as impressively as on the Power Mac side.

Other necessities (SZA). In addition to many of the utilities described throughout this chapter, there are others that are necessities of Mac life, so I want to mention them here even though they're dealt with in detail in other chapters.

- *Virus protection:* Whether you use a commercial package or one of the many shareware products around, protecting your files from nasty infections is necessary if you have high exposure—all of this is covered in Chapter 7. (I have to admit that I don't understand why people *buy* virus protection when the terrific Disinfectant is free.)

- *Backup software:* Sometime, when you least expect it, you're going to lose some files, or even access to your entire drive—and you're going to wish you had an extra copy of important documents put aside. Backup software makes making those copies a cinch. There's more about this in Chapters 5 and 7.

- *Memory manipulation:* RAM Doubler from Connectix is a staple of Mac use; see Chapter 4 for more information about it.

- *Disk repair and recovery tools:* The Disk First Aid program that comes with the system software is a good first step for preventing problems or fixing them afterward. But Norton Utilities, from Symantec (which first rose to fame in the PC world), keeps millions of Mac hard disks safe and fixes small problems before they become big ones. Actually, though, I've always preferred MacTools, which Symantec bought and, to everyone's surprise, kept in its product line instead of killing it. Serious Mac users, and especially consultants, keep both of these programs in their troubleshooting arsenal. Check Chapter 7 for more information on these.

- *Font utilities:* See Chapter 14 for details, but it boils down to this: If you use lots of fonts, you need Suitcase or MasterJuggler to handle them. I've always preferred Suitcase, and so do most of my friends—whom I haven't unduly influenced in this area, so far as I know.

Resource Editing

One of the nicest things about Macintosh software, and something that sets it apart from most PC software, is that the code that makes the program run is separate from the interface that's presented to the user—the dialog boxes, alerts, menus, icons, pictures, sounds, and so on, collectively known as *resources*. That means you don't have to be a programmer to futz around with the interface; all you need is a *resource editor.*

The two editors (EC). There are two good resource editors available for the Mac: Apple's **ResEdit** and Mathemaesthetics' excellent **Resorcerer**. Although both programs can do the job, Resorcerer offers many time-saving options that programmers will love. Resorcerer can find and replace text in resources, decompile the text in resources for spell checking or printing, and it has a great icon editor, just for starters. Resorcerer is also more stable, more flexible, and generally more powerful. Unfortunately, the difference in price—ResEdit is freeware, while Resorcerer costs $256—makes ResEdit the only choice for most home editors.

Used incorrectly, ResEdit or Resorcerer can make your program (or your system) inoperable. Make sure you *always* work on a copy, and in the case of system resources, make sure you have a disk you can boot up your Mac with, in case you damage the installed system.

ResEdit's uses (EC). You can change (or just copy) resources from practically any application, desk accessory, extension, control panel, or other nondocument file. A few programs, most notably those from Microsoft, cannot be looked at or tinkered with. (Spoilsports!)

What does all this mean? It means you can personalize your programs and the System and Finder by changing the wording of menu commands, adding keyboard shortcuts, and editing text and icons in dialogs and alerts. You can also transfer pictures and sounds from one program to another.

ResEdit basics (SZA). Despite the sometimes dire consequences of making a mistake with ResEdit and ruining a program, it's easy to use—easy enough that you can just play around with it and figure out how to change some resources.

When you use ResEdit's Open command and select an application or desk accessory, you get a window that displays the resources used in that program. Double-click on a resource icon, and you'll get a list of resources of that type (such as all the cursors, or all the icons). Double-click on an item in the list, and you'll be looking at the actual resource, with its (sometimes) editable contents. (As a general rule, the resources represented by pictorial icons rather than the block of ones and zeros are the ones you can edit easily.) The figure at left shows the main resource window for System 7.5's Find File desk accessory, the window that displays its CURS items (cursor resources), and the editing window for one of the cursors.

ResEdit has no Save command. Instead, when you close the main window of a file that you've worked on, you're asked if you want to save the changes.

Three steps to happy ResEditing (SZA/EC). If you follow these three steps (along with general Mac hygiene, such as regular saves and backups) you should be able to modify your resources without fear.

Working in ResEdit means working in a series of windows. To edit a cursor in the Find File desk accessory, for instance, you open Find File and double-click on the CURS resource icon. You'll get a window that shows all the cursor resources (there are two available in Find File); double-clicking on one opens that cursor in an editing window where you can alter it.

1. **Always, but *always*, work on a copy.** That has already been said, but it bears repeating: Never work on the original or sole copy of a program or the system. Instead, make a copy of the program and alter *that*. It's easy to damage a file so that it will never run again, and unless you have a clean copy, you'll have lost it forever.

2. **Be careful what you touch.** There are many different kinds of resources; some are more difficult to alter than others, and some are downright dangerous to mess around with. Generally speaking, you should limit yourself to these resources:

   - *DITL:* dialog box contents, with corresponding DLOG or ALRT resource that stores the window size and title

   - *MENU* and *CMNU:* menu resources

   - *STR#:* string resources attached to menus and dialogs

   - *PICT:* pictures used in the program

   - *CURS:* cursors in programs and the system

   - *ICON, ics4, ic18* (and other resources beginning with IC): icon families

   - *snd:* sound resources can't be altered easily but you can copy and paste them from one place to another

3. **Don't create, just modify.** Don't erase anything and don't create anything: only modify what's already there. Generally, you should stick to cosmetic changes—modifying a button's text, size, color, and shape is fine, but changing it from a button to a checkbox will probably cause the program to hang.

Other Desktop Tools

Not every utility is a power tool—but that doesn't mean that it's not extremely useful. There's a wide range of utilities that do everything from find files to change your desktop background.

Utility Collections

Because so many utilities are tiny, they have a hard time making it as commercial software. It finally occurred to someone to put a bunch of the tiny ones together and sell the collection. So, there are several utility collections available, although their contents are often of uneven quality and totally unrelated to one another.

The Now collection (SZA). Now Utilities is the premier utility collection for the Mac. Is it perfect? No. Is it great? No, not really. But it's good and there's no competition. Thousands of users can't work without it.

Now Utilities has two drawbacks, both of which you can live with or work around. First, it's pretty self-centered: Install all the components and you'll find that they've taken over your Mac. Press ⌘F in the Finder, and Now Find comes up instead of Find File. Carelessly select a menu item while a key is being pressed, and you'll find that you've added a keyboard equivalent accidentally. You can avoid unwelcome surprises by activating a single component at a time and learning all its ins and outs. Now Utilities' second problem is that it always seems to "break" under a system update, causing problems and conflicts; it also, because it's in such widespread use, has problems with some popular applications. To Now Software's credit, they are always on top of things, supplying fixes and updates on-line for all their customers; if you use Now Utilities, plan to stay in touch on-line.

Here's a roundup of Now Utilities' components. As I write this, **Now Utilities 6** ($90; $30 upgrade for **5.x** users) is only weeks away from release; these descriptions include the new **6.0** modules, although I haven't had a chance to try them out yet.

Now's premier components are:

- *Now Menus.* You get a hierarchical Apple menu in which you can customize the order of items and even add dividers (version 6 lets you go to ten levels of submenus instead of five). This capability alone is important, but Now Menus also lets you create other menus for instant access to all sorts of things—documents, applications, even file servers on a network. In addition, you can assign keyboard equivalents to any existing menu item.

GOOD FEATURE

- *Now SuperBoomerang.* This utility is something you can't live without once you've used it. It puts a menu bar inside every Open and Save dialog, providing lists of recently opened folders, files, and disks so you can get directly to them without moving up and down through intervening folders. The Options menu lets you assign permanent entries to the other menus, as well as edit what you see in the dialog's list—copy,

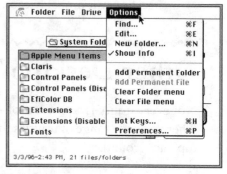

SuperBoomerang adds a menu bar to every Open and Save dialog. The Option menu lets you add items to its first three menus, as well as search for files and even move, copy, rename, or delete them.

move, rename, or delete items without moving to the Finder. Finally, it provides a Find feature which, although it's no better than the system's Find File, is right there in the dialog box.

- *Now Startup Manager.* This extensions manager is miles ahead of the system's control panel, and only a few steps behind the stand-alone gem Conflict Catcher.

Now's smaller but still handy utilities include:

- *Now FolderMenus.* This lets you click on a folder on the desktop and get a pop-up menu that lists its contents, with submenus for subcontents; select an item to open it. But you can do more than just view the contents: You just drag a desktop item directly into one of the submenus to put it in an inner folder without ever having to open the outer one.

- *Now Scrapbook.* If you need a scrapbook at all, the one that comes with the system software won't be sufficient. Store almost anything—including sound and QuickTime movies—in this scrapbook, on pages you can name for easier retrieval. You can use a catalog view to see more than one page at a time, and print the scrapbook contents as thumbnails or full-size.

- *Now QuickFiler.* The Find function in QuickFiler is no better than Find File, though Now claims that it's faster. But QuickFiler also compresses files, even breaking them into pieces to fit on floppies. (Its usefulness is limited, because it can't handle standard compressed files that StuffIt makes.)

Version 5 of Now Utilities also includes: **Now Save**, for automatic document saving at set intervals; **Now Profile**, for compiling a profile of your system, including extensions, control panels, and even applications that are available; and **WYSIWYG Menus** ("whizzy-wig"—What You See Is What You Get) that change all Font menus so that the names are listed in the fonts themselves. All these items are still in version 6.

The new items in Now Utilities 6 include:

- *Now Tabs.* With an apparent nod towards Windows 95, Now Tabs puts a tab bar at the bottom of the screen; dragging an item onto the bar creates a button which later lets you open the item.

- *Now AutoType.* AutoType will let you define shorthand entries that are automatically expanded as you type (type *ss*, for instance, and it turns into *spreadsheet)*; this is similar to Word 6's AutoText feature, or the Glossary feature in Casady & Greene's Spell Catcher (described in Chapter 8).

- *Now Shortcuts.* The Shortcuts in the title refers to saving time in the Finder, triggering such actions as duplicating, setting sharing options, and locking files with a single mouse click.

Super 7 Utilities (EC). **Super 7 Utilities** ($100, Atticus) provides a small list of capabilities: tear-off menus so you can put your regular menus anywhere on the screen; a printer menu; an alias trasher; a sound manager; a file finder; and a comments manager that lets you type comments in a Save dialog that gets stored in the item's Get Info window. I love tear-off menus, and Super 7's work quite well, but the printer menu is good only in environments with multiple printers. I couldn't get the file finder to work at all, and most of the other components are not overwhelmingly useful. In all, the product isn't worth its price tag.

Aladdin Desktop Tools (SZA). Aladdin, purveyor of fine utilities like the superb StuffIt, has succumbed to the "let's make a package" syndrome: Take one terrific can't-live-without-it tool that's too small to be sold on its own and surround it with a bunch of okay-but-don't-really-need-it enhancements. The core of **Aladdin Desktop Tools** ($90) is Desktop Shortcut, the one you can't live without. Shortcut puts a menu inside all Open and Save dialogs that lets you jump directly to any folder or file without traversing intervening folders. The menu keeps track of recently used files and folders and also lists any items you specifically add to it. You also get the convenience of a Find command, an erase option, and the ability to look *inside* a StuffIt archive of multiple items—and unstuff a file so you can open it.

As wonderful as Shortcut is, it's not worth $90, and none of the other utilities in the package adds to its value. In fact, two of them—Desktop SpeedBoost (for faster Finder copying) and Desktop Makeover (for adding keyboard commands to Finder menus)—wouldn't even install on my Mac because they're incompatible with system 7.5.3. While the Desktop Viewer application could come in handy (it lets you view many types of documents without opening the parent application), Desktop Printer (drag and drop a document to a desktop printer icon to send it to the printer) and Desktop Secure Delete (make erased files unrecoverable) don't add up to a well-rounded package. Find this at a blow-out sale price, though, and you'll wonder how you ever survived without Shortcut.

Connectix Desktop Utilities (SZA/EC). This package provides keyboard shortcuts for menus and dialog boxes, a cursor locator (meant for PowerBooks with passive-matrix displays, so it's not much use on a desk Mac), control panel management, desktop beautifiers, file synchronization (described in the PowerBook utilities section later in this chapter), limited security, and a screen dimmer. **Connectix Desktop Utilities**, or **CDU**, ($100, Connectix) is something of a jack-of-all-trades and master of none: It includes many utilities, but none is particularly spectacular. The screensaver only dims the screen (no fun pictures here), the security system can be overridden by booting from a floppy, and you can't customize the desktop beautifying schemes (except for the background picture). The package was obviously spun off from the company's CPU package for PowerBooks (described a little later in this chapter) and isn't worth half the price they're asking.

Search Tools

There are two basic ways to search for something on the computer: Look for an item based on its name or other outer attribute like a label or modification date, or according to the text stored inside the file. The first is a system-level capability, while the second takes a special utility that looks through the text of a file for key words or phrases.

Finding files (SZA). The Mac's anemic Find command underwent a total revamp in System 7.5, essentially killing the "find file" utility market. Apple took the best shareware find utility—Bill Monk's Find Pro—and licensed it for the system software.

Several utility packages, such as Now Utilities and Norton Utilities, include Find utilities. And two utilities described later in this chapter, DiskTools and Disk Top, have powerful Find functions. But there's only one commercial package that's strictly a file finder: Olduvai's **MasterFinder** ($150). While it's slick and fast, it's not *that* much better than the system's Find File utility, and its price certainly doesn't reflect the reality of the market.

Text retrieval (KC). The basic function of a text-retrieval package is to find a document stored anywhere on a disk or drive by searching the text that it contains. To do that job well, most text retrieval packages will let you:

- Search for part of a word, a word, or a string of words.
- Select a location—a disk or specific folder—to search.
- Use AND and OR to define multiple search criteria.
- Add special criteria for the search, such as the creation date of a file.
- Save your search criteria for use in later searches.
- Use your Mac for something else while it searches for your text in the background.
- Create and maintain an updated index of the files and folders on your disk, to expedite file searches.
- Read the contents of found files from within the search program.
- Search over a network.

Location, location (KC). **OnLocation 2.0.1** ($130, On Technology) is the best search tool available on the Mac, because of its speed (it creates indexes for fast searches) and its ability to work in the background.

But OnLocation's search criteria are paltry at best. The program offers text searching with the Boolean operators AND and OR as well as a half-hearted wild card search—it can match the root of a word to find related files. I harp on the lack of search criteria so much because OnLocation has the potential of returning a daunting list of files—particularly since it can work over a network and search remote volumes.

FetchIt (KC). **FetchIt 3** ($40, SilverWARE) is an extension that enhances the functions of the standard Save and Open dialog boxes by installing a pop-up menu containing several functions—most notably text retrieval.

FetchIt's Look 'Fer command lets you search for text strings in files in a given folder (and only in that folder) and is smart enough to automatically narrow the scope of the search to files the active program can read. A successful Look 'Fer will display a Context Window that shows you the part of the file where FetchIt found the match. The utility also lets you continue your search with Look 'Fer Next, which picks up where Look 'Fer left off, using the same criteria.

Additionally, FetchIt includes other utilities, such as Find, which looks for text in file and folder names. FetchIt also lets you change disks and rename, delete, copy, and move files and folders—all from within an application.

Alki Seek (KC). If it weren't for the fact that this program doesn't generate an index and doesn't search in the background, I'd tell you that **Alki Seek 2.1** ($40, Alki Software) is the best search package available for individual users. I have a soft spot for this program because it has so many ways to narrow down a search—without bogging down the user in the process.

The strongest feature of Seek is its "banter box." With so many options available for building a search string, this box is a necessity. It answers the question, "What was I looking for again?" by giving you a plain English description of what you had set up as your search criteria.

Alki Seek has a very elegant interface. The majority of the program's operations are handled in two main windows—one to set up a search and one to show the results. The search window has icons representing the different criteria you can select to define your search, and Alki Seek lets you search for files and folders by location, date, size, and application as well as by content.

Using Word for word searches (SZA). Word 6's Find File command can be used to find text inside non-Word documents, even if the document can't be opened by Word. So, if you use Word for word processing, you already have a general-purpose text retrieval tool.

HOT TIP

Just for PowerBooks

PowerBook users have some concerns that never bother desktop Mac users: making a battery last, figuring out how much battery charge is left, dealing with a "disappearing" cursor on a passive-matrix screen, and keeping track of where the most recently changed copy of a file resides. For software solutions to these concerns, read on.

POWERBOOK

CPU (SZA). **Connectix PowerBook Utilities** ($100), known as CPU, has quite a following because it was the first collection of PowerBook utilities available. It's loaded with features—but they're not all useful, and they sure load up your menu bar with icons. Fortunately, you can pick and choose among the modules and keep clutter to a minimum.

CPU provides the basics: battery management with "sets" of conservation settings for different situations, an instant Sleep command, and a cursor finder. It also gives you keyboard control over menus and dialog boxes—a welcome feature for the trackball-impaired. The Easy Sync utility provides bare-bones file-synching capabilities (see "That Synching Feeling" later in this chapter).

But Connectix doesn't seem to care much about this little collection anymore: there have been no updates, it's seldom demonstrated at trade shows except by special request, and it's rarely advertised. So, there's some question in my mind as to how long this product will be supported.

PBTools (SZA/RC). A serious geekhead workplace lurks beneath **PBTools'** appealing simplicity of design ($100, $40 for owners of VST's PowerBook batteries, VST Systems). One control panel offers easy access to battery analysis, security, and power and sleep adjustment. A compact menu bar icon displays more information than seems possible in such a tiny space. At a glance you can check the battery-charge level, AC connection, hard disk spin, and AppleTalk and Caps Lock status. Deep Discharge Battery easily reconditions nickel cadmium batteries. It even has a *key remapper*—by pressing (Control), you can use the (→)(←)(↑)(↓) keys as (Page Down), (Page Up), (Home), and (End). And it's all beautifully supported by extensive Help balloons.

GOOD FEATURE

Enter battery nerdhood with PBTools' PowerWatch station: Use adjustable graphs and diagnostic logs to track voltage thresholds, charge/discharge curves, and other matters for up to four different batteries (it's not half as difficult as it sounds). If you have a PowerBook, you need PBTools.

That synching feeling (SZA). The PowerBooks introduced a unique problem to millions of computer users: When a file is used in two places (on the PowerBook and on a desktop machine), it's important that, as one copy is changed, the other is updated—and it's just as important to know if both files have been changed since the copy was made. Keeping the files updated in both places is called *synchronization* or *synching*.

File Assistant is a simple synching program that comes with your system software—it's in System 7.5 and also in the 3.0 update to System 7.1. It's better than nothing—but not much better. **CPU** and **CDU** from Connectix (described earlier in this chapter) include the EasySync module. EasySync watches as you drag things from one folder (or disk) to another and interrupts the normal "An older item with the same name already exists at this location. Do you want to replace with the one you're moving?" dialog with one that gives you the option to synchronize the two files so that they're the same.

Of all the stand-alone file-synching programs that came out soon after the PowerBooks were released, only **PowerMerge** ($130, Leader Technologies) remains—and rightly so, in an atmosphere of "may the best program win." You can use a variety of controls to define which files, folders, and disks should be synchronized, and when. You can include or exclude a specific file from a sync run, or any file that meets certain criteria. You can set the sync to run at a specific time, or in reaction to a certain event (like mounting a volume or logging on to a network). PowerMerge is so smooth and easy to set up that I use it all the time for backing up my desktop work as well as for file synching.

The Clipboard and Beyond

The elegant simplicity of the Clipboard and its Copy and Paste commands just can't be left alone by utility programmers—and it's a good thing, too, because there are actually some improvements available.

KopyKat (EC). Copy up to ten items and store them in temporary clipboards with **KopyKat** (SilverWARE, $90). Paste the last item copied with ⌘V as usual, or hold down ⌘Option and click to have a pop-up menu appear with each of the items currently stored. The best thing about KopyKat is that you don't even notice you're using it—it is fast and works exactly like the regular system (with the Option key added). One problem: In Microsoft Word, KopyKat doesn't copy and paste formats correctly.

MultiClip Pro (SZA). With **MultiClip Pro** ($150, Olduvai), you can use repeated Cut or Copy commands and have all the selections piled up in the Clipboard—the MultiClipboard—for later access. Copied material can be saved in collections, and you can interact with the Scrapbook seamlessly. Items in collections can be viewed as thumbnails or searched for by name. MultiClip really does provide quite a bit of functionality, but it does have two flaws: the price is way too high for what you get, and the manual has just about the worst writing I've ever seen.

Captivate (SZA). Mainstay's two staple utilities, Capture and ClickPaste, have always been terrific; now they've been tweaked a little further, renamed, and combined into a single package along with another little program. How could you go wrong? You can't. **Captivate** ($90) includes Captivate Select (Capture), Captivate Store (ClickPaste), and Captivate View.

A *screen-capture* program lets you turn whatever's on the screen into an editable picture, either by putting it on the Clipboard for pasting or by saving it as a file for opening in a graphics program. Captivate Select is the perfect screen-capture utility. You can capture an entire screen or any portion of it just by activating Select (with a customizable keystroke) and then dragging across the area you want captured; it even works while menus are opened. You can set zillions (oh, all right, dozens) of options: a time delay for tricky captures, including the mouse pointer or not; capturing in color or black and white; sending the image to the Clipboard or a disk file; saving the

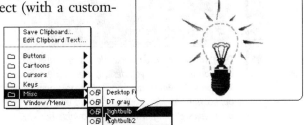

Captivate Select's pop-up menu lets you choose text or graphics that you've previously stored; whatever you select is automatically pasted in your document.

image in any one of several file types (PICT, TIFF, GIF, and so on); and even automatically capturing the same section of the screen that you grabbed the last time out.

Captivate Store is perhaps best described as a hierarchical pop-up scrapbook. Its pop-up menu lists the folders and subfolders where you have items stored; pointing to a menu item pops out a sample of the item so you know what's there. Selecting the item copies it to the Clipboard and automatically pastes it down in your current application. Captivate Store can handle text, PICT, sound, or QuickTime files that you've put in its folders from within the Finder; you can also paste just about anything into Captivate Store and it will create a file for that item.

The final component in the trio is Captivate View. As its name implies, it lets you view any type of graphic file, but it also provides some manipulative capabilities. You can crop, frame, flip, or rotate the image, print it, or save it in any of these formats: PICT, TIFF, GIF, Startup Screen, MacPaint, Stand-alone, or SimpleText.

A Few More Tools

In the interest of sampling as wide a range of tools as possible, here's a brief list of totally unrelated utilities!

DragStrip (SZA). At first glance, **DragStrip** ($60, Natural Intelligence) is a variation of the Launcher control panel and its clickable buttons for launching applications and opening documents. But, as with so many utilities, the more you're willing to put into it, the more you can get out of it. You can set up palettes of buttons that not only let you launch the item on the button, but also let you access subfolders (and, of course, their contents) connected to the button item. You can also treat the buttons as if they were icons in a Finder window, dragging a document onto an application's button to force it to open, for instance. In addition, you can make an application button "remember" the documents most recently used by the application so you can select them from

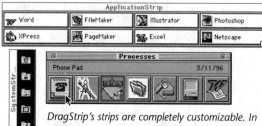

DragStrip's strips are completely customizable. In addition to the ones you design, there's a Processes strip provided which automatically tracks opened applications and lets you switch from one to another by clicking or with an assignable hot key.

a pop-up menu; or, you can manually add document names to a permanent list for the menu. DragStrip "strips" can be completely customized, including background color, the size of the icon buttons, and whether or not icon names should be included.

Although using DragStrip is both a convenience and a breeze, creating the strips is sometimes a drag. It starts off well enough—you can create a strip button by simply dragging a desktop icon onto the strip. But a strip doesn't automatically resize itself to accommodate a new button, and you can't easily rearrange existing buttons: Although you can move a button to a blank spot, you can't drag a button between two existing ones and have them move apart. Luckily, the setup is the smallest part of using DragStrip. At a street price of under $50, it's worth getting.

File-handling tools (SZA). It's beyond my apparently limited understanding why **DiskTools** (formerly from the MacPak collection from Fifth Generation Systems) and **Disk Top** (formerly from CE Software, more recently from PrairieSoft) didn't become commercial successes. Both let you do Finder operations—such as finding, copying, deleting, and getting info—without working on the desktop. More importantly, both let you view and manipulate some basic file attributes—like visibility/invisibility, file

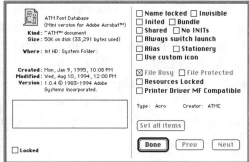

DiskTools' main window (left) and the Info window it provides for an item (right), in which you can view and manipulate a file's attributes.

type, and creator—that you can't do in the Finder. (Did you ever notice that System 7.5's Find command lets you search by both file type and creator, yet there's nothing in the system software that lets you see either of these attributes?)

BAD FEATURE

If you can find either of these programs, get it. At last sighting, Disk Top was still being distributed by PrairieSoft for a hefty $100; although it hasn't been updated since January of 1994, it still works under the latest system software. DiskTools, my personal favorite, was released as shareware in 1995, so troll around your favorite on-line service for it as soon as possible.

Opening unopenable files (SZA). Everyone winds up with a corrupted document sooner or later—one that just can't be opened or, if it can be opened, can't be scrolled or manipulated in any way without crashing the application. A backup copy is not always the solution for this problem, either, because often you'll have backed up the already damaged file. **CanOpener** ($65, Abbott Systems) lets you open almost any damaged file and copy out the text and pictures that you thought you'd lost.

Calculators (SZA/Raines Cohen). Although Apple's Calculator, preinstalled on your Apple menu, works just fine for the basics, several developers offer souped-up alternatives. When shopping for one, evaluate carefully which one matches your style of data entry (conventional or reverse-Polish notation, for instance) and provides the features you need without taking over your screen.

Tuesday Software's **CalcuPad** ($30) can save and print its calculations as documents. The application takes a unique approach: It thinks it's a Note Pad-type desk accessory, so you can enter comments (and variables) as well as numbers. The program includes 63 arithmetic, math, conversion, logical operation, and programming functions. You can customize the math symbols and use different languages, such as C programming, to operate the calculator.

Calc+ ($80, Abbott Systems) is unattractive—although you can change the font and size of its number readout, it's a plain gray box with ugly little buttons. On the other hand, it's highly functional: In addition to providing standard calculator functions, it works as a graphics calculator, doing conversions between inches, centimeters, picas, and ciceros. The "paper tape" area is missing scroll bars but can be manipulated by "rolling" it with the mouse pointer. A significant flaw is that typing = on the keyboard presses the percent key on the calculator (pressing Enter on the keypad works fine, though).

BAD FEATURE

If you really want a calculator that meets your specific needs, build it yourself. Dubl-Click Software's versatile **Calculator Construction Set** ($100) has been around for years, and its longevity may largely be attributed to its flexibility. You can create your own custom calculators using a toolbox similar to those found in painting programs. CCS contains emulations of popular scientific and business calculators (such as those from Hewlett-Packard and Texas Instruments), but you can modify them with no programming, or create your own task-specific calculator. CCS calculators are stand-alone desk accessories, and Dubl-Click encourages you to give them away or post them on-line.

Two calculators that come with Calculator Construction Set; if you don't like any of the sample calculators, you can build your own.

Desktop Diversions

Just as our real desks (the ones with legs and a wood top) are more inviting with a colorful sheet of blotter paper, a nicely framed photo of the spouse and kids, and a tasteful piece of artwork hanging nearby, our Mac desktops sometimes need personalization to offer just the right atmosphere for daily work.

Now Appearing on the Big Screen

From a black-and-white checked background that passed for gray on colorless monitors, the Mac's desktop (the surface itself, as opposed to the work area) has evolved to accommodate color, patterns, textures, outright artwork, and even animations, both as backgrounds and for taking over the screen when you're not working.

Wallpaper (SZA/RC). Until the advent of System 7.1, the desktop patterns that you could set through the General Controls control panel were limited to eight-color,

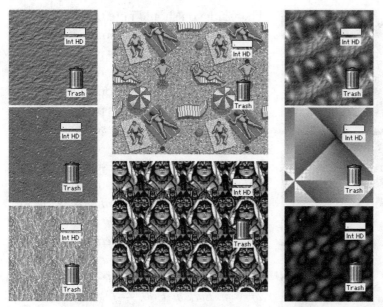

Desktop background patterns can be subtle (left), wild (middle), or weird (right).

8-by-8-pixel squares, repeated again and again across the screen. When **Wallpaper** ($60, Thought I Could) came out, it provided a much-needed improvement: 128-pixel squares and as many colors as your monitor could handle—and a pattern editor that let you create your own large patterns. With the larger basic pattern and greater color depth, you can get impressive backgrounds that simulate the rich warm feeling of marble, wood, rice paper, a field of clover, or a pool of water.

Large patterns and full color depth are now a standard part of the system, and the Desktop Patterns control panel comes with a wide selection of special patterns, so Wallpaper, revolutionary at the time, is now needed only if you want to do the pattern editing. But it's a terrific little utility with lots of patterns—including Patterns from Hell, which fill your screen with a host of phantom arrow pointers, folders, or trash cans—and a screensaver, Wallpaper in the Dark, which can run a patchwork slide show of desktop patterns or After Dark modules.

About screensavers (SZA/EC). Most computer monitors (like most TVs) use *cathode ray tubes*. They're coated on the inside with phosphor that glows when a beam of electrons hits it, creating the image on the screen. Leaving the same image on the screen for a long period of time can exhaust the phosphor in certain areas, causing it to shine less brightly, or not at all. That's why *screensavers* came into being—to prevent this "burn-in" for monitors where the user walks away and leaves the same thing on the screen for hours at a time.

Selections from After Dark's Totally Twisted collection: the Toxic Dump, a Shock Clock, and the Flying Toilets.

That said, you should note that burn-in was a problem only on early monitors, and even then it took days of a non-changing screen to actually wreck the phosphor coating. But screensavers have taken on a life of their own, with various products producing beautiful or amusing moving screens or even game-style components—extremely odd for a program that's only supposed to run when you're not at your computer to see it! *[Some screensaver modules can actually be useful when you're away from your Mac. For example, there are screensavers that enable you to customize the screen with a message such as, "I was here, but now am gone—left my Mac to carry on. Back at 1:00."—JJ]*

Although you can manually invoke a screensaver with a well-placed mouse click, most of them keep track of how long it's been since you did something on your Mac, and automatically activate themselves after a certain amount of idle time (which you specify); the screensaver provides an ever-changing landscape on the screen. Hitting any key or moving the mouse instantly puts your work windows back on the screen.

Before and after After Dark (SZA). The first Mac screensaver was Pyro, which put simple fireworks on the screen. But the standard is Berkeley System's **After Dark** ($30 per package), which comes in so many flavors it's staggering. Whether you want the old standbys that include Boris the Cat and Flying Toasters, or something thematic like Star Trek (original and The Next Generation), Marvel Comics, Looney Tunes, Disney characters, the Simpsons, or the Totally Twisted collection, you can have it. And you'll find plenty of other modules on-line for downloading.

An animated screensaver from After Dark's Disney collection.

Each package provides not only ready-made screens, but also the ability to edit them and combine features from different scenes.

After Dark isn't the only screensaver around, but it's the standard by which all others are measured: Other screensavers can run After Dark modules, and make sure that their modules work with After Dark.

The shareware route (RC). **Desktop Textures** and **Before Dark** are two solid shareware screensaver applications that don't have pattern editors but do let you choose patterns from an easy-to-access list—an excellent feature none of the commercial programs offers.

And now for something completely different (SZA/RC). Just for giggles, call Bit Jugglers and tell their tech support, "I have a technical question about UnderWare." **UnderWare** ($30) is a special kind of screensaver, something its slightly sick creators call the Dynamic Desktop. After a set period of time (usually just a few seconds), your desktop comes alive with a great variety of animated events. The configurable cartoon antics don't take over the screen, but instead interact with whatever's already there—ducking behind windows, jumping over folders, and sometimes smacking up against the inside edge of the screen. Robber is especially endearing: he breaks through your desktop and reappears later with your processor chip in his hands and the computer police hot on his trail. The fire-breathing dragon occasionally toasts a desktop icon (temporarily, of course!); Jindak the wizard is waiting to cast spells; and sometimes tiny ballerinas dance across the screen. And all this can happen *while* you're working in a window!

You may tire of UnderWare rather quickly, and not everyone has room for the 5.5MB of space that the 26 desktop dynamos require, but UnderWare is a front-runner in the arena of desktop procrastination.

Changing Interface Elements

With only one or two inexpensive software packages, you can totally negate the millions of dollars that went into the design of the elegant Macintosh interface!

Icon editors (SZA/RC). When you use System 7's built-in ability to alter an icon (described in Chapter 3), all you do is paste a picture onto the existing icon. You may have noticed that a pasted icon doesn't always behave the way a "real" icon works: viewing it in grayscale instead of its original color, or applying a color from the Label menu, or seeing it in a small icon view instead of at regular size may result in the icon's not looking right. That's because every true icon is actually made up of a family of eight icons that includes two color versions (16 and 256 colors), a black-and-white version, and a *mask* to alter the icon when it's selected or open; each of these icon designs comes in both regular and small icon sizes.

An icon editor allows you to custom-design *all* the members of an icon family. You can modify any existing icon or easily create new ones. Icon editors can also allow you to maintain icon libraries and simplify the process of replacing one icon with another. The cost of an icon editor may seem prohibitive considering the tiny piece of art you get out of it, but hand-crafted icons can look like little jewels on your desktop. *[I didn't write that last sentence. I can't imagine how people find the time to hand-craft icons. If I need some special icons, I'll take ones crafted by other hands.—SZA] [On the other hand, many Mac users are intensely individualistic and no amount of time is too great to make your Mac truly yours. Create icons in your own image, I say.—JJ]*

- **Icon 7** ($80, FOCUS Enhancements) is a system extension; all you have to do to open its editor is to open an icon's Get Info window and double-click on its picture in the window. Even though you're adding yet another system extension to your System Folder, this is a seamless approach to icon editing. Icon 7's text tool is particularly useful, because it's nice to be able to emblazon a folder with a big letter or a short word.

- **Icon Mania!** ($70, Dubl-Click Software) blows away the competition by integrating icon selection, editing, and library storage into an easy-to-navigate, single-window display. The window's three columns display icon libraries, the icons on your computer, and a pasteboard for temporary storage while you're working. Icon Mania! lets you create thumbnail icons of any graphic file; you can even select just a part of the file to be the representative icon. One of the best features is the ability to customize the system's default icons: New folders and alert icons can be enhanced, and you can choose from 30 new Trash icon styles or make your own.

- Zonkers, described on the next page, includes an icon editor. And check out the shareware editors **IconBOSS** and **iContraption** for a cheaper introduction to creating icon art, although neither program is as slick and trouble-free as its commercial cousins.

Total makeovers (SZA/RC). Redesign the Mac interface: menu bar, windows, scroll bars, buttons—everything's fair game. Make your Mac look like a NeXT machine, a System 8-based system, something from a circus, or even a Windows computer (if you're feeling particularly perverse). Then customize or even animate your cursors (perhaps turn the wristwatch cursor into a spinning Earth).

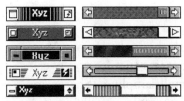

Some of the many styles available from ClickChange for title and scroll bars.

If you're planning on totally redecorating your Mac, it's a good idea to reduce the chance of system conflicts by having a single program make all the changes. **ClickChange** ($50, Dubl-Click Software) can do all these tricks, and more. It provides a menu-bar clock for pre-System 7.5 setups, substitutes icons for menu titles on your menu bar, puts color anywhere and everywhere, gives you a selection of desktop patterns, changes the style of window controls (including double-headed scroll arrows), offers alternatives for the standard button styles ... the list goes on and on.

Zonkers ($50, Nova Development) also provides window, menu, and cursor enhancements. And, it has more than 1,000 icons you can apply to system icons (such as floppy disks, hard disks, the Trash, and special system folders) or your own folders or documents. Assigning the icons is a cinch: Drag the one you want from the icon library to the Zonkers window that displays all the icons on your drive. To top it all off, there's a

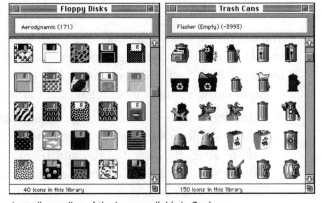

A small sampling of the icons available in Zonkers.

collection of desktop patterns, and a desktop pattern editor, along with a control panel that lets you choose several patterns that come up randomly on each startup.

Sounds galore (SZA). You already know that you can change the Mac's alert sound, or system beep, by selecting a new sound in the Sound control panel; you may even know how to put more sounds in there. But did you know that you can attach sounds to other events, such as emptying the trash, inserting a disk, and even clicking in a window's zoom box? Of course, you need a program to help you do that, and you need a lot of nifty sounds. **ClickTrax** ($50, Dubl-Click) includes 4MB of sounds and a control panel to assign them to various events. And these aren't just special effects sounds such as crashing planes and tinkling glass—they're wonderful impersonations of characters as varied as Ronald Reagan and Elvis Presley.

For even more sound control, there's **Kaboom!** ($30) and **More Kaboom!** ($40) from Nova Development. Aside from the 150 sounds in one and 100 in the other, and a control panel to assign them to events, you get a sound editor, Kaboom! Factory, that lets you tweak sounds (add echoes, play them backwards, loop a section, add fade-ins and fade-outs) until you can't recognize them anymore.

The Shareware Interface (SZA)

You don't have to buy a commercial package to twiddle with the looks of your Mac; there must be at least a zillion shareware and freeware programs that let you tweak the interface. The ones described in this section are just a small sampling. (Shareware programs come and go based on their popularity, how many people actually pay for them, and how busy the authors are. If you can't find these specific programs, look for others like them.)

Doing windows. The crux of the Mac interface is really the window, because that's where you do your work. So, there are plenty of programs that change the way windows look and behave.

You can drag a window by grabbing it anywhere along its title bar, but you can resize it only from the bottom right corner, and the top left—at the close box—is always anchored to the screen. With **Stretch2**, you can resize the window from any of its edges or corners simply by dragging the frame that gets added to every window.

- Mac windows seem to have conveniently placed scroll arrows but, in fact, if you want to scroll up and down, or back and forth, you have to move the mouse quite a bit to alternately use the top and bottom or left and right scroll arrows. Both **DoubleScroll** and **Scroll2** provide double scroll arrows at each end of both scroll bars—you won't believe how convenient this is!

- When you drag a window, it's just the outline that moves until you've let go of the mouse button. If you want the actual window to move as you drag, try **RealDrag**.

- **WindowWizard** keeps track of all your windows. You configure it to pop up in the menu bar, in window title bars or anywhere on the screen; its hierarchical menu lists every open application (including the Finder), and every window open in each one. Select a window from the menu, and it (and its application, of course) comes to the front.

- If you're using System 7.1 instead of System 7.5, the **WindowShade** control panel that lets you collapse a window down to just its title bar is still available as shareware; another shareware program, **Zoombar**, also shrinks windows down to their title bars.

Menu manipulation. You can change your menus as easily as you change the desktop pattern; make them drop down without clicking, add color, abbreviate their names, change the names to icons—the possibilities are seemingly endless.

POWERBOOK

- Slide up to the menu bar, point to a menu title, and have the menu drop down without a click; then, click on a menu command to activate it. **AutoMenus** provides this option, and it's especially handy on PowerBooks for the trackball- or trackpad-impaired.

- Use **Menuette** to change menu titles from the Chicago font that was specifically designed for easy readability to anything you'd like, or to change from text to icons for menu titles.

- Change any common menu title (File, Edit, Format, and so on) to an icon of your choice—even of your design—with the **MICN** utility.

- Change the standard system menu icons (, Help, and Application) to animated ones with **Zipple**.

- Although you wouldn't guess it from its name, **Greg's Buttons** lets you add color to the menu bar and menus. Its main focus, however, is altering the standard style of radio buttons and checkboxes.

Power Tool Tips

Tips for Macro Editors   (SZA)

Keyboard launchers. Both macro editors (QuicKeys and Tempo II Plus) have specific, easy ways to assign a key to a program or file launch, so the only thing you have to think about is which keys to use. And the macros work not only to launch the program initially, but also to move you from one open program to another.

Use the function keys (F5 , F6 , and so on) at the top of the keyboard as single-key launchers for the applications you use most. Avoid the first four keys because they work as single-stroke Undo, Cut, Copy, and Paste commands. You can even reserve the last three keys (off in a group by themselves) for special functions (mine are assigned to trigger a screen capture, hide all background applications, and move to the Finder) and still have eight keys left for launching applications.

I use those eight function keys to launch the applications I use the most; I've assigned eight other applications, which I use less often, to a combination of Shift and a function key. A combination of Option and a function key triggers something extra related to the application that usually launches from the key—a special template opens in Word, the telecommunication program logs on for my e-mail, or my database of Mac products opens in FileMaker.

Desk accessories and utilities are assigned to Control Option Shift (they're clustered together, so they're easy to press) and a number from the numeric keypad; so I can open the Chooser, or the Calculator, or my Phone Pad, from the keyboard.

Finder Menu Command-Key Equivalents

File Menu		View Menu	
New Folder	⌘N*	Small Icon	⌘Shift S
Open	⌘O*	Icon	⌘Shift I
Print	⌘P*	Name	⌘Shift N
Close Window	⌘W*	Size	⌘Shift Z
Get Info	⌘I*	Kind	⌘Shift K
Sharing	⌘H	Date	⌘Shift D
Duplicate	⌘D*	Label	⌘Shift L
Make Alias	⌘M*	Comments	⌘Shift C
Put Away	⌘Y*		
Find	⌘F*	**Label Menu**	
Find Again	⌘G*	None	⌘0
Page Setup	⌘J	Labels/Colors	⌘1 through 7
Print Window	⌘T		
Edit Menu		**Special Menu**	
Undo	⌘Z*	Clean Up	⌘U*
Cut	⌘X*	Empty Trash	⌘Shift Option T
Copy	⌘C*	Eject Disk	⌘E*
Paste	⌘V*	Erase Disk	⌘Shift Option E
Clear	⌘B	Restart	⌘Shift Option R
Select All	⌘A*	Shut Down	⌘Shift Option S
Show Clipboard	⌘K	Sleep	⌘L

Note: * = These command-key equivalents already exist.

Finder menu commands. Use a macro editor to add a keyboard equivalent to any Finder command that doesn't have one. There aren't enough alphabetic characters to go around in logical combinations, but you don't have to stick to using just the ⌘ key with a letter. The above table lists suggested keyboard combinations that cover every command available. Combinations with asterisks are the ones that already exist.

Making a better Make Alias command. The Finder's Make Alias command already has a keyboard equivalent, but you can improve upon the command itself, which creates the alias using the original icon's name with *alias* appended to it. To create an alias without that pesky suffix, record a macro that includes these steps (making sure you first select an icon that can be aliased):

1. Choose Make Alias from the File menu.

2. Press → to move the insertion point to the end of the alias's name (it's automatically selected when it's created).

3. Press Delete five times to erase the word *alias*.

That's all. By not erasing the space that comes before the word *alias*, the alias has a name that's different from the original's, so they can co-exist in the same folder—which is where the alias is created.

Keyboard button presses. Record macros that let you "click" buttons in dialog boxes so you don't always have to reach for the mouse; these are especially convenient when it's a simple dialog that just presents a few buttons and no other controls. Make sure you save them as universal macros so that they'll work no matter what application you're in. Here's a list of suggestions which will help you avoid the problem of assigning something like ⌃⌘C for Configure when that combination is often built-in for the Cancel button; in fact, even Control C isn't a good idea for Configure because of the potential confusion. And, don't forget—Return and Enter work for the highlighted button in a dialog, and ⌃⌘. and Esc trigger the Cancel button.

Control Y	Yes	Control T	Options
Control N	No	Control K	Configure
Control S	Save	Control R	Revert
Control D	Don't Save	Control H	Help

ResEdit Tips and Projects

Jumping around (EC). Because ⌃⌘O is used to open files, ResEdit lets you use Return and Enter to open practically everything else. Try it while you have a resource item selected in a list, or while you have a button selected in a dialog box, just to name a few spots. You can use ⌃⌘W to close, and the ↑↓ keys to move up and down the lists. You can also type in a resource item number (or a name if it has one) to jump to that resource item.

Aligning (EC). If you're really picky about aligning things, which most people who bother with ResEdit usually are, you'll find that entering values in the Top, Bottom, Left, and Right boxes is the fastest way to align items. The numbers entered refer to the number of pixels from the given edge. The ↑↓←→ keys also work nicely for moving one pixel at a time.

Hidden objects (EC). Sometimes you'll find that various objects are piled up one on top of another in a window that holds DITL resources. To see all the objects in a dialog box, hold down the Option key. Each item's ID number will be revealed. To select an object that's below another, use the Select Item Number command in the DITL menu, enter the appropriate number, and press Enter.

HOT TIPS

Use Get Info (EC). If you have an "orphaned" document on your Mac—one with a generic icon—and you want to know what program it was created with, open ResEdit and use the Get Info command in the File menu. It will tell you the Type and Creator of the document, which will often clue you in to which kind of program you'll be able to use to open the document. *[Of course, if you get DiskTools, described earlier, you won't have to do this.—SZA]*

Use the Get Resource Info command (EC). Many programmers don't bother to name their resources. When you open a resource type, you may just see the number and size. You can give a resource item a name (or a better name) to help you find it later. Simply press ⌘I and type in a name. When you close the Info box, the name appears in the list. You can change an item's name without problem, but don't touch anything else in the window; the ID number and type should not be modified. (On rare occasions, and almost never with DITL, DLOG, MENU, or STR# resources, a resource item name is used as text in the program itself. Changing the resource item's name will change the text in the software.)

Adding a keyboard equivalent (SZA). It's easy to add keyboard equivalents to menu commands so long as the application stores its menus as standard resources. The following example adds the standard ⌘B to the Clear command in the Stickies desk accessory's Edit menu.

1. Open Stickies in ResEdit and double-click on the MENU resource icon.

2. Double-click on the picture of the Edit menu to open the editing window.

3. Click on the Clear command in the menu at the left of the window. Type a *B* in the box labeled Cmd-Key. You'll see the keyboard equivalent immediately added to the picture of the menu. (The menu you're editing also appears in RedEdit's menu bar so you can pull it down and see what it looks like.)

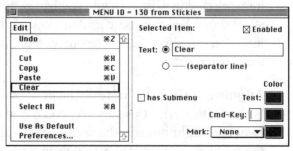

Type the letter B in the Cmd-Key box in the lower right to add the keyboard equivalent to the Stickies Edit menu.

4. Close all windows and click Yes when you're asked if you want the changes saved.

Grabbing a sound (SZA). You can move sounds from one application to another, or from an application into the Sound control panel so you can use it for your system beep. The following example gets the xylophone sound used in the Jigsaw Puzzle desk accessory and puts it into the Sound control panel.

1. Open the Jigsaw Puzzle in ResEdit, and double-click on the snd resource.

2. Select the "CongratsSnd" line from the list of sounds in the window that opens.

3. Use Copy from the Edit menu.

4. Open the Sound control panel and select Alert Sounds from the pop-up menu.

5. Choose Paste from the Edit menu, and name the sound in the dialog that appears.

That's all—don't forget to close the Jigsaw Puzzle file in ResEdit.

Creating a keyboard layout (SZA). It seems pretty simple: You press the N key, and an *n* appears on your screen; press Shift N and you get an *N*. But sometimes it's annoying: Hold down Shift when you want to type "N.Y." and you'll wind up with "N>Y>" instead. And working on a PowerBook presents a problem for numeric entry: Wouldn't it be nice if you could, say, hold down Option and use a cluster of alphabetic keys as numbers instead of having to use the ones spread out along the top row of the keyboard?

It's actually very simple to create a keyboard layout that maps the keys on your keyboard to any character you want. Here's how to get rid of the *N>Y>* problem:

1. Create a keyboard layout to work on: Double-click on your System file, and option-drag the *U.S.-System 6* keyboard layout to the desktop (this makes a copy of it). Rename the icon to something like *MyKeyboard*. If you can't rename it because it's locked, use the Duplicate command from the File menu, and rename the duplicate.

2. Launch ResEdit and open the new keyboard file; a window opens with four icons in it; double-click on the one named KCHR.

3. In the window that opens, double-click on the single line of information. This opens the layout window.

4. The only items you need to work with in the layout window are the 16-by-16 grid of characters and the sample keyboard. Hold down Shift on your real keyboard, and drag the . character from the grid to the > key on the sample keyboard. With Shift still down, next drag the . character to the < key.

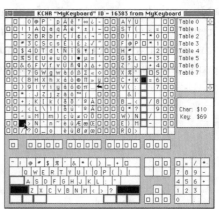

Dragging a character from the grid at the upper left onto the keyboard in the lower left changes how keys are mapped from your keyboard to the system.

5. To make sure you can still type <kbd><</kbd> and <kbd>></kbd>, you have to put them somewhere accessible: Hold down <kbd>Option</kbd> and <kbd>Shift</kbd> and drag the greater-than and less-than symbols from the grid to their usual positions on the keyboard.

6. Close all the windows you've opened; you'll be asked if you want to save changes when you close the last one. Click Yes, and quit ResEdit.

7. Drag the keyboard layout into your System Folder.

To use the new layout, open the Keyboard control panel and select it from there—that's it!

The keyboard layout menu (SZA). If you work with multiple keyboard layouts for foreign languages or other, simpler purposes, you don't have to use the Keyboard control panel to switch among them. Although it's disabled by default, there's actually a system menu that lists keyboard layouts.

For this trick, you'll be altering the System file itself, so start by duplicating it inside the System Folder, and open the duplicate in ResEdit.

1. Double-click on the itlc resource icon.

2. Double-click on the single line of information in the window that opens.

3. In the new window, look for radio buttons labeled Always Show. The zero button will be selected; click on the 1 instead.

4. Close the windows, saving your changes when prompted.

Next, you have to swap your System files: Drag the original out onto the desktop, and rename the altered duplicate to *System*. Restart, and you'll find a keyboard menu on the menu bar between the Help and Application menus. If everything's working fine, you can trash the original system file at this point.

14 Fonts

It might not be too much to say that fonts made the Mac what it is today. In addition to its graphical user interface, what really delighted the Mac's first users was that they could create something on a computer that didn't look like it came from a computer. The Mac's first typefaces, limited as they were, were far better than anything anyone had seen before on the desktop. People soon learned that the typefaces they used for a document had a big impact on the way it was received. And fonts made the Mac *fun.*

The Mac took that promising beginning even further when it adopted PostScript in its first LaserWriter printer, and desktop publishing was born. Desktop publishing made the Mac respectable and brought it into a lot of offices. And today, it's still the fonts—in a number, quality, and variety that the first Mac users never dreamed of—that can make people really passionate about their Macs. Now, as Apple introduces QuickDraw GX, type on the Mac enters a whole new dimension, as designers dream up animated fonts and other surprises.

In this chapter, we'll talk first about the technology of Macintosh fonts, then get into the fine points of using them.

Contributors

Ted Alspach (TA) is the chapter editor.

Gene Steinberg (GS) is a contributing editor to *Macworld,* and the author of *Using America Online* (Que).

Rob Teeple (RT) is president of Teeple Graphics, an AppleVAR and World Wide Web services company.

Erfert Fenton (EF) writes about fonts and graphics for *Macworld* and other magazines. She's also the author of *The Macintosh Font Book*, *third edition* (Peachpit Press).

Darcy DiNucci, (DD), Alastair Johnston (AJ), Kathleen Tinkel (KT), James Felici (JF), Arthur Naiman (AN), Sharon Zardetto Aker (SZA), and **Nancy E. Dunn (ND)** contributed to earlier versions of *The Macintosh Bible*, from which parts of this chapter were taken.

Contents

What Is a Font, Anyway? (JF/EF)

When you hear people talking about computer-based publishing, you'll hear the word "fonts." Just when you think you're getting the hang of the terminology, someone else will pipe up and say something about "typefaces." What's the difference?

Fonts, Faces, and Families: Some Basic Terms (JF/EF)

Alphabets come in different designs: skinny, fat, formal, casual, ghastly, and gorgeous. An alphabet (accompanied by a slug of numbers, punctuation marks, and so on) with a particular design is called a *typeface*. A *font* on the Mac is a jumble of computer code that creates text in a specific typeface, say Times or Helvetica.

HOT TIP

A typeface and a font are not the same thing, any more than a cookie and a cookie cutter are the same thing. So when you want to set some type in a specific typeface, you choose the corresponding font, and your Mac will make the letters and numbers you type appear in that typeface.

When you see a printed page then, you can say "What typeface is that?" or "What font did you use to make that?" But you can't say "What font is that?" because the font is in your computer, not on the page.

The next term you need to learn is *font family*, which is a group of typefaces that are designed with similar features so they'll look good together on the page. Like most families, font families all go by a single family name (such as Times or Helvetica). A typical font family consists of four members: a regular version (usually used for text) plus a heavier bold version, a slanted italic version, and a bold-italic version. When you're shopping for a font, then, you normally get a disk containing four of them, one for each typeface in the family.

But font families, like human families, come in all different sizes. The Helvetica family, for example, contains over 50 members, varying by degrees of boldness and character width, among other features. On the other hand, some typefaces are one of a kind, woeful orphans with no family to call their own.

If you decide to set a document in Palatino, chances are you won't use just the plain version of the face. Palatino also comes in bold, italic, and bold-italic versions, which you can access from a Style menu or keyboard command. These four *styles* make up the Palatino *family*, a set of related designs meant to be used together.

With these three bits of type jargon—*fonts, typefaces,* and *font families*—under your belt, you can wade into the wild world of Mac typography.

Serif and Sans Serif Faces (EF)

The typeface you're reading now is a *serif* face; it has small counterstrokes, called serifs, at the ends of the main strokes. Serifs are a holdover from type's predecessor, calligraphy, in which letters were capped with flourishes from the calligrapher's pen. Serif faces are often used for long passages of text, since most people find serif type easy to read.

A *sans serif* face doesn't have flourishes at the end of its strokes (sans serif means *"without serif"*). Unlike serif faces, the letters of sans serif faces tend to have a uniform stroke width, making them appear more modern, but also making them harder to read in long passages. (Some people set books or magazines in sans serif type, but this is the exception in the United States.) Most publishers like to use sans serif faces for headings, captions, or other relatively short elements of a publication.

Using Fonts on the Macintosh (DD/JF)

As the Mac has grown up, its techniques for handling fonts and type have gotten slicker and more sophisticated. Font technology has followed suit. There are now at least four kinds of Mac fonts out there—four distinct font formats, each with its own way of digitally encoding how letters should be drawn on your screen and on your pages. It can get a little confusing, but it's not as bad as it sounds. A little history will help sort out the story.

Bitmapped Fonts (DD/JF)

When the Mac was introduced in January 1984, it had just one font format. It used *bitmapped fonts* to display type on screen and to print to the only available Mac printer, the ImageWriter. The Macintosh screen and the ImageWriter both had the same resolution—72 dots per inch—and bitmapped fonts were built to match them.

A Mac font consisted of a set of 72-dpi dot-by-dot drawings of each letter in a typeface. A printed ImageWriter page, then, was essentially a dot-for-dot replication of what you saw on screen, so the font that created your screen type also created your printed type.

But because the position of each dot was pre-defined in the font, you needed a separate font

Manhattan 12

Manhattan 24

For bitmapped fonts to be really readable, a separate 72-dpi font must exist for each size you'll be using. If the right size isn't installed, the Mac will stretch the installed size to compensate. This example shows the difference between the screen versions of Manhattan at 12 points (for which a font is installed) and at 24 points (for which it's not).

for every size of type you wanted to create. If you requested a type size that wasn't installed, the Mac would just stretch or squash letters from an existing font—adding or subtracting bits here and there—which tended to produced some odd and very hard-to-read shapes.

These days, 72-dpi bitmapped fonts for printing are still available from only a couple of sources (most notably Dubl-Click Software, with its World Class Fonts line). For the most part, it's an outmoded format, superseded by the formats we'll talk about next.

PostScript (Type 1 and Type 3) (DD/JF)

Almost exactly one year after the Mac debuted, Apple introduced the LaserWriter printer and Adobe System's new *PostScript* font format (often referred to as Type 1 or Type 3). The LaserWriter and its 300-dpi resolution not only produced beautiful pages, it also changed the relationship between the Mac and its printer. Instead of simply passing off its screen images for printing, the Mac now passed off files (written in the PostScript programming language) that were reinterpreted by yet another computer inside the LaserWriter, which rebuilt the images at 300-dpi resolution.

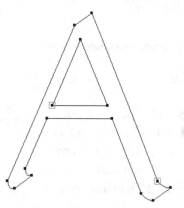

TrueType and PostScript fonts are outline fonts: The font information describes the shape of the letter, which can be scaled to any size and output at any resolution.

PostScript fonts broke the link between screen resolution and printer resolution. The Mac still used 72-dpi bitmapped fonts to create the type on screen, but when you sent the file to the printer, the Mac substituted matching PostScript fonts for use on the page. Instead of storing images of letters as distinct patterns of dots, PostScript fonts stored those images as mathematically described outlines—electronic stencils that could be scaled to any size and then "colored in" by a printer imaging at any resolution. To do the required computations, you needed a *PostScript interpreter*—a computer inside the printer—a feature that makes PostScript printers relatively expensive.

The practical effect of this for Mac owners (in addition to getting snappier-looking print) was that now they had to reckon with two kinds of fonts—72-dpi *screen fonts* plus resolution-independent *printer fonts* (also sometimes called *outline fonts*). This created (and still creates to this day) a lot of confusion. Only with System 7.5 and QuickDraw GX is the need for bitmapped screen fonts for PostScript fonts finally eliminated (see "QuickDraw GX Fonts" later in this chapter). With earlier systems, the only way for your Mac to make a PostScript font available to your applications is for you to install a corresponding bitmapped screen font.

TrueType

(DD/JF)

In 1991, in an attempt to wrest control of type away from Adobe, Apple introduced a new font format called *TrueType*. Like PostScript fonts, TrueType fonts use outlines that can be interpreted for any size and any resolution, on screen or for a printer. And like PostScript fonts with ATM (Adobe Type Manager, software for making text look good on screen at any size), TrueType doesn't need an interpreter in the printer; for TrueType, the interpretation is done by the Mac's own system software. Unlike PostScript fonts, though, TrueType fonts have never needed screen fonts to operate on a Mac, which has made them easier to install and manage.

OpenType

As this book went to press, Adobe and Microsoft announced what could turn out to be one of the most important business ventures since Apple started shipping TrueType fonts as part of their system software. Adobe and Microsoft have decided to combine their respective font technologies: Type 1 (Adobe) and TrueType (Microsoft with Apple), into one font format called OpenType.

The claim from both companies is that the best features of each format (such as font hinting) will be retained in the new format, while some of the less desirable features (Type 1's reliance on both screen and printer font files) will be removed. New features (such as Adobe's Multiple Master axis technology) may possibly be added as well.

The downside to this new format is that the fonts you now own will eventually (several years down the road) not be supported. The upside is that all applications and platforms will support the format, as it is being pushed by two of the biggest software publishers, who happen to own the entire font format industry.

You'll no doubt be hearing more and more about OpenType (or whatever it ends up being called) in the future as we all watch QuickDraw GX fonts become but a footnote in font history.

HOT TIP

TrueType runs automatically on Macs with System 7. If you're using System 6, you can use TrueType fonts (System 6.0.5 or later) if you add a TrueType system extension to your System Folder. (Apple does not sell the extension directly, but it is included with some QuickDraw printers such as the StyleWriter II.)

For typophiles, TrueType offers some sophisticated capabilities that potentially place it a cut above the PostScript format. We say *potentially* because most of these Epicurean features are strictly optional and don't always find their way into the TrueType fonts you buy. But TrueType fonts are theoretically capable of crisper resolution at low resolutions (such as on screen) and are built to take advantage of the Line Layout Manager feature of System 7.5, which can provide more professional-looking typesetting in heretofore typographically inept applications such as word processors and spreadsheets.

Almost every font manufacturer now sells its fonts in both TrueType and PostScript Type 1 formats (Adobe, of course, sticks strictly to PostScript), and this has made things more complicated for font users. (More about the problems in choosing one font format over the other, or in using both, are described in "Deciding on a Format" below.) Ironically, TrueType hasn't been very successful on the Mac—its real success has come on IBM PC compatibles running Windows, which also uses the format.

QuickDraw GX Fonts (TA)

QuickDraw GX and QuickDraw GX fonts were supposed to have made the Macintosh font community stand on its ear. Instead, they've all but been ignored by the bulk of Mac users.

The idea behind QuickDraw GX fonts is that they were supposed to remove the artificial limit of 256 characters per font, with a new "limit" of 16,000 characters. This would allow fonts to contain fractions and small caps and other special characters that don't fit into a single font at this time.

Unfortunately, developers and users alike have been slow to move towards this new format, possibly due to the confusion that already exists between using TrueType and PostScript fonts. Apple has not abandoned the platform, but then it isn't really pushing ahead with it very strongly either. If you're just getting into the desktop publishing or graphics markets, you'd do well to stay far, far away from QuickDraw GX fonts until they (if they ever do) become more commonplace; service bureaus and printers are strictly Type 1 (PostScript) as of this writing.

Deciding on a Format (TA/DD/JF)

There's no argument that TrueType and PostScript fonts provide better-quality printed output than do bitmapped fonts. Which of the two outline formats is better, however, is a source of much controversy. But if you judge the quality of a font format by the type you see on the page, there's little debate: Both formats are capable of producing great-quality type at any output resolution.

If you're not using QuickDraw GX, TrueType has an edge in simplicity. TrueType fonts require you to install only one file, compared to PostScript's two. And if you use PostScript fonts, you'll also need to get Adobe Type Manager to see clear screen type at all sizes and to get good quality type from non-PostScript printers.

On the other hand, for jobs that will be printed on high-resolution imagesetters, PostScript has the advantage. Because it had such a long head start on TrueType, PostScript became the standard for use in professional publishing applications. The result is that imagesetters have built-in PostScript interpreters. On those machines, printing using TrueType fonts can be very slow, because all the image processing has to be done by the Mac, in software—the TrueType image-processing program can't take full advantage of the PostScript computer. Most service bureaus, then, won't let you near their imagesetters with a TrueType font, although this is changing slowly.

A final problem with TrueType is that you can't use TrueType fonts at all if you're running a System version earlier than 6.0.5, or if you're using 6.0.5 or 6.0.7 but don't have the TrueType extension. Of course, if you're running a computer using such an old version of the system software, many of today's software packages won't even run on them, so using TrueType fonts is the least of your worries.

Multiple Formats on One Macintosh   (TA/DD/JF)

Most people end up with a variety of font formats in their systems because they tend to shop for specific typefaces, that is, specific designs, regardless of format. Even if you opt for PostScript as a standard (perhaps because most of your work is eventually output to PostScript imagesetters), you usually end up with a few TrueType fonts, if only because Apple's basic TrueType and bitmapped fonts are installed automatically each time you install or reinstall your system.

This generally causes a problem only when you have PostScript and TrueType versions of the same typeface installed. The Mac has built-in methods for choosing between font versions at print time (described in "Fonts and Printing," later in this chapter), which could result in your ending up with one version of the font when you expected the other. This could produce unexpected line endings or other untoward changes in your printed pages. In some cases, the printer can get so confused it doesn't print anything at all.

The best advice is to pick one font format to work with and stick with

> ### Why Bitmapped Fonts Won't Go Away   (RT)
>
> If you use PostScript fonts, you *have* to have the bitmap screen fonts installed in order to view those fonts and use them on your Mac. But if you use TrueType fonts, you shouldn't need a bitmap version, right?
>
> Well, sorta.
>
> One advantage that bitmaps have over outlines (PostScript printer fonts and TrueType fonts) is that they're custom drawn for that point size, making them more legible than fonts generated on the fly from ATM or using TrueType's screen representation generation algorithms. So a bitmapped 12-point font will be more readable on screen than a bitmap display generated from the outline of the font.
>
> Another advantage is that bitmap fonts will more accurately show widths than screen displays generated with outlines, due to the limited number of pixels available for type at small point sizes.

HOT TIP

it—it just reduces confusion. If you do mix font formats, try not to have different versions of the same typeface installed. (If you buy a font that supplies both TrueType and PostScript versions on the disk, copy just one onto your system.) The greatest confusion will arise with the most common typefaces—the ones supplied with the system (including Times, Helvetica, Courier, and Symbol) and the ones built into most PostScript printers (which are often supplied with Adobe Type Manager).

The consensus among graphics and DTP professionals is to use Type 1 PostScript fonts, which are both the standard and the most common of the two formats. Further, the standard manufacturer of these fonts is Adobe, which provides fonts to service bureaus at reduced rates, thus guaranteeing their compatibility.

Font Files

When you open a font disk, you may be greeted by an alarming array and variety of icons and files. Because each font format is handled differently by your Mac, each kind of font requires a different set of font files, and each vendor may organize its fonts differently on the disks it provides. The following is a guide to what you see on a font disk, and what to do with it all.

Suitcases (RT)

Fonts are usually grouped into *suitcases*, which contain several different fonts within a font family. For bitmapped and PostScript fonts, a suitcase usually contains several different point sizes for each font in the font family. For TrueType fonts, a suitcase contains one file for each font; different sizes are not necessary.

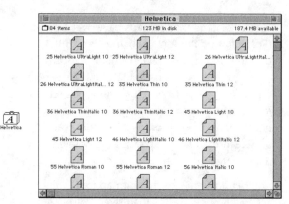

A suitcase that contains fonts is indeed a strange beast, unique among the Macintosh's typical files and folders. It works like a file, yet contains documents like a folder. Actually, the System file in your System Folder is another example of a suitcase, albeit a different breed of suitcase entirely.

A font suitcase (left) contains various files. In this example, the suitcase is for the PostScript Type 1 font Helvetica, so several bitmapped versions of the font (right) are inside the suitcase.

Font suitcases need to be stored in the Fonts folder in the System Folder to be accessed by your Macintosh under System 7.1 and later. To add a suitcase to the Fonts folder, just drag it into that folder. If you have applications currently running when you do this, those fonts may not show up in the applications until after you've quit them and run them again.

The Organized Type (RT)

Fonts are organized differently depending on their type. TrueType fonts consist of one font file, usually neatly packed into a suitcase. These files have to be in the Fonts folder in the System Folder to be used by your computer. Bitmap fonts also exist in suitcases, but due to their nonscalable nature, you'll need several different files for each font, one file for each point size. Usually all the files with the different point sizes are located in one folder.

PostScript fonts are a little trickier. Like bitmapped fonts, you'll have a suitcase containing several font files for different point sizes (usually two, one for 10-point and one for 12-point). But you'll also have a *printer font,* which is the outline the font refers to in order to achieve a smooth, even appearance when displayed at different point sizes on screen or when printed. Printer font files need to reside in the Fonts folder as well.

You can change the contents of suitcases simply by double-clicking on them and dragging font files in or out. For convenience, you might want to group the fonts by the way you use them, or maybe by client, or by some other method that makes sense for the way you work.

HOT TIP

To make a new suitcase in the Finder, you have to take an existing suitcase, duplicate it, empty out its contents, and rename it. Not the most intuitive thing in the world, but it works. Software such as Suitcase and MasterJuggler will create new font suitcases with the click of a button (see "Using Suitcase or MasterJuggler," later in this chapter).

Installing Fonts (RT)

The procedure for installing fonts varies depending on your system software. If you're still using System 6, you might discover that it's worth the hassle of upgrading to System 7.x just to avoid font installation hassles.

Installing Fonts With System 6 (RT/TA)

To load fonts into and out of your system when using System 6, you'll need a utility called Font/DA mover. Font/DA Mover (which comes with most versions of System 6) installs fonts *into* the System file itself. Fonts installed with Font/DA mover are not available until you restart.

TrueType and bitmapped fonts are installed completely this way, but to install PostScript fonts, you have to install the suitcase (screen font) portions of the fonts, and then drag the printer fonts into the System Folder.

Click Remove to remove the selected
font from the suitcase or System file.

Make sure the Font
button is clicked.

Click Copy to install
the selected font in
the suitcase the arrows
are pointing toward.

This list shows the
fonts installed in your
System file.

Select the font you
want to copy or
remove from the list.

You can close the
System file and open
another by clicking
this button.

When you're done,
click Quit.

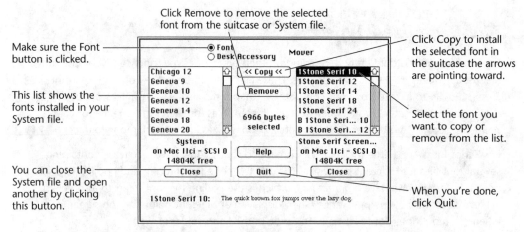

When you open Font/DA Mover, the fonts already installed in your System Folder are displayed in the box at left.
You open the new font suitcase with the Open button at the right, select the font you want to install, and click Copy.

There is no Fonts folder in System 6, so all printer font files must be installed directly
into the System Folder. This makes for a very messy System Folder, especially if you
have large numbers of fonts.

GOOD
FEATURE

Because few systems still run System 6, this is probably the last time System 6 font
installation will appear in an edition of *The Macintosh Bible*.

Installing Fonts With System 7 (RT)

The biggest difference between System 6 and System 7.0 font installation is that
the awful, annoying, buggy, troublesome Font/DA Mover has been put to rest, and
now fonts are installed (still into the System file) by dragging them. Printer font files
for PostScript printers are still installed by dropping them into the System Folder,
loosely, so they clutter up the folder substantially.

Because System 7 is much smarter than System 6, dragging both suitcases and printer
font files *on top of* your System Folder automatically stores them in the proper location.

To remove fonts, open the System file (double-click on it) and drag the fonts out of
the file. To do this you must have no applications running (just quit them all first).

Installing Fonts With System 7.1 or Later (RT)

System 7.1 introduced a quantum leap advance into the world of font management on
the Macintosh. A solution so simple you wonder why in the world they didn't think of
it sooner. Instead of sticking all the fonts and printer font files into the System Folder,
now all fonts go into the Fonts folder, located in the main level of the System Folder.

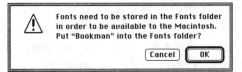

When you drag font files onto the System Folder, the system determines where the files should go but asks your permission before placing them there.

This little innovation not only made fonts easier to organize and use, but also cleaned up the much-too-messy System Folder in the process.

With System 7.1 and later, dragging font files (both screen and printer font files) to the System Folder automatically places them into the Fonts folder.

Managing Your Fonts (DD)

Installing fonts in the ways just described is easy enough, but depending on how many fonts you have, loading all of them directly into your system can start slowing you down. For one thing, every font you install takes up a small, but perhaps significant, amount of memory. The larger your system grows, the less memory you have to run programs, and because every time you launch a program it has to take inventory of all those fonts, your Mac will be slower starting up, slower opening programs, and slower executing some commands. And another thing: If your system is full of fonts you rarely use, you're probably wasting a lot of time scrolling through mile-long font menus to get to the one or two fonts you generally want.

In either case, it's time to start thinking about managing your fonts.

One way to simplify your font menus and pare down the amount of memory your fonts use is to be more selective about what font files you install. Dragging all the icons on a new font disk over the System Folder will install every file on the disk, but you may not need them all.

If you're using TrueType fonts, you don't need to install the bitmapped fonts at all (see the sidebar "Why Bitmap Fonts Won't Go Away," earlier in this chapter). If you're using PostScript fonts with ATM, you need to install just one screen font for each typeface (any size will do, so pick the smallest). ATM will use the printer fonts (which you *do* need to have available) to create type for the screen and for non-PostScript printers. That's the technical minimum.

Screen Fonts You Don't Need (RT)

Technically, you *can* get away with one point size worth of screen fonts for each font. However, you might be shortchanging yourself in both speed and display quality by not having all the different screen fonts available.

If you don't have the point size of the font you are currently using installed, ATM or QuickDraw has to generate the font on the screen for you on the fly. Due to the zippy performance of these routines, the slowdown isn't noticeable except on the slowest Macintosh computers, or on pages with several different fonts (more than ten). Having multiple screen fonts at different point sizes can speed up your screen redraw considerably if one of the above criteria is true.

However, the more important reason to have more than one point size of screen fonts installed is for display quality. Each bitmap font at each point size is custom designed to be as readable as possible at that point size. If the screen display is generated by ATM or QuickDraw, pixel variances can occur, and at small point sizes letters can become jumbled or illegible.

I usually recommend that you have all the screen fonts smaller than 16-point installed, for maximum readability. After all, they don't take up much disk space.

Using Suitcase or MasterJuggler   (GS)

If you've got just a handful of fonts installed on your Mac, you don't have to read any further.

But if you're a font junky like me, and you need a way to handle all those fonts, you'll want to consider two handy ways to turn your fonts on and off like a light switch.

Alsoft's **MasterJuggler** ($49) and Symantec's **Suitcase** ($99) both let you put the fonts you don't want to use all the time someplace other than the Fonts folder. With either of these programs working you can create a special folder for most of your fonts (on any hard drive that you have available to you when you start your Mac), and use the font manager program to activate the fonts when you need them and disable them when they are no longer needed.

Either program will let you group your fonts into *sets* (a collection of fonts). And some Mac programs, such as Adobe PageMaker and QuarkXPress will even recognize fonts that have been switched on or off, and update their font menus accordingly. The resemblance of Suitcase to MasterJuggler more or less ends there, though.

Suitcase 3.0 offers complete font management capability in a Finder-like interface. You can drag fonts from one set to another, have some fonts load when you boot your Mac, and have others load only when you launch a specific program.

MasterJuggler sports a klunky if serviceable interface that only a mother could love. But the newest version of Suitcase, version 3.0, has truly joined the '90s. Suitcase is now slick and sports all the latest Mac OS features, such as PowerPC native code, Apple events and AppleScript capability, and a Finder-like interface that you can use to drag your fonts from one set to another.

When you use a font management program, don't turn off a font till after you print your document. Otherwise, the font won't be available when the printer needs it, and you'll end up with the wrong font (probably Courier) when your document is printed. Also, if you're using a program that doesn't update a font menu automatically, such as Microsoft Word, be sure to quit the program before you make any alterations to the font lineup.

HOT TIP

Font Moving and Application Problems   (RT)

Moving fonts in and out of the Fonts folder/System file doesn't seem all that special, but to the Macintosh this is a major change in the way it works, and how it works with applications. Fonts added to the system don't necessarily appear in applications until after they've quit, and the Mac won't let you remove fonts while other applications are running.

I've found a clever way to get around this problem in System 7.1 and later, but it can wreak havoc with your system (à la crash) if you abuse it. Simply drag the Fonts folder from the System Folder. Create a new Fonts folder (you have to create it in a different location than where the current Fonts folder is, because no two folders can have the same name). Then copy the fonts from the Fonts folder into the new Fonts folder, and add or subtract fonts from the new Fonts folder until you've reorganized them just right. Then put the new Fonts folder into the System Folder. Many programs will automatically update their font lists. Some won't, and using a font that doesn't exist anymore is a sure way to send your system into oblivion until you restart. Be careful not to remove system fonts (Geneva, Chicago, Monaco) from the Fonts folder when using this method.

HOT TIP

Font Display on Your Screen   (RT)

It wasn't that long ago that when you increased the point size of type on your screen, that the type did indeed get larger, but it appeared blockier and blockier. At large point sizes (anything bigger than 48-point), type was pretty much unusable. In the fall of 1989, a little *init* (a file that loads at startup and becomes part of the system software) came along called Adobe Type Manager. ATM, as it is commonly known, changed the appearance of type on screen forever. ATM lives now as a control panel, looking to PostScript printer fonts to create perfectly smooth outlines of all your Type 1 type. If you have TrueType fonts, they're automatically rendered at the point size you choose. Bitmapped typefaces, however, only look as good as the largest point size installed.

Adobe Acrobat and SuperATM (RT/TA)

Occasionally, when you receive a document from someone, it may use fonts that you don't have installed on your system. This causes much pain and suffering, because then the font is usually replaced with Helvetica, which probably has a different width than the missing font. So not only does the document look bad because it has the wrong font, but the text also fails to wrap correctly, which in long documents can cause either loads of white space at the end of a story or missing text.

SuperATM was created to help prevent these types of problems. SuperATM relies on a few special fonts that are designed to replace your missing fonts, keeping the overall look and the character widths the same.

Adobe Acrobat uses this technology to ensure that documents saved as *PDF* (Portable Document Format) have fonts that closely match the correct fonts, both in appearance and widths. Acrobat is fast becoming the standard format for exchanging documents on the Internet, because it is cross-platform, and any existing document from any software can be translated into a PDF document.

Future versions of Acrobat are rumored to contain full font support, so PDF documents will actually contain font information as part of the file. This means that any platform will be able to see a document with the exact same fonts that were used to create it. (See Chapter 25 for more on Adobe Acrobat.)

Fonts Aren't Part of Most Files (RT)

While most documents *use* fonts, those fonts aren't actually part of the document file. This is what can cause the most trouble when transporting documents between different computers. When your friend saves a QuarkXPress file that uses New Century Schoolbook and Caxton, those fonts aren't part of the QuarkXPress file. If you open up that QuarkXPress file on your computer, and you *don't* have New Century Schoolbook and Caxton, you'll get a message telling you that "This document uses fonts that are not available on this system." You'll either have to install those fonts or convert the text that is in those fonts into other fonts that are installed on your system, never an enjoyable task.

Fonts and Printing (JF)

Whether you print using PostScript or TrueType, fonts play the same role: They supply character outlines used to create printable text. Generally, documents don't really *contain* any fonts—they simply call for particular fonts to be used and describe how the text should be sized and positioned. (The exception: There are some pure PostScript files, which you can use to deliver your documents to off-site printing services that don't have your fonts in-house. For details on that, see "Using Service Bureaus" in Chapter 21.)

You can create a document perfectly well using only bitmapped screen fonts—your application needs to know only how much space the letters take up (information stored in the screen fonts), not what the characters in the typeface actually look like. But at printing time, the printer fonts for every typeface called for in a document have to be available.

PostScript Printing versus QuickDraw Printing

Whether you use PostScript or TrueType fonts, the font information in your document must be *interpreted*, that is, rendered into a printable image. If you print using QuickDraw, this image processing is done inside your Mac, while PostScript printers use their own built-in image-processing computer. If you're printing with PostScript fonts on a QuickDraw printer, ATM does the interpreting inside your Mac. (ATM is described on page 405; the difference between PostScript and QuickDraw printers is described in Chapter 21.)

In either case, the interpreter has to have access to the fonts you used to create the original page. This is simple for QuickDraw printing, because everything is done in your Mac. The entire image of each page is assembled there and passed to the printer, which needs very little in the way of brain power to reproduce the page image being spoon-fed to it by your Mac.

But when printing with PostScript, you may need to get fonts from your Mac into the printer—a process called *downloading*—where the printer's on-board computer can get to them. (Downloading is described in more detail in the next section.)

Not all fonts need to be downloaded to the printer, because PostScript printers always come with some *resident fonts*—fonts built into the printer's ROM. This is usually a set referred to as the *LaserWriter 35* (see the sidebar "The LaserWriter 35: Fonts *Almost* Everybody Has," later in this chapter.). Every PostScript printer has at least the Times, Helvetica, Courier, and Symbol fonts built-in to provide a common set of fonts that all PostScript users can share, regardless of which program or printer they use. You can also attach a hard disk to some PostScript printers for permanently storing large numbers of fonts, in effect adding to the number of resident fonts.

Font Downloading   (JK/JF)

When you click OK in the Print dialog box, the Mac calls down to the PostScript printer, "Yo, file coming! You got Palatino down there?" The printer, consulting its list of built-in fonts, might answer, "Always! Send that file!" Whereupon the Mac might say, "You got Frutiger, too?" and get the answer, "Never heard of it; send it down." In which case the Mac downloads Frutiger to the printer, where it's stored in memory. It takes about 15 seconds to download a font over a standard AppleTalk network.

This Mac/printer dialogue and downloading continues until all the necessary fonts are in the printer (in which case your pages print), or until the printer runs out of memory (in which case the printer freaks out, sends an error message to the Mac, and quits in a huff).

This way of getting the fonts you need into the printer is called *automatic downloading,* and fonts sent to the printer this way stay in the printer's memory only until the document has been printed, after which the fonts are dropped to make room for those in the next print job.

Automatic downloading is the easiest way to handle fonts because you don't do anything special—just choose Print. It's also the logical strategy for a workgroup that uses many different fonts—one person's downloaded fonts are automatically cleared out to make room for those needed by a comrade's job.

HOT TIP

If you use the same fonts over and over again though, it's a waste of time to have them downloaded and deleted every time you print. It's smarter to download the fonts so they stay resident in memory, a process called *manual* or *permanent downloading.*

Manually downloading PostScript Fonts (JF). Manual downloading copies fonts into the printer's memory so they stay there "permanently" (until the printer is turned off). You manually download fonts with a special program, such as Apple's LaserWriter Font Utility (included with the system) or Adobe's Downloader (free with Adobe fonts). If your printer has a hard disk attached, these programs can also copy your fonts permanently onto it, where they'll stay until you erase them.

The benefit of manual downloading is that your pages print faster because you download the fonts just once (in the morning, say, when you start your printer), not every time you print. Manual downloading also helps your printer pack fonts more efficiently into memory.

The LaserWriter 35: Fonts Almost *Everybody* Has   (DD)

Most PostScript printers come with a set of PostScript typefaces, often referred to as the "LaserWriter 35" (they first appeared together in Apple's LaserWriter Plus), built into their ROMs (the printer manufacturers usually also provide the bitmapped versions of these fonts on disk for loading into your operating system). They're also available as part of Adobe's **Type Basics** pack ($200). Except for Symbol, Zapf Chancery, and Zapf Dingbats, all these fonts come in full, four-member families, including plain, bold, italic, and bold-italic versions (that's why they add up to 35 instead of the 11 shown here).

Courier
Helvetica
Palatino
Σψμβολ   (Symbol)
Times
ITC Avant Garde Gothic
ITC Bookman
Helvetica Narrow
New Century Schoolbook
ITC Zapf Chancery
☆✳✤ ✻❁□❃   (Zapf Dingbats)

The 11 base fonts stored in a laser printer.

How your printer looks for fonts (TA/JF). The Mac and PostScript printers have a fixed routine when it comes to finding the fonts they need to print a page. Here's how the search proceeds:

First, the printer checks the printer's ROM, where fonts that are built into the printer are permanently stored. Next, the printer's RAM is checked, in case the font has recently been downloaded, and is still available. If the printer has a hard drive attached directly to it, that is checked next for fonts. If the fonts are found in any of these places, the font is loaded very quickly, because no files need to be sent across the network. Finally, the printer looks in the System Folder of the Macintosh that originally sent the file to be printed.

If your system doesn't find the required PostScript font in any of those places, the Mac will look for an equivalent TrueType font in the System Folder.

But what happens when your printer or Mac can't find a font it needs for printing? One of two things:

• It will use the screen font to print lumpy-looking screen-resolution type.

• It will substitute another font, Courier, which is so ugly you can't miss the substitution.

If you're using Adobe's SuperATM, the program will create a substitute for the missing font using a generic Multiple Master serif or sans serif typeface. The substitute

> ## Never Rename Printer Fonts (RT)
>
> If you start digging through your Fonts folder, you might come across PostScript printer fonts with odd names, such as FuturBooObl and ZapfChaMedIta. These are the printer fonts for Futura Book Oblique and Zapf Chancery Medium Italic. They're named that way for a reason, and if you decide, on a whim, to change the names of these printer fonts, they won't hook up with the screen fonts, and they won't end up printing.
>
> *Any* alteration to the printer font name will "hide" it from the screen font, and both your on-screen display and printouts will suffer.

won't look exactly the same as the missing font, but at least it will have the correct character widths (also know as *font metrics*) so that your layout will be preserved with all original line endings intact.

Font Manufacturers and Buying Fonts (RT/KT/EF)

You can buy fonts from a dizzying variety of sources. Any given font is usually available directly from the manufacturer or from any number of retailers who have licensed it from its original maker. Software discounters such as CompUSA, MacConnection, MacWarehouse, Egghead, and MacMall all sell fonts, and so do some office supply stores. You can find the names of vendors in books like this one, in design and computer magazines, from on-line services such as America Online, or by word of mouth from your friends.

HOT TIP

What sometimes makes things confusing is that a company you tend to identify as a font maker—Adobe, for instance—also licenses fonts from other sources. The thing to remember is that just because you buy a font from Adobe (or Linotype-Hell or Monotype), that doesn't make it an Adobe (or Linotype-Hell or Monotype) font. All of these companies, and many more, license each others' fonts, though not all sell them at the same prices. We're also seeing a new phenomenon: font vendors, such as Precision Type, that make no fonts of their own but sell (usually at a low price) only fonts licensed from others.

How do you find out what typefaces each vendor offers? For starters, you can contact font vendors and ask for their catalogs. If you want to see font samples from many companies, combined with articles on various facets of typography, there are several publications you can read. *x-height* is a quarterly newsletter/catalog ($18 per year) from FontHaus. *U&lc*, ITC's quarterly journal ($14 per year), just celebrated its 20th anniversary. ITC also publishes ***The ITC Directory of New Typefaces***, which includes specimen pages of new faces from leading foundries and designers ($190 including quarterly updates). The *Directory*'s three-ring-binder format allows you to insert updates, and an index helps you locate faces by category, name, or designer. (See Appendix D for information on how to contact these companies.) ***Font & Function*** from Adobe showcases their newest fonts, contains type-related stories, and includes a complete catalog of their available typefaces.

In addition to selling fonts singly, most of the major manufacturers offer package deals that significantly reduce the cost per font. Adobe sells its **Type Basics** pack (the 35 basic PostScript printer fonts described on page 409, plus 30 more faces "specially chosen to complement the 35 printer fonts") for $200. Adobe's **Value Pack**, including 30 text, script, decorative, and display faces, sells for just $60, which works out to a couple of dollars per font. And those are the list prices: You can get these packages and similar ones from other vendors through mail-order companies for about 40 percent less.

Adobe, Monotype, Agfa, and the other vendors with large libraries also offer their entire libraries on CD-ROM. The CD itself is available for a nominal cost (Adobe's Type on Call is included free with most of their major software packages), and most of the fonts are encrypted (unreadable unless you have a code) until you call the manufacturer with your credit card number. In return, the vendor tells you the secret codes that unlock the fonts you want. Most of the font vendors offer bargains to customers who buy fonts this way, charging $25 or so for fonts that may normally retail for $100 or more. Most also offer unlocked CDs, giving you access to an entire library on your desktop. Other font libraries, such as FontHaus and URW, offer their entire libraries for as little as 20 cents per font.

Ares and ElseWare, with their synthetic font technologies, have a new twist on font sales. Their programs each create more than 200 fonts from compact font descriptors, so you buy a whole library of fonts when you buy the software. (At this writing, Ares was acquired by Adobe Systems; the Ares product line will reportedly be folded into the Adobe product line.)

On pages 423–431, we've pulled together a small sampling of fonts in four different categories: text fonts, display fonts, pictorial fonts, and special-purpose fonts. They should at least give you a taste of what's out there. Happy hunting.

Type Manufacturers   (TA)

There are several typeface manufacturers that both sell and design their own type-faces, from Agfa to Monotype to Letraset. One company, however, stands out from the rest of the pack, especially in regard to Macintosh fonts and related technologies.

Adobe Systems Incorporated carries one of the most complete lines of typefaces which can be purchased one family at a time by mail order, right from their Type On Call CD-ROM, or as one giant collection (Font Folio) for a few thousand dollars. Adobe fonts have become the standard for service bureaus, ad agencies, and prepress shops all over the world.

Shareware Fonts   (RT)

Some of the best bargains to be found when font hunting are from shareware-based fonts. Recently, font designers who elect to distribute their fonts as shareware have been charging $10 to $20 per font, a steep price when you consider the lack of extras in many of those fonts. Sometimes, however, you'll run across a gem of a typeface for only $5, such as the following:

Lefty Casual, a handwriting font that in-cludes three different weights (in addition to the standard "casual" weight, there is also LeftyBold and LeftyMarker), is great for a readable "I wrote it by hand" look.

RansomNote is a typeface that consists of mismatched letters and ransom-style words, which resemble words cut from a magazine. Great for hostage negotiations, to show that you're really serious.

The way shareware fonts work is that you get to install the font and use it for nothing. But if you decide you like the font enough to keep it, you're obligated to pay the share-ware fee. This encourages font designers to both update their current fonts and create new ones.

"You know, This is really a very relaxing, casual TypeFace."

"And IT even has a bold variaTion...whaT do you know?

I like This weighT, which looks like a Sharpie" marker!"

Lefty Casual is a $5 shareware font that sports three weights and professionally kerned pairs. The design is both readable and friendly enough to use in casual correspondence.

If you Ever WANT to see your preCious Pet ROCK alive again, Send LOTS of $$$ (MILLIONs) to ME! Now!

RansomNote consists of letters and words that appear to have been torn from a magazine.

You can find shareware fonts on on-line services such as America Online, or from huge shareware CD-ROM collections. The quality of the fonts ranges greatly from the professionally designed and kerned typefaces to really ugly, terrible, rotten fonts…you decide how good the fonts are by sending in (or not sending) your shareware fee to the manufacturer.

Specialty Faces (EF)

Specialty faces can be practical (pictorial fonts depicting credit cards, international symbols, or computer **Key Caps**, whimsical (alphabets made up of cats, flowers, or laundry), or ornamental (borders, Dingbats, or other decorative elements). Other specialty faces include foreign-language fonts and fonts for disciplines such as music, math, or chemistry.

theTypeBook (EF)

Even if you use one of the utilities described earlier to display a font's characters on the screen, you still can't tell what a typeface *really* looks like until you print a sample. That's where Rascal Software's **theTypeBook** ($50) comes in. This utility automates the process of printing type-specimen pages, allowing you to create a printed catalog of your PostScript and TrueType typefaces.

The program includes six page layouts, and lets you customize features such as point size and leading for the sample text blocks in the Sample Page layout, and the text of the catalog's headers and footers.

~~~~~~~~~~~~~~~~~~~~~~~~~~~~~~~~~~~~~~~

Font Styles

From the beginning, the Mac included not only different fonts but different ways you could style them. Like its font formats, though, the Mac's styles have come a long way since then, resulting in (as usual) both more possibilities and more confusion for users.

Bold and Italic: The Basic Styles (RT)

The most basic of all font stylings are the *bold* and *italic styles*. **Bold is a slight darkening and widening of the plain style.** *Italic is a slanted, curved version of the plain style.* The two can be combined to create ***Bold-Italic, which is a dark, wide, slanted and curved version of the original typeface***.

To apply bold or italic styles to a typeface, most applications have a style menu with Bold and Italic options. Depending on the font, you might be able to choose the bold or italic version of the font you are currently using, right from the font list. Often, these styles show up as "B Times Bold" or "I Times Italic" or "BI Times Bold Italic."

If the font doesn't have a bold or italic version, the Mac does some magic and automatically creates both a bold version (by printing the characters twice right next to each other) and an oblique version (by slanting each character slightly, commonly referred to as italic). Unfortunately, this results in rather ugly looking mutations of the original font. My advice is to avoid bold and italic stylings unless the font already contains those variations.

HOT TIP

Oddly enough, there are different names for bold and italic than just "Bold" and "Italic". Bold can be referred to as "Demi," and italic is often called "Oblique." Some fonts contain several weights, which range from very thin typefaces to very large, dark ones. For instance, weights of Helvetica include: Light, Thin, Medium, **Bold**, **Heavy**, and **Black**. Other fonts have weights such as Ultra Light and **Extra Black**.

The Custom Styles   (RT)

Of course, bold and italic aren't the only variations of fonts available. Many applications let you create *custom styles*. The styles include:

Underline
: This style places an underline under all the characters you type.

Word Underline
: This style places underlines under all characters except spaces.

Strikethru
: This style puts a line right "thru" all your characters. The practicality of this style eludes me to this day (unless, I guess, you're a lawyer).

Outline
: This style surrounds the font with an outline, leaving the middle empty.

Shadow
: This style places a 50 percent tinted shadow just below and to the right of the original text.

Condensed
: This style compresses the type into about 75 percent of its original width.

SMALL CAPS
: This style changes all lowercase letters to small versions of the uppercase letters.

ALL CAPS   This style changes all lowercase letters to uppercase letters.

Sentence caps   This style changes the first letter in a sentence to an uppercase character, while the rest of the characters in the sentence remain lowercase.

Superscript   This style reduces (usually) the size of the characters and moves them up from the baseline of the type.

Subscript   This is the inverse of Superscript: The characters are reduced (usually) and moved down from the baseline of the type.

Superior   This style dramatically reduces the size of characters and moves them up from the baseline slightly.

Most applications only allow you to apply a few of these styles, though text-intensive applications (word processors, page layout programs) let you apply more than others.

Applying Styles   (RT/TA)

To apply a style to characters, select the characters, and select the appropriate style from the Style menu. The standard keyboard command for bold is Cmd Shift B, and the standard keyboard command for making text italic is Cmd Shift I. Some programs allow you to avoid the Shift key, enabling you to press Cmd B for bold and Cmd I for italic.

A word of caution when using bold and italic styles: Because of the way fonts are designed, bolding a lighter font may not result in the next darker version of that font. For instance, applying a Bold style to Helvetica will result in Helvetica Bold, but applying Bold to Helvetica Light will result in (gasp!) Helvetica Black, a much darker font than Helvetica Bold.

Once again, when it comes to bold and italic, if your font doesn't have these styles built-in as separate fonts, don't apply the generic styles. I'd like to say the same thing about the "condensed" style, but oftentimes there are no condensed versions of type-faces available.

Another thing to be careful of is applying Bold to bold fonts and Italic to italic fonts. This can result in super-dark overprinting fonts, or extra-slanted italics, both of which look terrible.

Styles versus Specific Fonts (RT)

HOT TIP

If the font you're using has a separate listing for the Bold or Italic setting, should you select the bold or italic font, or apply the Bold or Italic option to the "base" font? The best thing to do is to apply the Bold and Italic options to the base font, because it makes editing the style in the future much easier. This method allows you to select all the type and change the font, while keeping both your bold and italic styles intact. This also works great if you're using an application's style sheets.

Managing the Font Menu (EF)

If you have more than a couple dozen fonts installed—and these days, who doesn't?—you may find yourself taking a leisurely scroll down the Font menu to select the font you need. (As far as the Mac is concerned, each weight or style in a font family is a separate font, and warrants its own listing in an application's Font menu.) You may give up on using Zapf Chancery because of the long trek involved to get there.

The following utilities can help you organize your Font menu to make selecting fonts easier and quicker.

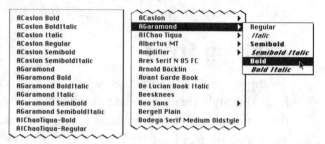

Font menus without (left) and with (right) Type Reunion installed.

Adobe Type Reunion. Adobe's **Type Reunion** ($65) extension shortens your Font menu by organizing fonts into families, placing all the styles for each family into a submenu. The figure above shows the same Font menu before and after Type Reunion is installed.

MenuFonts. Dubl-Click Software's **MenuFonts** ($70) is a control panel that groups fonts by family in the Font menu and displays fonts in their own type styles, in sizes from 9- to 24-point. (MenuFonts is smart enough to display pictorial fonts in

A MenuFonts font menu.

Chicago, so you can still read their names in the menu.) MenuFonts includes a number of other nifty features as well. It puts a bar along the edge of the menu that lets you access samples of a font in different sizes. It lets you know whether a font is PostScript, TrueType, or bitmapped by placing *Ps*, *Tt*, or *B* next to the name. And, to save you time when you have a long Font menu, MenuFonts lets you jump to any letter in the alphabetized Font menu simply by pressing a key on the keyboard (press Z and you're whisked to Zapf Chancery et al, for example).

Font Style Shorthand (SZA/EF/AN)

The weight or style of a typeface supplied by a particular font is often indicated by initials preceding the font name. Here are some of the initials you're likely to see, and what they stand for:

B	bold	*L*	light	*D*	demibold	*S*	semi
Bk	book	*N*	narrow	*E*	extended	*Sl*	slanted
Blk	black	*O*	oblique	*H*	heavy	*U*	ultra
C	condensed	*P*	poster	*I*	italic	*X*	extra

Sometimes you'll see them in combination—*XBO*, for example, stands for *extra bold oblique*.

TypeTamer. Like the font-menu organizers just described, Impossible Software's **TypeTamer** ($70) consolidates font families into submenus, making your Font menu easier to navigate. TypeTamer performs a few other handy tricks as well. It places an icon beside each font name, indicating whether the font is PostScript, TrueType, or bitmapped. It lets you zip to a font in the menu by typing the first few letters of its name. Best of all, the program's TopFonts feature places the names of the fonts you're using at the top of the Font menu, allowing you to reselect them without scrolling down the menu. TypeTamer also lets you create your own font categories for the Font menu, based on the way you work. For example, you might want to place all your script fonts in a category, or maybe divide fonts up by vendor or publishing project.

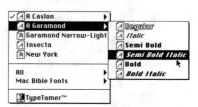

TypeTamer's effect on the Font menu.

Fontina. Eastgate Systems' **Fontina** ($70) control panel presents a novel way of displaying your Font menu: It squeezes all your font names into columns, showing the whole menu at once. (Weights and styles are in alphabetical order under each font family's name.) When you select a font, a sample is displayed in large type at the top of the screen. A feature called Personal Font Knapsack lets you place the names of frequently used fonts in the upper-left corner for easy access. If you have lots of fonts, Fontina's small type can be hard to read—but it does save you the trouble of scrolling down a lengthy Font menu.

Fontina's novel approach to font-menu organization can save you a lot of scrolling when searching for a font.

Special Characters

With the fabulous variety of fonts and styles on the Mac, you can get text to look just about any way you want it to. But what if your imagination—or your business—extends further than the Latin alphabet? Not to worry; the wide, wide world of fonts has something for everyone, and the special characters you need are often lurking right in the fonts you already own.

If you don't want to bother with utilities, the following table lists the keystroke combos that produce some of the most common accents, symbols, and other special characters.

Quick Reference for Special Characters (EF)

Press	For
Option E, then letter	é, á, etc.
Option I, then letter	ê, î, etc.
Option `, then letter	è, à, etc.
Option N, then letter	ñ, ã, etc.
Option U, then letter	ü, ï, etc.
Option C	ç
Option O	ø
Option [	"
Shift Option [	"
Option]	'
Shift Option]	'
Option ;	…
Shift Option -	—
Shift Option K	(not all fonts include this symbol)
Option 2	TM
Option R	®
Option G	©
Option 4	¢
Option 8	•

Mnemonics for Special Characters   (TA/SZA/AN/JK)

Understanding why certain special characters are placed on certain keys can help you remember where they are. (If the logic isn't obvious, look for a connection that means something to you.) The bullet (•) and the degree symbol (°) resemble the asterisk; all three are on the ⑧ key. The dagger (†), which you get with Option T, looks like a *T*. The diamond (◊) and the square-root symbol (√), both of which incorporate the V shape, are on the ⓥ key.

The copyright symbol can't be on the ⓒ key, since ç and Ç are already there, but its shape is similar to a G and that's the key you'll find it on. The ellipsis (…), which has three dots, is on the semi-colon/colon key, which you'll notice also has three dots. Other easy connections are π and ∏ on Ⓟ, ® on Ⓡ, μ (mu) on Ⓜ, ¢ on the dollar sign, and ¥ (the yen sign) on Ⓨ.

Of course, some keys seem to make no sense at all, such as £ on the 3 key, and ‡ on the 7 key. For these, you can construct your own meanings. For instance, £ is the English Pound symbol, and # (pound) is on the 3 as well. And ‡ has seven segments to it, and it is on the 7 key. I know, it's stretching, but whatever helps you to remember these symbols and their corresponding keys. *[I suppose that's the same as when I think "Velcro" for Paste, which is on the ⓥ key.—TA]*

How Do You Type That Character Again?   (EF)

How many times have you been typing along at lightning speed, only to come to a screeching halt because you can't remember how to type a particular accent, symbol, or other special character? You're not alone; many special characters require you to type finger-tangling key combinations. Fortunately, several utilities can help you find the characters you need.

Key Caps (EF). The easiest way to find special characters is to use Key Caps, an Apple desk accessory that comes with your Mac's system software. When you choose Key Caps from the menu, it displays a representation of a keyboard and puts a new menu title, Key Caps, on the menu bar. Select a font from the Key Caps menu, and that font appears in the Key Caps keyboard display.

When you hold down the Shift key, Key Caps darkens the Shift keys on its display and shows you the characters you get in the selected font when you hold down Shift and press another key.

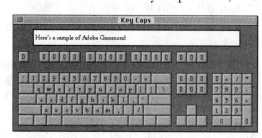

The Key Caps menu item.

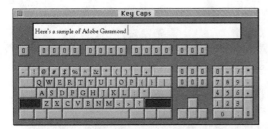

Pressing [Shift] while in Key Caps displays the Shift versions of the keyboard keys.

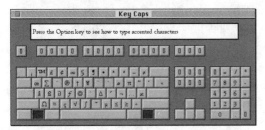

Pressing [Option] while in Key Caps displays the Option versions of the keyboard keys.

But you already know what the [Shift] characters are (except in fonts composed entirely of pictures or symbols). Where Key Caps really comes in handy is in showing you the characters generated by the [Option] and [Shift][Option] keys. When you hold down [Option], Key Caps displays the characters you get in the selected font when you hold down [Option] and press another key.

System 7's version of Key Caps outlines the keys that produce accents that you can apply to other letters. When you press one of these keys, the display outlines the letters to which you can apply the selected accent.

The accent produced by pressing [Option][E] is shown below.

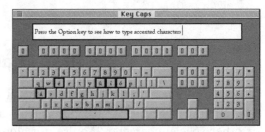

The é accent, accessed by pressing [Option][E] and [E] again.

You can enter sample text in the box at the top of the displayed keyboard by typing on the (real) keyboard or by clicking on keys in the Key Caps keyboard. You can cut or copy this text into a document, saving you the trouble of remembering a keystroke combination for a special character. (The pasted text won't appear in the font you chose in Key Caps, but you can change the font once you're back in your document.) If you need a string of special characters, you can type them in Key Caps, copy them to your document, and then change the font.

BigCaps (EF). Apple's Key Caps desk accessory is free, and it's right there when you install your system software, but it has its limitations. For example, you may have trouble seeing the characters for some fonts, since Key Caps displays them in only a single size. BigCaps, a utility that comes with Dubl-Click Software's MenuFonts (described in the "Managing the Font Menu" section), takes care of this problem. As its name implies, BigCaps can display fonts at a

The BigCaps display is larger and friendlier than the Key Caps display.

larger size than Key Caps. It has a few additional pluses as well: Its window is resizable, and it can display fonts even if you're not using them and they're not in the menu.

TypeTamer (EF). Impossible Software's **TypeTamer** ($70) control panel, described in the "Managing the Font Menu" section, provides a way to quickly view and insert special characters. TypeTamer can display a window that contains all the special characters in a font. You simply click on a character to insert it into your document. Unlike Key Caps, TypeTamer inserts the character in the correct font, saving you the trouble of changing it in your document.

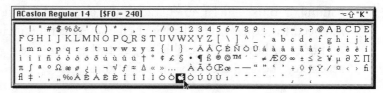

TypeTamer not only displays the character, but also automatically inserts it into your document in the correct font.

PopChar (EF). If you're on a budget, try **PopChar**, a freeware control panel from Günther Blaschek. PopChar inserts a tiny hot spot on the menu bar. When you want to find a special character, you point to that spot and a window showing every character in the selected font appears. Drag the pointer to the character you want, let go of the mouse button, and the character is inserted into your document.

PopChar enables you to quickly display characters in each font.

theFONDler (EF). One neat little utility, **theFONDler** ($70, Rascal Software), scans the inner workings of your fonts and reports any problems it finds. (The program's name comes from the *FOND* resource, which stands for font family descriptor.) You need to know a bit about fonts to use this utility effectively, because many of its messages are fairly technical (e.g., "Bad Width table offset"). However, theFONDler's manual makes an effort to explain what the diagnostic messages mean, and its ability to spot problems such as damaged or missing font files, duplicate font names or numbers, or poorly constructed fonts, can help even nonexperts cull defective fonts from their collections.

Special Character Font Sets (TA)

Because there are only so many special characters in most fonts, some fonts have been created that consist of *only* special characters and symbols. The following sections discuss the different categories of these font sets.

Dingbats (DD)

Fonts aren't limited to letters and numbers. There has recently been an explosion of *pictorial fonts*, which assign images to the different keys of your keyboard. They're available from almost any font vendor, and several font designers, such as Judith Sutcliffe at Electric Typographer, specialize in such fun and decorative images.

Expert Sets (EF)

Expert sets, or *expert collections*, are companion fonts for certain typefaces that provide special characters such as small caps, fractions, old-style numbers (the kind that dip below the baseline), and ornate alternate letters. Unfortunately, they exist for only a handful of fonts. The larger character sets allowed by TrueType GX will do away with the need for expert sets; all variant characters can be included in the main font. But it's not clear how you'll be able to get at them all unless Apple adds some additional access keys beyond the [Option] and [Shift] keys.

Foreign-Language and Special-Purpose Fonts (DD)

Some fonts are made just to supply those characters that the standard Latin alphabet fonts don't include. These include foreign-language fonts, such as Kanji, Arabic, Cyrillic, and other non-Latin alphabets, and *pi fonts* that include such utility characters as mathematical symbols, map-making symbols, musical notations, credit card logos, and other useful and decorative shapes.

What's That Funny Box? (RT)

Occasionally you'll be typing along just fine, and a silly little box will appear. This box is called a *missing character box*, which shows up any time you've typed a special character that isn't part of the font's real characters. For instance, system fonts like Geneva and Chicago don't have very many special characters. Several of the more common [Option]-based characters in those fonts display the missing character box. Oddly enough, the box doesn't appear when you print.

> What's that funny "box?"
>
> What□s that funny □box?□

Strange little empty boxes appear in certain fonts where there is no corresponding character.

Font Sampler: Text Fonts   (AJ)

A good text font should be basically invisible. If you read a book all the way through and don't notice the typeface, the typographer has done a good job. If, however, you keep noticing a weird *g* 6r odd swash capitals, your mind wanders and the author loses his or her grip on your attention.

That's not to say that text types are boring. In fact, there are some beautiful typefaces around that can clearly and unobtrusively display the characters of your text. For short copy such as advertisements, you can afford to get a little more allusive and experimental with the text type.

Text fonts can be divided into several categories, based on the historical period in which their basic design emerged. A flexible font library should include one or more from each category to accommodate all kinds of work.

Old Style

Sabon (Linotype-Hell/Monotype, various prices), designed by Jan Tschichold in 1966, is a quiet and refined version of the classic Garamond model.

Adobe Garamond ($150, expert set $100) is an excellent example of Old Style type that's a little lighter and appears slightly smaller than Sabon.

Old Style types begin with the romans of Francesco Griffo, cut for Aldus Manutius in Venice in the late 1490s. Griffo refined earlier models by increasing the contrast between vertical and horizontal strokes, reducing the height of the capitals, straightening the crossbar in the eye of the *e*, and substituting round dots (such as that over an *i*) for diamond-shaped ones. The Old Style model was perfected in France by the mid-16th century by two men: Claude Garamond and Robert Granjon.

Dutch Old Style

Kis (Bitstream, $50 per weight) is a condensed and tight-fitting version of Kis Janson.

Monotype's Ehrhardt ($95), redrawn in 1937, is a condensed type, more interesting than its Janson.

Dutch Old Style began when Christopher Plantin hired Granjon to design a type that would be more economical to print. To make the type sturdier, the face was made bolder. To fit more on a page, Granjon shortened the descenders and condensed the type somewhat. Then, because the tiny counters of the more-condensed *e* and *a* tended to fill with ink, he enlarged them. Dutch Old Style types make good workmanlike text faces. (This book is set in Adobe's Janson Text, a classic of Dutch Old Style.)

Font Sampler: Text Fonts (continued)

Transitional

Monotype's Bell ($145, expert set $50) is an elegant choice as a basic text type that also looks great in large, display sizes.

ATF Bulmer (Bitstream, $50 per weight) has contrast that points the way to modern types.

Transitional types were inspired by the Rococo copper-engraved lettering popular in the 18th century. The French were first to lighten type and restore some of its calligraphic modeling. These types have high contrast and a primarily vertical stress (the narrow parts of letter strokes in characters such as *o* and *e* are at the top and bottom of the letter, not off-center, as is the case with Old Style typefaces).

Modern

Walbaum is a German type that is lighter, wider, more curvaceous, and more readable than most moderns. The Berthold version (licensed by various vendors) is less severe than others.

Designed to reflect improvements in type cutting and printing technology, including smoother paper, modern types are generally hard on the eyes, having a strong vertical emphasis with marked contrast between thick and thin portions of the letters, and thin hairline serifs. Bodoni is the best-known example of this style.

Sans-Serif

Paul Renner's Futura (Elsner + Flake via FontHaus, $40 per weight) is a clean, modern type that works well in all its weights and styles.

Gill Sans (Monotype, $145 for the text weights) is a humanist type with a bit more personality than Futura.

Hans Ed Meier's Syntax (Linotype-Hell, $30 per weight) is another family group with great flexibility and readability.

Although any book on typography will tell you that sans-serif typefaces are difficult to read for long stretches, they are increasingly popular for setting text. The best of them (such as the faces shown here) have a lot of variations for setting work that requires different levels of headings as well as different kinds of emphasis.

Ahistoric Faces

Electra (Linotype-Hell, $30 per weight) is an elegant type from W.A. Dwiggins with an understated calligraphic quality.

Eric Gill's Joanna (Linotype-Hell, $30 per weight) is his greatest typeface. Its slab serifs make it appear flashy and angular in large sizes. (Also available in Adobe's Value Pack for $60.)

Bitstream Charter ($50 per style), designed by Matthew Carter, is a quiet type, constructed to be legible in extreme variations of weight.

Swift (Elsner + Flake via FontHaus, $170 for the family or $30 per weight) designed by Gerard Unger in 1985 for newspaper work, has a chiseled look, condensed capitals, and a large x-height.

Many 20th-century designers have devised faces that have no particular historic model in mind. Eric Gill, Jan Van Krimpen, and W.A. Dwiggins produced many wonderful types around mid-century that are still popular. Contemporary designers such as Gerard Unger, Matthew Carter, and Sumner Stone are also producing enduring models.

Fancy Text

Cochin (created by Monotype in 1917, digitized by Matthew Carter in 1977 for Linotype-Hell, $90 from Adobe) manages to look simultaneously like an engraved type from the Rococo period and an Art Deco face from the early 20th century.

Michael Harvey's 1990 Ellington (Monotype, $195) has the consummate confidence and control one would expect from a stonecutter. Its bold weights are also very distinctive.

Koch Antiqua (Alphabets, $25 per weight from FontHaus) or Eva-Antiqua (shown here), based on Koch's Eve (from Spiece Graphics via FontHaus, $40 per weight) are recent re-creations of types cut in Germany in the 1920s that show the heritage of pen-drawn lettering.

Some text faces are a little too fancy for book work but have great appeal for dust jackets or display work. Texts shorter than books, such as greeting cards, announcements, even works of poetry, could use one of these fancier types. You could also use these in headings to contrast with a more sober text type.

Font Sampler: Display Fonts   (AJ)

These are types designed to be used at large sizes to break up blocks of text and grab your attention. They range from quiet, enlarged versions of text types to the wildest faces a type designer can dream up. The strong personalities of display faces can instantly create a mood or impart a sense of time and place. Remember, the more personality a typeface has, the less versatile it will be—but the more appropriate for some specialized use.

The traditional categories are decorated, engraved, script, slab serif, and sans serif. When building a library, it's good to have some reliable standbys (such as the Smaragd shown here) as well as some more goofy ones (such as the Xavier Black or Ad Lib).

Smaragd (Linotype-Hell)

SEE THE TREASURES OF ROME

Gudrun Zapf von Hesse's Smaragd, from Linotype-Hell ($40), is a classy, all-caps in-line face, the subtlest kind of decorated type, which features a white line inside the stroke, making the type appear incised. From here the "decorated" category branches out to letterforms made out of other things, such as cactus, banana peel, Band-Aids, whatever.

Poetica (Adobe Systems)

The Pleasure of Your Company

As a rule, scripts are hard to read and should be restricted to short bursts of text. Sometimes script capitals used with a text face can create a nice effect. Adobe's Poetica ($150, $100 for the expert sets), shown here, is a beautiful calligraphic face with lots of variant forms.

Egiziano Classic Black Antique (FontHaus)

15 Men on a Dead Man's Chest

Dennis Ortiz-Lopez's Egiziano Classic Black Antique, from FontHaus ($40), is one of the best re-creations of an historic slab serif: a style based on geometric letter shapes with bold flat serifs grafted on. The style, which was popular in the late 19th century, can sometimes be extremely dull and heavy.

Bernhard Gothic (Spiece Graphics via FontHaus)

Fly to New York

Spiece Graphics' Bernhard Gothic, from FontHaus ($70 for one weight, $40 for additional weights), is an elegant sans serif dating from the 1920s. It has unusual variant characters, including swash italics and a Greek *e* and works well at all weights.

Xavier Black (Castle Systems)

RHUMBA TO CUGAT'S ORCHESTRA

The wacky Xavier Black, from Castle Systems, is a type you'll want to use for display work at least once. It comes by itself for $50.

Ad Lib (Bitstream)

Phil Silvers as Bilko

ATF's goofy Ad Lib ($25, Bitstream) looks something like Ben Shahn's lettering for "What's My Line?" It is extremely informal and very evocative of the '50s (it dates from '61)

Goudy Stout (Castle Systems)

BEWARE OF THE BULL

Fred Goudy claims that his Goudy Stout ($50, Castle Systems) was a typographic lapse, but I think it's one of his best types. This all-caps face looks like it was conceived after a night of drinking and tango-dancing.

Berthold Lo-Type (Linotype-Hell)

Serenade in Ragtime

Berthold Lo-Type ($110, Linotype-Hell) is a quirky German poster letterform from the turn of the century. Some very unusual characters, such as the *f, g,* and *t,* add to its charm. Its quirky details are best appreciated at large sizes. The Adobe package has several weights and styles.

Willow (Adobe Systems)

Wanted! Dead or Alive!

Willow ($100) is a highly condensed type, a member of Adobe's best-selling Wood Type package ($185). (They're called wood types because they're based on late 19th Century American typefaces, which were carved from wood rather than forged in metal.)

Font Sampler: Decorative and Pictorial Fonts (EF)

Pictorial fonts can be practical (pictures of credit cards, telephones, or cut-on-the-dotted-line scissors to use in ads), silly (kids' drawings or wacky birds), or simply ornamental (borders, fleurons, and other decorative elements). The following samples show just a few of the dozens of pictorial fonts available. (We didn't have the space to show a complete character set for every font, but the sample characters will give you the flavor of each.)

Adobe Wood Type Ornaments 2 (Adobe Systems)

Adobe's Wood Type Ornaments collections provide lots of old-fashioned ornaments. This font is included in the Adobe Type Basics package, which offers 65 fonts for $100, or sold with the Adobe Wood Type package for $95.

Adobe offers other pictorial fonts as well, including audio symbols, map symbols, ornaments, and yet more dingbats.

Credit Cards (Agfa)

If your business welcomes popular credit cards, you'll find this font handy for creating ads, menus, and the like. It costs $35 from Agfa.

Other pictorial fonts from Agfa illustrate astrology, animals, borders, ornaments, business, communications, games, sports, medicine, military, music, transportation, TV listings, logos, dingbats, and symbols.

DingBRATS (DS Design)

These dingbats from some of America's youngest type designers are a refreshing change of pace. The font includes 100 charming drawings by kids for $40.

Tommy's Type (The Electric Typographer)

Electric Typographer Judith Sutcliffe based this playful line o' type on some lettering sent to her by Santa Barbara historian Walker A. Tompkins ($45, includes Catastrophe, a font made up of cats). Other pictorial fonts from The Electric Typographer depict masks and petroglyphs.

Birds (FontHaus)

This antic aviary ($40) is just the thing for adding a spot of whimsy to a document. I like a font that makes me laugh.

FrankenFont (Handcraftedfonts Company)

Now you can create your own people without all the muss and fuss of stealing body parts from graveyards. FrankenFont ($45, per weight) consists of 74 parts that can be combined to make 1,000 human figures; each figure is assembled by typing a three-character combination.

Vine Leaves, Volume 1 (Lanston Type Co.)

The Lanston Type Company has brought many classic faces from Goudy, Caslon, and other respected designers into the digital age. To augment these traditional faces, Lanston offers old-style borders, initial caps, and ornaments, including the 128 vine leaves in this font ($75).

Organics (Letraset)

Letraset's Fontek Design Fonts series ($90 per font, $350 for six fonts) offers several pictorial fonts in a variety of styles, inspired by everything from woodcuts to paper cutouts. (Note: Although Letraset has improved the font's performance, placing too many of the intricate Organics on a page might hang up a printer with less than 4MB of memory.)

Linotype Game Pi (Linotype-Hell)

This set of game fonts ($30 per weight, $80 for the set) includes chess, checkers, dice, dominoes, and playing cards (French and English styles).

Other pictorial fonts from Linotype-Hell include dingbats, ornaments, maps, warnings, audio symbols, holiday motifs, astrology symbols, and borders.

Font Sampler: Special-Purpose Fonts (EF)

Macintosh fonts aren't limited to the Latin alphabet. If you speak a non-European language, chances are you can find a font for that language. For that matter, Mac fonts aren't even limited to words; you can find fonts for the languages of music, mathematics, and other symbolic systems. This section presents samples of several special-purpose fonts along with information on where to look for others (see Appendix D for company addresses and phone numbers). Because of space constraints, we haven't shown the complete character set for each font.

Carta (Adobe Systems)

Carta ($29) is the perfect font for mapmakers, or for those Mac users who suddenly find themselves in need of an Interstate symbol. It includes most of the symbols you need to make a map, including route signage, city and capital markers, and symbols for map-like markers such as rest stops, airports, and hospitals.

OCRA (Adobe Systems)

OCRA is a font designed to be easily and quickly read by scanning equipment. While most high-end OCR packages can read most fonts, OCRA will read at 100% accuracy, all the time. You can purchase a set for $79 that includes OCRA, OCRB, and MICR.

Torah Sans Script (Font World)

Font World doesn't simply offer Hebrew fonts; it offers hundreds of Hebrew fonts in a variety of styles. The company's designers have created 36 custom faces that are being used to typeset a new edition of the Talmud (which has been photographically reproduced until now). Font World provides many other fonts as well, including Arabic, Cyrillic, Georgian, Greek, Thai, Vietnamese, and many Western European and Central/Eastern European languages ($100 to $400).

Cyrillic (Linguist's Software)

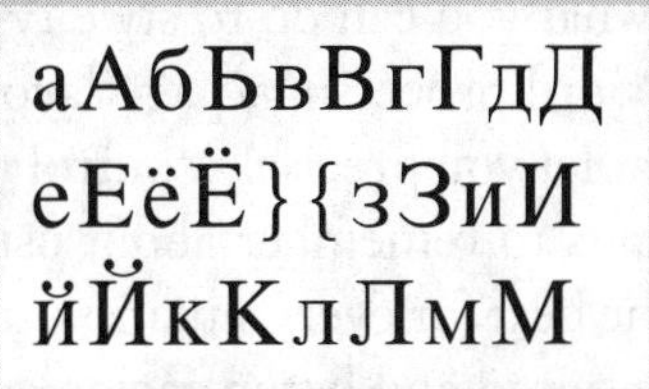

аАбБвВгГдД
еЕёË}{зЗиИ
йЙкКлЛмМ

Linguist's Software offers many language fonts, including Cyrillic (shown here), Arabic, Cambodian, Coptic, Georgian, Greek, Gujarati, Hebrew, Hindi, Inuit, Korean, Laotian, Persian, Punjabi, Thai, Tibetan, and Vietnamese. (Prices range from $80 to $200 per font.)

Stone Phonetic (Adobe Systems)

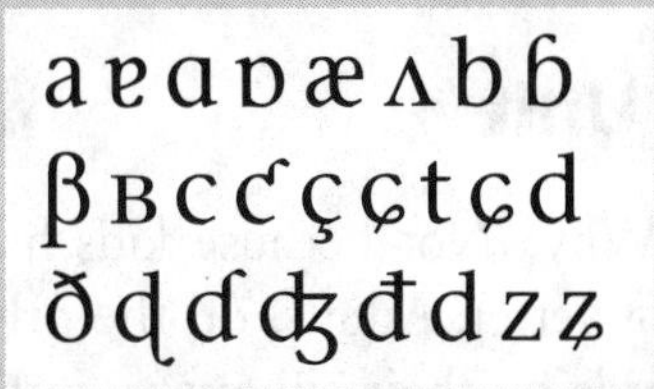

aɐɑɒæʌbɓ
βʙcɕçɕtɕɗ
ðdɖʤɖdzʑ

Adobe's Stone Phonetic ($95) provides the symbols and diacritical marks for the International Phonetic Alphabet (IPA), which represents the sounds of a wide number of languages (or 'I{~gwKDes, phonetically speaking). The font comes in a serif and a sans-serif version.

DruScott and Custom Handwriting Fonts (Lazy Dog Foundry)

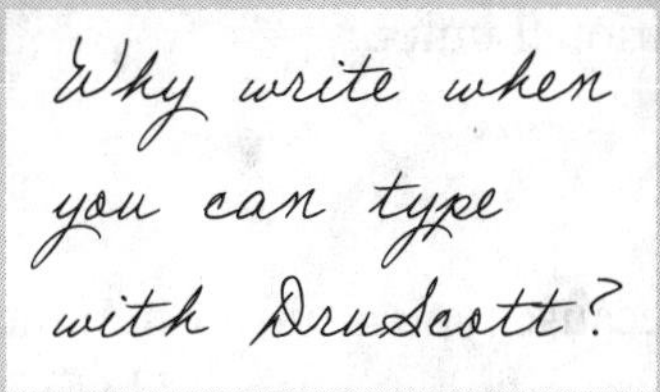

Why write when you can type with DruScott?

Remember the days when letters were written by hand? You can revive that quaint custom without abandoning your trusty word processor—just order a custom font made from your own handwriting from Lazy Dog. Depending on how many characters you want (you can probably live without most of the characters invoked by Option or Shift Option), the font will run you between $200 and $500. (Signature Software will also make a custom font from your handwriting, for $110 per font.)

If your handwriting isn't worth immortalizing, you might consider buying one of Lazy Dog's prefab handwriting fonts ($90 each). The DruScott font is shown here.

TF Crossword (Treacyfaces)

CROSSWORD PUZZLE
TREACYFACES

Create your own crossword puzzle (with or without the solution) with this clever font.

Typesetting

(AJ/DD)

Working from the Style menu is just the beginning of what you can do to style type. Macintosh software that's designed to work with type (word processing, page layout, and graphics programs) usually offers lots of features that let you precisely control the look of type on the page. There are two important things to remember about using these controls: 1) the default settings aren't necessarily the best for every situation, and 2) to badly apply these programs' controls over tracking, word and letterspacing, and leading can be worse than not adjusting them at all. To get you off on the right foot, here's a crash course in the principles behind good typesetting.

Shape Recognition: The Ideational Unit

Children's books are often set in large sizes of type. Why? Not because kids have poor eyesight. It's because children read words letter by letter. Adults, on the other hand, read whole words at a time, recognizing the words by their silhouette rather than by examining each letter. These letter clusters (called *ideational units*) have to fit together well in order to be easily legible. The best-quality fonts are designed with the proper letter fit to create smooth, easy-to-read ideational units.

Point Size

(RT)

The size of type is commonly referred to as *point size*, because type is most often measured by points ($\frac{1}{72}$ of an inch). Standard point sizes for reading are usually between 9- and 12-point. Headings are commonly 18- or 24-point. Oddly enough, even when type is several inches tall, it is still measured by points, not by inches or even feet.

Leading

(AJ/DD)

The space between lines of type—called *leading* (pronounced "ledding") by typesetters and in page layout programs, and called *line spacing* in some word processors—is often automatically set at 120 percent of the type size. (For 10-point type, for instance, the leading would be set at 12 points.) Although this setting may work fairly well in a lot of cases, it's often worth experimenting with to determine what looks best for the typeface and line length you're using. Typefaces with small x-heights (and longer ascenders and descenders) generally need less leading than do faces with comparatively large x-heights, and pages with short lines of text need less leading than do pages with long lines. (The white space between lines serves as a highway for your eyes to follow when moving from the right-hand margin back to the left.)

Type Size versus Real Size (RT)

It's one thing to have type measured by points instead of good old-fashioned inches, but it's another thing completely for those measurements to always be wrong. Let's say you made a 100-point capital "T" in Microsoft Word. When you'd print it out and measure it, the "T" would only be about 70 points tall!

This unusual behavior is the result of measuring type not from the baseline to the tops of letters, but instead from the *descenders* (such as the bottoms of lowercase g's and y's) to the *ascenders* (a fancy name for the tops of capital letters and lowercase letters like b's and h's). So, even though our "T" doesn't have any descenders, it is still being measured from where a descender would've been if it had one.

You can usually estimate the true height of a capital letter to be between 60 to 75 percent of the type point size.

Alignment (RT/AJ/DD)

People often consider a justified right margin (making all the lines exactly the same length, as in this book) the hallmark of professionally typeset text, probably because this feature was all but impossible to achieve with a typewriter. The truth is, though, that when you ask your Mac to justify your type it has no choice but to mess with the spaces between the letters or between the words in each line, making for inconsistent spacing that can make reading a chore. Many word processing and page layout programs allow you to control the maximum and minimum amounts you'll allow the program to stretch or compress the spaces, but the best amount is none at all. Remember, then, that if you must justify the right margin, you'll need to spend some time adjusting line breaks—and even rewriting sentences if necessary—to get your lines to set smoothly, with consistent-looking spacing.

Many times, you'll have several alignment options, such as Justified (this book), Flush Left (also referred to by old-school typesetters as "ragged right," but this term is frowned upon by the professionals of today), Flush Right (right side is even, left is "ragged"), and Centered (even space on both ends of the line. Typically, the best choice is Flush Left (Cmd Shift L in several applications).

Force Justifying (RT)

Force justifying is similar to justified type, except that instead of making both ends even by adding or subtracting a little bit of space, it adds a substantial amount of space, making a line of any length stretch out far enough to reach the end of the text area. This is often used for design purposes, and can often be very difficult to read.

Kerning and Tracking   (RT/AJ/DD)

Kerning is the act of adjusting the spacing between individual letters. This makes up for the fact that the letterspacing built into the font just can't work with every possible letter pair. Some fonts have built-in tables of *kerning pairs*—pairs of letters that require special letterspacing adjustments—but the software you use must also be sophisticated enough to put those adjustments into effect (most page layout programs are). In addition, most page layout and graphics programs offer features that let you manually kern pairs of letters individually.

Manual kerning must be done carefully: It's possible to kern too much as well as too little. And once you start kerning, it's hard to stop, because changing the fit of one pair of letters changes the relative relationships of everything else on the line. The best rule is to kern only when the line appears unsightly, when there are eye-catching gaps between letters, or when pairs of letters appear pinched together. It's also important to proof your hand-kerning work on a high-resolution printout; it's hard to judge kerning on screen.

HOT TIP

Tracking is also a form of adding or reducing the amount of space between characters, but tracking works on several characters at a time, affecting equally the space between all pairs it encounters. If your text needs both tracking and kerning, it is wise to do the tracking first, and then do the touch-up with kerning.

Horizontal Condensing/Expanding   (RT)

Type can be mathematically condensed or expanded in several applications. This method actually takes the characters and spaces and reduces or enlarges the width of both. Slight modifications such as these are often done for copyfitting purposes. Unfortunately, this mathematical process changes the width not only of the characters, but of the widths of the lines and shapes used to create those characters. This can result in awkward-looking letterforms with uneven strokes.

Small Caps   (RT)

When an application creates small caps as a style, it also mathematically scales the characters to make larger letters appear shorter (and in some cases, wider). Because you now have a reduced capital letter as the small caps character, the line weights that form the smaller caps are thinner than the line weights of the larger caps, resulting in the small caps looking "light" or "thin" in comparison to the rest of the text.

The best thing to do if you need small caps is to use a font that has a small caps variation (the Adobe Expert series of fonts has real small caps).

Creating Special Typographic Effects

There are lots of ways to get type to do crazy things. The PostScript outline format uses the same Bézier curves that create PostScript graphics in a program such as Adobe Illustrator. You can import your type into such graphics programs and stretch it, bind it to a path, or otherwise distort it. Programs specifically designed to manipulate type do a whole lot more (and more easily, too), as the following programs demonstrate.

LetraStudio (EF)

Letraset's **LetraStudio** ($250) lets you place TrueType or PostScript text into "envelopes" of various shapes. You can reshape an envelope to get the effect you want on a particular selection of text and save the modified envelope for later use.

You can also embellish text with color graphics or artwork imported from Illustrator or FreeHand, and LetraStudio's effects can be applied to these graphics as well. LetraStudio provides a limited set of drawing tools (including a line, a circle, and a rectangle); for more complex work, you can paste your text effect into a graphics program and work on it there.

Illustrator or FreeHand (RT)

If you have a PostScript drawing program such as Adobe Illustrator or Macromedia FreeHand, you can create all sorts of special typographical effects from ordinary PostScript or TrueType fonts.

Most of these special effects are due to the little feature in each program that allows you to change type from an editable line of text into editable PostScript outlines. These outlines can be manipulated in various ways to achieve all sorts of unusual and fantastic effects.

So, what types of things can you do to type converted into outlines? Actually, you can do anything you could do to any other artwork in either program. For instance, you can use FreeHand's Paste Inside command or Illustrator's Mask feature to place a full color TIFF image within a series of characters. Or maybe you want to give your type a rough look; use Illustrator's Roughen filter, or a third-party filter like Doodle Jr. to make jagged or rounded, bumpy text. (Illustrator and FreeHand are discussed in depth in Chapter 15.)

StrataType 3d (EF)

StrataType 3d 2.5 ($100, Strata) transforms PostScript or TrueType text into 3-D shapes, letting you then add textures (marble, wood, chrome, or ones you create yourself from scanned PICT images), adjust the size and shape of beveled edges, position text (on an arc or in a circle, for example), rotate letters, set a vanishing point, add a background, and position a light source. Then you sit back while the program renders the image.

You can save the image as a PICT, TIFF, or EPS file and transfer it to a graphics application or page layout program.

KPT Vector Effects (TA)

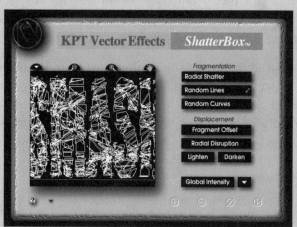

If you are manipulating type in Illustrator or FreeHand, don't stop with their built-in features. KPT Vector Effects ($199, MetaTools) has several effects filters for use in Illustrator and FreeHand that produce amazing effects such as 3D Extrusion, Shadows, and Neon. There's even a filter called KPT ShatterBox (Illustrator only) that smashes your text outlines into millions of pieces.

KPT Vector Effects' KPT ShatterBox gives your text that "glass type dropped from a 13-story building" look that so many designers crave.

Other Type Manipulation Software (TA)

There are several other packages available that do various manipulations to type. In olden times (the '80s), **TypeStyler** ($220, Brøderbund) was a favorite, but its frustrating interface and the lack of any significant upgrade for almost five years have turned it into a Macintosh has-been. **Effects Specialist** ($200, Postcraft International) is a set of several premade effects, each of them with wacky fun names such as Crash, Shaky, and Vibrate. **Typestry 2.1** ($300, formerly sold by Pixar) takes fonts and performs wonderful 3-D imagery on them. As we go to press, Pixar is shopping Typestry around for a buyer, so it may become available from another software vendor in the near future.

Font Creation and Design

The programs we describe in this section let you customize your fonts in a variety of ways. Some let you translate fonts into new formats for use on PCs or in illustration programs. Others let you add characters to existing fonts, remap your keyboard, or add graphics to your fonts. Yet others let you redesign the fonts you already have or make your own fonts from scratch. (These are the same programs used by many professional type designers to create commercial fonts.)

Metamorphosis Professional (KT/EF)

Metamorphosis Professional (or Meta Pro, as it's familiarly called) from Altsys ($150) converts fonts to and from common Mac and PC formats. It will also open many older Type 3 fonts, enabling you to convert them to Type 1 fonts. Metamorphosis also has the useful ability to fetch outline data from certain PostScript printer ROMs and hard disks (for modifying fonts that aren't even in your Mac). It also lets you convert font outlines into PICT or EPS graphic outlines so you can treat characters as graphic elements in programs such as Canvas, FreeHand, or Illustrator.

FontMonger (EF)

FontMonger ($150, Ares Software) is a multitalented utility that lets you convert PostScript fonts to TrueType and vice versa. (Although you can use PostScript and TrueType fonts together, many people like to standardize on one format or the other.)

You can also use FontMonger to add characters to a font. Let's say you're setting a scientific paper in Palatino and find yourself frequently needing certain Greek letters from the Symbol font, for example. Instead of constantly switching between the two fonts, you can add the Symbol characters to Palatino and then type both the text and symbols from the hybrid font.

FontMonger can also alter characters in existing fonts to create fractions, small caps, superscripts, subscripts, and narrow, wide, or slanted characters. Of course, these alterations won't look as good as characters created by a living, breathing type designer, but if you don't happen to have a type designer hanging around, this is an excellent alternative.

FontChameleon (EF)

Ares Software's **FontChameleon** is a unique program that creates *synthetic fonts* from a master outline and instructions called *font descriptors* (215 fonts in FontChameleon, $300; 47 in the FontChameleon Starter Kit, $55). You can use this remarkable program to generate fonts that look very much like traditional serif and sans serif designs, or you can alter the font descriptors to create your own custom fonts, altering weight, width, height, or slant—or even (horror of horrors!) concocting a blend of two fonts.

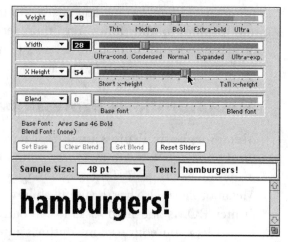

Although synthetic fonts can't match the quality of hand-crafted faces, they have some advantages. Because a single master outline can be used to create thousands of variations, the instructions that describe a particular font can be very small—only 5K or 6K. And because fonts can be generated from the master, you can send an electronic file to a colleague who has FontChameleon, without worrying whether that person has the same fonts you used.

Create synthetic fonts with FontChameleon.

Fontographer (SZA/KT)

Fontographer ($500, Macromedia) lets you create your own PostScript or TrueType fonts, letter by letter. If you don't want to start drawing from scratch, Fontographer offers many automatic creation tools (including autotracing of printed or hand-drawn artwork) or allows you to import an existing font and modify the character outlines individually or en masse.

With the current version (4.1), you can create *Multiple Master* fonts (fonts with several user-controlled variations, such as thickness and width), interpolate between weights or other features of two separate fonts, automatically clean up extra Bézier control points (often the result of autotracing), and accept input from pressure-sensitive graphics tablets to create calligraphic fonts. It also offers excellent automated production tools for adjusting font metrics (which define the way the characters fit together), *hinting* (to make the type clear and readable on the screen and on low-resolution printers), and building extensive kerning tables.

FontStudio (KT)

Like Fontographer, Letraset's **FontStudio** ($500) lets you import and alter existing font outlines or draw new fonts from scratch (in either PostScript or TrueType format). It can also save characters as PostScript graphics for modification in Illustrator or FreeHand.

Although it's gone a long time without an update, FontStudio still works, and it has a few advantages over Fontographer. It allows you, for instance, to create anti-aliased grayscale screen fonts, which use pixels of varying brightness to give them fuzzy edges, paradoxically making them easier to read. FontStudio also helps make the mysteries of font hinting understandable through a slick visual interface.

Ikarus-M (KT)

Ikarus-M ($600, URW) is the new Mac version of a font-building program that was used by professional font designers long before the Mac made the scene. It's for people who are really serious about commercial font production and are willing to spend some time learning its rules.

In contrast to the Bézier curve editing used by Fontographer and FontStudio, Ikarus-M relies on a carefully drawn paper-based design with data points marked out in advance and entered by means of a digitizing tablet. Alternatively, you can use the autotracing companion tool (**Linus-M**) for handling automatic input of scanned images ($350, or Ikarus-M and Linus together for $900). Because one person can lay out the points, and another, less-skilled person can enter them into the computer, Ikarus is an excellent tool for big production environments.

Adobe Illustrator (TA)

Taking on the task of creating a font can be overwhelming. Throw learning all about font editing software on top of that, and you might opt to keep your font safely stored somewhere in the dark recesses of your head. Fortunately, if you know Adobe Illustrator already, font design can be quite enjoyable. Illustrator has the most powerful editing and design tools available, and its Pen tool is considered the smoothest and most accurate drawing tool on any platform. Use Illustrator to create the outlines of the font, then import them into your font editing software.

HOT TIP

Font Troubleshooting Tips (DD/KT)

HOT TIPS

Let's be honest: Fonts are bound to cause you some trouble. Constant loading, unloading, and reloading of resources from lots of different manufacturers into your precious system is bound to cause some funny business once in awhile. The problems are rarely insoluble, and are usually the result of getting one typeface when you want another. Careful font management is the answer to most of them.

The following is a summary of the font problems we've run across most often, along with advice on how to solve them. We'll start with the easy ones.

Where's My Font? (SZA/AN/JK)

Sometimes you know you have a font installed, but it doesn't appear in the Font menu. The first thing to do is not to be so sure of yourself—double-check to see that the font is really installed correctly (this is the most common source of the problem). Remember that in Mac systems prior to System 7, fonts you install don't appear in the Font menu until after you've restarted the computer.

If you're using Suitcase or MasterJuggler, fonts may not appear in the menu as expected because you opened the suitcase file the font is in *after* you launched the application you're using. If that's not the case, the problem may arise because you have different fonts with the same ID number in separate open suitcases. (See the sidebar "Whatever Happened to Font ID Conflicts?" in the next section.)

Bitmapped Font Printouts (DD)

Sometimes you get output that looks almost right, but the characters in certain typefaces look a little shaky—jagged around the edges, bearing an eerie resemblance to screen type. This problem typically happens when you're using PostScript fonts, and it usually means that your system had the proper screen fonts on hand, but it couldn't find the corresponding printer fonts. In that case, your Mac will often simply copy the bitmapped version of the type from your screen onto your printed page.

To solve the problem, just make sure the printer fonts are installed correctly before you try printing again. Remember that fonts from different manufacturers (or in different formats) may have identical names, so you can have a Bodoni screen font from one manufacturer and a Bodoni printer font from another manufacturer, and they may not work together.

Whatever Happened to Font ID Conflicts? (RT)

Weird, unexplained phenomena involving fonts used to happen on a regular basis involving Font ID conflicts. Suddenly, the conflicts stopped (even before Mulder and Sculley could investigate). Well, it used to be that there were only 256 font ID numbers. Each font on a Mac has to have its own Font ID number. Apple reserved only the first 128 ID numbers for system fonts, leaving 128 left over. There are estimated to be more than 20,000 different fonts available for the Macintosh. Do the math, and you'll figure out that only having 128 ID numbers is a problem. So quite often, fonts with the same ID number would crop up, causing all sorts of trouble.

In 1988, Apple replaced a critical resource (FONT) with another one (NFNT), which was capable of containing up to 16,000 different font IDs. Occasionally there are conflicts, but they're so rare that they hardly ever cause problems.

The Twilight Zone of Typefaces (RT/DD/KT)

Many fonts are published by more than one company; Brush Script, for example, is available from seven publishers. Not all font names are trademarked, however, so although fonts with the same name may look a lot alike, they're not always identical. When you print your documents on someone else's system (say at a service bureau), you've got to be sure your fonts not only have the same name but that they are also from the same manufacturer.

This is further complicated by the fact that fonts from a single *manufacturer* may be sold by different *vendors* under their own labels. Companies that cross-license each others' fonts may not be selling exactly the same font. When you're telling an output service what fonts you've used in the documents you're sending them, give them the name of the typeface, the name of the vendor, and the creation date, if available. (You can get this by selecting the printer font file in the Finder and choosing Get Info from the File menu.)

Printed pages sporting the wrong version of the right font can be hard to spot, unless you're an ace typographer. You may notice, though, that the line breaks of the new output may be different from those on a proof print you created on your own printer, or that the type looks more crowded or more loose than in your original version.

The only way to be really safe is to bring copies of your own fonts to the printing site...a process frowned upon by most font vendors' legal departments.

Corrupted Screen Fonts (RT)

Some of the most baffling Macintosh system problems are caused by renegade, corrupted screen fonts. Because screen fonts are loaded into the system, they're an integral part of the way your Macintosh operates. When a screen font becomes corrupted, you might start experiencing Type 1 errors, random freezes and crashes, and document corruption. All the standard fix-it tips, like rebuilding the desktop, reinstalling the system software, and running a disk fixer like Norton Utilities have no effect on these little data gremlins. Simply removing these fonts from the Fonts folder can suddenly fix the problem. Of course, finding the bad font isn't always so easy; it's often a process of elimination.

15 } Graphics

From its first programs, MacPaint and MacDraw, to today's photo-realistic 3-D images, the Mac has always dazzled us with its graphics prowess. You can see evidence of the Mac's digital artistry everywhere you look: magazine ads, product packaging, posters, audio CDs, technical schematics, book covers, even TV commercials and hit movies.

Although a computer graphics program won't automatically make you an artist, it *will* let you do things that are time-consuming, expensive, or even impossible with traditional tools. With the appropriate software, you can easily draw infinite variations of a design, test different color schemes for a business logo, make an eye-catching chart for a presentation, adjust the sharpness and contrast in a scanned photograph, or create a 3-D mock-up of your latest invention.

Whether you're a first-time artist, business presenter, or professional designer, there's a graphics package to meet your needs. In this chapter, we'll show you the different kinds of graphics you can create on the Mac, help you pick the right applications, and reveal some tricks for getting the most out of your favorite programs.

Contributors

Ted Alspach (TA) is the chapter editor.

Rob Teeple (RT) is president of Teeple Graphics, an AppleVAR and World Wide Web services company.

Steven Frank (SF) is a Southern California-based writer and consultant specializing in Macintosh graphics and entertainment software.

Aileen Abernathy (AA) and **Ben Long (BL)** contributed to past editions of *The Macintosh Bible,* from which parts of this chapter were taken.

Contents

~~~~~~

Graphics on the Macintosh (TA)

Graphics created on the Macintosh can be broken down into three categories:

- *Pixel-based graphics* are images created by a grid of differently colored *pixels*. Pixels are never added or deleted from these images, but their colors are changed. These graphics are often referred to as *raster* images. Common pixel-based graphics include scans and photographs.

- *Vector-based graphics* are images that consist of outlines that form shapes. It takes less memory to define a shape using outlines than pixels. Vectors allow images to be printed at any resolution. Common vector-based graphics include logos and type.

- *3-D graphics* are graphics that exist in 3-D space. Because very few methods exist for viewing 3-D graphics, they are usually converted to either pixel-based or vector-based graphics for viewing or printing. With 3-D graphics software you can create architectural drawings and scale models. Many 3-D programs offer animation capabilities.

While these are the basic categories, most programs overlap into two or even three of these areas, but are primarily focused on one specific category. For instance, Adobe Photoshop is a pixel-based graphics program, but its Clipping Path feature is decidedly vector-based. Extreme 3-D is a 3-D program, but it can import vector graphics and can export finished images as pixel-based artwork.

Pixels (SF)

The word *pixel* (from the original *picture element*) refers to a single dot on a computer monitor (or, to be technically correct, the "smallest image-forming element of a video display"). A hundred pixels, placed end to end, create a line. A thousand pixels, all lumped together, create a filled circle, square, and so on. Each pixel is a separate element, but when viewed together, they form shapes that we recognize. When you were younger, you may have pressed your face against a television screen and noticed that the images you were seeing were really just a bunch of multicolored dots. These "multicolored dots" are pixels. (If you never did this as a kid, go ahead and try it now.)

A great way to picture exactly how pixel-based images are formed is to take a sheet of graph paper and start coloring in squares to form a picture of something. Up close, it looks very blocky, but if you hold it further away, the jagged edges become less clearly defined, giving your image a smoother overall appearance. This process of coloring in

The Need for Speed (TA/AA/BL)

If you plan to work with 24-bit images, 3-D graphics, or animation, you'll need a fast Mac, lots of RAM, a spacious hard disk, and a 24-bit display. If time is money, you might also want to boost your Mac's performance with a graphics accelerator board, particularly if you use Photoshop. There are two basic types of graphics accelerators: QuickDraw boards (also called *accelerated video cards*), which speed up screen redraws, and DSP (digital signal processor) cards, which ramp up certain processor-intensive operations.

QuickDraw Acceleration

A QuickDraw accelerator speeds up display tasks such as scrolling and zooming—particularly important if you're working in 24-bit color and/or on a large monitor. (The acceleration isn't limited to graphics—you'll also be able to scroll through a spreadsheet or word processing document much faster.) Prices vary, depending on the Mac model, monitor size, screen resolution (pixels per inch), and accelerator features. If your monitor is 16 inches or smaller, Radius' **PrecisionColor Pro 24XP** ($600) is a good buy. If cost isn't a factor, however, and you want super-fast screen redraws and goodies such as high-resolution CMYK acceleration, then an on-board DSP chip, SuperMac's **Thunder II GX•1360** ($3,300) is the way to go.

DSP Acceleration

The most time-consuming part of graphics work isn't screen redraw, however, it's the number-crunching routines used in special-effects filters, image resizing and rotation, JPEG decompression, and color-mode changes. Happily, DSP accelerators are tailor-made for those operations. Painter and Photoshop can use the DSP chips in AV Macs to boost performance, but don't despair if an AV Mac isn't in your future. DayStar Digital, Radius, and SuperMac offer DSP accelerators that make specific operations five to ten times faster on other Macs. SuperMac's **ThunderStorm for Adobe Photoshop** ($500) is arguably the best (and most economical) choice. At this writing, DSP accelerators are available only for Photoshop, although the optimized filters bundled with the cards will work in most programs that accept Photoshop plug-ins (see "Photoshop-Compatible Plug-Ins," later in this chapter). Some 3-D packages also can use specialized accelerator boards to rev up the rendering process; see "3-D Graphics and Animation," later in this chapter. (See Chapter 2 for more on graphics accelerators and DSP cards.)

Power Macs

For the ultimate speed boost, however, get a high-end Power Mac. A graphics application running in native mode on a Power Mac performs two to six times faster, on average, than it does on an '040 Mac such as the Quadra 800. And that's overall, not just for specific operations. Accordingly, all the serious software manufacturers have software that is Power Mac native. The increased computing power has allowed companies to add features to Power Mac programs that were not practical before.

POWER MAC

A typical pixel-based image (left) and a close-up of the framed area (right). Note the obvious squareness of the pixels.

squares (using various shades of red, green, and blue) is sort of how images are formed on your computer monitor. Images which are based on pixels are referred to as *bitmapped* images, because they can be defined as a "map" of individual "bits" of information (the pixels). The process of creating an image from this type of information is known as *rasterizing*—bitmapped (pixel-based) images are sometimes called *raster images* or *raster graphics*. The biggest disadvantage of pixel-based graphics is that the

Pixels versus Vectors   (RT)

As a user of both pixel and vector software for many years, I've developed a healthy respect for both formats, and I'm comfortable with the advantages and drawbacks of each. However, there are some radical graphic extremists out there declaring that their format is better, and that the other should be used only when absolutely necessary. To set the record straight, I've included the arguments from the two chief movements in the graphics arena:

Why Pixels are Better than Vectors (according to The Organization of Squareheads): "Pixels are the building blocks of images; each pixel can be individually colored or colored as a group. No pixels are ever added or subtracted from an image unless its size needs to be enlarged or reduced. There are no vector scanners. The ironic thing is, vectors by themselves are nothing. It's not until those vectors are filled in with pixels that an image exists at all! Have you ever seen a photograph made of vectors?"

Vectors: In Line With the Future as outlined by *Followers of the Path*: "Vectors are fast becoming the new graphics standard. While pixels have been around for years, vectors are finally getting the attention they deserve. Vectors are more compact than pixels; a 3-inch diameter circle created with vectors takes up less than 1K of memory. That same circle created with pixels takes more than 2MB at a reasonable resolution. Pixels are square, so they have to resort to trickery like anti-aliasing to achieve anything resembling a diagonal line, let alone a curve. When technology catches up to vectors, both scanners and photographic images will be created with vectors, not pixels. Talented artists, such as those at Thomas-Bradley Design, easily create photorealistic images with vectors. And, don't forget that vectors are infinitely scaleable, never losing any quality regardless of their size."

final quality of the image is determined by the quality (or *resolution*) at which it was drawn. Images drawn using a *72-ppi* (pixels per inch) grid will be printed at 72 dpi, even on a laser printer with 300-dpi resolution.

Although ppi is the proper technical term for the number of pixels across an inch on your screen, many people use dpi (dots per inch, usually referring to dots on a printed image) and ppi interchangebly. Throughout this book, we've standardized on the correct, technical terminology of ppi for on-screen images, and dpi for printed images.

Vectors (SF)

The word *vector* (from the Latin *vecte*, "mathematically defined," and *ores*, "computer-generated graphic") is used primarily when referring to a type of graphical object that can be described using precise measurements and complex mathematical formulas. These vector-based objects are composed of (you guessed it) vectors, which define the object's overall shape. In the world of computer graphics, vectors are at the opposite end of the spectrum from pixels. Whereas a pixel-based graphic can be described as a map of dots on a grid, the same graphic, if vector-based, would be described as a series of mathematical formulas, describing the starting coordinates of a line, its thickness and angle, how long it is, whether it curves anywhere along its length (and if so, how

much), and so on. And that's for just one line. Your average vector-based drawing might consist of dozens or even hundreds of such lines. While all of this may seem very complicated, rest assured that *you* don't have to keep track of any of it. (That's why you're drawing on a computer in the first place.)

The two biggest advantages of vector-based graphics are that mathematically described objects can be easily manipulated (to double the thickness of a line, all the computer has to do is multiply its current width by two), and that they are resolution-independent, meaning that they will display or print at the best quality that your monitor or

Images showing the basic outline framework that makes up a vector image (left) and the final, printed vector image (right).

Color, Color Everywhere (AA)

In choosing a graphics program, color depth is no longer a major factor. The era of 8-bit color—which limited graphics to 256 colors and prevented us from creating photorealistic images—is (almost) gone. Today even entry-level programs offer 24-bit color, allowing us to work with millions of colors and produce images ranging from photographs to drawings with smooth blends. Sometimes 24-bit color is called 32-bit color, which is actually more accurate. Those extra eight bits per pixel don't give you more colors; they're reserved for special operations such as masking or transparency effects.

Color management—the consistent matching of color from scanner to screen to printer—remains a persistent problem, however. Many companies, from Apple to Kodak, offer color-management strategies, but if you use Photoshop or QuarkXPress, one of the best (and cheapest) solutions is **EfiColor Works** ($200, Electronics for Imaging). This system-level software has direct hooks into the two programs, allowing you to achieve accurate image colors across a wide range of scanners, monitors, and output devices.

Still working with shades of gray? No worries. Graphics programs work just as well with black-and-white or grayscale images, and your color artwork will print fine in grayscale.

POWERBOOK

printer is capable of (because all of the image information is sent to the output device, which then displays or prints the image at the highest possible resolution).

Pixel-Based Graphics (RT)

Pixels, at first glance, seem to be the obvious way to go about creating images. Their main advantage is that any set of pixels can be any color at all, and there are so many pixels, even in a tiny document, that there are infinite variations. In large images, there may be millions of pixels, each with slightly different colors. This makes pixels perfectly suitable for photographs.

An Overview of Pixels (RT)

Pixel-based images exist on a grid of pixels. For instance, a 3-by-5-inch image created at 72 ppi has 77,760 pixels. You can figure out the number of pixels in any pixel image by multiplying the width in inches (3) times the ppi (72), multiplying the height (5) times the ppi (72), and then multiplying those two totals together ($216 \times 360 = 77,760$).

These high numbers of pixels can result in obscenely large files, so working with big pixel-based images can be an exercise in mail-ordering SIMMs (see Chapter 4 for more on memory). These images can also take up a good deal of your hard drive space; the following section discusses various formats that have been developed to reduce the size of saved image files.

Pixelized File Formats (RT)

There are several different file formats that pixel-based applications can use when saving files. Each application has its own set, though you'll find the high-end software (Photoshop, xRes) packages can read and write the most formats. The following formats are the most common ones you'll find in Open, Save, Import, and Export dialog boxes.

MacPaint. The first graphics program for the Macintosh, MacPaint had a format that most other applications could read (many still can). Unfortunately, there were two limitations in the original format: Pixels could be black or white only (not even shades of gray), and resolution and size were limited to 72 ppi and just a few inches wide and high. For the most part, this antiquated format has been laid to rest, a casualty of Photoshop and color scanners.

PICT. The PICT (short for picture) file format is the Mac's long-standing "classic" format. It actually comes in several flavors, often causing mass confusion. Two of the PICT variations (PICT and PICT2) are pixel-based, while the other PICT format is vector-based. PICTs are closely integrated into the workings of a Macintosh. Most of the graphics in applications are PICT-based, and when you take a screenshot (⌘ Shift 3) the resulting file is saved in PICT format. While PICTs are great for on-screen purposes, especially within programs, their bulky format and troublesome printing problems have lessened their use over the past few years.

TIFF. This familiar format (especially to desktop publishers) was developed by Aldus before Aldus was swallowed whole by Adobe. The acronym stands for *Tagged Image File Format*. TIFFs are common for printing, as the typical alternative to PICT. Don't spell it out, just say "tiff."

EPS. *Encapsulated PostScript* format is yet another format with a pixel-based version and a vector-based version. Technically, PostScript is a programming language for your printer. Encapsulated PostScript is this code mashed (usually) with a low-resolution preview (usually 72 ppi) into a file. EPS is a great choice when printing to a PostScript printer, especially when various transformations have to be done to the graphic (scaling, rotating, and so on). Oddly enough, unlike most of the other file formats, you don't say EPS as "eps" (like "steps") but instead you should say each letter separately: "E, P, S."

JPEG. The JPEG format is PICT's smarter, smaller brother. Several years ago, a bunch of pixelheads got together with the sole intention of creating a new graphics file format that would have built-in compression. These pixelheads were the Joint Photographic Experts Group, thus the name. JPEG is a true photographic standard, as it supports more than 32 million colors, with various levels of compression. The levels of compression are relative to the resulting quality of the images. Pronounce JPEG, "jay-peg."

GIF. Originally developed to be the standard compressed format for sending images via modem, the original GIF format was limited to 256 colors, and so-so compression. Some people say "jif" while others say "gif." It's on its way out, to be shortly replaced by GIF89.

HOT TIP

GIF89. This format, although still limited to 256 colors, is the new standard for on-line imaging, thanks to two significant improvements. First, alpha channels can be incorporated into the image to mask out certain portions. Second, GIF89 files load very quickly in super-low resolution, and are then refined continuously until the correct, high-resolution image is showing.

The progression of GIF89 as it is first read, becoming more refined as more detail of the image is loaded.

There are other pixel-based file formats in addition to the ones listed here, but either they're relatively unused, or they're PC-based. Also, keep in mind that several applications save images in their own proprietary format by default, which usually can't be read by other software packages.

Scanning Images   (RT)

One of the easiest ways to get images from the real world into your Macintosh is to scan them. Desktop *flatbed* scanners are fairly inexpensive; for less than $1,000 you can get a decent 600-ppi color, single-pass scanner. If you've got the cash, there are more and more inexpensive desktop *drum* scanners available for less than $20,000. The difference between flatbed and drum scanners? Only quality. It is actually easier to use a flatbed scanner than a drum scanner; to properly use a drum scanner requires training from an expert. But the difference is readily apparent when you compare scans from each device.

If you need super-high quality but can't lay out $20,000, many prepress and color houses offer Scitex or Crossfeld scanning services. The quality from these large drum scanners is better than the desktop variety as well, mainly due to better optics in the scanner, and more highly trained/skilled scanner operators.

Painting and Image Editing (RT)

Pixel-based graphics applications fall into two categories: painting and image editing. Painting applications usually have several "natural media" options (options which simulate traditional art tools such as paintbrushes, watercolors, and textured paper) and are designed for creating images from scratch (or a scanned template). Image editing applications are first and foremost designed to manipulate existing artwork, with the primary emphasis on photo retouching. The following sections discuss painting applications and tools; the later sections focus on programs for image editing.

Painting With Layers (BL/AA)

The latest advance in painting programs is the concept of *object-oriented* editing—the ability to manipulate bitmapped images as if they were objects in a drawing program. Instead of editing on a single digital canvas, you turn pieces of a painting into layers (à la Illustrator or Canvas), allowing you to select and manipulate them at will.

Say, for example, you import a scanned photo of a cat into a picture of a cozy cottage. Instead of the cat becoming a permanent part of the underlying painting as soon as you deselect it, you make it a discrete layer. Now you can reselect it at any time, perhaps to resize it and add a shadow. Then, by shuffling the image layers, you can place the crouching cat behind some flowerpots. All this, in a *painting* program.

Specular International created **Collage** ($350) specifically to composite photos and other images into seamless collages. Although it lacks painting and image-editing tools, Collage offers excellent masking features and object-oriented handling of imported graphics. And because you work with a 72-dpi screen proxy for each image, Collage is faster than working with large, high-resolution files. Painter 4, PixelPaint Pro3, and Photoshop 3 (covered later in this chapter) also offer object-oriented editing.

Fractal Design Painter (RT)

Painter 4 ($400, Fractal Design) is the king of the painting programs, possibly because the program ships in (of all things) a one-gallon paint can. When Painter first appeared on the scene several years ago, Macintosh users knew that this wasn't the latest in a long line of painting programs, but instead, a new way of life.

Before Painter, paint programs usually had a fairly standard arsenal of "painting tools" (see the "Painting Tools" section). But Painter upped the ante by providing artists with their dream arsenal of tools, from charcoal to crayons to a watery brush. That was impressive and useful, but Fractal Design had stuffed quite a bit more under the hood. Dozens of paper textures could be applied both to a blank canvas or to existing images.

An innovative autotracing method was developed, enabling existing images to suddenly look like they were watercolored, oil painted, or created by one of the masters, such as Georges Seurat (the guy who did those dotty paintings in a style called pointillism).

Painter has grown and matured, containing enough features to keep you busy exploring and painting for weeks. Its main drawback is what's come to be known as "palette clutter," a disease that seems to have stricken several graphics programs over the last few years (FreeHand is the most obvious offender). Keep in mind that while Painter has a feature set that rivals most other pixel-based applications, it still isn't an image editor.

Painting Tools (TA/BL/AA)

Painting and image-editing applications do have many features in common—such as selection marquees, erasers, and paint buckets—but each has specialized tools to call its own. The following tools are those most commonly found in painting applications:

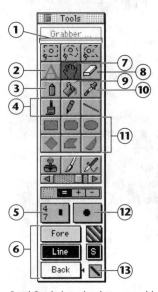

1. Selection tools, for selecting parts of an image

2. Text tool, for adding bit-mapped text

3. Spray can, for creating airbrush effects

4. Brush, pencil, and line tools, for freehand painting

5. Line-width control, with separate indicators for horizontal and vertical width

6. Color and pattern pop-up palettes, for specifying colors and patterns for the foreground, background, and lines

7. Grabber hand, for navigating around an image

8. Eraser, for erasing parts of an image

9. Paint bucket, for filling a selected area with a color or pattern

10. Eyedropper, for picking up a specific color from an image

11. Graphic primitives, for creating rectangles, circles, polygons, and curves

12. Brush-shape selector, for specifying the size and shape of brushes

13. Anti-aliasing control, for smoothing lines created with other tools

BrushStroke's tool palette resembles that of most paint programs.

In addition to the painting tools shown in the tool palette, look for the following features, many of which are also found in image-editing programs:

- *Image distortions*, such as resize, rotate, flip, and skew.

- *Fill patterns*, which you can customize or apply as-is to any area of an image.

- *Custom color palettes*, for saving special colors you want to use for particular jobs.

- *Multiple levels of undo*, so you can backtrack to earlier stages of an image—otherwise a difficult maneuver in paint programs.

- *Natural-media tools* that emulate oils, watercolor, chalk, paper textures, and other traditional media, and let you adjust parameters such as brush size, opacity, and number of brush hairs. Many programs support pressure-sensitive digitizing tablets, which provide for even more realistic painting.

- *Anti-aliasing tools* for combating *jaggies*, the stair-stepped look you get when you draw a diagonal or curved line in a bitmapped image. *Anti-aliasing* is a process that blends the colors of adjacent pixels to minimize these rough edges. When you paint with an anti-aliased brush, for example, the edges of your strokes are automatically blurred to produce smooth lines. Some programs also let you anti-alias (or *feather*) the edges of a selection so you can paste one image into another without unnatural-looking sharp edges.

  If your program doesn't have anti-aliasing tools, you can smooth away the jaggies after the fact with Ray Dream's **JAG II** ($130) utility.

HOT TIP

- *Variable resolution*, so you can print artwork with a resolution higher than the on-screen 72 dpi. Many programs can save bitmapped images at any resolution, ensuring sharp, crisp output even when you send files to a high-resolution printer or imagesetter.

Other Paint Programs (TA/AA/BL)

Besides Painter, several other painting packages are available, ranging from simple programs for general users to artistically inclined applications that let you imitate real-world oils, watercolors, and papers. There are even one-stop programs that provide both drawing and painting tools.

Thanks to the popularity of home-based color Macs, the low-end paint market is booming, with at least half a dozen programs in the under-$100 range. All offer the basic complement of painting tools and features—plus a few extra goodies—and work well in black and white and low-memory situations, making them good choices for PowerBook and monochrome Mac users.

POWERBOOK

Expert Color Paint ($50, Expert Software) combines simplicity with a well-rounded tool set, including a magic wand, brightness/contrast controls, anti-aliasing, and simple special effects (Blur, Sharpen, Invert). You can define custom tool sets and color palettes, and it offers multiple undos—a feature conspicuously missing in Photoshop. Another longtime favorite is Zedcor's **DeskPaint,** always bundled with its companion product, DeskDraw (see "Draw Software" later in this chapter). For a mere $30 (if you order directly from Zedcor), you get features similar to those in Expert Color Paint, albeit with a less elegant interface. DeskPaint has some nice special effects (such as Oil Painting and Mosaic), simple masks, and *autotracing*, which lets you convert a bitmapped graphic into an object-oriented one. Version 4 was a major overhaul that added capabilities such as image cataloging and support for QuickDraw GX, scanners, and Photoshop-compatible plug-ins.

If you'd like to mix fun with practicality, get **Prism** ($60, Delta Tao), the successor to the whimsically named, critically acclaimed Color MacCheese. It invites playful exploration with a water drop (for blurring), paint roller (for gradients), rake (for scattering pixels—say, to make a tree look more realistically leafy), and snowflake and tree tools (for instant doilies or fractal forests). Best of all, though, is the transmogrifier, which sprays color change, adding texture to solid colors. On the downside, Prism can't handle TIFF files.

If you're new to computers and digital painting—or just want an elegant, full-featured program at an entry-level price—Claris' **BrushStrokes** is a good bet. Trampling all over the memory of MacPaint (Claris' previous budget paint program), BrushStrokes has an astonishing array of features for $140, including gradients, some clever selection tools, and simple masking. Its attractive, easy-to-navigate interface is supplemented by an impressive on-line help system (the manuals are good, too). Handy feedback features take the guesswork out of painting: Preview windows let you see the results of filters before you apply them; the Tools palette shows current color and line settings; and when you use a brush, the cursor changes to reflect the color and brush shape you've selected.

GOOD FEATURE

In addition, when you save custom tool settings, they appear as thumbnail icons in a special palette for one-click retrieval—a novel approach.

If you want natural-media and image-editing tools in a single package, consider **PixelPaint Pro3** ($380, Pixel Resources). Besides supplying many (but not all) of the capabilities of those two genres—from an Impressionist brush and paper textures to contrast and brightness controls—PixelPaint has a few tricks of its own. It's the only painting program besides Painter 4, with built-in floating layers for object-oriented editing (for more on this capability, see the sidebar "Painting With Layers," earlier in this chapter) and support for Apple events scripting, allowing you to automate tasks such as applying filters or color corrections.

PixelPaint also has an unusual half-drawing/half-painting mode called Wet Paint that provides an easy way to paint specific shapes. As in a drawing program, you can create lines, curves, and shapes by clicking and dragging out objects. Once you've shaped an object, PixelPaint strokes it with the selected paint tool. If the resulting brush stroke doesn't look quite right, you can reshape the path and stroke it again. On the downside, PixelPaint can't handle 8-bit images, multiple undos, CMYK editing, or EPS images.

Artists in Training (AA)

Perhaps you don't just want to use a paint program, you actually want to learn to paint (or draw). A digital tutor does have advantages over traditional media: Making and matching colors is easier, you don't have to wait for oils to dry, there's nothing to spill, and you can delete mistakes without ruining the rest of your masterpiece.

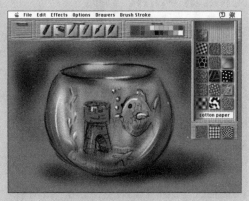

If this appeals to you (or to a young acquaintance), check out Fractal Design's **Dabbler 2** ($100) or Delta Tao's

Dabbler 2's tools are organized into drawers. Clicking a drawer shows its contents.

Apprentice ($60). The programs have several similarities, including natural-media tools (pencil, chalk, oils), the ability to create original artwork or draw over reference pictures (such as photos), and the option to play back your drawing sessions stroke by stroke.

Dabbler's simple interface may seem a bit precious to adults, but it's the more polished program, with a greater variety of painting tools as well as paper textures (both borrowed from big brother Painter). Precreated brush variants let you mimic artists such as Seurat and Monet, and it supplies animated drawing lessons and a how-to-draw manual from Walter Foster Publishing, a leading purveyor of art instruction books.

Basic Painting (RT)

Most often, Painting software starts you off with a dreaded white, blank canvas. With all those little white pixels staring at you, you might panic, but don't. Instead, start by selecting the Paintbrush tool and clicking and dragging around the screen. Most paint programs have at least one level of undo, and some (such as Painter) have several, so if you make a mistake, just press ⌘Z.

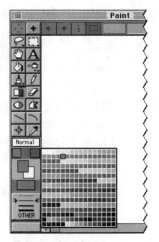

To change the current color, click on that color and hold. A pop-up palette should appear, which you can drag your cursor onto. Stop on the color you want to use, and now all your painting will be done in the new color.

Changing the color is as easy as clicking and releasing over the desired color.

Remember when you're painting that you're never adding any new pixels, you're just changing the color of the pixels that are already there. For instance, a blank image is actually stuffed to the gills with white pixels. Understanding this concept should make your painting more logical and productive.

General Paint Tips

These tips should work in most paint and image-editing programs and in the painting components of programs such as SuperPaint, Canvas, HyperCard, and ClarisWorks. Some will even work in draw programs. But remember: Life has no guarantees.

Tool palette shortcuts (AN/SZA/AA). Double-clicking on icons in the tool palette produces some handy shortcuts. For examples, see the chart at right.

Preselect your tools (AA). Be sure to choose all the parameters—color, pattern, line width, brush size, and so on—you want *before* you begin painting. Unlike a draw program, you can't change your mind about these things after the fact; your only choice is to undo or delete the area and start over.

Double-click on	To
⬚ or ⌇	Select the entire window
▱	Erase the entire window
▮	Bring up a palette for changing brush size and shape
🔍	Zoom to 8x magnification (or back to normal view)

Shift effects (AN/SZA). Holding down Shift while you use a tool usually constrains its movement and forces shapes to be of equal length and width. See the chart at right for some examples of its actions.

Lasso tricks (AA/AN). The lasso tool lets you select an irregularly shaped area (such as a flower) by tracing around it. (Some-

Shift +	Lets you
▮	Paint straight horizontal or vertical brush strokes
╲	Draw straight horizontal or vertical lines
✋	Shift the window contents horizontally or vertically
▱	Erase in straight horizontal or vertical swipes
▢ or ⬚	Create squares (instead of rectangles)
◯	Create circles (instead of ovals)

times you can select an object simply by double-clicking it with the lasso.) In many programs, you can choose whether the lassoed selection will shrink to exclude any surrounding background (the same is often true for the selection rectangle). Some programs, such as BrushStrokes and SuperPaint, let you opt to exclude all background areas—such as the interior of an *O*—from a selection; this is often called the *transparent* or *X-ray mode*.

Note that you don't have to draw a complete loop with the lasso to select an area. The program will automatically close the loop with a straight line between where you start and end the lasso drag.

Eraser alternatives (AN/AA). The eraser deletes parts of an image, changing erased areas to the background color (usually white). Here are three other ways you can erase bitmapped artwork:

- To quickly erase large areas, use a selection tool (the selection rectangle or lasso, for example), then hit (Delete).

- Use the paintbrush—in any convenient size and shape—to paint over the desired area with white paint (or whatever the background color is).

- For detailed, pixel-by-pixel erasing, go to a magnified view and use the pencil with white paint (or the background color).

Preventing paint bucket spills (AA). When you fill a selected area using the paint bucket, it fills the *entire* contiguous area. This can produce unexpected results if there's a pixel or two missing from the border of a supposedly enclosed shape. The paint will spill out through the gap into the surrounding area. If this happens to you, immediately choose Undo, then locate the gap in the outline and use the pencil to close it up.

Duplicating an image (SZA/AN/AA). The easiest way to copy an image isn't the cut-and-paste routine. Nope, all you have to do is press (Option) while dragging a selected area. Instead of moving the original image, you'll peel away an exact copy. If you also hold down (⌘), you'll leave a trail of images behind as you drag the selection. The more slowly you drag, the more copies there'll be. Holding down (Shift) as well (which means (⌘)(Option)(Shift) in total) keeps the dragged copies in a straight line. In some programs, you can adjust the spacing between copies by changing the current line width.

Resizing bitmapped images (AA). Enlarging a bitmapped image is generally a Bad Thing, because the image deteriorates into a jaggy mess. Instead, make the original image as large as possible, then scale it *down* to whatever size you need. Reducing the size of a bitmap effectively increases the resolution, thus improving its appearance. For optimum results, use a multiple of the original size—half or one-fourth the size, for example. (This approach is mandatory if you insist on enlarging the image.) Here are four ways to resize a bitmap:

- Select the image, hold down (Shift), and drag to shrink the image proportionally. This works in most programs, including page layout and presentation documents.

- Import the full-size image into a draw program (or the drawing component of a combination program) and reduce it there. This will minimize the loss of detail, particularly if there's text in the image.

- Boost the image's resolution in a program such as Photoshop. When you increase the resolution—say, from 72 dpi to 300 dpi—the image size will shrink proportionally.

- Open the Page Setup dialog box (File menu) and change the Reduce or Enlarge percentage to less than 100. The on-screen image won't change, but when you select Print, the image—along with everything else on the page—will be scaled down to the specified size. (Remember to return the percentage to 100 when you're finished.)

Global Nudge Commands (SZA/AN/AA). Every graphics (and page layout) program should let you move selected objects pixel by pixel (called *nudging*). But if yours doesn't, here's how to make your own nudge commands that will work in any program—paint, draw, page layout, you name it.

You need the Easy Access control panel in your Control Panels folder. (If it's not there, install it from your original system disks and restart the Mac.) Press ⌘ Shift Clear to activate one of its handiest features, Mouse Keys. Tap ⓪ on the numeric keypad twice to lock down the mouse button. Now you can use ②, ④, ⑥, and ⑧ on the keypad to move any selected object down, left, right, or up one pixel at a time. (Press the keypad's · twice to release the mouse button and press ⌘ Shift Clear to turn off Mouse Keys.)

Photoshop (RT)

Image editing on the Macintosh is defined by one program: **Adobe Photoshop** ($900, Adobe). In 1990, Photoshop 1 appeared, with much fanfare from Adobe. Unfortunately, the product didn't really take off until version 2, released about two years later. Photoshop arrived at just the right time, when Macs were finally ready to handle large image files (prior to System 7, it was impractical to have a system with more than 8MB of RAM). Desktop scanners also became more popular, fueling the photo-retouching flames.

Photoshop 3 currently supports *layers*, which enables images to be composited, saved, and later rearranged. It works great from tiny little files up to images that are several hundred megabytes. The catch? You need from three to five times as much RAM as the size of the largest image you'll be working with, or Photoshop will kick in its own virtual memory scheme, drastically slowing down your Mac's progress. Want a tip? Buy RAM. Lots of RAM. Then buy some more RAM.

Photoshop's main strength is in how it selects portions of a current image. Several tools (see "Photoshop Tips") assist in making selections, and these selections are versatile enough to select not just entire pixels, but portions of pixels as well.

Second to selecting, Photoshop's *filter* capabilities are just short of phenomenal. Filters add some function or feature to a program, such as the ability to blur, sharpen, or spherize selected artwork. The filters that ship with the product are good, functional, useful filters, but the incredible selection of third-party filters makes Photoshop a virtual image-editing operating system. (See "Photoshop-Compatible Plug-Ins," later in this chapter).

If Photoshop frightens you, with all its tools and other options, there are plenty of books out there to get you up to speed. More than 20 Photoshop books are currently available, from *The Complete Idiot's Guide to Photoshop* ($25, Que) to specific high-end books, such as *Photoshop Filter Finesse* ($45, Random House). *[Both of these, as well as Deke McClelland's* Macworld Photoshop 3 Bible *($40, IDG Books), are fantastic books.—TA]* Most of them (including the aforementioned titles) contain CD-ROMs with tons of sample images, filters, and more.

Photoshop Tips   (TA/EC/BL/AA)

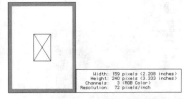

HOT TIPS

Most of these Photoshop 3 tricks work in earlier versions as well. For the ultimate in tips and techniques, get *The Photoshop Wow! Book* ($40, Peachpit Press).

Changing views. Photoshop has several shortcuts for zooming in and out. Double-click the zoom tool to see an image in 1:1 view (one image pixel is equal to one screen pixel). Keep in mind that the 1:1 view may not correspond to the image's actual dimensions. For example, if the image resolution is higher than the screen resolution (typically 72 dpi), the image will appear larger on screen than it actually is.

To instantly zoom part of an image to fill the screen, use the zoom tool to drag out a selection rectangle around the area you want to magnify. Access the zoom tool quickly by pressing and holding [Spacebar][⌃⌘]. Zoom out by pressing [Spacebar][⌃⌘][Option] and clicking.

Some viewing shortcuts don't use the zoom tool. Double-click the grabber hand, for example, to make the image fit in the window. To change the magnification and simultaneously change the window size, press [⌃⌘][+] or [⌃⌘][-].

Quick page previews. The file-size indicator at the lower left of a window has two pop-up screens of document details. Click and hold on the indicator to see a page preview that shows your image size relative to the printable page area. Depending on the options

Width: 159 pixels (2.208 inches)
Height: 240 pixels (3.333 inches)
Channels: 3 (RGB Color)
Resolution: 72 pixels/inch

Clicking on the size box in the lower left of a document window displays the box on the left (with an X in it). The box represents the size of the image when printed with the current print settings. Option-clicking that same area produces the box on the right, which gives more detailed document information.

selected in the Page Setup dialog box, you may also see registration marks, labels, and other elements. Hold down (Option) before clicking to view a summary of the document, including its size in pixels and in your current measurement units, as well as the number of channels and ppi.

Precision editing. Each tool has a cursor that looks like its icon. While cute, these cursors don't lend themselves to precision editing. If you want to know exactly where the paint bucket will drop its load, you can change the cursor into a crosshair by pressing (Caps Lock). This trick works for all the tools, including the magic wand and rubber stamp. (Press (Caps Lock) again to restore the original cursor.) If you'd like, you can turn on Precision editing all the time in the General Preferences dialog box (accessed by choosing Preferences from the Edit menu).

Multiple views. The New Window command (Window menu) lets you create one or more duplicate windows for an image. You can change the magnification and channel information for each window independently, giving you different simultaneous views of your artwork. Whatever editing changes you make in one window show up instantly in the other(s).

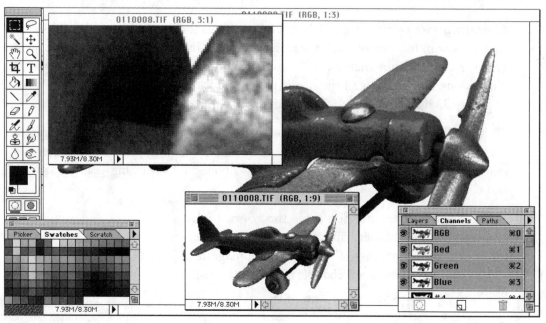

In Photoshop you can have several windows of the current document visible. This is useful for touch-up, as you can work on the detail without losing the overall look of the entire image.

Fine-tuning selections. Photoshop's selection tools (the selection rectangle and lasso) are more robust than those in most paint programs. You can eliminate part of a selection, for example, by pressing ⌘ while dragging with the desired selection tool. Shift-dragging adds to a selection, even if it's in another part of the image. You can make a polygonal (straight-sided) selection area with the lasso by holding down [Option] and clicking at the desired corner points. You move a selection by dragging it, of course, but you can move just the selection marquee instead if you hold down [⌘][Option] as you drag. Choosing Inverse from the Select menu switches the selected and unselected parts of the image—particularly handy because it's sometimes easier to first select the areas you *don't* want to change.

The Grow and Similar commands (Select menu) let you extend a selection based on color values. The color range they add depends on the tolerance value specified in the Magic Wand Options palette (double-click the magic wand icon to open it). The Grow command adds areas adjacent to the selected area that have similar color values. The Similar command enlarges the selection by including all areas in the image that are similar in color.

Hiding the palettes. Tired of the toolbox and the other palettes obscuring your handiwork? Press [Tab] to hide them all. Pressing [Tab] again will make them reappear.

Selecting colors. The eyedropper tool lets you select a color in an image that you want to be the foreground or background color. Normally, a click with the eyedropper changes the foreground color. If you hold down [Option] while clicking, however, the eyedropper will change the background color instead.

If you're using another tool, you can change the foreground color on the fly by pressing [Option]. This turns the current tool into the eyedropper. Click the color you want to use, let go of [Option], and continue painting using the newly selected color.

Fast fills. You don't have to use the Fill command or the paint bucket to paint a selected area with the foreground color. Just press [Option][Delete]. To fill a selection with the background color, press [Delete].

Dialog box shortcuts. In several of the image-correction dialog boxes—including Levels, Curves, Color Balance, Brightness/Contrast, Hue/Saturation, and Posterize—pressing [Option] displays a Reset button. By clicking Reset, you can restore the original image settings without having to close the dialog box with the Cancel button.

You can also reposition the image with these dialog boxes open by using keyboard shortcuts. You can zoom in or out with [⌘][Spacebar] or [Option][Spacebar], and press [Spacebar] to move around with the grabber hand.

HOT TIPS

Magic eraser. The Revert command (File menu) lets you undo all changes made to an image since the last time you saved it. But if you hold down [Option] as you drag the eraser, you'll restore just the underlying area to its previously saved condition.

You can use the magic eraser to give an image a hand-colored look. Open (or save) a color image, then convert it to black and white by choosing Grayscale from the Mode menu. Then select RGB Color to switch back to color mode for editing. Now you can use the magic eraser to paint the original color back onto selected areas.

Controlling letter spacing. Working with text in Photoshop can be difficult, because the characters are just a collection of bitmaps, but here's a quick way to adjust the spacing between individual letters (called *kerning*). Type some text, and while the type tool is still active, press [⌘]. The cursor will turn into the lasso. Now you can deselect any of the letters by circling them, then use the arrow keys to push the remaining letters closer to (or farther from) the deselected ones. By doing this several times, you can precisely control letter spacing. (Alternatively, you can press [⌘][Shift] and drag the lasso around the letters you want to remain selected.)

Use type from Illustrator. Illustrator provides some of the best type tools in any software. Set up your text exactly as you'd want it in Illustrator, and copy and paste it into your Photoshop document. Versions of Photoshop prior to 3.0.5 had trouble with the letter spacing from pasted Illustrator text, so make sure you have the latest version of Photoshop.

Applying filters to individual channels. You can achieve some interesting, subtle effects by using a filter on individual color channels rather than on the entire image. For example, try applying the Noise filter separately to each channel—R (red), then G (green), then B (blue)—in an RGB document. (You can selectively edit channels via the Channels palette.) Rather than the grainy, colorful noise you get by applying Noise to the entire RGB image, you'll get a film-grain-like effect.

Photoshop Wannabes   (RT)

The last few years have brought about an incredible number of new Photoshop clones, aimed at the "consumer market" (a fancy term for Performa owners and other Mac users who don't rely on Mac programs to survive). Most of these are adequate, but none come close to having the power of Photoshop. As expected, the prices on most of these knockoffs are phenomenally low, in the $40 to $200 range. Examples of these programs include **PhotoMaker** ($80, MacSoft) and even Adobe's own **PhotoDeluxe** ($150), a downgraded Photoshop.

Photo CDs (RT)

Can't afford a scanner? Tired of paying $35 per scan from your local color house? Photo CDs may be the way of the future for you. A Photo CD is a CD-ROM that contains photographs developed from recently shot 35mm film, or even from existing negatives. Up to 100 images can fit on a single CD. Each image has several sizes to choose from as well.

Many local film processing houses will accept your film for Photo CD processing, but don't expect a one-hour turnaround; there are only a few places in the U.S. that do image-to-Photo CD conversions. Instead, it will usually take a couple of days to get the CD-ROM processed.

You can put up to 100 photographs on a Photo CD (for about $1 per image).

Many programs will let you import Photo CD images without converting them into one of the standard file formats (listed in the "Pixelized File Formats" section, earlier in this chapter). If you have QuickTime 2.1 installed, you'll be able to view Photo CD images as PICTs just by double-clicking on their icons.

HOT TIP

One of the more popular of the low-end image-editing software is **Color It! 3** ($150, MicroFrontier), which uses Photoshop plug-ins and a fairly useful toolset for photo retouching.

The most serious contender for the Photoshop crown is **xRes 2** ($700, Macromedia), which contains features that often go beyond Photoshop's, including delayed image processing (which significantly reduces down time when manipulating large images). Oddly, Macromedia is marketing **xRes 2** as "the perfect Photoshop companion," when there's quite a bit of overlap present.

Going beyond Photoshop is **Live Picture 2.5** ($1,000, Live Picture). Formerly distributed by MetaTools (the Kai's Power Tools people), Live Picture has been selling its own product (without the Kai-designed interface) since the beginning of 1996. Live Picture uses FITS technology to virtually eliminate the bottlenecks that go along with working with large files. One of the most amazing features of Live Picture is that even after you've closed a file, you can open it up later and undo actions you did in previous sessions.

Photoshop-Compatible Plug-Ins   (RT)

To help satisfy the cravings of the typical Photoshop user (instead of "more power!" they shout "more filters!"), there are now several quality Photoshop plug-ins to choose from.

Adobe Gallery Effects ($100, Adobe) contains three sets of artistic and special effects filters. My favorite is Craquelure, which places your selection on a finely cracked surface.

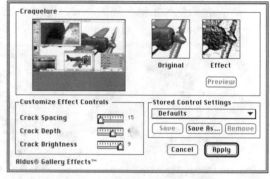

Andromeda Series Filters (Series 1 and 2, $120 each; Series 3, $160; Andromeda) provide such useful features as automatic image wrapping onto any surface.

Adobe Gallery Effects provides several different texture and artistic effects for Photoshop users.

PhotoLab ($100, Cytopia Software) contains a virtual darkroom of filters, perfect for final tweaks and adjustments. There's even a true negative-to-positive filter that instantly converts scanned film negatives to their proper positive values.

Kai's Power Tools ($200, MetaTools) is *the* Photoshop filter set, containing some of the most powerful filters ever created. Included in this package are Gradient Designer for creating complex custom gradients, Texture Explorer for discovering unique textures, Interform for combining textures, and Spheroid Designer to custom design various spheres. Other unique filters include Lens fx and several miniature "credit card" filters, each containing basic controls for a specific kind of effect.

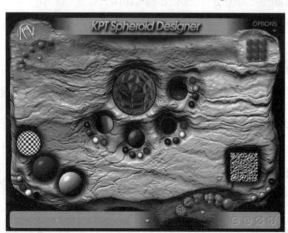

Kai's Power Tools contains several fascinating interfaces, including this one from KPT Spheroid Designer. The interface design is as much fun to play with as the filters are useful.

KPT Convolver ($100, MetaTools) is the productive portion of the MetaTools Photoshop-compatible filters. A single filter, Convolver contains an incredible collection of touch-up tools and controls for maximizing your image's appearance.

Ready-Made Patterns and Textures (AA)

Need a nice marble background for a book cover? How about some knotty pine for a 3-D model, or fabric swatches for an architectural rendering? Numerous companies offer packages of predesigned patterns and textures that you can use in artwork and presentations or wrap onto the surfaces of 3-D objects. Most are 24-bit images in PICT or TIFF format and will *tile* seamlessly, meaning that if the image isn't large enough to fill the area, it repeats itself without showing any joints.

Form and Function provides everything from paper and bricks to shrubbery and jelly beans in its **Wraptures** series ($130 each on CD-ROM). **Fresco** ($200 on CD-ROM, Xaos Tools) offers classy abstract designs. Pixar's **One Twenty Eight** ($300) CD-ROM has photographic textures, while Artbeats' **Marble & Granite** collection ($350 on CD-ROM) includes beveled buttons and mortises, seamless tiles, and bump maps for 3-D renderings (see "3-D Graphics and Animation" later in this chapter).

If you want to try your hand at texturing, check out **Pattern Workshop** ($50, Micro-Frontier), a Photoshop plug-in that lets you edit its 160 premade patterns or make your own. Another plug-in, **Terrazzo** ($200, Xaos Tools), provides 17 symmetry effects for turning any section of a bitmapped image into a tilable texture, and **TextureScape** ($200, Specular) generates seamless, high-resolution textures from EPS images created in Illustrator or FreeHand. The latter two programs let you add complexity to a texture by adjusting properties such as gloss, transparency, bumpiness, and color. TextureScape also has sophisticated lighting controls and can animate textures over time.

Intellihance ($100, Extensis) is a powerful filter that automatically "fixes" images, enhancing the colors and contrast automatically.

Paint Alchemy ($100, Xaos Tools) is a set of effects accessed through a unique brush system.

The Black Box 2 ($120, Alien Skin Software) contains some extremely powerful filters, including ones for creating drop shadows and bevels instantly.

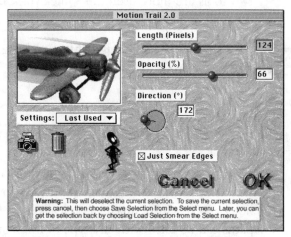

The Black Box filters provide instant bevels, drop shadows, and more.

Graphics on the Internet (RT)

There are three things to remember when sending, posting, or working with files on the Internet: (1) Keep the file size small; (2) Don't let the image become a giant file; and (3) Make sure that the file is fairly compact in size. There's a lesson here somewhere.

When sending files to others, use JPEG compression at the Medium or Low Quality setting. JPEGs allow for millions of different colors within a file, unlike GIFs, which are limited to 256 colors.

When creating images for the World Wide Web, use the GIF89 format. Currently, both Photoshop and Illustrator can export with that format.

For viewing graphics on the Internet (like image-heavy Web pages), you need either a 28.8 kbps (kilobits per second) modem or unlimited patience. Even at 28.8, graphics are slow to get from the source to your system.

Introductory Image Editing (RT)

Adjusting and manipulating photographs and other pixel-based images can be loads of fun. The key to image editing is getting the right portions of your image selected. Master the selection tools, selection commands, and masking (channel) capabilities of your software before trying to do any serious work. Selecting images correctly is two-thirds of the battle.

Although most image editing programs have a paintbrush and an airbrush, you probably want to stay away from them, at least as far as painting goes. In Photoshop, these two tools are more useful in QuickMask mode or within a channel than they are in the main image.

HOT TIP

Save often, especially right after waiting for your Mac to complete a 15-minute Unsharp Mask.

Vector-Based Graphics (RT)

Vector-based graphics are becoming more and more popular, as vector-based software has recently become significantly more powerful. Instead of having to deal with millions of pixels in an image, a typical vector file deals with a few thousand paths. These paths can be filled with any type of fill, from solid colors to gradients to patterns.

Managing Your Media (AA)

The Mac's graphics bounty does have a downside: Trying to track hundreds (or thousands) of images scattered across hard disks, floppies, CD-ROMs, and SyQuest cartridges can be a major time waster. The solution? A media-cataloging program—a specialized database that lets you create a master catalog of all your graphics, no matter what their format or location. A single catalog can hold 32,000 images or more; each cataloged image is represented by a thumbnail-size preview (which is linked to the original file) and identifying text. Using filenames, keywords, or other criteria, you can quickly find and retrieve graphics ranging from EPS illustrations to scanned photographs to QuickTime movies.

For individual users, Aldus' **Fetch** ($150 single user, $300 multiuser), **Cumulus PowerLite** ($200, Canto Software), and **Multi-Ad Search** ($250, Multi-Ad Services) are all good choices. They have excellent features, catalog a wide variety of file formats, and let you place cataloged images directly into PageMaker and QuarkXPress documents—with Cumulus, you simply drag and drop images from a catalog directly into a page layout. If you work with Photo CD images, both Fetch and Eastman Kodak's **Shoebox** ($140) provide special support features.

If you're managing graphics over a network, however, get Canto Software's **Cumulus PowerPro**. This client/server database is easy to use and—best of all—*fast,* even on a busy network. It can automatically catalog files dropped into designated folders and lets you automate tasks with Apple events scripting. Pricing starts at $1,500 for five users.

QuickDraw versus PostScript (AA)

Drawing programs are based either on *QuickDraw* (the Mac's native graphics language) or *PostScript* (Adobe's page description language). Traditionally, business users favor QuickDraw-based programs, and professional illustrators prefer PostScript. QuickDraw programs are more numerous, less expensive, and easier to learn and use. QuickDraw images can be printed on more (and less-expensive) printers, and no matter how complex the drawing, you never get output errors.

PostScript-based programs, on the other hand, can manipulate images in ways that are difficult (or impossible) in QuickDraw. PostScript is famous for producing sophisticated illustrations with fine lines (called *paths*), complex curves, seamless blends, special text effects, rotation, skewing, and transparency effects. PostScript illustrations are infinitely scalable, but for best results they must be output on a PostScript-compatible printer—and if a drawing is too complex (too many blends, for instance), it may not print at all. There are four major programs that offer PostScript features: the two heavyweights, FreeHand and Illustrator, plus CA-Cricket Draw III and Canvas (a program that also supports QuickDraw).

Bézier Curves (RT)

One of the toughest concepts to master regarding draw and PostScript programs is the *Bézier* (bez-ee-ay) *curve*. Created by Pierre Bézier, a French mathematician, to help

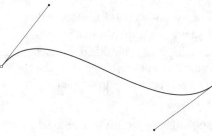

streamline the process of cutting car parts with automated machines, Bézier curves provide an inventive way to control curves. Using two *endpoints* (often called *anchor points*) and two control handles for each line segment, you can create a wide variety of curves.

A typical Bézier curve has two endpoints, two control handles, and a line segment between the two endpoints. Note how the curve seems to be magnetically pulled towards the control handles.

Unfortunately for Mr. Bézier, his curves are one of the least intuitive aspects of drawing ever to be loosed upon unwitting artists. The learning, er, *curve* is so steep it seems unclimbable at first. Eventually, after some practice, the magic of Bézier curves becomes apparent. Here are a couple of tips to keep in mind when using Bézier curves:

- The control handles should fall outside the curve.

- Keep the control handles about one-third of the distance of the entire line segment from the original endpoint.

HOT TIP

- Never set a new endpoint right on a control handle you've just dragged.

Draw Software (SF)

In the beginning (circa 1984), there was MacDraw, one of the two original graphics programs available for the Macintosh, and the first ever object-oriented Macintosh graphics program. In the past 12 years drawing software has grown by leaps and bounds, and today's drawing heavyweights can be used to create breathtakingly beautiful works of precision and sophistication. MacDraw led the way with tools to create discrete lines and shapes, commands for arranging and grouping these elements together, and options for altering the line weights, fill patterns, and line and fill colors.

Every drawing program since MacDraw has upped the ante in one way or another. Claris succeeded the original MacDraw with MacDraw II and MacDraw Pro, but has since replaced the MacDraw line with **ClarisDraw** ($200, Claris), an excellent all-around drawing program with versatile drawing tools and even some painting and image-editing capabilities. The undisputed heavyweight in the drawing arena these days is **Canvas** ($600, Deneba Software), a comprehensive, cross-platform program with powerful tools and too many features to count. While the learning curve is a little steep, Canvas has just about everything you could ever want in a drawing program (and then some). In fact, Canvas is so robust that it is more often grouped with the professional illustration leaders, Adobe Illustrator and Macromedia FreeHand, than it is with standard drawing programs.

In addition to ClarisDraw and Canvas, there are a number of other packages available which we can recommend. **DeskDraw** ($200, Zedcor) is part of a bundle (with DeskPaint) which gives you two lean, but very capable, software packages at a reasonable price. **CA-Cricket Draw III** ($200, Computer Associates), **IntelliDraw** ($100, Adobe), and **Expert Draw** ($50, Expert Software) also give you some nice features at bargain prices. In particular, Cricket Draw III gives you PostScript image manipulation capabilities for one-third the price of Illustrator or FreeHand. *[Price aside, the horror stories related to Cricket Draw printing are legion; I'd stick with the big guns (Illustrator and FreeHand) when it comes to PostScript printing.-TA]*

Shareware Extras   (Gregory Wasson)

Most of this chapter covers commercial software, but on-line services and user groups also offer a variety of shareware (and freeware) graphics programs. If you aren't ready to ante up for a commercial paint program, for example, the freebie **ColourPaint** provides a color alternative with simple MacPaint-like tools.

Stuck with a monochrome Mac? The black-and-white **LightningPaint** ($14) has the painting basics plus some really cool tools (spiral, starburst) and special effects (fish-eye lens, gradients). **NIH Image**, a freeware image-editing program, rivals some commercial programs. It was created for use with medical scans and X-rays, but you can easily use it for more artistic pursuits. I've also been dazzled by the freeware **MandelTV**, an entertaining DA that generates Mandelbrot fractals and saves them as PICT files.

POWERBOOK

On the drawing side, **DesignerDraw** (free) comes in handy if you need to produce simple organization or flow charts. Like some commercial products, it preserves line connections if you drag linked text boxes around. **AppleDraw** ($30) has most of MacDraw's tools and is a good choice for basic drawing tasks, such as logos, although it doesn't have the oomph for sophisticated illustrations.

There are also a few nifty utilities that can enhance your graphics experience. **Super Ruler** ($10) is a clever DA that displays a vertical or horizontal ruler on screen. It's great for page-layout measurements in word processors that lack vertical rulers. Creating perfect gradient fills with smooth transitions between colors is something of an art; the $5 **Blender DA** calculates the minimum number of steps you need to specify in programs such as Illustrator to attain that perfect smoothness. And if you have a lot of graphics to keep track of, **ImageCatalog** (free) lets you organize, annotate, and access PICT, TIFF, MacPaint, and some EPS graphics.

Drawing Tips   (SF)

Although every drawing package on the market is unique, following some funda-mental tips can make getting started a whole lot easier.

Give yourself room. Remember that where you draw something has nothing what-soever to do with where it will eventually end up. With this in mind, don't frustrate yourself by trying to draw individual components in the middle of a very complex drawing. Draw the pieces off to the side (where you'll have plenty of room) and then move them to their final destination.

Keep objects simple. Create groups of simple objects rather than single, complex objects. If you need to draw a house, first draw the walls, then the roof, then the door, then a couple of windows. And *then* move them together, line them up just so, and group them together as a single object.

Avoid object obsession. Don't worry if you mess up while drawing an object. Just keep going, finish the object, then clean up the one corner that wasn't quite right. I don't know how many times I've watched someone give up on five or ten minutes worth of work just because they made a mistake near the end of drawing the object. Finish, *then* fix. Remember that with drawn objects, every single line, curve, and corner is fully selectable and editable.

Illustration Software   (RT)

In the world of professional illustration there are two combatants: **Adobe Illustrator 6** ($600, Adobe) and **Macromedia FreeHand 5.5** ($600, Macromedia). There is no loser, and there is no winner, except you. These two programs have been one-upping each other for years, with each package getting bigger and tougher and more feature-packed with each release.

But they both have several similar features that make them valuable all by themselves. Because they're as close to a pure PostScript application as you can possibly get, printing to PostScript printers and imagesetters usually works very well (unless you have

Illustrator, the PostScript drawing choice of professional illustrators, allows you to create complex illustrations that you can scale to any size without loss of quality. Illustrator 6 also allows you to place and manipulate various pixel-based image formats.

FreeHand 4, the black mark of FreeHand releases). Each program provides full color separation capabilities. In addition, both packages come loaded with many, many extras such as free fonts and bundled applications.

PostScript Tips

HOT TIPS

Saving files. Save your files in EPS format in order to bring them into other programs, such as page layout (e.g. PageMaker and QuarkXPress). Photoshop 3.0.5 can rasterize Illustrator format files (all versions through 6), and both Illustrator and FreeHand can save files in an Illustrator format. When bringing files into other applications, you might want to convert larger text to outlines before saving. This eliminates the need for those fonts when the graphic is printed.

Limit use of paths. Be careful not to use too many paths in any one document. Not only will Illustrator and/or FreeHand slow to a crawl, but the files they generate may be too large to preview, or even too large to save, let alone print.

For fans of *Easter Eggs* (secret messages planted by the software engineers) there are two incorporated into Adobe Illustrator 6 that are worth mentioning. First, Option-click on the Info bar in the lower left of the screen to reveal several more options, including eyes that follow your cursor around, the current phase of the moon, and the current national debt (which depressingly increases as you watch it). Second, bring up the About Adobe Illustrator screen (from the top of the menu), and click on the Adobe logo; you're treated to a fascinating light show.

Illustrator or FreeHand?

The rivalry between these two programs has waged since the good folks at Aldus signed the licensing agreement with Altsys, the creators of FreeHand back in 1987. Illustrator was first out of the gate, and a few loyal users jumped on board, and more followed a year later with the release of Illustrator 88 (which continued to sell well into 1990). But Aldus FreeHand 2 gained both respect and sheer numbers of users due to its ability to work in preview mode. Illustrator users wouldn't get this feature until Illustrator 5, released in 1993.

At this point, each package had a loyal following, with the artists and professional designers favoring Illustrator, while corporate in-house artists and educators used FreeHand (with a little help from the corporate DTP warhorse and fellow Aldus product, PageMaker). FreeHand followers defected when FreeHand 4 turned out to be a dud (printing and file format errors abounded). Illustrator gained momentum in 1994 with a quick 5.5 follow-up to version 5.0, becoming one of the first major

Illustrator's capabilities are more suited to the traditional and high-end graphic artist, with such impressive features as the Ink Pen fill (above). FreeHand has superb pixel-based graphics support, and many page layout tools as well (right), resulting in a Swiss Army Knife graphics application.

products for Power Macintosh computers. 1995 was a good year for FreeHand (now owned by Macromedia), as version 5 began the year with support for Adobe's own filter spec, and ended the year with an upgrade to version 5.5, which by most indications seems to have been just a revenue generation machine, with little added substance. Finally, 1996 saw the release of the long-anticipated Illustrator 6, with a shiny new API (application program interface) that allowed third-party filter developers more access to Illustrator's workings, as well as giving them many tools.

So, which product is better? Well, Illustrator has more users. FreeHand has more palettes. Illustrator has tight integration with Photoshop. FreeHand has Live Blends. Illustrator has the best drawing tool with its Pen tool, as far as accuracy, feel, and smoothness are concerned. FreeHand has...well, FreeHand's Pen tool works adequately...and it has a Bezigon tool to boot.

After doing an informal poll, it seems that while almost all primarily-FreeHand users also use Illustrator, very few primarily-Illustrator users use FreeHand. As far as my client base goes, which consists mainly of advertising agencies, prepress and color houses, and printers and service bureaus, almost everyone has Illustrator. I could count on one hand those clients who have FreeHand. I believe the tide is turning towards Illustrator but I doubt that FreeHand will ever go away. In fact, I hope they're both in there for the long haul, providing incentive for the other to become a better product.

PostScript Plug-Ins (TA)

Before Illustrator 5, there were no such things as PostScript plug-ins. Now, you can't get away from them. Mirroring the flood of Photoshop filters, *plug-ins* (files that increase the features and capabilities of the host program) for Illustrator and FreeHand have arrived from various sources. There's already a book about them (*Illustrator Filter Finesse*, $45, Random House), and several developers are working on upgrades to the current slew of filters and other plug-ins. The following is a sampling of what's out there now:

Letraset Envelopes ($100, Letraset USA). This one-shot plug-in was the first to arrive, containing multiple preset envelope distortions and the capability to create new shapes for distorting artwork. Since then, it has substantially faded into the vector woodwork as better, more versatile plug-in packages have arrived.

Infinite FX1 ($100, BeInfinite). A polar opposite to Envelopes, this set contains 55 different (well, most of them are different) distortion filters, with no presets. An innovative (though frustrating) interface grabs your attention immediately.

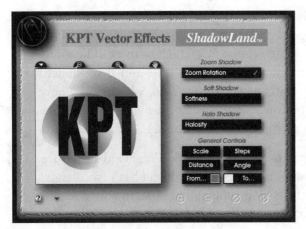

KPT Vector Effects provides boatloads of special effects, such as this shadow effect on "KPT".

KPT Vector Effects ($200, MetaTools). The makers of Kai's Power Tools grabbed what was once **Sree's Cool Tools** from Intrepid Systems, jazzed up the interface, and released a baker's dozen of the coolest vector filters yet. This package includes a 3-D filter, a filter for generating shadows, a much more powerful and useful distortion envelope than that found in Envelopes, and ten more filters. A must-have for Illustrator and FreeHand users alike.

DrawTools 1 ($100, Extensis). This set of productivity filters contains plug-ins for color control, shape wrapping, and object placement.

Stylist ($120, Alien Skin). This Illustrator 6-only plug-in from the Black Box 2 (plug-in for Photoshop) creators provides style sheets for Illustrator, both object and text, in a unique floating palette. One new concept that Stylist introduces is "complex constructions," which consist of several overlapping paths that create incredibly complex objects.

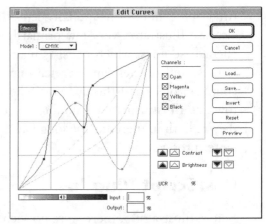

DrawTools Curves provides indispensable color adjustment capabilities within Illustrator and FreeHand.

Socket Sets 1 and 2 ($100, Cytopia Software). This incredibly powerful double set of filters (Illustrator only) is ideal for production environments. Included are filters for selecting and adjusting objects, and controlling color.

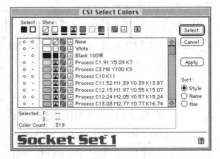

The CSI Select filters in CSI Socket Sets can substantially increase your Illustrator productivity by eliminating the tedious nature of complex selections.

Supplementary PostScript Software   (TA)

There are several packages that take Postscript artwork further than Illustrator or FreeHand can. Appropriately enough, the two most popular of the bunch are also made by Adobe.

Adobe Streamline 3.1 ($200). This program converts pixel-based images into vector-based ones by tracing different colors as individual shapes. The final results aren't photographic by any means, but Streamline is great for tracing spot color art, and for creating posterizations of other art.

Adobe Dimensions 2 ($200). This is a 3-D program for vectors. The most unique thing about Dimensions is that unlike other 3-D software, Dimensions renders to vectors, not pixels. Dimensions supports Copy and Paste to and from Illustrator via Adobe's PostScript Clipboard technology.

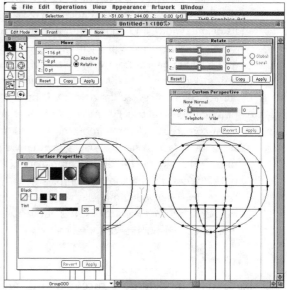

Adobe Dimensions drastically simplifies complex vector-based image creation.

3-D Graphics and Animation   (SF)

You can use sophisticated painting and drawing programs to create extraordinarily realistic images of just about anything that you might care to make, but there isn't a painting or drawing program in existence that can show you what the *other* side of your newly drawn apple, boat, or gear might look like. That's where 3-D modeling programs come into play. Three-dimensional graphics software programs are generally referred to as *modeling* programs because they allow you to create models of real, 3-D objects. You can then place these models together to form *scenes* (the standard term for files created in 3-D modeling programs) which you can view from any angle or distance, and then render in a format that can be used in a separate page layout or image-editing program.

Three-dimensional graphics programs are perfect for engineers, architects, illustrators, animators, or anyone who needs to create and view real-world objects (and whose profession starts with a vowel). The process of creating a 3-D image has three

Why 3-D Graphics Are So Complex (SF)

3-D graphics and animation software is more complex than 2-D graphics software because 3-D graphics are, by nature, more complex than 2-D graphics. There is considerably more information necessary to describe an image in three dimensions than in two dimensions. Imagine a 2-D shape such as a rectangle. To describe this, we need only know its height, width, and origin. With this information we can display the rectangle on screen. With a brick (the 3-D equivalent of our rectangle), we have to know its height, width, *depth*, and origin in order to draw it. So far, no big deal, right? But what if we want to make our brick more realistic? We introduce minor imperfections, such as some small chips in its surface (six surfaces, actually, on a 3-D brick). Just a dozen chips (each with at least three outer corners and usually one or more inner angles) changes our simple six-surfaced, eight-cornered brick into a monster with 30 or more corner angles and probably 50 or 60 separate surface planes. Now let's say that we want to add color, texture, light, and shadow to our brick. This increases the complexity of the brick exponentially. And this is for just one brick! It's easy to imagine the complexity of the calculations required to model an entire house. This is why 3-D modeling programs require powerful computers with plenty of memory and large hard drives. It is also why, even on a fast Mac, rendering your 3-D images can take hours (or sometimes even days).

basic steps: modeling, texture mapping, and rendering. These steps enable you to create a photorealistic image of an object with true, 3-D properties. In addition to these three steps, you will probably have to do some scene building (arranging multiple objects together, and setting viewing angles and light sources), and you may find yourself animating your 3-D scenes to create short clips for presentation to clients or colleagues, or for use in sophisticated, video editing programs.

Modeling (SF)

Modeling refers to the process of creating the actual 3-D objects. Most modeling is done using *primitives* (basic shapes such as spheres, cubes, and cylinders), *extrusion* (stretching a 2-D outline along a third axis), and *lathing* (spinning a 2-D outline around a central axis). These three techniques allow you to create just about any object (or object component) imaginable. After you create a basic object, you can manually stretch and pull individual points to warp your object into exactly the shape you need.

During the modeling phase, you usually work in a wireframe mode, where your objects are displayed as (relatively) simple wireframe outlines. This mode allows your 3-D program to update the screen as quickly as possible, letting you manipulate your object without having to wait for complex calculations and screen redraws. If you have a fast enough Mac you can work in a variety of shaded modes, giving you a more accurate idea of what your object will look like in the final image.

Modeled objects are generally saved in DXF format, which is the standard for 3-D objects. These days, though, many programs also support 3-DMF, a format that is steadily increasing in popularity. If you want to be able to exchange objects among different applications, make sure your 3-D program supports one (or both) of these formats.

HOT TIP

Texture Mapping (SF)

If you don't want all of your objects to look like they are made out of dull, gray plastic, you will need to do some sort of *texture mapping*. Texture mapping is the process of applying (mapping) a texture to the surface of a 3-D object. Generally speaking, these textures are wrapped around the "skin" of your object, although some programs give you other mapping options.

Your choice of textures is virtually unlimited, as any decent modeling program has its own library of textures to choose from (including everything from stone, wood, and natural fabrics to glass, chrome, and fire). You can also choose from among any of the commercial texture collections available, scan in your own textures, or modify the textures included with your 3-D program.

Generally speaking, you won't see the texture applied to your object until you render your scene, but many 3-D programs will let you create quick previews of your objects as you work, so you can get a good idea whether or not you like the flaming eyeball texture wrapped around that banana, for example.

Rendering (SF)

After you've created your objects, arranged them as desired, and applied textures, you are ready for the final step, *rendering*. When you render your scene, your 3-D program creates a final "picture" of your scene, at whatever angle and with whatever lighting effects you have specified. This final image is usually saved in either PICT or TIFF format, and can then be imported into an image editing program for further modification, or placed directly into your favorite desktop publishing or multimedia software program.

When you render your scene, you can choose from among several different levels of realism and complexity, such as flat shading, Gouraud or Phong shading, or ray tracing. Flat shading is the fastest method, but produces blocky, unrealistic images.

A 3-D World Through a 2-D Window   (SF)

One of the biggest stumbling blocks (a fully-rendered, 3-D stumbling block, mind you) to using 3-D software is getting used to working with 3-D objects in a 3-D environment on a 2-D computer screen.

In the real world, we perceive depth based on our stereoscopic vision (i.e., we see things simultaneously from two different perspectives, our left and right eyes) which lets us judge the relative distance of objects in a scene. We also use other cues, such as shadows, haze, the horizon line, and our own past experience, to decide, for example, whether one figure in a scene is further away than the other, or simply smaller in size. For objects on a computer monitor, we cannot use these standard techniques to judge depth and distance. Instead, we must depend on our 3-D software to give us alternative visual cues. These cues might include numeric coordinates (an accurate, but extremely nonintuitive method), multiple viewing angles (better, but still not entirely intuitive), or (my personal favorite) *cast shadows*. Many 3-D programs use cast shadows in some form or another to let you accurately judge an object's position in your scene. Ray Dream Designer, for example, shows your scene with a false floor and two back walls. These three planes won't be visible in your final scene, but by having your objects cast shadows against these planes, you can always tell exactly where things are.

Another problem area is in moving objects through three dimensions with a 2-D input device, such as a mouse or stylus. To rotate or stretch objects along three dimensions, most 3-D programs provide separate handles on objects for modifications along the x (width), y (height), and z (depth) axes. Moving objects in three dimensions is often best accomplished by changing the way you view your scene. To move objects closer to or further away from the "camera," you might use an overhead view, while placing one object on top of another is best accomplished by viewing your scene either head-on or from the side (or both).

For this reason, flat shading is generally only used for quick previews and crude animation. Gouraud and Phong shading are much better than flat shading, and can produce acceptable images in a reasonably short time (especially Phong shading). Ray tracing is absolutely the best rendering method if you want breathtaking scenes with realistic lighting and reflection effects. Keep in mind, though, that everything comes at a price, and ray-traced images can take hours, or even days, to fully render (depending on the complexity of your scene and the speed of your computer).

The Ultimate Renderer   (BL)

If you're serious about 3-D graphics, investigate Pixar's **MacRenderMan** (bundled with **Showplace** for $500, or $400 on CD-ROM). As its name implies, RenderMan is a rendering-only application, but it can achieve a photorealism that no other program can touch—and Pixar has the Oscar to prove it. If you've seen *Jurassic Park*, *Terminator 2*, or *The Abyss*, you've seen RenderMan's rendering techniques, called *procedural shaders*, in action. Pixar was also the force behind the amazing *Toy Story* animated feature. Procedural shaders are little programs that define the way light should interact with a model's surface, allowing you to generate effects ranging from stretching and flexing dinosaur skin to flowing liquid-metal cyborgs.

RenderMan is an application-independent, stand-alone rendering system—in fact, it works much like a PostScript printer driver. You select its renderers from the Chooser, and it uses a language, RIB (RenderMan Interface Bytestream), that's essentially PostScript for 3-D images. Several 3-D applications provide RenderMan support, including Macromedia Three-D, Swivel 3-D Professional, Presenter Professional, and Pixar's own Showplace and Typestry. These programs let you apply RenderMan shaders to your 3-D models, then send the finished scene (as a RIB file) to RenderMan for output.

The Power Problem (SF)

"I have a Mac LC with 4MB RAM and a 40MB hard drive. Which 3-D modeling program do you recommend?"

Ha, ha, ha, ha, ha, ha, ha, ha, ha, ha, ha, ha, ha, ha, ha, ha, ha, ha, ha, ha, ha, ha, ha, ha, ha, ha, ha, ha, ha, ha, ha, ha, ha, ha, ha, ha, ha, ha, ha, ha, ha, ha, ha, ha, ha.

Ahem. Sorry about that. I think I'm done now...

Ha, ha, ha, ha, ha, ha, ha, ha, ha, ha, ha, ha, ha, ha, ha, ha, ha, ha, ha, ha, ha, ha, ha, ha, ha, ha, ha, ha, ha, ha, ha.

Whew! Okay, *now* I'm done. Seriously, though, if you want to do 3-D modeling or animation, I wouldn't consider *anything* but a Power Mac. Your average, reasonably equipped Power Mac renders significantly faster than the most powerful Quadra, even with a gigabyte of RAM. An ideal system would be a PCI-based Power Mac (8500 or better) with 40-plus megabytes of memory and a big, big hard drive.

If even the fastest Power Mac is still not enough, there are some good accelerators on the market, notably YARC Systems' Hydra PCI co-processor boards ($3,000 to $12,000, depending on configuration). These accelerator boards can provide a dramatic improvement in processing and rendering times, and can be a great solution for sluggish rendering (if you've got the cash). An alternative solution is to let several networked Macs divide the work, provided each Mac has plenty of RAM, disk space, and, of course, the necessary software.

HOT TIP

Clip Art for 3-D   (SF)

If you want to create really cool 3-D scenes, but don't have hundreds of hours to spend creating detailed models, three companies may have just the thing you're looking for. ViewPoint DataLabs International and Acuris, Inc. have extensive libraries of 3-D objects in several popular formats for you to use in your own scene files. Zygote Media Group also offers 3-D objects for you to use in your scenes, but they differentiate themselves by specializing in the human form, and have some amazing business and recreational figures available. Many of these figures can be posed as desired, and they can even create custom figures to your specifications.

An example of the 3-D clip art available (3d-Active set from Plastic Thought, Inc.).

3-D Programs   (SF)

Every time Apple opens its doors, the power of the high-end Macintoshes goes up, while the price comes down. With more and more companies and individuals getting their hands on fast, robust Macs, the popularity of 3-D modeling and animation programs is steadily increasing, which means that more and more of these programs are finding their way onto store shelves every day.

At the entry-level end of the spectrum, **Ray Dream Designer** ($200, Ray Dream) reigns supreme. A full-featured and intuitive program, Ray Dream Designer lets you create 3-D scenes quickly and easily through a combination of a friendly user interface and features such as the Modeling Wizard, which guides novices through the process of creating sophisticated objects.

If you want to check out a couple of bargain programs of more limited scope, **LogoMotion** ($200, Specular International) is great for creating 3-D animations with type and logos, and **Fractal Design Poser** ($200, Fractal Design) lets you create reference models of the human form quickly and easily.

The mid-range of 3-D modeling is dominated by **Infini-D** ($900, Specular International), **Extreme 3-D** ($700, Macromedia), **Vision 3-D** ($700, Strata), and **Ray Dream Studio** ($500, Ray Dream). Infini-D, Extreme 3-D, and Vision 3-D are all excellent choices for professional designers and animators who need sophisticated 3-D modeling, rendering, and animation all in one package. Extreme 3-D and Infini-D have more intuitive interfaces (and slightly better animation), and Vision 3-D is the better modeler and renderer. Ray Dream Studio is basically Ray Dream Designer bundled with Ray Dream Animator, adding animation capabilities to Ray Dream's excellent modeling program.

At the high end of the spectrum, Vision 3-D's big brother, **Strata Studio Pro** ($1,500, Strata) is hard to beat. It has even better modeling and rendering capabilities than Vision 3-D, plus an excellent animation interface and impressive natural-media rendering and animation special effects. **Presenter Professional** ($2,000, Visual Information Development) has excellent modeling, sculpting, and rendering capabilities, plus excellent sound effect capabilities and support for Pixar's RenderMan.

The Bryce Breakthrough   (SF)

One 3-D modeling program that I must mention is a little gem from MetaTools, called **KPT Bryce** ($200). Originally designed as a simple, easy-to-use program for creating photorealistic landscapes, Bryce has achieved a large, very enthusiastic following for two reasons: First, it *really is* easy to use (a 12-year-old can easily create his or her own landscapes in 5 to 10 minutes); and second, the final images are astonishingly good. Bryce simply has one of the best rendering engines in the business.

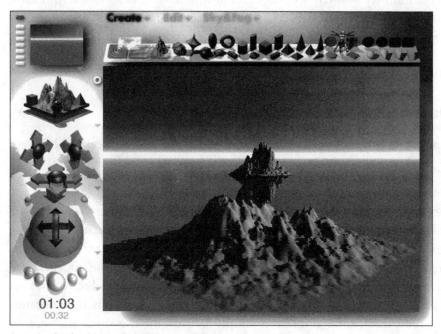

Bryce 2 takes landscape rendering to a new level.

Professionals and novices alike have bent Bryce to their own ends to create advertisements, logo treatments, movie backdrops, and more, simply because the final image quality is so good. By the time you read this, **Bryce 2** ($250) should be on the shelves, and it promises to make gorgeous, professional-caliber landscapes (and much more) more accessible than ever before.

CAD Programs   (SF)

CAD (computer-aided design) software fills a special niche not adequately covered by traditional 2-D drawing or 3-D modeling software. Used primarily by engineers, architects, and designers, CAD software provides levels of detail and precision not possible with other software (with the unfortunate trade-off that CAD software is generally harder to learn and more complex to use). CAD software comes in both 2-D and 3-D varieties, with 2-D CAD programs used primarily for blueprints and technical diagrams, and 3-D CAD programs used for producing complex architectural and industrial designs and models for manufacturing.

Some good 2-D CAD programs include **Blueprint** ($300, Graphisoft) and **MacDraft** ($450, Innovative Data Design). Blueprint is the bargain, but MacDraft is easier to use. **PowerDraw** ($800, Engineered Software) is expensive and frustrating to use, but is extremely flexible and has a wide variety of plug-in tools.

AutoCAD is the industry standard in 3-D CAD programs, but, unfortunately, release 12 ($3,750, Autodesk) is dated and no future Macintosh versions are planned. **MiniCAD** ($795, Graphisoft) matches AutoCAD practically feature-for-feature, is relatively inexpensive, and will probably be around on the Mac platform for some time to come. **Vellum** ($1,500, Ashlar) is another good choice for 3-D CAD work.

Animation Software   (SF)

Traditional animation (Disney, Warner Bros., and so on) has always been frame-based, wherein individual frames are drawn on clear *cels* (sheets of transparent celluloid), overlaid onto a background, and then photographed frame by frame.

Animation on the Mac is both easier and more complex than traditional methods. Easier, because you don't have to draw every single frame of your animation. In most cases, you can simply create *keyframes* at important points in your animation, and your animation software will use a process called *tweening* to create the intermediate frames. (Tweening refers to creating the "in-between" frames to produce a smooth transition between keyframes.) On the other hand, digital animation is sometimes more difficult than traditional animation simply because of the sheer number of parameters that you can control. Digital animation offers multiple light sources, sophisticated motion paths, motion blurs, and other techniques which would be impossible to replicate using traditional methods.

Your finished animation files are generally saved in either PICS or QuickTime format. PICS has traditionally been the industry standard format, but QuickTime is rapidly overtaking it due to its widespread support, cross-platform capabilities, and ability to always play back animations at the correct speed (even on slower computers).

If you go to your local computer software store and look for an Animation section, you probably won't find one. That's because most animation is done within 3-D modeling, video editing, or presentation software.

Most of the 3-D modeling programs discussed earlier also provide excellent animation capabilities. If animation is the most important part of your 3-D modeling work, Ray Dream Studio, Infini-D, and Strata Studio Pro are probably your best bets.

Video editing software such as Adobe After Effects or Adobe Premiere (see Chapter 17) have limited animation capabilities. In general, you can create animated special effects, but cannot create free-form, frame-based animations.

Macromedia Director ($1,200, Macromedia) is *the* program for professionals who need to create either stand-alone animated presentations or animation clips to be used in a video-editing program. With the new Netscape plug-in, **Shockwave for Director,**

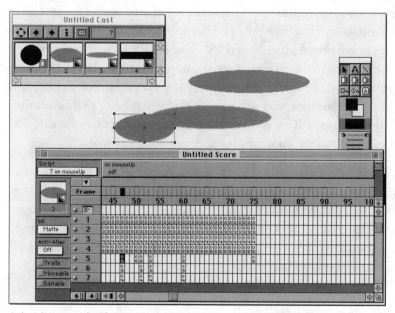

Animation created with Director isn't always easy as the myriad of windows shows, but the results can be incredible.

Director animations can now be viewed on the World Wide Web. **ADDMotion II** ($50, Motion Tool Works) is a great little program for creating HyperCard-based animations, and **Animation Works** ($200, Gold Disk), **Cinemation** ($300, Vividus), and **PROmotion** ($200, Motion Tool Works) are good entry-level animation programs.

Miscellaneous Graphics Programs   (SF)

In addition to painting, drawing, illustration, 3-D modeling, and animation software, there are a few miscellaneous software packages that bear mentioning. They are clip art and photographic image collections, and dedicated charting and graphing software.

Clip Art and Photo Samplers

Even if you have no artistic ability whatsoever, you can still add stunning visuals to your newsletters, proposals, and multimedia presentations with clip art and photos available in a wide variety of themes and formats.

Clip art. It is probably safe to say that there are more clip art images on the market than there are words in this book. Clip art is ready-made art that you can use in your own art pieces. With that kind of volume, it would be impossible to adequately cover even a small segment of them in these pages. (But I'll try.) First of all, you need to decide on the file format and resolution that you need. Most clip art comes in either TIFF, PICT, or EPS format, and in either 72- or 300-dpi resolution. TIFF format is used for scanned photos and painted images, and PICT and EPS formats are used for object-oriented graphics created in drawing or illustration programs. If your clip art is for an on-screen presentation, 72 dpi (the resolution of your computer screen) will look okay, but for most printed output, you will want 300-dpi art. Note that resolution is only an issue with TIFF images. PICT and EPS images are resolution-independent, and will print at the best quality that your printer is capable of producing.

Probably the largest selection of quality commercial clip art is in the **ClickArt** collections ($20 to $70, T/Maker), although there are many other quality packages available. (3G Graphics and Image Club also offer a wide variety of quality images at reasonable prices.) Clip art can also be obtained through on-line services, user groups, and educational sources, although the quality of most of these images is well below what you'll find in the commercial packages.

Clip Art Sampler

ARRO International
Series: ARROglyphs
Packages: Environment (left), $150;
   Wildlife (right), $70
Formats: EPS, TIFF, PICT

3G Graphics
Series: Images With Impact
Packages: Places & Faces (left), Accents & Borders 2
   (right), $54 each; 7-volume series $200 on
   CD-ROM
Formats: EPS, PICT

Creative Media Services
Package: Megatoons Part II, $100
Formats: TIFF

C.A.R.
Series: Master IBM/Mac Master CD
Package: Master CD, $190
Formats: PICT

Dream Maker Software
Series: Cliptures; MacGallery
Packages: MacGallery V: Holidays and
   Special Occasions (left), $50;
   Cliptures 4: World Flags (right), $100
Formats: PPI (MacGallery), EPS (Cliptures)

DS Design
Series: KidBAG
Package: Art by Kids, $80
Formats: EPS, TIFF

Clip Art Sampler (continued)

Image Club Graphics
Series: DigitArt
Packages: Sports & Leisure, $50;
   36-volume series $800 on CD-ROM
Formats: EPS

Metro Creative Graphics
Packages: Metro ImageBase on CD (left), $150;
   Metro Food CD (right), $40
Formats: TIFF

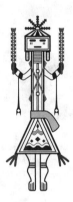

PhotoDisc
Series: PhotoDisc
Packages: Retro Americana (left),
   Business and Industry (right), $300 each
Formats: TIFF, JPEG

RT Computer Graphics
Package: Santa Fe Collection, $80
Formats: EPS

Totem Graphics
Series: Totem Color Clip Art
Packages: Fish (left), Domestic Animals (right), $40
   each; 18-volume series $500 on CD-ROM
Formats: EPS

T/Maker Company
Series: ClickArt
Packages: Beastly Funnies (left), $20; Studio: Business
   Art (right), $40
Formats: EPS

Some of the high-quality images available through KPT PowerPhotos.

Photo samplers. As CD-ROM drives become standard on more and more computers, CDs full of photographic images are becoming more widespread and economical. A single photo CD can contain hundreds of gorgeous, full-color photos at a very affordable price. These images can then be used in page layout programs, image editors, or even most word processors.

Digital Stock Corporation, PhotoDisc, and MetaTools offer very good packages of high-quality photos in the $150 to $300 range. These images are professionally shot specifically for image compositing (as opposed to many CDs which contain only stock photos which have no relationship to one another, and may or may not composite well together). The **PowerPhotos** ($200, MetaTools) series is especially nice, as all photos have the same perspective and lighting, and many include built-in alpha channels and opacity masks, allowing you to seamlessly composite them with each other or even with other images.

Graphing Software

There was a time when you could slap a simple pie chart and a couple of line graphs into a business presentation and wow a client with your "artwork." Those days are, thankfully, long past, and today's sophisticated clients require equally sophisticated charts and flawless, full-color output. While any spreadsheet program worth its columns and rows will give you a variety of chart and graph types, dedicated graphing software packages, with their depth, flexibility, and custom formatting capabilities, may give you the edge you need the next time you venture into a conference room. **DeltaGraph Pro** ($200, DeltaPoint) is the undisputed leader when it comes to sheer variety and flexibility, and produces great-looking charts. **CA-Cricket Graph III** ($130, Computer Associates) is also a solid program. While lacking some of the variety and sophistication of DeltaGraph Pro, CA-Cricket Graph III is easier to use and gives you quality output. For the ultimate in high-level graphing capabilities, **KaleidaGraph** ($250, Synergy Software) is perfect for scientists, engineers, or anyone else who needs visual representations of complex data sets.

16 Page Layout

Building a document is a lot like erecting a building. You start with a design and materials (plasterboard, flooring, and other materials for buildings—text, photos and other artwork for documents), wield the appropriate set of tools, and end up with a useful product. For page layout the tools you use to assemble and control text and graphics and print out the result are the functions in desktop publishing programs.

Word processing programs ease the once tedious process of typing, editing, and correcting text (and may support some graphics as well). Graphics programs enable you to create and modify pictures (and may also include limited text tools). Page layout programs are what you use to control all the elements of a document—text, graphics, and color.

Because page layout programs have been designed to meet the requirements of graphic designers, publishers, and commercial printers—including the ability to make fine typographic adjustments and create color separations for offset printing—they also work well for any other sort of publishing task you may have. In this chapter, we'll talk about how to choose a page layout application that suits your needs.

Contributors

Kathleen Tinkel (KT) is the chapter editor.

Richard Becker (RB) has been a graphic designer long enough to remember lead type and rubber cement.

Phil Gaskill (PG) is a New York-based book typesetter and nationally recognized typographic expert. He was a technical writer for Aldus Corporation in Seattle, was co-author of *QuarkXPress Tips and Tricks,* second edition (Peachpit Press), and was technical editor of *Real World PageMaker 5* (Peachpit Press).

Moe Rubenzahl (MR) is a Mac-head. If this has helped you get on the World Wide Web, tell me about it! Send your URL to me at <MRubenzahl@ videonics.com>. I'd love to see what you created!

Elyse Chapman (EC), Anne-Marie Concepcion (AC), Richard Pfeiffer (RP), Ray Robertson (RR), and **JB Whitwell (JW)** and other members of the Desktop Publishing Forum on CompuServe.

David Blatner (DB), Steve Roth (SR), and **Randy Anderson (RA)** contributed to earlier versions of *The Macintosh Bible* from which parts of this chapter were taken.

Contents

Page Layout and Desktop Publishing (KT)

Desktop publishing—the process of laying out pages of *WYSIWYG* (what-you-see-is-what-you-get) text and graphics on a personal computer—was born when three key developments came together with the year-old Macintosh computer: (1) Adobe Systems put its PostScript page description language in processors (*RIPs*) that could be used to print computer files to any sort of printing device; (2) Apple adopted Adobe's technology for its first 300-dpi laser printer and the major typesetting equipment manufacturerer, Linotype, used it in its first high-resolution imagesetter; and (3) Aldus Corporation introduced PageMaker, the first popular page layout program.

This potent combination sparked a revolution in the way words and pictures were prepared for printing—a revolution that rivals Gutenberg's invention of movable type in its economic and social impact. After 1985, any computer user could create usable camera-ready art without buying a lot of extra supplies and equipment, and without necessarily learning a bunch of specialized skills or being able to draw a straight line.

Thanks to desktop publishing, any computer user who has an idea and a design for a publication of any size or type can construct a document on screen and print it out on a laser printer or imagesetter to create camera-ready pages ready for printing. No more cutting up strips of type, no more messing with wax or rubber cement,

The Toolbox holds tools for selecting text and other elements, for drawing rules, rectangles, and circles, for cropping imported graphics, and for performing other tasks.

The Library palette lets you stash recurring elements, such as logos, that may be needed for several publications. This one has key word search capabilities built-in.

The Styles palette makes it easy to edit or apply typographic and paragraph styles to selected text.

You can place text, graphics, and rules (drawn lines) anywhere on each page.

The Scripts, Master Pages, and Colors palettes.

Page layout programs such as PageMaker 6 provide tools for placing and manipulating text and graphics on a page.

The Layout Process in a Nutshell   (KT)

Judging by the frequent questions we receive on the DTP Forum on CompuServe, it appears that many beginners are uncertain about what the layout process involves. Here are the basic steps:

1. Prepare text for typesetting. Delete extra spaces between sentences, words, and lines; replace typewriter marks with typographic (curly) quotes and apostrophes, double-hyphens with em-dashes, fi and fl combinations with ligatures; and so on. You can also apply style sheets here (or wait to do it in the layout). The easiest way to accomplish text preparation is to use special utilities (such as Overwood, Add/Strip, or Torquemada the Inquisitor) but you can also make repeated search-and-replace runs manually with a text editor or word processor.

2. Prepare graphics for placing in the file. Scan in or create electronic illustrations; edit (crop, rotate, colorize) clip art; and correct color and sharpen scans, saving the graphics in formats compatible with the layout program—usually as TIFF or EPS files.

3. Set up the document in your page layout program. Take specs from the design (page size, margins, allowances for bleeds, fold lines); establish defaults for the document (adjust settings for text, paragraphs, graphics, and other details); create basic text styles unless you plan to import style sheet information with the text files.

4. Place text in the document. If you didn't apply styles in the text cleanup process, do so now. Flow it onto the pages, and check the pages.

5. Place the graphics. Add captions; set text to run around graphics; and adjust graphic or text as needed.

6. Check the pages to make sure everything is in place, and print a proof copy.

7. Proofread and make corrections to the layout.

8. Tweak the type to finish the typesetting, and to adjust awkward text—widows, bad word breaks, poor spacing (too much space between words, usually), and any other visible problems. Then print another proof.

9. Proofread and correct, possibly printing out another proof to check again for final approval.

10. Make any final corrections and print proofs of any pages affected by changes.

11. Set file for output (checking any resolution- or device-dependent settings, turning on crop marks, and making any other adjustments that may be necessary).

12. If you're sending the file to a remote service for output, prepare a cover sheet listing all fonts used (typeface name, brand, and version if known), assemble all graphics, specify output resolution, line frequency for halftones and screened areas, request RC paper or film, indicate whether color is to be separated, and provide any other information required for output.

13. Mark up a life-size rough dummy for the printer to show bleeds, color breaks, and other details if there are any ambiguities in the job.

and no more razor blades or T-squares. The tools for professional-level publishing are no longer locked away in type and trade shops staffed by specialists. They're right in your Mac, ready to be wielded by any designer, editor, or other user who cares to learn how to design pages and use desktop publishing software.

Choosing the Right Program (KT/DB)

Appropriate tools make most kinds of work easier—and page layout is no exception. The first programs most people think of when they hear "desktop publishing" are Adobe PageMaker and QuarkXPress. They're the standards of the publishing industry and primary competitors. However, there are plenty of reasons for considering Ready,Set,Go! which, while inexpensive, was designed to compete with the big guys, and still retains functions that make it an ideal choice for some desktop publishers. Or you might consider Adobe FrameMaker, with its powerful tools for producing structured documents.

You may not want to stick with the tried-and-true programs, either. If you like to experiment with new software you may want to consider Viva Press Professional—it opens XPress files and has a similar approach to page layout, but it offers some new functions and enhances others. If you have an interest in Apple's QuickDraw GX (see the sidebar, "Page Layout with QuickDraw GX," later in this chapter)—particularly the fonts and text composition functions—you should look at the only two page layout programs so far to embrace the new technology: UniQorn (from SoftPress Systems); and Ready,Set,Go! GX. We'll discuss all these programs in the next section.

You don't need an all-purpose powerhouse of a program if you only occasionally need to produce a few simple documents—it may make sense for you to choose one of the easy-to-use (and less expensive) packages—Adobe Home Publisher or Brøderbund's Print Shop, for example. Or perhaps you can get the job done with software you already have—a word processor, an integrated "works" package, or a drawing program.

These page layout programs are meant to create documents designed for print. If you're mainly interested in laying out Web pages, see "Layout for the Web," later in this chapter; if you're trying to pull together elements for on-screen presentation, look in Chapter 17.

Versatile Workhorses: PageMaker, XPress, and Ready,Set,Go! (KT/DB/SR)

Page layout programs have been playing leapfrog for a decade, with each set of feature upgrades allowing one program to push ahead of its competitors for a time. The serious action is between **PageMaker 6.01** ($895, Adobe) and **QuarkXPress 3.32r3** ($995, Quark). But **Ready,Set,Go! 7.02** ($395, Manhattan Graphics; formerly marketed by Letraset USA as DesignStudio) isn't far behind, and its much lower price makes it an excellent value.

If these programs were cars, XPress would be an Italian sports car, offering performance and style but perhaps exhibiting a few quirks at times; PageMaker would be a German sports sedan, reliable and comfortable but still fun to drive; and RSG a sports utility vehicle, a bit homely, maybe, but with solid performance and no pretensions to high style. You wouldn't compromise on essentials by buying any of these types of vehicle—and you won't have to sacrifice essential functions with these layout programs, either. In the end, all three will do the job: All enable you to mix text, graphics, and drawn rules or boxes in complex documents, and all offer tools for sophisticated typography, graphics, color, and output that can meet the most exacting commercial standards. So all three are considered together here.

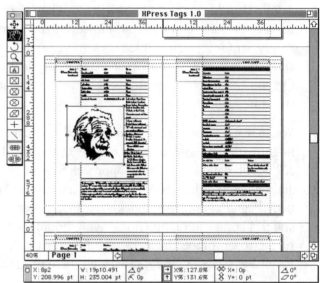

In QuarkXPress, you first create a text or picture box, either on the page or on the pasteboard area surrounding each page. You can then modify the boxes and import text and graphics into them.

Points of Distinction

It would take a book just to outline the major features of these programs, so we won't try to describe them in great detail. They don't differ all that much functionally and all are capable of producing a wide range of layout work. Many users seem to base their choice on what they're used to—whether the way the program works feels familiar or alien. Occasional specialties may require a particular add-on module that runs with only one of these programs—such as the Quark Publishing System XTension that makes XPress into a newspaper production system (see the sidebar, "Using Add-on Modules to Customize Your Layout Program" later in this chapter). Or you may find that the approach the software takes in accomplishing layout tasks is what makes the difference to you. We'll attempt to describe significant differences here.

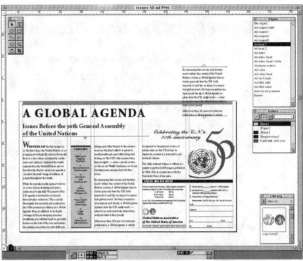

In PageMaker, you can place any object (graphic or block of text) on the pasteboard—there's no need to draw a box first.

General approach. XPress and RSG are based on frames—first you draw a box, then you fill it with text or a graphic. PageMaker is free-form—you can place any element anywhere. Frames can be convenient—you don't have to draw a separate box if you want to print a rule around or add a color panel behind text or graphics. On the other hand, if you don't need to do anything to the text, creating frames is an extra step and managing links between text boxes in RSG and XPress takes a bit more effort than PageMaker's approach.

Master pages. A *master page* is a sort of a template that lets you keep even a very large document consistent without a lot of repetitive work. You can set up master pages for different kinds of pages—chapter openers, regular pages, covers, or reference sections, for example. XPress supports up to 127 master spreads per document, PageMaker as many master pages and/or spreads as available memory will allow, and RSG 52 (26 each for right- and left-hand pages). All elements in RSG and PageMaker master pages are fixed on the document pages. In XPress, you can move, delete, or otherwise edit master page elements in document pages.

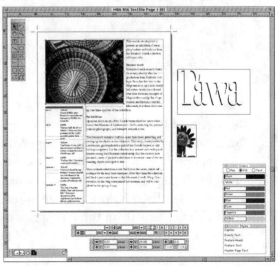

In Ready,Set,Go! 7, you must place all elements in predrawn boxes, but you also have free access to a document-wide pasteboard (upper right).

Guidelines for Non-Designers   (RB/KT)

Computers equipped with desktop publishing software can produce perfectly straight lines at your command and they never get the type cockeyed (unless you want it that way). But one thing hasn't been computerized in the rush to desktop publishing—graphic design. So far it still takes a human being to decide how a book, brochure, magazine, or newsletter should look—where (and how) those perfect lines and words should appear. That human being is the designer—and it may well be you.

Buying a page layout program doesn't magically turn you into a graphic designer. But basic design isn't rocket science, either—applying commonsense principles should enable you to produce decent-looking pages and documents that communicate clearly. Here are some specific guidelines:

- *Plan first.* Sketch your layout—or make a little dummy with all the elements shown diagramatically—before you sit down at the computer. It's easier to guide the logic of the piece when you're not lost in detail on the computer.

- *Question the status quo.* Rethink the form your document should take: Would it work best in a booklet? A multipanel folded brochure? A simple flyer? A series of postcards?

- *Work in spreads.* Lay out all the pages or panels that your reader will see together as a single visual unit—that's how your readers will see them.

- *Keep type in the family.* Limit yourself to just one or two typefaces for text, captions, headlines, and so on, and consider taking all from a single type family (using plain roman for text, bold-italic for captions, and perhaps extra bold for the title or major headlines, for example). Although you can pair a bold sans serif face for heads with a serif text face, there's no rule that says you have to—keeping all the type in a single family often works better. (See Chapter 14 for more information on using type.)

- *Be consistent.* Use style sheets to make sure that details such as captions, heads and subheads, and other bits of text are always

Page views. XPress shows as many pages as will fit in the window—you can scroll from spread to spread, and a spread can have more than two pages. PageMaker and RSG can show only a single page or spread at once. The *pasteboard* (an area you can use to temporarily store elements you haven't placed yet) in RSG and PageMaker is common to all pages, so you can park elements from one page that will later be dragged onto another. Each XPress page or spread has its own pasteboard. You can view pages in thumbnail view in all three programs, and print a page of thumbnails, a useful way to record a schematic overview of a publication.

Grids, guides, and measurements. All three programs use nonprinting guides to help you lay out pages and position objects. Only RSG supports full grids (with active horizontal as well as vertical guides). Both XPress and PageMaker allow you to use arithmetic operators (+, −, /, and *) and mixed measurement systems (3p5+1cm,

handled the same way—same size and style, same distance from other text and pictures, and so on.

- *Line things up.* Use nonprinting guides on master pages to establish a grid-like pattern to help you place elements on pages.

- *Honor the rhythm of the page.* Watch out for page elements that almost (but don't quite) align, photos or other illustrative elements that are almost (but not quite) the same size or shape, and other disruptions to the rhythm of the page. Don't change line spacing (leading) to make things fit—it irritates readers and looks amateurish.

- *Be cautious with color.* A little color goes a long way. Remember that most colors are less contrasty than black and are likely to make an element seem recessive, not emphasized. Colored type is also usually harder to read than black.

- *Help the reader navigate.* Use a logical hierarchy of type size, degrees of boldness, and space around heads and subheads to help

the reader navigate through text. Yes, you have to get your reader's attention, but don't sacrifice a logical layout to visual shock tactics.

- *Add nothing without good reason.* Every element has to earn its way onto the page. Question the urge to draw a box around type or to put color behind it. Meaningless graphic emphasis undermines your work and misleads the reader.

- *Strive for the occasional surprise.* Spice things up by introducing a few elements of surprise—an outsized initial cap or a headline hung in an otherwise empty column, a very small (or very large) graphic element, and so on. But watch the overall visual balance of the spread.

- *If the design works, it works.* That's an old designer's maxim. Once you're confident about laying out pages, don't become a slave to the rules—in the end, it's all about choice.

for instance)—though PageMaker's feature is limited to the Control palette. Both XPress and PageMaker allow you to force text to align across columns or spreads. In PageMaker, a paragraph-level control lets you set objects or guides to snap to custom vertical ruler increments. In XPress, you can elect to snap objects to a baseline grid, and can define an elegant first line offset that controls where the first line of text will begin, but these are document settings.

Tool palettes. Both PageMaker and XPress have a Master palette that lets you have precise numerical control over most attributes—element size and position, text formatting, and so on. PageMaker's Control palette is even more flexible (you can control paragraph as well as character attributes, for example). PageMaker's palette also includes a useful proxy for indicating what part of a selected object will be acted on. All three programs also have floating palettes for controlling specific functions—stylesheets, color, and so on.

GOOD FEATURE

Using recurring elements. All three programs have a place to store recurring elements (such things as logos, standing heads, or a copyright notice) for use in multiple documents. PageMaker and XPress call this a *library*, RSG a *glossary* item. PageMaker's library allows searching by keyword, description, and author name, and you can import libraries from Adobe Fetch, an image-archiving program. The XPress library doesn't provide searching (you can only select by item names), but you can have multiple libraries open.

GOOD
FEATURE

Long documents. PageMaker has good book-oriented functions for automating assembly of multiple chapters or sections for output, including control of left- and right-hand pages and consecutive numbering. PageMaker also has excellent automatic TOC and indexing systems. For XPress you need a third-party extension to create indexes and tables of contents (but Quark has promised better support for long documents, including auto-indexing in XPress 4). RSG has no special support for long documents, and there is no way to generate an index or TOC automatically.

Tables. Neither XPress nor RSG has any specific function for creating tables—you must use tabs and style sheets to arrange tabular material manually. PageMaker 6 ships with an enhanced stand-alone Table utility that produces EPS files (the old one just made PICTs). It's a bit clunky, though better than nothing (and the tables can be imported into XPress or RSG documents as well as PageMaker's).

The fact remains: If you use many tables, you should probably be looking at FrameMaker, which revels in them (see "FrameMaker" later in this chapter).

Color issues. In the past, XPress was the tool of choice for color work, but with version 6 PageMaker has more than caught up. Its automatic trapping tool is more capable than the one in XPress (PageMaker does a better job of trapping elements that overlap more than one background color, for example). It also offers better color management—the program ships with the Kodak Precision *Color Management System* (*CMS*), but will support others as they become available. XPress 3.x includes the EfiColor CMS XTension from Electronics for Imaging (EFI), but EFI no longer produces color management software, so Quark will probably have to replace it in the next major upgrade. The Kodak CMS gives PageMaker a bonus—one of the best Photo CD acquisition tools on the desktop (most users will be able to place images directly from the CD-ROM, safely relying on the Kodak software for auto-sharpening and color correction). RSG falls down here—it has manual object-level trapping and no color management system.

GOOD
FEATURE

Text runarounds. All three programs can be set to run text around other page elements, though all have irritating limitations. PageMaker runs text around all sides, but only works with graphics (which can include text that has been grouped). Then, the

Color: The Final Frontier

(DB/Darcy DiNucci)

One of the most important differences between major page layout programs and simpler software is their ability to handle color for *offset printing* (printing on a printing press rather than on a desktop color printer). Here is a guide to some of the issues.

Color Separation

On a printing press, each color is printed separately. To create color for printing, a page lay-out program must be able to separate the colors onto separate pages for output. Those separations are usually printed to film, from which the different printing plates can be made.

Spot versus Process Color

How the colors are separated depends on whether they will be printed as *process color* or *spot color*. Spot color is printed with an ink of the specified color, in a single pass through the press, and is generally used when the document includes just one or two colors, for dec-oration. You typically choose spot colors out of a swatch book, such as a Pantone Matching System (PMS) book, and some page layout programs include on-line versions of the Pantone and other color matching system palettes for easy color specification.

With process color, all colors are created by printing the image with different tints of four col-ors: cyan, magenta, yellow, and black (CMYK). Process color is more economical to use when the piece includes more than four colors, and it is always used to print color photographs.

Trapping

When paper is flying through the printing press, it often gets misregistered, and each color isn't printed exactly where it should be. This can cause gaps at the edges between colors where the white paper shows through. *Trapping* is the process of slightly overlapping colors at their edges so no gap will show when misregistration occurs. This is an area that even the best page layout programs haven't really mastered yet (and they may never do so). Even though several of the programs discussed here let you trap type and graphics created within the program (none of them can trap elements of an imported graphic), the best solution is often to have specialists at the service bureau that outputs the job take care of the trapping for you.

runaround window is rectangular—you have to create and resize irregular text wraps manually, which can be a frustrating process. Both XPress and RSG limit runarounds to one side of an element but they work with text boxes as well as graphics. You can modify the *standoff* (gutter) in XPress and PageMaker but not in RSG. XPress can be set to follow either the box or the irregular shape of a graphic.

GOOD FEATURE

Cropping imported graphics. All three programs support *cropping* of imported graphics. Both XPress and RSG allow you to crop graphics to a variety of shapes. Imported graphics in PageMaker are always square or rectangular, although you can sometimes use PageMaker's masking function to simulate irregular cropping.

Flowing elements with text. XPress's anchoring function allows you to attach graphic or text boxes so they stay connected to a specified bit of text. You can set the anchored boxes to align on the baseline or cap height of the main text. This is a powerful tool that neither of the other programs has. PageMaker does support inline graphics, a more limited approach.

Typographic defaults. All three programs can produce commercial-quality type but PageMaker's defaults give it the edge right out of the box. You should adjust typographic defaults before creating new documents in any of these programs. XPress ships with the optimum word space set to 110 percent—which has the effect of enlarging word spaces no matter how carefully a font was designed, and tends to create loose spacing in both ragged and justified text. RSG ships with only standard specs for justification and ragged typesetting; but even the professional specs only give you control of minimum and maximum settings so you cannot directly modify the word space in any font.

XPress also defaults to a spacing standard that is not shared by other typographic software; you can make fonts set the same in XPress as in other applications by clicking on the Standard em space in the typographic specifications dialog. As it ships, RSG will not auto-kern any type smaller than 12-point; you can change this threshold to 4 points (thus ensuring that all readable type will be kerned), which is the default setting in both PageMaker and XPress.

Tracking. All three programs support *tracking* for global control of type spacing and all include editable tracks. XPress uses a single editable track per font, and it applies to the entire document. Because of that, hardly anyone ever uses it, preferring instead to adjust spacing by "range-kerning" of selected text at the paragraph level. PageMaker and RSG 7 have editable paragraph-level tracks (five for PageMaker, three for RSG).

Drop caps. XPress has automatic *drop caps*; but you cannot adjust them or contour text around the cap, so many users prefer to use the anchored text function instead. PageMaker's drop caps are accomplished somewhat awkwardly through a plug-in (see the sidebar, "Using Add-On Modules to Customize Your Layout Program" later in this chapter), but you can contour text around the large character. PageMaker's drop cap has other problems: Hyphens disappear at the ends of lines, and editing the paragraph messes up line breaks. RSG has semi-automatic, noncontourable drop caps.

Creating PDFs and HTML files. This is one of the places where RSG and XPress show their age—they make no reference to Adobe Acrobat "portable document files" (PDFs—see Chapter 14 and Chapter 25 for more information on Acrobat) or

HTML for Web pages (Chapter 23). Quark has released Immedia—it's an XTension for creating Web and multimedia pages with XPress. PageMaker 6 ships with plug-ins for automating creation of both PDFs and Web pages. The PDF tool is useful because it simplifies the required print-to-disk process. The HTML Author plug-in is limited—but useful if you're trying to "repurpose" a PageMaker document for use on the Web.

Automation. All three programs support functions that aid automation of page layout—*templates*, *scripting*, and *tagging*.

- *Templates.* PageMaker's templates are ingenious little scripts that create publications (including style sheets) based on dialog box selections (page size, label template, and so on). Surprisingly, XPress's few in-the-box templates are for special purposes and lack style sheets (preset text formats), so they aren't of much use. RSG supports RSG Stationery.

- *Scripting.* All three programs are scriptable—that is, all or a useful portion of their functions can be automated by a small program written in a *scripting language*. XPress supports AppleScript only; RSG and PageMaker have their own scripting languages (or you can use a limited subset of AppleScript commands with PageMaker). For real hackers, AppleScript is much more powerful, but PageMaker scripts—accessible through an optional palette—are easier to write and use. The CD-ROM edition of PageMaker 6 includes a useful on-line scripting manual; scripting in RSG and XPress is documented minimally in their manuals.

- *Tagging.* All three programs support tags (codes that convey formatting information). XPress and PageMaker tags can encode character formatting; RSG tags are the simplest (style sheet tags only). PageMaker can read XPress tags directly, which allows PageMaker users to take advantage of a collection of shareware tools—including Mark My Words, XP8, and Torquemada the Inquisitor—designed by programmer Greg Swann to automate tagging in XPress. (These utilities are available from on-line libraries.)

Support. PageMaker and XPress both provide some period of telephone support when you first buy their products. During this interval the support is "free" but you pay for the call; and Adobe also offers telephone support after every major upgrade; Quark does not. After this, both companies offer complicated pay-as-you go and/or prepaid support plans. RSG's telephone support can be summarized very simply: It's always free, but you pay for the call.

Both Quark and Adobe are trying to move as much support as possible to on-line facilities: Both have Web pages as well as forums on CompuServe and America Online (see Chapter 22 for more on on-line services). On-line users get first crack at small updates (which can be downloaded), get answers within 24 hours during the week from on-line tech support personnel (and often get even faster answers at any time from other users of the on-line services).

PageMaker users receive *Adobe Magazine* for free as soon as you register your copy of PageMaker. Quark sends XPress owners the *XPressions* newsletter only if you pony up for extended support, but an independent publisher sends *X-Ray* magazine to all registered XPress users.

Using Add-On Modules to Customize Your Layout Program   (KT/DB/SR)

You can add functionality to XPress and PageMaker—to compensate for temporary deficiencies in the core features of the software, adapt the programs for specialized tasks, or expedite some layout processes—through *plug-in modules*. These are called *plug-ins* in PageMaker, *XTensions* (or *XTs*) in XPress. (RSG supports add-ons called *Annexes,* but the only ones available ship with the software and are fairly limited in use.)

Some add-ons are free, though most cost between $20 and $300. These include small utilities that accomplish one particular task efficiently, such as the CursorPos XT (Kytek, Inc.) that monitors the position of the cursor at all times, as well as more complex utilities such as QX Tools for XPress and PageTools for PageMaker (both from Extensis Corp.) that reorganize the XPress and PageMaker user interfaces and simplify access to most commands. Some high-end add-ons—such as the Quark Publishing System XT that turns XPress into a workgroup newspaper pagination system, or the ad-layout utilities for both programs from Managing Editor Software and Integrated Software—cost more than the programs themselves.

Some XTensions fundamentally change XPress's feature set (for instance, SXetchPad, which adds full drawing tools—including Bézier curves and putting text on a curve). By comparison, many of PageMaker's plug-ins resemble sophisticated macros with dialog boxes.

This discrepancy was more true of PageMaker's tentative early forays into add-ons (when they were called Additions) than it is now. Quark pioneered add-on technology and XPress has been extensible almost from the start. However, since Adobe's acquisition of Aldus in 1994, PageMaker's plug-in architecture is being changed to make it compatible with Photoshop, Illustrator, Acrobat, and other Adobe products, thus giving all the Adobe programs a common set of add-ons. It remains to be seen how far Adobe will go with this approach. In the meantime, add-ons help many users accomplish page layout more effectively.

Making Your Decision

There's no doubt about it: You can produce consummately professional publications of almost any type with any of these three programs—PageMaker, XPress, or Ready,Set,Go!

In the end, you'll probably base your decision on personal factors. PageMaker is a bit more flexible, and it's the right tool for book production (assuming you don't need FrameMaker, described later in this chapter). On the other hand, XPress is better understood at service bureaus and benefits from a wide array of available add-on tools. And RSG is a terrific value, giving you much of the power and dexterity of PageMaker and XPress at a much lower cost.

Intriguing Newcomers (KT)

Introducing new high-end page layout software takes courage at this stage of the game. Most publishers at every level have already invested cash, training, and time in a program (and probably have existing files to deal with, as a further disincentive to change).

Still, today's popular programs are not perfect and leave room for newcomers. Some problems are holdovers—even after all this time, none of the popular programs provides for the kind of typographic control taken for granted before desktop publishing wiped out the typesetting industry. And today's programs aren't too helpful in helping designers "repurpose" documents (convert them from conventional print jobs for distribution on-line or as Web pages). We also face new publishing technologies that didn't exist when PageMaker, XPress, and RSG were being developed, including these:

- *Stochastic screening.* Photos and other continuous-tone art must be converted to a halftone dot pattern for printing. Traditional halftones use an orderly pattern of rows of dots, but it's easier for computers to produce a frequency-modulated (randomized) pattern of halftone dots. This still experimental process can also produce higher visual quality from smaller files, especially when combined with high-fidelity color.

- *High-fidelity color.* Stochastic screening is sometimes combined with hi-fi color—the use of more than the traditional four process colors, in other words. So far, only PageMaker supports hi-fi color explicitly, through Pantone's Hexachrome color library.

- *Non-offset printing processes.* For the past 50 years most commercial printing has been done by photo-offset, but other techniques are starting to grow in popularity.

Page Layout with QuickDraw GX   (KT)

Apple's QuickDraw GX brings several gee-whiz features to users of System 7 (7.1 or later). This set of system extensions affects five areas: graphics, type and typography, printing, color management, and document portability, any of which can affect page layout functions, but the typographic features of GX have really captured the liveliest interest among desktop publishers.

Apple calls GX fonts "smart fonts" because they can automatically produce high-end typographic effects—glyph substitution (for ligatures, for example), hung punctuation, stylistic variations (beyond italics and bold), vertical fractions, swashes (beginning/end of line or beginning/end of word), and optical alignment—that are difficult (or nearly impossible) with conventional fonts, applications, and operating systems. And a single GX font can have a huge character set (more than 16,000 characters compared to the 256 of a standard Mac font).

Unfortunately, to take advantage of these stunning features you need not only QuickDraw GX and GX fonts but DTP applications that exploit them. So far, none of the industry stalwarts—PageMaker, XPress, Illustrator, FreeHand, or Photoshop—is compatible with GX. Because Apple has announced its intention to build GX permanently into System 8 (code-named Copland), we would expect to see functional compatibility, if not full-fledged support in the 1997 rounds of software upgrades.

Note: In System 7 you have to add the GX extensions manually—they're not installed automatically when you update your system.

Meanwhile, Ready,Set,Go! GX and UniQorn (a new program from England) take advantage of some of the GX features (both require GX to launch, in fact). You can experiment with GX today—all you need is one of these programs, a way to switch from standard to GX operations (to avoid problems with incompatible applications), and some GX fonts. In addition to the fonts Apple shipped with System 7.5, several companies—including ITC, Bitstream, Galapagos, and Linotype-Hell—have released collections of GX fonts.

Today's page layout programs basically assume all work will be reproduced by offset printing.

- *New system-level printing tools.* Apple's QuickDraw GX (see "Page Layout with QuickDraw GX") includes its own printing architecture as well as built-in high-end font and graphic capabilities. So far, mainstream page layout and graphic programs continue to rely on PostScript for image and output control. But there is at least a possibility that things might change, particularly if Apple and Microsoft were to collaborate on a single standard. And hope beats eternal in some developers' breasts.

Such changing circumstances as these combine to place new burdens on old page layout programs (and on their users), and open the door a crack so new competitors can enter the market. Enter Viva Press Professional, and two programs based on QuickDraw GX: UniQorn and Ready,Set,Go! GX. It remains to be seen whether any of these will make much headway, but they're interesting enough to consider right now.

UniQorn (PG)

UniQorn ($895, SoftPress Systems), a brand-new QuickDraw GX-based page layout program (from England), is a very impressive-looking piece of software.

In UniQorn, the Font Extras palette makes it easy to experiment with GX fonts. This dialog box shows a fraction being created.

When you launch UniQorn, the first thing that strikes you is that it looks a lot like XPress. Even better news—for the most part (besides incorporating all the QuickDraw GX features), UniQorn combines the best features of XPress and PageMaker.

There are some new things about the interface, though. Perhaps the strangest is that there's only one kind of frame or box. It can hold either text or graphics, but you don't have to specify this at the time you draw the box. If you start typing, it decides it's a text box; if you click on the border of the box so that you see the handles, it becomes a picture box.

Many of UniQorn's menus, menu items, and keyboard shortcuts are the same as in XPress.

Here's a brief list of some of UniQorn's features I like especially:

- Full underline control (position and thickness) for up to three (!) underscores.

- A nice sizing/cropping feature for imported graphics.

- An extremely clever "flexible presentation" feature that lets objects retain their proper relative size and position when the page size is changed. This feature is supposed to be an aid to Web publishing, but of course could have a million other uses.

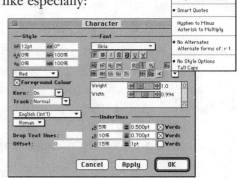

UniQorn has a logical and comprehensive Character Spec dialog, with all the controls in a single place.

- XPress-like multiple master pages—master items are editable on document pages.

- Compact and logical—even elegant—Character and Paragraph dialogs.

- Tracking—UniQorn has five PageMaker-like tracks (unlike PageMaker, however, these are uneditable).

- UniQorn's styles can control both character and paragraph attributes; it's an unusual implementation, but powerful once you get the hang of it.

- UniQorn exports tagged text—set by default to HTML for Web publishing, but alterable to other types of tags by the user.

- It also supports AppleScript. Even better—it's recordable (you can have it record your actions and build a script out of them).

BAD FEATURE

Shortcomings? It's a pretty short list, although one of them is a show-stopper: UniQorn doesn't support import of formatted text—only plain ASCII or text with Rich Text Formatting (RTF) tags. True, you can export text from most programs to RTF, but it's cumbersome and not foolproof. Other weaknesses: No vertical-alignment capability for text. And they very unfortunately adopted XPress's insane word- and letter-spacing defaults, the worst of which is the 110 percent desired word space.

Is UniQorn worth its $895 list price? If they'd fix the text import function, absolutely. I'd switch to it in a minute.

Ready, Set, Go! GX (PG)

The GX version of this venerable program fully supports GX fonts—it can only be run in a QuickDraw GX environment, in fact. Except for this, **Ready,Set,Go! GX** ($395) doesn't seem to differ much from the conventional version of the program (covered earlier in this chapter).

Don't get me wrong—GX compatibility is a major revision. First, it means that developer Manhattan Graphics had to rewrite all the code for the entire program. I'm impressed that this small company cared enough, and believed enough in GX, to make this kind of investment. Second, by supporting GX, RSG can take advantage of the dazzling features in GX fonts, including controls that let you trans-

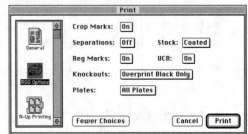

Because QuickDraw GX incorporates sophisticated printing controls, the Ready,Set,Go! GX Print dialog box is simple and easy to use.

form weight, width, and slant, and make use of typographic variations if they're available in the font. RSG will always be known as the first GX page-layout application, by a margin of more than a year. But if you're looking for dazzling new features besides the GX stuff, you'll likely be disappointed.

One change from the standard version of RSG disturbs my typographic sensibilities: They seem to have done away with word- and letter-spacing controls. This is enough to keep me from using the program for serious work. I hope they restore these controls soon.

A couple of especially nice things about RSG GX include: hyphenation controls that prevent breaking the last word of a paragraph; and PageMaker-like tracking—RSG GX has five tracks, just like PageMaker (except they're not editable). It also supports tagging (styles only).

And some random lackings include: no AppleScript dictionary, which means it's not scriptable; no "section" capability; and there's only one column per text block.

Is it worth the $395 list price? Probably. The best thing price-wise is that upgrades from previous versions are inexpensive (about $80; in fact, you can upgrade to RSG 7 and RSG GX from any older version for $80 each).

Viva Press Professional (KT)

If **Viva Press Professional** ($495) didn't seem so promising, I'd be inclined to ignore it, but it has some of the makings of strong competition for PageMaker and XPress (especially for the latter, which it much resembles). It does everything the other programs do—plus such innovative features as these:

- *Object guides*—any object can be a guide

- *Bézier curve drawing tools*, as if you had Illustrator or FreeHand built-in

- *Automatic indexes, TOCs, and tables;* and you can set up automated lists of pictures, abbreviations, and bibliographic references used in a document

- *The best typographic controls* of any WYSIWYG page layout program yet

- *XPress compatibility*—it can open XPress files (not convert them—open them, with all elements intact and editable)

In Viva Press Professional 2 you must draw frames before placing text or graphics objects, but (like UniQorn), there's a single frame-drawing tool—the contents determine what sort of box it is.

Unfortunately, Viva Press' US distributor InterPress seems to be having difficulty bringing this German product to market. The original version had a limited release in early 1995; version 2 should be out by the time you read this, having been delayed while the company defended itself against Quark's lawsuit over trade issues and possible copyright infringement. According to InterPress representatives, the lawsuit has been settled. The program still has room for improvement, but is surprisingly slick and capable. If it succeeds in reaching the marketplace, it might be a contender. (See the table, "Overview" for summary information on each page layout package.)

High-End Specialists

FrameMaker (KT/DB)

Standard page layout programs can produce most types of documents, but if you need to include lots of tabular material or footnotes, if you want to build cross-references into your file, or if you need files that flow seamlessly not just across from Mac to PC but possibly to Unix as well, you should probably consider **FrameMaker 5** ($895, Adobe), which was designed for just that sort of work.

You could use FrameMaker for short documents and brochures, but it's not really designed for that. It's set up for documents that have a fairly consistent layout from page to page. It can handle graphics and rules, but it doesn't have the typographic and graphics-oriented bells and whistles that PageMaker, XPress, or RSG have.

It really comes into its own for long documents such as technical manuals or in-house guides—jobs you might start out by producing in a word processing program (which is what FrameMaker most feels like). FrameMaker's built-in word processor has an excellent spelling checker, extensive find-and-replace features, automatic index and table of contents generation, footnotes, and so on. Many software companies—including Adobe—use FrameMaker to produce software manuals.

FrameMaker has the best table-handling of any program for the Mac, plus unique features such as automatic cross-referencing and conditional text (that is, insert if…, which lets you include or exclude certain text and different versions of a document). It's also got an impressive equation editor, for doing things such as math texts. Because FrameMaker is available on so many different platforms—including Windows—it's also great for large corporations that need to move documents around among Macs, PCs, and Unix-based systems. You can even use a Reader utility to read FrameMaker files over networks or on CD-ROMs.

Multi-Ad Creator (RA)

Multi-Ad Creator 3.8 ($650, Multi-Ad Services) is probably the best-kept secret in professional Macintosh publishing. While it's used by a zillion newspapers, magazines, and in-house ad departments, Multi-Ad's marketing is so bad that most people still don't know about this very cool program. Multi-Ad Creator is clearly designed to make ads, but you could make any one-page piece with it. Here are a few of my favorite features:

- *Importing graphics* is a snap, and you can easily make 1-bit TIFFs transparent or colorized.

- *Masking*—a Mask palette with FreeHand or Illustrator-like pen tools lets you easily auto-mask any imported image or trace areas in an image.

- *The Starburst tool* has no peer, even among drawing programs.

- *Powerful text handling*, especially the style sheets, go beyond—far beyond—anything you've ever seen, including not only character styles, but also algorithmic styles ("the first line of the paragraph should be in Helvetica, then change to Palatino; put a Zapf Dingbats bullet at the beginning of the paragraph," and so on).

- *Controlled export* of an entire ad (or just a portion of it) as an EPS or DCS (separated EPS) file for inclusion in a multipage layout program.

Trying to describe all of Multi-Ad Creator's features in one section like this is just plain cruel. If this is something that might make your life better, try a demo version (just write to Multi-Ad at the address in Appendix D).

Multi-Ad Creator can handle only single pages, but boy, can it handle those. It includes some of the best graphics and file-handling tools of any page layout program available.

Overview

Product	List	Distinguishing features
PageMaker 6.0	$895	Free-form layout program; good book-production tool (auto-indexing, TOC-generation, and book assembly function); excellent color tools (auto-trapping, color management, Photo CD).
XPress 3.32r2	$995	Well established in high-end agencies, design studios, and with output services. Many XTensions available for flexible off-the-shelf customization.
Ready,Set,Go! 7	$395	Supports layout grids; somewhat weak in typographic and color tools; excellent value for the price.
Ready,Set,Go! GX	$395	First page layout application to support QuickDraw GX (which is required).
UniQorn 1	$895	Has best features from both XPress and PageMaker plus QuickDraw GX (which is required).
Viva Press Pro 2	$495	Functions in most ways like XPress but with added functionality in both type and graphics. Opens XPress files.
FrameMaker 5	$895	Sold as a document-creation rather than page layout tool. Supports indexing, cross-references, tables, and other necessities for technical manuals.
Multi-Ad Creator 3.8	$650	One-page layout tool optimized for creation of ads and unparalleled in its ability to create starbursts and other spot illustrations.
Home Publisher 2.1	$ 49	Somewhat limited but easy-to-use page layout program with templates for common types of layout tasks; poor typographic control (no support for kern pairs, no control over word and character spacing). Includes collections of fonts and clip art.
Print Shop Deluxe	$ 80	Template-based, highly formatted utility for creating relatively simple informal pieces (banners, greeting cards, and so on). Includes collections of fonts and clip art.

Good Enough Page Layout

In the industry, we tend to hear this approach to page layout referred to as low-end, but perhaps a better term would simply be "appropriate technology." If you only occasionally prepare any sort of document, or produce only simple informal pieces, a program such as XPress or PageMaker would be overkill. But maybe one of the following would do.

Adobe Home Publisher   (KT/SR/DB)

This is the linear descendent of Personal Press, a surprisingly capable page layout program developed by one of the first Mac software companies, Silicon Beach—famous for developing SuperPaint, SuperCard, and Dark Castle. The company was acquired by PageMaker developer Aldus Corporation several years ago and the program, which had been designed for beginning and occasional page creators, was renamed Home Publisher. Adobe has revived the program as **Adobe Home Publisher,** put it on a CD, fluffed it up with a collection of useful templates, fonts, clip art, and preprinted specialty paper, and sells it for less than $50.

The program has some powerful features long missing from the big guys (in fact, it rotated text before PageMaker could). One clever feature is the Equals tool that makes two objects the same size and shape, and a Replicate function with options for replicating a page element a given number of times.

Text is handled relatively well—you can either type directly on the page or import text into a text box—and

Although simple to use, Adobe Home Publisher is capable of useful work. Here you see a simple fax sheet laid out in the program, along with several of its palettes.

there's a well-designed spelling checker and thesaurus to polish your prose. On the other hand, the type formatting controls are rudimentary, which is perhaps to be expected in a low-end page layout program. You can specify a number of typographic settings, but there's no automatic kerning, which would be an obvious way to help novice users create good-looking publications.

One of Home Publisher's most interesting features is AutoCreate—a sort of super-template that enables novices to build documents without wrestling directly with elements in the layout. It advises that "you need four stories and three graphics for this newsletter," and you choose appropriate text and images to fill the boxes. Home Publisher then builds the publication, pulling the files into the template.

Print Shop Deluxe (KT)

If the other programs sound too complex for your work, you might want to consider the template-based **Print Shop Deluxe** ($80, Brøderbund). It ships on a CD with a collection of clip art and fonts, and is even simpler—and more rigid—to use than the less expensive Home Publisher. But if you produce only relatively simple layout projects—greeting cards, banners, calendars, or signs, for example—and don't want to prepare for the task by taking a graduate degree in the graphic arts, Print Shop may be the right program for you.

~~~~~~

Layout for the Web   (MR/KT)

So you've decided to join Godiva Chocolates, the U.S. Congress, and your local pizza joint and create a page on the World Wide Web. Where do you begin? Well, you surf the Web, obviously, in search of advice, good examples—and to see what doesn't work. There are hundreds of pages of free information on how to design Web pages, write HTML, add graphics to your pages, and so on. We've listed a few here (see the sidebar "Great Web Sites for Learning HTML"), but you can find others on the Web via Yahoo, Excite, Alta Vista, or other Web search engines, searching with such keywords as "tutorial HTML" or "HTML tool macintosh" (see Chapter 23 for more on the World Wide Web and HTML).

Creating a Web Page

You work in *HTML*, a simple text-based language that Web browsers know how to interpret. Your page will include your message (*content* in HTML-speak) mixed with HTML *tags* (codes) that specify in general terms how the page elements will be handled. (For instance, <h1> and <h2> indicate two levels of heading.) HTML tags are something like the styles we use in word processors or page layout programs, but unlike style sheets, HTML doesn't specify exactly what an <h1> heading looks like. That's taken care of by the reader's browser program (an HTML interpreter). Its settings determine the font, type size, and other details. It's efficient—a whole page of HTML takes just seconds to appear on a reader's screen.

Writing HTML. You don't need special programs to design a Web page—you can enter HTML tags manually in any text editor. But it's much easier to use a program such as Adobe's WYSIWYG editor PageMill. It allows you to work more or less as you would in a very simple page layout program, then creates the HTML file automatically. Once you become an experienced Web author, you will probably learn to use more sophisticated tools, but PageMill 1 is useful for quick and dirty pages, and the recently announced version 2 promises to be even better. (Before discovering PageMill, I used the shareware program World Wide Web Weaver, but it's buggy, the user interface is quirky, and version upgrades carry additional shareware fees, even as basic problems remain unaddressed.) A PageMill file can be further refined in a text editor (I use BBEdit, shareware from Bare Bones Software).

A few other Web page development tools worth mentioning include NaviPress, HoTMetaL Pro, Netscape Navigator Gold, and Microsoft's (formerly Vermeer's) FrontPage. And Quark's Immedia will let you use the familiar XPress interface and toolset to create HTML. It's hard to make recommendations months ahead since the state of the art is shifting rapidly. For instance, final versions of Navigator Gold and FrontPage have not been released as I write—yet they could be obsolete by the time you read this.

Be realistic. "Keep it simple" is a good slogan for most page layout projects, but it's definitely the best strategy for creating HTML. Compared to print-oriented layout, you have little control over some aspects of Web pages. Readers may have older browsers that don't support advanced HTML features, or may have customized their browser oddly. No matter how you fuss, some readers may see an ugly page or, worse, may not see all of your content. Besides, some effects that seem cool at first, including blinking or flashing images, irritate many readers who respond by clicking themselves off to some other page. Other sophisticated features—such as forms that can be filled in and submitted on-line, text in multiple columns, data arranged in table format, and image maps (graphics with multiple hot spots you can click on to go to specific pages)—are impressive but some of these features require custom programming or support from the Web server.

Setting up some of your content in graphics rather than HTML does give you more control over the look of your Web page, and text-only pages are rare (and pretty boring). On the other hand, graphics can take a long time to load. A smallish image that occupies just part of a page can easily be 30K to 100K in size and take several minutes to load in many typical reader setups. (In contrast, the HTML text on a page is usually less than 10K; even a long article seldom exceeds 30K.)

A Web page and the HTML code that produces it.

But watch out—if your page loads too slowly, some Web surfers (especially those with limited browsers, slow modems, or poor phone line access to the Web) will just move on to the next site. So you need to balance pretty pictures with efficiency. One strategy is to divide your content among more pages. White space is free—and sparse pages let visitors begin to read quickly.

WARNING

Adding graphics. The Web supports two graphic formats, GIF and JPEG, both bitmapped. JPEG works best for large photos and graphics with many different colors (graduated fills and blends, for instance). But GIF works for small graphics or those with few colors—including icons, line drawings, and simple illustrations.

Great Web Sites for Learning HTML   (MR)

For more on designing Web pages, check out the following Web sites:

- Here's how to get to Yahoo: <http://www.yahoo.com> Then enter appropriate keywords.

- One site that lists many Web tools, both commercial and share/freeware:
<http://www.comvista.com/net/www/
        WWWDirectory.html>
It lists HTML editors, HTML converters, graphics tools, and much, much more.

- Here is a URL that has a nice listing:
<http://www.excite.com/Subject/Computing/
        Authoring/HTML/Basic_HTML/>

- A classic HTML tutorial can be found at NCSA (birth-place of NCSA Mosaic, the first popular browser):
<http://www.ncsa.uiuc.edu/General/Internet/
        WWW/HTMLPrimer.html>

- One of my favorites among the many that show HTML style guides is:
<http://www.dsiegel.com/home.html>

- How not to design a Web page—Mirsky's Worst of the Web. <http://mirsky.com/wow/worst.html>

The Web page of type designer David Siegel (he designed Tekton and Graphite).

Stick to the Mac's standard 72-dpi screen resolution—higher resolutions result in larger file sizes with no benefit to the reader.

GIF images can include transparent areas—by designating any single color as transparent, you can allow a background to show through (or around) an image. (There is no support for transparency in JPEG—all JPEG graphics are rectangular.) GIF also allows *interlacing*, a technique that paints an image in stages. Interlacing doesn't really save time, but it gives the reader a chance to see what the graphic looks like sooner.

The power tool of choice for most Web authors is Photoshop (3.0.5 or later) but you could also use Canvas or the Paint module in ClarisWorks. If your graphics program cannot create GIF or JPEG files directly, you can convert most bitmapped image files with such utilities as DeBabelizer or DeBabelizer Lite (Equilibrium Software) or the shareware GraphicConverter.

You can also use vector-based drawing programs—Illustrator, FreeHand, or Canvas, for example—and save your work as a bitmapped graphic. (Photoshop will open an Illustrator file and convert it to GIF or JPEG.)

Test Early and Often

Because there are so many unpredictable variables, it's a good idea to test your page with a variety of the most popular browsers—I check mine using Netscape Navigator, NCSA Mosaic, America Online's browser, and Microsoft Internet Explorer, for example. And take time to test with a modem—especially if you have the newest and greatest browser yourself and high-speed lines for accessing the Web. You may not realize that your pages load so slowly that few visitors will stick around to read them.

HOT TIP

Moe's Favorite Inspirational Web Sites (MR)

- Clnet is a weekly television show about computers, technology, and the Web. This site is one of the best I have seen when it comes to presenting massive amounts of data in a clean, organized fashion. <http://www.cnet.com>

- The TV Food network (a cable channel that consists mainly of cooking shows) installed a Web site because they were inundated with recipe requests—as many as 20,000 a week! The Web is an inexpensive way to let people fill their own requests. <http://www.foodtv.com>

Another nicely designed Web page, this one about music.

- Federal Express lets you track your packages. (UPS has a similar service). This frees up their operators and at the same time gives you faster results: <http://www.fedex.com/track_it.html>

- This small publisher gains a worldwide audience through an elegantly designed site. By offering samples of its publications, Rainwater Press reaches new customers and new markets. <http://www.rainwater.com>

- Need a book? This is one of many sites where one can order books through the Internet. I like this one because the search and order entry pages are exceptionally well done, making it easy to find and order with minimal hassle. <http://www.amazon.com/>

- There is no explaining Joe Holmes's Space Age Bachelor Pad Music. I just like it. <http://www.users.interport.net/~joholmes/ index.html>

- My own site—Videonics manufactures video editing equipment (including a Mac-based video editor called Video ToolKit). One of our ongoing challenges is to teach camcorder owners how to edit videos. The Web is perfect for this because we can deliver, at very low cost, as much information about how to edit videos as the customer wants. We serve about 3,000 files a day, which is like having a running trade show 24 hours a day, seven days a week! (Bias alert! This is the site I created!) <http://www.videonics.com/>

Page Layout Tips

XPress

Increase your productivity and general DTP know-how by using the following tips in QuarkXPress.

Seeing what you're moving (DB). When you drag something in XPress, what you see is an outline of the item; when you stop dragging and let go of the mouse, the item itself appears in the new position. But when you're trying to align something carefully, that just isn't good enough. If you hold down the mouse button for about half a second (until the object you're trying to move flashes once), you can actually see the object move instead of just a box.

Switching to the grabber hand (DB). One of the coolest subtle features of XPress is the grabber hand. Instead of clicking on the scroll bars all the time to move around your document, hold down the Option key while clicking and dragging somewhere on your page. A little hand icon appears and moves your page in the direction that you're dragging. This seems like a really little feature, but it speeds up life a lot!

Copying paragraph formats (DB). You can copy all the paragraph attributes of one paragraph to another by first putting the cursor in the new paragraph (the one you want to copy to), then Shift-Option-clicking on the old one (the paragraph you want to copy from). Tabs, indents, and even style sheets are copied.

Enlarging the spread view (RB). To see spreads as large as possible, choose the Application option from the Preferences submenu (Edit menu) and change "pasteboard width" to something less than the 100 percent default. A 50 to 75 percent setting will leave you with generally adequate working space and yield a much larger spread view.

Working with style sheets (RB). When appending styles from one document to another, always append Hyphenation and Colors before Styles. If you bring in Styles first, XPress will replace missing colors with black and missing hyphenation styles with Standard—not very helpful.

Aligning rules to guides (EC). To align a drawn rule to a guideline by its edge (rather than its center), step and repeat it with horizontal and vertical offsets set to zero. Marquee-select the two rules, group them, and move the group. When you come near a guide and have Snap to Guides turned on, the edge of the group (and therefore the rule) will snap to the guide. When you have the rule right where you want it,

HOT TIPS

ungroup it, deselect the group and select the cloned rule that's sitting on top of the original one. Delete it and you're back to just one rule whose edge is now aligned to the guide. After all that I usually lock the rule to make sure it stays where I put it, but that's optional, of course.

Item/content tool toggle (RP). A little-known shortcut: Pressing Shift F8 sets a permanent toggle between the item and content tools.

Setting tabs (AC). You can enter column widths in XPress' Tabs dialog (and/or do a kludgy implementation of Repeat Tab). Open the Tabs dialog, enter the position of the first tab and click Apply (or type ⌘ A). (If you wanted the first column to be 4p3, starting from the left edge of the text box to the first tab, you'd type in "4p3" and click Apply.) Everyone knows that. But let's say you want four more columns, each 6p2 in width. Here's the easy way.

After you set your first tab, click in the Position field to the right of the number representing the first tab's position. Now type "+[distance]". Using the above example, you'd click after the "4p3" that's showing in the Position dialog and type "+6p2". Click Apply. The second tab appears at 10p5. The Position field still says "4p3+6p2". Click again after the entry (because it's all selected, it's easier to just tap the Right Arrow key to deselect the entry and get your cursor to the end) and type "+6p2" again. A third tab appears at 16p7. And so on. The numbers "4p3+6p2+6p2+6p2" will be scrolling off the left of the field, of course, but as long as you can get your cursor to the end of the numbers string with the good ol' right arrow, you'll be fine.

PageMaker

Increase your productivity and general DTP know-how by using the following tips in PageMaker.

Seeing what you're moving (DB). When you drag something in PageMaker, what you see is an outline of the item; when you stop dragging and let go of the mouse, the item itself appears in the new position. But when you're trying to align something carefully, that just isn't good enough. If you hold down the mouse button for about half a second (until the object you're trying to move flashes once), you can actually see the object move instead of just a box.

Switching to the grabber hand (DB). One of the coolest subtle features of PageMaker is the grabber hand. Instead of clicking on the scroll bars all the time to move around your document, hold down the Option key while clicking and dragging somewhere on your page. A little hand icon appears and moves your page in the direction that you're dragging. This seems like a really little feature, but it speeds up life a lot!

Page Layout Resources (KT)

No one ever learns all this desktop publishing stuff without help. Learning on the job—as most typesetters and many designers did in the old days—is one of the best approaches, but today it's hard for most of us to find time, even assuming we can find a place to work on that basis. Hiring a trainer or attending classes is another possibility. But classes take time and money, and, besides, your teacher can't be there for you the night before your deadline. So here are some more accessible resources:

Going on-line

There's a vibrant community of desktop publishers and designers on-line. I'm most familiar with the smart and generous crowd on the DTP and Professional Publishing forums on CompuServe (where I'm on staff), but you'll also find helpful people on other forums and services—America Online, the Web, and other parts of the Internet. When you need fast advice at odd times, I'd go on-line first (then, if necessary, wrestle with a vendor's telephone support). Better yet, participate regularly in these forums so you'll know of bugs and common problems in advance—it's even more satisfying to avoid a crisis than to solve it. (As a bonus, you get to participate in an international community of kindred spirits.)

Going on-line is about the closest thing to an all-night consultant there is—the services never sleep. But it's not just for emergencies—it's the most reliable way to keep up to date on the computer aspects of design and publishing. Other users offer great (and relatively objective) tech support, but when you need information from a vendor, you'll probably get it faster on-line than over the phone. Adobe has support forums on both CompuServe and America Online (though the CompuServe forums are livelier), and on the Web. Quark monitors the Quark Users forum on CompuServe and has its own sections on America Online and on the Web. Most other vendors can also be reached on some on-line venue.

Helpful books (and a CD-ROM)

The Agfa Guide to Digital Color Prepress, Interactive Edition ($100, with five printed companion volumes, Agfa Prepress Education Resources). An on-line version of the highly regarded prepress series of booklets (which can be bought separately from the same source). Comprehensive and applicable information.

Design with Type by Carl Dair has timely and excellent advice on page layout and it's still in print (University of Toronto Press; ISBN 0-8020-1426-7; available through Swipe Books).

Graphic Idea Notebook, Inventive Techniques for Designing Printed Pages (ISBN 0-8230-2149-1) or other books by the prolific Jan V. White. Graphic Idea Notebook is one of my favorites, but it may be out of print (his books are often in libraries, though).

The Mac Is Not a Typewriter by Robin Williams ($10, Peachpit Press). Basic information in a very accessible format.

Make Your Scanner a Great Design & Production Tool by Michael Sullivan ($28, North Light Books). Insight into the use of scanners and scanned images, with real-world examples.

Quark Design, a step-by-step approach to page layout software by Nancy J. McCarthy ($35, Peachpit Press). Real design projects explained by the designers—including general techniques that could also be adapted for PageMaker or other software. Very helpful insights into the computer-aided design process.

The QuarkXPress Book ($30, Peachpit Press) by David Blatner. A must-have classic for XPress users.

QuarkXPress Unleashed by Brad Walrod ($40, Random House). *The* book on power techniques, and one of the best sources of information on how to use XTensions.

Stop Stealing Sheep & Find Out How Type Works by Erik Spiekermann and E.M. Ginger ($20, Adobe Press). Cute, clever, sometimes a bit sloppy in the details (surprisingly), but a good fast read that provides lots of helpful information.

Typefaces for Desktop Publishing—A User Guide by Alison Black (Architecture Design and Technology Press, London. ISBN 1-85454-841-7). One of the best of the books on design and type in the era of DTP.

Using PageMaker 6 by Rick Wallace ($40, Que, with CD-ROM). A bit of a compendium, but with rare and useful power tips on scripting, tagging, and other approaches to production automation in PageMaker.

Magazines

Adobe Magazine, though sponsored by a vendor, is both handsome and useful. Free to registered owners of any Adobe product.

Before & After is an excellent design-based full-color newsletter that shows you, step-by-step, how to get great-looking pages and cool graphic effects.

Dynamic Graphics Magazine (Dynamic Graphics), is a new magazine aimed at beginning desktop publishers.

Publish is the only independent desktop publishing magazine on the newsstand, and it's very useful, especially for intermediate to advanced desktop publishers.

Step-by-Step Electronic Design (Dynamic Graphics), is a monthly full-color newsletter with detailed instructions for achieving particular effects.

X-Ray is an authorized magazine, free to all registered owners of QuarkXPress.

Shrinking files (SZA/AN). By default, PageMaker files get bigger as you work on them. That's because the program appends changes to the existing file when you save, rather than replacing it with the new, edited version, which might be only half the size (or even smaller). You can avoid this by changing the defaults from "Save faster" to "Save smaller" in the Document Setup dialog. Or you can periodically use Save As (instead of Save) from the File menu. When you Save As with the same filename, the old file is completely replaced by the current one, ridding yourself of all those old appendages and reducing the file size.

Finding/changing multiple attributes (Elizabeth Castro). Did you know that you can look for more than one character style (bold, italic, and so on) at a time using the Find dialog box? Just select the first style and then select the second. When you let go of the mouse button, you'll see one of the styles with a plus sign, indicating that there is more than one style selected. To deselect either style without deselecting all of them, click it. To deselect all of the styles, select Any from the pop-up menu.

Switching documents (RR). With multiple documents open in PageMaker, Option-clicking on the title bar will switch to the next document. Open windows in the story editor are also included in the rotation. So with a single document and one story open, this is a handy way to switch from layout view to an open story editor window. (Pressing ⌘E displays a new untitled story window every time if nothing is selected in layout view. I don't always want this!)

Editing styles safely (JW). Here's a trick I've used ever since PageMaker included styles and color that still works great. Suppose you need to change a paragraph style, but you're not sure what other styles might be based on the style you want to change, when the same change might be undesirable in the subordinate styles.

To find out if the style change will ripple through to child styles—assign a weird color like fuchsia to the style you need to change. Fast perusal of the document after doing so will show quickly if based-on styles have been affected as well, enabling you to easily undo the unwanted change to the substyles. Once the dependent styles have been changed back, simply revert/remove the color attribute from the parent style.

Serial deletions (RR). In all layout programs (that I know of) that support deleting with the ⌦ key, holding down the ⌦ key continuously as you click on individual items will delete as you go. Be careful! (Lefties will have an easier time with this shortcut.)

Cross-Platform

Ease the process of transferring files between the Macintosh and Windows platforms by using the following tips.

Cross-platform file moves (DB). If you need to move either graphic files or documents between the Macintosh and Windows, you should typically use the lowest common denominators for everything. That means, use PC EPS and TIFF files (most graphic programs on the Macintosh can write them). And all your file names should be eight-dot-three (eight letters or numbers, followed by a period, followed by a three-letter extension). For example, you could use 8LTRPLUS.TXT.

Use .ZIP for cross-platform files (KT). You can avoid some common problems when sending files to a PC (particularly by modem) if you first compress them with a Zip utility, even if they're not very large. (Zip files (.ZIP) are the PC equivalent to our .sit or .cpt files.) The Zip wrapper seems to protect the contents from the vagaries of telecommunications and every PC user has an un-zipper. (You can download the shareware.)

Tell your PC pals to get an unStuffer (KT). Aladdin Systems has a freeware utility for PC users that will extract StuffIt archives. It's available from CompuServe, America Online, and other popular on-line venues.

Web Design Tips   (MR)

Graphic File Conversion

Make your graphics Web-compatible by using the following graphic conversion tips.

Use ScreenReady for Web graphics. If you're working with clip art or other EPS files, Adobe ScreenReady can convert EPS files to bitmaps at 72 dpi, which is perfect for the Web. ScreenReady anti-aliases the image, adding in-between colors to fill in the "jaggies," to deliver much smoother looking graphics. The only drawback is that it creates PICT graphics, but these are easily converted to GIF using GraphicConverter or other shareware and freeware tools.

GraphicConverter. The shareware utility GraphicConverter is an invaluable tool for converting graphics from a wide range of formats to Web-compatible JPEG or GIF. This Swiss Army Knife of an application can also add or alter transparencies and set interlacing, and includes a few image-editing tools. The author of this utility updates it frequently and supports it well.

General Graphics

Use the following graphics tips for finding graphics, as well as sprucing up your Web page.

Using screenshots as Web graphics. You can use screenshots as Web images. The Mac's native function records the entire screen, but third-party utilities allow you to capture specified areas. My favorite is the shareware FlashIt (good program, just don't say the name fast) by Nobu Toge.

Look for good Web pages. If you see pages you like, grab the raw HTML. Because it is text-based, you can study the pages to learn how the effects were created. (Save the file in "source" or "HTML" format in your browser and open it in a text editor or word processor.)

Snag graphics from the Web. You can also grab any image you see on the Web—most browsers have a command that lets you copy a graphic to the clipboard or to a file. (Be careful about copyright issues, though—you may not be able to use those images legally on your own Web pages.)

Editors' Poll:
What Feature Would You Most Like to Have
Added to Your Favorite Page Layout Program?

JH: Perfect WYSIWYG HTML capabilities.

JC: I think the software developers have a handle on just about every feature one can imagine. How about some predesigned templates for billing clients?!

SS: For PageMaker: captions that could be linked to figures/screenshots—just as they could in the old copy of Ventura Publisher that I originally used when I started doing layout work on the PC about eight years ago.

TA: Some sort of automatic disaster protection. If there's any software that gives me fits, it's QuarkXPress and PageMaker both. Lockups, bad document files, annoying problems, etc. make me grimace each time I launch them. And, no, XPress's wasteful and poorly engineered/designed automatic backups isn't what I had in mind....

ML: I'd like QuarkXPress to track figure/caption numbers automatically so that when I insert or delete a figure, all the ones after it are automatically renumbered. Heck, even Microsoft Word does this! I'd also like the text box to shorten itself, fitting itself automatically to the bottom of the text I enter.

KT: It's time for the developers to go back and pick up the pieces they skipped over in the first place—especially tools for typography, which are still not as capable as the systems that DTP supplanted a decade ago. We need better tools for setting unjustified text in soft (aesthetic) rags, ability to hang punctuation to both right and left with control over which characters and how far, and practical methods of contouring text next to a drop cap.

17 Multimedia

From Wall Street to Hollywood Boulevard, from Cannes to Katmandu, multimedia is raising both artistic spirits and investor dollars. Widely available and inexpensive computers that can smoothly blend text, sound, graphics, and video have transformed the worlds of business, government, education, and home entertainment. Quarterly business reports come on CD-ROM; automobile companies sell cars with mouse clicks; the Library of Congress distributes its archival movie collection on-line; encylopedias include interactive multimedia presentations; rock and rollers put interactive videos and games directly on their latest albums—even family photo albums now end up on disk accompanied by Aunt Emily's eloquent audio reminiscences.

The conventional wisdom about multimedia production was once "Don't try this at home." That is no longer true: Making multimedia now requires nothing more complicated than using what comes built-in to nearly every one of today's Macintosh computers. It is also one of the most exciting and satisfying things you can do with your Mac.

In this chapter, we'll look at the ingredients of multimedia and how they fit into the blend, and then look at how to blend those ingredients together into something rich and wonderful.

Contributors

Michael E. Cohen (MEC) has produced and programmed a number of multimedia products at Voyager (most notably, Voyager's *Macbeth*) and is currently the senior tech-nomancer at Calliope Media. He has been using computers since the standard input device was a card reader.

Fletcher Beasley (FB) is a composer/sound designer working in the Los Angeles area. He has been involved in multimedia and com-puter audio since the late 1980s and has worked on most of the CD-ROM and video game platforms avail-able on the market.

Suzanne Escoffier (SE) has been creating multimedia titles for home, industry, and education for more than a decade. Her most recent consumer CD-ROM title is *Farm Buddies*, reading-readiness activities in English and Spanish for kids aged three to seven.

Contents

Jack Kurtz (JK) is a seasoned multimedia programmer and developer. He has worked on commercial CD-ROM titles, interactive business presentations, and kiosks for companies such as Sony, NBC, Davidson, and SoftKey. He is currently working at Cloud 9 Interactive in Santa Monica, California, developing children's interactive titles.

Aileen Abernathy (AA) went from being a desktop publisher to writing about it for *MacUser* magazine. She currently writes for *MacUser*, *MacWEEK*, *Publish*, and corporate clients.

Shelley Cryan (SC) runs a consulting business in New York and writes frequently about presentation software for computer publications.

Michael D. Murie (MM), a multimedia consultant based in Massachusetts, is the author of *The QuickTime Handbook* and *Macintosh Multimedia Workshop*, both published by Hayden Books.

~~~~~~

How Did We Get Here? <span style="float:right">(MEC)</span>

When I was in elementary school, we had a special room called the "multimedia" room. This was a room stocked with a bunch of folding chairs, a small stage, and a big closet. Inside that closet was the magic: a clattering and tempermental 16mm film projector, a record player, a filmstrip projector, a portable movie screen, and an over-head projector.

The filmstrip projector and record player were a true interactive multimedia combi-nation: The projector might show a scratched and washed-out picture of cattle grazing in a field, while the record player would crackle, "This is the heart of the Wisconsin dairy industry." Then the record player would make a "bing!" noise (much like the sound the first Macs made when they started up), and one lucky kid would get to turn the knob on the filmstrip projector and show us the next slide. Okay, it wasn't inter-active multimedia for the rest of us, but it was for that lucky kid who got to control the show. (I was once chosen to be that lucky kid: I got excited and missed a couple of cues and was never chosen again. But I never forgot the thrill.…)

Today, that multimedia room is a little box or two sitting on your desk. We call it a Macintosh.

If There Were No Macintosh, It Would Be Necessary to Invent One

Q: Did the Mac create multimedia, or did multimedia create the Mac?

A: Yes.

Multimedia is certainly much older than the Mac or even the computer industry—in fact, a scholar I know says that multimedia is thousands of years old. It is certainly true that artists have been blending together materials from different media for a long time. But when the Mac came along, it was able to provide a single *medium* ideally suited for combining all the stuff that used to be on separate media (such as a filmstrip projector, a movie screen, and a record player). So you can think of your Mac as a tool that was designed to help create a lot of different media, and you can think of it as the place where all those different media can be blended together into something new. As a result, you can now listen to a Beethoven symphony with interactive commentary that appears in time to the music; you can read a real estate catalog that lets you take a tour of a new home entirely on your computer screen; your school-aged children can write reports on the Civil War complete with pictures, maps, and marching songs.

It's the Hardware; It's the Software

The very first Macs of 1984 were capable of showing text, playing sounds, displaying pictures, and performing animations. What they didn't have was the software needed to combine them into a single presentation (those very first Macs didn't have much software at all, come to think of it). It took a few years for things to change, but they changed quickly: Over the course of a few months in 1987, Apple released both its first CD-ROM player (which could also play *audio* CDs—very cool!) and HyperCard. From that marriage the multimedia industry was born.

Apple has continued refining and improving the Macintosh hardware. Most Macs now have microphones that let you record sounds directly; many have video inputs that let you transfer video from your camcorder directly to your hard disk; and most have built-in CD-ROM players as standard equipment that are four times as fast as the first ones.

The software has gotten better, too. Where once there was only HyperCard, there are now dozens of software packages for making multimedia. And nearly all that commercially available multimedia software relies on what is probably Apple's most important addition to the Mac System Folder to date: QuickTime.

QuickTime: the Soul of the Multimedia Machine (MEC)

QuickTime has become increasingly central to Apple's multimedia strategy over the last few years, which is not surprising when you consider that the QuickTime system extension underlies much of the Mac's multimedia power. The QuickTime extension is most famous, of course, for letting the Mac do video, but the latest version also does digital audio, MIDI (see "What is MIDI?" and "General MIDI on the Mac" later in this chapter), animation, virtual reality, still image compression, and text display.

The QuickTime Extension and Friends (MEC)

QuickTime currently consists of three parts: the QuickTime extension itself (version 2.1 as of this writing, though version 2.5 should be out by the time this goes into print), the QuickTime Musical Instruments extension (which allows QuickTime to play back MIDI using sound samples licensed from Roland), and the QuickTime Powerplug (required only for Power Macs). All Macs sold today come with QuickTime preinstalled.

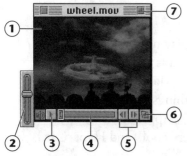

1. Movie frame

2. To adjust a movie's volume, click and hold the Volume Control button to bring up the Volume Slider.

3. Play/Pause button

4. The Slider indicates where you are in a movie. Drag its thumb to move around in the movie, or click a spot on the Slider to jump to that point in the movie.

5. Step Backward and Step Forward buttons. Control-click either button and a shuttle control will appear that lets you play a movie backward or forward at just about any speed. Dragging the shuttle's thumb adjusts the speed of playback as well as the direction.

6. The Resize Window button lets you click and drag to resize the movie frame. For optimum playback, use a multiple of the original frame size—twice as big, for example, or half the size. The frame automatically resizes in the appropriate increments if you hold down [Option] while dragging the button.

7. To restore a movie's original frame dimensions, click the Zoom box.

The Standard Controller provides a VCR-like interface for playing QuickTime movies.

HOT TIP

In addition to the QuickTime software that goes into the System Folder, you almost certainly want to acquire Apple's free **MoviePlayer** program. MoviePlayer lets you open up, edit, and save QuickTime movies. It also lets you convert audio tracks from an audio CD into AIFF files on your hard disk (see "Digitizing Sound" later in this chapter), as well as convert and play MIDI files. MoviePlayer can be obtained from Apple's Web site and from user groups. It is also available on the QuickTime Developer's Kit CD (see "The QuickTime Developer's Kit and the Apple Multimedia Program" later in this chapter).

QuickTime and Video (MEC)

QuickTime provides standard formats for storing and playing back video at acceptable speeds (hence the name *Quick*Time), it supplies a reliable timing system to allow pictures and sound to synchronize (hence the name Quick*Time*), and does it all at the system software level, which means that an ever-increasing number of programs can now incorporate video and sound—even word processors and spreadsheets. Whatever program you use to get video into the Mac (a process called *capturing* or *digitizing*) will almost certainly use QuickTime, and whatever program you use to edit your video will use QuickTime, too. Not only that, the programs you use to view the video will also use QuickTime.

HOT TIP

Because digital video and QuickTime are fast-changing technologies, you may want to periodically check out the QuickTime FAQ (frequently asked questions) by Charles Wiltgen, which is available on the Internet at <http://www.onshore.com/quicktime/>. This work, a labor of love by its author, compiles the latest tricks, tips, and techniques for dealing with QuickTime video on the Mac.

QuickTime and Audio (FB)

Aside from QuickTime's ability to synchronize events on a computer (which obviously has important ramifications for multimedia), the latest versions of QuickTime support *IMA compression*, a multimedia industry standard which allows relatively high-quality sound to take up much less disk space (IMA is the Interactive Multimedia Association). IMA compression, while not perfect, sounds much better than any compression previously available on the Mac. You can find out more about QuickTime's ability to compress audio and synchronize it with other media in "Using QuickTime For Compression and Synchronization" later in this chapter.

QuickTime VR (MEC)

QuickTime VR is Apple's neat technique for creating *virtual reality* experiences (hence the VR in its name). It makes it possible to use a QuickTime window as a view into a space, letting you turn around, move in more closely on objects, and so on, merely by clicking in the window. It does this using specially prepared QuickTime sequences, usually made from a 360-degree photographic panorama of an area, that are put together with a "stitcher" application (actually, a HyperCard stack) that Apple provides. QuickTime VR can also use sequences made from rendered 3-D images, making possible tours of spaces that never existed in the real world. This technology is still evolving, but it is already useful for games, simulations, and tours of real places. Licensing and development tools for QuickTime VR are available from Apple.

QuickTime Controller Shortcuts (MM)

The Standard Controller has several shortcuts for movie playback:

Play	Press ⟨Spacebar⟩ or ⟨Return⟩, or double-click in the frame
Pause	Press ⟨Spacebar⟩ or ⟨Return⟩, or click once in the frame
Mute the sound	Press ⟨Option⟩ while clicking the Volume Control button
Step forward	⟨→⟩
Step backward	⟨←⟩
Jump to end	Press ⟨Option⟩ while clicking the Step Forward button
Jump to beginning	Press ⟨Option⟩ while clicking the Step Backward button
Play in reverse	Press ⟨⌘⟩ while clicking the Step Backward button, or Shift-double-click in the frame
Play every frame	Hold down ⟨Option⟩ and begin playback

The QuickTime Developer's Kit and the Apple Multimedia Program (MEC)

If you are at all serious about Macintosh multimedia, you should obtain Apple's **QuickTime Developer's Kit** CD, which contains the latest versions of QuickTime, documentation, tools, and sample code. You can get the disk from Apple's Developer Catalog for $99. The catalog is available on-line at <http://devcatalog.apple.com>.

If you are really serious about multimedia development, you should also think about joining the Apple Multimedia Program. Registration is currently $300 a year, and it includes developer CDs (including the QuickTime Developer's Kit CD), marketing information, access to Apple's Third Party Compatibility Lab, conference invitations, and referral services. More information on this program is available by calling 408/974-4897 or by checking out Apple's Web site at <http://www.amp.apple.com>.

Ingredients of Multimedia (MEC)

To make multimedia, you need media—all sorts of media, and usually lots of it. You should also have good reasons for combining all this stuff together (note: impressing your friends or making money are good, or, at least, compelling *motives*, but they aren't *reasons*). In other words, you need to know which kinds of media are best for which purposes, and you have to figure out the best ways to blend them to get the response you want (e.g., the respect and admiration of your friends and associates, and tons of money from satisfied purchasers of your multimedia creation).

Text

While at first glance, text may seem to be boring and low-tech, it can actually be a powerful addition to a multimedia work. Text is good for lots of things in multimedia, and has at least one powerful advantage over some other forms of media: It is very compact. For instance, the text of an entire book takes up less room than, say, a medium-fidelity rendition of one top-40 song.

You can search text very easily, and you can use it to navigate through your work: Not only can a button with a text caption be more informative to your audience than a similar button that relies upon nontextual artwork, but many multimedia programs support "hot text" that can bring up pictures, play sounds, or display a different piece of text (such as a footnote or a sidebar). Although often overlooked by those who promote and review multimedia, there are few multimedia titles that don't have at least *some* text in them.

Unfortunately, the creators of many multimedia authoring programs have been rather backward in providing good text formatting and searching capabilities in their products. For example, Macromedia's Director, perhaps the authoring program most widely used by multimedia professionals, has only recently begun to provide sophisticated text support with its latest release, version 5. Even HyperCard, which began life as a sort of filing system that let users mix text and pictures on a virtual stack of cards, still only supports limited text formatting, though its abilities to search through text have rarely been surpassed. You should also know that producing good-looking text requires good-looking fonts; however, licensing and distributing fonts with your work can become costly, and often involves users in an installation process that can become cumbersome.

HOT TIP

Still, when you design your multimedia title, remember that text can help explain some things better than any other medium, takes up less disk space, and provides additional ways for the user to navigate beyond pointing and clicking on graphic buttons.

Graphics

Multimedia titles usually rely very heavily on graphics, using them as background "frames," user-interface elements (such as buttons, sliders, and scroll bars), illustrations of subject matter, or even *as* the subject matter. As a result, there are often several graphics on the screen at any one time. But, like sound, graphics take up disk space: The larger the picture and the more colors it requires, the more space it takes up. Furthermore, pictures take up available RAM as well as disk storage, since pictures have

Is a Picture Really Worth a Thousand Words? (MEC)

As far as your Mac's memory and disk space are concerned, it's usually worth more. One letter in a text file usually requires a single *byte* of storage. In this chapter the average word is about six characters long, which means that a thousand words takes up about 6,000 bytes, or 6K. A black-and-white picture that would fill the screen on the first 128K Mac requires about 22K to store, which is a little more than the amount of space that 3,500 words of text would take. Color pictures require much more storage space: If you display that same picture in 256 colors (also called 8-bit color), it takes about 175K, which makes it worth more than 29,000 words (about one-third the size of an average novel).

to be held in memory as long as they are visible. A 640-by-480 picture shown in 256 colors takes up about 300K of RAM while it is on the screen; the more pictures your title displays at one time, the more RAM your multimedia title will require in order to run. There are many different types of graphics that the Mac handles; see Chapter 15 for more details about graphic formats.

Sound

From the very beginning, Macintoshes have been able to produce relatively high-quality sound, and as the years have gone by each generation of Mac has gained even more sound capabilities. Today's Macs can record as well as play back sound; they can both talk and respond to spoken commands using Apple's Speech Manager and PlainTalk software (see "PlainTalk" in Chapter 3); they can play MIDI music without the addition of an external MIDI interface, courtesy of QuickTime (see "What is MIDI?" and "QuickTime" in this chapter); they can play audio CDs if a CD-ROM drive is attached; and even (again, courtesy of QuickTime) copy sounds from those CDs to standard Macintosh file formats. Right out of the box, the newest Macs are close to being a combination recording studio and hi-fi system.

You can use sound in a variety of ways and in a variety of resolutions in your multimedia title, from simple sound effects to high-fidelity music. For example, you can use sound to provide simple audible feedback to user actions (such as a click noise when the user presses a button), pronunciations (e.g., in a glossary), narrations, musical accompaniment to a picture presentation, and much more. Remember, though, that a sound effect can go from interesting to boring to downright annoying the more times the user hears it: You should only use sound effects when you *need* to use them, and not just because you *can* use them.

HOT TIP

Sound does take up considerable amounts of storage room on your hard disk or CD-ROM, and the better the sound quality, the more room it takes. You also need to know that different models of Mac produce different quality sound. Although the newest Macs can produce stereo sound that has the same quality as sound from an audio CD, older Macs can only produce monaural sound of much lower quality (lower, that is, to the audiophile—even the oldest Mac can produce sound that is quite acceptable for many multimedia uses).

Video and Animation

Video is really just a sequence of still pictures that, when shown one after another, creates the illusion of motion. The first Macs could do that much, although making pictures move on those early machines took some very tricky programming. Today, thanks to QuickTime, video is something that the Mac does very easily and very well.

Video can liven up almost any presentation. There is something about a moving image that attracts and focuses attention: Although video may not have completely killed the radio star, a talking head really does get noticed more than a disembodied voice. Video is especially good for showing processes (it is one thing to read about how to bone a chicken, but it is quite another to see Julia Child wielding her knife).

But video does have its drawbacks: It is expensive to produce, it takes up lots of disk space, and even with QuickTime's sophisticated assistance, it can still task the processing speed of many machines. On the other hand, it is one heck of a lot of fun to make and use. Don't we all really want to direct?

Rights and Wrongs: Using Copyrighted Media

No matter what mix of media you put into your title, there is one important area that you really must consider: Who owns the sound, pictures, images, text, and movies you are using? This is not critical if you are only making something for your own amusement, but if you plan to show your work in the classroom or boardroom, or if you plan to distribute your title to others, it is very important. People who produce original material have a long-standing legal right not to have their work used without permission, and they also have the right to be paid for any use of their work.

WARNING

Just because you have bought an album or a book, for example, does not mean that you have the right to reuse that material without permission. As the multimedia industry grows, "content providers" (those folk who used to be called publishers, or writers, or recording artists, or directors) are becoming increasingly savvy about copyright. So should you.

How do you get permission to use copyrighted media? It depends. You can get clip art collections, for example, that give you the right to use the artwork they contain, sometimes with limits, sometimes without. There are also clip collections of sounds, and even video, that allow the same permission to reuse their contents. But in many cases, you have to ask permission of the individual publishers, record companies, museums, and studios that have produced or that own the material you wish to use—this is a slow process, and sometimes expensive, but you cannot shirk this responsibility. The world is full of lawyers, and you don't want to find yourself on the short end of a copyright infringement suit.

HOT TIP

Macs for Playing and Making Multimedia (MEC)

Although other computer companies tout their specialized "multimedia PCs," nearly *all* of Apple's Macs do multimedia. This does not mean that every Mac is suitable for every multimedia task, though. Here we'll look at what you'll need in your Mac to play and to make multimedia.

Playing Multimedia

If you are planning to use your Mac to look at multimedia, you need a Mac that is almost unbelievably more powerful than the first little toaster box that came out in 1984. To run most multimedia titles you need a machine with at least 8MB of RAM (64 times the amount of RAM in the first Mac!), a color monitor that displays at least 640 by 480 pixels at once and can show 256 or more colors, at least a double-speed CD-ROM drive, and some very powerful software installed in the System Folder; in other words, a standard desktop Mac. Apple has come to realize that multimedia is one of its core businesses, so you can expect that most of the desktop machines that they sell from now on, as well as an increasing number of their notebook machines, will be ready for multimedia right out of the box.

Doubled RAM Isn't Multimedia RAM (MEC)

Many people today use commercial products such as RAM Doubler or system features such as *virtual memory* to make their Macs act like they have more *RAM* than they really do (see Chapter 4 for definitions of virtual memory and RAM). After all, RAM chips are expensive, and you can do a lot with a RAM-doubled Mac or with a Mac running virtual memory. These RAM-stretching tricks, however, tend to give multimedia titles fits—as in fits and starts.

Playing audio or video requires the constant attention of your Mac's CPU. Utilities such as RAM Doubler, however, use compression schemes to pack temporarily inactive portions of your Mac's memory into smaller spaces, and compressing and decompressing memory takes the CPU time to accomplish. While your Mac is busy doing that, it can't also be decompressing the video playing from your CD-ROM. Virtual memory also ties up the CPU, and then aggravates the problem by involving the Mac's hard disk: With virtual memory, your Mac copies temporarily dormant portions of memory to a hard disk, and reads those portions back into RAM when they become active again. Hard disks are a *lot* slower to access than RAM, and when the swapping is going on, your ordinarily fleet machine grinds away like a glacier on an Arctic night.

If you bought a new Mac within the last year, you are probably already set up to view the majority of current multimedia titles. If you have an older machine with a 68020 processor or better, you can probably upgrade your system to meet multimedia requirements as well. However if you're one of those folk with an old trusty Mac SE or Plus or Classic you are out of luck as far as multimedia is concerned—though your machine is still certainly a useful machine, today's multimedia titles demand performance and capabilities that will be forever beyond those brave little toasters.

Making Multimedia   (MEC)

Making multimedia tends to require considerably more computing power and resources than does playing it back. Image-editing programs, for example, benefit from lots of RAM and fast CPUs. Video and audio editing are virtually impossible without copious disk storage as well. If you plan to make multimedia titles on a regular or even semi-regular basis, you will want some serious computing horsepower.

Memory (MEC). The bare minimum is really 24MB of RAM, and more is better (I get by with a 40MB machine, and I still occasionally feel the need for even more RAM). To hold that memory, you will want a fast machine; look at a Mac that has a fast PowerPC 601 CPU (by "fast," I mean a chip that runs at a speed of at least 100 MHz) or one of the newer, faster PowerPC 604 CPUs. For more details on memory, see Chapter 4.

Hard disk storage (MEC). If you are planning to create a CD-ROM title, you will want fast hard disk storage and lots of it: at least two gigabytes of hard disk storage, and probably more. In my experience, you want to have from four to six times the amount of storage that your final product will take up, just to hold the assets for your project and to give you room to manipulate them. If you are going to digitize your own video, you will need much more disk storage: Raw, uncompressed video takes up huge amounts of room; you can easily fill up a gigabyte with just a few minutes of it. For video capture, you probably want to have very fast *RAID* disks (RAID stands for "Redundant Array of Inexpensive Disks," and is a way of increasing storage speed and reliability), or at least, fast disks designed for video capture—not all hard disks are up to the challenge. For more information about your storage options, see Chapter 5.

Slots (MEC). You also want a machine with slots, because chances are you will want to add in some special boards for video digitizing or sound sampling. Until recently, *slots* meant NuBus slots, a special board interface that hardly anyone in the computer industry other than Apple used. The newest Macs, though, use the industry standard PCI slot: Most board manufacturers for the Mac are now issuing their products in

PCI format, and many of the high-end video and audio PCI boards used in the Windows world are now becoming available for the Mac as well. You can expect NuBus boards to become rarer in years to come, so plan on getting a Mac with PCI slots if you are buying a new machine for making multimedia.

CD-ROM drive (MEC). A CD-ROM drive is something you must have for both playing and making multimedia, and you want a fast one. Apple currently sells *quad-speed* drives (that is, drives that are four times as fast as the first CD-ROM drives) and other manufacturers make even faster ones. If your production process requires you to access a lot of material from a variety of CD-ROM sources, it may even be worth your while to investigate some of the multiple disk CD-ROM drives (often known as CD-ROM jukeboxes).

CD-R (MEC). A CD-R device (that is, a device for making single CD-ROMs; it means "CD-Recordable") is almost essential for the serious multimedia developer. The price of CD-R "burners" has fallen rather quickly over the last few years, and you can get one capable of making a CD in about an hour for about $1,000. Blank recordable CDs cost about $10. With a CD-R and some blank media, you have a good way to produce CDs for testing and archive purposes. Make sure that the CD-R mastering software

AV Macs for Making Multimedia (MEC)

Apple has manufactured a number of Macintoshes in recent years that are specialized for creating multimedia: the AV Macintoshes (AV, of course, stands for Audio-Video). The first two machines of this type, the 660AV and the 840AV, used the Motorola 68040 CPU and incorporated special chips, called DSPs (for Digital Signal Processing), to give them a speed boost when processing the huge amounts of digital information that multimedia—particularly video—requires.

The more recent AV machines use the PowerPC processor and lack the specialized DSP chips used in the 660AV and the 840AV. Apple figures that the PowerPC is fast enough to handle most digital signal processing tasks without any assistance, and it makes the machines less complicated, and therefore cheaper, to construct.

Today, what makes a Mac an AV Mac is simply the addition of ports for inputting and outputting video and high-quality stereo audio. For relatively small projects, these machines can serve your needs rather well. However, the video *throughput* (that is, the number of megabytes of video information per second) these machines can handle unassisted does not meet most professional production needs, being limited to quarter-screen size (i.e., 320 by 240 pixels) and half the number of frames per second of normal television (i.e. 15 frames rather than 30).

Not Just Multimedia Software (MEC)

Aside from the software discussed in this chapter, there are other types of tools you want to have for making multimedia, including such things as a good database and a spreadsheet.

Sure, these are more the tools of the business world than the artistic world, but they are very useful nonetheless in multimedia production. Most multimedia projects involve lots of *assets*: image files, sound files, MIDI files, video files, text files, and so on. Keeping track of all of your assets can become a nightmare unless you get organized early and stay organized, and a good database program can help you do that.

Even though a CD-ROM can hold a lot, it can't hold everything. You'll also want to keep track of how much room each asset takes, and you might want to try juggling different sets of assets to make things fit. A spreadsheet can help you with this. You don't need anything super-sophisticated, though; an integrated program such as **ClarisWorks** is all you need: It is a word processor, database, and spreadsheet program rolled into one—it even serves as a competent drawing and painting program, and can also do slide show presentations! ClarisWorks is covered more fully in Chapter 12, and information about other spreadsheet and database programs can be found in Chapters 9 and 11.

you get for your CD-R is capable of producing *hybrid* disks, that is, CDs that can be read on both the Mac and Windows. If it is also capable of creating "Red Book" CDs (i.e. audio CDs) that's even better. You will want to get as flexible a system as you can.

Tape backup (MEC). A tape backup system of some sort is crucial. The amounts of data involved in most multimedia projects make floppy-disk backup completely impractical (heck, for most Mac users, floppy backup is becoming increasingly impractical). A DAT backup drive, on the other hand, can usually back up a gigabyte of data in less than an hour on a single $15 tape. See Chapter 5 for details on backup alternatives and strategies.

Monitor (MEC). No multimedia developer should be without a good large-screen monitor. This is not just because you deserve the very best (although, of course, you do), but because it is worth it in time and trouble saved. With a large-screen monitor, you can view both the work you are developing and the tools you are using to build it. Because most multimedia titles are designed for a 640-by-480 display, you should get a screen that can show more than that: 832-by-624 (the resolution of a 17-inch monitor) at least, and preferably more. A *multiscan* monitor, capable of multiple resolutions is a very good choice. With it, you can switch between various resolutions without rebooting, allowing you to see your title in 640-by-480 resolution (as your audience will), and then switching back to higher resolution as you do your development work.

And make sure to get the *VRAM* (that is, Video RAM) to support at least thousands of colors (16-bit color) at the highest resolution; the serious professional will want millions of colors (24-bit color) at all screen resolutions (see Chapter 4 for details about VRAM).

Speakers (FB). Let's face it folks, that little speaker on your Mac just doesn't cut it. To appreciate the output your Mac is capable of, you need a set of decent speakers. Apple sells a nice, inexpensive pair of speakers specifically designed to be hooked up to your Mac. These are self-powered speakers, which means that they don't need an amplifier to power them, they plug into the speaker output of the Mac, and provide decent quality stereo sound. They actually seem to take the edge off 8-bit sound, which is quite a feat indeed. There are many other multimedia speakers available on the market now and all will work on your Mac. My only recommendation is to listen before buying because they range greatly in quality.

Graphics for Multimedia   (MEC)

Although Chapter 15 covers Macintosh graphics in considerable detail, a few words need to be said here about graphics as they relate to multimedia.

The most important point to remember is that your graphics are all destined to end up on the screen. You don't need to worry about bleeds, trapping, Pantone colors, or all the other arcana associated with producing print graphics digitally. What you do need to worry about are bit depths, color palettes, and graphic formats. You also need a passing familiarity with a couple of drawing and painting programs.

Bit Depths

The *bit depth* of a graphic refers to how many bits of storage are required to show each pixel in the graphic. The deeper the bit depth, the more memory is required to show the graphic and the more colors the graphic can show. The first Macs had only one bit depth: Because the bit representing each pixel could be either 1 or 0, it meant the picture could only show two colors; by convention, these two colors were black and white. The more bits used per pixel, the more colors (or shades of gray) are possible. Some PowerBooks, for example, can only handle bit depths of 4, which, in turn, means 16 colors or shades of gray, since you can arrange 4 bits in 16 possible combinations.

Most multimedia titles require a minimum bit depth of 8: that is, 256 possible colors. While that is a lot of colors, it is by no means enough to represent what the eye can see. It takes at least 16 bits (which can show thousands of colors) or more before the number of colors available is sufficient to rival photographic quality, and, although some Macs are capable of showing that many colors, many are not. Multimedia authors want to reach the widest possible audience, and, for now, staying with a 256-color limit is the best means for reaching that audience.

Multimedia developers cope with the 256-color limit by using two techniques to make 8-bit pictures seem to show more colors than they can. The first method is called *dithering*, which reduces the resolution of the picture by using more than one actual pixel to represent a single point in the picture. For example, a bluish pixel and an adjacent reddish pixel will be blended by the eye to form a larger, purplish pixel. Dithering can fool the eye to some extent, but at the cost of making the picture look less sharp. The second method is to choose the right set of 256 colors that best shows the picture: This is called using a *custom color palette*.

Color Palettes

The Mac uses a standardized set of 256 colors (called the *standard color palette*) when it is set to a bit depth of 8. When it has to show a picture that has a different set of 256 colors associated with it, one of two things will happen: Either the Mac will dither the picture to match its standard color palette, reducing the picture's resolution and fidelity, or it will use the color palette attached to the picture, which will change the colors on all the other parts of the screen. If the Mac uses this second method, it usually causes the screen to flash unattractively as the color palette changes. Most multimedia titles use a combination of dithering and custom color palettes: A few palettes are chosen that are the best for the bulk of the pictures in the program, and the rest are dithered to look as good as possible in that set of colors. Titles that do this also tend to take over the entire screen so that no color changes will be noticed on the desktop.

Graphic Formats and Image Conversion Software

The world of graphics program developers has spawned a menagerie of special file formats for graphics, each one tailored to suit a specific need. The standard format for all Macintosh graphics onscreen, however, is the PICT format. Because of the plethora of picture formats, and the large number of possible palettes for 256-color PICTs, converting graphics to the right format and set of colors you need for your project can often be frustrating. But every need carves a niche, and the graphics-conversion niche holds some remedies for this mess. One tool, **DeBabelizer** ($270, Equilibrium), is famous among digital graphic artists for its power (and infamous for its confusing user interface). This program excels in converting batches of graphics from one format to another, from one size to another, from one color depth to another, and from one color palette to another. You won't need this product every day, most likely, but when you need it, you will really need it. DeBabelizer is covered more fully in Chapter 25. Another useful package in this niche is Adobe's recently released ScreenReady, which converts graphics intended for print output, such as PostScript line art (for example, EPS files), into attractive screen-ready PICTs.

Painting Software

You should have at least one high-quality painting program in your suite of tools. Adobe's Photoshop is nearly a standard among those who create and manipulate images on the Mac for a living, and Fractal Painter is much loved by artists who like its abilities to create digital art that looks like it was created with real-world media. There are other programs that might suit your needs just as well, though, and you can find out all about them in Chapter 15.

Drawing Software

A good drawing (as opposed to painting) program is also a handy tool in the multimedia development environment. Although such tools are really optimized for print needs where the resolution is much higher, they can also produce output that looks good onscreen. If you need line art or specialized text treatments, you might want to look at Adobe Illustrator or Macromedia FreeHand. These and other drawing tools you might find useful are also discussed in Chapter 15.

Digital Audio on the Macintosh (FB)

You can produce audio on the Macintosh in one of two ways, either through the use of MIDI (see "Music (MIDI)" later in this chapter), or through the use of digital audio. *Digital audio* is recorded audio waveforms that are stored as bits and bytes like all other forms of digital media. There are two basic concepts that are important for understanding how digital audio works—the bit rate and the sample rate.

Bit Rates

Digital audio is commonly found in either 8- or 16-bit formats. The *bit rate* refers to the number of possible values used to describe the *dynamic range* of an audio file (that is, the range between the loudest and softest sound). The 8-bit files have 256 possible values whereas 16-bit files have 65,536 possible values, which results in a marked difference in sound quality between 8-bit and 16-bit sound files. Also, 8-bit files tend to have a grainy quality with a lot of noise and, as one would imagine, don't handle dynamic ranges well, whereas 16-bit files are the standard for high-quality audio and are used for audio CDs.

So now you are asking yourself, "why would anyone use 8-bit files?" As always in the world of computer multimedia, the issue comes down to CPU overhead and what the hardware is capable of playing. The 16-bit files are twice as large as 8-bit files and 68K Macintoshes (non-AV) that are not running Sound Manager 3 (or later) cannot play them without additional hardware. (Sound Manager is the system extension which controls how sound is played back, recorded, and routed on a Mac.) Sound Manager 3 can interpret 16-bit files and play them back in 8-bit format on 68K (non-AV) Macs. Sound designers don't use 8-bit files because they like the way they sound, they use them because they will play back on every Macintosh and are small enough not to grind your presentation down to an untenable crawl while the computer attempts to play back the music along with it.

This is not as much of an issue if you are creating a project that is designed to run solely on a higher-end Power Mac. The Power Mac and AV Macs have the capability of playing back 16-bit audio in true 16-bit mode. If your project is designed to be played back solely on a high-end Power Mac, go nuts and use the best quality audio you can. The sad reality is that if your project must run on everything from an IIx to a Power Mac you will probably have to use 8-bit sound.

HOT TIP

Sample Rates

The process of recording sound onto a computer is often referred to as *sampling* (digital files are sometimes called *samples*) because when you record audio onto a computer it samples that audio signal thousands of times per second to re-create the waveform digitally. The sample rate determines the frequency range at which the digitized audio can be reproduced. For example, audio CDs are sampled 44,100 times per second or at 44.1 KHz. Due to something called the *nyquest average*, digital audio plays back a maximum frequency that is half the sample rate. In other words, audio that has been sampled at 44.1 KHz plays back at a maximum frequency of 22.050 KHz, which is well beyond the range of human hearing.

All this really isn't as complicated as it sounds so long as you remember the basic rule that the playback rate of digital audio is half the sample rate. Much as we would all like to have CD quality audio on our multimedia projects, the cold harsh reality is that it takes far too much computer overhead to play 16-bit, 44.1 KHz audio while playing an animation or displaying a high-resolution graphic file. In fact, Macintoshes of the 68K (non-AV) variety can't play 16-bit, 44.1 KHz audio without additional hardware even if the computer isn't doing anything else.

HOT TIP

Having said all of this, I must put in my plug for high-quality sound. There are few things that can make a multimedia presentation shine as much as good quality audio. Good sound will smooth out the rough edges of a mediocre animation and make the whole show seem that much livelier. Multimedia producers often forget, in their zeal for beautiful graphics, how important audio is to the perceived quality of a project. Often it is worth opting for 256-color images if it means the sound won't suffer for it. Whew, had to get that out of the way. Now we can move on to other things.

Audio Formats

Like text or graphics, audio can come in a variety of different formats which allow a user to move files back and forth between various applications and platforms. The most common generic *audio format* on the Mac is *AIFF* or Audio Interchange File Format. On the PC, the most common format is Microsoft's *Wave* or .WAV. On the Internet, it is common to see audio files in Sun Microsystems's *uLaw* format. The main thing to remember is that when you are using audio files across different platforms you should save the file in a format the platform can read. Most audio programs can now save audio files in a wide variety of formats and there are plenty of shareware programs available on the Internet such as Balthasar and Brian's Sound Tool that can do this.

Mixers

For those who wish to get into serious multimedia audio production, you probably want to buy an external mixer so that you can mix your different sources of audio. A *mixer* is a piece of hardware that allows you to mix multiple audio sources. Mackie Designs makes an excellent mixer that it is gearing toward the multimedia market, called the MS1202-VLZ. It features 12 channels, balanced inputs and outputs, and excellent sound quality.

Why Can't I Hear the Audio From My CD on My External CD-ROM Drive? (FB)

Macs that come with internal CD-ROM drives make it easy for the user. You put in an audio CD, you play it using the AppleCD Audio application and you hear it coming out of your Mac speaker. This is because the CD's output is routed to the same output as the Mac audio chip. If you have an external CD-ROM, it can be a little confusing because you won't hear an audio CD's output coming through your Mac. An external CD-ROM drive has two RCA jacks on the back of the unit. These are the same kind of jacks that you find on your home stereo and, not surprising, require the same kind of cables which can be found at any store that sells stereo equipment. When you play an audio CD in an external CD-ROM, you will either need to hook the RCA cables up to external speakers or listen through headphones connected to the CD-ROM drive itself. The headphone jack is almost always found on the front of the unit.

The Miniplug (FB)

When you are connecting external speakers or a mixer to your Mac you need to be aware of the kind of cable that is required. The Mac output uses something called a *miniplug*. The miniplug is an ⅛-inch jack that outputs a stereo signal. You can tell that the jack is stereo if it has two rings around the end. Most multimedia speakers include a cable when you buy them but if you go the mixer route you will need to purchase a cable that has a miniplug on one end and two male RCA plugs on the other end. If you buy a mixer such as the Mackie, it will probably have ¼-inch inputs. In that case, you will need to get ¼-inch-to-RCA adapters to get all your cables to plug in properly. All of these can be found at Radio Shack, which is an excellent place to find solutions to your cabling nightmares.

If you decide to go with a mixer, you will probably want to get a decent amplifier and pair of speakers. There are many amplifiers and speakers out on the market so we won't mention anything specifically except to say that the speakers that 90 percent of the studios in the world use are the Yamaha NS10. This is not because they are the best (sort of like Windows), but because they are considered representative of the kind of speakers most people listen to music on.

Digitizing Sound

Most Macs sold nowadays come with a microphone which plugs into the microphone input on the back of the computer. The 68K Macs support 8-bit audio input while the Power Mac and AV machines support both 8- and 16-bit input. The Mac also comes with a cable that has female RCA plugs on it allowing you to digitize a *line level* source such as a tape deck or VCR. For those of you who need to record and edit 16-bit sound on a 68K (non-AV) Mac, you will need to purchase a NuBus card designed for this purpose. Digidesign's Audiomedia II card features a higher *signal-to-noise ratio* than the Power Mac or AV Macs (meaning it's less noisy) and has digital inputs and outputs.

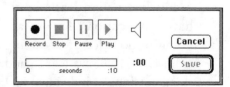

You can digitize sound using the Mac's internal *DAC* (digital to analog converter) by going into the Sound control panel, choosing Alert Sounds from the pop-up menu, and clicking the Add button. You then will be prompted with an interface that looks a bit like

You can record short sounds using the Sound control panel's Add function. Sounds are saved in the System file, but you can double-click on the System file to open it up and drag the sounds out.

the buttons on a standard tape deck. Simply click on the Record button and begin speaking into the microphone or playing your line level source. You can then save

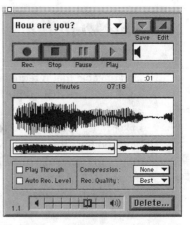

your sound as a System 7 sound and it will be added to alert sounds in the System file. A System 7 sound can be played by double-clicking on it right from the desktop.

HyperCard's Audio palette has a similar interface to the Sound control panel for adding sounds to a HyperCard stack. The Audio palette can be found under Audio in the Edit menu. This brings up an interface which works much the same way as the previous example. The Audio palette has the added benefit of allowing you to edit the sound.

The HyperCard Audio palette lets you edit sounds as well as record them. Sounds are saved as resources in the HyperCard stack, so you will need to use ResEdit to move them elsewhere (see Chapter 13 for more information about ResEdit and other resource editing tools).

WARNING

One of the best ways of adding sound to a presentation is to digitize it directly from a CD. (Of course, if you plan to sell your multimedia presentation, you *must* make sure that you have licensed the right to use the audio you pull from the CD.) To digitize directly from a CD, you must have QuickTime installed on your Mac. Using MoviePlayer (see "The QuickTime Extension and Friends" earlier in this chapter), choose Import from the File menu and highlight the track from the CD that you wish to digitize. Click on the Options button to choose the bit- and sample-rate and to home in on the exact portion of the track that you wish to save. Finally, name your file and click on the Convert button. MoviePlayer will save the track as a QuickTime movie file, which you can then save again as an AIFF file by choosing Export from the File menu. Other programs such as Opcode's Audioshop and version 2 of Macromedia's SoundEdit 16 will also allow you to digitize tracks directly from an audio CD.

Disc-To-Disk ($199, Optical Media International) is a must-have application if you are going to do a lot of digitizing from CDs. It allows you to add small portions of individual CD tracks to a list and then save the items on the list directly to audio files so that you can edit them in your favorite sound editor. You can also see previews of the waveforms for fine-tuning your edit points when saving.

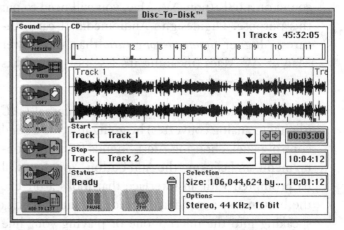

Disc-to-Disk enables you to save portions of audio CDs to your hard disk.

Sound Manager 3.0 and 3.1 (FB)

The audio world breathed a collective sigh of relief when Apple released Sound Manager 3.0 as an addition to the Mac's system software. With Sound Manager 3.0, 68K (non-AV) Macs can now play 16-bit stereo sound files, albeit converted to 8-bit mono. In addition, Sound Manager 3.0 allows the user to route Mac sound through 16-bit sound cards such as the Audiomedia II and increases QuickTime performance by taking over many of the audio chores. Sound Manager 3.1 adds support for IMA compression (see "Using QuickTime For Compression and Synchronization"), as well as increasing performance on Power Macs.

Sound Editors

As you start getting into editing sound, you'll probably find it worthwhile to buy a dedicated sound editing program. Sound editors all show audio in a similar way so you won't have to relearn everything when going from one program to another. The horizontal axis always represents time moving from left to right while the vertical axis represents amplitude or volume.

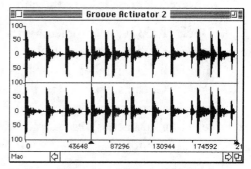

Most sound editors show audio waveforms the same way: The horizontal axis measures time and the vertical axis measures volume.

SoundEdit 16 version 2 ($280, Macromedia) is a fairly complete 8- and 16-bit sound editor that lets you apply a number of audio effects such as reverb and echo to a sound file (though these effects are not of professional quality). With SoundEdit 16 you can save files in a number of formats (including the Windows .WAV) and it lets you convert a number of files between different file formats, sample- and bit-rates all at once (known as *batch processing*). You can also digitize directly from an audio CD.

Audioshop ($150, Opcode Systems) is a nice, inexpensive sound editor that sports several unique and, frankly, nifty features. In addition to the standard audio editing functions, it allows you to play CDs and digitize directly from them. One of my favorite features is Audioshop's ability to make a list of any audio files you may have on your drive and play them back with a click of a button. This is an excellent feature if you need to compare volume levels between files or are just trying to find a sound file whose name you forgot.

GOOD
FEATURE

Sound Designer II ($495, Digidesign) is a professional quality sound editing package that comes bundled with Digidesign's Audiomedia II card; it requires the Digidesign card to work. The program is designed to work with 16-bit sound files, and is a must-have for anyone who is serious about sound design. One of its nice features is the ability to digitize from a DAT tape entirely in the digital realm through an *S/PDIF* or *AES/EBU* connection (these are digital connection formats used in professional sound studios). Sound Designer II can apply serious *DSP* (digital signal processing) functions to a sound file, such as equalization and time-compression, with professional quality results. It also supports third-party plug-in applications such as the L1 Maximizer from Waves Software, which is the best 16- to 8-bit sound converter available on the market.

Alchemy ($300, Passport Designs) is worth mentioning because it has many of the features of Sound Designer II, but it doesn't require the Digidesign hardware in order to work. Alchemy is one of the best pieces of software available for looping sound files. It also does an excellent job of sample rate conversion, allowing you to specify any sample rate between 1 KHz and 48 KHz (most programs only allow conversions from and to a limited selection of sample rates). The program does require a lot of RAM, however, because it loads the entire sound file into RAM for editing.

Deck II ($329, Macromedia) isn't really a sound editor: it is a 16-bit *multitrack* recorder and editor that lets you mix multiple audio tracks together. You are only limited by the number of tracks your computer will support; for example, the faster PowerPCs can support up to 16 tracks for editing and playback. It also sports professional features such as syncing to SMPTE (a time-code system used in the movie and television industries), *nondestructive* editing (which leaves the original files intact until you save), and *automated mixdown* (which lets you specify a number of mixing options

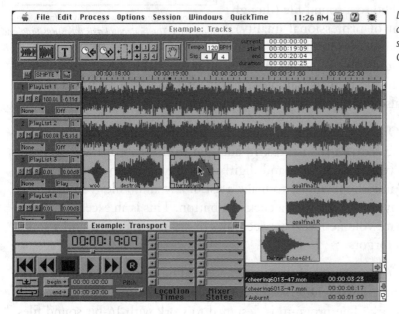

Deck II lets you mix multiple audio tracks together and synchronize sound effects to QuickTime videos.

and run them automatically). It is particularly useful for synchronizing music and sound effects to QuickTime videos, because it allows the user to import QuickTime movies and edit them.

Session ($250, Avid) is an affordable multitrack editor which has many features similar to those found in Deck II.

Pro Tools III ($7,000, Digidesign) is the cream of the crop among multitrack audio editors, and is used in many professional recording studios. Like Sound Designer II, it comes with its own hardware. It features software-based professional-quality audio effects as well as automated mixdown and nondestructive editing. Though even the base-level system is beyond the price range of most low-end multimedia producers, it is worth mentioning because soon after this book is published Digidesign will introduce a version of the Pro Tools software that will run on PowerPC Macs without requiring additional hardware.

Using QuickTime For Compression and Synchronization

Although most people think of video when they think of QuickTime, this system extension offers a lot to anyone working with digital audio.

First off, QuickTime 2.1 supports IMA compression of audio files. IMA compression yields 4 to 1 results on 16-bit files, which means that your 16-bit, 22 KHz stereo file will compress down to the same size as an 8-bit, 11 KHz monaural file. It doesn't work well with every piece of music, so you'll have to experiment with it. Apple's SoundConverter and Macromedia's SoundEdit 16 are two programs that allow you to save files using IMA compression. Sound Manager 3.1 now supports IMA compression as well, so almost any program can play back IMA compressed audio if Sound Manager 3.1 is installed (previously, you had to use a QuickTime player to hear IMA compressed audio).

GOOD FEATURE

One of the wonderful things about QuickTime is that it allows audio and visual data to play back in synchronization. That may not seem like a big deal, but it has been problematic in the past to get visual and audio events to play back in sync. For example, in Director, if you have a sprite dance across the screen while you play an audio file at the same time, the sprite will probably dance at a different speed on a Power Mac 8100 than on a Mac LC III. The audio, however, *will* play back at the same speed on the two computers. This presents a major problem if you want the music to reach a climax at a certain point in the animation. QuickTime helps solve this problem because it keeps the different events running in sync, no matter what Mac it is playing back on.

A quick way of adding an audio soundtrack to a movie is to use Apple's free MoviePlayer program. Open both the movie to which you want to add the soundtrack and the AIFF file you want to add. Make the AIFF file's window active, choose Select All from the Edit menu, and copy the sound to the clipboard. Bring the movie's window to the front and, while holding down (Option), choose Add from the Edit menu (when (Option) is held down, the Paste command changes to Add). This will add your soundtrack to the movie.

The best tools for synchronizing sound and video are Deck II (see "Sound Editors" earlier in this chapter) and Adobe Premiere (see "Editing Video" later in this chapter). Both yield similar results although the two programs have rather different emphases. Deck II is first and foremost a multitrack editor. It has no video editing capabilities but is a very powerful audio editor and is very good for fine-tuning frame-accurate sound effects. Premiere is first and foremost a video editor, but it also can accurately synchronize sound effects. With Premiere, you synchronize audio and video by lining up the audio visually to the video frame, whereas Deck II gives you a SMPTE time-code readout to go by.

Future Possibilities

An increasingly important center for multimedia activity is the World Wide Web, and audio is just beginning to become very important on it. At many sites on the Web, audio files are available for the user to download and then play back later. But, as *helper* applications such as RealAudio and programming languages such as Java become more common, and as the Internet begins to support faster connections and increased bandwidth for the average Mac user, you will see an increasing use of real-time audio across the Net. See Chapter 23 for more about the Internet and the World Wide Web.

Audio File Sizes for One-Minute Audio Files

Sample size, sample rate, and the number of channels all affect the amount of disk space that audio data takes up. This table can help you figure out what the best combination is for your project.

Sample Size	Sample Rate	Channels	File Size
16-bit	44.1 KHz	Stereo	10.59MB
16-bit	44.1 KHz	Mono	5.3MB
16-bit	22.254 KHz	Stereo	5.34MB
16-bit	22.050 KHz	Stereo	5.3MB
16-bit	22.254 KHz	Mono	2.67MB
16-bit	22.050 KHz	Mono	2.65MB
16-bit	11.127 KHz	Stereo	2.67MB
16-bit	11.025 KHz	Stereo	2.65MB
16-bit	11.127 KHz	Mono	1.34MB
16-bit	11.025 KHz	Mono	1.32MB
8-bit	44.1 KHz	Stereo	5.3MB
8-bit	44.1 KHz	Mono	2.65MB
8-bit	22.254 KHz	Stereo	2.67MB
8-bit	22.050 KHz	Stereo	2.65MB
8-bit	22.254 KHz	Mono	1.34MB
8-bit	22.050 KHz	Mono	1.32MB
8-bit	11.127 KHz	Stereo	1.34MB
8-bit	11.025 KHz	Stereo	1.32MB
8-bit	11.127 KHz	Mono	0.67MB
8-bit	11.025 KHz	Mono	0.66MB

〜〜〜〜〜〜〜〜〜〜〜〜〜〜〜〜〜〜〜〜〜〜〜〜〜〜〜〜〜〜〜〜〜

Music (MIDI)   (FB)

What is MIDI?

If you've been involved with computers for awhile or if you've thumbed through any of the multimedia magazines that are now available at your local newsstand, you've probably seen the term "MIDI" bandied about. *MIDI* stands for Musical Instrument Digital Interface; it's a protocol which is used for passing digital musical data between electronic musical devices. With the right hardware and software, computers can also understand MIDI data. On computers, MIDI is typically used to play music back. Rather than storing a digital recording of music, you use the MIDI protocol to store information about the musical *performance* and let the playback device, usually a synthesizer or sound card, take care of producing the actual sounds. In other words, MIDI handles which notes are played, when they are played, how loud they are played, and for how long they are played. Because MIDI is only sending performance data, it takes very little CPU overhead.

MIDI was designed for musicians to use as a means of making music. Musicians use programs called *MIDI sequencers* to write music using the MIDI protocol. A song played back using MIDI is referred to as a *sequence*. MIDI uses the serial port on a computer to transmit MIDI data to synthesizers, which then play back the data they receive using their own internally generated sounds. There are 16 *MIDI channels* per serial port; a channel supports a single musical part with a unique musical voice. That means that you can get up to 16 individual musical parts per serial port. On a Macintosh, without using additional hardware, you can get 32 channels of MIDI if you use both serial ports.

In addition to specifying the notes that are played, MIDI data also contains information about what sound or *patch* that synthesizer should play. By convention, patches are numbered from 0 to 127. Patches, however, vary from synthesizer to synthesizer, and the MIDI protocol does not specify which patches are available on any specific synthesizer. All it can do is carry *program change* messages that tell the synthesizer which sound to use based on the number the sound is located at in the synthesizer's internal bank. The MIDI protocol also allows for *continuous controllers* which are messages that musicians use to enhance the performance of a piece of music. For example, Controller 7 controls volume. A musician can send a Controller 7 message that causes a musical phrase to rise or fall in volume in time with the music. There are many other MIDI messages which allow for a great deal of control over a sequence and, through something called *System Exclusive* data, control over features unique to individual synthesizers.

How a synthesizer interprets System Exclusive (or *SYSEX)* data depends on the individual synthesizer, and the same SYSEX message will probably mean very different things to two different synthesizers from two different manufacturers.

You should realize that MIDI isn't only used for music. Because it is merely a protocol for sending data, MIDI can be used for other, nonmusical purposes. For example, MIDI is often used to synchronize sound effects to a video source. A sound designer might load her *sampler* with sound effects (a sampler is a device that has RAM to store snippets of digital audio that it can play back in response to MIDI commands), and then use a MIDI sequencer to line up the sound effects with a video. When she plays a key on her keyboard, the resulting sound might be an explosion or a footstep, depending upon how she has mapped her sound samples to the keyboard. MIDI can also be used to control lights in theaters using a variation of the MIDI protocol called *MIDI Show Control*. If you are interested in exploring MIDI, there are many good books available that go into it in much more detail than I have room for here.

General MIDI

The original MIDI specification let each musician decide which sounds he could use for which program numbers. Unfortunately, if a musician wanted to give someone a MIDI sequence, he would have to tell that person which kind of sound should be heard on each track in order to get the sequence to sound right. *General MIDI* was created to address this issue and to make it possible for musicians to create sequences that would sound the same on different systems. *General MIDI* defines a standard *instrument bank* so that if a sequence sends out a program change message the instrument that is chosen is predefined. For example, General MIDI specifies that program 0 is a piano, program 12 is a vibraphone, and that MIDI channel 10 is reserved for a drum kit in which specific notes are reserved for different percussion sounds (see the table, "General MIDI Programs"). In order for a General MIDI sequence to play correctly, the synthesizer that plays it back must support the General MIDI standard.

General MIDI Program Names   (FB)

Many synthesizer manufacturers now sell inexpensive synthesizers that are designed specifically for General MIDI. One of the most popular is the Sound Canvas series made by Roland. General MIDI pieces will probably sound best when played back on a Sound Canvas, since it was the first General MIDI device available on the market and, as a result, has become the de facto standard on which composers create General MIDI sequences. The Sound Canvas even comes with a port to connect it directly to a Mac via a serial cable (normally you'd have to get a MIDI interface in order to connect a synthesizer to your Mac).

General MIDI Programs

The General MIDI standard specifies 128 different instruments, or *programs*, that all MIDI-savvy devices should understand. You may not need all of the instruments in this list, but isn't it nice to know that they are there?

1	Acoustic Grand Piano	44	Contrabass	87	Lead 7 (fifths)
2	Bright Acoustic Piano	45	Tremelo Strings	88	Lead 8 (bass and lead)
3	Electric Grand Piano	46	Pizzicato Strings	89	Pad 1 (new age)
4	Honky-Tonk Piano	47	Harp	90	Pad 2 (warm)
5	Electric Piano 1	48	Timpani	91	Pad 3 (polysynth)
6	Electric Piano 2	49	String Ensemble 1	92	Pad 4 (choir)
7	Harpsichord	50	String Ensemble 2	93	Pad 5 (bowed)
8	Clav	51	Synth Strings 1	94	Pad 6 (metallic)
9	Celesta	52	Synth Strings 2	95	Pad 7 (halo)
10	Glockenspiel	53	Choir Aahs	96	Pad 8 (sweep)
11	Music Box	54	Voice Oohs	97	FX 1 (rain)
12	Vibraphone	55	Synth Voice	98	FX 2 (soundtrack)
13	Marimba	56	Orchestra Hit	99	FX 3 (crystal)
14	Xylophone	57	Trumpet	100	FX 4 (atmosphere)
15	Tubular Bells	58	Trombone	101	FX 5 (brightness)
16	Dulcimer	59	Tuba	102	FX 6 (goblins)
17	Drawbar Organ	60	Muted Trumpet	103	FX 7 (echoes)
18	Percussive Organ	61	French Horn	104	FX 8 (sci-fi)
19	Rock Organ	62	Brass Section	105	Sitar
20	Church Organ	63	Synth Brass 1	106	Banjo
21	Reed Organ	64	Synth Brass 2	107	Shamisen
22	Accordion	65	Soprano Sax	108	Koto
23	Harmonica	66	Alto Sax	109	Kalimba
24	Tango Accordion	67	Tenor Sax	110	Bagpipe
25	Acoustic Guitar (nylon)	68	Baritone Sax	111	Fiddle
26	Acoustic Guitar (steel)	69	Oboe	112	Shanai
27	Electric Guitar (jazz)	70	English Horn	113	Tinkle Bell
28	Electric Guitar (clean)	71	Bassoon	114	Agogo
29	Electric Guitar (muted)	72	Clarinet	115	Steel Drums
30	Overdriven Guitar	73	Piccolo	116	Woodblock
31	Distortion Guitar	74	Flute	117	Taiko Drum
32	Guitar Harmonics	75	Recorder	118	Melodic Tom
33	Acoustic Bass	76	Pan Flute	119	Synth Drum
34	Electric Bass (finger)	77	Blown Flute	120	Reverse Cymbal
35	Electric Bass (pick)	78	Shakuhachi	121	Guitar Fret Noise
36	Fretless Bass	79	Whistle	122	Breath Noise
37	Slap Bass 1	80	Ocarina	123	Seashore
38	Slap Bass 2	81	Lead 1 (square)	124	Bird Tweet
39	Synth Bass 1	82	Lead 2 (sawtooth)	125	Telephone Ring
40	Synth Bass 2	83	Lead 3 (calliope)	126	Helicopter
41	Violin	84	Lead 4 (chiff)	127	Applause
42	Viola	85	Lead 5 (charang)	128	Gunshot
43	Cello	86	Lead 6 (voice)		

General MIDI has become very popular in the PC world for game and multimedia applications because just about every PC sound card currently sold supports General MIDI. Because MIDI data takes so little CPU power, it is very appealing to developers, although it is not used nearly as commonly on the Mac as digital audio.

General MIDI on the Mac

Although PC users must have sound cards installed in order to play General MIDI data, General MIDI data can be played back on the Mac using QuickTime. In order to do this, you need the QuickTime Musical Instruments extension, which comes with QuickTime 2.1. The Musical Instruments extension contains the sound samples you need to play back a General MIDI sequence. If you simply want to hear a General MIDI sequence you must convert it into a QuickTime movie (although some programs are now beginning to appear that use QuickTime's MIDI capabilities directly).

HOT TIP

An easy way to convert a General MIDI file into a movie is to use MoviePlayer. Choose Open from the File menu and select the General MIDI sequence file you wish to hear. (There are many General MIDI sequences available both commercially and on the Internet.) Highlight the MIDI sequence and the Open button will change to Convert; click to convert the sequence to a QuickTime movie. You can then play the sequence back as a QuickTime movie in MoviePlayer. If you choose Options before converting, you can change the instruments that play on the different tracks. Once a sequence is converted, you can still change the instruments using MoviePlayer: Choose Get Info from the Movie menu, select the music track and instruments, and then double-click the instrument you wish to

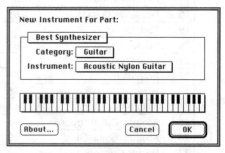

The standard QuickTime Musical Instruments dialog box lets you change the instruments used in a QuickTime MIDI movie.

change. This will bring up the same dialog box as when you choose Options during the conversion process. Note, however, that MoviePlayer will only convert sequences whose file type is "Midi" which is how most Mac sequencing programs save MIDI files—if it isn't, which might be the case for files that come from a PC or from the Internet, you must first change the file type with a utility such as ResEdit (see Chapter 13 for more about ResEdit). Luckily, there is an even easier way to convert a MIDI sequence using the freeware program **All MIDI** by Paul C.H. Ho: Just drop the MIDI sequence on All MIDI and the file will be instantly converted.

You may be disappointed with the way your movie sounds. The QuickTime Musical Instruments are a limited sound set and don't actually contain the full set of General MIDI programs. For example, QuickTime Musical Instruments will substitute a single trumpet for a brass section. Unfortunately, all the instruments must be stored as sound samples in memory and it would take more memory than most users are willing to sacrifice to fit all the General MIDI instruments into RAM. QuickTime General MIDI tends to sound best on pieces that aren't heavily orchestrated, such as a Bach piece for solo harpsichord. To get the best sound out of General MIDI, I recommend getting a dedicated General MIDI box such as the Roland Sound Canvas.

HOT TIP

Creating MIDI With Your Mac

General MIDI is a great way to get started writing music on your Mac. General MIDI synthesizers don't tend to be as expensive as professional quality synthesizers and they allow the beginner to dissect sequences others have created. So what do you need to start creating your own music? In addition to your Mac, you will need a MIDI sequencing program, a MIDI interface to connect your Mac to your synthesizer, a synthesizer (this doesn't have to be General MIDI-compatible), and a MIDI controller, which usually takes the form of a piano-like keyboard. The last two items can be found as a single entity.

There are many manufacturers of MIDI hardware; *Keyboard* and *Electronic Musician* magazines often have good articles about buying synthesizers, so I recommend looking there as a place to start. Your local music store should also be able to help you select a suitable synthesizer.

As for software, there are several manufacturers of MIDI software that address the needs of musicians at all levels. Opcode Systems makes a good starter kit for the burgeoning electronic musician called the **Easy Music Starter Kit** ($299). It includes **Musicshop** ($100), their entry level sequencing and notation program, the **MIDI Translator II** ($45) MIDI interface, and **Band In a Box**, an auto accompaniment program.

Mark of the Unicorn has an entry level sequencing program called **Freestyle** ($200) which features a unique interface designed to be more intuitive for those who are less technically oriented. It also has notation features. Two other entry level sequencing programs are Emagic's **MicroLogic** ($159) and Steinberg-Jones' **Cubasis** ($99).

On the professional end, there are several high-end sequencing programs that address most composers' needs. These include **Vision** ($495, Opcode), **Performer** ($495, Mark of the Unicorn), **Cubase** ($799, Steinberg-Jones), **MasterTracks Pro** ($80, Passport), and **Logic** ($799, Emagic). Most of these manufacturers also make a version of their sequencer that allows the user to record digital audio along with MIDI.

Another area for MIDI software is applications that are designed for music notation. While many sequencers have notation features, composers who wish to write complicated music scores need to explore programs that are designed for that purpose. **Finale** ($550, Coda) is considered by many to be the final word in notation programs. It supports almost every conceivable type of notation but has a steep learning curve. **Encore** ($350, Passport) would probably suit the needs of most composers. Its interface is more intuitive than Finale's but it doesn't support some obscure forms of notation.

For those who wish to edit the sounds on their synthesizers, there are editor/librarian programs to help with the job. Opcode makes **Galaxy Plus Editors** ($399) which has been the premiere patch editor/librarian program for some years. To edit a sound for your particular synthesizer, you need to purchase the appropriate editor from Opcode (some of the more popular synthesizers are included when you buy the program) as a plug-in module. This allows you to edit the parameters of the synthesizer's sounds on your computer screen and save your sounds in a library for easy accessibility. Patch editors use system-exclusive data to edit the parameters of a synthesizer. Mark of the Unicorn's **Unisyn** ($395) is another editor/librarian with similar features.

A unique piece of software is **Max** ($495, Opcode). Max is a MIDI construction kit that allows the user to create their own MIDI programs by patching together icons that control MIDI parameters. Max is a very powerful development environment that can be used for everything from algorithmic composition to creating your own patch editors.

MIDI in Multimedia Applications

Although one could argue that every piece of software that has been mentioned in this section is a multimedia application, there has been scant support in multimedia development environments for MIDI on the Macintosh. Macromedia's **Director** ($1,195) dropped MIDI support in version 4 and HyperCard has little for the MIDI enthusiast that's readily available. **HyperMIDI** is a HyperCard stack that is an exception to that. It provides a bit of everything—SYSEX dumps, recording, analysis, keyboard play, and a programmable patch editor. This is your best bet for complex MIDI implementation within a HyperCard stack. Version 1 is available as shareware on the Net, but it is about eight years old. If you are interested in the latest version, it is available for $125 from the author, Nigel Redmond. It may be possible to use HyperMIDI's XCMDs in Director, though I haven't tried it so I can only speculate.

Your best bet for MIDI in multimedia is to use QuickTime. At present, you can play General MIDI sequences back without the use of an external synthesizer. QuickTime 2.5 (which should be available by the time you read this) will add many enhancements to its MIDI capabilities. Version 2.5 will give synthesizer developers the capability of creating custom software synthesizers and instruments which should greatly improve the sound quality of QuickTime MIDI scores. It will also allow you to route musical information to external MIDI devices. With these sorts of enhancements, QuickTime will become an increasingly viable option for creating music on a Macintosh.

Digital Video (MEC)

How times change: A few years ago people would say that adding video to computer-based multimedia was a thankless, nearly impossible task. Today, video is almost *required* for a multimedia title to get any attention. To use video, you need to know two things: how to get the video into the Mac, and how to manipulate it once you do.

Digitizing (a.k.a. Capturing)

Capturing video is a task that requires more computing speed and storage than almost any other task you may do on your Mac. You'll either want a Mac that is "video-ready" or one that you can make video-ready.

AV Macs and digitizing boards. The Macs that Apple labels with "AV" are set up to do basic video capturing right out of the box. Some other Macs (for example, most Power Macs) can be made video-ready by installing Apple's **Power Macintosh AV** card ($530). A few consumer-level Macs (such as the Power Mac 5200/75, LC, or the Performa 630) can use Apple's **Video System** card ($120), which is cheaper, but which can't handle very large frame sizes or frame rates (that is, the number of frames of video it can capture per second). Fast Macs with NuBus slots might also be able to use a **Spigot II Tape** ($750, Radius) digitizing card. Any of these solutions will enable you to create credible video for most multimedia purposes. If, however, you want to capture professional quality, full-screen, full-motion video, you will need additional help in the form of a proprietary third-party capture board, and you should be prepared to spend a few thousand dollars and a lot of time reading professional video magazines and journals—this field is changing so rapidly that any recommendations I might make here will be obsolete by the time you read this.

Video sources. Getting the Mac set up to capture video is one thing; getting the video to capture is quite another. (Note: unless you are doing all this merely for your own amusement, you don't want to capture video from commercially produced videotapes, television broadcasts, cablecasts, or laser disks—you'll be violating copyright laws and leaving yourself open to a very expensive legal education.) Your video source will

WARNING

probably be some sort of videotape: VHS, Hi-8, or, if you are verging on the professional, Beta-SP. Whatever your source, make sure that it is the highest quality possible; the more video "noise" in your original, the harder it will be to compress well. Furthermore, as the Mac's video capabilities improve, you may eventually want to recapture your video, and you will be grateful for a high-quality original when you do.

Making the capture. A number of video editing programs support video capturing, which is not surprising, since the bulk of the work of capturing is handled by QuickTime itself. In most cases, the process is no more elaborate than choosing "Record" or "Capture" from a menu or dialog box. Before you do, though, you should set your frame rate and compression choices from QuickTime's standard dialog box. The menu which brings up the box is not standard; it will vary from program to program. You also want to set the capture window size. Once you have these things set, you can start capturing. After that, sit back, relax, and watch the free space on your hard disk start to disappear!

HOT TIPS

Tips For Capturing Video (MEC)

- *Capture your video without any compression if your hardware supports it and you have the room.* Most codecs (compressor/decompressor; see "Compressing Video") are just too slow to compress video in real time, and besides, you will want to play around with compression settings to get the best possible results.

- *Capture video in short segments.* The longer the segment, the longer it will take to compress, the more disk space it will take up, and the more chance that something will go wrong in the process, forcing you to recapture.

- *Defragment your hard disk before you capture video.* If your Mac has to search all over your hard disk looking for empty sectors, it takes precious processing time away from the video capture, and will almost certainly result in your losing some frames.

- *Turn off CPU-hungry extensions and network connections.* Some extensions work continually in the background, taking small chunks of processing time away from the capture process. Also, if you have AppleTalk turned on, the Mac will be checking the network periodically and, while it is doing that, it won't be working on your video. (Some programs, such as **Adobe Premiere** will even offer to turn AppleTalk off for you before it starts to capture.)

- *Capture your video at the final frame size you wish to use.* If you are planning to show your video in a 180-by-120 window, for instance, it doesn't make sense to capture it at a larger size: This will merely consume disk space and processing time. Worse, if you plan to show your video in, say, a 320-by-240 window and you capture it at 180-by-120, it will look terrible when scaled up.

Video Connectors (MEC)

Attaching a video source to your Mac requires some sort of cable and connector (attaching the audio source requires a different cable and connector and is explained in "The Miniplug" earlier in this chapter). There are two different connector types for video connections: a high-quality *S-Video connector* (which looks a lot like an ADB connector) and a *composite video connector* (which looks like the RCA connectors on the backs of most stereo amplifiers). The 840AV has both sorts of connectors; the AV Power Macs have only an S-Video connector, but come with an adapter cable that converts a composite connector to S-Video. The Apple Video System card for consumer Macs has only composite video connectors.

- *Capture your video at the final frame rate you wish to use.* The television standard in America (NTSC) shows frames at about 30 per second (actually, it is 29.97 frames per second...go figure). You should capture video at some even fraction of this rate for the best playback: 15 frames per second is usually a good choice. Capturing at an uneven fraction of the standard rate can result in jerky motion, dropped frames, and other oddities.

- *Put a floppy disk in your floppy disk drive (and a CD in the CD drive, and a cartridge in your cartridge drive).* Seriously. Every so often your Mac likes to check all attached drives to see if something has been put in them. This check takes a little time, and time is something you don't have to spare when capturing video. Once a disk is in a drive, the Mac doesn't check anymore until the disk is removed.

Compressing Video

The still pictures that make up a video take up a lot of room: A single picture measuring 320 by 240 pixels at a bit depth of 16 takes up over 150K. If you wanted to show 30 pictures like that a second (about the same rate as television), a minute of video would take up over 250MB! Luckily, there are ways to compress that same video so that it might only take up 1MB...a significant savings.

There are a lot of different methods for compressing video. The most practical ones are called "lossy" compression schemes; that is, they deliberately discard some of the video information, which reduces the picture quality of each frame. A good lossy compression scheme must choose the information to throw away that least reduces the picture quality. Video compression schemes must also allow the compressed video to be decompressed quickly enough to be shown on screen.

One type of lossy scheme uses something called *frame differencing*. In this scheme, *key frames* are chosen and stored periodically. Non-key frames only contain those pixels that differ significantly from those in the key frame. This sort of compression works well for video that doesn't contain a lot of motion; a field of wheat rippling in the wind, for example, would not work well with frame differencing. Another scheme reduces the number of pixels stored in each frame by collecting adjacent pixels of similar color and making them all the same color. This scheme can make the picture look blocky and less distinct. In practice, both schemes are usually used when compressing video. It takes a certain amount of experience and experimentation to balance these different compression methods for the best results.

One of QuickTime's jobs is to manage video compression. It does this through software packages called *codecs*, which stands for "Compressor/Decompressor." Codecs are little chunks of software that handle the compression and decompression of video, graphical, and audio data. Some codecs are built into the QuickTime extension in your Extensions folder; while other, more specialized, codecs are dropped into that folder separately. QuickTime manages them all, even codecs that are designed to work only with special hardware add-ons to your Mac.

The standard QuickTime Compression dialog box includes a pop-up menu that lets you choose which codec to use. Here are some of QuickTime's built-in codecs that appear on this menu.

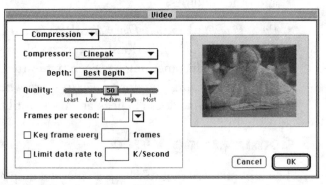

The QuickTime Compression dialog box lets you adjust a variety of compression settings. Because it is a standard part of QuickTime, this dialog box will appear in most digitizing programs.

- **None**—As its name implies, this codec actually does no compression at all. But it is not worthless; using this codec you can convert video from one bit depth to another. You may also want to use this codec for capturing video that you want to compress later, since uncompressed video is usually the highest quality you can get—but you'll only do this if you have very fast hardware and lots of disk space.

- **Animation**—You should choose this codec for material that is made up of images generated on the Mac, such as computer-generated video or sequences of screen shots—in other words, animations as opposed to camera work. If you choose Most quality from the Compressor dialog, it supports lossless compression. The codec is very sensitive to changes between images, so even the subtlest video noise will reduce its effectiveness.

Choosing Video Compression Settings (MEC)

Aside from letting you choose a compressor, the standard compression dialog offers you other choices. Cinepak, the typical compressor for live-action video, offers you a number of things you can set. Unfortunately, it is not always clear what effect a particular combination of settings will have on the final product. The "Quality" slider is rather difficult to interpret because it actually controls a number of low-level compression features (e.g. balancing "spatial" versus "temporal" compression techniques).

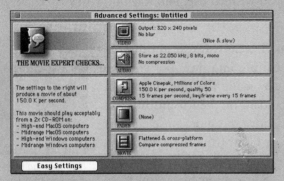

MovieCleaner Lite, an excellent shareware package, eliminates this confusion. This program (which also comes in a more full-featured commerical version) distills the experience of digital video experts, and presents

The shareware program MovieCleaner Lite provides software smarts to help you deal with the complexities of video compression.

you with informed compression choices. The latest version of Adobe Premiere also has a number of customized batch compression settings designed to help you make informed compression choices.

- **Apple Video**—This was the very first video codec that came with QuickTime 1.0 (during development it was known as "Road Pizza," a sobriquet it still wears among digital video veterans). This codec provides fast enough decompression for many video playback needs, and the compression is a good deal faster than Cinepak's (see below), taking about seven times as long to compress video as to decompress and play it back. The (relatively) fast compression speed makes it useful for doing editing experiments before final editing and compression. In addition, this codec can compress video as much as 25 to 1 with the right settings.

- **Cinepak**—This codec is most commonly used for video in multimedia titles. It compresses even more tightly than Apple Video and decompresses much faster. Furthermore, it lets you specify the data rate for your video (that is, how much data is processed each second); this is particularly useful for video that will play from a CD-ROM, where the maximum data transfer rate may be relatively low. Cinepak, however, offers these features at a price: Compression is very slow, often taking the better part of an hour to compress a mere 30 seconds of video.

Editing Video

The field of video editing packages runs the price gamut from free to extremely costly. Nearly all video editors have certain interface elements in common: a time line that lets you select portions of the movie and places to insert clips, a Clip palette that lets you choose from the unedited clips you wish to use, and a window to play back the current state of your movie.

MoviePlayer 2.1, Apple's free video viewer (you can get it from their Web site) does not have a real editing interface, but you can do rudimentary video editing with it by using the traditional cut, copy, and paste commands that are standard on the Macintosh. You simply hold down the [Shift] key as you move the slider to select part of the movie, then choose Cut, Copy, or Clear from the Edit menu. When you finish editing, choose Save As… from the file menu and make sure to select the Make Movie Self-contained option from the Save dialog; otherwise, it will simply save a tiny file that points to the original movie, and if you move that file to a different disk, you will lose your edits.

The utilitarian MoviePlayer from Apple lets you select, cut, copy, and paste QuickTime video. It does a whole lot more, too, and the price is right: it's free.

QuickFlix ($150, Radius) is a low-cost way to do real video editing. It provides some rudimentary effects and transitions that you can apply to your clips, and it supports direct video capture.

Videoshop ($260, Avid) has more features than the first two editing packages. You can trim individual clips and layer multiple video tracks. Videoshop has a storyboard as well as a time line so you can see which clips, in which order, are currently in your movie, and it has a more robust set of effects, transitions, fades, and filters.

Premiere ($500, Adobe) is probably the standard of multimedia video professionals, as well as having a place in the world of broadcast video editing. It has a huge number of standard transitions and effects, supports batch compression, lets you "matte" one video onto another, and much more. Its weakest feature may be its manual, which is skimpy and sometimes misleading, but if you can afford to buy it, you should have it.

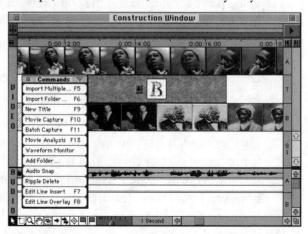

Adobe Premiere's Construction Window is typical of video editing programs, showing the movie and the soundtrack as separate time lines that can be adjusted and edited.

Animation (JK)

The word *animate* literally means "to make alive," and because most Mac owners tend to think of their machines as living, breathing things anyway, it's only natural that they use their Macs for creating animations. Actually, one of the biggest reasons why the Mac is the machine of choice for most multimedia developers is the availability of animation tools, as well as image manipulation and sound editing software for the Mac. All of these programs work hand-in-hand to create successful animations, animations that can range from a simple button that comes alive when you click it to talking, walking, lifelike 'toons in an interactive children's book.

Most computer animation falls into one of two categories—two-dimensional or *cel* animation (2-D) and three-dimensional (3-D) animation. Each has its specific place in the multimedia world, and each has an extensive set of tools available on the Mac. The biggest difference between 2-D and 3-D animation is how they are made.

No matter which type of animation you intend to make, the process usually starts with recording the soundtracks: It is almost always easier to synchronize an animation to a soundtrack than the other way around. The soundtracks are mixed down to *DAT* (digital audio tape) and then digitized and edited using programs such as Sound Designer or SoundEdit 16 (see "Digital Audio" earlier in this chapter). The real work starts after you finish the soundtracks.

2-D Animation

In 2-D animation, you draw the parts of the image that will move: Some animators use illustration programs such as Adobe Illustrator or Macromedia Freehand, but most animation artists still prefer to draw the old-fashioned way. Whether you do your drawing on screen or on paper though, you'll need to create at least ten separate drawings for each second of animation if you want it to look smooth. At the same time, you'll need to create the background art over which the moving image will appear. If you've been doing your drawings on paper, you'll then scan and colorize them using a flatbed color scanner and a 2-D image manipulation program such as Adobe Photoshop. The whole process is not too different from the way animation has been done since the Road Runner was an egg.

Even with your Mac's help in reducing some of the drudgery of making all those pictures, 2-D animation is still a lot of work. That's why most 2-D animation projects require a small team of artists. If your project will require more than just a few seconds of animation, you'll probably want to farm out that work to a company that specializes in animation. Still, trying your hand at this venerable form can be a lot of fun, too, and the buy-in price is right: The inexpensive **Dabbler** ($70, Fractal Design), lets you create animations and even provides interactive multimedia tutoring on the art of cartooning.

3-D Animation

Although most 2-D animation work still starts with pencil and paper drawings, 3-D animation is almost completely created on the computer. The two main stages in creating 3-D art are *modeling* and *rendering*.

In the modeling stage, you start by making *wireframe* images on the screen (so called because the pictures are made up of a series of lines that look like wire frames, which require much less processing time than generating a filled-in image), and fine tuning them to simulate real-life characteristics and movements. Once you've made your wireframe images, you'll apply surfaces, textures, and lighting effects to them, often using the same software that you used to generate the wireframe images. The character or scene can be modeled from various viewing angles, allowing you to create different versions of the same image. You'll also specify movements of the image over time in this stage.

The rendering process takes the choices you've made about surfaces, textures, motions, and lighting effects and turns them into a finished 3-D image. The rendering process also saves your images on disk, using one of the standard file formats (such as PICT, PICS, or QuickTime) that multimedia applications will be able to use. Rendering, however, can take a long time and it requires your Mac to do a lot of highly complex math work, so you really should use the fastest Power Mac that money can buy. In other words, your good old Mac IIsi would probably not be a wise choice for 3-D rendering, unless you have a couple of days to kill.

HOT TIP

3-D packages range vastly in price and sophistication. On the lower end of the spectrum, many developers use **StudioPro** ($1,500, Strata) or **Infini-D** ($900, Specular). Macromedia recently released a good 3-D product, called **Extreme 3D** ($500), which offers time-based 3-D animation capabilities in addition to good 3-D modeling and rendering. On the higher end, **Electric Image** ($7,500, Electric Image) is the program of choice for the serious 3-D artist.

Integrating Animation into Multimedia

How you integrate your animation into your multimedia project depends very much on the multimedia authoring program that you use. In many cases, you'll want to save your animation as a QuickTime movie, since nearly all multimedia authoring programs can use it. Some programs, however, let you do more than just plop a QuickTime animation onto the screen.

Macromedia Director (see "Interactive Multimedia Authoring" later in this chapter) is one of the most frequently used tools for constructing animations because it uses a time-based metaphor, and also has its own programming language called "Lingo" for developing interactivity. With it, you can make animated sequences come and go when you choose and interact with other objects on the screen.

Some developers have recently started using mFactory's mTropolis (see "Interactive Multimedia Authoring" later in this chapter) as their authoring tool, because of its ability to efficiently animate numerous objects simultaneously, and because it uses a more object-oriented authoring environment than Director's (something the programmers you work with might appreciate). mTropolis also allows you to create something called *mToons*, which are animation files used exclusively for titles developed in mTropolis. mToons are similar to QuickTime movies, since they can use the same types of compression used in QuickTime.

Of course, standard authoring and animation tools don't always meet the needs of high-end multimedia developers, some of whom develop their animated titles using proprietary software created by their own in-house programmers (who probably don't get very much sleep). Luckily, most high-end in-house proprietary tools usually find their way onto the market sooner or later. As it is, there are numerous possibilities available for creating animations on the Mac, whether you're a seasoned animator with a big budget, or a weekend hacker with some "off the shelf" software and a good machine.

Presentations (AA)

If multimedia is defined as the blending of different types of media, then presentation software is its very essence. That's right: Those slide-making programs that marketing and business folks use everyday for sales, education, and training are actually powerful multimedia tools. With a presentation program, you can combine text, charts, and illustrations—and, if you wish, animation, video, and sound—into eye-opening visuals that keep the audience awake and get your points across in style.

You can choose from a variety of output options, including on-screen presentations, 35mm slides, overhead transparencies, audience handouts, and videotape.

What to Look For   (SC)

Presentation software comes in two basic flavors. *Traditional presentation programs*, such as PowerPoint and Persuasion, are essentially slide-making tools for business presentations chock full of charts and bullet points. If you're doing an on-screen slide show, you can add QuickTime movies and sounds.

Multimedia presentation programs output only to the screen (or videotape), but they offer more pizzazz. Not only can you combine elements from a variety of sources—including sounds and movies—but you can also define precisely when and how they will come and go over time. For example, you could have a pie chart roll onto the screen and break apart. Then each slice could tumble off the screen in a different direction while theme music pounds in the background. Two seconds later, the company logo fades in while a narrator adds a pithy comment. Most multimedia programs also offer rudimentary interactivity, allowing you (or a client) to jump to different points in the presentation at will.

Whether you opt for an old-fashioned or newfangled presentation program, here are some key features to look for.

Import capabilities. You'll probably create most of your media elements elsewhere, so be sure the program imports the file formats you need for text, graphics, animation, video, and sound. Typically, traditional programs offer better support for spreadsheet data, while multimedia programs can handle more sound and animation formats.

Media creation and editing. You don't want to import everything, so look for text-formatting features (including a spelling checker!) and basic drawing tools. Traditional programs can create graphs from scratch, while some multimedia presenters have sound editors. But if, for example, you require a truly sophisticated chart, you'll have to produce it in a dedicated program such as DeltaGraph Pro (see Chapter 15).

Run-time player. This is critical if you want to hand out copies of presentations. A run-time player is a limited version of the program that plays back presentations but can't create them. You can freely distribute it with your presentations, so that clients can view them without the full program installed on their computer.

HOT TIP

Don't forget to include external source files (such as QuickTime movies) when you distribute the presentation. And stick to core fonts such as Helvetica and Times so the text will look good on everyone's Mac.

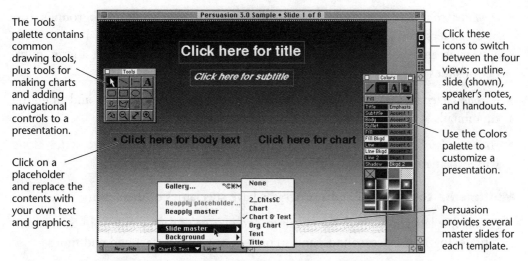

The Tools palette contains common drawing tools, plus tools for making charts and adding navigational controls to a presentation.

Click on a placeholder and replace the contents with your own text and graphics.

Click these icons to switch between the four views: outline, slide (shown), speaker's notes, and handouts.

Use the Colors palette to customize a presentation.

Persuasion provides several master slides for each template.

Presentation programs such as Persuasion provide a variety of templates—predesigned slides with color-coordinated backgrounds and formatted text.

Templates. A healthy selection of predesigned slides or scenes makes creating consistent, professional-looking presentations faster and easier. The backgrounds, color schemes, text placement and formatting, charts and graphics, and (in some cases) animation are already in place. Just substitute your material for the placeholders, and away you go.

Transition effects. For on-screen presentations, you can vary the way one slide or scene is replaced by another. Wipes, fades, and dissolves can add subtle interest. Some programs offer funkier effects such as checkerboards and vertical blinds.

Use a program's build feature to reveal bullet points or chart elements one slide at a time; it adds drama and helps ensure that the audience will be listening to you instead of studying the slide.

HOT TIP

Cross-platform compatibility. If you work in a mixed-platform environment, look for programs with Windows versions that allow users to open and edit presentations created on the Macintosh, and vice versa. Most slide-based presentations should convert with only minor changes, such as text reformatting (due to font differences).

Traditional tools. Slide-making programs have a few other key features:

- *The outliner*—a defining feature of these programs—lets you quickly enter or import text. Outline entries should be linked directly to slides, so that any text changes you make show up in the slide, and vice versa. It also should be easy to change the order and hierarchy of items in the outline.

- *A master slide* acts as a guide for individual presentation slides. Backgrounds, text placeholders, and graphics (such as a company logo) that you put on a master slide appear on any slide tied to that master. This lets you quickly format a large number of slides and ensure a consistent look for the presentation.

- *A slide sorter* lets you quickly rearrange a presentation by clicking and dragging thumbnails.

- *Audience handouts and speaker's notes* often contain thumbnails of the slides along with explanatory text.

Multimedia tools. Multimedia programs have specialties of their own:

- *A time line* lets you control the comings and goings of each element in the presentation—logos, movies, sounds, and so on—by specifying start and end times.

- *Slide-import capabilities* let you convert a traditional slide presentation into a multimedia extravaganza.

- *Basic animation tools* let you add motion to text and graphics. For example, you could direct a circular corporate logo to bounce around a scene, then come to rest on top of an *i*.

- *Interactivity* means you can add buttons that let you (or another viewer) decide where to go in a presentation or when to play a QuickTime movie. This makes multimedia programs good choices for producing training materials and kiosk displays.

Presentation Programs (SC)

Slide-making applications are the workhorses of business presentations, meeting the needs of most of the people most of the time. You can't go wrong with either Persuasion or PowerPoint. Both offer good outliners and text handling, drawing tools, robust charting capabilities, numerous templates and transitions, a run-time viewer, and hot links to other programs—which means you could, for example, double-click on a table imported from Excel to open it directly into Excel for editing.

Persuasion. After a couple of years in PowerPoint's shadow, **Persuasion** ($260, Adobe) is again king of the hill, at least temporarily. Version 3 is easier to use, with floating palettes and better navigation icons, and its improved color handling ensures that color slides convert nicely to grayscale or black and white, so that audience handouts are legible. Beefed-up options for on-screen presentations include bare-bones animation; more control over transitions; and an autojump feature that lets you branch to other slides, presentations, or programs. And, unlike PowerPoint, Persuasion can juggle several master slides in a single presentation. For example, you could use one master for bullet-point slides, another for charts, and a third for titles. Persuasion's biggest drawback is its clumsiness in exchanging presentations with the Windows version.

PowerPoint. The original presentation program has that familiar Microsoft look and feel: a handy toolbar up top and hot links to other programs. **PowerPoint 3** ($295) has

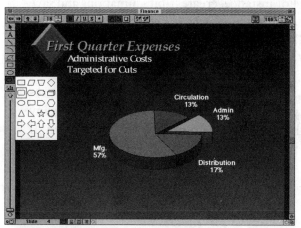

only a single master slide, but the ability to format slide text in outline view is a real time-saver. A versatile shape tool lets you quickly draw perfect stars, arrows, and triangles, and the artistically challenged will appreciate the color coach, which helps you select coordinated colors for your presentations. PowerPoint's near-flawless ability to transfer presentations to and from its Windows version is a definite advantage over Persuasion. Version 4 sports more production aids and design features, such as improved toolbars, easier creation of organizational charts, and limited interactivity.

PowerPoint is a full-featured traditional slide-making program with a variety of tools neatly arranged around the window. It offers excellent graphing capabilities, and a handy shape tool (left) helps you draw perfect polygons.

Astound. You don't have to choose between a traditional slide show and multimedia presentation program: Get **Astound** ($170, Gold Disk), the only program that offers the best of both worlds. Like traditional programs, it uses a slide-based approach and supports outlines, 35mm slides, overheads, and speaker's notes. You can even create charts and edit text (including spelling checks). Yet Astound also provides a full range of multimedia tools, including a timeline, rudimentary animation tools, interactive buttons, and a sound editor. To top it off, Astound has a well-designed interface that's relatively easy to use, and its transition effects are positively stunning.

If you're presenting mostly charts and graphs, also consider **DeltaGraph Pro**, a super graphing program with decent presentation features to boot.

HOT TIPS

Presentation Tips

Keep it simple (AA). Transitions, animations, movies, and sounds liven things up, no doubt about it, but too many will distract, instead of impress, your audience. Too much activity may also overstress your Mac, causing the presentation to become slow and jerky. Try using just one or two eye-catching effects to guide the audience to specific points.

Color concerns (AA). Use 8-bit color whenever possible, because the Mac can process it much faster than 24-bit color. For instance, create 8-bit animations and save them with the QuickTime animation compressor set at highest quality (this also reduces file sizes). (For more on QuickTime compressors, see "Compressing Video" earlier in this chapter.)

File management (AA). Keep all the source files in the same folder with the presentation so they'll be available when you run it. This is important because many programs create a link to movies, sounds, and graphics instead of importing them. If you're distributing the presentation, keep in mind the space limitations of floppy disks and don't forget the run-time player!

Presentations to go (SC). If you plan to take your show on the road with a PowerBook, here are a few tips:

- Several programs provide templates specially designed to look good on a PowerBook screen.

- Keep it simple. QuickTime movies, jazzy sounds, and intricate drawings won't cut it on most PowerBooks.

- If you don't have a color PowerBook, test-drive the presentation in black and white or grayscale to be sure contrasting colors and text show up well. (Persuasion 3 has a built-in grayscale preview.)

- Stick to core fonts (see "The LaserWriter 35: Fonts *Almost* Everyone Has" in Chapter 14). You'll save hard disk space and, in an emergency, won't have problems running the presentation on someone else's Mac.

- Bring backup—PowerBook batteries and floppies with an extra copy of your presentation and the run-time player.

- A PowerBook screen works only for a handful of viewers. For larger groups, hook up an external monitor, video projector, or LCD projection panel.

Interactive Multimedia Authoring   (MEC)

Presentations that simply combine text, video, audio, and graphics can do a lot, but sometimes you need your Mac to do even more. When you really need to *involve* your audience, to put them in control of the material you've assembled, you no longer have just a presentation: You have an interactive multimedia experience.

Stacks, Stages, and Scripts

Considering all the material that goes into a typical multimedia title, it helps to have some overall structure to arrange and contain it. Many interactive multimedia authoring packages choose one of two metaphors to provide that structure: the *stack* metaphor, or the *stage* metaphor.

The stack metaphor arranges the title as though it were a stack of index cards. You can flip through these cards like the pages in a book, but, more importantly, you can sort them in different orders. In this metaphor, each card contains information: pictures, text, buttons, and so on. The card metaphor is particularly good for titles that are more like books or databases than like movies, such as an interactive cookbook, or an encyclopedia.

The stage metaphor arranges the title as a collection of various movies. The screen is a stage upon which objects appear, move, interact, and disappear. This metaphor is particularly good for titles that are time-oriented and have stories to tell. Interactive fiction, games, and simulations often use the stage metaphor.

The distinction however, between stage and card is not clear: The cards in card-based programs can act a lot like stages, and the stage in stage-based programs can be made to look and act a lot like a card.

Whatever metaphor you choose, you may find yourself severely limited in the sorts of interactivity you can provide if the package does not provide some sort of *scriptability* (that is, the ability to do custom programming using the package's *scripting language*). Clever scripts can often lift the products you make with an authoring package far above what the package's creators thought possible, as well as allowing you to work around some of the package's limitations. As a simple example, most authoring programs let you create buttons that, when clicked, take you someplace, or play a sound, or show a video. But a program that lets you customize a button's actions with a script can let you do things such as detect whether the user clicked near the left or right side of the button and then use that information to control the speed of a video or the direction in which it plays.

Authoring Packages (SE)

HyperCard ($100, Apple). This is the original easy-to-use multimedia authoring tool. First released by Apple in 1987, it has traveled through many versions (and software companies) since then. HyperCard is at version 2.3 as of this writing, and has been accelerated for Power Macintosh, though you can use HyperCard with practically any 68000-series Macintosh that has at least 2MB of RAM and a hard disk.

HyperCard uses the stack metaphor for creating multimedia. To build a program, you create cards containing data to be viewed (or heard) and interactive elements (such as buttons that may take the user from one card to the next). HyperCard has built-in tools for making or entering text, graphics, buttons, user-input fields, time-based events, or location-based events. HyperCard's automated button tasks make it easy to create jumps between cards or trigger multimedia events such as playing back audio files or QuickTime movies. HyperCard also supports AppleScript (see Chapter 3) so that you can run Apple events from within your stack. And if all the ready-to-use tools don't accomplish what you need, you (and your favorite programmer) can use the HyperTalk scripting language to accomplish practically anything you can dream up.

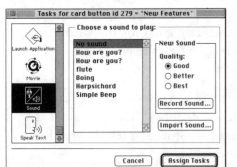

HyperCard's new button tasks automate a number of multimedia tasks that used to require scripting in earlier versions.

Over the years, HyperCard has incorporated support tools that it now ships as part of the package. For example, a 24-bit painting program is built-in so you can create and edit your graphics directly in HyperCard. Similarly, HyperCard's QuickTime movie tools are a boon for anyone who needs to do some quick movie editing.

Although the program has fallen out of favor with many commercial developers, HyperCard is still widely used by the rest of us to create elegant and effective multimedia applications. Its card-and-stack metaphor makes it simple for school kids to visualize and create their projects using real-world index cards while it helps them acquire important logical skills (that will come in handy when they need to build that corporate presentation that is due Monday morning). HyperCard is an excellent authoring platform for interactive kiosks, computer-based training programs, presentations, and multimedia databases.

HOT TIP

If you expect to distribute your product, HyperCard is also an economical choice. HyperCard stacks can be compiled into self-running applications that you can distribute royalty-free. (Note: Always be sure to check with Apple before distributing a HyperCard product for retail sale as the rules regarding royalty and credit are subject to change.)

SuperCard ($400, Allegiant). This authoring package has been around almost as long as HyperCard, and likewise has gone through some tough times. Like HyperCard, it has been sold and bought by a number of software companies; luckily, it is now owned by Allegiant, a small company that doesn't see it as just another inventory item. At this writing, SuperCard is at version 2.5. It requires System 7, a hard disk, and 2MB to 4MB of RAM to get started.

SuperCard also uses a stack approach like HyperCard, but relies more heavily on scripting to add sophisticated interactivity. Although most work is done using the SuperTalk scripting language, don't let this put you off. SuperCard includes a lot of support for scriptwriting, including a help system that inserts the correct syntax for any script command. With SuperTalk, you can create the exact environment you need to meet your project needs, easily controlling the contents of menus, interactivity with QuickTime movies, and sound playback.

GOOD FEATURE

You can give your applications a professional look by adding a backdrop window to your application: This will blot out the desktop, regardless of monitor size. A *backdrop window* can save you from the chuckles that will accompany your presentation if your hard disk named "Snuggles" is floating at the upper right of that large screen you weren't expecting to use. Better still, when creating computer simulations, you can be sure the simulation window is the only thing visible onscreen.

SuperCard is an efficient user of system memory, so if your users are on less robust machines, your application won't drag along like it is in need of stimulants. SuperCard also uses a *player* approach to running stand-alone versions: Your application contains just the data and scripts and the SuperCard Player contains the kernel of software necessary to make your application run. This is particularly useful when you are putting a number of applications on a single computer—instead of duplicating the kernel with each application (taking up precious hard disk space), you only need one copy of SuperCard Player.

You'll find that SuperCard is a good, professional tool and a real workhorse. Its reliance on scripting means you will need to make an investment of time to become an expert user, but you will be well-rewarded for that effort. With SuperCard, you will be able to create sophisticated computer simulations or other specialized interactive environments in addition to more run-of-the-mill applications such as multimedia databases, presentations, and kiosks. It can even be used as a prototyping tool.

Because you will need to distribute a copy of SuperCard Player with your project, you should check with Allegiant Technologies for their current royalty and credit requirements.

Oracle Media Objects ($100 introductory price, Oracle). This software was introduced as part of Oracle's interactive multimedia suite in 1995. Part of a grand design that includes client/server software, a custom extensions development kit, and players for a variety of platforms, Oracle is worth considering if you will be delivering time-sensitive data over a local network or interactive television.

Oracle Media Objects uses the stack metaphor. In this case, though, the metaphor presumes that content will be created separately from interactivity, and that the author will simply glue data and interactive objects into stacks to create applications (although those who have developed interactive titles know this isn't always the case). You'll probably want to brush up on your object-oriented programming skills to make efficient use of this metaphor (or defer to a programmer-author). Oracle also includes a scripting language, Oracle Media Talk, that will look familiar to anyone who has ever used HyperTalk or SuperTalk. For those brave enough to create their own object classes, a Custom Extensions Standard Developers Kit (SDK) is available.

Oracle's object-oriented approach makes it possible to build links to content files as well as embed data within a stack. Linked objects are easy to edit during development (you can change the contents of the linked object without modifying your stack), and they make it possible to establish dynamic links to live data sources such as media servers. Dynamism plays another role in the Oracle Media Objects world. Even after you create a stand-alone application, it can be modified as the user runs it. When this is combined with the ability to pull in live data, you've got the makings of an application that never goes out of date.

Although too new to have a long list of finished products to its name, Oracle Media Objects provides an interesting combination of abilities. Its stack metaphor makes it useful for simple presentations and interactive titles. But its ability to work in a client/server model and its strong object orientation make it extremely useful in corporate environments as a front-end for media databases. By integrating tightly with Oracle's own server architecture, it could even be possible to build on-demand titles such as interactive television and Web sites.

Media Objects' biggest shortcoming currently is a less-than-robust way of handling text, and the lack of any text searching abilities. This is expected to change, however.

Oracle sells run-time player applications for a variety of platforms. Contact them directly regarding royalties and credits for commercially distributed products.

Apple Media Tool ($475). Apple released **Media Tool** several years ago as a simple solution for those who wanted to create simple multimedia presentations quickly and without programming. Although never heavily promoted, reviewers have begun to notice that the Apple Media Tool is, as intended, a very good choice for authors who want to get a simple cross-platform multimedia product up and running quickly. The current version is 2.0.

The Media Tool is built upon the concept of a map. You create locations (which represent a screen) on this map by clicking on the map window with a + tool, and then dragging and dropping media elements and interactive elements onto those locations. Each of these screens is like a cross between a Director stage and a HyperCard card.

Each screen has its own Objects window, which lists all the objects in that screen. Unlike some authoring programs that import the media into the title that is being developed, the media in a Media Tool title remains separate from the title itself: Pictures remain in graphic files, sound in sound files, and so on. This way, you can build a production using placeholder media, and substitute the final versions at a later time.

Interactivity is provided by adding "actions" to objects on a screen: Actions are listed in an Action window, which changes its contents depending upon the selected object. To add an action to an object, you simply drag the object from the Objects window and drop it onto an action. The built-in actions that the Media Tool supports are well chosen for those who wish to create a basic

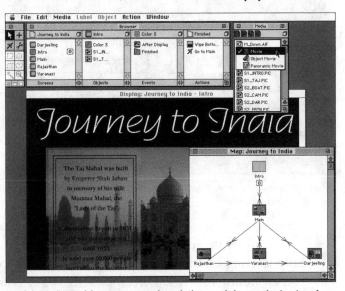

Apple's Media Tool features a map-based, drag-and-drop authoring interface.

point-and-click interface. It does not, however, allow you to create things such as forms, or in fact, any part of a presentation that involves typed-in text.

Media Tool's capabilities can be enhanced, albeit at substantial cost and complexity, through the **Media Tool Programming Environment** ($995). The Programming Environment is for serious programmers. With it, programmers export Media Tool titles as text files that are in the Apple Media Language, and then add the custom enhancements that are required. The Media Tool is available in a Power Mac native version, and it can create cross-platform titles.

Licensing fees vary depending upon the use: Fees can be waived for educational and non-profit uses, but for commercial uses (such as a for-sale CD-ROM, or in-house corporate training productions created with Media Tool), Apple charges a $500 per title licensing fee.

Director ($1,200, Macromedia). Ah, **Director**, the authoring tool everyone loves to hate. Director has been the flagship of Macromedia for many years, and has kept well in tune with regular and significant upgrades. Currently at version 5, you need a high-octane Macintosh to run Director at a comfortable speed. A 68030 Macintosh running System 7, a 13-inch or larger monitor, at least 8MB RAM, and up to 32 MB free hard disk space will allow you to open the program, but you will probably want

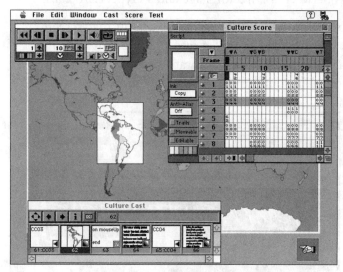

to invest in a Power Mac with at least 32MB RAM if you don't want to spend a lot of time watching the watch.

Director uses a stage approach to authoring, which means that you have to remember that you can only occupy one physical space in the universe at any one time (although you may have placed copies of yourself at strategic locations all over, just in case). A background in theater also makes the Director metaphor a bit easier to understand. In Director, you create

Director's stage-based, score-driven interface is especially well-suited for animations and simulations.

"movies" that comprise cohesive units of your application. A Director movie contains cast members that can be controllers, graphics, text, QuickTime, or sound. By physically locating cast members on your screen and controlling them through scripts, you create interactivity. Director's scripting language is called Lingo, and like any programming language, what you do with it can be as simple or as complex as your imagination allows (and a programmer can code).

Director includes a paint program and palette editor to speed your work with graphics. With 50 transitions available, you can get from screen to screen in a variety of ways that range from elegant to obnoxious.

Director has made great strides in creating a cross-platform tool for both development and delivery. This means that you need only author your application once. Then, with a bit of tweaking to accommodate for differences such as XObjects (custom code chunks for the Mac that programmers write) and DLLs (custom code chunks for Windows), you can export a version that will run under Windows, on the Internet (see the sidebar, "On the Horizon" later in this chapter), or with a 3DO set-top system. Should you be courageous enough to try this, be sure to carefully plan things such as filenames and file types beforehand, to accommodate the weird rules that apply to the various platforms.

Director's major drawback has always been that it doesn't handle text very well. For years, it has viewed text as just another form of graphic, which means that things such as full-text search or true text hyperlinks were practically impossible to achieve. Version 5 corrects some of that, with new features that support paragraph styles, line spacing, and automatic anti-aliasing of large type.

Director is great for controlling objects in motion over time. You can easily create presentations, interactive products, simulations, and kiosks with Director. If you check the credits of your favorite CD-ROM product, you'll probably find that it was created with Director. Director's cross-platform portability makes it a natural choice if you need to present your application on both the Mac OS and Windows.

Authorware ($5,000, Macromedia). This authoring tool has its roots in training and education, and it shows. Bought by Macromedia a few years ago, Authorware provided a cross-platform tool when few were available. Currently at version 3, Authorware includes a complete toolbox (including sound and video editors, 3-D modeler, and clip art library), and compatibility with Macromedia's more famous authoring tool, Director. Its high price does make Authorware a significant investment.

Using a flowchart approach that has its roots in computer-based training development, Authorware employs icons to represent data types, individual screens, and user input, and it lets you connect them in charts that specify all the possible paths through your application. To work on your application, you open an icon on the flowchart to manipulate its contents or specify its settings.

The program includes a number of interactivity templates where all you have to do is arrange them in order and add data. This makes developing standard applications (such as a presentation or quiz) a breeze.

GOOD FEATURE

Authorware understands that words are still the basis of most communication. You can import text files in *RTF* format (Microsoft's standard Rich Text Format which most word processors can import and export) and instantly create a series of screens based on the page breaks in the document. You can identify a word or phrase as a hyperlink, and you can easily implement full-text and keyword-search features for your users.

If you need to gather feedback from your users or score correct results, Authorware will save you days of programming. You can easily track a user's progress through your application or present remedial information if a user answers a quiz incorrectly.

Although its own animation tools are pretty rudimentary, you can create animations in Director and play them back in your Authorware application. As of this edition, the Authorware application even includes a copy of Director.

This package is the Cadillac of computer-based training development tools, and its price tag makes it clear that its market is the Information System Development departments of major corporations. You will also find many copies in the halls of academe (thanks to a reasonably-priced academic version). Kiosks, videodisk training systems, and database query tools will benefit from Authorware's flowchart metaphor. Templates make it possible to create lecture presentations, quizzes, and computer-based training courses that look good and work.

You can save your Authorware application as a stand-alone that will run under either the Mac OS or Windows. Although royalty-free as of this edition, if you are distributing your product commercially, check with Macromedia regarding their current requirements for credit and royalties.

mTropolis ($5,000, mFactory). A new arrival on the scene, mTropolis heralds what is likely to be a wave of products that create a new, object-oriented development approach to multimedia authoring. First released in late 1995, mTropolis requires a Macintosh 68040 or Power Mac with a double-speed CD-ROM drive and at least 8MB RAM. Far from being for the rest of us, this is a serious tool for serious developers.

The mTropolis approach is object-oriented which means you will spend as much time defining the vehicles that deliver your content as the content itself. Object orientation best suits those who like building models. The approach really makes sense for applications that explore multimedia worlds because you won't have to re-create the sound of planetary dust under each footstep or that neat visual effect each time a new door opens. A footstep object would include its sound, a door object would include its open and close effects (and the accompanying sounds). You keep track of your store of objects using a palette, picking up copies and positioning them as needed on the screen.

mTropolis promises to port your application effortlessly to the many flavors of Windows platforms available today. It is also positioned to handle the new on-line delivery by implementing streaming of your application (so it can be fed in bite-size pieces to a Web browser).

Given its set of features, the package appears to have been created by the programmers and graphic artists who create leading-edge interactive fiction and action/adventure applications. It is definitely the tool to use to create new worlds and new visions, but its support of text is quite limited. *[But now that Adobe owns a piece of the company, this*

On the Horizon (MEC)

Java. While billed as an Internet tool (and cooed over by Wall Street analysts as the biggest thing to happen to computing since the bit), this complex programming language from Sun Microsystems has the potential to turn Internet web browsers into multimedia applications. Java programs are cross-platform "applets" that you download from an Internet server and then run on your machine. Some applets will certainly be designed to do multimedia tasks directly in your Web browser.

Shockwave. This technology from Macromedia allows Director movies to be viewed on the Internet. Using Shockwave's compression utility, called Afterburner, animations and simulations can be downloaded and run at acceptable rates for those with relatively slow Internet connections. Shockwave should provide yet another niche for multimedia developers to exploit.

OpenDoc. OpenDoc is a system that sees documents, rather than applications, as the center of the computing experience. Rather than using a word processor, for example, you create a document from stationery and use an "editing part" to create your text, a "spell-checking part" to check it, and so on. OpenDoc should make it possible to create multimedia experiences in nearly any sort of document by using a combination of small multimedia parts to manage and display the media. OpenDoc should become a standard part of the Mac OS by the time you read this.

shortcoming may disappear in subsequent releases.—MEC] Although too new to boast a long list of released titles (such as Director), we can expect to see more mTropolis-developed titles in the next couple of years.

mTropolis creates a stand-alone application for the platform of your choice. If you are distributing your application commercially, be sure to check with mFactory for current royalty and credit requirements.

Editors' Poll:
What Does Multimedia Mean to You?

JH: Games! Okay, also the Web. Past those two, I haven't had any use or need for multimedia.

ML: It is the communication of information and ideas in a format far more interesting than any single medium.

SZA: Multimedia is for presenting information in a way that engages more than a single one of our senses so that it's more interesting, effective, and memorable.

TL: Games (including "edutainment"), demos, and presentations mostly, at least so far as I have seen. Also, the WWW looks like fertile ground for multimedia to explode (witness Shockwave, JAVA, RealAudio, and so on).

BW: At its best it's for letting a viewer choose their own points of entry into a given subject and perhaps come away with better comprehension. At its worst it's for selling "information" to folks whose lives revolve around the TV.

KT: Multimedia is a term, still being defined, for the general class of communication based on stimulation of more than one sense—often sight and sound, but at least in theory also potentially including touch, smell, motion, and others. It usually draws on multiple techniques or styles—moving as well as still image, and spoken as well as written text, for example. It tends to be expressive rather than objective and is warm rather than cool.

JC: For me multimedia is the integration of sound and pictures (moving or still) that can be used in a number of ways. For example, using a Mac's multimedia capabilities for presentation puposes (a way to liven up a dull sales presentation). Or, to educate by involving the user in an interactive manner. To be creative—making QuickTime movies and animation—creating and editing sound or music. To have some fun!

SS: When used effectively, video and sound can present information that can't be handled by text and static pictures. However, at this writing, its effective use is severely limited by our inadequate computer hardware and video's massive storage requirements. Consumers are led to expect full-screen, movie-quality video. Instead they get small, choppy QuickTime clips. Until we move beyond the inadequate speed and storage capacity of today's CDs, multimedia (at least so far as video is concerned) will remain only a mildly interesting, content-poor phenomenon.

18 Education & Reference

One of the earliest promises of computers was that they would put a vast amount of information at your fingertips. With CD-ROM technology, the promise has been fulfilled. Millions of megabytes of information, covering a vast array of subjects, have been collected, compiled, sorted, indexed, and annotated for your pleasure and edification.

And the really good news is this: Following the laws of supply and demand, the prices of CDs have dropped precipitously in the last few years. Many of the programs mentioned in this chapter that were also discussed in the last edition of this book are now less than half the price.

Contributors

Sharon Zardetto Aker (SZA) is the chapter editor.

Dr. Steven Blazar (SB) is an orthopedic surgeon who had the third edition of *The Macintosh Bible* dedicated to him.

Connie Guglielmo (CG) is a writer for such publications as *MacWEEK* and *Wired*, and was this chapter's editor for the last edition.

Dr. Richard Wolfson (RW) is a Mac maven who teaches educational technology at Montclair State University.

Contents

Classic Reference Works

The advantage of quick searches through tons of material puts computer-based reference works ahead of their paperbound counterparts. Some CD-based references rely on this fast-search capability alone to get you to switch from the volume on your bookshelf, while others take more advantage of the medium, bringing words and concepts to life with graphics and animations.

Encyclopedias   (SZA)

A disappointing classic. The $600 **Encyclopedia Americana** from Grolier Electronic Publishing should be a joy of a reference tome: all 30 volumes of the paperbound edition on a single CD. But that's all it is: the text of the paper version slapped onto a disk, with a minimal interface, a few hyperlinks, some basic charts and graphs … in all, quite a disappointment.

BAD FEATURE

For the price of this package, you have the right to a little pizzazz, even if it's not a full multimedia approach. Instead, you get a screen font that's virtually unreadable, especially when italics are used. You also get a clumsy design, including *More* and *Continued* buttons to move back and forth as you read through some entries. The documentation claims the articles are chopped into small pieces because of the constraints imposed by putting vast amounts of information into electronic form. Nonsense.

While I'm sure the *content* of this CD is accurate, the first nonencyclopedic material I looked at (the on-line help) contained an obvious spelling error. The wonderful search engine, and the compactness of 30 volumes on one CD just don't make up for the overall presentation. For the money, I'd much rather be poring over the printed version of this reference work.

The multimedia approach. From the minute you launch the **Grolier Multimedia Encyclopedia** ($60, Grolier Electronic Publishing), you know you're looking at something that was designed for the computer. You can choose from six basic types of information presentations, including Articles, Gallery, Atlas, and Timelines; a pop-up menu provides subcategories for each. When you're viewing information, it's easy to move to related topics because all you have to do is click on a tab such as Picture, Media List, or Related Articles. Although the setup encourages you to browse, finding specific information in the more than 34,000 entries is made easy by a good search engine and a filter option that lets you browse through materials within a certain subject area.

GOOD FEATURE

Some CD Tips (SZA)

If you use reference CDs frequently (or plan to), there are several points you should keep in mind—only some of which the CD's documentation or Read Me file will bother to tell you.

- You need, at minimum, a double-speed CD-ROM drive; quad-speed units are better, not all that much more expensive, and will soon be the minimum necessary. (See Chapter 5 for details on CD-ROM drive speeds.)

- Most multimedia CDs need the monitor set to 256 colors; you may get "out of memory" errors or crashing otherwise.

- Many multimedia titles need virtual memory turned off in the Memory control panel.

- Most programs on CDs create and maintain a Prefs file in your Preferences folder (inside the System Folder); if you don't use a CD anymore, you can get rid of the Prefs file.

Many multimedia titles have Install programs on the CD that put all sorts of things on your hard drive. Most of the installers aren't all that smart: they often, for instance, replace a newer system file (like a QuickTime extension) that's on your drive with the older one that's on the CD. Whenever possible, use the "Custom" option in an installer and disable the older extension installation; sometimes you can skip the installation completely if you already have the extensions you need. Here's what a typical installation for a multimedia CD might drop in your System Folder:

- QuickTime extension

- QuickTime PowerPlug extension (only needed for PowerPC-based Macs)

- Sound Manager extension

- Apple Multimedia Tuner extension

- QuickTime Musical Instruments extension

- Special fonts that the program uses for display

Lots of reference CDs require that you copy some portion of the program to your hard drive and run it from there, although you'll still need the CD; the main program (which runs much faster when it's on your hard drive) then accesses information on the CD.

The "multimedia" part of the encyclopedia is its extensive support in the way of photographs and music clips, and a few well-done animations. Printed reference material seems almost archaic when you look up the entry on "animation" and then get a movie to see how it's done. (Proper English seems almost archaic, too, when you hear the voice-over referring to "less frames per second...".)

What you may not like about this encyclopedia is its Windows-like interface and immovable windows; it's too bad that the care put into the top layer of the interface wasn't lavished all the way through. Still, you get a lot of well-presented information at a great price—a very good family encyclopedia.

Another winner. When you fire up **Compton's Interactive Encyclopedia** ($150, Compton's NewMedia), you won't be impressed—at least, not at first. Its unfortunate multiwindow interface is a little awkward to work with, and even its floating button palette doesn't follow the rules—it doesn't stay active, and you have to click on it to activate it before you can click on any of its buttons.

But you can forgive a lot of interface transgressions because of the material it presents. You can approach your research from articles, timelines, or a list of movies, sounds, and pictures. As befits a computer-based reference, you can search easily based on specific words or general ideas. Type in *carbonation*, for instance, and you get dozens of article suggestions including such seemingly disparate topics as *soda fountain*, *jewelry*, *glass*, *varnish*, *rubber*, and *Ouagadougou*. Look up that last item, and you'll be glad there's a built-in atlas available.

Once you have sound support in an encyclopedia, you'll wonder how people have depended on printed references for so long. Look up alligators, and you can get a sample of their hissing; look up Martin Luther King, Jr., and you get a snippet of the "I have a dream" speech. QuickTime movies are as varied as a Greek and Roman art slide show—Babe Ruth plodding around the bases, and news footage of the Los Angeles riots after the Rodney King verdict.

GOOD FEATURE

This is a wonderful family resource for general reference.

Microsoft's entry. It's hard to love an encyclopedia that lists *Microsoft Windows* as the first, default topic when you look up *computer*, but I was willing to give **Microsoft Encarta** ($100) a chance, anyway. Encarta finds a good balance between breadth and depth for a general encyclopedia, although it needs more memory (4MB) and disk space (10MB on your hard drive, in addition to the CD itself) than any of the other CD encyclopedias reviewed here. And although I'd like to be enthusiastic about the wealth of material included, it's difficult to get past what is, finally, a terrible interface.

Encarta's Windows interface provides some unpleasant side effects, like the half-hidden lines of text at the top and bottom of scrolling areas, and menus that slowly stretch out on the screen to show hard-to-read white text on dark backgrounds.

I'm not condemning it because it has a Windows look and feel, although it is hard for a dyed-in-the-wool Mac person to work with that inelegant approach; the real problem is the hard-to-read screen font, and lines of text that are cut off at the top, bottom, and even sides as you scroll through it.

The best and worst of times. After looking at dozens of CD-based encyclopedias, it becomes obvious that the best ones are generally those that narrow their scope somewhat, because despite the capacity of a CD, good graphics, sound, and video take up a lot of room. **Our Times** ($70, Vicarious) is subtitled "Multimedia Encyclopedia of the 20th Century"; while that's not a very narrow focus considering the political, industrial, and technological wonders of this century, it's just enough to provide in-depth coverage in a zillion categories decade-by-decade and even year-by-year. The graphics are great, the interface is slick, and the package is perfect as a handy reference or as a browse-through learning experience.

Dictionaries (SZA)

Funky. Even my teenagers—no great arbiters of taste or aesthetics—said "Ugh!" when the **Funk & Wagnalls Standard Desk Dictionary** ($50, Inductel) arrived: That's how ugly the type is—a type-only "design" that looks like a fourth-grader did it on his Mac. The fact that it comes on eight 800K floppy disks with amateurish labels didn't help the initial impression, either; nor did the printed-in-someone's-basement look of the manual.

In a terrific piece of software rudimentary aesthetics can be forgiven; this software, however, is nowhere near terrific. Its more than 100,000 entries are presented with as much elegance as its outer packaging. It doesn't even include a pronunciation guide for the defined words. This one's a waste of time and money.

Back talk. The **American Heritage Talking Dictionary** ($30, SoftKey) answers the question I've had about other computer-based dictionaries: Why should we have to figure out those arcane pronunciation symbols when we're using a computer? And it answers the question out loud—because this dictionary, true to its name, does indeed speak more than a third of its 200,000 entries. It provides links to similar words and synonyms, and includes lots of pictures and a sprinkling of QuickTime movies. The main dictionary resides on your hard drive for speed (it comes in both 68K and PowerPC versions), while the multimedia elements stay on the CD for space reasons; you don't need the CD to run the basic dictionary. Like any good dictionary, this one includes place names and biographical data; extras include a word-hunt feature using wild cards for when you don't know the proper spelling of the word you're looking for, and an anagram maker.

The Perfect Tool   (SZA)

The perfect educational tool on the Mac is one that's never claimed to be one: **Spell Catcher** (formerly Thunder 7) from Casady & Greene. This interactive spelling checker, described in detail in Chapter 8, watches as you type and immediately alerts you to a misspelled word. You can backspace and retype, or press a key and get a list of suggestions as to the correct spelling. (Not that there's a question as to how to spell each word, but there might be a question as to just what that word was supposed to be: Type *accomodate* and you'll get *accommodate,* type *mispell* and you'll get *misspell*—but type *ontoward* and you'll have to choose from *untoward, on toward,* and *onto ward.*)

While Spell Catcher is meant as a writer's tool, it's the perfect spelling teacher for kids. From an educational point of view, there's nothing better than immediate feedback—and Spell Catcher's menu-bar flash or beep is instant. If your child spells something incorrectly, she can try again by backspacing to the mistake in the word and typing again from there or by double-clicking to select the word and then retyping it. After a second try, or if she's stymied the first time around, she can open the Spell Catcher window that displays both the misspelled version and the correct one—exactly what an attentive, patient teacher would do in the same circumstances.

Atlases

Breadth with a little depth (Cindy Luker). The **Quick Reference Atlas** ($60), from the company whose name is synonymous with maps, Rand McNally, is a perfect blend of good graphics, easy interface, and useful information. You can look at the world as topological, geopolitical, climatic, or even as time zones. No matter where you are, extra information is only a click away; a text window nicely synopsizes all the pertinent facts about a country. Because it's only about 35MB of information, you can drag the whole thing to your hard drive and run it more quickly from there. Of course, the main reason it's so compact is that there aren't as many maps as you might like: You can't zoom in for any view smaller than a whole country, which is frustrating in an otherwise excellent package.

Maps, facts, flags, and anthems (Cindy Luker). Brøderbund's **Maps 'n' Facts** ($35) is more than just a collection of geographic information; it includes things such as populations, per capita income, country flags and anthems (which you can listen to), capitals, and even point-to-point distance calculations. The package that all of this comes in is a little clumsy: If you're looking at a political map of the Middle East and want to switch to the physical map of the same region, you have to pick that region from a separate dialog box instead of just changing views. Another small glitch is that

The Most Important Educational Tool   (SZA)

Do yourself a favor: Learn to type! No more hunt-and-peck, no matter how fast. Do it the right way and everything's faster, from word processing to e-mail. And as soon as the kids' hands are big enough, make them learn touch-typing, too. There are lots of packages out there, and many are even aimed at kids; prices range from $20 to $60, and it will be worth every penny. Here are a few suggestions:

- **Typing Tutor**, Davidson
- **Stickybear Typing**, Optimum Resource
- **Dinosoft Typing Tutor**, Dinosoft
- **Kid's Typing**, Sierra
- **Mario Teaches Typing**, InterPlay
- **Mavis Beacon Teaches Typing** and **Mavis Beacon Teaches Typing for Kids**, Mindscape
- **UltraKey**, Bytes of Learning

zooming in and out doesn't always work the way you'd want it to. But this is still a handy and complete reference work for school kids of any age.

More maps (CG). Applied Optical Media offers two CD-ROM-based atlases. **The American Vista Atlas** ($50) charts out the United States using maps from Hammond and incorporates data from the 1990 U.S. Census. **The World Vista Atlas** ($50) is an international atlas based on maps from Rand McNally and contains standard phrases in the major languages of each of the more than 200 countries included.

Other Reference Works

A whole bookshelf (RW). Microsoft—often the bane of Mac users—has a terrific product in **Microsoft Bookshelf** ($100), a compendium that includes a great collection of reference tools, such as an encyclopedia, dictionary, thesaurus, almanac, atlas, and a book of quotes. Everything's easy to find: The interface, though Windows-inspired, is easy to work with, and although each edition is labeled with a year (Bookshelf '96, for instance), only the "year in review" section is time-sensitive. The whole package strikes a good balance in the breadth-versus-depth dilemma and deserves a spot in any home with school-age children.

The fastest, biggest, smallest... (Carol Aiton). The **Guinness Multimedia Disc of Records** ($50, Grolier Electronic Publishing) is the paper version brought to life with the use of movie clips and sound, and, of course, plenty of pictures. It's one thing to read about the tallest man who ever lived and see a photograph or two, but to see movies of him at the age of 13 playing leapfrog with his tiny-in-comparison friends, or as an adult reaching to steady a swaying traffic light while standing on a street corner, is utterly fascinating.

GOOD FEATURE

There are lots of ways to look things up on the CD, and browsing is encouraged by a special "Guess what?" mode where you're asked to name, for instance, the country with the highest life expectancy. This is a wonderful CD, thoughtfully put together and with a well-designed interface.

Phraseology (SZA). With so many colorful multimedia titles available, the basically black-and-white **5000 Quotes** ($50, Books-On-Disk) HyperCard stack—which might have been ground-breaking five years ago—seems dull and awkward. But then, as Alexandre Dumas said, "The custom and fashion of today will be the awkwardness and outrage of tomorrow—so arbitrary are these transient laws." If you're someone who needs to look up quotes for writing or speech-making, this stack, with its Find function, is still a lot easier than thumbing through a paperback. *[Forget about writing and speech-making; learning new quotes and turns of phrase can be great fun and will enable you to impress your friends with your enhanced eloquence, too. Sometimes you can even learn more about yourself, as I did with this gem from Nicholas von Hoffman: "We are the people our parents warned us against."—JJ]*

The opening screen of the Guinness Multimedia Disc of Records promises that you're in for a treat, and it doesn't break that promise.

SF, not Sci-Fi (SZA). Grolier's **Multimedia Encyclopedia of Science Fiction** ($50) is a work of art. It's beautiful to look at, easy to use—whether you want to look something up or just browse—and it's filled with all sorts of information, from Buck Rogers to cyberpunk. The designers and editors did a beautiful job, with an upbeat attitude that never plunges into wide-eyed, admiring fandom. The articles about authors and books are dead-on (for example, on Asimov's *Foundation's Edge*: "Fourth volume of the Foundation series, uncomfortably extending its themes and beginning the work of

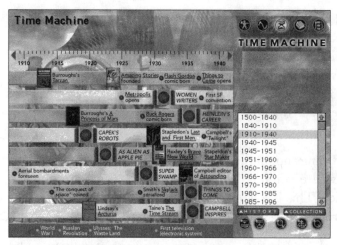

This one section of the timeline in the Multimedia Encyclopedia of Science Fiction gives an idea of the scope of its coverage.

binding it into a common future history with Asimov's robot stories." In regard to McCaffrey's *Pern* books: "Despite the commercial success of later volumes, the quality and originality of the books decline somewhat as the series proceeds, although the most recent addition, *All the Weyrs of Pern*, represents something of an improvement."). There are a few film clips, author movie clips, and sound bytes, all of which leave you wishing for more.

A home run (SZA). Get yourself some peanuts and Cracker Jacks to go with **Baseball's Greatest Hits** ($40, Voyager), an enjoyable collection of well-presented player and game stats, photos, sound bytes, video clips of disappointing quality, and, of course, a trivia challenge. You won't find anything on Cal Ripkin's record-breaking game streak because the most recent "footage" is of Joe Carter's game-clinching three-run homer for the Blue Jays in the '93 World Series, but baseball nuts seem to prefer their facts and trivia slightly aged. I'm not a big baseball fan, but I've raised one, and he'll be happy with this CD for a long time.

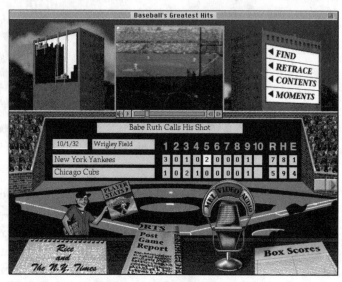

Baseball's Greatest Hits has a QuickTime video of one of baseball's greatest hits.

Literature, Art, and Music

Whether your preferred reading material is Shakespeare, comic books, or the latest issue of *People*, you can put the equivalent on your Mac. Great art? Poetry? The Beatles? If it's out there in the "real" world, there's a good chance you can find the electronic version.

Literature and Books

The Bard (Carol Aiton). It's a rare person who reads Shakespeare for pleasure—perhaps as a result of the Elizabethan speech and some high-school teacher's uninspired reading assignment. Besides, if you want to read for pleasure, sitting at a computer screen doesn't do much to enhance the experience. But if you want to research Shakespeare himself or study his plays, a computer-based program could be handy because of its searching capability.

Unfortunately, **Romeo and Juliet** and **Macbeth** ($70 each, Learning Tomorrow) ignore this most compelling feature of all, and provide only a black-and-white HyperCard stack containing the text of the play and some related material such as glossary definitions and brief historical background. **Shakespeare and the Globe Theatre** ($130) is no better; even the "pictures"—of Shakespeare and Queen Elizabeth I, for instance—are strictly MacPaint-type black-and-white constructs. All these items are clumsy early-issue HyperCard stacks that are as far out of date as a Mac Plus, and not worth half their price.

BAD
FEATURE

Voyager's Expanded Books (CG). Voyager's Expanded Book series of fiction and nonfiction books on disk (originally designed with PowerBooks in mind) have redefined portability for the digital age. Click on the arrow to turn the page, or use the search tools to trace a character through a novel: The thoughtful layout and design make these books highly readable, and after a while, you forget that you're reading a book on disk rather than on paper. The more than 60 titles in the series sell for under $30 apiece, with the majority carrying a $20 list price. The range of titles is impressive: **Jurassic Park, The Autobiography of Malcolm X, The Pelican Brief, Of Mice and Men**, the complete works of Jane Austen, lots of science fiction, and even children's favorites such as **A Wrinkle in Time**.

Poetry (CG). For literary commentary in an interesting and interactive form, check out **Poetry in Motion** ($30, Voyager), a CD-ROM with audio, graphics, and over 90 minutes of QuickTime video that gives 18 modern poets (including Allen Ginsberg, William S. Burroughs, and Tom Waits) a chance to recite/perform their work and comment on it (interviews with some of the authors are also included).

Art and Music

Galleries on CD (Ted Lippincott). Anyone who appreciates art would prefer to appreciate it in person. That's not always possible, but an art CD is a reasonable alternative. DCI (Digital Collections, Inc.) provides several collections for your viewing pleasure, including my longtime favorite, **The Frick Collection**, and the Brooklyn Museum's **Ancient Egyptian Art** collection ($80 each).

The DCI collections are not full-fledged art history lessons on CD; they are, instead, a meticulous exploration of the art in each collection. You'll find all the information you'd see in a very thorough museum catalog—in some cases, even a biography of the artist. You can view each item as a thumbnail or in various larger sizes, sort them in any order (by artist or date, for instance), and create a slide show. You can even select and sort based on keywords ("still life" or "ocean"). And, with a good monitor, the quality of the painting on-screen rivals that of a high-quality art book.

The **Microsoft Art Gallery** ($50) includes 2,000 works from London's National Gallery, and takes a more instructional approach for those unfamiliar with both the collection and art in general. You get detailed biographies of the artists, and information about the historical and social context of their works. There's a historical atlas that organizes the art according to place and time—something you could manually create for the DCI collections but is ready-made here. There are even lessons with helpful animations in areas such as composition and perspective.

Musical voyages (CG). Voyager's **CD Companions** are HyperCard stacks that let you listen to an entire composition as a text commentary scrolls by; or you can click to bring up a glossary of music terms and theory, or read about the life of the composer. Titles ($40 to $60) in the series include: **Ludwig van Beethoven: Symphony no. 9**; **Igor Stravinsky: "The Rite of Spring"**; **Antonín Dvořák: Symphony no. 9 "From the New World"**; and **Franz Schubert: "The Trout Quintet."**

The three titles in Voyager's **So I've Heard** series ($25 each) are designed to be music samplers, offering you commentary and sound clips from an array of composers. **Volume 1: Bach and Before** takes you from the music of ancient Greek rituals to Bach; **Volume 2: The Classical Ideal** is an earful of the work of 18th-century composers such as Mozart and Haydn; and **Volume 3: Beethoven and Beyond** explores Beethoven's impact on the classical music scene.

The great thing about all of Voyager's offerings is their interface: You'll find the screens easy to read, punctuated with elegant illustrations, and designed with search tools and icons that make it a pleasure to explore the topic at hand.

Pop Culture

People (Cindy Luker). What could be more representative of pop culture than Voyager's **People: 20 Years of Pop Culture** ($40) from *People* magazine? It provides plenty of low- to mid-brow fun through its 20 years of cover stories, as well as diversions such as Face-To-Face (like-minded covers morphing into one another) and Di-o-Rama (following the beleaguered princess through her triumphs and trials). This certainly isn't a must-have, but it's fun and would make a good gift, too.

The fab four (SZA). Even a die-hard Beatle fan who spent her adolescent years in love with John Lennon can't find Voyager's **A Hard Day's Night** ($40) particularly enjoyable. You get a tiny QuickTime window that plays the entire movie while you can read through some mildly interesting but overblown commentary (it states, for instance, that the opening of the movie was as cinematically ground-breaking as that of *2001: A Space Odyssey*). Yes, you can read the script of the movie, and play around with its QuickTime controls, and pick up fascinating little tidbits, but there's just not enough here to keep you at your computer. If you want a trip down memory lane, or into rock and roll history, I suggest you do what I did: rent the movie.

Comics as history and art (RW). If you think of Superman when you think of comics, or if Archie and Veronica are more comic book characters than Internet buzz-words for you, you may be disappointed in **Comic Book Confidential** ($40, Voyager). Some of the most famous comics—published as books or in newspapers—are never mentioned here, presumably because of copyright and permission problems. But even if you don't know or care about many of the comics covered here, you'll still find some of the accompanying information utterly fascinating—such as the Congressional hearings in the 1950s that "proved" the link between comic books and juvenile delinquency (I think it was a separate commission that proved the link between juvenile delinquency and rock and roll). Although you could wish for wider coverage, what's here is enjoyable and well-presented.

Beyond the Arts

There are so many educational-category CDs out there that it was impossible to cover even a large fraction of them; so we settled for a representational sampling. (You'll find some suggestions for how to check current software and CD offerings in Appendix B.")

Science and Nature

The Way Things Work (RW). The transfer of **David Macaulay's** wonderful book **The Way Things Work** ($70, DK Multimedia) has lost nothing in the transliteration to CD—in fact, it has gained a little (if that's at all possible). This volume is a guide to "machines, inventions, and technology" suitable for a wide range of ages (from about ten years on up). There's a wealth of wonderfully illustrated diagrams for items from dishwashers to telescopes; there are lots of links between related items and you'll find an animated sequence every time you need one.

Eyewitness Encyclopedia of Nature (SZA). The Eyewitness series of encyclopedias has always been a staple at my house, and I've added to the collection over a period of years. I was skeptical about these excellent volumes being translated well onto CD, but, based on the **Eyewitness Encyclopedia of Nature** disc ($35, Vicarius), the computer series is even better than the paper versions. The graphics are crisp and clean, and the interface is intuitive, designed so that you can delve deeper into the subject at hand or go off on a tangent exploration. All the text can be spoken aloud if you wish, and there's a selection of movie clips that demonstrates things such as jellyfish locomotion.

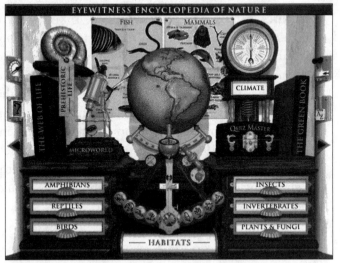

The inviting opening screen of the Eyewitness disc has the same feel as the book series of the same name.

On Evolution (SZA). After years (oh, all right, *decades*) of being a Stephen Jay Gould fan, I finally know what he looks and sounds like because Voyager's "expanded book" **On Evolution and Natural**

History ($40) includes a QuickTime video of one of his lectures, along with the complete text of one of his essay collections, *Bully for the Brontosaurus*. In addition, the CD boasts the illustrated text of Darwin's *Origin of the Species* and *The Voyage of the Beagle*.

If you need to research this subject or these texts, the Find function and the links between them would certainly be helpful. But if you're reading for enjoyment, I recommend the traditional paper copy, and a comfortable chair, couch, or bed.

Outer space (CG). Sumeria's **Space: A Visual History of Manned Spaceflight** ($50) contains more than 90 minutes of footage taken from the NASA video and film library, provided in QuickTime format. Also included are mission histories for the Mercury, Gemini, Apollo, and Space Shuttle projects, and descriptions of space-based science experiments, life in zero gravity, satellite deployment, and space stations.

In Multicom's **Americans in Space** ($40), 500 photographic images and one hour's worth of full-motion video in QuickTime format tell the story of America's efforts in space, beginning with early experimental rockets and the X-15 program and ending with plans for space stations still on the drawing board. An interface modeled on a Mission Control room serves as command center for accessing the disc.

Flora and fauna (CG). If you're interested in underwater adventures, you can journey through the Atlantic with a humpback whale and learn about more than 100 other species in **A World Alive** ($40, Voyager), an interactive documentary on CD-ROM that also includes a game to test what you've learned.

Audubon's Mammals ($50, Creative Multimedia) offers the illustrations that John James Audubon produced in 1840, along with sound and text describing the animals' habitats. For bird watchers, there's also **Birds of America** ($50), containing the complete text (and 500 color bird lithographs) from the 1840 edition of Audubon's book.

For an authoritative overview of animal (and plant) life, Educorp offers **The Encyclopedia of Life** ($50). The easy-to-use interface lets you delve into 3,700 text entries, launch 130 QuickTime video clips, choose from among 600 color images, and search through the glossary covering the millions of plants and animals that inhabit the planet.

Operation: Frog ($100, Creative Multimedia) dissects a frog for you. Pick a body part, and you get to cut through the various layers and organs in exquisite (and annotated) detail. At least you don't have to smell the formaldehyde.

Endangered species are the topic of **Last Chance to See** ($50, Voyager), a CD-ROM version of the book by Douglas Adams (better known for his *Hitchhiker's Guide to* *the Galaxy*) and photographer Mark Carwardine. Adams reads the entire text on the disc, which includes more than 700 color photos and information about the status of each species.

Physics the fun way (SZA). The blurb on **The Cartoon Guide to Physics** ($50, Harper Collins) says it's for "anyone with a passing interest in physics—or with an interest in passing physics." That pretty much sums up the attitude of this fun yet mildly educational CD. The title itself might ring a bell, since cartoonist Larry Gonick has been at this on paper in the pages of *Discover* and other magazines for years. I could do without the guide, Lucy, doin' her rap thing during some explanations, but she's easy enough to ignore.

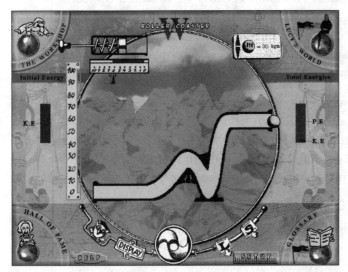
You can play with a roller-coaster tube in The Cartoon Guide to Physics, but you're really learning about kinetic and potential energy.

Oh, and in case you don't think about physics much—or much about physics—don't forget that its rules keep planes up, and roller coasters going, and apples falling on people's heads; it's not just dry formulas. Through interesting interactivities where, for instance, you get to set the starting point and initial force of a ball in a winding tube, you get a feeling for how potential and kinetic energy work in a roller coaster.

Health

How Your Body Works (SZA/SB). Mindscape's **How Your Body Works** ($70) is touted as a fun and easy-to-use journey through the human body, but it falls a little short on both counts. While there are plenty of interesting movie clips on bodily processes, there are just as many "talking heads"—videos of some expert sitting there giving a lecture on the topic at hand—or, even worse, a section where you look at a radio while listening to some snippet of information. And navigation from one area to another is not as simple as it first seems. There's a body you can click on to start your tour, but such large portions are selected at a time that, for instance, half the chest and most of an arm are highlighted for the topic "respiration." Even the laboratory starting point can be frustrating because clicking on some items leads you to genuine

Testing, 1, 2, 3, Testing... (RW)

Practice may not always make perfect, but it can certainly make you better. For those standardized tests that get us to various educational stages—the SATs, GREs, GMATs, and so on—a little practice can boost the score just enough to make a difference—often as much as 100 points.

Many companies provide test-practice software for your highschooler to practice those SAT questions, or for grad school wannabes, including:

- **SAT Verbal** ($80, Smartek)

- **Personal Trainer** series (**ACT**, **SAT**, and **GRE**; $60 each, Davidson)

- **RoadTrip** series (**SAT**, **GRE**, **GMAT**, and **LSAT**; $50, Kaplan Interactive)

And if you'd like to practice on-line, here're two World Wide Web sites where you can take some practice tests:

http://www.cdean.com/

http://www.testprep.com/

information, while other spots get you cute little animations—but you can't tell ahead of time which is which.

The CD is, for the most part, a good general introduction to human anatomy and is appropriate for basic research or learning on a high-school level. But it veers uncomfortably from introductory, relatively linear material to more complicated items such as microscope slides of a macrophage or a striated muscle segment with no definitions, explanations, or relationship to other material in the program.

Two A.D.A.M. offerings (SZA/SB). Both these packages from A.D.A.M. Software— **A.D.A.M. The Inside Story** ($30) and **A.D.A.M. Essentials** ($300)—include detailed anatomical drawings of almost breathtaking quality that are precise down to the last capillary.

The Inside Story is suitable for students in junior or senior high school, or any family member who's curious about the structure of the human body. Although most of the program merely identifies components of various systems (such as skin, organs, and skeletal structure), it also includes four hours of video and animation demonstrating many bodily processes. Looking up information about a specific body part is frustrating, and sometimes fruitless: The organization of the program is very hierarchical (you have to move up and down through topic branches instead of directly where you want to go), and sometimes there just isn't the depth of information you're looking for. But it's a captivating piece of work that invites exploration by anyone even mildly interested in anatomy.

The audience for A.D.A.M. Essentials, which provides much more information, is from advanced high school to introductory college biology; due to its price, it's bound to be a classroom rather than a home program. It's fascinating to work your way through a body, peeling it off in layers (skin, fat, connective tissue, muscle, and so on), and detouring to explanatory text at any time.

Both programs have odd little interface glitches, but you can put up with them to get at the great illustrations. With the configurable body on the screen—you can choose male or female, or white, black, Asian, or Hispanic features and skin tones—these packages are both anatomically and politically correct.

BodyWorks (SZA/SB). One of the best of the body "tours" available on CD provides a wealth of information unmatched by the other products reviewed here. **BodyWorks 3** ($70, SoftKey) is suitable for high school to early med school anatomy. Its drawings are not as beautiful as the ones in A.D.A.M.'s software, but they are accurate and easy to

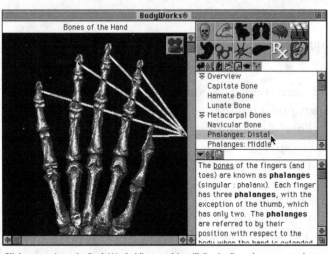

read. One of the most welcome features is the way items are identified: Click on a name and a line is drawn from the name to the correct spot in the picture, while a text explanation appears in the window below.

BodyWorks presents information in many ways—text, pictures, diagrams, movies—for many topics, from specific ones such as the skeletal and respiratory systems to more general ones such as health and fitness. When you think

Click on an item in BodyWorks' list, and it will "point" to the proper places.

you've mastered something, you can take an interactive quiz in any one of many categories. The overall excellence of this software is marred only by its use of the mechanical-sounding Macintalk for speaking words in the glossary and reading explanatory text, and by several careless misspellings.

A.D.A.M.'s Eve (SZA). A.D.A.M. Software's **Nine Month Miracle** ($40) is a disappointing effort that covers conception, pregnancy, and childbirth from a myriad of directions, resulting in a choppy presentation of facts, figures, pictures, and video.

To view a developing fetus, for instance, you have to suffer through a "family album" with a sappy scenario of a couple expecting their first baby; there's a section for each month, and to get to the good part, you have to listen to boring, stilted dialog first. There's lots of information here, and even a section for very young children, but even the most advanced of medical information is often buried in a package suitable for a junior-high sex education class.

Geography, History, and Social Studies

World Discovery Deluxe (Carol Aiton). This is a well-done geographical teaching tool that can be used at home or in a classroom on almost any level, although most of it is a little too difficult for the lower end of the suggested range of grades three through 12. (It's a good tool for geographically challenged adults, too.) Through any of a dozen configurable games, a user can test his or her geographical knowledge on a global scale, including basic history, political, and economic facts. Many of the tests, such as dragging state outlines to their proper places on a map (or country outlines onto a continent), also serve to teach basic geography.

Painful history lessons (SZA). MultiEducator puts out a series of history CDs that focus on different periods and areas. **American History** is without a doubt the ugliest piece of software I've ever seen; it looks as if it had been designed by a ten-year-old (and one without any taste, at that). It's also rife with typos and grammatical errors. It's impossible to get past these factors to learn anything from the actual content of the CD.

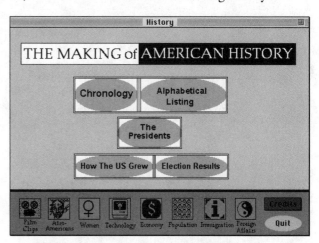

World History: 20th Century has a different design, but it's no better. It's amateurish, hard to read, and, overall, a very bad experience. **Civil War: America's Epic Struggle** is, design-wise, only a slight improvement over the others—if you don't mind glaring red text on a bright blue tweed background (which is better than the areas

The crude presentation and implementation of this package should make us hope we're not doomed to repeat American History.

where there's blue text on blue background!), and buttons and lists that aren't aligned. But it's just as well that you can't quite read it, because if you could, you'd find things like "Dredd-Scott Decision," with its egregious double D and hyphen, listed as choices.

If the graphics, design, and spelling in an educational product are so poor, how could you possibly depend on the quality of its content?

American history (CG). **Who Built America?** ($50, Voyager) is a thoughtfully designed CD-ROM put together by the American Social History Project. It explores, through words and pictures, the people and events that shaped U.S. history from 1876 to 1914. With its background audio and stylized photographs, this presentation has the look and feel of a PBS documentary—a good one.

19 Kids' Stuff

You have a computer. You have a kid (or two, or…). They go together perfectly when you get just the right software. Good programs are entertaining and often informative even when they're not primarily educational. The computer is infinitely patient and won't have to swallow back a frustrated sigh when asked to read the same story, or play the same game, for the umpteenth time in a single week. And if you follow a few simple guidelines to protect the hardware and your own "grown-up" software and files, the whole family can happily share the computer.

That's what this chapter's all about. You'll find lots of software covered here, including games and educational software for the pre-high school crowd.

Contributors

Sharon Zardetto Aker (SZA) is the chapter editor, and mother of two computer-savvy kids lucky enough to have their own machine so that they'll leave hers alone.

Carolyn Said (CS), senior news editor for *MacWEEK,* collaborated on her reviews with her son B.B. and their friends.

Contents

Kids and Computers

When it comes to your kids and your computer, you have two goals that are occasionally at cross-purposes: Get the kids interested, and keep the computer (and your information) safe!

Issues   (SZA)

How old is old enough? I'm not suggesting that if a child doesn't start early enough on a computer, he'll forever lag behind his peers educationally. Nor am I recommending that you get a computer specifically for a young child. But if you have, or you're getting, a Mac, and you happen to also have a child, you'll find that most three-year-olds have the motor skills necessary for pointing and clicking, and the cognitive skills to know that what they're doing with the mouse is affecting what's happening on the screen. Two-and-a-half isn't too early to let them play with the simplest of programs; although purposefully maneuvering a mouse and using its button is beyond many two-year-olds, most can be taught to press one key at a time to get some feedback from the screen.

The care and not feeding of a computer. The computer area should be taboo for certain combinations—such as kids and food, or kids and drink. The potential problem with liquids is probably obvious, but cookie crumbs can sift down into the keyboard, too.

The youngest kids need to be taught that while the computer is something you can play on, it is *not* a toy, and needs to be treated gently—the same way you might teach a young one to press piano keys one at a time and not just bang away at it.

Data protection. Because few families can afford multiple computers, it's important to keep your grown-up stuff from being messed up by the youngsters in the family. For older kids, it's a simple matter of making some folders off-limits. But for the younger ones, who behind your back might accidentally move from a program to the desktop, and then have fun dragging lots of little pictures into the cute little garbage can, you need to set up a "fire wall" (as it's called in big business). There are several approaches, with different levels of security:

• Use the General Controls control panel settings to lock the System Folder and your Applications folder when the kids use the machine. You can even store your documents inside a subfolder in the Applications folder to protect them.

- If your child isn't an explorer, setting up the Launcher control panel with her program icons in it, and keeping other desktop folders closed, is probably sufficient protection against software accidents.

- Consider using **At Ease** ($50, Apple), which replaces the Finder with a giant folder with buttons for launching programs; you can get back to the desktop only with the proper password.

- Edmark's **KidDesk** ($30) acts like At Ease in that you get launching icons for selected programs and a password-protected desktop, but it's aimed at kids, providing a friendlier screen as home base. You can choose from several desk styles; each comes with a collection of useful little gadgets such as a calendar, note pad, and calculator—and even a private mail system that sends messages to the desks of other family members! Application icons appear on the desk surface, and the only way to access the real desktop is through a password.

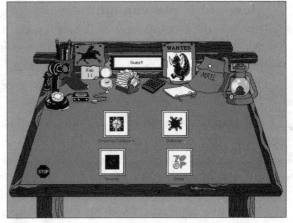

One of KidDesk's desktops. The accessories work—even clicking on the lamp dims or brightens the screen.

- **Launch Pad** ($30) from Berkeley Systems goes beyond just providing a password-protected special desktop. The metaphor here is that of a car; each family member has his own ignition key and chooses the "scenery" for his background. Application icons appear on the dashboard, but can be dragged anywhere on the screen. Other dashboard items, such as a clock and calculator, also work. The extraspecial features of Launch Pad, though, are the ones that interrupt any application's Print and Save commands so the child is routed to simpler dialogs and special folders. (Saved documents are accessed through the car's glove compartment!) There's even a special kids' trash can that saves items for a week before actually deleting them.

GOOD FEATURE

Educational? Hey, for a four-year-old, *everything* is educational. So, although we cover educational software later in this chapter—things that foster specific learning skills or cover particular subject areas for young children—don't get hung up on educational software just because you're embarrassed to admit you're letting a preschooler *play* on a $2,500 machine. There's nothing wrong with playing; in fact, many psychologists will tell you that playing is a child's job.

Not Made For Kids (SZA)

There are lots of programs not specifically designed for kids that make great kids' software nonetheless. A "programmable" screensaver, for instance, is a perfect little activity for the nine-to-twelve set. The basics of a "grown-up" paint program or word processor are well within the capabilities of many preteens. Both these groups can also doodle for hours with interface components, changing the desktop backgrounds and window colors; and if you have a program such as Dubl-Click's ClickChange (see Chapter 13), that's all the more items to play with (so long as you can trust the kids not to mess with your files, and can put up with "awesome" color combos on your desktop).

Ejecting CDs. Even young kids catch on quickly—before you know it, they'll be clicking their way out of a program and getting the CD out of the drive. But if they do it incorrectly, leaving the ghost icon of the CD on the desktop, they'll be asked to insert the CD at annoying intervals. First, make sure your child knows how to quit out of every program—"officially," not just by clicking on the exposed desktop if it's available. Next, set up a way to eject the CD properly. Unfortunately, one of the "proper" ways is to drag it to the Trash—not a habit you want the little ones to get into. So, make an alias of the Trash, change its icon to something more appropriate, and teach the kids to use it for ejecting CDs. (See Chapter 3 for more information about creating and using aliases.)

Spit It Out!

Make an alias of the Trash and edit its icon to create a CD-eject icon.

HOT TIP

Equipment (SZA)

Where to put the computer. Not many families buy a computer *just* for the kids, and even fewer buy separate ones for them. So, most setups are centrally located in a family room or living room where everyone can access it.

But if you do have a "kids" computer, I'm adamantly against putting it in a child's room (I wouldn't put a TV in there, either). I prefer to draw my kids out of their rooms rather than give them more excuses to shut their doors on the rest of the family, especially now that they're teenagers. For the youngest children, you'll want the computer more centrally located, since they both need help and always want to share the experience ("Look, mom!") anyway.

The CD-ROM explosion. If you have a computer and a kid, you need a CD-ROM drive. That's all there is to it. If your Mac didn't come with one, get one. All the best kid stuff is on CD-ROM; good reference material for older kids (through college!) is also on CD-ROMs.

Quiet! To have kids, software, and sanity all at the same time, you need earphones; standard Walkman-style work just fine. When you've heard "Find the letter A" in a cloying tone for the umpteenth time, or had to listen to preschool background music for hours on end, you'll be glad to spend a few dollars on sound insulation. (You'll also appreciate it if you have older kids, or a spouse, who's into noisy games.)

Books and Activities

Not all kids' software is hard-core educational—that is, specifically designed to teach a particular skill; there are plenty of titles that foster imagination and thinking just through the enjoyment of an activity.

Interactive Storybooks

Living Books (Anita Maining). If you have young children, Living Books from Brøderbund Software are a must; they set the standard for interactive CD books. They're beautifully produced, and faithful to the original titles (a paperback version of each book is included).

The original package, Mercer Mayer's **Just Grandma and Me** ($40) still holds its own as one of the best for the three-to-six set. It captures the playfulness of the book and adds to it, following Little Critter's day at the beach with his grandmother.

The longer, wordier text of Marc Brown's **Arthur's Teacher Trouble** ($50) can hold some three-to-fives, but is better suited to slightly older kids. Poor Arthur is stuck with a demanding teacher (Mr. Ratburn), a list of words to memorize for a spelling contest, and an irrepressible little sister who won't let him forget how much he has to study. But silliness abounds, too: Click and a dragon toy spits fire, the fire extinguisher goes berserk, and the little sister falls off the bed in the midst of taunting Arthur.

Discis Book series (Dan Ruby/Twyla Ruby). Discis Knowledge Research has a collection of titles ($30 to $40) designed for kids over six, including classics such as **Aesop's Fables** and **The Tale of Peter Rabbit**, as well as contemporary titles such as **Scary Poems for Rotten Kids**. With color illustrations, dramatic narration, music, and sound effects, they provide a rich learning experience for beginning readers. But they don't include animation, so although they're useful for teaching vocabulary and spelling, they have limited appeal for kids who can already read.

Puddle Books (SZA). I used only one book in Davidson's Puddle Book series—**A Day at the Beach with the Fuzzooly Family**—but it's so superb that I recommend you get it and every other title in the line ($20 each). These volumes use a variation on the usual interactive book approach: Every page is linked to another screen that fleshes out a particular part of the story with animations and games. So, you get to help Pop carry all the stuff down to the beach when the rest of the family leaves him at the car; in another scene, you can build sand castles. And the scenes and dialog change slightly each time you visit!

Building sand castles with the Fuzzooly kids.

Quick Takes (Cindy Luker). Here're three more storybooks worth reading:

- **The Escape of Marvin the Ape** ($20, T/Maker) puts the book of the same name on CD, provides minimal but effective animation, and lets a child wander into coloring and matching activities during the course of the imaginative story.

- **Baba Yaga and the Magic Geese** ($40, Davidson) brings the Russian folktale witch, Baba Yaga, to life in a tale about carelessness and its consequences. Lots of animation, good sound effects, music, and songs add up to a great experience. (Note that the haunted woods may be a little *too* haunted for timid three- to five-year-olds).

- **Four Footed Friends** ($20, T/Maker) is charming, with lots of little extra activities, but they're so hard to get that a young child will probably need help every time. There are also some confusing things for the young set, such as offering American and British spelling variations (armor/armour)—as if American spelling weren't difficult enough!

Creative Endeavors

Kid Pix (SZA). From a black-and-white shareware program to a full-color multiactivity CD, **Kid Pix Studio** ($50, Brøderbund) has come a long way—and it's a must-have for ages three to 12. Activities include a fun paint program that uses tools that have plenty of weird options and make strange noises, a puppet show where pressing different keys makes various body parts move, and a stamp-your-own scene builder where the stamps are animated. This will hold any child's interest for a very long time.

Creative writing (CS). Children can make up stories and illustrate them with MECC's **Storybook Weaver** and **My Own Stories** ($35 each). The programs provide elementary word processing and hundreds of images and background scenes, as well as dozens of sounds. Storybook Weaver draws its images (knights, trolls, treasure chests) from folklore; My Own Stories offers contemporary symbols (shopping malls, Frisbees, fire trucks, and so on).

Flying Colors (SZA). Davidson's **Flying Colors** ($40) is the perfect dabbling paint program for about seven years on up (up to adulthood). Choose backgrounds ranging from a dungeon to a country glade to a barren planet. Complete the picture with paint tools and a wide variety of stamps that can be resized and reversed. But what puts this package ahead of the rest is the "cycling color" option that adds a dash of pseudo-animation to any item. With candle flames or campfires cycling through yellows and oranges, for instance, you get flickering flames; the contents of laboratory bottles bubble ominously through greens and blues; and you can get twinkling stars and other out-of-this-world effects for your planetary pictures.

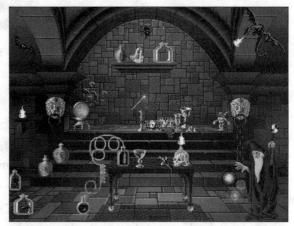

One of the scenes you can build in Flying Colors; many of the items here are sparkling on the screen.

Quick takes (SZA). Wait! There's more:

- Take a paint program, add animation and sound, combine it with a screensaver—and you get Bit Jugglers' **Kids World** ($30). It may sound complicated, but it's a breeze to use and can offer endless fascination to the ten-and-up gang.

- **Print Shop Deluxe CD Ensemble** ($80, Brøderbund) is a classic that keeps growing in capabilities. Create and print greeting cards, posters, calendars, certificates—just about anything, within a simple interface. This CD version includes more than 1,000 pieces of clip art and a few dozen fonts, too. Terrific—and not just for kids, either.

- **Kid Works Deluxe** ($60, Davidson) is mildly disappointing but still worthwhile. Write your story on one side, illustrate it on the other, occasionally using "stickers" instead of words. It's a confusing design for the younger end of the four-to-nine target age range; the stickers, for instance, are presented in small groups and you have to open a sticker book to change the group. For the older half of the recommended age range, this program is very close to being very good.

Use Kid Works Deluxe to create an illustrated storybook.

Each title in the **Imagination Express** series ($23 each, Edmark) provides a theme (ocean, neighborhood, castle, and so on) and related pictures and information for a child to write a story about. The approach is wonderful, but way too complicated for the lower half of the recommended kindergarten-through-eighth-grade range. It would be great in a classroom where a project could be worked on over a period of months, but probably wouldn't work very well at home.

Fun Stuff

Thinkin' Things (SZA). Edmark offers three **Thinkin' Things Collections**, numbered 1 through 3 for age groups three to seven, six to 11, and eight to 13. They're all terrific CDs that offer four or five interesting activities that foster such important learning areas as critical thinking skills, memory, problem solving, logic, and spatial dexterity. Sounds like heavy-duty stuff, but the kids will never notice because they'll be enjoying themselves too much.

Places to go, things to do (CS). Brøderbund offers three packages ($35 each) that let your child just wander around and get involved in various activities; any one of these packages would make an excellent first introduction to the Mac. **The Playhouse** and **The Backyard** are for ages three to six, while **The Treehouse** is for the five-to-eight crowd.

Each program is chock full of things to do. Clicking around The Treehouse turns up plenty of interesting reactions: Clouds change shape and the opossums and birds can be fed. Players pick an opossum playmate with whom to explore a bevy of activities, such as a musical maze, a theater where you make up silly sentences, and a counting game. The Playhouse features a clock that teaches how to tell time, an ABC book, and a counting board game. The Backyard offers activities that teach animal habitats, mapping and directional skills, strategy, and logic.

Two duds (SZA). Kids Count Entertainment's first title, **Jack's House** ($40), is a disappointing effort. The sound and graphics are fine, but the approach is frequently flawed. You click your way around Jack's house, but some of the most tempting objects, such as a half-opened drawer, do nothing. Click on the wooden blocks, and they pile up while being counted—but the letters and numbers on the face of each block don't match the number being spoken, a *big* educational no-no for the pre-school set. Move outside, and you'll find a frustrating garden that has some rigid rules about what you can do, and in what order. In all, wait for the second version of this one.

Great Wave's **KidsTime** ($50) was great when it came out about ten years ago, but it hasn't changed much except that it's in color now. It's an uneven collection of activities, some suitable for three-year-olds, and others for ten-to-twelves. It runs in a window instead of taking over the screen and has cheesy, minimal animation. Yuck.

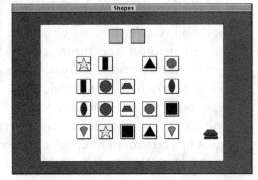

A typical screen from KidsTime, with its unappealing, outdated graphics.

Voyager's voyages (Susan McCallister/Connie Guglielmo). Two colorful CDs from The Voyager Company will lead your kids on adventures through worlds beautifully conceived by their creators.

Peggy Weil's **A Silly Noisy House** ($35) is an imaginative adventure designed for three-year-olds and up. The game begins with a cross section of a large house: Just click on a room to zoom in. Each room is loaded with objects that, as promised, do silly, noisy things: A rocking horse makes galloping sounds; a pie erupts with black-birds as you hear *Sing a Song of Sixpence*. Some objects are unpredictable, responding to clicks in different ways at different times.

Rodney's Wonder Window ($40), created by artist Rodney Alan Greenblatt, provides 24 interactive episodes filled with animations and sounds—and you don't have to be a kid to enjoy it. It's wacky, weird, wild, and fun: Order "Data Shorts" in your favorite fabric (including plaid, knotty pine, and X-ray); take a trip to the "Probe and Poke Pet Shop"; watch a movie of Chip and Peg's adventures in ShapeLand.

Educational Software

Let us just repeat this note: *Everything* is educational for a young child, and there's nothing wrong with playing. But when you want to provide experience in specific learning areas, there's lots to choose from.

Reading and Math

Reader Rabbit (SZA). Reader Rabbit was one of the first educational games on the Mac. It has been continually upgraded and improved, and—as suits its namesake—has multiplied into many products. Now on CD, **Reader Rabbit Deluxe 1** (ages three to six), **2** (ages five to eight), and **3** (ages six to nine) concentrate on building reading skills with simple but colorful and fun activities. Even within each package ($50 each), you can set the skill level that's appropriate for your child—and change it as your child grows. So, a three-year-old can play Word Train concentrating on sounds that words begin with, but a year later can work with ending sounds, or even vowel sounds in the middle. You can't go wrong with this series.

ReadingMaze (SZA). **ReadingMaze** ($50, Great Wave) is aimed at the three-to-eight classroom crowd and should be rated AA: absolutely awful. With a goal of finding an object in a multi-room house, you click on the target and hear the word "bull." Find the room with the bull, click on it again, hear the word "bull"—and get switched to a screen with the word "ladder" on one side and the letters "l", "d", and "b" on the other. It's bad enough that the first step has nothing to do with the second conceptually, and that the sounds you hear have nothing to do with the letters you look at, but then you can click on a wrong answer until the end of eternity, and you get no feedback or help.

BAD FEATURE

Super Solvers OutNumbered! (Nancy Dunn). My eight-year-old installed **Super Solvers OutNumbered!** ($45) himself and started playing without one look at the instruction booklet. It's a great game that combines arcade-style action and logical problem-solving, and unlike many educational games, it induces you to drill by making that a prerequisite for more play. The problems are interesting—more like puzzles than drills—and there's even an on-screen calculator to help make sure the focus is on arithmetic. It's from The Learning Company, for ages seven to ten.

Stradiwackius (Cindy Luker). One of T/Maker's **VroomBooks** titles, **Stradiwackius** ($20) takes a musical approach to working with numbers (and learning about musical instruments at the same time). It has plenty of music, charming graphics, and a few little activities, such as painting the various instruments. But there's a dubious educational approach: You get a screen, for instance, that says (both in print and in voice-over) "Four tiny violins…". Using the word instead of the numeral is not the right approach for the preschool set—and there's only a single violin at the bottom of the screen!

Quick takes (SZA). Here's a quick look at a few other packages:

- In **Math Rabbit** ($50, The Learning Company), the famous Reader Rabbit changes his subject area without losing any of his charm or effectiveness. For ages four to seven.

- **NumberMaze, Decimal & Fraction Maze**, and **Kid'sMath** ($50 each, Great Wave) are all creaking with age. They're on floppies, so there's not much room for good graphics or animation, or decent sound. And some of the design is downright clunky, such as a plain dialog box with "Good" printed in it as a reward for the right answer—and didn't it occur to someone that if a child can't count to six successfully, she probably won't be able to read the dialog "Please try again"?

- Knowledge Adventure has three titles in its **Jump Start** series: **Preschool, Kindergarten**, and (predictably) **First Grade.** Each offers a collection of activities that help develop necessary learning skills, starting with counting, letter and number recognition, shape identification, and the concepts of "same" and "different." By the time you're in the First Grade package, you've progressed to science concepts, language arts basics, and telling time.

Geography, History, and Social Studies

Carmen Sandiego series (SZA/Mary Toth). The software program that spawned a TV Series—Brøderbund's **Where In The World is Carmen Sandiego?**—also includes titles that take Carmen (and your kids) to Europe, through the U.S.A., and even into space. You learn about geography and history as you track Carmen and her band of thieves. You have to collect enough clues to get an arrest warrant and find the suspect, using information offered by witnesses and informants. If you find that the suspect stole something from Francisco Pizarro, you'd have to travel to 16th-century Peru—and if you didn't just happen to know that, you'd be able to look it up in the standard reference book that comes with the software. (Depending on the package, you might get a paperback edition of the *World Almanac and Book of Facts, Fodor's U.S.A.* travel guide, the *New American Desk Encyclopedia*, or *What Happened When*.) Titles range from $40 to $60, with those still available on floppy disks being on the lower end of the range.

And, for the jealous younger sibling, there's **Carmen Sandiego, Junior Detective** ($40), a program aimed at five- to eight-year-olds with minimal or no reading skills. A "case" is in a single country, the clues are all visual, and there's plenty of on-line help at hand.

MECC's Trail books (CS). MECC has taken to heart the saying, "The journey is the reward." The company offers educational games for ages ten to adult in which players "travel" a route packed with adventures, information, and colorful characters.

In **The Oregon Trail** ($60), players follow the covered wagon route pioneers trekked in 1848 from Missouri to Oregon's Willamette Valley. After "stocking up" on supplies, they head west, dealing with difficulties such as river crossings and wagon breakdowns as well as day-to-day decisions such as how much food to consume. Players can stop along the way to trade, buy supplies, or hunt. Top-notch edutainment, with geographical and historical information skillfully interwoven throughout.

The Amazon Trail ($60) is a canoe trek up the Amazon River. The scenario: A mysterious disease has afflicted a hidden Inca village and a secret medicinal plant hidden in the rain forest is the villagers' only hope for salvation. You must find the plant and then the people, along the way stocking up on other items the Inca king might desire. The trip weaves in and out of time, allowing the traveler to meet up with explorers, scientists, and others who shaped the development of the Amazon. The color animations are absolutely stunning, and digitized photographs and speech and authentic South American music provide nice touches of realism.

Headline Harry (CS). In addition to learning U.S. geography, players get the lowdown on important historical events and pick up some news-gathering skills from **Headline Harry** ($60, from Davidson for ages ten and up). It pairs the player with ace reporter Harry, who's racing to scoop the competition on important news stories circa 1950 to 1990.

How Would You Survive? (Cindy Luker) Grolier's **How Would You Survive?** ($35) is a superb package based on the book of the same name. Although the title might imply some sort of action adventure, it actually covers the daily life of three ancient cultures: Aztec, Egyptian, and Viking. You can see how women were treated, what children did, what kinds of foods were eaten, and what monetary systems were used. You can explore a single culture in depth, or go back and forth and compare certain facets of each society. There's no built-in game here, but that's no drawback: It's a wonderful reference book brought to life that will fascinate the ten-to-fifteen age group.

Unearth ancient civilizations in How Would You Survive?

Science   (SZA)

Explorers. Two finely crafted pieces of software come in a single package
from Compton's New Media: **Zoo Explorers** and **Ocean Explorers**
($60). They present a plethora of information in an easy-to-understand
format that young kids (three to eight) will return to again and again. From
the bright cartoon main screens, you can get a QuickTime movie of the
animal you click on or move to a related activity. The picture here, for
instance, shows a fishy game—you build a fish by selecting from wildly
colored component parts. Both these titles—which come in a double package—are a joy to behold.

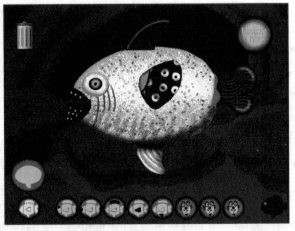

The build-a-fish activity is just one of the many fun things inside the ultra-informative Ocean Explorers CD.

What's the Secret. The **What's the Secret** series ($40 each), from 3M Learning
Software, is based on Public Television's Newton's Apple show, and it lives up to both
its pedigree and your highest expectations. The first volume covers things as diverse as
the world of bees and the human heart; the second includes things such as how glue
works and cockroaches. Both present tons of information in varied forms, including
QuickTime clips from the TV show. There are some minor activities, but there's no
game approach; since the package is aimed at seventh graders and higher, that's not a
problem. Kids are encouraged to keep wandering around: There are 45 "patches"—
like scout merit badges—scattered through the material that are meant to be collected
in a special knapsack.

Quick takes. Just a few more:

- **Sammy's Science House** ($35, Edmark) provides a mild introduction to science
skills for ages two to five. Activities revolve around weather, observation, sorting,
and sequencing.

- Why do I sneeze, and what happens to the food I eat, and why do I get the hiccups,
and why don't haircuts hurt? These questions and more are answered in **What is a
Bellybutton?** ($35, IVI Publishing), a gentle animated book about a child's bodily
functions that includes straight, simple answers, and simple activities for ages three
to eight.

20 | Games & Hobbies

Despite what your boss might have you believe, computers can be excellent tools for relaxation and enjoyment. Some estimates suggest that up to 80 percent of computer owners use their machines for some recreational activity. In 1995–96, this fact alone transformed the trickle of recreational software into a tsunami, making kicking back on your Mac easier than ever.

Whether it's taking in a few rounds of golf at a world-class course or carefully planning the garden that tickles your fancy, the Mac has become an impressive instrument for exploring your favorite diversions. In this chapter, we'll help you get the most bang for your buck when it comes to entertainment and hobby software.

Contributors

Bart Farkas (BF) is the chapter editor.

Chris Breen (CB) is a San Francisco Bay Area writer and musician and the coauthor of *The Macintosh Bible Guide to Games* as well as a contributing editor for *MacUser* magazine.

Karen Kaye (KK) is the Senior Editor of *Inside Mac Games* magazine and a staff writer for *MacSense* magazine. She sublets her apartment from three gracious cats, who give her a break on the rent in return for services and various domestic chores.

Greg Kramer (GK) is a freelance writer and editor currently living in Calgary, Alberta, Canada. His column, "Cerebreality", appears monthly in *MacSense* magazine and he is a regular contributor to *Inside Mac Games* magazine.

Contents

Games

Computers have long been touted as excellent tools for writing, bookkeeping, and graphic design. With those honorable intentions foremost in mind, people sit at their computers ready to attack the mounds of pending work. But as they boot up the machine they notice that copy of X-Wing that's been sitting on the bookshelf. "Maybe I'll just have a quick look at this," they mumble as they pick up the box. "Just five minutes, then I'll take care of that spreadsheet."

Four and a half hours later, the sun rises and they realize that although the Rebel Alliance has successfully quelled an Imperial attack on an Alliance fleet, those spreadsheets sit untouched. Thus is the nature of computer games. There are few computer owners without one or two games stashed on their hard disks. Whether for the kids, the spouse, or yourself, games have become an integral part of owning a computer. With the introduction of the Power PC-based Macintoshes, there has been an influx of quality games in the market. So loosen up your wrists and fire up the old noggin' as we take a look at the world of Macintosh games. It's recreation time!

Game Doctrine (BF)

The world of Macintosh entertainment software has its own special rule set. Here are a few details that might help you in your quest for great gaming.

Shareware, freeware, and other ways to get gaming. Many great games are available as either shareware or freeware. Freeware can be described pretty much just as is sounds. Games distributed this way are free for the taking, and usually only require you to say a good word about the author. Shareware, on the other hand, is a "pay as you play" system that requires you to send a nominal fee (usually $5 to $20) if you decide you like playing the game. Some commercial games (such as DOOM) are released as shareware or freeware with extra levels and features available for an additional fee.

Where to get more. For a desk reference on Mac gaming, check out *The Macintosh Bible Guide to Games* ($35, Peachpit Press), a 500-page book complete with a CD-ROM chock full of games and demos. If you are looking for a monthly way of keeping up on Mac gaming, you can subscribe to the *Inside Mac Games CD-ROM*. IMG regularly reviews new titles and includes the latest demos and shareware. On-liners can inspect the *Macintosh Entertainment Forum* on CompuServe. In fact, most on-line services have a heaping helping of Mac gaming resources.

The best World Wide Web option is the *Macintosh Entertainment Software* page, at <http://www.usyd.edu.au/~dchallis/MacES.html>. This resource can direct you to nearly every important Mac gaming page on the Web. (For more details on the Internet, see Chapter 23.)

Hardware. Two major rules apply to Macintosh gaming today:

1. Faster is better. The speedier your Mac's processor and the more RAM you have, the more games you can play to their fullest. Games are always pushing the technology envelope, and even the top-of-the-line machines are only able to keep up with modern games for a short two years. There are still games for every Mac, however, regardless of speed and memory confines.

2. Get a CD-ROM drive. Over 75 percent of new games ship on CD-ROM. This is most likely due to a combination of burgeoning game sizes and the built-in copy protection offered by the medium (most of us don't own CD duplicating equipment).

Arcade/Action Games

Watch out for Carpal Tunnel Syndrome (see Appendix A) and repetitive stress injuries in this department. These games are about rapid fire, quick reflexes, and a supernatural sense of timing.

Prince of Persia I and II (CB). Ever since the days of Dark Castle, Mac gamers have shown a proclivity for catapulting their digital alter egos off high perches and across deep chasms. **Prince of Persia** ($35), and its sibling **Prince of Persia II: The Shadow and the Flame** (Brøderbund) are superior examples of the run 'n' jump genre. The graphics are excellent and character movement is quite lifelike. You'll find yourself gasping as you propel the Prince across a seemingly impassable void. Prince of Persia II features an expanded story line and even more challenges than its predecessor.

Macworld Game Hall of Fame (BF). This $40 five-game CD-ROM from Casady & Greene packs several great classic action games on one disc including the eternally addictive **Crystal Quest** and its sibling, **Crystal Crazy**. These two humorous titles have you flying a cow-laden ship around an enclosed screen, gobbling up crystals and yummies while avoiding nasty critters. Crystal Crazy incorporates many new twists into gameplay such as puzzle assemblage and sinking pool balls. It's a blast. Rounding out the disk are **Sky Shadow**, **Glider 4.0**, and **Mission Thunderbolt**, a perennial favorite sci-fi dungeon adventure/action game. Thunderbolt is now being marketed as shareware under the moniker **Jaunt Trooper: Mission Thunderbolt** ($30, Megacorp International).

Joysticks

For years Mac users had to attack their favorite games with a keyboard or a measly mouse. Anyone who has had to play an arcade game with a mouse knows this is no way to go through life. Thankfully, an explosion of good Mac joysticks and gaming peripherals has hit the market in recent years.

CH Products has an impressive line of Macintosh peripherals. The **Flightstick Pro** ($79, CH Products) is probably the best all-around stick on the market. By the time you read this, CH will have also released a **Pro Throttle, F-16 Combat Stick** and **Virtual Pilot Pro** to compete directly with Thrustmaster. A good low-end joystick is the **Mac Alley Joystick** ($35), and those with Sega/Atari or PC joysticks can look to Kernel Productions' **ChoiceStick** for a way to

The Flightstick Pro from CH Products is one of the best all-around joysticks for the Mac.

take advantage of existing hardware. Although only the Sega/Atari model is available as I write, the PC version should be on the market by the time you read this.

For hard-core flight simulator junkies there's the **Thrustmaster Flight Control System** ($109), **Weapons Control System** ($59), and **Rudder Control System** ($125). These are best suited for real flight aficionados though, and the rather hefty price tag should deter all but the most obsessed.

Breaking out of this world of senseless violence is a truly pleasurable shoot-'em-up arcade game. **Power Pete** ($35, MacPlay) is probably the cuddliest arcade game going. You are Power Pete, a battery operated protagonist stuck in a toy store full of evil teddy bears, gingerbread men, heinous cavemen, and nasty little candies that want nothing more than to drain your batteries. Although this game contains some elements of violence, it is restricted to toothpaste guns and exploding birthday cakes. All in all, it's a great deal of fun. Its only drawback is the need for a Power Macintosh to make it run properly.

PegLeg (BF). If a simple arcade shoot-'em-up is the best medicine for what ails you, then I must recommend **PegLeg** ($35, Changeling Software). This is a bizarre mix of Asteroids and Space Invaders that will have you playing for hours—and will inflict serious damage on your trigger finger if you're not careful.

Apeiron (BF). The best Centipede clone on the market is **Apeiron** ($25, Ambrosia Software). Cartoon-like graphics and great gameplay punctuate this classic from Ambrosia.

ShadowWraith (BF). By far the best top-down view shoot-'em-up is **ShadowWraith** ($35, StarPlay Productions). Wraith includes ultracrisp graphics, speedy gameplay, and a CD-quality soundtrack. Any or all of these games are sure to be a blast (pun intended).

Pinball Simulations   (CB)

Little Wing Productions. Although the PC offers far more pinball games than the Mac, few PC pin games match the elegance of design or accurate physical modeling found in the products made for the Mac by Little Wing (published by StarPlay

Solid State PINBALL *Loony Labyrinth*

Loony Labyrinth from Little Wing is elegance personified and is just about as close to a real wood-and-glue pinball machine as you can get.

Productions)—**Eight Ball Deluxe**, **Crystal Caliburn**, and **Loony Labyrinth**. Developed by Yoshikatsu Fujita and Reiko Nojima, these three games are so close to the real thing that you'll be tempted to shove quarters into your floppy drive slot.

Published by Amtex, **Eight Ball Deluxe** is a re-creation of a classic '70s pinball machine. In contrast, Crystal Caliburn and Loony Labyrinth are completely original tables featuring gorgeous graphics, driving sound, ramps, and multiball play. All three games allow you to strategically nudge the table with the press of a key.

3-D Ultimate Pinball. Another option is Sierra On-Line's **3-D Ultimate Pinball**. What this title lacks in realism—the ball floats oddly about the table and is nearly impossible to trap in an upturned flipper—it makes up for in frenetic action. A hybrid pinball/arcade game, 3-D Ultimate Pinball comes with three highly animated tables that feature ramps, tunnels, hidden levels, exploding tractors, electric fences, and seemingly endless scoring options. To get the most out of this game you need a fast 68000-series or PowerPC processor.

3-D Action Games   (BF)

The last couple years have seen a plethora of new first-person perspective shoot-'em-ups break onto the Mac market.

Marathon II. The big daddy of this genre is **Marathon II** ($45, Bungie) which uses high-resolution graphics and smooth 3-D scrolling to produce fantastic gameplay. Where M2 really excels, however, is in network gaming.

DOOM and DOOM II. Another classic of the genre is **DOOM** ($25) and its sibling **DOOM II** ($50, GT Interactive). These best-selling titles, ported from the PC world, have engrossing and hyperkinetic action, but also have particularly violent and disturbing themes.

Dark Forces. All the awesome technical achievements of the **DOOM** titles are featured in **Dark Forces** ($49, LucasArts) while keeping the violence at a more acceptable level, consistent with the original Star Wars movies.

System Shock. For a 3-D game of a different breed, there is **System Shock** ($59, Origin). Instead of killing everything in sight, you must play this game like an adventure, carefully assembling items and defeating puzzles to reach victory. The only drawback to System Shock lies in its high system requirements. Without an 80 MHz PowerPC 601 and 16MB of RAM, you can forget about playing this one. Lastly (but certainly not leastly), be sure to check out **Descent** ($48, MacPlay).

POWER MAC

The Path to Adventure (BF)

Adventure games are the backbone of every computer platform. From solving spine-tingling mysteries to saving the Rebel Alliance, the Mac has become a premier computer for these games.

Myst. If you want to start at the beginning and get indoctrinated in adventure gaming in true style, then take a look at the huge-selling monster known as **Myst** ($49, Brøderbund). Be prepared to spend many an hour attempting to solve the strange puzzles of Myst Island. Myst has a highly engrossing story line and one of the best musical scores ever produced for a computer game.

Journeyman Project II: Buried in Time. If you prefer to play something a little more recent, **Journeyman Project II: Buried in Time** ($59, Sanctuary Woods) should fit the bill. In this three-CD thriller you must travel through time to find the person (or persons) who has altered time to turn you, the hero, into the villain.

Dust. PowerPC technology has allowed computer games to venture ever closer into the realm of virtual reality. No game comes as close as **Dust** ($59, CyberFlix), a virtual Western drama which drops you smack-dab in the dusty hamlet of Diamondback, New Mexico, with its cast of 40 interactive characters.

Frankenstein: Through the Eyes of the Monster. Another alternative for the virtual reality experience is **Frankenstein: Through the Eyes of the Monster** ($49, MacPlay) in which you assume the persona of Mary Shelley's most famous creation. With photorealistic backdrops and Tim Curry as the over-the-top Dr. Frankenstein, Frankenstein is as visually stunning a game as you'll find.

The Riddle of Master Lu. Part of a new generation of adventure game that incorporates lifelike video characters into detailed computer designed sets is **The Riddle of Master Lu** ($59, Sanctuary Woods). Master Lu takes you on an Indiana Jones type adventure to capture a powerful talisman before it can fall into the clutches of evil. This title's breathtaking graphics and animation make it a solid choice for anyone feeling adventurous.

The Riddle of Master Lu is one of a new generation of ultra-realistic adventure games, but as with many new games, you can't play it without a powerful Mac.

Rebel Assault II. Many titles are becoming interactive movies, and none fit the bill more than Rebel Assault II ($49, LucasArts). This game has minimal arcade participation, but has beautifully rendered artwork and cut scenes.

Sinkha and Gadget. If a passive movie experience is more your style then check out **Sinkha** ($35, Mojave) or **Gadget** ($35, Synergy). These titles can best be defined only as 3-D multimedia novels. When it comes to just kicking back in front of the computer, these are a feast for the senses.

Role-Playing (Elf Games) (BF)

There has never been a great selection of these games in the Mac world. There are, however, several titles worthy of mention.

Might and Magic: World of Xeen ($59, New World Computing) is perhaps the best of the lot, with great graphics, sound, and puzzles. Xeen is unique because it combines both M&M IV and M&M V on one CD, leaving it up to you to decide which areas to explore.

Other Options. The very serious role-playing gamer should also take a look at **Curse of Dragor** ($59, Domark), which combines an intuitive interface with challenging gameplay. **Ultima III** ($25, LairWare) and **Odyssey: The Legend of Nemesis** ($25, MacSoft) are both excellent examples of less sophisticated but nonetheless entertaining role-playing games.

Puzzle/Card Games (BF)

Tang Chi. One of the newest on the market is **Tang Chi** ($45, Capcom). This delightful and unique brain game consists of 50 puzzles which require you to assemble several geometric shapes into a given design. Believe me, it's not as easy as it sounds. Fortunately, there's a help feature to give you a boost, and when a puzzle is solved you're treated to a 3-D rendered movie.

Shanghai: Greatest Moments. Speaking of movies, **Shanghai: Greatest Moments** ($59, Activision) is a classic game reworked yet again. Loosely based on the ancient Chinese game Mah-Jongg, Shanghai required you to remove stylized tile pairs from a multilayered palette. Greatest Moments rewards you with highly entertaining video clips for every tile pair removed.

Hearts Deluxe and Power Poker (GK). One of the great benefits of computer gaming is being able to play multiplayer parlor games without having to muster the required number of opponents. Countless games, both shareware and commercial products, attempt to capture the complexity and excitement of these games with varying degrees of success. Two of the most notable are **Hearts Deluxe** ($15, Ian Lynch Smith) and **Power Poker** ($35, Electronic Arts). Featuring realistic gameplay, a full complement of rule variations, and entertaining playing partners, Hearts Deluxe is almost as much fun as a real late-night session of cutthroat Hearts. Smith and some third parties also offer a number of plug-ins (for about $10 each) which change your opponents to, among others, a trio of skeletons and the attendees at the Yalta Conference (Roosevelt, Churchill, and Stalin). For the green visor set, Power Poker is a truly superior poker simulation. With QuickTime rendered opponents and a dizzying variety of preset and customizable games, this title is perfect for the card shark and struggling beginner alike.

Eric's Ultimate Solitaire. For those who prefer Lady Luck as their opponent, **Eric's Ultimate Solitaire** ($35, Delta Tao) is perhaps the simplest and best all-around product on the market. You can even run this game from a floppy disk. Just about every solitaire game you can think of is represented in EUS, from Poker Square to plain old Klondike.

You Don't Know Jack ($35, Berkeley Systems) is a game show-like affair that almost defies description or categorization. To say Jack is entertaining is a profound understatement. Whether Nate, the host, is forcing you to answer questions because you're so far ahead of your competitors, or the questions posed to you seem truly demented, you won't go through a game without experiencing the gamut of emotions. It's infuriating,

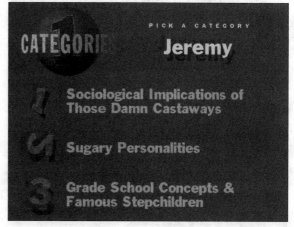

You Don't Know Jack from Berkeley Systems is a fast-paced, hilarious trivia game. If it's attitude you're looking for, this game won't disappoint.

addictive, side-splittingly funny and intense. It's a beautiful rarity to come across a computer game so engrossing, so humorous, and with such replay value. You Don't Know Jack is the best $35 you'll spend all year.

Simulations

This is were you can find out what it's *really* like to fly an F/A-18 Hornet supersonic jet, or be mayor of a city for a couple hundred years. Sound like Fantasy Island? Well you won't need Mr. Rourke to enjoy these games.

Sim City 2000 (BF). Maxis has—and probably always will—dominated the sim genre of gaming. The crowning achievement is **Sim City 2000** ($60, Maxis), which allows you to micro manage a city literally from the ground up. Dealing with the complexities of supplying housing, power, and water will pale in comparison to the headache you'll get with your first bona fide earthquake. **Sim Farm, Sim Tower, Sim Earth,** and **Sim Ant** offer up varying levels of sim gaming, though none of these games have been able to capture the glory of the flagship products Sim City and Sim City 2000.

Flight Unlimited (BF). Modern computers have brought the average person incredibly close to the realities of flight. From a World War II dogfight to an imaginary mission in an A-10 Warthog, today's flight simulators offer a spectacular experience. If going for a casual flight in a private plane without the worries of getting shot down is more your speed, then check out **Flight Unlimited** ($69 Looking Glass). This flight enthusiast's nirvana includes multiple aircraft, 3-D photorealistic landscapes, and real-world physics. Flight Unlimited will permanently unseat the anemic Microsoft Flight Simulator as the leading noncombat flight sim.

A-10 Attack! and F/A-18 Hornet. There are currently two excellent combat sims

Flight Unlimited from Looking Glass Technologies should easily unseat Microsoft's pathetic Flight Simulator as the king of nonviolent flight programs.

coexisting in the Mac market. **A-10 Attack!** ($49, Parsoft) is easily the most complex of the current sims, and the graphics and physics of gameplay are the best available. The new Cuba missions should propel A-10 to the forefront of combat gaming. Not far behind is **F/A-18 Hornet 2.0** ($49, Graphic Simulations). Hornet is an order of magnitude simpler to fly, and the excellent networking features and fabulous graphics make it a better alternative for flight enthusiasts who don't have rudder pedals. Star Wars fans will be thrilled with **X-Wing: Collector's CD** ($60, LucasArts) which is superior in every way to its DOS counterpart. This is the cream of the crop in spaceflight simulations. The force is with us!

Links Pro CD and PGA Tour Golf III. (CB). Fans of the mashie niblick, brightly colored polyester shirts and spiky, two-toned shoes are in luck. Golf is well-represented on the Macintosh by **Links Pro CD** ($40, Access Software) and **PGA Tour Golf III** ($35, Electronic Arts). Both games place you behind the little white ball and demand that—with a couple of well-timed mouse clicks—you propel your digital Dunlop down the fairways of a variety of lush courses.

The trophy winner as the end-all and be-all of Macintosh golf simulations is Links Pro CD. Above par features include spectacular graphics, voice command with Apple's PlainTalk technology, narrated aerial flybys of the holes accompanied by a corporate-jazz soundtrack, and the optional caustic remarks of your virtual golfing buddy, comedian Bobcat Goldthwait. The game contains two courses, South Carolina's Harbour Town Golf Links and Banff Springs Resort Course.

Another worthwhile golf game is PGA Tour Golf III. This title boasts wonderful graphics and sound, flybys, a suitably hushed announcer who describes your lie on each green, three separate courses, and an optional caddie feature that recommends clubs for each shot. Regrettably, PGA Tour Golf III is not networkable nor are add-on courses available.

For those who don't have the kind of hardware muscle to drive these professional golf sims (you need at least a fast 68040 to run these babies), or who crave the simple pleasures of miniature golf, take a peek at Bob Mancarella's delightful $15 **GopherGolf**.

War Games

(KK)

World at War. Traditional strategy board game designers favored famous land battles, and it should come as no surprise that these dominate the computer war game segment as well. The finest example of this genre is the **World at War** series. Available in three installments, **Operation Crusader, Stalingrad, and America Invades** ($42, Avalon Hill), each of these stand-alone titles designed by ATOMIC covers all aspects of a major operation during World War II. The nuclear boys are currently working on **Close Combat**, a squad-level war game to be published by Microsoft later in the year. Arsenal will shortly be shipping **Panzers East**, a much more sophisticated and graphically pleasing tactical combat simulator of the Russian Front during World War II. **Onslaught** ($46, Frontal Assaultware) is another worthy design that will appeal more to the casual gamer. This product is a cross between a war game and a conquest-type game like Empire. Two opponents fight it out with 1950s vintage military hardware in an attempt to control a continent.

TacOps. Some war gamers prefer to stay in the present instead of rehashing the past. The lethality of the modern battlefield is aptly illustrated by **TacOps** ($49.95, Arsenal). The graphics in this contemporary tactical war game are minimalist, but the overall combat simulation is amazing in its detail. Multiple two-player options are supported, and the illustrated weapon system database alone is worth the price of purchase.

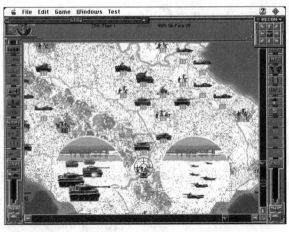

Although combat animations in Allied General look nifty, they do not add to the game's depth.

Allied General. The above games are essentially board games translated to a computer format. **Allied General** ($49.95, SSI), however, was designed with no such preconceptions and is not burdened with the conventions of standard war games. Players command one of the Allied armies of World War II in a series of interconnected battles which determine the outcome of the war. Very easy to learn and use, this could be the product that redefines the concept of the computer war game in the coming years.

Drumbeat: U-Boat II. Submarine gamers have fewer choices of platforms when stalking beneath the waves. **Drumbeat: U-Boat II** ($44.95, Deadly Games) is a gripping simulation of World War II submarine operations where players get to compete with the great U-Boat aces of the war. The game captures the claustrophobic tension through realistic intercom sounds and actual photographs of the interior of a German submarine.

Hobbies

Although it may seem difficult to believe, there are *actually* many Mac users that do not play games, but nonetheless enjoy recreational software. This is where the fairly obscure category of hobby-related software comes in handy. As with the Mac entertainment titles, the field of recreation has seen a recent proliferation of new and exciting software. From fixing up your home to taking a journey through the essence of your personality, there's some sort of recreational software for everyone.

Home Sweet Home   (KK)

Despite the associated taxes and the never ending maintenance work, home ownership remains an essential part of the American dream. A dizzying array of software titles promise to provide assistance on everything from home design to interior decorating.

Key CAD Complete. The best bargain of the bunch is **Key CAD Complete** ($30, SoftKey). It is a competent tool for mechanical and architectural drawings, and at this price it does not disappoint. **Design Your Own Home: Architecture** ($49, Abracadata) is a streamlined title that doesn't require excessive resources but still offers up the ability to work on most areas of home design. Multilevels, utilities (electrical wiring, water works), and even preset household fixtures make this a bargain for the designer with an older Mac.

Better Homes and Gardens: Planning Your Home. Because most of us have little free time and even less architectural prowess, it might be better to stick with a title such as **Better Homes and Gardens: Planning Your Home** ($40, or $50 with book, Multicom). Instead of offering an architectural angle, this software offers guidance on planning and selecting a professional home design based on needs and preferences. Over 500 floor plans are included, and several of these can be toured as 3-D photorealistic walkthroughs, providing a unique opportunity to explore your future home.

The Home Depot: Home Improvement 1-2-3. With the cost of professional repair work skyrocketing, more and more people are doing work around the home themselves. **The Home Depot: Home Improvement 1-2-3** ($40, or $50 with book, Multicom) is a first-rate guide to over 250 projects, from installing hardwood floors to weatherproofing storm windows. Each job is described in detail either through animation or a narrated slide show. The program lists all the necessary tools, offers time estimates for the job, and includes useful safety tips.

In order to get the most out of Home Improvement 1-2-3, you'll want to print instructions and diagrams so that they are available right where you're working.

Landscaping and Gardening (KK)

One of the best ways to raise the value of your home is to make it more appealing on the outside. Even if you're unsure of the difference between a dibble and a crevice trowel, you can beautify the grounds around your home with the aid of your Mac.

FLOWERscape. ($50, Voudette) is as handy as a good garden fork in helping you plant a beautiful garden. FLOWERscape contains a library of over 200 plants—each depicted as a digitized photograph—that can be searched by a variety of filters, such as required exposure to sun, planting season, and resistance to drought. The program takes into account the local climate and soil pH and is able to display the garden during any month of the year.

Mum's the Word Plus 2. Gardeners who require a more comprehensive land-scaping program should consider **Mum's the Word Plus 2** ($95, Terrace Software). It contains an extensive database of over 600 plants, shrubs, and trees that can be searched through a myriad of options. The landscaped area can be depicted during various seasons and from several different perspectives. Unfortunately, the program is more akin to a CAD tool and uses abstract icons to depict the plants. Therefore, it may be of more use to the professional or avid gardener with access to other reference materials.

Better Homes and Gardens Complete Guide to Gardening. Neophytes who are ready for the seed of their ideas to mature to full bloom need the assistance of a manual such as the **Better Homes and Gardens Complete Guide to Gardening** ($40, or $50 with a book, Multicom). Although nothing that claims to be complete ever is, this well-illustrated CD-ROM is packed with a slew of valuable gardening information on everything from annuals to wildflowers. Best of all, the program contains video instruction on such knotty gardening jobs as planting a hedge and using a pruning saw.

Genealogy (KK)

Genealogy takes us from roots in your garden to your family roots. The study of genealogy has become a popular hobby for anyone interested in exploring their family tree, thorns and all. It should be noted, however, that none of these programs is a reference tool for locating long lost ancestors; they are primarily database shells that provide you with a convenient way to store and display family information.

Gene. First-time explorers of dusty attics and county archives should consider a basic and inexpensive shareware solution called **Gene** ($15, Diana Eppstein). It is a convenient way to catalog the members of a family and to display the complex relationships in easy-to-understand charts. Although the defined fields in the database are limited, the program redeems itself by providing the option to link an individual to a scanned picture. Gene is simple and efficient, and it may be all the genealogy tool that most of us need.

Reunion. In order to go further back to your roots, you will also have to dig deeper into your pockets. **Reunion** ($100, Leister Productions) is a bit pricey, but it is the granddaddy of lineage hunting software. Reunion lets the user link scanned images to various entries, providing a means to create a visual record that complements the family tree. Leister is known for excellent support and also maintains a Web page to assist those looking for reference materials <http://www.leisterpro.com>.

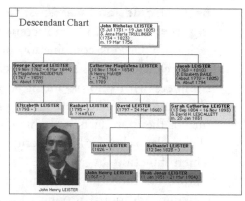

Reunion is not only attractive because it allows you to create colorful Descendant Charts with pictures, but also because data entry is the most intuitive of all the genealogy programs.

The Culinary Mac

The computer is an excellent medium for counting calories, getting the most out of your kitchen cupboards, or just learning to cook. The last several years have witnessed a gastronomical surge in culinary software on the Mac. So cleanse your palate and prepare to be impressed.

MasterCook Deluxe. ($40 Sierra) is a highly polished cooking companion which helps you manage meals, nutrition, and shopping (to quote Sierra). MasterCook contains a wide variety of recipes and offers great photos of dishes and snappy graphics. As with most titles in this category you can have an in-depth analysis of recipes including important nutritional information. **MasterCook Cooking Light** ($40) offers 1,250 low-fat recipes for your recipe collection.

Mangia! ($50 Upstill) is a perennial favorite on the Mac and, although not as flashy as some of the newer titles, offers many great features. From keeping track of your kitchen's supplies to adding and categorizing recipes, this is a great, flexible, and classic program.

Mealtime II. ($35 Chris Hostetter) is the blue-collar member of the cooking programs, but still has the ability to do what all other programs do (including scaling recipes). What Mealtime lacks in graphical prowess it makes up for in expandability and usability.

Better Homes and Gardens: Cooking for Today. ($32 Multicom) is a series of CD/book combination products each with a solid lineup of recipes complete with photos and a simple glossy interface. The most striking feature of these products is the inclusion of video help clips for kitchen etiquette, which function as an added safety feature for those just learning about cooking. Additional products include Stir Fries, Pasta, Chicken, and Great American Cooking. If you have the money for all the segments, this is an excellent collection.

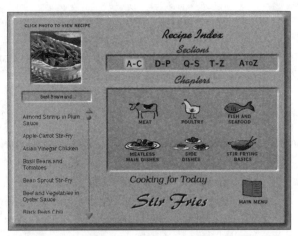

Better Homes and Gardens: Cooking for Today is perhaps the best-looking cooking program for the Mac and has several add-on CDs.

If the Spirit Moves You   (KK)

From brewing your own beer to expanding your wine knowledge, this is an area that has undergone an excellent aging process.

The Beer Hunter. Beers of all varieties, especially from small independent breweries, are suddenly all the rage. In order to understand the origins of this beer renaissance—or simply to find out where and how to get in on the action—take a look at **The Beer Hunter** ($40, Discovery Channel Multimedia). The program educates the user with tasting notes on all major styles of beer and identifies U.S. microbreweries where the best samples of each can be found. Beer lovers who prefer their brew in a stein as opposed to a frosty mug should check out the **World Beer Hunter**.

Microsoft Wine Guide. Those who prefer the drink made from the fruit of the vine will find a bold, vibrant experience with a sophisticated finish in the **Microsoft Wine Guide** ($35, Microsoft). This slick multimedia title is liberally illustrated with the enthusiastic video commentary of Australian wine aficionado Oz Clarke, whose humorous observations reinforce his belief that enjoyment of wine ought to be a fun social experience. This title is also an invaluable reference tool with a superb atlas of wine-growing regions, and a searchable database of over 6,000 wines complete with tasting notes. Oenophiles may be attracted to the significantly larger listing of wines found in the **Wines of the World** ($40, or $50 with a book, Multicom). Sadly, bigger is not always better. It can take upwards of five minutes to search through the 28,000 items in the database.

Travel   (KK)

While none of the titles discussed in this section can easily replace a printed travel guide from a reputable company, they do offer an invaluable source of travel-related information by taking advantage of the multimedia capabilities of CD-ROMs.

Nile: Passage to Egypt. The first software title that can claim the honor of being a true travel experience is **Nile: Passage to Egypt** ($50, Discovery Channel Multimedia). Billed as a journey of 4,000 miles and 5,000 years, this program unlocks a world otherwise not available to the majority of us. The sights are explored through a series of narrated photographs and video segments guided by such experts as Dr. Robert Fernea. Those considering a trip to Egypt would be well served to initially explore the cradle of civilization on this stunning CD-ROM.

Passage to Vietnam. A splendid chronicle, **Passage to Vietnam** ($40, Against All Odds) is both a physical journey and a spiritual one. The work of photographer Rick Smolan, the title seamlessly integrates over 400 photographs and an hour of full motion video organized along such topics as the central role of the Perfume river and the legacy of the American war. This is an unflinching portrait of the hardships and perseverance of the people of Vietnam—occasionally shocking or disturbing, but never manipulative.

Route 66. The station wagon and the trailer may have been replaced by the minivan and the condo, but the desire to pack up the family and hit the road seems little changed from previous generations. **Route 66** ($80, Route 66 Geographic Information Systems) is a route planner that lets you select the shortest, fastest, and cheapest course from one destination to another. The program calculates expenses and travel time based on the user's specific gas mileage and cruising speed. When the other entries are complete, the software constructs an itinerary which indicates all significant points along the trip—complete with a corresponding time and distance chart.

Photography   (KK)

Travel and photography seem to go together as naturally as chocolate and peanut butter. While camcorders are increasingly popular, the camera remains our favorite means of capturing precious moments. Unfortunately, what most of us see through the lens is not always what appears in print.

Better Photography: Understanding Exposure. This instructional package ($60, or $80 with a book, DiAMAR) is aimed at the amateur who is ready to move beyond the bland, overexposed snapshots found in most family albums. The program is not a dry, abstract textbook, rather it is more like a photography seminar held by the author, Bryan Peterson. An award-winning professional, Mr. Peterson builds his instruction

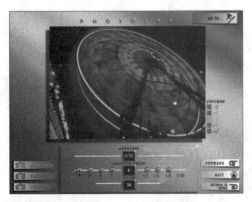

Understanding Exposure features a number of photography exercises where the user can instantly see the results of changing a camera setting—in this case shutter speed.

around an understanding of the three fundamental elements of a great photograph: film speed, aperture setting, and shutter speed. This is one of the most flexible titles of its kind, and among other things, it allows users to create custom workshop sessions on topics of particular interest.

Better Photography: Learning to See Creatively. Although no more complex than the product mentioned above, **Better Photography: Learning to See Creatively** ($60, or $80 with book, DiAMAR) seems to focus on enthusiasts who are ready to pursue their hobby more seriously. Learning to See Creatively unlocks the secrets of award-winning photographers by teaching the elements of their art as individual topics in separate sessions. The program also reveals the most hallowed secret of the great masters: Instead of taking just one or two shots of a scene, professionals will hedge their bets by taking entire rolls of film!

Movie Magic (BF)

Finding just the right video in the sea of titles in most video rental stores can be challenging to say the least. These products are designed not only to help you pick out a movie gem, but they're often highly enlightening as well.

Movie Select. One of the original movie-related CD-ROMs was **Movie Select** ($60, Paramount Interactive). Movie Select's movie database is somewhat lacking when it comes to European flicks and the video clips promote only a few titles, but there is one feature where this product excels. The Movie Select Recommends command is an excellent way to make a list of potential rentals to suit your taste. Print your list, and you're off to the video store.

HOT TIP

Cinemania 96. The current champion of the movie circuit and the classiest of the bunch is **Cinemania 96** ($69, Microsoft), which not only has photos and clips of many titles in its database, but also includes reviews by such critics as Leonard Maltin, Pauline Kael, and Roger Ebert.

Corel All-Movie Guide. The final product in this genre is the **Corel All-Movie Guide: The Ultimate Guide to the Movies** ($69, Corel). The All-Movie Guide allows you to create your own special lists of movies as well as order obsolete titles from within the program. There are also a few built-in games including a trivia game and a crossword game.

Collector's Heaven (BF)

Although collecting is a relatively obscure software category, there is one company that covers all the bases.

Although this software department essentially has only one player, Ninga Software's products are worthy of mention. **Hobbysoft Comic Keeper** ($50) offers up the perfect alternative to a log book for comic book fanciers. With separate categories for DC and Marvel Comics this program has everything a collector could want in an electronic record. If stamps or coins are your preference, Ninga has both the **Hobbysoft Coin Collector** and the **Hobbysoft Stamp Collector** ($50). These titles have recently been upgraded from their rather ugly DOS roots, and although they won't be winning any awards for glitz, they serve a great practical purpose.

The Ego, Id, and IQ (BF)

Personal exploration has recently become a software niche on the Mac. There is one thing that seems to be of interest to all people: themselves. Several titles have recently emerged in the introspective fields of IQ and personality testing, allowing Mac users to explore the inner workings of their minds.

IQ Test ($29, Virtual Entertainment) offers a CD-ROM based IQ test that will give you a reasonable idea of what your intelligence quotient is. Perhaps the most impressive feature is inclusion of video clips of experts describing just what an IQ test is and is not. It's a fun little diversion but folks should be cautioned not to take the results too seriously. **IQ Test 2.0** ($8, White Sands) is a shareware program that, surprisingly, produced similar scores to Virtual's IQ Test. This is a great program for those who want to check out their IQ without too much glitz and glamour.

Personality Test 2.0 ($17, White Sands) offers a different, perhaps more interesting glimpse at your inner self. Personality Test 2.0 is based on several respected personality tests developed in the early '80s. It offers truly fascinating and accurate insight into your behavior patterns based on your answers to a series of questions. If you pay the share-

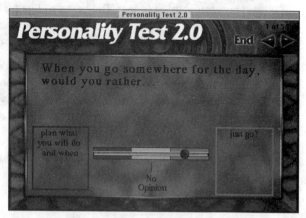

After a series of 50 questions, Personality Test 2.0 from White Sands Multimedia can tell you a lot about your inner workings.

ware fee, you are given a code that lets you unlock the General Personality test, the Stress Indicator test, the Leadership Potential test, and the Entrepreneurial Drive test.

Editors' Poll:
What Are Your Favorite Games?

ML: My favorite game is Myst. The reason? Because I can't win.

KT: I turn to computer games to defrazzle myself, so I like contemplative things. Basically, I like solitaire games and image-matching games.

SA: I fall into the "Doesn't play computer games" category.

SS: My favorite games at the moment are Warcraft: Orcs and Humans, and Dust: A tale of the Wired West. I like Warcraft because of the challenge, and Dust because of the storyline.

TL: My all-time favorite game is Dark Forces, but it's not terribly replayable after you've finished it. For a never-ending source of fun, my favorite game is Cyrstal Caliburn. I still play it several times a week. Spectacular.

JC: My current favorite is Ambrosia Software's Swoop. Fans of the old-fashioned arcade game Galaga will enjoy this game.

BF: There are so many quality games available for the Mac now that it's hard to decide. However, I'd have to say that A10-Cuba (Parsoft), You Don't Know Jack, and any Ambrosia game would rate up there fairly high.

MEC: I don't get much chance to play games, but I tend to enjoy Apeiron, Crystal Crazy, Maelstrom, and Shanghai when I do get the chance.

TA: Marathon 2 is the best network game on the Mac. I usually play until I feel the tendons in my arms starting to tear. The best party game is You Don't Know Jack, unfortunately you need at least two people to play. Finally, Strategic Conquest is a classic military strategy game without the complexity of Civilization or the time crunch of Warcraft.

JH: My favorite game of all time is Myst; it's so involving that, over the three or four weeks I played it, I actually came up with solutions to some parts in my dreams! To this day, there are sounds I hear that remind me of the game. Nothing like it. A close second are the pinball games from Starplay (Crystal Caliburn and Loony Labyrinth).

BW: I don't play computer games per se. However, I do play a game of my own called "Thesaurus". Look up a word in the thesaurus, and then choose a synonym, and a synonym of that synonym. Then judiciously choose synonyms or antonyms to see if you can get back to the original word. Any electronic thesaurus will do.

PART

3

Extending Your Reach

Editors' Poll: What On-Line Services Do You Subscribe to? Favorite Forums?

TA: America Online. Because it's the biggest, the best, and I just happen to be an AFC in the Mac Graphics Forum. The Illustrator SIG is the best place to learn all about Adobe Illustrator, with more secrets, tips, tricks, and techniques than you'll find anywhere else.

KT: I subscribe to CompuServe and America Online, and my favorite forum, bar none, is the DTP Forum on CompuServe. (Naturally—I'm a sysop there, and on the Professional Publishing Forum as well.)

SS: I've had an America Online account for the last six years and just recently signed up with my city's first ISP for a "real" Internet account. The AOL forums I use most often are StockLink (for tracking my meager portfolio) and Computing & Software (for software updates and new freeware/shareware utilities).

MEC: I subscribe to America Online, and I have a shell account at Netcom that I use with TIA for a SLIP connection. I hardly ever check any forums on AOL anymore, and I only keep it for a mail address. I do subscribe to a number of newsgroups through my Netcom account; if you want to consider a newsgroup as a form of forum, my favorite would be alt.fan.cecil-adams: a hopelessly trivial experience.

JH: As a sysop (system operator—see my Telecom chapter) I'm incredibly biased, but CompuServe is my home and hands-down favorite. Specifically ZDNet, where all the Ziff Davis magazines are based as well as plenty of online-only attractions. End of plug!

My favorite forum on CompuServe is Roger Ebert's message section in the Showbiz Forum. Nothing like dropping in on Roger to debate his review of your favorite—or most despised—film of the month.

TL: CompuServe and America Online. America Online has by far the better graphical interface and is more fun to use. But I still prefer CompuServe more. I especially like the way its forums are organized. It is much easier to follow a threaded discussion and track replies to messages with CompuServe Information Manager (CIM) than with AOL (I only wish the current version of CIM worked better with PCI Macs). The other advantage of CompuServe (although AOL is catching up here) is that it was the first to allow PPP connections to the Internet, which meant that you could use Netscape or any other Internet software of your choice with your CompuServe account. This was a much better alternative than AOL's more limited Web browser and general Internet access.

When I am on CompuServe, I spend most of my time in the ZMac forums (*MacUser, MacWEEK,* and Download forums). The bulletin boards and download libraries in ZMac are all excellent. CompuServe's Internet forums are also good. And I frequently check out Roger Ebert's movie reviews.

21 } Printing

While pundits jabber about the World Wide Web and global electronic information exchange, most of us still pass the paper when it's time to show off what we've created on our Macs. And though paper's not getting cheaper, printers are! The current trend in desktop printers is color, better, and easier. Color inkjet printers costing under $500 now kick out better-looking text and color graphics than inkjets costing over $1,000 did just a few years ago. And you can have a color laser printer—once a $10,000-plus budget buster—for under $5,000, less than the price of the original Apple LaserWriter Plus monochrome PostScript laser printer.

For the home and small office, it looks like color inkjets are supplanting black-and-white models as the entry-level printers of the '90s. But if it's monochrome you need, think about moving up to the speed of a laser printer: the Apple Personal LaserWriter 300 mail orders for around $630, for example—more than inkjet, but faster.

In this chapter, we'll help you find the printer that does what you want—hopefully at a price you can afford, including everything from dirt-cheap inkjets to high-speed/high-resolution laser printers, to expensive dye-sublimation photo-quality color printers. In addition, you'll learn what it takes to get a printer up and running on your Mac, and how to get the most out of it.

Contributors

Bob Weibel (BW) is the chapter editor.

Jim Felici (JF), ex-managing editor of *Publish* magazine, is now a free-lance writer and *bon vivant* residing in Fontès, France.

Randy B. Singer (RS) is a practicing attorney and Apple Legal Fellow who leads user groups for attorneys using the Mac.

Sharon Zardetto Aker (SZA), **Nancy E. Dunn (ND)**, **Darcy DiNucci (DD)**, **John Kadyk (JK)**, and **Arthur Naiman (AN)**, edited previous editions of *The Macintosh Bible,* from which parts of this chapter were taken.

Contents

How Printing Works

You've seen it on screen, now you need it on paper. The Mac makes printing easy—if you've got it set up right—by invisibly merging your software with the printer hardware to kick out a proper page. When you *don't* have your printer set up properly, the Mac's a misery, because there's really a lot going on behind the scenes when you click that Print button. The Mac has to convert its method of storing and representing text and graphics into a form the chosen printer expects. It then has to guide this printer data out of the right port on your Mac and down the correct type of cable into the printer, which itself must be turned on, stocked with ink/toner and paper, and ready to print! For added complexity, printers differ in their graphical capabilities, and each generation of Mac system software offers new ways of printing. But don't worry; we'll make it easy to understand.

Printer Drivers   (JK/SZA/AN/ND/RS/BW/Susan McCallister)

Printer drivers are programs that tell the Mac how to prepare print data for your printer. Without them, each application would need additional programming to handle all the types of printers you might use.

So, in addition to physically connecting your printer to the Mac, you also need a printer driver to connect your software to the printer. Apple supplies drivers for the ImageWriter, the StyleWriter, and the LaserWriter. Some third-party printers have their own drivers, supplied on diskettes packaged with the printer, although many are designed to use Apple's drivers.

You may not need a separate driver for each type of printer you use; sometimes a single driver works for several related printers. For example, Apple's LaserWriter driver works for any PostScript laser printer.

Printer drivers go into the Extensions folder in your System Folder; if you drag them onto the System Folder icon (not the window), the Finder will put them in the Extensions folder automatically. (In System 6, printer drivers go in the System Folder, but not into any folder within it.) Most installation software will automatically put driver files in the correct folders.

Once your printer drivers are installed in the Extensions folder, you still have to tell your Mac which one to use. The standard way to do that is to select Chooser from the ❤ menu and click on the printer you want to use. (Apple's QuickDraw GX, and LaserWriter driver version 8.3.3, which we discuss later in this chapter, offer

Click on the icon
of the printer you
want to use.

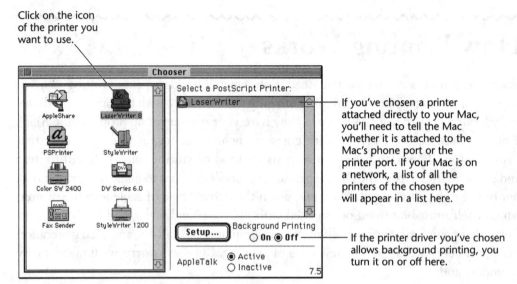

If you've chosen a printer
attached directly to your Mac,
you'll need to tell the Mac
whether it is attached to the
Mac's phone port or the
printer port. If your Mac is on
a network, a list of all the
printers of the chosen type
will appear in a list here.

If the printer driver you've chosen
allows background printing, you
turn it on or off here.

You use the Chooser to tell your Mac which printer you want to use.

alternate scenarios.) The printer driver you select in the Chooser will display Page Setup and Print dialog boxes reflecting the capabilities of your printer. Many applications substitute their own dialog boxes for these basic ones to give you even more printing options.

HOT TIP

When you use the Chooser to switch from one type of printer to another—from a StyleWriter to a LaserWriter, say—you need to let any open applications know that. That's because different kinds of printers use different print areas on the page, and even different character spacing. To an make an application hip to the change, open its Page Setup dialog box and then close it again (you don't have to change any settings). You should also do the same thing to activate a newly installed printer driver. (A dialog box will warn you when you need to do this.)

If you have a PostScript printer (see "PostScript" later in this chapter), Apple's LaserWriter driver version 8.3.3 and later has a niftier way of presenting your printer choices, using features borrowed from QuickDraw GX, which we also describe later. With LaserWriter 8.3.3 installed you select your printer from the Chooser. Just select from the Chooser those to which you might print, and then either double-click or push the Setup button and a Desktop Printer icon will appear on your desktop as well as next to the printer's name in the Chooser. The one you most recently used becomes your "default" printer; but, that's easily changed by just selecting the desired printer icon on the desktop and selecting Set Default Printer from the Printing menu which appears in the Finder whenever one of the printer icons is selected.

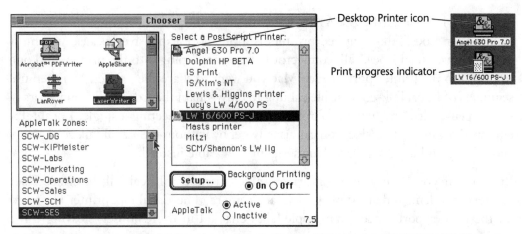

Apple's LaserWriter driver version 8.3.3 and later adopts the Desktop Printer concept of QuickDraw GX. When you first choose a PostScript printer from the Chooser a Desktop Printer icon appears on the desktop and in the Chooser. A small page appears at the Desktop Printer to show you a print job's progress.

When one of your files is printing, the icon changes to show a small page in the lower-left quadrant, indicating the progress of your print job. You can also resume interrupted print jobs, either from the beginning or from any page, so long as the job is still in the queue. This saves a lot of time when paper or labels jam. Have you ever sent a job to a printer and found someone with a large job in front of you in the queue? Well, here, you just select your job in the queue and drag it to a different printer icon. All of the other features previously available in Backgrounder are now available directly in the icon and from the Printing menu.

The Cable Connection   (BW/RS)

Most, but not all, printers come with a cable for connecting to your Mac. You should usually connect the power and printer cables before running the printer's software driver installation program. One end of the cable goes in the printer, but there are two choices at the Mac end, the printer port and the modem port. Many inexpensive printers sport a serial interface, and can plug into either the printer or modem port. The printer port actually doubles as a serial port and a LocalTalk network port, depending on whether you turn the AppleTalk option off (serial printer port) or on (network port) in the Chooser. (See Chapter 24 for more on LocalTalk and AppleTalk.)

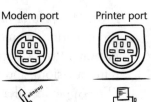

The Macintosh printer port doubles as a serial printer port or LocalTalk network connection which can also connect a LocalTalk-interface printer. The modem port is strictly serial and can connect a modem or a serial interface printer.

LocalTalk serves as a shared wire, along which you can string (daisy-chain) many devices, including LocalTalk-equipped printers *and* other Macs, making it easy for several Macs to share one printer. Many printers, even inexpensive ones such as the Hewlett-Packard DeskWriter 660C come with LocalTalk ports of their own. Cabling for LocalTalk-equipped printers is a bit more expensive because you must first purchase small LocalTalk connector boxes, one to plug into the printer, and one to plug into the printer port of each Mac you want to share the printer. You then use segments of LocalTalk-compatible cabling to daisy-chain the LocalTalk connectors—in an open-ended line, not in a circle. If you're only connecting a single, LocalTalk-equipped printer to the Mac, you can usually get by without the LocalTalk connectors and cabling and use a standard Mac serial printer cable instead.

But what if you have a serial-interface inkjet printer, a LocalTalk-interface laser printer, a modem, and an Apple QuickTake camera. The LocalTalk printer has to go on the printer port (check that AppleTalk's enabled in the Chooser), leaving three other peripherals to share the modem port. You'll soon tire of plugging and unplugging devices as you need them, and you risk wearing out the connectors. Instead, purchase a manual switch box that lets you keep everything plugged in, and turn a knob to select a device. They range from $20 to $50 in catalogs, depending on whether you order the two-, three-, or four-port model. (Try Microcomputer Cable at 313/946-9700.) For around $100 you can snag Momentum's four-connector **Port Juggler**, a small box that automatically switches to the correct device depending on which application you're using.

HOT TIP

Background Printing   (RS/BW/SZA/AN/JK)

Macs can send out print jobs faster than most printers print them, too, often leaving the computer waiting for the printer. You can drastically cut the wait with a type of program known as a *print spooler*, which temporarily stores print jobs and takes over feeding the printer in the background. Because the Mac creates this print file quite quickly, you can get back to work and leave the computer and the printer to talk to each other in the background. *(Spool* is an acronym for simultaneous print operations on-line.)

Most Mac printer drivers let you simply click an On or Off radio button to turn background printing on or off. Two system files work behind the scenes during background printing: PrintMonitor, for System 7 (which installs as both a control panel and a system extension), and Backgrounder, required for background printing under System 6. (The Apple installer for the LaserWriter driver should do this automatically, although the System 7 installer will also work.)

PrintMonitor keeps track of which document is printing, how many pages are left to go, which other documents are waiting to be printed, and so on. It's launched automatically when you start a print job, and you can check a job's status by choosing PrintMonitor from the Application menu. When the printer needs attention (because it's out of paper, for example), the PrintMonitor flashes its icon in the upper-right corner of the screen.

Note that QuickDraw GX (see "Printing with QuickDraw GX"), bundled with System 7.5, and slated to be part of System 8 (code named "Copland"), includes an enhanced print spooler/monitor know as Desktop PrintMonitor. It'll let you rearrange the order of printing jobs, redirect them to different printers, delay printing to a scheduled time, and lots of other cool stuff. Because it works with current printer drivers and software, the old PrintMonitor becomes obsolete once you've moved up to Desktop PrintMonitor. You can get Desktop PrintMonitor itself, with QuickDraw GX, from Apple's Software Update libraries on the Internet (ftp.info.apple.com or ftp.support.apple.com). It's now also included with the LaserWriter 8.3.3 driver, as we described earlier.

[An all-too-common background printing tale: A new Mac owner starts printing a 16-page report, and when nothing happens right away, hits the Print command again, and again, and then shuts off the Mac. Someone else later starts the Mac and pages of the "mystery report" come pouring out! They don't realize that background printing takes time to spool before printing starts, so they line up several jobs, and quit the scene, leaving someone else to reap the grief—especially if they don't know to cancel the jobs in PrintMonitor. For this reason I turn Background Printing off for first-time or occasional Mac users.—BW]

QuickDraw and PostScript Printing (BW)

QuickDraw is a graphics description language, the part of the Macintosh operating system that handles the screen display—drawing lines, managing color, controlling windows, basically handling all the graphics. The *PostScript* page description language is also a graphical programming language, used mostly for imaging on printers (it was introduced with the first LaserWriter printer). PostScript handles a greater variety of graphical functions, and with greater precision, than QuickDraw.

Macintosh printers fall into two types: those that use QuickDraw's description of the image to be printed, and those that use PostScript information translated from QuickDraw by a PostScript printer driver (or generated by an application such as Illustrator or QuarkXPress).

In either case, the QuickDraw or PostScript information must go through one more translation before printing: It must be converted to a *raster*—the pattern of dots that actually hits the page. For QuickDraw printers, the Mac does this translation in its own processor. For most PostScript jobs, it's done by a computer—called a *raster image processor* or *PostScript interpreter*—within the printer itself.

Note well: though you *can* print QuickDraw graphics to a PostScript printer, you *can't* print PostScript graphics to a QuickDraw printer (the special interpreter is missing), unless you run a PostScript interpreter on your Mac, (see "PostScript" later

HOT TIP

in this chapter). A special exception is made for fonts. By using ATM (available from Apple or Adobe, or installed automatically with System 7.5), you can turn the Mac's processor into a PostScript font interpreter, as described in Chapter 14.

Printing with QuickDraw GX   (BW)

QuickDraw came up the river, had a child, and Apple called it *QuickDraw GX*. It grew strong and came of age in 1994 with graphical imaging and typographic features that put it more in league with PostScript. Apple provides it as a system extension with System 7.5, and it can be used with any system version after 7.1. (We discuss the basics of QuickDraw GX in Chapter 3 and how it affects typography in Chapter 14.) As we've hinted earlier, it also has lots of repercussions for printing, introducing, among other things, a new Chooser, new drivers for Apple printers, and Desktop PrintMonitor, which replaces PrintMonitor. Here are some of the new features you'll see:

- A desktop icon appears for each printer you select using the new Desktop PrintMonitor. To change printers just select a desktop printer icon and choose Set Default Printer from the Printing menu that Desktop PrintMonitor adds to the Finder. You can print a file by simply dragging it onto a printer icon.

- With new GX drivers, the Print dialog box lets you select, at print time, any printer for which you've created a desktop icon, as above—no last-minute trips to the Chooser.

- You can share over a network any printer connected to your Mac, even via the serial port.

- The GX Print One command ($\boxed{\text{⌃}}\boxed{\text{⌘}}\boxed{\text{P}}$) prints a single copy of your document using your latest Print dialog box settings.

- Printing software extensions will add custom print tools, such as the ability to print the word *Copy* screened across each page. Third-party vendors can also develop printer extensions.

- Each desktop printer has its own print queue, which you can move to a different printer if you want. Double-clicking on a job name will let you see a print preview.

- The myriad of new graphics functions of QuickDraw GX will translate into greater graphical potential for QuickDraw printers, though, unfortunately few application vendors have jumped on the GX bandwagon so far.

Types of Printers

You need the right printer for the right job. Picking the wrong type of printer is a waste of money, no matter how good a deal you got. It's all a question of reconciling what you *think* you need with what certain types of printers can *really* do, and with what you can afford. That's where our "Price a Printer" table comes in handy (see page 650), once you grasp the basic printer technologies described in this section.

Black and White   (BW/RS)

Elegant, basic black: still the cheapest, most common form of printed matter. Even people who own a color printer use black-and-white printers to cheaply print copy for proofing and informal communications.

Inkjet printers (RS/BW). *Inkjet printers* form characters out of little dots—created by tiny jets of ink. Inkjet technology has largely taken over the market once occupied by dot-matrix impact printers: They're inexpensive, quieter, often faster, and produce better-looking text and graphics than dot-matrix impact printers. Apple's StyleWriters and Hewlett-Packard's DeskWriters are two well-known lines of ink-jet printers compatible with the Mac. (See "Price a Printer" for prices.)

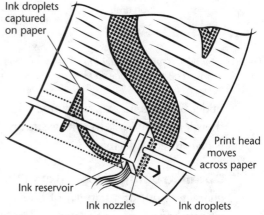

Inkjet printers squirt tiny drops of ink from an array of tiny nozzles that pass back and forth across the paper.

Laser printers (RS/BW). Printers such as Apple's LaserWriters print images by beaming flashes of laser light onto a photoelectric drum, though some "laser" printers use rows of tiny light-emitting diodes (LEDs). A dry ink powder called *toner* sticks electrostatically to the imaged portion of the drum, as in a photocopying machine. A hot fuser roller presses and bonds the toner to the paper after it's transferred from the drum. Laser printers are bigger, heavier, and more expensive than inkjet printers, but print quality is usually better. We cover this major market in greater detail later in this chapter.

Thermal fusion (RS). *Thermal fusion printers* employ tiny heated elements in the print head that push a ribbon against the page, bonding a waxy ink to the paper. Desktop and portable varieties of thermal fusion printers compete with black-and-white

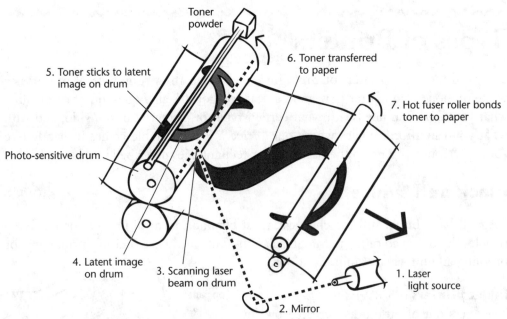

Toner
powder

5. Toner sticks to latent
image on drum

6. Toner transferred
to paper

7. Hot fuser roller bonds
toner to paper

Photo-sensitive drum

4. Latent image
on drum

3. Scanning laser
beam on drum

2. Mirror

1. Laser
light source

Laser printers print indirectly. They first create an image on a photo-sensitive cylinder (drum). Electrostatic toner powder sticks to the image on the drum and is then bonded to the paper.

inkjet printers. Cost per printed page is generally higher than for inkjet printing, but there's no liquid ink to run or smear. (See "Portability" for the Mac-compatible models worth considering.)

Dot-matrix impact printers (AN/JK/BW/RS). Dot-matrix impact printers form characters out of a pattern of dots created by a row of pins hammering on an inked ribbon lying against the paper. The number of pins can vary, with 9-pin and 24-pin being two common configurations; the more pins, the better the print quality. Speed is measured in cps (characters per second), instead of pages per minute or ppm.

HOT TIP

If you're printing multiple forms that use carbon or NCR paper, neither laser nor inkjet printers will do the job—you need impact! But get *this:* vendors, including Apple, no longer make or market Macintosh-compatible dot-matrix impact printers. You can check around for used ImageWriter IIs, which last sold new for around $450, or scout and scheme for one of the discontinued ImageWriter-compatible printers, such as Seikosha's 9-pin, 150-cps **SP-2400AP,** or wide-carriage **SP-2415AP,** which listed for $400 and $570, respectively. GCC's **WriteImpact** 9-pin, 192-cps dot-matrix, at $600, was pricier, though somewhat faster. Your best bet may be to snag a bargain dot-matrix designed for the PC, along with a Mac-to-PC compatibility kit, as described in the sidebar "Adapting PC Printers for the Mac."

Adapting PC printers for the Mac (RS)

You *can* use a PC printer with a Mac; you just need a Macintosh driver and a serial-to-parallel converter cable. The best kit is GDT Softworks' **PowerPrint** ($149 list, $100 mail order). It includes a serial-to-parallel converter, intended for printers that only have a PC standard Centronix parallel port. The converter draws power from both the printer and from your Mac ADP port, no wall plug needed. The PowerPrint software has print drivers for just about every dot-matrix, inkjet, and laser printer. The latest version of PowerPrint has a built-in spooler, grayscale capability, and color printer support, multiple feeder trays, text rotation, scaling, and multiple paper sizes.

Color Printers (BW/RS)

In the past you were lucky if an affordable color printer could handle up to a dozen colors. Fortunately, that's changed, thanks to improved technology and the economics of mass marketing.

Color inkjet (BW). It didn't take long for engineers to design inkjet printers sporting three or four separate print heads, each spraying a different color of ink. The four colors normally used in process color printing are cyan, magenta, yellow, and black. Even cheaper models print a large array of colors, good for simple charts, diagrams, and graphs. More expensive models print faster, and may include PostScript interpreters for printing elaborate color text, and graphics for presentations and design comps. To approximate different colors and shades, the printer driver must *dither* (that is, create patterns of dots, or halftones for each color). At 300 dpi resolution, these patterns can have a rather coarse appearance, like cheap comic books, but improvements in printer drivers over the last couple of years have smoothed things out considerably.

Thermal-wax transfer (RS). Using rolls of plastic film coated with four different colors of wax-based pigments, these printers lay down each of three or four primary colors when printing a page. Heating elements melt the wax and transfer it to the paper. Any wax that wasn't used in printing the page is left on the plastic film, which you'll later throw away. (There are also "phase-change" thermal-wax printers that melt sticks of wax pigment and apply it much as inkjets do.) Both types apply each color in a separate pass, which means that the page being printed must go through the printer several times. Like color inkjet printers, thermal-wax printers must also use halftone or dithering techniques to simulate a wide range of colors and shades.

Thermal-wax printers create attractive, glossy prints that are slightly raised from the page. As such, they're popular for printing hard-copy and overhead-transparency presentations and color design comps. The wax-transfer variety usually requires special paper, though some companies, such as Tektronix, have options that allow you to use plain paper, which the printer primes during printing. Choose the phase-change variety when you plan to print text as well as graphics: They print on a wider array of paper, and don't waste any wax.

Dye sublimation (RS/BW). *Dye-sublimation printers* work in much the same way as thermal-wax printers, but instead of melting wax-based pigments, dye-sublimation pigments become gaseous (sublime) when heated by the print head. The sublimed dye then penetrates the paper's special coating. Dye-sublimation printers don't have to use dithering or halftones to create different colors or shades of colors. They can blend the correct amount of each primary color (cyan, magenta, yellow, or black) to create just the right color at each printed dot. That's why they're called continuous-tone printers. A good dye-sublimation print looks like a color photograph. Not too long ago $40,000 was cheap for a dye-sublimation printer. Now, many cost less than $5,000, and some are below $1,000.

There are two classes of dye-sublimation printers on the market: those designed primarily for rendering retouched photos and computer-generated art, and those designed primarily for proofing pages containing continuous-tone images, type, and graphics. Shutterbugs and retouchers go for the former: The printers lack built-in PostScript interpreters and LocalTalk interfaces, using data-munching SCSI or GPIB connections instead. The accent is on high-quality media and color balance, so these printers typically are used to get a photo-quality proof of an edited color photo or computer-rendered scene, or a hard-copy version of a computer video presentation or multimedia display, rather than for proofing desktop published publications.

For the document-proofing market, several dye-sublimation printers sport built-in PostScript processing, 300-dpi resolution (or higher), and typical Mac interfaces such as LocalTalk, in addition to SCSI. The higher dpi rating makes for better text and possibly a crisper image in a few cases.

HOT TIP

PostScript is important if you're going with imagesetter color separations as your final production process. With type and graphics as well as scanned photos supported by PostScript, this type of printer is also very good for comping package design and color point-of-sale displays that employ all three elements.

Color laser (BW). The least expensive color laser printers, such as the QMS **Magicolor LX**, are now under $5,000, easily half the price they were two years ago. They're sold as "business" machines, having finally crossed the price threshold of general business users, with not much more than what they were willing to spend for black and white. You can still hook your Mac to a $40,000-plus Canon CLC copier, as some big-budget firms do, and with sufficient memory, the Canon CLC can print continuous-tone images, a benefit of the transparent toner the machines employ. Lower-priced color lasers, such as the QMS Magicolor LX, Hewlett-Packard Color DeskJet, and the Apple Color LaserWriter (see "Price a Printer" for prices), use opaque toner, so continuous-tone images and tints are printed as halftones. At 300 dpi, they look rather rough, anything but photographic.

What Type of Printer Do You Need?

There's what you want and there's what you need. Your printouts might look nice in color, but can you afford the expensive inks, and possibly slower printing? Can your software easily format the reports in color? If you need only four colors, then there's little point in paying for a printer that prints millions. This section should put your basic options in perspective.

Color or Black and White?   (BW)

This used to be a simple question to answer: "You wanna print color pictures, charts, graphs? Get a color printer." No one doubts that good color design makes information graphics easier to comprehend while putting a slick spin on your image.

But the interest in color is spilling over into a hybrid area now dominated by black-and-white desktop printing. In the glut of sales and promotional documents competing for attention these days, a document sporting colored headlines, callouts, illustrations, and charts is more likely to catch someone's attention. That requires a printer that's good at both black text *and* color, but that isn't too pricey.

Print Quality   (BW)

Subjective judgments aside, we usually rate print quality in terms of *resolution*. All the printers cited in this chapter use tightly packed arrays of dots to create the shapes we see on paper. The tighter the array of dots, that is, the more dots per inch (dpi), the higher the resolution, and the finer the images appear. Inkjet printers typically produce 300 to 720 dpi, a respectable resolution that rivals laser printing quality.

Only entry-level "home" laser printers kick out a mere 300 by 300 dots per inch. The new standard for "office" printing is 600 by 600 dots per inch, but there's also a growing market in affordable graphic arts laser printers that boast 1,200 by 600, and even

Price a Printer

Model	Street Price	List Price	Printing Method	Capabilities	B/W Speed (ppm)	Color Speed (ppm)	B/W Max. Resolution	Color Max. Resolution	Printing Language	Max. Page Size	Serial Port	LocalTalk Port	PC Parallel Port	Weight (lbs.)	Notes
Apple Computer															
StyleWriter 1200	$200	$219	Inkjet, 1-cartridge color	Monochrome text and halftone grayscale	3	n/a	720x360	n/a	QuickDraw	Legal	●	○	○	6.6	
Color StyleWriter 1500	$289	$289	Inkjet, 2-cartridge color	Good text, halftone	0.3	3	720x360	360x360	QuickDraw	8.5x14	●	○	○	7.5	
Color StyleWriter 2200	$395	$419	Inkjet, 2-cartridge color	Good text, halftone colors, almost photo quality	0.3	5	720x360	360x360	QuickDraw	8.5x14	●	○	○	3.1	4
Color StyleWriter 2500	$389	$389	Inkjet, 2-cartridge color	Good text, halftone colors, almost photo quality	0.3	5	720x600	360x360	QuickDraw	8.5x14	●	Opt.	○	7.9	
Personal LaserWriter 300	$629	$652	Laser, monochrome	Good text, newspaper quality grayscale halftones	4	n/a	300x300	n/a	QuickDraw	8.5x14	●	○	○	15.4	
LaserWriter PS 4/600	$895	$929	Laser, monochrome	Great text, adequate halftoned grayscale	4	n/a	600x600	n/a	Adobe PostScript-2	8.5x14	○	●	○	15.4	5
LaserWriter 16/600 PS	$2,298	$2,429	Laser, monochrome	Great text, adequate halftoned grayscale	16	n/a	600x600	n/a	Adobe PostScript-2	8.5x14	○	●	●	40	5
Color LaserWriter 12/600	$6,500	$6,989	Laser, color	Great text, adequate halftoned grayscale and color	12	3	600x600	600x600	Adobe PostScript-2	8.5x14	○	●	○	110	5
Brother Int.															
HL 660PS	$800	$1000	LED/toner, monochrome	Great text, adequate halftoned grayscale	6	n/a	600x600	n/a	BR-Script,[3] PCL	8.5x14	○	●	●	16.6	
HL 655M	$400	$700	LED/toner, monochrome	Good text, coarse-looking grayscale halftones	6	n/a	300x300	n/a	QuickDraw	8.5x14	●	○	●	16.6	
Epson America															
Stylus Color II	$350	$649	Inkjet, 2-cartridge color	Good text, halftone colors almost photo quality	1	4	720x720	720x720	QuickDraw,	8.5x14	●	○	○	11	
Stylus Color Pro	$600	$999	Inkjet, 2-cartridge color	Good text, halftone colors almost photo quality	1	4	720x720	720x720	QuickDraw,	8.5x14	●	Opt.	○	16.5	6
Stylus Color Pro XL	$1,800	$2,125	Inkjet, 2-cartridge color	Good text, halftone colors almost photo quality	1	3	720x720	720x720	QuickDraw,	13x19	●	Opt.	○	22	6

Fargo Electronics

Product			Technology	Quality					Language	Max size					
FotoFun	$400	$600	Dye sublimation, color	Photo-quality color	0.4	0.4	n/a	300x300	Fargo	4x6	●	○	○	7	7
Primera Pro	$1,495	$1,895	Dye sublimation and thermal wax transfer	Photo-quality, and presentation quality, not great for text	0.1[1]	0.6[2]	600x300	600x300	Adobe PostScript-2 optional	8.5x11	●	○	○	42	
Pictura 310	$3,800	$4,995	Dye sublimation and thermal wax transfer	Photo-quality, and presentation quality, not great for text	.08[1]	0.4[2]	300x300	300x300	Adobe PostScript-2	12x20	Opt.	○	○	42	8

GCC Technologies

Product			Technology	Quality					Language	Max size					
Elite 600	$1,375	$1,479	Laser, monochrome	Great text, adequate halftoned grayscale	10	n/a	600x600	n/a	Adobe PostScript-2	8.5x14	●	●	●	28.6	5
Elite XL 608	$2,400	$2,499	Laser, monochrome	Great text, adequate halftoned grayscale	8	n/a	600x600	n/a	Adobe PostScript-2	11x17	●	●	●	39.6	5
Elite XL 1208	$4,500	$4,999	Laser, monochrome	Typeset-quality text, almost-magazine-quality grayscale images	8	n/a	1200x1200	n/a	Adobe PostScript-2	11x17	○	●	●	39.6	5

Hewlett-Packard

Product			Technology	Quality					Language	Max size					
DeskWriter 600	$240	$365	Inkjet, 1-cartridge color	Good text; halftone color, good	1	4	600x300	300x300	QuickDraw	8.5x14	●	●	●	11.6	
DeskJet 340CM	$310	$390	Inkjet, 1-cartridge color	Good text; halftone color, good	0.5	3	600x300	300x300	QuickDraw	8.5x14	●	●	○	5.4	4
DeskWriter 660C	$350	$499	Inkjet, 2-cartridge color	Good text, halftone colors almost photo quality	1.5	4	600x300	300x300	QuickDraw	8.5x14	●	●	●	11.6	
DeskJet 855C for Mac	$460	$658	Inkjet, 2-cartridge color	Good text, halftone colors almost photo quality	2	6	600x600	300x300	QuickDraw	8.5x14	○	●	●	14.3	
LaserJet 5MP	$1,000	$1,299	Laser/toner, monochrome	Great text, halftone grayscale newspaper quality	6	n/a	600x600	n/a	Adobe PostScript-2, PCL	8.5x14	○	●	○	24.5	
DeskJet 1600CM	$1,965	$2,479	Inkjet, 4-cartridge color	Good text, halftone colors almost photo quality	4	9	600x600	300x300	Adobe PostScript-2, PCL	8.5x14	○	●	●	25	5
Color LaserJet 5M	$6,000	$7,395	Laser, color	Great text, halftone colors	2	10	300x300	300x300	Adobe PostScript-2	8.5x14	○	●	●	102.5	5

Lexmark Int.

Product			Technology	Quality					Language	Max size					
Color Jetprinter 4079+	$2,995	$3,199	Inkjet, 4-cartridge color	Good text, halftone colors almost photo quality	1.7	1	360x360	360x360	Lexmark PostScript-2	11x17	●	●	●	22	6

NEC Technologies

Product			Technology	Quality					Language	Max size					
Silentwriter 640	$399	$735	LED/toner, monochrome	Good text, newspaper-quality grayscale halftones	6	n/a	300x300	n/a	QuickDraw	11x14	○	●	○	18	

Price a Printer (continued)

Model	Street Price	List Price	Printing Method	Capabilities	B/W Speed (ppm)	Color Speed (ppm)	B/W Max. Resolution	Color Max. Resolution	Printing Language	Max. Page Size	Serial Port	LocalTalk Port	PC Parallel Port	Weight (lbs.)	Notes
QMS															
Magicolor CX/8	$4,900	$6,499	Laser, color	Great text, halftone colors	12	3	600x600	600x600	QMS Script	8.5x14	●	●	●	86	6
Tektronix															
Phaser 240	$3,200	$3,695	Thermal Wax Transfer	Okay text, halftone colors comic-book quality	1	1	300x300	300x300	Adobe PostScript-2, PCL5	8.5x11	○	●	●	40	6
Phaser 340	$4,700	$4,995	Solid ink (wax), color	Halftone color, comic-book quality	4	4	300x300	300x300	Adobe PostScript-2, PCL5	8.5x11	○	●	●	68	6
Phaser 440	$6,950	$7,995	Dye-sublimation, color	Photo-quality images, not great for text	0.9	0.5	300x300	300x300	Adobe PostScript-2	9.6x13.3	●	●	●	46	6
Phaser 480x	$13,500	$14,995	Dye-sublimation, color	Photo-quality images, not great for text	0.8	.43	300x300	300x300	Adobe PostScript-2	12.6x18.3	●	●	●	85	6
Texas Instruments															
microLaser 600	$680	$850	Laser, monochrome	Good text, adequate halftoned grayscale	5	n/a	600x600	n/a	Adobe PostScript-2, PCL5	8.5x14	●	●	●	34	
Xante															
Accel-a-Writer 812	$1,699	$2,995	Laser, monochrome	Typeset-quality text, almost-magazine-quality grayscale images	8	n/a	1200x1200	n/a	PostScript	11x17	●	●	●	37	10
LaserPress 1800	$6,999	$8,495	Laser, monochrome	Typeset-quality text, magazine-quality grayscale images	8	n/a	1800x1800	n/a	PostScript	11x17	●	●	●	51	10

Symbols:
● = Model has this port
○ = Model does not have this port

Notes:
1. Dye-sub speed
2. Wax transfer speed
3. PostScript-2 clone
4. Battery portable
5. Ethernet connection
6. Ethernet optional
7. PC model available
8. Uses bundled NuBus adapter printer interface
9. SCSI connection
10. Ethernet, SCSI connection

Subjective judgments aside, we usually rate print quality in terms of *resolution*.

300-dpi laser; GCC BLP II

Subjective judgments aside, we usually rate print quality in terms of *resolution*.

600-by-300-dpi inkjet; Hewlett-Packard DeskWriter 660C

Subjective judgments aside, we usually rate print quality in terms of *resolution*.

600-by-600-dpi laser; Apple LaserWriter Select 360

Subjective judgments aside, we usually rate print quality in terms of *resolution*.

1,800-dpi laser; Xante LaserPress 1800

Although actual printed samples look different, these do show the type quality you can expect from an offset printing press when using printer output as "camera-ready art." How do they compare to high-resolution imagesetter text on the rest of this page?

1,800 by 1,800 dots per inch. Many of these also offer various forms of enhanced resolution, which smoothes jagged edges and/or sharpens grayscales to give the appearance of higher-dpi output. Though these high-end printer resolutions rival those of high-resolution imagesetters, their print quality isn't as good.

Portability

The PowerBook has liberated Mac users from their desktops, and fortunately battery-powered portable printers are affordable companions. The best of these are inkjet printers, such as the **Color StyleWriter 2200** ($400, Apple) or **DeskWriter 340** ($380, Hewlett-Packard), and their print quality is practically indistinguishable from that of laser printers. But road warriors pay a penalty for portability because these printers tend to be quite a bit slower than equivalent desktop options.

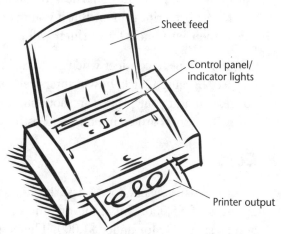

(BW/RS)

Sheet feed

Control panel/
indicator lights

Printer output

Portable printers generally lack paper cassettes and output trays, though a simple sheet feed typically holds 10 to 30 sheets of paper.

If you need *tiny*, the $400, thermal-fusion **Citizen Notebook Printer II** fits easily into a coat pocket. The waxy ink doesn't spread on the page like that of inkjets, giving its 360 dpi an impressive laser-like crispness (if you use the higher-quality ribbon). Another thermal-fusion pup, the **MobileWriterPS** ($1,000, Mannesmann Tally) is decidedly more expensive and less portable than the rest, but it provides Adobe PostScript, six-page-per-minute printing, and print quality indistinguishable from a desktop laser printer. *[As inkjet inks evolve greater smear-resistance, these thermals lose some advantage, though the Notebook Printer II is the smallest printer I've ever seen, and built-in PostScript, if you need it, gives the MobileWriterPS an edge.—BW]*

PostScript   (RS/AN/JK/BW)

As previously mentioned, there are two basic kinds of printers—those with PostScript (Adobe's page description language) built into their processors, and those without. PostScript used to be a very pricey luxury, but now the difference between the PostScript and non-PostScript versions of a printer can be as little as $500. You'll find many color inkjet, thermal-wax, dye-sublimation, and laser printers that use PostScript.

If you're creating pages ultimately destined for a high-resolution imagesetter, you'll need a PostScript printer for proofing your pages. The same holds true if you intend to use EPS (Encapsulated PostScript) format clip art or other PostScript-based graphics.

HOT TIP

You can also print PostScript graphics on a non-PostScript printer by using an interpreter program such as GDT Softworks' $149 **StyleScript** (for Apple StyleWriter models only), or **T-Script** ($145, TeleTypesetting), though this approach tends to really slow printing. For professional desktop publishing and graphics work, there's no substitute for a PostScript printer. But if you mainly print text and non-PostScript graphics, a less expensive QuickDraw printer will probably give you everything you need.

One more issue to consider when deciding between PostScript and QuickDraw printers is speed. Because QuickDraw printers rely on the Mac's own processor to rasterize the image, you and your printer are both sharing the Mac's processor, slowing each other down. The on-board computer of a PostScript printer relieves the Mac of that task.

Cost   (BW)

You get what you pay for: A fast, high-resolution, PostScript color printer can cost upwards of $5,000. But trade off one or more of those qualities, and you can do quite respectably for under $1,000. The best buys are inkjets, with 300-dpi resolution for under $300. The trade-off there is speed. The "Price a Printer" table shows this clearly.

Speed (BW)

Most printers have some sort of rated speed, but those textbook figures rarely factor in the time the printer spends processing the print data prior to actually spitting out paper. This is especially true for PostScript printers, which bear the awesome task of crunching complex PostScript programs. A four-page-per-minute laser print engine, for example, with a high-speed PostScript processor, may well outpace an eight-page-per-minute model with a slow processor.

Inkjet Printers

Inkjet printers have become the home and personal business printer of choice, given their low price, small size, crisp print quality, and the other traits we discussed in "Types of Printers" earlier in this chapter. Inkjet speeds were once typically rated in characters per second, such as dot-matrix printers, but Hewlett-Packard and most other vendors now rate speeds in pages per minute. For the Mac, dot-matrix printers are a specialty item, mainly for printing multipart forms. Some people prefer the inkjets' output to that of laser printers because the blacks are blacker—although the output is also less crisp since the ink tends to bleed into the paper.

Keep in mind that no printout from an inkjet printer is as smear-proof as prints from a laser printer, but inkjet ink's gotten more waterproof. I've soaked pages printed in Hewlett-Packard's pigment-based inkjet ink in a bucket of warm water without substantial smearing. And many new models, such as the Apple Color StyleWriter 2500 now also boast smear-resistant ink. (If your inkjet print absolutely must be smear resistant, you can spray it with artists' fixative, available from art supply stores, but this is not an economical practice and overspraying will also cause it to smear.) *[If you use a fixative, make sure you use it in a well-ventilated area. Last time I tried one, the room smelled like overripe bananas for a couple of weeks. It probably causes cancer, too.—DD]*

HOT TIP

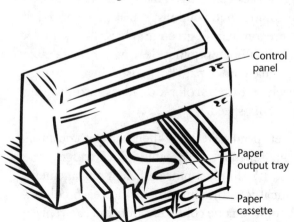

Control panel

Paper output tray

Paper cassette

The HP DeskJet 660C offers great text and color graphics for its $430 price tag, and is easily shared via its built-in LocalTalk port.

The Cartridge Count   (BW)

PostScript options aside, there are really three types of color inkjet printers: single-cartridge color, dual-cartridge, and four-cartridge. The least expensive color inkjets listed in our product table, in the $200 to $350 range, let you print with either an all-black ink cartridge or a single, three-color cartridge that has separate chambers for cyan, magenta, and yellow ink for color printing. You pop in the black cartridge when printing black-and-white documents. To print color graphics, you pop out the black cartridge, store it in an air-tight container provided with the printer, and then pop in the three-color cartridge. We call it a single-cartridge system, because there's always only one cartridge in the printer, black or color.

This is all fine until you're printing a color budget chart, for example, which contains black text and color graphics. In this situation, a single-cartridge printer has to mix cyan, magenta, and yellow inks to create the black color for the text. This "composite black" usually isn't as black as a true black ink, and generally doesn't look as crisp. Neither does it give the best results on certain graphics, especially scanned images, where many different color shades include some level of black.

Color inkjets in the $350 to $1,500 range use a dual-cartridge system: They keep both a black and a three-color cartridge mounted in the printer so you don't have to manually swap one for the other. Conveniently, the printer automatically switches to the black cartridge when text or even color graphics need a shot of true black ink; and both text and graphics look better for it.

Nevertheless, there are two drawbacks to the dual-cartridge system. First off, and this applies to single-cartridge color as well, it wastes color ink. That's because when one ink chamber in the three-color cartridge empties out, you must replace the entire ink cartridge. If you've been printing some predominantly green graphics, for example, it's likely that the cyan and yellow chambers will empty first, leaving a considerable amount of magenta ink to throw away—ink you've paid for! Also, dual-cartridge inkjets spend extra time juggling the black and three-color cartridges into printing position, so this setup isn't optimal for printing speed.

In fact, one reason the $1,500 and up inkjets print faster than their cheaper cousins is that they use a four-cartridge system: four separate, replaceable ink cartridges, one each for cyan, magenta, yellow, and black. It's simply a more efficient arrangement, with room for a larger number of individual jets (tiny ink nozzles) for each color—more ink hitting the page each second. Also, when one color runs out, you can replace just that cartridge, and avoid throwing out any unused ink. If you're going to spend most of your time printing color graphics then you should save up your money for one

HOT TIP of these. (See the table "Price a Printer" earlier in this chapter.)

Inkjet Printer Ink Supplies   (BW/RS)

Printing with inkjet ink costs more per page than with laser printer toner. An ink cartridge for Apple's StyleWriter 1200, for example, costs around $25 and prints about 466 pages of text. That's more than five cents a page, compared to about two cents a page for a $90 LaserWriter printer cartridge. Printing high volume or lots of high-ink-coverage graphics could empty a cartridge every two or three days. Vendors all quote monochrome and color "page yields" for their printers' inkjet cartridges (i.e., the number of pages you can expect to print per cartridge). Note however, that they may presume different levels of ink coverage for the typical "page," anywhere from five percent to 25 percent ink coverage, so comparing products is tough. Figure that a $27 DeskJet 660C color cartridge prints 313 color pages at 15 percent ink coverage, which means a nice, juicy full-color page at 90 percent could cost you at least 50 cents in ink.

Inkjet cartridges (RS). Mail-order ink-cartridge pricing is typically about 20 percent less than list, not nearly as dramatic as discounts on many toner cartridges. There are ways to cut ink costs further, though, as we explain below.

You can save a lot of money by refilling your printer's ink cartridges instead of buying new ones. Most cartridges are good for ten or more refills. JetFill and American Ink Jet sell syringe-like devices (the eponymic **JetFill** and the **CompuJet**, respectively) that come with smear-resistant black ink ($10) or colored ink ($11), about $10 less than buying a new DeskWriter or StyleWriter cartridge. *[Uh, Randy? This "refill" business is just a little too tricky for most people and voids most printer warranties, which is why it amounts to a very small portion of the inkjet cartridge trade, and mainly for black ink. So, let me also recommend "remanufactured" inkjet cartridges, which are professionally refilled and sold, with a guarantee, for less than half the price of a new cartridge. Mobile Toner is a typical vendor: Just send in your used cartridges with your order.—BW]*

HOT TIP

Monochrome proofs (BW). This may sound obvious, but use a monochrome printer to proof the basic text and graphic layout of your color documents. The cost per page is invariably cheaper than that of a color printout, and you'll spot a lot of errors that don't relate to color.

Inkjet paper (BW). With their improved ink formulations, the current crop of color inkjets look better than ever when printing on cheap ol' plain paper. That said, they look even better printing on special coated papers that keep the ink on the paper surface. Uncoated papers let the color ink sink in, leaving the surface slightly uncovered, producing a slightly washed out look. You can buy generic or printer-vendor-branded coated papers for five to 20 cents a sheet. If you're willing to spill a buck a sheet for special glossy stock, such as HP's **LX JetSeries Glossy** (which is more a plastic than a paper), you can print scanned photos that look truly photographic, just to give you an idea how much better color inks look on this deluxe media.

Inkjet Printer Troubleshooting (ND)

I printed just a few pages on a new inkjet cartridge and later found it was "out of ink!" What happened? Try to avoid opening a new ink cartridge if you know you're not going to be using your printer for awhile—the ink may dry up before you get a chance to use it. Standard DeskWriter cartridges normally print about 300 pages, but a friend of mine let a newly opened cartridge languish for six months, and he then ran out of ink after only 50 pages. Take his advice and change the cartridge *after* your vacation!

Why am I getting unwanted stripes in my inkjet printouts? Sometimes ink clogs some of the fine holes in inkjet print heads, so you see blank stripes in whatever you're printing. To clear the holes, you can try using the Prime feature on the DeskWriter or StyleWriter, but that doesn't always work—and it shortens the life of the cartridge.

Instead, try printing a heavily inked page one or more times. You can make a suitable page to print by going into a graphics program, drawing a box that fills a whole page, and filling it with black (or a dark pattern). If this fails, you can try soaking just the print head (not the whole cartridge) in some alcohol.

Laser Printers

Apple Computer cofounder Steve Jobs decided that Apple's first laser printer should also launch Adobe Systems' PostScript page description language into the consumer sphere. The first LaserWriter listed for over $6,000 in 1985, but people paid it. For graphic artists and publishers, PostScript was probably *the* best reason for buying a Mac (and, of course, PageMaker).

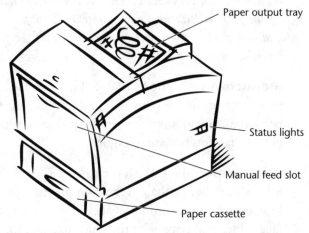
Paper output tray

Status lights

Manual feed slot

Paper cassette

Today's popular laser printers are capable of 600-dpi output and cost a fraction of what they did just two years ago.

Choosing a Laser Printer (BW/RS)

The Macintosh laser printer market has exploded, with more models on the market than we could possibly describe in detail here. Check the "Price a Printer" table for some specific models. Prices continue to free-fall, while printing speed, resolution, and convenience have soared. Here's an overview of laser printer features and the issues surrounding today's laser printer market.

PostScript clones (BW). Some printer manufacturers felt shut out of the PostScript printer market because of Adobe's initially stringent licensing policies. That, or they wished to add features (such as resolution enhancement) that Adobe's PostScript hardware/software designs had failed to address. As a result they developed or licensed PostScript-compatible interpreters that performed like Adobe's patented PostScript. Over the years they've gotten pretty reliable. Adobe's lightened up its licensing policies in the last couple of years, so fewer vendors than before feel compelled to employ clone PostScript. When a printer has the price and features you want, and it's a clone, don't hesitate to buy it unless there's a genuine Adobe-licensed equivalent. Most companies make it easy to upgrade the PostScript-compatible interpreter via software, and they generally stay on top of compatibility problems. Adobe-licensed PostScript printers have had bugs, too!

HOT TIP

Resolution and resolution enhancement (RS/BW). The new standard in quality is the 600-dpi resolution provided by relatively inexpensive laser engines such as the Canon EX found in printers such as the Apple LaserWriter Pro 630 and the Hewlett-Packard LaserJet 4M. Once costing over $10,000, some 600-dpi printers are now breaking $700, not much more than last year's 300-dpi printers. You'll definitely notice the difference between 300-dpi and 600-dpi printing. The jaggies almost disappear from text, and it's even more dramatic when printing graphics and scanned-in photos.

Vendors such as Apple, LaserMaster, NewGen, Xante, and others sell printers with controller circuitry that manipulates the laser beam to create a higher apparent resolution, beyond the 600 dpi of a standard laser engine. For comparative purposes, enhanced resolutions are hard to quantify because different vendors use different electronic techniques. One vendor's "800 by 800" enhanced resolution may look as good as another's "1,000 by 1,000." If you're looking for better text quality, start looking at HP's LaserJet 4 and LaserJet 5 printers, which combine true 600-by-600-dpi resolution with HP's resolution enhancement technology, and compare it with higher-resolution models from Xante, LaserMaster, NewGen, and so on.

HOT TIP

Resolution enhancement that improves text and graphics doesn't always improve grayscale images, so vendors now provide additional grayscale enhancement. Apple's

PhotoGrade grayscale enhancement, introduced with LaserWriter IIg, and now in the Personal LaserWriter 300, is quite good; in fact, the IIg did better grayscale at 300 dpi than most grayscale printing at 600 by 600. Other vendors have been upgrading their grayscale enhancements quicker than we can test them, so if grayscale's your game, check out the current models.

HOT TIP

Just remember that 1,200 dpi on a toner-based printer doesn't compare with the sharpness of a 1,200-dpi photoimagesetter. The laser-drum-toner process produces a rather sloppy, nonuniform dot in comparison to the photo-chemical process of imagesetters. Also, it's very important to test different toner density settings on "enhanced-resolution" printers, since density, which tends to wander, can make a huge difference in print quality.

Speed (RS/BW). Laser printers' rated speeds range from about four pages per minute to 40 and beyond. That speed indicates how fast the printer can push through blank pages. But it doesn't account for the time it takes to process the page prior to printing—and for PostScript printers, that can be considerable. Vendors are now incorporating fast *RISC* (Reduced Instruction Set Computer) processing chips, which are optimized to execute one or more instructions per computer clock cycle. Compare that to general-purpose processors such as the 68000 series, which use several cycles to execute more complex instructions that aren't easily optimized for printing. The faster RISC chips help printers process pages for printing at a rate closer to the actual page-per-minute speed of the printer engine—especially important for complex graphics and large scanned images.

RAM (JF/BW). Even monochrome PostScript printers need a lot of memory. They use almost a megabyte to hold the image of a page before it's printed and nearly another half-megabyte to do the calculations which create those page images. Any leftover memory is used for storing fonts and for caching images of letters it has already drawn, so it doesn't have to draw them from scratch again next time they're needed. In a PostScript printer with 2MB of memory, less than 400K is available for font storage—enough for perhaps ten typical PostScript fonts (less for the porkier TrueType variety). If you use many fonts, your best bet is a printer that has more than 2MB of RAM (for a letter-size printer). Adding a hard disk to your printer is an expensive option, but it's popular mainly among graphic arts and publishing pros. Note that some newer printers include some form of RAM compression or "doubling" in their processors, and can get away with less actual RAM. A case in point is the Hewlett-Packard LaserJet 5MP, which uses Adobe's Memory Booster to make its seemingly meager 3MB of RAM as useful as 6MB would be on a LaserJet 4MV Plus, for example.

With enough RAM to hold all the fonts and forms for a print job, your printer won't waste time automatically downloading them during printing (see "Font Downloading" in Chapter 14). Some printers will also use additional RAM for *double-buffering*, wherein one page gets ready while a previously processed page is fed to the print engine.

You can now add RAM to most printers, usually by installing RAM SIMMs (Single In-line Memory Modules). There are several types of SIMMs on the market, so check out which one your printer accepts before buying any.

Resident fonts (BW). Most PostScript laser printers come with at least 13 built-in fonts, typically Times, Helvetica, and Courier (each in regular, bold, italic, and bold italic weights), plus Symbol. Many come with 35 fonts, adding Bookman, Avant Garde, Palatino, New Century Schoolbook, and Zapf Dingbats to the basic 13. A few come with more. These fonts are coded into ROM (Read-Only Memory) chips inside the printer.

Some printers, such as the LaserMaster Unity models, may include more than 100 fonts stored on a hard drive mounted inside the printer, to which you can add or delete fonts. Most Accel-a-Writer printers from Xante have 512K of *flashROM* (expandable to 1MB) to which you can download your own set of fonts that are then stored as though they were built-in.

Paper handling (BW). A heavily used shared printer should have at least one paper tray holding at least 240 sheets. Most of the faster (12- to 20-page-per-minute) printers on the market have ample paper-handling options.

And consider paper size. Laser printers capable of printing tabloid-size (B-size) pages were once *beaucoup* pricey: $15,000 and up. Now they start at around $5,000, thanks to Canon's 600-dpi BX laser engine. Even if your final production is letter-size, you'll want a B-size printer if you need to show crop marks and bleeds that extend off the page.

Toner Tips

If you've been paying close to list price for brand-new toner cartridges down at the corner store, you can probably guess why we're offering a few smart buying and conservation techniques. Use 'em and cut your toner costs in half.

Adjusting toner density (JF/RS/BW). If you print mainly text, you can crank the print density way down on your laser printer. Only at the very lowest setting does type start to look pale, although large, solid areas of black will begin to suffer below a midrange setting. This can extend the life of your toner cartridges considerably.

Working Software makes a neat product called **Toner Tuner** ($25 list) that lets you adjust the darkness of a print from the Print dialog box prior to printing. It's not only more convenient than most utilities, but it's also a good option for printers lacking toner-density adjustment. Toner Tuner works with any type of printer, even inkjets.

If you're shopping for new printers, be aware that special hardware in Hewlett-Packard's LaserJet 4ML and 4MP lets you select an "EconoMode" that saves toner by printing 50 percent fewer printer dots. Somewhat more refined than Toner Tuner, EconoMode prints solidly along the leading edge of text and graphics, more lightly for the remainder. *[I tried this but found it unacceptably light, even for drafts. However, the HP LaserJet Utility offers a Print Density setting that lets you choose between five density levels, and I've found the lightest one to be just right.—DD]*

Getting the last drop (JF). As your toner cartridge approaches the end of its useful days, there are a couple of ways to extend its life.

- When the "low toner" light comes on, remove the cartridge and give it a few brisk shakes from end to end to jog the remaining toner around. Don't turn the cartridge upside down; just make motions like you're sifting flour. You should be able to do this a dozen times or more before the "low toner" light refuses to turn itself off and the cartridge is really getting empty.

- If you're running out of toner when stores are closed, you can use a can of aerosol acrylic fixative from an art supply store (it's used for fixing pastel and charcoal drawings) and spray any pages on which the image is becoming faint. The spray dissolves and darkens the toner, resulting in richer blacks. It'll do until you can buy more toner.

Discount toner cartridges (BW). The Canon SX toner cartridge in your old LaserWriter IINT prints about 4,000 text-based pages and lists for $130. At 100 pages per business day, that amounts to around $750 a year in toner. Fortunately, without much effort you can get that figure down to around $300.

First off, don't end up buying cartridges one at a time from corner retailers; buy at discount stores such as OfficeMax or Office Depot, if you insist on new cartridges. My local Connecting Point computer store, for example, charges $100 for a brand-new SX cartridge, whereas OfficeMax office supply superstores sell it for $74. Mail-order SX cartridges cost around $85 each, down to about $80 if you buy a dozen, including shipping.

Recycled toner cartridges (BW). If you really want to save on toner, you should consider remanufactured cartridges. These have been disassembled, cleaned, and inspected. Worn parts, including the imaging drum, are replaced as necessary, and often given an extra-large dose of toner. As a result, remanufactured engines commonly come with guarantees. Avoid cartridges that have simply been "recharged," that is, refilled without inspection. Recycled SX cartridges, for example, price out at $40 to $70, instead of from $70 to $100—way less than new, and better for the environment. Quality varies on remanufactured cartridges, so test a brand out before ordering it in bulk.

Disposing of toner cartridges (RS/BW). Our best advice: Don't throw out toner cartridges, even if you buy only new cartridges. Many cartridge recyclers will buy CX, SX, LX, NX, EX, and other cartridges. Apple not only has a cartridge recycling program, it'll donate one dollar to a conservation charity for each empty cartridge you return. *[HP has my loyalty. New HP cartridges come with a prepaid UPS shipment label in the box. You just pack your old cartridge in the new wrapper and box, slap on the sticker, and hand it to a UPS driver.—DD]*

Because not all used cartridges are in demand, you may have to throw one away. Place the cartridge back in its shipping bag or another plastic bag (ZipLocs are handy) and tie or tape it completely shut to prevent residual toner from escaping. Some cartridges may be hot when they come out of the machine, so let them cool down in the printer before removing.

Laser Printer Troubleshooting

How do I stop the printer test page from printing every time I turn on the printer? (BW). Most PostScript printers churn out a time- and paper-wasting startup test page when you turn them on, but there are several ways to stop that from happening. First, check your printer manual to see if there's a "no startup page" option you can set using the printer's front-panel controls. If that's not an option, you can suppress the startup page on many printers by pulling the paper tray part way out when you power up. Then slide the tray back in after the printer has finished its internal self-test and other warm-up routines.

A more elegant solution is to use software commands to change the printer's internal configuration so that the startup page won't print. The LaserWriter font utility and most other font-downloading utilities for the Mac include an option to turn off the startup page. You can also prepare and download a short PostScript-language program that instructs the printer to stop printing the startup page. It's not as hard as it sounds. Here's how to do it:

1. Using any word processor type the following four lines of code and save them as an ASCII or text-only file:

```
serverdict begin 0 exitserver
statusdict begin
false setdostartpage
end
```

   Give the file a descriptive name, such as STOPTEST.PS.

2. Download the file to the printer, using the Download PostScript File command in the File menu of Adobe's Font Downloader (included with every font package from Adobe), Apple's LaserWriter Utility which comes with LaserWriters and the Mac system software, or other PostScript utility. Note that during the download you'll get a message "exitserver: permanent state may be changed." That's just what you want to see, since the start page won't print when you turn on the printer until you send another message to turn it on again.

The test page does tell you some important things such as the printer lifetime page count, installed memory, and the version number of the PostScript interpreter. You need to print a test page again in order to see this. To print it again, just change the word "false" to the word "true" in the above PostScript code, and download the file again. Or fire up the same PostScript utility used for disabling the test page, and elect the option to enable the startup page.

Why do some PostScript print jobs print quickly while others take forever, even without graphics? Chances are your document uses several fonts, which are automatically downloading, sometimes repeatedly, as the document prints. Manual downloading copies fonts into the printer's memory so they stay there until the printer is turned off. If you're going to print several times using the same fonts, you'll save time by manually downloading them, even if you'll be using other fonts later in the day. When you've finished using one set of fonts, restart your printer to clear its memory; then download the next batch. The time it takes to manually download the fonts is paid back each time you print using those fonts by saving about 15 seconds per font used in each document.

You manually download fonts with a special program, such as Apple's LaserWriter Font Utility (included with the Mac system software) or Adobe's Downloader (free with Adobe fonts). If your printer has a hard disk, these programs can copy your fonts permanently onto it, where they'll stay until you erase them.

If you're stuck with a 2MB-or-less printer, your best strategy is to manually download each day the handful of fonts you most commonly use (four to six fonts for a 2MB printer, one to two for a 1.5MB model). This will leave enough memory for printing most typical jobs (using three fonts or fewer) using automatic downloading. If you're starved for printer memory, avoid TrueType fonts, which munch more RAM than PostScript fonts do.

Only in the most desperate circumstances should you select "Unlimited Downloadable Fonts in a Document" in the Page Setup dialog box. This causes the Mac to download only a single font to the printer, deleting it when another font is called for. This means a 30-second delay for every typeface change, even if it's only for italicizing a single word.

How can I avoid getting "ghost images" on portions of my laser-printed pages? (JF). If you're using your laser printer to make many copies of a page, you may notice that you get a ghost image of one part of the page invading another part of the page, especially in large areas of solid black. To avoid this, crank up the print density setting to near its maximum.

My laser printer is supposed to print envelopes, but they get all wrinkled when printed, and occasionally jam. Is this normal? (JF/AN/SZA/DD). It can happen with many envelopes, since they have to squeeze through some tight places in the printer. To minimize wrinkling and paper jams when printing envelopes, use your fingernail as a brayer to flatten out all the seams of the envelope before printing, particularly the edge of the envelope that first meets the rollers.

Note that unless it's made especially for laser printers or copiers, don't print on any material that contains glue. The heat in the printer can cause labels to peel off inside the printer and can seal envelopes. If your laser printer lets you switch to a straight-through paper feed—the printed sheet goes straight out the back of the printer instead of curving out toward the top—your labels are less likely to peel. If you've *got* to print envelopes in your printer (of course you do), just make sure to be waiting at the output end, to peel them open before they seal permanently.

Avery makes labels specifically designed for laser printers. Because a special adhesive is used, the labels don't peel off when subjected to the high heat inside the printer. We've used them at the office and haven't had any problems with jamming. They come in three sizes: 1-inch by 2-inch (product codes 5160 and 5260), 1-inch by 4-inch (product codes 5161 and 5261), and 1.25-inch by 4-inch (product codes 5162 and 5262), and are available at most office supply stores.

My brand-new laser printer toner cartridge started printing with gray bands across the page. What happened? (BW). Even though toner cartridges look light-tight, they're not. Stuffing them back into their light-proof shipping bags when you take them temporarily out of the printer will prevent damage to the photo-electric drum inside. Once overexposed to light, the cartridge may start showing one or more bands of overly light printing across the page, caused by exposure lines on the drum. All you can do then is buy a replacement.

Why does my PostScript laser printer sometimes refuse to print? (AN/RS). Laser printers sometimes get confused and hung up (just like the rest of us). When this happens, restart the printer with the LaserWriter Utility (or some similar program). If that doesn't help, restart your Mac (with the Restart command on the Special menu).

If there's still a problem, turn both the Mac and the printer off and wait five minutes before turning them back on (check all the cable connections while they're both off). If *that* doesn't help, replace your printer drivers. If *that* doesn't help, reinstall your system software as described in Chapter 3. If it's still no-go, you may actually have a hardware problem. See if a blank page will print. If so, try simplifying the document you're trying to print. (See "Using Service Bureaus" for troubleshooting PostScript printing problems.)

Color Printing Troubleshooting

Solid blacks printed on my thermal-wax transfer printer aren't quite solid. What can I do? (BW). Sometimes the straight black from a thermal-wax transfer printer may have a matte texture or tiny gaps in coverage. You can get a glossier, more solid-looking black by specifying 100 percent of cyan, magenta, and yellow, in addition to black (provided your software lets you specify colors that way).

Why does color text on my printer look rougher than black text, and how can I improve it? (BW). When you're printing color text in small point sizes, you're better off using a single color ink: cyan, magenta, or yellow. Most other colors use a halftone or dither pattern made of different-color ink dots, which makes small type look unacceptably coarse.

Why can't I get consistently good color when designing poster ads on my inkjet printer? (BW). Because of peculiarities in ink formulations or color dithering and halftone techniques; some colors and shades simply look better than others on a given printer. If a specified color just doesn't print well, experiment with slightly different values. When you find one that works, record its color specs so that you can re-create it, or save a sample of the color in a document to retrieve later.

Special Purpose Printers

Beyond the mainstream you'll find some interesting breeds of printer, designed for special tasks and circumstances. Check 'em out.

Label and Address Printing   (Karen Faria/JK/BW)

CoStar's **LabelWriter XL** and **XL Plus** print quietly on thermal paper printers. You'll find them mail order for around $160 and $250, respectively. The XL prints standard 1¼-inch-wide shipping labels, and the XL Plus prints wider, 2¼-inch labels for shipping, floppy disks, video cassettes, and so on. A roll of 700 address labels costs $17, available from CoStar, or through MacWarehouse and other mail-order firms. Its bundled software stores up to 1,600 addresses, and the addresses can even include PICT graphics. It also generates and prints a postal bar code for each address. The bar code not only speeds up delivery of your mail, but it can also save you up to 20 percent on bulk mailings. On the budget side, Seiko's **Smart Label Printer EZ30** goes for around $130, and prints 1 by 3.5-inch labels, also on thermal paper.

[Why buy a label printer? Word and WordPerfect have good templates for standard labels. Plus there are great utilities such as DynoPage and DynoDex for easy label printing on any printer. TouchBase also includes excellent templates for labels. I personally recommend the shareware package Easy Envelopes by Andrew Welch for doing envelopes with bar codes. It's dead easy to use, and cheap.—RS]

[Anyone who does a variety of correspondence or fulfillment during the day wants push-button labeling. I use templates and addressing utilities myself, and guess what? They're meant for printing sheets of labels, not one or two at a time! And I still end up fiddling with the darn things instead of getting work done. I only send two or three letters a day, otherwise I'd blow my next royalty check on an AddressWriter.—BW]

Using Service Bureaus

When you need better-quality printing than you're equipped to handle, you can often get the job done at a service bureau. Most service bureaus offer laser printing, dye-sub, and large-format color printing as well as high-resolution (1,200 to 3,600 dpi) image-setter output to film or paper. Some offer do-it-yourself access to their equipment, while others ask you to drop off your files for processing.

Before You Deliver Your Files (BW)

Getting files printed at a service bureau isn't quite as casual as dropping off your laundry. You've got to make sure that the service bureau has the files it needs, that it has the fonts and software you need, and that everyone is clear on what to expect. Here are some guidelines and tips.

Setting up your files. When you deliver your files to a service bureau, make sure to include not only the document files, but also any graphics files included in the documents.

The Service Bureau Form

A standard service bureau work-order form. At $7 or more a page, don't spare the details when ordering high-resolution imagesetting of your files. One missing font, for example, can mean a useless job and money down the drain.

The Service Bureau
Imagesetting Services
100 Pi Alley • Boston, MA 02100
(617) 555-1234 • Pager: 555-2345 • Fax/Modem 555-3456

WORK ORDER

Project #:

Date:
Name:
Address:

Attention: Fax:
Phone: RUSH!
Need by: ☐IBM ☐Macintosh
Computer System:
Client Project# / Job # / PO #:
File Name(s):

Pages to Process:
Page Size(s):
Print Percentage: 100%☐   Other %
Software Used:

Fonts Used: (includ. mfg.)

NOTE: THERE WILL BE A $10.00 CHARGE FOR FONTS NOT LISTED
DUE TO THE TIME IT TAKES TO OPEN A FILE, READ THE FONT INFO,
AND THEN LOAD THE FONTS FOR DOWNLOADING TO THE RIP!

Colors used in document:

Overprint Black? ☐ YES ☐ NO
Placed Graphics: Linked?
Comments:

Crop/Reg. Marks? ☐ YES ☐ NO
Bleeds?   ☐ YES ☐ NO
Screening: ☐ Balanced ☐ Accurate ☐ Postscript

Agfa 9800:
RC Positive ☐   RC Negative ☐   Up ☐   Down☐
Resolution: ☐1200   ☐2400
LPI: ☐1200   ☐2400
AccuSet 1000: Film Only
LPI:____ Resolution: ☐1200 ☐800 ☐2400 ☐3000
Negative☐   Emulsion Up☐ Down☐
Positive☐   Emulsion Up☐ Down☐

Color Prints: Tektronix 480 Dye Sub Prints ☐
3M Matchpints☐   Tektronix 300i Color Prints ☐
Deskjet 1200C ☐

Scanning:
Color: ☐   Black/White: ☐   Line Art:☐
Flatbed ☐   Transparencies ☐
Slides ☐   Drum Scanning ☐
Scan for Separations:
        Size:____ DPI____ LPI____
Scan to: ☐CD ☐Disk ☐Zip Disk ☐Syquest

CD Archiving or Photos:
Instructions:

ALL FILES ARE IMAGED "AS IS" AND IT IS THE CLIENT'S
RESPONSIBILITY TO MAKE SURE THAT FILES ARE CORRECT FOR
IMAGING, AND THAT ALL GRAPHICS, FONTS, ETC. ARE INCLUDED.
Note: Fonts contained in EPS files will not download if not
on the system to rip to the imaging equipment.

FOR OFFICE USE ONLY
1 2 3 4   File Name   Cost

TOTAL

1. Make sure you include your name and address as well as a phone number at which you can be reached for any emergency questions while the bureau handles your job.

2. Let them know you're using a Macintosh. The specific model and configuration isn't necessary.

3. Be very precise about the names of the files you want processed. It's best not to send extraneous files.

4. Include the name and version number of the software you used to create your documents. "Quark", for example, isn't specific enough; "QuarkXPress 3.31" is. Different versions may handle text and graphics differently, and the bureau must know what to expect.

5. Specify the font vendor, such as Bitstream or Adobe, along with the actual font name listed in your Mac's font menus, also stating whether it's TrueType or Type 1 PostScript. Don't forget fonts included in EPS graphics.

6. For color documents, a separate imagesetter page is printed for each color, known as a "separation" (one for each printing press ink). Specify the color on any special inks, such as those of Pantone, or other "spot-color" systems. If you've never sent in color documents for imagesetter printing, talk to the bureau *before* you prepare your files.

7. Let them know whether you've placed graphics in the document. Large graphics files are often only "linked" to a DTP document file, not embedded within it. The bureau must know this in order to insure that the graphics files are properly linked to print.

8. Many bureaus have imagesetters for different purposes, some calibrated expressly for magazine-quality color separations. Specify which type of imagesetting you need and whether you want it on film or resin-coated paper. When in doubt, ask.

9. Most service bureaus provide additional services such as 35mm slide printing, dye-sublimation printer proofs, scanning, and even CD-ROM creation. Make sure to specify what you want.

Fonts and software. Service bureaus usually have the major applications installed—PageMaker, QuarkXPress, Photoshop, and so on—with which to load and print your documents. The service bureau also needs to have the fonts you used in your document. The assumption is, of course, that they, too, own those fonts. If they don't, you're faced with a moral dilemma. You'd be violating your license agreement to copy a font for your service bureau to use, but circumstances often force people to do it.

Always let the service know the exact font name, version number, and vendor of the fonts you've used. It's a good idea to include a suitcase of the screen fonts—critical if you're using any custom kerning-pair adjustments.

If a service bureau you want to use doesn't have the fonts and software you need, there is a way around it: Print your file to disk as described in "Printing to PostScript Files."

Filling out the form. Unless you're renting the equipment by the hour and doing the output yourself, most service bureaus require you to fill out a form that describes the files you are supplying and the type of output you want. (See the sidebar, "The Service Bureau Form".)

If you're asking for film, confirm how your print shop wants it—film positive or negative, right-reading emulsion up or down—and make sure the service bureau knows what that means.

And one more thing: If a service bureau has more than one type of laser printer and/or imagesetter, make sure you know the rate for the one you want to use. Rates may be higher for higher-resolution imagesetting, film, complex (long-running) jobs, and faster turnaround, among other things. So ask, don't presume.

Printing to PostScript Files (SZA/JK/Larry Pina/AN/BW)

You can turn any Mac document into a PostScript text file that can then be printed on any PostScript device without using the application that originally created the document. Because the PostScript file can include font, graphic, and image file data, this process saves you from having to provide all those files separately—a nice tidy package, though possibly a huge one.

Generating a PostScript file in version 7 or later of the LaserWriter driver is easy. Just open the document and choose Print from the File menu. In the Print dialog box, click the PostScript File button (the File button in the Destination options for version 8 of the Apple and Adobe drivers). The Print button becomes a Save button. Click on it and you'll get a dialog box that asks you where you want to put the file and what you want to call it.

Version 8 of the Apple and Adobe drivers give you additional options:

- You can choose to capture the job as a PostScript print job or as an EPS file with standard bitmapped, scalable PICT, or no preview image.

- You can select between PostScript Level 1 or Level 2 compatibility.

- You can elect to include or not include fonts, or to simply exclude the basic 13 fonts built into most PostScript printers.

- You can choose between ASCII and the more compact binary-encoded PostScript formats.

With earlier versions of the LaserWriter driver, there was no PostScript File button to click; instead, you had to click the OK button and press ⌘P within about a second. (If you didn't press ⌘P fast enough, the document would print rather than be saved as a PostScript file.)

The PostScript file created by either of these methods can be opened (and altered, if you're a PostScript programmer) in any word processor. To print it, you don't open it and then choose Print; that will just give you a printout of all the PostScript commands in the file. Instead, you *download* the PostScript file to the printer the same way you do fonts, with the LaserWriter Font Utility or a similar program.

Service Bureau Tips

HOT TIPS

Proof your pages on a laser printer before getting high-resolution output (BW). Remember, you're spending $7 to $15 or more for each page of image-set paper or film. It's always worth it to get a laser proof, and check it carefully, before you send your files for final output.

Set up the page for PostScript output (BW). On your own machine, open the Chooser and select the LaserWriter icon (or whatever printer driver icon corresponds to the laser printer you'll use). Select Page Setup from the File menu, make any changes you want (or no changes), and click OK. Now go through your document to make sure it still looks right. Remember that different printers use different margins than the LaserWriter, and there are other incompatibilities, so you may need to make some changes.

Lock your floppies (BW). Service bureaus are notorious sources of viruses. Make sure your disks are locked when you deliver them to avoid any accidental contamination.

Optimize the document (David Van Ness/JK). To keep the file size down, delete any extraneous art from the pasteboard margins. Similarly, check illustrations for undefined colors or unnecessary placed art by choosing the Select All command, Shift-clicking to deselect everything you recognize and then investigating any remaining objects.

Ask for help with trapping (David Van Ness/JK/DD). If your job has color separations, find out from the company that's going to print the job how much color *trapping* it needs (that's making darker colors overprint lighter colors by a certain distance, to avoid unsightly gaps where they meet). It sounds easy, but it's really complicated; if you don't know what you're doing, ask for help.

Avoid the Imagesetter RIP killers (BW). PostScript imagesetters have a far tougher job than laser printers given their higher resolution, and consequently they work differently inside. What's hard for a PostScript printer to swallow will likely choke an imagesetter's raster image processor. Be kind, in the following ways:

- Don't embed one EPS file within another if you can avoid it, especially when there's a font specified within. The font spec can get lost or the resulting PostScript code may get too convoluted to process.

- Don't drastically scale down a large scanned image to obtain a thumbnail size. Use an image-editing program to resample the image to the proper pixel resolution.

- Beware of complex PICT graphics. PICT is a notoriously ambiguous file format and its PostScript processing has caused many tears.

- Avoid long paths and excessively large, complex masks. The calculations involved may simply overwhelm the processor. Break complex curves into simpler ones and/or remove unnecessary control points. Use several simpler masks instead of one complex one.

- Avoid scaling and rotating complex EPS graphics in your page layout program. Doing so can lengthen print time or choke the imagesetter processor. Do the required scaling or rotating in your graphics program, and then re-import it into your layout.

Getting negative, right-reading film (AN/SZA/JK). If you need to adjust a PostScript printout to conform to a print shop's requirement of right-reading film with emulsion up, or down, and so on, clicking on the Options button in the Page Setup dialog box gives you several relevant choices. (Clarus, the dog-cow, will appear to demonstrate the effect of each option as you select it, though a lowercase *a* does it on Adobe's PSPrinter driver.) For example, you can flip the entire image on the page vertically or horizontally, and also "invert" a printout, changing whites to blacks and blacks to whites to create a negative image. Note that Microsoft applications may present these features somewhat differently.

Editors' Poll:
What Printer Do You Use, and How Do You Like It?

JH: Apple LaserWriter 4/600, monochrome laser. It's a beauty, but moving up from my eight-year-old reliable HP DeskWriter inkjet, I was surprised to discover how slow and jam-prone a laser printer can be.

Apple StyleWriter II, monochrome inkjet. I don't like it because it's slow, it has poor envelope handling, and the ink still isn't waterproof.

JC: Apple LaserWriter Select 360, monochrome laser. Tastes great, less filling! The speed and print quality are outstanding.

KT: Apple LaserWriter Pro 630, monochrome laser. I like it, but... it's got a tricky paper path that restricts materials, which occasionally causes jams. It's not as rock-solid-reliable as the LaserWriter Plus or the LaserWriter II NTX that preceded it, but a good printer nonetheless.

MEC: Apple LaserWriter IINT. It's too slow for some graphics-intensive work, but, hey; it stood up to having a bookcase fall on it during the Southern California Northridge Earthquake of 1994.

SZA: Apple LaserWriter Pro 630, monochrome laser. I love it! It produces great printouts, and the engine is a real workhorse—just keeps going with a minimum of care.

SS: Apple LaserWriter IINT, monochrome laser. It's incredibly sturdy, and although I could replace it with a 600-dpi, PostScript Level 2 model for a fraction of this printer's original cost, it still works as well as it did when I bought it—and I've spent *nothing* on maintenance!

TA: Apple LaserWriter Pro 630. The 630's built-in Ethernet connection makes it more useful than many other printers. This faster interface allows for zippy font downloading and faster printouts overall.

TL: Apple Color StyleWriter 2400, color inkjet. I got it last year to replace my ImageWriter, and it's lived up to its billing. However, I hardly ever use it, because there just aren't that many times that I need to print in color!

Apple Personal LaserWriter NTR, monochrome laser. It's getting a bit old, and new 600-dpi, speedier printers are looking more and more attractive. But the NTR is still so solid that I am reluctant to spend money to replace it. I haven't had a single complaint about it.

22

~~~~~~~~~~

Telecommunications

Telecommunications—the transfer of information between computers over wires and cables—can take you and your Mac beyond the confines of your desktop and your office. Just plug in a modem, fire up some communications software, and you're headed into a whole new way of working with people and information.

The traffic regulations and road signs may be confusing at first, but with a little patience you'll be on your way. Whatever your destination—be it a colleague's computer or the World Wide Web, a local bulletin board or a national on-line service, or maybe just the office network—odds are you'll soon find your Mac and modem an indispensable way to keep in touch. Before long you could be chatting familiarly with electronic friends you've never met, trading messages and files with associates around the world, getting answers to your computer questions (and maybe even offering a few tips to others), and decking out your Mac with the latest free and shareware software.

Contributors

Joseph O. Holmes (JH)
is the chapter editor.

Jonathan Oski (JO) is
vice president, manager
of network and technol-
ogy planning at BOT
Financial Corporation in
Boston. He is also a
contributing editor for
MacWEEK.

David J. Swift (DJS) is
a photographer, writer,
musician, and computer
consultant who, thanks
to telecommunications
and overnight-any-
where delivery, lives in
Jackson, Wyoming with
impunity.

Steven Bobker (SB)
has been editor-in-chief
of *MacUser,* a sysop
on CompuServe and
eWorld, and even met
his wife on-line.

Henry Norr (HN)
edited the previous
version of this chapter,
from which parts
were taken.

Contents

All About Modems

To telecommunicate, you need a *modem* ("MOE-dem"), a small piece of hardware that lets you hook up your computer to a phone line and transmit and receive data. Strictly speaking, a modem is no longer required—see the sidebar "Once and Future Telecom Technologies" later in this chapter. The name is short for modulator-demodulator. On the sending end, a modem translates (modulates) digital information from your computer into sounds, which then travel over telephone wires; the modem on the receiving end translates (demodulates) the sounds back into digital data.

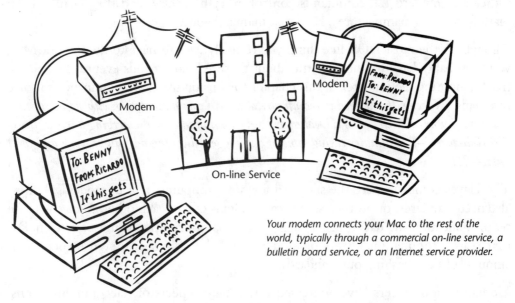

Your modem connects your Mac to the rest of the world, typically through a commercial on-line service, a bulletin board service, or an Internet service provider.

Internal, External, and PC Card Modems   (HN)

POWERBOOK

Modems can be either external or internal (installed in an expansion slot inside your Mac or plugged into a PC Card slot on the side of a PowerBook). Internal modems are the norm among PowerBook users because you don't have to carry around another device when you're on the road, and because there's one less power outlet to search for. A recent addition is the PC Card (formerly PCMCIA) modem which, amazingly, fits all the electronics necessary for today's fastest connections inside a card not much bigger than a credit card. They're more expensive than other kinds and lack useful status lights, but the size and weight outweigh the drawbacks. The only Apple products that use these modems are the later PowerBooks and the Newton MessagePad. *[Get used to PC Card modems; they are the way of the future, even on desktop Macs.—SB]*

Connection Protocols (HN/JH)

Modems actually have to make two different connections. First, your Mac has to communicate with the modem to send commands that operate the modem and to pass along and receive the data.

A modem can't do a thing without instructions from your Mac, instructions based on a set of commands originally developed by Hayes Microcomputer Products and thus called the *Hayes command set* or *AT command set* (because AT starts each command as a way to tell the modem to pay ATtention). The official Hayes commands are used by nearly all modems today to control the basics: dialing, resetting, and hanging up. Other nonstandard AT commands control everything else, and they change from manufacturer to manufacturer; keep that manual handy.

Though it's the most DOS-like thing you're likely ever to have to do on your Mac, you'll probably have to know a little about these AT commands eventually. See the troubleshooting section later in this chapter for tips on using AT commands to solve problems. *[No way. If you need to reconfigure a modem command string, either find a better string on-line or call tech support. Dealing with AT commands is not something worthwhile.— SB] [I disagree—five minutes trying some of our suggested commands might work and can't hurt.—JH]*

The Hayes commands are the standard for how computers talk to modems, but we also need standards, or protocols, for how modems talk to each other. A *protocol* is the set of connection and data transfer rules which a pair of computers must agree on. For that reason the manufacturers of modems and the chip sets they use spend vast amounts of time hashing out standards.

Modem manufacturers have addressed three main aspects of telecommunications: transmission speed (measured in bits per second), error checking, and data compression. Its standards are identified by a "V." followed by a number (and sometimes the word *bis* or *ter*, French for "second" and "third"). Here's what they mean and why you do (or don't) need to pay attention to them.

Speed (JH). The speed at which modems transfer data is measured in *bits per second* or *bps*, as in "Don't buy a modem that doesn't do at least 14,400 bps." *[Don't buy a modem that does less than 28,800 bps!—SB]* (See the sidebar "Baudy Tales" for the lowdown on speed nomenclature.)

Modems were first widely available at 300 bps, then at 1,200, 2,400, 9,600, and 14,400. The fastest official standard today is V.34, for a modem that can transfer data at 28,000 bps, though an even newer version of V.34, nicknamed V.34 plus, supports 33,600 bps, and is already available on some modems.

Baudy Tales (JH)

There are actually three common ways to refer to data transfer speeds. You'll most commonly see *bps*, for bits per second, and sometimes *cps*, for characters per second. The only difference between bps and cps is a factor of 10: a 9600-bps modem can move data at 960 cps. For super-fast connect speeds, you'll also see *kbps*, thousands of bits per second, and even *mbps*, megabytes per second! (See the sidebar "Once and Future Telecom Technologies.")

You'll also hear the term *baud*, but it's wrong. Baud refers to the number of signal changes per second, but every modem transfer protocol since antique 300-baud modems conveys more than one bit per signal. A 9,600-*bps* modem is actually a 2,400-*baud* modem. But forget the details—in common usage, baud means bps.

Standard modem speeds won't continue to grow at that pace. Technology has squeezed all it can from standard telephone lines, which have a theoretical limit of 35,000 bps. My V.34 modem seldom does better than 26,400 bps. If you're making a local call and your phone lines are good you may do better. To exceed those speeds though, you'll need to move to a digital line such as ISDN (see the sidebar "Once and Future Telecom Technologies" later in this chapter).

The major standards for data and fax modem communications are listed in the table at right.

Error correction (HN). Today's modems are amazingly accurate, but they do make mistakes. (How would *you* like to interpret 28,800 sounds a second transmitted over a noisy copper wire?) That's why they need *error detection* and *error correction*—ways to verify that the receiver received what was sent and to request a retry if that didn't happen. Software-based file-transfer protocols incorporate their own error checking, but with high-speed devices the hardware helps carry the burden.

The current error-correction standard, V.42, incorporates several previous technologies. An additional error-correction technique not included in V.42 is Microcom's

Modem Modulation Standards (HN/JH)

Standard	Maximum Speed (bps)
Bell 102	300
Bell 212A	1,200
V.22bis	2,400
V.32	9,600
V.32bis	14,400
V.32terbo*	19,200
V.34, V.Fast*, or V.FC*	28,800
V.34 plus*	31,200 and 33,600
V.27ter	4,800
V.29	9,600 fax
V.17	14,400 fax
*Unofficial interim standards	

MNP Level 10, designed for adverse conditions such as exceptionally noisy lines and cellular connections. Look for it if you're shopping for a cellular modem to connect to your PowerBook.

Data compression (HN). To the extent that data can be compressed before transmission, you can get more effective *throughput*—in other words, send and receive your files faster—with any modem, whatever its transmission speed. That's why most Mac files in on-line libraries are compressed with software such as Aladdin's **StuffIt** or the shareware **Compact Pro** (see "Compression" in Chapter 13). The idea behind hardware compression is similar, but it's simpler because it requires no effort on the part of either sender or receiver—the modems compress and decompress the data automatically.

But hardware compression only works if both devices are using the same technology, so modem vendors have agreed on a standard, V.42bis (not to be confused with the

Once and Future Telecom Technologies   (JH)

To think that at one time folks were happy tootling along at 300 bps! Nowadays, a 28,800-bps connection can feel unbearably slow as it's struggling to download massive multimedia files on the World Wide Web. Though that's the top speed you'll attain over standard telephone lines (nicknamed *POTS*—Plain Old Telephone Service—by telecom fanatics and the phone companies), there are faster, though more expensive alternatives available right now, and even faster alternatives coming.

ISDN

At this writing, the only commonly available and relatively affordable step up is *ISDN*, Integrated Services Digital Network, available in about 70 percent of the country. Basic-rate ISDN service is fast, theoretically up to 128,000 bps or about four and a half times faster than a V.34 or 28,800 bps modem. It runs for the most part over existing telephone wires, but through tweaking and equipment upgrading by the phone company, turns the entire connection digital, from your Mac to the computer at the other end. That means of course no modem, because there's no longer a need to modulate the digital signal into analog and demodulate it back to digital.

One neat thing about ISDN is that, because it uses two *channels,* or independent data connections, it can carry a fast 64-kbps over one channel while you simultaneously use the other channel for telephone, fax, or modem calls. Or, through a process known as *multilinking,* ISDN can carry data at 128 kbps over its combined channels.

ISDN service is much more expensive than regular POTS. Your Mac will need an ISDN terminal adapter, such as Motorola's **BitSurfer** ($499), but that will stick you with the serial port bottleneck of 57.6 kbps. For $1,000, maybe less, you can get the full speed from an internal NuBus card.

V.42 error-correction protocol). Exactly how effective it is depends on many factors, including the nature of your data, but V.42bis generally seems to increase throughput by 50 to 100 percent. (And most V.42bis modems are smart enough not to waste time trying to compress data you've already compressed with a utility.)

Vendors regularly imply that compression is much more efficient than it really is. For V.42bis, for example, they generally assume a 4:1 compression ratio. These claims may not be literally false, but they're bogus because they are based on ideal conditions—you'll probably never achieve those levels of throughput.

[Something else to consider is serial port speed. If you buy a 28,800 bps modem and expect to get 115 kbps or greater rates through compression, make sure that your Mac's serial port can handle this higher data rate. Third-party cards, such as Creative Solutions's Hustler card, add high-speed serial ports to your Mac that can handle higher transfer rates, even on older Macs such as the Mac II.—JO]

Next, getting ISDN service installed in your home by the phone company costs anywhere from $50 to $500 depending on your location, with monthly fees from $30 to $100, plus a per-minute usage charge of a penny or so. Finally it'll all be for naught if you aren't calling something ISDN-equipped at the other end. Many Internet service providers offer ISDN connections for prices starting at $30 to $60 a month, and CompuServe has 56 kbps ISDN available at nine locations throughout the country, for no surcharge at all.

Be warned: The setup is very tricky. Pick vendors based on support as well as price. *[Get your vendor to commit to an ISDN connection in writing. I had an ISDN line put in at my vendor's verbal urging. No connections have become available. In fact, there are no ISDN connections available in my very large metro area. What a joke.—SB]*

WARNING

Cable Modem
Though it's only being tested in a few markets right now, cable modem, an even faster technology, is likely to supplant ISDN, at least for home use. Cable modem uses a standard coaxial TV cable to deliver a (theoretical) maximum of 10 mbps, though closer to 2.5 mbps in the real world—that's *megabytes* per second, and almost 20 times faster than ISDN, almost 90 times faster than a 28,800 bps modem. The technology now operates *asymmetrically*, that is, somewhat one-sidedly by using a super-fast connection to bring graphics and sound data downstream into your computer, while the upstream connection, which typically carries just mouse clicks and some text, is a leisurely 14,400 bps to 1 mbps.

Of course cable modem will only be available in areas where TV cable is or can be installed. It probably won't be widely available for a year or two, but several small test markets are already up and running, including Elmira, New York. Keep your eyes peeled.

Figuring Actual Transfer Rates (HN)

When you are shopping for a modem, it's important to pay attention to the speeds and standards supported by the various models—a 14,400-bps modem really is a lot faster than a 9,600-bps model. But many factors other than a modem's speeds and standards influence actual transfer rates, or throughput, that you'll experience in real-life telecommunications.

A 2,400-bps modem, for example, can transfer 2,400 bits or 300 bytes per second—in theory. But there is always extra overhead involved in telecommunications—setup negotiations between the two modems, special stop bits that sometimes mark the beginning and end of bytes of data, and occasional retries when some data is not received properly. All of this reduces real data-transfer rates. As a very rough rule of thumb, assuming no data compression and normal amounts of line noise, divide the bps rate by 10 to approximate the actual transfer rate in bytes or characters per second. (Remember that in the binary system computers use, it takes eight bits, or one byte, to represent a character.)

In other words, two 2,400-bps modems will typically transfer about 240 bytes per second, or around 14K per minute; with 14,400-bps modems, you can expect to average 1,400 to 1,500 bytes or characters per second (84K to 90K per minute). You'll have to check the actual connect speed of a 28.8 modem to make the calculation, since they typically connect at 24,000 or 26,400 bps, not 28,800.

Remember, though, your mileage may vary. A noisy line or bad connection can drastically reduce your throughput. And if you download a file from a BBS or on-line service at a time of day when the system is crowded, expect lower-than-optimal transfer rates even if the connection is clean, because the computer at the other end of the line may sometimes leave your modem sitting idle while it services other users.

On the other hand, you can boost effective throughput to significantly higher levels by using data compression: If you can compress a 1MB file down to, say, 500K, you can send it over the phone in half the time (see "Compression," in Chapter 13). *[That's not always true, especially if you have a V.42 or MNP10 connection. Precompressed files are not compressed (well maybe one percent) by hardware compression modems.—SB]*

Buying a Modem

New modems: 28.8 versus 14.4 (HN/JH). Simply put, telecommunicating is slow. In fact, it requires more waiting than almost anything else we do with our Macs. Worst of all, when you log onto a commercial on-line service or dial a long-distance number, you have to pay to wait! That's why there's no such thing as a modem that's too fast—provided that you can use and afford the speed.

We've finally reached a technological—and price—plateau, so the choice is much simpler than it used to be. V.34 modems, which connect at 28,800 bps, are today's

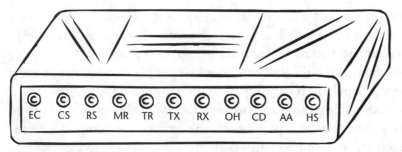

The status lights on the front of an external modem can be very useful. TX: Data is being sent out; RX: Data is coming in; OH: The modem has taken the telephone line "off hook"; AA: Auto-answer is turned on, usually by the fax software; CD: A connection has been made with a remote modem.

modem of choice and are likely to remain so for awhile. You can pick up a decent one for under $200, a fancy one for twice that. The only alternatives in new modems are V.32 14,400-bps modems, but at roughly $100 to $150, they aren't typically cheap enough for you to pass up the faster modems. (Though they're more expensive, the same ratio applies to PC Card modems.) You should only consider a V.32 if you can't connect at faster speeds today and won't for the next year or so. A 14,400-bps modem may suit your light e-mail needs just fine, but once you begin to explore the service that provides your e-mail account, you can eat up the price difference in short order.

Used modems: older protocols (JH). No one makes the slower 9,600- and 2,400-bps models any longer, but with no moving parts, modems last a long time, and you can still find used ones for sale. For some folks, especially those who plan to use only e-mail, a slower modem is a sensible choice. But remember: A 2,400-bps modem can spend as much as 12 times more time *downloading* a file—copying a file onto your Mac from a remote location—as a 28,800-bps modem *[And that includes e-mail of course.— SB]* Consider on-line charges and the value of your time.

Avoid the nonstandard protocols. The interim standard *V.32terbo* allows communication at up to 19,200 bps as long as it connects with another V.32terbo modem. Another standard, *V.FastClass* or *V.FC* supports speeds up to 28,800 bps when connecting with another V.FC modem. Although modern modems promise backward compatibility with these standards, you're more likely to have problems.

Reliability, Compatibility, and Support (HN)

Specs and standards don't tell you everything about a modem—between two units with seemingly identical features, subtle differences, especially in their ROMs, can make the difference between smooth sailing and constant hassles. Some modems only have problems with certain other manufacturers' units.

Unfortunately, it's not easy to get a handle on such issues; magazine reviews usually aren't much help. Your best bet is to talk to others who are already using the model in question. Ask around among friends or at a user group, or go on-line. Most major modem makers have their own BBS (bulletin board service) or a customer-support forum on CompuServe (popularly referred to as "CIS"), America Online (known as "AOL"), or elsewhere. Scanning those forums provides invaluable insight—both in terms of the problems users may be reporting and the attitude the company's representatives display. Tech support is important—odds are you'll need it sooner or later. An on-line forum with knowledgeable reps providing prompt and friendly support is both a valuable resource in its own right and a telling sign about the company's culture; if it doesn't offer on-line support, or messages go unanswered for days, I'd stay away.

And don't forget to find out in advance about the vendor's return and warranty policy.

Tester's Choice

Real telecom fanatics passionately believe in their chosen modems. Here are four of our personal favorites. Note that street prices are much lower than the list prices we show here.

Practical Peripherals MC288LCD V.34 ($460) (JH). Practical Peripherals has long been my favorite modem manufacturer, because with one exception, each of the four I've owned (2,400, 9,600, 14,400, 28,800) has run perfectly. The single time I had a problem, the company sent me a user-installable firmware upgrade immediately and without charge. My current **PM288LCD V.34** consistently performs perfectly.

GOOD FEATURE

The MC288LCD is pricey, but it's worth paying extra for the backlit 24-character LCD display, which constantly rotates information about the connect speed, carrier, quality of connection, connection protocols, up-to-the-second transfer rates, and time connected. It even tells me the time of day. I find it indispensable when debugging connection problems; the readout reports "Ready, Dialing, Silence, Far Ring 1, Handshaking, Negotiating, Online." And it comes with a lifetime warranty.

HOT TIP

A $10 shareware application called **SetLCDclock** from Adept Solutions sets your PM288LCD's clock to match your Mac's clock: Drop it into your Startup Items folder. Download it from the Practical Peripherals forum on CompuServe or from other on-line services.

Global Village PowerPort Platinum ($240) (DJS). I fax. A lot. In broad daylight I can fax a two-page document from the Wyoming mountains to New York for a lot less moolah than a letter. Thus, my printer's toner cartridge is not one cycle closer to replacement, I don't wince with the thought of cutting my tongue licking an envelope, and fewer trees have died.

If you fax as a way of life, you use the Global Village. Simple as that. Mine's a Gold. I wish it were the Platinum.

Hayes Smartmodem Optima 288 ($580) (JO). When it comes to personal computer modems, Hayes practically invented them almost 15 years ago. Though the company has had a series of financial difficulties of late, they still make rock-solid modems and ultimately define the term "Hayes-compatible." Hayes includes a low-end version of Smartcom II, their scriptable terminal-emulation program and fax software, but these pale in comparison to the better third-party products. Don't buy the modem for the bundled software. The Optima 288 is not the least expensive modem you can buy, but its wide support is bound to save you compatibility debugging headaches. *[This modem is no better than its cheaper cousins and Hayes has abandoned Macs. I'd skip this one.—SB] [Hayes still sells Mac modem bundles, and they're probably the best supported and most widely used modem today.—JO]*

Global Village PowerPort Series ($400) (JO). Internal modem or PC Card, the best PowerBook modem comes from the line of Global Village PowerPort modems. Global Village charges a bit more, but they go to great lengths to ensure a high-quality user experience. The Mercury line, which works with the 100-, 200-, and 500-series PowerBooks supports speeds up to 19.2 kbps. The newer Platinum series modems are full-fledged V.34 modems that support 28.8 kbps transfer rates. Included with all their products is the acclaimed GlobalFax software which is probably the finest on the market. If you are planning to use your PowerBook to send and receive even a modest number of faxes, the PowerPort choice becomes even more compelling.

POWERBOOK

Penny Wise?

These modems are less expensive, and less feature-rich, but we still recommend them.

SupraExpress 288 V.34 ($170) (DJS). I bought Supra LC144s by the six-pack back when 14.4 was fast. I've watched cheap (and cheaper) Supras sit there for years and do nothing but shag calls or download daily weather maps or surf for wire photos, glib as can be. Because of their square-jawed reliability and fine documentation, I'd not hesitate to foist on anyone the 288 SupraExpress if faxing is not a factor. I like Supra for one more reason: You can download a continually updated list of their extended (to near-infinity) AT command set. Global Village has never offered this courtesy. *[The SupraExpress lacks the $250 Supra FaxModem's flash ROM, LED display, and extras such as caller ID.—JH]*

GOOD
FEATURE

MultiTech MultiModem 2834ZDX ($300) (JO). The little-known MultiModem ZDX, with a street price of about $190, is a fine economical V.34 modem. It is considerably smaller and lighter than most desktop modems, so it's easy to take with you. (The external power pack is also nice and small.) It's a Type 2 fax modem, as opposed to most others which are Type 1, which seems to result in some better performance since the modem handles more of the responsibility for the fax transmission. On the downside, it's hard to find a Macintosh-specific bundle for this modem at most mail-order houses. If you don't care about the software or cable, the MultiModem is fast and travels well.

POWERBOOK

Duo Express Modem ($345 installed) **and Global Village PowerPort Mercury for the Duo** ($400) (DJS). This is a specialized intelligence: the Duo modem. There are only two Duo internals available: the singular Global Village PowerPort-for-Duo Mercury (19.2 kbps) and Apple's Duo Express Modem (14.4 kbps). Both send and receive faxes. Apple's modem was much maligned, so if you find a used one, it's a deal at $100 or $200 less than a new GV. (You simply do not find used GV Duo modems.) I've lived with both; the Apple modem is less fussy. The Express Modem's original problem? Software. Apple fixed things with releases 1.5 and up. Install Telecom 2.x (free on-line) and the Express Modem is downright swell. *[Judging by the complaints I see on-line, the Express Modem certainly has more than its share of dissatisfied customers. And by today's standards, it's slow. My recommendation is to buy this modem only if it's included in a used PowerBook you're buying.—JO]*

Communications Software

There was a time, not long ago, when everyone used general-purpose telecommunications programs to connect remotely to other computers. The same program could be used to reach your friend's modem, your favorite BBSs, on-line services, and even industrial computers.

Those days are gone. We still use general-purpose programs, but for the most part, we use service- and function-specific programs to telecommunicate. Most services now require you to use their special software. The situation on the Internet, where a general program used to be enough, is even more chaotic. You'll likely use a different program for each major function you perform: For example, I use a mail manager/reader, a news reader, a Web browser, a Telnet remote connection program, and a special uploading program to maintain my Web page (for more on Web pages, see Chapter 23). That's five programs to do what one program used to do. The new way is easier and far more friendly, however.

The MacBinary Imperative (HN)

Virtually every Mac telecommunications program has a setting for enabling something called *MacBinary.* It should be on by default, and you should leave it on unless you have some very special reason to turn it off.

MacBinary is not a protocol but a file format. It was devised by Mac telecommunications pioneers to deal with some unique Mac features, including the fact that the Mac divides files into two segments (called the *data fork* and the *resource fork*) and stores some information about files, such as type and creator codes, creation and modification dates, and icons, in the Finder rather than the file itself. MacBinary solves these problems by combining both forks in a single block and adding a 128-byte header with the Finder information; when receiving a file, MacBinary-aware applications recognize the header, decode the file, and restore it to standard format.

When MacBinary is turned on and you initiate a file transfer, your software will convert the file into the MacBinary format. If it's sent to a PC or a mainframe, it will stay in MacBinary format, but if it reaches a Mac via a Mac communications program, it will automatically be converted back to its original format. If you download a Mac file to a PC and take it to a Mac on a floppy or over a network, you'll have to convert it yourself before it's usable. (To find out how to do that, see Chapter 25.)

General-Purpose Packages (SB)

Why do we even keep general-purpose programs around? They're still the best way to reach many computers. Their bare bones interface is very fast and efficient. You may never need a general-purpose telecom program, even if you live your life on-line. If you do need one, here's what to look for:

- Compatibility with and the ability to use the *Mac Communications Toolbox*—Apple's system-level communications tools (see the sidebar "The Communications Toolbox")—and *Open Transport,* Apple's latest modern networking and communications architecture.

- Scripting or button-creation ability. The time you spend connected to other computers is valuable, so never do the same operation twice manually. Create scripts or buttons using the software's built-in tools to log on, navigate, perform tasks, and log off. Any time spent creating these aids will repay itself many times over.

- Be sure your software supports high-speed transfers. Having a program that can move data at 28.8 kbps may seem likely enough if you connect via a modem, but that's today's standard and tomorrow's will be faster. Look for the ability to move

The Communications Toolbox   (HN)

If you look into a lot of recent Mac communications programs, you may notice that the configuration dialog boxes in many of them look suspiciously similar. Is this evidence that developers are simply copying each other's look and feel?

Not exactly. What you are seeing are dialogs created with the help of the Macintosh Communications Toolbox (a.k.a. the Comm Toolbox, or CTB), a piece of Apple system software that was introduced as an add-on to System 6 and then rolled into System 7. It provides a uniform framework for communications (including nicely designed dialog boxes) and a set of basic communications tools, all of which are available to any application that supports the toolbox. The goal was to make it easier for developers to add communications capabilities to their software, enable multiple applications to share the same tools, and spare users from having to confront a new interface in each program.

In addition to standard dialog boxes, the Comm Toolbox defines three standard types of tools:

- *Connection tools,* which define how the Mac is to be connected to another computer. In addition to the Apple Modem Tool, there's a Serial Tool for direct connections, a Telnet tool for TCP/IP connections, and several other tools for different kinds of network connections.

- *Terminal tools,* which define the types of terminals that communications programs can emulate—TTY, VT102, or VT320, for example.

- *Transfer tools,* which implement file-transfer protocols such as Xmodem or Zmodem.

Under System 7 these tools get installed in the Extensions folder, and you have access to them from any Communications Toolbox-based application. If, for example, you install Aladdin's SITcomm program, you'll have a Zmodem tool that's also available for use in, say, ClarisWorks' communications module, even though that program did not come with Zmodem support.

data at least 57.6 kbps and preferably faster. If you have a direct, that is, modemless, link to another computer or network, look for the ability to move data at 115 kbps and up.

- File downloading uses special protocols to speed up an otherwise tedious process. When using the Comm Toolbox, adding protocols is simply a matter of getting and using new Tools. The fastest protocol is Zmodem. CompuServe users should use QuickB, a proprietary protocol.

Consider the following programs:

MicroPhone Pro ($300, Software Ventures) is the top of the widespread MicroPhone family. It is the most versatile and feature-laden Mac telecom program. It even has the ability to set up a dial-in BBS, and use custom graphical front ends for CompuServe, GEnie, and MCI Mail. There are some add-on and separate Internet tools also in the box. The upside is real telecom power; there's not much you can't do. The downside is complexity. The learning curve is steep, and the demands on hard disk space RAM are not small. The lesser versions cut out features and are worth it only if free. *[For heavy scripters, there's nothing like MicroPhone Pro.—JH]*

Smartcom II used to be the best, joining simplicity with power. Its publisher (Hayes) dropped all Mac development and support over a year ago. The final version runs well on all Macs including PCI Macs, supports the Comm Toolbox brilliantly, is unmatched at high speeds, and has more than adequate scripting and button-creating ability. I'd consider Smartcom worth about what good shareware is worth: $20 or $30. Just don't expect support from Hayes.

SITcomm is a basic program ($120, Aladdin Systems) with okay performance. A nice Zmodem tool is included, but there's nothing truly special here. While SITcomm can handle high connection speeds and has excellent Comm Toolbox support, there's no built-in scripting, except via AppleScript. *[SITcomm is straightforward and easy to use; I highly recommend it for simple needs.—JH]*

CrossTalk ($195, Attachmate) has the same name as the best Windows telecom program, but is an entirely different beast. The original developer (DCA) has sold it, and the performance and the feature set are not up to snuff for today's users. Its only advantage is that it can use Windows' scripts and button sets (QuickPads).

ZTerm ($30, Alverson Software) is the most common general-purpose telecom program. It's reasonably priced shareware and comes bundled with many other packages. It works well at very high speeds, takes up little disk space and RAM, and supports all common transfer protocols. Scripting is rudimentary but effective (and easy!). ZTerm is capable of higher connection speeds than any other program, making it invaluable for directly connecting computers. Unfortunately, there isn't any Comm Toolbox support yet. Still, the price and feature set make this a must-have. This program was in beta for literally years; be sure to get the release version (1.01 or later).

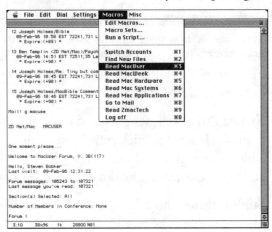

ZTerm's macros come in sets of ten; you can have as many sets as you like.

ClarisWorks 4 ($129, Claris) has a built-in tele-com module that fully supports the Comm Toolbox and is not the joke that the telecom modules in earlier versions were. Indeed, if you have ClarisWorks, you likely have all the general-telecom power you need today.

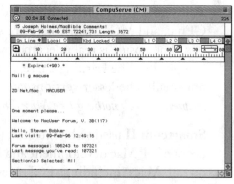

ClarisWorks's telecom interface is really bare-bones, but it's easy to use and works very well.

E-Mail Managers   (JH)

If you only send or receive a few e-mail messages a day, your on-line service's software will suffice. (We have a lot to say about e-mail—what it is and why you'll love it—later in the chapter.) But if you get lots of e-mail, or if you need to sort it into categories, store it, and retrieve it easily, you should consider an e-mail manager, an application which automatically goes on-line to send and retrieve all your mail, letting you read and reply to it off-line at your leisure.

Eudora Pro ($90, Qualcomm). Eudora began life as a free e-mail manager, and later spawned an expanded commercial version, Eudora Pro. It sends and retrieves e-mail

Eudora Pro enables you to automatically file e-mail in "mailboxes" you create, which can be several layers deep.

only through a TCP/IP Internet account, not from the commercial services or from a local network.

Eudora Pro will check for mail on demand or at regular intervals. After picking up e-mail, Eudora files the messages in user-created "mailboxes," which can be nested one or more folders deep. Mail can be filed in the mailboxes automatically by filters, filing according to words in various fields of the message. Filters can also change a message's subject, label, or priority, but cannot automatically forward a message or send a reply.

BAD FEATURE

Eudora Pro is well-designed and powerful, if a tad quirky. There's no address book, for example. Instead a "nickname" system allows a short name to stand for a full e-mail address or a group of addresses. There's no way to import addresses from existing address books from other applications, and no way to sort or search the addresses.

Still for those who rely on a TCP/IP-based service for e-mail, Eudora Pro is easy to use and stable. The free Eudora Light is still supported; it lacks filtering, spell checking, and other features, but it makes a terrific first e-mail manager. *[Eudora is also wired for AppleScript, so you can further automate its operations with simple or complex scripts.—JO]*

At this writing, Qualcomm announced Eudora 3.0, which, among other improvements, offers a more robust address book, though there's still no way to import addresses from other applications.

Claris Emailer ($90, Claris). A newcomer, this package is the best all-around e-mail manager, less powerful than Eudora Pro at filing messages, but covering most other areas better. Emailer will retrieve e-mail from CompuServe, America Online, RadioMail, AppleLink, and an Internet service provider, on demand or on days and

times you preset. Emailer is a natural choice for those with accounts on more than one service, but it has several slick features that make it a terrific utility even if you retrieve e-mail from just a single service.

First, like Eudora, Emailer files messages in user-created "filing cabinets," though there are no subfolders. Also like Eudora, Emailer automatically files mail according to "mail actions," looking in specific fields for designated words. Mail actions will also automatically send a prewritten reply ("I'm on vacation…"), forward an incoming message to another recipient or account, or set a priority label. It's good at

Claris Emailer makes it easy to switch among locations, changing access information such as phone numbers as well as modem settings if you move between modems.

searching messages for names or words, too. *[If you subscribe to listservs (see "Mailing Lists," later in this chapter), be careful with that auto-reply business. You might earn a lifetime of scorn in one week.—DJS]*

Emailer can also easily switch locations settings. I use Emailer at work and at two locations at home, for example, and I can quickly switch between the locations, changing the settings for my three modems and two phone numbers.

GOOD
FEATURE

If you have TCP/IP access to the Internet, Emailer makes checking your mail on America Online and the Internet incredibly fast. Set up an Emailer TCP location for your Internet account and for each screen name in America Online. When your TCP connection is live, Emailer takes about three seconds to check each service.

HOT TIP

Emailer's biggest drawback is that, as of version 1.0.v2, it cannot retrieve mail from local area networks such as QuickMail and First Class, and it sorely needs a more sophisticated database for storing and retrieving mail.

[Getting mail from a dial-up Internet service provider on an automatic schedule is difficult to impossible. Otherwise Emailer is fine.—SB]

PowerTalk (bundled with System 7.5). This software is Apple's attempt to create mail and fax management at system level, so that e-mail and fax capabilities are available throughout the Mac environment.

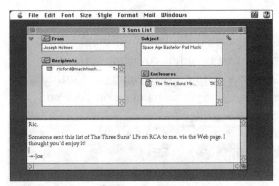

Although it's potentially powerful, and some of it is elegantly designed, it's mostly a nightmare of confusing interface, made up of half a dozen components whose exact relationships are a puzzle. Its fatal flaw, though, turns out to be that, in a classic chicken-and-egg situation, each service is required to develop its own PowerTalk extension. No extension, no connection. And only CompuServe has developed a PowerTalk extension.

Some components of PowerTalk, such as AppleMail, the universal e-mail application, are simple and well designed, even if the overall package is confusing and poorly documented.

Because of the poor showing from the on-line services, Apple announced in January 1996 that it had halted further development of PowerTalk, at least until the next major system release. Still, PowerTalk is bundled with System 7.5, and the CompuServe plug-in is free, so you should try it if you have a CompuServe account. Once it's set up, it works as advertised.

Setting Up the Connection (HN)

Because of multiple telecommunications standards, any versatile communications application must offer an array of configuration choices—most telecommunications programs need at least minimal fiddling with their settings to get everything working correctly. (That's what makes telecommunications one of the most difficult computer tasks to master.) To make matters worse, most manuals that come with modems and telecom software are poor.

The good news is that once you have your software set up and running properly, you can normally forget about most of these settings and put the manual on the shelf—at least until you get a new modem, switch to another program, or try a new on-line service.

Bits per second. Modems connect at their top speed and also at several slower speeds; a 28,000-bps modem, for example, can also connect at 14,400, 9,600, 2,400, and 1,200 bps (see the sidebar "Baudy Tales," earlier in this chapter). When two modems connect, they negotiate to determine the highest transfer rate they have in common; if line noise or other problems make it impossible to carry on at that rate, they should drop down automatically to a lower rate. Some (but not all) modems are even smart enough to move back up to a higher rate if line conditions improve.

But no modem can use a higher speed than your software is set for, so be sure your software is set to the speed you want—actually, higher than the fastest modem speed you can use, to make use of the modem's compression (see Data Compression, earlier in this chapter).

Flow control. Modems generally can't transmit data over the phone line as fast as your Mac can send it to the modem over a serial cable, and sometimes your Mac can't keep up with the incoming data from the modem. If either device feels it's in danger of gagging on excess data, it can signal to the other to stop sending data until the backlog has been processed. This coordination process is called *flow control* or *handshake*.

Lower-speed modems (2,400 bps and slower) usually rely on a flow-control technique called *Xon/Xoff*. They send the computer on and off codes between chunks of data. Make sure to turn on the Xon/Xoff switch that you'll find in some settings dialog box or menu in your communications program.

Modems that work at 9,600 bps and faster support hardware handshaking, a scheme that uses dedicated wires in the serial cable for signaling. Hardware handshaking is faster and more reliable than Xon/Xoff, so be sure to turn it on if you have a high-speed modem. *[Internal modems, by their nature, are all hardware handshaking.—SB]*

Cables that come bundled with high-speed modems are hardware-handshaking; if you have to purchase a cable separately, specify that you need hardware handshaking. If you upgrade from an older (2,400-bps) modem, you probably don't already have a hardware-handshaking cable.

HOT TIP

Other Terminal Settings: 8-1-No. Depending on the program or service you are communicating with, you may need to send and receive data in chunks of either seven or eight bits; your software should offer a choice under the heading *data bits*. The end of one byte and the beginning of another is marked by *stop bits*. Finally, *parity* is an old-fashioned way of checking that the other computer received exactly what you sent. Far and away the most common setting is eight data bits, one stop bit, and no parity, nicknamed 8-1-no. Those are the default settings in most Mac telecommunications programs; don't change them unless you know what you're doing.

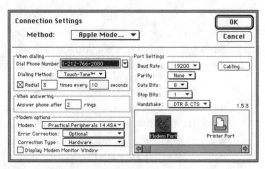

In the Apple Communications Toolbox, under "Port Settings," you'll find the common settings for parity, data bits, and stop bits. Here, flow control is called "handshake." The dialog box may look different depending on the application you're using.

```
┌────────────────────────────────────┐
│  Transfer Options for 'CIS 28.8 - Home'  │
│  Default Protocols                       │
│  Send: [ ZModem... ▼]  Receive: [ XModem ▼] │
│  Kermit Error Checking: [Checksum-1 (6 bit) ▼] │
│  Kermit Packet Size: [94    ]            │
│  X/YModem error checking:                │
│    [ Try CRC, fallback to Checksum ▼]    │
│  Sent filenames (Y/ZModem):              │
│    [ Remove funny chars ▼]               │
│  ☒ CIS B+ / Quick-B Protocol             │
│              [  OK  ] [ Cancel ]         │
└────────────────────────────────────┘
```

This dialog from ZTerm allows you to set various aspects of file transfer protocols, but the only areas you need to bother with are the two menus under Default Protocols, and the checkbox for CIS B+, which you need to check only when using CompuServe.

File Transfer Protocols. You can send plain-text (ASCII) files via modem with no special protocol or error checking; any communications program can send an unformatted text file character by character, as if you were typing it out. But there are lots of problems with text transfers. Characters may get dropped or garbled, for example.

To send anything but plain text, or even if you just want to make sure a text file arrives intact, you need to use a *file-transfer protocol*—a set of conventions for how much data will be packaged, sent, and verified. These protocols are independent of the computer, the modem, and even the communications software you are using. When a Mac user sends a file using the Zmodem protocol, any modem connected to any computer

Xmodem, Ymodem, Zmodem   (HN/Randy Singer)

Here's a guide to some commonly used transfer protocols (in order of preference):

- *Zmodem* should be your choice whenever possible. It's the fastest, can send multiple files in a batch, includes the files' names and other information about them, and can resume interrupted transfers right where it left off, so you won't have to cover the same ground twice.

- *Ymodem* (and an even faster variant called Ymodem-G) also supports batch transfers and filenames. Ymodem-G contains no error-checking protocol. It's a very fast way to transfer files, but use it only with modems that do error correction in hardware or when two computers are hardwired together directly.

- *CompuServe B+* is the latest in a series of proprietary "B" protocols the CompuServe Information Service developed for its use on its own network. It's useless anywhere else, but it's your best choice if you are downloading from CompuServe. (It's not quite as fast as Zmodem, but CompuServe doesn't support Zmodem.)

- *Xmodem* is an older protocol that is still widely used, in part because it's supported by virtually all communications programs, while its Y and Z cousins are not. But because it sends data in smaller packets it's relatively slow, and, unlike Zmodem and Ymodem-G, it waits for acknowledgment of a packet before starting to send another. It uses an error-detection technique called *checksumming,* but some implementations give you another option called *CRC,* for cyclical redundancy checking. Choose the latter if available.

- *Kermit* works with a wide range of computers and telecommunications equipment, including mainframes that don't support newer protocols. Because of its versatility and easy configuration, it's still a favorite among many government and university users. But it's generally slower than the alternatives, and it's not supported on most services.

running any program that can handle Zmodem transfers will be able to receive the file correctly. Not all communications programs and services support all protocols, though, so you may not be able to stick with just one.

Troubleshooting Connections (DJS)

Fact is, modems work. Like the rest of your equipment, once they are trained properly they tend to stay trained.

Unlike the rest of your equipment, the modem is useless until it's in cyberspace, the huge and messy on-line universe. A modem requires a component that is subject to untold pressures—the phone system. No wonder modems get snarled at times.

Be patient and be methodical.

General Rules of Engagement

Cozy up to basic telecom software. Type AT. The modem should answer OK. Behold both a revelation and a warning: You can learn a lot from, and do a lot to, a modem by using bare-bones telecom software. *[Remember, however, this is as far as any sane person should go with AT commands. If the modem is working, get outside help. If you don't get the OK in response to AT <return>, solve what is likely a hardware problem such as a loose cable.—SB]*

- Connect a phone to the line to confirm a dial tone. Use the modem's phone extension connector if possible. Dial the number and listen for modem shrieks.

- If you hear undue background crackles and pops, your modem does too. Modems hate that. *[Call up your phone company and complain!—JH]*

- *Make sure* the RJ-11 plug is in the proper hole. One goes to the wall, the other to an optional phone or another modem.

- *Make sure* there's power and good phone cords attached.

- *Make sure* the cable is good. Be wary of checking the cable against older modem cables. Today's high-speed modems require a cable with an extra connection for hardware handshaking.

- Turn the modem off and on. Then your computer.

- Determine what has changed before trouble started. New extension? New system? New on-line service?

- Test with all extensions off, except for PowerBooks with internal modems.

- With AppleTalk turned off, put the modem cable in the printer port. Tell your software you've changed ports.

- Remember, your modem is making a call just like you do: listening for a dial tone, dialing, waiting for something to answer, and jabbering in a common language.

- If someone picks up an extension line while your modem is chitchatting, ka-blooey! The connection is done, crashed, kaput. Restart the session.

HOT TIP

- *[Radio Shack sells a "Data Guard," item 43-107, which blocks other phones when your modem is in use. $10 per other phone.—JH]*

- If you're at all serious, get a second phone line. Ma Bell frequently cuts deals on them. Benefits: testing; walking a partner through a direct connection; no more trashing a modem connection with an impulse to reach out and touch someone; displays unquestionable futurist credentials.

Diagnosing Connection Problems

HOT TIPS

If your trusty connection no longer connects.

- Your software is ill.

- The phone line has gone sour.

- The answering modem isn't.

- Your modem is dead. Dead modems are quite rare but you've had Why Me? days before.

If a new service won't connect. It could be any of the above. More likely, the cause is:

- The on-line vendor's software is faulty or poorly prepared.

- Your end of the bargain—configuring software—is not completed.

- Is the User ID spelled right? Capitals and lowercase?

- Is the Password entered carefully? Is the Caps Lock on?

- What about the modem init string? This can get tricky. More on this later.

- What about dialing string? Should there be a 9 or 8, or other access code first? An access code afterward?

You connect but soon lose it. This is probably a modem init string problem. Compare notes with someone who, with the same modem, successfully connects to the same service. Or talk to tech support at your on-line service. Chances are the problem has cropped up before, and a gearhead located the problem, issued an alert, and the techies are aware of a modem init string modification.

Is call waiting disabled? This is essential. Start by dialing your telco's Call Waiting Disable code, most typically "*70."

I was doing great until I signed up for the Internet. If you're using a SLIP or PPP dial-up Internet connection, you are attempting the most daunting modem connection in all the realm—with the possible exception of the fax I once tried to send to a steamship off Taiwan.

The problem is easy to summarize: Your fancy, technologically endowed Macintosh is playing "Look Ma, I'm a Unix Low-Bit Dumb Terminal." IP (Internet protocol) was not designed with dial tones in mind.

Your Internet provider surely issued detailed instructions about how to set up MacTCP and the SLIP or PPP software. *[None of my several Internet service providers had much of a clue about Macs. But fear not. All you need from your ISP are the router and name server addresses in numeric form (these are the same for PC users so your ISP won't mess these up) and the access node phone number that your modem must call (reason=ditto). Then get the FreePPP FAQ (bundled with the freeware FreePPP) and follow the explicit directions. They'll even work if you are using a SLIP connection!—SB]* There are many configuration nooks. Fill them meticulously.

Taming a fussy Internet connection usually consists of reinstalling the connection software, then comparing setups with someone who has a similar setup. You can easily find such a person, um, on the Internet.

- MacTCP in particular is easily broken. Always keep fresh spares handy.

- New PCI Mac? You can't run MacTCP and the newer TCP/IP control panel at the same time.

My computer keeps hanging when using Netscape. Everybody's Netscape does that. Now and then, completely empty Netscape's Cache folder. Give Netscape all the memory you can. The Mac escape sequence, Cmd Option Esc, works for emergency Net-escape but restart ASAP.

The screen says CONNECT 38,400! Wow! I'm jammin'! Joke's on you. Today's modems like you to aim high and sort things out for themselves. That's why we routinely set data rates a notch or two higher than what's possible. If upon connection

HOT TIPS

your modem dutifully responds with "connect 38,400" it's really saying, "Connected as you ordered, *sir!*" The modems have agreed on a mutual speed (note the cycle of different pitches) that could be 28,800, could be 4,500. To get a real reading, add Q0 V1 W2 to your modem init string. When you get a CARRIER message—CARRIER 9,600, for example—that is the real speed.

I got a telecom bill for $120. You too? Some telecom programs like to force the action. Check your preferences! My first Internet account was on a server 200 miles away. Eudora, the e-mail program, has a "Check Mail every *n* minutes" preference that defaults to 10. I left the house for six hours. Eudora made the call but did not know about hanging up.

Every time Net software such as Newswatcher or Netscape tries to force an Internet connection, my session is history. I must restart the computer.

My Duo keeps whining "serial port is in use." Duos are wonderful until you get to the trade-off part: the single port. Make sure your telecom software is configured for an internal modem if that's what you have. If not, turn off AppleTalk. Duo port madness is best solved by getting a MiniDock or better.

Apple Remote Access works no more. The ARA installer actually hacks the System file itself. Replace the System and you must reinstall ARA. Recheck your file sharing info. Make sure AppleTalk is on.

1-800-D-D-DEAD. If a commercial on-line service won't connect, try another number, even if it's long distance. CompuServe (800/544-3095) and AOL (800/716-0023; in Canada: 800/318-2265) charge for their 800 numbers but a minute or three won't hurt if it helps determine where the problem is. *[CompuServe Information Manager and the proprietary AOL software have the ability to make an 800 call to find a local number. This is a good test. Just be sure to set the modem speed to 2,400 bps (which is mandatory for these calls) before you try.—SB]*

PowerBook modem notes.

- Internal modems require an assortment of software extensions and settings. Rerun the modem's Installer package. Check all settings.

- Duos are fussy about their single port. See "My Duo keeps whining 'serial port is in use'" above.

- In the PowerBook Setup control panel, the nonsensical modem picker settings Normal (internal) and Compatible (external) were better labeled in earlier versions. See "Telecommunications Tips" for a harmless way to rename them.

General modem notes.

- Run the modem without Now Toolbox (this disables all Now Utilities). Corrupt Now preference files have a history of interfering with certain extensions.

- Desktop Macs make perfectly good use of any modem—Global Village users, take note—even if none of the supplied extensions are running. All that stuff is for faxing.

- Nevertheless, GV modem extensions result in a menu display declaring that the modem is on-line. A splendid reminder.

PCI (postmodern computing info). The new generation of PCI Macs ship with OpenTransport, a rewrite of the networking and communications architecture. It's brand new, buggy, and changing fast as this book goes to press. Be not afraid, however, because when it goes it goes faster.

- Global Village Teleport software v2.5.5 and earlier is incompatible with SerialDMA extension. Upgrade to Teleport 2.5.6.

I'm getting annnn-gry... If you can sense a pattern to the failure, you might be able to solve it by examining the AT command set for ways to modify the modem init string. "Useful AT Commands" includes a few of the handier codes to play with.

Useful AT Commands

&F or &F1, depending on your modem, resets it to the factory default high-speed setting.

Q0 returns a result code.
When used with V1, the modem blabs out its various experiences (busy, no dial tone, connect, and so on) while trying to connect.

X0 is Blind Dialing. The modem dials no matter what it hears, a desperation move if you're on a strange phone system.

%E1 is Enable Auto Retrain. The right modem on the other end will better set mutual speed.

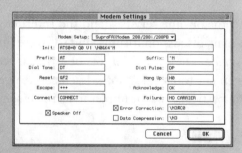

Every telecom application has a buried place where you can customize the "modem init string" with AT commands, your only way to change the deep workings of your modem. Remember: custom AT commands are an art, not a science.

&D2 cured a problem on my GV Teleport Gold. After hanging up it failed to completely disconnect from some servers until I added this.

[&Q0, which disables error correction, keeps my Express Modem from dropping the CompuServe line.—JH]

By, the, way, A comma in the dialing string gives pause, two or three seconds by factory default. This value can be changed within your modem with telecom software by changing the modem's S8 register.

There's good reason to alter a comma's pause value. If short-sighted software limits the number of characters in a dialing string, you can halve the number of commas by doubling the comma's pause value. Adding S8=6 to the init string changes the comma to give six-second pause.

The On-Line Universe

Despite the light-speed growth of the Internet, there's still plenty of interest in all the various other on-line services: the commercial services—big names such as CompuServe and America Online which charge a monthly fee for access to well-maintained conferences, databases, and more—as well as less well-known alternatives such as large bulletin board systems. The next chapter will give you the lowdown on the Internet, but for now we'll introduce the kinds of features you can expect to find on all of the services.

The Essentials (JH)

All the on-line services (and the Internet as well) offer the Three On-line Essentials: e-mail, discussion forums, and software libraries, plus live conversation usually known as *chats*. They also offer lots of extras: live conferences, major magazines, money management tools, and more. Each service gets its unique character and feel more from the particular way it implements the essentials than from its selection of extra services.

E-Mail

Many folks buy a modem just to use e-mail, and it's no wonder. E-mail is fast and relatively simple to use: Bang out a letter, tell your software to send it, and it's (usually) ready to be picked up by the recipient within minutes. Unlike "snail mail," as the paper kind is often called, you may exchange several letters with a friend in the space of a day.

Writing an e-mail message is not the same as writing a paper letter—it's often more like a telephone call, a short informative message (though e-mail, unlike phone calls, can be archived). Most people eliminate the salutation and closing, and of course there's no need to type in the date or inside address because the message's header

E-Mail Communication Between On-line Services   (JH)

The commercial services allow you to send and receive e-mail among them by routing the mail over the Internet. Here's a cheat sheet on how to address e-mail for each service. *[Note that dots replace commas when CIS addresses hit the Net. And then there's CompuServe's move from numbers to real user names.—DJS]*

From:	To:	Address
CIS		
	CIS	12345,677
	AOL	Internet:[user]@aol.com
	Prodigy	Internet:[user]@prodigy.com
	Internet	Internet:[user]@Internet.address
AOL		
	CIS	12345.677@compuserve.com
	AOL	[user]
	Prodigy	[user]@prodigy.com
	Internet	[user]@Internet.address
Prodigy		
	CIS	12345.677@compuserve.com
	AOL	[user]@aol.com
	Prodigy	[user]
	Internet	[user]@Internet.address
Internet		
	CIS	12345.677@compuserve.com
	AOL	[user]@aol.com
	Prodigy	[user]@aol.com
	Internet	[user]@Internet.address

Note: Brackets indicate where sender should type recipient's user name.

provides those. There are advocates of extreme informality, so don't be offended if otherwise intelligent people send you e-mail with typos and misspellings.

[Because of e-mail's ease of use and the speed with which it can be sent, you may find a sharp increase in your expectations for a quick response (and, more horribly, an increase in the expectations of those who e-mail you). You're now entering the e-mail Twilight Zone, where an hour in the on-line world is equivalent to a day off-line. Those letters to pen pals you used to procrastinate sending via "snail mail"…? You'd better go write them now!—JJ]

My dear friend 'user name'. Whenever you join any on-line service, you'll pick a *user name* (also known as a *user ID* or *screen name*) to identify yourself. Your user name doubles as your e-mail address, so pick something short that will remind people of you, and try to use something similar on every service you join. Though services such as America Online allow wild (and even stupid) screen names, refrain.

If you join more than one service, you'll have a different e-mail address for each service. Pick one service, the service you access most often or that you're likely to keep the longest, as your main public e-mail receptacle. Then you'll have one address to give out or put on a business card. If you get a lot of e-mail, or if you get e-mail on several services, you should look into e-mail management software (see "E-Mail Managers," earlier in this chapter).

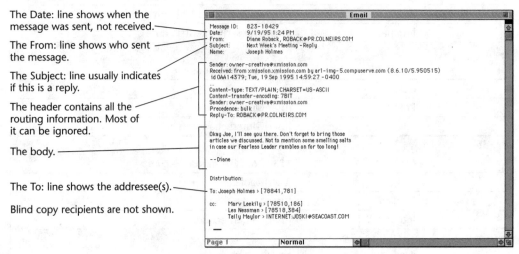

The Date: line shows when the message was sent, not received.

The From: line shows who sent the message.

The Subject: line usually indicates if this is a reply.

The header contains all the routing information. Most of it can be ignored.

The body.

The To: line shows the addressee(s).

Blind copy recipients are not shown.

The different parts of a typical e-mail message.

Every on-line service implements e-mail in a different way, but they all have some things in common. Mail always has a header filled with information including who sent the message and when. You must supply the *subject*—a descriptive title—the addressees' correct e-mail addresses, and of course the body of the message. When you reply to a message, everything is supplied automatically except the body. Some software automatically append the word "Re:" to the subject, the date and time are updated, and you are listed as the sender.

Attaching files to e-mail. Every commercial on-line service makes it easy to send a nontext file—an application, graphic, formatted text—to someone on the same service. But sending files between services, that is, over the Internet, is more complicated. Here's the short lesson: *Binhex* the file, which turns any file into plain text which you can simply append to the text of your e-mail. Use a commercial utility such as StuffIt Deluxe or John Stiles' $10 shareware HQXer (found on most on-line services). A Binhexed file must then be decoded by the recipient, and the free StuffIt Expander does the job very well. Recognize Binhex files by the suffix ".hqx." Some e-mail managers do this coding and decoding for you automatically. *[Auto-Binhexing might be the best reason to get Eudora Pro or Claris Emailer.—DJS]*

Mailing lists. E-mail is also a nifty way to sign up for mass mailings on various topics—everything from exotic music to technical support to Apple Computer press releases. Some lists mail out all the messages, or digests of them, contributed by all the folks who subscribe to the list, making a sort of e-mail-based discussion forum. Other lists are little more than electronic junk mail. *[Be warned: Some lists can flood your mailbox with 50 to 100 messages a day. If you don't have the time to plow through all the mail you'll be getting, try one or two lists, or better yet, get the digest, typically a weekly compendium of all the traffic on a server.—JO]*

Signing up typically involves sending a message to a list server (not the mailing address) with a subscribe command in the body and the name of the mailing list. (Lists usually include unsubscribe instructions at the end of every mailing.) The following table has a few to get you started.

Starter Mailing Lists

Mail List	To Subscribe
The Apple EvangeList: news to hearten Mac users.	E-mail MACWAY-REQUEST@SOLUTIONS.APPLE.COM. Any message will work.
The KidLink Connection: worldwide discussions for kids 10 to 15 years old.	E-mail LISTSERV@VM1.NODAK.EDU with only the words GET KIDLINK GENERAL *in the body.*
Robert Seidman's *Online Insider*, covering all the on-line services and the Internet.	E-mail LISTSERV@PEACH.EASE.LSOFT.COM and in the body of the message type SUBSCRIBE ONLINE-L FIRSTNAME LASTNAME (substituting your name) *in the body of the message.*
A word and a quote a day from Wordsmith.	E-mail WSMITH@WORDSMITH.ORG with SUBSCRIBE YOURFIRSTNAME LASTNAME *as the subject.*
Brock Meeks's CyberWire Dispatch.	E-mail CWD-L-REQUEST@CYBERWERKS.COM with only the word SUBSCRIBE *in the body.*

Discussion Forums

Forums are where public discussions occur. Also known as *roundtables*, *message boards*, *SIGs* (for special interest groups), or *conferences* (which confusingly also refers to live chats on some services), each discussion forum is devoted to a topic and divided up into subsections on subtopics. CompuServe's show business forum, for example (GO SHOWBIZ), is divided into 24 subsections, including Recent Films, Classic Films, Cult TV/Films, Soap Operas (one section for each network!), and Daytime

Talk Shows. Forums are run by *sysops* (SYStem OPerators), *forum leaders*, or *moderators*, who stir up conversations, enforce the rules, and answer questions. For many people (including yours truly), discussion forums are the heart and soul of on-line services.

Forum discussions don't occur in *real time*, as conversations do face-to-face. Instead a visitor composes a message, gives it an informative subject or title, addresses it to a specific person or to "All," and *posts*

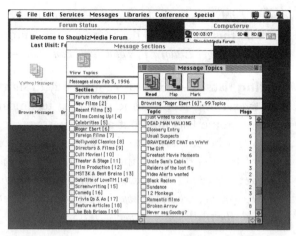

Browse the current subjects under discussion in Roger Ebert's message section, one of 24 message sections in CompuServe's Showbiz forum.

it in the appropriate forum and section. You might for example post a question about *Pulp Fiction* in CompuServe's Showbiz forum, in the section devoted to Recent Films, and title it "Pulp Fiction Briefcase?" (CompuServe allows only 24 characters in message titles).

Other visitors interested in films then *browse* the Showbiz forum by reading the list of message subjects, choosing to read the full text of messages that interest them. A visitor can then compose a reply to any message, or even to the replies themselves. The original message and the string of replies and replies to replies, all keeping the same subject, make up a *thread*. As powerful and useful as message threading is, not all services use it.

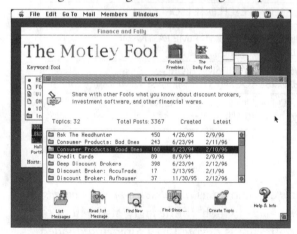

America Online's message board windows display the current topics under discussion. Messages can be browsed, but because AOL lacks message threading, it's not possible to follow the messages in order of replies, or to have a reply to your message displayed to you automatically.

These forum discussions sometimes take on the character of religious debates, and some especially inflammatory messages become known as *flames*. But for the most part, forum discussions are civil, and often lively and informative. They can go on for days and even weeks.

Something like 90 percent of the people who regularly visit forums are *lurkers*—people who read messages but never post any. What a shame. Lurkers miss out on the best part of on-line life.

Telephony (JH)

One promising technology that never quite got off the ground is Macintosh *telephony*—software and hardware that can make your Mac perform some telephone functions. A few mildly interesting telephony applications have come and gone, but with one exception the field has remained fairly barren.

Some time ago Apple introduced the *GeoPort,* a higher-speed serial port on AV and Power Macs, inaugurating what was to be a new cross-platform standard for voice, data, fax, and video over both analog and digital telephone lines. GeoPort never really took off as a standard, but Apple eventually—finally—released the **GeoPort Telecom Adapter Kit** ($125), which gives a GeoPort-equipped Mac the capabilities of a speakerphone, digital answering machine, and 14,400-bps fax modem tied to a limited personal information manager, and other software niceties. At this writing, Apple announced the availability of a V.34 28,800-bps modem.

The software/hardware bundle gives a Mac sophisticated telephony capabilities; the heart of the package is the 30-day demo version of **MegaPhone** by Cypress Research Inc., which adds the features of an advanced office phone system to your Mac, including speed dialing, call logging, a digital answering machine with remote message retrieval, and a speakerphone. When the 30 days runs out on the demo version of MegaPhone, a full version can be purchased for $50. It requires 2MB RAM, 10MB of hard disk space, speakers, and a microphone.

But before you dive, consider: Are you really making the best use of your multi-thousand dollar Macintosh to replace a $20 telephone and a $40 answering machine?

Discussion forums are also where software and hardware manufacturers offer on-line technical support. The best of these are staffed by folks who read your questions and leave you a reply within a day or so. Support questions can be addressed directly to the sysop or forum leader. This is a terrific resource, and all the reason you need to join an on-line service.

Libraries (JH)

All the services offer software you can download. The on-line universe is bursting at the seams with games, utilities, reading material, fonts, Mac System updates, demo versions of commercial software, and Frequently Asked Questions (FAQs) documents.

Downloadable software divides neatly into a few basic categories. *Freeware* is, of course, free—no strings attached. *Shareware* is Honor System software; it's fully functional, and, after you've tried it, you must either delete it or send the fee to the author. Closely related is *demoware*—demonstration versions of software which stop working after 30 days or so, or are crippled in some way, usually by disabling printing or saving.

No matter what you hear, computer viruses can't be transmitted by an e-mail message; viruses hop onto your hard drive when you download files. All of the commercial services do an excellent job of keeping their libraries clean, but bulletin boards aren't always so safe. Invest in a good virus detection utility, or download Disinfectant, a terrific freeware virus utility, available on all the services. (See Chapter 7 for more details on viruses.)

HOT TIP

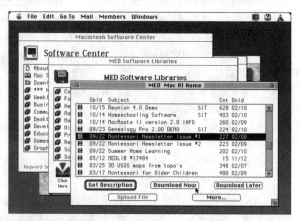

America Online's library windows display the number of times a file has been downloaded (under "Cnt"), one way to judge the popularity of a download.

To check for the most recently uploaded files:

- On America Online, select Search Software Libraries under the Go To menu, click the Past Week radio button, then click List Matching Files.

- On CompuServe, each forum has its own library. Using CompuServe Information Manager, go to a forum, select Search from the Libraries menu, leave the text fields blank, check the One Week Ago radio button, and click Search.

- On Prodigy, alas, there's very little software for the Mac. But give this a try: "Jump" "Download" to display a list of places that offer software; sometimes a button will display recent files.

Chat   (JH)

To enjoy a live chat, you'll have to develop some of the skills of a cryptanalyst to piece together the threads of conversations. The more participants, the more difficult to follow.

Most services also offer some form of *chat*, a live discussion between two people or a whole "room" full of people, all conducted by typing furiously. Chats are much more informal than forum discussions, and they're filled with arcane shorthand and short expressions which stand for such things as hugs and grins. They're often a kind of virtual singles bar, especially on America Online. Your enjoyment of chats will probably depend on your typing speed and ability to read sentence fragments. *[Tracking a single conversation amidst the thrashing ASCII is a splendid mental exercise.—DJS]*

Other Features

(JH)

Finally, each service touts a slew of special features, including on-line shopping, news, weather reports, sports info, airline reservations, on-line versions of popular magazines

and newspapers such as *People*, *Sports Illustrated*, *The New York Times*, and *Scientific American*, movie, book, and restaurant reviews, encyclopedias, interactive multiplayer games, stock quotes and financial services, and a myriad of others. Don't sweat the details on these—all the services offer more features than you'll be able to use in a lifetime, and many of the features are duplicated in a slightly different form on each service.

All the services offer a variety of travel services (such as America Online shown here), including airline reservation systems and on-line travel guides. Travel services are some of the most useful services available on-line.

Remember that the look and culture and feel of each service, and the kinds of people who populate it, are more likely to determine your satisfaction than the presence of a particular magazine or encyclopedia.

Commercial Services: The Choices

(JO)

America Online. Recently America Online (AOL) surpassed CompuServe in total subscribers. This is undoubtedly due to its advanced marketing strategy that involves

sending sign-up kits to every man, woman, and child on earth who has ever mentioned the word computer. These tactics aside, America Online has improved by leaps and bounds since its inception. More than any other service, AOL has made on-line services easier to use by virtue of a very graphically oriented user interface. AOL does not require you to enter any commands to use the service. On-line navigation can be performed by clicking on buttons or icons which take you to a specific location or another window full of more icons. This can get a bit tedious at times, and cause your screen to become

America Online's main window is your launching pad to the rest of the service. Unfortunately, as you navigate your way to your final destination, windows are not closed behind you, leading to clutter and memory consumption.

cluttered with a stack of windows. You can also navigate using keywords which are a much more efficient way to get to a specific forum or place on AOL. Because of this, it is best to learn the keywords for the places you frequent on AOL.

On-Line Etiquette: Ten Rules   (JH)

If you've ever visited France and watched American tourists shouting English orders at scowling Parisians, you know that it pays to do your homework and learn the local lingo. Violate the rules of on-line behavior and you'll be branded a *clueless newbie*, a newcomer who doesn't have the decency even to pick up the basics. Okay, you're warned. Study these few rules and you just may be mistaken for a veteran.

1. DON'T TYPE IN ALL CAPS! It's hard to read and it looks like YOU'RE SHOUTING!

2. *[It's OK to type like a banshee e.e. cummings; all lowercase is fine if perhaps a trace too hip. Always put two carriage returns at the end of each paragraph. And keep the grafs short.—DJS]*

3. Quote a relevant piece of a message to which you're replying, just enough to give needed context, but not the entire message. Nothing looks more idiotic than quoting an entire enormous message, followed by your reply: "Thanks for the tip!"

4. Don't delete messages to which you reply. In a public message forum, the original message helps others follow the conversation.

5. Address people by their first names—it may not be proper in a business letter, but it's standard on-line.

6. Stay out of flame wars. Just stay out. Life's too short and nothing ever, not ever, gets settled. Remember: The best way to extinguish a flame is to deprive it of fuel. Corollary: You'll never have the last word, because there's always a fool with even more time to waste.

7. Reread your messages before you post them. You'll be surprised how often you reconsider and decide to tone down the language.

8. Use smileys and emoticons, but sparingly (see the sidebar "Of Acronyms and Emoticons" later in this chapter). It's sometimes important to give readers a clue to your state of mind, but you might try writing so that they're not needed. You don't see Dave Barry peppering his column with little smiley faces, do you?

9. Give back as you take. Seek help, but don't forget to help others.

10. Finally, give the clueless newbies a break.

The AOL interface allows you to perform very limited customization. Unlike other services, you cannot create a window of frequently accessed places to speed navigation to them. You can however, store the keywords for up to ten of your favorite places and get to them using a menu or command-key combination. It is relatively easy to perform system-wide searches for items such as reference materials and files, making the service well-suited to novice users.

Everyone wants to check out the Internet hype, and America Online has been a pioneer in providing Internet connectivity. AOL members can browse the World Wide Web, access Usenet newsgroups and ftp servers directly from the service.

(See Chapter 23 for more details on these services.) AOL will also let members create and manage their own personal Web pages. Though their proprietary Web browser is weak (at the time of this writing), AOL was about to offer a choice of Netscape Navigator or Microsoft's Internet Explorer in its place.

America Online also allows parents to limit the areas that their children can access on the service, but AOL has made some other blundering moves in its attempt to preserve its "family values" image. Recently, it tried to ban the use of a word (breast) from its conference and discussion areas not realizing that this limited the ability to freely discuss a form of cancer.

[I, like many other telecom old-timers, despised AOL in the past. That's changed. It's now one of my favorite places on-line. I like the way I can access its own content and then, with a quick click, go straight onto the World Wide Web. The Web browser is more than okay, and the rest of the Internet tools are superb. For me, there is no better news reader. AOL Mail is fast, reliable, and capable of carrying multiple files as attachments. The news features are complete and posted fast. I get more breaking news from AOL than from any other source. There are still problems (message forums are awful), but overall, AOL is now the best general-purpose on-line service.—SB]

[As any AOL user can attest, what truly makes AOL unique (or irritating) is that folksy, enthusiastic "You've got mail!" greeting that booms out when mail is waiting. Also, many of the chapters of this book were originally submitted to the editor using AOL, enabling us to spirit these pages to your waiting arms.—JJ]

CompuServe. Once the king of the on-line services, CompuServe has seen its market share erode considerably. Competition from America Online, Prodigy, and Internet service providers has led to some welcome changes, most notably in cost and user interface. Its cryptic character-based interface is gradually being put out to pasture in favor of some more modern graphical user interfaces.

Among CompuServe's biggest assets are its forums. Its software is the only one that allows the creation of message threads. A thread of messages can branch in various directions based on the message being replied to.

MacPlanet (GO CIS:MacPlanet) is a gathering place on CompuServe for the Macintosh community. From here you can quickly access any of the Macintosh-related areas on CompuServe and ZD Net/Mac.

GOOD FEATURE

America Online's message areas strictly add messages to the end of the topic making it harder to follow the train of thought in a discussion. *[Impossible is a better word than harder. In this respect CompuServe stands way above every other service.—SB]*

CompuServe has recently overhauled CIM, its principle browser, which now sports an integrated Web browser. The new CIM 3 provides a number of improvements including support for multitasking (i.e. you can download and browse at the same time), improved search capabilities, and tracking recent places you have visited. CIM is a good tool for casual browsing or when you need interactive access to the service. Navigator is an off-line reader that, once you get the hang of it, is equally valuable. When using Navigator, you do not interact directly with CompuServe; instead you tell Navigator what you want it to do for you, let it do its thing, and then browse through the results once it has logged off. This has the potential of lowering your on-line costs since Navigator does things much faster than you can on-line. Navigator falls down, however, when it comes to browsing, since you do not directly interact with the service. For browsing, stick with CIM.

Like America Online, CompuServe offers access to the Internet, including the Web, newsgroups and ftp servers. At present, it lags behind AOL in ease-of-use and direct access to some of these features. Promised improvements are on the way so you should check in with CompuServe to get an update on Internet accessibility.

One big reason for Macintosh users to consider CompuServe is that it's home to many of the Mac's most renowned gurus. The editors and staff of leading Macintosh journals as well as those who slave to create many of the applications and utilities we use each day frequent CompuServe and contribute greatly to its wealth of content. It is home to MacPlanet, MAUG and ZD Net/Mac. If the folks on CompuServe cannot find the answer to *any* Mac-related question, there probably isn't one. CompuServe also publishes a monthly magazine sent to all service subscribers. It typically highlights some of the things that are happening on the service and provides useful tips for getting more out of CompuServe—and spending more time and money on-line.

Also-rans. Despite heavy hype at one time, Prodigy has not lived up to its promises. It still enjoys a strong following among Windows and DOS users, but the service has failed to show any strong commitment to the Macintosh as evidenced by its clumsy client software and lack of Mac-related content. If you are looking for an information-only service, Prodigy will probably do a good job of keeping you up to date with national, world, and financial news—but you will have to bear with the constant stream of advertisements that are displayed at the bottom of your screen. Prodigy does

Fun Locations On-Line (JH/DJS)

America Online: The Motley Fool

America Online; Keyword: Fool. The Fool is "a forum dedicated to the individual investor," but it's not nearly as dull or nerdy as that sounds. As serious as the advice is, the emphasis is on fun and humor. With lots of info and guidance for the novice investor, this popular AOL area has hundreds of stock folders, but the heart of the Fool is its nightly chat, where the floor is open for all kinds of discussions, from the ridiculous to the sublime. The Fool also runs The Fool Portfolio, a real on-line portfolio, and visitors are invited to trade along. As with the best forums, it's more like joining an on-line community than just learning about investing.

CompuServe: Motorcycle Forum

CompuServe; (GO RIDE). On-line communities come in two versions, conjecture (idealism) and reality (narcissism). Few forums have achieved the on-line ideal like CIS' Motorcycle Forum, GO RIDE. Its regulars are civil but hardly wishy-washy. They laugh a lot and quickly iron out the clowns who start those idiotic your-bike-sucks threads. Many friendships cultivated on-line have blossomed into asphalt-based meetings during which mountain roads are neatly carved. Traditionally, motorcyclists travel a lot and help each other. GO RIDE is a seamless extension of this tradition.

CompuServe: Apple Support Forum

CompuServe; (GO APLSUP). The term "support" is to be taken advisedly. *Apple does not answer questions here!* Still, Apple is a model company when it comes to making its software available on-line. The CIS version (they are as effective on AOL and the Web) includes every piece of software that's not retailed plus the excellent bi-monthly Information Alley. The Technical Library? Whoooo-wee. You'll be there for days.

CompuServe: Roger Ebert's gigs

CompuServe; (GO EBERT and GO SHOWBIZ). Except for the fact that he's clueless about Terry Gilliam being one of the century's great artists, Roger Ebert is the sharpest movie guy there is. His passion has made him famous and rich but not snooty. He hangs with celluloid homeboys in GO SHOWBIZ. His own forum, GO EBERT, has no give-and-take but is a hefty database of just about everything he's written.

allow you to customize the interface to the degree that you can set your preferred starting location and favorite places, but these aren't enough to attract many Mac users due to the lack of Mac-related content.

Two other obscure services are Delphi and GEnie. At present, it appears that Delphi is pursuing a second life as an Internet service provider while the future of GEnie will depend on its ability to update its stale character-based interface and improve its marketing to the Mac community.

The BBS Alternative   (JH)

Bulletin boards—small, usually inexpensive, specialized, and local on-line services—were once the only destination for a modem user. As the major commercial on-line services grow more enormous and the Internet becomes a household word, bulletin boards are now fading from view. Yet there are still good reasons for making use of a bulletin board system, or *BBS*.

Local bulletin boards. A local BBS can be a bargain. Many are free, and others charge a yearly fee of well under $100. You should especially seek out your local Mac user group's BBS, which is a terrific resource for Mac software and tech support from local experts. (Call 800/538-9696 for the name of your nearest Mac user group.) A local BBS is also a great resource for local people, news, and events. *[Always check your phone-in costs very carefully and go easy until you see an actual phone bill. If a "local" BBS isn't local by phone company measurements, it can quickly cost you the price of a new luxury car in phone bills.—SB]*

WARNING

GOOD FEATURE

Unlike the old days (just ten years ago!), small bulletin boards are no longer synonymous with an arcane command-line interface. More and more boards use graphical interfaces, the most popular of which is SoftArc's First Class. After downloading the First Class Client software (available from any First Class BBS by logging on with any standard communications software), you can dial into any First Class BBS and use easy icon and menu-based navigation. Libraries, mail, and discussion areas are grouped in nested folders against attractive graphics.

First Class is a far cry from the old type-a-menu-choice BBS software of the past. Not only is it incredibly easy to navigate the folders and lists, but it's darned attractive as well!

There are two other popular graphical BBS interfaces: Spider Island's TeleFinder and ResNova's NovaLink Professional. As with First Class, each makes use of client software which you launch on your Mac. The client software for TeleFinder and NovaLink must be downloaded first from an on-line service or the Internet—you can't log onto a TeleFinder or NovaLink BBS before you have the client software.

Each of these BBS systems also allows you to log onto the bulletin boards via a TCP/IP Internet connection. (More on TCP/IP connections in Chapter 23.) This means that with a local call to your Internet provider, you can dial into any distant BBS using this feature. You can, for example, dial into Planet BMUG, a California-based First Class BBS operated by the world's largest Mac user group, from anywhere in the world just by calling a local number and launching the properly configured First Class Client software. (Full access requires a paid membership; e-mail Planet BMUG at BMUG@aol.com for details.)

ECHO and The WELL. A select few bulletin boards, notably California's **The WELL** and New York City's **ECHO**, are justifiably famous for the consistently high quality of discussions. Though each charges prices similar to commercial services, each offers a sense of intelligence and community spirit not easily found anywhere else.

Originally established by *Whole Earth Catalog* founder Stewart Brand, The Well ran for years as the West Coast home of an intense and closely knit community of

The Well's conferences on the World Wide Web are easy to access, are attractive, and are easy to use.

computer users interested in serious conversation on a broad range of subjects. The board grew famous for its fanatical Grateful Dead following and its vocal hacker community. Membership has grown dramatically, but the strong identity remains. In 1995, with blurring distinctions between on-line services and the Internet, the board developed proprietary software to move its discussion conferences into a members-only area on

GOOD FEATURE

the World Wide Web called Well Engaged. Now The Well conferences are not only easy to use, they're accessible to anyone with Web access. Voice: 415/332-9200; data: 415/332-8410 ($20 registration fee; $15 per month for unlimited hours in conferences).

ECHO (East Coast Hang Out), on the other hand, while also aiming for that same high level of community and grown-up discussion, is stuck in command-line hell,

If you can stand to memorize obscure commands like "ffs" and "ind," you'll find the discussions on ECHO to be a cut above those found on most BBSs and commercial services.

requiring memorization of arcane commands such as "sh item 5" which must be typed at the ubiquitous "And Now?" prompt. Still, it succeeds well in offering plenty of smart and lively conversation in such diverse conferences as Over 40, High Times, Games/Toys, Angst, Parenting, and Writing. And, like The Well, it manages to extend itself out into the real city beyond the computer monitor by regularly scheduling gatherings around New York. For that reason, ECHO turns out to be a great

BAD FEATURE

Of Acronyms and Emoticons   (JH)

People can't talk and write on-line like they do in the rest of the world. They *emphasize* words with asterisks, for instance, because there's no accepted standard for bold or underlining in the primitive world of telecom. In addition, each on-line service has its own culture, with customs, mores, and lingo slightly different from the others. Here's a quick and dirty guide to common usage.

Emoticons

These are unbearably cute little faces created from standard typographical characters, used to show an emotion that isn't otherwise obvious. It's sometimes important, for instance, to show that you're only kidding: Don't be an idiot! :-) To see the smiling face, turn your head on its left ear and look for the eyes, nose, and mouth. The most common three:

:-)	Just kidding!
:-(	Bummer!
;-)	Wink

There are dozens, even hundreds of these, but you'll mostly see variations on these three. Some folks use less common variations, such as <G> which means "grin." You can put various indications within such brackets. <blush!>

=%?)	*{There is room for creativity when emoting.—JJ}*

Acronyms

There seems to be an infinite number of on-line acronyms, but here's a sample of the most common:

BTW	by the way
GR&D	grinning, running, and ducking
IMHO	in my humble opinion
LOL	laughing out loud
MorF	male or female? (popular in AOL chats)
OTOH	on the other hand
ROFL	rolling on the floor laughing
RTFM	read the #@%$&! manual
PMFJI	pardon me for jumping in; I don't care for this one because it makes no sense in a public forum where jumping in is the whole idea.
TNOWEMN	the name of which escapes me now. (I made this one up; there's no sign it's catching on.)

way to meet people the old-fashioned way—face to face. (Voice: 212/292-0900. $19.95/month for 30 hours, $1.00 each additional hour up to 60 hours; no charges after 60 hours.)

Now How Much Would You Pay?   (JH)

It's difficult to predict exactly what on-line services will cost. It can depend on your exact usage pattern and whether you use areas that carry surcharges, such as CompuServe's searchable magazine database. But here's a comparison to get you started. In the following table we've done a calculation of *roughly* what it will cost you to use each service for five hours, ten hours, 20 hours, and 40 hours (easy to exceed, especially if you have two or more users).

Commercial Services Price Comparison

	CIS 1	CIS 2	AOL	Delphi 1	Delphi 2
Base Monthly Fee	$9.95	$24.95	$9.95	$10.00	$20.00
"Free" Hours	5	20	5	4	20
$ per Additional Hour	$2.95	$1.95	$2.95	$4.00	$1.80
Est. Cost 5 Hours	$9.95	$24.95	$9.95	$14.00	$20.00
Est. Cost 10 Hours	$24.70	$24.95	$24.70	$34.00	$20.00
Est. Cost 20 Hours	$54.20	$24.95	$54.20	$74.00	$20.00
Est. Cost 40 Hours	$113.20	$63.95	$113.20	$154.00	$56.00

	Prodigy 1	Prodigy 2	GEnie[1]	The Well BBS[2]	ECHO BBS	ISP[3]
Base Monthly Fee	$9.95	$29.95	$8.95	$15.00	$19.95	$25.00
"Free" Hours	5	30	4	unlimited	30	60
$ per Additional Hour	$2.95	$2.95	$3.00	none	$1.00	$2.00
Est. Cost 5 Hours	$9.95	$29.95	$11.95	$15.00	$19.95	$25.00
Est. Cost 10 Hours	$24.70	$29.95	$26.95	$15.00	$19.95	$25.00
Est. Cost 20 Hours	$54.20	$29.95	$56.95	$15.00	$19.95	$25.00
Est. Cost 40 Hours	$113.20	$59.45	$116.95	$15.00	$29.95	$25.00

Notes:

1 Rates are higher during certain hours.

2 $20 registration fee.

3 For comparison, typical rates of an average Internet service provider.

Fax   (JO)

Virtually every modem you can buy today also has some fax capability built-in. At the very least, they can send faxes and most can also receive.

For many people, it's hard to grasp the concept behind computer-based fax. Having a fax modem is not quite the same as having a stand-alone fax machine. You cannot, for example, hold a piece of paper up to your screen to fax it. (Don't laugh—I've actually had someone ask this.) One way to think of computer-based fax is as a means of printing your documents remotely. The most common way to send a fax from your Mac is to use a print driver. Open the Chooser and select the fax icon as your output device. Then simply print from within an application. *[A common shortcut is to hold down Ctrl Shift while dropping the Edit menu. "Print" becomes "Fax."—JH]* An altered print dialog prompts you for fax information: the recipients, the phone numbers of their fax machines, and perhaps a cover page of your choosing.

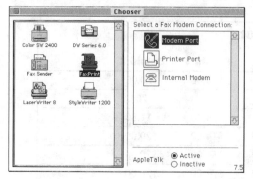

Fax software acts like a printer driver, and so it's controlled by a fax driver which you access from within the Chooser, under the menu.

Receiving faxes on your computer also presents challenges. First, your computer must be turned on and your fax software must be set to answer calls. If you have only one telephone line, this process takes some coordination with the person sending the fax, since you probably don't want your fax modem answering all of your calls. When you receive a fax, you can either view the image on your screen or print it. Faxes are stored as images on your hard disk and can be quite large; printing them can be time consuming. Some fax software ships with a companion program that will perform optical character recognition (OCR) on your received faxes. In essence, OCR turns a fax into a word processing or spreadsheet document that you can then work with.

Fax Utilities

There are a few additional products you can buy to make faxing easier. If you want to fax things such as newspaper or magazine clippings, an inexpensive scanner will let you capture these images for faxing. Visioneer's **PaperPort** ($300) is an excellent product for this use. If you're worried about having your fax modem answer calls, you can buy a phone line adapter from stores such as Radio Shack ($75) that will answer your calls, detect a voice or fax call, and route the call to your phone or fax modem. There are also software utilities included with some fax modems to route incoming calls to your fax software or Apple Remote Access if necessary.

Fax Applications

With few exceptions, the fax software that comes bundled with a modem either has very limited capabilities, conflicts with some other software on your Mac, or its user interface is so poor that it makes you want to avoid faxing altogether. There are exceptions, of course. In a few cases, the software bundled with your modem is good, even great. This includes **GlobalFax** from Global Village, which is included with its TelePort and PowerPort line of modems, and **FAXcilitate** from PSI, bundled with Supra modems. Both of these are full-featured and should be more than adequate for a variety

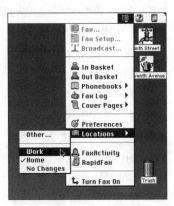

FAXcilitate adds a menu to the menu bar, making it easy to access its features.

of faxing needs. GlobalFax is particularly well-designed and extremely easy to use and customize. The same software can also be used with Global Village's line of network-based fax servers, so you can use the same fax software on your PowerBook, at home, or at the office.

If you need to look beyond the software bundled with your modem, or if you bought a PC modem that doesn't include Mac fax software, your best choices are Delrina's **FaxPro**, STF Technologies' **FAXstf**, or a shareware product called **ValueFax** which is available from CompuServe and other on-line services.

These applications are flexible and support a wide variety of modems, so you can upgrade your modem without replacing your fax application. Delrina, a big

The STF Manager application is a central application for managing all FAXstf-related activities and settings, calling up other "applets" to perform such tasks as viewing faxes or changing preferences. FAXstf allows multiple address books and supports import and export of names and phone numbers.

player in the Windows market, has earned an undeserved bad reputation for porting the software from Windows. Although some of the dialog boxes are a bit busy, the program works well and is compatible with other software. It's easy to import and export fax addresses, and you can maintain a number of different fax address books. You cannot, however, add comments to the cover page of a fax, an annoying omission.

FAXstf version 3.2 has addressed some of its former stability problems, but it's still apparently incompatible with some extensions. The software is also a bit pokey, even on faster 68K and PowerPC-based Macs. The user interface is only so-so: The program is broken down into so many components that it's hard to determine which part you are using at any given time.

GlobalFax is the winner here, but unfortunately, it works only with Global Village modems. Some day another maker will wake up and emulate Global Village's attractive features in a general-purpose package.

Telecommunications Tips

HOT TIPS

Mac Bible on-line (Arthur Naiman/Randy Singer). *The Macintosh Bible* has its own forum on America Online (Keyword: macbible). You can (among other things) leave messages for your favorite Peachpit authors and ask questions in the Message Center.

Closing the serial port (Randy Singer/HN). Sometimes when you switch from one communications program to another, or even if you try to start the same program after a crash while it was on-line, you get an error message that the modem port is in use and that the program you are launching cannot use it; under some circumstances the program may even crash. That's because the first program told the Mac operating system it was using the port, and the system, for obvious reasons, won't let two programs try to send data out the same port at the same time. Restarting your Mac, or using the free utility CommCloser, will solve the problem.

The free CommCloser will close a stuck serial port without making you restart your Mac.

Fax (JH). Many folks are stuck with a fax modem at home that cannot scan newspaper articles and pictures, and a stand-alone fax machine at work, where you're not allowed to make long-distance calls. Here's a two-step trick to get around the rules. At work, fax the newspaper article from the stand-alone fax machine to the fax modem on your Mac at home. For most folks, that's a local call. When you get home, fax that document long distance on your own phone bill using your fax software's "fax forwarding" feature.

If your home Mac is a long-distance call, fax the document to your office Mac and carry the file home on a floppy. Use StuffIt Deluxe or Compact Pro to make the fax files small enough for a floppy or split them up on more than one disk.

Auto-mail retrieval in CompuServe Information Manager (JH). CompuServe Information Manager has Send & Receive All Mail and Get New Mail commands (under the Mail menu), but CIM stays on-line after checking for mail. Hold down ⌘ while selecting Send & Receive All Mail, or ⌘ Option while selecting Get New Mail, and CIM will do its thing and then log off automatically.

CompuServe Navigator (JH).
* Copy Table, found in the Edit menu, acts like a normal clipboard copy except that every series of spaces is converted into a tab. This is very useful when copying text that has been formatted with spaces substituted for tabs and indents.

* Shortcut: Highlight the thread subject in the Session View window and—avoiding the Summary menu—type E to retrieve the entire thread so far, O for this one message, B for this branch, and T for all new thread messages next session only.

* If you need a CompuServe local access number when you're traveling, use Navigator in terminal mode (or any telecommunications application) and dial 800/346-3247. At the Host Name prompt, type PHONES and then follow the prompts.

Stop that annoying AOL graphics delay! (JH). If you're really tired of waiting for America Online to send graphical elements to your hard drive just so the splash screens look pretty, locate and install a copy of ArtValve. It's a control panel that stops AOL from performing that annoying interruption, and it substitutes a generic icon for the missing graphics. You can find it on America Online.

Me and my buddy want to play Network Candyland with a modem but ... (DJS). Thanks to today's point-and-shoot telecom software, knowledge of basic terminal programs such as ZTerm and (violins swell) MacTerminal is a dying art. Wrangling a terminal program is a handy craft for no other reason than for the day when you are called on to perform an emergency instantaneous file transfer between Kalispell and Paris: *We need that serum formula now or fungus will eat the Matisse!* Knowing how to use a terminal program is your ticket to heroism.

* The other modem must be attuned to your parameters. There are lots. Certain ones are standard: No Parity, 8 Data Bits, 1 stop bit. Set them as you wish but make sure they're the same on both ends.

* Data transfer rate? Shoot for the moon. The modems will decide the real speed.

* The host modem (the one taking the call) must be in Answer mode.

- Once the connection is made both ends are on equal ground. Type toodle-oos to each other. Be sure to press ⟨Return⟩ every 60 characters or so.

- To transfer files, one end chooses a Send command, the other Receive. As before, make sure you pick the same protocol, be it Ymodem, Zmodem, *ad nauseam*.

How to get your modem to dial out using your calling card number (DJS). Your mileage may vary. Fine-tune your dialing string like this:

1. Using head and hands, make the connection—up to the point where you pay. Punch the numbers, time the pauses.

2. Compose your dial string and run it.

3. Listen on the computer speaker and note how closely you've placed your pauses. Fine-tune it.

4. Save variations—different card numbers, different originating area codes.

The comma is the crucial item. It's a two-second pause, probably.

To check and change its value:

1. With a telecom program, type ATS8? and return.

2. If the modem returns 002, a comma indeed begets two seconds.

3. To change a comma to three seconds, enter ATS8=3.

```
9, 1 800 225 5288 ,,,,,,,, 1 ,,, 307 733 1716 ,, 307 773 0987 ETC

Gets out of              Auto-Lady          Bong!
motel, pauses.           asks for "1".

     Dials AT&T access,        Dials server's       Calling card number,
     waits for prompt.         modem.               coyly presented.
```

Here's the dialing string that one day, from a motel in Mexican Hat, Utah, made whoopee with a server 800 miles away.

How to log on with ARA without lifting a finger (DJS). Okay, so you lift one finger. Twice.

There's no better illustration of Macintosh elegance than the combined power of Apple Remote Access and aliases. The way our forefathers logged on to a remote server is a complicated task no one should be asked to perform. You can set up a Mac

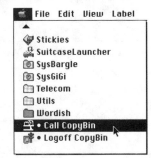

to reduce this alchemy to two menu items. One logs on and mounts the remote volume. The other logs off.

1. Using ARA, log on to the server.

2. Mount the folder you regularly access.

3. Make an alias of it. Log off.

4. Rename the new alias •**Call CopyBin**. (Press Option 8 to get the bullet.)

5. Rename (or make an alias of) the Apple menu item **Remote Access Disconnect** so it's •**Logoff CopyBin**. The bullets force them downward together and give them, as David Byrne might say, specialness.

6. Drop both into the Apple Menu Items folder.

7. Now test the loveliness of it all. Selecting the •**Call CopyBin** menu item kicks ARA into gear. It makes the call and mounts the folder. All you have to do is type your password.

Bullets group items at the bottom of the ⌘ menu.

To log off, select •**Logoff CopyBin** from the ⌘ menu.

How to convert your PowerBook's setup dialog to logical verbiage. No one, but no one, can remember what "Compatible" and "Normal" means. This is Apple-ese for telling your PowerBook whether you're using an internal or external modem. *[Don't fret if you can't find the offending control panel. Later versions use improved language.—JH]*

Don't ask.

1. Make a copy of PowerBook Setup if a clean retreat path sounds like a good idea.

2. Launch ResEdit. Open the PowerBook Setup control panel.

3. Double-click the STR# resource.

Open the STR# resource with ResEdit.

HOT TIPS

4. Double-click ID number -4046. Behold the offending text.

5. Change the wording to something you like.

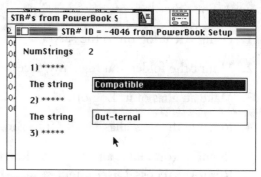

Wield etymological empowerment here.

6. Quit ResEdit and save your changes. Check it out.

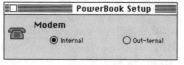

Now we're talking.

23 { The Internet

Unless you've been hiding in a cave on a mountain top in Tibet, you already know terms such as *World Wide Web* and *Netscape* and *Information Superhighway*, if only from reading the newspaper or watching TV. The Internet may be the most overhyped technology since the videophone debuted at the 1964 World's Fair, but unlike the videophone, millions of people use the Internet every day. (In fact, as you'll read later in this chapter, an Internet technology called CU-SeeMe acts like a videophone.) But in this case, despite the steep learning curve and the barricades to access, the hype actually has a hard time keeping up with the reality.

The Internet is more than just an entertaining place to spend a little time. In the near future, it's likely to become deeply integrated into our day-to-day computer use, so much so that it may eventually become an extended part of most operating systems. Your desktop Mac will become more and more like a single client on the world's largest network, and every distant file on the Internet will be as accessible as any other file in a folder on your Mac.

But we're getting a bit ahead of ourselves! In this chapter we'll stick to the basics, passing along information about what's currently out there and how to get to it.

Our Pledge: The terms *Information Superhighway* and *Cyberspace* will not appear in this chapter.

Contributors

Joseph O. Holmes (JH) <http://www.inter port.net/~joholmes/> is the chapter editor.

Jonathan Oski (JO) is vice president, manager of network and technology planning at BOT Financial Corporation in Boston. He is also a contributing editor for *MacWEEK*.

David J. Swift (DJS) is a photographer, writer, musician and computer consultant who, thanks to telecommunications and overnight-anywhere delivery, lives in Jackson, Wyoming with impunity.

Steven Bobker (SB) <http://www.voicenet. com/~rawfish> has been editor-in-chief of *MacUser,* a sysop on CompuServe and eWorld, and even met his wife on-line.

Contents

A Quick and Dirty Overview (JH)

Even more than with other computer technologies, connecting to and using the Internet can overwhelm you with arcane details and obscure terminology. To help you keep the forest in view even as you work among the trees, here's a brief overview of what's involved in getting and keeping connected. And remember to read up on the basics of Telecommunications in Chapter 22.

The Internet is nothing more than a few million computers—at homes, offices, and universities, all connected together over telephone lines and communicating using a variety of different *protocols*, or rules, to transfer text, pictures, files, and even sound. We start off the chapter with the story of the Internet. It's not just an interesting tale—understanding how the Internet evolved and what it's made of will help you better understand how to use it.

Your Mac may already be set to connect to the Internet if you're on a network that's attached to the Net—office workers and university folks should talk to their official computer wranglers for details. If you're lucky, you'll just need to pick up the various Internet applications—see the applications we recommend under each of the subsections of "The Main Features of the Internet" later in this chapter.

But from home, you'll almost certainly connect using a modem—that's called a *dial-up account*—and you'll do that by using the modem to dial up an Internet service provider, or *ISP*. We'll help you choose an ISP in "How to Get There From Here" and in the sidebar "Ten Questions to Ask an ISP."

The Internet communicates through a special Internet protocol known as TCP/IP. Some connections—*PPP* or *SLIP* connections (see "The Net Gets Legs" later in this chapter)—require you to install special TCP/IP software, typically the MacTCP control panel plus either a MacPPP or MacSLIP extension, and these things take careful configuration. Check out "How to Get There From Here" and the sidebar "Setting Up TCP: The Basics." A commercial on-line service such as America Online, on the other hand, offers a simple preconfigured connection without extra control panels or extensions.

Finally, Internet addresses will be a lot easier to understand after you read the sidebar "How to Read a URL."

You may notice that we place Internet addresses throughout this chapter in brackets like so: <http://www.apple.com>. This is to make the beginning and end of each address unambiguous, so, for instance, you'll know that the period which ends the sentence isn't part of the address—type everything within but not including those brackets. We also usually provide an address to the directory of a downloadable file, rather than to the file itself. Filenames and versions change so often that a pointer to the file itself would be quickly outdated.

Don't worry if all this doesn't make complete sense the first time through. Come back if you get confused. We'll be right here when you need us.

What is it? How Do it Know? (DJS)

The Internet is a 24-hour conference call among every computer in the world that wants to take part. The Internet used to be an exclusive club of smart people using dumb computers but that situation has changed drastically.

In some cases it's been reversed.

One Million B.P.C.

The Internet's roots grew and flourished in the Cold War, B.P.C. (before personal computers). Scientists felt compelled to develop fail-safe telecommunications (in case of a nuclear attack). There were no dial-up connections then; if a computer was turned on, it was on-line. This led to Internet protocol (IP), a common code developed so all computers could recognize all others at any moment. Therefore, all *packets*, or bits of information sent, would find their destinations, even if one packet got there by way of Livermore and Austin while the next packet found its way through Los Alamos by way of Chicago.

Such is the liquid essence of the Internet: push here, it expands there. Defense (military, factory, and of course

The Internet was designed to survive the loss of individual nodes by spreading out the responsibility for passing the information along to its destination.

university) computers would remain linked—alive!—and chattering under engagement even as unlucky computers took direct nuke hits. (This impenetrability would come back to haunt politicians, but that's another story.) By 1969, the rudiments of today's Internet were in place, wholly owned by the Department of Defense, and known as ARPANET.

IP had no trouble spreading far and wide. By the 1980s, the National Science Foundation responded to the growth of on-line computers by absorbing, upgrading, and expanding the Department of Defense's Internet structure. And NSF permitted initial forays by commercial Internet providers such as FidoNet and DECnet.

However, IP was designed for dumb terminals (keyboards and screens attached to mainframes rather than PCs) using the modest Unix character set. As more types of computer operating systems (or *platforms)* took to the Internet, malleable software innovations appeared to accommodate them.

The Net Gets Legs

It wasn't enough that computers on the Net could "talk" to one another. Tinkerers developed strong, uniform protocols to upload and download files (FTP); a graphical navigation tool for accessing directories among disparate platforms (Gopher); ways to route, reroute, and account for e-mail (SMTP); and word-based, rather than numerical, domain addresses (a private, nonprofit organization, InterNIC, became the clearinghouse).

The new breed of self-booting and frequent-flyer computers needed to log onto the Internet from anywhere. This brought us dial-up connections via *SLIP* (Serial Line Internet Protocol) and *PPP* (Point-to-Point Protocol), a boon for the burgeoning ranks of commercial Internet access providers.

While the Internet was plodding along in relative seclusion from the public eye, a growing number of PC users felt brave enough to try getting a modem to work. Most were unaware of the Internet but knew of proprietary on-line services, the largest being CompuServe. Such services grew at a solid rate by selling access to a wealth of on-line databases and chatty customers. America Online, a bold startup, used aggressive marketing and slick dedicated software to turn on-line services into a consumer product explosion.

Nonetheless, CompuServe and AOL were not "on the Internet" in the strictest sense; the Internet was "free." The borders between proprietary on-line services and the Net began dissolving in the early '90s, however. Everyone with an e-mail address could swap messages inside or outside the traditional Internet.

The Essential—and Essentially Free—Internet Tool Kit

Two reasons to pick up all these recommended utilities and applications: First, they all make life on the Net easier. Second, they're free! Dig in!

Internet Config by Quinn and Peter N. Lewis (free)
<ftp://ftp.share.com//pub/Internet-configuration/>

Numerous Internet applications demand the same arcane setup info. Internet Config is a single repository of your profile and preferences for the increasing number of applications that look for IC before bothering you. Quinn's Read Me is a stitch, too.

Internet Config lets you configure (almost) all of your Internet tools by filling in the blanks just once.

ICeTEe by Quinn and Peter N. Lewis (free, Bundled with Internet Config)

Command-clicking a URL in most text applications (but not big word processors) will automatically launch or switch to the appropriate Internet tool and take you straight to that address. Neat!

Eudora Light from Qualcomm (free)
<ftp://ftp.qualcomm.com//quest/mac/eudora/Light/>

A well-designed e-mail application that includes supreme interactive help. Learn good e-mail habits such as organizing and trashing messages, and neatly accumulating e-mail addresses. Learn it before buying Eudora Pro or Claris Emailer. You'll make a wiser decision. (Eudora Pro and Claris Emailer are reviewed in Chapter 22.)

Acrobat Reader from Adobe (free)
<http://w1000.mv.us.adobe.com/Acrobat/>

Acrobat displays fully formatted text and graphics that are identical to the original document no matter the platform. Spot Acrobat files by their .pdf (portable document format) tags and huge size—a single page of text can be 150K instead of 2K. (Acrobat files will be fine once we have the bandwidth.) Meanwhile, Acrobat Readers let you read as well as print PDF files, and you will prefer the latter.

StuffIt Expander from Aladdin (free)
<http://www.aladdinsys.com/obstufex.htm>

The Net is going to toss another file format at you: Binhexing, which is tagged .hqx or .bin, turns all sorts of coding into Internet-friendly text characters. Mac files (except raw text) must be encoded to a least-common-denominator form to pass through the Internet.

(DJS/JH)

It's common to get a file that has been stuffed, then binhexed. No matter how it has been encoded, dragging the file's icon onto the StuffIt icon will turn it inside out properly. Amazing beast, this.

Macintosh Drag-and-Drop from Apple (free)
<ftp://sam.austin.apple.com/Apple.Support.Area/Apple.Software.Updates/US/Macintosh/
    System/Other_System/>
(You need this extension if you have System 7.1. System 7.5 has Drag-and-Drop built-in.)

My editor asked me to include a URL manager, but those I've seen are too huge and convoluted considering the simplicity of the problem. The idea of URL storage is to eliminate typing; a single error and the destination's a goner. Drag-and-Drop not only eliminates typing, it turns the formerly miraculous Copy-Click-Paste into a single swipe of the mouse. Netscape Navigator and Microsoft Internet Explorer effectively store most URLs as bookmarks. After that, Drag-and-Drop plus a list manager is the answer: Stickies, Note Pad, and Scrapbook support it. Most new applications do, too.

Tex-Edit Plus by Tom Bender ($10)
<http://hyperarchive.lcs.mit.edu/HyperArchive/Archive/text/>

A jewel of a text-wrangler. A good portion of Net surfing is saving text for off-line reading. A lot of that text ends up ugly. Tex-Ed contains a huge, savvy assortment of one-pass tweaks that straighten out and further format text. It supports system-wide Drag-and-Drop, shows PICTs, and is fast as all get-out.

MacWeather 2 by Chris Kidwell ($10)
<http://hyperarchive.lcs.mit.edu/HyperArchive/Archive/comm/tcp/>

Okay, less than essential but a delight. Nothing to talk about? Flying somewhere? MacWeather logs onto a server that displays the latest weather information from hundreds of cities.

MacTCP Switcher by John Norstad (free)
<ftp://mirror.apple.com/mirrors/Info-Mac.Archive/
    comm/tcp/conn>

Say you're home from the office and your PowerBook needs to switch to different TCP/IP settings? This utility makes it a snap, but unless you're using Open Transport (Apple's newest networking/communications architecture), you'll need to restart between switches.

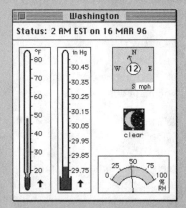

MacWeather can serve as your own little Internet Weather Channel.

How to Read a URL (JH)

Before you dig any deeper into this chapter, you'll need to know a little about Internet addresses, known as *URLs*, for *Uniform Resource Locators*. Most people pronounce it "You Are Ell," though some folks pronounce it "Earl" (which is why otherwise literate people may sometimes write "an URL"). Every accessible resource on the Net has its own unique URL, and you can learn a bit about what a URL points to by reading it piece by piece. This is a distinctly useful talent.

URLs are divided into three parts. First comes the *protocol*, a few letters that specify both the resource at the address as well as the tool that will reach it. After a separator—either // or the "at" sign (@)—comes the *domain*, which spells out the host computer or network on which the resource is located. Finally, beginning with a slash, you'll find the *file path* through the machine's hierarchy of directories all the way down to the resource itself.

E-mail—Look for the @

If the separator is an @, it's an e-mail address.

Every Internet e-mail address begins with the addressee's user name, the unique name assigned at the service or company. For example, Bob Cratchit may have picked his own user name, "bcratchit," on his Internet service provider, Dickens Internet Services. On the other hand, his office network at Scrooge, Inc., may have assigned him the user name "bobc".

The portion following the @ separator is the host on which that user has an e-mail account, known as the *domain*. The domain breaks down into *subdomains*, specifying first the organization or company, then typically the machine, and then a final three-letter *domain type* : "com" indicates a commercial organization; "net," an Internet service provider; "gov," a U.S. government site; "edu," an educational institution, such as a college or university; "org," a nonprofit organization; and "mil," for the military. (You can find a guide to country codes at <http://ics.uci.edu/WebSoft/wwwstat/country-codes.txt>.) Thus Tiny Tim's e-mail address at Oxford University may be ttim@oxford.edu.

Domains aren't picked just willy-nilly—a host must purchase and register a domain with an organization known as InterNIC <http://www.internic.net>. If you'd just love to have ebeneezer@scrooge.com as your e-mail address, don't print up your business cards just yet. Someone else may already have registered the domain name "Scrooge."

You can e-mail someone from anywhere in the on-line universe by addressing a message to: username@service.xxx. Thus write to Bob Cratchit at bcratchit@dickens.net or bobc@scrooge.com. You must know Cratchit's *exact* user name and the exact name of his service. One little typo and your message will bounce back to you undelivered or disappear into the ether forever. Thus, your friend Tiny Tim may have an account on America Online, but simply guessing at his e-mail address, ttim@aol.com, will probably miss the mark.

Now let's say that, by coincidence, someone else also picked the user name "bobc." That creates no confusion so long as he's on a different service, because his e-mail address

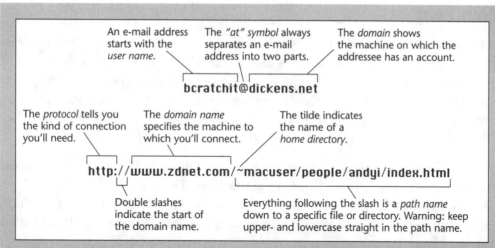

An e-mail address starts with the *user name*.

The *"at"* symbol always separates an e-mail address into two parts.

The *domain* shows the machine on which the addressee has an account.

bcratchit@dickens.net

The *protocol* tells you the kind of connection you'll need.

The *domain name* specifies the machine to which you'll connect.

The tilde indicates the name of a *home directory*.

http://www.zdnet.com/~macuser/people/andyi/index.html

Double slashes indicate the start of the domain name.

Everything following the slash is a *path name* down to a specific file or directory. Warning: keep upper- and lowercase straight in the path name.

Anatomy of two URLs.

remains unique: If Bob's provider is Heaven Connections, Inc., his address is the unique bobc@heavens.net. And no service will allow two users to pick identical user names.

Two notes: You needn't worry about uppercase and lowercase in e-mail addresses. BCratchit@scrooge.com and bcratchit@Scrooge.COM are considered identical in e-mail addresses. And, a space in an on-line service's user name ("bob cratchit" on America Online) is simply dropped for Internet purposes ("bobcratchit").

Other Internet URLs—Look for the //

If the URL is separated by a double slash (//), then the leading protocol tells you what sort of address it is: "http:" indicates a World Wide Web page; "ftp:" is an FTP site from which you can download a file; "gopher:" is a Gopher site, and "wais:" is a searchable text database called WAIS, for *Wide Area Information Services.* (See "The Main Features of the Internet," later in this chapter for details on these Internet services.) Web site domains usually begin with "www" such as: <http://www.peachpit.com>. Similarly, FTP sites usually begin with "ftp." Many Web browsers will understand a URL which is missing the protocol "ftp://" or "http://" so long as the domain begins with "ftp." or "www," but that's an exception. As with e-mail addresses, a single typo in a URL and you're nowhere.

Finally, slashes after the domain are used to show the path down through various directories (such as the Mac's folders) to the location of the file. Thus if you FTP to the address <ftp://ftp.acns.nwu.edu/pub/newswatcher/> you'll see a list of all the files that reside inside the "newswatcher" directory, which is in the "pub" (for public) directory at the Northwestern University FTP site. When you see a *tilde* (~) at the beginning of a Web URL path, you've spotted the Unix identifier for the home directory of the account. While case, upper or lower, doesn't matter on most of the URL, it *does* matter in the path name. That's the first thing to examine when you get a "404 Not Found" error in your Web browser.

HOT TIP

Web Feat

In Internet circles the popularity of the Mac-like graphical, hyperlinked interface led to a 1989 paper by Tim Berners-Lee at CERN, a physics lab in Switzerland. He proposed an astonishingly simple technique for displaying and navigating through information in similar style on each and every screen, no matter the platform, called *HTTP* (Hypertext Transfer Protocol). *[Read a history of the World Wide Web at <http://www.w3.org/hypertext/WWW/History.html>.—JH]*

HTTP's cleverness is in the way its priorities are aligned. The easy part—sending minimal text—is handled over slowpoke phone lines. The heavy lifting—drawing pictures, formatting text, playing sounds, *ad nauseam*—is handled locally, by the client's speedy computer. By 1991, HTTP was appearing on the Net and the World Wide Web was born.

The World Wide Web's ease of use gave birth to the Brave New Internet: a burgeoning consumer product that no one quite knows what to do with, which is why they're doing everything.

Timing was right. The national news media, enchanted by the Web (and investing heavily in its future), made the Internet, apparently, the story of the decade. Consumers paying $1,500 for home computers, complete with modems, demanded to be "on the Internet." Now-has-been Delphi, then American Online, and a slower-reacting CompuServe, responded with kludgey additions to their software to allow "real" Internet access.

The Body Electric

The Web allows all but the most mentally infirm to cruise the nether regions of the Internet world with nothing but mouse clicks. Today's Web browsers are sophisticated enough to handle numerous Net functions—FTP downloads, e-mail, newsgroup reading, Gophering—in one package. (Don't fret—we define these terms later.)

New technologies such as Java and Shockwave are creating an industry of software that not only takes a Web page from a server to your screen—it shoves a Web page in your face with animations and interactions that have yet to be imagined.

We're back in familiar territory, really. Like all wildly popular software packages, Net browsers are becoming infested with feature-itis. Meanwhile, modern personal computers are suddenly being asked to behave more like the dumb terminals of 1969. They'll just sit there to collect information from all over the world, although the color is better. Well, there's one important new wrinkle: Distant computers now ask for your credit card number.

How to Get There From Here

Champing at the bit to get started? You've got a bit of work to do first. Take a deep breath.

Get Thee Wired (JO)

It's relatively easy to get connected (or "wired" in Internet-speak) to the Internet—you just have to decide which kind of access is best for your needs—and your pocketbook. The good and bad news is that, for most folks, there are quite a few options; deciding which is best for you may involve some trial and error. The problem with writing about this topic is that the options change almost daily, so what you read now is bound to have been eclipsed by something new and different—and maybe even better. Nonetheless, we'll stick to the basics to give you essential information that will apply no matter what changes sweep the field.

Ultimate Multitasking (JH)

One of the beautiful aspects of connecting to the Internet over a TCP/IP connection is that it allows you to run several different applications, connecting to completely different services, all at once. If you're already familiar with bulletin boards or one of the commercial services, you know that you're almost always limited to doing one thing at a time. All telecommunications can be tied up, for example, by a single long download. Not so on the Internet.

A TCP/IP connection becomes the pipeline for several different connections, though you'll need a fast modem to make the best use of it. Over my 28.8-kbps PPP connection to my local provider, I use Fetch, for example, to download a large file while simultaneously browsing my favorite Web sites with Netscape Navigator. And when I tire of waiting for a large graphic to display in the Navigator browser window, I switch to NewsWatcher to read articles in my favorite newsgroups.

I've also logged onto CompuServe over my PPP connection with CompuServe Information Manager (using the Apple Communications Toolbox Telnet tool) and, as CIM downloaded large files, I logged onto CompuServe a second time with SITcomm to do a little sysop work in the forum I run. The possibilities are mind-boggling. Log onto AOL and CompuServe at the same time; open two or three windows in your Web browser to create no-waiting browsing; or have Claris Emailer check all your services for mail in the background while you browse the Web. If you have two monitors, I guarantee telecommunications heaven.

Of course all that activity will slow down your downloads, but you might prefer to check your e-mail at the expense of a quick download. Once you get used to this kind of freedom, you'll be frustrated with anything less.

Regardless of the mode you choose, some basics are common to all. To connect from your home you'll need a modem, some additional software, and an account with an Internet service provider (ISP), which can take the form of a local provider or the Internet access provided by one of the large commercial services.

Using the Internet is akin to using a commercial on-line service such as America Online or CompuServe, so many of the same ground rules apply. For example, if you plan to spend a lot of time on-line, you should investigate adding a second phone line so that you don't tie up your main phone line (let's be hip and call it your *voice line*)

Setting Up TCP: The Basics   (SB)

Internet pros *really* know about this subject. Unlike most Mac installations, which are truly "plug 'n play," setting up a SLIP or PPP TCP/IP connection is "plug 'n pray." Simple setups almost always work best, so type in as little data as your ISP suggests you can get away with. Adding data just adds to the chances of failure.

Use your software's installer—don't drag bits yourself. With Apple's new Open Transport networking and communications architecture, lots of small bits need to be placed in the right place (shades of Windows). Even the old standby (and soon to go away) MacTCP should be installed via a scripted installer.

There is one way around TCP/IP, sort of. You can avoid dealing with it (and SLIP or PPP) by using an ISP that gives you proprietary software that buries the protocol stuff, and still works. The trouble is you're locked into that particular provider and that particular software with its limited capabilities.

The configuration looks daunting, but your ISP will give you detailed instructions on exactly what to fill in where. Your control panel may look different. This one is part of Apple's Open Transport. Notice how much simpler it appears than the MacTCP control panel you may have worked with.

To do the TCP/IP setup yourself, you'll need a crib sheet from your ISP. On it you should find your *dial-in number* (don't hesitate to ask for a list of numbers; the one the ISP selects may not be optimal), a *router address* (which is a bunch of numbers such as 192.204.28.8), a *nameserver address* or two (same kind of numbers), and a *domain name* like peachpit.com. Be sure you've been set up with "dynamic server addressing." Some ISPs may suggest "manual addressing." It's faster connecting, but ultimately will fail you as traffic builds.

[While you have all that info in front of you, grab a copy of Internet Config and fill in all the blanks. That will save you from having to type in info every time you configure a new Internet application. See the sidebar "The Essential Internet Tool Kit" earlier in this chapter for more on Internet Config.—JH]

while you're cruising the Internet. You should also consider investing in the fastest modem you can afford. (A 28.8 kbps, or V.34, modem is *highly* recommended if you plan on accessing the Web.) See Chapter 22, for more information on the basics of getting connected.

Communication over the Internet is based on a protocol called *TCP/IP*. To use TCP/IP you'll need to install either MacTCP or Open Transport TCP/IP, both of which are included with System 7.5 or later. If you have the choice of using Open Transport, which became nearly universally available with the release of System 7.5.3, use it. It simplifies things to some extent and many connections seem to run faster.

You will also need an additional extension that allows you to use PPP or SLIP proto- cols. (These are two means of using TCP/IP over a dial-up connection. PPP is a bit better and has more or less become the de facto standard.) A service provider may provide you with the PPP or SLIP extension, but they're also available via on-line services and included with Internet starter kits. Check out the sidebar "Setting Up TCP: The Basics" for advice on setting up the TCP software.

Internet Service Providers

The Internet service provider market is probably one of the most volatile markets in existence. Everyone from garage-based small companies to multinational cable and telephone companies are clamoring for your business. At this writing, pundits are declaring that the small local ISPs are endangered by AT&T's entry into the ISP busi- ness. In fact, nearly everyone with any sort of connection to your home is struggling for a way to offer connection to the Internet, including, in the next year or two, tele- vision cable companies. (See the sidebar "Once and Future Telecom Technologies" in Chapter 22.)

There are literally hundreds of ISPs in existence today, and the list keeps growing. An ISP provides your conduit to the Internet. Fee structures are usually similar to those of commercial on-line services, but they're frequently cheaper. You can usually opt to pay a flat monthly fee or pay by the hour for connect time. You'll typically pay $20 to $35 a month for anything from 20 hours to unlimited access, or a smaller monthly base fee, perhaps $5, and an additional hourly fee in the $2 to $3 range. Because there are many vendors competing for your business, shop around to get the cheapest, yet most reliable, service provider (see the sidebar "Ten Questions to Ask an ISP"). Some ISPs offer attractive bundles that feature unlimited connect time if you are willing to pay up-front monthly, quarterly, or annual fees. *[AT&T's announcement that it wants to be a super-ISP caused one of my local ISPs to announce a $90-per-year rate for an unlimited dial-up PPP or SLIP account. That's $7.50 a month and ain't competition wonderful?—SB]*

Ten Questions to Ask an ISP (SB)

Unless your company or school provides free Internet access, the most important factor in efficiently and effectively using the Net is finding the best possible Internet service provider. When picking an ISP, you need to get the right answers to several questions. Here are the top 10 questions (plus a bonus) and some answers.

1. What's the monthly cost? $20/month for unlimited hours is fair. Hourly connect time charges should be considered only if there isn't an unlimited hours ISP local to you.

2. Does the ISP provide at least 5MB of memory for a personal home page?

   [In my experience, 5MB is generous. 2MB seems to be typical.—JH] [It is also worth finding out who manages your Web pages. Can you upload changes directly, or does someone on the ISP staff publish them after you have copied them to the server?—JO]

3. What is the server software? It's likely to be some flavor of Unix, but you might get lucky and find an ISP running a Mac-based operation. If you plan an elaborate Web site, running it on a Mac-based server will be very beneficial.

4. What are the technical support hours and policies? Are there specialists in Mac technical support?

5. Who supplies the software, and can generic tools such as Eudora, NewsWatcher, and Netscape Navigator be used, or are you restricted to proprietary software? Although using the generic tools is slightly more difficult, they offer many more options and the ability to quickly stay on top of the technology as it advances.

6. Are there dial-in locations that are local calls for me? Is 800-number service or some low-cost method available for checking in while traveling? How many dial-in numbers are there?

7. Does the news feed get all Usenet groups and does it ever "miss" messages? Most ISPs miss some; you want to miss as few as possible. *[I've also noticed that some ISPs try to play censor and refuse to carry certain newsgroups. If you want them all, make sure the provider doesn't censor any.—JO]*

8. Do all call-in nodes support V.34 modems at 28.8 kbps? You don't want anything else, even if you currently have a slower modem.

9. Can you run CGI scripts—scripts which run on the server to enable more powerful capabilities such as forms—and, if so, in what language? The programming language PERL is ideal on Unix-based servers.

10. Is there a trial period? What happens if you sign up and get solid busy signals from dawn to midnight?

Bonus: Are ISDN connections available, and what do they cost? Even if you don't have ISDN now, ask about this; it'll tell you how the ISP views the future.

The easiest way to get a list of providers in your area is to get a copy of Peter Kaminski's PDIAL list which contains a list of dial-up access providers by state. (Send e-mail to <kaminski@netcom> with the word "PDIAL" in the message body.) You can also browse through the racks of your favorite bookstore where there are apt to be quite a few titles devoted to the Internet, many of which include a massive list of ISPs in an appendix.*[Also check your local newspaper. Every one has a technology section at least one day a week and every ISP worth considering will have at least a classified ad in that section.—SB]* Get an e-mail address for each ISP in your local calling area and do a mass mailing requesting information from each provider on rates. Be sure to ask about startup or setup fees.

HOT TIP

You can also buy prepackaged Internet connectivity kits, such as Software Ventures' **Internet Valet** ($50) or Adam Engst's **Internet Starter Kit** ($35). (See "Everything You Need to Get on the Internet. Really?" later in this chapter.) These kits include the software and startup account information you need to get on-line with relative ease.

Using a large, nationwide ISP such as Netcom or EarthLink rather than a local provider has its pluses and minuses. You should expect to get better customer support and reliable performance from a national ISP, but you may have to make a long-distance call to connect to the service, which can quickly add to the cost. Luckily, the number of *POPs* (local telephone call *points of presence*) for large service providers is growing. This means that if you are located near a metropolitan area, you should be able to connect via a local telephone call.

Using a Commercial Service to Access the Internet

Major on-line services such as CompuServe and America Online can also be considered ISPs. If you already have an account on one of these services, you can already access the Internet. Though the Web is probably the hottest Internet-based service, you can also use FTP, Gopher, Usenet newsgroups, and Telnet as well.

America Online has a well-developed Internet interface that is accessible directly with the America Online client software and its companion Web browser. At press time, AOL planned to offer you a choice of Netscape Navigator or Microsoft's Internet Explorer, a major plus since AOL's original Web browser was buggy and lacked many useful features. From America Online's main menu, you can easily connect to the Internet to use Gopher, WAIS, FTP, Telnet, Usenet, or browse the Web.

America Online provides adequate access to the Internet if your needs are fairly casual. It's best suited to those who already have an AOL account and expect to use AOL's content as much as the Internet. As a conduit to the Internet, AOL is typically slower than a local ISP because you must use AOL's integrated Internet access tools rather than other best-of-breed applications. For example, AOL's Usenet news reader software limits your ability to read large news messages and download entire threads. For serious news reading, there are better MacTCP alternatives, such as NewsWatcher. (See "Usenet Newsgroups," later in this chapter.) But a benefit of AOL's approach is that it's all integrated into one package.

CompuServe's approach at this writing is not as cohesive as AOL's. You must make a separate PPP connection if you want to browse the Web, which involves setting up your TCP and PPP software and launching individual Internet applications—in that way, CompuServe is acting like a local ISP, though Telnet, FTP, and Usenet newsgroups are all accessible directly from within the CompuServe Information Manager. Again, this approach is less integrated, takes more work to set up, but ultimately provides the flexibility of a local ISP. In addition, because CompuServe has local dial-up numbers across the world, you'll be able to access the Internet with a local call as you travel, something a local ISP can't provide.

GOOD FEATURE

Other Means of Access

There are some other alternatives that may also be available to you. Many large companies and organizations are directly connected to the Internet via leased lines. In these cases, you can typically access the Internet, in all of its glory, from your desk via a local area network (LAN). In this case, your computer operations or information services staff plays the role of service provider. See them to get your workstation set up for Internet access.

HOT TIP

You may also be able to access the Internet from home by way of such a network link. To do this, you will need Apple Remote Access to connect to your organization's network and then to the Internet. Many universities also provide access to students and faculty, and again, you'll have to talk to the information services folks for access info.

These methods, though a bit more complicated to configure, have the obvious benefit of eliminating the costs of an ISP.

~~~~~~

"Everything You Need to Get on the Internet." Really? (DJS)

"Everything you need to get on the Internet." This lovely promise is rampant but, at this writing, only one kit keeps it in spirit if not in fact.

Unless you buy the Internet Valet, you must:

- Find a reputable ISP with a local number.

- Learn if the dial-up connection is SLIP or PPP.
  [Virtually all dial-up connections these days can handle PPP or SLIP: it's up to you on your end. PPP is more robust as a connection method; I've found SLIP software much steadier and more freeze-free.—SB]

- Obtain detailed instructions, including user name and password, for setting up connective software.

That said, behold three kits that are worthy of your cash for reasons that vary:

You Want to Get on, Right Now!

Internet Valet ($50; Software Ventures) is the only kit (at this writing) that can get you on the Internet right away. I went from shrink-wrap to PSINet's home page in 15 minutes. Valet heroically configured PPP and other onerous stuff. All I did was fill in a few blanks about who I am. You'll need a credit card number.

Valet installs three floppies' worth of tried-and-true Internet software including the essential MacTCP control panel, a handsome Enhanced Mosaic Web browser, Eudora for e-mail, clients for both FTP and Gopher, a news reader, and more. It organizes them on a small clickable palette, too.

The only catch is PSINet, a quality nationwide ISP, may not be a local call. If you live in a metropolitan area, PSINet probably is. If not, the Valet is still a decent kit that only needs SLIP software if that's what your ISP demands.

You Have a Provider and Want the Best

Apple's **Internet Connection Kit** ($99) comes with Netscape, Claris Emailer Lite, the amalgam of client software (FTP, Gopher, et al), and bonuses such as RealAudio, Acrobat Reader, a QuickTime movie player, and more. (It takes ten floppies to hold this kit; thankfully it comes with a CD-ROM, too.) No SLIP, however.

Like Valet, ICK organizes all its goodies on a palette, configures PPP, and handles messy signup chores if you have a credit card number.

Alas, ICK's palette is the clunkier Launcher palette that no one, but no one, uses. The kit tries to marry you to an Internet service provider via an 800 number but I could not get it to connect using two different computers.

These are minor complaints in the long run. For all the software you get and all the downloading it saves, the Internet Connection Kit is a deal.

Another point in the Apple kit's favor: As I type, Apple is releasing Open Transport 1.1—a version that works! Open Transport is taking over networking and telecom duties in the Mac OS, especially in the realm of PowerPCs. MacTCP is replaced with the TCP/IP control panel. It's a safe bet that future releases of ICK will keep users abreast of recently released network and telecom software.

Internet Search   (JH)

The Internet has no central directory of resources or addresses. Instead, you'll mostly rely on two kinds of help. The first is a *search engine:* Type in a keyword or words and the engine will return the names and locations of all the sites on which those words appear. Each of the various search engines boasts of how many millions of pages are in its index, but just as important is the intelligence of the search engine itself. We've listed many below so you can sample them all to find one that suits your preferences.

Excite provides a powerful search engine. Note the advertisement at the bottom of the page. These ads are why the search engines are free.

The other way of locating an Internet resource is through a *directory,* a selective hierarchical listing of resources, resembling a vast table of contents to the Internet. The benefit is that you don't have to wade through every little useless home page containing your keywords. Of course that can also be a drawback, especially if it means you miss interesting but minor sites not included in the directories.

GOOD FEATURE

Search Engines
One of the best search engines is Digital Equipment Corporation's Alta Vista
<http://www.altavista.digital.com>.
Other excellent search sites are Lycos <http://www.lycos.com>,
Infoseek <http://www.infoseek.com>, and Excite <http://www.excite.com>.

You Want to Roll Your Own

Adam Engst's supreme book-and-disk package, **The Internet Starter Kit** ($35, Hayden Books), is a pure roll-your-own proposition, the best value if you need MacTCP 2.0.6 going in. If you want to learn all about the Internet too, there's no contest.

The single floppy contains a complete suite of Net-cruising shareware including both SLIP and PPP extensions. Included bookmark files point to lots more Net tools for easy download using the included FTP tool Anarchie. (The cost of these shareware tools is not included in the purchase price, so you should pay the shareware fees if you use them.)

Yes, *The Internet Starter Kit* comes with a "free trial" Internet connection to a Seattle-area provider. That's an expensive call unless you happen to live in Seattle.

A roundup of several search sites is kept at Netscape's Web site <http://home.netscape.com/home/Internet-search.html>, at W3 Search Engines <http://cuiwww.unige.ch/meta-index.html>, and at All-in-One Search Page <http://www.albany.net/~wcross/all1srch.html>.

GOOD FEATURE

For a *really* comprehensive search, MetaCrawler <http://www.cs.washington.edu/research/projects/metacrawler/www/index.html> plugs keywords into several of the best search engines and returns results from all. The same principle is behind SavvySearch <http://www.cs.colostate.edu/~dreiling/smartform.html>.

And finally, the best *directory* of search engines is at Yahoo! <http://www.yahoo.com/Computers_and_
        Internet/Internet/World_Wide_Web/
        Searching_the_Web>,
(which also offers a good search engine itself).

Directories
The father of all directories is Yahoo! <http://www.yahoo.com>, and another excellent directory is Magellan <http://www.mckinley.com>, which includes professionally written reviews of Web sites.

The White Pages
To search for people on the Internet, see "E-Mail" later in this chapter.

Yahoo! locates thousands of Web sites by leading you through a hierarchical listing by subject. It's searchable as well.

There's no complaining about Valet and Apple manuals; both are clear and concise. *The Internet Starter Kit*, on the other hand, is a whopping 600-plus pages of facts, discussions, history, side trips, and obscure technical points. Run into a uuencode glitch, lately? It's in the hefty index.

[As we went to press, CompuServe's Spry/Internet division was slated to release a Mac version of its "Internet in a Box." For details, check <http://www.spry.com>.—JH]

[EarthLink, another metro-based ISP, now touts its quick-connect kit. You can download it from <ftp://ftp.earthlink.net/total_access/mac/tamcv110.bin> or call 800/ 395-8425.—DJS]

The Main Features of the Internet

Internet access can be neatly divided into a few basic areas, each based on the particular thing you want to do on the Net: send and receive e-mail, join public discussions, download files, or browse the World Wide Web. Each different kind of activity comes with its own protocols and its own tools.

You can search the White Pages at Switchboard for names, phone numbers, and home addresses, but you won't find a whole lot of e-mail addresses.

E-Mail

E-mail on the Internet works much like it does on the commercial services—be sure to read "E-mail" in Chapter 22 for the details. But you don't need a commercial on-line service to send and receive e-mail. Every Internet service provider will set you up with an e-mail account. Your user name plus the ISP's address serves as your e-mail address: user name@service.provider.etc (see the sidebar "How to Read a URL" earlier in this chapter).

HOT TIP

There's no true "White Pages" for e-mail addresses, but point your Web browser to Four11 <http://www.Four11.com/> for a fairly big list, or Netfind <http://www.nova.edu/Inter-Links/netfind.html> if you have a last name and a domain. For true White and Yellow Pages, try Switchboard <http://www.switchboard.com>, which offers millions of names, phone numbers, and home addresses, but fewer e-mail addresses.

We reviewed e-mail management software in the previous chapter (see "E-Mail Managers").

And now a word from our sponsor… At the time of this writing, a new concept in e-mail was being unveiled—*free* e-mail. (Can we coin the phrase *free-mail*?) Okay, fee-free but not string-free—It's *sponsored* e-mail. At this writing, two companies have begun offering e-mail accounts on their proprietary (so far Windows-only) software with no monthly charges. The software you use to compose, send, and receive your mail displays an advertisement. If you'd rather ignore a plug for pimple cream than pay a monthly fee, keep your eyes peeled for Mac versions of this service. Check with Juno <http://www.juno.com/> and Freemark <http://www.freemark.com/>. If you're now paying an on-line service only to use its e-mail services, consider these. On the other hand, if you use any other services of your current provider, there's little incentive to try these.

[Another interesting concept is the "permanent" e-mail address. As ISPs come and go, many of us switch. But that means a new address with many attendant hassles. A group called PO Box offers addresses that can be aliased to whatever your current real address is. It's cheap, and it works. Check out <http://www.pobox.com>.—SB]

HOT TIP

And while we're on the subject of e-mail, take a moment to subscribe to Adam and Tonya Engst's terrific Macintosh newsletter, *TidBITS*, e-mailed weekly. It's considered essential reading for nearly everyone who worked on this book. Drop a message to <info@tidbits.com>.

The World Wide Web

For years, the Internet was little more than text, text, and more text. Then just a couple of years ago the World Wide Web changed everything. It was as if the telegram had been followed directly by the invention of glossy color magazines. And because it's so simple to compose a home page, a personal Web site, the content has grown tremendously fast (see "Your First Home Page" later in this chapter). Imagine what cable TV would be like if every person with a video camera could schedule a TV show—that's the Web in a nutshell.

There's still plenty of text, of course, but the Web presents it in formatted *pages*, literally resembling a magazine page, with color illustrations, backgrounds, and even animation and sound (though for the most part, sound involves downloading the sound sample and playing it with a *helper* application). The Web's most revolutionary innovation, however, is its use of *hyperlinks*—click on highlighted text or pictures and you're whisked off to some spot on that page or elsewhere on the Web. It feels as if the entire Web is just one enormous, if slow, multimedia magazine.

GOOD FEATURE

All this is accessed by a Web *browser*, an application which efficiently scoops up the text from Web pages and then reads special tags embedded within the text to do all the heavy duty formatting locally, on your Mac. That's how attractively formatted Web pages appear much more quickly than if a fully formatted page had to be downloaded from scratch through your modem. All sorts of extra attractions—sound, QuickTime movies, animations—are downloaded and either passed off to helper applications or displayed right on the page with various plug-ins.

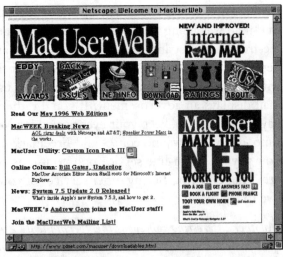

The Web has grown incredibly fast, and there are now hundreds of thousands of sites to visit. If you imagine the commercial services as big shiny malls, offering a carefully selected array of services, the Web is the

There are three kinds of clickable hyperlinked spots on this Web page: the highlighted words (underlined), the magazine cover (which would be outlined in the highlight color if this were a color illustration), and the six icons below the banner, which comprise a map of clickable areas. Each hyperlink takes you to another place in this Web site.

world's largest parking-lot flea market. The U.S. Postal Service, Time/Warner, and Apple Computer are literally right next door to the home page of the 11-year-old with scanned photos of his Star Trek models.

Because it's so easy and inexpensive to put up your own home page on the Web (see "Your First Home Page" later in this chapter), the Web is a showcase for every genius and every crackpot-with-a-vision. There's almost no passing fad, cult interest, or obscure object of desire that doesn't have at least one multimedia altar on the Web. (Proof? "Mr. Neff's Mambo Karaoke Steakhouse" at <http://www.teleport.com/~zoetek/mambo_karaoke/entrance.html>, "I Just Want To Be Friends" at <http://www.phantom.com/~joelogon/platonic.html>, and a personal favorite, "Andy Ihnatko's Colossal Waste of Bandwidth" at <http://www.zdnet.com/~macuser/people/andyi/>.)

Andy Ihnatko's Colossal Waste of Bandwidth.

The Web is without question the killer app of the Internet. Go forth and browse.

Terrific Destinations on the Internet

The Philadelphia Inquirer and the Daily News   (SB)
<http://www.phillynews.com>

Much to my horror and amazement, I now start each day by reading my local papers, *The Philadelphia Inquirer* and the *Daily News* on-line. Although their on-line personas still show

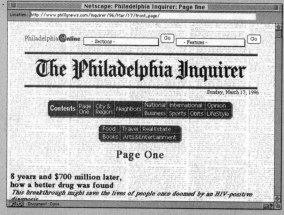

signs of experimentation (and some real howlers), they use a model that works. Each article is represented by a head (or maybe a graphic), the lead paragraph or two, and a link that simply says "… more." I rapidly scan whole sections, more efficiently than I can scan the pages of the hard copy versions and read only what I want. That's how most of us actually read newspapers. Ads are spaced throughout, but are not overwhelming; you need to expand the ad position holder graphics to see the full ads or link to the Web

The Philadelphia Inquirer is remarkably easy to browse.

site of the advertiser. There's also an interactive crossword, really great customizable comics, and a super restaurant database with searching capability. It's really nice having the future of news now.

Andy Ihnatko's Colossal Waste of Bandwidth   (JH)
<http://www.zdnet.com/~macuser/people/andyi/>

There are two types of humor on the Web. There's the post-modern/ironic/winking kind which worships PEZ or karaoke with a straight face. And there are the jokes pages, which usually make me feel like I'm visiting somebody's Uncle Ike, who still regrets he never took his Elks Lodge standup act to the Catskills instead of marrying Aunt Linda. Andy Ihnatko's Web site falls into the third category.

Like all personal home pages, there's not a detail of Andy's life that isn't up for scrutiny: The odometer on Andy's 1982 Plymouth Grand Fury reaches 100,000 miles, and here's the picture to prove it; The Clint Howard Project is a nearly complete database of Clint Howard's major and cameo appearances in big and little films; plus, of course, here's Andy's take on all things Macintosh and Internet. Is this the most self-indulgent home page ever or the most crafty spoof of home pages yet?

Some Web sites evoke a smile and a knowing nod; some evoke a grimace. Andy's site makes me laugh so hard my wife looks up from her book to ask me what's so funny.

Terrific Destinations on the Internet (continued)

MacInTouch   (JH)

<http://www.macintouch.com>

Ric Ford writes the indispensable MacInTouch column for *MacWEEK* magazine, but at the MacInTouch Web site, Ric doesn't reprint the column. Instead, he goes *MacWEEK* one better

and offers a nearly daily update of essential Mac info, guiding Mac users to Apple and third-party resources and software found all over the Internet and beyond. There's no better place to get up-to-the-minute details on system software updates, bugs, and every other kind of Mac info. There aren't any heavy graphics to slow you down, and Ric provides hyperlinks directly to the resources—a click will download the software MacInTouch points to.

MacInTouch also maintains vast quantities of essential information, including the finest rundown of bugs, problems, and incompatibilities anywhere, and a choice

Ric Ford's MacInTouch offers a daily dose of well-linked hard-core Mac news and tips.

list of links to Internet Mac file libraries, Apple sites, and other resources.

MacInTouch should be on every Mac user's daily must-visit list.

The New York Times <http://www.nytimes.com/>   (DJS)
and HotWired <http://www.hotwired.com/>

The New York Times went all Webby just before deadline. Nonetheless, its site looks thorough,

especially its edgy CyberTimes coverage. 'Tis a future to behold. *[CyberTimes is on my daily visit list.—JH]*

Nonetheless, I'll stick with HotWired as my favorite Net site. Downside: It's as gaudy as its print cousin *Wired*, too ostentatious in its attempt to be leading-edge, with-it, hep-to-the-jive.

Once you're familiar with the site, however, you can customize your opening HotWired page. Art, fads, movies, books and Net culture!—there's little that HotWired misses.

The New York Times' CyberTimes includes articles on the Internet not printed in the daily paper version.

HotWired's newest travel offering.

HotWired contains the magic ingredient: content. The writing is uniformly to the point. Its collective voice is a prototypical mixture of literacy, iconoclasm, and snottiness that seems to be becoming the standard tone of Net prose.

HotWired's political reporting is already outstripping all but the best daily papers. And it's murdering TV news coverage, no contest. The best thing about HotWired: It proves we should eliminate TV and not look back.

(JO)

Switchboard <www.switchboard.com>
and MapQuest <http://www.mapquest.com>

Do you ever wish you had a phone book for the entire U.S.? How about one that also had e-mail addresses? Switchboard is a White and Yellow Pages directory for the U.S. that quickly searches and finds telephone numbers and addresses, including electronic mail and

home page addresses for anyone who has taken the time to update their entry. Once you've registered, you can update your own entry, control access to your entry (i.e. make it unlisted), or add other affiliated entries (i.e. for your family members).

An interesting twist is the ability to allow people to send you electronic mail without knowing your e-mail address. Coordinate, the Banyan, Inc. subsidiary that runs this page/service, calls this feature "knock-knock."

Plug in your starting and ending points, and MapQuest's TripQuest calculates the exact instructions for your trip. The Internet increasingly offers more and more free and useful services such as this one.

Once you have located someone's phone number and address, how would you like directions and a map to get there? Another Web site, MapQuest, is an interactive atlas that has street-level detail for the entire U.S. If you know someone's address, you can have MapQuest create a detailed street map and a set of instructions on how to get there. Or, say you're looking for hotels and restaurants near an attraction you're planning to visit. MapQuest can create a map that points out these places.

GOOD FEATURE

Browser wars. There are two good choices for a Web browser. Ever since it overtook the original free browser, Mosaic, **Netscape Navigator** <http://home.netscape.com/> has had a near-total lock on the market. It's well designed, feature-rich, and free (for educational and nonprofit use). But most significantly, Navigator has always supported many nonstandard Web styles.

At one point Navigator was the only browser to display formatted tables on a page, centered text, and *frames*—independent windows within the main browser window— among other things. Web page authors, eager to make pages more interesting and attractive, made full use of the Navigator nonstandard standards, often displaying a notice, "This page best viewed with Netscape Navigator!" At the same time, because only Navigator could display such features, it became a virtual requirement for visiting the cutting-edge sites. And that's how most folks came to abandon other browsers for Navigator.

At this writing, Navigator's most serious competition is from software giant Microsoft. After ignoring the Internet for a long time, the company is in hot pursuit of the browser market with its free **Internet Explorer** <http://www.microsoft.com/>. Based on the original Web browser, Mosaic, Microsoft's product is a fine alternative to Navigator, generally less buggy, but not quite up to Navigator's feature set.

Although both America Online and CompuServe offer Netscape Navigator as an alternative browser for access to the Web from within their services, Microsoft's Internet Explorer is the primary browser for each.

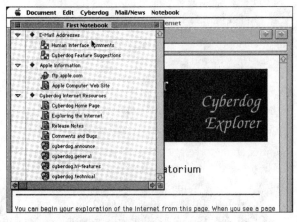

And, finally, you should keep your eyes on the progress of Apple's suite of Internet tools, code-named **Cyberdog**, developed to demonstrate OpenDoc, Apple's component software technology. Where Netscape Navigator and Internet Explorer accept plug-in components for viewing specialized Web features, CyberDog is nothing *but* components. To change the feature set, Apple promises, you need only replace a component.

Apple's Cyberdog is a showcase of the OpenDoc technology.

For the latest scoop on the browser wars, see Dave Garaffa's site <http://www.ski.mskcc.org/browserwatch/index.html>.

"We're Sorry, but the Number You Have Dialed Is Not in Service at This Time ..."

Here are some common Internet error messages and a bit of explanation to help you cure them:

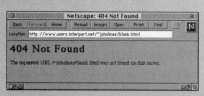

The dreaded 404 Not Found Error—it's not as hopeless as you might think.

Web Browser

404 Not Found—Your URL got you as far as the right host computer, but the document you asked for isn't there. First check your typing. Remember to keep your upper- and lowercase straight, be sure you've spotted and included the tilde (~) you find in many addresses, and check for typos. Sadly, magazines routinely misprint URLs. Write a letter to the editor. You might also try deleting everything following the final slash and try again. If you're lucky, you'll find a list of documents to choose from. Finally, of course, it's possible that the page you want is simply gone: removed or renamed.

403 Forbidden (or Access Denied)—You don't have the password or other permission to go to this document. If that makes no sense, check your URL for typos.

503 Service Unavailable—Too busy! Try again or wait until a less busy time of day—between 9:00 p.m. and 7:00 a.m. Pacific time.

File Contains No Data—You might be led to believe that the Web page turned out to be blank, but try this trick: Add :80 just before the first pathname slash, like so:

    http://www.sophia.com:80/just/testing.html

E-Mail

Most e-mail errors, such as all addressing errors, result from a typo in the address. Examine the header of the bounced mail. You can sometimes decode the error message. "Host unknown" suggests there's no host computer of the name you specified in the address domain. Other error messages will tell you that there's no user by that user name on the machine you've reached.

It's especially frustrating to get e-mail returned when you've simply replied to a message and there's no chance for a typo. The problem in this case probably lies at the other end— for any number of reasons the recipient's network refused the mail. There's little to do if you can't contact the recipient some other way. Try resending in a few days or weeks.

FTP

Invalid host—You've either mistyped the FTP site's URL or the site is down and can't respond. Check the URL and try again. You can also try getting another machine to check the FTP site for you. Send e-mail to <dns@grasp.insa-lyon.fr> and in the body put only the message `ip site name` (where "site name" is the name of the FTP site you can't con-tact). An automatic response will be returned with the numeric address of the site. No response means no such site.

HOT TIP

Usenet Newsgroups

In Chapter 22, we discussed on-line discussion forums. *Usenet newsgroups* are the Internet's discussion forums, despite the misleading word "news" and the fact that posted messages are confusingly called *articles*. At last count there were something like 16,000 newsgroups—and it's still growing—so you can imagine that you can easily find some incredibly obscure topics: how about alt.fan.karl-malden.nose? (Don't be surprised if you can't find that particular group. Minor groups come and go.)

HOT TIP

You don't need a full Internet connection to participate in newsgroups. Even smaller bulletin boards often offer access to some subset of the groups. To search the contents of all newsgroups, use a Web search site such as Infoseek (see the sidebar, "Internet Search" earlier in this chapter).

Because most newsgroups aren't supervised, discussions on the commercial services are usually more focused and civil. Pick your newsgroups carefully if you're easily offended. And because millions of users have access to the groups, groups usually lack the intimate feel of the best forums on the commercial services. You aren't nearly as likely to make friends, for example, on newsgroups.

BAD FEATURE

You're also likely to be bombarded with completely inappropriate messages in a newsgroup. *Spamming* is the unseemly practice of saturating many newsgroups with a message inappropriate for the topics, and commercial spamming is becoming very common. Some of the more common spams include ads for services resembling the 900-number phone sex lines. Forewarned is forearmed.

The newsgroup address can tell you a bit about what you'll find there. The address is organized into hierarchies, from the broadest to the most specific, separated by periods. The first part specifies the general category. The most common are "alt." (the alternative—often wilder and weirder—groups), "biz." (business), "comp." (computers), "k12." (kindergarten through 12th grade), "misc." (miscellaneous), "rec." (hobbies and recreation), "sci." (science), "soc." (social, cultural, religious), and "talk." (controversial topics). There are many others, including geographical address, such as "ca." for California and "ba." for Bay Area.

Read the remainder of the address for a clue about the specific contents of the newsgroup: comp.newton.misc contains miscellaneous discussions about the Newton MessagePad; any group name ending with ".binaries" includes *uuencoded* (specially coded for transmission over the Internet) images, sounds, or even applications. (Your news reader or StuffIt Expander can decode these for you.)

Play by the rules. Almost every newsgroup posts a current *FAQ*, a *Frequently Asked Questions* document, which contains guidelines and rules for the newsgroup, and often a FAQ covering the subject of the group as well. (A list of FAQs is kept at <http://www.cis.ohio-state.edu/hypertext/faq/usenet/>.) Read the FAQ before posting messages or risk looking like a newbie.

It's important to remember the global nature of newsgroups. Unless you post an article in a local group ("ba." groups, for instance, are related to the San Francisco Bay Area), don't post messages—er, articles—of purely local concern. Your offer to sell your car will bring a rain of derision down on you. It's also considered good form to set the preference in your news reader application to reply in e-mail to the sender as well as to the entire newsgroup, because many folks don't catch the reply posted to the group. (But don't do this on the commercial services' forums.) Finally, don't post a test message to any group except test groups like alt.test or misc.test.

HOT TIP

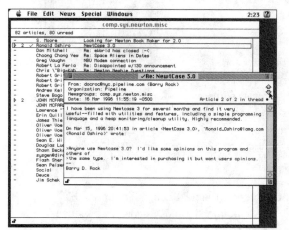

NewsWatcher makes reading newsgroups really easy.

I read the news today, oh boy. There are a few fine news readers, but the best is John Norstad's free **NewsWatcher**. NewsWatcher is beautifully implemented, and so simple to use that you probably won't need to crack open the instructions. NewsWatcher's only serious disadvantage is that it doesn't let you read and reply off-line. One clue: John has implemented Drag and Drop very nicely—make use of it.

GOOD FEATURE

A commercial news reader, **NewsHopper**, ($60, Landware) has one big advantage: It allows off-line reading. Download the articles you'd like to read and browse through them at your leisure after disconnecting from the Internet. You can find a demo version of NewsHopper at <http://www.demon.co.uk/sw15>, which is fully functional except that you're limited to reading just five groups and the demo is not a native PowerPC application.

GOOD FEATURE

MacSoup is another off-line reader ($20 shareware, Stefan Kurth) <http://www.inx.de/~stk/macsoup.html>.

For the terminally lazy, a browser such as Netscape Navigator will read newsgroups too, though without the bells and whistles of the best stand-alone readers.

Hot New Internet Technologies

The Internet is fertile ground for new technologies. Here's a rundown of just a few of the latest and hottest.

Java

The hot Web technology of the moment promises to turn the Web from glossy magazine to interactive TV. A Java-enhanced Web browser downloads tiny platform-independent applications associated with Web pages. These *applets* can do amazing things on the Web page. For instance? Time will tell. At this writing, cool-but-forgettable demos of the technology abound. Play Tetris, do a crossword puzzle, gaze at 3-D modeling, or read a live stock ticker tape. Visit the Web site Gamelan <http://www.gamelan.com> for samples.

A game of Tetris—er, Quatris—played live over the Internet (including sound effects) with the help of the Netscape Navigator Shockwave plug-in.

Shockwave for Director

Macromedia Director creates multimedia for the Mac, and Macromedia's free AfterBurner software will convert and compress those files so you can add them to Web pages. Drop the free Shockwave plug-in into your browser and you can experience slick interactive animation over the Web. Visit Macromedia's Web site at <http://www.Macromedia.com>.

Amber

All we have at this writing is the code name, but Amber is the next generation of Acrobat (see the sidebar "The Essential—and Essentially Free—Internet Tool Kit," earlier in this chapter for info about Acrobat). The Amber plug-in for Netscape will let you display Adobe PDF pages from within the browser as well as download individual pages rather than entire documents. Visit the Amber Web site at <http://w1000.mv.us.adobe.com/Amber/>.

RealAudio

Radio over the Internet, piped live into your Mac. No more waiting through a five minute download just to hear a single 20-second sound sample. From a growing list of RealAudio Web sites you can listen to sports and concert coverage, news broadcasts, and rebroadcasts of archived speeches and music. Don't expect FM-quality sound—the fi isn't yet hi—but version 2 improved on the original release greatly. The RealAudio client software for listening is free. Visit the RealAudio Web site at <http://www.realaudio.com/>.

[Xing Technology (<http://www.xingtech.com/>) offers a similar application, Streamworks. View live movies in real time with audio. It's hungry for bandwidth and jumpy at 28.8 kbps, but the fact that you can watch and listen to multiplexed audio and video makes TV over the Internet pretty darn close.—JO]

NetPhone

Electric Magic Company's **NetPhone** ($60) turns your microphone-equipped Mac into a telephone and the Internet into your long-distance provider. You can make long-distance phone calls to anywhere in the world over your TCP/IP Internet connection, though the sound is less than telephone quality, and you must call a similarly-equipped Mac running NetPhone. Visit the Electric Magic Web site at <http://www.emagic.com/>. Several other companies promise similar applications. Check Trel's Commercial Internet Products site (<http://www.lpac.ac.uk/Trel/1Phone_products.html>) for a current list of other Internet phone products.

CU-SeeMe

CU-SeeMe is not a hot new technology. It's a hot *old* technology, developed in 1992 at Cornell University. CU-SeeMe is video-conferencing over the Internet—videophone!—using an inexpensive Mac video camera such as the $100 Connectix QuickCam (see Chapter 6 for more details) and the video digitizing capabilities of an AV Mac or a video digitizing card. You'll actually see live pictures of everyone in the conference, though it's more like a slide show than video. Visit Cornell University's Web site at <http://cu-seeme.cornell.edu/>.

The CU-SeeMe Welcome page shows off some samples of the sorts of images you can see, though honestly, they're often a bit less clear.

VRML (Virtual Reality Modeling Language)

This programming language can set the user down in a 3-D environment. Many Mac VRML browsers or viewers are in the works. Visit the following Web site for more information: <http://rosebud.sdsc.edu/SDSC/Partners/vrml/software/browsers.html>

Other Innovations

The Internet also has lots of smaller tricks up its sleeve. MVP Solutions's **Talker** <http://www.mvpsolutions.com/> uses a Netscape plug-in and Apple's Plain Talk extension to read Web pages aloud through your Mac's speaker. **Emblaze Creator** by GEO Interactive Media Group promises full-screen color animation via a free Netscape plug-in <http://www.geo.co.il>. The list goes on and on …

FTP

Not surprisingly, the Internet offers the universe's largest collection of software, available for download by a process known as *FTP*, which stands for *file transfer protocol*, a set of rules dating back to the early days of the Internet. You can FTP files from thousands of sites all around the Internet, most of them universities, which make software libraries available to the general public.

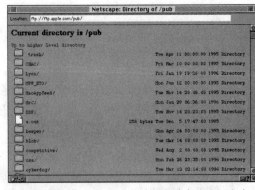

A typical FTP directory, as seen in a Web browser window. Click on "Up to a higher level directory" to go back up the hierarchy.

HOT TIP

You can access public FTP sites on which you have no account by means of *anonymous FTP*—use "anonymous" as your user name and your e-mail address as your password. Then just supply the URL—the host name and the path to the file you're seeking. If you're not allowed in, try this trick: Use "anonymous" for your user name, and the "at" sign (@) for your e-mail address.

After the software takes you to the FTP site, don't worry if you don't immediately spot the file. Most FTP sites are organized in nested *directories*, similar to the Mac's folders, enabling you to navigate up and down the hierarchy to look for files. Clicking on a period takes you to the *root* or top directory, and clicking on a double period takes you up one level higher in the hierarchy. Feel free to poke around. Look for directories named "pub" (for public), "incoming," and of course "Mac." Look for files titled "readme" for useful information.

HOT TIP

FTP Etiquette: It's common courtesy to limit your downloading to off hours—evenings, and weekends as measured locally at the FTP site. Try to use a local site. And, when possible, download from a *mirror* site, a less busy copy of the original site.

Help for serious downloaders. Several utilities are available to ease the process of searching for and downloading software. Most Web browsers allow you to FTP files—just pop the FTP address into the URL text box—but a dedicated utility is much easier and faster. My favorite by far is the shareware classic **Fetch** ($25) <ftp.dartmouth.edu/pub/software/mac/>, which is extremely easy to use. Fetch displays lots of information in a friendly way, so you know just what's happening (though don't take its estimate of remaining download time too seriously). It makes terrific use of Drag-

Fetch, a download utility, displays lots of information on the progress of a download.

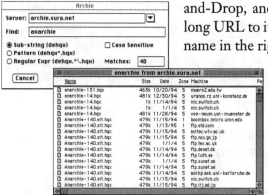

Anarchie locates files on anonymous FTP servers all over the world. It'll also download any of them on command.

and-Drop, and I often find it's smarter than me—drag a long URL to its dialog box and it splits it up to put the path name in the right text box. Fetch can also do almost all the uploading and maintenance work for maintaining a Web page.

Where in the World Is carmen.sgo?

Archie is the name of the special databases that keep track of the locations of files on Internet sites all around the world. These databases reside on a few publicly accessible servers. While you can search an Archie server manually (ugh!), there's one terrific utility that automates the process: Peter Lewis's **Anarchie** ($10) <ftp://ftp.share.com//pub/peterlewis/anarchie-160.sit.bin>. Anarchie not only searches Archie servers for files, but lets you download the file once you've found it. *[I Command-clicked on an FTP site's directory window title. I gasped. Sure enough, the remote directory path flopped down just like the Mac's window titles do. Anarchie makes FTP uploads and downloads a matter of dragging icons the way we've always used the Finder. A smart, deep, and fast program.—DJS]*

All the Rest

There are plenty of other things you can do on the Internet, but because they're less commonly used, we'll just give them a quick glance. Turn to the Read Me file or manual included with each of the tools' software for more details and instructions.

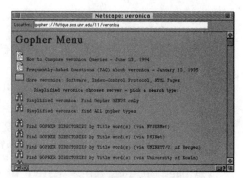

Before there was a World Wide Web, there was Gopher, a slick way to present a directory of resources on the Internet.

Gopher. Before the World Wide Web, people moved through hierarchical menus of resources by way of *Gopher*, a slick and still very useful method of creating a directory of resources. Your Web browser makes a fine Gopher application, though the old standby Turbo Gopher <ftp://ftp.aloha.net/pub/Mac/> is fine. For a sample, visit the "mother of all Gophers" at <gopher://gopher.umn.edu>. You can also use keywords to search all Gopher databases using an application called Veronica <gopher://futique.scs.unr.edu/11/veronica>. (If you think it's a coincidence that there are Internet tools called Archie and Veronica, think again.)

MUDs. A *MUD* (*Multi-User Dimension* or *Dungeon*) is what you get if you cross Dungeons and Dragons with the old text-only adventure games—role-playing virtual worlds which can be dragon-filled adventures or simulations of small fantastic towns. MUDs typically have elaborate social structures and an open-ended user-created structure. Some people become so obsessed that real life takes a back seat. Info on MUDs is available in the alt.mud and rec.games.mud newsgroups.

GOOD
FEATURE

Internet Relay Chat. In the last chapter we introduced the concept of live conversations known as chat. The Internet version is *Internet Relay Chat*, or *IRC*, in which live conversations take place over *channels*. Unlike chat on the commercial services, IRC is often thrilling for immediate news of world-shaking events. Eyewitness accounts of the Oklahoma City bombing and the Gulf War were first transmitted over IRC. Homer is software for IRC <ftp://ftp.aloha.net/pub/Mac/> and as a bonus, it converts text to sound!

Telnet. Telnet is a primitive but sometimes necessary method of remotely logging onto another computer. Telnet will usually plop you at the remote computer's command-line prompt, at which point you'll need to enter a user name and password, but from there you can, for instance, join in a MUD, search for resources, or use a few Unix commands to maintain your Web pages. Check out NCSA Telnet <ftp://ftp.aloha.net/pub/Mac/>.

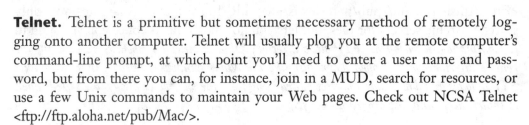

Your First Home Page

The Web is stuffed to the gills with *home pages*, personal Web sites set up by individuals and dedicated to personal obsessions, a favorite cause, or sometimes almost nothing at all. Creating a home page is easy. No, really. Not "easy" like AppleScript or HyperCard programming. Easy.

A page on the Web is written in *HTML*, *Hypertext Markup Language*, but it's not a programming language. It's called a markup language because it's just a set of short tags (such as <i>) inserted into the text of a page so a Web browser can understand how to display the styled, formatted text, graphics, and sound.

The <i> tag, for instance, tells a browser that the text following it should be displayed in italics. A matching closing tag, in this case </i>, tells the browser to end the italics style. Once you learn a couple of dozen or so markup tags, you know enough to make your first simple home page. You can do all the writing in any word processor (though later in this section we'll recommend some applications to automate some of the process). And you can prepare your first page in just an hour or two—then the fun is

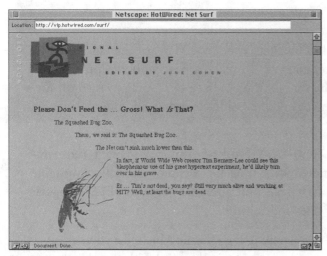

The advanced page layout used by HotWired's webmasters takes some painstaking and creative use of HTML.

enhancing your page with more advanced formatting.

Don't worry about memorizing everything at first. Read this section, follow the instructions for setting up and viewing the template, and then use these instructions again as a reference for more creative enhancements. Copy the template, inserting your own content. Study the way the tags affect what's displayed in your browser.

It's usually considered fair game to find a Web page you admire, save the HTML source code with your browser's Save As Source command, and steal the author's ideas for layout—but certainly not the text or images! Examine the tags used to format the page, and copy what you like. I learned a lot of tricks by examining the behind-the-scenes HTML work of sites such as HotWired <http://www.hotwired.com/>. HotWired's webmasters really know how to use HTML tags to do new, unsupported tricks.

When you finish a page, you can upload it, plus any graphics and sounds you've linked on the page, to a provider who gives you home page space, such as AOL and many ISPs. Each service offers specific instructions on how to upload the files.

Okay, let's go!

My Incredibly Interesting Home Page

Start with a blank document in your favorite word processor, and title it "index.html"—that's the title of the default document, the page that will be displayed first to a visitor, on most Web servers. Be sure to save the file in plain text format. Launch your Web browser and use the browser's Open Local or Open File command to open the file you're working on. Then switch to the browser as you work to see how your document looks: Save your document in the word processor, switch to the browser, and click the browser's Reload button.

Important note: Forget your desktop publishing training—don't use "curly quotes" anywhere in your HTML document. Stick to straight quotes only!

Markup Tags

All HTML *markup tags* are encased in brackets <like so>. Many of the tags you'll be using simply turn text formatting on and off. To make a passage bold, for instance, place the bold tag <b> just before the start of the boldface text. A tag to turn off formatting is identical except for a slash. To end the boldface, simply add this closing tag: </b>. It would look like <b>this</b>.

HOT TIP

That's how you'll specify *italics* (<i> and </i>), **bold** (<b> and </b>), centered paragraphs (<center> and </center>), and other simple formatting. The following table shows the common formatting tags. You can find a terrific guide to HTML tags at <http://home.mcom.com/assist/net_sites/index.html>.

Every HTML document begins with the opening tag <html>. Much like yourself, your document will be divided into a head and a body. Start the head with the <head> tag, then specify `<title>The Home Page Window Title</title>`. That will appear as the title of the window in the browser, not as a title in the text of the page.

Close the head </head> and open the body <body>, where you'll be putting the content of your page. At the end be sure to close the body with </body> and close the entire document with </html>. Confused yet? See "The Official Macintosh Bible Home Page Template" to see how these first tags are placed.

You can specify six levels of headers (though only the first three look good in my opinion). Headers open with the <h1> through <h6> tags and close with matching </h1> through </h6> tags. A level-one or level-two header belongs right at the top of the body; levels three and four make good section headers.

A Sampling of Useful HTML Tags

These tags are among the most useful.

<h1>Heading 1</h1>
<h2>Heading 2</h2>
<h3>Heading 3</h3>
New line
Paragraph<p>
Horizontal rule <hr size=xx width=xx>
Anchor <A href="http://xx">hyperlinked text</A>
Image <img src="xx.gif">
Unordered list <ul>
List items <li>
Close unordered list </ul>

A browser will ignore normal paragraph breaks completely. You'll have to specify every simple line break <br> and paragraph <p>.

One of the more useful tags <hr> inserts a line across the page, known in publishing as a *horizontal rule*. Some browsers, such as Netscape Navigator, know how to read the width and thickness of the rule, specified in pixels <hr size=xx width=xx>. Examine some of the illustrations of Web pages in this chapter for useful horizontal rules.

The Official Macintosh Bible Home Page Template

Copy this template for the beginnings of your first page, fill in your own content, open in your browser, and then expand on it as you learn more HTML.

Here's how the Official Macintosh Bible Home Page Template will look through the eyes of Netscape Navigator.

```
<HTML>
<HEAD>
<TITLE>The Home Page Template</TITLE>
</HEAD>


<BODY>
<A name="top">
<H2>Your Macintosh Bible Home Page Template!</H2>
```

The difference between a break tag "br" and a paragraph tag "p" is the space after the line break. The break tag simply starts a new line, like so
while the paragraph tag keeps a blank line between paragraphs, making clear paragraph breaks.

Notice that the return inserted in the original text after the previous sentence was ignored by the browser.<p> The "p" tag inserted before this sentence makes it a paragraph set off by a blank line.

```
<A name="middle">
<hr>
<h3>Middle of the Page</h3>
```

You can jump directly to a spot in the middle of a page specified by a "name" anchor. Create a link pointing to a name anchor, like so: `mypages/text.html#info`. This is especially useful for creating a table of contents at the top of a page.

```
<hr>
<ul>
<li>Each item in a list
<li> Is separated by the list tags
<li> Without any need for
<li> Paragraph or break tags.
</ul>
<A HREF="index.html#top">Return to the Top</A><p>
<A HREF="index.html#middle">Go to the Middle</A><p>
```

And don't forget to invite visitors to <A href="mailto:72241.731@compuserve.com"> e-mail</A> you!

```
</BODY>
</HTML>
```

Tags can also set up several kinds of lists, the most useful being the unordered (that is, unnumbered) list. Each list entry is preceded by the tag <li> (for list item—and there's no closing tag for list items), and the entire list must be surrounded by the opening tag <ul> (for unordered list) and matching closing tag </ul>. No paragraph breaks are needed—the <li> tags take care of them.

Now you know enough to put a bare-bones text page on the Web. Next, let's create some links.

Linking Logs

Some tags specify hypertext *links*—colored or underlined text or graphics which, when clicked on, will take you immediately to another document or picture, or even download a file such as a sound. Many people use links to create a page of favorite Cool Sites elsewhere on the Web.

To turn any text into a link, surround it with special *anchor* tags:
<A href="http://www.zdnet.com/~macuser/people/andyi/">Colossal Waste!</A>.
The text between the opening and closing tags will be highlighted, and clicking on that text will send the visitor to the URL specified between the quotation marks.

To display a graphic, you'll need an *image* tag, which displays the graphic located at the URL specified by a *source* attribute, like so:
<img src="graphics/baaroom.gif">.
Here, the source portion, src="graphics/baaroom.gif", tells the browser where to find the graphic "baaroom.gif," in this case in a local subdirectory titled "graphics." You must include the exact path name and the exact title of the document.

You can add a couple of more useful attributes to the image anchor:
<img width=484 height=479 src="graphics/baaroom.gif" alt="Music for Bang Baaroom and Harp">.

HOT TIP

Specifying the exact pixel height and width of the graphic will let some smart browsers automatically set aside that space for the graphic and then go ahead and fill in the text on the page. That way a visitor can read the text without first waiting for the graphic to download. Please make use of this attribute!

You'll also notice the "alt" tag, which tells the browser what text to display if the graphic can't be shown. This is useful for some text-only browsers, or in case your link to the graphic is broken for some reason.

Study this example to see how to make a hyperlinked graphic image:
<A href="http://www.zdnet.com/~macuser/people/andyi/">
  <img src="graphics/baaroom.gif"></A>.
See the anchor tags surrounding the image tag?

HTML Troubleshooting in 50 Words or Less

The best HTML troubleshooting tip I can offer is that, when things look screwy, double check to be sure you've included a matching closing tag for every opening tag. If you've forgotten to close a bold tag, for example, the rest of the page will be bold!

HOT TIP

Internet Tips (JH)

Because it's tough to gracefully surf the Internet with seaweed all tangled in your toes, we've provided some ideas to consider for maximizing your surfing pleasure.

Netscape

Real estate. Give yourself a larger Web browser window. Many browsers allow you to disable the toolbars and other doohickeys that clutter the window frame. In Netscape Navigator, for instance, turn off Show Toolbar and Show Directory under the Options menu. Study up—you can substitute command keys for most toolbar buttons and make your switch to a larger window permanent. Leave Show Location turned on, though—it's just too useful.

Real estate, part two. Remember that you can open more than one window in Netscape Navigator. If you're waiting for enormous graphics or a huge page to load in one window, press ⌘N for a new window, where you can go exploring elsewhere rather than twiddle your thumbs. Switch back and forth between windows as needed.

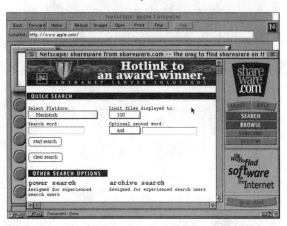

In one picture we illustrate three tips! The foreground window displays more of the Web page because the toolbars have been turned off. We're about to search for some shareware while the window in the background continues to download some heavy graphics.

Professional Help for Budding Webmasters

Once you get your HTML sea legs, you'll want to begin investigating applications, add-on utilities, and books that help automate HTML coding.

Guidance of the Web, by the Web, for the Web (JH)

Netscape offers pointers to lots of HTML and Web page authoring sites at <http://home.netscape.com/assist/net_sites/index.html>. And HotWired lists an essential tool kit of Web tools at <http://www.hotwired.com/surf/special/toolkit/toolkit.html>.

The Software (JH)

One of the best shareware HTML editors is **HTML Pro** by Niklas Frykholm ($5). You might also consider the HTML writing add-ons in **Microsoft Word 6.0.1** and **WordPerfect 3.5** or Lindsay Davies's $120 set of BBEdit **HTML Extensions** <http://www.barebones.com>. **Netscape Navigator Gold 2** for Macintosh <http://home.netscape.com> includes page authoring extensions. And SoftQuad's **HoTMetaL Pro** ($195) <http://www.sq.com> adds spell checking and tools for working with images and graphics.

The most serious HTML tool is Adobe's **SiteMill** ($600), and its little sister **PageMill** ($100). PageMill smoothes the hassles and drudgery of simple HTML coding, and allows for instantaneous switching to viewer mode, so there's no need to switch back and forth to a Web browser. Adding images to a page is positively easy. While version 1 was directed strictly at novice page authors, version 2, due out as we go to press, promises to be a much more powerful and complete tool, offering support for tables, search and replace, Drag-and-Drop sound importing and conversion, and spell checking.

Adobe SiteMill does PageMill one better—it manages all the documents of an entire Web site, taking over such drudgery as updating all the hypertext references throughout your site when you change the name of one document or move it to a new location. SiteMiil is a serious and useful tool, and for the price, it's obviously aimed at professional webmasters.

The commercial HTML editor HoTMetaL Pro adds niceties such as a spelling checker.

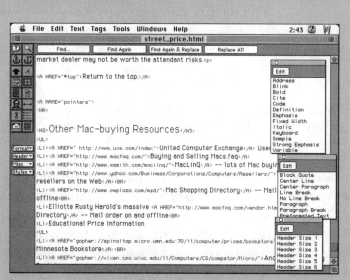

World Wide Web Weaver is an inexpensive and powerful HTML editor.

*[PageMill 1 is junk and will lead you seriously astray. Yeah, you can do a fast home page (five minutes or less) but the HTML created is bad, and not particularly portable. The program fails to use or even allow important tags, and when you open a well-coded page in it, it instantly changes all the good code to its own poor, sometimes buggy HTML, with no option thank you. Version 2 has been announced, but wasn't shipping when I wrote this. If the press release doesn't exaggerate, then PageMill 2 will be a great and useful tool. Much better now, and still great even when PageMill 2 shows, is the cheaper **World Wide Web Weaver** ($50) <http://www.northnet.org/best/Web.Weaver/WWWW.html>.—SB]*

At this writing, Microsoft was slated to release a Mac version of **FrontPage** ($700) which will allow both WYSIWYG Web page editing and Web site management. Keep your eye out for news.

The Best Web Page Book (SB)

Creating a personal home page on the Web is a snap. Anyone can do it. Not everyone can do a great page though. The language of pages, HTML, isn't difficult, but there are too many tricks to just fly by the seat of your pants. Book publishers have noticed that and there are dozens of titles that help you with your own pages. Most are average, some are useless, and *The Web Page Design Cookbook* by Horton, Taylor, Ignacio, and Hoft (ISBN 0-471-13039-7; $34.95 with CD-ROM; John Wiley & Sons) is just wonderful. It's readable, you will learn from it (even if that's not your goal), and it has a CD-ROM of templates, samples, and goodies that every Web page designer should use.

Other Tips

Target practice. Web page authors: This sly trick will help keep visitors from wandering off exploring the links on your page, never to return. Insert the "target= window" tag (Netscape Navigator 2 and later only) inside your pointer anchors like so:

```
<A target=window
href="http://www.macintouch.com">MacInTouch</a>.
```

Your visitors will visit the pointed-to site in a new window, with your original page still waiting patiently in the background.

Internet shareware database. It keeps getting more and more difficult to get useful results from Archie servers, the databases that track the location of all the software on the Internet. They're either too busy or the search just doesn't turn up anything useful. To locate shareware on the Internet, try this neat new alternative. The commercial Web site c/net offers a massive searchable database of shareware, including abstracts of each piece of software and the sites that carry it <http://www.shareware.com/>.

Forgo the graphics. Though the graphics are nice, sometimes you just need to get around the Web fast. Use the option in your Web browser to turn off the loading of graphics, which will instead show you the text quickly with just a small place holder for missing graphics. Click on any of the place holders to load individual graphics anytime you like.

Turning off graphics. The small page symbols represent the spots where graphics were to be loaded.

24 Networking

With today's emphasis on getting "wired" it's hard to imagine a time when folks bought personal computers precisely because they didn't *have* to be connected to another computer! Your newly purchased Apple II+, for example, was *yours*, to do *any* dang thing with—no mainframe system administrator looking over your shoulder.

Networking is nothing more than getting computer devices to work together. And as soon as you get more than one at a location you may want to tie them together. Maybe you simply want both Macs to share a single PostScript laser printer. Maybe someone at one Mac wants to look at a file on your Mac without leaving their seat or tossing diskettes across the room. Maybe they want to send you phone messages or meeting schedules. Perhaps you need to tie into the office Macs downtown. Or maybe you only want to play the network version of DOOM! In this chapter, we'll make you hip to setting up your Macs to handle these tasks.

Fact is, no one says you *have* to connect your Mac to another computer, but if you want to, that ability is built right into it, and has been since the introduction of the Mac Plus over a decade ago.

Contributors

Bob Weibel (BW) is the chapter editor.

Ron Colvin (RC) designs and maintains big, BIG networks, for the U.S. Army, NASA, the U.S. Veterans Administration, and commercial clients.

John Rizzo (JR) is a computer columnist and author of several books including *How Macs Work* (Ziff-Davis Press). He's also an on-line and networking specialist, and teaches computing at San Francisco's Center for Electronic Art.

Paul Hurley (PH) is director of computer services for a large law firm in Sacramento, California.

Sharon Zardetto Aker (SZA), Nancy E. Dunn (ND), Stephen Howard (SH), Arthur Naiman (AN), John Kadyk (JK), and **Charles Rubin (CR)** contributed to earlier editions of *The Macintosh Bible*, from which parts of this chapter were taken.

Contents

Why Network? (BW)

You haven't "wired" your Macs, and you're doing just fine. Your partner doesn't mind pausing her work to print a document you've handed over on disk; after all she gets that nice laser printer at her station. And what's wrong with strolling down the hall with a diskette to share a file with someone on another Mac—yellow Post-it notes attached? Those hand-written messages taped to the fridge or water cooler have a certain communal charm, and shouting down the hall is cool, too. Then you take on an extra project and suddenly your old, informal system of sharing documents and ideas isn't up to the new pace. You can't print anything because Suzy's too busy: She's spent too long doctoring the wrong revision of an important document thrown onto a shared diskette. Soon you've got new printers, modems, and other relatively expensive pieces of equipment to share.

It's time to get networked—time to connect those Macs so that someone can send a document or just a brief reminder to someone else; get easy, organized access to collaborative documents; or maybe just print something without jumping up and interrupting someone.

In the following sections, we'll describe the main benefits of networking. If the features described seem attractive to you, it's time to set up a local area network (LAN) for your Macs. We'll deal with network wiring and organization further on in the chapter.

File Sharing

If the "In" tray next to your Mac still bears interoffice memos with attached routing slips, ask yourself why. Everything you need in order to share files is built right into System 7. When you've finished your part of a project you can quickly invoke file sharing so that others on the production line can use their Macs to read or copy the file from your hard disk. No more sprints between desks.

System 7 Peer-to-Peer File Sharing (JK/CR/SH)

System 7's file sharing lets Macs on a network access each other's files. It's a great way to copy files from one Mac to another—much easier and faster than carrying floppies back and forth. You can also work on a file located on another Mac without copying it to your own, but that generally slows down both Macs.

Using System 7 file sharing starts with a trip to the Sharing Setup control panel. Click the Start button to activate file sharing on your Mac. The names you enter under Network Identity will appear on everyone's Chooser.

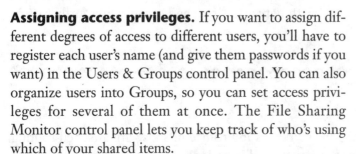

To set up access privileges for a file, folder, or disk volume, select it on the desktop and choose the Sharing command in the Finder's File menu. This dialog box will appear.

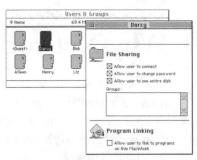

The Users & Groups control panel lets you grant sharing privileges to different users or groups of users.

Turning on file sharing. Your files are private until you turn on file sharing by clicking the Start button in the Sharing Setup control panel. Then you select a disk, folder, or file to share and choose the Sharing command from the File menu. In the dialog box that appears, you can set up access privileges for other users on your network, restricting them to merely looking at your files, or allowing them to make changes, rename, move, or delete them.

Assigning access privileges. If you want to assign different degrees of access to different users, you'll have to register each user's name (and give them passwords if you want) in the Users & Groups control panel. You can also organize users into Groups, so you can set access privileges for several of them at once. The File Sharing Monitor control panel lets you keep track of who's using which of your shared items.

Once you've set up file sharing on your Mac, you can use the File Sharing Monitor control panel to see which files, folders, or disks you've shared, and who's currently using them.

To gain access to files on a server or another user's Mac, select the shared volume in the Chooser.

Accessing files on another Mac. To access shared files on someone else's Mac, you open the Chooser, click on the AppleShare icon, select the Mac's name in the box on the right, and click OK. In the next couple of dialog boxes, you'll be asked to enter the name under which you were registered and your password (if any), and to select the shared item you want to use. When you've clicked OK in the last dialog box, the shared item's icon shows up on your desktop, just like another disk.

In the same way, you can access all the contents of your own Mac's hard disk from another networked Mac; just enter your owner's name and password (you entered them in the Sharing Setup control panel when you turned file sharing on).

Are You Being Served?

(Martin Labelle/James Reynaldo/BW)

There are two ways to set up network services. In a *peer-to-peer* arrangement, say for file sharing, each networked Mac is capable of sharing files. In a *server-based* setup, all shared files must be kept on a central file-sharing computer. Before your housemates or coworkers can access a file, you must copy it from your computer to the file server, which then shares the file. System 7's file-sharing feature is peer-to-peer. Apple's AppleShare file-sharing software represents the server-based approach. (Both approaches are described in "File Sharing," earlier in this chapter.)

Because "service" is the raison d'être of computer networking, whether it's print spooling, file sharing of centralized databases or documents, e-mail, or shared modems, your network is likely to require at least one type of server. Although you can run several services from a single Mac if you have to, matching the right Mac with the right server software is a tricky business. You need to consider the number of people accessing the server at any one time, how many and what kind of services you've installed, the kinds of files you're sharing, and the speed of your cabling (LocalTalk versus Ethernet, for example). Given the number of interrelated factors, we'll throw out a nonlinear potpourri of considerations to help you weigh the alternatives:

- If you store thousands of 100K or smaller files on a file server, then the server should be able to complete file requests quickly. If, on the other hand, you're storing multi-megabyte image files, you'll want a dedicated Mac with a fast CPU and faster network cabling than LocalTalk. Still, if people don't use the server a lot, then you won't need the fastest CPU. Get the idea?

- In our experience, AppleShare version 3 running on older 68030 Macs (LC III, IIci, IIsi) with at least 8MB of RAM is the minimal setup for a workgroup of 25 users. If you have a 68040-based Mac or Power Mac as a server, there's no reason not to go with AppleShare 4 (it's faster). And get the biggest, fastest hard drive you can afford—you'll never regret it.

- You usually know your server setup is too slow when users start consistently complaining about it. If only a couple of people tend to complain, find out whether they're inadvertently doing hog-city stuff. Launching applications from a server will definitely slow you down over LocalTalk, as will double-clicking a Word document from a mounted server drive or sharing font suitcases. LocalTalk just can't take it. It's good practice to always copy files to your desktop before opening them.

- Different types of server software can often work together on the same Mac. For example, you can run Apple's Apple Remote Access on the same machine as your AppleShare file server, no problem. (And that way, ARA can just tap into the AppleShare user list, so you don't need another utility to create a user's account for the ARA server.)

- It's not a good idea to allow the file server, such as AppleShare, to also act as a print server on a LocalTalk LAN. The aggravation of having to restart the server every time the spooler hangs up isn't worth it.

- You're better off upgrading (for example, purchasing faster drivers or CPU accelerators) the server hardware you already own and handing the newly purchased Macs over to individual users. Any network—whether it's five users or 5,000—is only as good as the people on it. The real work is done by the workers, and it is done better with better tools.

Safe Service/Fault Tolerance

It's the information age, and chances are greater than ever that you or your business sells information, not widgets. All day long you're dipping into the company's vital information, stored on an AppleShare file server. How much business would you lose if the hard disk failed during business hours. Oh sure, you've got rigorous data backups on tape or disk—right?—but it could take three or more hours to pop in a replacement disk, format it, and restore all the data from last night's backup. Plus you'd have lost the day's current work! There are situations in which you just can't afford to go down, and fortunately, with a specialized form of disk storage known as *RAID* (Redundant Array of Independent Disks), you can greatly diminish the chance of disk failure.

Disk arrays gang together several separate hard drives so that they function as a single drive. And in numbers, there's security. It's like flying the Pacific in a jet: With only one engine, you'll crash if the engine fails. But a four-engine jet can keep flying on three engines should one fail. This is the concept of "redundancy," having more than one critical component in line in case one part should fail in action. In computer talk this concept is lumped under the term *fault tolerance*.

Disk arrays can achieve this fail-safe ability, or fault tolerance, in several ways depending on how the separate disks are designed to function together. The developers of RAID devised several types, or *Levels,* of RAID, each designed with certain strengths in mind. They trade off security and performance in different ways. Following are the basics of the commercially attractive Levels, so you can decide which type to buy (Level 2 is obsolete, and Level 4 isn't commonly implemented, hence their omission):

Level 1: Known as *disk mirroring,* Level 1 simply writes two complete copies of the files you save, each copy on a separate disk in the array. If one drive in the array fails, the other takes over. Level 1 arrays read data as fast as a single disk, and write data slightly more slowly.

Level 3: Known as *parallel access,* Level 3 splits your files up into sections, and spreads those sections across several different drives—typically three—as it writes. A fourth drive is reserved for storing information know as *parity data.* Parity is simply special data that's mathematically derived from the file data spread across the first three or more drives. It can be used to reconstruct the data on any one of the other drives in the array, should one fail—although it won't work if two drives fail at once. Also, since a Level 3 array reads and writes data from three drives at once, it's faster than a single drive, making it good for storing and retrieving large files, such as those used in desktop publishing production, or image editing.

Level 5: Known as *independent access,* Level 5 also uses parity for data backup, but in a different way. Instead of storing all the parity data on the same disk, Level 5 arrays spread the parity data across several disks, mixing it in with your file data. That means that Level 5 arrays don't have to wait in line to write the parity data to one particular disk, since all the disks are available for that purpose. That level of independence makes RAID Level 5 good for servers that handle lots of users writing small files, such as you'd encounter in a busy order-entry system, dating service, or sales transaction setup.

Although only System 7 Macs can share their files, Macs running System 6 can access files on other Macs—all they need is the AppleShare workstation software, which comes on all System installation disks since version 6.0.4 (or later).

AppleShare file sharing (BW/SZA/SH/JK). *AppleShare*, Apple's file-server software, can turn any Mac on a network into a dedicated, centrally managed depot for storing and sharing files—a.k.a. a file server. With AppleShare running, the file server's hard disk appears to everyone on the network as another icon on the desktop, with its own window, folders, and files. AppleShare predates System 7 file sharing (described earlier) and has some similar security features; each file or folder can have an *owner* and only someone with appropriate access privileges can get at it. A network administrator can set up workgroups with various levels of access privileges. AppleShare also includes the AppleShare Print Server, which spools print jobs (see "Background Printing" in Chapter 21).

AppleShare 3 now shares the lineup, along with AppleShare 4, a speed-optimized version that only runs on 68040 and higher Macs using System 7.1 or later. A separate version, AppleShare 4.1, is available with Apple Workgroup Servers supplanting AppleShare Pro, or as an upgrade from version 4. A Power Mac native version, version 4.2, should be available by the time you read this. AppleShare 4.2 replaces AppleShare Pro, which ran on Apple's Unix implementation, A/UX (Apple's Unix-based operating system). This new version provides big speed improvements on existing Power Mac servers.

POWER MAC

Current AppleShare Versions: Capacities and Requirements

Features	AppleShare version		
	AppleShare 3.0.1	AppleShare 4.0.1	AppleShare 4.2.1
Number of users logged in at the same time	100	150	250
Open files	346	346	3,000
System required	7.0	7.1	7.5.1
Minimum RAM	4MB	8MB	16MB
Mac processor	68030	68040	PowerPC

File Sharing Tips

File sharing has two main disadvantages: It uses up memory in and slows down the *host Mac* (the one that's sharing files). Here are a few tips on how to minimize that tendency, and simplify its use overall:

Create aliases. You can bypass most of the procedure for getting a shared item onto your desktop by making an alias of it once you get it there the first time. The next time, just double-click the alias and click OK in the dialog box that appears. (See "System Tips" in Chapter 3 for more on setting up aliases.)

Consolidate shared items. You can share up to ten separate items (files, folders, or disk volumes), but unless you're setting up different access privileges for each of them, it's much easier to gather everything you're sharing into one folder and share it.

Ask those you share with to be considerate. The fewer people with whom you share files, the less time your Mac will spend responding to their requests. Ask the people with whom you share files to free up your Mac by disconnecting as soon as they've copied what they need.

Limit number of shared files. Share as few files as possible. The fewer files you share, the fewer opportunities there will be for someone else to accidentally delete or rename your files or see something they shouldn't.

Use as little security as possible. You should be able to control access to your sensitive files by being careful about which folders you share. As soon as you start creating users and groups and setting privileges for them, you'll find yourself tangled in a web of security that you'll constantly be asked to change. A lot of people will forget their passwords, and there's no place to look them up—you can only create new ones.

If you do register users, make sure all owners of file-sharing Macs on the network register users with the same names. If someone named Margaret were registered as Meg on one Mac, Peggy on another, and Maggie on a third, she'd have to remember which Mac had her set up under which name.

Network E-Mail

Here we're talking network e-mail, not to be confused with dial-in electronic mail services of America Online, CompuServe, or the Internet (see Chapters 22 and 23 for more on these). With the right software you can run your own mail system, customized for your needs; and lots of people do just that. That's because if file sharing is the network circulatory system for documents, *e-mail* is the nervous system, serving to trigger activity, to stimulate thought, and respond to crises. When, for example, your contribution to a group project is complete and the file is ready for sharing, you still need to notify your next-in-line salary slave before you can put your feet up. A simple electronic mail system might only flash a message on someone's screen. More sophisticated systems store messages in electronic mailboxes and notify people to check and retrieve their mail. Many even allow you to attach document files to messages, and thus serve as a means of file sharing as well.

Memos and reminders are perfect fodder for e-mail: No more slips of important paper blowing in the wind or getting buried in the heap on your desk. You can quickly nudge a single individual or a whole department, checking electronically to see if everyone has received the message. Most mail systems make replying to a message quick and easy—a great catalyst for decision making.

In its classic "store-and-forward" form, e-mail consists of e-mail server software running on a server computer, and a *client* (or *front-end*) portion running on each individual's Mac. The *mail server* acts as a sort of electronic post office where messages come in, are sorted, and are then stored in each individual user's personal mailbox. Using the front-end client software, you can open your mailbox at your convenience and retrieve your mail. An alternate, "broadcast" form of e-mail shoots messages straight to individual desktops, often a good option for small (five-to-ten-person) networks or for network conferencing.

E-Mail Features   (PH)

Given the number of features competing vendors have added to the basic mail packages of yesteryear, there's more to e-mail than you might realize. Here are some of the things you can expect to find:

- *Mail messaging*. This is the typical method of posting messages to one or more electronic mailboxes.

- *Transport medium for files*. You can attach one or several document files to a single message, which means your mail system can also serve for file exchange.

- *Conferencing.* Some e-mail packages provide a message-passing system with a conference screen. Several people can get an interactive conference session going, not unlike what you'd find on CompuServe or America Online (described in Chapter 22).

- *Remote mail access.* Some e-mail packages let remotely located Macs dial in to send and receive mail messages through a modem connected to the mail server.

- *Gateways.* The boundaries of your e-mail activity may extend beyond your local network into the realms of public e-mail services such as AppleLink, CompuServe, MCI Mail, and America Online. Some e-mail packages provide *gateway software* that lets you automatically exchange mail with these services. With a gateway, you don't have to quit your local e-mail to log on to the outside service.

The Shrinking World of Mac E-Mail (PH/BW)

If you're ready to take advantage of the e-mail features we describe, you should be aware that your choices of Macintosh e-mail server software, which you'd use to set up an e-mail post office on a dedicated Mac computer, have shrunk a bit in the last few years. For example, Microsoft bailed out on its Microsoft Mail server for Macintosh, stating its policy to no longer upgrade or develop the Mac-based mail-server portion. Instead, Microsoft is recommending that users move to a new MS Mail server that will run on PCs using the Windows NT multitasking operating system. Microsoft had planned to develop Mac e-mail service as a PowerTalk module, but Apple kind of pulled the plug on PowerTalk after noticing that only a small percentage of users bothered to install and use it. That'll all take a while to get rolling, so for now, MS Mail is in a state of flux.

Many of the popular mail products for the IBM PC, including Lotus's cc:Mail and DaVinci eMAIL, now are including a Macintosh desktop front-end client, as well as front-end clients for DOS, Windows, and OS/2. Note, however, that these products require a PC to run the mail server.

That leaves QuickMail as the leading Mac-based e-mail server, as well as SoftArc's FirstClass, which is aimed at larger corporate mail requirements. But you'll get plenty of mileage out of some economy-class e-mail packages such as WordPerfect Office (described in Chapter 12) and Casady & Greene's Snap MAIL, described later in this chapter.

QuickMail (PH)

In CE Software's **QuickMail** ($450 for five users), you'll always have a Mac as the mail server, even if you have PCs connecting via QuickMail's PC client software. It's a natural choice for Macintosh networks that have a few PCs attached. And thanks to the Mac-like interface, QuickMail is very easy to administer, so it makes a good overall mail package even if half the connected machines are PCs. Version 3.6 now runs native on Power Macs, and the extra processing speed means QuickMail can handle more mail without the server bogging down.

QuickMail is what we call a "full-featured" mail system, meaning that it includes all the bells and whistles outlined in "E-Mail Features" earlier in this chapter. On the network I manage, QuickMail does more than handle mail messages. For example, we can attach up to 16 files to a single QuickMail message, allowing us to send the file(s) along with a message that explains what to do with them, and when.

We're also using the QuickMail message-passing system, which lets us call up a QuickConference screen, select the person or persons we want to beam a message to, type in a message, and shoot it directly to their Mac, where it pops up on screen.

Several people can also get an interactive conference session going in QuickMail. We find it useful in conferencing between offices located in different cities, because they're connected via a high-speed backbone network. Everyone can follow the conference, selecting and saving relevant text from the screen.

Remote dial-in mail. When someone doesn't have his or her own e-mail account but wants to get into our network, the QuickMail dial-in feature lets us set them up with a QuickMail mailbox that they can access via a modem. They dial in, enter a password, and with standard terminal emulation (and Xmodem or Zmodem file transfer protocols), they can send and receive messages and attached documents using standard telecommunications software. If they're using an IBM PC, Unix workstation, or any system sporting the required terminal emulation and file transfer protocols, all they see are simple ASCII screen prompts. If the person remotely connecting to QuickMail has a Mac, the standard QuickMail package includes an excellent program called QM Remote, which provides the same interface as the standard QuickMail client software. As an added advantage, QM Remote lets you create your QuickMail messages off-line and then send and receive all your waiting mail messages at once, in the evening, for example, when phone rates are cheaper.

GOOD
FEATURE

E-mail gateways. With QuickMail's built-in e-mail gateways you can send or receive electronic mail from MCI Mail, AppleLink, and CompuServe without leaving QuickMail to log on to these services directly. Third-party gateways from StarNine

Technologies are also available for linking e-mail systems for Novell MHS, IBM AS/400 systems and mainframes, and even the Internet. The gateway software automatically connects to the outside mail system, appropriately reformats the message, and handles enclosed files. You can set it to automatically connect and exchange mail once a day or every few minutes, as you wish. My firm uses QuickMail's AppleLink gateway quite frequently, so instead of signing onto AppleLink we just create a normal QuickMail message, enclose a document if necessary, and then send it to our AppleLink account.

It is also very easy to exchange QuickMail messages between remote QuickMail sites. We use a QuickMail-to-QuickMail gateway to exchange messages with several of our clients who use QuickMail. To address a message to a remote QuickMail site, you simply include the person's name and his or her QuickMail phone number.

You'll need to set up a gateway mail center on your QuickMail server. That setup does require you to run the QuickMail administration software all the time, because it's that software that actually controls the modem. It runs as a separate task under System 7, so you'll need to have sufficient RAM for it.

If you have several QuickMail servers (we have 12, in order to handle our 200 local users, since each QuickMail server can handle up to 32 active users at one time), pick one to handle the gateways. In my office, the one that's least busy has the modem attached, and that's the one that communicates with the outside world.

E-Mail Contenders

(BW)

Although QuickMail dominates the Mac e-mail server market, there are other products worth considering. As we explained earlier, while most e-mail programs offer Mac software for sending and receiving e-mail at your Mac (called the desktop, or client portion), only a few offer a Mac-based server portion. Here are three more programs that do.

Snap MAIL. Casady & Greene's Snap MAIL ($200 for five users) may be poised to move into the vacuum created by Microsoft's repositioning of MS Mail. It has many of the features of full-blown packages, including message encryption for information privacy, but for external mail gateways and compatibility with non-Mac systems you need to purchase Information Access Technologies' HoloGate gateway software ($135, $162, and $500 for 5-, 10-, and 50-user packs.) Snap MAIL's easy to administer, and it doesn't necessarily require you to dedicate a Mac as a mail server. At $200 for a five-user package, it also costs only about half as much as programs such as QuickMail.

HOT TIP

The Snap MAIL software comes configured to work without a dedicated Mac as a server (though you can change this later). Instead of going through a server, the Snap MAIL software installed on *your* Mac sends your message straight to the Mac of the recipient. If that destination Mac isn't on when the message arrives, your Mac holds onto the message until the destination Mac makes its appearance on the network. This distributed e-mail setup saves you the expense of a dedicated Mac, and works fine in small, informal work settings.

As things get more hectic, though, this setup can backfire. If, for example, you turn off your Mac as you leave for lunch with an undelivered message waiting for delivery, the recipients won't get the message when they return and fire up their Macs while yours is turned off. That's why in larger offices or busy situations, you might want to recon-figure Snap MAIL to keep everyone's mail on a single Mac dedicated as mail server.

Like most mail programs, you can quickly launch Snap MAIL via the menu or by pressing a "hot key" of your choice. A nice resizable window pops up with the usual in-box, out-box, and a list of mail recipients. For sending notes, though, the program offers fill-in-the-blank templates for creating standard messages—phone notes, prod-uct orders, and so on—but you can also create your own custom forms. You can also use Snap MAIL's Talk mode to set up text-based "chats" with other Snap MAIL users on your network. Also, you'll find keyboard command shortcuts for every function, so you don't have to take your hands off the keyboard.

FirstClass. Although priced at only $495 for server software and license for five users, SoftArc's FirstClass is designed to fill the needs of industrial-strength corporate e-mail. That doesn't mean that you can't start small and simple with FirstClass, because FirstClass' strength is the ease with which you can scale up the power and range of its functions as your enterprise grows. You can add modules for handling additional net-work types (protocols) such as Novell and TCP/IP, as well as e-mail gateway modules for cc:Mail, Novell MHS, Internet, while a Microsoft Mail gateway is a standard fea-ture. SoftArc should release a native Power Mac version (3.5) of the server software by the time you read this, along with an upgrade to its Windows NT server product. If you're planning on growing your small enterprise, and the sky's the limit, investigate FirstClass further.

cc:Mail. Although **Lotus cc:Mail** is the predominant e-mail system used on personal computers, it has only one foot in the Mac-based e-mail server market. True, its **cc:Mail Desktop for the Macintosh** ($455 for 10 users) lets you set up a single e-mail mailbox on a Macintosh server. But all of the software provided for adminis-tering that server (which includes setting up additional mailboxes) must run on DOS or Windows-based computers, which access the Mac server. There's nothing wrong with that, provided you've got PCs networked along with your Macs.

From its beginning, cc:Mail was particularly strong at providing reliable e-mail between networked Macs and PCs, and that, among other strengths, including compatibility with Lotus Notes, the leading corporate groupware product, has put cc:Mail in its strong position. Still, for a smaller, "pure Mac" office, it may not be your top choice, given that you can't take full advantage of the cc:Mail Desktop for Macintosh server without a networked PC to run the administration software. However, if your small office is part of a larger organization that uses cc:Mail, they'll probably recommend you run with cc:Mail.

Sharing Other Resources

There's more to computer networks than sharing files and e-mail; you can also share equipment such as printers and modems (in fact, AppleTalk's main task in the early Mac days was connecting expensive LaserWriter printers). Most Macintosh-compatible printers come with the same built-in LocalTalk ports as do Macs, so when you connect a printer to your Mac with LocalTalk, it will appear in your Chooser, ready to use, even if it's down the hall.

Print Serving   (BW)

With LocalTalk circuitry built-in, your printer becomes a print station: It sits by itself informing everyone that it's there, ready for service to anyone on the AppleTalk network who'll select it from the Chooser. Granted, it's not quite what we'd call a *printer server*, in that it doesn't *spool* files (see the section on print spooling in Chapter 21). Apple's AppleShare file server software also includes print service. When you print to a printer connected to the AppleShare server, your print job moves quickly off your desktop and over to the AppleShare server Macintosh, which stores jobs waiting to print, automatically feeding each job to the printer. If a printer doesn't have network circuitry, such as LocalTalk, built-in, connecting the printer to a print server is one good way of sharing it over the network. Be aware that many Mac-compatible printers, such as Apple StyleWriters, come with software that, when installed on the computer to which the printer's attached, lets other people on the network share the printer. If you're sharing the printer this way, though, you may experience interruptions or slowdowns on the serving Mac when others on the network print to the shared printer.

Dial-Up Connections (PH/BW)

One thing about a good network—it's awfully hard to leave behind. Whether you're roving with your PowerBook or handling some office business from home, heaven forbid, you can still reach their file servers, printers, and e-mail over the phone lines. AppleTalk dial-in access has been around for years: You establish a modem connection between your remote Mac and another Mac or black-box device on the office network, and the two Macs use the regular AppleTalk network to pass data back and forth. The telephone connection basically substitutes for the network cabling, though at much slower modem speeds. Early products used proprietary drivers to send AppleTalk protocols over the wires via modem. Now Apple has set the standard with the Apple Remote Access protocol, which finally integrates dial-in access at the Mac system level.

The first product, AppleTalk Remote Access 1, originally shipped with early PowerBooks. It then became a separate product, and has now been superseded by Apple Remote Access 2, with version 3 waiting in the wings as of this writing.

There's now a large array of hardware and software products that let you take advantage of ARA. Apple's **Remote Access Personal Server** ($190) gives you everything you need to set up a remote Mac and a networked Mac for dial-in access. For larger organizations Apple offers a $1,300 software/hardware combo called **Remote Access MultiPort Server**. It includes a NuBus four-port serial card to which you can attach four modems, allowing multiple dial-in access sessions. You can add up to three additional $1,500, four-port expansion cards to control a maximum of 16 remote connections. Naturally, these prices don't include the Macintosh you'll have to dedicate as an ARA server machine.

Several companies make stand-alone ARA server hardware—no server Mac required. Shiva's **LanRover/PLUS** ($5,300) is a popular model, and other ARA server boxes are available from Asanté, Ascend, Telebit, Global Village, and others.

Communications Servers (BW)

Though it sounds pretty highfalutin', a *communications server* can be as simple as a computer or black-box device that lets folks on your network share modems, or other forms of high-speed links to remote sites or services. Most people on a network don't use a high-speed modem often enough to justify buying one for each—although that's changing as the world gets wired to the Web—but with a little specialized hardware and software, you can access a shared modem as if it were connected directly to your Mac.

Putting Together a Network

Now that you know *why* you might want to network your Macs, you face another big question: How do you do it? In some ways, networking Macs is easier done than said: It's easier to plug your Macs together in a simple AppleTalk network and start sharing files and printers than it is to even begin explaining what's actually going on. That's because the AppleTalk network technology is designed to handle many network issues automatically, behind the scenes.

AppleTalk: Plug-and-Play (BW)

The plug-and-play beauty of the Macintosh makes it easy to start building a small network of two to 20 Macs. Beyond that, it becomes a bit more like "plug-and-pray," because you'll start needing to understand more about the inner workings of your network—the very things that AppleTalk has been handling automatically—and you'll need to purchase additional products to keep it humming. Example? Imagine that your 10-person organization grows to 40 people. All this time your network has been slowing down, and some people regularly find that it doesn't work at all! Unless you hire a network consultant, you'll have to learn about AppleTalk *zones* and *network numbering*. You'll need to know what *routers* are, and how they can reduce network traffic jams. Likewise, terms such as *Ethernet* and *EtherTalk* should spell relief, in terms of speeding up your traffic. And what's all this talk about *protocols*, anyway? Well, relax. The second part of this chapter will at least give you a framework for building an AppleTalk network, at least up to the point where your organization would hire someone with a professional understanding of networks.

AppleTalk: a Protocol (BW)

In the early days of the Mac the built-in network circuitry as well as the required inter-Mac cabling was called AppleTalk. That tended to make people think the wiring *was* the network, when in reality it's just a minor part. As mentioned in the "Network Protocols" sidebar, when we say "AppleTalk protocol" we're really talking about a large group of protocols that govern AppleTalk networks. The low-speed network circuitry and wiring that used to be called *AppleTalk*, is now called *LocalTalk*, to distinguish it from the other types of wiring and transmission schemes over which your Mac's AppleTalk protocols can operate. Ethernet is another transmission/wiring scheme over which AppleTalk protocols operate, one that you simply can't ignore these days, since Ethernet circuitry has been built into Macs since the Macintosh Quadra. (See "Ethernet Transmission" later in this chapter.)

Network Protocols (RC/BW)

In local area networks, all the computers are strung along a single wire, a sort of "party line" over which all the digital communication takes place. That saves on cabling, but it creates the potential for incredible chaos. Imagine if all the phones on your block were connected in a single, huge party line. Picture the interruptions, the eavesdropping, the total jam you'd be in. Sooner or later you and your neighbors would start developing rules and procedures (let's call them *protocols*)—hang up if the line is busy and try again later, keep calls short, hang up if an incoming call is not intended for you, and so on—to guarantee at least a semblance of orderly communication.

Solving this "party line" problem is the crux of networking. Although you can see and touch network cabling, it's the invisible sets of complex rules and digital procedures—the protocols—that really make a network run. In fact, for any network there may be dozens of separate protocols at work, many operating in different ways at the same time.

Protocol layers and functions

I once overheard this snippet of conversation at a truck stop on I-5: "What kind of network they got, anyway?" "I think it was an Ethernet," came the frank reply. I later asked a magazine art director what kind of network she had. The answer: "AppleTalk." Soon after, someone on the elevator was talking about a specific kind of network in his office, called 10BaseT.

But here's the point: All these people could have been talking about the same network. These three terms, Ethernet, AppleTalk, and 10BaseT, could actually describe different parts of a single network. How? The functions they name are all separate, each only describing a part of the whole network. Network folks tend to think of these different parts as occupying separate "layers," based on their function: wiring and raw signaling capability is one functional layer, protocols that organize those signals into a meaningful data flow form another distinct functional layer, and protocols that ensure reliable data transmission across the network form yet another discrete layer, and so on.

10BaseT, for example, is a wiring scheme, using twisted-pair cabling similar to phone wire. Ethernet, on the other hand, is a somewhat broader term, defining how computers and other devices should access the wiring—i.e. a distinct layer. Ethernet can and does run on other types of wiring, not just 10BaseT, or 100BaseT. And AppleTalk refers to an entire group of protocols created by Apple that governs almost every other aspect of networking, that is, how computer messages are organized and sent so that they arrive where they're supposed to without error.

If you've got a Mac-only network, you can pretty much safely stick to AppleTalk (lucky you). If you've got to connect with other kinds of computers, however, you'll need to know about—and coexist with—other protocol suites.

As we hinted above, AppleTalk, as a network protocol, breaks some real ground by merit of its plug-and-play nature, automatically handling a lot of techie things such as assigning workstation and network addresses, routing messages between networks, and so on. Instead of dealing with cryptic numbers, you can assign names to workstations, or to sections of your network, called zones. Zones are unique to AppleTalk and are part of why it's so easy to use.

LocalTalk transmission. Look on the back of any Mac dating from the original Mac Plus, and you'll find a connector marked with a printer icon. That connector does more than connect printers: It's also a LocalTalk network port. You can connect Macs and other LocalTalk-equipped devices, such as printers, by stringing special LocalTalk cabling between the LocalTalk connectors, called *ports*. There's a particular way to do this, and it's referred to as a *daisy-chain* setup.

If you ran the right kind of wire from the LocalTalk port of one Mac straight into the LocalTalk port of another Mac they'd be networked all right, but they'd also be the only two Macs on the network, since there'd be no way to string on other Macs. Instead of connecting Macs port to port, you must first plug a small plastic transformer box called a *LocalTalk connector* (or *compatible device)* to the Printer (i.e. LocalTalk) port. That LocalTalk connector is a sort of cable Y connector, which con-

ditions the signal and splits the single LocalTalk port on the Mac, providing *two* LocalTalk connections. To connect a series of LocalTalk devices, you simply plug a series of separate cable links between the connectors, forming a chain: One link of cable goes from one of the LocalTalk connector ports to the computer or device on one side, and another link of cable runs from the second port of the LocalTalk connector to the computer or device on the other side of a Mac in the chain. The chain

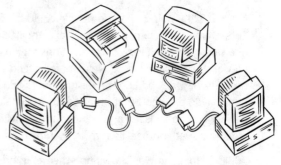

In a daisy-chain connection, such as those used with LocalTalk networks, a separate piece of cable runs between each connected Mac or other device. In LocalTalk networks, the wires plug into LocalTalk connector boxes, which plug into each Mac's printer port.

can be straight or twisted into a pretzel, as long as you don't connect the two ends together—no circles or loops. For the computers at each end of the wire, there's only one cable connection; a *terminating plug*, which reduces signal reflection back down the wires, is sometimes fitted into the remaining empty connector.

The original version of Apple's LocalTalk cable supported only up to 1,000 feet of total wiring with a maximum of 30 nodes (i.e. connected devices). Phone-type LocalTalk (called *PhoneNET*) was originally developed by Farallon to use standard

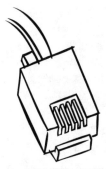

The RJ-11 phone jacks used in home and office phone systems are also used in PhoneNET-type LocalTalk cabling.

GOOD FEATURE

telephone cabling (and telephone RJ-11 connectors) instead of the more expensive LocalTalk shielded cabling. PhoneNET extended AppleTalk's total wiring limit to 3,000 feet, and through the use of star *repeaters*, used to boost signal strength, and quality wiring, it is possible to put 50 or 60 *nodes* on a PhoneNET network without too much distortion. And since RJ-11 plugs lock into place, they don't accidentally disconnect, as many Apple-style LocalTalk connectors are prone to do.

If you have a network of any size, PhoneNET-type hardware can save you lots of money, and imitations of it can save you even more. Trimar's **CompuNet** costs just $15 per connector, or $10 each if you buy ten or more. Focus Enhancements sells its LocalTalk **TurboNet ST** connectors for about the same price as the Trimar product, providing a signal boost that lets you extend your network up to 5,000 feet without using repeaters. (If you already have LocalTalk cabling, just switch over to PhoneNET-type hardware for any additional needs. Farallon makes an adapter for connecting LocalTalk to PhoneNET systems, so you won't lose whatever you have invested.)

Ethernet Transmission   (JR)

Once you start adding dozens of busy people to a network you'll need faster network wiring. Even folks at home and small offices are scanning photos, shuttling QuickTake images around, and occasionally running multiuser applications which must reside on a central server. LocalTalk, with a maximum transmission speed of 230.4Kbps is just too slow. Enter Ethernet, a data transmission and access scheme invented in 1973 at Xerox by Bob Metcalf, who went on to found 3Com Corporation, an influential networking company. Ethernet boasts a transmission speed of 10 megabits per second, and the new FastEthernet hits 100 megabits per second. That's like moving up from a cow path to a multilane freeway. Graduating to Ethernet entails getting the right hardware to connect to the Ethernet cabling at your location (check the "Ethernet Cabling" sidebar for details), and installing Ethernet driver software, which we discuss later.

A lot of Macs have Ethernet ports built into them, and several Macs have *two* Ethernet ports. In most cases, especially with 10BaseT and FastEthernet (also known as 100BaseT), you connect to your network a bit differently than you do with LocalTalk. The basic Ethernet port built into most Macs is called an *AAUI* (Apple Attachment Unit Interface), specific to the Mac. To use that port you plug in a small, $40 transceiver box that connects between the AAUI and the specific kind of wiring you're using. Think of the AAUI port as kind of general-purpose port that lets you plug into

POWER MAC

Open Transport   (JR)

Open Transport is a group of extensions that's replacing the network system software the Mac's been using up until now. Most Macs have some networking software, called *AppleTalk Manager,* built into ROM (Read Only Memory), and Open Transport basically replaces that. Think of it as a complete revision of the Mac's network system software.

Before Open Transport, AppleTalk was the Mac's native networking language, and everything else was just an add-on. That even goes for TCP/IP, the networking protocol used over the Internet: Even though you could (and still can) install MacTCP, AppleTalk had privileged access to the operating system resources. Open Transport reverses this situation, making every protocol—whether TCP/IP, Netware, or DecNet—an "equal-opportunity" protocol. It uses industry standard *API*'s (Application Programming Interface), so that an application that's written for Open Transport or these industry standard APIs can use any network protocol. Before this, network software developers had to crank out their own software for each protocol they wanted to support. Now they only have to write one interface to Open Transport, and Open Transport will handle the different protocols. In fact, Open Transport comes with TCP/IP network protocols.

Open Transport's other strength, aside from compatibility, is speed performance: It's Power Mac native networking, which speeds up everything. AppleTalk speeds up, and TCP/IP speeds up a lot. That's especially important if you're moving up to 100BaseT cabling on your network. The old system network software is just too inefficient to take advantage of FastEthernet's enhanced speed.

HOT TIP

You can now download Open Transport with the latest system software upgrade. The first version of Open Transport came out with the Power Mac 9500, though it now ships with all PCI Macs. The first version had notorious problems connecting to the Internet over a modem, and would cause intermittent system crashes. Also, if you'd established an Internet session and closed it, you couldn't launch another Internet session without restarting. So make sure you've upgraded to version 1.1 at least, which fixes these problems.

several types of Ethernet cabling, provided you buy the type of transceiver that corresponds to the cabling used in your network. If you get a 10BaseT transceiver you can plug into a 10BaseT-wired network. If you get a 10Base2 transceiver you can plug into a 10Base2 network. It's that simple.

Some of the newer Macs (the Power Mac 8500 and PCI Macs, for instance) have two Ethernet connectors, an AAUI, *and* a built-in 10BaseT connector. You don't need a transceiver at all with the 10BaseT connector. You simply plug the standard RJ-45 10BaseT plug (which looks like a fat phone plug) straight into the 10BaseT connector on the Mac. It's fairly plug-and-play Ethernet at that point, even more plug-and-play than LocalTalk, because you don't have to buy anything extra.

For older Macs without Ethernet circuitry built-in, you'll need to buy a *network interface card* (NIC) that plugs into your Mac. They're pretty cheap these days, generally under $100. The major vendors are Asanté, Dayna, Farallon, and Apple. You'll find adapters for NuBus, PCI, and even processor-direct slots (PDS) for computers like early Performas that didn't have NuBus expansion slots. You'll find a wide variety of NICs. Some simply provide an AAUI, others a specific transceiver, such as 10BaseT, or 10Base2. Others provide several different kinds of Ethernet ports on the same card, and you can use the one that best applies to your current cabling, and still be able to use the same card if your cabling changes.

FastEthernet (JR). Ten megabits per second sounds like a lot of data under the bridge but it may work out to less than you think. About one-third of that is carrying the network protocols that keep data messages organized. And, of course, this 10-megabits-per-second is shared with other systems on the network, further cutting into what *you* get for your actual data. In short, even Ethernet bogs down, which is why a lot of folks are moving to 100-megabit-per-second Ethernet, or FastEthernet.

There are a couple of competing 100-megabit-per-second standards: 100BaseT (FastEthernet), and VG AnyLan, designed by Hewlett-Packard. At least on the Mac scene, 100BaseT has basically won out: HP, which still sells VG AnyLan products now also sells 100BaseT products. Most Mac 100-megabit-per-second network equipment you see advertised is 100BaseT (FastEthernet), usually the 100BaseTX variety which requires Category 5 shielded twisted-pair wiring. VG AnyLan and 100BaseT4 (see "Ethernet Cabling" later in this chapter), will run over lower grades of twisted-pair wiring.

To move on up to FastEthernet you'll need:

- *A good reason.* If your conventional Ethernet setup is serving you well, why upgrade?

- *A 100BaseT network adapter card for your Mac.* You can't move up without one.

- *A 100BaseT hub or concentrator* (see "Ethernet Cabling" for an explanation of these terms).

- *Macs that can make use of the extra network speed.* That generally means PCI-bus Power Macs. NuBus expansion slots generally can't move data fast enough to take full advantage of a NuBus 100BaseT interface.

- *The Open Transport network system software upgrade.* Older network extensions just can't keep pace, but the redesigned, Power Mac native Open Transport software can. (See the "Open Transport" sidebar.)

POWER MAC

If you currently have a 10BaseT network installed, you might want to consider one of the dual-speed 10/100BaseT cards on the market. They go for around $250 and can operate at both 10BaseT and 100BaseT speeds. Buy one now, and when you upgrade to 100BaseT wiring and hubs, you won't have to replace your card. Most 10/100BaseT cards can sense whether you're connected to a 10BaseT or 100BaseT hub, and will downshift or upshift as needed.

Ethernet drivers (JR). You have to have some kind of Ethernet *network driver*. If the Mac comes with a built-in Ethernet port, then the driver will come with the System. Otherwise, the driver comes with the *NIC* (network interface card) you buy. These EtherTalk drivers are system extensions that go in the Extensions folder when you drop them onto the System Folder, and they show up in the Network control panel. In the Network control panel you'll see a driver for LocalTalk, and the Ethernet driver shows up as EtherTalk, or for Token Ring networks, there's one called TokenTalk.

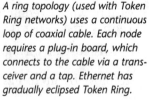

Apple's Ethernet driver works with most NICs but not all. Sometimes the NIC manufacturer says that you must use the driver they provide. This can cause a problem if you're a network manager installing network software on dozens of Macs. If you go to install a new Apple Ethernet driver on all the Macs, for example, and you're not aware that some cards in some Macs won't work with that Apple driver, you'll soon be getting calls from folks who suddenly can't get on the network.

A ring topology (used with Token Ring networks) uses a continuous loop of coaxial cable. Each node requires a plug-in board, which connects to the cable via a transceiver and a tap. Ethernet has gradually eclipsed Token Ring.

Some vendors' drivers may offer a performance boost for their cards. For that reason it's probably a good idea to use the card manufacturer's Ethernet driver. Some manufacturers actually just give you the Apple driver, but for a particular piece of hardware, the vendor's own specialized driver will do a better job.

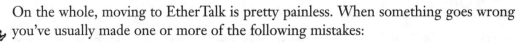

On the whole, moving to EtherTalk is pretty painless. When something goes wrong you've usually made one or more of the following mistakes:

- You didn't use the manufacturer's EtherTalk driver when the card will only work with that driver, and won't work with the Apple-supplied EtherTalk driver.

- You're plugging 10BaseT wiring directly between Macs without going through a hub.

- You're not using a transceiver along with the AAUI port, or using the wrong type of transceiver for the kind of Ethernet cabling that's installed.

Ethernet Cabling (JR/BW)

Ethernet, like LocalTalk, is really a set of protocols that describes how digital signals are transmitted and how computers access the cable. In that sense, it's not specific to any one kind of cabling, and several kinds of cable are currently used, as we describe below. And as we pointed out earlier, Ethernet isn't specific to any particular set of protocols either. It's purposely designed to handle multiple protocols, including AppleTalk, TCP/IP, Netware, and others.

There are five main types of Ethernet cabling currently in use:

• *10BaseT (twisted-pair) Ethernet.* 10BaseT has become the most popular Ethernet wiring, since it uses inexpensive twisted-pair wire similar to that strung throughout buildings for telephone connections. In short, it's cheaper and easier to install than the earlier types we discuss below. (The T in 10BaseT stands for telephone.) Unless you're using the new daisy-chainable Farallon EtherWave units (discussed on the next page), you'll have to set up your 10BaseT network as an active star topology that uses something called a 10BaseT *hub*, or *concentrator*, into which you connect a wire running from each separate Mac. These hubs are basically signal repeaters, a dumb apparatus that rebroadcasts the network signals down each run of wire so that they don't run out of steam. There are a lot of companies that make "mini-hubs" or "hublets".

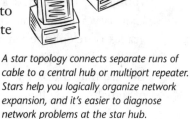

A star topology connects separate runs of cable to a central hub or multiport repeater. Stars help you logically organize network expansion, and it's easier to diagnose network problems at the star hub.

On a 10BaseT star network, each run of wire is limited to a maximum of 100 meters, or just over 300 feet. The number of devices depends on the make of the hub; high-end hubs can support more than 100. The hub needn't be a big, expensive affair. An 8-port mini-hub usually costs about $150 mail-order.

When shopping for 10BaseT wiring, look for Category 5, the highest grade. Call Black Box Corporation for its nifty networking catalog and order a spool of it. It's not much more expensive than lower-rated cabling and could be used for higher-speed wiring such as FastEthernet (100BaseT) described below.

RJ-45 jacks (top) and twisted-pair cabling are the standard cabling elements for 10BaseT Ethernet networks.

• *100BaseT (shielded twisted-pair) FastEthernet.* FastEthernet is a new standard that provides ten times the raw signaling speed of conventional Ethernet. At 100 megabits per second, large video, audio, and

Speed, Length, and Node Limits for Different Types of Cable

Network cabling and transmission schemes vary in speed, maximum cable length, and in the number of devices you can connect on a single run of cable. The table below tells you what to expect from the predominant types of Mac network cabling.

Cable Type	Maximum number of nodes per segment	Maximum cable run without repeaters	Maximum transmission speed
Apple LocalTalk	30	1,000 feet	230.4K/sec
PhoneNET LocalTalk	30	3,000 feet	230.4K/sec
10BaseT Ethernet (twisted-pair)	1*	100 meters	10MB/sec
10Base2 Ethernet (thin-wire)	30	189 meters	10MB/sec
10Base5 Ethernet (thick-wire)	100	500 meters	10MB/sec
100BaseT Ethernet (FastEthernet)	1*	250 feet	100MB/sec

Note: * One device per cable run is optimal, though you can add more and decrease reliability.

graphics files simply zip along the wire. There are actually two specifications for 100BaseT, one called 100BaseTX, which requires cabling comparable to the Category 5 wiring mentioned above. The other, called 100BaseT4, runs on lower grades of telephone wiring, including the common Category 3 used for 10BaseT. 100BaseT4 equipment isn't compatible with 100BaseTX and is less widely available. Beware that 100BaseT won't run with a 10BaseT hub, since it uses a different kind of signaling. You'll need to buy a 100BaseT hub.

- *Daisy-chained 10BaseT.* An alternative to the hub approach is Farallon's EtherWave, which lets you daisy chain 10BaseT Ethernet the way you would LocalTalk. Daisy-chained EtherWave networks are limited to a maximum of 100 meters, and each EtherWave daisy chain can support up to seven devices. EtherWave AAUI transceivers cost about $90 mail-order.

- *10Base2 (thin-wire) Ethernet.* 10Base2 Ethernet allows up to 30 daisy-chained devices per each 189-meter segment of coaxial cable (a type that uses a single-wire conductor surrounded by layers of electrical shielding). (The 2 in 10Base2 stands for the 200-meter maximum cable length; they rounded up.) Thin-wire Ethernet can use a daisy-chain topology or, with a *multiport repeater*, an active star layout. The use of thin-wire star topologies is rapidly disappearing in favor of 10BaseT.

Thin-wired Ethernet (10Base2) connections are daisy chained via BNC "tee" connectors and shielded coaxial cable.

- *10Base5 (thick-wire) Ethernet.* 10Base5, or thick-wire Ethernet, is a stiff twin-axial (one wire inside another wire) cable about ⅜ inch in diameter, with a 15-pin D-style connector. (The 5 in 10Base5 stands for the 500-meter maximum cable length.) The cable is terminated at both ends with special fittings that minimize signal reflections that would otherwise degrade communications, so it permits a maximum of 200 devices on a 1,640-foot segment. Thick-wire Ethernet has often been used as a central backbone connecting secondary networks throughout a building, although FastEthernet and fiber-optic links are rapidly replacing thick-wire as a backbone media.

Connecting PowerBooks (BW)

You rove with your PowerBook, creating reports and lots of other fresh data, all of which need to get onto your company's file server back at the office. You'll also want to tap directly into the office e-mail when you're back in town. Basically, you want that PowerBook to feel right at home with a network connection of its own. Fortunately there are many ways to do that, for every make and model of PowerBook.

POWERBOOK

PowerBook LocalTalk. Every PowerBook has LocalTalk networking built-in, so you can hook it to a LocalTalk (or PhoneNET) network just as you would any Mac, as we describe earlier in the chapter. Once you've got a LocalTalk connector in place along the daisy chain, you disconnect and reconnect the lead between the connector and the PowerBook, leaving the connector itself in place along the daisy chain. When you return to the office, plug the LocalTalk connector lead into the Printer port on the PowerBook and fire up the computer; you'll be on the network. Naturally, you'll need to have AppleShare and e-mail client software installed on the PowerBook in order to use those services.

PowerBook Ethernet. You've got several options for connecting to an Ethernet network, depending on the model of PowerBook you own. Here's a rundown:

- The Duo Dock II, 500-series, and later PowerBooks have built-in AAUI ports, just like most Macs sold these days. All you need is the appropriate transceiver to link the AAUI to the specific form of Ethernet cabling installed at the site, as we described in "Ethernet Transmission" earlier in the chapter.

- You can also buy 10BaseT Ethernet docks for Mac Duos. Newer Technology (316/685-4904, 800/678-3726) sells its **MicroDock** ($235) with a 10BaseT connector and an ADB port. Don't forget that you can always add a NuBus Ethernet card to the original full-size Duo Dock.

- For 100-series PowerBooks and expansionless Macs (such as the Plus and Classic) SCSI Ethernet adapters can still get them out on the Ethernet. Note that they're only about half as fast as a standard Ethernet adapter. One of the cheapest is Focus Enhancements' **EtherLAN SC** ($200). Asantè's **Mini EN/SC** ($413) works with both thin-wire Ethernet and 10BaseT, as does the **DaynaPort Pocket SCSI/Link** ($249).

- For Duos without docks, you can use serial-port-to-Ethernet adapters such as Farallon's **EtherWave PowerBook Adapter** ($379) and Dayna's **DaynaPort E/Z** ($309). They're slower than a straight Ethernet connection, but convenient.

- You can also plug an Ethernet adapter into the PC Card slot on the PowerBook 5300 and 190. Farallon's **EtherMac PC Card** for 10BaseT mail orders for around $170. A combination 10Base2/10BaseT version goes for $230, and the **EtherWave PC Card** for $250.

GOOD
FEATURE

- If you've got one of the PowerBook 5300 series or later that sports a built-in IR (infrared) transceiver, you can exchange files with an IR-equipped Mac or PowerBook, just as you would with any Mac wired up to a LocalTalk network. For $70 mail-order you can equip your stay-at-home desktop Mac with Farallon's AirDoc so that it can handle the PowerBook infrared signals. The compact AirDoc pod plugs into a free serial port on the desktop Mac, and with the bundled AirPath software installed, gives infrared PowerBooks access to LocalTalk, Ethernet, and even Token Ring networks.

Networking Tips

HOT TIPS

The following are a few ounces of prevention that could go a long way in helping you sidestep common networking mishaps.

Equipment

Shield for electrical noise (BW). Apple-specified LocalTalk cabling is shielded, meaning that one of the electrical conductors within the cable consists of braided strands of wire or a metal foil which, in either case, wraps completely around the other insulated conductors. This shielding reduces signal distortion from external electrical noise generated by AC power lines, motors, generators, signaling equipment, and other devices that generate electromagnetic frequencies. PhoneNET wiring is usually unshielded, so if you must run wiring through a conduit that also carries AC power, or pass it near large motors in factories or elevators, for example, you should probably use shielded LocalTalk cabling.

Avoid hazardous cabling (BW). Most inexpensive cabling uses PVC (polyvinyl chloride) insulation, which gives off poisonous gases when burned. If you're in a modern office building and intend to run network cabling through the air space above the ceiling tiles (called the plenum air return), then you must use a plenum-grade cabling made with Teflon or other nontoxic insulation. Most local building codes require it, though it's more expensive.

HOT TIPS

Make sure it's twisted (BW). You can buy preassembled, modular PhoneNET-style cabling from many sources, and in many lengths, with the connecting jacks already attached at each end. Trouble is, the pairs of wires in many of these modular cables aren't twisted around each other. That can be a problem once you get past 30 to 50 feet because it's the twist in twisted-pair wiring that helps cancel out the electrical interference to which unshielded cabling is vulnerable. If you can't find truly twisted modular PhoneNET cabling for long cable runs, either assemble the cabling yourself from twisted-pair wiring (in which case you'll need a crimper tool to properly attach the RJ-11 jacks), or order the lengths you need from a custom cable shop in your area.

Other Tips

Place networked printers properly. Printers with built-in LocalTalk or EtherTalk circuitry can theoretically plug in anywhere on the network. I've known some folks though, who've insisted on locating the network printer physically closer to the boss's office on the assumption that she'll thereby gain both priority and speed in printing, but networks don't really work that way. In fact, you don't even have to directly connect a network printer to the Macintosh that's functioning as its print server (see "Print Serving" earlier in the chapter), since the server can also find it on the network and send it spooled jobs.

However, many large networks use devices known as *routers* to subdivide a network into separate physical subnetworks. The router device stands between the two subnetworks it connects, and you must make sure to locate a network printer and the print server Mac on the same side of the router, i.e., within the same subnetwork. Otherwise, the router will get clogged with the constant print traffic that's forced to hop through the router. Physical proximity can be misleading, so check the wiring map to make sure that the run of cable just over the aisle from your print server, for example, isn't really on the other side of a router tucked away in the ceiling or in a wiring closet.

Know thy vendor (RC). Once you get beyond installing simple LocalTalk plug-and-play networks, stay on good terms with a local vendor, unless you're a true network expert or wish to become one. Mail order is nice, but nothing can replace a good relationship with a local vendor in times of trouble.

Editors' Poll:
Who Would You Rather Have as
Your Network Administrator, and Why?

(a) *Daffy Duck*

(b) *Donald Duck*

(c) *David Letterman*

MEC: Letterman, because he knows what late night work is all about.

ML: David Letterman, so we can get the "Top Ten Reasons why the network went down today."

JC: Donald Duck, because while Donald is "quacking up", Huey, Dewey, and Louie are doing all the real work.

JH: Letterman, because he'd never say I was "Dessssssthpicable!"

SZA: Donald Duck, because with e-mail, I could finally understand what he's saying.

JJ: I favor David Letterman because "stupid pet tricks" are just what you need when your server takes your data for a joyride and leaves your soul yearning.

TL: David Letterman. Even if he couldn't get anything to work, I'd still have a fun time just listening to him tell me about it.

TA: David Letterman, because his style is well-planned, fun, and usually goes over without a hitch. (I can imagine my system coming up with a sad Mac face while Daffy is bouncing around my office "woo-hoo"ing and spitting on my screen exclaiming, "that's dessssssthpicable." Donald throws a tizzy whenever things go wrong. As a 'toon net admin, Road Runner is always one step ahead of pitfalls and other trouble ....

25 Sharing Files

Let's say you've been using Microsoft Word 6 to create a lengthy report for work. You've spent days working on it and you're just about done. All you need to finish the job is some feedback and additional information from a colleague who works out of his home somewhere in the Arizona desert. You e-mail the report to him with instructions to make necessary changes and additions right in the file and send it back to you by noon. When he returns it, you'll take one last look at it, print it, and have it on your boss' desk when she gets back from lunch.

There's a problem, though. Your colleague has a Mac, but he doesn't use Word 6. When he attempts to open it with his word processor, all he gets is gibberish mixed in with plain, unformatted text. All the formatting you labored over—fonts and font styles, tables, borders, and graphics—is gone. Even if he adds the missing information to the file, the whole thing will have to be reformatted from scratch. You'll never get it done in time.

This problem isn't uncommon, but it can be prevented. In this chapter, we cover some of the ways to work around the problems of sharing files between different programs.

Contributors

Maria Langer (ML) is the chapter editor.

Dennis Cohen (DC) is a senior software engineer at Claris Corporation and a longtime forum consultant on America Online's Macintosh Developer Forum. He writes occasionally for *MacTech,* and provides technical editing and review services for a number of Macintosh publishers.

Aileen Abernathy (AA), **Darcy DiNucci (DD)**, **Jamie Brown (JB)**, **Henry Norr (HN)**, and **Ross Scott Rubin (RSR)** contributed to the fifth edition of *The Macintosh Bible*, from which parts of this chapter were taken.

Contents

Understanding File Formats   (DD/JB)

Text is text, right? Why wouldn't your desert-dwelling friend be able to open a word processing document in whatever word processor he happens to use?

Well, if the file contained just text, he could. Most English-language programs use a standard code called ASCII (see the section "ASCII") to spell out the letters of the alphabet and basic punctuation. Unfortunately, most word processing files don't just contain ASCII text characters—they also include special codes that tell the program how to display and print the information with the formatting you've applied. These codes vary from program to program. As a result, each program is said to have its own *file format*.

Trying to open a file in a program other than the one in which it was created can cause problems. In some cases, you won't be able to open the file at all. In other cases,

You Also Need the Fonts   (DD)

HOT TIP

Even if you've got the right application to open a shared file, it may still look funny when it opens on your screen. If you don't have its fonts installed, the text will show up in the application's default font (usually Geneva, Helvetica, or Times). Your first hint that something is wrong might be a table whose columns don't line up or a headline that doesn't fit its measure.

There are a few ways to make sure this doesn't happen. One is to format any documents you intend to share with fonts you know the other person has. Using the basic fonts that come with the system software is always a safe bet. Most people have these fonts installed, and if they don't, they've usually got them around somewhere.

Adobe Systems sells a product called **SuperATM** ($80) that solves the problem by creating fonts on the fly that match the metrics of the original document fonts. The product is based on Adobe's ATM (Adobe Type Manager) product, which interprets PostScript fonts for screen display. The Super version adds a database of Adobe PostScript font metrics and installs two Multiple Master fonts (a serif and a sans-serif). With this information, SuperATM synthesizes fonts that match the character widths and essential style of the original fonts. They don't look perfect, but at least when you open the document, your line breaks are right and you get a sense of what the original creator intended.

Another method is to use a document format specifically designed for the electronic distribution of files, such as those described in "Electronic Publishing Tools," later in this chapter. Those programs have ways of making sure that readers who don't have the right fonts will still see something approaching your original design on screen.

you'll be able to open the file, but it will be full of all sorts of extra characters that'll look like gibberish.

ASCII   (JB/HN)

ASCII (pronounced "as-key") is an acronym for the American Standard Code for Information Interchange, which is a universal system of numbering characters. Every text character, tab mark, paragraph mark, punctuation mark, and other common text symbol has its own ASCII number, which all Macintosh programs understand. When you press a key, the code is stored in your document, so any other program can match it to the corresponding symbol in any font.

The Mac uses an extended (256-character) version of the ASCII standard. Many other platforms support only the original 128-character version. That's why some characters you can create in a Mac text editor, like é or ©, may not be displayed if you paste the text into an on-line service.

Most applications use ASCII to code the text you type in, adding their proprietary formatting and layout codes around it. If you want to share files between programs, ASCII is always a safe way to get the raw text (and nothing else) across.

Interchange Formats   (ML)

Some file formats, like ASCII, can be read by almost any application. The native formats of the industry's top programs—Microsoft Word and Excel, Claris FileMaker Pro and MacWrite, and WordPerfect, for example—are usually supported by translators in their competitors' programs. There are also a few intermediate or *interchange* formats that are recognized as standard paths between programs. You may lose some formatting when you rely on interchange formats to move a document from one file format to another, but they're your best bet when native formats don't work.

Text formats (DD/HN). For text, ASCII is a sure bet. It can be read by any text-processing program. If all you need is the text, but no formatting (not even bold and italic styles), ASCII is as good as any other format. Its small file size is a bonus.

RTF, or *Rich Text Format* (sometimes called *Interchange Format*), preserves formatting instructions, along with the document's contents, as text. Many word processing applications support this format and can interpret its instructions to re-create the formatting. Programs that don't support RTF, however, will just be confused by the extra information.

Microsoft Word offers another option in its Save As dialog box to turn a formatted word processing file into ASCII text without losing its formatting: *Text with Layout.*

File Types and Creators   (JB/HN/ML)

When you double-click a file icon in the Finder, how does the Mac know what program to open?

The Finder keeps track of which programs created which files through a system of four-character codes called *Types* and *Creators*. A four-letter Type code identifies the nature of the file, regardless of the application that created it. All applications have the same Type code, APPL, regardless of the kinds of files they create; all ASCII text documents have the code TEXT; and dozens of different programs can create graphics files of the Type PICT, for example. Some applications, however, use proprietary type codes for their files.

Creator codes tell the Finder which program "owns" the document: They distinguish a text file created with Microsoft Word (MSWD), for instance, from one created with MacWrite Pro (MWPR). This determines which program's icon is displayed for the document and which program is launched when you double-click the file's icon, among other things.

HOT TIP

When none of your programs can open a file, you can assign a new Creator to the file using a utility designed for that purpose (see Chapter 13). This will allow you to at least open the file, although the results may not be very satisfactory: You may still end up with gibberish. Changing codes can be useful if you have to get the actual ASCII text from a file and have no other way to open or translate the file.

If you want to try changing the creator code, there are several shareware programs that'll let you do it: **FixCreator Pro** (free), **FileTyper** ($10), **File Kit** ($15), and **Changeling** ($5). Power users might prefer doing the job with **ResEdit** (free), Apple's resource editing tool, or Norton Disk Editor, which is part of Symantec's Norton Utilities package.

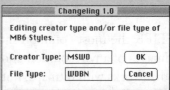

Changeling offers a straightforward way to change the type and creator code of a document.

When selected, Word saves the file as text, inserting spaces to re-create spatial formatting like indents, tabs, tables, and line and paragraph spacing. This makes it possible to have a plain text file with the white space that was present in the original formatted document.

Spreadsheet and database formats (RSR/HN/JB). ASCII is also a standard format for transferring information from spreadsheets and databases, but these programs need more information than just the text. They need to be told what text goes into each field and how to separate groups of fields into records. The standard way to do this is to place either tabs or commas between the fields (or columns), and returns between the records (or rows), in a format called *tab-delimited text* or *comma-delimited text*. Nearly all spreadsheet and database applications, including personal information managers, let you import and export data in these formats.

There are several other standard tabular formats that retain more information than the ASCII formats. *SYLK*, *DIF*, and *DBF* are among the most frequently used. SYLK, the *SYmbolic LinK* format, is designed to store numbers and is used primarily by spreadsheet programs. It preserves text, numbers, formulas, and text formatting. DIF (*Data Interchange Format*) and DBF (the format for dBase) are used mostly for databases. They preserve the field names but no text formatting. Most applications support one or more of these formats, but they do not include the formatting and layout information you would get by saving in an application's native format. They are used primarily to get data from one program to another and keep it in the right place.

Graphics formats (AA). As discussed in Chapter 15, graphics programs are generally split into two camps. Paint programs use *bitmapped* graphics, that is, they record images as a grid of colored pixels or bits. Draw programs use *object-oriented* graphics—they store each element of an image as a discrete object that can be manipulated separately. Most graphics programs can save both in their own native formats and in a number of other formats that can be used to transfer images among programs.

The most common graphics interchange formats on the Mac are *TIFF* (*Tagged Image File Format*), *EPS* (*Encapsulated PostScript*), and *PICT* (not an acronym). Each has its own uses and limitations.

- TIFF, the most common interchange format for bitmapped graphics, can contain images of any resolution and color depth. It's supported by every graphics program that works with bitmaps, but because the format has several variations, occasionally an application may have trouble opening a TIFF file created by another program.

- EPS is the standard format for storing high-resolution PostScript illustrations. Unlike pure PostScript files, EPS files usually have two parts: the PostScript language description of the graphic, readable by the *raster image processor* (RIP) on PostScript output devices, and a bitmapped PICT image used for on-screen display. A drawing saved in EPS format can be imported into other documents and scaled and cropped, but its contents would often no longer be editable, even by the program that created it. (Illustrator and FreeHand can open EPS files for editing; Photoshop can too, although it translates EPS into its own, bitmapped format along the way.)

- PICT files are encoded in QuickDraw, the Mac's native graphics language, and can contain both bitmapped and object-oriented graphics. PICT is the standard format for graphics that are cut or copied to the Clipboard and for drawings that won't be output on PostScript printers.

Opening Documents Created With Applications You Don't Have   (ML)

When you double-click an icon for a document created with an application you don't have, one of two things happens, depending on which version of the system software you've got installed. If you've got any version prior to System 7.5, your Mac may display a dialog box telling you that it can't open the document because the application that created it "could not be found." Sometimes, it'll generously offer to open it with TeachText or SimpleText, which is a satisfactory way to get a look at the contents of a file.

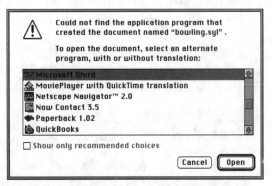

If your Mac is running a version of the system software prior to System 7.5, when you double-click an icon for a document created with an application you don't have, a dialog box like this appears.

If you've got System 7.5 or later and Macintosh Easy Open (which comes with System 7.5) is installed, your Mac will display the Easy Open dialog box, which lets you select an installed application to open the file. In this section, we tell you about Easy Open and similar programs that you can use to open documents created with programs you don't have. We also tell you about some translation programs you can use to change file formats so they open with the programs you do have.

If your Mac is running System 7.5 or later and Macintosh Easy Open is enabled, when you double-click an icon for a document created with an application you don't have, you get a comprehensive list of the installed applications that may be able to open the file.

Macintosh Easy Open   (DC/ML)

Usually called just Easy Open, this control panel ships as part of System 7.5 (it's also available separately for System 7.1 and later). In spite of the name, Easy Open does not actually open or translate any of your documents. What it does is replace the "Application not found" alert with a dialog box that lets you choose an alternate application to open a document for which you do not have the creator application.

You configure Easy Open with the Macintosh Easy Open control panel. In addition to the radio buttons to turn Easy Open on or off and a checkbox to specify whether it should work with plain TEXT files, there are three Translation Choices Dialog box options:

Use the Macintosh Easy Open control panel to configure Easy Open for the way you want it to work.

- *Always show dialog box.* If you turn this on, you'll see an application selection dialog box every time you try to open a document whose creating application isn't installed on your Mac. The problem with that is that every time you double-click a document icon for which you don't have the creator application installed, that box appears. If you leave this option turned off, the dialog box appears only the first time you open a document with that creator. From that point forward, Easy Open tells the Finder to open all documents with that creator using the application you picked the first time.

- *Include applications on servers.* If you turn this on, Easy Open will laboriously search all mounted disks, including file server volumes, for applications which can open the document type. The attached speed penalty will usually cure you of utilizing this capability except in special cases.

- *Auto pick if only 1 choice.* Although this seems like a logical option to turn on, if the only choice is a bad choice, and the "Always show dialog box" option is turned off, you'll be stuck with it each time you open a document with that creator.

Translation Systems   (JB/HN)

In addition to built-in translation capabilities, many applications let you add extra "plug-in" translators. There are two main systems: *Claris XTND* and *Microsoft External Converters* (ECs). When properly installed, XTND and EC translators appear in pop-up menus in the Open and Save As dialog boxes of programs that support them, allowing you to open and save files in any of the supported formats.

XTND
XTND (pronounced "extend"), which was developed by Claris, and is available for licensing from Apple, is shipped with all Claris applications and a variety of programs from other developers. Claris and other developers provide a number of conversion filters that work with the system, and DataViz, the leading commercial developer of translators (see the section "MacLinkPlus"), has adapted its translators to work with programs that support XTND.

Microsoft EC
The Word and Works EC systems were developed by Microsoft and aren't as widespread as XTND filters. Microsoft Word ships with many translators, and you can add converters from other vendors at your discretion. A number of EC translators also come in DataViz's MacLinkPlus package.

As you use Easy Open, you build up a list of document-application relationships that make opening documents created with uninstalled applications just as easy as opening documents created with installed applications. As you add or remove applications, however, this list may become outdated. Unfortunately, you can't just edit the list to get rid of the bad preferences. Instead use the Delete Preferences button to throw away the whole list and start over.

MacLinkPlus (HN/ML)

DataViz, the pioneer developer of format-translation tools for the Mac, has developed filters for more than 1,000 format combinations, including word processing, graphics, database, and spreadsheet formats. The DataViz translators work with Easy Open, Claris XTND, Microsoft EC systems (see the "Translation Systems" sidebar), and DataViz's own translation utility. As a result, with DataViz translators installed, you get more options in Easy Open and the Open and Save As dialog boxes of many popular applications.

There are three versions of MacLinkPlus. The basic version, **MacLinkPlus/Easy Open** ($70), includes the full set of filters plus Apple's Easy Open extension. (This version shipped with the System 7.5 upgrade and the System 7.5 software that came with some Macintosh models, such as Performas.) **MacLinkPlus/Translators Pro** ($100) adds Macintosh PC Exchange, the Apple extension for mounting DOS floppies on the Mac desktop. The top-of-the-line **MacLinkPlus/PC Connect** ($130) adds a serial cable and software for linking a Mac and PC directly.

[My favorite feature of MacLinkPlus is its ability to create drag-and-drop document converters. Once set up, simply drag a document icon onto the document converter to have it automatically convert the document to the format you specified.—ML]

Adobe File Utilities (ML)

A relative newcomer on the file translation scene is **Adobe File Utilities** ($130), which combines some older products that may be familiar to Mac users. The file translation component, Word for Word, converts word processing, spreadsheet, graphics, and database files among over 250 Macintosh, Windows, DOS, and Unix formats, as well as Hypertext Markup Language (HTML), the language of the World Wide Web. It maintains character, paragraph, table, and page formatting whenever possible and tags the formatting it can't maintain. DocuComp, an automatic document comparison program, is also part of the package. Both utilities were formerly distributed separately by Mastersoft, which has since become part of Adobe.

Graphics Conversion Utilities   (RSR/HN/Ben Long/Greg Wasson)

Service bureau operators and others who have to deal with a wide variety of graphics files often rely on Adobe Photoshop for translation, since it can read and write so many formats. Dedicated graphics-conversion packages, including Equilibrium Technologies' appropriately named **DeBabelizer Toolbox** ($290), a streamlined sibling called **DeBabelizer Lite** ($100), and TechPool's **Transverter Pro** ($400), offer a broad range of PC and Mac graphics format translations.

GOOD FEATURE

DeBabelizer also supplies tools for batch processing and editing, which you can use, for example, to automatically open a series of scanned images, remove moiré patterns, sharpen each image, and save them all as TIFF files. The DeBabelizer products are designed mainly for bitmapped graphics such as scanned images, while Transverter Pro is oriented toward PostScript art, though it can convert files to other formats.

CanOpener   (HN/ML)

GOOD FEATURE

Abbott Systems' **CanOpener** ($75) is an extremely handy utility for digging text, graphics, and sounds out of files. Although it won't preserve any fancy formatting, it lets you extract the contents of a file—even if the file is damaged and can't be opened any other way. It can also search for a word or phrase inside any file on your disk, making it a good, basic file management tool.

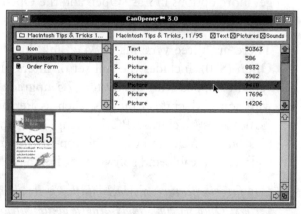

CanOpener makes it possible to view and extract text, pictures, and sounds from files such as this damaged DOCMaker format file.

Built-In Translation   (ML)

If all this talk about file translation utilities is getting you down, don't despair! There's a good chance that you may already have the translation capabilities you need right inside your favorite applications.

Many programs have built-in translators for files created with other applications. If the translator you need is present, you'll be able to open the file with all the information and formatting intact. All you need to do is open the file from within your application, using the Open dialog box's File Type pop-up menu to display the file formats the program supports.

Shareware Alternatives (JB/HN/ML)

There are some shareware utilities that do some of the same things as Easy Open and MacLinkPlus—and more. Adam Stein's **System 7 Pack** ($30) and Victor Tan's **SpeedyFinder 7** ($20 [Australian currency]) both include features that let you associate new programs with file types and pick a new program when the original creator isn't available.

If you need to translate graphics from one format to another, be sure to check out Thorsten Lemke's **GraphicConverter** ($35) and Kevin Mitchell's **GIFConverter** ($45). Both packages offer basic translation features, as well as more advanced graphics manipulation features, which make them good general-purpose graphic utilities.

For electronic publishing (discussed later in this chapter), try Green Mountain Software's **DOCMaker** ($25). It supports formatted text, embedded graphics, table of contents, searching, and hypertext links. The resulting document is an application all its own. You can even create a custom About box, which document readers can open by choosing About… from the Apple menu when the document is open.

Sharing Information (ML)

Sometimes just opening files isn't enough. Sometimes you need to incorporate information from one file into another file.

As any experienced Macintosh user can tell you, the Copy and Paste commands make it possible to copy information in one document and paste it into another. This works in almost every application and almost every document. But nowadays there are more powerful information sharing techniques, including methods that let you create live links between documents.

Macintosh Drag-and-Drop

System 7.5 improved Macintosh Drag-and-Drop, a feature of the operating system that lets you drag selected text and graphics from one document window to another—even when the two windows are for different applications. The selection is immediately copied to the destination document, leaving the original as is.

Although Macintosh Drag-and-Drop is a big improvement over copy and paste, there's a minor problem: Not all applications support it. Some applications that do support it include SimpleText, Scrapbook, Stickies, Note Pad, ClarisWorks, Claris Emailer, and WordPerfect. If you're not sure whether your favorite application supports Macintosh

Drag-and-Drop, try dragging a selection from its document window to a SimpleText window or the desktop. If the selection doesn't end up where you dragged it, the application doesn't support Drag-and-Drop.

HOT TIP

You can use Macintosh Drag-and-Drop to create text or picture *clipping files*. Simply drag selected text or graphics from a document window to the desktop. A tiny clippings file icon appears. You can then drag the clipping document icon into the window of any application that supports Macintosh Drag-and-Drop to insert the text or picture. Think of it as scraps without the Scrapbook. One thing to remember: The Clipping extension must be installed in the Extensions folder inside your System Folder for this to work.

Publish and Subscribe

Copy and Paste and Macintosh Drag-and-Drop have one thing in common: They can take information from one document and put it in another. After the information is pasted or dragged into the destination document, it no longer has any connection with the source document. If the source changes, the destination remains the same.

Publish and Subscribe, a Macintosh feature since System 7, lets you share information between documents while maintaining a link between them. You begin by selecting text or graphics within a source document and choosing Create Publisher from the Edit menu (or a Publishing submenu) to *publish* it as a separate *edition file*. A standard Save As dialog box appears so you can name and save the edition file. You then open a destination document, position the insertion point where you want the contents of the edition file to appear, and choose Subscribe To from the Edit menu (or a Publishing submenu) to *subscribe* to the edition file. A standard Open dialog box appears so you can locate and open the edition file. The edition file's contents appear at the insertion point. That's all there is to it.

While this might seem like just another way to copy and paste information between documents, it's really much more. The source and destination files are linked via the edition file. Any change in the original selection within the source file is carried forward to the edition file, which then passes the change on to the destination file. The result: When the source changes, the destination changes automatically.

Like Macintosh Drag-and-Drop, Publish and Subscribe is only available within applications that support it. Because Publish and Subscribe has been around for years, however, lots of programs support it in one way or another. You can usually set publisher or subscriber options to determine whether the edition file is updated manually or automatically and break the link if necessary.

There's one thing to remember when working with Publish and Subscribe: You must maintain an intermediary file—the edition file. Although the edition file is especially useful when sharing information with others who access the same file server, if that file is accidentally deleted, the link is destroyed.

Object Linking and Embedding (OLE)

As you might expect, Microsoft wasn't satisfied with Publish and Subscribe. Instead, it developed its own way to share information between files: *Object Linking* and *Embedding* (OLE).

OLE is similar to Publish and Subscribe in that it lets you maintain a live link between documents. But rather than going through the bother of selecting part of a document to make available as a separate file, OLE lets you embed an entire document. This document, which is called an *object*, can be an existing file on disk or a brand new doc-ument you create from within the destination application.

Here's an example. Say you're creating a report with Microsoft Word and you want to include a Microsoft Excel worksheet within it. You begin by position-ing the insertion point where you want the worksheet to appear and selecting Object from the Insert menu. If the Excel work-sheet already exists, you can use the From File button to display a standard Open dialog box that you can use to locate and open the spreadsheet. Be sure to turn

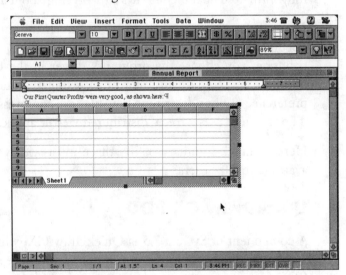

With Object Linking and Embedding, you can embed one kind of document within another—and edit its contents by double-clicking it.

on the Link File checkbox if you want to maintain a live link between the two docu-ments. If you want to create a new Excel worksheet within the Word document, choose Excel Worksheet from a scrolling list of installed OLE-compatible applications and click OK. A worksheet grid appears in the Word document and the menus and toolbars change to offer Excel commands. When you're finished creating the worksheet, click outside the spreadsheet grid to continue working with the Word document.

The main benefit of OLE over Publish and Subscribe is that OLE doesn't require an intermediary file. In addition, simply double-clicking the embedded object opens it with the application that created it—if that application is installed on your Mac and you have enough available RAM to open it while the document containing the embedded file is open. But like Publish and Subscribe, OLE is only available within programs that support it—such as all Microsoft applications.

Electronic Publishing Tools (ML)

Of course, you can never count on the people you share files with to have the right application to open the files you want to share with them. And you can never count on them to have the file opening and translation tools discussed in this chapter to open foreign files. That's where electronic publishing tools such as QuickDraw GX, Adobe Acrobat, and Common Ground come in. They make it possible to distribute beautifully formatted documents without worrying about applications, fonts, and translators.

Most of these programs work pretty much the same way. You begin by creating a document in your favorite application. Then, to make a version available for distribution, you choose the program's driver in the Chooser (or hold down a special modifier key) and "print" it to disk using the standard Print command. Various preference options determine how files are compressed and what fonts are embedded. The recipient uses a freely distributed viewer application to read the files.

Here's a quick summary of the three most widely used electronic publishing tools available to Mac users.

QuickDraw GX PDD

A component of System 7.5 is QuickDraw GX, which lets you create *portable digital documents* (PDDs). If you've got System 7.5, you've already got all you need to create PDD files that can be read by anyone who also has QuickDraw GX installed.

That's the main benefit of QuickDraw GX PDDs—it's included with the system software. But there are drawbacks. First of all, not everyone who uses System 7.5 opts to install QuickDraw GX, primarily because of compatibility issues. (I'm a good example: I only install it when I need to write about it and I usually deinstall it as soon as I'm finished with it.) So even if you use QuickDraw GX, there's a chance that the Mac user receiving your file won't be using it.

The other drawback, which may or may not be important to you, is that QuickDraw GX PDD files work only on Macs. If you need cross-platform compatibility (to communicate with the unfortunate souls using DOS, Windows, or Unix), a QuickDraw GX PDD is not the answer.

Of course, if you use QuickDraw GX and the people you need to share files with use QuickDraw GX, you can't beat the price or convenience of PDD files.

Adobe Acrobat

What began as yet another entry into the electronic publishing arena has exploded into what some people would consider the industry standard. Nowadays, you'll find Adobe Acrobat *portable document format* (PDF) documents everywhere—on disks and CD-ROMs, on on-line services, and even on World Wide Web pages. With Acrobat's feature set and widespread availability of the freely distributed Acrobat reader in Mac, Windows, Silicon Graphics IRIX, SunOS, Sun Solaris, and HP-UX versions (wow!), it's no wonder that many organizations and individuals have chosen it to electronically publish their documents.

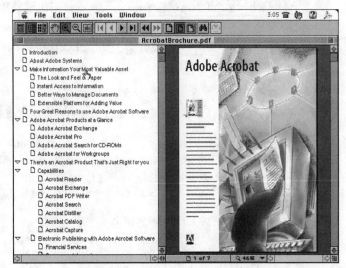

An Adobe Acrobat document can include graphics and text formatting, as well as a table of contents (called "bookmarks") to help readers find the information they need quickly.

In addition to being able to distribute your documents with graphics and formatting intact on almost any computer platform, Acrobat PDF files can be searched, annotated, and indexed. You can include links to other documents, QuickTime movies, and uniform resource locators (URLs) for documents on the World Wide Web.

If you set up the Acrobat Reader application as a Helper application for Netscape Navigator, a popular World Wide Web browser, when you click a link to a PDF file on a Web page, Netscape will automatically launch Acrobat Reader to display the file.

HOT TIP

My favorite feature of Acrobat is part of its Acrobat Distiller application: I can set up a watch folder and, with Distiller running, any PostScript file I save into that folder is automatically converted to a PDF file while I continue working on other things. Very cool.

GOOD FEATURE

The Acrobat family of products is extensive—too extensive to cover in detail here. To get started, you'll need **Adobe Acrobat Exchange** ($180), which includes Acrobat Exchange and Acrobat PDF Writer to create PDF document files. To create PDF files from PostScript documents, you'll need **Adobe Acrobat Pro** ($450), which includes everything in Acrobat Exchange plus Acrobat Distiller to work with PostScript files. Both packages also include Adobe Acrobat Reader, Adobe Type Manager, 14 Adobe Type 1 fonts, and an Acrobat CD Sampler. Other packages include Acrobat for Workgroups, Acrobat Search for CD-ROMs, Acrobat Catalog, and Acrobat Capture.

The main drawback to Acrobat (other than the price, which might be prohibitive for the average user) is the system requirements. Acrobat Reader or Exchange requires a Mac with a 68020 or better processor with 2MB of application RAM or a Power Mac with 4.5MB of application RAM. Acrobat Distiller requires a Mac with a 68020 or better processor with 6MB of application RAM or a Power Mac with 8MB of application RAM.

MarkUp: For Detailed Collaboration   (DD)

Mainstay offers an electronic publishing solution for editors and others who want to comment on electronic documents with precision and old-fashioned proofreading marks instead of posted notes. **MarkUp** ($195) uses the same print-to-disk method as the other electronic publishing apps, and it lets you embed a viewer for recipients who don't own the program.

GOOD FEATURE

What MarkUp offers that the others don't are carets, transposition marks, and other symbols dear to copyeditors, along with the ability to add boxes for lengthier comments. Each reviewer's comments are added in a separate overlay, which can be viewed altogether or separately, and marks can be coded with any of eight colors. MarkUp users can also create a change log showing the time of each editing session.

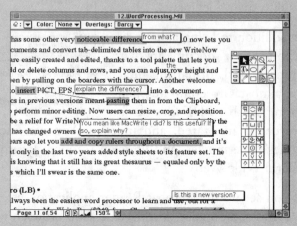

MarkUp offers copyediting marks, a highlighter tool, and text boxes for editing and annotating electronic documents.

[In reviewing Darcy's comments about MarkUp, I checked it out for myself. Although the product has not changed since the fifth edition of The Macintosh Bible, *it's a very cool program that no writer/editor team should be without.—ML]*

Common Ground

One of the first entries into the world of electronic publishing was **Common Ground** ($100). Developed by Common Ground Software (which went by the name No Hands Software back then), its DigitalPaper (DP) format documents can now be distributed among Mac, Windows, or Unix users.

Like QuickDraw GX PDD and Acrobat PDF files, Common Ground DP files retain all the formatting and graphics you put into the original document. Like Acrobat PDF files, Common Ground DP documents can be indexed, annotated, and searched. DP documents can include hypertext links and PostScript format graphics.

But the best feature of Common Ground (at least as far as I'm concerned) is the ability to embed its MiniViewer application right in the DP file. Even though the MiniViewer can be freely distributed among Mac, Windows, and Unix users, by embedding the viewer within the document file, they don't have to have it to read the file.

GOOD FEATURE

Other benefits of Common Ground over Acrobat include file size and system requirements. The MiniViewer is less than 600K (as opposed to almost 2MB for Acrobat Reader and its associated files). Both the MiniViewer and Common Ground software will work with a Mac with a 68020 or later processor (including Power Mac) and System 6.0.5 or later. You'll need only 1MB of application RAM for the MiniViewer and 2MB for Common Ground. The free MiniViewer and other related products, such as Web Publisher and CD-ROM Publisher, are also available from Common Ground Software.

Editors' Poll:
What Techniques Do You Use to Move Files Created With One Application to Another Application?

SZA: Simple copy and paste whenever possible.

TA: PDF is the god of all file formats. Acrobat Exchange coupled with Illustrator (where you can save a page of the PDF file as an EPS image for importing into other software).

DC: I use file formats that transfer easily, such as plain text, where possible. I stay away from specific product file formats when I can. I also use integrated applications (ClarisWorks and Microsoft Office) where I can.

JC: Import and Export commands built into most programs seem to offer the quickest and easiest method for large amounts of data such as mailing lists. For smaller tasks I still use the copy and paste function but prefer the drag-and-drop ease of clippings files whenever possible.

MEC: Drag-and-Drop, usually between BBEdit, where I do the scripting for a project, and ClarisWorks, where I keep the list of pictures, videos, and so on.

BF: I usually use ClarisWorks (because of its excellent translator set) to move files between programs. If worse comes to worse I'll save the file as an intermediate (such as text), then open it in the other program from the intermediate.

JH: I can't say I move files between applications.

ML: I always try opening a file with the destination application before turning to translators such as MacLinkPlus.

SS: I use Export/Import/Place commands or copy and paste.

BW: Most applications these days save and import files in a variety of formats, so I can usually find a match-up between them. MacLinkPlus translators fill the gap.

KT: I do a lot with ASCII/text files. I try to avoid cutting and pasting between documents or between applications as much as possible—it doesn't leave a good paper trail, for one thing; and it too often doesn't work right, for another.

By the way, the text editor in CompuServe Information Manager (the AOL-like CIS utility that is in many ways very annoying) is a great tool for checking and fixing text files. Because it's inherently cross-platform it seems to pick up quickly on file detritis that might otherwise cause problems if moved to a new setting.

26 | Coexisting With PCs

If this were a perfect world, all personal computers would run the Macintosh operating system. Unfortunately, that isn't the case. And odds are that a time will come (if it hasn't already) when you'll want to read some files created on a PC or send some data to someone who uses one. Or perhaps you'll want to put both kinds of machines on the same office network. Or maybe you have a program written for the PC platform's DOS or Windows operating system and want to run it on your Mac.

Not long ago, most of those things were out of the question because of major differences in hardware architecture and operating systems. But today, exchanging data between computer families—or "across platforms"—is commonplace and simple. And Macs and PCs can now share more than data files—look-alike versions of most major applications are available for both systems; you can plug them both into the same networks and electronic mail systems; and they can share peripherals. You can even run DOS or Windows on your Mac.

Contributors

Maria Langer (ML) is the chapter editor.

Ross Scott Rubin (RSR) has written or edited nine computer books. His work has appeared in *MacWEEK*, *MacUser*, *PC/Computing*, *Publish*, *Web Week*, and other publications.

Cheryl Schneider (CS) is a consultant, lecturer, and president of The Mac Works, a Macintosh-centric networking and support company in New York City.

Henry Norr (HN) was the chapter editor for the fifth edition of *The Macintosh Bible*.

Contents

What's the Difference?

The difference between Mac and PC hardware boils down to these things: disk formats, file formats, and the way the two systems read and understand information. Here's a brief overview of the obstacles you can expect to run into—and overcome—when dealing with PCs.

Disk Formats   (CS)

Formatting, or initialization, is the process by which a computer prepares a disk so files can be stored and retrieved quickly and accurately. The trouble is, Macs and PCs format disks using different filing systems. Without special software, PC-formatted disks cannot be read by a Mac and Mac-formatted disks cannot be read by a PC.

If your Mac isn't prepared to read a non-Mac disk, it displays a dialog box like this one when you insert a DOS disk. With special software such as PC Exchange, AccessPC, or DOS Mounter 95, you can mount DOS disks just like Mac disks.

DOS File Extensions   (RSR/HN)

Macs and PCs use different schemes to associate data documents with applications. PCs just ignore the four-letter type and creator codes on Mac documents (see "File Types and Creators" in Chapter 25). The Mac has no way of interpreting the three-character filename extensions that identify the creating application in the PC world. (See the sidebar "Mapping DOS Extensions later in this chapter.")

Mac File Forks   (ML)

All Mac application files and many Mac document files consist of two parts: the *resource fork* and the *data fork*. The Mac looks for and uses information about the file in one or both forks. Unfortunately, PCs don't have the same kind of file structure so they don't know how to deal with it. (See the sidebar "Fork It Over later in this chapter.")

Other File Format Considerations   (ML)

The internal structure of a document may include other information added and understood by the application that created it. This information may confuse other programs. Chapter 25, which deals with sharing files between Macs, discusses this in detail, but this also applies when sharing files between Macs and PCs.

Special Characters   (RSR/ML)

WARNING

Macs and PCs use different character sets—Macs use an extended ASCII character set of 256 characters, including symbols and accents not normally available on PCs. If you use special characters in a Mac document, they may not display properly when the document is opened on a PC.

Text Characters   (RSR/ML)

PC text files often include additional characters such as *line feeds* at the beginning of lines. These characters may appear as little boxes when the file is viewed with a Mac text editor. Line feeds, as well as hard returns (if present) must be stripped out of a document for proper word wrap. (See Chapter 8 for more information about hard returns.)

Exchanging Files

There are many ways to move data between a Mac and a PC—probably more than you think. Which approach you should choose depends on the distance between the machines, the size and nature of the files you have to transfer, how often you expect to be doing transfers, and your budget.

PC Disks in Mac Drives   (RSR/HN)

Probably the most common method of transferring information between Mac and PC is "sneakernet"—walking a floppy disk from one machine to the other. When PCs used 5.25-inch floppies, this wasn't easy, since the PC disks didn't fit into the Mac's 3.5-inch floppy drives, and vice versa. In the late 1980s, the PC world finally caught on to the advantages of the smaller disks, and now all new PCs have at least one 3.5-inch drive. But although the physical incompatibility was no longer an issue, the 400K or 800K floppy drives used in early Macs were incapable of reading or writing PC floppies.

With the 1988 introduction of the *SuperDrive*—the 1.4MB floppy mechanism now used in all Mac models—Macs and PCs could share floppy disks. But since the Mac can't read PC directories without help, you need special software to be able to see a DOS disk's contents in standard Finder windows and Open and Save As dialog boxes.

Mapping DOS Extensions (RSR/HN)

All three of the DOS disk mounters discussed in this chapter offer a feature called *extension mapping*. Using a control panel, you can associate a particular Type and Creator code with any DOS extension. You can, for example, assign the Creator "MSWD," which designates Microsoft Word on the Mac, to all PC files ending in .DOC, the extension Word uses in its PC and Windows versions; the Type can be set to "TEXT" (plain text) or "W6BN" (Word version 6).

HOT TIP

What you get in exchange for the time you spend setting up these mappings is the ability to open a PC file with the Mac application you want just by double-clicking. Otherwise, you'd have to launch the application and use the Open dialog box to open the file.

DOS Suffix	Application Program	Document Type
.DOC	Microsoft Word	W6BN
.GIF	Adobe Photoshop™ 3.0.4	GIFf
.TIF	Adobe Photoshop™ 3.0.4	TIFF
.TXT	SimpleText	TEXT
.WK3	Microsoft Excel	XLS5
.ZIP	ZipIt	ZIP

(PC Exchange window: "Each assignment below determines which Macintosh application program is used when you open DOS documents with a particular suffix." Buttons: Add... Change... Remove... Options... On/Off radio buttons)

PC Exchange, a control panel which is now a part of the system software, is one of several programs which lets you map DOS extensions to Macintosh file Types and Creators.

PC Exchange is a control panel from Apple that's part of System 7.5. When properly installed, it can mount DOS, OS/2, and ProDOS disks on any Mac equipped with a SuperDrive. You work with data on "foreign" disks the same way you work with data on Mac disks.

PC Exchange may be the free way to mount DOS disks, but it has limitations when compared to two third-party alternatives—Insignia's **AccessPC** ($90) and Software Architects' **DOS Mounter 95** ($100). AccessPC works with System 6 as well as System 7. DOS Mounter 95 allows Mac users to see 31 of the 256 characters possible in the new long file-names that Windows 95 supports. All three can handle SCSI devices such as hard disks, SyQuest, and Zip drives.

Apple File Exchange (RSR/HN)

Apple's original solution to the problem of reading non-Mac disks was **Apple File Exchange** (AFE), which came free with System 7.1 and earlier. This application let you read DOS and ProDOS disks and translate data to Mac-readable formats. AFE included a text file converter and a MacWrite to DCA/RFT (Document Content Architecture/Revisable Form Text) converter. Other companies, such as DataViz, developed additional translators that show up as options in AFE. (See "Reading Files" later in this chapter.) Apple File Exchange was not particularly user friendly, and it's now possible to do everything it does more easily with modern utilities. But it can still be useful if you're using older system software, and you can't beat the price.

Dealing With Other Media (HN)

Unfortunately, 3.5-inch disks aren't the only kind of removable media you may have to deal with. With files getting bigger and bigger, high-capacity removable media are becoming more and more common—on both platforms.

Recent versions of Apple's PC Exchange, Software Architect's DOS Mounter 95, and Insignia Solutions' AccessPC can mount PC-formatted removable Zip, Jaz, SyQuest, and Bernoulli cartridges on the Mac desktop. DOS Mounter 95 and AccessPC include software that lets you format DOS cartridges from the Mac; they even let you divide cartridges into separate Mac and DOS partitions. The most versatile cross-platform formatter, however, is Software Architects' **FormatterFive** ($200), which can apply PC formatting to hard drives as well as to removable media from the Mac.

GOOD
FEATURE

Mac Disks in PC Drives (CS/HN/RSR)

PC developers have also been busy coming up with utilities that let you read, write, and format high-density Mac floppy disks on a PC.

GOOD
FEATURE

Pacific Micro's **Mac-in-DOS Plus for Windows** ($140) and REEVEsoft's **MacSee** ($35 shareware, $80 commercial) are applications—you need to launch them and use their commands to move files. **MacDisk** ($50) from Insignia Solutions, **Here & Now** ($90) from Software Architects, and the Windows 3.1 version of **MacOpener** ($80) from DataViz, are not applications, but *TSRs* (terminate-and-stay resident programs)—the PC equivalent of a Mac system extension.

The benefit of a TSR-based solution is that it enables you to open files on a Mac disk from within DOS directories, the Windows File Manager, and the Open dialog boxes of Windows applications. Mac filenames are truncated, but blame DOS for that.

Here & Now and MacDisk are the most transparent utilities under Windows 3.1. MacOpener is included with DataViz's **ConversionsPlus** ($150), a PC-Mac format translation package for DOS and Windows that is similar to MacLinkPlus (see Chapter 25). You might find this package an economical solution for doing a lot of Mac to PC translations on a PC.

Direct Cable Connections (RSR/HN)

Sneakernet is a simple data exchange solution if your files are small and you have 3.5-inch floppy drives on both platforms. But it can be a pain if you have large amounts of data to move, or downright impossible if a 3.5-inch floppy drive isn't available on one or both of the computers. That's when it's time to consider another solution: a direct cable connection between the Mac and PC.

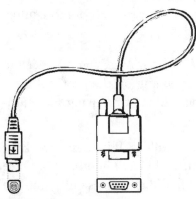

A null modem cable, which you can use to attach a Mac and a PC for direct data transfer, has a round 8-pin connector on the Mac end and a 9-pin, trapezoid-shaped connector on the PC end.

HOT TIP

The cable. A *null modem cable* has a round 8-pin end that can connect to a serial port of a Mac and a trapezoid-shaped 9-pin end that can connect to the serial (COM1) port of a PC. Both the modem and printer ports of a Macintosh are serial ports, but in order to use the printer port for a null modem cable, use the Chooser to disable AppleTalk.

The software. Each machine must have software capable of moving text or files through the serial ports and across the cable. Such programs are called *terminal emulators*.

If the PC is running Windows, you may already have what you need. Microsoft includes Terminal with Windows 3.1 and HyperTerminal with Windows 95. Both programs are simple and low-powered, but you can't beat the price. If the machine runs only DOS, you'll need to use a program such as ProComm or CrossTalk.

On the Mac side, any standard communications program will do. If you don't already have one, **ZTerm** ($35 shareware) is a great bargain.

The connection. With your software and cable in place, set up the connection.

1. Match the settings. Set the communications settings in both programs to 8 data bits, 1 stop bit, and no parity (sometimes abbreviated 8N1). (See Chapter 22 for more information about telecommunications software settings.) Then set the port speed to the highest speed both programs support. When both programs are properly set up and running, you should be able to type comments from one machine to the other.

2. Initiate the transfer. To send files from the Mac, look for a command called "Send File" or something similar. This should display a dialog box similar to the

standard Open dialog in other Mac programs. Then just double-click the file you want to send.

3. Pick a protocol. A *file transfer protocol* is a kind of language both sides agree to speak when executing a transfer. The most common are XModem, YModem, and ZModem. Sending files via ZModem is usually fastest and easiest. (For more information on file transfer protocols, see Chapter 22.)

GOOD FEATURE

Receiving files. When receiving files sent from a PC to your Mac, you may need to choose "Receive XModem" or a similar command depending on the protocol used. Software Ventures' **MicroPhone Pro** ($150), for one, can start receiving files automatically regardless of the protocol used.

This whole procedure sounds more complicated than it really is. If it doesn't work for you the first time, invoke some primal scream therapy and give it another try. Once you succeed and you get used to the procedure, you'll find that it takes only a minute to set up and works pretty well. If you find yourself using a cable connection often, however, it's time to consider getting a permanent one—a network link.

Modem Connections   (RSR/HN)

By sending computer data across telephone lines, modems let users share files over long distances and across geographic boundaries. They can also help you overcome the barriers that divide computer platforms, even if they're in the same office. Just use modems to connect the two machines or exchange files by e-mailing them to accounts on on-line services or local BBSs. (Remember, however, that sending large files by e-mail can get expensive when you pay for a service by the hour.)

HOT TIP

Connecting a single Mac and PC via modem is similar to linking them via direct cable, with a few extra considerations. Before you start communicating, one person will need to dial the other. You can set up your modem to wait for a call by typing *ATS0=0* in your terminal emulator. You'll be limited to the maximum speed of the slower of the two modems. The communications software on the Mac side should have MacBinary enabled unless you are sending just text files (see the sidebar "Fork It Over"). See Chapter 22 for more information about exchanging files via modem.

Network Connections   (RSR/ML/HN)

If you frequently need to pass files between Macs and PCs in the same location, and the files are large, and you can afford to spend a few hundred dollars, tying your Macs and PCs together on a *local area network (LAN)* is worth considering. Although networking Macs is discussed in Chapter 24, here are a few special considerations for adding PCs to the picture.

Hardware. There are several ways to add LocalTalk to PCs. Farallon Computing and CoOperative Printing Solutions produce add-on cards that give PCs a LocalTalk connector. For people who are hesitant to go through the bother of installing a card, Apexx Technology's **PCTalk** ($200) is a LocalTalk adapter that fits into the parallel port on a PC. Once the PC has a LocalTalk connector, you can add it to a Mac network with Farallon **PhoneNET** ($20) connectors (or equivalents from other companies) and telephone wire.

GOOD FEATURE

Fork It Over   (HN/ML)

All Mac applications and some Mac documents are divided internally into two parts: the *resource fork* and the *data fork*. That's a piece of techie trivia that may be important if you store Mac files on a PC. The trouble is, non-Mac OS computers don't know a thing about forks, Creator and Type codes, or the information the Mac uses to display Finder icons.

If you are just sending a document from your Mac to a PC, don't worry about the extra information—PC programs ignore it anyway. But if you're dealing with a file that's going to be used someday on a Mac, then it's either convenient (for data documents) or absolutely critical (for applications) that all elements of the file be preserved so the file can be reconstructed on a Mac.

WARNING

MacBinary, a file format created by communications developers, provides a standard way to keep Mac files intact when sending them through on-line services. When you upload a file with MacBinary enabled (turned on), the data and resource forks are combined, along with Finder attributes, into the MacBinary header at the beginning of the file. When you download a file with MacBinary enabled, your terminal emulation software decodes the header, returning the file to standard Mac form.

Mac files posted in on-line libraries are usually in MacBinary format. When you download such files to a Mac with MacBinary enabled, your communications software processes them as they arrive. But when you download MacBinary format files to a PC, it's up to you to make sure the reprocessing gets done. One way to do this is to transmit the file from the PC to the Mac using a communications program on the Mac side that has MacBinary enabled. The effect is the same as if you'd downloaded it from the BBS to the Mac in the first place.

HOT TIP

Alternatively, you can bring the file back to the Mac in MacBinary format and do the reprocessing there. Many Mac utilities will do the job, among them a classic application called **BinHex** ($10 shareware), an Apple File Exchange translator called **MacBinary to Mac** ($5 shareware), a System 7 drag-and-drop utility called **MacBinary II+** (free), Cyclos Software's **Compact Pro** ($35 shareware) compressor, and shareware and commercial versions of Aladdin Systems' popular **StuffIt** compression utility. (Compression utilities are described in Chapter 13.)

[For ease of use, I've found StuffIt Expander to be my compression package of choice. Expander lets you keep an icon on your desktop to which you can drag a MacBinary file for instant translation and decompression of the file.—JJ]

Both Macs and PCs can also use Ethernet, a faster networking scheme. This option makes sense if you plan to transfer large files frequently, especially if you have a new Mac with Ethernet support built-in. Farallon's EtherWave line and Tut Systems' Silver Streak Connectors make setting up and configuring Ethernet networks *almost* as much a plug-and-play proposition as LocalTalk. Apexx's **EtherChain** ($300) is an Ethernet adapter that, like PCTalk, fits into the parallel port on a PC, eliminating the need for an internal Ethernet card.

Software. Just connecting the Mac and PC isn't enough. You also need software capable of sending and receiving information over the physical connection.

From the Mac perspective, the easiest way to do this is by making the PC speak AppleTalk. Apple's **AppleShare Client for Windows** ($200), CoOperative Printing Solutions' **COPSTalk for Windows** ($180), Miramar Systems' **Personal MACLAN Connect** ($200), and Farallon's **PhoneNET PC** (packaged with Timbuktu for Windows, $150) let Windows users share disks and print-ers with Mac users in a System 7 file sharing-like environment. Both of Apexx's network adapters, PCTalk and EtherChain, are available as "kits"

that include Personal MACLAN Connect for an additional $100, mak-ing them economical solutions to networking needs.

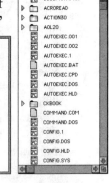

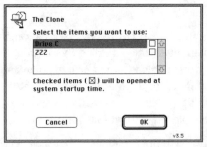

Once you configure a PC for a Macintosh network, it appears in the Chooser. Opening one of its disks or subdirectories displays a standard Finder window of its contents.

For Macs and PCs connected to a TCP/IP or Novell/IPX network, Farallon's **Timbuktu Pro for Networks** ($150 for the single-pack Macintosh Edition; $140 for the twin-pack Windows Edition) is an

amazing program that lets the user on either machine see the screen of the other in a window on the desktop. In effect, you can put a Windows screen on the Mac, and vice versa—and remotely control the machine whose window you see.

PC Server-Based Networks   (CS/HN)

In predominantly PC settings, it's the Mac that must adhere to PC standards. A PC network will most likely be running Novell Netware, the PC world's most popular networking software. Novell offers **Netware for Macintosh** ($500 for five users; $3,000 for 200 users), a special add-on that teaches Netware how to communicate with Macs. Once it's installed on a Netware server, Mac users can access the server through the Chooser, and Netware directories look just like Mac folders. You can also take advantage of Novell print queues so that printing can be centrally managed.

While Netware for Mac gives you the closest interaction with a Novell server, there are less expensive options. Novell's **Netware Client for MacOS** (distributed free on-line) and Insignia Solutions' **SoftNode** (included with SoftWindows) connect your Mac to a Netware server by emulating a PC on the network.

Microsoft's **Windows NT Server** ($1,000 for 20 users) is rapidly gaining popularity as the server of choice for networks. NT Server is much easier to set up and maintain than Novell's Netware and comes with built-in support for Macintosh clients.

Reading Files

Just moving a file from PC disk to Mac disk doesn't guarantee that Mac programs can read the file, because the information on it might be stored in a way Mac programs can't understand. Ditto with Mac documents copied to a PC disk.

The problems that arise when dealing with the differences between Mac and PC documents are similar to those discussed in Chapter 25, which deals with sharing files among Macs. In fact, many of the products and interchange formats you might use to solve file-exchange problems among Macs can also help you move files between Macs and PCs.

There are four primary strategies:

- Cross-platform applications—relying on applications that have versions on both platforms

- Translation—using utilities and filters to translate between formats

- Intermediate file formats—saving files in interchange formats understood on both sides

- Electronic publishing or collaboration tools—generating platform-independent versions of your documents

Cross-Platform Applications   (RSR/ML/HN)

Today most major applications are available for both Macintosh and Windows users. In most cases these programs have similar (if not identical) feature sets and file formats on both platforms, so the Mac version can read PC-created files, and vice versa. Choosing the same application on both the Mac and the PC makes sense if you plan to share files across platforms.

There are some caveats, however. First, sharing features and file formats does *not* guarantee that documents will look precisely the same on both platforms. Font differences, which can foul up the formatting of word processing and desktop publishing files, is just one example of the kind of problem you might encounter. And cross-platform sharing isn't always as easy as just opening the other file; you may have to use a special intermediate file format, which makes going back and forth from Mac to PC much less convenient.

Still another complication is that software publishers often allow long lags between Mac and Windows releases of new versions of the same product. The user with the newer version may have to save files in the older format—and therefore may not be able to take advantage of the newest features—if the document has to be portable. If you are running a cross-platform operation, it might be worth holding off on upgrading one side until the other side catches up.

Finally, remember that cross-platform compatibility isn't everything. If you and the Windows user in your life already own different programs, have each mastered the software you've got, and can manage to share the data you need to, then it may not be worth investing time and money in new software.

Translation   (RSR/HN)

A *translation utility* is a software package that reads in files in one format and generates an equivalent—ideally, an exact replica—in a different format. Translators for many common DOS and Windows formats come with some major Mac applications in every category (see the sidebar "Instant Translations" in Chapter 25). If those translators don't meet your needs, dedicated translation utilities such as DataViz's MacLinkPlus packages, Mastersoft's Word for Word, Equilibrium Technologies' DeBabelizer and DeBabelizer Lite, and TechPool's Transverter Pro (all described in Chapter 25) offer many additional filters.

Intermediate File Formats   (RSR/HN)

Intermediate or *interchange* file formats, which are described in Chapter 25, give you considerable flexibility in moving a document among applications and across platforms. Unfortunately, they sometimes require sacrificing some of the original formatting and detail.

Here's some interchange format information that's specific to Mac-to-PC and PC-to-Mac translations. Don't forget to check Chapter 25 for additional information.

Text and word processing. Although most Mac word processors don't provide a simple way to get rid of line feeds and other extra characters often inserted by PC word processors, text-processing utilities and text editors such as Bare Bones Software's **BBEdit** typically do. An elegant solution is **DOSWasher** ($5 shareware), a drag-and-drop utility that converts DOS text to Mac text and vice versa. Microsoft Word 6.0 is one of the few word processors that recognizes cross-platform text issues and corrects them automatically.

GOOD FEATURE

If you're dealing with formatted word processing documents, you can save documents in major word processing document formats like Word or WordPerfect as a kind of bridge across platforms. Most Mac and PC word processors support the popular formats. Word for Word and MacLinkPlus also translate among hundreds of formats; they are particularly useful if you need to convert files from older programs.

HOT TIP

Spreadsheet and database information. Tab- or comma-delimited text is a standard format for transferring information from spreadsheets and databases—nearly all such applications let you import and export data in one or both of those formats. The data is stored as ASCII text, the delimiter character separates fields or columns, and return characters normally mark the ends of records or rows.

DIF (data interchange format) preserves values but loses formulas. WKS, the original Lotus 1-2-3 format, preserves formulas. SYLK (symbolic link) format preserves both formulas and text formatting.

Graphics formats. A good way to transfer graphic files between platforms is to rely on applications that read and write multiple formats, like Adobe Photoshop and Deneba Software's Canvas. Another approach is to turn to a utility such as DeBabelizer, Transverter Pro, or Thorsten Lemke's **GraphicConverter** ($35 shareware).

PICT is not widely supported in the PC world, although a few PC programs can read it and most conversion utilities can translate it into something more universal.

Tag Image File Format (TIFF), the standard for scanned images and bitmaps, is platform-independent, but subtle differences exist between the Mac and PC versions. Photoshop, MacLinkPlus, and **FlipTIFF** (freeware) can help when you are translating TIFF files between platforms.

The EPS (Encapsulated PostScript) format allows Mac and Windows users to save preview images along with PostScript files. Those previews don't travel well across platforms, so don't include them if you'll be handing them to a Windows user.

WARNING

CGM (Computer Graphics Metafile) is a platform-independent graphics format. It's increasingly common on the PC, but its acceptance has been slow on the Mac. Deneba Software's Canvas is one program that can read and write CGM files.

Compression standards. As with other products, the Mac and the PC have different standards when it comes to compression. **PKZip** ($50 from PKWare) is the most popular PC equivalent to Aladdin Systems' StuffIt family and Cyclos' shareware Compact Pro on the Mac.

If you receive a file with the suffix *.zip*, it has almost certainly been compressed with PKZip and you will need to decompress it before you can use it. **StuffIt Deluxe** ($120) has an Unzip command in its Translate menu. **ZipIt** ($10 shareware) is unique in its ability to create as well as decompress Zip archives.

If you don't have ZipIt and want to compress a file before sending it to a PC user (to save time on long-distance charges, for instance), the developers of StuffIt and Compact Pro have created decompression-only utilities for expanding their archives on PCs: StuffIt Expander for Windows and EXTRAC.EXE.

Electronic Publishing and Collaboration Tools   (ML/HN)

Electronic publishing products such as Adobe Systems' **Acrobat Exchange** ($140) and Common Ground Software's **Common Ground** ($150) solve the problem of formatted electronic document distribution. These programs let you create cross-platform versions of files that look just as good on a PC as on a Mac. (See Chapter 25 for details on how these programs work.)

Collaboration tools, like ON Technology's **Common Knowledge** ($790), make it possible for networked computer users on both platforms to create and share documents. The document creator or "owner" allows others to make changes to it. The changes can then be compiled to create a finished document.

With electronic publishing tools such as Adobe Acrobat, you can open a document created on a Mac in Windows (or vice versa) and view or print it with all formatting intact.

Running PC Software on the Mac

The availability of cross-platform applications and the increasing ease of data exchange has greatly diminished the need for Macs and PCs to run each other's applications. But there may still be times when you'd like to run some DOS or Windows software. These days, you can do it right on your Mac.

SoftWindows   (RSR/ML)

Insignia Solutions' **SoftWindows for Macintosh** and **SoftWindows for PowerPC** ($300) use *software emulation* to run DOS and Windows applications on a Mac. These programs fool DOS and Windows into thinking they are running on a system with PC-standard hardware, including an Intel processor—the same processor used in most PCs. Behind the scenes, they translate the instructions issued by the PC software into terms understood by the Mac. The result is that DOS and Windows software can run in a window on a Mac.

GOOD FEATURE

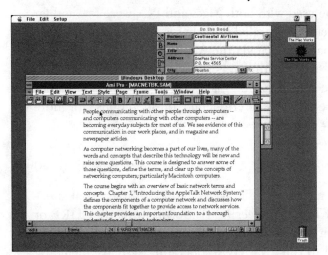

With SoftWindows, you can run Windows applications in a window on your Mac.

There are two main versions of SoftWindows and they have important differences. SoftWindows for Macintosh is for 68040-based Macs, including all Quadra and Centris models and many Performas and PowerBooks. It emulates an Intel 80286 processor, which makes it neither speedy nor compatible with all Windows software. SoftWindows for PowerPC emulates an Intel 80486 processor, which makes it faster and able to run all Windows software. You'll need a PowerPC processor inside your Mac to run it. Both versions come with DOS and Windows. Insignia also offers SoftPC and SoftWindows for Performa, two versions that run on older Mac models.

POWER MAC

The biggest problem with SoftWindows—and the most often-voiced complaint—is its performance. When working with demanding DOS or Windows software packages, you may simply find SoftWindows too slow.

BAD FEATURE

DOS Cards (ML)

GOOD FEATURE

Several vendors offer DOS cards that fit inside various Mac models. Apple's PC Compatibility Card (formerly the DOS Compatibility Card), Orange Micro's Orange PC, and Reply Corporation's DOS on a Mac card are three examples. These cards put a PC board, complete with processor, inside a Mac, so you have two computers in one box. A simple keystroke toggles you from one operating system to the other. A variety of configurations—processor, ports, SoundBlaster support, etc.—are available on the Orange Micro and Reply cards. A hardware solution like this may be more expensive—typically $700 or more—but it generally offers better compatibility and performance than software emulation.

Sharing Peripherals

In the past, peripherals that could be used with both Macs and PCs were few and far between. Many PC peripherals attach via a parallel port that is absent on Macs. Mac keyboards and mice, on the other hand, attach via the Apple Desktop Bus, which is absent on PCs. But now, more and more peripherals are learning to work on both sides of the fence. If you have a Mac and a PC, you may want to look for peripherals that can be used with either one. See the table "Peripheral Considerations" for more information.

Converging Hardware (RSR)

In the beginning of the chapter, we mentioned that Macs and PCs differ. That situation will change with the release of PPCP (PowerPC Platform, formerly CHRP or Common Hardware Reference Platform) machines due out in the second half of 1996. These machines are intended to run a variety of operating systems, including the Mac OS and Windows NT. They will include PC standards like a parallel port and a two-button mouse as well as Mac standards like ADB and the ever-underutilized GeoPort. With a PPCP computer, you can choose the operating system you want to run—and use either Mac or PC peripherals with it.

Peripheral Considerations

(RSR/HN)

HOT TIP

Peripheral	Consideration	Products
Modems	Modems have long been one of the least choosy devices when it comes to platform; generally, you just need to specify a Mac or PC cable.	No specific products required.
Printers	Most PC printers require a parallel port. To use a serial PC printer with your Mac, you'll need to get the corresponding Mac printer driver. (See Chapter 21 for more on printing.)	If you're stuck with a PC-only printer, GDT Softworks offers **PowerPrint** ($120), a package that provides a serial-to-parallel converter cable, print-spooling software, and drivers for most common PC printers. **Chuck's Printer Driver** ($20 shareware) supports many Epson-style printers and can even print in color.
Monitors	Most of Apple's recent Mac models can drive many standard PC monitors (VGA SuperVGA). PowerComputing offers a standard VGA connector on all its computers. Most major monitor manufacturers—including Apple—offer *multisync* monitors that can accommodate video signals from Macs as well as many different PC video cards.	To use a VGA monitor with your Mac, you need a cable adapter such as James Engineering's **MacVGA** ($20).
SCSI Devices	Although SCSI has been a standard way to connect hard disks, CD-ROM drives, and scanners to the Mac since the Mac Plus, it's only recently becoming more common on PCs. If your PC has a SCSI card, there's a chance that it will work with SCSI devices marketed for the Mac. You will, however, still need to get PC drivers, either from the hardware manufacturer or a third party.	No specific products required.
EIDE Devices	The method of choice for attaching internal hard disks and most CD-ROMs to PCs is EIDE (Enhanced Integrated Drive Electronics). EIDE peripherals are usually less expensive than their SCSI counterparts. Most Power-Books and Performas use EIDE hard disks internally, but there have been no EIDE CD-ROM drives for the Mac yet.	No specific products required.
Input Devices	The Mac's Apple Desktop Bus makes it easy to connect all sorts of graphics tablets, keyboards, joysticks, and track-balls. Many PC-centric vendors, however, have chosen not to use ADB.	Silicon Valley Bus Co.'s **KeyStone** lets you use PC keyboards and mice with the Mac. Kernel Productions' **ChoiceStick**, which boasts superb software, supports many joysticks and other controllers for the Sega Genesis.

Editors' Poll:
What Technique Do You Use to Transfer Mac Files to a PC or PC Files to a Mac?

SA: So far, I've managed to avoid this.

JC: DataViz seems to have it down to a science with MacLink Plus. It's been updated several times over the years and includes translators for practically every application.

TA: Pop in a PC floppy or Zip cartridge.

ML: AppleTalk network with MacLAN on the PC side. Added benefit: My PC can use my Mac's printer.

MEC: Novell Netware file server.

SS: I transfer all files via floppy disk, although I'm planning to run a cable between the two systems' serial ports and use MacLinkPlus/PC for all future Mac/PC projects.

JH: I never use PC files.

DC: I keep both on an Ethernet network (using MacLAN Connect on the PCs) and filesharing is a snap.

BF: For transfering between platforms, I used to use AccessPC. But now that it's built into the system I just use ClarisWorks or GraphicConverter to convert the files from a PC format.

BW: I either save the Mac files onto a 1.44MB DOS diskette and read that on the PC, or I read a Mac high-density diskette on the PC using a utility such as Mac-in-DOS or MacSee, the latter being shareware. I've also used network connections which offered filesharing for both Macs and PCs. This is most convenient for large files.

KT: I've had good luck opening PC WordPerfect files in Microsoft Word. Then I save them as plain text, jettisoning the formatting my clients insist on adding, open them in a text-cleaning utility (Overwood, Add/Strip, or Torquemada the Inquisitor—all available on the DTP Forum on CIS, by the way) and dispose of extra spaces, dumb quotes, hyphens where dashes should be, and so on. What's left is good Mac text, ready for whatever.

Going the other way, I try to use floppies that my clients have formatted on their PCs. I delete the old files and either Save As onto the floppy or drag-copy onto it. Not very sophisticated but it almost always works.

27 | The Perfect Mac Home Office

Your friends work at home. The neighbor next door who could never program his VCR has become conversant in Internet-ese. Everyone at work is chit-chatting in the lunchroom about their new tax deductions.

A world gone mad?

Nope, it's a world gone home—home to its Mac offices for fun, convenience, and profit, and we intend to help you get in on the action.

In this chapter, we'll discuss how a perfect Mac home office can benefit you, such as providing you with more leisure time, helping you organize your affairs, and even possibly adding to your bottom line.

In that spirit, ask yourself these questions just to see if you need a home office: Do you keep track of your budget, money, and taxes by hand? Do you bring office work home with you each night? Do you collect things and keep list after list trying to catalog them? Does your home business involve considerable record-keeping?

If you answered yes to any of these questions, read on!

Contributors

Don Crabb (DC) is the chapter editor.

Rochelle Garner (RG) is the former executive editor of *MacWEEK* and *Corporate Computing*. She is currently a contributing editor of *PCWEEK*, as well as a frequent contributor to *ComputerWorld* and *Forbes*. She has been building and rebuilding her own home office for more than five years. You may reach her at rgarner@well.com.

Karla Huebner (KH) is a freelance writer and editor whose writing has appeared in *The Northwest Review, Chevron USA Odyssey, Yellow Silk, Fantasy Macabre, Women Artists News*, and other magazines that have little in common with one another. She revamped her home office design a few months ago and is now lusting after a faster computer.

John Christopher (JC) is a data recovery engineer at DriveSavers in Novato, CA. He writes for various publications and has been a Mac fanatic for over ten years.

Contents

Defining and Managing the Macintosh Home Office

SOHO (Small Office Home Office): What a dumb acronym. But we are stuck with it, I'm afraid. Some wags have even proclaimed 1996 as the year of SOHO. And it's certainly the case that more folks than ever will be taking the SOHO plunge in 1996, especially smart SOHOers-to-be, a.k.a. Macfolk. Re-equipping existing home offices. Starting new home office-based businesses. Telecommuting from their home office into their corporate HQ. And generally, doing more work at home and requiring the right office environment to make that work. All driven by the Macintosh and Mac OS, thank you very much.

Any home office can be made better by the addition of any PC, of course. In fact, the best place to start is with a computer. And the best computer to start with is one running the Mac OS (otherwise, you'd be reading *The PC Bible*, right?). You start with a Mac, of course, because it's a multipurpose device capable of handling many chores, and the whole point of any home office is to maximize your working potential while minimizing your need to hire temporary or permanent help.

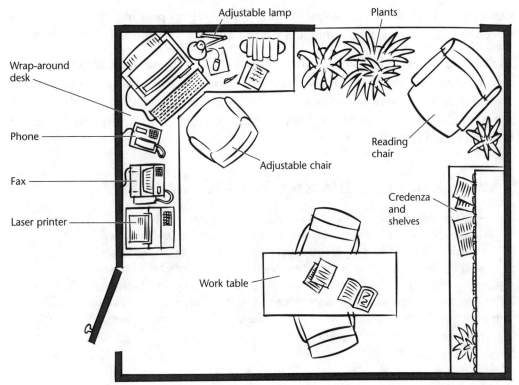

Why A Mac-Based Home Office?

Without too much effort or expense, you can equip your Mac with the appropriate hardware and software so it can handle everything from telecommunications to printing to access to the World Wide Web (see Chapter 23 for more on the World Wide Web). In this chapter, we'll take a look at how and why you do all that, as well as lay out some basic advice, tips, and help in setting up every aspect of the Perfect Mac Home Office.

Running a business from your home gives you considerable freedom and a de facto comfortable environment, but to really maximize the experience (both in terms of efficiency and comfort) you need to spend some time deciding on just how to equip your home office. Ask yourself some basic questions:

- What sort of business do I plan to run?

- How dependent am I upon timely and accurate information?

- Will I be keeping all of my business and financial records myself?

- How much space do I have to devote to a home office?

- How big is my budget?

Once you have answered these questions as completely as possible, you will be well-armed to take on the task of equipping your workspace with the right technology.

In the table, "SOHO Hardware," you will find a listing of the kinds of gear that you may want to consider for your particular Mac home office. Not every office needs each of these items, and some offices will need ones we have not included. But this list is a good place to start your shopping process. The table, "SOHO Software" lists the best and most useful SOHO Mac software.

What Kinds of Businesses Run Well at Home?

The kind of business you can run at home is only limited by your imagination, but a few do particularly well in the home domain, where electronic connections can practically define the business. These include electronic (World Wide Web, Internet, or BBS-based) and direct marketing, virtually any kind of consulting, freelance writing, graphic design and prepress, as well as accountancy, and most professional activities. If you have a business or plan a business that will require lots of client contact, though, consider carefully before setting up a home office. Home offices are often not well-suited for meeting lots of clients, unless you can arrange the proper room with proper outside access.

Top Ten Reasons You Should Create the Perfect Mac Home Office

10. You're tired of working on tray tables in front of the TV.

9. Your clients are tired of sitting in your living room while you interview them.

8. You're taking that big early retirement package at Big Bucks Corporation and putting the money into a real home business.

7. You're embarrassed that you kicked your daughter off her Mac (right in the middle of her search for Carmen Sandiego, no less) so you could reconcile the budget report due in the morning to your boss.

6. You've been running your freelance consultancy out of your car for so long that you have permanent seat imprints where the sun don't shine.

5. Your accountant has hounded you for years to quit your day job and really put that Psychic Friends Network connection to work for you.

4. How are you going to take the home office deduction if you don't have a home office?

3. It will let you fit in and stand out.

2. So you can buy all that cool office stuff out of the *Hammacher Schlemmer* catalog and have a nice place to put it.

1. Because it's really tough to run a proper home business without a home office!

But before we get to any of those tables and the verbiage behind them, though, consider why you'd want a Mac home office at all (see "Top Ten Reasons for Why You Should Create the Perfect Mac Home Office").

Don't forget the budget. As you're getting yourself all worked up to create that Perfect Mac Home Office, don't forget the money. How much will it take to do what you want? How much do you have? And how easy will it be for you to get your expectations in line with your fiscal realities? The Perfect Macintosh Home Office ain't cheap, but it doesn't have to bankrupt you either.

SOHO Hardware

Device	Key Vendors	Benefit	Price Range
Thermal fax	Panasonic, Murata, AT&T, HP, Brother, Toshiba	lower cost than plain paper	$250–$500
Plain paper fax	Same as above	higher quality than thermal units	$500–$3,000
V.34 data/fax modems	Best, IBM, Supra, Hayes, Global Village, US Robotics, AT&T, Intertec, Motorola	turns Mac into fax machine	$90–$350
V.34 data modems	Same as above	enables you to connect to the Internet and on-line services	$50–$250
Laser printers	Panasonic, IBM (LexMark), Apple, HP, Texas Instruments, Brother, Epson, Okidata, Canon	quiet, high quality text and graphics	$300–$5,000
InkJet printers	Same as above	quiet, good quality text and graphics, cheaper than laser printers	$200–$900
Label printers	CoStar, Seiko	quiet, fast at labels, handy where labelmaking is important	$150–$900
Personal copiers	Xerox, Canon, Panasonic, Minolta, Ricoh	handier and cheaper than running to a copy center	$150–$2,000
Electronic organizers (PDAs)	Apple, Casio, HP, Pilot, Sony	portable organizational tools that interface with your computer	$250–$800

Creating a Home Office

You can have a home office without a home business. But you can't have a good home office without a good home office plan. If you plan to run a home business out of that home office, you'll also need a business plan. Fortunately, once you have a basic office set up—a Macintosh, a phone, and some software—you can create a business plan that will get you seed money, incorporation, and even partners, if you need them. *[Of course, if your home business is a fairly straightforward one without employees, subcontractors, or inventory—and if you don't have big plans to expand that business—there's no rush to spend hours putting together a business plan.—KH]*

The key is to have the right idea and then find and use the right software to build a formal business plan from that idea. We can't give you the right idea, but we can tell you about the right software. That software is Tim Berry's **Business Plan Toolkit**, version 6, which works as a set of linked Microsoft Excel templates and it works very well, indeed. Once you have it, read the manual thoroughly, and you'll see immediately how to take your hot home business and turn it into a plan.

Getting Help for Your Home Office (DC/KH)

Sorting out a proper home office will take more work than reading this chapter, or even in reading a dozen more. Before you spend your cash on a home setup, consider getting professional advice, either from a home office consultant (a good place to look for such people is by checking with your local Mac user group) or through vendor-supplied consultants. Depending upon your needs and situation, home office products vendors will provide free consultations. Ameritech, Apple, AT&T, Sears Business Centers, HP, Nynex, OfficeMax, Office Depot, PacTel, and other vendors offer such services either over the phone or through their walk-in storefronts. Keep in mind that any product vendor is likely to be biased in their appraisal of technologies and products that compete with their own. For that reason, it's a good idea to consult an independent home office consultant even if you decide to get vendor help, too.

Talk to your friends, your suppliers, and your clients—in fact, talk to anyone you know who works in an office of any kind. People who work in basements may long for sunshine, your neighbor may have designed a nifty corner workstation out of plywood, and one of your clients may need projects delivered via Zip rather than SyQuest disks. Listen to what people say about shelving and comfy chairs, about disability insurance and how to keep children or pets from wreaking havoc. Ask people in the appropriate on-line forums; that's quicker than trawling the Web. Ask everyone for their favorite tip (whether software or desk height) and for the thing they'd most gladly change or get rid of (whether their modem or the long walk to the bathroom). Always keep three things in mind, and not necessarily in this order: efficiency, comfort, and enjoyment!

You'll also want to check the World Wide Web to find out what all the other home office folks already know. A good place to start is the *Chicago Sun-Times* Web site (http://www.suntimes.com), where you will find an access link to the columns of syndicated financial columnist and broadcaster Terry Savage, who has much to say about home offices, as well as the Small Business column of syndicated columnist Jane Applegate.

If you want to actually build or remodel home space for your new home office, there is no substitute for learning from the experts, such as Robin Hartl and Dean Johnson of PBS's popular *Hometime* program. You can get that help on the Web at <http://www.hometime.com/ps/95/ps2offce.html>.

SOHO Informational Resources

Believe it or not, this *Macintosh Bible* chapter doesn't offer the last word on creating the Perfect Mac Home Office. The following are other resouces you should check out:

Books

The Macintosh Way and *How to Drive Your Competition Crazy* by Guy Kawasaki (Harper-Collins and Hyperion, respectively)

The Macintosh in Small Business by Cynthia Harriman (Brady Books)

Fear Computers No More by Danny Goodman (Brady Books)

The Home Office Guide by the editors of *Home Office Magazine* (Home Books Press)

The Internet for Busy People by Christina Crumlish (Osborne McGraw-Hill)

Working From Home by Paul and Sarah Edwards (Macmillan)

Organizing Your Home Office for Success by Lisa Kanarek (Prentice-Hall)

Lighting Handbook by The General Electric Corporation (GE Books)

Healthy Computing: Risks and Remedies Computer User Needs to Know by Dr. Ronald Harwin and Colin Haynes (Prentice-Hall)

US West Home Office Resource Guide by US West (US West Publications).

Magazines

You'll also want to subscribe to a variety of topical magazines, including *MacHome Journal* (monthly), *Mobile Office Magazine* (monthly), *PC/Computing* (monthly), *MacUser* (monthly), *MacWEEK* (weekly), *ComputerLife* (monthly),and *HomePC* (monthly)

Getting the basics. The Perfect Mac Home Office should incorporate the following:

- Adequate space and storage. Don't pick a small room and hope you'll make do. Remodel space if necessary to get it right. You'll need copious shelf, cabinet, work-table, and other storage space, too. *[Still, you have to start somewhere. Maybe you can't have the Perfect Mac Home Office in your current sardine can; maybe you're starting a home business in order to escape the place next year, or maybe your landlord went berserk last time you defiled his wall by nailing into it! Even if you have your heavenly Mac in an infernal space, find out how to best arrange the space you've got.—KH]*

- Isolation from family and home activities. This is workspace, remember?

- A reasonable, efficient equipment layout. It's not a good idea, for example, to have your copier at the opposite end of your office from your printer.*[Likewise, if you're putting the computer itself under your desk to create a clear workspace, make sure you can easily reach to turn it on and off, insert disks, and that sort of thing.—KH]*

- Well-balanced and generous lighting. Both overhead and spot lighting. *[And, if you can manage it, sunlight! But watch out for glare on the monitor, no matter what your lighting source.—KH]*

- Enough separate phone lines (never mix them with your home lines) for voice, data, fax, fax modem., and so on. The key is to get the most flexibility you can out of your phone system. *[If you're just starting out and are low on funds, and especially if you don't have a lot of clients calling or a small child who delights in answering the phone, you can get away with just one phone line. But keep a log of your business calls (some people use separate long-distance companies for business and personal calls), and be sure to set your telecommunications software so that call waiting doesn't cause a problem when you're online or faxing. You'll also want to limit your on-line time to hours when clients are least likely to call.—KH]*

The home office and the IRS. According to our friends at the Internal Revenue Service, if you use your home office regularly and exclusively for business purposes (*please* note the restrictions the IRS imposes in their instructions), you may be entitled to a tax deduction for the business use of your home and depreciation of your equipment. *[A few quick tips: First, don't make it obvious that your home office doubles as a guest bedroom! Second, get those games off your computer before the IRS drops in for a visit, or it's likely they'll reject your deduction for an otherwise Perfect Mac Home Office. The IRS is very strict in its definition of what constitutes a deductible home office, and neither beds nor recreational software are included unless your business depends on one or the other.—KH]*

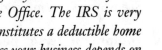

Your accountant, tax attorney, or the IRS can give you much better advice than we can on how to qualify for this deduction and whether you should take it. To get the basics, read these IRS publications:

Publication 529 (Miscellaneous Deductions: Home Office, Depreciation sections)

Publication 587 (Business Use of Your Home)

Publication 534 (Depreciation)

Publication 946 (How to Begin Depreciating Your Property)

You can get these and other publications from the IRS at little or no cost by calling 800/829-3676.

When you're done reading, call those tax advisers and make them give you a straight answer!

Perry Mason 101. There is a lot more to starting a home business than simply creating a home office and hanging out a shingle. You need to hook up with a good small business attorney to determine the following issues:

- Where and when do you file a *DBA* (doing business as) statement?

- How do you file for an *Employer's Identification Number* (EIC) from the Social Security Administration?

- How do you file your tax return? As a sole proprietorship under Schedule C?

- Is it worth it to incorporate? How do you do it? What does it buy you and what are the legal and tax consequences?

- How do you protect yourself from legal business liabilities?

- Can you even legally run a small business out of your home? You need to check with the local civil zoning board and also find out about permits, business taxes, and the like.

See why we recommend an attorney for this stuff?

Equipment versus people. It's easy to think you'll never need to use other professionals or hired help in your quest for The Perfect Macintosh Home Office. But you simply can't do everything with Macs, nor can you with all the other goodies you'll use to equip your office. The time will come when you have to hire other pros (especially an attorney to take care of incorporation and zoning issues, an accountant to keep you square with the IRS, and a contractor to remodel your office space).

Don't try to turn such needs into an adversarial relationship with your office and equipment. They did not let you down and they are not to blame. Once you get that chip off your shoulder, you can go about the most important aspect of creating a home office—buying the right Mac and software.

Buying the Right Mac(s). Whether you're buying a single Mac or several, the process you should go through is the same. Macs allow you to manage virtually every aspect of your home business, including your cash at hand, your federal and state small business income tax returns, and your business investments, and to organize your business's overall financial life. You really can't have a well-functioning SOHO without at least one Mac to anchor it.

A secondary computer purchase is also a good idea if you plan to travel a lot with your home office-based business. That secondary machine ought to be one of the next-generation PowerBook Epic-class notebook-sized machines that can be had for $1,500 to $4,000 (See Appendix C for more on buying a Mac).

Finally, once you have the Mac or Macs at home safely ensconced in your new home office, make sure that you spend some time configuring the system(s) to handle all of your home office needs.

Taking Your Office on the Road (JC)

If your business often takes you away from your office, you might consider adding a Macintosh PowerBook to your arsenal of hardware. PowerBooks are capable of doing everything your desktop Mac does including sending and receiving faxes, or e-mail. Imagine working on a proposal, or a customer database while flying at 50,000 feet (an airplane is required).

PowerBooks are also the perfect vehicle for showing multimedia presentations. Using presentation software such as Microsoft PowerPoint you could show your business associates charts, graphs, and pictures, and even run QuickTime movies of your new products. For the finale hook up a tiny video camera and teleconference with the company bigwigs.

When you're at home you can connect your PowerBook to your desktop Mac through the SCSI bus or network and effortlessly transfer your data using Apple's File Assistant software.

At the very least owning a PowerBook can drastically change your computing environment. Why sit at your desk when you could be working outside on the lawn, or on the floor with your children? PowerBooks are the home office unbound, they go anywhere and do it all—just don't take one with you on your honeymoon!

Equipage: You've Got the Mac, So...

Okay, you've got a room and it's got a Mac in it. What else do you need, from a hardware point of view? See the table, "SOHO Hardware," and then read on....

Even if you had an unlimited home office budget, you couldn't begin to buy all the stuff that crowds the big office supply stores. Try cruising stores such as OfficeMax, Office Depot, and others, and you will see what I mean. The sheer volume of cool stuff is enough to make a gadget freak never want to leave!

But leave we must, if we are to get back to our home offices, to make some more money, so we can go out and buy some more office gear. But while you're there, searching for that perfect combination of first-time home office gear, we have some recommendations. We'd buy the stuff in the order we have listed, because it forms a sort of home office gear triage, if you will:

HOT TIP

- Buy the best worktable/desk you can afford. Look for adjustable height, plenty of surface area, built-in monitor stand and bookshelves, a sturdy keyboard drawer large enough to also hold your mouse, and rock-solid feel. *[Don't be taken in by all those cute little so-called computer desks that infest office supply stores. There must be some good ones, but I haven't seen them. If you're tempted by one of these ready-mades, sit down at it with a tape measure and determine whether there's even room to fit your gear on it, let alone arrange that gear efficiently and ergonomically. The three best computer desks I've seen were all L-shaped, with the user facing the corner, and two of those desks (both of which extended along all or most of the adjoining walls, thus creating table space) were homemade. The third, my own, came from a store specializing in used office furniture. I'll bet it cost a lot new, but it only cost me $125.—KH]*

- Buy the best work chair you can afford. Look for adjustable lumbar and shoulder support, adjustable arms (height and width), adjustable height and tilt, and sturdy construction. Also, go for a five-point star base on wide casters. Make sure the fabric or leather (perforated, your backside will thank you) is high quality and will hide dirt well. Finally, invest in a large chair mat so you can roll around your desk and office without marring the floor or tearing up the carpet.

- Buy a V.34 voice/data/fax modem. And connect it!

Just the Fax—Modem? (JC)

Fax modems do a great job of sending and receiving faxes, but what happens when you get a document that requires your signature or handwritten notes on the page? Your Mac can handle some of these tasks but you might end up thinking you need a stand-alone fax machine too.

Before you contemplate just where you're going to fit another machine, consider purchasing a desktop scanner instead. Both the **ScanJet 4s** ($330 mail-order), by Hewlett-Packard and the Visioneer **PaperPort Vx** ($300 mail-order), are small enough to fit in front of your Mac and take up very little space.

These desktop scanners integrate nicely as the missing link to your fax modem by allowing hard copies of documents to be faxed. Dollar-wise they compete in price with low-cost fax machines but they do offer the additional benefit of storing scanned documents on your Macintosh.

- Buy a multiline telephone and have your local phone company install a second (and maybe third) phone line in your house. Use the second line only for home office business. If you really want to get fancy, install a third line only in your home office, and connect either a fax machine or a fax/data modem to it, along with an answering machine. If you plan to make data and fax connections at the same time, install a fourth line (it's much cheaper than you think). Make sure you set the fax machine or modem to answer the phone if it's a fax machine calling; if not, set it to let the line ring through to an answering machine. You can also buy a special black box to direct incoming calls to the right device. Most phone retailers carry these babies. *[If you spend much time on the phone, or anticipate many calls where you'll be put on endless hold (i.e. computer technical support), get a speakerphone and/or a hands-free headset. You'll save yourself a lot of frustration and prevent painful neck and shoulder injuries.—KH]*

HOT TIP

- Buy a multiline digital answering machine or sign up for voicemail on all your phone lines. Make sure you can retrieve messages remotely using just a touch-tone phone. The new digital models that use computer memory (instead of tape that can break or wear out) are the easiest to set up and maintain. Voicemail can also be provided through your Mac using Cypress Research's **PhonePro**, **MegaPhone**, **MegaDial**, and **Voice Messenger** software and either an Apple Geoport or voice-capable V.34 modem (a better choice).

- Buy a cellular phone and pager. You need to get calls on the road. Most cellular companies have special monthly airtime packages that accommodate home office folks nicely. Make sure that you buy a phone and pager with enough special features (such as call forwarding or page forwarding) to meet your needs. Don't cheap out when it comes to cellular products, as price and capability do have a lot in common. *[The idea that you need a cellular phone and a pager doesn't always ring true. The last thing a lot of us need is a cellular phone eating up our cash and contributing to the amount of time our cars spend in the local body shop. Some people—drug dealers and real estate agents, for example—really need cellular phones and pagers. So does a friend of mine who's a private investigator. But I'd say that most writers, musicians, therapists, desktop publishers, translators, word processing mavens, court and medical transcriptionists, and even a lot of computer consultants, just don't need cellular phones. If you really need one, you know you really need one. Otherwise, save your money—KH]*

- Buy a home personal copier. Nothing beats the convenience of making critical copies at home at 3 a.m., rather than running out to a 24-hour copy center. You can also find a copier that doubles as a fax machine and laser printer. If not, buy a home copier that uses the same kind of toner cartridges as your home laser printer. *[Again, think about whether you really need your very own copier. Sure, they're nice (and a lot safer than cellular phones since you aren't likely to use one on the freeway). But how often do you make those 3 a.m. copies? Once a week or once every five years? Some businesses couldn't exist without their own copiers, while others could do nicely without them.—KH]*

- Buy good home office or business insurance to cover all these goodies, plus your computer setup, and to cover your liability as a business owner. For liability coverage, don't settle for anything less than one million dollars per incident. Five million would be better. *[Don't forget health and disability insurance if you're self-employed. Search for good disability insurance, because if you use your computer much, you may well need it. No matter how ergonomic your setup, fast typing and mouse use cause injuries. If your business depends on your using the computer, you need disability insurance now!—KH]*

HOT TIP

To further protect yourself, videotape everything in your home office (and home, for that matter). Then inventory all your gear, so that when some cretin decides to break in, you have proof positive for your insurers of just what was stolen. To be extra safe, keep three copies of the tape and inventory (one with your attorney, one at home, and one in a bank safe deposit box). In addition, I'd install a high-quality monitored alarm system (which includes fire and smoke protection, as well) throughout your home. Both the alarm and the inventory help keep the insurance rider that covers all this stuff from becoming too high. Make sure that you shop around to find the best-priced coverage, which may *not* be from your current home insurer.

Finally, as you set about equipping your home office, keep in mind this simple advice: You can always buy that shiny fax/modem next week (or month, or year…) if you can't afford it today. No matter how much you like a piece of home office equipment, don't get caught up in a feeding frenzy. We know about that problem, only too well!

Working Smarter

Besides these hardware basics, there are a number of enabling technologies that you can invest in that let you get more bang from your home office buck and use your time more efficiently. The first of those is ISDN. The second are the new combo fax/printers on the market.

ISDN. As you use your SOHO more and more, nothing will be as important to you as reliable, fast access to the Internet and World Wide Web for electronic mail and WWW surfing. One way to insure that is to install an *ISDN* (Integrated Services Digital Network) phone line. ISDN lines typically offer two channels of digital data transmission at speeds of 64K bits per second. You can strap both channels together for over 128K bits per second, which is roughly five times faster than the fastest analog line/v.34 28.8K bits per second modem can operate at.

But ISDN can be expensive to install (check with your local service provider) and you have to pay a monthly line charge, as well as message units for the on-line data and voice calls you make. In addition, you'll need a digital "modem" to connect the ISDN line to your Mac, and that will set you back more than $500 (your existing analog modem won't work on ISDN, because it's an all-digital connection). A good compromise is a combo V.34/digital modem, like the I-Modem from U.S. Robotics ($699 with software). Finally, if your Internet Service Provider (ISP) or on-line service does not provide ISDN service, the whole point will be moot, since you have to have ISDN connections at both ends of the call. Check out the specifics of pricing and availability of ISDN before you take the digital connection plunge—keeping in mind, though, that it can be a big SOHO win.

Combo Fax/Printers. One new category of SOHO hardware deserves separate discussion—the combo fax/phone/modem/scanner/copier/printers such as the **OfficeJet** ($680, Hewlett-Packard), **MFC-4500ML** ($899, Brother), **TF601** ($650, Toshiba), **WorkGroup 250** ($499, Xerox), and **MultiPASS 1000** ($700, Canon). The Brother uses a laser printing engine, while the others use inkjet printing engines. All produce good (HP, Canon, Toshiba, Xerox) to excellent (Brother) printed, copied, or faxed output.

So far, though, the Canon is the most flexible of these machines, because it comes with Windows-based software that really ties it into your PC in a productive way. The MultiPASS 1000 can print, fax, scan, copy, make and receive voice phone calls and even store incoming faxes in digital memory, rather than printing them out, using its PC fax mode. The Xerox and Toshiba also show great promise in this area.

Lessons from the Home Front (RG)

Three years ago, the siren call of the freelance writers' market beckoned to me. Goodbye, commuting. So long, insane hours from 7:30 am to 9:00 at night. Hello life.

Now all I needed was a working home office.

True, I already had a gleaming teak desk from a brief freelancing stint seven years earlier. But my Mac was an asthmatic SE/30, and my printer was an eye-straining and ear-splitting dot-matrix. Clearly, both had to go. And just as clearly, I knew that today's editors expect their writers to submit copy electronically, turn in crisply printed invoices, and correspond by fax when the need arises. So I made a list of the basics I absolutely had to have before I could turn in my first article: faster computer, large color monitor, laser printer, and modem. Only the computer had been necessary seven years before, Now, they were all fundamental.

And expensive.

To reduce equipment costs, I constantly had to curb my technolust. Sure, I wanted the fastest, the best, and the sexiest, but I couldn't afford it. But I also knew better than to go for the bottom of the technical food chain: Money saved today would be spent much too soon on upgrades. So to balance my needs-to-cost ratio, I continuously asked myself how I would use the equipment. The question is critical. As a writer, for example, I don't use graphic-intensive software, such as QuarkXPress or Adobe Illustrator. I don't perform spreadsheet acrobatics. And I don't need to archive massive files. These factors ruled out a computer with through-the-walls power.

But as a professional writer, I wanted a machine I could use at home, on the road, or at Spago's while interviewing the subject of my next profile. I needed a laptop. My quandary: whether to buy a laptop and a desktop computer.

I opted for just the laptop. Specifically, I chose the PowerBook 160 (this was three years ago, remember) because I could create a desktop system just by plugging in a large-screen monitor. But which monitor? To find out, I read all of the large-screen monitor reviews I could lay my hands on. The upshot? All of those charts about pitch size and color fidelity were meaningless. But I did learn one important point: Buy the monitor that looks best to your eyes, running the same sorts of tasks you run, under the same lighting conditions. Bingo. Useful advice. I chose a 17-inch Sony Trinitron Multiscan HG.

Next purchase: A printer. Fortunately, I have lots of friends who had already made the jump to freelancing, and had done their research beforehand. I asked about reliability, printing speed, and PostScript Levels 1 and 2. Their advice: The Dataproducts LZR 960, a PostScript Level 2 laser printer that has been trouble-free the three years I've owned it. Unless something goes terribly, terribly wrong, I don't expect to upgrade my 300-dpi printer for many years.

And the fax? This is where I went the cheap, er, inexpensive route. Because I needed a data modem anyway, I decided to forego a separate fax machine and bought a data/fax modem instead. Three years ago, my choice was easy, because 9,600 bps was pretty much the standard. Sure, faster modems were available, but they were problematic. I bought a Global Village Teleport Gold, which transmits data at 9,600 bps and faxes at 14,000 bps. And, oh yes, its fax software was outstanding. That modem would share the same line with my telephone and answering machine. Now I could earn some money.

Upgrade Saga

I soon learned that a data/fax modem just wasn't going to be adequate for my faxing needs. The problems were logistical. For starters, I'd have to manually trigger the "receive" mode for each incoming message (the result of trying to protect telephone callers from a piercing fax squeal). That became particularly tiresome when folks on the East Coast insisted on faxing me in California at 5 a.m.

That's one problem with having a fax modem. Another problem: Sending something that isn't on your hard disk—such as your signature on the contract that just came in. For that, you need a fax machine.

Fax machines range in price, from about $300 to close to $900. At the low end, you get those endless rolls of paper that curl into office confetti. At the high end, plain paper fax and a built-in copier would allow me to photocopy my expenses, article clips, and contracts. I bought the Hewlett-Packard Fax-900. And although it doesn't slice or dice, it does hold 50 pages at a time and—attached to my newly installed second telephone line— answers faxes unattached. And, oh yes, I upgraded my modem to a 28.8 Kbps model, from Supra. Life was looking sweet.

The Ergonomic Zone

That is, until I developed repetitive strain injury (RSI) in both my wrists. My first signs were fatigue, followed by burning at the wrists, then nonstop pain. The irony is, I could have prevented my injury if I hadn't been so penny wise and pound stupid. My first problem? That lovely teak desk, with a carriage-return height of 29 inches. My second: My chair, with absolutely no adjustments for back or seat tilt. And my third problem was my wrist rest. (See Appendix A for more on RSI.)

Having your keyboard more than 26 inches off the ground is deadly. If your desk is higher than that, buy an under-the-desk keyboard tray. This is vital. I just paid $235 for a slide-out Proformix tray. For that I get a slideout tray for the mouse and a copy holder. It's also infinitely adjustable. When that tray arrives, it will hold my new ergonomic keyboard from Adesso. Identical to the Microsoft Natural Keyboard, it has a hump in the middle that acts as the Great Divide: The left-hand keys occupy one side of the slope, the right-hand keys the other. And on the advice of my occupational therapist, I replaced my mouse with the Kensington TurboMouse. (That clicking and dragging wears down the tendons.) Also on my therapist's advice, I threw out my wrist rests. Surprised? So was I. But it turns out that wrist rests should only be used when you're at rest. I'd mistakenly used the pads while typing.

The chair is a biggie. Because I already have the symptoms, I've opted for a mid-range chair from BodyBilt, with all of the adjustments a body could want. Lumbar support, adjustable arms, tilt seat, back height adjustment, back width adjustment, and height adjustment. All for a low, low price of $475. And yes, this is the mid-range.

These machines work surprisingly well, despite their jack-of-all-trades underpinnings. And sadly, none yet comes with software that tie them to a Macintosh directly (although that is about to change), but Mac home office folk can still put these convenient workhorses to work, either as standalones, or by running them with Insignia's **SoftWindows** or a PC coprocessor card.

Future technology in the home office. How will the Mac home office of the future be laid out? Will it be along the lines of George Jetson's fanciful cartoon workplace, all plastic and synthesized voices? Or will it have a retro touch to it, returning to a time when wood was wood, and gear didn't mean electronics?

If we knew the answer to that, we'd be inventing the future home office, rather than speculating about it! But we can say what kinds of devices and goodies the future Mac home office will have in it and what we can look forward to in a few years.

The big trend in home office electronics is miniaturization. Smaller this, littler that. That trend will continue, and combined with another trend—the combination of similar devices into one Swiss Army Knife device—means you will be able to get better functioning home office goodies that take up less space and cost less money than the single-purpose stand-alone devices they replace. Expect Apple to be a trendsetter in this domain.

Take the laser printer, for example. It's pretty much de rigeur around most Mac corporate offices these days. But at home, it's still often considered a luxury. No more, not with the new combo printers and inexpensive small laser printers that have and will continue to come out.

Cellular phone technology's also becoming much more pervasive in the home office. Within the next couple of years, we'll see PowerBooks and notebook Mac OS clones that come with built-in cellular phones at less cost than today's machines without the phones. Cellular technology also may eventually replace wired telephones in many homes, as it becomes cheaper for phone companies to put up cell towers, rather than burying cables in the ground. Expect combination pager/phone units within a year that offer better range and sound quality than today's units.

The other breakthrough technology for home offices revolves around wireless networks and personal digital assistants (PDAs) like Apple's **Newton MessagePad 130** and Sony's **Magic Link PIC-2000**. Soon, you will be able to set up an instant wireless RF or IR network in your home, that connects together your home computers and any PDAs you might have purchased. The advantage to such a setup is that it extends the home office way beyond its walls.

Say you are making dinner for the family downstairs. Your spouse is out, calling on her own clients, and you have charge of the kids. The office phone rings, and you just can't get to it, but you know it's an important customer calling back. No problem. Your Mac answers the call with a modem and gives the caller a brief message telling them they are transferring the call to you. The computer switches the call to your in-house wireless network and pages your Newton you have stuffed in your shirt pocket. You hit the communicate button and the PDA then becomes an extension phone, a voice transcriber (digitizing your conversation and storing it for later retrieval), and a window into your Mac. You can carry on the critical conversation with your customer, refer to her computer file through your PDA, and later review the conversation (which can be then stored as text on your computer).

The technology for this seemingly Buck Rogers scenario is in place now. Expect it to take a couple more years to become affordable and popular.

Mac SOHOware

Having great Mac hardware alone does not a perfect home office make. You also need good software. Where do you start looking? At software categories (see the table, "SOHO Software"). Chances are pretty good you'll *need* access to the Internet and World Wide Web, as well as word processor, spreadsheet, and database software.

Back It Up! And you need to use a *daily* backup program. Buy Dantz's **Retrospect** and do a full backup of all your data and software. Then do incremental backups daily on the data. Create a rotating set of backups so that you always have at least three backups (preferable on large scale removable media such as DAT tape) of all your data at any one time (one at the home office, one in your safe deposit box, and one at a trusted friend or relative's house—make sure you keep the home office tape locked in a fireproof container). Don't come crying to us when you lose your data and don't have a proper backup in place. (See Chapter 5 for more on backing up.)

The Internet and World Wide Web. We'll make this simple. You need e-mail. You need WWW access. Get 'em. Either through an Internet Service Provider (InterAccess, Iquest, Netcom, AT&T, SpryNet, etc.) or on-line service (America Online, CompuServe, Prodigy). Once you contact these folks, they'll set you up with the right access and e-mail software. Run it and use it. The Net will help you service your clients better, prospect for new ones, and generally get more work done in less time. (See Chapter 22 for info on telecommunications and Chapter 23 for info on the Internet.)

Buying Software

Buying the right software is a sufficiently complex and personal decision. To make it work, you have got to be prepared to invest some real time and effort. Start thinking about what your computing needs are, what your computing expectations are, and what your computing desires are.

Make a Plan and Categorize

You've got to decide just exactly what it is that you want out of your Mac. Do you expect to prepare your federal income tax returns each year? Perhaps you want to manage your investments, or correspond with your portfolio manager? Maybe you want to prepare and stick with a personal or business budget? Or you might want to catalog and list the stuff important to your home business or just your life. Regardless of what it is you need your Mac to do, unless you can clearly define those needs, you have no place to start from.

Take some time now to sit down and think about what you need your machine to do for you in your new home office. Based on those needs, you will want to categorize your potential software purchases. Some categories are nobrainers: Income tax returns should be done using tax software; catalogs and lists require databases; budgets can be done with spreadsheets or bookkeeping software; correspondence should be done with a bailiwick of a word processor.

But what about the less obvious categories? What kind of software, for example, will you use to handle your need to produce a monthly newsletter for business customers? Yes, you could use a word processor, or go full-bore and try a desktop publishing package, but what about programs that split the difference? Categorizing your software needs often requires the help of "experts"; even your next door neighbor who has been using a home office Mac for a few months longer than you is bound to be an expert about one kind of software. Use this help when you make up your own categories and assign them to your needs.

The Case of Roberta

Consider the case of a home direct marketeer, Roberta. She wants to produce a monthly newsletter for her business, her clients, and potential clients. She has some experience with WordPerfect on her Mac. She has used almost no other software on her Mac, but she has seen PageMaker and QuarkXPress running on a friend's Mac and thinks it might suit her needs. How does she make a software decision?

Well, her computing needs are already pretty well defined, or so it would seem. She needs to produce this newsletter, right? But how big is this thing going to be? How will it be printed? Will it include pictures and graphics? What's the basic design going to look like?

See my point? Roberta knows that she needs to produce a newsletter, so she knows she needs some kind of software to write, edit, design, and print that newsletter. But beyond that, she hasn't worked out the specifics of her needs. She must do that before even thinking about categorizing the software that meets those needs and before she invests any time in thinking about her expectations for that software.

But once she has considered her needs in depth, and worked up a software category listing, she can think about how the software she wants to buy should work to let her do the job she wants to do. Her software expectations will help drive her selection process, because not all the word processors or DTP programs will work in just the way she decides is best for her.

When she's done ruminating about her software expectations, she will have a short list of programs that will run on her Mac that will do the basic job she wants (newsletter production) in the way she wants to do it. Then it's time for Roberta to consider her software desires.

Desires as Motivation

Desires are tougher to pin down than either needs or expectations, because they reflect the intangible parts of using a computer. Yet meeting your software desires often has more to do with your ultimate software happiness than either needs or expectations (which most people eventually get right anyway). Thinking about your software desires should take you a step back and away from the immediate process.

Ask yourself what is the software that you currently use that gives you the greatest satisfaction. Forget about what it does or how it does it and concentrate on how it satisfies you (at whatever level you can measure). What are those satisfaction qualities? It may be something as superficial as the way the menus look, or as deep as the way the program saves and opens files. Whatever it is, you should think about it and apply it as a criteria to check your software shortlist against (that you created when you ran through your needs and expectations).

Once you've done all this thinking and reflecting, then you'll decide, just as Roberta did, that all you have to worry about now is getting the best price on that one program that will be perfect for you and your needs.

Getting Good Software Service

We hear this lament, often: "I can never seem to get good service from the stores where I buy my Mac software. I either get a line of baloney or worse. What can I do to fix that?"

Buy from stores that actually keep Mac software gurus on staff. Many mass marketers do not, although there are exceptions. Before you patronize a store selling software, ask to speak with their computer techie. If they stare at you blankly, try a different store. Once you find someone who knows a CRT from a BLT, sit down with them and discuss your software needs and decide if their comments make sense and are affordable. If so, lock that store into your software acquisition heart of hearts. Keep in mind that good service costs good money, so don't be surprised if you have to pay fees beyond basic help, or that software costs more at stores where service is a reality and not just a marketing slogan.

Word processing and works software. You also need to write, which means you need a word processor. Ask yourself some basic questions: Do I need to do mass mailings? Then you'll need mail merge facilities in your word processor. Do I need to produce complex documents, with tables of contents, indices, and footnotes? Then make sure that the word processor you buy offers those features. In short, buying a word processor, like buying any software, is an exercise in common sense. Go to your friendly neighborhood software store and start trying out the wares. When you find the package that does what you need to do, and it runs on your computers, and you can afford it, then buy it. The major names to look for are Microsoft Word, WordPerfect, and NisusWriter. Don't forget that your Mac will also come with a basic text processor (a.k.a. SimpleText or TeachText) as part of its "accessories" software.

You can also get a decent word processor if you buy a good integrated package such as ClarisWorks, that combines word processing with spreadsheet, graphics, and communications capabilities in an easy-to-learn-and-use context. In fact, many SOHOers can get along nicely with just ClarisWorks. (See Chapter 8 for more on word processors.)

If you need a number of secondary applications (such as desktop publishing, or communications) to get your home office work done, then you should definitely consider buying an integrated works package first. What you give up over separate, stand-alone single-purpose programs, are some features and some versatility. But you may very well find that the compromise is worth it, since works packages have gotten more feature-laden in recent years. (See Chapter 12 for more on integrated software.)

Spreadsheet and bookkeeping. Besides word processing, most home office setups will need spreadsheet and bookkeeping software for handling all those financial records. Spreadsheets work alike; they really only differ in the fanciness of their features (the more you pay the more built-in financial functions you get). Buy the simplest one that you can get by with. Major offerings include Microsoft Excel, Lotus 1-2-3, and the spreadsheet function in integrated software, the best of which is ClarisWorks.

Bookkeeping or accounting software can be tedious to learn and use and expensive. Unless you buy **QuickBooks Pro** from Intuit. This one is so much better than its competitors it almost hurts. Even fiscal boneheads like us can fly with QuickBooks.

(See Chapter 9 for more on spreadsheets and Chapter 10 for more on personal and business management applications.)

SOHO Software

Software	Category	Price Range
*Microsoft Word	Word processing	$250–$350
*NisusWriter	Word processing	$180 and up
WordPerfect Mac	Word processing	$250–$350
WorldWrite	Word processing	$190–$250
*Microsoft Excel	Spreadsheet	$150–$395
Lotus 1-2-3	Spreadsheet	$250–$395
Casady and Greene's Let's KISS	Spreadsheet	$149
Business Plan Toolkit	Spreadsheet	$150
*ClarisWorks	Works package	$99–$149
Microsoft Works	Works package	$99 and up
*Claris's FileMaker Pro	Relational database	$90 and up
ACI US 4th Dimension	Relational database	$500 and up
Mainstay Phyla	Object-oriented database	$195 and up
*Symantec's Norton Utilities	Utilities	$70 and up
*Hard Disk Toolkit	Utilities	$90 and up
*Synergy's VersaTerm Pro	Communications	$140 and up
*QuickBooks Pro	Bookkeeping	$90–$130
*Netscape	WWW Browser	Free to $39
*Eudora	Electronic Mail	Free to $99
Claris Emailer	Electronic Mail	$49 and up

* = Best in category

Keep it in a database. Another category of home office software that I recommend is a simple relational or flat-file database. With it, you can keep track of your contacts, of your inventory, and all of the other bits of info that any home office has to track that may not fall nicely into QuickBooks, ClarisWorks, or Excel. Most good databases also can use any of a number of third-party templates so that predefined tasks are a snap. Ask your dealer to take a look at Claris's FileMaker Pro, the best of the bunch. (See Chapter 11 for more on databases.)

Office suite software. If you want big productivity, the conventional wisdom goes, get big software. And biggest of the big are the office suite packages. The two exemplars are **Microsoft Office** and Lotus's **SmartSuite**. Unfortunately, the brain trust at Lotus has not migrated SmartSuite to the Mac. So, the choice for now is Microsoft Office. It's big and powerful, but surprisingly easy to use, and a bargain over what it would cost to buy the individual applications it comprises. MS Office has good integration (relying on MS's object linking and embedding [OLE] technologies). MS Office also offers a Power Macintosh version, which you'll want if you own a Power Mac, since the 68K Mac version is pig slow.

POWER MAC

HOT TIP

If you think you'll use both Microsoft Word and Excel, buy Microsoft Office instead. It's cheaper, it also comes with the excellent PowerPoint presentation package, as well as an e-mail client, and some other goodies for $299. Make sure you buy the CD-ROM version. Installing the jillion-floppy version would drive a teetotaller to hard liquor.

Extending Your Business

Once you've defined your Perfect Mac Home Office, built it, and have been managing it and your allied business for a few months it's time to think about extending your business and the reach of your Mac home office. But first, do a reality check.

Can you honestly say that you have done your best to protect and secure your business data you keep on your Mac? Have you organized your daily and weekly work schedule as well as you can? Are you keeping track of your customers and potential customers as well as you can? Are all your connections with the outside world working OK?

If you answered yes to each of these questions, move ahead and consider how to grow.

Net and Web and Keeping in Touch

The places to start are with a local area network and with the Internet and World Wide Web. If you have but one Mac, consider getting a second and maybe even a third and networking them together with Ethernet and the built-in filesharing of System 7.5.x. You can buy an inexpensive four-port Ethernet minihub from Farallon, for example, for about $100.

Along with RJ-41 type connectors and four-pair twisted pair wires, you can connect each of these Macs (assuming they have built-in Ethernet ports) to this minihub, fire up the Network control panel and pick Ethernet, turn on personal filesharing on each machine while setting up a standard access name for each machine to the other and you are on your way. That way, you can grow your business with temporary employees, high school and college kids working as interns, or even permanent staffers. You can lock your hired help out of sensitive files via the Sharing command in System 7.5.x or you can go for something more bulletproof, by installing file security software, such as Folderbolt Pro, on those sensitive Macs.

By connecting to and using the World Wide Web, you can prospect for customers, tap into rich reference and research sources, and become familiar with who you are trying to market yourself to. For that you need as fast a network connection as you can muster (V.34 28.8 Kbps modem or ISDN line) and the Netscape browser.

Using clever Web utilities such as Nisus Software's **MailKeeper**, CE Software's **WebArranger**, or the new Now Software **Now Up-to-Date Web Publisher** and **Now Up-to-Date Contact 3.6**, you can use the Net and Web as your business's organizational tour de force.

Of course, you can also choose to keep organized with less sophisticated strategies and software that don't use the Web. Good calendar/organizer programs include Attain's **In Control 3.0** and Claris Organizer.

Each of these programs makes it easy to record and display your appointments in monthly, weekly, and daily views along with to-do lists for managing your daily tasks. They all provide multiple alarms to remind you of upcoming events, so long as you remember to input your schedule and to-do lists conscientiously.

Project Control and Management

Another way to grow your business is by managing each project more carefully. In Control can handle outlining projects task by task, determining the order in which to complete tasks, and assigning your staff to complete these project tasks.

If you need more project management prowess than In Control, you can switch over to something such as **Microsoft Project** or even Claris's **MacProject Pro**. Project management software, of course, is the real thing. It takes a very formulaic, structured approach to planning, scheduling, and task completion, but it can help you get real growth into your business by letting you tackle more complex client work.

Keeping Your Customers Informed and Happy

Maintaining good rapport with customers and potential customers is a must for any business, large or small. To do it right, you need to supplement your calendar software with a contact manager.

If you're using Now Up-to-Date the choice is easy—Now Contact. And the new version 3.6 can be published on the Web (just like Now Contact 3.6) so that you can keep your business's calendar and contact list current while traveling, without file copying and synchronization—just open your private Web page!

If you are not a Now devotee, you can go with a full metal jacket contact database such as **ACT!** from Symantec, or use a slimmer all-in-one such as **Claris Organizer** or even the TouchBase/Datebook combo.

No matter what sort of contact software you choose, however, you've got to be nearly religious about using it if you're to reap its business growth benefits.

HOT TIP

Keeping Yourself Happy   (KH)

Whether you're putting together your first home office or revamping the old one that no longer answers your needs, always ask yourself what's really appropriate for your needs. Think about your needs today; balance that with what your needs may be one or five years from now. If your home office today is really an adjunct to an office elsewhere, you probably won't need to equip it as heavily as if it were the nerve center of a business—but maybe you want to start your own business in that same office. In that case, think about future needs. And if your current home business is a modest one, it may not be wise to go into debt expanding—but at the same time don't hamstring yourself by buying equipment that you'll immediately outgrow. Remember, you aren't General Motors, Standard Oil, or Apple Computer, but if your work requires QuarkXPress, 4th Dimension, and a speed-of-sound laser printer, you won't be well served by cheaper alternatives.

No matter what your line of work, your home office should be a pleasant and comfortable place. Make sure you have light that's easy on the eyes *and* makes the room look appealing to you. If you meet customers in your home office, think of the impression you want to make on them, but don't forget that ultimately it's *your* office. Make it please *you!* Paint the walls a color you like (a tip: sponge-painting in a couple of shades is quick, easy, really cheap, and looks like you hired a designer); add pictures or plants if those please you, and add an armchair or rocking chair if there's space. Always keep comfort, efficiency, and your own tastes in mind and you can't help but create a

HOT TIP

great Mac home office.

[If nothing else has convinced you of the benefits a Mac home office can provide, consider this: Nearly everyone who had a hand in creating this book—from editors and contributors to illustrators and layout specialists—has a Mac home office. Coincidence? I think not.—JJ]

Appendices

Editors' Poll:
Have You Ever Suffered From a Repetitive Stress Injury? If Yes, What Did You Do?

JH: Only once, and it was after playing a Nintendo Gameboy for way too long.... The cure was simple, of course. No more Gameboy.

MEC: No. I have this annoying (to my coworkers) habit of getting up and walking about every 20 minutes or so, and it may have saved me from RSI.

ML: I occasionally get tendonitis in the thumb of my right hand from extensive mousercize. I take ibuprofen. When it's really bad, I make a fist with my hand and put a sock over it—exactly what my doctor suggested to keep it immobile. Rest usually takes care of it within a day or so.

TL: No. Well, not exactly. The main symptom I get is incredible eye strain, which develops into pounding headaches and has resulted in a deterioration of my vision.

I ignored the eye strain, took coffee and apsirin for the headache, and got stronger eyeglasses for the vision problem. My wife said that I should simply not stare at the computer so much. I haven't yet tried her solution—it's too rash!

JC: I sometimes suffer from tendonitis. I've uncovered a number of ways to relieve the pain as well as prevent the problem from recurring. First, go see a doctor and get the opinion of a professional, don't just take the advice of some Mac-goobers. Most doctors will prescribe a combination of physical therapy, stretching exercises, and a pain killer if necessary. Personally, I've found working on my PowerBook instead of my desktop Mac helps alleviate the pain and helps prevent the problem. For flareups, ibuprofen is a good pain killer.

BF: About two years ago I had mild carpal tunnel caused by overuse of my fingers and wrist in my right hand. The solution was a rigid brace to wear during the night to prevent hyper-extension of my wrist, and spandex partial gloves to wear when typing. These gloves keep your wrist warm and improve circulation when you are typing (your hands are elevated when you type and circulation is impaired). They also provided a small measure of support as well as a constant reminder to take it easy.

KT: Yes. My orthopedist called it "Mac elbow." I brought on the acute form by typing about 300 pages of manuscript because I thought I could use the money myself instead of paying a typist, as is my usual practice. (Never again, by the way.)

My orthopedist gave me phenylbutazone—the stuff they give horses!—and huge doses of ibuprofen instead of exercises, and after a week the acute pain went away.

I've learned to use both hands when possible (or menus) just to avoid bad pivoting. I move the position of the keyboard and mouse up and down to avoid doing the same things in the same way. And I have tried using a trackball instead of a mouse (hated it) and tried one of those "ergonomic" keyboards, which I also hated.

A | Staying Healthy at the Mac

As you spend more and more of your time in front of computers, keeping an eye on health issues can save you time, money, and aggravation. The computer revolution is producing its own genre of health-related problems which were previously experienced only by a small percentage of workers exposed to repetitive work environments. From eye problems to a myriad of spinal complaints, there is a serious need for computer users to become familiar with these potential problems.

Most of the interventions for keeping healthy while working with your computer remain relatively simple, and yes, even economical. In this appendix, we'll discuss preventative measures you can take to avoid the kinds of health problems associated with spending long hours at the computer.

Contributors

Bart Farkas (BF) is the chapter editor.

Don Sellers (DS) is a Seattle-based computer writer, editor, educator, documentary filmmaker, and author of the book *Zap! How your Computer Can Hurt You—And What You Can Do About It* (Peachpit Press).

John Kadyk (JK) remembers proofreading the two-page plan for the first *Macintosh Bible* at Won Thai restaurant in Berkeley in June 1986. He likes playing music and riding bikes when he's not writing, editing, or consulting about Macs.

Contents

~~~~~~

Eye Problems and Headaches

Eyestrain and headaches are two of the most common medical complaints of computer users. Rarely is computer use the entire cause of the problem, but it is certainly a significant contributing factor.

The Symptoms (DS)

Eyestrain results from forcing our eye muscles to work too hard. Like any other muscle, if they are overworked they stop functioning properly until they are allowed to rest. Because most of us take our eyesight for granted, we often work through spells of eyestrain, simply accepting them as a part of life, until the strain becomes unbearable and a headache ensues. Signs of eyestrain include the inability to focus, double vision, headaches, and color confusion. The causes of eyestrain are basically anything that causes the eye muscles to work harder than they normally would. Be mindful of factors that cause your eyes to have to refocus more than usual: glare, reflections, dust on the screen, bright lights, dimly lit reading materials, or frequent distance changes.

Headaches are still somewhat of a mystery. They are caused by such a vast array of factors that preventing them is still an inexact science. On any given day, your headache may be caused by diet, air quality, weather, stress, eyestrain, a combination of any or all of these, or something entirely different. Obviously the frequency, intensity, and quality of your computer use can impact your chances for a headache. The best defense is vigilance; if you notice that your headaches coincide with your computer use, there may be more than just a casual connection.

Unfortunately, working heavily on a computer demands a lot of our eyes and it may be impossible to avoid overexerting them, but there are a number of things you can do to minimize the discomfort and avoid more serious problems.

Taking Preventative Action (DS)

You can avoid and reduce eyestrain in many ways, from changing work habits to changing hardware.

Monitors matter. If you have the freedom to select your own monitor, there are a number of features you should look for.

Resolution directly impacts the amount of work your eyes have to do to focus on small images. When picking out a monitor, reduce the text down to about 5-point and decide if it's legible. If you can read the text, you can be fairly sure the monitor will display 12-point type quite well. Also inquire about the *dot pitch* of a monitor. Dot pitch is the distance between pixels on your screen and the smaller the dot pitch, the more precise the image (.28 mm or less is considered very sharp).

Brightness, contrast, and sharpness can all cause problems if they are not properly set. Because light levels vary significantly from workplace to workplace (and from computer store to workplace) make sure that all controls, especially brightness, are easily and widely adjustable.

There should be no flicker on your screen as it causes the eye to constantly readjust. Ask about the *refresh rate* on any monitor you will be using (70 Hz is fine for most people, but some are more sensitive than others) and remember that the larger the monitor, the faster the necessary refresh rates. Most of all, stare at the screen carefully to look for flicker; if you see it, the refresh rate is not correct.

Avoid reflections on the screen. Reflections on your screen are the result of strong light sources or reflections off items facing your monitor. Make every effort to minimize these reflections as your eyes will work harder to see through the glare. You can accomplish this through a combination of monitor position, light control, and screen colors. The easiest way to avoid glare is to change the position of lights in your work area. If you cannot change them, monitor positioning is your next best tactic. Finally, the background color of your monitor can affect reflections. Use a white background whenever possible as it reduces the effect of glare.

You may also want to consider using a glare filter, but you should choose it carefully as many can actually cause worse problems than glare. Every type of filter involves a trade-off of one or more elements (i.e., brightness) in exchange for reduced glare, so try many different types of filters and be sure you can return them if you don't like them. Your safest guide may be right on the package; the American Association of Ophthalmologists evaluates and approves glare screens. Their seal is one indicator of a filter's quality and effectiveness.

Use readable type. Obviously, the smaller the image, the more your eyes have to work to focus on it. Position your monitor about 18 inches away from your eyes and experiment with type sizes and document magnifications that reduce eyestrain. Don't get carried away with colors.

Get your eyes checked. Computer work is particularly demanding on the eyes, so it may lead you to discover eye problems that wouldn't otherwise bother you. If you already wear glasses or contacts, consider getting your eyes rechecked—many forms of eyesight correction can cause rather than correct problems at the computer. You may need custom eyesight correction for the times you're at work.

Dry Eyes: Annoying, but Treatable (BF)

Dry eyes (when your eyes feel gritty, itchy, or generally irritated) is a fairly common condition where the natural lubricating mechanisms of your eyes are not functioning up to snuff, or cannot rise to the challenge of environmental factors. Some people even experience some transient blurring of vision, but this usually clears with blinking.

Computer users are more likely than most to suffer from dry eyes for a couple of reasons. First, staring at *anything* (a book, a computer screen, a TV) for extended periods of time dramatically reduces the natural rate of blinking, which, in turn, lowers the amount of natural tears bathing the surface of the eye. Second, computers have an addictive quality compelling some people to stare unblinkingly at them for long periods of time, compounding an untreated problem.

The above factors substantially reduce the eye's natural ability to properly lubricate its surface. The result is a dry corneal surface. This causes the "gritty" and dry feeling that many of us have experienced from time to time. Add in the fact that many work environments have a low humidity, and you've got some irritated eyes. This is a very easily treated condition. Ask your pharmacist for a good eye lubricant. These are nonmedicinal lubricants that can be used liberally without fear of damaging your eyes. Don't confuse the eye-clearing medications for the lubricants. Getting the red out is not going to do you any good for this problem.

Take breaks and exercise. The National Institute of Occupational Safety and Health recommends getting away from the screen for 15 minutes every one or two hours of intense work at the computer. If that's not realistic for you, take breaks as often as you can. Spend the interval doing noncomputer work, or—as one doctor recommends—put your feet up, your head back, and close your eyes and relax (general stress increases the strain on your eyes, too). Exercise your eyes every ten minutes or so by focusing on as distant an object as possible for five or ten seconds.

Neck and Back Pain (DS)

Neck and back pain can be particularly debilitating for anyone who works with computers. Because most if not all of us work with our computers while in a sitting position, we are particularly prone to neck and back injury.

The Symptoms

Humans are not designed to sit for long periods of time; even perfect posture can't eliminate the 30 percent increase in pressure on your lumbar vertebrae caused by being seated. That, along with the massive demand sitting puts on tendons, muscles, and nerves, makes sitting a terribly strenuous activity which can lead to an array of back and neck ailments, and other problems as well.

Muscle fatigue, lower back pain caused by poor posture, upper back and neck pain from slouching or twisting, spinal irritation or nerve compression, nerve pinches, stiffness, muscle spasm, and radiating pain can all affect anyone who sits in front of their computer for any period of time.

Taking Preventative Action

Good posture. Good seating posture is not necessarily sitting bolt upright on a hard-back chair. Above all you should be comfortable and use the support your chair offers; if the chair doesn't do it, your muscles have to. There are, however, some specific guidelines that should be followed.

Always keep your feet flat on the ground or on an elevated footrest. Don't slump your shoulders (Mom was right) and keep your chin slightly tucked in. Maintain your lumbar curve; most office chairs provide some support for this natural curve but you should

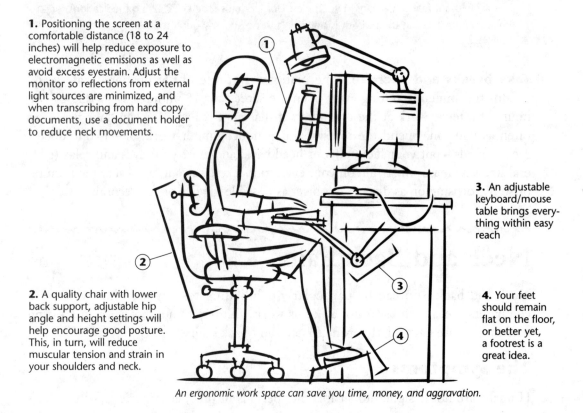

1. Positioning the screen at a comfortable distance (18 to 24 inches) will help reduce exposure to electromagnetic emissions as well as avoid excess eyestrain. Adjust the monitor so reflections from external light sources are minimized, and when transcribing from hard copy documents, use a document holder to reduce neck movements.

2. A quality chair with lower back support, adjustable hip angle and height settings will help encourage good posture. This, in turn, will reduce muscular tension and strain in your shoulders and neck.

3. An adjustable keyboard/mouse table brings everything within easy reach

4. Your feet should remain flat on the floor, or better yet, a footrest is a great idea.

An ergonomic work space can save you time, money, and aggravation.

Selecting a Chair (DS/JK)

The point of an adjustable chair isn't to let you find the one perfect position you can sit in all day without budging: A good chair should make you comfortable in a number of different postures. Get one with a backrest that adjusts up or down and whose tilt you can change (it should also be tall enough to support your upper back when you lean against it). The seat should also be adjustable to tilt forward or backward. Because the positions of the seat and backrest are related, you should be able to adjust both at once *while you're sitting*, by just moving around until you find a comfortable position and then setting it with a lever.

You should also be able to adjust the seat height so that when you sit with your hands on the keyboard, your feet are flat on either the floor or a footrest, and your elbows are level with your wrists and hands. Arm rests are often recommended, but it's unclear whether it helps to use them while typing.

Not all chairs—even those that appear to be on the forefront of design—are based on modern ergonomic principles, and there's no perfect chair for everyone; you need to try some out to find one that's right for you.

Kneeling chairs have forward-tilting seats and support for the knees, which bear a lot of body weight. These chairs have their advantages, but they put a lot of stress on the knees, tire the back, and are difficult to get in and out of. Many experts in ergonomics feel these flaws outweigh the advantages of kneeling chairs.

be prepared to supplement it if your chair is insufficient. Don't overwork your neck muscles by twisting, jerking, or repeatedly bending it. Fidget often (Mom didn't know everything); small changes in your position help to distribute the muscular work load.

Beyond posture, there are other things you can do to keep your back and neck fresh. Stand up as much as possible and take every opportunity to walk. It also helps to take active breaks; only sit when you absolutely have to.

Adjust your workstation. In addition to altering the position of your body, you can reduce neck and back problems by altering your work area to cause the least possible stress. Keep your monitor and reading material directly in front of you at eye level or below. If you answer the phone a lot, keep it within easy reach and do not cradle it between your cheek and shoulder. Adjust your chair to allow you to sit comfortably and with good posture.

Wrist and Arm Problems (DS)

The dangers and likelihood of wrist and arm injuries have been exaggerated by the extensive publicity they have gotten. They are, however, far from harmless, and pain in the wrists and arms should be carefully monitored.

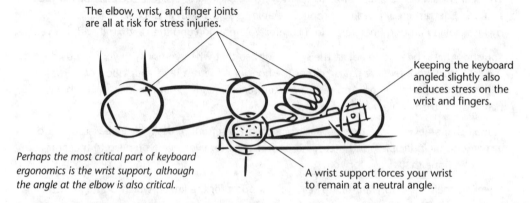

The elbow, wrist, and finger joints are all at risk for stress injuries.

Keeping the keyboard angled slightly also reduces stress on the wrist and fingers.

Perhaps the most critical part of keyboard ergonomics is the wrist support, although the angle at the elbow is also critical.

A wrist support forces your wrist to remain at a neutral angle.

The Symptoms

Cumulative Trauma Disorders (CTDs) are caused by the repeated infliction of small traumas which, in time, accumulate to become large and potentially debilitating injuries. The most commonly talked about disorder in relation to computer use is *Carpal Tunnel Syndrome* (CTS), which affects the median nerve that runs through the wrist. CTS and other CTDs are caused by a number of factors including awkward posture, constant hand flexing, working in cold temperatures, and typing with twisted or cocked wrists. There is a wide variety of symptoms which point to a CTD: burning pain when away from the computer, local pain, dull aches, radiating pain, numbness, or loss of muscle coordination. If any of these symptoms occur or become chronic or persistent, seek medical attention.

Taking Preventative Action

Minor CTDs can be self-treated with hot or cold treatment or over-the-counter anti-inflammatory medications. Persistent or acute problems, however, should only be treated by a professional, preferably with a CTD background.

The best treatment, however, is prevention. Wrist rests can be helpful in reducing stress. Make sure they are flat (curved ones are as bad as a desk edge), well-cushioned, and level with or just slightly above the level of the keyboard. You can also prevent CTDs by exercising good keyboard form: Forearms should be parallel to the floor, hands should be flat and even with the forearms, wrists should float or rest on a cushion (a folded hand towel does nicely) but should never rest on a hard desk edge, and arms and hands should be relaxed.

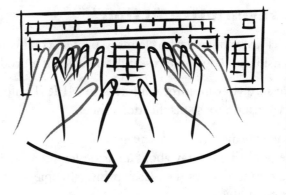

Your hands naturally want to point slightly inward. Conventional keyboards force you to constantly fight this natural position. Adjustable "split" keyboards help to alleviate this stress.

Many CTDs do not result from keyboard use but from a less talked

An ergonomic "split" keyboard can dramatically reduce wrist problems by keeping your hands at a natural angle.

about source: the mouse. The same rules of keyboard form apply to mouse form with a few extras: Don't grip the mouse too tightly, don't hold onto it when you are not using it, and keep it as close to your keyboard as possible. If you still have problems with your mouse, try one with a *drag lock* feature, try switching hands, use keystrokes instead, or try out a trackball (see Chapter 6 for more on trackballs).

Radiation

Computer monitors radiate electromagnetic radiation in two forms known as *ELF* (extremely low frequency) and *VLF* (very low frequency). Although it is not known for certain whether or not these emissions pose any danger, you can take minimal precautions if you are concerned. The most important thing to do is carefully scrutinize any claims made about computer monitor radiation and judge the risks soberly and with a healthy skepticism.

The Symptoms

Studies in recent years have called into question the assumption that the radiation produced by computer monitors is totally harmless. A number of theories have been advanced, but none has definitively proven any ill effects unique to computers. To a certain extent, computers are no more or less harmful than any other electrical equipment. Unlike other electrical equipment, however, computers produce both electrical *and* magnetic fields; some believe that it may be the *magnetic* fields that merit study. Whatever the answer, there are things you can do to minimize any potential risk without giving in to hysteria.

Taking Preventative Action

First, be suspicious of anyone who claims to protect you by making you part with your money. Be sensible and do some research to decide if a product is really of any use.

Second, make sure your monitor conforms to MPR II guidelines; you will find their approvals in your monitor's specifications sheet.

Lastly, limit your exposure to *electromagnetic fields* (EMFs). Turn off your monitor when you are not using it. Stay about an arm's length away from the screen. Arrange other EMF emitting devices (i.e., laser printers, copiers) so you are not bombarded while at your computer.

General Advice (DS)

Don't Wait Until You're Suffering

People constantly adjust to awkward or constrained positions, chairs of the wrong height, or bosses who put them in lousy moods. The body and mind compensate for these problems, minimizing the immediate results. But the worse the computer-related injuries get, the harder they are to fix. So listen to your body, and when something hurts, do something about it. If you don't take the time to be healthy now, you may have to use it to be sick later.

Make Sure Products Are Really Ergonomic

Don't believe labels, be a smart consumer. Consult the American National Standards Institute (ANSI) and the U.S. Occupational Safety and Health Administration (OSHA) for recommendations, but remember that they are only *recommendations* and neither organization actually certifies products. Most of all, pick products that work for you.

Other Resources

The material in this appendix under Don Sellers' name is adapted from his book, *Zap! How Your Computer Can Hurt You—And What You Can Do About It* (Peachpit Press), which gives much more thorough coverage of computer-related health threats than we have space for here. It also provides a huge list of related resources, including other books, periodicals, and organizations, plus sources of ergonomic hardware, software, and furniture.

B Where to Find More Information

When you're trying to find the right program, or figure out which Mac is best for you, or how to hone your Mac skills, there are three main routes you can try: books, magazines, and other users.

This appendix covers those routes, and more.

Contributors

Sharon Zardetto Aker (SZA) is the chapter editor.

Elizabeth Castro (EC) fell in love with the Mac while living in Barcelona, and founded the publishing house *Pagina Uno*. She was this chapter's editor for the fifth edition.

Contents

Magazines and Newsletters

You'd think that with millions of Mac users out there, there'd be more than two or three major magazines devoted to the Mac. But you'd be wrong. Luckily, there are many publications beyond the major ones.

Mainstream Publications

Shortly after the dawn of creation—that is, January of 1984—journalists and publishers jumped on the trail of the Mac. And here's the result:

Macworld (SZA/EC). *Macworld* magazine ($4 an issue, $30 a year) devotes a considerable amount of space to product reviews and lab tests, but also includes articles of a more general nature, including interviews with Mac movers, and a consumer column. *Macworld* maintains a presence on-line in America Online, where you can look up product ratings, read recent articles, and send letters to the editors and writers. *Macworld* also has a Web site at <http://www.macworld.com>.

MacUser (SZA/DD). *MacUser* ($3 an issue, $27 a year) has top-notch product testing and reports, lots of software reviews, and has recently mitigated its somewhat high-end

---

Can You Trust Them? (SZA)

There's a general assumption that major magazines have to pull their punches when reviewing products because they might otherwise risk their advertising revenue from the manufacturer. As an insider, I know that's just not true. I've written for all the major magazines, including *Macworld, MacUser,* and *MacHome Journal.* Not once in 11 years of reviewing products have I ever, ever, *ever* been asked to change comments or temper my criticisms—and I can be quite critical.

One scathing review I did of a software program for *MacUser* did cause a little ruckus when it was turned in; the editors asked if I was *really, really* sure of everything I said, since it was pretty nasty. But it went to print the way I wrote it. The fallout came more than a year later when the new version came out: *MacUser* called for a review copy and was told they couldn't have it if they were going to send it to "that housewife in New Jersey." *MacUser* declined to review it with any strings attached.

The editorial and advertising departments of professional magazines are completely independent at reputable publications. And you have the added benefit, in reviews from major magazines, of the usually higher level of expertise and exposure that the professional writers have—it's hard to do a good review of a program if one is working in the vacuum of not having used other, similar, programs, too.

business focus by adding short columns on games and even kids' stuff. *MacUser*'s on-line presence is on ZD Net, which you can access separately or through CompuServe; you can get product reviews, interact with editors, and download software utilities written especially for ZD Net users (which can then be freely shared with friends and user groups—you just can't post them on other on-line services).

MacWEEK (SZA/EC). *MacWEEK* is, obviously, a weekly publication, but its value is not so much in its frequency as in its timeliness, since the monthlies go to press about three months before you see them. It's the best source for the latest news, gossip, and product announcements, as well as what's happening on the business end of the market. A subscription is $100 a year—which is actually in line with the magazine subscriptions, because of the number of issues. Zillions of complimentary subscriptions are available, however, for the right people—those who manage or purchase *lots* of Mac hardware or software.

MacHome Journal (SZA). As the venerable *Macworld* and *MacUser* focus more and more on high-end, cutting-edge business use of the Mac and related products, the home and family user is getting left out. *MacHome Journal* ($2 an issue, $24 a year), not as slick or technical as the two others, is filling the gap. You won't find "lab test" product reviews, but you will find plenty of family- and home-based business information in this magazine, which has significantly improved with almost every issue since its inception.

Other Mac Publications

There's more support available in print than just the glossy monthlies (and weekly).

Macintosh Multimedia & Product Registry (SZA). Despite its name change from the simpler *Macintosh Product Registry*, this Redgate Communications publication ($15 an issue, $40 a year) still provides a comprehensive listing of all sorts of products, not just multimedia. A paragraph of description is included for every product whose manufacturer agrees to pay for the listing; a separate section has a brief listing for every conceivable product the editors could find, regardless of whether or not the manufacturer is a paying advertiser.

The CD-ROM version ($60) has all the information in a HyperCard stack that has an annoyingly clunky and slow interface.

The Macintosh Multimedia & Product Registry on CD is so complete it even includes itself.

It's great for finding information when you already know a product or company name, but the general Find function is a little weak; you can search through descriptions for specific words, but there's no formal keyword setup so you can search in categories like "preschool education" or "arcade games".

BMUG Newsletter (EC). This 500-page "newsletter" is published twice a year by the folks at BMUG—the Berkeley Mac User Group. It's jam-packed with reviews, commentary, and tips written by honest-to-goodness users. There's not a single ad, which frees BMUG's staff to say exactly what they think about the products they talk about (see "Can You Trust Them?" in this chapter). The newsletter is included free with membership, but I'd buy it even it weren't. (You don't have to be a member of the group to get the newsletter; back issues are available for $7 directly from BMUG.)

TidBITS (Adam Engst). TidBITS is a free electronic newsletter that covers the computer industry with an emphasis on the Macintosh and the Internet. It's distributed to about 150,000 readers each week on the Internet and on most commercial services. Issues are 30K of straight text, with topics ranging from the latest Macs to software reviews to editorials on the future of Apple and the Internet. TidBITS has been around for over 300 issues and six years, and sports one of the largest Internet newsletter mailing lists. TidBITS is widely quoted and republished; nonprofit, noncommercial publications are welcome to reprint articles with proper credit to the author and TidBITS. For subscription information, send e-mail to info@tidbits.com or check the Web page at <http://king.tidbits.com/>. *[Adam's the editor of TidBITs—who better to write the description? It's a great newsletter, and you can't beat the price.—SZA]*

> ## Books   (SZA)
>
> There's a wealth of Mac books out there; I know, because I've written many of them myself over the years. Aside from general-purpose Mac books such as this one, you'll find books that are more focused on certain aspects of Mac computing—such as font-handling or troubleshooting—as well as books on every major software program around.
>
> Browse the bookstores. As a general rule, if you like one book by a specific author or publisher, you can trust other books by that author or from that publisher. A good book is the best, and cheapest, investment you can make to get the most out of your Mac.

Special Interest Publications

You don't need Mac-only publications to glean helpful hints and information for your Mac. Newsletters and magazines that focus on special programs, such as Microsoft Word, or special activities, such as desktop publishing—even when it's a cross-platform approach—can be exactly what you need.

Cobb Group newsletters (ND). The Cobb Group publishes several excellent monthly newsletters for Mac users. *The Mac Authority* ($50 a year) contains general Mac techniques and tips. Four others, with prices ranging from $40 to $50 a year, focus on popular Microsoft products: *Inside Word, Excellence, Inside Microsoft Works,* and *Inside FileMaker Pro. Inside HyperCard* ($60 a year) is aimed at stack developers.

For desktop designers (Carol Aiton). One of the benefits of subscribing to magazines and newsletters aimed at designers is that they're so well-designed; it makes reading them a pleasurable, as well as educational, experience. Three of my favorites:

- *Before & After* (bimonthly, $36 a year) is a truly delightful 16-page newsletter packed with truly *usable* design information. Not only does writer John McWade give good, sound advice on the concepts of great design, he also provides realistic, technical "how-to" info in terms that are easy to understand and apply. It's a great source for expert and novice alike.

- *The Board Report* (newsletter, $69 a year; complete monthly $96 a year) is stuffed with information, all of it easily archivable with a built-in filing system for easy reference. Seemingly everything is included: tips, techniques, surveys, marketing reports, and fresh ideas and concepts. It's astute, knowledgeable, and a pleasure to read.

- *Color Publishing* (bimonthly, $20 a year) is a sound publication with articles from acknowledged leaders in the color publishing arena. The magazine keeps you abreast of trends in the graphics industry, supplies reviews of what's already in the marketplace, and talks about what's on the way.

More for desktop designers (Lorraine Bebee). There are many notable design periodicals for a Mac designer to choose from. Some of them don't have the computer as the main focus, concentrating mostly on important design issues. Of the eight that I subscribe to, there are two that I read cover-to-cover the minute they arrive:

- *Communication Arts* is one of the oldest, and, in my opinion, the best, in the design publication arena. It features a variety of work from the fields of graphic design, illustration, advertising, and photography. The focus is on good design, regardless of the tools used; it also includes regular columns on legal affairs, design issues, freelance questions, design technology, technology reviews and resources, and book reviews. A subscription includes four regular issues, four annuals, and an interactive design CD-ROM ($53 a year; $99 for two years; $39 a year for students).

- *Step-By-Step Electronic Design* (12 issues, $48 a year, $90 for two years) is a monthly four-color newsletter that focuses on specific production techniques used by leading computer graphic designers and illustrators. There're plenty of detailed "how-to"

Mac History Books   (EC)

If you're interested in how two guys in a garage started a billion-dollar company, and how one of them got kicked out halfway through, check out:

Steve Jobs: The Journey is the Reward, Jeffrey Young (pro-Jobs, pro-Wozniak)

Accidental Millionaire, Lee Butcher (anti-Jobs, pro-everyone else)

West of Eden, Frank Rose (pretty even)

Odyssey, John Sculley (pro-Sculley, doesn't talk much about anyone else)

Hackers, Steven Levy (an amazing book that explains where Woz came from)

pieces, and a good question-and-answer section for the most popular applications. All issues are three-hole-punched, making them easy to keep in a binder for later reference.

Other Resources

Some of the best help for Mac users comes in forms other than the printed word.

User Groups

A user group is a club whose members are interested in computers in general, or in a particular kind of computer, or even specific software. They're typically nonprofit and independent of manufacturers and publishers.

Meetings are usually free. Membership, with its perks of a newsletter, access to shareware libraries, and sometimes even discounts on major products, usually runs $20 to $60 a year. Subgroups, called *SIGs* (Special Interest Group), meet for members who share a particular focus, such as beginners or musicians.

Finding a local user group (EC). Unless you live in a very remote area, finding a local user group shouldn't be hard—especially if there's a college nearby. Call Apple's user group hot line (800/538-9696) to find out about user groups near you. If you can't find a group in your community, get together with some other Mac users and start one of your own.

There are a few user groups that are so big, or so old, that they serve as an example for all the rest. Even if you don't happen to live near them, their enormous software libraries (from which you can generally order by mail), incredible newsletters, member discounts, and tech support make long-distance membership very tempting.

Boston Computer Society (EC). There are more than 45 SIGs in the country's largest user group, the Boston Computer Society, and each of them publishes a newsletter (in addition to the slick main magazine). When you join ($40 a year), you get to choose two SIGs to belong to (more than two costs extra). BCS' Mac SIG has more than 10,000 members and its newsletter, *The Active Window*, is excellent. In addition, it offers great tech support, advice on buying software and hardware, and occasional discounts to members for third-party items.

BMUG (EC). BMUG's motto is "We give away information." With more than 12,000 members all over the world, and offices in Berkeley and Boston, BMUG is truly a Mac institution. BMUG maintains an extensive shareware library, sends out a 500-page newsletter twice a year to its members, and offers tech support, hard disk salvaging, and a great BBS.

And Don't Forget...

The list of learning resources goes on and on....

On-line (SZA). Gone are the days when a modem was an "extra," bought only by professionals or the nerdiest of hobbyists. A modem is now, if not an absolute essential, certainly part of almost every basic computer setup.

Once you have a modem, you can get on-line. And once you're on-line, you can join tens of thousands of other Mac users asking questions, providing answers, and generally sharing information. Of the major on-line services, America Online is the biggest Mac-oriented company you can find. CompuServe's MAUG (Micronetted Apple User Group) section is incredibly active and staffed by a great collection of experts in all Mac fields. ZiffNet is Ziff Publications' on-line service—they're the people who bring you *MacUser* and *MacWEEK*.

The Mac Expo (SZA). There are trade shows for everything from motorcycles to florist supplies. The one that's devoted to the Macintosh, Macworld's Mac Expo, is held twice a year: January in San Francisco and August in Boston. The show is three to four days of vendors showing their wares, and experts showing their stuff at seminars. The price is a little stiff if you want to attend the seminars (almost $60 for unlimited attendance) but is usually well worth it.

C | Buying Macs and Mac Products

There's nothing worse than buying computer equipment—except, maybe, buying a used car. You're never sure who's telling the truth, or who is truthful but misinformed, or if your purchase will be worth next to nothing the day after tomorrow when the SuperDuper models come out.

There's not much you can do about plummeting computer values, but we've designed this chapter to prepare you to deal with all other aspects of Mac-related shopping.

Contributors

Sharon Zardetto Aker (SZA) is the chapter editor.

Elizabeth Castro (EC) fell in love with the Mac while living in Barcelona, and founded the publishing house *Pagina Uno*. She was appendix editor for the fifth edition of *The Macintosh Bible*.

Michael Hetelson (MH) is a Mac maven and entrepreneur; he was formerly general manager at CompUSA.

Contents

Buying a Mac

In 1984, buying a Mac was easy because there was only one. These days, a dozen models are introduced each year, and there may be as many as 20 current models available at any time. Check out Chapter 2 for information on the kinds of Macs you'll be choosing from (at least when this was written).

Buying a New Mac

Shopping for a new computer is a lot like shopping for any big-ticket item: Prices vary from one place to the next, and you have to shop around and be willing to bargain to get the best price. That said, there are a few special considerations to keep in mind as you begin your Mac hunt.

Apple's falling prices (SZA/EC). There's something about buying a Mac that you have to understand: If you wait three months, the price will probably go down, and if you wait three more months, it'll go down further. But you could wait forever while prices keep falling, and you'll never have a Mac.

Also keep in mind that Apple introduces new models, and discounts or discontinues older ones, every three to six months. Check on-line services or *MacWEEK* to see if there are any hints about the imminent demise of a computer you're interested in—that's when it makes sense to wait a little to see if the price will drop. The electronic newsletter *TidBITS* is also a great source of information about new products and falling prices.

Less than "cutting edge" is less (SZA/EC). If you can bear to forgo the "very latest" in Mac technology, you can often get a great deal by buying a model that's just been, or is about to be, discontinued.

HOT TIP

But whether or not a discontinued model is a bargain depends on why it was discontinued. If it was replaced by another model with similar features, it's a good buy. But if it's discontinued because it's dead-end technology (such as the Mac II with its 68020 processor) then it's not such a bargain.

Warranties for new Macs (EC). Apple offers a one-year warranty on every hardware product it sells. That means that Apple or an Apple Authorized Service Provider will fix any hardware problem you have free of charge. Whether they will fix it on-site or when you bring it in depends on the problem you have. Apple will even send replacement parts by courier service—before you even send in your old one.

This is an Apple guarantee, and it's valid even if you buy your Mac from a mail-order company or from another person—as long as nobody but an authorized technician has touched your Mac's innards and you have a dated sales receipt with your equipment's serial number on it.

One of the nice things about the Apple guarantee is that it is good throughout the world. So if you are in Barcelona on a business trip and your PowerBook dies, you'll be happy to know you can bring it to any authorized service provider for service. (You may have to pay for out-of-country repairs, but Apple will reimburse you when you get back to the U.S.)

Buying a Used Mac

Though hardware prices continue to fall, a Mac is still a pricey item; when the choice is "used Mac" versus "no Mac," all of a sudden "used" doesn't sound so bad. In fact, when the choice is "new Mac" versus "used but *lots* cheaper," well, "used" can still sound pretty good.

Buying a used computer isn't like buying a used car. You're not getting something with high mileage and components ready to fall apart; most faulty hardware problems show up in the first couple of months of use, while under warranty. Still, there are many things to consider if you're not buying new.

[Unlike with a used car salesman, if the computer you buy turns out to be one sour lemon, you may eventually get satisfaction from the seller, or at least be able to vent your frustration, sullying the seller's reputation by word of foul mouth (my father tells anyone who'll listen how his no-good son sold him a no-good Mac). Of course, Mac martyrdom will only get you so far, as the seller will have probably already turned her attention to moving that '79 Gremlin, er, Mac Plus, sitting in the back lot. Caveat emptor, as they say.—JJ]

Upgrading old versus buying new (SZA/EC). If you're considering buying an older Mac and then upgrading it—either with an Apple upgrade to a newer model or with an accelerator, memory, and larger hard drive—be sure to check prices on the new Macs first. Prices sometimes drop so drastically that you might spend less on a new, faster Mac than on a used, souped-up model.

Where to look (SZA/EC). One of the best places to find a used Mac is through the classified advertisements in a user group newsletter (see Appendix B for more on user groups). Another great place to find out what's available is on-line. Some dealers may have second-hand Macs and may even provide some limited guarantee.

Is an Old Mac Usable? (SZA)

Well, it depends on how old the Mac is and what you want to do with it. After all, an eight-track tape player is usable if it comes with all the tapes you'll ever want to listen to. Likewise even the oldest Mac, if it has its original software, is still usable. You could type in the original MacWrite, play in MacPaint, and print on an ImageWriter printer. But you couldn't get support for those programs or the system software if you have a problem, and you couldn't run any new software on it. And you couldn't share information with any other users with newer Macs—the disks they're using won't work in your machine and, in all likelihood, you're not using software that's compatible anymore, either.

As for middle-aged Macs, once again, it depends. If your activities on the Mac are self-contained, and you already have all the software you need, you can just keep plugging away. You won't be able to upgrade to the latest and greatest applications or system software, which require both lots of memory (you may have an 8MB or 10MB limit on your machine) and more advanced processors (at least an 68030—sometimes even at least a PowerPC!). Newer programs that can run on your machine may do so very slowly unless it has at least a 68040 processor. You may have problems trading information with other Macs or even installing new software if you have only an 800K instead of a 1.4MB floppy drive.

In general, if you can get a Mac that will do what you need, don't worry about "better and faster" unless that's in your budget. But if you're on a tight budget and you're buying used equipment, don't buy more than one (or possibly two) generations behind the current models.

No matter who you buy a computer from, if it's less than a year old, the original Apple guarantee will still be valid so long as you have the original dated invoice that includes the computer's serial number.

Checking out a used Mac (SZA/LP/MH/AN). Buying a used Mac is probably easier than buying a used car, but you still have to kick the tires and look under the hood. You don't have to assume that someone's trying to cheat you—but neither should you assume that the seller always knows as much as he or she claims to know, even about equipment that's been used for years. When you pop the hood and go in for a closer look, you should be sure the following items are included:

- *Memory.* Choose About this Macintosh on the menu to make sure you're getting all the RAM you think you are.

- *Hard drive.* Run a utility such as SCSI Evaluator to check for speed and bad sectors; if there are many bad sectors, the disk may not be reliable. If it's an older machine with a small hard drive that you plan to replace, this may not be an issue.

- *Keyboard.* Check every single key—and the supporting "feet" that hold the keyboard up at an angle. Sticky keys may just need a cleaning, but having to replace the keyboard adds about $100 to your purchase.

- *Mouse.* Check out its basic functioning. Test it by wiggling both ends of the cable as you move the pointer around the screen and click. If the pointer isn't moving smoothly, there may be a problem with the connector or the inside of the cable. (Or, it may be just a dirty mouse—see Chapter 6.)

- *Floppy drive.* Don't settle for less than a SuperDrive that handles 1.4MB disks. Bring several with you and make sure it can read them all.

- *Screen.* To assess wear and tear on a very old screen, turn off the power and see if there's a ghosted image of the menu bar on the black screen; if there is, don't buy it. For middle-age screens, make sure the display, when on, is still bright; fiddle with any available brightness and contrast controls.

- *Video card.* If there's a separate video card in the Mac, use the Monitors control panel to see what it is. If it's strictly a black-and-white affair, you'll certainly notice without the control panel; but it's hard to tell, just by looking, whether you've got, say, four or 16 shades of gray, or 256 or thousands of colors, or millions of colors. The list in the control panel will be clear. Clicking the Options button in the control panel will identify the specific video card in use.

POWERBOOK

Buying a used PowerBook (SZA). If you're shopping for a used PowerBook (which can be a great bargain if all you need is a traveling word processor and e-mail machine), there are some additional things to keep in mind:

- *Hardware and memory limitations.* The oldest PowerBooks have small hard drives, severe restrictions on addressable memory (see Chapter 2), and laughable 2,400-baud modems. Figure in the cost of a new modem and possibly another hard drive; you can't do much about memory limitations.

- *Power drain.* Rechargeable batteries aren't immortal; if the PowerBook is two years old or more, you're going to need a new battery (or two). You may also want to buy a newer, more efficient power adapter.

~~~~~~

Buying Other Stuff

This book is filled with specific evaluations and comparisons of Mac programs. What follows are some general guidelines to keep in mind while you're shopping.

General Considerations (SZA/EC)

Here are some rules of thumb that apply to both hardware and software purchases.

Go for the best. If you can figure out which is the best program, buy it. It's often a false economy to tell yourself, "Well, I don't want to spend *that* much," or "I can really get by with less." You may end up paying to replace the defective or inadequate product, and you also lose the time you've invested learning to use the first one.

Take reviews (including ours) with a grain of salt. One problem with reviews is that most reviewers aren't like most users. They tend to have much more experience with Mac programs and sometimes suffer from "expertosis." And they're not always given adequate time to really get to know the software they're evaluating.

Still, reviews are a great place to learn about products. Just don't treat them as gospel—even when they appear in the *Mac Bible*.

Compatibility. Make sure that the product you want to buy is compatible with the ones you already own. This goes for both hardware and software, especially if you have some nonstandard hardware such as an accelerator card. Make sure you know what you have, and check reviews, and with the vendor to see if they'll all work together.

Make sure there's support. In real estate, the three most important things to consider when buying property are location, location, and location. Likewise, the three most important things to consider when buying a computer product are support, support, and support. But support from the vendor who sold the product is an almost impossible dream. Support from the people who publish the program is sometimes unavailable, and sometimes expensive (for some high-end products, it costs hundreds of dollars a year to be on a list of supported users).

But support isn't impossible. First, many vendors have Web pages and/or on-line support on the commercial services, where you can post questions and download bug fixes. But the most important source of support is the one that makes it smart to

SOS-APPLE (EC)

Apple has a free technical support line (800/SOS-APPL) which is unfortunately *very* popular: Sometimes you spend up to 45 minutes listening to minimalist music while you're on hold. (I can almost stand the wait, but the music makes me go berserk.) Here's a tip that will be worthless once everyone starts using it: They say the best time to call is Tuesday through Thursday, 9 a.m. to 10 a.m. and 3 p.m. to 5 p.m. (central time).

buy the popular program instead of a quirky little application in the same category: other users. If you use the same program thousands of others use, you'll find lots of help through a user group, on-line, in the major magazines, at the bookstore, and in specialty newsletters.

Don't pay full retail. When it comes to hardware, shop around and be prepared to try some bargaining. Prices vary from region to region, and from dealer to dealer; the best prices, especially for hardware, are usually found in big metropolitan areas. For software, the best prices are often found in mail-order catalogs. Whether you're buying a printer or a word processor, you would do well to check around before you buy.

Buying Hardware

Here are some things to remember when you're looking for hardware of all sorts.

Get what you need (SZA/EC). If you want something special—a big screen instead of a standard one, for example—you'll be happier if you figure out some way to justify getting it. Few people say, "I really shouldn't have bought this [expensive piece of equipment]." But an awful lot of them say, "How did I ever live without this?" after splurging a little.

Get more than you need (SZA/EC). There are some things you can never get too much of: hard disk space, RAM, Ben and Jerry's Cherry Garcia ice cream. If you're buying a hard disk, buy 50 percent more space than you think you need. If you're buying RAM, get as much as you can afford—and then charge a few extra megabytes.

Get a long warranty (EC). Look for a good long warranty—at least a year. Lots of companies offer two-, three-, or even five-year warranties. (Of course, those companies may not be around in five years, or even two, and that's definitely something else to consider.)

The three-year plan (SZA). My father's car-buying philosophy was to buy a new car every three years—before the current one started having trouble and/or had racked up enough mileage to really drop its trade-in value.

My computer-buying strategy is somewhat the same: A three-year-old machine can bring in a decent sum, and there will be buyers for it—it's not *that* out of date, and there will always be new computer buyers on a tight budget. The money you get for the computer can help finance a new one for you. Wait four years, however, and you'll probably not be able to sell it at all.

Because my livelihood depends on my hardware, I follow this strategy, with a twist. Every 18 months or so, I get a new Mac, and give mine to the kids; the kids' computer is the one that gets sold. That way, I stay current, there's a second not-so-old machine at my disposal in times of trouble, and I can still sell a machine at a decent price to take the edge off the new purchase.

Check out the OEM (EC). When buying hardware, remember that what really counts is often not the name on the box, but the *original equipment manufacturer* (OEM, pronounced "oh-ee-em"). Overall quality is determined by the OEM; service and tech support depend on who you buy the equipment from.

Buying Software (SZA/EC)

Use the following guidelines to find good software. (Of course, we realize that some of these things won't be obvious until *after* you've bought it, so try—at a store, at a friend's, at a user group—to really see the program running before you buy it.)

Public Domain, Shareware, and Freeware (SZA)

Public domain is an oft-misused phrase, because it means the author of the piece has given up all rights to it; it's commonly, though mistakenly, used to refer to *shareware* and *freeware*, great concepts that got started in the computer community.

Shareware is a program that you obtain for free (from a friend, user group, or on-line) so you can try it out. If you like it, you pay for it by sending the author a small fee, usually $5 to $25. *Freeware* is just what it sounds like—there's no fee involved at all.

If you use shareware, make sure you pay for it—that's what keeps programmers upgrading the programs and creating others in their spare time.

Trust good publishers. Because movie reviewers spend most of their time telling you the plot instead of saying whether the movie is any good, one of the best ways to decide if a movie is worth seeing is to find out who directed it. Similarly, a good way to predict if a program is worth buying is to check who publishes it. If you like one piece of software by a publisher, you'll probably like the others.

Try before you buy. Some computer stores let you sit at a computer and play with whatever's on its hard drive so long as no one else wants to get at the machine. Trying a program in a store will often give you enough of a feel for it to decide if you want to buy it.

Some software manufacturers offer free or low-cost demo versions so you can try out the program at home before deciding on your purchase. Typically, a demo version works like the real thing except it won't save or print, or it expires after a few weeks of use.

Things to look for in software. Great software packages—okay, even *good* software packages—have certain things in common. Be mindful of the following:

- *Ease of use:* Because all Mac programs are designed with a similar interface, a good program should look familiar even if you've never seen it before—you should be able to create, open, and save documents, and enter basic information without resorting to directions. Although you don't always need all the latest bells and whistles, programs that include the latest innovations—such as drag-and-drop editing—often make working with them easier and more efficient.

- *The right tool:* You don't need a bazooka to kill a fly, nor do you need PageMaker 6 to compose your e-mail. A small, snappy little program dedicated to a specific task can run circles around the big guys.

- *Speed counts:* The speed aspect of a program's performance is one of the most difficult things to ascertain ahead of time because a review's statistics, or even a hands-on store demo, is unlikely to be done on the equivalent of your own setup. But remember that waiting a few seconds hundreds of times a day is a lot of wasted time.

- *Customizability:* If you can change a program's keyboard commands or toolbars to match the way you work, you'll be able to work more efficiently.

- *File formats:* Make sure the program you're looking at can save its documents in several different formats and can import things from other programs.

- *Documentation:* As programs become more powerful, it's hopeless to expect to be able to learn it just from *using* it. Programs need good documentation: a well-written manual with lots of illustrations and a good index. On-line help is great as supplemental documentation; for simpler programs, on-line help is sometimes the only help you'll get, so it should be thorough and easy to get at.

Beware of vaporware. So much software has been promised that never saw the light of day (or saw it on a day many months after it was supposed to) that there's even a name for it: *vaporware.*

So when someone tells you that a new product will be along "real soon now" (which has its own acronym—RSN), don't depend on it. Few computer products come out on time, and some end up being nothing more than vaporware.

Thou shalt not steal. Pirating software is a shortsighted solution to your economic woes. Even if you save a couple bucks by copying your friend's program, you won't get the upgrades, manuals, or the support that comes with being a legitimate user.

If companies can't make money developing software because everyone is stealing their software instead of buying it, soon there won't be any good programs at all. Then what'll you do?

Being a Smart Consumer (SZA/MH)

While many shopping and buying techniques are common to any kind of high-priced purchase, there are some things specific to buying computer equipment—and some even more specific to buying a Mac product.

Commission? Incentive? While shoppers assume salespeople push higher-priced items if they're working on a commission basis, there's something more insidious in computer merchandising. Quite often, there are special incentives for salespeople who can sell a specific model or bundle—incentives that take the form of cash or merchandise. So, be wary of someone who tries to sell you what you didn't ask for to start with.

You don't need a MAP. Apple, and some other vendors, restrict their resellers with something called *MAP—minimum advertised price.* That means that no matter what the store may be willing to sell the computer for, they can't advertise below Apple's set price. How does knowing this help you?

- The price in the store might be lower than the one advertised in the newspaper; don't compare prices based just on ads.

- A store may make up a "bundle," or offer a great price on a second, non-MAP item, when you buy the computer at the advertised price.

- The salesperson, or the manager, may be willing to sell it for less than the marked price; it can't hurt to ask.

Lead time. Magazines and newspapers set up their advertising in advance, and things often change between the time the ad was designed and when you see it. For magazines, the lead time is two to three months—that's why so many ads for things with volatile prices, such as memory chips, say "call for price." As for local newspapers and stores, ads go in on Thursday for the Sunday paper—so if Apple announces a new machine or price cut on Friday, it won't be reflected in the ad. And supplemental circulars are prepared *months* in advance, so the prices on older models may be entirely different by the time you see the ad.

Dicker. Don't assume the price written on a tag is also carved in stone. Offer a little less—or a lot less, if that's your bargaining philosophy. If you've seen the same machine for sale for less somewhere else, offer that price—even stores that don't advertise "we'll match our competitor's prices" often will.

Roll your own bundle. The profit margin on Macs these days is relatively small, and so there may not be much bargaining room when you start with its sticker price. But smaller items usually have larger profit margins, so you might suggest a roll-your-own bundle that includes cables, printer paper, and some software, at 20 to 30 percent off their sticker prices.

This is also a good reason to plan to buy lots of stuff all at once instead of the computer first, and peripherals and supplies later.

Comparisons are sometimes fruitless. Apple has three basic merchandising channels: educational for schools, and through college stores; mass merchant, such as Sears and Staples; and superstore, such as Computer City and CompUSA. (Mail-order companies tie in to one of the latter two.) Trying to compare prices from one to another is like comparing apples and oranges. (Sorry.)

Models in these different channels have slightly different configurations. So if you bring a Sears ad to CompUSA and say, "Look, this is $200 less down the street," they can say, "Look, this is actually a different model." Was this done because different types of customers, with different needs, go to college stores, Sears, and computer stores? Or was it done to protect merchants from price-comparison shopping? Hmm....

Money-back guarantee. Don't buy from a store that doesn't offer a money-back guarantee for hardware, no questions asked, for two weeks to a month. And make sure the following considerations are addressed in the fine print on that guarantee:

- *Extent of guarantee.* Items such as printers are often excluded from this guarantee because once you try them, they're used and can't be resold.

- *Extra fees.* Are you going to be charged a "restocking" fee if you return the item?

- *For mail order:* Do they pay the shipping on the return? Do they reimburse you for the original shipping? Is there a "handling fee" separate from shipping, and is it nonrefundable?

- *Refund policy.* If you pay by check originally, will you have to wait weeks for a cash refund?

Get price protection. Shop at a store that offers 30-day price protection. That means if the price drops within 30 days of your purchase, you are refunded the difference. Make sure you keep your receipts, and check the price just before the 30-day period is up.

Even if a store doesn't advertise this policy, you may find that they're willing to do it—especially if they offer a return policy, because otherwise you could return the item at the original, high price and just buy another computer at the new, low price. (Sometimes it helps to point this out to sales or management!)

Already-opened boxes. If the box you're buying has obviously been opened and re-closed, don't accept the explanation of its condition as a "stock" or "check" procedure. Assume the box has been opened and emptied: Open the box in the store, make sure the inner packaging is in shape and that everything, including cables, manuals, and registration cards, is still there.

Which brings us to another point: Often items are returned to stores simply because a customer changed his mind, or didn't like it, or decided on something even better—it's not necessarily because there's something wrong with the item. You can ask if there's any returned merchandise available at a discount—the store can't always return it to Apple, nor can it sell it as new, and is often willing to sell it at some discount.

A few more points. Some final admonitions:

- If the price seems too good to be true, it probably is. Dealer costs are almost always the same. Check the fine print.

- An Apple warranty always applies to a new Mac no matter where you buy it, but service and support vary from one store to another.

- Avoid shopping at crowded, rushed times: weekends, holiday sales, the hour before closing. You'll get undivided attention and bargaining time if you choose less popular hours.

- If a salesperson says an item is out of stock and he doesn't know when it will be available, that's the truth—Apple never tells when back orders will be filled. If you get the reverse ("We'll have it next week" or "It will be three months"), don't count on it.

- Using a credit card for the purchase is always your best defense, no matter where you're shopping, because you can stop a disputed payment. Using anything other than a credit card for mail order merchandise is the height of foolishness.

D } Contact Information

This appendix provides the information you need to get ahold of the software publishers and hardware manufacturers of products mentioned in this edition of *The Macintosh Bible.* By calling the numbers listed here, you can find out about the current availability of products you're wondering about, their current list price, and local sources. You could probably also order the product, but, as explained in Appendix C, that may not be a great idea, since you can usually find the product from outside sources at prices much lower than the manufacturer's list price.

The information was up to date at press time, but, as proven by the trouble we had tracking down some of these companies, these things can change fast. We've included e-mail addresses for companies that advertise them as part of their customer marketing materials. In those cases, we've used these abbreviations: AOL=America Online, AL=AppleLink, CIS=CompuServe Information Service, INT=Internet address, and MCI=MCI Mail. We've also included phone numbers for private bulletin board services (BBSs), and World Wide Web URLs for the companies that supply them.

A

Abbott Systems
62 Mountain Rd.
Pleasantville, NY 10570
800/552-9157, 914/747-4171,
fax 914/747-9115
AL: d5679; AOL: abbott sys

Abracadata
P.O. Box 2440
Eugene, OR 97402
800/451-4871, 541/342-3030,
fax 541/683-1925
CIS: 70751,620

Access Software
4750 Wiley Post Way
Bldg. 1, Suite 200
Salt Lake City, UT 84116
800/800-4880, 801/359-2900,
fax 801/596-9128
CIS: 72662,61

ACI US
20883 Stevens Creek Blvd.
Cupertino, CA 95014
800/384-0010, 408/252-4444,
fax 408/252-4829
AL: d4444; CIS: go acius;
INT: http://www.acius.com

Activision
11601 Wilshire Blvd., Suite 300
Los Angeles, CA 90025
800/477-3650, 310/473-9200,
fax 310/479-4005
CIS: go gambpub

Acuris
1098 Washington Crossing Rd.
Washington Crossing, PA 18977
800/OK-ACURIS, 215/493-4302
INT: http://www.acuris.com

A.D.A.M. Software
1600 River Edge Pkwy., Suite 800
Atlanta, GA 30328
800/755-2326, 770/980-0888,
fax 770/988-0611
INT: http://www.adam.com

Addison-Wesley Publishing
One Jacob Way
Reading, MA 01867
800/447-2226, 617/944-3700,
fax 617/944-9338

Adesso
5110 W. Goldleaf Circle, Suite 50
Los Angeles, CA 90056
213/294-4300, fax 213-294-7451

Adobe Systems
1585 Charleston Rd.
P.O. Box 7900
Mountain View, CA 94039-7900
800/833-6687, 415/961-4400,
fax 408/562-6775,
BBS 408/562-6839
AL: acd.techsup; AOL: adobe acp;
CIS: go adobe

Affinity Microsystems
1900 Folsom St., Suite 205
Boulder, CO 80302
800/367-6771, 303/442-4840,
fax 303/442-4999
AL: d0001; AOL: affinity;
CIS: 76344,1750;
INT: affinity@henge.com

Against All Odds
110 Caledonia St.
Sausalito, CA 94965
415/331-6300

Agfa Division of Bayer
90 Industrial Way
Wilmington, MA 01877
800/424-8973, 508/658-5600,
fax 508/687-5328

Aladdin Systems
165 Westridge Dr.
Watsonville, CA 95076-4159
800/732-8881, 408/761-6200,
fax 408/761-6206
AL and AOL: aladdin;
CIS: 75300,1666;
INT: info@aladdinsys.com

Aldus (see Adobe Systems)

Alien Skin Software
800 St. Mary's St., Suite 100
Raleigh, NC 27605-1457
919/832-4124, fax 919/832-4065
INT: Alien-skinfo@alienskin.com;
http://www.alienskin.com/alienskin

Alki Software
300 Queen Anne Ave. N.
Suite 410
Seattle, WA 98109
800/669-9673, 206/286-2600,
fax 206/286-2785
CIS: 72400,3720;
INT: support@alki.com;
http://www.alki.com

Allegiant Technologies
9740 Scranton Rd., Suite 300
San Diego, CA 92121
619/587-0500, fax 619/587-1314
AL and AOL: allegiant;
INT: info@allegiant.com;
http://www.allegiant.com

Alps Electric (USA)
3553 N. First St.
San Jose, CA 95134-1898
800/825-2577, 408/432-6000,
fax 408/432-6035
INT: http://www.alpsusa.com

Alsoft
P.O. Box 927
Spring, TX 77383-0927
800/257-6381, 713/353-4090,
fax 713/353-9868
INT: alsoft@applelink.apple.com

Altsys (see Macromedia)

Alysis Software
1231 31st Ave.
San Francisco, CA 94122
800/825-9747, 415/566-2263,
fax 415/566-9692
AL: alysis; CIS: 75300,3011;
INT: alysis@aol.com

Ambrosia Software
P.O. Box 23140
Rochester, NY 14692
800/231-1816, 716/325-1910,
fax 716/325-3665
CIS: 74777,1147;
INT: ambrosiasw@aol.com;
http://www.ambrosiasw.com

American Ink Jet
13 Alexander Rd.
Billerica, MA 01821
800/332-6538, 508/667-0600,
fax 508/670-5637

America Online
8619 Westwood Ctr. Dr.
Vienna, VA 22182-2285
800/827-6364, 703/448-8700,
fax 703/448-0760

Amtex Software
P.O. 572
Belleville, ON, K8N 5B2, Canada
613/967-7900, fax 613/967-7902

Andromeda Interactive
1050 Marina Village Pkwy.
Suite 107
Alameda, CA 94501
800/769-1616, 510/769-1616,
fax 510/769-1919

Apexx Technology
506 S. 11th St.
Boise, ID 83702
800/767-4858, 208/336-9400,
fax 208/336-9445

Apple Computer
1 Infinite Loop
Cupertino, CA 95014
800/776-2333, 408/996-1010,
fax 408/974-6726,
fax on demand 800/505-0171,
tech support 800/767-2775
CIS: go aplsup

AppleLink
Apple Online Services,
1 Infinite Loop, MS: 41-D,
Cupertino, CA 95014
408/974-3309

Applied Optical Media
(see ROMTech, Inc.)

APS Technologies
P.O. Box 4987
6131 Deramus
Kansas City, MO 64120-0087
800/233-7550, 816/483-1600,
fax 816/483-3077

Ares Software (see Adobe)

ARRO International
P.O. Box 167
Montclair, NJ 07042
800/243-1515 ext. 485 (orders
only), 201/746-9620,
fax 201/509-0728

Arsenal Publishing
44901 Falcon Place, Suite 108
Sterling, VA, 20166-9815
703/742-3801, fax 703/742-6020

Artbeats
P.O. Box 1287
Myrtle Creek, OR 97457
800/444-9392, 541/863-4429,
fax 541/863-4547
AL: artbeats, CIS: 74221,125

Asanté Technologies
821 Fox Ln.
San Jose, CA 95131
800/662-9686, 408/435-8388,
fax 408/432-1117
INT: sales@asante.com

Ascend Communications
1275 Harbor Bay Pkwy.
Alameda, CA 94502
800/ASCEND-4, 510/769-6001,
fax 510/814-2300
INT: http://www.ascend.com

ASD Software
4650 Arrow Hwy., Suite E-6
Montclair, CA 91763
909/624-2594, fax 909/624-9574
INT: asd@applelink.apple.com

Ashlar
1290 Oakmead Pkwy., Suite 218
Sunnyvale, CA 94086
800/877-2745, 408/746-1800,
fax 408/746-0749
AL: govellum; CIS: 71333,1060

AT&T Paradyne
P.O. Box 6457
Salinas, CA 93912
800/554-4996, 813/530-2000,
fax 813/530-2398

Attachmate
3617 131st Ave. SE
Bellevue, WA 98006
800/426-6283, 206/644-4010,
fax 206/649-6484
CIS: go attachmate;
INT: support@attachmate.com;
http://www.attachmate.com

Attain
48 Grove St.
Somerville, MA 02144-2500
800/925-5615, 617/776-1110,
fax 617/776-1626
AL: attain; CIS: 72662,134;
INT: info@attain.com;
http://www.attain.com

Atticus Software
456 Glenbrook Rd.
Stamford, CT 06906
203/348-6100, fax 203/964-8271
AL: atticus; AOL: atticus sc;
CIS: 75300,3173

Autodesk
111 McInnis Pkwy.
San Rafael, CA 94903
800/964-6432, 415/507-5000
CIS: asoft;
INT: http://www.autodesk.com

Automated Graphics
1911 W. Wabansia Ave.
Chicago, IL 60622
312/384-3833, fax 312/384-4539

The Avalon Hill Game Co.
4517 Harford Rd.
Baltimore, MD 21214
800/999-3222, 410/254-9200,
fax 410/254-0991

Avery Dennison
20955 Pathfinder Rd.
Diamond Bar, CA 91765-4000
818/969-3311,
tech support 214/389-3699
CIS: go avery

Avid Technology
Metropolitan Technology Park
One Park West
Tewksbury, MA 01876
800/949-2843, 508/640-6789,
fax 508/640-1366
AL: avidnewmedia;
AOL: avidnewmed;
CIS: 71333,3020

B

Bare Bones Software
P.O. Box 1048
Bedford, MA 01730-1048
508/651-3561, fax 508/651-7584
AL: bare.bones; AOL: barebones;
CIS: 73051,3255;
INT: bbsw@barebones.com;
http://www.barebones.com

B.C. Software, Inc.
11965 Venice Blvd., Suite 405
Los Angeles, CA 90066
800/231-4055
AOL: bcsoftwre;
INT: info@bcsoftware.com;
http://www.bcsoftware.com/
bchome

BeInfinite
4651 Woodstock Rd., Suite 203
Roswell, GA 30075-6624
800/554-6624, 770/552-6624,
fax 770/339-3864
INT: http://www.beinfinite.com

Berkeley Data Access
2560 Bancroft Way, Suite 3
Berkeley, CA 94704
510/644-9999 or 2396,
fax 510/649-9542

Berkeley Systems
2095 Rose St.
Berkeley, CA 94709
800/877-5535, 510/540-5535,
fax 510/540-5115
AL: d0346; AOL: brklysystm;
CIS: 75300,1376;
INT: http://www.berksys.com

Best Data Products
21800 Nordhoff St.
Chatsworth, CA 91311
800/632-BEST, 818/773-9600,
fax 818/773-9619,
BBS: 818/773-9627
INT: http://www.bestdata.com

Best!Ware
300 Roundhill Dr.
Rockaway, NJ 07866
800/322-6962, 201/586-2200,
fax 201/586-8885
AOL: forum myob;
CIS: forum myob;
INT: http://www.bestprograms.com

Big Software
2111 Grant Rd.
Los Altos, CA 94024-6954
415/919-0200, fax 415/919-0205,
tech support 415/919-0215
AL: automatic;
INT: info@bigbusiness.com;
http://www.bigbusiness.com

Bit Jugglers
785 Castro St., Suite C
Mountain View, CA 94041
415/968-3908, fax 415/968-5358

Bitstream
Athenaeum House
215 First St.
Cambridge, MA 02142-1270
800/237-3335, 617/497-6222,
fax 617/868-4732
CIS: 71333,223;
INT: http://www.bitstream.com

Black Box
P.O. Box 12800
Pittsburgh, PA 15241
800/552-6816, 412/746-5500,
fax 800/321-0746 or
412/746-0746

BMC Software (formerly Trimar)
2101 CityWest Blvd.
Houston, TX 77042-2827
800/841-2031, 713/918-8800,
fax 713/918-8000,
tech support 800/537-1813

**BMUG (Berkeley
Macintosh Users Group)**
1442A Walnut St., Suite 62
Berkeley, CA 94709-1496
800/776-2684 (sales only),
510/549-2684, fax 510/849-9026,
BBS 510/849-2684
AOL and AL: bmug;
CIS: 73237,501

Books-On-Disk
311 Harvard St.
Brookline, MA 02146
617/734-9700, fax 617/734-3974
AL: d2158; CIS: 72662,13

**Boston Computer
Society (BCS)**
1972 Massachusetts Ave.
Cambridge, MA 02140
617/864-1700, fax 617/864-3501,
BBS 617/864-3375

Brøderbund Software
500 Redwood Blvd.
P.O. Box 6121
Novato, CA 94948-6121
800/521-6263, 415/382-4400,
fax 415/382-4419
AOL: bbund tec1;
CIS: 70007,1636;
INT: http://www.broderbund.com

Brother International
200 Cottontail Ln.
Somerset, NJ 08875-6714
908/356-8880, fax 908/469-5167
tech support for printers
800/276-7746; tech support for
faxes 800/284-4329

Bungie Software Products
1935 S. Halsted St., Suite 204
Chicago, IL 60608
312/563-6200, fax 312/563-0545
AL: bungie; AOL: bungie1;
INT: http://www.bungie.com

Bytes of Learning
150 Consumer's Rd., Suite 203
Willowdale, ON, M2J 1P9, Canada
800/465-6428, 416/495-9913,
fax 416/495-9548

Caere
100 Cooper Ct.
Los Gatos, CA 95030
800/535-7226, 408/395-7000,
fax 408/354-2743

CalComp
2411 W. La Palma Ave.
Anaheim, CA 92801
800/932-1212

Canon Computer Systems
2995 Redhill Ave.
Costa Mesa, CA 92628
800/848-4123, 714/438-3000,
fax 714/438-3099

Canto Software
330 Townsend St., Suite 212
San Francisco, CA 94107
415/905-0300, fax 415/905-0302
AL: canto; INT: canto@sirius.com

Capcom Entertainment
475 Oakmead Pkwy.
Sunnyvale, CA 94086
408/774-0500

C.A.R.
4661 Maryland Ave., Suite 200
St. Louis, MO 63108
800/288-7585, 314/454-3535,
fax 314/454-0105

Cartesia Software
5 S. Main St.
P.O. Box 757
Lambertville, NJ 08530-9977
800/334-4291, 609/397-1611,
fax 609/397-5724

Casa Blanca Works
148 Bon Air Ctr.
Greenbrae, CA 94904
415/461-2227, fax 415/461-2249
AL and AOL: cbworks;
CIS: 72662,142

Casady & Greene
22734 Portola Dr.
Salinas, CA 93908-1119
800/359-4920, 408/484-9228,
fax 408/484-9218
AL: d0063; AOL: casadygree;
CIS: 71333,616;
INT: http://www.casadyg.com

Casio
570 Mt. Pleasant Ave.
Dover, NJ 08701
800/96-CASIO, 201/361-5400
INT: http://www.metaverse.com/
grammy/casio

Castle Systems
1306 Lincoln Ave.
San Rafael, CA 94901
415/459-6495 (also fax)

Central Point Software
(see also Symantec)
15220 NW Greenbrier Pkwy.
Suite 150
Beaverton, OR 97006
800/964-6896, 503/690-8088,
fax 503/690-8083,
BBS 503/984-5366
CIS: go central

CE Software
P.O. Box 65580
1801 Industrial Circle
West Des Moines, IA 50265
800/523-7638, 515/221-1801,
fax 515/221-1806
AL: ce.sales; AOL: cesoftware;
CIS: 76136,2137;
INT: http://www.cesoft.com

CH Products
970 Park Center Dr.
Vista, CA 92083
619/598-2518

Chang Labs
10228 N. Stelling Rd.
Cupertino, CA 95014
800/972-8800, fax 408/252-3081
INT: d0185@applelink.apple.com

Changeling Software
2507 Albata Ave.
Austin, TX 78757-2102
800/769-2768, 512/419-7085
AL: changeling; AOL: changelins;
CIS: go gamcpub

CharisMac Engineering
66 P&S Ln., Suite D
Newcastle, CA 95658
800/487-4420, 916/885-4420,
fax 916/885-1410

The Chip Merchant
4870 Viewridge Ave.
San Diego, CA 92123
800/426-6375, 619/268-4774,
fax 619/268-0874

Citizen America
2450 Broadway, Suite 600
Santa Monica, CA 90404
800/477-4683, 310/453-0614,
fax 310/453-2814,
BBS 310/453-7564

Claris
5201 Patrick Henry Dr.
Santa Clara, CA 95052-8168
800/325-2747, 408/727-8227,
fax 408/987-3932
AOL: claris; CIS: go claris;
INT: info@claris.com;
http://www.claris.com

The Cobb Group
9420 Bunsen Pkwy., Suite 300
Louisville, KY 40220
800/223-8720, 502/491-1900,
fax 502/491-8050

Coda Music Technology
6210 Bury Dr.
Eden Prairie, MN 55346
800/843-2066, 612/937-9611,
fax 612/937-9760
AOL: codatech; CIS: go coda

Common Ground Software
303 Twin Dolphin Dr., Suite 420
Redwood City, CA 94065-1409
800/598-3821, 415/802-5800,
fax 415/593-6868
AL and AOL: nohands;
CIS: 74740,2142;
INT: support@commonground.com;
http://www.commonground.com

Communication Arts
410 Sherman Ave.
Palo Alto, CA 94306-1826
415/326-6040

Communication Intelligence
275 Shoreline Dr.
Redwood Shores, CA 94065
800/888-9242, 415/802-7888,
fax 415/802-7777
CIS: go cic

Compton's NewMedia
2320 Camino Vida Roble
Carlsbad, CA 92009
800/862-2206, 619/929-2500,
fax 619/929-2511

CompUSA
15167 Business Ave., Suite 194
Dallas, TX 75244-9659
800/266-7872, 214/888-5770,
fax 800/329-2212 or
214/888-5706

CompuServe
P.O. Box 20212
Columbus, OH 43220
800/848-8199, 614/457-8600,
fax 614/457-0348

**CompuServe
(SPRY/Internet Div.)**
3535 128th Ave. SE
Bellevue, WA 98006
800/SPRY-NET, 206/957-8000,
fax 206/957-6000, tech support
206/447-0958, BBS 206/447-9060
INT: http://www.spry.com

**Computer Associates
International**
One Computer Associates Plaza
Islandia, NY 11788-7000
800/225-5224, 516/342-5224,
fax 516/342-5734
AL: ca.cricket; CIS: go ca

Connectix
2655 Campus Dr.
San Mateo, CA 94403-2520
800/950-5880, 415/571-5100,
fax 415/571-5195
AL and AOL: connectix;
CIS: 75300,1546;
INT: info@connectix.com;
support@connectix.com

Conner Storage Systems
(division of Conner Peripherals)
450 Technology Park Dr.
Lake Mary, FL 32746
800/724-3511, 407/263-3500,
fax 407/263-3555, technical
BBS 407/263-3662
INT: http://www.conner.com

**CoOperative Printing
Solutions (COPS)**
5950 Live Oak Pkwy., Suite 175
Norcross, GA 30093
404/840-0810, fax 404/448-7821
AL: cops; AOL: copstech;
CIS: 70671,3371

Corel
The Corel Bldg., 1600 Carling Ave.
Ottawa, ON, Canada, K1Z 8R7
800/772-6735, 613/728-8200,
fax 613/728-9790
INT: http://www.corel.com

Corex Technologies
233 Harvard St., Suite 207
Brookline, MA 02146
800/942-6739, 617/492-4200,
fax 617/277-5069

CoStar
599 W. Putnam Ave.
Greenwich, CT 06830-6092
800/426-7827, 203/661-9700,
fax 203/661-1540
AL: costar1; AOL: costar;
CIS: 75300,2225;
INT: support@costar.com;
http://www.costar.com

Creative Media Services
2936 Domingo Ave., Suite 5
Berkeley, CA 94705
800/358-2278, 510/843-3408,
fax 510/549-2490

Creative Multimedia
513 NW 13th Ave., Suite 400
Portland, OR 97209
800/262-7668, 503/241-4351,
fax 503/241-4370,
BBS 503/241-1573

Creative Solutions
4701 Randolph Rd., Suite 12
Rockville, MD 20852
800/367-8465, 301/984-0262,
fax 301/770-1675

Cyberflix
4 Market Sq.
Knoxville, TN 37902
423/546-1157, fax 423/546-0866
AOL: cyberflix

CyberSound
2445 Faber Place, Suite 102
Palo Alto, CA 94303-3315
415/812-7380, fax 415/812-7386

Cyclos Software
P.O. Box 31417
San Francisco, CA 94131-0417
415/821-1448, fax 415/821-1168
AOL: cyclos; CIS: 71101,204;
INT: support@cyclos.com;
http://www.cyclos.com

Cypress Research
2901 Tasman Dr., Suite 208
Santa Clara, CA 95054
408/752-2700
AL: cypress;
INT: tech@cypressres.com;
http://www.cypressr.com

Cytopia Software
1735 E. Bayshore Rd., Suite 30B
Redwood City, CA 94063
800/588-0274, 415/364-4594,
fax 415/364-4592
INT: http://www.cytopia.com

D

Dantz Development
4 Orinda Way, Bldg. C
Orinda, CA 94563-9919
510/253-3000, fax 510/253-9099

DataDesk International
9524 SW Tualatin-Sherwood Rd.
Tualatin, OR 97062
800/477-3473, 503/692-9600,
fax 503/691-1101
AL: dantz.tech; CIS: 73367,2416

Datastorm Technologies
3212 Lemone Blvd.
P.O. Box 1471
Columbia, MO 65201
800/315-3282, 314/443-3282,
fax 314/875-0585,
tech BBS 314/875-0503

DataViz
55 Corporate Dr.
Trumbull, CT 06611
800/733-0030, 203/268-0030,
fax 203/268-4345
AL: d0248; AOL: datavizinc;
CIS: 75410,3306;
INT: info@dataviz.com;
http://www.dataviz.com

DataWatch
P.O. Box 13984
Research Triangle Park
NC 27709-3984
919/549-0711, fax 919/549-0065
AL: d0588; AOL: virex1

Davidson & Associates
19840 Pioneer Ave.
Torrance, CA 90503
800/545-7677, 310/793-0600,
fax 310/793-0601

Dayna Communications
849 W. Levoy Dr.
Salt Lake City, UT 84123-2544
800/531-0600, 801/269-7200,
fax 801/269-7363

DayStar Digital
5556 Atlanta Hwy.
Flowery Branch, GA 30542
800/962-2077, 404/967-2077,
fax 404/967-3018
AL: daystar.info; AOL: daystar ol;
CIS: 75300,1544

Deadly Games
P.O. Box 676
Bridge Hampton, NY 11932-0676
516/537-6060, fax 516/471-4676
AOL: deadly g

Decision Maker's Software
1910 Joslyn Pl.
Boulder, CO 80304
fax 303/449-6207
AL: d0391; AOL: jgcman;
CIS: 70337,2143

Delphi
1030 Massachusetts Ave.
Cambridge, MA 02138
800/695-4005, 617/491-3393,
fax 617/491-6642

Delrina
6830 Via Del Oro, Suite 240
San Jose, CA 95119-1353
800/268-6082, 408/363-2345,
fax 408/363-2340
INT: http://www.delrina.com/
index.htm

DeltaPoint
2 Harris Ct., Suite B-1
Monterey, CA 93940
800/446-6955, 408/648-4000,
fax 408/648-4020
AOL and AL: deltapoint;
CIS: 76004,1522;
INT: http://www.deltapoint.com

Delta Tao Software
760 Harvard Ave.
Sunnyvale, CA 94087
800/827-9316, 408/730-9336,
fax 408/730-9337
AOL: deltavee

Deneba Software
7400 SW 87th Ave.
Miami, FL 33173
305/596-5644, fax 305/273-9069
AOL and AL: deneba;
CIS: 76004,2154;
INT: http://www.deneba.com

**DGR Technologies
(Bottom Line Distribution)**
4544 S. Lamar Blvd., Suite D100
Austin, TX 78745-1500
800/235-9748, 512/892-4070,
fax 512/892-4455

DiagSoft
5615 Scotts Valley Dr., Suite 140
Scotts Valley, CA 95066
408/438-8247, fax 408/438-7113

DiAMAR Interactive Corp.
600 University St., Suite 1701
Seattle, WA 98101-1129
800/234-2627, 206/340-5975,
fax 206/340-1432
INT: http://www.cyclos.com

Digidesign
1360 Willow Rd.
Menlo Park, CA 94025
800/333-2137, 415/688-0600,
fax 415/327-0777

Digital Collections, Inc.
1301 Marina Village Pkwy.
Suite 320
Alameda, CA 94501
510/814-7200

Digital Eclipse Software
5515 Doyle St., Suite 1
Emeryville, CA 94608
800/289-3374, 510/547-6101,
fax 510/547-6104
AL: desi; AOL: declipse;
CIS: 71333,254

Digital Equipment Corp. (DEC)
146 Main St.
Maynard, MA 01754
800/344-4825, 508/493-5111,
fax 800/234-2298

Digital Stock
400 S. Sierra Ave., Suite 100
Solana Beach, CA 92075
800/545-4514, 619/794-4040,
fax 619/794-4041

Discis Knowledge Research
45 Sheppard Ave. E., Suite 410
Toronto, ON, M2N 5W9, Canada
800/567-4321, 416/250-6537,
fax 416/250-6540

Discovery Channel Multimedia
7700 Wisconsin Ave.
Bethesda, MD 20814-3579
800/762-2189, 301/986-0444

DK Multimedia
95 Madison Ave.
New York, NY 10016
212/213-4800

Domark Software
1900 S. Norfolk St., Suite 110
San Mateo, CA 94403
800/695-GAME, 415/513-8929,
fax 415/571-0437
INT: http://www.domark.com/
domark

Dream Maker Software
925 W. Kenyon Ave., Suite 16
Englewood, CO 80110
800/876-5665, 303/762-1001,
fax 303/762-0762

DS Design
2440 SW Cary Pkwy., Suite 210
Cary, NC 27513
800/745-4037, 919/319-1770,
fax 919/460-5983

Dubl-Click Software
22521 Styles St.
Woodland Hills, CA 91367-1730
800/266-9525, 818/888-2068,
fax 818/888-5405
AOL: dublclick;
INT: dublclick@dublclick.com;
http://www.dublclick.com

Dynamic Graphics
6000 N. Forest Park Dr.
Peoria, IL 61614
800/255-8800

E

EarthLink Network
3171 Los Feliz, Suite 203
Los Angeles, CA 90039
213/644-9500

Eastgate Systems
P.O. Box 1307
Cambridge, MA 02238
800/562-1638, 617/924-9044,
fax 617/923-4575
AL: eastgate; AOL: eastgates;
CIS: 76146,262;
INT: info@eastgate.com;
http://www.eastgate.com

Eastman Kodak
343 State St.
Rochester, NY 14650
800/235-6325, 716/724-4000
AL: kodakepseng;
CIS: go kodak or 72662,412;
INT: http://www.kodak.com

Eccentric Software
P.O. Box 2777
Seattle, WA 98111-2777
206/628-2687, fax 206/628-2681
AOL: dgoldstein; CIS: 73677,1537

Edmark
P.O. Box 3218
Redmond, WA 98073-3218
800/426-0856, 206/556-8400,
fax 206/556-8998
INT: edmarkteam@edmark.com;
http://www.edmark.com

Educorp
7434 Trade St.
San Diego, CA 92121-2410
800/843-9497, 619/536-9999,
fax 619/536-2345

Electric Magic Company
209 Downey St.
San Francisco, CA 94117-4421
415/759-4100, fax 415/566-6615
INT: http://www.emagic.com

The Electric Typographer
501 First Ave.
P.O. Box 224
Audubon, IA 50025-0224
712/563-3799

Electronic Arts
1450 Fashion Island Blvd.
San Mateo, CA 94404-2064
games 800/245-4525, children's
titles 800/543-9778,
415/571-7171, fax 415/571-7993
CIS: go gamapub;
INT: http://www.ea.com/osi/
welcome.html

Electronics For Imaging
2855 Campus Dr.
San Mateo, CA 94403
800/285-4565, 415/286-8600,
fax 408/848-5784

Emagic
P.O. Box 771
Nevada City, CA 95959
916/477-1051, fax 916/477-1052

Engineered Software
615 Guilford-Jamestown Rd.
P.O. Box 18344
Greensboro, NC 27419
910/299-4843, fax 910/852-2067

Epson America
20770 Madrona Ave.
Torrance, CA 90503
310/782-0770, fax 310/782-5220
INT: http://www.epson.com

Equilibrium Technologies
3 Harbor Dr., Suite 111
Sausalito, CA 94965
800/524-8651, 415/332-4343,
fax 415/332-4433
AL: equilibrium; AOL: equilibriu;
CIS: 76420,310;
INT: info@equil.com;
http://www.equil.com

EveryWare Development
6543 Mississauga Rd.
Mississauga, ON, L5N 1A6, Canada
905/819-1173, fax 905/819-1172
AL: everyware;
INT: info@everyware.com;
http://www.everyware.com

Expert Software
800 Douglas Rd., Suite 750
Coral Gables, FL 33134-3160
800/759-2562, 305/567-9990,
fax 305/443-0786
AL: expert; AOL: expertsoft

Extensis
55 SW Yamhill St., 4th Floor
Portland, OR 97204
800/796-9798, 503/274-2020,
fax 503/274-0530

F

Farallon Computing
2470 Mariner Square Loop
Alameda, CA 94501-1010
800/998-7761, 510/814-5000,
fax 510/814-5020

Focus Enhancements
800 W. Cummings Park
Suite 4500
Woburn, MA 01801
800/538-8866, 617/938-8088,
fax 617/938-7741
AOL: focus tech; CIS: 71075,1262

FontHaus
15 Perry Ave., Suite A7
Norwalk, CT 06850
800/942-9110, 203/846-3087,
fax 203/849-8527

Font World
2021 Scottsville Rd.
Rochester, NY 14623-2021
716/235-6861, fax 716/235-6950

Form and Function
1595 17th Ave.
San Francisco, CA 94122
415/664-4010, fax 415/664-4030
AL: x1968

Fractal Design
335 Spreckels Dr.
Aptos, CA 95003
800/297-2665, 408/688-8800,
fax 408/688-8836
AL and AOL: fractal; CIS: go fractal;
INT: support@fractal.com;
http://www.fractal.com

Frontal Assaultware
48 Grove Street, Suite 203
Somerville, MA 01801
617/623-6006, fax 617/623-6466

**Fujitsu Computer Products
of America**
2904 Orchard Pkwy.
San Jose, CA 95134
800/626-4686

FWB
1555 Adams Dr.
Menlo Park, CA 94025
415/325-4FWB
AL: fwb; AOL: fwb.inc;
CIS: 71320,1034;
INT: http://www.fwb.com

G

Galapagos Design Group
256 Great Rd., Suite 15
Littleton, MA 01460-1916
508/952-6200, fax 508/952-6260

GCC Technologies
209 Burlington Rd.
Bedford, MA 01730-9143
800/422-7777, 617/275-5800,
fax 617/275-1115

GDT Softworks
4664 Lougheed Hwy., Suite 188
Burnaby, BC, V5C 6B7, Canada
800/663-6222, 604/291-9121,
fax 604/291-9689
AL: gdt.mkt; CIS: 72137,3246

GEnie
401 N. Washington St.
Rockville, MD 20850
800/638-9636

**Global Village
Communication**
685 E. Middlefield Rd., Bldg. B
Mountain View, CA 94043
800/736-4821, 415/390-8200,
fax 415/390-8282,
BBS 415/390-8334
AL: globalvillag; AOL: globalvill;
CIS: 75300,3473

Gold Disk
3350 Scott Blvd., Bldg. 14
Santa Clara, CA 95054
800/982-9888, 408/982-0200,
fax 408/982-0298

Granite Digital
3101 Whipple Rd.
Union City, CA 94587
510/471-6442, fax 510/471-6267

Graphic Simulations
1200 E. Collins, Suite 214
Richardson, TX 75081
214/699-7400, fax 214/699-0972
AOL: graphic

Graphsoft
10270 Old Columbia Rd.
Suite 100
Columbia, MD 21046-1751
410/290-5114
AL: d0313; AOL: mcadtech;
CIS: 72662,1320;
INT: marketing@graphsoft.com;
http://www.graphsoft.com

Great Wave Software
5353 Scotts Valley Dr.
Scotts Valley, CA 95066
408/438-1990, fax 408/438-7171

Green Mountain Software
9404 Valley Ln.
Huntsville, AL 35803-1326
205/883-0373
AOL: mswall; CIS: 73047,1233;
INT: http://www.hsv.tis.net/pub/
users/~greenmtn/

Grolier Electronic Publishing
Sherman Turnpike
Danbury, CT 06816
800/285-4534, 203/797-3530,
fax 203/797-3835

GT Interactive Software
16 East 40th St.
New York, NY 10016
212/726-6500
INT: http://www.gtinteractive.com

H

HandcraftedFonts
P.O. Box 14013
Philadelphia, PA 19122-0013
215/922-5584

HarperCollins Interactive
10 E. 53d St.
New York, NY 10022
800/424-6234
INT: http://www.harpercollins.com

Hayden Books
201 W. 103d St.
Indianapolis, IN 46290
317/581-3500

**Hayes Microcomputer
Products**
P.O. Box 105203
Atlanta, GA 30348-5203
800/254-2937, 404/840-9200,
fax 404/441-1238

Heizer Software
1941 Oak Park Blvd., Suite 30
P.O. Box 232019
Pleasant Hill, CA 94523
800/888-7667, 510/943-7667,
fax 510/943-6882
AOL: heizersw;
INT: http://www.webcom.com/
~heizer/

Helix Technologies
744 Pinecrest Dr.
Prospect Heights, IL 60070
800/364-3549, 708/465-0242,
fax 708/465-0252
AL and AOL: helix.tech;
CIS: 71154,350;
INT: support@helixtech.com;
http://www.mcs.net/~hxtech

Hewlett-Packard
Direct Marketing
P.O. Box 58059, MS: 511L-SJ
Santa Clara, CA 95051-8059
800/752-0900, 208/323-2551,
fax 800/333-1917 or
208/344-4809

Chris Hostetter
1800 E. Market St.
Long Beach, CA 90805
310/422-6909

I

IDG Books Worldwide, Inc.
919 E. Hillsdale Blvd., Suite 400
Foster City, CA 94404
800/434-3422, 415/312-0650

Image Club Graphics
729 24th Ave. SE
Calgary, AB, T2G 5K8, Canada
800/387-9193, 403/262-8008,
fax 403/261-7013
AL: cda0573; AOL: imageclub;
CIS: 72560,2323;
INT: http://www.imageclub.com

Imation
1185 Walters Blvd.
Vadnais Heights, MN 55110
800/219-9022, 612/733-1110

Impossible Software
P.O. Box 52710
Irvine, CA 92619-2710
714/470-4800
AOL: typetamer; CIS: 74673,1010;
INT: info@impossible.com;
http://www.impossible.com

Inductel
5339 Prospect Rd., Suite 321
San Jose, CA 95129-5028
408/866-8016, fax 408/243-1762
INT: http://www.liberty.com/
        home/inductel

Infogrip
1145 Eugenia Pl., Suite 201
Carpinteria, CA 93013
800/397-0921, 805/566-1049,
fax 805/566-1079

**Information Access
Technologies**
46 Shattuck Sq., Suite 11
Berkeley, CA 94704
510/704-0160, fax 510/704-8019
INT: info@hologate.mailer.net;
http://www.holonet.net

Innovative Data Design
1820 Arnold Industrial Way
Suite L
Concord, CA 94520
510/680-6818, fax 510/680-1165
AL: d0610

Inside Mac Games
3862 Grace Ln.
Glenview, IL 60025
847/486-0636, fax 312/850-0430
AOL: imgames; CIS: 71554,2761

Insignia Solutions
1300 Charleston Rd.
Mountain View, CA 94043
800/848-7677, 415/694-7600,
fax 415/694-3705
AL: insignia.tch; AOL: insigniats;
CIS: 71333,2643;
INT: mactech@isinc.insignia.com;
http://www.insignia.com

**International Typeface
Corp. (ITC)**
866 Second Ave.
New York, NY 10017
212/371-0699, fax 212/752-4752

InterPlay Productions
17922 Fitch Ave.
Irvine, CA 92714
800/969-4263, 714/553-6655,
fax 714/252-2820,
BBS 714/252-2822
INT: http://222.interplay.com

Interpress Technologies
250 W. 49th St., Suite 202
New York, NY 10019
212/245-2700, fax 212/245-2784

Intuit
2650 E. Elvira Rd., Suite 100
Tucson, AZ 85706
520/295-3110, fax 800/756-1040
or 520/295-3015
CIS: go intuit;
INT: http://www.intuit.com

Iomega
1821 W. 4000 S.
Roy, UT 84067
800/456-5522, 801/778-1000,
fax 801/778-3748

IVI Publishing
7500 Flying Cloud Dr.
Eden Prairie, MN 55344-3739
800/432-1332

J

Jabra
9191 Towne Centre Dr., Suite 330
San Diego, CA 92122
800/327-2230, 619/622-0764,
fax 619/622-0353
AL and AOL: eartalk Jabra;
INT: info@jabra.com;
http://www.jabra.com

James Engineering
6329 Fairmount Ave.
El Cerrito, CA 94530
510/525-7350, fax 510/525-5740

JetFill
10815 Seaboard Loop
Houston, TX 77099
800/695-4538, 713/933-1900,
fax 713/933-1909

Jian
1975 W. El Camino Real, Suite 301
Mountain View, CA 94040
415/254-5600, fax 415/254-5640

K

Kaplan Interactive
444 Madison Ave.
New York, NY 10017
800/KAP-ITEM, 212/752-1840,
fax 212/752-1845
INT: http://www.kaplan.com

Kensington Microware
2855 Campus Dr.
San Mateo, CA 94403
800/535-4242, 415/572-2700,
fax 415/572-9675

Kent-Marsh
3260 Sul Ross, Kent-Marsh Bldg.
Houston, TX 77098
800/325-3587, 713/522-5625,
fax 713/522-8965
AL: kml.support; AOL: kentmarsh;
CIS: 73730,274;
INT: support@Kentmarsh.com;
http://www.kentmarsh.com

Kernel Productions
24 Kensington Ln.
Newark, DE 19713
302/456-3026, fax 302/456-3124
AOL: kernelpup

Key Tronic
P.O. Box 14687
Spokane, WA 99213
800/262-6006, 509/928-8000,
fax 509/927-5224

Kinesis
915 118th Ave. SE
Bellevue, WA 98005-3855
800/454-6374, 206/455-9220,
fax 206/455-9233

L

La Cie
8700 SW Creekside Pl.
Beaverton, OR 97008
800/999-1455, 503/520-9000,
fax 503/520-9100

Lanston Type
P.O. Box 60
Mount Stewart
Prince Edward Island, C0A 1T0,
Canada
902/676-2835, 800/478-8973,
fax 902/676-2393

LaserMaster
7156 Shady Oak Rd.
Eden Prairie, MN 55344
800/950-6868, 612/944-9330,
fax 612/944-0522

Lazy Dog Foundry
275 E. 4th St.
St. Paul, MN 55101

Leader Technologies
(see SoftKey International)

The Learning Company
6493 Kaiser Dr.
Fremont, CA 94555
800/852-2255, 510/792-2101,
fax 510/792-9628

Learning Tomorrow
One E. Main St.
Bloomsburg, PA 17815
800/722-1978, 717/387-8270,
fax 717/784-4160

Leister Productions
P.O. Box 289
Mechanicsburg, PA 17055
717/697-1378, fax 717/697-4373
AOL: leisterpro; CIS: 74774,1626;
INT: info@LeisterPro.com;
http://www.LeisterPro.com

Letraset USA
40 Eisenhower Dr.
Paramus, NJ 07653
800/343-8973, 201/845-6100,
fax 201/845-5351
INT: http://www.letraset.com

Lexmark International
740 New Circle Rd.
Lexington, KY 40511
800/358-5835, 606/232-2000,
fax 606/232-2380

Linguist's Software
P.O. Box 580
Edmonds, WA 98020
206/775-1130, fax 206/771-5911
CIS: 75507,1157

Linotype-Hell
425 Oser Ave.
Hauppauge, NY 11788
800/842-9721, 516/434-2000,
fax 516/434-2706
INT: http://www.linotype.com

Logitech
6505 Kaiser Dr.
Fremont, CA 94555
800/231-7717, 510/795-8500,
fax 510/792-8901
CIS: go logitech;
INT: techsupport@logitech.com

Looking Glass Technologies
100 Cambridge Park Dr.
Suite 300
Cambridge, MA 02140
617/441-6333

**Lotus Development Corp.
(cc:Mail Div.)**
800 El Camino Real
Mountain View, CA 94040
800/343-5414, 415/961-8800,
fax 415/961-0215,
tech support 415/966-4900,
BBS: 415/691-0128
AL: d5429; CIS: go lotus cc:Mail;
INT: http://www.lotus.com

LucasArts Entertainment
P.O. Box 10307
San Rafael, CA 94912
800/782-7927, fax 415/721-3394,
tech BBS 415/257-3070
INT: http://www.lucasarts.com

M

MacConnection
6 Mill St.
Marlow, NH 03456-9987
800/800-2222, fax 603/446-7791

MacHome Journal
612 Howard Street, Sixth Floor
San Francisco, CA 94105
editorial 415/957-1911,
subscriptions 800/800-6542

**Macintosh Multimedia &
Product Registry**
660 Beachland Blvd.
Vero Beach, FL 32963

Mackie Designs
16220 Wood Red Road NE
Woodinville, WA 98072
800/258-6883, 206/487-4333,
fax 206/487-4337,
BBS 206/488-4586
CIS: go mackie

MacMall
2645 Maricopa St.
Torrance, CA 90503-5144
800/222-2808, fax 310/225-4000

MacPeak Research
3701 Bee Cave Rd.
Austin, TX 78746
512/327-3211, fax 512/327-9553
AL: macpeak.usa

MacPlay
17922 Fitch Ave.
Irvine, CA 92714
714/553-3521
INT: http://www.macplay.com

Macromedia
600 Townsend St.
San Francisco, CA 94103
800/945-4061, 415/252-2000,
fax 415/626-0554
AL: macromediats; AOL: mmtech;
CIS: go macromedia;
INT: http://www.macromedia.com

MacSoft
3850 Annapolis Ln., Suite 100
Plymouth, MN 55447
612/559-5140

MacToolkit (see B.C. Software)

MacUser
950 Tower Ln., 18th Floor
Foster City, CA 94404
editorial 415/378-5600,
subscriptions 800/627-2247,
303/447-9330, fax 303/443-5080
CIS: go macuser or 72511,422;
MCI: 584-5561

MacWarehouse
P.O. Box 3013, 1720 Oak St.
Lakewood, NJ 08701-3013
800/255-6227, 908/370-4779,
fax 908/905-9279,
BBS 203/855-1155
CIS: go mw

MacWEEK
301 Howard Street, 15th Floor
San Francisco, CA 94105
editorial 415/243-3500,
subscriptions 609/786-8230,
fax 415/243-3651
CIS: go macweek; MCI: 323-1203

Macworld
501 Second St.
San Francisco, CA 94107
editorial 415/243-0505,
subscriptions 800/288-6848 or
303/604-1465, fax 415/604-7644
AL: macworld1; AOL: macworld;
CIS: 70370,702

The Mac Zone
15815 SE 37th St.
Bellevue, WA 98006
800/248-0800, 206/883-3088,
fax 206/881-3421

Mainstay
591-A Constitution Ave.
Camarillo, CA 93012-9812
805/484-9400, fax 805/484-9428
AL: d0397; AOL: mainstay1;
CIS: 76004,1525

Manhattan Graphics
62 Candlewood Rd.
Scarsdale, NY 10583
800/572-6533, 914/725-2048,
fax 914/725-2450
AL: rsg; AOL: rsg tech

Mannesmann Tally
(see State of the Art)

Mark of the Unicorn
1280 Massachusetts Ave.
Cambridge, MA 02138
617/576-2760, fax 617/576-3609
INT: http://www.motu.com

Mastersoft (see Adobe)

Mathemæsthetics
P.O. Box 298
Boulder, CO 80306-0298
303/440-0707, fax 303/440-0504
AL and AOL: resorcerer;
CIS: 70521,1114

Maxis
2121 N. California Blvd., Suite 600
Walnut Creek, CA 94596
800/336-2947, 510/933-5630,
fax 510/927-3736,
BBS 510/927-3910
AL: d4459; AOL: maxis;
CIS: go gambpub or go Maxis

MaxOptix
3342 Gateway Blvd.
Fremont, CA 94538
800/848-3092, 510/353-9700,
fax 510/353-1845

Maxtor
211 River Oaks Pkwy.
San Jose, CA 95134-1913
800/2-MAXTOR, 408/432-1700,
fax 408/432-4510
INT: http://www.maxtor.com

MECC
6160 Summit Dr. N.
Minneapolis, MN 55430
800/685-6322, 612/569-1500,
fax 612/569-1551
AOL: mecctech;
INT: mecc@mecc.com;
http://www.mecc.com

MegaCorp
1257 Worcester Rd., Suite 280
Framingham, MA 01701

MetaTools Inc.
6303 Carpinteria Ave.
Carpinteria, CA 93013
800/972-6220, 805/566-6200

Metro Creative Graphics
33 West 34th St.
New York, NY 10001
800/223-1600, fax 212/967-4602

mFactory
1440 Chapin Ave., Suite 200
Burlingame, CA 94010
415/548-0600

Microcomputer Cable
12200 Delta Dr.
Taylor, MI 48180
313/946-9700

MicroFrontier
3401 101st St., Suite E
Des Moines, IA 50322
800/388-8109, 515/270-8109,
fax 515/278-6828
AL and AOL: mfrontier;
CIS: 72662,1123 or go frontier;
INT: http://www.microfrontier.com

Microlytics
2 Tobey Village Office Park
Pittsford, NY 14534
800/828-6293, 716/248-9150,
fax 716/248-3868

MicroMat Computer Systems
7075 Redwood Blvd.
Novato, CA 94945-4136
800/829-6227, 415/898-6227,
fax 415/897-3901
AL: micromatcomp;
AOL: microtmat; CIS: go macaven;
INT: micromat@nbn.com;
http://www.sonic.net/mmcs

MicroNet Technology
80 Technology
Irvine, CA 92718
800/800-3475, 714/453-6000,
fax 714/453-6001

Micro Planning International
3801 E. Florida Ave., Suite 507
Denver, CO 80210
303/757-2216, fax 303/757-2047

Micropolis
21211 Nordhoff St.
Chatsworth, CA 91311
818/718-5308
INT: http://www.micropolis.com

MicroQue
5211 Greenpine Dr.
Murray, UT 84123
801/263-1883, fax 801/263-2886
INT: http://www.maclinq.com/
microque

Microsoft Corporation
One Microsoft Way
Redmond, WA 98052-6399
800/426-9400, 206/882-8080,
fax 206/936-7329
INT: http://www.microsoft.com

MicroSpeed
5005 Brandin Ct.
Fremont, CA 94538-3140
800/GET-SPEED, 510/490-1403,
fax 510/490-1665
INT: http://www.microspeed.com

Mindscape
88 Roland Way
Novato, CA 94945
800/234-3088, 415/897-9900,
fax 415/897-2747,
BBS 415/883-7145
AOL: mscape; CIS: 74431,2476;
INT: http://www.mindscape.com

Minolta
101 Williams Dr.
Ramsey, NJ 07446
201/825-4000

Miramar Systems
121 Gray Ave., Suite 200B
Santa Barbara, CA 93101
800/862-2526, 805/966-2432,
fax 805/965-1824
AL: miramar;
INT: miramar@pacrain.com;
http://www.miramarsys.com

Mojave
2nd West St. George Blvd.
St. George, UT 84770
801/652-5267, fax 801/652-5447

Momentum
7 Waterfront Plaza
500 Ala Moana Blvd., Suite 400
Honolulu, HI 96813
808/543-6426, fax 808/522-9490

Monotype Typography
150 S. Wacker Dr., Suite 2630
Chicago, IL 60606
800/666-6897, 312/855-1440,
fax 312/855-9475
AL: monotype; AOL: monotypelg;
CIS: 71333,2361

**Motion Tool Works (USA)
Corp.** (see Motion Works Group)

Motion Works Group
1020 Mainland St., Suite 130
Vancouver, BC, V6B 2T4, Canada
604/685-9975, fax 604/685-6105
AL: mw.usa

Motorola
3501 Ed Bluestein Blvd.
Austin, TX 78721
512/933-SRAM

**Motorola PCMCIA Products
Division**
50 E. Commerce Dr., Suite M-5
Schaumburg, IL 60173
847/538-5200

Multi-Ad Services
1720 W. Detweiller Dr.
Peoria, IL 61615-1695
800/447-1950, 309/692-1530,
fax 309/692-5444

Multicom Publishing
1100 Olive Way, Suite 1250
Seattle, WA 98101
206/622-5530, fax 206/622-4380

MultiEducator
244 North Ave.
New Rochelle, NY 10801
800/866-6434, 914/235-4340,
fax 914/235-4367

Multi-Tech Systems
2205 Woodale Dr.
Mounds View, MN 55112-9907
800/328-9717, 612/785-3500,
fax 612/785-9874, tech
BBS 800/392-2432
INT: http://www.multitech.com

Murata/Muratec
5560 Tennyson Pkwy.
Plano, TX 75024
214/403-3300, fax 214/403-3400,
tech support 214/403-3350

N

Natural Intelligence
725 Concord Ave.
Cambridge, MA 02138
800/999-4699, 617/876-7680,
fax 617/492-7425
AL and AOL: natural;
CIS: 72427,177;
INT: info@natural.com;
http://www.natural.com

NaviSoft
8619 Westwood Center Dr.
Vienna, VA 22182
800/748-1800, 703/448-8700,
fax 617/433-0595

NEC Technologies
1255 Michael Dr.
Wood Dale, IL 60191
800/388-8888, 708/860-9500,
fax 800/366-0476 or
708/860-5812

**NETCOM On-Line
Communications Services**
3031 Tisch Way, 2d Floor
San Jose, CA 95128
800/NETCOM1

Netscape Communications
501 E. Middlefield Rd.
Mountain View, CA 94043
800/NETSITE, 415/528-2600,
fax 415/528-4120
INT: http://home.netscape.com

Newer Technology
4848 W. Irving
Wichita, KS 67209
800/678-3726, 316/943-0222,
fax 316/685-9368

NewGen Systems
3545 Cadillac Ave.
Costa Mesa, CA 92626
800/756-0556, 714/641-8600,
fax 714/641-2800

New World Computing
P.O. Box 4302
Hollywood, CA 90078-4302
800/325-8898, 818/889-5650,
fax 818/889-5682

Night Diamonds Software
P.O. Box 1608
Huntington Beach, CA 92647
714/842-2492, fax 714/847-1106

Nikon Electronic Imaging
1300 Walt Whitman Rd.
Melville, NY 11747-3064
516/547-0247
AL and AOL: nikontech;
CIS: go nikon

Ninga Software
1240 Kensington Road NW
Suite 410
Calgary, AB, T2N 3P7, Canada
800/265-5555, 403/265-6611,
fax 403/265-5760

Nisus Software
107 S. Cedros Ave.
Solana Beach, CA 92075
800/922-2993, 619/481-1477,
fax 619/481-6154
AL: nisus.mktg; AOL: nisustech;
CIS: 71620,2565;
INT: info@nisus-soft.com;
http://www.nisus-soft.com

Nova Development
23801 Calabasas Rd., Suite 2005
Calabasas, CA 91302-1547
800/395-6682, 818/591-9600,
fax 818/591-8885

Novell
122 E. 1700 S.
Provo, UT 84606-6194
800/453-1267, 801/429-7000,
800/733-9673
CIS: go novforum;
INT: http://www.novell.com

Now Software
921 SW Washington St., Suite 500
Portland, OR 97205-2823
800/237-2078, 503/274-2800,
fax 503/274-0670
AL: nowsoftware; AOL: now;
CIS: 71541,170;
INT: support@nowsoft.com;
http://www.nowsoft.com

Okidata
532 Fellowship Rd.
Mt. Laurel, NJ 08054
800/OKI-TEAM, 609/235-2600,
fax 609/273-0300, tech support
609/273-0300, BBS 609/234-5344
INT: http://www.oki.com

Olduvai
9200 S. Dadeland Blvd., Suite 525
Miami, FL 33156
800/822-0772, 305/670-1112,
fax 305/670-1992
AOL: olduvaigy; CIS: 76004,2077;
INT: http://www.shadow.net/
      ~olduvai

ON Technology
One Cambridge Center, 6th Floor
Cambridge, MA 02142
800/548-8871, 617/374-1400,
fax 617/374-1433
AL: on.tech; AOL: on tech;
CIS: go ontechnology;
INT: xpsupport@on.com;
http://www.on.com

Opcode Systems
3950 Fabian Way, Suite 100
Palo Alto, CA 94303
800/557-2633, 415/856-3333,
fax 415/856-3332
AL and AOL: opcode;
CIS: go midiaven;
INT: http://www.opcode.com

Optical Media International
51 E. Campbell Ave., Suite 170
Campbell, CA 95008
408/376-3511

Optimum Resource
5 Hiltech Ln.
Hilton Head, SC 29926
800/327-1473, 803/689-8000,
fax 803/689-8008
INT: stickyb@stickybear.com

Oracle
500 Oracle Pkwy.
Redwood Shores, CA 94065
800/633-0596, 415/506-7000,
fax 415/506-7200
INT: http://www.oracle.com

Orange Micro
1400 N. Lakeview Ave.
Anaheim, CA 92807
714/779-2772, fax 714/779-9332

Origin Systems
5918 W. Courtyard Dr.
Austin, TX 78730
800/245-4525, 512/434-4263,
fax 512/794-8959
INT: http://www.ea.com/
      origin.html

OSC (see Macromedia)

Pacific Micro Data
16751 Millikan Ave.
Irvine, CA 92714
800/933-7575, 714/955-9090,
fax 714-955-9490

Palo Alto Software
144 East 14th Ave.
Eugene, OR 97401-9990
800/229-7526, 541/683-6162,
fax 541/683-6250
INT: Sales@pasware.com or
info@pasware.com;
http://www.pasware.com

Pantone
590 Commerce Blvd.
Carlstadt, NJ 07072
888/726-8663, 201/935-5500,
fax 201/896-0242

Paramount Interactive
700 Hansen Way
Palo Alto, CA 94304
800/821-1177, 415/812-8200,
fax 415/813-8055

Parsoft Publishing
101 W. Renner Rd., Suite 430
Richardson, TX 75082
214/479-1340, fax 214/479-0853
AOL: Parsoft

Passport Designs
1151 Triton Dr., Suite D
Foster City, CA 94404
800/443-3210, 415/349-6224,
fax 415/349-8008
AL and AOL: passport;
CIS: 71333,1433;
INT: http://www.mw3.com/
      passport

PC Computing
P.O. Box 58229
Boulder, CO 80322-8229
800/365-2770,
CIS: 76000.21@compuserve.com

Peachpit Press
2414 Sixth St.
Berkeley, CA 94710
800/283-9444, 510/548-4393,
fax 510/548-5991
AOL: macbible

Peachtree Software
1505-C Pavilion Pl.
Norcross, GA 30093
800/247-3224, 404/564-5800,
fax 404/564-5888
AL: peachtree; AOL: peachmac;
CIS: 73740,1627

PhotoDisc
2013 4th Ave., 4th Floor
Seattle, WA 98121
800/528-3472, 206/441-9355,
fax 206/441-9379

PictureWorks Technology
649 San Ramon Valley Blvd.
Danville, CA 94526
800/303-5400, 510/855-2001,
fax 510/855-2019

Pinnacle Micro
19 Technology
Irvine, CA 92718
800/553-7070, 714/727-3300,
fax 714/727-1913

Pixar
1001 W. Cutting Blvd.
Richmond, CA 94804
800/888-9856, 510/236-4000,
fax 510/236-0388
AL: pixarmktg; AOL: pixartech;
INT: cusp@pixar.com

Pixel Resources
P.O. Box 921848
Norcross, GA 30092-7848
800/851-1427, 404/449-4947,
fax 404/449-3789
AL: pixl; AOL: pixel resources

Plextor
4255 Burton Dr.
Santa Clara, CA 95054
800/886-3935, 408/980-1838,
fax 408/986-1010

Portrait Display Labs
6665 Owens Dr.
Pleasanton, CA 94588
510/227-2700
INT: pdlcal@surfnet.com;
http://www:portrait.com

Power Computing
2555 N. Interstate 35
Round Rock, TX 78664-2015
800/410-7693, 512/388-6868,
fax 512/388-6799

Practical Peripherals
P.O. Box 921789
Norcross, GA 30092-7789
770/840-9966, fax 800/225-4774,
tech BBS 770/734-4600
INT: http://www.practinet.com

Prairie Group (formerly Advanced Software)
P.O. Box 65820, 1650 Fuller Rd.
West Des Moines, IA 50265
800/346-5392, 515/225-9620,
fax 515/225-2422
AL: prairiesoft; CIS: 72662,131;
INT: advanced@aol.com

PrairieSoft
(see Prairie Group Inc.)

Precision Type
47 Mall Dr.
Commack, NY 11725-5703
800/248-3668, 516/864-0167,
fax 516/543-5721

Prodigy
445 Hamilton Ave.
White Plains, NY 10601
800/776-3449, 914/993-8000

ProVue Development
18411 Gothard St., Unit A
Huntington Beach, CA 92648
800/966-7878, 714/841-7779,
fax 714/841-1479
AOL: provue

Publish
501 Second St.
San Francisco, CA 94107
editorial 415/243-0600,
subscriptions 800/685-3435 or
615/377-3322, fax 415/495-2354
AL: publish.mag; CIS: 76127,205;
MCI: publish

Q

QMS
One Magnum Pass
Mobile, AL 36618
800/633-4300, 334/633-4300,
fax 334/633-0116
INT: http://www.qus.com

Qualcomm
6455 Lusk Blvd.
San Diego, CA 92121
800/238-3672, 619/587-1121,
fax 619/452-9096
INT: quest-rep@qualcomm.com;
http://www.qualcomm.com

Quantum
500 McCarthy Blvd.
Milpitas, CA 95035
408/894-4000, fax 408/894-3282,
tech support 800/826-8022,
BBS 800/472-9799

Quark
1800 Grant St.
Denver, CO 80203
800/788-7835, 303/894-8888,
fax 303/894-3399
AL and AOL: quarktech; CIS: go
quark; INT: http://www.quark.com

Que Software (Macmillan Publishing)
201 W. 103 St.
Indianapolis, IN 46290
800/992-0244, 317/581-3500,
fax 800/448-3804

R

Radius
1710 Fortune Dr.
San Jose, CA 95131
800/227-2795, 408/434-1010,
fax 408/434-0770

Rand McNally-TDM
8255 N. Central Park Ave.
Skokie, IL 60076
800/333-0136, 708/329-8100,
fax 708/674-4496

Random House Reference & Electronic Publishing
400 Hahn Rd.
Westminster, MD 21157
800/733-3000, 410/848-1900,
fax 800/659-2436

Rascal Software
25223 Wheeler Rd.
Newhall, CA 91321
805/255-6823, fax 805/255-9691,
tech support 714/542-5518

Ray Dream
1804 N. Shoreline Blvd.
Mountain View, CA 94043
800/846-0111, 415/960-0768,
fax 415/960-1198
AL: ray.dream; AOL: rdreamtech;
INT: support@raydream.com

REEVEsoft
2449 Spring Lake Dr.
Marietta, GA 30062
770/971-3217, fax 404/977-7165
CIS: 71521,2200;
INT: Reevesoft@aol.com

Reply
4435 Fortran Dr.
San Jose, CA 95134
408/942-4804

ResNova Software
5011 Argosy Dr., Suite 13
Huntington Beach, CA 92649
714/379-9000; fax 714/379-9014
AOL: resnova;
INT: support@resnova.com

Ricoh
5 Dedrick Pl.
West Caldwell, NJ 07006
800/241-RFMS, 201/882-2000,
fax 201/882-2506,
tech support 800/955-3453
INT: http://www.ricoh.co.jp/
index_e.html

Roland
7200 Dominion Circle
Los Angeles, CA 90040
213/685-5141, fax 213/722-0911

ROMTech (formerly Applied Optical Media)
1450 Boot Rd., Bldg. 400,
West Chester, PA 19380
800/321-7259, 610/429-3701,
fax 610/429-3810

Route 66 Geographic Information Systems
7216 Coronado Dr., Suite 2
San Jose, CA 95129
800/569-0878

RT Computer Graphics
602 San Juan De Rio
Rio Rancho, NM 87124-1146
800/891-1600, 505/891-1600,
fax 505/891-1350

S

Samsung
105 Challenger Rd.
Ridgefield Park, NJ 07660
800/933-4110

Sanctuary Woods
1825 S. Grant St., Suite 410
San Mateo, CA 94402
415/286-6000

Scholastic Software
P.O. Box 7502
Jefferson City, MO 65102
800/541-5513, 573/636-5271,
fax 573/635-5881

Scitex America
Eight Oak Park Dr.
Bedford, MA 01730
617/275-5150

Seagate Technology
920 Disc Dr.
Scotts Valley, CA 95066-4544
408/438-6550, fax 408/438-7852,
tech BBS 408/438-8771
INT: http://www.seagate.com

Second Wave
2525 Wallingwood Dr., Bldg. 13
Austin, TX 78746
512/329-9283, fax 512/329-9299

Seiko Instruments
1130 Ringwood Ct.
San Jose, CA 95131
800/888-0817
INT: info@seiko.com

Seikosha America
10 Industrial Ave.
Mahwah, NJ 07430
800/338-2609, 201/252-1040,
fax 201/818-9135

Shana
9744 45th Ave.
Edmonton, AB, T6E 5C5, Canada
403/433-3690, fax 403/437-4381,
tech support 403/433-3690 ext. 242
AL: cda0004; AOL: shanacorp;
CIS: 76260,3551;
INT: http://www.shana.com

Shiva
28 Crosby Dr.
Bedford, MA 01730
800/458-3550, 617/252-6300,
fax 617/270-8599

Shreve Systems
1200 Marshall St.
Shreveport, LA 71101
800/227-3971, 318/424-9791,
fax 318/424-9771

Sierra On-Line
3380 146th Pl. SE, Suite 300
Bellevue, WA 98007
800/649-4904, 206/649-9800,
fax 206/641-7617,
BBS 209/683-4463
INT: http://www.sierra.com

Signature Software
489 North 8th St., Suite 201
Hood River, OR 97031
800/925-8840, 503/386-3221,
fax 503/386-3229
INT: sigsoft.netcom.com

Silicon Valley Bus Co.
475 Brown Rd.
San Juan Bautista, CA 95045
800/775-0555, 408/623-2300,
fax 408/623-4440

SilverWARE
3010 LBJ Fwy., Suite 740
Dallas, TX 75234
214/247-0131, fax 214/406-9999,
BBS 214/247-2177
INT: http://rampages.onramp.net/
~silver

Smartek Software
P.O. Box 366
2223 Avenida De La Playa
Suite 208
La Jolla, CA 92037
800/858-WORD, 619/456-5064,
fax 619/456-3928
INT: http://www.wordsmart.com

SoftArc
100 Allstate Pkwy.
Markham, ON, L3R 6H3, Canada
905/415-7000, fax 905/415-7151
AL: cda0674; AOL: softarc;
CIS: 70511,2065;
INT: info@softarc.com

SoftKey International
One Athenaeum St.
Cambridge, MA 02142
800/227-5609, 617/494-1200,
fax 617/494-1219
CIS: go softkey

SoftPress
8 Blenheim Office Park, Lower Rd.
Long Hanborough, Oxfordshire
OX8 8LN, UK
+44 1993 882588,
fax +44 1993 883970
AL: uk0102; CIS:100322,1271;
INT: info@softpress.com;
support@softpress.com

SoftQuad
56 Aberfoyle Crescent, Fifth Floor
Toronto, ON, M8X 2W4, Canada
800/387-2777

Software Architects
19102 N. Creek Pkwy., Suite 101
Bothell, WA 98011-8005
206/487-0122, fax 206/487-0467
AL: softarch; INT:
support@softarch.com

Software Ventures
(merged with Intercon)
2907 Claremont Ave.
Berkeley, CA 94705
510/644-3232, fax 510/848-0885
AL and AOL: svctech;
CIS: 76004,2161;
INT: microphone@svcdudes.com;
http://www.svcdudes.com

Sonnet Technologies
18004 Sky Park Circle, Suite 260
Irvine, CA 92714-6428
800/945-3668, 714/261-2800,
fax 714/261-2461

Sony Electronics
Computer Peripheral Products
3300 Zanker Rd.
San Jose, CA 95134
800/352-7669, 408/432-0190,
fax 408/955-5171

Specular International
479 West St.
Amherst, MA 01002
800/433-7732, 413/253-3100,
fax 413/253-0540
AL and AOL: specular;
CIS: go multiven;
INT: http://www.specular.com

Spider Island Software
4790 Irvine Blvd., Suite 105-347
Irvine, CA 92720
714/669-9260, fax 714/669-1383
AL: d4955; AOL: spiderisla;
CIS: 73457,2756;
INT: info@spiderisland.com;
http://www.spiderisland.com

SSI (Strategic Simulations, Inc.)
675 Almanor Ave., Suite 201
Sunnyvale, CA 94086-2901
408/737-6800,
tech support 408/737-6850

Stac Electronics
5993 Avenida Encinas
Carlsbad, CA 92008
800/522-7822, 619/431-7474,
fax 619/431-9616
AL: stac; AOL: stacmactec;
CIS: go stacker

StarNine Technologies
2550 9th St.
Berkeley, CA 94710
510/548-0391, fax 510/548-0393
AL: starnine;
INT: info@starnine.com

StarPlay Productions
1200 28th St., Suite 201
Boulder, CO 80307
800/203-2503, 303/447-9562,
fax 303/447-2739

State of the Art
8211 Sierra College Blvd.
Suite 440
Roseville, CA 95661
916/791-7730, fax 916/791-5525

Steinberg-Jones
9312 Deering Ave.
Chatsworth, CA 91311
818/993-4091, fax 818/701-7452,
tech support 818/993-4161

STF Technologies
P.O. Box 81
Concordia, MO 64020
800/880-1922, 816/463-2021,
fax 816/463-7958,
BBS 816/463-1131
AL: d1870; AOL: stftech;
CIS: go stftech

Strata
2 W. Saint George Blvd.
Suite 2100
Saint George, UT 84770
800/678-7282, 801/628-5218,
fax 801/628-9756
AL: strata3d; AOL: strata 3d;
INT: http://www.strat3d.com

Sumeria
329 Bryant St., Suite 3D
San Francisco, CA 94107
800/478-6374, 415/904-0800,
fax 415/904-0888

SunStar Interactive
203/785-8111

SuperMac Technology
215 Moffett Park Dr.
Sunnyvale, CA 94089
800/334-3005, 408/541-6100,
fax 800/541-7680 or
408/541-6150
AL: smt.tech; AOL: supermac;
CIS: 76004,2330

Supra
7101 Supra Dr. SW
Albany, OR 97321
800/727-8772, 541/967-2410,
fax 360/604-1401

Symantec
175 W. Broadway
Eugene, OR 97401
800/441-7234, 541/345-3322,
fax 541/334-7400
CIS: go symantec;
INT: http://www.symantec.com

Synergy Software
2457 Perkiomen Ave.
Reading, PA 19606
800/876-8376, 610/779-0522,
fax 610/370-0548
INT: http://www.synergy.com;
tech@synergy.com

SyQuest Technology
47071 Bayside Pkwy.
Fremont, CA 94538
800/245-2278, 510/226-4000,
fax 510/226-4100

T

TechWorks
4030 Braker Ln. W., Suite 350
Austin, TX 78759
800/688-7466, 512/794-8533,
fax 512/794-8520
INT: http://www.techwrks.com

TechPool Studios
1463 Warrensville Center Rd.
Cleveland, OH 44121-2676
800/925-6998, 216/291-1922,
fax 216/382-1915

Teknosys
3923 Coconut Palm Dr., Suite 111
Tampa, FL 33619
800/873-3494, 813/620-3494,
fax 813/620-4039
AL and AOL: teknosys;
CIS: 71333,710

Tektronix
P.O. Box 1000, MS 63-630
Wilsonville, OR 97070-1000
800/835-6100, 503/682-7377,
fax 503/682-7450

TeleAdapt
51 E. Campbell Ave.
Campbell, CA 95008
408/370-5105, fax 408/370-5110
CIS: 100111,2713

Telebit
One Executive Dr.
Chelmsford, MA 01824
800/835-3248, 800/989-8888,
508/441-2181, fax 508/441-9060
INT: info@telebit.com;
http://www.telebit.com

TeleTypesetting
311 Harvard St.
Brookline, MA 02146
617/734-9700, fax 617/734-3974

Terrace Software
P.O. Box 271
Medford, MA 02155
617/396-0382

Texas Instruments
P.O. Box 202230
Austin, TX 78720-2230
800/527-3500, 512/794-5970,
fax 512/250-7329
CIS: 75056,1733

Thought I Could
107 University Pl., Suite 4D
New York, NY 10003
212/673-9724, fax 212/260-1194
CIS: 75056,1733

3G Graphics
114 Second Ave. S., Suite 104
Edmonds, WA 98020
800/456-0234, 206/774-3518,
fax 206/771-8975

3M Learning Software
  (see Imation)

ThrustMaster
10150 SW Nimbus Ave.
Portland, OR 97223-4337
503/639-3200, fax 503/620-8094
AOL: thrustmaster;
CIS: 76520,3325

Timeslips
17950 Preston Rd., Suite 800
Dallas, TX 75252
800/285-0999, fax 214/248-9245
AOL: Timeslips; CIS: 75300,2047

T/Maker Company
1390 Villa St.
Mountain View, CA 94041
800/395-0195, 415/962-0195,
fax 415/962-0201

Toshiba America
9740 Irvine Blvd.
P.O. Box 19724
Irvine, CA 92713
800/456-3475, 714/583-3000,
fax 714/583-3140

Totem Graphics
6200-F Capitol Blvd.
Tumwater, WA 98501
206/352-1851, fax 206/352-2554

Treacyfaces
P.O. Box 26036
West Haven, CT 06516-8036
800/800-6805, 203/389-7037,
fax 203/389-7039

Tuesday Software
215 Via Sevilla
Santa Barbara, CA 93109
800/945-7889, 805/962-7889,
fax 805/564-8955

Tut Systems
2446 Estand Way
Pleasant Hill, CA 94523
800/998-4888, 510/682-6510,
fax 510/682-4125

U

Upstill Software
1442A Walnut St.
Berkeley, CA 94709
800/568-3696, 510/486-0761,
fax 510/486-0762
AL: cookware; CIS: 70521,1264

U.S. Robotics
8100 N. McCormick Blvd.
Skokie, IL 60076
847/982-5010, fax 847/933-5800

URW America
P.O. Box 700
Barrington, NH 03825
603/664-2130, fax 603/664-2295

V

ViaCrypt
9033 North 24th Ave., Suite 7
Phoenix, AZ 85021-2847
602/944-0773, fax 602/943-2601
INT: http://www.viacrypt.com

Vicarious
3 Lagoon Dr., Suite 300
Redwood City, CA 94065
800/465-6543, 415/610-8300
INT: techsupport@vicarious.com;
http://www.vicarious.com

**Viewpoint DataLabs
International**
625 S. State St.
Orem, UT 84058
800/DATASET, 801/229-3000,
fax 801/229-3300
INT: http://www.viewpoint.com

Virginia Systems
5509 W. Bay Ct.
Midlothian, VA 23112
804/739-3200, fax 804/739-8376
AL: vasys

Virtual Entertainment
200 Highland Ave.
Needham, MA 02194
800/301-9545, 617/449-7567,
fax 617/449-4887
INT: http://www.virtent.com

Visioneer
2860 W. Bayshore Rd.
Palo Alto, CA 94033
415/812-6400

**Visual Information
Development (VIDI)**
136 W. Olive Ave.
Monrovia, CA 91016
818/358-3936, fax 818/358-4766

Vividus
378 Cambridge Ave., Suite I
Palo Alto, CA 94306
415/321-2221, fax 415/321-2282
AL: cornish1;
INT: info@vividus.com;
http://www.wco.com/~infov/

Voudette
Village Station, Box 24935
Los Angeles, CA 90024
310/474-7142, fax 310/474-7516

The Voyager Company
578 Broadway, Suite 406
New York, NY 10012
800/446-2001, 212/431-5199,
fax 212/431-5799
CIS: go voyager;
INT: 3sixty@voyagerco.com;
http://www.voyagerco.corel

VST Technologies
1620 Sudbury Rd., Suite 3
Concord, MA 01742
508/287-4600, fax 508/287-4068

W

Wacom Technology
501 SE Columbia Shores Blvd.
Suite 300
Vancouver, WA 98661
800/922-6613, 360/750-8882,
fax 360/750-8924
AL: d4993; AOL: wacom;
CIS: go wacom;
INT: http://www.wacom.com

Waves
6716 Central Avenue Pike, Suite 8
Knoxville, TN 37912
800/264-0109, 423/689-5395,
fax 423/688-4260
INT: http://www.waves.com

WestCode Software
15050 Avenue of Science
Suite 112
San Diego, CA 92128
800/448-4250
AOL: WestCode
INT: westcode@westcodesoft.com;
http://www.WestCodeSoft.com

White Sands Multimedia
1817 California St., Suite 203
San Francisco, CA 94109
AOL: wsmedia

Wired
544 Second St.
San Francisco, CA 94107-1427
subscriptions 800/769-4733,
415/904-0660, fax 415/904-0669
INT: editor@wired.com;
subscriptions@wired.com

WordPerfect (see Corel)

Working Software
P.O. Box 1844
Santa Cruz, CA 95061-1844
800/229-9675, 408/423-5696,
fax 408/423-5699
AL: d0140; AOL: workingsw;
CIS: 76004,2072;
INT: working@working.com;
http://webcom.com/~working

Xante
P.O. Box 16526
Mobile, AL 36616-0526
800/926-8839, 334/342-4840,
fax 334/342-3345

Xaos Tools
600 Townsend St., Suite 270-E
San Francisco, CA 94103
800/289-9267, 415/487-7000,
fax 415/558-9886
AL: d7093; AOL: xaos tools;
INT: macinfo@xaostools.com

Xerox
80 Linden Oaks Pkwy.
Rochester, NY 14625
716/423-5090
CIS: go xerox

Xing Technology
1540 W. Branch St.
Arroyo Grande, CA 93420-1818
800/294-6448, 805/473-0145,
fax 805/473-0147,
BBS: 805/473-2680
INT: http://www.xingtech.com

Yamaha
Consumer Products Division
P.O. Box 6600
Buena Park, CA 90622
714/522-9937, fax 714/228-3913

Z

Zedcor
3420 N. Dodge Blvd.
Tucson, AZ 85716
800/482-4567, 520/881-8101,
fax 520/881-1841
AL and AOL: zedcor

Ziff-Davis Publishing (ZiffNet)
950 Tower Ln.
Foster City, CA 94404
415/378-5600

Zygote Media Group
1 E. Center St., Suite 215
Provo, UT 84601
800/267-5170, 801/375-7220,
fax 801/375-7374
INT: http://www.zygote.com

Glossary

This glossary contains definitions for commonly used Macintosh terms (plus a few extras). For explanations of terms and products relating to a specific subject, such as fonts or networking, see the relevant chapter or locate them through the Index.

When a word that's defined below occurs in the definition of another term, we usually put it in italics so you know you can look it up (but we don't always do that for common terms such as *file* and *software*). Words are alphabetized as if spaces and hyphens didn't exist; thus *database* comes before *data fork*, and *e-mail* falls between *ELF radiation* and *emulation*.

A

accelerator board A *card* containing a faster *processor*, more *memory*, or other electronic wizardry that speeds up a particular aspect of the computer's operation. The three main types are *CPU* accelerators, which speed up the Mac's overall operation; graphics accelerators (or accelerated *video cards*), which provide faster screen redraws; and *DSP* cards, which ramp up the processor-intensive operations common to graphics programs.

active-matrix See *LCD*.

active window The currently selected window, where the next *command* (or anything you type) will be applied. The active window is always on top of overlapping *windows*, its *title bar* has stripes, and its *scroll bars* are active.

adapter Electronic circuitry that adapts a *device* (such as a *monitor*, *printer*, or *network* cable) so that it's compatible with the Mac. An adapter can be a *card* (such as an *Ethernet* adapter) or a cable (such as the one required to attach a PowerBook to a desktop Mac in *SCSI disk mode*).

ADB Apple Desktop Bus, the standard connection for *input devices* such as keyboards and *mice* for all Macs from the SE onward. ADB connections are different from those on the Plus and earlier Macs.

AIFF Audio Interchange File Format, the standard *file format* for sound files.

alert box A box that pops on-screen, announced by one or more beeps, to give you information or a warning. Alert boxes don't require any information, but you may have to click a *button* such as OK or Cancel. Also called a message box. Compare *dialog box.*

alias A duplicate file *icon* (about 2K in size) that serves as a remote control for opening a *file, folder,* or *disk.* You can put an alias anywhere—on the *desktop,* in a folder, or on the *menu*— and it will find and open the original item when you *double-click* it or *select* it from the menu.

allocation block size This is the size of the blocks recorded on the *hard disk media* that are used to store your *files.* The Mac permits only one file in an allocation block. So if the file is small but the allocation block is big, the rest of the allocation block goes to waste. The allocation block size grows larger for every 32MB of hard disk capacity so you should consider *partitioning* your *drive* if you have many small files.

animation program Software that adds motion to images created in *paint, draw, presentation,* and *3-D graphics* programs.

anti-aliasing A technique for smoothing the rough edges (the infamous *jaggies*) of *bitmapped graphics,* usually by blurring the edges.

Apple events A System 7 feature that allows one *application* to invoke the features of another (on a single Mac or across a *network*) by sending it a *command* called an Apple event. It's the technology behind *AppleScript* and most *hot links,* and is part of Apple's overall scheme for interapplication communication (*IAC*), which also includes *OpenDoc.*

Apple Guide An *interactive* help system built into System 7.5. You tell Apple Guide what you want to do, and it shows you how to do it by walking you through the process.

** (Apple) menu** The *menu* at the left end of the *menu bar* in the *Finder* and within most *applications.* In System 7 you can make any *file, folder,* or *hard disk* appear on the menu by adding it (or its *alias*) to the Apple Menu Items folder; in System 6 the menu only gives you access to *desk accessories* and *control panels.*

ApplePrice The price that Apple believes one of its products will be sold for. Unlike list prices given by other companies, the ApplePrice is usually pretty close to the *street price.*

AppleScript Apple's *scripting language* (distributed as a system *extension*) that lets you write *scripts* to automate common tasks. Some *applications* incorporate AppleScript support, allowing you to create and run scripts within those programs.

AppleShare 1. A *Chooser extension* that lets you access shared files on networked Macs or AppleShare file *servers.* 2. Software that turns a Mac with a *hard disk* into a centralized file server, enabling other Macs on the *network* to access its files.

AppleTalk The *network protocols* built into every Mac. The Mac uses AppleTalk to talk to *laser printers* and other Macs connected to it via a cabling scheme such as *LocalTalk* or *Ethernet.* Compare *TCP/IP.*

application *Software* that does relatively complex tasks and that lets you create and modify *documents*. Common application types include *word processors, spreadsheets, database managers*, and *graphics* programs. Most programs are called applications, unless they're *utilities* or *system software*.

application heap The portion of a Mac's *memory* used by *applications*. Compare *system heap*.

Application menu In System 7, the *menu* at the right end of the *menu bar* that lets you switch between *programs* (and lets you hide the *windows* of programs you're not currently using). The menu's *icon* changes to match whichever program is currently active.

ARA AppleTalk Remote Access, a *protocol* (and product) that provides system-level support for dial-in (*modem*) connections to an *AppleTalk network*. With ARA, you can call your desktop Mac from a PowerBook and remotely access all the available services—*files, printers, servers, e-mail*, and so on.

Archie A service that collects names and locations of *ftp* files on the *Internet* and makes them available for searching at certain Internet sites.

archive 1. A copy of a *file* that's stored on a separate *disk* for safekeeping. 2) A group of files compressed and combined into a single file on the disk.

ASCII The American Standard Code for Information Interchange is a system for referring to letters, numbers, and common symbols by code numbers. (A is 65, for example.) This widely used *file format* is useful for transferring files between Macs and PCs. On the Mac, ASCII files are often called *text files*. Pronounced "askee."

authoring program Software for creating *interactive* software such as presentations, training materials, and games. It typically combines features found in *presentation programs* with a *scripting language*.

A/UX A version of *Unix* designed by Apple for use on the Mac. Pronounced as separate letters.

average access time The length of time in milliseconds that it takes a *drive's heads* to move to the desired track plus latency (the average wait for the desired sector to come around under the heads once they get to the right track).

average seek time The length of time in milliseconds that it takes a *drive's heads* to move to a desired track.

B

background printing A feature provided by the *system software* (accessed via the *Chooser*) and by *print spoolers* that lets you keep using the Mac while it's sending *documents* to the printer "in the background."

backing up Copying some or all of the *files* on your Mac to different *disks* or tape, so you won't lose the information if the original versions are damaged, lost, or stolen. The copied files are called backups.

backup The process of making copies of your important data on another kind of storage medium (another *hard disk*, removable cartridge, *floppy disks*, or tape.)

bad blocks Areas of a *disk* or platter that have become demagnetized through constant use.

balloon help When you point to items on the screen, this System 7 feature pops up cartoon-like message balloons to explain them. You turn it on or off from the *Help menu*.

bandwidth The amount of information that can travel between two points in a given time. The "broader" the bandwidth, the faster the *data* flows. Commonly used to describe how fast data can travel over a *bus*, or from *disk* into *memory*, or from one *modem* to another.

baud The number of signal changes per second transmitted by a modem.

baud rate A measure of the speed at which a *modem* sends and receives *bits* of *data*. Technically, baud is not the correct term for transmission speed (except in ancient 300-baud modems); you should say *bps* (bits per second) instead.

bay See *storage bay*.

BBS Bulletin Board Service, a noncommercial dial-up service usually run by a *user group* or *software* company. By dialing up a BBS with your *modem*, you can exchange messages with other users (or the *sysop*) and *download* (or *upload*) software. A BBS has fewer features than a commercial *on-line service*, but it's usually free (except for the phone call).

beta version A prerelease version of a *program*, which is still getting the *bugs* worked out.

Bézier curve A type of curve used in *draw programs* that consists of mathematically defined line segments connected by control points. By adjusting the points, you can create complex shapes.

Binhex The method of converting a *data file* into text for transmission to another computer for decoding; used where only standard text characters are accepted for transmission, for example, over the *Internet*.

bit Short for binary digit, this is the smallest unit of information the computer can work with. It can represent only one of two things: yes or no, on or off, 0 or 1 (as it's expressed in the binary numbers used by computers). The computer usually groups bits together into bigger chunks such as *bytes*, *kilobytes*, and so forth.

bit depth Refers to the number of *bits* the Mac's *memory* assigns to each *pixel* on the screen or each sample point on a *scanner*. One-bit color gives you just black and white; 8-bit gives you 256 colors or shades of gray; 16-bit gives you over 32,000 colors or shades of gray; and 24-bit gives you over 16.7 million colors.

bitmap An image made up of dots (or *pixels*).

bitmapped font A font in which each character is made up of a pattern (map) of dots. To display it correctly, you must have a separate set of character maps for each size (10 point, 12 point, and so on)—otherwise, you'll have a bad case of the *jaggies*. Also called a fixed-size or *screen font*. Compare *outline font*.

bitmapped graphic An image made up of dots (*bits*) rather than discrete objects. Typically produced by *paint*, *image-editing*, and *3-D graphics programs*. Sometimes called a *raster* image. Compare *object-oriented graphic*.

board A piece of fiberglass or pressboard on which *chips* and other electronic parts are mounted. The connections between the chips are normally printed with metallic ink, so it's called a printed circuit (or PC) board. The main board in a computer is called the logic board or *motherboard*. A board that plugs into an *expansion slot* is called an add-in board or *card*.

board See *card*.

bomb Another word for *crash*. Bombs are usually heralded by an *alert box* with a picture of a bomb, indicating you must restart the Mac. Compare *hang*.

Boolean operator Words such as *and*, *or*, and *not*, that you place between text strings to refine a search. For example, you could search a *database* for "men *and* cook *or* clean *but* not married." Also see *wild card*.

boot blocks Parts of a Mac's *startup disk* that hold information about the *System file* and *Finder*. When you start up the Mac, it checks this area for a pointer toward a valid *System Folder*.

booting Starting up a computer, which loads the *system software* into *memory*. (The idea is that the computer is "pulling itself up by its own bootstraps.") Restarting the computer is called rebooting or a warm boot.

bps Bits per second, the correct way to express the data-transfer speed of a *modem*. Today's modems generally range from 9,600 bps to 28,800 bps; compression can increase the effective *throughput* to higher levels. Compare *baud*.

browse 1. To read messages posted in the public message area of a *bulletin board service*, or the libraries in such a service. 2. To surf pages on the *World Wide Web* and *Usenet* newsgroups.

browser An *application* which reads and displays *World Wide Web* pages.

buffer An area of *memory* set aside for the storage of transient *data*. On the Mac it's called the *disk cache*, but other devices, such as *printers* and *modems*, also have buffers, which allow them to process data more quickly.

bug A mistake, or unexpected occurrence, in a piece of *software* (or, less commonly, in a piece of *hardware*). Bugs often cause the Mac to *hang* or *crash*.

bulletin board See *BBS*.

burst transfer rates The rate of speed in milliseconds that a *drive* can pump out a small amount of *data* loaded into *memory buffers* on the drive's controller.

bus A path over which electronic impulses (*data*) travel between various computer *devices*. Examples include the Apple Desktop Bus (*ADB*), which connects keyboards and *mice* to the Mac, and the *SCSI bus*, which connects *hard disks* and other *peripherals*.

button A control inside a *dialog box* that lets you give a command or select options. The standard rounded-rectangle shape commonly referred to as a "button" is actually a *push button*; *radio buttons* and *checkboxes* are other kinds of buttons.

byte Eight *bits*. A byte typically represents one character (letter, number, or other symbol) on the screen.

C

cache A temporary storage place for information. Also see *disk cache*.

cache card A *card* that speeds up the Mac by supplying a small amount of high-speed *memory* (called static RAM, or *SRAM*) that the *processor* can use to quickly store and retrieve *data* while it's working.

CAD Computer-Aided Design, a category of high-end *draw programs* used by engineers, architects, and designers. Pronounced "cad."

card A kind of *board* that has connectors on its edges, so you can plug it directly into an *expansion slot* on the Mac. Cards add functionality, such as *24-bit color* or an *accelerator*. Also called an add-in board.

carpal tunnel syndrome A nerve problem that causes pain, numbness, or tingling in the hands (and often in the forearms). Advanced cases can cause permanent nerve damage. It's one type of repetitive stress injury.

cathode ray tube The picture tube inside a Mac's *monitor*. Often abbreviated as *CRT*.

CCDs Charge-Coupled Devices. Light sensors that convert the light energy to electricity. Used in *scanners* and the Connectix QuickCam.

CD-ROM Compact disk, read-only memory. A type of *storage device* that looks just like an audio CD (in fact, you can play audio CDs on a CD-ROM *drive*) and stores as much *data* as a large *hard disk* (600MB or so), making it a popular means of distributing *fonts*, photos, electronic encyclopedias, games, and *multimedia* offerings. As the name indicates, however, you can't save or change *files* on a CD-ROM, only read them. Pronounced "see-dee rom."

cdev Control panel device, the System 6 name for a *control panel*.

chat A live discussion between two or more people via typing on an *on-line service* or in an *e-mail application* such as QuickMail.

checkbox A *button* that works as a *toggle*—that is, you turn on an option by *clicking* once in the empty checkbox (an x will appear); and click again to turn it off. Unlike *radio buttons*, any or all of a group of checkboxes can be on at once.

chimes of doom A heart-stopping sequence of chords played during startup (instead of the usual *boing*) when a serious problem prevents the Mac from completing the startup procedure. You'll usually also see the *Sad Mac*.

chip The most essential electronic component of a computer: a tiny piece of silicon (about the size of a baby's fingernail) with an electronic circuit embedded in it. The Mac's *processor* and *memory* (*RAM* and *ROM*) are chips, which are normally mounted on *boards* or *SIMMs*.

Chooser A *desk accessory* that displays which *printers* and, on a *network*, which file *servers* and shared *folders* are available to you. You select a printer or other item by clicking its *icon*. The Chooser is also where you turn *background printing* and *AppleTalk* on and off.

Chooser extension An *extension* that displays an *icon* in the Chooser *window*. It's what enables the Mac to communicate (through its *modem* and *printer ports*) with *networks* and with *devices* such as printers and modems. Two common Chooser extensions are the *LaserWriter driver* and *AppleShare*.

CISC Complex instruction set computing; pronounced "sisk." The *processor* design used in the 68000-series Macs. Compare *RISC*.

clean install Installing a *system* so that it makes a new *System Folder* instead of altering the existing one.

clicking Pressing and immediately releasing the *mouse* button. To click on something is to position the *pointer* over it and then click.

client The computer which makes use of the services of a *network server* machine. Your Mac is a client, for example, when it uses a Web *browser* to access a Web server, the computer which makes Web pages available on the *Internet*.

clip art Precreated graphics—from simple line art to full-color photographs—that you can use, royalty-free, in publications and presentations. Also called clip media.

Clipboard A temporary *storage* area in the Mac's *memory* that holds what you last cut or copied. *Pasting* inserts its contents into a *document*. Some programs have a *menu* item that lets you see what's in the Clipboard.

clipping A file that's created by dragging a selection to the *desktop* (or to a *Finder* window), using System 7.5's *Drag and Drop* capabilities.

clock rate A measure of the performance of a computer's *CPU* (or *processor*). The CPU's operations are synchronized to a quartz crystal that pulses millions of times each second. The rapidity of these pulses—measured in *megahertz*—is the clock rate (or speed).

clones Macintosh computers made by companies other than Apple—which have licensed the technology for a legitimate product.

close box A small box at the left end of the *title bar* in the *active window*. Clicking it closes the window. Compare *size box* and *zoom box*.

code The actual statements or instructions (written in a programming language) that make up a piece of *software*.

color management Any of several approaches—including Apple's ColorSync *extension*—that attempt to provide a consistent match between the image colors you see on screen (or that are input from a *scanner*) and those that are printed on paper.

color management system (CMS) A method of providing more accurate representations of color across *devices*—computer *monitors*, proofing *printers*, *imagesetters*, and others—that have varying abilities to reproduce a full range of colors.

command The generic name for anything you tell the Mac to do. Commands are usually listed on *menus* or are invoked using *keyboard shortcuts*.

commercial software Programs sold for profit in stores or by mail-order, with the purchaser paying before taking possession. Compare *shareware*, *freeware*, and *public-domain software*.

communications program Software that enables you to send and receive information through a *modem*.

communications slot A slot made specifically for an internal *modem*.

compact Mac An all-in-one Mac such as the Classic II, SE, or Plus, which have a nine-inch *monitor* built into the same box as the *CPU*. Compare *modular Mac* and *portable Mac*.

compatible Said of *software* and/or *hardware* that work together correctly (that is, without *crashes* or other problems). Also refers to PCs made by other companies that work just like IBM PCs.

compression Making a *file* smaller (using a special *utility* for the purpose) so that it will take up less room on the *disk*.

configuration 1. The components that make up a computer system (which model of Mac and what *peripherals*). 2. The physical arrangement of those components (what's placed where). 3. The *software* settings that enable two computer components to talk to each other (as in configuring *communications software* to work with a *modem*).

contact manager A *database program* that keeps track of the names, addresses, phone numbers, and so forth of your personal and business contacts. TouchBASE is one example of this genre, which is part of a larger software category called *PIMs*.

control panel In System 7, a control panel (lowercase) is a *utility* that lets you set basic parameters such as the speaker volume, *desktop* pattern, date and time, and so on. Control panels are kept in a *folder* called Control Panels (capitalized, plural); one way to open it is by *selecting* Control Panels from the menu. In System 6, control panels are called *cdevs*, and they're accessed through the Control Panel (capitalized, singular) command on the menu.

Control Strip A collapsible *palette* that comes with current PowerBooks and provides convenient, on-screen access to features such as battery charge, sleep mode, sound volume, *AppleTalk*, file sharing, and the PowerBook *control panel*.

convergence When the three color beams (red, green, and blue) inside a *monitor's* display tube are adjusted, they converge to hit the right spots on the screen, affecting its sharpness. A few monitors let you adjust for convergence.

Copland The code name for System 8.

coprocessor A *chip* designed specifically to handle a particular task, such as math calculations or displaying graphics on-screen. A coprocessor is faster at its specialized function than the main *processor* is, and it relieves the processor of some work. A coprocessor can reside on the *motherboard* (an *FPU* is one example) or be part of an *expansion card*, as with an *accelerator*.

copy protection Any of the various annoying schemes that companies employ to prevent the unauthorized (and illegal) copying of their *software*.

cps Characters per second. Used to describe the speed of *inkjet* and *dot-matrix printers* or characters per second transmitted by, for example, a *modem*.

CPU Central Processing Unit, the brains of the computer. The CPU interprets and executes the actual computing tasks; one measure of its performance is the *clock rate*. In the Mac, the entire CPU resides in the *processor chip*, which is located on the *motherboard*. Also used to refer to the box that holds the motherboard and its CPU. Sometimes people (including us) use CPU as another word for the processor, motherboard, or the entire computer.

crash A problem (often caused by a *bug*) that causes a *program*, or the entire *operating system*, to unexpectedly stop working. If a program crashes, you sometimes can recover with the *force quit* command, but you often have to restart the Mac. Also see *bomb* and *hang*.

creator The four-letter *code* that a file uses to tell the *Finder* which program "owns" it. It distinguishes a *document* created with Microsoft Word (MSWD) from one created with MacWrite Pro (MWPR), for example, so that the correct file *icon* appears and the correct *application* is launched when you *double-click* the icon. Compare *file type*.

cropping Trimming a photo or other image to eliminate irrelevancies or control the area of major emphasis.

cross-platform Refers to *software* (or anything else) that will work on more than one *platform* (type of computer).

CRT Cathode Ray Tube, the display technology used in virtually all desktop computer *monitors* and television sets. (Portable computers typically use an *LCD* (liquid-crystal display.) Compare *cathode ray tube*.

curly quotes See *smart quotes*.

cursor 1. The little shape that moves around on the screen when you move the *mouse*. The most common is the *pointer*, the black arrow that you use to select things on the *desktop* and from *menus*. 2. The blinking vertical bar that indicates the insertion point in text. (There's really no such thing as a cursor on the Mac—it's used on more primitive computers—but people often say cursor when they mean pointer.)

D

DA The common name for a *desk accessory*; pronounced as separate letters. See *desk accessory*.

daisy chain A *hardware* configuration in which *devices* are connected to each other (via *cables*) in a linear series. Typically used to describe a *network* setup (such as the *nodes* on a *LocalTalk* network), or the arrangement of *SCSI devices* attached to your Mac.

DAT Digital Audio Tape, the most common type of tape backup. Commonly used to back up large quantities of *data*. DAT tapes can hold as much as 8GB of data. See *backing up*.

data The generic name for anything you input to a computer, or anything it outputs to you. It's the plural of datum, a single piece of information.

database A *file* created by a *database manager* that contains a collection of information organized into *records*, each of which contains labeled categories (called *fields*). It's sort of like an electronic Rolodex, or a set of 3-by-5-inch file cards.

database manager A *program* that lets you create a *database*, enter *data*, and then search, *sort*, and output it. There are several categories of database managers, including flat-file, relational, and *contact managers*. Also called a database engine, database management system (DBMS), or simply (and confusingly) a database.

data bus The circuitry in a processor which handles the transfer of data as opposed to instructions between memory and processor.

data encryption See *encryption*.

data file A file on disk which contains information used by a program, but is not itself a program. Memos and letters, address lists, and budget information would be stored in data files and manipulated using word processors, database managers, and spreadsheet programs, respectively.

data fork The part of a Mac *file* that holds user-created data, such as text and graphics. *Documents* always have a data fork; *applications* sometimes do. Compare *resource fork*.

data path The "roadway" along which information travels in a computer; a wider path can mean faster operation. Also called the *data bus*.

data transfer rate The data transfer rate is a measure of how fast a *drive* can deliver *data* to the Mac once it gets to the sectors it's looking for. The transfer rate is counted in megabytes per second (or sometimes, just to confuse things, megabits per second). Today's drives usually have transfer rates between 1.5 and 5 megabytes per second.

daughterboard A *board* that attaches to (rides piggyback on) another board, such as the *motherboard* or an *expansion card*. For example, you can often add a daughtercard containing additional *memory* to an *accelerator card*.

DAV slot Stands for Digital Audio Video. A special *expansion slot* on the AV Macs that gives direct access to their digital-processing *hardware*.

default The option that will be used unless you change it. It often refers to preset parameters such as the margins in a *word processor* or the volume in the Sound *control panel*. Also see *default button*.

default button In a *dialog box*, the button with a heavy border that's activated when you hit Return or Enter.

defragmenter A *utility* program that optimizes *disk* performance by shuffling fragments of files around until each forms a neat, contiguous whole. Also known as a disk optimizer.

demo version A sample copy of commercial *software* (and sometimes *shareware*) that has limited capabilities (usually you can't save or print), but allows you to see how the program works.

desk accessory A mini-application (such as the Alarm Clock) that's normally accessed from the *menu*. In System 6 that's the only way to get to them, but in System 7 they can be kept anywhere. Desk accessories usually only open one *document* at a time and quit automatically when you close their *window*. Commonly called *DAs*.

desktop What you see on the screen when you're in the *Finder*: the *menu bar*, background pattern, *Trash*, disk *icons*, *files*, *folders*, and so forth. It's the Mac's version of home base.

Desktop file An invisible file on every *disk* that stores *data* such as *icons*, the size and location of *windows*, and the information available with the Get Info command. System 6 has one desktop file; System 7 has two. Compare *directory*.

desktop publishing The process of designing printed documents (brochures, newsletters, magazines, books, and so on)—often using a *page layout program*—on a personal computer.

device Another word for *hardware*.

dialog box A box that appears on the screen (often after you issue a *command*) and requests information or a decision. Compare *alert box* and *window*.

DIF Data Interchange Format, a standard file format for *databases* (and sometimes *spreadsheets*). It preserves *field* names and *data* but not formulas or text *formatting*. Compare *SYLK*.

digital signal processor See *DSP*.

digitize To turn something from the real (analog) world into digital data on a computer. You might use a *scanner* to *digitize* pictures or text, a sound digitizer to record music or a human voice, or a video-digitizing board to input video from a VCR or camcorder. Also see *sampling*.

dimmed When something, such as a *menu* item, is dimmed (gray) on the Mac's screen, it means that you can't currently access it. When you eject a *disk*, its *icon* is dimmed, as are all *windows* and icons associated with it.

direct memory access A *chip* that handles data transfers between *memory* and various *devices* (*hard disks*, *floppy-disk drives*, and anything connected to the Mac's *ports*), freeing up the main *processor* for other tasks. The AV Macs and Power Macs have a DMA chip.

directory An invisible *file* on every *disk* that keeps track of the name, size, and location of all other files. If this critical file becomes damaged, you can lose access to your *data*. Compare *desktop file*.

dirty ROMs See *32-bit clean*.

disabled folders Folders created by *extension managers* to hold *extensions* and *control panels* that are turned off through the extension manager control panel.

disk A thin round platter on which computer *data* is stored in either magnetic or optical form. Although the disk is circular, its case is usually rectangular. The main types are *floppy disks*, *hard disks*, and *CD-ROMs*.

disk cache An area of *RAM* reserved for *data* recently read from *disk*, which allows the *processor* to quickly retrieve it if it's needed again. You adjust the cache's size in the Memory *control panel* (96K or 128K is usually optimal). In System 6 it's called the RAM cache. Also see *cache card* and *RAM disk*.

disk drive See *drive*.

disk driver The disk driver is an invisible *program* written to a *hard disk* or removable cartridge during *formatting*. Disk drivers transfer *data* from *memory* to storage media.

display Another word for screen or *monitor*.

display card A *card* that controls an external *monitor*. Also called a *video card*.

display port A *port* where you can plug in a *monitor*. They were formerly called video ports, but some Macs now have ports for connecting to camcorders, TVs, and VCRs, which are also called video ports.

dock 1. (noun) A piece of *hardware* that attaches to a PowerBook Duo and gives it desktop-Mac features (such as a *floppy-disk drive*, *ports*, and *expansion slots*). 2. (verb) To connect a PowerBook to a desktop Mac in *SCSI disk mode*.

document The *file* that you create and modify with an *application*. Examples are a letter, a drawing, and a mailing list.

dogcow His name is Clarus, and he appears in the Page Setup *dialog box* (File menu). The dogcow demonstrates the options (like Flip Vertical) by acting them out when you *select* them. Clarus says "Moof!"

DOS Pronounced "dahss," it refers to MS-DOS or PC-DOS, the (disk) *operating systems* used on IBM personal computers and *compatible* machines.

dot-matrix printer An impact printer, such as Apple's ImageWriter II, that forms images from a pattern of dots, which are created by an array of pins striking an inked ribbon against the paper.

dot pitch On a *monitor*, it is the distance between individual dots of phosphor on the screen, and affects the overall clarity of the image. Generally, anything below .30mm is acceptable.

double-clicking Positioning the *pointer* and quickly clicking the *mouse* button twice without moving the mouse. You double-click to open *applications* and *documents* (when the pointer is an arrow) and to *select* entire words (when the pointer is an *I-beam*).

double-sided disk A double-density *floppy disk* that stores information on both surfaces (top and bottom) and can hold 800K of *data*. Compare *single-sided* and *high-density disks*.

download 1. To retrieve a *file* from another computer using a *modem*. For instance, you might download some *shareware* from an *on-line service*. Opposite of *upload*. 2. To send a *font* or *PostScript file* from the Mac to a *printer*. In general, any font installed on your Mac is a downloadable font, and downloading can be done automatically or manually. Compare *resident font*.

dpi Dots per inch, a measure of the *resolution* of a *printer*, *scanner*, or *monitor*. It refers to the number of dots in a one-inch line. The more dots per inch, the higher the resolution.

drag To move the *pointer* while holding down the *mouse* button. Depending on the situation, dragging can move an object, *select* an area (indicated by a *selection rectangle*), or move you down a *menu*.

Drag-and-Drop 1. The capability, introduced in System 7.5, that lets you *drag* selected items directly from one *document* to another (even across *applications*) or onto the *desktop*. 2. Also refers to the editing option in some *word processors* that lets you drag selected text and drop it elsewhere within the same document. 3. Formerly used to identify the ability to drag a document *icon* onto an application icon and have it open.

DRAM Dynamic Random Access Memory, commonly called *RAM*.

draw program *Software* that lets you create finely detailed illustrations and save them as *object-oriented graphics*. Some draw programs are based on *PostScript*, and there are specialized applications for charting and *CAD*. Compare *paint program*.

drive A motorized *device* that reads information from, and writes information onto, *disks* or tapes. The main types are *floppy disk drives* and *hard disk drives*, but there are also drives for *CD-ROMs*, *removable media*, and tape.

drive heads The magnetic attachments on the positioning arms which read and write the binary information on a disk (floppy or hard).

driver A piece of *software* that tells the Mac how to operate an external *device*, such as a *printer*, *hard disk*, *CD-ROM drive*, or *scanner*. For instance, you can't print unless you have a printer driver (such as the LaserWriter file) installed in the Extensions *folder* inside the *System Folder*. Hard-disk drivers are invisible *files* that are loaded into *memory* when you start the Mac, while scanner drivers are usually *plug-ins* accessed from within a particular *application*.

drop caps Enlarged initial capital letters whose baselines drop down a few lines to mark the beginning of a section. Drop caps are decorative and functional, serving to guide the eye to the beginning of a section.

droplet A special type of *application* created with *AppleScript* that acts upon the items dropped onto its *icon*.

DSP Digital Signal Processor, a *coprocessor* that specializes in heavy-duty number crunching, making it ideal for speeding up the *processor*-intensive operations associated with graphics, video, and audio programs. The 68040-based AV Macs have a built-in DSP *chip*, or you can buy DSP *cards* for things such as Photoshop *acceleration* and JPEG *compression*.

dual-scan See *LCD*.

dumb quotes Straight quotation marks (and apostrophes) such as those found on a typewriter. They look like this: " '. They're a big faux pas on a computer unless you're referring to feet, inches, hours, or minutes. Compare *smart quotes*.

DXF Drawing Interchange Format, a standard *file format* for 3-D *graphics* and *CAD* programs.

dye-sublimation printer A *printer* that creates images by heating special pigments that become gaseous (sublime) and then diffuse into the paper's special coating. Also called dye-diffusion or continuous-tone printers.

E

edutainment A combination of the words education and entertainment, it usually refers to children's *software* that provides educational value in an entertaining way—for example, by using games, animations, and sounds.

8-bit color See *bit depth*.

ELF radiation Extremely Low Frequency electromagnetic radiation (between 60 Hz and 75 Hz), which is generated by computer *monitors* and other electrical *devices* (including hair dryers). Compare *VLF radiation*.

e-mail Electronic mail—that is, private messages sent between users on different computers, either over a *network* or via a *modem* connection to an *on-line service* or *BBS*.

emulation A way to allow *software* to run on a *processor* it was not designed for. When you run an *application* written for a *68K processor* (such as the Quadra) on a Power Mac (which has a *PowerPC chip*), it runs in emulation mode (which is slower than native code would be). Emulation mode requires an emulator, a piece of software that imitates the native processor. For example, the Power Macs have a 68LC040 emulator built into their *ROM* chips and can come with SoftWindows, an emulator that lets you run PC programs. Compare *native*.

Enabler See *System Enabler*.

encryption Scrambling the *data* in a *file* to prevent unauthorized access. Accessing the information requires a password.

Energy Star A government program that requires all computer equipment the feds buy to drop their power consumption below 30 watts when not in use. Most manufacturers are redesigning their products to meet this energy saving standard.

EPS Encapsulated PostScript, a standard *file format* for high-resolution *PostScript* illustrations. It usually has two parts: the PostScript *code* (which tells the *printer* how to print the graphic) and a *PICT* image (for on-screen previews).

ergonomics The study of the relationship between people and their work environment. Working ergonomically means minimizing work-related health threats and setting up a comfortable, efficient workplace.

Ethernet A *network* cabling scheme for *AppleTalk* networks (as well as other types of networks) that's much faster than *LocalTalk*. Ethernet support is built into some Macs (otherwise you must install an Ethernet *card*), and it can be used with a variety of wiring systems.

expansion card See *card*.

expansion slot A connector inside the Mac where you can plug in a *card* that adds capabilities such as *acceleration* or *24-bit color*. The number and types of *slots* vary among Macs; the main types are *NuBus*, *processor direct (PDS)*, *DAV*, and (soon) *PCI*.

export To save *data* from one *application* in a *file format* that another program can *import* or *open*. Some programs have an Export *command* that's separate from the Save command.

extension Software (including many popular commercial *utilities*) that extends the *system's* capabilities by, say, enabling it to display QuickTime movies or use a particular type of *printer*. There are two main types: system *extensions* (*QuickTime*, *AppleScript*, and so on) and Chooser extensions (such as printer drivers and *AppleShare*). Extensions in the Extensions *folder* in the active *System Folder* are automatically *loaded* into *memory* when the Mac starts up. (Some extensions are also *control panels*.) Called an *init* in System 6.

extension manager A *utility* that lets you control which extensions are loaded at startup.

F

fat binary The name given to *software* that contains *code* for both *68K* and *PowerPC processors*. A fat-binary *application* automatically uses whichever type of code is appropriate for the Mac it's running on.

fax modem A type of *modem* that can send (and, in most cases, receive) faxes in addition to transferring *data files*. Unlike regular fax machines, fax modems can't send printed documents—only *disk* files.

FDHD Refers to the 1.4MB *SuperDrive* that comes with current Macs. FDHD stands for *Floppy Disk, High Density*, and it's pronounced "fud-hud."

field The smallest element of a *database* record; a container in a database designed to store one particular type of information, such as a last name, ZIP code, or salary amount.

file A discrete collection of information on a *disk*, usually a *document* or a *program*, that's represented by an *icon*. Mac files usually consist of a *resource fork* and a *data fork*.

file server See *server*.

file format The structure that the *data* for a particular *document* is stored in (e.g., ASCII, RTF, PICT, TIFF). Most *applications* can save documents in one or more standard formats as well as in their native format. Also see *file type*.

file-transfer protocol A set of conventions for determining how *files* will be packaged, sent, and verified over telephone lines. An ftp (such as Zmodem or Kermit) is independent of the computer, *modem*, and *communications software*. See *ftp*.

file type The four-letter code that identifies the nature of a *file* to the *Finder*. All *applications* have the file type APPL; *text files* have the code TEXT; and many graphics are *PICT* (the same as their *file format*). Compare *creator*.

filter A piece of *software* that an *application* uses for *file-format* conversion or special effects. PageMaker, for example, has a filter that lets it import Microsoft Word files, while Photoshop has dozens of filters for effects such as image blurring. Filters can be part of the main application or external programs called *plug-ins*, as with Claris *XTND* system.

Finder The basic program that generates the *desktop* and lets you access and manage *files* and *disks*. Together with the *System file* and the *ROMs*, it comprises the Mac's *operating system*. There are Finder substitutes, such as Apple's At Ease, that perform the same basic tasks (and usually give you other capabilities as well).

FireWire Apple's new interface standard for connecting *peripherals* to the Mac. It will be phased in over the next few years, gradually replacing the current *SCSI* standard.

flame A derisive message posted in the public area of a *bulletin board system*, *on-line service*, or in a *Usenet* newsgroup on the *Internet*.

flicker Also called strobe. Seen if a screen refreshes too slowly. See *redraw*.

floating-point processor A *coprocessor* (or part of a main *processor*) that handles sophisticated calculations, such as those used in *spreadsheet*, *CAD*, and scientific programs. The functions of the chip, called an FPU (floating-point unit) or a *math coprocessor*, are built into the 68040 (but not the 68LC040) and PowerPC chips.

floppies Commonly used name to describe *floppy disks*.

floppy disk A 3.5-inch removable disk that's flexible (although it's usually protected by a hard plastic case). Newer floppy disks can store up to 1.4MB of *data*. Also called a diskette. Compare *hard disk*.

floptical A technology for *removable media* that stores *data* magnetically but uses optical techniques to position the *read/write head*. Floptical disks, which resemble *floppy disks*, currently hold up to 21MB. Also see *magneto-optical*.

folder A grouping of *files* and/or other folders that's represented by a folder-shaped *icon* on the *desktop*. (Its equivalent on DOS machines is a subdirectory.) Also see *HFS*.

font The *software* that creates a *typeface* on the Mac. In olden (precomputer) times, it referred to a single size and style of a typeface, such as 9-point Times Italic.

font family A group of *typefaces* that's designed to work together. A typical family (say, Palatino) has four members: regular, bold, italic, and bold italic.

footer Similar to *header*, but at the bottom of a page. The page number of a document often appears in a footer.

footprint The amount of space a piece of *hardware* takes up on your desk (and its dimensions).

force quit A System 7 feature that lets you return safely to the *Finder* (usually) when a program *hangs* or *crashes*. The *command* is ⌘Option Esc . You lose unsaved work in the crashed *application*, but you'll usually be able to save work in other programs before restarting the Mac.

format All *storage* devices and *media* must be formatted or initialized to prepare the disk to store Macintosh data. See *file format*.

formatting 1. For text, all the information above and beyond plain text that's added to a *document*, including character *styles* (bold, italic), spacing, indents, tabs, and so on. 2. Another term for initializing a *disk*.

forum leader See *Sysop*.

FPU Floating-Point Unit, a specialized *math coprocessor*. See *floating-point processor*.

fragmentation A condition in which parts of a *file* are stored in different locations on a *disk*. When a file is fragmented, the *drive's read/write head* has to jump from place to place to read the *data*; if many files are fragmented, it can slow the drive's *performance*. The problem can be resolved using a disk optimizer or defragmenter.

freeware Software that may be freely copied and used, but the copyright for which is retained by the author, who usually forbids you to alter or sell the program. Compare *public-domain software* and *shareware*.

ftp File-transfer protocol. The *protocol*, or set of rules, by which files are transferred over the *Internet*. Use it as a verb: "I'll ftp that file."

G

generic icon An icon that has lost all its identifying features, and possibly its link to its parent *application*. A generic *document* icon looks like a page of paper with its upper-right corner turned down.

GeoPort A special type of *printer port* or *modem port* that can serve as a built-in *modem*, *fax modem*, speakerphone, and answering machine.

gigabyte A measure of computer *memory*, *disk* space, and the like that's equal to 1,024 mega-bytes (1,073,741,824 bytes), or about 179 million words. Sometimes a gigabyte is treated as an even billion bytes (giga means billion), but that's almost 74 million bytes short. Abbreviated G, GB, or gig. Compare *kilobyte* and *megabyte*.

gopher A method of presenting information on *Internet* resources in a directory for easy navigation.

graphics The display of pictures, shapes, and colors to convey information, to decorate, or to amuse.

graphics tablet An *input device* that lets you draw with a *stylus* (pen) on a flat piece of plastic. You can make more precise movements than with a *mouse*, making it a great adjunct to *draw* and *paint programs*, particularly if the stylus is pressure-sensitive. Also called a *digitizing* or pressure-sensitive tablet.

grayscale Anything that contains shades of gray as well as black and white, such as a grayscale *monitor*, which typically displays 256 grays.

GUI Graphical User Interface. See *user interface*.

GX font An *outline font*, in either *PostScript* or *TrueType* format, that takes advantage of *QuickDraw GX*. GX fonts can have larger character sets and can include special programming that lets the fonts decide for themselves when to use alternate characters (such as ligatures) or include other special features.

H

halftone A way of converting (*rasterizing*) a *grayscale* or color image (a photograph, say) into a pattern of dots for output on a *printer* or *imagesetter*.

handshaking The process computers and *modems* go through in order to establish a connection and agree on the speed and *protocols* for *data* transmission.

hang A *crash* where the Mac ignores input from the *mouse* and keyboard. Sometimes you can escape with the *force quit command*; otherwise you must restart the Mac. Also called a freeze. Compare *bomb*.

hard disk A rigid (usually nonremovable) *disk*, and/or the *drive* that houses it. Actually, *hard disks* usually have several disks (or platters, made of aluminum and which are magnetically coated), and they store much more data and access it more quickly than *floppy disks*. Also called a hard drive or hard-disk drive.

hard disk formatter A *program* used to prepare *hard disk* and removable cartridges for use on the Macintosh.

hard drive See *hard disk*.

hardware The parts of your computer system you can bump into—physical components such as *hard disks*, *printers*, *modems*, *scanners*, *cards*, keyboards, *mice*, and the Mac itself. Compare *software*.

HDI-30 High-Density Interface, the special, smaller *SCSI connector* used on PowerBooks.

header 1. Identifying text (such as the date or page number) that appears at the top of each *document* page (versus the *footer*, which is at the bottom). 2. The part of a document's *code* that tells a program how to interpret its contents; the header defines the *file format*, for example.

Help menu The menu near the right end of the *menu bar* that lets you turn *Balloon Help* on and off and, in System 7.5, access *Apple Guide*. (Its title is a question mark inside a balloon.) In some programs, you can also use it to access on-line help.

Hertz Times Or cycles per second.

HFS Hierarchical File System, the Mac's method of organizing files on a *disk*, in which *files* and *folders* can be nested (contained) within other folders. See *folder*.

hierarchical menu A menu that has *submenus* (indicated by arrows) attached to it.

high-density disk A floppy disk that can store 1.4MB of data when used on a Mac with a *SuperDrive*. Compare *single-sided* and *double-sided disks*.

highlight To make something stand out from its background in order to show that it's *selected* or active. The Mac usually handles this by reversing the colors (for example, switching black and white) or, in the case of text, by placing a colored bar over the words.

home page The default page, which Net surfers first see when visiting a *World Wide Web* site.

hot link A special "live" link between *applications* that lets you select an element in a *document* (say, an illustration in PageMaker) and, using a special key combination, open it directly into the program that created it (such as FreeHand). You can make changes to the element, then return to the original document and instantly see those changes.

hot spot The single spot on a *mouse* cursor that "counts" when you're pointing or dragging.

HTML Hypertext Markup Language. A programming/formatting language for creating *platform*-independent pages on the *World Wide Web*.

HyperTalk A programming language used to interact with *HyperCard* stacks.

hypertext A text-linking strategy that lets you jump between related information in a *document* by clicking on a *button* or highlighted word. *On-line* help systems often use hypertext links, as do some programs designed for the electronic distribution of documents (see *PDD*). On the *Internet*, Web pages use hypertext, typically to link to text at another location, locally or at another site, but also to link to graphics, downloadable files, and so on.

I

I/O Input/Output. Used to describe the *ports* on the back of the Mac.

IAC Interapplication Communication. An underlying technology in System 7 whereby one *application* can send a message to another, either to exchange information or to make something happen. *Apple events* and *OpenDoc* are two implementations of IAC.

I-beam The shape (I) the *pointer* normally takes when dealing with text. You use the I-beam to create an insertion point or to select a range of text. Also called the text cursor.

icon The little picture that represents a *file*, *folder*, *disk*, or tool. It's a key component of the Mac's user *interface*. Click it once to *select* it; *double-click* it to open a file, folder, or disk.

icon parade The *extension* and *control panel* icons that appear one at a time across the bottom of the screen during startup, indicating they are *loading* into *memory*.

IDE Integrated Drive Electronics. IDE drives are installed inside Macs such as the PowerBook 150 and 190 and the Duo 2300 and 5300 series.

image-editing program Software that lets you alter existing images, such as photographs captured with a *scanner*, and saves them as *bitmapped graphics*. Compare *paint program*.

imagesetter A high-quality (usually *PostScript*) *printer* that can output pages (on paper or film) at resolutions of 1,200 *dpi* or greater. They're usually found at *service bureaus*.

impact printer See *dot-matrix printer*.

import To bring *data* into a *document* from another document, often generated by a different *application*. For instance, you can import text and graphics into a page layout program, or import *spreadsheet* data into a *word processor*. This data sharing is made possible by the applications' support of common *file formats*. Compare *open*.

init What an *extension* is called in System 6. It's short for initialization program and pronounced "in-it."

initialize To set up a *disk* (any kind) to receive information. When a disk is initialized, its magnetic media is divided into tracks and sectors, and a *directory* and *Desktop* file are created. Also called *formatting*.

inkjet printer A *printer* that forms text and images out of little dots created by tiny jets of ink.

input device Anything you use to directly input information to the computer: a *mouse*, keyboard, *trackball*, *graphics tablet*, joystick—even a *scanner* or digital camera. Also see *pointing device*.

insertion point The place in a *document* or *dialog box* where the next keystroke will add or delete text. The insertion point is represented by a blinking vertical line and is placed by clicking with the *mouse*.

installer A *utility* that copies *system software* or an *application* from *floppy disks* or a *CD-ROM*, *server*, or another *hard disk* to your hard disk. An Installer may also decompress the new *files*, remove obsolete files, place *extensions* and *control panels* in their proper *folders*, and/or create new folders.

integrated software A single *application* that includes several types of basic programs, such as a *word processor*, *spreadsheet*, *database manager*, *draw*, *paint*, and (often) *communications*.

interactive Said of *software* (particularly *multimedia*) that gives you some control over what's going on. You might click *buttons* to play a movie or jump to a different point in a presentation, or type in questions or answers that cause the program to respond in different ways. System 7.5's *Apple Guide* is an interactive help system.

interchange format A file format that's supported by most programs of a certain type (such as *word processors* or *paint programs*), allowing you to exchange files among them. *ASCII* is the standard interchange format for text, for example, while *PICT* and *TIFF* are common graphics formats. Compare *native*.

interface Sometimes referred to as *user interface*, the way a computer user interacts with their computer. For example, the Mac OS provides a graphical user interface that uses pictures (icons) to simplify overall computer use.

interleave ratio Setting the interleave ratio for a *hard disk* can be achieved using a hard disk formatter. The Mac Plus requires an interleave ratio of 3:1; for the SE, the Classic, and the PowerBook 100, the requisite ratio is 2:1. All recent Macs use a 1:1 ratio.

Internet A worldwide super-network that links thousands of individual *networks* and *on-line services*. You can gain access to the Internet—and its millions of users and thousands of newsgroups (discussion forums), *databases*, directories, and other digital goodies—if your computer is on one of the corporate, government, or university networks it connects to, or if you have an account with an *Internet service provider*. You also can send *e-mail* across the Internet from almost any on-line service.

Intranet A *network* inside an organization based on Internet protocols. Network users thus use Internet tools such as Web *browsers* to access network *documents*.

IRC Internet Relay Chat. Live discussion between two or more people on the *Internet*, much like chat on the commercial *on-line services*.

ISDN Integrated Services Digital Network, a type of telecommunications service based on an all-digital line between the local computer and the remote host.

ISP Internet Service Provider. Any enterprise which supplies access to the Internet, typically through a dial-up connection. ISP usually refers to a local independent provider.

J

jaggies The blocky, stair-stepped look common to *bitmapped graphics* and bitmapped *fonts*. *Anti-aliasing* can minimize this effect.

JPEG A sophisticated technique (it's not really a file format, per se) for compressing full-color *bitmapped graphics*, such as photographs. It stands for Joint Photographic Experts Group.

K

K An abbreviation for kilobyte, as in "an 800K file."

keyboard layouts A *system resource* that defines what character is typed when you press a key on your keyboard.

keyboard shortcut A combination of keystrokes (almost always involving ⌘ and often Shift, Option, and/or Control as well) that executes a command without your having to choose it from a *menu*. Also called a key combination or keyboard equivalent.

kilobyte A measure of computer *memory*, *disk* space, *document* size, and the like that's equal to 1,024 bytes, or about 170 words. Abbreviated *K*. Compare *megabyte* and *gigabyte*.

L

label One of seven descriptive names and colors that you can attach to *files* and *folders* using the Label *menu* in the *Finder*. You can sort files and folders by label to group related files and folders together (to do so, choose By Label from the View menu). To change the names and colors of labels, use the Labels *control panel*.

LAN Local Area Network. A *network* that's physically connected (via cables) and confined to a relatively small area, like one office or one building. Often just called a network. Compare *WAN*.

landscape Most *monitors* display a landscape view, which is wide from left to right with a short height.

laserdisc A 12-inch disk that's similar to an audio CD but holds visual images (such as high-quality movies) as well as music. Some laserdisc players can be hooked up to the Mac. Also called a videodisc.

laser printer A *printer* that creates images by drawing them on a metal drum with a laser. An ink powder, called toner, sticks to the imaged portion of the drum and is then transferred and fused to the paper (as with a photocopying machine). Apple established the popularity of *PostScript*-based laser printers with its LaserWriter line.

LaserWriter 35 The standard set of 35 resident *fonts* that most *PostScript laser printers* have built into their *ROM*. So named because they first appeared in Apple's LaserWriter Plus.

latency The time in milliseconds it takes for a spinning *disk* platter to bring the desired sector to the *read/write heads*.

Launcher A *control panel* that arranges the *icons* of selected *applications* and *documents* in a special *window*. To open a *file*, you click once on its icon.

launch Open (start) an *application*—that is, load it into *memory* from a *disk*.

layout An arrangement of *fields*, field labels, *graphics*, and static text in a *database*. Different layouts are used to display or print different things, such as data entry information, help text, mailing labels, and reports.

LCD Liquid-Crystal *Display*, the screen technology used in PowerBooks. *Active-matrix* LCDs are clearer and faster; *passive-matrix* LCDs are not quite as sharp and are sometimes slow to respond. Dual-scan passive-matrix screens, refreshed at twice the rate of standard ones, offer considerable improvement.

LiIon Lithium-ion, a battery technology for laptop computers.

list box A box with *scroll bars* that appears within a *dialog box* and lists things—*files, fonts,* or whatever.

list view One of five text-based ways—Name, Size, Kind, Label, and Date—that you can view a *folder's* contents in the *Finder*. In System 7, these are also called outline views because they can display a folder's contents in outline form, without opening another *window*.

load Get something ready to use. It can mean install (as in loading new *fonts*) or open (as in loading *extensions* into *memory* when the Mac starts up).

LocalTalk This refers to the networking *hardware* built into the Mac as well as to Apple's cabling scheme for connecting Macs on a *network*. Compare *PhoneNet* and *Ethernet*.

lock To prevent a *file* or *disk* from being changed. You can lock (or unlock) a file or *floppy disk* by clicking the Locked *checkbox* in its Get Info *window*. You also can lock a floppy disk by moving the plastic tab in the upper-left corner of its back side so that you can see through the little square hole. Locked disks are also called write-protected.

logic board See *motherboard*.

log on Establish a connection to a *server, BBS,* or *on-line service*, usually by entering a *user name* (or identification number) and a password. Disconnecting is called logging off.

lurkers People who read public messages in any *on-line service* but don't post any.

M

MacBinary A format for transferring Mac *files* over a *modem* or to another type of computer that ensures that all component parts (including the *data fork, resource fork,* and *icons*) stay together, so that you wind up with a usable file. Virtually all file-transfer and communications programs support MacBinary.

macro A user-defined *keyboard shortcut* that executes a series of *commands*. Macros are easy to create; all you need is a macro *utility* to record your keystrokes and *mouse* clicks. If you want to automate complex tasks, however, you'll probably need a *scripting language*.

magneto-optical A technology for *removable media* that combines magnetic and optical techniques. MO disks resemble *floppy disks*, but in terms of capacity and speed they're more like *hard disks*. Also called erasable-optical disks.

mail merge The merging of *database* information (such as names and addresses) with a letter *template* in a *word processor*, in order to create personalized letters.

marquee The rectangle of moving dots (called "marching ants") that surrounds a *selected* area in some programs.

marching ants See *marquee*.

math coprocessor Another name for *floating-point processor*.

MB An abbreviation for Megabyte.

MTBF Abbreviation for Mean Time Between Failures. The number of average power-on hours a *drive* will last before some component gives out.

media 1. The physical component of a *floppy disk*, *hard disk*, cartridge, tape, or *CD-ROM* that stores computer *data*. The main storage strategies are *magnetic* and *optical*. 2. The various ways of communicating, including print, video, and audio. See *multimedia*.

megabyte A measure of computer *memory*, *disk* space, *application* size, and the like that's equal to 1,024K (1,048,576 bytes) or about 175,000 words. Abbreviated MB or meg. Compare *kilobyte* and *gigabyte*.

megahertz A million cycles (occurrences, alterations, pulses) per second. Used to describe the speed at which a computer's *processor* (or *CPU*) operates. A 25-MHz processor can handle 25 million operations per second.

memory In general, another word for dynamic *RAM*, the *chips* where the Mac stores *system software*, *programs*, and *data* you are currently using. Other kinds of memory you may encounter are parameter RAM (*PRAM*), video RAM (*VRAM*), and static RAM (*SRAM*). Most computer memory is volatile—that is, its contents are lost when the computer shuts down. Also see *ROM*.

memory buffer A block of memory set aside for an emergency or special use.

menu A list of *commands*. To select one, *drag* down the menu until the desired command is highlighted, then release the *mouse* button. (If a command is unavailable, it will be *dimmed*.) Also see *pop-up menu*, *pull-down menu*, and *submenu*.

menu bar The horizontal strip across the top of the screen that contains the *menu* titles.

MHz An abbreviation for Megahertz.

microprocessor See *processor*.

MIDI Musical Instrument Digital Interface, a technology that enables a computer to record and play musical performances. The MIDI standard provides a common language and *interface*, so that the Mac and the electronic instruments and *software* can reliably connect and communicate with one another. Pronounced "middy."

mirror An *ftp* site on the *Internet* which contains an exact copy of another site, helping to increase the bandwidth to accommodate mass downloading.

modem A piece of *hardware* that lets computers talk to each other over telephone lines (you also need a *communications program*). The modem translates back and forth between the computer's digital data and the sounds carried over the phone lines. (The word is a contraction of modulator/demodulator.) Also see *fax modem*.

modem port A *serial port* on the Mac's back panel that's ordinarily used for attaching a modem. You also can use the port to attach other serial *devices*, such as a *graphics tablet* or *inkjet printer*. Compare *printer port* and *GeoPort*.

moderator See *Sysop*.

modifier key A key that modifies the effect of the character key being pressed. In most Mac *applications*, for example, ⌘S saves the document you're working on. The standard keyboard has five modifier keys: Shift, Option, ⌘, Control, and Caps Lock.

modular Mac A desktop Mac whose *monitor* isn't built into the same box as the *CPU*. Most Macs sold today are modular, except for the PowerBooks and 500-series Performas and LCs. Compare *compact Mac* and *portable Mac*.

monitor The piece of *hardware* that contains the screen that you look at while you work. It's also called a *display* or *CRT* and can be *monochrome* (black and white), *grayscale*, or color. You connect it to the Mac's *display port* or to a *video card*.

monochrome Anything that contains just one color (and shades thereof). A monochrome *monitor*, for example, is either black and white (black is the color, white is the background) or *grayscale*.

MooV The *file format* for *QuickTime* movies. It can include video, audio, and animations.

morphing A special effect used in graphics, video, and animation that produces a smooth transformation of one shape into another, such as a pop star turning into a panther.

motherboard The heart, soul, and brains of the Mac. This plastic *board* resembles a miniature city, but its buildings are actually *chips* for things such as the *processor*, *RAM*, and *ROM*, and the tiny roads connecting them are circuit traces. Also called the logic board. See *daughterboard*.

mount Make a *storage device* available as an *icon* on the *desktop*. The Mac can't access a *disk* until it's mounted on the desktop; to dismount a disk, you drag its icon to the *Trash*.

mouse The standard *pointing device* supplied with every Mac. Moving the mouse causes the pointer on-screen to move in the same direction.

MUD Multiuser Dungeon or Dimension. An open-ended virtual world in which the users can typically extend the rules or capabilities of the "game."

MultiFinder A System 6 program that allows several *applications*, including the *Finder*, to be open at the same time. (This capability is built into System 7.)

multimedia Any presentation or program that combines several media, such as *graphics*, sound, video, animation, and/or text. Multimedia is everywhere these days—business presentations, *CD-ROM* games, educational *software*, and training systems—and it's often *interactive*.

multiscan monitor A *monitor* that can operate at different *resolutions* and *scanning* frequencies, allowing it to be used on a variety of computers. Multiscan monitors are not to be confused with MultiSync monitors, which are a brand name monitor used by NEC Technologies. See *MultiSync*.

MultiSync A brand name monitor used by NEC Technologies for *multiscan monitors*.

multitasking Said of a computer that can do more than one thing at a time, such as sorting a *database* and recalculating a *spreadsheet*. The Mac isn't a true multitasking machine (yet).

multiuser Said of an *operating system* (such as *Unix*), *application*, or piece of *hardware* that can be used by more than one person at one time.

N

nanosecond A billionth of a second. Used to measure the speed of *memory* (*RAM*) *chips*, among other things. Abbreviated ns.

native 1. Said of *software* that's written specifically to run on a particular *processor*. For example, a program optimized for a *68K* processor runs in native mode on a Quadra, but it runs in *emulation mode* (which is slower) on a *PowerPC*-based Power Mac. 2. The *file format* in which an *application* normally saves its *documents*. The native format is generally readable only by that application (other programs can sometimes translate it using *filters*). Compare *interchange format*.

network In general, a group of computers set up to communicate with one another. Your network can be a small system that's physically connected by cables (a *LAN*), or you can connect separate networks together to form larger networks (called *WANs*). The *Internet*, for example, is made up of thousands of individual networks.

network protocol The rules describing the transfer of data and communication between devices on a network.

NiMH Nickel-Metal Hydride, a battery technology for PowerBooks.

node Any *device* that's directly connected to a *network*. This usually includes computers, *printers*, and file *servers*.

noise Inaccurate *data* picked up by a *scanner* and produced by the *CCD*. The less noise there is in relation to total data collected, the more usable information the scanner can deliver.

NuBus A type of *expansion slot* within the Mac where you can insert NuBus *cards* that add capabilities such as *acceleration* or *24-bit color*. The number of NuBus slots varies among Mac models.

null modem cable A *serial-port* cable that lets you connect a Mac directly to another computer, such as a PC, for direct data transfers.

object-oriented graphic An image made up of individual, mathematically defined objects, rather than a collection of *bits*. Typically created by *draw programs*, which are based on either *PostScript* or *QuickDraw*. Also called a *vector graphic*; compare *bitmapped graphic*.

OCR Optical Character Recognition, a technology that lets you scan a printed page (with a *scanner*) and convert it into a text *document* that you can edit in a *word processor*. Some OCR software also works with files received by a *fax modem*.

OEM Original Equipment Manufacturer. A company that produces a product that isn't sold on its own but instead is incorporated into another company's product. For example, Quantum is an OEM that makes *hard disks* sold under different names by other companies. Sometimes OEM is used as a verb: "Quantum OEMs *disk drives* for Apple."

OLE (OLE 2) Object Linking and Embedding. A Microsoft technology that gives programs a standard way to incorporate objects, such as *graphics* and *spreadsheet* charts, into *documents*. Objects can be embedded into documents or merely linked (a reference to the original object is stored in the document rather than a copy of the actual object).

on-line Actively connected to other computers or devices. You're on-line when you've *logged on* to a *network*, *BBS*, or *on-line service*. A *device* such as a *printer* is on-line when it's turned on and accessible to the Mac. (It can even refer to *software*: An on-line help system is one you can call up via your software, as opposed to opening a manual.) If you're not on-line, then you're off-line.

on-line service A commercial service that (for a price) provides goodies such as *e-mail*, discussion forums, tech support, *software* libraries, news, weather reports, stock prices, plane reservations, even electronic shopping malls. To access one, you need a *modem*. Popular on-line services include America Online and CompuServe. Compare *BBS* and *Internet*.

one-pass scanner A *scanner* that only needs to scan the original once, rather than once each for red, green, and blue.

OOP Object-Oriented Programming. A programming technology in which program components are put together from reusable building blocks known as objects.

open 1. Start up an *application* and/or make a *document* visible on the screen—that is, *load* its contents into *memory* from a *disk*. Compare *import* and *save*. 2. Expand a *folder* or disk into a *window* by *double-clicking* on its *icon*. Also see *Drag-and-Drop*.

OpenDoc An architecture that lets you use several *applications* to work on different types of *data* within a single *document* (called a compound document because of the multiple formats it contains).

operating system The basic *software* that runs the computer itself. On the Mac, it consists of the *System file*, the *ROMs*, the *Finder*, and related *system software*. Often called the OS (pronounced as separate letters) or just the system.

optimizers See *defragmenter*.

outline font A font in which each character's shape is stored as a mathematical outline. It can be scaled to any size with no loss of quality and will print at the highest available resolution. *PostScript*, *TrueType*, and *GX fonts* are outline-font formats. Also called a scalable font. Compare *bitmapped font*.

P

page A *window* full of text and graphics on the *World Wide Web*, as displayed by a Web *browser*.

Paged memory management unit See *PMMU*.

page layout program Software designed to combine text and graphics on a virtual *page*, giving you extensive control over the design and typography. The cornerstone of *desktop publishing*.

Paint A nearly obsolete *file format* (file type PNTG) that holds low-resolution black-and-white *bitmapped graphics*. Compare *TIFF*.

paint program Software that lets you create digital paintings from scratch and saves them as *bitmapped graphics*. Compare *image-editing* and *draw programs*.

palette A floating *window* within an *application* that sits above open *documents* so that you can easily access its contents. It can contain tools, *buttons*, colors, *styles*, or whatever is appropriate to the program. Also called a windoid.

parallel port A type of *port* that transmits *data* in parallel—several *bits* side by side. The Mac doesn't have parallel ports, but they are common printer interfaces on PCs.

parameter RAM See *PRAM*.

partition A section of a *hard disk* that's *formatted* so the Mac will treat it as a separate *disk*. Partitioning can reduce wasted space and make file management easier, especially on a large disk. Also called a volume.

passive-matrix See *LCD*.

paste To insert something into a *document* from the *Clipboard* by choosing Paste from the Edit *menu* (or typing ⌘V).

patch A small piece of *code* added to an existing program to enhance *performance* or fix a *bug*.

path menu The *menu* that appears when you hold ⌘ and press on the title of a *Finder* *window*. It lists the *folder* that window belongs to, and the folder that folder's in, and so on, describing the path up to the *disk*.

PC Personal Computer. While the Mac is, of course, a PC, the term refers almost exclusively to those other computers: IBM PCs and their *compatibles*.

PCI Peripheral Component Interconnect. A new kind of *expansion slot* built into new Power Macs. PCI replaces Apple's *NuBus* expansion *bus*.

PCMCIA A standard format for credit-card-size *expansion cards*, used to add features (such as *hard disks*, *modems*, and *memory*) to 500-series PowerBooks, hand-held computers such as the Apple Newton MessagePad, and (in the future) desktop computers. The unpronounceable acronym stands for Personal Computer Memory Card International Association (whew!), but an easier mnemonic is People Can't Memorize Computer Industry Acronyms.

PDD Portable Digital Document. A *file format* introduced with *QuickDraw GX*. A *document* saved as a PDD file can be viewed and printed accurately on any Mac that has QuickDraw GX (or System 7.5), even if that Mac doesn't have the file's original *application* or *fonts*.

PDS See *processor-direct slot*.

peer-to-peer A *network* setup that allows every Mac to both offer and access *network* resources, such as shared files, without requiring a centralized *AppleShare server*.

performance In computer parlance: speed. (How well your computer actually performs, however, is based on much more than its raw speed.)

peripheral A piece of *hardware* that's outside (peripheral to) the main computer. In practice, it usually refers to external hardware—such as *disk drives*, *printers*, and *scanners*—sold by a third party.

PhoneNet A popular implementation of *LocalTalk* cabling that uses ordinary telephone wire to connect devices on an *AppleTalk network*.

Photo CD A technology developed by Eastman Kodak for *scanning* and storing photographs on *CD-ROM*. Many film developers will turn a roll of 35mm film into high-quality digital photos that you can access using a Photo CD-compatible CD-ROM drive.

PICS A standard *file format* for animation files.

PICT A standard *file format* for graphics files. It can contain both *object-oriented* and *bitmapped graphics*, and is the standard format for graphics that are cut or copied to the *Clipboard*.

PIM Personal Information Manager. Used to describe programs that keep track of information you need to conduct day-to-day personal business. They usually offer some combination of an address book (or *contact manager*), calendar and scheduling, and to-do lists.

piracy Copying commercial *software* (or *shareware*) without permission and without paying for it. Also called theft.

pixel One of the little points of light that make up the picture on a computer (or TV) screen. (The name is short for picture element.) The more pixels there are in a given area—that is, the smaller and closer together they are—the higher the *resolution*. Often, pixels are simply called dots.

PlainTalk A voice-related *system enhancement* that has two parts. Text-to-speech enables *applications* that support it to read text aloud. Voice recognition works in conjunction with *AppleScript* to let you control the Mac with spoken commands.

platform Usually refers to a particular type of computer running a particular *operating system*. The Mac is one platform, a PC running *Windows* is another, and a *Unix* machine is still another. Also see *cross-platform*.

platters A rigid *disk* typically made out of aluminum and magnetically coated to retain saved data.

plug-in A software module that adds capabilities to an *application*. Pop a plug-in *file* into the appropriate *folder*, and the *program* will sprout new features.

PMMU Paged Memory Management Unit, the *chip* that makes virtual memory possible (provided the appropriate *software* is installed). Its functions are built into the 68030, 68040, and *PowerPC processors*.

pointer The little *icon* that moves on the screen when you move the *mouse* (or other *pointing device*). Its most common shapes are the arrow (▶), the I-beam (Ⲓ), and the wristwatch (⌚). It takes on other shapes and names—such as the lasso (𝒫)—in other applications.

pointing device A *mouse*, *trackball*, or other *input device* that moves the *pointer* on-screen.

POP Post Office Protocol. An *Internet protocol* for handling *e-mail*.

pop-up menu A *menu*, typically found in a *dialog box* or *palette*, that pops up (or down or to the side) when you press the *mouse* button on its title (a box with a drop shadow around it). Compare *pull-down menu*.

port A connection for plugging in external computer *devices*. Most Macs have an *ADB* port, a *SCSI* port, a *display* port, a *printer* port, a *modem* port, and so forth.

portable Mac A smallish, (relatively) lightweight Mac, such as a PowerBook or the Portable, that includes the *CPU*, *monitor*, and keyboard in a single, fold-up unit. Compare *compact Mac* and *modular Mac*.

portrait monitor A *monitor* designed to show a full letter-size page. The word portrait indicates the monitor's tall, rectangular shape. Portrait monitors are most commonly called full-page displays.

post To *upload* a message to the public message area of a *bulletin board system* or *on-line service*.

PostScript A programming language developed by Adobe that's designed to describe, in precise detail, how the text and graphics on a printed page should look. It's often referred to as a page-description language and is used on many types of *printers* and *imagesetters*. Compare *QuickDraw*.

PostScript font An *outline font* format defined in PostScript. With *system software* versions before 7.5, *PostScript fonts* (also called *printer fonts*) must be used in conjunction with *bitmapped fonts* (the *screen fonts*). Compare *TrueType font*.

PowerPC A type of *processor chip*, based on powerful *RISC* technology and made by IBM and Motorola. Apple introduced PowerPC chips with the Power Macs and plans to phase out the *68K* processors used in other Macs.

PPP Point-to-Point Protocol. A *protocol* that allows your Mac to make an *Internet* connection by dialing up an *ISP*.

PRAM Parameter RAM (pronounced "pee-ram"), a small portion of the Mac's *RAM* set aside to hold basic information such as the date and time, speaker volume, *desktop* pattern, and keyboard and *mouse* settings. PRAM is powered by a battery, so it doesn't lose the settings when you shut down. Sometimes, however, the PRAM data gets corrupted, causing *crashes* or other problems. That's where zapping the PRAM comes in.

pre-emptive multitasking An efficient method of dividing up the *processor's* attention to accomplish several tasks at a time.

preferences The user-adjustable features of a *program*. Many programs create separate Preferences (or Prefs) *files*, which are usually stored in the *System Folder*.

presentation program Software that lets you combine text, charts, and illustrations—and, if you wish, animation, video, and sound—into electronic slide shows or *multimedia* presentations. You also can output the results to 35mm slides or videotape.

printer A *device* that takes the text and graphics sent from the Mac and puts them on a piece of paper. Most are computers in their own right, with *CPUs* and *memory*. The range of printer types includes *laser, inkjet, dot-matrix, thermal-fusion, dye-sublimation*, and *imagesetters*.

printer driver See *driver*.

printer font Another name for a *PostScript font*, which is an outline font designed to be used by printers. For screen display, you use a companion *screen font*.

printer port A *serial port* on the Mac's back panel that lets you connect to a *printer* or *LocalTalk network*. Compare *modem port* and *GeoPort*.

PrintMonitor A *print spooler* that comes with the *system software*; it shows you which *files* are printing as background tasks.

print spooler Software that intercepts a *document* on its way to the *printer*, temporarily storing it on *disk* until the printer is ready for it. It feeds the printer while you continue to work, providing *background printing*. System 7 has a built-in spooler, *PrintMonitor*; you can also buy a spooler *utility*.

processor The all-important *chip* that contains the computer's brains, or *CPU*. Sometimes called a microprocessor, it's located on the *motherboard*. Also see *coprocessor*.

processor-direct slot A type of *expansion slot* that connects to the *CPU* directly, rather than via a *bus* as with *NuBus slots*. Abbreviated *PDS*.

program Another word for *software*.

programmer's switch A small piece of plastic that comes with your Mac. It contains the reset button (which lets you restart the Mac in virtually any situation) and the interrupt button (used mainly by programmers). Also see *force quit*.

protected memory An approach that lets the system and each running *application* exist in *memory* so that if one *crashes*, the others are not affected.

protocol The set of connection and data transfer rules which a pair of computers must agree on.

public domain Software to which the author has given up all legal rights. Public domain software is actually extremely rare; the phrase is usually mistakenly applied to *shareware* and *freeware*.

Publish and Subscribe A data-linking strategy built into System 7 that's sometimes called "live cut and paste." You can *select* and publish (make available) *data* in one *document*, then subscribe (create a link) to it from one or more other documents. Whenever you change the original information, all the copies are automatically updated.

pull-down menu The kind of *menu* you find on the *menu bar*. It pops down when you click on its title; to keep it extended, you hold down the *mouse* button. Compare *pop-up menu*.

push button See *button*.

Q

QuickDraw The Mac's native graphics language, which tells it how to draw everything on the screen: text, images, *dialog boxes*, *menus*, *icons*, you name it. QuickDraw, which is built into the Mac's *ROM*, is also responsible for producing *PICT graphics* and for outputting text and images to non-PostScript *printers*. Compare *PostScript*.

QuickDraw GX A *system enhancement* that makes big improvements in the way the Mac handles printing, graphics, *fonts*, and exchanges of formatted *files* between Macs.

QuickDraw printer A non-PostScript printer, which relies on the Mac's *QuickDraw* language to tell it how to print text and images.

QuickTime Apple's technology for recording and playing back time-based *data* (video, animation, and sound). Physically, QuickTime is an *extension* that provides a standard *user interface*, a special *file format* (MooV), and *compression* (movies can be huge).

quitting Leaving a *program* and returning to the *Finder* (or its equivalent).

R

radio button One in a group of buttons of which only one can be on at a time (such as the presets on a car radio). When you select one radio button, the others are automatically deselected. Compare *checkbox*.

RAM Random Access Memory, the *chips* in a desktop Mac that contain most of its *memory*. RAM is the most common type of computer memory, and it's where the Mac stores *system software*, *programs*, and *data* you are currently using. It's formally called dynamic RAM (*DRAM*) because it's volatile—that is, the contents are lost when you turn off the Mac (or *crash*). It's pronounced "ram" and measured in megabytes. Compare *PRAM*, *SRAM*, and *VRAM*, and *ROM*.

RAM cache See *disk cache*.

RAM disk It's not a disk at all, but rather a portion of *memory* set aside to act as a temporary disk. The Mac sees it as a *hard disk*, but because RAM is faster, the *files* and *programs* stored on it will run faster. (You get to decide how big the RAM disk is and what *files* it contains.) It's especially useful in PowerBooks, because the Mac won't waste battery power spinning up the *hard disk* if the needed data is on the RAM disk.

rasterizing The process of converting the outlines of an *object-oriented graphic* or *font* into the *bitmap* (a pattern of dots or *pixels*) required for display on a *monitor* or output on a *printer*. In printers, this step is usually handled by a *RIP*.

readme file A disk document that accompanies *software* and gives you information that's either very important or was left out of the printed manual.

read-only Refers to something you can view and print but not write (save changes) to. Locked *files* or *disks* are read-only, as are *CD-ROMs*.

read/write head The part of a *drive* mechanism that actually deposits information on (writes) and extracts information from (reads) the *disk*.

reboot See *booting*.

recent folders Folders created by the Apple Menu Options *control panel* to hold *aliases* of recently used *documents*, *applications*, and *file servers*. With the *folders* listed in the menu, you can select recent items from their *submenus*.

record A grouping of all defined *fields* for one subject of a *database*, such as a single person, recording artist, or recipe. In an address database, for example, a record would consist of all address data for one person, such as Mike Jones.

redraw The process of a graphics program re-displaying a graphic on the screen, for example, after you've made a change to the object. Also called refresh.

refresh rate The rate that an image is redrawn on the *monitor*. The lower the refresh rate the better.

removable media Any storage *media* you can insert and remove from a *drive*. SyQuest, Iomega Zip, and *magneto-optical* cartridges are examples of removable media.

rendering The process of drawing the final image in some *graphics programs* (such as 3-D graphics), which includes applying the specified colors, textures, shadows, movements, and so forth, and outputting the image at the specified *resolution*.

resident font A *font* that's built into a *printer's ROM* (or stored on an attached *hard disk*), so it's always available for printing. Compare *download*.

resolution The granularity of output or display. Usually presented in dots per inch and dot pitch (width of the dots).

resource A special component of Mac *software* that's separate from the main programming instructions that make the software work. Resources include *dialog boxes*, *icons*, *fonts*, and sounds.

resource fork The part of a Mac *file* that holds program-specific resources such as *menus*, *dialog boxes*, sounds, *icons*, and formatting instructions. *Applications* always have a resource fork. Compare *data fork*.

RGB monitor A generic name for a color monitor, which uses three separate signals—red, green, and blue—to create the screen image.

RIP Raster Image Processor, *hardware* or *software* that converts (*rasterizes*) *object-oriented graphics* and *fonts* into the *bitmaps* required for output on a *printer* or *imagesetter*.

RISC Reduced Instruction Set Computing; pronounced "risk." A type of *processor* design that uses a relatively small set of instructions for faster operation. The *PowerPC chip* in the Power Macs is based on RISC technology. Compare *CISC*.

ROM Read-Only Memory; rhymes with "mom." ROM is permanent *memory* that's programmed on a *chip* (called the RAM chip) and can't be altered. It contains parts of the *system software* responsible for very basic things, such as starting up and drawing images on the screen. Compare *RAM*.

RSN Real soon now. Used disparagingly to describe the timeline of oft-promised but late-arriving products and upgrades.

RTF Rich text format, a *file format* for text files that includes *formatting* instructions. Also called *interchange format*.

run-time player A limited version of an *application*, such as a *database manager* or *presentation program*, that lets you access a database or play back a presentation, but not modify it or create new ones. You often can freely distribute the run-time player with *documents*, so others can use them without having to install the full program.

S

Sad Mac The glum Mac face that appears on-screen (accompanied by the *chimes of doom*) when the Mac can't start up due to a serious problem with its *hardware* or *system software*. When everything is OK, the Happy Mac appears during startup.

sampling Taking audio snapshots (called samples) of a sound wave (such as music or a voice) at regular intervals and turning them into a digital recording on the computer. The number of samples taken per second is called the sampling rate. Also see *digitize* and *sequencing*.

save To transfer information (usually a *document*) from *memory* to a *disk*. Compare *open*.

scanner A *device* that converts images (such as photographs) into digital form, so that they can be stored and manipulated on computers. When used in conjunction with *OCR software*, a *scanner* can convert a page of text into an editable document.

Scrapbook A *desk accessory* where you can permanently store material (text, graphics, sounds, movies) and then easily access it from within any *program*.

screen font Another name for a *bitmapped font*. Screen fonts are required for the on-screen display of *PostScript fonts*. With *TrueType fonts*, they're often supplied to speed up the screen display of common type sizes.

screen name See *user name*.

screensaver A *utility* that temporarily replaces the current screen image with a blank screen or an amusing/attractive/silly moving image. It's designed to prevent a static image from being permanently burned into the screen phosphor.

script A series of *commands* (saved as a *file*) that automates everyday tasks, such as file backups, or adds capabilities to a program or presentation. A script is, in essence, a simple program that you write using a *scripting language*. Also see *macro*.

scripting language A simple programming language, such as *AppleScript* or HyperCard's *HyperTalk*, that you use to create scripts.

scroll arrow A *scroll bar* component.

scroll bar The rectangular strip that appears on the right and/or bottom edges of a *window* when there's more information than is currently displayed. You can click in its gray area and/or use the *scroll arrows* and *scroll box* to move the window's contents.

scroll box A *scroll bar* component.

scrolling Moving through the contents of a *window* or *list box* in order to see things not currently displayed. It's normally done with the *scroll bar*.

SCSI Small Computer Systems Interface; pronounced "scuzzy." The standard *interface* for connecting *peripherals* to the Mac. You can attach up to seven SCSI *devices* to your Mac in a *daisy chain*. SCSI *ports* have been built into all Macs (except dockless Duos) since 1986. Compare *FireWire*.

SCSI connector The parts at each end of a SCSI cable which attach to the matching connector on your computer or other SCSI device.

SCSI device A *peripheral* that you connect to the Mac via a SCSI *port*. Examples include *hard disks*, *CD-ROM drives*, tape backup units, *scanners*, and some personal *printers*.

SCSI disk mode A way of connecting a PowerBook to a desktop Mac so the PowerBook behaves as if it were an external *hard disk*, allowing you to swap files back and forth. It's supported by most PowerBook models, but you need a special *adapter* cable.

SCSI ID The number assigned to a SCSI *device* so the Mac can distinguish it from other SCSI devices. Each device must have a unique number in the range from 0 to 6 (most *peripherals* let you change the ID with a switch or dial); the Mac itself is number 7. Also called the SCSI address.

select To choose something (text, graphic, object, region) that you want to change. You do this by clicking on an object or button, Shift-clicking on several objects, or dragging across an area. The chosen area (the *selection*) is either *highlighted* or surrounded by a *marquee*. Selecting by itself doesn't change anything, it just tells the Mac what you want to be affected by the next command or action. You deselect something by clicking elsewhere.

selection rectangle The dotted box that appears (in the *Finder* and many *applications*) when you click on an empty spot and *drag*. When you release the *mouse* button, the box disappears (or becomes a *marquee*) and everything within it is *selected*.

self-extracting archive A compressed *file* that contains all the information needed to decompress itself so that a user doesn't need a special program to access the file; *double-clicking* on a self-extracting archive decompresses it. Most such archives have names ending in ".sea".

sequencing To record music instrument by instrument (track by track). You record and edit the music in a *program* called a sequencer, and the resulting *MIDI file* is naturally called a sequence.

serial port A type of port that transmits *data* serially, one *bit* after another. The Mac's *modem* and *printer* ports are serial ports. Compare *parallel port*.

server A computer that provides shared, centralized resources—such as *files, e-mail, databases, modems*, and *printers*—to other computers on a *network*. Server can also refer to the *software*, such as *AppleShare*, that runs on such a computer. Compare *peer-to-peer*.

service bureau A business that can output your *documents* on specialized (read "expensive") equipment such as *laser* and *dye-sublimation printers*, large-format color printers, and *imagesetters*. Most service bureaus also let you rent time on computers, send faxes, and do photocopying.

sfil The standard *file format* for System 7 sound resources, which are stored in the *System file* and appear in the Sound *control panel*. To hear one, *double-click* its *icon*.

shareware Software you can try before you buy. It's distributed on the honor system, passed around through *user groups, on-line services*, and *BBSs*. If you like it enough to keep using it, you send the (usually nominal) fee to the author. Compare *freeware* and *public domain*.

Shift-click To hold down the [Shift] key while clicking the *mouse* button. Shift-clicking lets you select multiple objects or large amounts of text, depending on the program.

SIG Special Interest Group, a subgroup of a computer *user group*.

SIMM Single In-line Memory Module, a small *card* that holds memory *chips*. To add more *RAM* to your Mac, you buy SIMMs and plug them into *slots* on the *motherboard*. Pronounced "sim."

single-sided disk An older type of double-density *floppy disk* that stores just 400K of *data* on one surface. Compare *double-sided* and *high-density disks*.

68K Shorthand for Motorola's 68000 series of *processor chips*—the 68000, 68020, 68030, 68040, and 68LC040—used in every Mac model prior to 1994. Also called the 680x0 series. They're being replaced by *PowerPC chips*.

size box A small box found in the bottom-right corner of most *active windows*. Clicking and dragging it lets you change the window's size and shape. Compare *close box* and *zoom box*.

sleep A powered-down state that saves energy. A fact of life for PowerBook users running on battery power, but it's now available on several desktop Macs.

slot See *expansion slot*.

smart quotes True (curly) quotation marks that should be used for professional-looking text. They look like this: " '. Most *fonts* have them as ⌾Option characters. Compare *dumb quotes*.

SMTP Simple Mail Transport Protocol. A protocol for transferring *e-mail* on the *Internet*.

snd The *resource* responsible for making the sounds you hear in programs and HyperCard *stacks*. In System 7, system sounds are *sfil* resources.

sneakernet A file-sharing strategy that uses hand-carried *disks* as the exchange *media*. Transfer speed depends on the efficiency of your footwear.

software The instructions that tell a computer what to do. It takes many forms, from an *application* on a *disk* to the *code* in a Mac's *ROM*. Also called *programs* or, redundantly, *software programs*. Compare *hardware*.

software suite Programs sold by a software company as a group. The intent is to provide users with all the major *applications* needed for common business functions in one package. A *spreadsheet* and *word processor* typically form the core of a software suite. (Programs in a suite are usually not as well-integrated as those found in an integrated package.)

sort To order selected information (in a *database*, say, or a *word-processing* document) by one or more criteria, such as alphabetically.

spreadsheet program Software that processes number-related information, allowing you to apply calculations and formulas to *data* that's organized in rows and columns of cells. Its documents are sometimes called worksheets.

SQL Structured Query Language. An English-like language designed to obtain information from and to modify *data* in large relational *databases*.

SRAM Static RAM, a speedy but expensive form of *memory* found in *cache cards*. It boosts the Mac's performance by reducing the time the *processor* spends waiting for data from the slower dynamic *RAM*.

stack A *document* created by HyperCard.

startup disk The disk containing the *System file* and *Finder* that the Mac is currently using (which is usually the *disk* it started up from). If you have several disks mounted at the same time, you can designate which will be the startup disk using the Startup Disk *control panel*.

stationery A feature of System 7 (and some *applications*) that lets you create *templates—documents* that, when *double-clicked*, open an exact duplicate of themselves, leaving the original untouched. In System 7, you can turn most *documents* into stationery by clicking the Stationery Pad *checkbox* in their Get Info window.

storage Any type of *media* that you can store *files* on, including a *hard disk*, *floppy disk*, SyQuest cartridge, *magneto-optical* disk, or DAT tape.

storage bay A space inside the Mac where you can install additional *disk drives*. There are two sizes: 3.5-inch (the standard size for *floppy-disk drives*, *hard disks*, and some cartridge drives) and 5.25-inch (*CD-ROM* drives, some hard disks, and cartridge drives).

street price The average price that a product sells for through mail order or dealers. It's usually significantly less than a company's official list price. Also see *ApplePrice*.

style Formatting that's applied to text in a *document*. A character style is an attribute—such as *font* and size, and whether it's bold or italic—that affects only individual letters. A paragraph style also includes information such as line spacing, indents, and tab settings.

style sheet 1. A list of the style definitions used in a *document*. 2. A collection of character and paragraph styles that has a name, allowing you to quickly apply several formatting changes at once.

stylus A small, tipped object, similar in appearance to a pen or pencil used to emulate a writing/drawing device on a *graphics tablet* or similar medium.

submarining An unsettling effect sometimes found on *passive-matrix* PowerBook screens: If you move the *pointer* too fast, it disappears until you stop moving it.

submenu The secondary *menu* that appears next to an existing menu when you choose a command name that has a small, right-pointing arrow.

suitcase A file that stores *fonts*, sounds, or *desk accessories*; its *icon* looks like a little suitcase. In System 7, suitcases operate like *folders*: You can *double-click* them to open a *window* showing their contents, and drag items into and out of them. In System 6, you move items into and out of a suitcase file with Font/DA Mover.

SuperDrive The 1.4MB floppy-disk *drive* that comes with all current Macs. It can read and write *single-sided* (400K) disks, *double-sided* (800K) disks, and *high-density* (1.4MB) disks. With the appropriate *software*, it can also read 3.5-inch disks from PCs and Apple II machines. It used to be called the *FDHD* (floppy disk, high density) drive.

support 1. Help with *hardware* or *software* problems, usually in the form of advice from the technical support staff at the company that sold you the product. 2. To say that a piece of hardware or software supports something means that it works with it, or enables it to work. For example, System 7 supports *TrueType fonts*, and System 6 doesn't (normally).

surge protector A *device* that protects computer equipment from being damaged by variations in electrical current.

sustained transfer rates The speed at which a *drive* can deliver large amounts of *data*. Burst rates are much higher, so some vendors focus on those, but for most purposes the sustained rate is more important.

SYLK Symbolic Link format, a standard *file format* for *spreadsheets* (and sometimes *databases*). It preserves formulas and text formatting as well as *data*. Compare *DIF*.

sysop A person who manages a *BBS* or moderates a forum (discussion group) on an *on-line service*. Short for system operator and pronounced "siss-op."

system 1. A computer setup. 2. Short for *operating system*.

system disks A *CD* or set of *floppy disks* that contain *system software* installation information. Compare *startup disk*.

System Enabler A file in the *System Folder* that makes the Mac *compatible* with the current version of the *system software* (starting with System 7.1). Different Mac models have different enablers.

system enhancement A *program* (often an *extension*) that extends the capabilities of the *system software*, such as *AppleScript*, *QuickDraw GX*, or *QuickTime*. Some work in the background, adding features (such as movies) to *applications*, while others—such as At Ease and PowerTalk—are stand-alone programs that you can access directly.

System file The program the Mac uses to start itself and to provide certain basic information to all *applications*. Together with the *Finder* and *ROM*, it comprises the Mac's *operating system*.

System Folder The all-important *folder* on a Mac *disk* that contains the *System file*, *Finder*, and other *system software*. Only disks with a System Folder can be *startup disks*.

system heap The portion of a Mac's memory reserved for the *system software*. Compare *application heap*.

system resource Resources which are used by and "belong to" the System, such as fonts.

system software A catchall term for the basic programs that make the Mac work. It creates the *desktop*, provides universal commands such as Open, Save, and Cut, and includes features such as the *Clipboard*. Part of the system software is in *ROM*, and the rest is on disk in the *System Folder*.

T

TCP/IP The *network protocols* used on the *Internet* and on many multiplatform networks (especially those with *Unix* machines). It stands for Transmission Control Protocol/Internet Protocol. The Mac can speak TCP/IP using the MacTCP *extension*. Compare *AppleTalk*.

tear-off Refers to a *menu* (or *palette*) that you can detach from the main menu (or main palette) and move around on the screen like a palette. A tear-off menu/palette stays fully extended and remains in front of open *document windows*.

telecommunications The transfer of information between computers over telephone lines. Just plug in a *modem*, fire up some *communications software*, and you can make contact with the office computer, an *on-line service*, a *BBS*, or the *Internet*.

Telnet A function of the Internet that allows you to log onto a remote computer.

template A master *document* that you can use repeatedly without altering the original contents. Many *applications* provide templates (and/or let you create them). System 7 has a seldom-used template feature called *stationery*.

terminator A small *device* that eliminates echoes and other unwanted electrical signals from a *SCSI bus* or *network*. In a SCSI chain, it usually plugs into the *SCSI port* of the last device in the chain.

text box An area, usually in a *dialog box*, where you insert text. Also called a text field.

text editor A simple, no-frills *word processor* that works with plain *ASCII* text.

text file An *ASCII file*—just characters, no *formatting*.

text tool Another name for the *I-beam pointer*.

thermal-fusion printer A *printer* that produces output via tiny heated elements in the print head that push a ribbon against the page, bonding a waxy ink to the paper.

thermal-wax transfer printer A printer that creates images using tiny heated elements that push rolls of plastic film against a page, bonding a waxy ink to the paper. Also called heat-fusion or *thermal-fusion printers*.

third party You are the first party; Apple (the maker of your computer) is the second party; and the companies that make *hardware* and *software* for the Mac are third parties. It also refers to companies who make add-on software for major *applications*—for example, a *plug-in* for Adobe Photoshop (the second party in this case).

32-bit addressing A method of handling *memory* in System 7 that enables most Macs to work with as much *RAM* as the machine can hold. Without it, Macs have 24-bit addressing, which limits total RAM to 8MB.

32-bit clean A phrase used to describe *software* (including what's in *ROM*) that's written to work correctly—that is, without crashing—with *32-bit addressing*. A few older Macs, such as the IIcx, aren't 32-bit clean and are said to have "dirty ROMs."

32-bit color Color that uses 32 *bits* to store each *pixel's* color value. Like 24-bit color (see *bit depth*), it offers 16.7 million colors; the extra 8 bits per pixel don't offer more colors; they're reserved for special operations such as masking.

thread A message posted in a public area of a *bulletin board system* or *on-line service*, plus the replies and replies to replies.

3-D graphics Graphics that are made to look three-dimensional by using shading, perspective, and other techniques to give the illusion of depth in addition to the height and width (two dimensions) actually available on a computer screen.

throughput The rate at which *data* can be transferred between two computers or other *devices*. With *modems*, it refers to the number of *bits* exchanged per second. See *bps*.

TIFF Tagged Image File Format, the standard *file format* for high-resolution *bitmapped graphics*, including those generated by most *scanners*.

tile 1. To arrange *windows* side by side, as if they were floor tiles. 2. To print an oversized image across several pieces of paper (which can then be taped together). 3. To repeat a pattern or texture across an image in a *graphics program*.

title bar The horizontal strip across the top of a *window* that contains its name. When the window is *active*, its title bar has horizontal stripes, a *zoom box*, and a *close box*. To move a window, you *drag* it by the title bar.

toggle A feature that changes its status (on or off) each time you use it. For example, the common type *styles* (bold, italic, and so on) are toggles, because the first time you choose them they turn on, and the next time they turn off. Other toggles include *checkboxes* and certain *menu* items (e.g., Show Ruler, Hide Ruler).

toolbox 1. A special *palette* containing *buttons* and tools that floats above a *document* for easy access. Also called a tool palette, unless it's a toolbar (a ribbon across the top of the screen). 2. The Toolbox is a collection of predefined software routines (*code*) built into the Mac's *ROM* that performs basic tasks such as drawing *dialog boxes* and displaying *menus*.

trackball A pointing *device* that resembles an upside-down mouse. Instead of sliding a *mouse* across the desk, you roll a ball in a stationary holder.

tracking speed The relationship between the motion of a *mouse* or on a *trackpad* and how fast the cursor moves on the screen.

trackpad The touch-sensitive *pointing device* built into late-model PowerBooks. Instead of moving about the screen by rolling a *trackball*, you run a fingertip across the trackpad.

Trash The *icon* on the *desktop* into which you put *files* to be deleted; they aren't actually deleted, however, until you choose Empty Trash from the Special *menu*. You can also eject a *floppy disk* or dismount a *hard disk* (or *AppleShare* volume) by dragging its *icon* to the Trash.

TrueType An outline *font* format developed by Apple and supported by System 7. Unlike *PostScript fonts*, a single TrueType font file works for both the screen and any *printer*.

Tune-Ups Free *utilities* from Apple that fix *bugs* and enhance features of System 7 and 7.0.1. For System 7.1, they're called System Updates.

24-bit color See *bit depth*.

Type 1 font The primary format for *PostScript fonts*, developed by Adobe Systems.

typeface A collection of letters, numbers, punctuation marks, and symbols with an identifiable and consistent design. A typeface, such as Helvetica or Times, can include many different weights (light, semibold, bold, and so on) and styles (regular, italic, and so on). Compare *font*.

typography The craft of setting type so it is both readable and attractive. It includes selection of appropriate *typefaces* and control over horizontal and vertical spacing.

U

Undo The Mac's most beloved *command* ($\boxed{\text{⌘}}\boxed{\text{Z}}$), it lets you, well, undo the last thing you did in a *program*. Undo is often a *toggle*, so you can flip back and forth between two versions of something, and the cool programs have multiple undo, allowing you to go back more than one step.

Unix This multiuser, multitasking, multiplatform *operating system* was developed by Bell Labs and is pronounced "you-nix." Apple's implementation of Unix is called *A/UX*.

upload To send a *file* to another computer using a *modem*. Opposite of *download*.

URL Uniform Resource Locator. A unique address that specifies the exact location of every accessible resource on the *Internet*.

Usenet News The discussion forums of the *Internet*.

user group A bunch of people who get together to share help and advice about their computers and *software*. Mac-specific user groups are often called MUGs, the largest of which are BMUG (in Berkeley, California) and the Boston Computer Society.

user interface The way a computer (or a *program*) interacts with the user. For example, the Mac's interface uses graphical elements—*icons*, *windows*, *buttons*, *menus*, *dialog boxes*—which is why it's called a graphical user interface, or GUI (pronounced "gooey").

user name Also known as a user ID or screen name. A name you use to identify yourself on an *on-line service*.

utility A program that provides support to the *system software*, other *applications*, or even the Mac *hardware*. You don't need utilities unless you're using your Mac to do other things. Spelling checkers, *disk* recovery tools, *extension* managers, *screensavers*, and *compression* programs are all utilities.

V

value list A set of values associated with a *database field* from which the user can choose rather than typing an entry. Associating a value list with a field can speed *data* entry and help ensure consistency.

vaporware A product that a company keeps promising to deliver but never does (or at least is very, very late in shipping).

VAR Value Added Reseller. A person or company that buys *hardware* and *software*, packages it all together, and sells it to you as a complete system. A VAR will discuss your needs, make the buying decisions, install the system, train you, and provide support. For a price, of course.

vector graphics Another term for *object-oriented graphics*.

video card 1. A card that controls an external *monitor*. It can include features such as *24-bit color* and/or a graphics *accelerator*. 2. A card that *digitizes* the video signal from a TV, VCR, or camcorder. Also called a digitizing board or a digitizer.

video editor Software that lets you create and edit *QuickTime* movies, record video and audio (with the appropriate *digitizing* hardware), and output the movies in various formats.

video port 1. A port where you can attach an external *monitor*. Now called the *display port*. 2. A port where you can attach a VCR, camcorder, or TV. Video-in ports let you *digitize* the video signal coming from one of these *devices*, and video-out ports send digital data to them.

virtual memory A System 7 strategy that expands the available *memory* by treating vacant space on a *hard disk* as if it were *RAM*.

virus A program that replicates itself from one *file* or *disk* to another without your consent. Viruses can spread through *floppy disks*, *networks*, and *on-line services* and can go undetected (unless you have an antiviral *utility*) until something goes wrong. Some viruses deliberately destroy *data*, and even those designed to be "benign" can cause *crashes*, slowdowns, and file corruption.

VLF radiation Very Low Frequency electromagnetic radiation (between 10KHz and 30KHz), which is emitted by the *CRTs* in *monitors* and televisions. Compare *ELF radiation*.

voice recognition The ability of the Mac to interpret and execute spoken commands (and even, with the right *software*, to take dictation). PlainTalk is one implementation.

VRAM Video RAM, a type of *memory* dedicated to handling the image displayed on a *monitor*. VRAM is built into many Macs, and it also comes on *display cards*.

W

WAN Wide Area Network, a network that spans geographically separated areas, usually by using *modems* and dedicated, high-speed telephone lines. Compare *LAN*.

Web Short for *World Wide Web*, a graphical portion of the *Internet*.

wild card A character (usually * or ?) that can stand for one or more unknown characters during a search. Searching for some text or a *file* using Mac* would find Macintosh, MacUser, and macadamia.

window A rectangular frame on the Mac's screen that has a *title bar* and *scroll bars*. Disks and *folders* open into windows, and *documents* appear in windows when you're working on them. Compare *dialog box*.

Windows Microsoft *software* that adds a Mac-like graphical *user interface* to PCs.

WorldScript A technology that enables the Mac to handle non-Roman-based language systems.

word processor Software that lets you enter, edit, and *format* text. Not only that, but it also provides goodies such as spelling checkers, outlining, tables, footnotes, and tables of contents.

World Wide Web The portion of the *Internet* which allows the display of *formatted* pages of text and graphics.

wristrest A little cushion that provides support for the wrists and helps prevent repetitive stress injury.

wristwatch The *icon* the *pointer* normally turns into while you wait for the Mac to do something.

WYSIWYG Means "what you see is what you get"—that is, the image you see on-screen matches what will print on paper. Pronounced "wizzy-wig."

Z

zoom box A small box at the right end of the *title bar* in most *active windows*. Clicking it expands the window to display all the contents; clicking again restores the previous size and shape. Compare *close box* and *size box*.

Index

A

U

A 32-signature salute to Peachpit Press
founder and publisher, Ted Nace.
So long, and good luck!